T0212361

Lecture Notes in Computer Science 11139

Commenced Publication in 1973
Founding and Former Series Editors:
Gerhard Goos, Juris Hartmanis, and Jan van Leeuwen

Věra Kůrková · Yannis Manolopoulos
Barbara Hammer · Lazaros Iliadis
Ilias Maglogiannis (Eds.)

Artificial Neural Networks and Machine Learning – ICANN 2018

27th International Conference on Artificial Neural Networks
Rhodes, Greece, October 4–7, 2018
Proceedings, Part I

 Springer

Editors
Věra Kůrková
Czech Academy of Sciences
Prague 8
Czech Republic

Lazaros Iliadis
Democritus University of Thrace
Xanthi
Greece

Yannis Manolopoulos
Open University of Cyprus
Latsia
Cyprus

Ilias Maglogiannis
University of Piraeus
Piraeus
Greece

Barbara Hammer
CITEC Bielefeld University
Bielefeld
Germany

ISSN 0302-9743   ISSN 1611-3349   (electronic)
Lecture Notes in Computer Science
ISBN 978-3-030-01417-9   ISBN 978-3-030-01418-6   (eBook)
https://doi.org/10.1007/978-3-030-01418-6

Library of Congress Control Number: 2018955577

LNCS Sublibrary: SL1 – Theoretical Computer Science and General Issues

This Springer imprint is published by the registered company Springer Nature Switzerland AG
The registered company address is: Gewerbestrasse 11, 6330 Cham, Switzerland

Preface

Technological advances in artificial intelligence (AI) are leading the rapidly changing world of the twenty-first century. We have already passed from machine learning to deep learning with numerous applications. The contribution of AI so far to the improvement of our quality of life is profound. Major challenges but also risks and threats are here. Brain-inspired computing explores, simulates, and imitates the structure and the function of the human brain, achieving high-performance modeling plus visualization capabilities.

The International Conference on Artificial Neural Networks (ICANN) is the annual flagship conference of the European Neural Network Society (ENNS). It features the main tracks "Brain-Inspired Computing" and "Machine Learning Research," with strong cross-disciplinary interactions and applications. All research fields dealing with neural networks are present.

The 27th ICANN was held during October 4–7, 2018, at the Aldemar Amilia Mare five-star resort and conference center in Rhodes, Greece. The previous ICANN events were held in Helsinki, Finland (1991), Brighton, UK (1992), Amsterdam, The Netherlands (1993), Sorrento, Italy (1994), Paris, France (1995), Bochum, Germany (1996), Lausanne, Switzerland (1997), Skovde, Sweden (1998), Edinburgh, UK (1999), Como, Italy (2000), Vienna, Austria (2001), Madrid, Spain (2002), Istanbul, Turkey (2003), Budapest, Hungary (2004), Warsaw, Poland (2005), Athens, Greece (2006), Porto, Portugal (2007), Prague, Czech Republic (2008), Limassol, Cyprus (2009), Thessaloniki, Greece (2010), Espoo Helsinki, Finland (2011), Lausanne, Switzerland (2012), Sofia, Bulgaria (2013), Hamburg, Germany (2014), Barcelona, Spain (2016), and Alghero, Italy (2017).

Following a long-standing tradition, these Springer volumes belong to the *Lecture Notes in Computer Science Springer* series. They contain the papers that were accepted to be presented orally or as posters during the 27th ICANN conference. The 27th ICANN Program Committee was delighted by the overwhelming response to the call for papers. All papers went through a peer-review process by at least two and many times by three or four independent academic referees to resolve any conflicts. In total, 360 papers were submitted to the 27th ICANN. Of these, 139 (38.3%) were accepted as full papers for oral presentation of 20 minutes with a maximum length of 10 pages, whereas 28 of them were accepted as short contributions to be presented orally in 15 minutes and for inclusion in the proceedings with 8 pages. Also, 41 papers (11.4%) were accepted as full papers for poster presentation (up to 10 pages long), whereas 11 were accepted as short papers for poster presentation (maximum length of 8 pages).

The accepted papers of the 27th ICANN conference are related to the following thematic topics:

AI and Bioinformatics
Bayesian and Echo State Networks
Brain-Inspired Computing

Chaotic Complex Models
Clustering, Mining, Exploratory Analysis
Coding Architectures
Complex Firing Patterns
Convolutional Neural Networks
Deep Learning (DL)

– DL in Real Time Systems
– DL and Big Data Analytics
– DL and Big Data
– DL and Forensics
– DL and Cybersecurity
– DL and Social Networks

Evolving Systems – Optimization
Extreme Learning Machines
From Neurons to Neuromorphism
From Sensation to Perception
From Single Neurons to Networks
Fuzzy Modeling
Hierarchical ANN
Inference and Recognition
Information and Optimization
Interacting with the Brain
Machine Learning (ML)

– ML for Bio-Medical Systems
– ML and Video-Image Processing
– ML and Forensics
– ML and Cybersecurity
– ML and Social Media
– ML in Engineering

Movement and Motion Detection
Multilayer Perceptrons and Kernel Networks
Natural Language
Object and Face Recognition
Recurrent Neural Networks and Reservoir Computing
Reinforcement Learning
Reservoir Computing
Self-Organizing Maps
Spiking Dynamics/Spiking ANN
Support Vector Machines
Swarm Intelligence and Decision-Making
Text Mining
Theoretical Neural Computation
Time Series and Forecasting
Training and Learning

The authors of submitted papers came from 34 different countries from all over the globe, namely: Belgium, Brazil, Bulgaria, Canada, China, Czech Republic, Cyprus, Egypt, Finland, France, Germany, Greece, India, Iran, Ireland, Israel, Italy, Japan, Luxembourg, The Netherlands, Norway, Oman, Pakistan, Poland, Portugal, Romania, Russia, Slovakia, Spain, Switzerland, Tunisia, Turkey, UK, USA.

Four keynote speakers were invited, and they gave lectures on timely aspects of AI.

We hope that these proceedings will help researchers worldwide to understand and to be aware of timely evolutions in AI and more specifically in artificial neural networks. We believe that they will be of major interest for scientists over the globe and that they will stimulate further research.

October 2018

Věra Kůrková
Yannis Manolopoulos
Barbara Hammer
Lazaros Iliadis
Ilias Maglogiannis

Organization

General Chairs

Věra Kůrková	Czech Academy of Sciences, Czech Republic
Yannis Manolopoulos	Open University of Cyprus, Cyprus

Program Co-chairs

Barbara Hammer	Bielefeld University, Germany
Lazaros Iliadis	Democritus University of Thrace, Greece
Ilias Maglogiannis	University of Piraeus, Greece

Steering Committee

Vera Kurkova (President of ENNS)	Czech Academy of Sciences, Czech Republic
Cesare Alippi	Università della Svizzera Italiana, Switzerland
Guillem Antó i Coma	Pompeu Fabra University, Barcelona, Spain
Jeremie Cabessa	Université Paris 2 Panthéon-Assas, France
Wlodzislaw Duch	Nicolaus Copernicus University, Poland
Petia Koprinkova-Hristova	Bulgarian Academy of Sciences, Bulgaria
Jaakko Peltonen	University of Tampere, Finland
Yifat Prut	The Hebrew University, Israel
Bernardete Ribeiro	University of Coimbra, Portugal
Stefano Rovetta	University of Genoa, Italy
Igor Tetko	German Research Center for Environmental Health, Munich, Germany
Alessandro Villa	University of Lausanne, Switzerland
Paco Zamora-Martínez	das-Nano, Spain

Publication Chair

Antonis Papaleonidas	Democritus University of Thrace, Greece

Communication Chair

Paolo Masulli	Technical University of Denmark, Denmark

Program Committee

Najem Abdennour	Higher Institute of Computer Science and Multimedia (ISIMG), Gabes, Tunisia

Tetiana Aksenova	Atomic Energy Commission (CEA), Grenoble, France
Zakhriya Alhassan	Durham University, UK
Tayfun Alpay	University of Hamburg, Germany
Ioannis Anagnostopoulos	University of Thessaly, Greece
Cesar Analide	University of Minho, Portugal
Annushree Bablani	National Institute of Technology Goa, India
Costin Badica	University of Craiova, Romania
Pablo Barros	University of Hamburg, Germany
Adam Barton	University of Ostrava, Czech Republic
Lluís Belanche	Polytechnic University of Catalonia, Spain
Bartlomiej Beliczynski	Warsaw University of Technology, Poland
Kostas Berberidis	University of Patras, Greece
Ege Beyazit	University of Louisiana at Lafayette, USA
Francisco Elanio Bezerra	University Ninth of July, Sao Paolo, Brazil
Varun Bhatt	Indian Institute of Technology, Bombay, India
Marcin Blachnik	Silesian University of Technology, Poland
Sander Bohte	National Research Institute for Mathematics and Computer Science (CWI), The Netherlands
Simone Bonechi	University of Siena, Italy
Farah Bouakrif	University of Jijel, Algeria
Meftah Boudjelal	Mascara University, Algeria
Andreas Bougiouklis	National Technical University of Athens, Greece
Martin Butz	University of Tübingen, Germany
Jeremie Cabessa	Université Paris 2, France
Paulo Vitor Campos Souza	Federal Center for Technological Education of Minas Gerais, Brazil
Angelo Cangelosi	Plymouth University, UK
Yanan Cao	Chinese Academy of Sciences, China
Francisco Carvalho	Federal University of Pernambuco, Brazil
Giovanna Castellano	University of Bari, Italy
Jheymesson Cavalcanti	University of Pernambuco, Brazil
Amit Chaulwar	Technical University Ingolstadt, Germany
Sylvain Chevallier	University of Versailles St. Quentin, France
Stephane Cholet	University of Antilles, Guadeloupe
Mark Collier	Trinity College, Ireland
Jorg Conradt	Technical University of Munich, Germany
Adriana Mihaela Coroiu	Babes-Bolyai University, Romania
Paulo Cortez	University of Minho, Portugal
David Coufal	Czech Academy of Sciences, Czech Republic
Juarez Da Silva	University of Vale do Rio dos Sinos, Brazil
Vilson Luiz Dalle Mole	Federal University of Technology Parana, Brazil
Debasmit Das	Purdue University, USA
Bodhisattva Dash	International Institute of Information Technology, Bhubaneswar, India
Eli David	Bar-Ilan University, Israel
Konstantinos Demertzis	Democritus University of Thrace, Greece

Antreas Dionysiou	University of Cyprus, Cyprus
Sergey Dolenko	Lomonosov Moscow State University, Russia
Xiao Dong	Chinese Academy of Sciences, China
Shirin Dora	University of Amsterdam, The Netherlands
Jose Dorronsoro	Autonomous University of Madrid, Spain
Ziad Doughan	Beirut Arab University, Lebanon
Wlodzislaw Duch	Nicolaus Copernicus University, Poland
Gerrit Ecke	University of Tübingen, Germany
Alexander Efitorov	Lomonosov Moscow State University, Russia
Manfred Eppe	University of Hamburg, Germany
Deniz Erdogmus	Northeastern University, USA
Rodrigo Exterkoetter	LTrace Geophysical Solutions, Florianopolis, Brazil
Yingruo Fan	The University of Hong Kong, SAR China
Maurizio Fiasché	Polytechnic University of Milan, Italy
Lydia Fischer	Honda Research Institute Europe, Germany
Andreas Fischer	University of Fribourg, Germany
Qinbing Fu	University of Lincoln, UK
Ninnart Fuengfusin	Kyushu Institute of Technology, Japan
Madhukar Rao G.	Indian Institute of Technology, Dhanbad, India
Mauro Gaggero	National Research Council, Genoa, Italy
Claudio Gallicchio	University of Pisa, Italy
Shuai Gao	University of Science and Technology of China, China
Artur Garcez	City University of London, UK
Michael Garcia Ortiz	Aldebaran Robotics, France
Angelo Genovese	University of Milan, Italy
Christos Georgiadis	University of Macedonia, Thessaloniki, Greece
Alexander Gepperth	HAW Fulda, Germany
Peter Gergel'	Comenius University in Bratislava, Slovakia
Daniel Gibert	University of Lleida, Spain
Eleonora Giunchiglia	University of Genoa, Italy
Jan Philip Goepfert	Bielefeld University, Germany
George Gravanis	Democritus University of Thrace, Greece
Ingrid Grenet	University of Côte d'Azur, France
Jiri Grim	Czech Academy of Sciences, Czech Republic
Xiaodong Gu	Fudan University, China
Alberto Guillén	University of Granada, Spain
Tatiana Valentine Guy	Czech Academy of Sciences, Czech Republic
Myrianthi Hadjicharalambous	KIOS Research and Innovation Centre of Excellence, Cyprus
Petr Hajek	University of Pardubice, Czech Republic
Xue Han	China University of Geosciences, China
Liping Han	Nanjing University of Information Science and Technology, China
Wang Haotian	National University of Defense Technology, China
Kazuyuki Hara	Nihon University, Japan
Ioannis Hatzilygeroudis	University of Patras, Greece

Keynote Talks

Cognitive Phase Transitions in the Cerebral Cortex – *John Taylor Memorial Lecture*

Robert Kozma

University of Massachusetts Amherst

Abstract. Everyday subjective experience of the stream of consciousness suggests continuous cognitive processing in time and smooth underlying brain dynamics. Brain monitoring techniques with markedly improved spatio-temporal resolution, however, show that relatively smooth periods in brain dynamics are frequently interrupted by sudden changes and intermittent discontinuities, evidencing singularities. There are frequent transitions between periods of large-scale synchronization and intermittent desynchronization at alpha-theta rates. These observations support the hypothesis about the cinematic model of cognitive processing, according to which higher cognition can be viewed as multiple movies superimposed in time and space. The metastable spatial patterns of field potentials manifest the frames, and the rapid transitions provide the shutter from each pattern to the next. Recent experimental evidence indicates that the observed discontinuities are not merely important aspects of cognition; they are key attributes of intelligent behavior representing the cognitive "Aha" moment of sudden insight and deep understanding in humans and animals. The discontinuities can be characterized as phase transitions in graphs and networks. We introduce computational models to implement these insights in a new generation of devices with robust artificial intelligence, including oscillatory neuromorphic memories, and self-developing autonomous robots.

On the Deep Learning Revolution in Computer Vision

Nathan Netanyahu

Bar-Ilan University, Israel

Abstract. Computer Vision (CV) is an interdisciplinary field of Artificial Intelligence (AI), which is concerned with the embedding of human visual capabilities in a computerized system. The main thrust, essentially, of CV is to generate an "intelligent" high-level description of the world for a given scene, such that when interfaced with other thought processes can elicit, ultimately, appropriate action. In this talk we will review several central CV tasks and traditional approaches taken for handling these tasks for over 50 years. Noting the limited performance of standard methods applied, we briefly survey the evolution of artificial neural networks (ANN) during this extended period, and focus, specifically, on the ongoing revolutionary performance of deep learning (DL) techniques for the above CV tasks during the past few years. In particular, we provide also an overview of our DL activities, in the context of CV, at Bar-Ilan University. Finally, we discuss future research and development challenges in CV in light of further employment of prospective DL innovations.

From Machine Learning to Machine Diagnostics

Marios Polycarpou

University of Cyprus

Abstract. During the last few years, there have has been remarkable progress in utilizing machine learning methods in several applications that benefit from deriving useful patterns among large volumes of data. These advances have attracted significant attention from industry due to the prospective of reducing the cost of predicting future events and making intelligent decisions based on data from past experiences. In this context, a key area that can benefit greatly from the use of machine learning is the task of detecting and diagnosing abnormal behaviour in dynamical systems, especially in safety-critical, large-scale applications. The goal of this presentation is to provide insight into the problem of detecting, isolating and self-correcting abnormal or faulty behaviour in large-scale dynamical systems, to present some design methodologies based on machine learning and to show some illustrative examples. The ultimate goal is to develop the foundation of the concept of machine diagnostics, which would empower smart software algorithms to continuously monitor the health of dynamical systems during the lifetime of their operation.

Multimodal Deep Learning in Biomedical Image Analysis

Sotirios Tsaftaris

University of Edinburgh, UK

Abstract. Nowadays images are typically accompanied by additional information. At the same time, for example, magnetic resonance imaging exams typically contain more than one image modality: they show the same anatomy under different acquisition strategies revealing various pathophysiological information. The detection of disease, segmentation of anatomy and other classical analysis tasks, can benefit from a multimodal view to analysis that leverages shared information across the sources yet preserves unique information. It is without surprise that radiologists analyze data in this fashion, reviewing the exam as a whole. Yet, when aiming to automate analysis tasks, we still treat different image modalities in isolation and tend to ignore additional information. In this talk, I will present recent work in learning with deep neural networks, latent embeddings suitable for multimodal processing, and highlight opportunities and challenges in this area.

Contents – Part I

Spiking

Learning

Classification

Facial/Emotion Recognition

Short Papers

Contents – Part II

Kernel

Reinforcement

Pattern Recognition/Text Mining/Clustering

Optimization/Recommendation

Computational Neuroscience

SOM/SVM

Anomaly Detection/Feature Selection/Autonomous Learning

Signal Detection

Contents – Part III

Deep Learning

Social Media

CNN/Natural Language

Fast CNN Pruning via Redundancy-Aware Training

Xiao Dong[1,2], Lei Liu[1(✉)], Guangli Li[1,2], Peng Zhao[1,2], and Xiaobing Feng[1]

[1] State Key Laboratory of Computer Architecture,
Institute of Computing Technology, Chinese Academy of Sciences,
Beijing 100190, China
[2] University of Chinese Academy of Sciences, Beijing 100049, China
{dongxiao,liulei,liguangli,zhaopeng,fxb}@ict.ac.cn

Abstract. The heavy storage and computational overheads have become a hindrance to the deployment of modern Convolutional Neural Networks (CNNs). To overcome this drawback, many works have been proposed to exploit redundancy within CNNs. However, most of them work as post-training processes. They start from pre-trained dense models and apply compression and extra fine-tuning. The overall process is time-consuming. In this paper, we introduce redundancy-aware training, an approach to learn sparse CNNs from scratch with no need for any post-training compression procedure. In addition to minimizing training loss, redundancy-aware training prunes unimportant weights for sparse structures in the training phase. To ensure stability, a stage-wise pruning procedure is adopted, which is based on carefully designed model partition strategies. Experiment results show redundancy-aware training can compress LeNet-5, ResNet-56 and AlexNet by a factor of $43.8\times$, $7.9\times$ and $6.4\times$, respectively. Compared to state-of-the-art approaches, our method achieves similar or higher sparsity while consuming significantly less time, e.g., $2.3\times$–$18\times$ more efficient in terms of time.

Keywords: In-training pruning · Model compression
Convolutional neural networks · Deep learning

1 Introduction

In recent years, convolutional neural networks (CNNs) have been playing an important role in the remarkable improvements achieved in a wide range of challenging computer vision tasks such as large-scale image classification [11], object detection [3], and segmentation [6]. Deploying CNN models in real-world applications has attracted increasing interests.

However, the state-of-the-art accuracy delivered by these CNNs comes at the cost of significant storage and computational overheads. For instance, AlexNet [11] has 61 million parameters, takes up more than 243 MB of storage and requires 1.4 billion floating point operations to classify a 224×224 image.

© Springer Nature Switzerland AG 2018
V. Kůrková et al. (Eds.): ICANN 2018, LNCS 11139, pp. 3–13, 2018.
https://doi.org/10.1007/978-3-030-01418-6_1

As a result, deploying CNNs on devices with limited resources, such as mobile phones and wearable devices, could be infeasible.

Since large CNNs are highly over-parameterized [2], many methods have been proposed to compress them. Pruning methods have attracted much attention due to its simplicity and effectiveness. However, most of these methods work as post-training processes. Based on dense pre-trained models, unimportant connections and neurons are pruned to reduce the model size and the computational complexity. The following fine-tuning step is responsible for compensating the accuracy loss. The pruning and fine-tuning steps may be repeated several times for a good balance between accuracy and sparsity (the ratio of pruned weights). Some methods introduce sparsity-inducing regularizers to learn sparse structures from a pre-trained dense model. The overall process consumes significant time to get sparse models, resulting in poor time efficiency as summarized in Table 1.

In this paper, we propose *redundancy-aware training*, which can exploit redundancy efficiently by *learning both sparse neural network structures and weight values from scratch*. Besides minimizing training loss, it prunes unimportant connections for sparse structures. Varying structure may bring difficulty in achieving good accuracy. Redundancy-aware training solves this problem by adopting a stage-wise pruning procedure. It leverages novel partition strategies to divide the network into layer classes. The pruning starts from one class in the first stage and extends to the left classes in following stages. Our training method yields sparse and accurate models when it finishes. Evaluations on several datasets, including MNIST, CIFAR10 and ImageNet, demonstrate our redundancy-aware training can achieve state-of-the-art compression results. Meanwhile, our method is much more efficient in terms of time as it requires neither extending normal training iterations nor any post-training compression procedure.

Table 1. Time breakdown of some pruning methods. For post-training methods, we show epochs spent in the training phase (*Training*) and the post-training phase (*Post-Training*). For in-training pruning methods (denoted by ∗), we report the epochs taken by the method (*Training*) and the normal training epochs (*Normal*).

Method	CNN	Dataset	Training	Post-training	Normal
DC [5]	AlexNet	ImageNet	90	>960	
DNS [4]	LeNet-5	MNIST	11	17	
NISP [18]	GoogLeNet	ImageNet	60	60	
LSN∗ [14]	LeNet-5	MNIST	200		11
NSN∗ [10]	ResNet-56	CIFAR10	205		164

2   Related Work

According to whether pre-trained models are required, we divide existing pruning methods into two categories: post-training methods and in-training methods.

Post-training Pruning. Deep compression [5] prunes trained CNNs through a magnitude-based weight pruning method, showing a significant reduction in model size. DNS [4] improves deep compression [5] by allowing the recovery of pruned weights. NISP [18] prunes unimportant neurons based on its neuron importance estimation. SSL [17] makes use of group lasso regularization to remove groups of weights, e.g., channels, filters, and layers, in CNNs. Compression-aware training [1] takes post-training compression into account in the training phase. A regularizer is added to encourage the weights to have lower rank. These methods often suffer from poor time efficiency. Table 1 lists time taken by some pruning methods. We can see the post-training compression procedure takes considerable time. Redundancy-aware training adopts in-training pruning, thus improving the time efficiency significantly.

In-training Pruning. AL [15] introduces binary parameters to prune neurons and layers. A binarizing regularizer is used to attract them to 0 or 1. Similar approach as [15] is adopted to prune weights in [16]. The above two methods only evaluate the *in-training compression ability* on small datasets. Method attempting to use L_0 regularization to directly learn sparse structures is proposed in [14]. To enable gradient-based optimizations, approximation of the non-differentiable L_0 norm is added to the loss. But more training iterations are required (See Table 1). Redundancy-aware training adopts pruning approach to remove redundant weights. By incorporating stage-wise pruning within training process, our method outperforms other in-training pruning works in terms of both compression results and time efficiency.

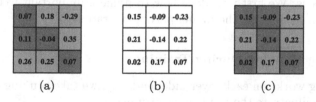

| (a) | (b) | (c) |

Fig. 1. Pruning *(b)* with $u = 0.2$ and $l = 0.1$. Weights marked *red* are pruned. The pruning states of the last iteration and this iteration are shown in *(a)* and *(c)* respectively. (Color figure online)

Algorithm 1. Redundancy-Aware Training

Input: CNN to train *network*
the maximum number of training iterations *max_iterations*
the interval of extending pruning to the next class *extending_interval*
Output: network trained by redundancy-aware training
 1: divide *network* into layer classes based on the partition strategies:
    classes ← {$c_1, c_2, ..., c_m$}
 2: i ← 0
 3: *pruning_classes* ← {}
 4: initialize *network*
 5: **while** $i <$ *max_iterations* **do**
 6:   **if** $mod(i, extending\_interval) = 0$ **then**
 7:     c ← *classes.pop()*
 8:     append c to *pruning_classes*
 9:   **end if**
10:   forward and backward through *network*
11:   update weights in *network*
12:   **for** each class c in *pruning_classes* **do**
13:     **for** each layer l in c **do**
14:       pruning layer l
15:     **end for**
16:   **end for**
17:   i ← $i + 1$
18: **end while**

---

3   Redundancy-Aware Training

In this section, we introduce our redundancy-aware training method. The overview of the proposed method is displayed in Algorithm 1. For a given CNN, redundancy-aware training first divides it into layer classes based on the partition strategies. In each training iteration, it prunes layers in *pruning_classes* after the update of weights. More classes will be appended into the *pruning_classes* as training proceeds. We first introduce how to prune unimportant weights during training. Then, we present the model partition strategies.

3.1   Pruning Weights During Training

As the pruning works on each layer independently, we take pruning one layer as an example to illustrate the in-training pruning.

Let us denote the parameters of a layer by K. Redundancy-aware training adopts a magnitude-based pruning approach. Specifically, two thresholds u and l are introduced. In each iteration, weights with absolute value below l are pruned, while others with magnitude above u are kept. Weights with absolute value in the range of $[l, u]$ are skipped in this iteration and their pruning states stay unchanged. To reduce the risk of pruning important weights wrongly, we use the update scheme in [4] where pruned weights can also be updated in the back-propagation. This scheme enables the recovery of wrongly pruned weights. Figure 1 shows an example.

To avoid tuning u and l for each layer manually, we choose to compute them based on K as shown in Eq. 1. μ and σ represent the mean and the standard variation of K, respectively. Two hype-parameters $range$ and ϵ are introduced to provide more flexibility. Increasing $range$ will make l larger, resulting in pruning more weights from network. ϵ is a small positive value and controls the difference between u and l. We analyze how μ and σ influence the compression results in Sect. 4.2.

$$u = max(\mu + \sigma(range + \epsilon), 0)$$
$$l = max(\mu + \sigma(range - \epsilon), 0). \tag{1}$$

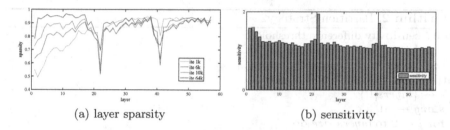

| (a) layer sparsity | (b) sensitivity |

Fig. 2. Sparsity and sensitivity of layers in ResNet-56. The shapes of sparsity lines of different training time are quite similar, indicating the difference of sparsity between layers stays stable during training. Based on the sensitivity, ResNet-56 is divided into three classes as shown by the black vertical lines in *(b)*.

3.2   Model Partition

In-training pruning allows learning sparse structures during the training phase. However, pruning all layers in network simultaneously causes instability and slows down the learning process, resulting in difficulty in reaching as good accuracy as the normal training.

Redundancy-aware training adopts a stage-wise pruning procedure. The pruning scope in each stage is orchestrated by our model partition strategies. When layers within the pruning scope are being pruned, the left layers can adapt to it and alleviate the impact through updating their weight values. Formally, we call the unit of adjusting the pruning scope 'class'. A class contains several consecutive layers. Based on our model partition strategies, redundancy-aware training divides the CNN into classes. Then, the in-training pruning starts from the first class and extends to one more class at the beginning of each of the following stages. Both layer by layer pruning and pruning all layers together are special cases of our approach.

Partition Strategy. We propose two heuristic strategies for two different types of CNN. The first type is called simple CNN, which refers to networks composed of stacked convolution layers and several fully-connected layers. LeNet-5 [12] and AlexNet [11] fall into this category. For simple CNN, the partition strategy is:

Strategy1: Layers with the same type are divided into the same class.

Thus, simple CNNs will be divided into two classes. The first class contains convolution layers and fully-connected layers belong to the second class. Strategy1 is not applicable to recently designed CNNs, which tend to avoid using fully-connected layers. For example, ResNet [7] has only one fully-connected layer to produce the possibilities over given number of classes. Inspired by [13] which prunes filters based on the analysis of layer sensitivity to pruning, we propose the second strategy for these CNNs:

Algorithm 2. Partition Strategy2

Input: sensitivity difference threshold δ
         layers' sensitivity to pruning $s[...]$
         layers in given network $layers[...]$
Output: the partition result of network
1: $c \leftarrow \{layers[1]\}$
2: $s\_avg \leftarrow s[1]$
3: **for** $l \leftarrow 2$ **to** $layers.size$ **do**
4:     $diff \leftarrow abs(s[l] - s\_avg)$
5:     **if** $diff > \delta$ **then**
6:        set c a new partition class
7:     **end if**
8:     add $layers[l]$ to c
9:     update s_avg to the average sensitivity of layers in c
10: **end for**

Strategy2: Divide model at layers which are quite sensitive to pruning.

Algorithm 2 illustrates how this strategy works. The sensitivity to pruning is determined through our proposed 'probe' phase which is described in the next section. We also analyze the impact of δ in Sect. 4.2.

Determine Layer's Sensitivity Efficiently. The in-training pruning zeros out unimportant weights. Layers with relatively low sparsity should be important and sensitive to pruning. *Thus, we define layer's sensitivity as the reciprocal of its sparsity achieved by the in-training pruning.* A naive but inefficient approach to determine the sensitivity works as follows. We train the CNN with all layers under in-training pruning and use the layer's sparsity after training to compute the sensitivity. Based on a key observation, we propose a more efficient approach. Figure 2a shows the sparsity of ResNet-56 at different time of training. The relative sparsity between layers is actually quite stable in training. As the partition result only depends on the difference of sparsity between layers, we can use the sparsity at early training time to obtain the partition result.

More precisely, we introduce a probe phase where the CNN is trained with all layers under the in-training pruning. When the probe phase finishes, we compute layer's sensitivity based on its sparsity, which is then used by the strategy2. In our experiments, we find tenth of the training time is sufficient for the probe phase. Figure 2b shows the sensitivity of layers in ResNet-56. It's noticeable that layers of residual blocks where the number of output channels changes are sensitive to pruning. This discovery is consistent with the results reported in [13].

Table 2. Comparison to other compression works. Results of our method are denoted by *RA-range-ε*. The result of *DC* for ResNet-56 is provided in [10]. The result of *PF* is based on our implementation. The *scratch-train* models show notable accuracy drops, demonstrating the difficulty of training a sparse network from scratch.

Network	In-training methods	Baseline accuracy	Accuracy change	Sparsity	Post-training methods	Baseline accuracy	Accuracy change	Sparsity
LeNet-5	LNA [15]	99.3%	−0.23%	90.5%	SSL [17]	99.1%	−0.1%	75.1%
	LSN [14]	99.1%	0	90.7%	DC [5]	99.2%	+0.03%	92%
	TSNN [16]	99.2%	−0.01%	95.8%	DNS [4]	99.1%	0	99.91%
	RA-2-0.1	99.1%	0	**97.7%**	Scratch-train	99.1%	−1.5%	97.7%
ResNet-56	NCP [10]	93.4%	−0.5%	50%	CP [8]	92.8%	−1.0%	50%
	NWP [10]	93.4%	−0.6%	66.7%	PF [13]	92.4%	−1.04%	62%
	RA-1.8-0.1	92.4%	−0.1%	**87.4%**	DC [5]	93.4%	−0.8%	66.7%
	RA-3.0-0.1	92.4%	−1.0%	**92.1%**	Scratch-train	92.4%	−2.8%	87.4%

4   Evaluation

In this section, we evaluate redundancy-aware training on MNIST, CIFAR10, and ImageNet with LeNet-5, ResNet-56, and AlexNet, respectively. First, we compare the compression result and the time efficiency with state-of-the-art compression methods. The compression result includes achieved sparsity and accuracy loss. Sparsity is defined as the percentage of the zeroed out weights. We compare the time efficiency based on the number of iterations or epochs required to obtain sparse models. Then, we analyze the effectiveness of the model partition and the effect of hyper-parameters in Sect. 4.2. We implement our method in Caffe [9].

4.1   Compression Result and Time Efficiency

The comparison to other methods on LeNet-5 and ResNet-56 is summarized in Table 2. We also train models with the same sparsity as the models trained through redundancy-aware training from scratch (the *scratch-train*).

LeNet-5. Redundancy-aware training reduces the model size of LeNet-5 by
43.8× without accuracy loss and outperforms all in-training methods by a
notable margin, validating its ability to reduce redundancy in the training phase.
Compared to post-training methods, redundancy-aware training achieves higher
or similar sparsity. Our method prunes more weights in every layer than [14]
and [5]. As for time efficiency, our method only takes 11 epochs which is equal
to the normal training time and is about 18× more efficient than the in-training
method in [14] and 2.5× more efficient than the method in [4].

ResNet-56. Based on the strategy2 in Sect. 3.2, ResNet-56 is divided into
three classes. We extend the in-training pruning at 10k and 20k iterations.
Redundancy-aware training achieves a 7.9× reduction with only 0.1% top-1
accuracy drop. Importantly, our method achieves this without any post-training
procedures. By using a larger *range*, we can achieve a 12.6× compression at the
cost of 1.13% accuracy loss, which can be reduced to 1% after a fine-tuning of 20k
iterations. As far as we know, our method achieves state-of-the-art compression
result for ResNet-56. In terms of time-efficiency, our method takes 70k iterations
(64k for training and 6k for the probe phase), which is about 2.3× more efficient
than NWP in [10] and PF in [13].

Table 3. Layer-by-layer comparison to deep compression on AlexNet.

Method/layer	conv1	conv2	conv3	conv4	conv5	fc1	fc2	fc3	Total
DC	16%	62%	65%	63%	63%	91%	91%	75%	89%
Ours	31%	65%	69%	63%	61%	88%	81%	80%	84%

AlexNet. Finally, we experiment with AlexNet on ImageNet. We train the
bvlc_alexnet in Caffe and get 78.65% top-5 accuracy on validation dataset with
single-view testing. Redundancy-aware training reduces the model size by 6.4×
with 0.36% accuracy loss. We further fine-tune it for 45k iterations and obtain a
model with 78.54% accuracy. We display sparsity achieved by our method and
DC [5] in Table 3. Our method takes 99 epochs in total, which is 9.69× more
efficient in terms of time.

4.2   Ablation Study

Hyper-parameter Sensitivity. We make use of ResNet-56 to measure the
impact of varying *range* and ϵ. The result is shown in Fig. 3.

Increasing *range* leads to larger l and more weights will be pruned in training.
Thus we can make trade-offs between the sparsity and the accuracy through
adjusting *range*. Note the accuracy does not drop dramatically (2.2% drop)
when *range* increases from 0 to 3.5. Since increasing ϵ makes l smaller, weights

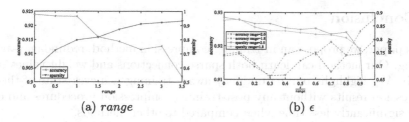

(a) *range*   (b) ϵ

Fig. 3. Impact of hyper-parameters *range* and ϵ. The model is divided into three partition classes.

are less likely to be pruned and the sparsity decreases. We can observe that the accuracy does not change drastically for a wide range of ϵ.

Table 4. Accuracy with varying δ.

δ	+∞	0.5 * s_avg	0.4 * s_avg	0.3 * s_avg
# partition classes	1	2	3	5
Accuracy	91.3%	91.7%	92.3%	90.2%

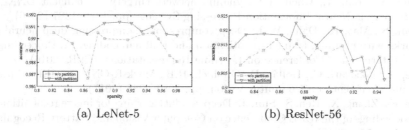

(a) LeNet-5   (b) ResNet-56

Fig. 4. Effect of partition with varying *range*s.

Effectiveness of Partition Strategies. We first analyze the impact on accuracy with different number of partition classes. To this end, we fix *range* = 1.8 and ϵ = 0.1 and vary δ to change the partition result. Results are shown in Table 4. When δ is set to +∞, all layers belong to the same class and the network is pruned all through the training phase, which shows a 1.1% accuracy drop. Dividing ResNet-56 into two or three classes improves accuracy. The model with five classes has inferior accuracy, implicating too many classes result in insufficient training iterations in each stage.

We also verify the effectiveness of model partition with varying *range*s. Results are shown in Fig. 4. The model partition helps to improve accuracy over a wide scope of *range*s, confirming the benefit of our model partition approach in stabilizing training and helping in good convergence.

5   Conclusion

In this paper, we propose an in-training compression method, redundancy-aware training. Our method can learn both sparse connections and weight values from scratch. We highlight our redundancy-aware training achieves state-of-the-art compression results without any post-training compression procedures and consumes significantly less time when compared to other methods.

Acknowledgments. This work is supported by National Key R&D Program of China under Grant No. 2017YFB0202002, Science Fund for Creative Research Groups of the National Natural Science Foundation of China under Grant No. 61521092 and the Key Program of National Natural Science Foundation of China under Grant Nos. 61432018, 61332009, U1736208.

References

1. Alvarez, J.M., Salzmann, M.: Compression-aware training of deep networks. In: Advances in Neural Information Processing Systems, pp. 856–867 (2017)
2. Denil, M., Shakibi, B., Dinh, L., de Freitas, N., et al.: Predicting parameters in deep learning. In: Advances in Neural Information Processing Systems, pp. 2148–2156 (2013)
3. Girshick, R.B.: Fast R-CNN. In: 2015 IEEE International Conference on Computer Vision, ICCV 2015, Santiago, Chile, 7–13 December 2015, pp. 1440–1448 (2015)
4. Guo, Y., Yao, A., Chen, Y.: Dynamic network surgery for efficient DNNs. In: Advances in Neural Information Processing Systems, pp. 1379–1387 (2016)
5. Han, S., Mao, H., Dally, W.J.: Deep compression: Compressing deep neural networks with pruning, trained quantization and Huffman coding. In: Proceedings of the International Conference on Learning Representations, ICLR (2016)
6. He, K., Gkioxari, G., Dollár, P., Girshick, R.B.: Mask R-CNN. In: IEEE International Conference on Computer Vision, pp. 2980–2988 (2017)
7. He, K., Zhang, X., Ren, S., Sun, J.: Deep residual learning for image recognition. In: Proceedings of the IEEE Conference on Computer Vision and Pattern Recognition, pp. 770–778 (2016)
8. He, Y., Zhang, X., Sun, J.: Channel pruning for accelerating very deep neural networks. In: Proceedings of the IEEE Conference on Computer Vision and Pattern Recognition, pp. 1389–1397 (2017)
9. Jia, Y., et al.: Caffe: convolutional architecture for fast feature embedding. In: Proceedings of the 22nd ACM International Conference on Multimedia, pp. 675–678. ACM (2014)
10. Kim, E., Ahn, C., Oh, S.: Learning nested sparse structures in deep neural networks. arXiv preprint arXiv:1712.03781 (2017)
11. Krizhevsky, A., Sutskever, I., Hinton, G.E.: ImageNet classification with deep convolutional neural networks. In: Advances in Neural Information Processing Systems, pp. 1097–1105 (2012)
12. LeCun, Y., Bottou, L., Bengio, Y., Haffner, P.: Gradient-based learning applied to document recognition. Proc. IEEE **86**(11), 2278–2324 (1998)
13. Li, H., Kadav, A., Durdanovic, I., Samet, H., Graf, H.P.: Pruning filters for efficient ConvNets. In: Proceedings of the International Conference on Learning Representations, ICLR (2017)

14. Louizos, C., Welling, M., Kingma, D.P.: Learning sparse neural networks through l_0 regularization. In: Proceedings of the International Conference on Learning Representations, ICLR (2018)
15. Srinivas, S., Babu, R.V.: Learning neural network architectures using backpropagation. In: Proceedings of the British Machine Vision Conference. BMVA Press (2016)
16. Srinivas, S., Subramanya, A., Babu, R.V.: Training sparse neural networks. In: 2017 IEEE Conference on Computer Vision and Pattern Recognition Workshops, CVPR Workshops, pp. 455–462 (2017)
17. Wen, W., Wu, C., Wang, Y., Chen, Y., Li, H.: Learning structured sparsity in deep neural networks. In: Advances in Neural Information Processing Systems, pp. 2074–2082 (2016)
18. Yu, R., et al.: NISP: pruning networks using neuron importance score propagation. arXiv preprint arXiv:1711.05908 (2017)

Two-Stream Convolutional Neural Network for Multimodal Matching

Youcai Zhang, Yiwei Gu, and Xiaodong Gu$^{(\boxtimes)}$

Department of Electronic Engineering, Fudan University, Shanghai 200433, China
xdgu@fudan.edu.cn

Abstract. Mulitimudal matching aims to establish relationship across different modalities such as image and text. Existing works mainly focus on maximizing the correlation between feature vectors extracted from the off-the-shelf models. The feature extraction and the matching are two-stage learning process. This paper presents a novel two-stream convolutional neural network that integrates the feature extraction and the matching under an end-to-end manner. Visual and textual stream are designed for feature extraction and then are concatenated with multiple shared layers for multimodal matching. The network is trained using an extreme multiclass classification loss by viewing each multimodal data as a class. Then a finetuning step is performed by a ranking constraint. Experimental results on Flickr30k datasets demonstrate the effectiveness of the proposed network for multimodal matching.

Keywords: Multimodal matching · Two-stream network
Convolutional neural network

1 Introduction

Multimodal analysis has received ever-increasing research focus due to the explosive growth of multimodal data such as image, text, video and audio. A core problem for multimodal analysis is to mine the internal correlation across different modalities. In this paper, we focus on the image-text matching. For example, given a query image, our aim is to retrieve the relevant texts in the database that best illustrate the image. There are two major challenges in multimodal matching: (1) effectively extracting the feature from the multimodal data; (2) inherently correlating the feature across different modalities.

Previous works for multimodal matching prefered to adopt off-the-shelf models to extract the features rather than learn modality-specific features. For the image, some well-known hand-crafted feature extraction techniques such as SIFT [1], GIST [2] were widely used. Inspired by recent breakthroughs of convolutional neural network (CNN) in visual recognition, CNN visual features were also introduced to multimodal matching [14]. For the text, latent Dirichlet allocation (LDA) [3] and *word2vec* [18] models were two typical choices for vectorization. Despite their contributions to the multimodal matching, off-the-shelf

V. Kůrková et al. (Eds.): ICANN 2018, LNCS 11139, pp. 14–21, 2018.
https://doi.org/10.1007/978-3-030-01418-6_2

models suffer from some weaknesses. They are not specific designed for the task of multimodal matching. That is, these features are not discriminative enough, which limits the final matching performance.

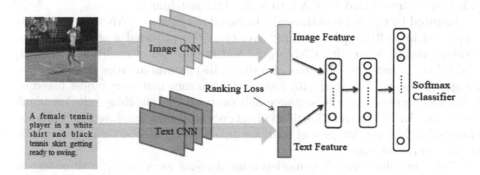

Fig. 1. Overview of the proposed two-stream convolutional neural network.

Another challenge is to correlate these multimodal features. Most deep learning based methods [4,5] are highly dependent on the categorical information for network training. However, such high-level semantic information is absent in most scenarios and requires much manual labels. Furthermore, the explosive increase of data makes it unrealistic to label each data with a certain category. Luckily, co-occurred data usually delivers correlated information (i.e. image-text pair information). The pair information is relatively easy to be obtained via the web crawler and should be fully explored for multimodal matching.

To address above issues, we propose a novel two-stream convolutional neural network as shown in Fig. 1, which extracts visual and textual representations and simultaneously performs the task of multimodal matching. Thus the similarity between images and texts can be measured directly according to the learned representations. More specifically, CNN is the backbone to extract the feature from the raw images and texts respectively. The outputs of the two stream are concatenated and followed by several shared fully connected layers. The final output of the network is the class probabilities after a softmax regression. To train the network, we adopt an extreme multiclass classification loss and a ranking loss both based on the pair information.

The remainder of this paper is structured as follows. Section 2 reviews the related work. Section 3 presents our two-stream network for multimodal matching and its learning process, followed by experimental results in Sect. 4. Section 5 draws an overall conclusion.

2   Related Work

The core issue for multimodal matching is to learn discriminative and joint image-text representations. Canonical correlation analysis (CCA) [7] and cross-modal factor analysis (CFA) [8] were two classic methods. They linearly projected vectors from the two views into a shared correlation maximum space. Andrew *et al.* proposed deep CCA [12] to learn the nonlinear transformation through two deep networks, whose outputs are maximally correlated. Yan *et al.* [13] further introduced DCCA into image-text matching.

Inspired by recent breakthroughs in visual recognition, CNN was also widely employed in multimodal matching. Wei *et al.* [14] provided a new baseline for cross-modal retrieval with CNN visual features instead of traditional SIFT [1] and GIST [2] features. CNN has also shown its powerful abilities in natural language processing. Hu *et al.* [10] proposed a sentence matching model based on CNN that represented the sentence and captured the matching relation simultaneously. In [9], convolutional architectures were first employed to learn the correlation between image and sentence by encoding their separate representations into a joint one.

There are also some deep models related to our work. In [6], a three-stream deep convolutional network was proposed to generate a shared representation across image, text, and sound modality. Wang *et al.* [15] presented a two-branch network to learn the image-text joint embedding. The network was trained by an extended ranking constraint and only received the input of feature vectors. Mao *et al.* [16] proposed a multimodal Recurrent Neural Network (m-RNN) model for image captioning and cross-modal retrieval. [17] presented a selective multimodal network that incorporated attention and recurrent selection mechanism based on long short term memory.

3   Two-Stream CNN

3.1   Network Architecture

Overall Architecture. As exhibited in Fig. 1, the overall architecture of the proposed network contains two parts. The color part with two streams focuses on the feature extraction from the raw image and text. The gray one integrates the feature vectors from different modalities with shared weights and fully connected layers for further multimodal matching. In general, to generate a joint representation, the color part is specific to modality but gray one is shared across modalities.

Image Stream. We adopt a 50-layer ResNet model [11] pretrained on ImageNet classification tasks as the visual CNN. We discard the top fully connected layer designed for ImageNet. Thus, given a raw image resized to 224×224, a 2048-*dim* vector considered as the image representation is produced by the model after average pooling.

Text Stream. Since each image can be represented by a fixed-length vector with CNN, we also design a textual CNN with three convolutional layers to vectorize the text as shown in Fig. 2. Text is first encoded into a $1 \times n \times d$

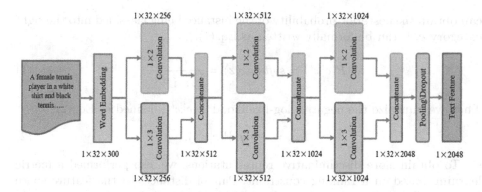

Fig. 2. Overview of the textual CNN stream.

numerical matrix $\mathbf{T}$, where n is the length of the sentence and d is the size of the vocabulary. The vocabulary contains all tokens appeared in the corpus. Let w_i be the i-th word in the vocabulary, thus w_i can be converted into a one-hot high-dimensional sparse vector $\mathbf{v_i}$ where the i-th element is set to be 1 and rests to be 0. Then the embedding layer turns each $\mathbf{v_i}$ into a low-dimensional dense word embedding $\mathbf{e_i}$ with the length of k via a lookup table. Thus, each sentence is encoded into a $1 \times n \times k$ matrix.

Though embedding layer encodes the semantic information of each word into vectors, simply concatenating word vectors ignores many subtleties of a possible good representation, e.g. consideration of word ordering. Therefore, following convolutional layers are employed to extract the word sequence information of the words. In each convolutional layer, the context in the sentence is modeled using two convolution kernels of size 1×2 and 1×3, respectively. And the outputs of two convolutional operations are concatenated directly, fed into following layers. At the end of network, a pooling layer with dropout is used to produce final output, which matches the size of image features. Convolutional layers combined with word embedding ensure that the output feature contains most necessary information to effectively represent sentences for further multimodal matching.

3.2 Network Learning

Objective Function. Supervised semantic labels usually play an important role in deep neural network learning. However, the lack of labels poses a unique challenge to multimodal matching: how to effectively utilize the only image-text pair information. In this paper, we transform the multimodal matching into an extreme multiclass classification task where the matching becomes accurately classifying a specific data among tens of thousands classes. Here, each multimodal document including an image and corresponding text is viewed as a pseudo class. Given an instance x^i, we apply the *softmax function* to the output of the network $\mathbf{z} \in \Re^{1 \times n}$ (n is the number of multimodal document). Thus, we can obtain the posterior probability of the instance being classified into the right category c. It can be formally written as Eq. (1).

$$P(c|x^i) = softmax(\mathbf{z}) = \frac{e^{\mathbf{z}_c}}{\sum_{j=1}^{n} e^{\mathbf{z}_j}}. \tag{1}$$

Then we minimize the negative log-likelihood $P(c|x^i)$, defined as Eq. (2).

$$L_{cls} = -log(P(c|x^i)). \tag{2}$$

To obtain more discriminative representations, we also performed a metric learning based on a ranking constraint. Pair of distances in the feature space between x^p and x^n against the anchor x^a should be pulled apart up to a margin α ($\alpha = 0.1$ in our case) as $d(x^a, x^p) + \alpha < d(x^a, x^n)$. Instances sharing the same pseudo class with x^a are defined as x^p, otherwise, x^n. We compute the cosine distance between the feature vectors $(\mathbf{v}_i, \mathbf{v}_j)$ of two instances (x^i, x^j) as $d(x^i, x^j) = 1 - \frac{\mathbf{v}_i \cdot \mathbf{v}_j}{\|\mathbf{v}_i\|_2 \|\mathbf{v}_j\|_2}$. We further define the bi-directional ranking constraint with a hinge loss for the given image reference $(x_{img}^a, x_{txt}^p, x_{txt}^n)$ and the text reference $(x_{txt}^a, x_{img}^p, x_{img}^n)$ respectively as Eq. (3).

$$L_{rank} = max\{0, d(x_{img}^a, x_{txt}^p) - d(x_{img}^a, x_{txt}^n) + \alpha\} \\ +max\{0, d(x_{txt}^a, x_{img}^p) - d(x_{txt}^a, x_{img}^n) + \alpha\}. \tag{3}$$

The final objective function is a weighted combination of the classification loss and ranking loss as Eq. (4).

$$L = \lambda_1 L_{cls} + \lambda_2 L_{rank}. \tag{4}$$

Training Scheme. Network training is done in three steps. Firstly, we fix the image stream and train the remaining part using the classification loss ($\lambda_2 = 0$, only text data is used). The reason behind is that pre-trained weights on Imagenet can be used for image stream but weights of the remaining part have to be learned from scratch. Secondly, we update the weights of the entire network after step 1 converges ($\lambda_2 = 0$, both text and image data are used). Considering that ranking loss usually converges very slowly or even does not converge especially in two-stream network learning, we fine-tune the entire network using the combination of the classification loss and ranking loss ($\lambda_1 = 1, \lambda_2 = 1$) only in the last step.

4   Experiment

4.1   Datasets and Evaluation Metrics

We choose widely-used Flickr30k [19] for experiments. Flickr30k contains 31,783 images collected from website Flickr. Each image is described with five sentences. We follow the partition scheme in [16,17], where 29,783, 1,000, and 1,000 images are used for training, validation, and test respectively. $R@k$ and $Med\ r$ are adopted as evaluation metrics. $R@k$ is the average recall rate over all queries in the test set. Specifically, given a query, the recall rate will be 1 if at least one ground truth occurs in the $top\text{-}k$ returned results and 0 otherwise. $Med\ r$ is the median rank of the closest ground truth in the ranking list.

4.2   Implementation Details

For Flickr30k, the vocabulary size d is 20,074, and each word is encoded into a $300\text{-}dim$ dense vector. To ensure that each input sentence has the same length of 32, we use 0 vectors as paddings for those short sentences. And we use the pre-trained vectors of the $word2vec$ [18] model to initialize our embedding layer. The network is optimized by backpropagation and mini-batch stochastic gradient descent with the momentum fixed to 0.9. For the three training steps, learning rate is set to 0.001. 0.0001 and 0.00005 respectively. The maximum epochs are set to 180, 60 and 20 accordingly. In our experiments, we observe convergence within 150, 30, 10 epochs.

4.3   Experimental Results

We consider two basic multimodal tasks: Img2Txt (an image query to retrieve texts) and Txt2Img (a text query to retrieve images). Table 1 presents the experimental results of different methods in terms of $R@k$ and $Med\ r$. The proposed network outperforms other methods in the Img2Txt task with the highest $R@1$ of 48.4%. In the Txt2Img task, $R@1$ obtained by our method is only 0.7% lower than the best method RBF-Net [20]. The results indicate that the learned features are effective for multimodal matching. The superiority of our network can be explained by the following two aspects: (1) We simultaneously perform feature extraction and multimodal matching. Compared with off-the-Shelf models, the learned features are more targeted for the matching task instead of previous generic representations; (2) We fully explore the image-text pair information via the classification and ranking loss to generate more discriminative representations.

We also conduct experiments to analyze the effect of the training scheme. Step 1 only trains the text stream using the classification loss and directly adopts the image features extracted from pre-trained ResNet-50. Step2 trains the entire network using the classification loss, which encourages instance from the same document to fall into one category. Thus, results obtained from step 2 gains a great increase of about 10%, 6% on $R@1$ in the bidirectional retrieval respectively. Step 3 combines ranking constraints to further finetune the network, which provides a higher performance for the final model.

Another issue to be noticed is that the improvement brought by step 2 is not as impressive as that by step 3. On the one hand, that illustrates the effectiveness of posing multimodal matching as a classification problem. On the other hand, considering the effectiveness of ranking loss in previous works, there could be space for improvement in our network especially the weakness of $R@5$ and $R@10$.

Table 1. Bidirectional image and text retrieval results on Flickr30K.

Methods	Img2Txt				Txt2Img			
	R@1	R@5	R@10	Med r	R@1	R@5	R@10	Med r
DCCA [13]	16.7	39.3	52.9	8	12.6	31.0	43.0	15
m-CNN [9]	33.6	64.1	74.9	3	26.2	56.3	69.6	4
m-RNN [16]	35.4	63.8	73.7	3	22.8	50.7	63.1	5
2-branch [15]	40.3	68.9	79.9	-	29.7	60.1	72.1	-
sm-LSTM [17]	42.5	71.9	81.5	2	30.2	60.4	72.3	3
RBF-Net [20]	47.6	**77.4**	**87.1**	-	**35.4**	**68.3**	**79.9**	-
Ours (step 1)	38.4	68.4	79.3	2	28.4	56.1	68.2	4
Ours (step 2)	46.8	75.7	85.6	2	33.5	63.0	74.9	3
Ours (step 3)	**48.4**	77.2	85.9	2	34.7	64.9	76.4	3

Ranking loss requires a careful triplet sampling strategy from the extremely unbalanced positive and negative ones, which points out the direction of our future work.

5 Conclusion

This paper mainly addresses the issue of multimodal matching via a novel two-stream convolutional neural network. The proposed network can extract the features from the raw image and text. To guarantee the features shared between different modalities, a classifier and ranking constraint are adopted for network learning by utilizing the pair information. Experimental results on Flickr30k datasets demonstrate the effectiveness of viewing each multimodal document as a discrete class. For further research, the ranking constraint will be polished to perform a more effective metric learning. Also, more detailed experiments on the Microsoft COCO datasets will be conducted to further validate the validity of our network.

Acknowledgments. This work was supported by the National Natural Science Foundation of China under Grants No. 61771145 and No. 61371148.

References

1. Lowe, D.G.: Distinctive image features from scale-invariant keypoints. Int. J. Comput. Vis. **60**(2), 91–110 (2004)
2. Oliva, A., Torralba, A.: Modeling the shape of the scene: a holistic representation of the spatial envelope. Int. J. Comput. Vis. **42**(3), 145–175 (2001)
3. Blei, D.M., Ng, A.Y., Jordan, M.I.: Latent Dirichlet allocation. J. Mach. Learn. Res. **3**, 993–1022 (2003)

4. Wang, B., Yang, Y., Xu, X., Hanjalic, A., Shen, H. T.: Adversarial cross-modal retrieval. In: ACM International Conference on Multimedia Conference, pp. 154–162 (2017)
5. Huang, X., Peng, Y.: Cross-modal deep metric learning with multi-task regularization. In: IEEE International Conference on Multimedia and Expo, pp. 943–948 (2017)
6. Aytar, Y., Vondrick, C., Torralba, A.: See, hear, and read: deep aligned representations. arXiv preprint arXiv:1706.00932 (2017)
7. Hardoon, D.R., Szedmak, S., Shawe-Taylor, J.: Canonical correlation analysis: an overview with application to learning methods. Neural Comput. 16(12), 2639–2664 (2004)
8. Li, D., Dimitrova, N., Li, M., Sethi, I.K.: Multimedia content processing through cross-modal association. In: ACM International Conference on Multimedia, pp. 604–611 (2003)
9. Ma, L., Lu, Z., Shang, L., Li, H.: Multimodal convolutional neural networks for matching image and sentence. In: IEEE International Conference on Computer Vision, pp. 2623–2631 (2015)
10. Hu, B., Lu, Z., Li, H., Chen, Q.: Convolutional neural network architectures for matching natural language sentences. In: Advances in Neural Information Processing Systems, pp. 2042–2050 (2014)
11. He, K., Zhang, X., Ren, S., Sun, J.: Deep residual learning for image recognition. In: IEEE Conference on Computer Vision and Pattern Recognition, pp. 770–778 (2016)
12. Andrew, G., Arora, R., Bilmes, J., Livescu, K.: Deep canonical correlation analysis. In: International Conference on Machine Learning, pp. 1247–1255 (2013)
13. Yan, F., Mikolajczyk, K.: Deep correlation for matching images and text. In: IEEE Conference on Computer Vision and Pattern Recognition, pp. 3441–3450 (2015)
14. Wei, Y., et al.: Cross-modal retrieval with CNN visual features: a new baseline. IEEE Trans. Cybern. 47(2), 449–460 (2017)
15. Wang, L., Li, Y., Lazebnik, S.: Learning deep structure-preserving image-text embeddings. In: IEEE Conference on Computer Vision and Pattern Recognition, pp. 5005–5013 (2016)
16. Mao, J., Xu, W., Yang, Y., Wang, J., Huang, Z., Yuille, A.: Deep captioning with multimodal recurrent neural networks (m-RNN). arXiv preprint arXiv:1412.6632 (2014)
17. Huang, Y., Wang, W., Wang, L.: Instance-aware image and sentence matching with selective multimodal LSTM. In: IEEE Conference on Computer Vision and Pattern Recognition, pp. 2310–2318 (2017)
18. Mikolov, T., Sutskever, I., Chen, K., Corrado, G.S., Dean, J.: Distributed representations of words and phrases and their compositionality. In: Advances in Neural Information Processing Systems, pp. 3111–3119 (2013)
19. Plummer, B.A., Wang, L., Cervantes, C.M., Caicedo, J.C., Hockenmaier, J., Lazebnik, S.: Flickr30k entities: collecting region-to-phrase correspondences for Richer image-to-sentence models. In: IEEE International Conference on Computer Vision, pp. 2641–2649 (2015)
20. Liu, Y., Guo, Y., Bakker, E.M., Lew, M.S.: Learning a recurrent residual fusion network for multimodal matching. In: IEEE Conference on Computer Vision and Pattern Recognition, pp. 4107–4116 (2017)

Kernel Graph Convolutional Neural Networks

Giannis Nikolentzos[1]([✉]), Polykarpos Meladianos[2], Antoine Jean-Pierre Tixier[1], Konstantinos Skianis[1], and Michalis Vazirgiannis[1,2]

[1] École Polytechnique, Palaiseau, France
{nikolentzos,anti5662,kskianis,mvazirg}@lix.polytechnique.fr
[2] Athens University of Economics and Business, Athens, Greece
pmeladianos@aueb.gr

Abstract. Graph kernels have been successfully applied to many graph classification problems. Typically, a kernel is first designed, and then an SVM classifier is trained based on the features defined implicitly by this kernel. This two-stage approach decouples data representation from learning, which is suboptimal. On the other hand, Convolutional Neural Networks (CNNs) have the capability to learn their own features directly from the raw data during training. Unfortunately, they cannot handle irregular data such as graphs. We address this challenge by using graph kernels to embed meaningful local neighborhoods of the graphs in a continuous vector space. A set of filters is then convolved with these patches, pooled, and the output is then passed to a feedforward network. With limited parameter tuning, our approach outperforms strong baselines on 7 out of 10 benchmark datasets. Code and data are publicly available (https://github.com/giannisnik/cnn-graph-classification).

1 Introduction

Graphs are powerful structures that can be used to model almost any kind of data. Social networks, textual documents, the World Wide Web, chemical compounds, and protein-protein interaction networks, are all examples of data that are commonly represented as graphs. As such, graph classification is a very important task, with numerous significant real-world applications. However, due to the absence of a unified, standard vector representation of graphs, graph classification cannot be tackled with classical machine learning algorithms.

Kernel methods offer a solution to those cases where instances cannot be readily vectorized. The trick is to define a suitable object-object similarity function (known as a kernel function). Then, the matrix of pairwise similarities can be passed to a kernel-based supervised algorithm such as the Support Vector Machine to perform classification. With properly crafted kernels, this two-step approach was shown to give state-of-the-art results on many datasets [12], and has become standard and widely used. One major limitation of the graph kernel + SVM approach, though, is that representation and learning are two *independent* steps. In other words, the features are precomputed in separation from the training phase, and are not optimized for the downstream task.

© Springer Nature Switzerland AG 2018
V. Kůrková et al. (Eds.): ICANN 2018, LNCS 11139, pp. 22–32, 2018.
https://doi.org/10.1007/978-3-030-01418-6_3

Conversely, Convolutional Neural Networks (CNNs) learn their own features from the raw data during training, to maximize performance on the task at hand. CNNs thus provide a very attractive alternative to the aforementioned two-step approach. However, CNNs are designed to work on regular grids, and thus cannot process graphs.

We propose to address this challenge by extracting patches from each input graph via community detection, and by embedding these patches with graph kernels. The patch vectors are then convolved with the filters of a 1D CNN and pooling is applied. Finally, to perform graph classification, a fully-connected layer with a softmax completes the architecture. We compare our proposed method with state-of-the-art graph kernels and a recently introduced neural architecture on 10 bioinformatics and social network datasets. Results show that our Kernel CNN model is very competitive, and offers in many cases significant accuracy gains.

2   Related Work

Graph Kernels. A graph kernel is a kernel function defined on pairs of graphs. Graph kernels can be viewed as graph similarity functions, and currently serve as the dominant tool for graph classification. Most graph kernels compute the similarity between two networks by comparing their substructures, which can be specific subgraphs [13], random walks [16], cycles [6], or paths [2], among others. The Weisfeiler-Lehman framework operates on top of existing kernels and improves their performance by using a relabeling procedure based on the Weisfeiler-Lehman test of isomorphism [12]. Recently, two other frameworks were presented for deriving variants of popular graph kernels [18,19]. Inspired by recent advances in NLP, they offer a way to take into account substructure similarity. Some graph kernels not restricted to comparing substructures of graphs but that also capture their global properties have also been proposed. Examples include graph kernels based on the Lovász number and the corresponding orthonormal representation [7], the pyramid match graph kernel that embeds vertices in a feature space and computes an approximate correspondence between them [11], and the Multiscale Laplacian graph kernel, which captures similarity at different granularity levels by considering a hierarchy of nested subgraphs [9].

Graph CNNs. Extending CNNs to graphs has experienced a surge of interest in recent years. A first class of methods use spectral properties of graphs. An early generalization of the convolution operator to graphs was based on the eigenvectors of the Laplacian matrix [3]. A more efficient model using Chebyshev polynomials approximation to represent the spectral filters was later presented [4]. All of these methods, however, assume a fixed graph structure and are thus not applicable to our setting. The model of [4] was then simplified by using a first-order approximation of the spectral filters [8], but within the context of a *node* classification problem (which again, differs from our *graph* classification setting). Unlike spectral methods, spatial methods [10,15] operate directly on the

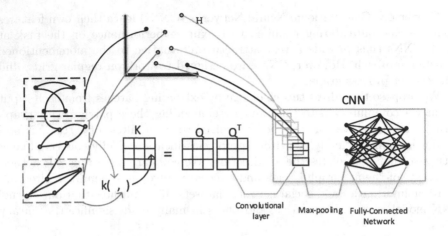

Fig. 1. Overview of our Kernel Graph CNN approach.

topology of the graph. Finally, some other techniques rely on node embeddings obtained as an unsupervised pre-processing step, like [14], in which graphs are represented as stacks of bivariate histograms and passed to a classical 2D CNN for images.

The work closest to ours is probably [10]. To extract a set of patches from the input graph, the authors (1) construct an ordered sequence of vertices from the graph, (2) create a neighborhood graph of constant size for each selected vertex, and (3) generate a vector representation (patch) for each neighborhood using graph labeling procedures such that nodes with similar structural roles in the neighborhood graph are positioned similarly in the vector space. The extracted patches are then fed to a 1D CNN. In contrast to the above work, we extract neighborhoods of varying sizes from the graph in a more direct and natural way (via community detection), and use graph kernels to normalize our patches. We present our approach in more details in the next section.

3 Proposed Approach

In what follows, we present the main ideas and building blocks of our model. The overarching process flow is illustrated in Fig. 1.

3.1 Patch Extraction and Normalization

Many types of real-world data are regular grids, and can thus be decomposed into units that are inherently ordered along spatial dimensions. This makes the task of patch extraction easy, and normalization unnecessary. For example, in computer vision (2D), meaningful patches are given by instantiating a rectangle window over the image. Furthermore, for all images, pixels are uniquely ordered along width and height, so there is a correspondence between the pixels in each patch, given by the spatial coordinates of the pixels. This removes the need for normalization. Likewise, in NLP, words in sentences are uniquely ordered from left to right, and a 1D window applied over text provides again natural regions. However, graphs do not exhibit such an underlying grid-like structure. They are irregular objects for which there exist no canonical ordering of the elementary units (nodes). Hence, generating patches from graphs, and normalizing them so that they are comparable and combinable, is a very challenging problem. To address these challenges, our approach leverages *community detection* and *graph kernels*.

Patch Extraction with Community Detection. There is a large variety of approaches for sampling from graphs. We can extract subgraphs for all vertices (which may be computationally intractable for large graphs) or for only a subset of them, such as the most central ones according to some metric. Furthermore, subgraphs may contain only the hop-1 neighborhood of a root vertex, or vertices that are further away from it. They may also be walks passing through the root vertex. A more natural way is to capitalize on *community detection* algorithms [5], as the clusters correspond to meaningful graph partitions. Indeed, a community typically corresponds to a set of vertices that highly interact with each other, as expressed by the number and weight of the edges between them, compared to the other vertices in the graph. In this paper, we employ the Louvain clustering algorithm, which extracts non-overlapping communities of various sizes from a given graph [1]. This multilevel algorithm aggregates each node with one of its neighbors such that the gain in modularity is maximized. Then, the groupings obtained at the first step are turned into nodes, yielding a new graph. The process iterates until a peak in modularity is attained and no more change occurs. Note that since our goal here is only to sample relevant local neighborhoods from the graph, we could have used any other state-of-the-art community detection algorithm. We opted for Louvain as it is very fast and scalable.

Patch Normalization with Graph Kernels. After extracting the subgraphs (communities) from a given input graph, standardization is necessary before being able to pass them to a CNN. We can define this step as that of *patch normalization*. To this purpose, we leverage graph kernels, as described next. Note that since the steps below do not depend on the way the subgraphs were obtained, we use the term *subgraph* (or *patch*) rather than *community* in what follows, to highlight the generality of our approach.

Let $\mathcal{G} = \{G_1, G_2, \ldots, G_N\}$ be the collection of input graphs. Let $\mathcal{S}_1, \mathcal{S}_2, \ldots, \mathcal{S}_N$ be the sets of subgraphs extracted from graphs $G_1, G_2, \ldots, G_N$ respectively. Since the number of subgraphs extracted from each graph may depend on the graph (like in our case with the Louvain community detection algorithm), these sets vary in size.

Furthermore, let S_i^j be the jth element of $\mathcal{S}_i$ (i.e., the jth subgraph extracted from G_i), and P_i be the size of $\mathcal{S}_i$ (i.e., the total number of subgraphs extracted from G_i). Let then $\mathcal{S} = \{S_i^j : i \in \{1, 2, \ldots, N\}, j \in \{1, 2, \ldots, P_i\}\}$ be the set of subgraphs extracted from all the graphs in the collection, and P its cardinality. Let finally $K \in \mathbb{R}^{P \times P}$ be the symmetric positive semidefinite kernel matrix constructed from S using a graph kernel k. Since the total number P of subgraphs for all the graphs in the collection is very large, populating the full kernel matrix K and factorizing it to obtain low-dimensional representations of the subgraphs is $\mathcal{O}(P^3)$. Fortunately, the Nyström method [17] allows us to obtain $Q \in \mathbb{R}^{P \times p}$ (with $p \ll P$) such that $K \approx QQ^\top$ at the reduced cost of $\mathcal{O}(p^2 P)$, by using only a small subset of p columns (or rows) of the kernel matrix. The rows of Q are low-dimensional representations of the subgraphs and serve as our normalized patches.

3.2   Graph Processing

1D Convolution. To process a given input graph, many filters are convolved with the normalized representations of the patches contained in the graph. For example, for a given filter $w \in \mathbb{R}^p$, a feature c_i is generated from the jth patch of graph G_i z_i^j as:

$$c_j = \sigma(w^\top z_i^j)$$

where σ is an activation function. In this study, we used the identity function $\sigma(c) = c$, as we observed no difference in results compared to nonlinear activations. Therefore, when applied to a patch z_i^j, the convolution operation corresponds to the inner product $\langle w, z_i^j \rangle$. We will show next that any filter w with $\|w\| < \infty$ learned by our network belongs to the Reproducing Kernel Hilbert Space (RKHS) $\mathcal{H}$ of the employed graph kernel k.

Theorem 1. *The filters live in the RKHS of the kernel k that was used to normalize the patches.*

Proof. Given two subgraphs S_i^j and $S_{i'}^{j'}$ extracted from G_i and G_i' and their associated normalized patches z_i^j and $z_{i'}^{j'}$, it holds that:

$$\langle z_i^j, z_{i'}^{j'} \rangle = k(S_i^j, S_{i'}^{j'}) = \langle \phi(S_i^j), \phi(S_{i'}^{j'}) \rangle_{\mathcal{H}}$$

Let $\mathcal{Z} = \{z_i^j : i \in \{1, 2, \ldots, N\}, j \in \{1, 2, \ldots, P_i\}\}$ be the set containing all patches of the input graphs. Then, $\mathrm{Span}(\mathcal{Z})$ is either the space of all vectors in $\mathbb{R}^P$ if the rank of the kernel matrix is P or the space of all vectors in $\mathbb{R}^P$ whose last t components are zero if the rank of the kernel matrix is $P - t$ where $t > 0$. Then, given a patch z_i^j, vector w is contained in $\mathrm{Span}(\mathcal{Z})$, hence:

$$\sigma(w^\top z_i^j) = \langle w, z_i^j \rangle = \langle \sum_{i'=1}^{N} \sum_{j'=1}^{P_i} a_{i'}^{j'} z_{i'}^{j'}, z_i^j \rangle$$

$$= \sum_{i'=1}^{N} \sum_{j'=1}^{P_i} a_{i'}^{j'} \langle z_{i'}^{j'}, z_i^j \rangle = \sum_{i'=1}^{N} \sum_{j'=1}^{P_i} a_{i'}^{j'} k(S_{i'}^{j'}, S_i^j)$$

which shows that the filters live in the RKHS associated to graph kernel k. For other smooth activation functions, one can also show that the filters will be contained in the corresponding RKHS of the kernel function [20].

Note that the proposed approach can be thought of as a CNN that works directly on graphs. In computer vision, convolution corresponds to the element-wise multiplication between part of an image and a filter followed by summation. Convolution can thus be viewed as an inner-product where the output is a single feature. In our setting, convolution corresponds to the inner-product between part of a graph (i. e. a patch) and a filter (i. e. a graph). Such an inner-product is implicitly computed using a graph kernel, and the output is also a single feature.

By convolving w with all the normalized patches of the graph, the following feature map is produced:

$$c = [c_1, c_2, \ldots, c_{P_{max}}]^\top$$

where $P_{max} = \max(P_i : i \in \{1, 2, \ldots, N\})$ is the largest number of patches extracted from any given graph in the collection. For graphs featuring less than P_{max} patches, zero-padding is employed.

Note that this approach is similar to concatenating all the vector representations of the patches contained in a given graph (padding if necessary), thus obtaining a single vector representation of the graph, and sliding over it a unidimensional filter of size the length of a single patch vector, without overspanning patches (i.e., with stride equal to filter size).

Pooling. We then apply a max-pooling operation over the feature map, thus retaining only the maximum value of c, $\max(c_1, c_2, \ldots, c_{P_{max}})$, as the signal associated with w. The intuition is that some subgraphs of a graph are good indicators of the class the graph belongs to, and that this information will be picked up by the max-pooling operation.

3.3   Processing New Graphs

When provided with a never-seen graph (at test time), we first sample subgraphs from it (here, via community detection), and then project them to the feature space of the subgraphs in the training set. Given a new subgraph S^j, its projection can be computed as $z^j = Q^\dagger v$ where $Q^\dagger \in \mathbb{R}^{p \times P}$ is the pseudoinverse of $Q \in \mathbb{R}^{P \times p}$ and $v \in \mathbb{R}^P$ is the vector containing the kernel value between S^j and all P subgraphs in the training set (those contained in set $\mathcal{S}$). The dimensionality p of the emerging vector is the same as that of the normalized patches in the training set. Thus, this vector can be convolved with the filters of the CNN as previously described.

3.4   Channels

Rather than selecting one graph kernel in particular to normalize the patches, several kernels can be jointly used. The different representations provided by each kernel can then be passed to the CNN through different channels, or *depth* dimensions. Intuitively, this can be very beneficial, as each kernel might capture different, complementary aspects of similarity between subgraphs. We experimented with the following popular kernels:

- **Shortest path kernel (SP)** [2]: to compute the similarity between two graphs, this kernel counts how many pairs of shortest paths have the same source and sink labels, and identical length, in the two graphs. The runtime complexity for a pair of graphs featuring n_1 and n_2 nodes is $\mathcal{O}(n_1{}^2 n_2{}^2)$.
- **Weisfeiler-Lehman subtree kernel (WL)** [12]: for a certain number h of iterations, this kernel performs an exact matching between the compressed multiset labels of the two graphs, while at each iteration it updates these labels. It requires $\mathcal{O}(hm)$ time for a pair of graphs with m edges.

This gave us two single channel models (KCNN SP, KCNN WL), and one model with two channels (KCNN SP + WL).

4   Experimental Setup

4.1   Synthetic Dataset

Dataset. As previously mentioned, the intuition is that our proposed KCNN model is particularly well suited for settings where some regions in the graphs are highly discriminative of the class the graph belongs to. To empirically verify this claim, we created a dataset featuring 1000 synthetic graphs generated as follows. First, we generate an Erdos-Rényi graph with number of vertices sampled from $\mathbb{Z} \cap [100, 200]$ with uniform probability, and edge probability equal to 0.1. We then add to the graph either a 10-clique or a 10-star graph by connecting the vertices with probability 0.1. The first class of the dataset is made of the graphs containing a 10-clique, while the second class features the graphs containing a 10-star subgraph. The two classes are of equal size (500 graphs each).

Baselines. We compared our model against the shortest-path kernel (SP) [2], the Weisfeiler-Lehman subtree kernel (WL) [12], and the graphlet kernel (GR) [13].

Configuration. We performed 10-fold cross-validation. The C parameter of the SVM (for all graph kernels) and the number of iterations (for the WL kernel baseline) were optimized on a 90/10 split of the training set of each fold. For the graphlet kernel, we sampled 1000 graphlets of size up to 6 from each graph. For our proposed KCNN, we used an architecture with one convolution-pooling block followed by a fully connected layer with 128 units. The `ReLU` activation was used, and regularization was ensured with dropout (0.5 rate). A final `softmax` layer was added to complete the architecture. The dimensionality of the normalized patches (number of columns of Q) was set to $p = 100$, and we used 256 filters (of size p, as explained in Subsect. 3.2). Batch size was set to 64, and the number of epochs and learning rate were optimized by performing 10-fold cross-validation on the training set of each fold. All experiments were run on a single machine consisting of a 3.4 GHz Intel Core i7 CPU with 16 GB of RAM and an NVidia GeForce Titan Xp GPU.

Results. We report in Table 1 average prediction accuracies of our three models in comparison to the baselines. Results validated the hypothesis that our

Table 1. Classification accuracy of state-of-the-art graph kernels: shortest path (SP), graphlet (GR), and Weisfeiler-Lehman subtree (WL); and the single and multichannel variants of our approach (KCNN), on the synthetic dataset.

SP	GR	WL	KCNN SP	KCNN WL	KCNN SP + WL
75.47	69.34	65.88	98.20	97.25	**98.40**

proposed model (KCNN) can identify those areas in the graphs that are most predictive of the class labels, as its three variants achieved accuracies greater than 98%. Conversely, the baseline kernels failed to discriminate between the two categories. Hence, it is clear that in such settings, our model is more effective than existing methods.

4.2 Real-World Datasets

Datasets. We also evaluated the performance of our approach on five bioinformatics (ENZYMES, NCI1, PROTEINS, PTC-MR, D&D) and five social network datasets (IMDB-BINARY, IMDB-MULTI, REDDIT-BINARY, REDDIT-MULTI-5K, COLLAB)[1]. Notice that the bioinformatics datasets are labeled (labels on vertices), while the social interaction datasets are not.

Baselines. We evaluated our model in comparison with the shortest-path kernel (SP) [2], the random walk kernel (RW) [16], the graphlet kernel (GR) [13], the Weisfeiler-Lehman subtree kernel (WL) [12], the best kernel from the deep graph kernel framework (Deep Graph Kernels) [19], and a recently proposed graph CNN (PSCN $k = 10$) [10]. Since the experimental setup is the same, we report the results of [19] and [10].

Configuration. Same as Subsect. 4.1 above.

Results. The 10-fold cross-validation average test set accuracy of our approach and the baselines is reported in Table 2. Our approach outperforms all baselines on 7 out of the 10 datasets. In some cases, the gains in accuracy over the best performing competitors are considerable. For instance, on the IMDB-MULTI, COLLAB, and D&D datasets, we offer respective *absolute* improvements of 2.23%, 2.33%, and 2.56% in accuracy over the best competitor, the state-of-the-art graph CNN (PSCN $k = 10$). Finally, it should be noted that on the IMDB-MULTI dataset, every variant of our architecture outperforms *all* baselines.

Interpretation. Overall, our Kernel CNN model reaches better performance than the classical graph kernels (SP, GR, RW, and WL), showing that the ability of CNNs to learn their own features during training is superior to disjoint feature computation and learning. It is true that our approach also comprises two disjoint steps. However, the first step is only a *data preprocessing* step, where we extract

---

[1] The datasets, further references and statistics are available at https://ls11-www.cs.tu-dortmund.de/staff/morris/graphkerneldatasets.

Table 2. 10-fold cross validation average classification accuracy (± standard deviation) of the proposed models and the baselines on the bioinformatics (top) and social network (bottom) datasets. Best performance per dataset in **bold**, among the variants of our Kernel CNN model underlined.

Method	Dataset				
	ENZYMES	NCI1	PROTEINS	PTC-MR	D&D
SP	40.10 (± 1.50)	73.00 (± 0.51)	75.07 (± 0.54)	58.24 (± 2.44)	>3 days
GR	26.61 (± 0.99)	62.28 (± 0.29)	71.67 (± 0.55)	57.26 (± 1.41)	78.45 (± 0.26)
RW	24.16 (± 1.64)	>3 days	74.22 (± 0.42)	57.85 (± 1.30)	>3 days
WL	53.15 (± 1.14)	80.13 (± 0.50)	72.92 (± 0.56)	56.97 (± 2.01)	77.95 (± 0.70)
Deep Kernels	**53.43** (± 0.91)	**80.31** (± 0.46)	75.68 (± 0.54)	60.08 (± 2.55)	NA
PSCN $k = 10$	NA	76.34 (± 1.68)	75.00 (± 2.51)	62.29 (± 5.68)	76.27 (± 2.64)
KCNN SP	46.35 (± 0.39)	75.70 (± 0.31)	74.27 (± 0.22)	**62.94** (± 1.69)	76.63 (± 0.09)
KCNN WL	43.08 (± 0.68)	75.83 (± 0.25)	**75.76** (± 0.28)	61.52 (± 1.41)	75.80 (± 0.07)
KCNN SP + WL	48.12 (± 0.23)	77.21 (± 0.22)	73.79 (± 0.29)	62.05 (± 1.41)	**78.83** (± 0.29)
	IMDB BINARY	IMDB MULTI	REDDIT BINARY	REDDIT MULTI-5K	COLLAB
GR	65.87 (± 0.98)	43.89 (± 0.38)	77.34 (± 0.18)	41.01 (± 0.17)	72.84 (± 0.28)
Deep GR	66.96 (± 0.56)	44.55 (± 0.52)	78.04 (± 0.39)	41.27 (± 0.18)	73.09 (± 0.25)
PSCN $k = 10$	71.00 (± 2.29)	45.23 (± 2.84)	**86.30** (± 1.58)	49.10 (± 0.70)	72.60 (± 2.15)
KCNN SP	69.60 (± 0.44)	45.99 (± 0.23)	77.23 (± 0.15)	44.86 (± 0.24)	70.78 (± 0.12)
KCNN WL	70.46 (± 0.45)	46.44 (± 0.24)	81.85 (± 0.12)	**50.04** (± 0.19)	**74.93** (± 0.14)
KCNN SP + WL	**71.45** (± 0.15)	**47.46** (± 0.21)	78.35 (± 0.11)	44.63 (± 0.18)	74.12 (± 0.17)

neighborhoods from the graphs, and normalize them with graph kernels. The features used for classification are then learned *during training* by our neural architecture, unlike the GK + SVM approach, where the features, given by the kernel matrix, are computed in advance, independently from the downstream task.

Our two single-channel architectures perform comparably on the bioinformatics datasets, while the KCNN WL variant was superior on the social network datasets. On the REDDIT-BINARY, REDDIT-MULTI-5K and COLLAB datasets, KCNN WL also outperforms the multichannel architecture, with quite wide margins. The multi-channel architecture (KCNN SP + WL) leads to better results on 5 out of the 10 datasets, showing that capturing subgraph similarity from a variety of angles sometimes helps.

Table 3. 10-fold cross validation runtime of proposed models on the 10 real-world graph classification datasets.

	ENZYMES	NCI1	PROTEINS	PTC-MR	D&D	IMDB BINARY	IMDB MULTI	REDDIT BINARY	REDDIT MULTI-5K	COLLAB
KCNN SP	28"	4' 26"	42"	22"	54"	36"	1' 41"	5' 29"	15' 2"	7' 2"
KCNN WL	53"	4' 54"	48"	22"	1' 33"	41"	58"	5' 22"	14' 23"	8' 58"
KCNN SP + WL	1' 13"	5' 1"	53"	25"	1' 46"	45"	1' 44"	9' 57"	24' 28"	10' 24"

Runtimes. We also report the time cost of our three models in Table 3. Runtime includes all steps of the process: patch extraction, path normalization, and 10-fold cross validation procedure. We can see that the computational complexity of the proposed models is not high. Our most computationally intensive model (KCNN SP + WL) takes less than 25 min to perform the full 10-fold cross validation procedure on the largest dataset (REDDIT-MULTI-5K). Moreover, in most cases, the running times are lower or comparable to the ones of the state-of-the-art Graph CNN and Deep Graph Kernels models [10,19].

5   Conclusion

In this paper, we proposed a method that combines graph kernels with CNNs to learn graph representations and to perform graph classification. Our Kernel Graph CNN model (KCNN) outperforms 6 state-of-the-art graph kernels and graph CNN baselines on 7 datasets out of 10.

References

1. Blondel, V.D., Guillaume, J.L., Lambiotte, R., Lefebvre, E.: Fast unfolding of communities in large networks. JSTAT **2008**(10), 1–12 (2008)
2. Borgwardt, K.M., Kriegel, H.: Shortest-path kernels on graphs. In: ICDM, pp. 74–81 (2005)
3. Bruna, J., Zaremba, W., Szlam, A., LeCun, Y.: Spectral networks and locally connected networks on graphs. In: ICLR (2014)
4. Defferrard, M., Bresson, X., Vandergheynst, P.: Convolutional neural networks on graphs with fast localized spectral filtering. In: NIPS, pp. 3837–3845 (2016)
5. Fortunato, S., Hric, D.: Community detection in networks: a user guide. Phys. Rep. **659**, 1–44 (2016)
6. Horváth, T., Gärtner, T., Wrobel, S.: Cyclic Pattern Kernels for Predictive Graph Mining. In: KDD, pp. 158–167 (2004)
7. Johansson, F., Jethava, V., Dubhashi, D., Bhattacharyya, C.: Global graph kernels using geometric embeddings. In: ICML, pp. 694–702 (2014)
8. Kipf, T.N., Welling, M.: Semi-supervised classification with graph convolutional networks. In: ICLR (2017)
9. Kondor, R., Pan, H.: The multiscale laplacian graph kernel. In: NIPS, pp. 2982–2990 (2016)
10. Niepert, M., Ahmed, M., Kutzkov, K.: Learning convolutional neural networks for graphs. In: ICML (2016)
11. Nikolentzos, G., Meladianos, P., Vazirgiannis, M.: Matching node embeddings for graph similarity. In: AAAI, pp. 2429–2435 (2017)
12. Shervashidze, N., Schweitzer, P., Van Leeuwen, E.J., Mehlhorn, K., Borgwardt, K.M.: Weisfeiler-Lehman graph kernels. JMLR **12**, 2539–2561 (2011)
13. Shervashidze, N., Vishwanathan, S., Petri, T., Mehlhorn, K., Borgwardt, K.M.: Efficient graphlet kernels for large graph comparison. In: AISTATS, pp. 488–495 (2009)
14. Tixier, A., Nikolentzos, G., Meladianos, P., Vazirgiannis, M.: Classifying graphs as images with convolutional neural networks. arXiv:1708.02218 (2017)

15. Vialatte, J.C., Gripon, V., Mercier, G.: Generalizing the convolution operator to extend CNNs to irregular domains. arXiv preprint arXiv:1606.01166 (2016)
16. Vishwanathan, S.V.N., Schraudolph, N.N., Kondor, R., Borgwardt, K.M.: Graph kernels. JMLR **11**, 1201–1242 (2010)
17. Williams, C.K., Seeger, M.: Using the Nyström method to speed up kernel machines. In: NIPS, pp. 661–667 (2000)
18. Yanardag, P., Vishwanathan, S.: A structural smoothing framework for robust graph comparison. In: NIPS, pp. 2125–2133 (2015)
19. Yanardag, P., Vishwanathan, S.: Deep graph kernels. In: KDD, pp. 1365–1374 (2015)
20. Zhang, Y., Liang, P., Wainwright, M.J.: Convexified convolutional neural networks. In: ICML, pp. 4044–4053 (2017)

A Histogram of Oriented Gradients for Broken Bars Diagnosis in Squirrel Cage Induction Motors

Luiz C. Silva$^{(\boxtimes)}$ (ID), Cleber G. Dias (ID), and Wonder A. L. Alves (ID)

Informatics and Knowledge Management Graduate Program,
Universidade Nove de Julho, São Paulo, SP, Brazil
lumaleo2016@gmail.com

Abstract. The three-phase induction motors are widely used in a lot of applications both industry and other environments. Although this electrical machine is robust and reliable for industrial tasks, for example, conditioning monitoring techniques have been investigated during the last years to identify some electrical and mechanical faults in induction motors. In this sense, broken rotor bars is a typical fault related to the induction machine damage and the current technical solutions have shown some drawbacks for this kind of failure diagnosis, particularly when motor is running at very low slip. Therefore, this paper proposes a new use of Histogram of Oriented Gradients, usually applied in computer vision and image processing, for broken bars detection, using data from only one phase of the stator current of the machine. The intensity gradients and edge directions of each time-window of the stator signal have been applied as inputs for a neural network classifier. This method has been validated using some experimental data from a 7.5 kW squirrel cage induction machine running at distinct load levels (slip conditions).

Keywords: Induction motors · Broken rotor bars · Stator current
Neural network classifier

1 Introduction

During the past decades, conditioning monitoring techniques have been applied by several researchers for failure detection in induction motors (IM), as well as in predictive maintenance programs at industry. Today, the induction motors are responsible for many load drivers and also capable of applying its power in a variety of energy conversion processes [1]. However, the IMs have some technical limitations, such as mechanical stresses or electromagnetic strengths that are usually related to damages in stator and rotor cage [2]. For larger machines, for example, longer downtime per failure usually occurred with induction motors starting more than once per day, or in applications of pulsating load or direct on-line startups [3].

A noninvasive technique, called motor current signature analysis (MCSA), is currently applied for broken bars detection and has been used over the last decades, particularly due to its noninvasive characteristic and attractive applications in industrial environment, but MCSA has some drawbacks related to rotor failures diagnosis, such

V. Kůrková et al. (Eds.): ICANN 2018, LNCS 11139, pp. 33–42, 2018.
https://doi.org/10.1007/978-3-030-01418-6_4

as detection at very low slip (low load or no load) and nonadjacent broken bars, as cited by [4–6]. The sideband frequencies (features extracted from stator current) which are related to MCSA are usually near the fundamental frequency for a motor running at low load, thus it is quite difficult to distinguish between a healthy and failure rotor. Therefore, in many cases MCSA is responsible for both false positive and negative alarms in the rotor broken bars evaluation [4].

Other signal processing and feature extraction methods have been used for failure diagnosis on induction motors using time and/or frequency domain data, such as described by [7–11]. In general, such works have disclosed the use of Fast Fourier Transform (FFT), Hilbert Transform (HT), Esprit and Empirical Mode Decomposition (EMD) to extract some information from stator current and other signals from a IM with broken bars. However, most of them require a long data acquisition time and a high frequency resolution to ensure the failure detection efficiency.

In addition, other studies have demonstrated the use of some machine learning and artificial intelligence approaches to detect no only broken rotor bars, but also other types of failures in induction motors as cited by [12–15]. A recent work published by [16], for example, has disclosed the current methods used for fault diagnosis on rotating machinery, such as artificial neural networks, clustering algorithms, deep learning and hybrid techniques.

Based on the aforementioned state of the art, the present work proposes a new approach for broken rotor bars diagnosis, using histogram oriented gradients (HOG) method [17], using only one single phase data of the stator current. The main features of stator current data have been extracted from the intensity gradients and edge directions for a multilayer perceptron classifier (MLP). In addition, this paper discusses the present approach for broken bars detection when induction motors are operating at reduced load or low slip.

2   Theoretical Background

An analog signal is a physical process that depends on time and can be modeled by a real function on a variable real that representing time.

In this paper, this function models the stator current from an induction motor which represents a sinusoidal and periodic signal of the electrical machine. The amplitude of this signal depends on the load torque applied to the shaft of the motor. The stator current signals can be digitized by a process called sampling which approximate the stator current signals taken at regular time intervals.

Thus, the digital stator current signals is represented by a function $u : \mathcal{D} \subset \mathbb{Z} \to \mathcal{R}$, in which a sample $x \in \mathcal{D}$ is an integer number representing a discrete instance in a sampled time of T_S seconds. In addition, this signal, which is periodic, can be divided into cycles with duration of $1/f$ seconds, since f is the fundamental frequency set to 60 Hz. Thus, we consider $W = \{W_1, W_2, \cdots, W_{T_W}\}$ a partition on $\mathcal{D}$ such that for any $1 \leq i \leq T_W$, follows that a time-window W_i contains the samples of some complete cycles of signal u. Thus, the time-window W_i contains W_{cycle} complete cycles with $\frac{1}{60} \times W_{cycle}$ samples of a sample time $T_S = W_{cycle} \times \frac{1}{60} \times T_W$ seconds. Note that, W is a set non-empty, its elements are disjoint and the union of its time-windows is W.

2.1 The Histogram of Oriented Gradients as a Feature Descriptor

The HOG is a feature descriptor, introduced by Dalal and Triggs, for the detection of pedestrians in photographs [17] and later used for other object detection problems, as the solutions disclosed by [18] and [19]. The HOG is a technique for describing the original signal u through a histogram of the gradient direction. The gradient $\nabla(u)$ can be computed by a simple difference schema, as follows:

$$\forall x \in D, [\nabla(u)](x) = \frac{u(x-1) - u(x+1)}{2} \tag{1}$$

The gradient direction $\theta(\nabla(u))$ at point $x \in D$ is expressed as an angle in intervals of $[0, 2\pi]$ radians and can be computed, as follows:

$$\forall x \in D, [\theta(\nabla(u))](x) = \tan^{-1}(\nabla(u)) \tag{2}$$

Then, each sample $x \in D$ contributes to the histogram with a value proportional to its gradient magnitude that can obtained by:

$$\forall x \in D, [\rho(\nabla(u))](x) = \sqrt{\nabla(u)^2} \tag{3}$$

The histogram is constructed for a small number n_{bins} of bins corresponding to regular intervals of gradient direction. Besides that, a sample x localized in k-th bin can contribute to two angle range in the histogram according to the distance ratio between the bin angle center θ_k and the sample angle $[\theta(\nabla(u))](x)$. This proportion is given as follows:

$$\omega_k(x) = \max\left\{0, \left[1 - \frac{|[\theta(\nabla(u))](x) - \theta_k|}{n_{bins}}\right]\right\} \tag{4}$$

Therefore, we compute a histogram HOG for each time-window $W_i \in W$ as follows:

$$[HOG(u, W_i)](k) = \sum_{x \in W_i} \omega_k(x)\rho(x), \quad for\ k = 1, 2, \cdots, n_{bins} \tag{5}$$

where $\omega_k(x)$ is defined in Eq. (4) and $\rho(x)$ is defined in Eq. (3).

3 The HOG-MLP Method for Broken Bars Detection

The proposed method is based on divide-to-conquer approach. The idea is to divide the problem into sub-problems and then the sub-problem solutions are combined to give a solution to the original problem. In this sense, our original problem is to classify broken rotor bars through the stator current signal. So, we divide the stator current signal into time-windows given by the partition W. Then, each time-window W_i is classified through a multilayer perceptron. Thus, we combine the results of the MLP into a single classification through the bayesian classifier.

The proposed method for the diagnosis of broken rotor bars consists of six stages (see Fig. 1) which comprise: *(i)* Acquisition of stator current signal; *(ii)* Signal simplification; *(iii)* Signal segmentation in cycles; *(iv)* Feature extraction; *(v)* Classification of time-window; and *(vi)* Fault detection.

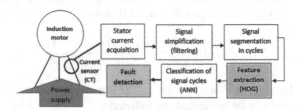

Fig. 1. Squematic view for broken bars detection using HOG and MLP.

Acquisition of Stator Current Signal: A table representing the function $u : \mathcal{D} \subset \mathbb{Z} \to \mathcal{R}$, is constructed from the stator current data. These data have been collected from motor running at four distinct load torque conditions, i.e., the braking system has been supplied with 40 V (slip = 0.66%), 50 V (slip = 0.077%), 60 V (slip = 1%) and 70 V (slip = 1.16%), thus the motor was running at very low slip in all cases (close to or lower than 1%). It is important to highlight that large motors usually run at low slip even for rated load, and small motors often operate at below rated load in many industrial applications. The slip s can be defined as the difference between the flux speed Ns and the rotor speed Nr and is usually expressed as a percentage of synchronous speed (Ns), i.e., $s = \frac{Ns-Nr}{Ns} \times 100\%$. The stator current was sampled at a time of 10 s (i.e., $T_s = 10$ s), thus, considering the fundamental frequency of 60 Hz and a sample frequency of 10 kHz.

Signal Simplification: After collecting the data from motor, the stator current was filtered to reduce the noise and to contribute for signal processing in the time domain. A Butterworth sixth order low pass filter was used in a cutoff frequency of 200 Hz, since this value was able to extract the waveform distortion according to the rotor failure. It is important to highlight that the distortion of the sinusoidal wave (stator current) is greater in the presence of broken bars, since this failure produces harmonic components with higher amplitudes (rotor slots harmonics).

Signal Segmentation in Cycles: As the sample time is 10 s, the fundamental frequency is 60 Hz and sampled frequency is 10 kHz. Then, each sample time has 600 cycles and each cycle contains 167 samples. In addition, the partition W is constructed in the following ways: either 600 time-windows of a single cycle each (i.e., $W_{cycle} = 1$) or 20 time-windows with 30 cycles each (i.e., $W_{cycle} = 30$).

Feature Extraction: The feature extraction was performed for each time-window of partition W and thus it was constructed a set of feature vectors from a stator current signals u, i.e., $k(u) = \{HOG(u, W_i) : W_i \in W\}$. From the descriptors extracted from the stator current signals we constructed the training and validation datasets, in which 6400 labeled examples were used for the training dataset.

Moreover, the datasets were constructed using balanced samples, that is, both classes contain the same amount of samples. It is worth remembering that we have constructed a pair training/validation dataset for each of our approach parameters that is discussed in Sect. 4.

Classification of Time-Window: A typical MLP classifier is built to using a training set $S = \{(p_k, c_k) \in \mathbb{R}^{n_{bins}} \times \{0,1\} : k = 1, 2, \cdots, 60 \times T_W\}$ of labeled feature vectors. The features vector is given by $HOG(u, W_i) \in k(u)$ of a time-window $W_i \in W$ of a stator current signal u into time-window of a healthy stator current signal (labeled "0") or time-window of an unhealthy stator current signal (labeled "1"), i.e., $MLB : \mathbb{R}^{n_{bins}} \rightarrow \{0,1\}$.

The ANN was trained with 37 input features extracted from HOG, using the Levenberg-Marquardt algorithm and only one hidden layer was used in its topology. The training error obtained for the MLP classifier is about 1.7×10^{-3} using the traditional k-fold-cross-validation (with $k = 10$) technique to evaluate the classifier performance.

Fault Detection: The last stage comprises the combining each time-window classification for the rotor fault detection. This procedure is performed using bayesian classifier. Thus, given a stator current signal u, we detected the rotor condition as follows:

$$Bayesian\ Classifier = \begin{cases} failure, & if\ P(y = 1|k(u)) > P(y = 0|k(u)) \\ non\text{-}failure, & otherwise \end{cases}$$

$$Bayesian\ Classifier = \begin{cases} failure, & if\ P(y = 1|k(u)) > P(y = 0|k(u)) \\ non\text{-}failure, & otherwise \end{cases} \tag{6}$$

where the posterior probabilities $P(y = 1|k(u)) > P(y = 0|k(u))$ are designed using MLP classifier as follows:

$$P(y = 1|k(u)) = \sum_{X_i \in k(u)} \frac{\frac{MLP(X_i)}{T_W} \times P(y = 1)}{P(k(u))} \tag{7}$$

and $P(y = 0|k(u)) = 1 - P(y = 1|k(u))$. The priori probabilities $P(y = 1)$ and $P(y = 0)$ are discussed in Sect. 4.

4 Experimental Results

As mentioned before, a current sensor (CT - current transform) was used to measure the stator current from a 7.5 kW squirrel cage induction motor (rated speed = 1800 rpm). This signal has been collected using a PC and an USB digital Oscilloscope Hantek, model HT6022BE, with bandwidth in 20 MHz and maximum real-time sample rate of 48 MS/s. The data was collected from some tests performed at laboratory, considering the motor running at rated frequency (60 Hz) and under distinct load levels. Figure 2 shows the experimental setup of the induction motor.

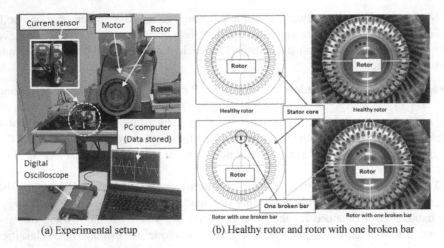

| (a) Experimental setup | (b) Healthy rotor and rotor with one broken bar |

Fig. 2. (a) Experimental setup and (b) Two rotor conditions.

For experimental tests and rotor evaluation, the stator current data have been collected from motor running at four distinct load torque conditions, i.e., the braking system has supplied with voltage equal to 40 V, 50 V, 60 V and 70 V. The stator current was sampled at a sampled time of 10 s (i.e., $T_S = 10$ s). Thus, considering the fundamental frequency of 60 Hz and a sample frequency of 10 kHz, each sampled time has 600 cycles. The classification error and the accuracy were obtained using a 10-fold-cross-validation, by considering some stator signal parameters variation. The performance of the MLP classifier is better described as follows.

4.1   Analysis of Parameters for the Proposed Method

In this subsection we show an analysis based on receiver operating characteristic (ROC) to find of the best parameters for ours approach. The parameters studied were (1) the angle range of HOG, i.e., the parameter n_{bins}; (2) the time-window length, i.e., the parameter W_{cycle}; and (3) the threshold value for output classification.

We study the gradient directions used in the HOG and we realized that the angles are in intervals of −90°, +90° giving a total of 37 angles. Thus, we analyzed the parameter n_{bins} varying of [1, 5] the quantity of angle by bin of HOG using a ROC curve. Analogously, we analyzed the parameter W_{cycle} for some time-window lengths. Figure 3 shows respectively the ROC curve results for a time-window of only one cycle and also for 30 cycles, according to the HOG bin angle variation.

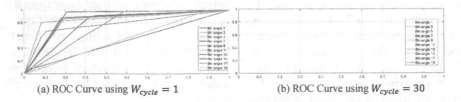

| (a) ROC Curve using $W_{cycle} = 1$ | (b) ROC Curve using $W_{cycle} = 30$ |

Fig. 3. Analysis of ROC curves to determine the better W_{cycle} and n_{bins} parameters.

It is possible to note that the ROC curves generated from a stator signal processed with 30 cycles has demonstrated a better performance than those obtained for only one cycle, even for distinct HOG angles, thus, in this paper the time-window of 30 cycles (i.e., 0.5 s) was chosen for broken rotor bar detection using MLP classifier. As mentioned by [20], the more the ROC curve is to the upper left corner the better the classifier performance is. Using the parameters selected, a typical bin angle distribution for a healthy motor and a damaged rotor is shows in Fig. 4. It is possible to note some HOG bin angle amplitudes variation according to the two classes conditions (healthy and faulted rotor).

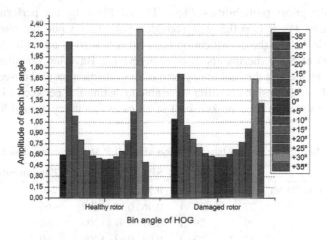

Fig. 4. Typical HOG for a healthy motor and a damaged rotor.

4.2 Fault Detection Using HOG, MLP and Bayesian Approach

In this work, the HOG angle of 5° was chosen as the best value for histogram descriptor distribution. It should be noted that, the MLP has been trained with 60 stator current signals. In the previous section, the MLP topologies were trained to defined the best parameters for rotor fault detection using HOG (threshold of sigmoid neuron is 0.7, $n_{bins} = 37$ and $W_{cycle} = 30$). The input layer is related to the number of n_{bins}, thus the input of each MLP topology was built with 37 bin angles. In this paper, a single hidden layer with 50 neurons was used for rotor fault detection.

Table 1 shows the results obtained for four load conditions of the rotor evaluation, after applying MLP classifier. These results are true positive values (TP), false negative (FN), true negative values (TN), false positive values (FP), specificity (SP), sensitivity (SN) and accuracy for both learning and validation datasets. In this case, the experiments numbered between 41 and 70 have been used for validation purposes.In the last stage, the rotor fault detection was performed using time-window classification and Bayesian classifier, as mentioned in Sect. 3.

Table 1. Results for time-window classification after applying MLP classifier.

Load condition	TP	FN	TN	FP	SP	SN	Samples	Experiments	Acc (%)
All loads (training data)	3128	72	3137	63	0.98	0.97	6400	320	0.98
All loads (validation data)	**2129**	**271**	**2100**	**300**	**0.87**	**0.88**	**4800**	**240**	**0.88**
40 V (validation data)	513	87	528	72	0.88	0.85	1200	60	0.87
50 V (validation data)	537	63	529	71	0.88	0.90	1200	60	0.89
60 V (validation data)	556	44	505	95	0.84	0.93	1200	60	0.88
70 V (validation data)	591	9	561	39	0.93	0.98	1200	60	0.96

For find the priori probabilities $P(y = 1)$ and $P(y = 0)$ we performed a ROC analysis and thus $P(y = 1) = 0.5$ was considered the best value for rotor condition diagnosis. Table 2 show the classification (i.e., either faulted or a healthy condition for rotor structure) of the experiments after applying the Bayesian classifier. For load scenarios, i.e., by feeding the braking system of the induction motor between 40 V and 70 V, the MLP and Bayesian classifier were able to distinguish between a healthy rotor and a damaged structure (one broken bar) in all cases (accuracy around 94%).

Table 2. Results for broken bars detection after MLP and Bayesian classification.

Load condition	TP	FN	TN	FP	SP	SN	Samples	Experiments	Acc (%)
All loads (40 V to 70 V)	**112**	**8**	**114**	**6**	**0.93**	**0.95**	**4800**	**240**	**0.94**
40 V	27	3	29	1	0.96	0.90	1200	60	0.93
50 V	29	1	29	1	0.97	0.97	1200	60	0.97
60 V	28	2	27	3	0.93	0.93	1200	60	0.91
70 V	28	2	29	1	0.93	0.93	1200	60	0.95

5 Conclusions

This paper proposes a new approach for broken rotor bars detection in squirrel cage induction motors, by using a histogram of oriented gradients (HOG). A HOG bin angle variation was evaluated for a healthy motor and a damaged rotor with one broken bar, using only stator current as a measurement signal from electrical machine. The amplitude of each bin angle, after applying HOG on each time-window, has been used as inputs for a Multilayer Perceptron Neural Network to detect fully broken rotor bars. For better failure classification, a bayesian classifier was applied to detect each experiment after time-window subset MLP evaluation. The experimental results have shown a good accuracy (around 94%) for failure diagnosis, even when IM was running at low load condition, thus at very low slip (close to 1%). Therefore, this time-domain approach, using HOG instead of other frequency domain techniques, could be very interesting for a rotor failure detection in the future. Further researches are going on to better detect the broken bars for other load conditions and also to evaluate the fault severity (more broken bars).

Acknowledgments. The authors would like to thank UNINOVE and FAPESP - São Paulo Research Foundation (Process 2016/02547-5 and 2016/02525-1) by financial support.

References

1. Zhang, P., Du, Y., Habetler, T.G., Lu, B.: A survey of condition monitoring and protection methods for medium-voltage induction motors. IEEE Trans. Ind. Appl. **47**, 34–46 (2011)
2. Bonnett, A.H., Soukup, G.C.: Cause and analysis of stator and rotor failures in three-phase squirrel-cage induction motors. IEEE Trans. Ind. Appl. **28**, 921–937 (1992)
3. Thorsen, O.V., Dalva, M.: Failure identification and analysis for high-voltage induction motors in the petrochemical industry. IEEE Trans. Ind. Appl. **35**, 810–818 (1999)
4. Lee, S.B., et al.: Identification of false rotor fault indications produced by online MCSA for medium-voltage induction machines. IEEE Trans. Ind. Appl. **52**, 729–739 (2016)
5. Riera-Guasp, M., Cabanas, M.F., Antonino-Daviu, J.A., Pineda-Sánchez, M., García, C.H. R.: Influence of nonconsecutive bar breakages in motor current signature analysis for the diagnosis of rotor faults in induction motors. IEEE Trans. Energy Convers. **25**, 80–89 (2010)
6. Sizov, G.Y., Sayed-Ahmed, A., Yeh, C.-C., Demerdash, N.A.O.: Analysis and diagnostics of adjacent and nonadjacent broken-rotor-bar faults in squirrel-cage induction machines. IEEE Trans. Ind. Electron. **56**, 4627–4641 (2009)
7. Puche-Panadero, R., et al.: Improved resolution of the MCSA method via Hilbert transform, enabling the diagnosis of rotor asymmetries at very low slip. IEEE Trans. Energy Convers. **24**, 52–59 (2009)
8. Xu, B., Sun, L., Xu, L., Xu, G.: Improvement of the Hilbert method via ESPRIT for detecting rotor fault in induction motors at low slip. IEEE Trans. Energy Convers. **28**, 225–233 (2013)
9. Sapena-Bano, A., Pineda-Sanchez, M., Puche-Panadero, R., Martinez-Roman, J., Kanović, Ž.: Low-cost diagnosis of rotor asymmetries in induction machines working at a very low slip using the reduced envelope of the stator current. IEEE Trans. Energy Convers. **30**, 1409–1419 (2015)
10. Valles-Novo, R., de Jesus Rangel-Magdaleno, J., Ramirez-Cortes, J.M., Peregrina-Barreto, H., Morales-Caporal, R.: Empirical mode decomposition analysis for broken-bar detection on squirrel cage induction motors. IEEE Trans. Instrum. Meas. **64**, 1118–1128 (2015)
11. Dias, C.G., Chabu, I.E.: Spectral analysis using a Hall effect sensor for diagnosing broken bars in large induction motors. IEEE Trans. Instrum. Meas. **63**, 2890–2902 (2014)
12. Sadeghian, A., Ye, Z., Wu, B.: Online detection of broken rotor bars in induction motors by wavelet packet decomposition and artificial neural networks. IEEE Trans. Instrum. Meas. **58**, 2253–2263 (2009)
13. Singh, H., Seera, M., Abdullah, M.Z.: Detection and diagnosis of broken rotor bars and eccentricity faults in induction motors using the Fuzzy Min-Max neural network. In: The 2013 International Joint Conference on Neural Networks (IJCNN), pp. 1–5 (2013)
14. Carbajal-Hernández, J.J., Sánchez-Fernández, L.P., Landassuri-Moreno, V.M., de Jesús Medel-Juárez, J.: Misalignment identification in induction motors using orbital pattern analysis. In: Ruiz-Shulcloper, J., Sanniti di Baja, G. (eds.) CIARP 2013. LNCS, vol. 8259, pp. 50–58. Springer, Heidelberg (2013). https://doi.org/10.1007/978-3-642-41827-3_7
15. Chandralekha, R., Jayanthi, D.: Diagnosis of Faults in Three Phase Induction Motor using Neuro Fuzzy Logic. Int. J. Appl. Eng. Res. **11**, 5735–5740 (2016)
16. Lei, Y.: Intelligent Fault Diagnosis and Remaining Useful Life Prediction of Rotating Machinery. Butterworth-Heinemann (2016)

17. Dalal, N., Triggs, B.: Histograms of oriented gradients for human detection. In: IEEE Computer Society Conference on Computer Vision and Pattern Recognition, CVPR 2005, vol. 1, pp. 886–893 (2005)
18. Yu, Y., Cao, H., Liu, S., Yang, S., Bai, R.: Image-based damage recognition of wind turbine blades. In: 2017 2nd International Conference on Advanced Robotics and Mechatronics (ICARM), pp. 161–166 (2017)
19. Meng, L., Wang, Z., Fujikawa, Y., Oyanagi, S.: Detecting cracks on a concrete surface using histogram of oriented gradients. In: 2015 International Conference on Advanced Mechatronic Systems (ICAMechS), pp. 103–107 (2015)
20. Martin-Diaz, I., et al.: An experimental comparative evaluation of machine learning techniques for motor fault diagnosis under various operating conditions. IEEE Trans. Ind. Appl. **54**(3), 2215–2224 (2018)

Learning Game by Profit Sharing Using Convolutional Neural Network

Nobuaki Hasuike and Yuko Osana[✉]

Tokyo University of Technology, 1404-1, Katakura, Hachioji, Tokyo 192-0982, Japan
osana@stf.teu.ac.jp

Abstract. In this paper, Profit Sharing using convolutional neural network is realized. In the proposed method, action value in Profit Sharing is learned by convolutional neural network. This is a method that learns the value function of Profit Sharing instead of the value function of Q Learning used in the Deep Q-Network. By changing to an error function based on the value function of Profit Sharing which can acquire probabilistic policy in a shorter time, the proposed method is able to learn in a shorter time than the conventional Deep Q-Network. Computer experiments were carried out on Asterix of Atari 2600, and the proposed method was compared with the conventional Deep Q-Network. As a result, we confirmed that the proposed method can learn from the earlier stage than Deep Q-Network and can obtain higher score finally.

Keywords: Profit Sharing · Convolutional neural network

1 Introduction

In recent years, as a method which shows better performance than the conventional method in the field of image recognition and speech recognition, the deep learning has been drawing attention. Deep learning is a hierarchical neural network with many layers, and the Convolutional Neural Network (CNN) [1] is one of the representative models.

On the other hand, various studies on reinforcement learning are being conducted as learning methods to acquire appropriate policies through interaction with the environment [2]. In reinforcement learning, learning can proceed by repeating trial and error even in an unknown environment by appropriately setting rewards.

The Deep Q-Network [5] is based on the convolutional neural network which is a representative method of deep learning and the Q Learning [4] which is a representative method of reinforcement learning. In the Deep Q-Network, when the game screen (observation) is given as an input to the convolutional neural network, the action value in Q Learning for each action is output. This method can realize learning that acquires a score equal to or higher than that of a human in plural games. The combination of deep learning and reinforcement learning is called Deep Reinforcement Learning, most of which is based on Q Learning.

© Springer Nature Switzerland AG 2018
V. Kůrková et al. (Eds.): ICANN 2018, LNCS 11139, pp. 43–50, 2018.
https://doi.org/10.1007/978-3-030-01418-6_5

As a deep reinforcement learning using a method other than Q Learning, we have proposed a Deep Q-Network using reward distribution [6]. This method learns to not take wrong actions, by distributing negative rewards in the same way as Profit Sharing [3]. Although this method can perform learning with the same degree of precision and speed as Deep Q-Network, it shows that the score that can be finally obtained is same level as Deep Q-Network.

In this paper, we propose a Profit Sharing using convolutional neural network. In the proposed method, action value in Profit Sharing is learned by convolutional neural network. This is a method that learns the value function of Profit Sharing instead of the value function of Q Learning used in the Deep Q-Network. By changing to an error function based on the value function of Profit Sharing which can acquire probabilistic policy in a shorter time, the proposed method is able to learn in a shorter time than the conventional Deep Q-Network. Computer experiments were carried out on Asterix of Atari 2600, and the proposed method was compared with the conventional Deep Q-Network. As a result, we confirmed that the proposed method can learn from the earlier stage than Deep Q-Network and can obtain higher score finally.

2   Deep Q-Network

Here, we explain the Deep Q-Network [5] that is the basis of the proposed method. The Deep Q-Network is based on the convolutional neural network [1] and the Q Learning [4]. In the Deep Q-Network, when the game screen (observation) is given as an input to the convolutional neural network, the action value in Q Learning for each action is output. This method can realize learning that acquires a score equal to or higher than that of a human in plural games.

2.1   Structure

The structure of Deep Q-Network is shown in Fig. 1. As seen in Fig. 1, the Deep Q-Network is a model based on the convolutional neural network, consisting of three convolution layers and two fully connected layers. The play screen of the game (observation) is input to the convolutional neural network, and the action value for each action corresponding to the observation is outputted. For the first to fourth layers, rectified linear function is used as an output function. The number of neurons in the last finally connected layer which is the output layer is the same as the number of actions that can be taken in the problem to be handled. Since the problem learned by Deep Q-Network can be regarded as a regression problem to learn the relationship between each observation and the action value of each action in the observation, the output function of the output layer is an identity mapping function.

2.2 Learning

Since the action value in Q Learning is used as the output, the following error function used in learning is given by

$$E = \frac{1}{2} \left(r_\tau + \gamma \max_{a' \in C^A(o_{\tau+1})} q(o_{\tau+1}, a') - q(o_\tau, a_\tau) \right)^2 \tag{1}$$

where r_τ is the reward at the time τ, $C^A(o_{\tau+1})$ is the set of actions that an agent can take at the observation $o_{\tau+1}$, γ is the discount factor, $q(o_\tau, a_\tau)$ is the value of taking action a_τ at observation o_τ.

When the game screen o_τ is given to the Deep Q-Network, the value of all actions in observation o_τ is output in the output layer. Based on the output action value, action is determined by the ε-greedy method. In the ε-greedy method, one action is selected randomly with the probability ε $(0 \le \varepsilon \le 1)$, the action whose value is highest with the probability of $1 - \varepsilon$.

The probability to select the action a in observation o_τ, $P(o_\tau, a)$ is given by

$$P(o_\tau, a) = \begin{cases} (1 - \varepsilon) + \dfrac{\varepsilon}{|C^A|} & \left(\text{if } a = \operatorname*{argmax}_{a' \in C^A} q(o_\tau, a') \right) \\ \dfrac{\varepsilon}{|C^A|} & (\text{otherwise}) \end{cases} \tag{2}$$

where, $|C^A|$ is the number of action types that the agent can take, which is the same as the number of neurons in the output layer of the Deep Q-Network.

The selected action a_τ is executed, and the state transits to the next state $o_{\tau+1}$. Also, by taking the action a_τ, the reward r_τ is given based on the score, game state and so on.

Learning is unstable merely by approximating the action value of Q Learning using the convolutional neural network, so in the learning of the Deep Q-Network, some ideas called Experience Replay, Fixed Target Q-Network, Reward Clipping are introduced.

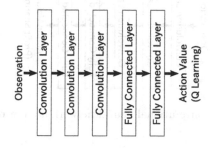

Fig. 1. Structure of Deep Q-Network.

3   Profit Sharing Using Convolutional Neural Network

Here, the proposed Profit Sharing using Convolutional Neural Network is explained.

3.1   Outline

In the proposed method, action value in Profit Sharing is learned by convolutional neural network. This is a method that learns the value function of Profit Sharing instead of the value function of Q Learning used in the Deep Q-Network. By changing to an error function based on the value function of Profit Sharing which can acquire probabilistic policy in a shorter time, the proposed method is able to learn in a shorter time than the conventional Deep Q-Network. However, in the Profit Sharing, since temporally continuous data is meaningful in episodes, experience replay used in the Deep Q-Network is not used in the proposed method. The Q Learning uses fixed target Q-Network because the value of other rules is also used when updating the value of the rule. In contrast, the Profit Sharing uses the value of the rule included in the episode in updating the connection weights. Therefore, the proposed method does not use fixed target Q-Network.

3.2   Structure

The structure of the convolutional neural network used in the proposed method is shown in Fig. 2. As similar as the conventional Deep Q-Network, the convolutional neural network used in the proposed method consists of three convolution layers and two full-connected layers. The input to the convolutional neural network is the play screen of the game. The output of the convolutional neural network is value of each action for that state.

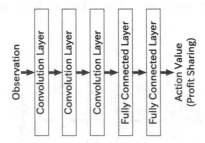

Fig. 2. Structure of convolutional neural network used in proposed method.

3.3 Learning

In the proposed method, the convolutional neural network learns to output the value of each action corresponding to the play screen of the game (observation) which is given as input. Here, the action value is updated based on the Profit Sharing. So, the error function E is given by

$$E = \frac{1}{2}\left(r_\tau F(\tau) - q(o_\tau, a_\tau)\right)^2 \tag{3}$$

where r is reward, $q(o_\tau, a_\tau)$ is the value of taking action a_τ at observation o_τ. $F(\tau)$ is the reinforcement function at the time τ and is given by

$$F(\tau) = \frac{1}{(|C^A| + 1)^{W-\tau}} \tag{4}$$

where C^A is the set of actions that an agent can take at the observation, $|C^A|$ is the number of actions that an agent can take, W is the length of an episode.

The action is selected based using the ε-greedy as similar as the conventional Deep Q-Network.

4 Computer Experiment Results

To demonstrate the effectiveness of the proposed method, computer experiments were conducted on a game of Atari 2600 (Asterix). The results are shown below.

4.1 Task

Asterix is an action game shown in Fig. 3. A player can operate own machine up and down, left and right. From the left and right of the screen, jars and harps fly. You can score 50 points by taking a jar. Taking the harp will reduce the remaining machines. At the start of the game, there are three machines. When the remaining machine runs out, the game ends. The score of the game is the sum of the scores acquired by the end of the game.

The actions of the agent are five kinds of movement; moving to up, down, left and right, and not moving. The agent gets a positive reward (1) when it gains score. In addition, the agent acquires a negative reward (−1) when a remaining machine decreases.

4.2 Experimental Conditions

Table 1 shows the conditions for the convolutional neural network used in the proposed method and the conventional Deep Q-Network. The game screen used in this research is an RGB image of 400×500. In the experiment, the RGB image is grayscaled, reduced to 84×84 pixels, and an image grouped for 4 frames is used as input.

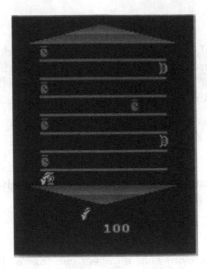

Fig. 3. Asterix.

Table 2 shows other conditions related to learning. An action is selected by ε-greedy. At the start of learning, ε is set to 1 so that actions are randomly selected. After that, ε is decreased until it becomes $1/10^6$ every action (one step). The agent gradually emphasizes the action value and selects an action.

In the proposed method, since Profit Sharing is used, as the length of the episode becomes longer, the value of the denominator on the right side of Eq. (4) becomes too large and the reward can not be distributed sufficiently. Therefore, only five steps before acquisition of the score are regarded as episodes.

4.3   Transition of Obtained Scores

Here, a game of atari 2600 (Asterix) are learned by the proposed Profit Sharing using convolutional neural network, and we compared the transition of the score with the conventional Deep Q-Network.

Figure 4 shows the transition of obtained scores in each method. This figure is the average of scores every 50 thousand times.

Table 1. Experimental conditions (1).

	Filter size	Stride	Output size	Output function
Input	–	–	$84 \times 84 \times 4$	–
Convolution layer 1	8×8	4	$20 \times 20 \times 32$	ReLU
Convolution layer 2	4×4	2	$9 \times 9 \times 64$	ReLU
Convolution layer 3	3×3	1	$7 \times 7 \times 64$	ReLU
Full-connected layer 1	–	–	512	ReLU
Full-connected layer 2	–	–	5 (the number of actions)	Identity function

Table 2. Experimental conditions (2)

The number of learning steps		1.0×10^7
Initial value of ε	ε_{ini}	1
Decrease amount of ε	ε_r	$1/10^6$
Minimum of ε	ε_{min}	0.1
ε in evaluation episodes	ε'	0.05
Size of replay memory	D_{max}	10^6
Size of mini batch	M	32
Discount Rate	γ	0.99
Update interval of target network	T_{update}	10^4

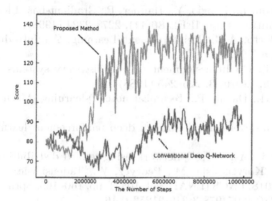

Fig. 4. Transition of obtained scores.

Asterix is a problem which is considered to be difficult to learn on the conventional Deep Q-Network, and the acquired score is not stable up to 5 million steps. However, after that, the acquired score rises, and the average score of acquisition at 10 million steps is about 90 points. In the proposed method, the score increases up to the first 5 million steps, and after that, it is able to obtain a high score stably. ε in the ε-greedy method is set to be the minimum value (0.1) at the time of 5 million steps. Considering that the score is stable in both methods after 5 million steps, we think that it may be possible that the progress of learning may change by changing the way of decreasing ε. According to the result of Fig. 4, we confirmed that learning can be done from the earlier stage than the conventional Deep Q-Network in the proposed method and the score obtained finally becomes high.

5 Conclusions

In this paper, we have proposed the Profit Sharing using convolutional neural network. In the proposed method, action value in Profit Sharing is learned by convolutional neural network. This is a method that learns the value function of Profit Sharing instead of the value function of Q Learning used in the Deep Q-Network. By changing to an error function based on the value function of Profit Sharing which can acquire probabilistic policy in a shorter time, the proposed method is able to learn in a shorter time than the conventional Deep Q-Network.

Computer experiments were carried out on Asterix of Atari 2600, and the proposed method was compared with the conventional Deep Q-Network. As a result, we confirmed that the proposed method can learn from the earlier stage than Deep Q-Network and can obtain higher score finally.

References

1. LeCun, Y., Bottou, L., Bengio, Y., Haffner, P.: Gradient-based learning applied to document recognition. Proc. IEEE **86**(11), 2278–2324 (1998)
2. Sutton, R.S., Barto, A.G.: Reinforcement Learning: An Introduction. The MIT Press, Cambridge (1998)
3. Grefenstette, J.J.: Credit assignment in rule discovery systems based on genetic algorithms. Mach. Learn. **3**, 225–245 (1988)
4. Watkins, C.J.C.H., Dayan, P.: Technical note: Q-learning. Mach. Learn. **8**, 55–68 (1992)
5. Mnih, V.: Human-level control through deep reinforcement learning. Nature **518**, 529–533 (2015)
6. Nakaya, Y., Osana, Y.: Deep Q-network using reward distribution. In: Rutkowski, L., Scherer, R., Korytkowski, M., Pedrycz, W., Tadeusiewicz, R., Zurada, J.M. (eds.) ICAISC 2018. LNCS (LNAI), vol. 10841, pp. 160–169. Springer, Cham (2018). https://doi.org/10.1007/978-3-319-91253-0_16

Detection of Fingerprint Alterations Using Deep Convolutional Neural Networks

Yahaya Isah Shehu[1]([✉]), Ariel Ruiz-Garcia[1], Vasile Palade[1], and Anne James[2]

[1] Faculty of Engineering, Environment and Computing, Coventry University, Priory Street, Coventry CV1 5FB, UK
{shehuy2,ariel.ruiz-garcia, vasile.palade}@coventry.ac.uk
[2] Faculty of Science and Technology, Nottingham Trent University, Clifton Campus, Nottingham NG11 8NS, UK
anne.james@ntu.ac.uk

Abstract. Fingerprint alteration is a challenge that poses enormous security risks. As a result, many research efforts in the scientific community have attempted to address this issue. However, non-existence of publicly available datasets that contain obfuscation and distortion of fingerprints makes it difficult to identify the type of alteration. In this work we present the publicly available Sokoto-Coventry Fingerprints Dataset (SOCOFing), which provides ten fingerprints for 600 different subjects, as well as gender, hand and finger name for each image, among other unique characteristics. We also provide a total of 55,249 images with three levels of alteration for Z-cut, obliteration and central rotation synthetic alterations, which are the most common types of obfuscation and distortion. In addition, this paper proposes a Convolutional Neural Network (CNN) to identify these alterations. The proposed CNN model achieves a classification accuracy rate of 98.55%. Results are also compared with a residual CNN model pre-trained on ImageNet, which produces an accuracy of 99.88%.

Keywords: Central rotation · Convolutional neural networks · Distortion Fingerprint alteration · Obfuscation · Obliteration · Z-cut

1 Introduction

The field of forensic science is the use of applied science and technical approaches to provide answers to issues in criminal, civil and administrative law. Fingerprints can be altered through abrading [1], cutting [2], burning [3] and distortions, such as skin grafting [4], where an unusual and unnatural change in the patterns of the friction ridge occurs. The most common alteration types are in the form of Z-cut, central rotation and obliteration. In this paper, we present a novel fingerprint dataset with unique attributes, such as gender, finger type (like index finger, thumb, ring finger, middle finger and little finger) for both left and right hand of the subject, respectively. Furthermore, we present preliminary experimental results on the detection of the alteration type using a deep CNN and a residual CNN model. The two presented models classify the

V. Kůrková et al. (Eds.): ICANN 2018, LNCS 11139, pp. 51–60, 2018.
https://doi.org/10.1007/978-3-030-01418-6_6

fingerprint images into Z-cut, central rotation, obliteration and real, i.e. non-altered fingerprint. The real fingerprints from our SOCOFing dataset [5], with a total number of 6000 fingerprints from 600 subjects, were synthetically altered to central rotation, Z-cut and obliteration, which are the common types of alteration, resulting in a total of 55249 altered fingerprints. The SOCOFing dataset is publically available for replication and further experimental research work with the sole aim of improving upon the security of biometric fingerprints, such that criminals in the watch list could be identified and apprehended even if their fingerprints have been altered.

2   Related Works

Boarder Control is one of the major beneficiaries of biometrics, where fingerprints are used to detect and recognise individuals. Those that are having past criminal records and those that have committed high profile crimes used to undergo certain alterations of their fingerprints to avoid detection, especially in refugee and asylum seeker camps [6]. Such mutilations come in either burning the fingers or using surgery to cut some part of the fingers or body and place them onto another finger ('grafting), some come in a Z-shape, rotated centrally or obliterated, just to evade detection or linking the individual with their past [6]. Fingerprints of a little proportion of visitors visiting foreign countries are matched against a database of well-known criminals or terrorists. Biometrics has helped in identifying and apprehending over 1600 wanted individuals for felony crimes [7]. This is a sign that those wanting to hide their identity in pursuit of their criminal motives may alter their fingerprints in order to break border and enter into any country without their true identity being detected. However, it is essential to detect such alteration types and link the altered fingerprint images to their original ones. Furthermore, determining the alteration type is an essential first step to reveal a subjects' identity.

Fingerprints can be obliterated or mutilated to systematically evade identification by the biometric system [2]. Fingerprint can as well be altered or grafted to various patterns, shapes, sizes, via surgical operation which comes in either a Z-cut or central rotation. Other types of alteration can be achieved by burning the fingerprints 'obliteration', which in turn changes the fingerprint patterns that the biometric system uses to match and identify individuals based on what was previously stored as the original fingerprint [8]. Various software application and hardware solutions are proposed [9, 10] to tackle this situation. However, the authors focus on spoofing and distortion by rotating fingers on the scanner. Obfuscation is the purposeful exertion of an individual of concealing their identity by altering ridge patterns of their fingerprint [3]. Generally the alterations are categorised into three fundamental classes in view of the changes made to the ridge patterns of the fingerprint (i) obliteration or decimation (ii) distortion or bending and (iii) imitation or impersonation of fingerprint [3]. The most common alteration types based on the examination of ridge patterns presented by [3] are obliteration and distortion, which make up 89% and 10% of such alterations, respectively, whereas only 1% is reported as imitation. This shows that most of the alterations are either obliteration or distortion, which we seek to address in this paper. In [3], the proposed algorithm and reported technique identify and detect such fingerprint alterations with an accuracy of 66.4%. They also emphasize on the lack of public available databases that comprise obliterated and distorted fingerprints, to be used for experimentation purposes to improve upon the detection alteration algorithms. The datasets used by the authors in [3] is not publically available as it is highly secured due to the sensitivity of the data and is mostly owned by law enforcement agency. This makes it difficult for the research community to proffer better solutions and robust detection or matching algorithms that can detect with high accuracy.

The authors in [11], proposed various methods to generate synthetically altered fingerprint images, which also include a variety of noise such as scar or blurring in order to create a more realistic fingerprints. The authors utilised these dataset to develop a framework for detection or matching of altered fingerprints, where the alterations are obliteration, central rotation and Z cut. The authors of [2] focused on the position of the alteration which is often chosen at random, since the main objective is to avoid being identified [2]. This alteration can be achieved by a publically available tool proposed by [12]; SynThetic fingeRprint AlteratioNs GEnerator (STRANGE).

Based on previous studies in the area of fingerprints alteration, analysis and detection, significant gap in knowledge was identified. In Yoon et al. (2012), a case study compilation with automatic detection, classification and evaluation of altered fingerprints is done with the view of reducing the number of individual wanting to evade identification. This study extends [3] in determining alteration types automatically as well as introducing a new fingerprint dataset comprising real fingerprints and altered fingerprints for experimental purposes and replication of other academic researches on fingerprint alteration detection algorithms. The dataset also has some attributes that can open more research avenues due to its uniqueness in identifying gender, fingers name and either a left hand or a right hand, which has received little or no attention in the past. These form the current research contribution to addressing alterations of fingerprints, using the specific sets of fingerprints dataset in addition to determining the alteration type.

3 Dataset

SOCOFing dataset comprises a total of 6,000 real fingerprints collected from 600 subjects, are provided for experimental and other academic research purposes. We used the STRANGE tool to alter fingerprints by applying Easy, Medium, and Hard settings according to a quality threshold during fingerprint comparison [11]. The quality threshold is determined by the image resolution which by default is set to 500 dbi. These categories are parameters that are tuned according to the performance drop during fingerprint comparison. Furthermore, each category mentioned above is divided into three types of synthetic alteration, i.e. obliteration, central rotation and Z-cut. Each image will have three types of alteration in the three categories; hence each image was presented with nine altered images.

The dataset is divided into altered and real fingerprints. A total of 5977 real fingerprints are altered using easy parameter setting while 5689 real fingerprints are altered as medium and finally a total of 4758 fingerprints real images are altered with hard parameter settings. Each of the three real fingerprint parameter settings produced

54   Y. I. Shehu et al.

three types of alteration: obliteration, central rotation and Z-cut. For instance 5977 real images produced 5977 obliterated fingerprints, 5977 central rotation and 5977 Z-cut alteration. This means that for 5977 real fingerprints there is going to be 17931 altered fingerprints presented as fake in easy category. Likewise in medium category a total number of 17067 are presented as altered and, finally, 14274 fingerprints are altered in the hard category. However, for the purpose of training and testing of the convolutional model, the alteration types of the fingerprint images are combined together irrespective of the settings. A total of 55249 fingerprint images were randomly divided into 50% training set and 50% testing set. Note that the STRANGE tool did not find some fingerprint images fit for alterations with specific parameters; hence the altered images for each category are less than the total number of real images. Figure 1 below shows a sample of real fingerprint from a left hand of one subject.

Fig. 1. Sample of real left hand of one subject.

After applying the STRANGE tool for the three types of alterations, Fig. 2 below displays the altered fingerprint of the left hand of the same subject in Fig. 1.

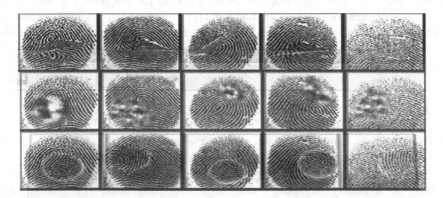

Fig. 2. Sample of altered left hand fingerprint into Z-cut, obliteration and central rotation, respectively, of the same subject.

4   Methodology and Experimental Setup

In this paper, we propose a deep CNN for feature extraction and classification. Deep CNNs have proven to be efficient in image processing related tasks and, therefore, are suitable for detecting fingerprints alteration types. We train and evaluate this model on the real and synthetically altered images of the SOCOFing dataset described above.

Each class, including real images, is randomly split into 50% training and 50% testing subsets. The images are also resized to 200 × 200 using bipolar interpolation.

4.1 Convolutional Neural Network Model

Convolutional neural networks retain spatial information through filter kernels. In this work, we exploit this unique ability of CNNs to train a model to classify images from the SOCOFing into four categories: central rotation, obliteration, Z-cut and real, where real images are those without any alteration.

The deep CNN model has five convolutional layers with 20 3 × 3, 40 3 × 3, 60 3 × 3, 80 3 × 3 filter kernels. All convolutional layers use a stride of one and zero padding of size two. Moreover, the output of every convolutional layer is shaped by a rectifier linear unit (ReLU) function. Max pooling is applied to the first three convolutional layers for dimensionality reduction. The convolutional layers are followed by two fully connected layers with 1000 and 100 hidden units, respectively. Furthermore, we employ batch normalization to standardize the distribution of each input feature across all the layers and thus speed up training and avoid exploding gradients [13].

The deep CNN is trained using stochastic gradient decent (SGD) and with Nesterov momentum of 0.5. We trained on min-batches of size 70 and set the learning rate, LR, to 0.01. LR was decayed with a factor of 0.01 according to:

$$LR = \frac{\lambda}{1 + (\omega \times \theta)} \tag{1}$$

where λ denotes the initial LR, ω the decay factor and θ the current epoch. The loss is defined by a SoftMax operator and the cross-entropy y is determined according to:

$$y = -x_c + \log\left(\sum_j \exp(x_j)\right) \tag{2}$$

where c is the class ground-truth. Training was done for 100 epochs as further training led to overfitting.

4.2 Residual Convolutional Neural Network Model

Residual Neural Networks (ResNets) have demonstrated to be exceptionally effective models on image classification [14]. ResNets have an identity shortcut connection that allows for very deep architectures to be trained and, therefore, more complex features to be learned, leading to improved classification performance. For this reason we decided to compare our model with a ResNet18, that is, with 18 parametrized convolutional layers, provided by [15, 16].

This network was originally trained and evaluated on ImageNet [17]. The authors also provide deeper architectures, of up to 200 layers, pre-trained on the same dataset. However, because fingerprint images have a relatively smaller number of features and the nature of the problem being addressed here is not as complex as classifying ImageNet which has 1000 classes, we did not consider deeper architectures.

The ResNet18 model is fine-tuned on the training subset of the SOCOFing presented in this paper for only 5 epochs. No modifications were done to the network other than the replacement of the output layer to only predict four classes. Training was also done using SGD, a Nesterov momentum of 0.75 and a learning rate of 0.001. This ResNet model is then evaluated on the test subset.

5 Results and Discussion

The confusion matrices below show the total number of each alteration types detected and also the number of fingerprint images misclassified. The results are presented in Tables 1 and 2 with the three types of alteration, the real fingerprint images and the percentage accuracy of the detection of the alteration types.

Table 1. Confusion matrix of our CNN.

Central rotation	Obliteration	Real	Z-cut	Accuracy (%)
7995	33	0	183	97.37
19	8148	0	44	99.23
0	0	2988	0	100
116	6	0	8089	98.51
98.34%	99.52%	100%	97.27%	98.55

Table 2. Confusion Matrix of the pre-trained and fine-tuned ResNet18.

Central rotation	Obliteration	Real	Z-cut	Accuracy (%)
8206	1	1	3	99.94
0	8195	15	1	99.81
0	0	2986	2	99.93
4	0	11	8196	99.82
99.95%	99.98%	99.10%	99.93%	99.86

As indicated in Table 1, 2988 cases of real fingerprint images are correctly classified as real fingerprints. The proposed model was able to detect and classify 100% of the entire real fingerprints correctly. However, 98.55% of the overall predictions across all four classes are correct. In addition, 183 altered fingerprint images in central rotation are mixed up with Z-cut alteration and 116 Z-cut altered fingerprint images are mixed up as central rotation. This can be explained because some of the angles in the parameter setting of the tool used rotate the altered part of the images in a similar pattern coupled with the ridges pattern, radial and ulnar loop. Radial loop is a loop that comes from the side of the thumb and looped out to the pinky side of the hand, while ulnar is the opposite, i.e., from the pinky side of the hand towards the thumb of the fingerprint images [18]. These angle rotation contributed to the misclassification of the alteration between the central rotation and Z-cut, which results in getting a high number of up to 183 and 116 altered fingerprint images presented as Z-cut and central rotation, respectively.

Table 2 shows the pre-trained confusion matrix for the ResNet-18 model that achieves a global accuracy of 99.86%. It misclassifies two real fingerprint images as Z-cut, while the proposed CNN model classifies all the real fingerprint images correctly. Furthermore, 15 of the obliterated fingerprint images are misclassifies as real, while 11 Z-cut altered fingerprint are also misclassifies as real. This may be because some of the real images are not of good quality and appear as obliteration. However, some loop ridges in the fingerprint when rotated to some certain degrees might result into some pattern changes that might look like Z-cut shape, hence classify them as Z-cut. In addition, there exist some natural cut in some of the fingerprints, which the models equally detect as a Z-cut shown in Fig. 3 central rotation classified as Z-cut. Some fingerprints also appeared to look blurring and haze, which the model classified as obliteration, indicated in Fig. 4 where central rotation are misclassified as obliteration. Figure 5 shows altered Z-cut fingerprint classified as obliteration because of the blurring defect of the real fingerprint at the top most of the images. As some of the images are from female fingers, we cannot also ruled out the possibility of them wearing henna as shown in the last image of Fig. 5.

Evaluating the confusion matrixes above, we found that the accuracy rate of central rotation is 97.37% and 99.94% of the pre-trained model. This shows that the pre-trained model performs better in terms of detecting altered images with central rotation alteration type. Likewise, it also does better in the recall, with 99.95% against 98.34%. The pre-trained ResNet-18 model performs better in almost all the categories. However, even though the detection accuracy is high on real images, with a precision of 99.93% and recall of 99.10%, the CNN model we proposed does better with 100% detection for both precision and recall scores.

The two CNN models achieved a high accuracy in the classification of altered fingerprint. Nevertheless, some images are still misclassified, particularly the altered fingerprint images.

Fig. 3. Central rotation misclassified as Z-cut.

Fig. 4. Central rotation misclassified as obliteration.

Fig. 5. Z-cut misclassified as obliteration.

From the misclassified fingerprints illustrated in Figs. 3 and 4, we can see that the easy alteration category fingerprints are misclassified more by the CNN model because they physically appeared with little proportion of the fingerprints altered, then followed by the medium category. The hard category fingerprints are less misclassified unless in the case of patterns rotational degrees that mixed central rotation with Z-cut.

Selvarani et al. [19] use singular points to distinguish between real fingerprints and altered ones, by extracting sets of features from the ridge orientation field of an input fingerprint and then apply a fuzzy classifier to classify it into real or altered 'Z-cut'. Similarly, [20, 21] introduced a classifier that detects altered fingerprint images with Z-cut and central rotation only using extracted features and a support vector classifier. This was tested using synthetic fingerprints and achieved 92% accuracy above the well-known fingerprint quality software, NFIQ, as it only recognised 20% of the altered fingerprints. We cannot therefore provide a comparison on other alterations, since, to the best of our knowledge, no prior work has been done on detecting these three types of alterations together.

One of the main advantages of the deep CNN proposed in this work is that the ResNet18 was pre-trained on the ImageNet dataset, which has over one million images spanning over 100 classes, compared to our model, which was only trained on our dataset and for only 100 epochs. Our model also has a significantly smaller number of convolutional layers, and thus an exponentially smaller number of hyperparameters. Moreover, because the CNN proposed here has a precision and recall rate of 100% on real images, it can be more suitable for use in applications where detecting whether a fingerprint has been altered or not is most important. Furthermore, the performance of the ResNet models provided by [15] heavily relies on the image pre-processing steps, such as aspect ratio resizing and luminance adjustments.

6   Conclusion

Fingerprint alteration detection is still an issue that requires more attention in detecting and identifying altered fingerprints. In this paper, we have introduced a novel finger-prints dataset, SOCOFing, for wider research accessibility. We highlighted the importance of fingerprint alteration research and the need for digital automatic detection of altered fingerprints. We also discussed the most common types of obfuscation and distortion: central rotation, obliteration and Z-cut. The presented dataset includes three different levels of alterations for each one of these types. Furthermore, the novel dataset presented in this paper has a number of unique attributes, such as the name of the fingers, which hand does the fingers belong to as well as the gender of the fingerprint owner. We have also proposed a CNN model that is not only able to detect whether a fingerprint has been altered or not but also detect the type of alteration. The proposed CNN achieved an accuracy rate of 98.55% on the testing subset of the SOCOFing dataset. This was compared against a ResNet18 model pre-trained on ImageNet and fine-tuned and tested on our dataset, achieving a state-of-the-art accuracy rate of 99.86%. One of the main differences in performance for our model and the ResNet18 model was that even though the ResNet18 slightly outperformed our model, our model achieved a precision and recall rate of 100% on real images, thus it can be more suitable for real-time applications.

To the best of the authors' knowledge, no prior work has addressed these three types of alterations. However, one of the limitations of this work is that the proposed CNN was evaluated on synthetically altered images due to the lack of publicly available datasets containing actual altered images. Nonetheless, we hope that the results presented in this work can serve as a benchmark in identifying fingerprint alterations and that the novel presented dataset can assist the research community in developing more robust biometric fingerprint technology for the automatic detection of altered fingerprints.

Future work will also investigate the reasons why the ResNet18 model confuses non-altered fingerprints with altered ones. Moreover, we will also test our model on different datasets, with different alteration types, to see if it retains 100% precision and recall rates on real images.

References

1. Burks Jr., J.W.: The effect of dermabrasion on fingerprints. AMA Arch. Dermatol. **77**, 8–11 (1958)
2. Cummins, H.: Attempts to alter and obliterate finger-prints. Am. Inst. Crim. L. & Criminol. **25**, 982 (1934)
3. Yoon, S., Feng, J., Jain, A.K.: Altered fingerprints: analysis and detection. IEEE Trans. Pattern Anal. Mach. Intell. **34**(3), 451–464 (2012)
4. Wertheim, K.: An extreme case of fingerprint mutilation. J. Forensic Identif. **48**(4), 466 (1998)
5. Shehu, Y.I., Ruiz-Garcia, A., Palade, V., James, A.: Sokoto coventry fingerprint dataset. arXiv preprint arXiv:1807.10609 (2018)
6. Petrovici, A.: Simulating alteration on fingerprint images. In: IEEE Workshop on Biometric Measurements and Systems for Security and Medical Applications, BIOMS, pp. 1–5. IEEE, September 2012
7. Salter, M.B.: Passports, mobility, and security: how smart can the border be? Int. Stud. Perspect. **5**(1), 71–91 (2004)
8. Feng, J., Jain, A.K., Ross, A.: Detecting altered fingerprints. In: 20th International Conference on Pattern Recognition, ICPR, pp. 1622–1625. IEEE, August 2010
9. Antonelli, A., Cappelli, R., Maio, D., Maltoni, D.: Fake finger detection by skin distortion analysis. IEEE Trans. Inf. Forensics Secur. **1**(3), 360–373 (2006)
10. Nixon, K.A., Rowe, R.K.: Multispectral fingerprint imaging for spoof detection. In: Biometric Technology for Human Identification II, vol. 5779, pp. 214–226. International Society for Optics and Photonics, March 2005

11. Papi, S., Ferrara, M., Maltoni, D., Anthonioz, A.: On the generation of synthetic fingerprint alterations. In: International Conference of the Biometrics Special Interest Group, BIOSIG, pp. 1–6. IEEE, September 2016
12. Biolab.csr.unibo.it: Biometric System Laboratory (2018). http://biolab.csr.unibo.it/research. asp?organize=Activities&select=&selObj=211&pathSubj=111%7C%7C21%7C%7C211& R eq=&. Accessed 3 Apr 2018
13. Ioffe, S., Szegedy, C.: Batch normalization: accelerating deep network training by reducing internal covariate shift. arXiv preprint arXiv:1502.03167 (2015)
14. Szegedy, C., Ioffe, S., Vanhoucke, V., Alemi, A.A.: Inception-v4, inception-ResNet and the impact of residual connections on learning. In: AAAI, vol. 4, p. 12, February 2017
15. He, K., Zhang, X., Ren, S., Sun, J.: Deep residual learning for image recognition. In: Proceedings of the IEEE Conference on Computer Vision and Pattern Recognition, pp. 770–778 (2016)
16. Facebook: facebook/fb.resnet.torch (2018). https://github.com/facebook/fb.resnet.torch. Accessed 29 Apr 2018
17. Krizhevsky, A., Sutskever, I., Hinton, G.E.: ImageNet classification with deep convolutional neural networks. In: Advances in Neural Information Processing Systems, pp. 1097–1105 (2012)
18. Maio, D., Maltoni, D.: A structural approach to fingerprint classification. In: Proceedings of the 13th International Conference on Pattern Recognition, vol. 3, pp. 578–585. IEEE, August 1996
19. Selvarani, S.M.C.A., Jebapriya, S., Mary, R.S.: Automatic identification and detection of altered fingerprints. In: 2014 International Conference on Intelligent Computing Applications, ICICA, pp. 239–243. IEEE, March 2014
20. Feng, J., Jain, A.K., Ross, A.: Detecting altered fingerprints. In: 2010 20th International Conference on Pattern Recognition, ICPR, pp. 1622–1625. IEEE, August 2010
21. Yoon, S., Zhao, Q., Jain, A.K.: On matching altered fingerprints. In: 2012 5th IAPR International Conference on Biometrics, ICB, pp. 222–229. IEEE, March 2012

A Convolutional Neural Network Approach for Modeling Semantic Trajectories and Predicting Future Locations

Antonios Karatzoglou[1,2](✉), Nikolai Schnell[1], and Michael Beigl[1]

[1] Karlsruhe Institute of Technology, Karlsruhe, Germany
{antonios.karatzoglou,michael.beigl}@kit.edu,
nikolai.schnell@student.kit.edu
[2] Robert Bosch, Corporate Sector Research and Advance Engineering,
Stuttgart, Germany
antonios.karatzoglou@de.bosch.com

Abstract. In recent years, Location Based Service (LBS) providers rely increasingly on predictive models in order to offer their users timely and tailored solutions. Current location prediction algorithms go beyond using plain location data and show that additional context information can lead to a higher performance. Moreover, it has been shown that using semantics and projecting GPS trajectories on so called semantic trajectories can further improve the model. At the same time, Artificial Neural Networks (ANNs) have been proven to be very reliable when it comes to modeling and predicting time series. Recurrent network architectures show a particularly good performance. However, very little research has been done on the use of Convolutional Neural Networks (CNNs) in connection with modeling human movement patterns. In this work, we introduce a CNN-based approach for representing semantic trajectories and predicting future locations. Furthermore, we included an additional embedding layer to raise the efficiency. In order to evaluate our approach, we use the MIT Reality Mining dataset and use a Feed-Forward (FFNN) -, a Recurrent (RNN) - and a LSTM network to compare it with on two different semantic trajectory levels. We show that CNNs are more than capable of handling semantic trajectories, while providing high prediction accuracies at the same time.

Keywords: Convolutional Neural Networks · Semantic trajectories
Location prediction · Embedding layer

1 Introduction

With the rise in the use of smartphones, wearables and other IoT devices over the past decade, applications that use location data have become increasingly popular. In addition, in recent years, providers attempt progressively to predict

© Springer Nature Switzerland AG 2018
V. Kůrková et al. (Eds.): ICANN 2018, LNCS 11139, pp. 61–72, 2018.
https://doi.org/10.1007/978-3-030-01418-6_7

the locations to be visited next by the users, in order to be able to offer them timely and personalised services. This makes the location prediction research particularly important. Patterns mined from location data can provide a deep insight into the behaviour of mobile users. The usage of semantic knowledge helps diving even deeper into their behaviour. So called *semantic trajectories* encapsulate additional knowledge that can be crucial for the predictive model.

The purpose of our paper is to present and evaluate a Convolutional Neural Network (CNN) architecture in a semantic location prediction scenario. First, we describe some related work that has been done in the realms of semantic location prediction, semantic location mining and CNNs. Next, we elaborate on the way CNNs work, by providing some relevant term definitions at the same time. In Sect. 4 we outline our own architecture together with some basic implementation details. Finally, in Sects. 5 and 6, we discuss our evaluation outcome and draw our final conclusions with regard to our findings.

2   Related Work

Spaccapietra et al. depict as one of the first in their work [12] the importance of viewing trajectories of moving objects in a conceptual manner. They show that, by defining and adding semantic information, such as the notion of application-specific *stops* and *moves*, to the raw trajectories, they can significantly enhance the analysis of movement patterns, and provide further insights into object behaviour. Elragal et al. depict in [5] the benefits of integrating semantics into trajectories as well. It is shown that semantic trajectories help improve both pattern extraction and decision-making processes in contrast to raw trajectories. For this reason, several papers have emerged in recent years presenting approaches to transforming raw location data into so called *semantic locations* (Sect. 3.1). Alvares et al. for instance introduce a semantic enrichment model aiming at simplifying the query and analysis of moving objects [1]. Bogorny et al. [2] extend the previous approach by introducing a more general and sophisticated model, capable of handling more complex queries, while providing different semantic granularities at the same time.

The notion of semantic trajectories has also grown in importance in the field of location prediction during the last years. Ying et al. [13] for example present a location prediction framework based on previously mined semantic trajectories from the users' raw geo-tracking data. Their prefix tree decision based algorithm shows good performance, especially in terms of recall, f-score and efficiency.

In their recent work, Karatzoglou et al. [7], explore the modeling and prediction performance of various artificial neural network (ANN) architectures, e.g., Feed-Forward (FFNN), Recurrent (RNN) and Long-Short-Term-Memory (LSTM) network on semantic trajectories. Similar to Ying et al. they evaluate their models using the MIT Reality Mining dataset [4], with the LSTM achieving the best results with up to 76% in terms of accuracy and outscoring the other methods on f-score and recall as well. In addition, they investigate the role of the semantic granularity of the considered trajectories in the overall performance of the networks. They show that the higher the semantic level, the better the modeling quality of the networks.

Lv et al. explore in [10] the possibility of using Convolutional Neural Networks (CNNs) (Sect. 3.2) to predict taxi trajectories. Their approach projects past trajectories upon a map and models them in turn as 2D images, on which the CNN is finally applied to estimate about future trajectories. By modeling trajectories as 2D images, they are able to make use of the inherent advantage of CNNs, namely their good performance in image analysis. This is also confirmed by their results. However, their approach is applied on raw, non-semantic GPS trajectories.

To our knowledge, there is no work exploring the performance of CNNs on semantic trajectories. Moreover, it seems that there is no work using trajectories (semantic or non-semantic ones) in combination with CNNs directly, e.g., without transforming them in an intermediate step into 2D images, but handling them in their raw form instead, as 1D vectors. In the presented work, we examine exactly these two points in terms of prediction performance in a semantic location prediction scenario. For this purpose, we focused on the Natural Language Processing (NLP) use case where, similar to our case, the data are also 1D and some work has already been done in combination with CNNs. Particularly interesting is the work of Collobert et al. [3], who propose a CNN architecture for solving several NLP problems including named entity recognition and semantic role labelling. Their framework features an unsupervised training algorithm for learning internal representations, e.g., by using an embedding layer and learning low-dimensional feature vectors of given words through backpropagation, yielding a good performance both in terms of accuracy and speed. The benefit of using embeddings has been recently shown also in connection with modeling human trajectories by Gao et al. in [6].

3   Theoretical Background

In this section, we give a brief insight into the fundamental components of our work.

3.1   Semantic Trajectories

Movement patterns, so called *trajectories*, describe sequences of consecutive location points visited by some object or person. In ubiquitous and mobile computing, trajectories refer usually to GPS sequences like the one displayed in Eq. 1, whereby $long_i$, lat_i and t_I refers to longitude, latitude and point of time respectively.

$$(long_1, lat_1, t_1), (long_2, lat_2, t_2), \ldots, (long_i, lat_i, t_i) \qquad (1)$$

In the attempt to add more meaning when modeling movement, researchers like Spaccapietra et al. [12] and Alvares et al. [1] went beyond such numerical sequences and lay focus on conceptual, semantically enriched trajectories,

so called *semantic trajectories*. A semantic trajectory is defined as a sequence
of semantically significant locations (*semantic locations*, e.g., "home", "burger
joint", etc.) as follows:

$$(SemLoc_1, t_1), (SemLoc_2, t_2), \ldots, (SemLoc_i, t_i) \qquad (2)$$

A significant location usually refers to a location at which a user stays more
than a certain amount of time, e.g. 20 min. Some researchers add further thresholds, like popularity, in order to extract the most significant common or public
locations (see [13]). Locations can be described hierarchically over a number of
various semantic levels, e.g., "restaurant" → "fast food restaurant" → "burger
joint". In this work, we evaluate the modeling performance of CNNs on two
different semantic levels.

3.2   Convolutional Neural Networks (CNNs)

The most popular application area of Convolutional Neural Networks (CNNs)
is the image classification and recognition [9]. However, CNNs can be applied
to other areas as well, such as speech recognition and time series [8]. A CNN
example architecture concerning the image classification use case can be seen in
Fig. 1.

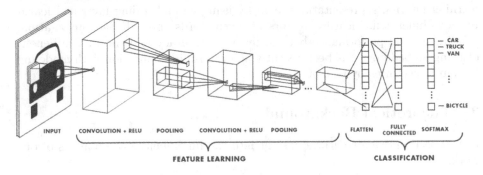

Fig. 1. Typical CNN architecture for Image Classification (source: [11]).

Here, the CNN first receives an image, which is supposed to classify, as its
input. Next, a set of convolution operations takes place in order to for the features to be extracted. These operations are realised by filter kernels of fixed size,
containing learnable weights, which are sled over the input image to "search"
for certain features. Each convolution filter output results in a new layer that
contains the findings of that filter in the input image. These layers are then further processed by a pooling operation set. Pooling operations combine multiple
outputs from filter kernels in a feature layer into a single value (e.g. by taking
the average or maximum value of the outputs in question). The resulting pooled

layers can then be further processed, as shown here, by more Convolution + Pooling operations and as such features of a higher level can be extracted. The last pooled layer is flattened i.e. transformed into a single long vector containing all of its weights. These are then connected to a fully connected layer, which is further connected to the output of the network, which in this case is a Softmax layer, containing a field for every classifiable object, and as such representing the classification estimation of the network for the given input.

4   CNNs for Semantic Trajectories - Our Approach

As already mentioned, our network (CNN) takes semantic trajectories as input, like the ones defined in Sect. 3.1. For this purpose, each semantic location is given a unique index. After being fed into the CNN, each index value in the trajectory gets passed to a hash table (*embedding layer*) which assigns each index, and as such each semantic location, a k-dimensional feature vector (*embedding*), whereby k represents a hyperparameter set by us (Sect. 5). At the very beginning, our feature vectors in the lookup table are randomly initialized. These vectors are then trained on the available training data via backpropagation in order to become optimal task-specific representations. In tangible terms, for our case, this means that we give our model the freedom to find the optimal semantic location representation by itself. The resulting representations will be used as input for our core model. A similar idea was proposed by Collobert et al. in [3] to learn feature vectors that represent words in a text corpus for solving NLP problems. After the hash table operation, our semantic location set, initially represented by a $n \times 1$ vector, becomes $n \times k$ matrix. This can be seen on the left in Fig. 2 and as *self.embedded_locs_expanded* in Listing 1.1.

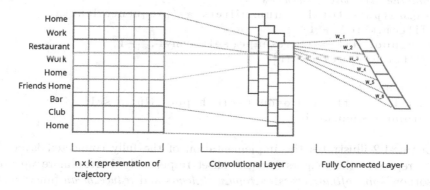

Fig. 2. An abstracted view on the core layers of our CNN.

In the next step, a set of convolutional filters is applied on the resulting matrix. These filters span along the entire feature vector dimension and across multiple locations of the trajectory as can be seen in Fig. 2. The number of filters is a hyperparameter that can be also set by the user. Like the size k of the embeddings dimension described above, it can affect the performance of the prediction.

The outputs of the filters are then concatenated and flattened (*self.h_pool_flat* in Listing 1.1) to make up a fully connected layer, linked to a Softmax output layer, which provides the final prediction about the next semantic location to be visited by a user. We decided against using pooling layers on the filter ouputs, since this led to the loss of significant feature information (e.g., locations in the latter part of the trajectory being more important to location prediction as the older ones).

In order to train our model, we used backpropagation with the Adam optimizer. The Adam optimizer maintains an individual learning rate for each network weight and adapts them separately. This is especially effective since our data is quite sparse compared to other more typical problems addressed by CNNs such as image recognition. We used Python and the Tensorflow[1] library to implement our model. To prevent overfitting, dropout is used on this flattened vector as shown in Listing 1.1 in line 14.

Listing 1.1. Convolution output and flattened layer.

```
# Convolution Layer
self.conv1 = tf.layers.conv2d(
    inputs=self.embedded_locs_expanded,
    filters=num_filters,
    kernel_size=[filter_size, embedding_size],
    padding="VALID",
    name="conv1")

# Combine all the features
filter_outputs_total = num_filters * ((sequence_length -
    filter_size) + 1)
self.h_pool_flat = tf.reshape(self.conv1, [-1,
    filter_outputs_total])

# Add dropout
self.h_drop = tf.nn.dropout(self.h_pool_flat, self.
    dropout_keep_prob)
```

Listing 1.2 illustrates the implementation of the fully connected layer. W and b represent the weights and the offset respectively. Furthermore we used Tensorflow's *nn.softmax_cross_entropy_with_logits* and *reduce_mean* functions to calculate the loss. The calculated loss is used by the Adam optimizer to adjust the weights of the Tensorflow graph, and as such to complete a single training step.

---

[1] https://www.tensorflow.org

Listing 1.2. Fully connected layer and loss calculation.

```
# Final (unnormalized) scores and predictions
W = tf.get_variable(
    "W",
    shape=[filter_outputs_total, num_classes],
    initializer=tf.contrib.layers.xavier_initializer())
b = tf.Variable(tf.constant(0.1, shape=[num_classes]), name="b
    ")
self.scores = tf.nn.xw_plus_b(self.h_drop, W, b, name="scores"
    )
self.predictions = tf.argmax(self.scores, 1, name="predictions
    ")

# Calculate mean cross-entropy loss
losses = tf.nn.softmax_cross_entropy_with_logits(logits=self.
    scores, labels=self.input_y)
self.loss = tf.reduce_mean(losses)
```

5   Evaluation

In order to evaluate our approach, we used the MIT Reality Mining dataset [4], which contains the semantically enriched tracking data of approximately 100 users over a period of 9 months. Filtering the inconsistencies out and keeping the most consistent annotators left us with the two-semantic-level evaluation dataset of 26 users of [7]. Figure 3 illustrates the overall location distribution. We then extracted trajectories of a fixed length and considered the subsequent location to be the ground truth prediction label (see Fig. 4). We shuffled the resulting (trajectories, label) pairs and took 90% of them for training and 10% for testing. We trained and evaluated both the separated single-user models, as well as a multi-user model that contained the trajectories of all users. In the

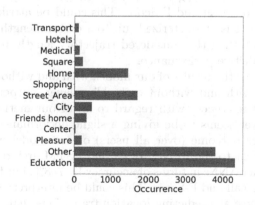

Fig. 3. Distribution of high-level semantic locations.

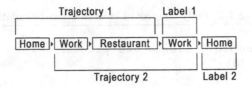

Fig. 4. Data Extraction exemplified with a trajectory length of 3.

case of the multi-user model, a single trajectory composed of all the available single-user trajectories was fed into the model as if it came from a single user. We further used the FFNN, the RNN and the LSTM from [7] as our baseline. In addition, since there is a timestamp present for every location visit in the Reality Mining data, we also tested the performance of our model when we include time as an extra feature. For this purpose we aggregated the available timestamps into hourly time slots. Finally, we evaluate a version of our model with the embedding layer missing. All models were evaluated in terms of *Accuracy, Accuracy@k, Precision, Recall,* and *F-Score.*

We tested several trajectory lengths (2, 5, 10 and 20) on different configurations of the following hyperparameters:

Filter Size: Width of the filter kernel, i.e. how many trajectories it encompasses.
Number of Filters: The number of different filters the CNN learns.
Embedding Dimension: The dimension of the learned location features.
Dropout Probability: The percentage of neurons in the fully connected layer that are dropped (used to minimize overfitting).

At the same time, we did a grid search to find the following optimal parameters as well: **Learning Rate, Number of training Epochs** and **Batch Size**. Both the results and the corresponding optimal parameter set can be found in Fig. 5.

In general, it seems that the longer the trajectory the better our model performs with regard to almost all of our metrics, e.g., accuracy, precision, recall and F-Score. However, if they get too long, e.g., >10, the performance drops. Especially in terms of recall and F-Score. This could be attributed to the fact that human movement is characterized, up to a certain length, by a long-term behaviour and thus raising the considered trajectory length in the model leads to an improved predictive performance.

In Fig. 6 we can see the results of our model, with and without an embedding layer. Both CNNs, with and without embedding layer, outperform the FFNN of [7] (used here as reference) with regard to all of our metrics. Additionally, the Embedding Layer seems to be giving a slight performance boost. Figure 7 contains the average outcome (over all users) of our model in the single-user model case in contrast to the FFNN, RNN and LSTM architecture. Our CNN outperforms the other ANNs in terms of accuracy by 7–8%, but falls a bit short in terms of precision, recall and F-Score. This could be interpreted as an indication that the CNN is worse at predicting location transitions that show up sparsely

Trajectory Length	Accuracy	Accuracy@4	Accuracy@10	Precision	Recall	F-Score
2	0.783	**0.976**	0.994	0.455	0.433	0.443
5	0.790	0.973	0.995	0.466	**0.439**	**0.451**
10	**0.792**	0.971	0.994	**0.467**	0.435	0.45
20	0.788	0.968	0.993	0.454	0.425	0.438

Fig. 5. Impact of trajectory length. Filter Size: **2**, Embedding Dimension: **100**, Number of Filters: **50**, Dropout Probability: **0.4**, Batch Size: **100**, Learning Rate: **0.001**, Number of Epochs: **10**.

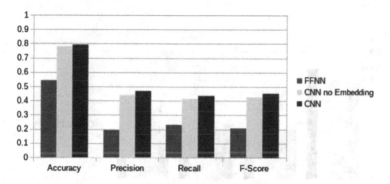

Fig. 6. Comparison of evaluation results of our architecture with and without embedding layer vs. FFNN.

in a dataset (in our case the respective single-user datasets) compared to the other ANNs. On the higher semantic level the accuracy discrepancy between the various models is similar to the low semantic version. However, in terms of precision, recall and F-Score the CNN seems to perform much worse than on the lower semantic version. It seems to disregard locations that occur relatively seldom in the dataset almost completely, which leads us to this result. In both

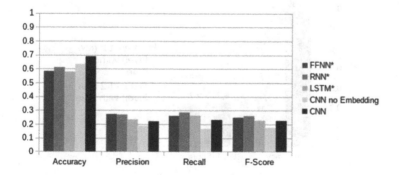

Fig. 7. Comparison of evaluation results of our architecture (CNN) vs. Karatzoglou et al. [7] (*) on the low semantic level (single user).

versions of the dataset (low- and high semantic level) the embedding layer seemed to make a small, but still significant difference.

Figure 9 contains the comparison results between the single-user and the multi-user modeling method. While the multi-user evaluation achieves much lower accuracies (as expected), it outperforms by far the single-user dataset in terms of precision, recall and F-Score. This can be attributed to the fact that the additional user information in the multi-user model fills the gap of missing locations and trajectories that can be often found in the single-user models (Fig. 8).

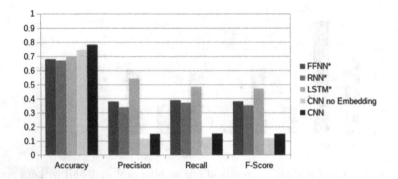

Fig. 8. Comparison of evaluation results of our Architecture (CNN) vs. Karatzoglou et al. [7] (*) on the high semantic level (single user).

Dataset 2 type	Accuracy	Accuracy@2	Accuracy@5	Precision	Recall	F-Score
Multi User	0.688	0.885	0.969	**0.53**	**0.428**	**0.474**
Single User	**0.78**	**0.919**	**0.993**	0.149	0.151	0.149

Fig. 9. Comparison of our multi- and single-user CNN models.

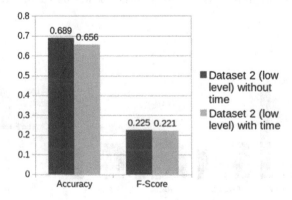

Fig. 10. Impact of time in the case of the low-level semantic representation.

Finally, in Fig. 10 it can be seen how adding time as an additional training feature affects the behaviour of our models. Similar to the results of [7], time seems to be having a negative influence on the prediction performance of our CNN model, both in terms of accuracy and F-Score.

6   Conclusion

In this paper, we investigate the performance of CNNs and embeddings in terms of modeling semantic trajectories and predicting future locations in a location prediction scenario. We evaluate our approach on a real-world dataset, using a FFNN, a RNN and a LSTM network as a baseline. We show that our CNN-based model outperforms all the above reference systems in terms of accuracy and is thus capable of modeling semantic trajectories and predicting future human movement patterns. However, our approach seems to be sensitive to sparse data. In addition, we show that, similar to the outcomes of [7], both the semantic representation level and the overall number of users considered for training the model can have a significant impact on the performance, especially with regard to precision and recall. In our future work, we plan to explore further the use of CNNs in the location prediction scenario by feeding additional semantic information into the model such as the users' activity and their current companion.

References

1. Alvares, L.O., Bogorny, V., Kuijpers, B., de Macedo, J.A.F., Moelans, B., Vaisman, A.: A model for enriching trajectories with semantic geographical information. In: Proceedings of the 15th Annual ACM International Symposium on Advances in Geographic Information Systems, p. 22. ACM (2007)
2. Bogorny, V., Renso, C., Aquino, A.R., Lucca Siqueira, F., Alvares, L.O.: Constant-a conceptual data model for semantic trajectories of moving objects. Trans. GIS **18**(1), 66–88 (2014)
3. Collobert, R., Weston, J., Bottou, L., Karlen, M., Kavukcuoglu, K., Kuksa, P.: Natural language processing (almost) from scratch. J. Mach. Learn. Res. **12**(Aug), 2493–2537 (2011)
4. Eagle, N., Pentland, A.S.: Reality mining: sensing complex social systems. Pers. Ubiquit. Comput. **10**(4), 255–268 (2006)
5. Elragal, A., El-Gendy, N.: Trajectory data mining: integrating semantics. J. Enterp. Inf. Manag. **26**(5), 516–535 (2013). https://doi.org/10.1108/JEIM-07-2013-0038
6. Gao, Q., Zhou, F., Zhang, K., Trajcevski, G., Luo, X., Zhang, F.: Identifying human mobility via trajectory embeddings. In: Proceedings of the 26th International Joint Conference on Artificial Intelligence, pp. 1689–1695. AAAI Press (2017)
7. Karatzoglou, A., Sentürk, H., Jablonski, A., Beigl, M.: Applying artificial neural networks on two-layer semantic trajectories for predicting the next semantic location. In: Lintas, A., Rovetta, S., Verschure, P.F.M.J., Villa, A.E.P. (eds.) ICANN 2017. LNCS, vol. 10614, pp. 233–241. Springer, Cham (2017). https://doi.org/10.1007/978-3-319-68612-7_27
8. LeCun, Y., Bengio, Y., et al.: Convolutional networks for images, speech, and time series. In: The Handbook of Brain Theory and Neural Networks, vol. 3361, no. 10 (1995)

9. LeCun, Y., Kavukcuoglu, K., Farabet, C.: Convolutional networks and applications in vision. In: Proceedings of 2010 IEEE International Symposium on Circuits and Systems (ISCAS), pp. 253–256. IEEE (2010)
10. Lv, J., Li, Q., Wang, X.: T-CONV: a convolutional neural network for multi-scale taxi trajectory prediction. arXiv preprint arXiv:1611.07635 (2016)
11. Mathworks: Convolutional neural network (2018). https://www.mathworks.com/discovery/convolutional-neural-network.html. Accessed 19 Feb 2018
12. Spaccapietra, S., Parent, C., Damiani, M.L., de Macêdo, J.A.F., Porto, F., Vangenot, C.: A conceptual view on trajectories. Data Knowl. Eng. **65**(1), 126–146 (2008). https://doi.org/10.1016/j.datak.2007.10.008
13. Ying, J.J.C., Lee, W.C., Weng, T.C., Tseng, V.S.: Semantic trajectory mining for location prediction. In: Proceedings of the 19th ACM SIGSPATIAL International Conference on Advances in Geographic Information Systems, pp. 34–43. ACM (2011)

Neural Networks for Multi-lingual Multi-label Document Classification

Jiří Martínek[1,2], Ladislav Lenc[1,2], and Pavel Král[1,2(✉)]

[1] Department of Computer Science and Engineering, Faculty of Applied Sciences,
University of West Bohemia, Plzeň, Czech Republic
{jimar,llenc,pkral}@kiv.zcu.cz
[2] NTIS - New Technologies for the Information Society, Faculty of Applied Sciences,
University of West Bohemia, Plzeň, Czech Republic

Abstract. This paper proposes a novel approach for multi-lingual multi-label document classification based on neural networks. We use popular convolutional neural networks for this task with three different configurations. The first one uses static word2vec embeddings that are let as is, while the second one initializes it with word2vec and fine-tunes the embeddings while learning on the available data. The last method initializes embeddings randomly and then they are optimized to the classification task. The proposed method is evaluated on four languages, namely English, German, Spanish and Italian from the Reuters corpus. Experimental results show that the proposed approach is efficient and the best obtained F measure reaches 84%.

Keywords: Convolutional neural network · CNN
Document classification · Multi-label · Multi-lingual

1 Introduction

Nowadays the importance of multi-lingual text processing increases significantly due to the extremely rapid growth of data available in several languages particularly on the Internet. Without multi-lingual systems it is not possible to acquire information across languages. Multi-label classification is also often beneficial because, in the case of real data, one sample usually belongs to more than one class.

This paper focuses on the multi-lingual multi-label document classification in a frame of a real application designed for handling texts from different sources in various languages. There are several possibilities how to perform a classification in multiple languages. Most of them learn one model in a mono-lingual space and then use some transformation method to pass across the languages. The usual document representation are word embeddings created for instance by the word2vec approach [8]. Contrary to this idea, we suggest one general model trained on all available languages. Therefore, this model is able to classify more languages without any transformation.

© Springer Nature Switzerland AG 2018
V. Kůrková et al. (Eds.): ICANN 2018, LNCS 11139, pp. 73–83, 2018.
https://doi.org/10.1007/978-3-030-01418-6_8

We use popular convolutional networks for this task with three different settings. The first one uses static word2vec embeddings that are not trained. The second one initializes the embeddings with word2vec and fine-tunes it on the available data. The last method initializes embeddings randomly and then they are, as in the previous case, optimized to the given task using available data. All these methods use the same vocabulary.

To the best of our knowledge, there is no previous study, which uses one classifier on multi-lingual multi-label data as proposed in this paper. The proposed approach is evaluated on four languages (English, German, Spanish and Italian) from the standard Reuters corpus.

2   Related Work

This section first presents the usage of neural networks for document classification and then focuses on multi-linguality.

Feed-forward neural networks were used for multi-label document classification in [16]. The authors have modified the standard backpropagation algorithm for multi-label learning which employs a novel error function. This approach is evaluated on functional genomics and text categorization.

Le and Mikolov propose [8] so called *Paragraph Vector*, an unsupervised algorithm that addresses the issue of necessity of a fixed-legth document representation. This algorithm represents each document using a dense vector. This vector is trained to predict words in the document. The authors obtain new state of the art results on several text classification and sentiment analysis tasks.

A recent study on the multi-label text classification was presented by Nam et al. [12]. The authors use the cross-entropy algorithm instead of ranking loss for training and they also further employ recent advances in deep learning field, e.g. the rectified linear units activation and AdaGrad learning with dropout [11,14]. Tf-idf representation of documents is used as a network input. The multi-label classification is done by thresholding of the output layer. The approach is evaluated on several multi-label datasets and reaches results comparable or better than the state of the art.

Another method [7] based on neural networks leverages the co-occurrence of labels in the multi-label classification. Some neurons in the output layer capture the patterns of label co-occurrences, which improves the classification accuracy. The architecture is basically a convolutional network and utilizes word embeddings as inputs. The method is evaluated on the natural language query classification in a document retrieval system.

An alternative multi-label classification approach is proposed by Yang and Gopal [15]. The conventional representations of texts and categories are transformed into meta-level features. These features are then utilized in a learning-to-rank algorithm. Experiments on six benchmark datasets show the abilities of this approach in comparison with other methods.

Recent work in the multi-lingual text representations field is usually based on word-level alignments. Klementiev et al. [5] train simultaneously two language models based on neural networks. The proposed method uses a regularization which ensures that pairs of frequently aligned words have similar word embeddings. Therefore, this approach needs parallel corpora to obtain the word-level alignment. Zou et al. [17] propose an alternative approach based on neural network language models using different regularization.

Kovčisky et al. [6] propose a bilingual word representations approach based on a probabilistic model. This method simultaneously learns alignments and distributed representations from bilingual data. This method marginalizes out the alignments, thus captures a larger bilingual semantic context. Sarath Chandar et al. [1] investigate an efficient approach based on autoencoders that uses word representations coherent between two languages. This method is able to obtain high-quality text representations by learning to reconstruct the bag-of-words of aligned sentences without any word alignments.

Coulmance et al. [2] introduce an efficient method for bilingual word representations called Trans-gram. This approach extends popular skip-gram model to multi-lingual scenario. This model jointly learns and aligns word embeddings for several languages, using only monolingual data and a small set of sentence-aligned documents.

3   Multi-lingual Document Classification

3.1   Multi-lingual Document Representation

The documents are represented as sequences of word indexes in a shared vocabulary V which is constructed in a following way. Let N be a number of the available languages. V_n represents the vocabulary of most frequent words in the given language. The shared vocabulary V is then constructed by the following equation

$$V = \bigcup_{n=1}^{N} V_n \tag{1}$$

The convolutional network we use for classification requires that the inputs have the same dimensions. Therefore, the documents with fewer words than a specified limit are padded, while the longer ones must be shortened. This is different from Kim's approach [3] where documents are padded to the length of the longest document in the training set. We are working with much longer documents where the lengths vary significantly. Therefore, the shortening of some documents and thus losing some information is inevitable in our case. However, based on our preliminary experiments, the influence of document shortening is insignificant to document classification score.

3.2   Neural Network Architecture

Neural network learns a function $f : d \rightarrow C_d$ which maps document $d \in D$ to a set of categories $C_d \subset C$. D is the set of classified documents and C is the set of all possible categories.

We use a CNN architecture that was proposed in [9]. This architecture utilizes one-dimensional convolutional kernels which is the main difference from the network proposed by Kim in [3] where 2D kernels over the entire width of the word embeddings are used. The input of our network is a vector of word indexes of the length M where M is the number of words used for document representation. The second layer is an embedding layer which represents a look-up table for the word vectors. It translates the word indexes into word vectors of length E. The document is then represented as a matrix with M rows and E columns. The next layer is the convolutional one. We use N_C convolution kernels of the size $K \times 1$ which means we do 1D convolution over one position in the embedding vector over K input words. The following layer performs a max-pooling over the length $M - K + 1$ resulting in N_C $1 \times E$ vectors. The output of this layer is then flattened and connected to a fully-connected layer with E nodes. The output layer contains $|C|$ nodes where $|C|$ is the cardinality of the set of classified categories.

The output of the network is then thresholded to get the final results. The values greater than a given threshold indicate the labels that are assigned to the classified document. The architecture of the network is depicted in Fig. 1. This figure shows the processing of two documents in different languages (English and German) by our network. Each document is handled in one training step. The key concept is the shared vocabulary and the corresponding shared embedding layer.

4   Experiments

4.1   Reuters RCV1/RCV2 Dataset

The Reuters RCV1 dataset [10] contains a large number of English documents. The RCV2 is a multi-lingual corpus that contains news stories in 13 languages. The distribution of the document lengths is shown in Fig. 2. We use four languages, namely English, German, Spanish and Italian. We prepare two settings: single- and multi-label ones.

Single-Label Configuration. The single-label setting was prepared so that we can compare the proposed approach with the state of the art. Similarly as the other studies, we follow the set-up proposed by Klementiev et al. [5]. Four main categories are used in this setting: *Corporate/industrial – CCAT, Economics – ECAT, Government/social – GCAT* and *Markets – MCAT*.

Documents containing more than one or zero main categories are filtered out. In total we randomly sample 15,000 documents for each language. 10,000 documents are used for training while the remaining 5,000 is reserved for testing.

Multi-label Configuration. In this setting we use all 103 topic codes available in the English documents. The number of documents for each language corresponds to the minimal number across the utilized languages which is Spanish

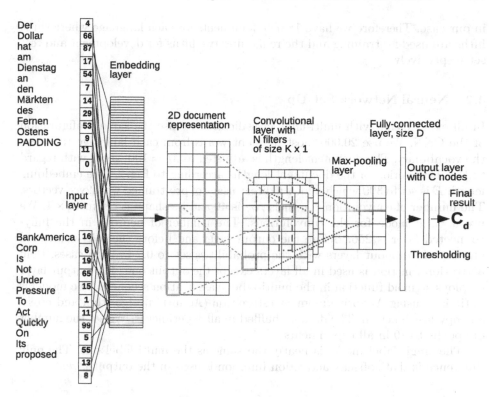

Fig. 1. The architecture of the CNN network used for multi-lingual classification. Two example documents are used as network input. Each document is handled in one training step.

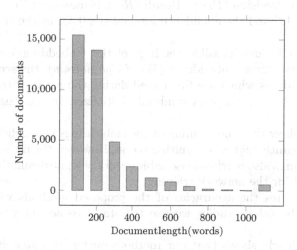

Fig. 2. Distribution of the document lengths in word tokens.

in our case. Therefore we have 18,655 documents for each language where three fifths are used for training and the remaining two fifths for development and test set respectively.

4.2   Neural Network Set-Up

In all experiments with multi-label classification we use the same configuration of the CNN. We use 20,000 most frequent words from each language to create the vocabulary. The document length is adjusted to $M = 100$ words with regard to the distribution of the document lengths according to Fig. 2. The embedding length E is set to 300 which allows a direct usage of pre-trained word2vec vectors. The number of convolutional kernels N_C is 40 and its shape is set to 16×1. We use a *valid* mode for the convolutions. The number of neurons in the fully-connected layer is 256. Before the output layer and before the fully-connected one we add dropout layers with the probabilities set to 0.2 in both cases. Relu activation function is used in all layers except the output one. The output layer employs sigmoid function in the multi-label classification scenario. The model is optimized using Adaptive moment estimation (Adam) [4] algorithm and cross-entropy loss function. The data is shuffled in all experiments. We set the number of epochs to 10 in all experiments.

The single-label model is nearly the same as the multi-label one. The only difference is that softmax activation function is used in the output layer.

4.3   Single-Label Results

Table 1 summarizes the results of the single-label classification experiments. We use the standard Precision ($Prec$), Recall (Rec), F-measure ($F1$) and Accuracy (ACC) metrics [13] and the confidence interval is $\pm 0.3\%$ at the confidence level of 0.95.

We present all three possible settings of the embedding layer. The first one uses static word2vec embeddings (*Word emb notrain*), the second one uses word2vec embeddings which are fine-tuned during the network training (*Word emb train*) and the last one uses randomly initialized vectors that are trained (*Random init*).

The results show that the training of the embeddings is beneficial and allows achieving significantly higher recognition scores. However, the usage of static pre-trained embeddings also reaches reasonable accuracy while dramatically lowering the time needed for the network training.

Table 2 compares the accuracies of the proposed methods with the state-of-the-art. As the other studies we use the standard accuracy metric in this experiment.

This table clearly shows that our methods outperform significantly all the other approaches. This is particularly evident in the case of English language where the increase of accuracy is almost by 20%. We must note that the set-up of the other approaches slightly differ. However, the reported methods are the

Table 1. Results of the single-label classification experiments [in %].

	Word emb notrain				Word emb train				Random init			
	Prec	Rec	F1	ACC	Prec	Rec	F1	ACC	Prec	Rec	F1	ACC
en	93.0	89.7	91.3	90.2	96.1	93.9	95.0	94.4	96.6	96.3	96.4	96.3
de	95.3	94.8	95.1	95.0	97.0	96.9	96.9	96.8	96.6	96.3	96.4	96.3
es	98.7	98.1	98.4	98.3	99.9	99.9	99.9	99.9	99.9	99.9	99.9	99.9
it	88.8	86.7	87.8	86.9	91.9	91.6	91.7	90.7	91.5	91.2	91.3	90.6
avg	94.0	92.3	93.2	92.6	96.2	95.6	95.9	95.5	96.2	95.9	96.0	95.8

most similar set-ups we found. Moreover, to the best of our knowledge, there are no studies with exactly the same configuration as we use.

Table 2. Comparison with the state of the art [accuracy in %].

Method [ACC in %]	de	en
Klementiev et al. [5]	77.6	71.1
Kovčisky et al. [6]	83.1	76.0
Sarath Chandar et al. [1]	91.8	74.2
Coulmance et al. [2]	91.1	78.7
Word emb notrain	95.0	90.2
Word emb train	**96.8**	**94.4**
Random init	96.3	96.3

4.4 Multi-label Results

Table 3 shows the results of our network in the multi-label scenario. We use the standard Precision (*Prec*), Recall (*Rec*), F-measure (*F1*) metrics in this experiment. The confidence interval is ±0.35% at the confidence level of 0.95.

We can summarize the results in this table in a similar way as the previous one for the single-label classification. The training of the embeddings improves the obtained classification results. However, the training of randomly initialized vectors has worse results than the fine-tuned word2vec vectors. The best obtained F-measure 86.8% is, as in the previous case, for Spanish using word2vec initialized embeddings with a further training.

4.5 Word Similarity Experiment

The last experiment analyzes the quality of the resulting embeddings obtained by the three neural network settings.

Table 3. Precision (*Prec*), Recall (*Rec*), F-measure (*F*1) of the multi-label classification [in %].

	Word emb notrain			Word emb train			Random init		
	Prec	Rec	F1	Prec	Rec	F1	Prec	Rec	F1
en	84.3	62.7	71.9	85.4	89.2	82.2	83.6	75.1	79.2
de	84.2	69.8	76.3	87.5	81.2	84.2	86.5	77.3	81.6
es	90.4	77.1	83.2	89.4	84.3	86.8	89.4	81.5	85.3
it	84.9	68.4	75.8	86.5	81.2	83.8	85.2	77.8	81.3
avg	86.0	69.5	76.8	87.2	81.5	84.3	86.2	77.9	81.9

Table 4. Ten closest words to the English word "accident" based on the cosine similarity; English translation in brackets including the language of the given word.

Word emb notrain		Word emb train		Random init	
Word	Cos sim	Word	Cos sim	Word	Cos sim
accidents	0.860	accidente	0.685	ruehe	0.248
incident	0.740	unglück (*de*, misfortune)	0.632	bloccando (*es*, blocking)	0.239
accidente (*es*, accident)	0.600	estrelló (*es*, crashed)	0.609	compelled	0.236
incidents	0.574	accidents	0.599	numerick	0.219
accidentes (*es*, accidents)	0.546	geborgen (*de*, secure)	0.585	fiduciary	0.217
disaster	0.471	absturz	0.584	barriles (*es*, barrels)	0.216
explosions	0.461	unglücks (*de*, misfortunes)	0.576	andhra	0.214
incidence	0.452	abgestürzt (*de*, crashed)	0.567	touring	0.212
personnel	0.452	trümmern (*de*, rubble)	0.560	versicherers (*de*, insurers)	0.209
unfall (*de*, accident)	0.450	unglücksursache (*de*, ill cause)	0.551	oppositioneller (*de*, oppositional)	0.203

Table 4 shows 10 most similar words to the English word "accident" across all languages based on the cosine similarity. These words are mainly in English when word2vec initialization without any training is used (the first column). Further training of the embeddings (middle column) causes that also German and Spanish words with a similar meaning are shifted closer to the word "accident" in the embedding space. On the other hand, when training from randomly initialized vectors, the ten most similar words have often quite a different meaning. However, as shown in the classification results, this fact has nearly no impact on the resulting F-measure. We can conclude that word2vec initialization is not necessary for the classification task. This table further shows that the similarity between Germanic (English and German) languages is clearly visible.

Table 5 shows 10 most similar words to the English word "czech" using the cosine similarity. The table is very similar to the previous one. For instance, if we take a look at the *Word emb train* column, we observe that there is (as in the previous case) a significant decrease of the cosine similarity. However on the other hand, some new words, which are more related to the word "czech", are included. The inapplicability to find similar words of randomly initialized embeddings has been confirmed. It is worth noting that although the Czech language is not a part of our corpus, some Czech words (*praha, dnes, fronta*) are also included due to the Czech citations available.

Table 5. Ten closest words to the word "czech" based on the cosine similarity; English translation in brackets including the language of the given word.

Word emb notrain		Word emb train		Random init	
Word	Cos sim	Word	Cos sim	Word	Cos sim
czechoslovakia	0.757	czechoslovakia	0.399	festakt (*de*, ceremony)	0.273
slovakia	0.634	praga (*es*, prague)	0.335	val	0.250
polish	0.569	republic	0.329	provence	0.235
hungary	0.539	brno (*cz*, brno - czech city)	0.315	sostiene (*es*, hold)	0.222
hungarian	0.537	slovak	0.314	larry	0.216
prague	0.533	praha (*cz*, prague)	0.313	köpfigen (*de*, headed)	0.212
slovak	0.509	dnes (*cz*, today)	0.307	überschreiten (*de*, exceed)	0.206
praha (*cz*, praha)	0.509	checa (*es*, czech)	0.307	aktienindex (*de*, share index)	0.205
austrian	0.506	fronta (*cz*, queue)	0.304	councils	0.205
lithuanian	0.496	tschechoslowakei (*de*, czechoslovakia)	0.297	bancario (*it*, banking)	0.205

5 Conclusions

In this paper we presented a novel approach for the multi-label document classification in multiple languages. The proposed method builds on the popular convolutional networks. We added a simple yet efficient extension that allows using one network for classifying text documents in more languages.

We evaluated our method on four languages from the Reuters corpus in both multi- and single-label classification scenarios. We showed that the proposed approach is efficient and the best obtained F-measure in multi-label scenario reaches 84%. We also showed that our methods outperform significantly in the single-label settings all the other approaches. Another added value of this approach is also that no language identification is needed as in the case of the use of the single networks.

Acknowledgements. This work has been partly supported from ERDF "Research and Development of Intelligent Components of Advanced Technologies for the Pilsen Metropolitan Area (InteCom)" (no.: CZ.02.1.01/0.0/0.0/17_048/0007267), by Cross-border Cooperation Program Czech Republic - Free State of Bavaria ETS Objective 2014–2020 (project no. 211) and by Grant No. SGS-2016-018 Data and Software Engineering for Advanced Applications.

References

1. Sarath Chandar, A.P., et al.: An autoencoder approach to learning bilingual word representations. In: Ghahramani, Z., Welling, M., Cortes, C., Lawrence, N.D., Weinberger, K.Q. (eds.) Advances in Neural Information Processing Systems 27, pp. 1853–1861. Curran Associates, Inc. (2014)
2. Coulmance, J., Marty, J.M., Wenzek, G., Benhalloum, A.: Trans-gram, fast cross-lingual word-embeddings. arXiv preprint arXiv:1601.02502 (2016)
3. Kim, Y.: Convolutional neural networks for sentence classification. arXiv preprint arXiv:1408.5882 (2014)
4. Kingma, D., Ba, J.: Adam: a method for stochastic optimization. arXiv preprint arXiv:1412.6980 (2014)
5. Klementiev, A., Titov, I., Bhattarai, B.: Inducing crosslingual distributed representations of words. In: Proceedings of COLING 2012, pp. 1459–1474 (2012)
6. Kočiský, T., Hermann, K.M., Blunsom, P.: Learning bilingual word representations by marginalizing alignments. In: Proceedings of the 52nd Annual Meeting of the Association for Computational Linguistics (Volume 2: Short Papers), vol. 2, pp. 224–229 (2014)
7. Kurata, G., Xiang, B., Zhou, B.: Improved neural network-based multi-label classification with better initialization leveraging label co-occurrence. In: Proceedings of NAACL-HLT, pp. 521–526 (2016)
8. Le, Q.V., Mikolov, T.: Distributed representations of sentences and documents. In: ICML 2014, pp. 1188–1196 (2014)
9. Lenc, L., Král, P.: Deep neural networks for Czech multi-label document classification. In: Gelbukh, A. (ed.) CICLing 2016. LNCS, vol. 9624, pp. 460–471. Springer, Cham (2018). https://doi.org/10.1007/978-3-319-75487-1_36
10. Lewis, D.D., Yang, Y., Rose, T.G., Li, F.: RCV1: a new benchmark collection for text categorization research. J. Mach. Learn. Res. **5**(Apr), 361–397 (2004)
11. Nair, V., Hinton, G.E.: Rectified linear units improve restricted Boltzmann machines. In: Proceedings of the 27th International Conference on Machine Learning (ICML 2010), pp. 807–814 (2010)
12. Nam, J., Kim, J., Loza Mencía, E., Gurevych, I., Fürnkranz, J.: Large-scale multi-label text classification - revisiting neural networks. In: Calders, T., Esposito, F., Hüllermeier, E., Meo, R. (eds.) ECML PKDD 2014. LNCS (LNAI), vol. 8725, pp. 437–452. Springer, Heidelberg (2014). https://doi.org/10.1007/978-3-662-44851-9_28
13. Powers, D.: Evaluation: from precision, recall and f-measure to ROC, informedness, markedness & correlation. J. Mach. Learn. Technol. **2**(1), 37–63 (2011)

14. Srivastava, N., Hinton, G., Krizhevsky, A., Sutskever, I., Salakhutdinov, R.: Dropout: a simple way to prevent neural networks from overfitting. J. Mach. Learn. Res. **15**(1), 1929–1958 (2014)
15. Yang, Y., Gopal, S.: Multilabel classification with meta-level features in a learning-to-rank framework. Mach. Learn. **88**(1–2), 47–68 (2012)
16. Zhang, M.L., Zhou, Z.H.: Multilabel neural networks with applications to functional genomics and text categorization. IEEE Trans. Knowl. Data Eng. **18**(10), 1338–1351 (2006)
17. Zou, W.Y., Socher, R., Cer, D., Manning, C.D.: Bilingual word embeddings for phrase-based machine translation. In: Proceedings of the 2013 Conference on Empirical Methods in Natural Language Processing, pp. 1393–1398 (2013)

Multi-region Ensemble Convolutional Neural Network for Facial Expression Recognition

Yingruo Fan[✉], Jacqueline C. K. Lam, and Victor O. K. Li

Department of Electrical and Electronic Engineering,
The University of Hong Kong, Pokfulam, Hong Kong
yrfan@hku.hk, {jcklam,vli}@eee.hku.hk

Abstract. Facial expressions play an important role in conveying the emotional states of human beings. Recently, deep learning approaches have been applied to image recognition field due to the discriminative power of Convolutional Neural Network (CNN). In this paper, we first propose a novel Multi-Region Ensemble CNN (MRE-CNN) framework for facial expression recognition, which aims to enhance the learning power of CNN models by capturing both the global and the local features from multiple human face sub-regions. Second, the weighted prediction scores from each sub-network are aggregated to produce the final prediction of high accuracy. Third, we investigate the effects of different sub-regions of the whole face on facial expression recognition. Our proposed method is evaluated based on two well-known publicly available facial expression databases: AFEW 7.0 and RAF-DB, and has been shown to achieve the state-of-the-art recognition accuracy.

Keywords: Expression recognition · Deep learning
Convolutional Neural Network · Multi-region ensemble

1 Introduction

Facial expression recognition (FER) has many practical applications such as treatment of depression, customer satisfaction measurement, fatigue surveillance and Human Robot Interaction (HRI) systems. Ekman et al. [2] defined a set of prototypical facial expressions (e.g. anger, disgust, fear, happiness, sadness, and surprise). Since Convolutional Neural Network (CNN) has already proved its excellence in many image recognition tasks, we expect that it can show better results than already existing machine learning methods in facial expression prediction problems. A well-designed CNN trained on millions of images can parameterize a hierarchy of filters, which capture both low-level generic features and high-level semantic features. Moreover, current Graphics Processing Units (GPUs) expedite the training process of deep neural networks to tackle big-data problems. However, unlike large scale visual object recognition databases such

© Springer Nature Switzerland AG 2018
V. Kůrková et al. (Eds.): ICANN 2018, LNCS 11139, pp. 84–94, 2018.
https://doi.org/10.1007/978-3-030-01418-6_9

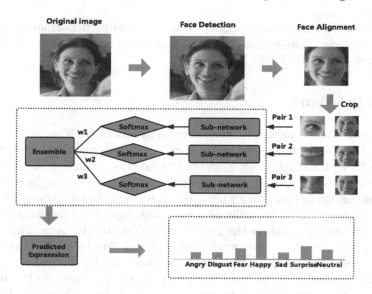

Fig. 1. An overview of our approach: Multi-Region Ensemble CNN (MRE-CNN) framework.

as ImageNet [10], existing facial expression recognition databases do not have sufficient training data, resulting in overfitting problems.

CNN approaches topped the three slots in the 2014 ImageNet challenge [10] for object recognition task, with the VGGNet [11] architecture achieving a remarkably low error rate. With a review of previous CNNs, AlexNet [5] demonstrated the effectiveness of CNN by introducing convolutional layers followed by Max-pooling layers and Rectified Linear Units (ReLUs). AlexNet significantly outperformed the runner-up with a top-5 error rate of 15.3% in the 2012 ImageNet challenge [10]. In our proposed framework, one of the network structures is based on AlexNet and the other one VGG-16 is a deeper network based on VGGNet [11].

The goal of automatic FER is to classify faces in static images or dynamic image sequences as one of the six basic emotions. However, it is still a challenging problem due to head pose, image resolution, deformations, and illumination variations. This paper is the first attempt to exploit the local characteristics of different parts of the face by constructing different sub-networks. Our main contributions are three-fold and can be summarized as follows:

- A novel Multi-Region Ensemble CNN framework is proposed for facial expression recognition, which takes full advantage of both global information and local characteristics of the whole face.
- Based on the weighted sum operation of the prediction scores from each sub-network, the final recognition rate can be improved compared to the original single network.

– Our MRE-CNN framework achieves a very appealing performance and out-performs some state-of-the-art facial expression methods on AFEW 7.0 Database [1] and RAF-DB [6].

2   Related Work

Several studies have proposed different architectures of CNN in terms of FER problems. Hu et al. [4] integrated a new learning block named Supervised Scoring Ensemble (SSE) into their CNN model to improve the prediction accuracy. This has inspired us to incorporate other well-designed learning strategies to existing mainstream networks bring about accuracy gains. [8] followed a transfer learning approach for deep CNNs by utilizing a two-stage supervised fine-tuning on the pre-trained network based on the generic ImageNet [10] datasets. This implies that we can narrow down the overfitting problems due to limited expressions data via transfer learning. In [7], inception layers and the network-in-network theory were applied to solve the FER problem, which focuses on the network architecture. However, most of the previous methods have processed the entire facial region as the input of their CNN models, paying less attention to the sub-regions of human faces. To our knowledge, few works have been done by directly cropping the sub-regions of facial images as the input of CNN in FER. In this paper, each sub-network in our MRE-CNN framework will process a pair of facial regions, including a whole-region image and a sub-region image.

3   The Proposed Method

The overview of our proposed MRE-CNN framework is shown in Fig. 1. We will start with the data preparation, and then describe the detailed construction for our MRE-CNN framework.

3.1   Data Pre-processing

Datasets. Recently, Real-world Affective Faces Database[1] (RAF-DB)[6], which contains about 30000 real-world facial images from thousands of individuals, is released to encourage more research on real-world expressions. The images (12271 training samples and 3068 testing samples) in RAF-DB were downloaded from Flickr, after which humans were asked to pick out images related with the six basic emotions, plus the neutral emotion. The other database, Acted Facial Expressions in the Wild (AFEW 7.0)[1], was established for the 2017 Emotion Recognition in the Wild Challenge[2] (EmotiW). AFEW 7.0 consists of training (773), validation (383) and test (653) video clips, where samples are labeled with seven expressions: angry, disgust, fear, happy, sad, surprise and neutral (Fig. 2).

---

[1] http://www.whdeng.cn/RAF/model1.html.
[2] https://sites.google.com/site/emotiwchallenge/.

Fig. 2. The first row displays cropped faces extracted from images in RAF-DB, and the second row represents faces sampled across video clips in AFEW 7.0.

Face Detection and Alignment. For each video clip in AFEW 7.0, after using a face tracker [3], we sample at 3–10 frames that have clear faces with an adaptive frame interval. To extract and align faces both from original images in RAF-DB and frames of videos in AFEW 7.0, we use a C++ library, Dlib[3] face detector to locate the 68 facial landmarks. As shown in Fig. 3, based on the coordinates of localized landmarks, aligned and cropped whole-region and sub-regions of the face image can be generated in a uniform template with a affine transformation. In this stage, we align and crop regions of the left eye, regions of the nose, regions of the mouth, as well as the whole face. Then three pairs of images are all resized into 224 × 224 pixels.

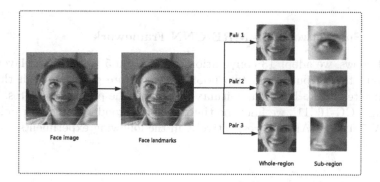

Fig. 3. The processing of the cropped whole-region and sub-regions of the facial image.

3.2 Multi-Region Ensemble Convolutional Neural Network

Our framework is illustrated in Fig. 1. We take three significant sub-regions of the human face into account: the lefteye, the nose and the mouth. Each particular sub-region will be accompanied by its corresponding whole facial image, forming

---

[3] dlib.net.

a double input subnetwork in Multi-Region Ensemble CNN (MRE-CNN) framework. Afterwards, based on the weighted sum operation of three prediction scores from each sub-network, we get a final accurate prediction.

Particularly, to encourage intra-class compactness and inter-class separability, each subnet adopts the softmax loss function which is given by

$$Loss(\theta) = -\frac{1}{m} \left[\sum_{i=1}^{m} \sum_{j=1}^{k} l\{y^{(i)} = j\} \right] log \frac{e^{\theta_j^T x^{(i)}}}{\sum_{l=1}^{k} e^{\theta_l^T x^{(i)}}}, \tag{1}$$

where $x^{(i)}$ denotes the features of the i-th sample, taken from the final hidden layer before the softmax layer, m is the number of training data, and k is the number of classes. We define the i-th input feature $x^{(i)} \in R^d$ with the predicted label y_i. θ is the parameter matrix of the softmax function $Loss(\theta)$. Here $l\{\cdot\}$ means $l\{$a true statement$\} = 1$ or $l\{$a false statement$\} = 0$.

Data Augmentation. Despite the training size of RAF-DB, it is still insufficient for training a designed deep network. Therefore we utilize both offline data augmentation and on-the-fly data augmentation techniques. The number of training samples increases fifteen-fold after introducing methods including image rotation, image flips and Gaussian distribution random perturbations. Besides, on-the-fly data augmentation is embedded in the deep learning framework, Caffe, by randomly cropping the input images and then flipping them horizontally.

3.3   The Sub-networks in MRE-CNN Framework

As Fig. 4 shows, we adopt 13 convolutional layers and 5 max pooling layers and concatenate the outputs from two pool5 layers before going through the first fully connected layer. The final softmax layer gives the prediction scores. When employing VGG-16 [11], we finetune the pre-trained model with the training set of AFEW 7.0 and RAF-DB, respectively, in the following experiments.

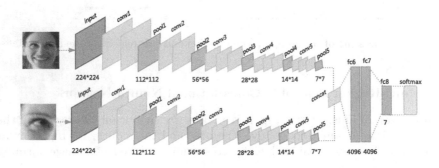

Fig. 4. The VGG-16 sub-network architecture in MRE-CNN framework.

To validate the proposed MRE-CNN framework, our modified AlexNet architecture do not use any pre-trained models during its training process. For AlexNet sub-network, we use 5 convolutional layers and 3 max pooling layers, the same as in the traditional CNN architecture. Different from the original AlexNet, the last two fully connected layers have 64 outputs and 7 outputs, respectively, making it possible to retrain a deep network with limited data. The following experiment results indicate its effectiveness in the MRE-CNN framework structure, despite its simplified network architecture.

Finally, we combine the three predictions from three sub-networks by conducting the weighted sum operation. The predicted emotion $P_{MRE-CNN}$ is defined as

$$P_{MRE-CNN} = \sum_{n=1}^{z} \alpha_n \sum_{i=1}^{m} \frac{1}{\sum_{l=1}^{k} e^{\theta_l^T x^{(i)}}} \begin{bmatrix} e^{\theta_1^T x^{(i)}} \\ e^{\theta_2^T x^{(i)}} \\ \dots \\ e^{\theta_k^T x^{(i)}} \end{bmatrix}, \tag{2}$$

where α_n denotes the weight for a single sub-network and z is equal to 3 as we utilize three sub-networks. Other parameters are the same as those in Eq. 1.

4 Experiments

4.1 Experimental Setup

All training and testing processes were performed on NVIDIA GeForce GTX 1080Ti 11G GPUs. We developed our models in the deep learning framework Caffe. On the Ubuntu linux system equipped with NVIDIA GPUs, training a single model in MRE-CNN took 4–6 hours depending on the architecture of the sub-network.

4.2 Implementation Details

In data augmentation stage, we augment the set of training images in RAF-DB and frames in AFEW 7.0 by flipping, rotating each with $\pm 4°$ and $\pm 6°$, and adding Gaussian white noises with variances of 0.001, 0.01 and 0.015. We then train our VGG-16 sub-networks for 20k iterations with the following parameters: learning rate 0.0001–0.0005, weight decay 0.0001, momentum 0.9, batch size 16 and linear learning rate decay in stochastic gradient descent (SGD) optimizer. For AlexNet sub-networks, we train them for 30k iterations with the batch size of 64 and the learning rate begins from 0.001. In the ensemble prediction stage, the specific weights of MRE-CNN (VGG-16 Sub-network) are 4/7 (lefteye weight), 2/7 (mouth weight) and 1/7 (nose weight) and those of MRE-CNN (AlexNet Sub-network) are 2/5 (lefteye weight), 2/5 (mouth weight) and 1/5 (nose weight), respectively.

4.3 Results on RAF-DB

RAF-DB is split into a training set and a test set with the idea of five-fold cross-validation and we performed the 7-class basic expression classification benchmark experiment. In the RAF-DB test protocol, the ultimate metric is the mean diagonal value of the confusion matrix rather than the accuracy due to imbalanced distribution in expressions. In this experiment, we directly train our deep learning models with our processed training samples from RAF-DB, without using other databases. In details, after filtering the non-detected face images and applying data augmentation techniques, 95465 cropped face images are generated, accompanied by lefteye images, mouth images and nose images.

Table 1. Confusion matrix for RAF-DB based on MRE-CNN (VGG-16 sub-network). The term Real represents the true labels (0 = Angry, 1 = Disgust, 2 = Fear, 3 = Happy, 4 = Sad, 5 = Surprise, 6 = Neutral) and Pred represents the predicted value.

Real	Pred						
	0	1	2	3	4	5	6
0	0.0088	0.0632	0.0000	0.0221	0.0706	0.0338	**0.8015**
1	0.0213	0.0182	0.0334	0.0030	0.0122	**0.8602**	0.0517
2	0.0209	0.0565	0.0084	0.0167	**0.7992**	0.0105	0.0879
3	0.0110	0.0211	0.0051	**0.8878**	0.0127	0.0110	0.0515
4	0.0811	0.0000	**0.6081**	0.0270	0.0676	0.1757	0.0405
5	0.1125	**0.5750**	0.0063	0.0813	0.0750	0.0187	0.1313
6	**0.8395**	0.0802	0.0185	0.0185	0.0123	0.0062	0.0247

Analyzing the confusion matrix based on MRE-CNN (VGG-16 Sub-network) in Table 1, our proposed model performs well when classifying happy, surprise and angry emotions, with accuracy of 88.78%, 86.02%, 83.95%, respectively. For comparison, in Table 2 we show the results of the trained DCNN models followed by different classifiers which are proposed in [6]. We find that our proposed MRE-CNN (VGG-16) framework outperforms all of the existing state-of-the-art methods evaluated on RAF-DB. In addition, the MRE-CNN (AlexNet) framework also achieves a very appealing performance although we retrain the AlexNet sub-networks with limited data.

Furthermore, we separated the sub-network modules from MRE-CNN framework and demonstrated their individual results on the test set of RAF-DB. Results can be viewed in Table 3. The result of the first row shows the average accuracy of Face+LeftEye while applying VGG-16 sub-network in MRE-CNN framework, and they are higher than that of Face+Mouth. Thus we assign higher weights to Face+LeftEye subnet when combining the three predictions with an appropriate ensemble method. Face+Nose subnet is slightly less effective, probably due to less information related to emotions; Nevertheless, it is still superior to the VGG-FACE model given in Table 2 with only the whole face region as input.

Table 2. Performance of different methods on RAF-DB (The metric is the mean diagonal value of the confusion matrix).

	Angry	Disgust	Fear	Happy	Sad	Surprise	Neutral	Average
DLP-CNN+mSVM [6]	71.60	52.15	62.16	92.83	80.13	81.16	80.29	74.20
DLP-CNN+LDA [6]	77.51	55.41	52.50	90.21	73.64	74.07	73.53	70.98
AlexNet+mSVM [6]	58.64	21.87	39.19	86.16	60.88	62.31	60.15	55.60
AlexNet+LDA [6]	43.83	27.50	37.84	75.78	39.33	61.70	48.53	47.79
VGG+mSVM [6]	68.52	27.50	35.13	85.32	64.85	66.32	59.88	58.22
VGG+LDA [6]	66.05	25.00	37.84	73.08	51.46	53.49	47.21	50.59
Singe VGG-FACE	82.19	56.62	55.41	86.38	79.52	83.93	71.18	73.60
Our MRE-CNN (AlexNet)	77.78	65.62	58.11	87.75	75.73	81.16	77.21	74.78
Our MRE-CNN (VGG-16)	83.95	57.50	60.81	88.78	79.92	86.02	80.15	**76.73**

Table 3. Sub-region comparison (the metric is the mean diagonal value of the confusion matrix).

Architecture	Average
Face+LeftEye (Single VGG-16 sub-network)	76.52
Face+Nose (Single VGG-16 sub-network)	75.64
Face+Mouth (Single VGG-16 sub-network)	76.13
Our MRE-CNN (VGG-16)	**76.73**

Table 4. Comparisons with the state-of-the-art methods on AFEW 7.0 (the metric is the average accuracy of all validation videos).

Network architecture	Training data	Validation (%)
C3D [9]	16 frames for each video	35.20
Resnet-LSTM [9]	16 frames for each video	46.70
VGG-LSTM [9]	16 frames for each video	47.40
Trajectory+ SVM [13]	30 frames for each video	37.37
VGG-BRNN [13]	40 frames for each video	44.46
C3D-LSTM [12]	Detected face frames	43.20
Our MRE-CNN (AlexNet)	Detected face frames	40.11
Our MRE-CNN (VGG-16)	Detected face frames	**47.43**

4.4   Results on AFEW 7.0

To validate the performance of our models, we also conduct experiments on the validation set of AFEW 7.0. The task is to assign a single expression label from seven candidate categories to each video clip from the validation set (383 video clips). Note that all our CNN models in MRE-CNN framework are trained on the given training data (773 video clips) only without applying any outside data. Considering the temporally disappearance or occlusion in some videos, we only use detected face frames for training and prediction. In our experiments, the predicted emotion scores of each video are calculated by averaging the scores of all its detected face frames. We can see from Table 4, for the validation set of AFEW 7.0, our MRE-CNN (VGG-16) framework gets great results which are superior to some state-of-the-art methods.

4.5   Discussions

A series of feature maps are shown in Fig. 5 for VGG-16 sub-network in our MRE-CNN framework, which can reflect the differences in the filters of the first three convolutional layers. It can be observed that shallower layer outputs capture more profile information while deeper layer outputs encode the semantic information. Shallower layers can learn rich low-level features that can help refine the irregular features from deeper layers. Furthermore, by combining features from the whole region and sub-regions of the human face, the resulting architecture provides more rich feature maps, which raises the recognition rate for FER problems.

Fig. 5. Visualization of the feature maps of the first three convolutional layers for the input image on the left of each row.

Generally, our method explicitly inherits the advantage of information gathered from multiple local regions from face images, acting as a deep feature ensemble with two single CNN architectures, and hence it naturally improves the final predication accuracy. The disadvantage of our approach is that we use grid searching to determine the contribution portions of individual sub-networks, which is relatively computationally expensive. We shall utilize ensemble methods like Adaboost to determine the best weights for different subnets. Although facial expression recognition based on face images can achieve promising results, facial expression is only one modality in realistic human behaviors. Combining facial expressions with other modalities, such as audio information, physiological data and thermal infrared images can provide complementary information, further enhancing the robustness of our models. Therefore, it is a promising research direction to incorporate facial expression models with other dimension models into a high-level framework.

5   Conclusion

We have proposed a novel Multi-Region Ensemble CNN framework in this study, which takes full advantage of different regions of the whole human face. By assigning different weights to three sub-networks in MRE-CNN, we have combined the predictions of three separate networks. Besides, we have investigated the effects of three different facial regions, each providing different local information. As a result, our MRE-CNN framework has achieved a very appealing performance on RAF-DB and AFEW 7.0, as compared to other state-of-the-art methods.

Acknowledgements. This research is supported in part by the Theme-based Research Scheme of the Research Grants Council of Hong Kong, under Grant No. T41-709/17-N.

References

1. Dhall, A., Goecke, R., Lucey, S., Gedeon, T., et al.: Collecting large, richly annotated facial-expression databases from movies. IEEE Multimed. **19**(3), 34–41 (2012)
2. Ekman, P., Friesen, W.V.: Constants across cultures in the face and emotion. J. Person. Soc. Psychol. **17**(2), 124 (1971)
3. He, Z., Fan, Y., Zhuang, J., Dong, Y., Bai, H.: Correlation filters with weighted convolution responses. In: 2017 IEEE International Conference on Computer Vision Workshop (ICCVW), pp. 1992–2000. IEEE (2017)
4. Hu, P., Cai, D., Wang, S., Yao, A., Chen, Y.: Learning supervised scoring ensemble for emotion recognition in the wild. In: Proceedings of the 19th ACM International Conference on Multimodal Interaction, pp. 553–560. ACM (2017)
5. Krizhevsky, A., Sutskever, I., Hinton, G.E.: ImageNet classification with deep convolutional neural networks. In: Advances in Neural Information Processing Systems, pp. 1097–1105 (2012)
6. Li, S., Deng, W., Du, J.: Reliable crowdsourcing and deep locality-preserving learning for expression recognition in the wild. In: 2017 IEEE Conference on Computer Vision and Pattern Recognition (CVPR), pp. 2584–2593. IEEE (2017)
7. Mollahosseini, A., Chan, D., Mahoor, M.H.: Going deeper in facial expression recognition using deep neural networks. In: 2016 IEEE Winter Conference on Applications of Computer Vision (WACV), pp. 1–10. IEEE (2016)
8. Ng, H.W., Nguyen, V.D., Vonikakis, V., Winkler, S.: Deep learning for emotion recognition on small datasets using transfer learning. In: Proceedings of the 2015 ACM on International Conference on Multimodal Interaction, pp. 443–449. ACM (2015)
9. Ouyang, X., et al.: Audio-visual emotion recognition using deep transfer learning and multiple temporal models. In: Proceedings of the 19th ACM International Conference on Multimodal Interaction, pp. 577–582. ACM (2017)
10. Russakovsky, O., et al.: Imagenet large scale visual recognition challenge. Int. J. Comput. Vis. **115**(3), 211–252 (2015)
11. Simonyan, K., Zisserman, A.: Very deep convolutional networks for large-scale image recognition. arXiv preprint arXiv:1409.1556 (2014)

12. Vielzeuf, V., Pateux, S., Jurie, F.: Temporal multimodal fusion for video emotion classification in the wild. In: Proceedings of the 19th ACM International Conference on Multimodal Interaction, pp. 569–576. ACM (2017)
13. Yan, J., Zheng, W., Cui, Z., Tang, C., Zhang, T., Zong, Y.: Multi-cue fusion for emotion recognition in the wild. In: Proceedings of the 18th ACM International Conference on Multimodal Interaction, pp. 458–463. ACM (2016)

Further Advantages of Data Augmentation on Convolutional Neural Networks

Alex Hernández-García$^{(\boxtimes)}$ and Peter König

Institute of Cognitive Science, University of Osnabrück, Osnabrück, Germany
{ahernandez,pkoenig}@uos.de

Abstract. Data augmentation is a popular technique largely used to enhance the training of convolutional neural networks. Although many of its benefits are well known by deep learning researchers and practitioners, its implicit regularization effects, as compared to popular explicit regularization techniques, such as weight decay and dropout, remain largely unstudied. As a matter of fact, convolutional neural networks for image object classification are typically trained with both data augmentation and explicit regularization, assuming the benefits of all techniques are complementary. In this paper, we systematically analyze these techniques through ablation studies of different network architectures trained with different amounts of training data. Our results unveil a largely ignored advantage of data augmentation: networks trained with just data augmentation more easily adapt to different architectures and amount of training data, as opposed to weight decay and dropout, which require specific fine-tuning of their hyperparameters.

Keywords: Data augmentation · Regularization · CNNs

1 Introduction

Data augmentation in machine learning refers to the techniques that synthetically expand a data set by applying transformations on the existing examples, thus augmenting the amount of available training data. Although the new data points are not independent and identically distributed, data augmentation implicitly regularizes the models and improves generalization, as established by statistical learning theory [31].

Data augmentation has been long used in machine learning [27] and it has been identified as a critical component of many models [6,21,22]. Nonetheless, the literature lacks, to our knowledge, a systematic analysis of the implicit regularization effect of data augmentation on deep neural networks compared to the most popular regularization techniques, such as weight decay [12] and dropout [29], which are typically used all together.

In a thought-provoking paper [34], Zhang *et al.* concluded that *explicit regularization may improve generalization performance, but is neither necessary nor*

© Springer Nature Switzerland AG 2018
V. Kůrková et al. (Eds.): ICANN 2018, LNCS 11139, pp. 95–103, 2018.
https://doi.org/10.1007/978-3-030-01418-6_10

by itself sufficient for controlling generalization error. They observed that removing weight decay and dropout does not prevent the models from generalizing. Although they performed some ablation studies with data augmentation, they considered it just another explicit regularization technique. In a follow up study [16], it is argued that data augmentation should not be considered an explicit regularizer and it is shown that explicit regularization may not only be unnecessary, but data augmentation alone can achieve the same level of generalization.

Here, we build upon the ideas from [16] and, using the same methodology, we extend the analysis of data augmentation in contrast to weight decay and dropout. In particular, we focus here on the capability of data augmentation to adapt to deeper and shallower architectures as well as to successfully learn from fewer examples. We find that networks trained with data augmentation, but no explicit regularizers, outperform the networks trained with all techniques, as is common practice in the literature. We hypothesize that weight decay and dropout require fine-tuning of their hyperparameters in order to adapt to new architectures and amount of training data, whereas the new samples generated by data augmentation schemes are useful regardless of the new training conditions.

1.1   Related Work

Data augmentation was already used in the late 80's and early 90's for handwritten digit recognition [27] and it has been identified as a very important element of many modern successful models, like AlexNet [21], All-CNN [28] or ResNet [15], for instance. In some cases, heavy data augmentation has been applied with successful results [32]. In domains other than computer vision, data augmentation has also been proven effective, for example in speech recognition [19], music source separation [30] or text categorization [24].

Bengio *et al.* [3] focused on the importance of data augmentation for recognizing handwritten digits through greedy layer-wise unsupervised pre-training [4]. Their main conclusion was that deeper architectures benefit more from data augmentation than shallow networks. Zhang *et al.* [34] included data augmentation in their analysis of the role of regularization in the generalization of deep networks, although it was considered an explicit regularizer similar to weight decay and dropout. The observation that data augmentation alone outperforms explicitly regularized models for few-shot learning was also made by Hilliard *et al.* in [18]. Only few works reported the performance of their models when trained with different types of data augmentation levels, as is the case of [11].

Recently, the deep learning community seems to have become more aware of the importance of data augmentation. New techniques have been proposed [7,8] and, very interestingly, models that automatically learn useful data transformations have also been published lately [2,13,23,26]. Another study [25] analyzed the performance of different data augmentation techniques for object recognition and concluded that one of the most successful techniques so far is the traditional transformations carried out in most studies. Finally, a preliminary analysis of the implicit regularization effect of data augmentation was presented in [16], showing that data augmentation alone provides at least the same generalization performance as weight decay and dropout. The present work follows up on those results and extends the analysis.

2 Experimental Setup

This section describes the procedures we follow to explore the potential advantages of data augmentation to adapt to changes in the amount of training data and the network architecture, compared to the popular explicit regularizers weight decay and dropout. We build upon the methodology already used in [16].

2.1 Network Architectures

We test our hypotheses with two well-known network architectures that achieve successful results in image object recognition: the all convolutional network, All-CNN [28]; and the wide residual network, WRN [33].

All Convolutional Net. The original architecture of All-CNN consists of 12 convolutional layers and has about 1.3 M parameters. In our experiments to compare data augmentation and explicit regularization in terms of adaptability to changes in the architecture, we also test a *shallower* version, with 9 layers and 374 K parameters, and a *deeper* version, with 15 layers and 2.4 M parameters. The three architectures can be described as follows:

Original	$2\times96C3(1)-96C3(2)-2\times192C3(1)-192C3(2)-192C3(1)-192C1(1)$
	$-N.Cl.C1(1)-Gl.Avg.-Softmax$
Shallower	$2\times96C3(1)-96C3(2)-192C3(1)-192C1(1)$
	$-N.Cl.C1(1)-Gl.Avg.-Softmax$
Deeper	$2\times96C3(1)-96C3(2)-2\times192C3(1)-192C3(2)-2\times192C3(1)$
	$-192C3(2)-192C3(1)-192C1(1)-N.Cl.C1(1)-Gl.Avg.-Softmax$

where $KCD(S)$ is a $D \times D$ convolutional layer with K channels and stride S, followed by batch normalization and a ReLU non-linearity. $N.Cl.$ is the number of classes and Gl.Avg. refers to global average pooling. The network is identical to the All-CNN-C architecture in the original paper, except for the introduction of batch normalization. We set the same training parameters as in the original paper in the cases they are reported. Specifically, in all experiments the All-CNN networks are trained using stochastic gradient descent (SGD) with batch size of 128, during 350 epochs, with fixed momentum 0.9 and learning rate of 0.01 multiplied by 0.1 at epochs 200, 250 and 300. The kernel parameters are initialized according to the Xavier uniform initialization [9].

Wide Residual Network. WRN is a residual network [15] with more units per layer than the original ResNet, that achieves better performance with a smaller number of layers. In our experiments we use the WRN-28-10 version, with 28 layers and about 36.5 M parameters. The details of the architecture are the following:

$$16C3(1)\text{-}4 \times 160R\text{-}4 \times 320R\text{-}4 \times 640R\text{-}BN\text{-}ReLU\text{-}Avg.(8)\text{-}FC\text{-}Softmax$$

where KR is a residual block with residual function BN–ReLU–KC3(1)–BN–ReLU–KC3(1). BN is batch normalization, Avg.(8) is spatial average pooling of size 8 and FC is a fully connected layer. The stride of the first convolution within the residual blocks is 1 except in the first block of the series of 4, where it is 2 to subsample the feature maps. As before, we try to replicate the training parameters of the original paper: we use SGD with batch size of 128, during 200 epochs, with fixed Nesterov momentum 0.9 and learning rate of 0.1 multiplied by 0.2 at epochs 60, 120 and 160. The kernel parameters are initialized according to the He normal initialization [14].

2.2 Data

We train the above described networks on both CIFAR-10 and CIFAR-100 [20]. CIFAR-10 contains images of 10 different classes and CIFAR-100 of 100 classes. Both data sets consist of 60,000 32×32 color images split into 50,000 for training and 10,000 for testing. In all our experiments, the input images are fed into the network with pixel values in the range $[0, 1]$ and floating precision of 32 bits. Every network architecture is trained with three data augmentation schemes: no augmentation, light and heavier augmentation. The light scheme only performs horizontal flips and horizontal and vertical translations of 10% of the image size, while the heavier scheme performs a larger range of affine transformations, as well as contrast and brightness adjustment. We use identical schemes as in [16], where more details are given in an appendix. It is important to note though, that the light scheme is adopted from previous works such as [10,28], while the heavier scheme was first defined in [16], without aiming at designing a particularly successful scheme, but rather a scheme with a large range of transformations.

2.3 Training and Testing

We train every model with the original explicit regularization, that is weight decay and dropout, as well as with no explicit regularization. Besides, we test both models with the three data augmentation schemes: light, heavier and no augmentation. The test accuracy we report results from averaging the softmax posteriors over 10 random *light* augmentations.

All the experiments are performed on the neural networks API Keras [5] on top of TensorFlow [1] and on a single GPU NVIDIA GeForce GTX 1080 Ti.

3   Results

In this section we present and analyze the performance of the networks trained with different data augmentation schemes and with the regularizers on and off. We are interested in comparing data augmentation and explicit regularization regarding two different aspects: the performance when the training data set is reduced to 50% and 10% of the available examples and the performance when the architecture is shallower and deeper than the original. The presentation of the results in Figs. 1 and 2 aims at enabling an easy comparison between the performance of a given network on a particular data set, when it has been trained with weight decay and dropout and when it has no explicit regularization (red and purple bars, respectively). The figures also allow a comparison of the performance between the different levels of regularization (color saturation).

3.1   Reduced Training Sets

The performance of All-CNN and WRN trained with only 50 and 10% of the available data is presented in Fig. 1. From a quick look at the accuracy bars it

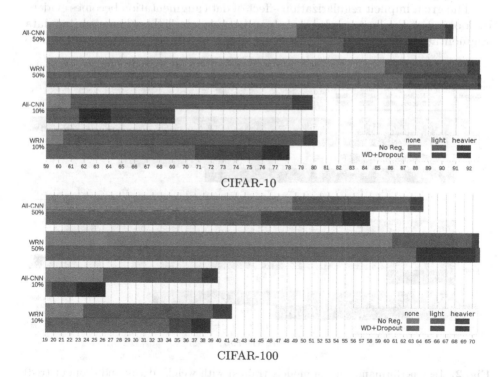

Fig. 1. Test performance of the models trained with weight decay and dropout (red) and the models trained without explicit regularization (purple) when the amount of available training data is reduced. In general, the latter outperform the regularized counterparts and the differences become larger as the amount of training data decreases. (Color figure online)

already becomes clear that the models trained without any explicit regularization (purple bars) outperform the models trained with weight decay and dropout (red bars). This is true for almost all the models trained with heavier data augmentation (darkest bars). Only in the case of WRN trained with 50% of CIFAR-10, the accuracy of the regularized model is marginally better (<0.001). Otherwise, it seems that turning off the explicit regularizers not only does not degrade the performance, but it helps achieve even better generalization.

The differences become even greater as the amount of training examples gets smaller, in view of the results of training with only 10% of the data. In these cases, the non-regularized models clearly outperform their counterparts. We hypothesize that this may occur because the value of the hyperparameters of weight decay and dropout, which were tuned to achieve state-of-the-art results with 100% of the data in the original publications, are not suitable anymore when the training data changes. It may be possible to improve the performance of the regularized models by adapting the value of the hyperparameters, but that would require a considerable amount of time and effort. On the contrary, it seems that the same data augmentation scheme helps generalize even when the training data set gets smaller.

The great implicit regularization effect of data augmentation becomes evident by looking at the large performance gap between the light scheme and no data augmentation. It seems that just a small set of simple transformations help

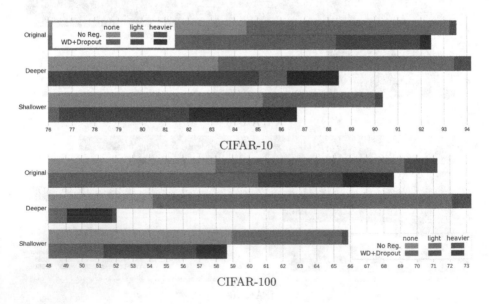

Fig. 2. Test performance of the models trained with weight decay and dropout (red) and the models trained without explicit regularization (purple) on shallower and larger versions of All-CNN. In all the models trained with weight decay and dropout, the change of architecture results in a dramatic drop in the performance, compared to the models with no explicit regularization. (Color figure online)

the networks reduce the generalization gap by a large margin. In all cases the regularization effect is much larger than the one of weight decay and dropout.

3.2 Shallower and Deeper Architectures

Figure 2 shows the accuracy of All-CNN when we increase or reduce the depth of the architecture. If no explicit regularization is included (purple bars), we observe that the deeper architecture improves the results of the original network on both data sets, while the shallower architecture suffers a slight drop in the performance. In the case of the models with weight decay and dropout (red bars), not only is the performance much worse than their non-regularized counterparts, but even the deeper architectures suffer a dramatic performance drop. This seems to be another sign that the value of hyperparameters of weight decay and dropout largely depend on the architecture and any modification requires the fine-tuning of the regularization parameters. That is not the case of data augmentation, which again seems to easily adapt to the new architectures because its potential depends mostly on the type of training data.

4 Discussion and Conclusion

This work has extended the insights from [16] about the futility of using weight decay and dropout for training convolutional neural networks for image object recognition, provided enough data augmentation is applied. In particular, we have focused on further exploring the advantages of data augmentation over explicit regularization, in terms of its adaptability to changes in the network architecture and the size of the training set.

Our results show that explicit regularizers, such as weight decay and dropout, cause significant drops in performance when the size of the training set or the architecture changes. We believe that this is due to the fact that their hyperparameters are highly fine-tuned to some particular settings and are extremely sensitive to variations of the initial conditions. On the contrary, data augmentation adapts more naturally to the new conditions because its hyperparameters, that is the type of transformations, depend on the type of training data and not on the architecture or the amount of available data. For example, a model without neither weight nor dropout slightly improves its performance when more layers are added and therefore the capacity is increased. However, with explicit regularization, the performance even decreases.

These findings contrast with the standard practice in the convolutional networks literature, where the use of weight decay and dropout is almost ubiquitous and believed to be necessary for enabling generalization. Furthermore, data augmentation is sometimes regarded as a hack that should be avoided in order to test the potential of a newly proposed architecture. We believe instead that these roles should be switched, because in addition to the results presented here, data augmentation has a number of other advantages: it increases the robustness of the models against input variability without reducing the effective capacity and may also enable learning more biologically plausible features [17]. We encourage future work to shed more light on the benefits of data augmentation and the handicaps of ubiquitously using explicit regularization, specially on research projects, by testing new architectures and data sets.

Acknowledgments. This project has received funding from the European Union's Horizon 2020 research and innovation programme under the Marie Sklodowska-Curie grant agreement No. 641805.

References

1. Abadi, M., et al.: TensorFlow: large-scale machine learning on heterogeneous systems (2015). http://tensorflow.org/
2. Antoniou, A., Storkey, A., Edwards, H.: Data augmentation generative adversarial networks. arXiv preprint arXiv:1711.04340 (2017)
3. Bengio, Y., et al.: Deep learners benefit more from out-of-distribution examples. In: International Conference on Artificial Intelligence and Statistics, pp. 164–172 (2011)
4. Bengio, Y., Lamblin, P., Popovici, D., Larochelle, H.: Greedy layer-wise training of deep networks. In: Advances in Neural Information Processing Systems, pp. 153–160 (2007)
5. Chollet, F., et al.: Keras (2015). https://github.com/fchollet/keras
6. Ciresan, D.C., Meier, U., Gambardella, L.M., Schmidhuber, J.: Deep big simple neural nets excel on handwritten digit recognition. Neural Comput. **22**(12), 3207–3220 (2010)
7. DeVries, T., Taylor, G.W.: Dataset augmentation in feature space. In: International Conference on Learning Representations (2017)
8. DeVries, T., Taylor, G.W.: Improved regularization of convolutional neural networks with cutout. arXiv preprint arXiv:1708.04552 (2017)
9. Glorot, X., Bengio, Y.: Understanding the difficulty of training deep feedforward neural networks. In: International Conference on Artificial Intelligence and Statistics, vol. 9, pp. 249–256, May 2010
10. Goodfellow, I.J., Warde-Farley, D., Mirza, M., Courville, A.C., Bengio, Y.: Maxout networks. In: International Conference on Machine Learning, pp. 1319–1327 (2013)
11. Graham, B.: Fractional max-pooling. arXiv preprint arXiv:1412.6071 (2014)
12. Hanson, S.J., Pratt, L.Y.: Comparing biases for minimal network construction with back-propagation. In: Advances in Neural Information Processing Systems, pp. 177–185 (1989)
13. Hauberg, S., Freifeld, O., Larsen, A.B.L., Fisher, J., Hansen, L.: Dreaming more data: class-dependent distributions over diffeomorphisms for learned data augmentation. In: Artificial Intelligence and Statistics, pp. 342–350 (2016)
14. He, K., Zhang, X., Ren, S., Sun, J.: Delving deep into rectifiers: surpassing human-level performance on ImageNet classification. In: IEEE International Conference on Computer Vision, pp. 1026–1034 (2015)
15. He, K., Zhang, X., Ren, S., Sun, J.: Deep residual learning for image recognition. In: IEEE Conference on Computer Vision and Pattern Recognition, pp. 770–778 (2016)
16. Hernández-García, A., König, P.: Do deep nets really need weight decay and dropout? arXiv preprint arXiv:1802.07042 (2018)

17. Hernández-García, A., Mehrer, J., Kriegeskorte, N., König, P., Kietzmann, T.C.: Deep neural networks trained with heavier data augmentation learn features closer to representations in hIT. In: Conference on Cognitive Computational Neuroscience (2018)

18. Hilliard, N., Phillips, L., Howland, S., Yankov, A., Corley, C.D., Hodas, N.O.: Few-shot learning with metric-agnostic conditional embeddings. arXiv preprint arXiv:1802.04376 (2018)

19. Jaitly, N., Hinton, G.E.: Vocal tract length perturbation (VTLP) improves speech recognition. In: ICML Workshop on Deep Learning for Audio, Speech and Language, pp. 625–660 (2013)

20. Krizhevsky, A., Hinton, G.: Learning multiple layers of features from tiny images. Technical report, University of Toronto (2009)

21. Krizhevsky, A., Sutskever, I., Hinton, G.E.: ImageNet classification with deep convolutional neural networks. In: Advances in Neural Information Processing Systems, pp. 1097–1105 (2012)

22. LeCun, Y., Bengio, Y., Hinton, G.: Deep learning. Nature **521**(7553), 436–444 (2015)

23. Lemley, J., Bazrafkan, S., Corcoran, P.: Smart augmentation-learning an optimal data augmentation strategy. IEEE Access **5**, 5858–5869 (2017)

24. Lu, X., Zheng, B., Velivelli, A., Zhai, C.: Enhancing text categorization with semantic-enriched representation and training data augmentation. J. Am. Med. Inf. Assoc. **13**(5), 526–535 (2006)

25. Perez, L., Wang, J.: The effectiveness of data augmentation in image classification using deep learning. arXiv preprint arXiv:1712.04621 (2017)

26. Ratner, A.J., Ehrenberg, H.R., Hussain, Z., Dunnmon, J., Ré, C.: Learning to compose domain-specific transformations for data augmentation. In: Advances in Neural Information Processing Systems, pp. 3239–3249 (2017)

27. Simard, P., Victorri, B., LeCun, Y., Denker, J.: Tangent prop-a formalism for specifying selected invariances in an adaptive network. In: Advances in Neural Information Processing Systems, pp. 895–903 (1992)

28. Springenberg, J.T., Dosovitskiy, A., Brox, T., Riedmiller, M.: Striving for simplicity: the all convolutional net. In: International Conference on Learning Representations (2014)

29. Srivastava, N., Hinton, G.E., Krizhevsky, A., Sutskever, I., Salakhutdinov, R.: Dropout: a simple way to prevent neural networks from overfitting. J. Mach. Learn. Res. **15**(1), 1929–1958 (2014)

30. Uhlich, S., et al.: Improving music source separation based on deep neural networks through data augmentation and network blending. In: IEEE International Conference on Acoustics, Speech and Signal Processing, pp. 261–265 (2017)

31. Vapnik, V.N., Chervonenkis, A.Y.: On the uniform convergence of relative frequencies of events to their probabilities. Theory Probab. Appl. **16**(2), 264–280 (1971)

32. Wu, R., Yan, S., Shan, Y., Dang, Q., Sun, G.: Deep image: scaling up image recognition. arXiv preprint arXiv:1501.02876 (2015)

33. Zagoruyko, S., Komodakis, N.: Wide residual networks. In: Proceedings of the British Machine Vision Conference, BMVC, pp. 87.1–87.12 (2016)

34. Zhang, C., Bengio, S., Hardt, M., Recht, B., Vinyals, O.: Understanding deep learning requires rethinking generalization. In: International Conference on Learning Representations, ICLR, arXiv:1611.03530 (2017)

DTI-RCNN: New Efficient Hybrid Neural Network Model to Predict Drug–Target Interactions

Xiaoping Zheng[1], Song He[2], Xinyu Song[2], Zhongnan Zhang[1(✉)], and Xiaochen Bo[2(✉)]

[1] Software School, Xiamen University, Xiamen 361005, China
zhongnan_zhang@xmu.edu.cn
[2] Beijing Institute of Radiation Medicine, Beijing 100850, China
boxiaoc@163.com

Abstract. Drug-target interactions (DTIs) are a critical step in the technology of new drugs discovery and drug repositioning. Various computational algorithms have been developed to discover new DTIs, whereas the prediction accuracy is not very satisfactory. Most existing computational methods are based on homogeneous networks or on integrating multiple data sources, without considering the feature associations between gene and drug data. In this paper, we proposed a deep-learning-based hybrid model, DTI-RCNN, which integrates long short term memory (LSTM) networks with convolutional neural network (CNN) to further improve DTIs prediction accuracy using the drug data and gene data. First, we extracted potential semantic information between gene data and drug data via a LSTM network. We then constructed a CNN to extract the loci knowledge in the LSTM outputs. Finally, a fully connected network was used for prediction. The results comparison shows that the proposed model exhibits better performance. More importantly, DTI-RCNN is stable and efficient in predicting novel DTIs. Therefore, it should help select candidate DTIs, and further promote the development of drug repositioning.

Keywords: DTIs · Hybrid model · LSTM · CNN · Drug repositioning

1 Introduction

In the technology of new drugs discovery and drug repositioning, a critical step is the prediction of drug-target interactions (DTIs). Although the technology of biological experiments has made great progress, the discovery of new DTIs is still a challenging work [1]. The currently known DTIs account for a very small proportion of the total DTI data [2], so finding an efficient method of screening effective new DTIs from a large number of drug-target data is a very meaningful task.

The first two authors should be regarded as Joint First Authors.

© Springer Nature Switzerland AG 2018
V. Kůrková et al. (Eds.): ICANN 2018, LNCS 11139, pp. 104–114, 2018.
https://doi.org/10.1007/978-3-030-01418-6_11

In the past decade, machine learning methods have been adopted to the discovery of DTIs. The importance of structured knowledge and collective classification for drug-target prediction was discussed by Fakhraei et al. [3]. Bleakley and Yamanishi used a support vector machine framework to predict DTIs based on a bipartite local model (BLM) [4]. Mei et al. further improved this framework by introducing a neighbor-based interaction-profile inferring (NII) procedure into BLM (called BLMNII), which can extract DTI features from neighbors and predict interactions for new drug or target candidates [5]. Laarhoven et al. proposed a Gaussian interaction profile (GIP) kernel to represent the interactions between drugs and targets, and they combined RLS with the GIP kernel for DTI prediction problems [6, 7]. Wang and Zeng proposed a method based on the RBM model that could be used to predict multi-type associations and has shown its powerful performance in multi-type DTI prediction [8]. These prediction methods mainly focus on exploiting information from homogeneous networks and have performed well in some datasets. Recently, a number of computational strategies based on deep learning have also been introduced to address the problem. For example, Wen et al. extended the RBM to deep learning by creating a DBN called DeepDTIs, that can predict interactions from different data sources including chemical structures and protein sequence features [8, 9]. Unterthiner et al. combined multi-task learning with deep networks, which was applied to good effect on the ChEMBL database [10, 11]. These methods use a variety of data sources, but the associations between drug and gene data were less considered. Xie et al. developed a deep neural network to predict new DTIs based on the L1000 database [12] and obtained good performance [13]. However, Xie's model only combined drug with gene data simply, and did not consider the connection between these two features.

In this study, we proposed a deep-learning-based hybrid model, named DTI-RCNN, that integrates a long short term memory (LSTM) networks with a convolutional neural network (CNN) to further improve DTIs prediction accuracy using drug and gene data. The main novelty lies in that we introduce the LSTM network to obtain the relationship between the drug and gene data. Then, the features of the LSTM network output are input into the CNN to extract the knowledge between different loci. With this hybrid architecture, DTI-RCNN has excellent prediction performance. Furthermore, it can provide a practical tool for predicting unknown DTIs from the L1000 database, providing new insights for drug discovery or repositioning and understanding of drug action mechanisms.

2 Methods

2.1 Data Source

The Library of Integrated Network-based Cellular Signatures (LINCS) project is a Common Fund program administrated by the U.S. National Institutes of Health (NIH). The funds for this project enabled the generation of approximately one million gene expression profiles using the L1000 technology [14]. It reduces the number of gene expressions that need to be measured from more than 20,000 to 978. We can obtain a unified and extensive source of transcriptome data from this database. For the work described in this paper, we collected drug perturbation and gene knockout perturbation data from the following seven cell lines: A375, A549, HA1E, HCC515, HEPG2, PC3, VCAP.

The DrugBank database is a comprehensive drug data source, that records chemical, pharmacological, and pharmaceutical feature [15]. In order to obtain the complete DTI data, the PubChem ID was used as a drug identifier.

2.2 Construction of Positive and Negative Samples

In this study, we modeled the DTI prediction problem as a binary classification task and applied DTI-RCNN to it. From the L1000 and DrugBank databases we were able to obtain drug perturbation, gene knockout trails, and DTI pairs for the above listed seven cell lines. Some of gene knockout trails are target proteins while others are not. We treat each drug target reaction pair as a positive sample while considering the combination of drug data and non-target protein gene data as a negative sample. In order to avoid the fact that too many negative samples lead the final training model to be more inclined to predict the sample as negative, we extracted negative samples uniformly to keep the ratio of the positive to the negative samples as 1:2.

As mentioned above, the dimension of the gene expression profile obtained by the L1000 biotechnology is 978, and a sample includes both drug perturbation and gene knockout trail. However, unlike other methods, we do not directly concatenate drug data with gene knockout trail into one vector. Instead, we place gene disturbance data and drug data in order to form a 2×978 matrix, so that the LSTM network can fully learn the semantic correlation information between the gene knockout trail and drug data. The feature matrix for each input sample is denoted as follows:

$$x_i = \begin{bmatrix} g_i^1, g_i^2, \ldots, g_i^j, \ldots, g_i^n \\ d_i^1, d_i^2, \ldots, d_i^j, \ldots, d_i^n \end{bmatrix} \tag{1}$$

where x_i denotes the ith sample, g_i^j and d_i^j represent the jth drug feature and the jth gene feature of the ith sample respectively, and n is the dimension of the drug and gene features.

2.3 Hybrid Model Construction

In this paper, we developed a hybrid model DTI-RCNN, integrating a LSTM network and a CNN to solve the DTIs prediction problem. Figure 1 shows the architecture of our DTI-RCNN, which is a two-part network structure. The first part is a simplified version of the LSTM network, and the second part is a CNN.

When the positive and negative samples were generated, the input feature of each sample collected was a gene-drug pair, which is a 2×978 matrix. To deal with the semantic relationship between genes and drug characteristics, the recurrent units in the recurrent neural network (RNN) were replaced by the LSTM network, allowing the gene and drug information to fully fuse. In the LSTM network, the hidden layer contains multiple memory cells. Since the units of hidden layer also play a role in encoding features, the number of units (N) is generally smaller than the dimensions of the input features. A gene-drug pair is input into the LSTM network as a short sequence of two, so gene feature is processed first, followed by drug feature. It should be noted that when gene and drug features enter the LSTM network, they will be multiplied by the same set of parameter matrices, that is, their parameters are shared. The output of the gene feature after the LSTM process will be input into the network together with the drug feature. It is because of this operation that we can analyze the semantic information between gene and drug features. Finally, each of the gene and the drug features will output one vector after the LSTM process. We then combine the two vectors together to form a $2 \times N$ matrix and use it as input to the CNN.

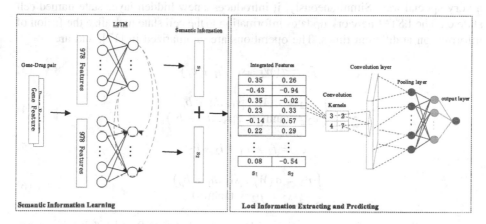

Fig. 1. DTI-RCNN architecture.

2.4   Learning Semantic Information via a LSTM Network

Recurrent neural networks (RNNs) are a variant of neural networks in which units are connected along a sequence [16]. RNNs were proposed to process sequence information. The specific manifestation is that the network will memorize the previous information and apply it to the calculation of the current output, that is, the units between the hidden layers are connected, and the input of the hidden layer includes both the output of the input layer and the output of hidden layers at the last moment. Considering the characteristics of RNNs, we used a RNN to learn the relationship between drug and gene data.

In standard RNNs, the recurrent hidden module has only a very simple structure that is a non-linear activation function. Given a sequential sample $x_i = (g_i, d_i)$, RNNs will update its hidden state s_t by

$$\begin{cases} s_1 = f(Ug_i) \\ s_2 = f(Ud_i + Ws_1) \end{cases} \tag{2}$$

where U is the hidden layer parameter matrix of the current input feature, and W is the parameter matrix of the hidden-layer output s_1 in the last time step, and $f(\cdot)$ is generally a non-linear activation function, such as tanh or a ReLU function.

However, from the Eq. (2) we can see that the fusion of gene and drug data is only achieved through simple dot multiplication and addition operation that are similar to the calculation after a simple splicing operation, and cannot learn the correlation between the drug and the data thoroughly. A LSTM network, first proposed in Ref. [17], can fully integrate the prior information and the current input data in the hidden-layer module because of its special hidden-layer structure. Unlike a single neural network layer, a LSTM network's hidden-layer has four network layers that interact in a very special way. Simultaneously, it introduces a new hidden layer state named cell state c_t. The LSTM network updates information to the cell state to realize the fusion of information at different times. The operations are summarized in [17], and are

$$f_2 = \sigma\left(W_f \cdot [s_1, d_i] + b_f\right) \tag{3}$$

$$\begin{cases} i_2 = \sigma(W_i \cdot [s_1, d_i] + b_i) \\ \tilde{c}_2 = \tanh(W_c \cdot [s_1, d_i] + b_c) \end{cases} \tag{4}$$

$$c_2 = f_2 * c_1 + i_2 * \tilde{c}_2 \tag{5}$$

$$\begin{cases} p_2 = \sigma\left(W_p \cdot [s_1, d_i] + b_p\right) \\ s_2 = p_2 * \tanh(c_2) \end{cases} \tag{6}$$

where $\sigma(\cdot)$ denotes a sigmoid function with an output between 0 and 1, b is a bias term, d_i is the drug feature of the ith sample, s_1 is the state of the hidden layer at the last moment whose only input is only gene feature g_i, and W is the parameter matrix of s_1 and d_i.

In the LSTM network calculation process, all parameter matrices are shared regardless of whether the input are gene features or drug features.

2.5 Extracting Loci Information Through a CNN

A CNN is a deep network structure that has been widely used in the fields of computer vision, speech recognition, text processing and other artificial intelligence processes. In recent years, it has also been used in drug-drug interactions prediction tasks [18]. The purpose of using a CNN is to fuse the same locus features.

For the context feature generated by a LSTM network, we designed a convolutional layer and a pooling layer according to the dimension of the matrix. In the convolutional layer, we designed multiple convolution kernels as encoders to fully extract the information of the features in multiple perspectives. The convolution process plays a role in re-encoding that can reduce the error caused by the redundant information and can enhance the effect of effective information. As mentioned above, the context feature output after passing through the LSTM network is a $2 \times N$ matrix. Based on this, we design the convolution kernel of size $2 \times L$ as the encoders, with a value of L greater than 2 and less than N. In the end, each convolution kernel is assigned a set of $(N - L + 1) \times 1$ vectors. The value of each cell y_k in the vector is calculated as follows:

$$y_k = \sum_{i=1}^{L} \sum_{j=1}^{2} L_{i,j} S_{k+i-1,j} \tag{7}$$

where $1 \le k \le N - L + 1$. In this paper, we set up M different convolution kernels, and then the result of the convolution is a matrix of $(N - L + 1) \times M$.

The convolutional layer generally is followed by the pooling operation. CNNs in computer vision generally use a max-pooling layer to guarantee the translation invariance of the image. Instead, we use mean-pooling operation to fuse features extracted from the convolutional layer in the pooling layer.

2.6   Assessment of the Model Performance

For binary classification tasks, the indicators used to evaluate the performance of the model mainly include AUC and Precision, which are also adopted in this paper.

AUC is the area under the receiver operating characteristic (ROC) curve. It can well measure the overall performance of the model. The higher the AUC value, the better the classification performance of the model.

Unlike AUC, Precision focuses on valuation of the accuracy of prediction models for positive samples.

3   Results

We sampled the positive and negative samples from the seven cell lines uniformly at a ratio of 1:2, and placed them in the model for training and testing. The performance of the model under different parameters was mainly discussed, and the best model parameters were obtained in each experiment according to the tenfold cross-validation method. Finally, the model with the best performance after training was used for DTIs prediction.

3.1   The Impact of Hyper Parameters on Model Performance

Here, we discuss the effects of several hyper-parameters on the performance of the model. In order to find high-performance model parameters, we designed multiple sets of different experiments for each parameter to verify the prediction results. For all experimental results reported in Figs. 2 and 3 we used the same network structure summarized in Table 1 except for the number of neurons in the LSTM hidden layer and the size of the convolution kernel.

The LSTM hidden layer can extract association information associated between gene and drug data. In addition, it can encode gene and drug features. Considering that the features of the gene and drug put into the model are represented as a vector of length 978, and the number of units in the hidden layer is generally smaller than the number of input features, we designed seven different numbers of LSTM hidden-layer units, fully considering the effect of the LSTM hidden-layer units in different quantities

Table 1. Parameter settings for hybrid model

Parameters	Range
LSTM neurons	[100, 200, 300, 400, 500, 600, 700]
Number of LSTM layers	2
Convolution kernel size	[5, 10, 15, 20, 25, 30, 35]
Number of convolution kernel	300
Fully connected neurons	10
Epoch	80
Batch size	64
Optimizer	Adam
Learning rate	0.001

on model performance. In this group of experiments, we set the size of the convolution kernel to 30. The experimental results are shown in Fig. 2.

As show in Fig. 2, when the number of LSTM hidden-layer units is equal to 400, DTI-RCNN can achieve the best classification performance in most cell lines. For most cell lines, the model's classification performance was enhanced with increasing number of neurons, but when the number exceeds a certain threshold, the classification performance gradually degrades. We speculate this is because when the number of neurons increases, the model can better learn the correlation information between gene and drug features. However, when the number of neurons is too large, the LSTM model cannot extract the high dimensional features of gene and drug data, and too much redundant information blurs the association between them. When the number of neurons is equal to 100, DTI-RCNN in some cell lines can also learn higher dimensional correlation information and feature representations.

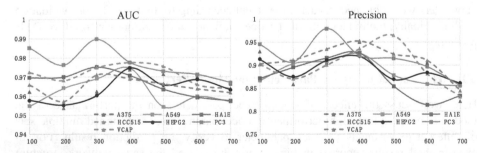

Fig. 2. Impact of the number of LSTM hidden-layer units. The abscissa is the number of LSTM hidden-layer units. The number of LSTM hidden-layer units is set in the range [100, 200, 300, 400, 500, 600, 700].

Since different sizes of convolution kernels can learn different feature representations, we tested the model performance of multiple $2 \times k$ convolution kernels. Considering that the feature dimension of the LSTM network output is above 100, we set the initial value of k to be relatively large, i.e., equal to 5. Meanwhile, in order to obtain more suitable parameters, we gradually increase the size of the convolution kernel, and carried out experiments for k in the range [5, 35]. The number of LSTM hidden-layer units is 400 in these experiments. The effect of different k values on model performance is shown in Fig. 3. We can see that different convolution kernels influence the model performance. When the k value is equal to 30, DTI-RCNN achieves the best classification results in the four cell lines (A375, A549, HEPG2, and PC3).

For cell lines HA1E and VCAP, the model achieved the maximum AUC and Precision when k is equal to 25, and the best classification is obtained when k is equal to 20 for cell line HCC515.

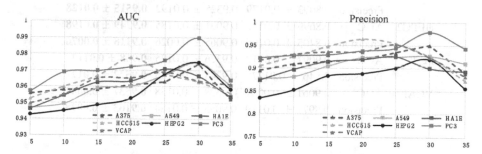

Fig. 3. Impact of the convolution kernel size. The abscissa is the size of the convolution kernel, which is set in the range [5, 10, 15, 20, 25, 30, 35].

It can be seen that the hybrid model classification ability is enhanced with increasing k value, but after k exceeds a certain threshold, the performance of the model starts to degrade. In general, when the k value is between 20 and 30, the convolutional network can well learn both the global and the local features of the LSTM output features. When the k value is less than this range, the amount of feature information extracted by the convolutional network is insufficient; when it is larger than this range, the convolutional network will focus on learning the high-dimensional global information; while ignoring the information of the same locus between the gene and the drug data. This leads to a decrease in the classification performance of the model.

3.2 Comparison with Other Models

Based on the above experimental results, we have found a set of parameters that exhibit relatively good classification performance. These parameters are listed in Table 1. And according to Figs. 2 and 3, we set the number of LSTM hidden layer units of the hybrid model to 400 and the convolution kernel size to 30.

In addition, we compared DTI-RCNN with other deep learning methods, including DNN and RNN. The prediction results of the three methods are shown in Table 2.

From Table 2, the AUC and Precision indicators of the simple RNN model for the seven cell lines are better than those of the DNN, indicating that the RNN can well learn the potential relationship between gene and drug data. The classification performance of DTI-RCNN is better than that of RNN, indicating that the CNN can indeed

Table 2. Comparison of prediction results of three deep learning algorithms (the results of the algorithm proposed in this paper are rendered in bold type).

Cell lines		DNN	RNN	DTI-RCNN
A375	AUC	0.8892 ± 0.015	0.9329 ± 0.0165	**0.9429 ± 0.0076**
	Precision	0.8036 ± 0.0164	0.8775 ± 0.0066	**0.9377 ± 0.0145**
A549	AUC	0.891 ± 0.01	0.9202 ± 0.0134	**0.9371 ± 0.0176**
	Precision	0.8339 ± 0.0166	0.9168 ± 0.0068	**0.9261 ± 0.0098**
HA1E	AUC	0.8817 ± 0.0203	0.9116 ± 0.0181	**0.9358 ± 0.0149**
	Precision	0.8714 ± 0.0105	0.9042 ± 0.007	**0.936 ± 0.0095**
HCC515	AUC	0.8812 ± 0.0101	0.9433 ± 0.0138	**0.9613 ± 0.0163**
	Precision	0.8093 ± 0.0179	0.9325 ± 0.0192	**0.9515 ± 0.0128**
HEPG2	AUC	0.8699 ± 0.0185	0.9091 ± 0.0185	**0.9249 ± 0.0198**
	Precision	0.8405 ± 0.0106	0.9065 ± 0.0026	**0.9118 ± 0.0076**
PC3	AUC	0.9097 ± 0.0112	0.9326 ± 0.0175	**0.968 ± 0.0117**
	Precision	0.846 ± 0.0127	0.9248 ± 0.0135	**0.9522 ± 0.017**
VCAP	AUC	0.9061 ± 0.0061	0.9328 ± 0.0138	**0.9537 ± 0.0047**
	Precision	0.8977 ± 0.0119	0.9055 ± 0.0184	**0.9163 ± 0.0078**

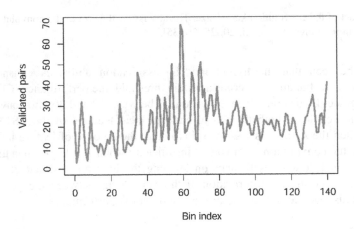

Fig. 4. Overlap between DTIs predicted by hybrid model and DTIs recorded by CTD database.

learn the locus information between gene and drug features. The results show that the proposed DTI-RCNN is superior to other deep learning models.

3.3   Prediction of Novel DTIs

We used DTI-RCNN to predict novel DTIs. Using the predicted DTIs in the PC3 cell lines as example, we examined the novel DTIs using the CTD database, which is a comprehensive database including chemical-gene interactions [19]. We ranked all novel DTIs by predicted score and computed overlapping pairs between the novel DTI predicted by DTI-RCNN and the interactions from the CTD database. Next, we counted the number of overlapping pairs in the sliding bins of 1,000 consecutive interactions (Fig. 4). In addition, we used the hypergeometric test to investigate the statistical significance of the overlap between predicted DTIs and those (P Value = 1.75×10^{-10}). The result indicates that DTI-RCNN could indeed discover a certain part of novel DTIs validated by known experiments.

4 Conclusions

In this work, we proposed a DTIs prediction framework, designated DTI-RCNN, which is based on the RNN-CNN hybrid model, and used the drug perturbation transcriptome data and gene knockout trails in the L1000 database to train the model. DTI-RCNN can learn the associated semantic information between gene and drug data effectively, and can make full use of its locus feature to predict the data. The results show that the proposed model's classification performance is superior to that of other deep learning methods and has the ability to discovery more reliable DTIs. The data from multiple cell lines demonstrate the superiority and robustness of DTI-RCNN. This also suggests that our hybrid model can effectively integrate gene and drug transcriptome data and effectively shorten the DTIs prediction process within the drug discovery process.

Acknowledgements. This work was supported by the Science and Technology Guiding Project of Fujian Province, China (2016H0035).

References

1. Whitebread, S., Hamon, J., Bojanic, D., et al.: Keynote review: in vitro safety pharmacology profiling: an essential tool for successful drug development. Drug Discov. Today **10**(21), 1421–1433 (2005)
2. Dobson, C.M.: Chemical space and biology. Nature **432**(7019), 824–828 (2005)
3. Fakhraei, S., Huang, B., Raschid, L., et al.: Network-based drug-target interaction prediction with probabilistic soft logic. IEEE/ACM Trans. Comput. Biol. Bioinform. **11**(5), 775–787 (2014)
4. Bleakley, K., Yamanishi, Y.: Supervised prediction of drug-target interactions using bipartite local models. Bioinformatics **25**(18), 2397–2403 (2009)
5. Mei, J.P., Kwoh, C.K., Yang, P., et al.: Drug-target interaction prediction by learning from local information and neighbors. Bioinformatics **29**(2), 238–245 (2013)
6. Van Laarhoven, T., Nabuurs, S.B., Marchiori, E.: Gaussian Interaction Profile Kernels for Predicting Drug-Target Interaction. Oxford University Press, Oxford (2011)
7. Laarhoven, T.V., Marchiori, E.: Predicting drug-target interactions for new drug compounds using a weighted nearest neighbor profile. PLoS ONE **8**(6), e66952 (2013)
8. Wang, Y., Zeng, J.: Predicting drug-target interactions using restricted Boltzmann machines. Bioinformatics **29**(13), 126–134 (2013)
9. Wen, M., Zhang, Z., Niu, S., et al.: Deep-learning-based drug-target interaction prediction. J. Proteome Res. **16**(4), 1401 (2017)

10. Unterthiner, T., Mayr, A., Klambauer, G., et al.: Deep learning for drug target prediction. In: Conference Neural Information Processing Systems Foundation, NIPS 2014, Workshop on Representation and Learning Methods for Complex Outputs (2014)
11. Gaulton, A., Bellis, L.J., Bento, A.P., et al.: ChEMBL: a large-scale bioactivity database for drug discovery. Nucleic Acids Res. **40**(Database issue), 1100–1107 (2012)
12. Duan, Q., Flynn, C., Niepel, M., et al.: LINCS Canvas Browser: interactive web app to query, browse and interrogate LINCS L1000 gene expression signatures. Nucleic Acids Res. **42**(Web Server issue), W449 (2014)
13. Xie, L., Zhang, Z., He, S., et al.: Drug—Target interaction prediction with a deep-learning-based model. In: IEEE International Conference on Bioinformatics and Biomedicine, pp. 469–476. IEEE Computer Society (2017)
14. Peck, D., Crawford, E.D., Ross, K.N., et al.: A method for high-throughput gene expression signature analysis. Genome Biol. **7**(7), R61 (2006)
15. Law, V., Knox, C., Djoumbou, Y., et al.: DrugBank 4.0: shedding new light on drug metabolism. Nucleic Acids Res. **42**(Database issue), 1091–1097 (2014)
16. Medsker, L.R., Jain, L.C.: Recurrent Neural Networks. Design and Applications, vol. 5. CRC Press, Boca Raton (2001)
17. Hochreiter, S., Schmidhuber, J.: Long short-term memory. Neural Comput. **9**(8), 1735–1780 (1997)
18. Liu, S., Tang, B., Chen, Q., et al.: Drug-drug interaction extraction via convolutional neural networks. Comput. Math. Methods Med. **2016**, Article no. 6918381 (2016)
19. Davis, A.P., King, B.L., Mockus, S., et al.: the comparative toxicogenomics database: update 2011. Nucleic Acids Res. **41**(Database issue), D1104–D1114 (2011)

Hierarchical Convolution Neural Network for Emotion Cause Detection on Microblogs

Ying Chen[✉], Wenjun Hou, and Xiyao Cheng

College of Information and Electrical Engineering,
China Agricultural University, Beijing 100083, China
{chenying, houwenjun, chengxiyao}@cau.edu.cn

Abstract. Emotion cause detection which recognizes the cause of an emotion in microblogs is a challenging research issue in Natural Language Processing field. In this paper, we propose a hierarchical Convolution Neural Network (Hier-CNN) for emotion cause detection. Our Hier-CNN model deals with the feature sparse problem through a clause-level encoder, and handles the less event-based information problem by a subtweet-level encoder. In the clause-level encoder, the representation of a word is augmented with its context. In the subtweet-level encoder, the event-based features are extracted in term of microblogs. Experimental results show that our model outperforms several strong baselines and achieves the state-of-the-art performance.

Keywords: Hierarchical model · Convolution Neural Network
Emotion cause detection

1 Introduction

Emotions are one of the most fundamental feelings of human experiences, thus emotion analysis has great value in a wide range of real-life applications. In the research community of Natural Language Processing (NLP), there are mainly two kinds of emotion analyses: emotion classification and emotion cause detection. The former focuses on the category of an emotion and the latter works on the cause of an emotion. In this paper, we work on the emotion cause detection task of Cheng et al. (2017).

A microblog focuses on an event, and a clause in a microblog often contains only some information about the event, so the extraction of event-based features for a clause needs to access the focused event in the microblog. In this paper, we propose a hierarchical approach which contains two steps (clause-level and subtweet-level) to extract event-based features. Given a Chinese microblog, a clause-level encoder combines several neural networks to extract local features in each clause. Then, a subtweet-level encoder treats those local features as a sequence and then extracts sequence features for each clause through Convolution Neural Networks (CNNs; Kim 2014). Moreover, because of the feature sparse problem in our small-scaled experimental data, our clause-level encoder extracts two kinds of local features to complement each other: salient features from CNN and weighted features from attention network.

V. Kůrková et al. (Eds.): ICANN 2018, LNCS 11139, pp. 115–122, 2018.
https://doi.org/10.1007/978-3-030-01418-6_12

The contributions of this paper are summarized as follows:

- We propose a hierarchical model to extract event-based features, which uses a clause-level encoder to extract rich local features in a clause and then use a subtweet-level encoder to extract sequence features of the whole microblog.
- We propose a context-aware attention encoder to address the feature sparse problem, which uses context-based representations of words to learn word weights.

2   Related Work

Due to the increasing attention to emotion cause detection recently, there are a few emotion cause corpora available. Most of them are manually annotated, either for formal texts (Lee *et al.* 2010; Gui *et al.* 2016; Xu *et al.* 2017) or for informal texts (Gui *et al.* 2014; Gao *et al.* 2015; Cheng *et al.* 2017). Based on these emotion cause corpora, intensive studies have explored the extraction of effective features for two kinds of emotion causes: explicit causes which are expressed with explicit connectives (e.g. "to cause", "for"), and implicit causes which are inferred from the given texts. In the former case, different linguistic rules are proposed to extract linguistic expression patterns using the context of the current clause (Chen *et al.* 2010; Xu *et al.* 2017; Ghazi *et al.* 2015). In the latter case, different event-based features which reflect the causal relation are examined, such as the convolutional deep memory network (ConvMS-Memnet; Gui *et al.* 2017), Long Short-Term Memory Network (LSTM; Cheng *et al.* 2017) and so on. Because implicit emotion causes play a dominant role in Chinese microblogs (Cheng *et al.* 2017), we focus on event-based feature extraction for implicit emotion cause detection in this paper.

3   Our Approach

3.1   Task Definition

In this paper, we use the emotion cause corpus provided by Cheng *et al.* (2017) as our experimental data, in which emotion causes in Chinese microblogs are manually labeled (namely Cheng emotion cause corpus). Moreover, to better explain our work, we adopt twitter's terminology used in Cheng *et al.* (2017).

In Cheng emotion cause corpus, a tweet can be considered as a sequence of subtweets ordered by their published time. E.g. in Fig. 1, there are five subtweets sequentially published by five users (*I'm Jay*, *Desdis Yun*, *I'm eggette*, *Little Koala*, and *the owner of the tweet*) in the example. Furthermore, given an emotion keyword in a subtweet, Cheng *et al.* (2017) found that the corresponding emotion causes usually locate either in the current subtweet or in the original subtweet. Therefore, there are two emotion cause detection tasks: current-subtweet-based emotion cause detection and original-subtweet-based emotion cause detection. The experimental result of Cheng *et al.* (2017) showed that the current-subtweet-based emotion cause detection task is more challenging, and thus we focus on this emotion cause detection task in this paper.

Chinese: 噢耶… //@小树熊：升工资了升工资~~开心ing   //@我是鸡蛋仔： 😊

//@Desdis韵：刚离职的*情何以堪*!!!!

[原帖]@我是Jay：什么不挂科消息都比不上我这个哈哈哈~~

English Translation: Oh yeah… //@Little Koala: Salary is increased, salary is increased~~happying   //@I'm eggette: 😊 //@Desdis Yun: It is *awkward* for me who was re-signed just now*!!!!*

[original subtweet] @I'm Jay: Nothing even exam fails can compare my message hahaha~~

Fig. 1. An example of a tweet.

In order to extract features from the perspective of the whole subtweet, an instance is a pair of (X, Y), where the input X consists of an emotion keyword (*EmoKW*) and a sequence of clauses in a subtweet, and the output Y is a sequence of binary labels which indicates the causal relation between a clause and the emotion keyword. E.g. in Fig. 1, there are two clauses in the current subtweet for "*awkward*" (the emotion keyword): "It is", and "for me who was resigned just now". The corresponding labels for the two clauses are '*0*' and '*1*'. Furthermore, in order to provide complemental information to a clause, each clause in the input X is attached with a context (i.e. the text between *EmoKW* and the current clause). Finally, the input text of an instance includes an *EmoKW*, a sequence of clauses (*ClauseSeq*) and a sequence of contexts (*ContextSeq*).

3.2 Overview

Our emotion cause detection approach is based on a neural network which mainly includes two components: an encoder which extracts a feature representation and a decoder which assigns a label to each clause according to the representation. As shown in Fig. 2, a hierarchical CNN encoder is applied to each input sequence (*ClauseSeq* or *ContextSeq*) and generates a sequence of hierarchical features (h_{hier_Clause} or $h_{hier\_Context}$). Then, the final representation of each clause is the concatenation of the feature of *EmoKW* (h_{EmoKW}) and the two hierarchical features separately from h_{hier_Clause} and $h_{hier\_Context}$. In the classification decoder, a linear layer takes the final representation as the input, and generates a label with *softmax* function.

To better explain the hierarchical CNN encoder in the following section, we assume the input sequence is the sequence of clauses *ClauseSeq* = $(C_1,..., C_T)$, where C_i is the i-th clause. As shown in Fig. 2, there are two-level sub-encoders in the hierarchical CNN: a clause-level encoder which extracts local features ($h_{local\_Context}$ or h_{local_Clause}) for C_i based on the words in the clause, and a subtweet-level encoder which extracts the hierarchical feature ($h_{hier\_Context}$ or h_{hier_Clause}) for C_i based on all local features in the subtweet. Each sub-encoder is a combination of several encoder layers. Given an input sequence X, an encoder layer yields a middle representation h through Eq. 1.

$$h = encoder(X) \tag{1}$$

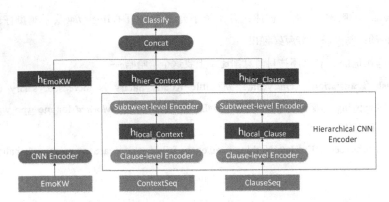

Fig. 2. Overview of our hierarchical emotion cause detection model.

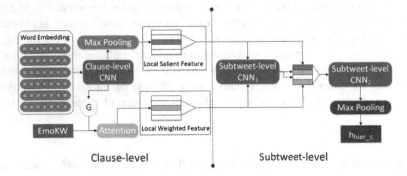

Fig. 3. Illustration of our hierarchical CNN encoder with the clause-level encoder and subtweet-level encoder. G is the Gated Linear Unit.

3.3   The Clause-Level Encoder

As shown in Fig. 3, the clause-level encoder sequentially uses different kinds of encoder layers to extract two local features for C_i ($i = 1 ......T$). In order to alleviate the feature sparse problem, CNN is used to extract abstractive features over the focused clause. In the clause-level CNN, convolutional filters are used to extract high-level features from the sequence of words in C_i and then in order to further handle the feature sparse problem, two ways are used to extract the two local features for C_i: a max-pooling layer with rectifier linear unit activation function (ReLU; Glorot *et al.* 2011) to obtain a local salient feature, and a context-aware attention network which learns the weights of words to obtain a local weighted feature.

In the context-aware attention network, Gated Linear Unit (Dauphin *et al.* 2017) is used to generate a representation of the context of each word and produce a context-based representation for the word, and then an attention layer (Ma *et al.* 2017) is applied to obtain a weighted feature for C_i. In this attention layer, the weight of the j-th word w_j ($j = 1 ......N$) in C_i is obtained through Eq. 2, where h_{w_j} is the representation of word w_j, h_{EmoKW} is the representation of *EmoKW*, [;] is the concatenation between matrices, W_α and v_α are the weight matrices. Secondly, the weights are normalized to construct a probability distribution over the words (see Eq. 3). Lastly, the local weighted feature of C_i (i.e. h_{att}) is a weighted summation over the representations of all words in C_i (see Eq. 4).

$$e_j = v_\alpha^T \tanh\left(W_\alpha\left[h_{EmoKW}; h_{w_j}\right]\right) \tag{2}$$

$$a_j = \frac{\exp(e_j)}{\sum_{k=1}^N \exp(e_k)} \tag{3}$$

$$h_{att} = \sum_{j=1}^N a_j h_{w_j} \tag{4}$$

3.4   The Subtweet-Level Encoder

Based on all local features in a subtweet, which are either local salient features or local weighted features, the subtweet-level encoder uses two CNNs to extract a hierarchical feature. Firstly, the local salient features (or the local weighted features) are ordered into a sequence according to their corresponding clauses, and then subtweet-level CNN_1 with ReLU is used to extract hierarchical salient features (or hierarchical weighted features) over the sequence of local features. Secondly, a clause is represented by a set of features: a local salient feature, a local weighted feature, a hierarchical salient feature, and a hierarchical weighted feature. The sets of features are ordered into a sequence according to their corresponding clauses, and then subtweet-level CNN_2 with ReLU and max-pooling layer are used to extract the final features (h_{hier_C} in Fig. 3).

4   Experiments

4.1   Experimental Setup

Datasets and Metrics. As mentioned in Sect. 3.1, Cheng emotion cause corpus is used in our experiments, which contains $\sim 4,300$ instances and $\sim 12,600$ clauses. We use 5-fold cross-validation to evaluate all the methods. Because a subtweet often contains several emotion keywords, the instances containing one of the emotion keywords have overlaps in their input texts. Therefore, when creating the folds, we ensure instances from the same subtweet are not shared between the folds. This is important as repeating subtweets in both the train and the test sets could potentially make a model performs better than it actually does. Similar to previous work (Cheng *et al.* 2017; Gui *et al.* 2017), only the precision, recall and F1-score of label '1' are reported as evaluation metrics.

Model Settings and Training Details. The dimension of word vector in our model is 20; the kernel widths of the clause-level CNN and subtweet-level CNN_1 are 3, and the kernel numbers are 128. The kernel widths of subtweet-level CNN_2 are 1 and 4, and the kernel numbers are both 64. Dropout is set to 0.5 and is only applied to the final representation. Adam optimizer (Kingma and Ba 2015) is used to optimize the parameters, the learning rate is 0.001, the weight decay is 0.0001, and the batch size is 20. All the parameters are initialized with Xavier Initialization (Glorot and Bengio 2010).

Baselines. We compare our hierarchical CNN approach (Hier-CNN) with the following baselines which use different approaches to encode an instance, where CNN and ConvMS-Memnet use the emotion keyword and the current clause as input, and LSTM uses the same input as Cheng *et al.* (2017) (i.e. local text defined in Sect. 2).

- CNN: the CNN-based encoder is applied to obtain the representation of local text.
- LSTM: it is the emotion cause detection approach proposed by Cheng *et al.* (2017).
- ConvMS-Memnet: it is the state-of-the-art emotion cause detection approach proposed by Gui *et al.* (2017).

4.2   Method Comparison

Table 1 shows the performances of different emotion cause detection approaches. From Table 1, we observe that our hierarchical CNN approach (Hier-CNN) significantly outperforms the three baselines and yields the highest performance. Compared with the two state-of-the-art emotion cause detection approaches (LSTM and ConvMS-Memnet), our hierarchical CNN encoder chooses a multi-channel structure to separately use three sequences of input words in local text (the emotion keyword, the current clause and the context), and uses a hierarchical CNN encoder to effectively extract event-based features for the emotion cause detection on Chinese microblogs.

Table 1. The performances of different methods for the emotion cause detection.

Encoder	Precision	Recall	F1
CNN	48.2	57.2	52.3
LSTM	51.5	63.4	56.7
Convs-Memnet	41.4	61.0	49.2
MChanCNN	54.0	62.8	58.0
MChanLSTM	52.9	64.7	58.1
MChanLSTM-ATT	53.1	61.9	57.1
MChan Convs-Memnet	**54.7**	47.1	50.5
Hier-CNN	52.9	**68.8**	**59.7**

4.3   Model Analysis

In this section, we make an in-depth analysis of our hierarchical CNN encoder in terms of two lines: the multi-channel structure and the components of our hierarchical CNN encoder.

Multi-channel. We integrate the multi-channel structure with one of the three baseline encoder (CNN, LSTM and ConvMS-Memnet), and list their performances in Table 1 (MChanCNN, MChanLSTM, and MChan ConvMS-Memnet). When the multi-channel structure is applied to each baseline encoder, the performance is improved. E.g. the F1-score is increased by 5.7% for CNN, 1.4% for LSTM, and 1.3% for ConvMS-Memnet. This indicates that the multi-channel structure can effectively detect the causal relation between an emotion and an event through separately using the information in the current clause and the complemental information in the context. Moreover, the slight improvement for LSTM and ConvMS-Memnet shows that these encoders suffer the feature sparse problem in Chinese microblogs.

Table 2. The detailed performances of our hierarchical model.

Encoder	Precision	Recall	F1
Hier-CNN	**52.9**	**68.8**	**59.7**
R-HF	51.7	65.9	57.3
R-LF	52.8	61.3	56.5
R-WF	**52.9**	67.6	59.1

Components. In Table 1, although LSTM significantly outperforms CNN (56.7% vs. 52.3% in F1-score), the performance difference between MChanCNN and MChanLSTM is rather small (58.0% vs. 58.1% in F1-score). CNN and LSTM have different advantages in terms of feature extractions: CNN outperforms in capturing high-level features and LSTM is advantageous for capturing sequence features. Moreover, we observe that applying attention mechanism to MChanLSTM (MChanLSTM-ATT) does not improve the performance (58.1% vs. 57.1% in F1-score).

Compared with MChanCNN and MChanLSTM, Hier-CNN achieves the best performance (59.7% in F1-score). This indicates that the hierarchical CNN encoder can effectively integrate the clause-level information and subtweet-level information. Moreover, in terms of attention mechanism, Hier-CNN significantly outperforms the MChanLSTM-ATT (59.7% vs. 57.1 in F1-score). This indicates that Hier-CNN can better capture the key information of a clause.

In order to investigate the effect of local salient features (SF), local weighted features (WF) and hierarchical features (HF), we build another three classifiers listed in Table 2, where R-HF, R-FL and R-WF are the Hier-CNN whose HF, LF and WF are removed respectively. As shown in Table 2, if LF is removed, the recall drops significantly, which directly pulls down the overall performance. Moreover, if WF is removed, the recall drops slightly. This indicates that combining LF and WF, the feature sparse problem can be effectively alleviated. Furthermore, it can be observed that, after removing the HF, the overall performance degrades. This indicates that the subtweet-level information of a clause can effectively augment event-based features from local clauses, and thus improve the performances.

5   Conclusion

In this paper, in order to extract more event-based features for emotion cause detection on Chinese microblogs, we propose a hierarchical CNN approach, which extract the rich local features using the clause-level encoder and more event-based features using the subtweet-level encoder. We show that our hierarchical CNN approach can effectively utilize information in a subtweet for emotion cause detection.

References

Chen, Y., Lee, S., Li, S., Huang, C.: Emotion cause detection with linguistic constructions. In: Proceedings of COLING (2010)

Cheng, X., Chen, Y., Cheng, B., Li, S., Zhou, G.: An emotion cause corpus for Chinese microblogs with multiple-user structures. ACM Trans. Asian Low-Resour. Lang. Inf. Process. TALLIP **17**(1), 6 (2017)

Dauphin, Y.N., Fan, A., Auli, M., Grangier, D.: Language modeling with gated convolutional networks. In: Proceedings of ICML (2017)

Gao, K., Xu, H., Wang, J.: A rule-based approach to emotion cause detection for Chinese microblogs. Expert Syst. Appl. **42**(2015), 4517–4528 (2015)

Ghazi, D., Inkpen, D., Szpakowicz, S.: Detecting emotion stimuli in emotion-bearing sentences. In: Gelbukh, A. (ed.) CICLing 2015. LNCS, vol. 9042, pp. 152–165. Springer, Cham (2015). https://doi.org/10.1007/978-3-319-18117-2_12

Glorot, X., Bengio, Y.: Understanding the difficulty of training deep feedforward neural networks. In: Proceedings of AISTATS (2010)

Glorot, X., Bordes, A., Bengio, Y.: Deep sparse rectifier neural networks. In: Proceedings of AISTATS (2011)

Gui, L., Yuan, L., Xu, R., Liu, B., Lu, Q., Zhou, Y.: Emotion cause detection with linguistic construction in Chinese weibo text. In: Zong, C., Nie, J.Y., Zhao, D., Feng, Y. (eds.) Natural Language Processing and Chinese Computing. CCIS, vol. 496, pp. 457–464. Springer, Heidelberg (2014). https://doi.org/10.1007/978-3-662-45924-9_42

Gui, L., Wu, D., Xu, R., Lu, Q., Zhou, Y.: Event-driven emotion cause extraction with corpus construction. In: Proceedings of EMNLP (2016)

Gui, L., Hu, J., He, Y., Xu, R., Lu, Q., Du, J.: A question answering approach to emotion cause extraction. In: Proceedings of EMNLP (2017)

Kim, Y.: Convolutional neural networks for sentence classification. In: Proceedings of EMNLP (2014)

Kingma, D., Ba, J.: Adam: a method for stochastic optimization. In: Proceedings of ICLR (2015)

Lee, S.Y.M., Chen, Y., Huang, C.-R.: A text-driven rule-based system for emotion cause detection. In: Proceedings of NAACL (2010)

Ma, F., ChittŠa, R., Zhou, J.: Dipole: diagnosis prediction in healthcare via attention-based bidirectional recurrent neural networks. In: Proceedings of KDD (2017)

Xu, R., Hu, J., Lu, Q., Wu, D., Gui, L.: An ensemble approach for emotion cause detection with event extraction and multi-kernel SVMs. Tsinghua Sci. Technol. **22**(6), 646–659 (2017)

Direct Training of Dynamic Observation Noise with UMarineNet

Stefan Oehmcke[1]([✉]), Oliver Zielinski[2], and Oliver Kramer[1]

[1] Computational Intelligence Group, Department of Computing Science,
University of Oldenburg, Oldenburg, Germany
[2] Institute for Chemistry and Biology of the Marine Environment,
University of Oldenburg, Oldenburg, Germany
{stefan.oehmcke,oliver.zielinski,oliver.kramer}@uni-oldenburg.de

Abstract. Accurate uncertainty predictions are crucial to assess the reliability of a model, especially for neural networks. Part of this uncertainty is the observation noise, which is dynamic in our marine virtual sensor task. Typically, dynamic noise is not trained directly, but approximated through terms in the loss function. Unfortunately, this noise loss function needs to be scaled by a trade-off-parameter to achieve accurate uncertainties. In this paper we propose an upgrade to the existing architecture, which increases interpretability and introduces a novel direct training procedure for dynamic noise modelling. To that end, we train the point prediction model and the noise model separately. We present a new loss function that requires Monte Carlo runs of the model to directly train for the uncertainty prediction accuracy. In an experimental evaluation, we show that in most tested cases the uncertainty prediction is more accurate than the manually tuned trade-off-parameter. Because of the architectural changes we are able to analyze the importance of individual parts of the time series of our prediction.

Keywords: CNN · LSTM · Predictive uncertainty · Time series

1 Introduction

Recent research proposed the combination of dropout and Monte Carlo (MC) runs to approximate the predictive uncertainty for regression and classification tasks [3,4]. Instead of predicting a single point, the model expresses its uncertainty through intervals. This is particularly useful for tasks that want to evaluate the prediction in terms of reliability and robustness, e.g. mixing the measured and predicted uncertainty state to control a robot [13]. We apply this predictive uncertainty method to the marine virtual sensor task based on the combined *Biodiversity-Ecosystem Functioning across marine and terrestrial ecosystems* (BEFmate) [2] and the *Time Series Station Spiekeroog* (TSS) [1] real-world dataset [14]. The goal is to replace a real sensor that failed due to the harsh environmental conditions in the Wadden sea, such as the daily tidal forces,

© Springer Nature Switzerland AG 2018
V. Kůrková et al. (Eds.): ICANN 2018, LNCS 11139, pp. 123–133, 2018.
https://doi.org/10.1007/978-3-030-01418-6_13

salt water exposure, and occasional storms. This replacement sensor is virtual and represents a nowcasting task in which current values of different origin are used as input to predict the current target value. In our case, surrounding sensors are used to model a missing sensor at the same time step. For comparison, forecasting tasks predicts future target values based on current values, e.g. room temperature forecasts [16].

Previous work introduces the MarineNet architecture [14], which combines convolutional as well as recurrent layers, incorporates input quality information, and employs the above mentioned uncertainty prediction method. It assumes heteroscedastic, or dynamic uncertainty in the observations, which is reflected by varying noise in the data. The original method [3,14] trains this observation noise through approximation by tuning a hyper-parameter that cannot be learned directly. Moreover, MarineNet applies a unique time dimensionality reduction approach, exPAA, which splits a time series into parts that aggregate different amounts of time steps. An importance analysis of these exPAA parts for the final prediction is difficult, but could be useful for the prediction.

In this work, we propose to address the shortcomings of MarineNet with:

1. an architectural upgrade, allowing to analyze exPAA parts and
2. a novel training procedure to directly learn the dynamic observation noise.

The first contribution is achieved by replacing the last fully connected (dense) layer with a convolutional layer followed by averaging over the time series and more residual connections. We also adjusted the number of neurons of individual layers and finally require less weights to achieve similar performance. The second contribution is attained by separating prediction and observation noise training. We introduce a new loss function for the noise training that directly compares the predicted and the actual uncertainty of the model. In an experimental evaluation, we achieve equal or better performance with the proposed changes and are able to analyze the exPAA parts.

The paper is structured as follows. Section 2 introduces the MarineNet architecture with the most relevant mythological concepts. In Sect. 3 we describe our upgrade to the architecture as well as the new direct training of the observation noise. These upgrades are evaluated in Sect. 4. Finally, we draw conclusions in Sect. 5.

2   Original MarineNet

The MarineNet is a neural network architecture utilizing multiple concepts [14]. A macroarchitectural overview is presented in the upper part of Fig. 1. Convolutional layers filter the time series to create useful temporal features with kernel sizes of one and three (conv1 and conv3). These are grouped into four fire modules from SqueezeNet [10]. Then, the exPAA layer [15] follows, which creates δ' parts from δ time steps, whereby the number of time steps per part is decreasing over time, depending on a hyper-parameter exponent e. Consequently, earlier parts aggregate more time steps, while more information are retained in later steps. Next, the biLSTM layer [6, 8] is fed the aggregated time series, which is then processed by a dense layer. Finally, the sensor output and the dynamic noise is predicted in final linear regression layers.

The dropout mechanism [5, 17], where multiple neurons are deactivated for one iteration, is employed before each trainable layer. It acts as a regularizer and helps to avoid overfitting. Batch normalization [11] is applied after the activation function and if applicable after dropout to further reduce overfitting and to speed up convergence.

Another important part is the implementation of predictive uncertainty via MC dropout inspired by Gal [3, 4]. Predictive uncertainty is the confidence of our model about its current prediction and consists of two parts. First, the data uncertainty, which is reflected in the training distribution, e.g. predictions are unreliable if an unseen sample is on the far end of the training distribution or the available data is noisy. Second, the model uncertainty that affects the internal structure and expression of weights. For example, if a model weight is greater for one or another input and thus give it more importance. The predictive uncertainty can be expressed as an interval around the point prediction. To create this interval, multiple forward passes of MarineNet are calculated with different dropout realizations. These MC dropouts are conducted at test time and give two outputs, a predictive mean $\mathbb{E}[y]$ with variance $\widetilde{\mathrm{Var}}[y_t]$ of m MC model runs $f_i \in F$:

$$\mathbb{E}[y_t] \approx \frac{1}{m} \sum_{i=1}^{m} f_i(x_t)$$

$$\widetilde{\mathrm{Var}}[y_t] \approx \frac{1}{m} \sum_{i=1}^{m} g_i(x_t) + f_i(x_t)^2 - \mathbb{E}[y_t]^2. \tag{1}$$

With a higher number m of MC runs, the approximation is stabilizing. The standard uncertainty interval is represented by squaring the predictive variance (e.g. $\widetilde{\mathrm{Var}}[y_t]^2$ is the 68.27% uncertainty interval).

The observation noise g is modeled dynamically, because in the employed marine application varying noise is introduced, inter alia, by tides and seasons. This noise is equal to the inversion of the models' precision and represents a function $g(x_t)$, which is part of the loss function during training:

$$L := \alpha \cdot (y_t - f(x_t))^2 \cdot (g(x_t) + 1) - (1 - \alpha) \cdot \log(g(x_t)), \tag{2}$$

with the trade-off variable $\alpha \in [0, 1]$ to calibrate the uncertainty scale. Since the noise is not allowed to be smaller than or equal to zero, softplus is used as activation function.

Lastly, the qDrop layer [14] adapts the dropout chance per input dimension after the input layer depending on the current time step and sensor quality. The sensor quality results from the number of consecutively imputed values, since the imputation quality decreases with the length of the data gap. This has direct impact on the uncertainty predictions at test time. For example, when we drop some of the inputs due to low quality, we increase the uncertainty if the dropped

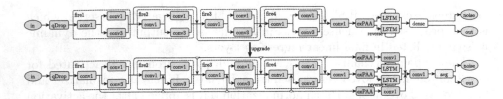

Fig. 1. The macroarchitectural view of MarineNet (top) and UMarineNet (down).

features are important for the prediction. During the training phase, less reliable features are automatically dropped more often based on their quality and thus the network learns to favor trustworthy features to a greater extent.

3 MarineNet Upgrade

We found two shortcomings of MarineNet. First, there is no easy way to analyze the importance of individual exPAA parts. If these information were available, the time series aggregation could be adapted to focus on the more crucial time steps. Second, the scaling of the observation noise greatly depends on the hand-tuned parameter α in Eq. 2. To address these shortcomings, we updated the architecture to return explainable time step impact. Further, we change the training process of MarineNet to acquire accurate uncertainty predictions without calibration of α.

3.1 Changes to the Architecture

The architectural changes to MarineNet are shown on the lower part of Fig. 1. As a first change, we substitute the only dense layer by a convolutional layer with kernel size of one (conv1 layer), followed by an averaging of the outputs over the steps, but not the neurons. We drew inspiration for this change from multiple publications [7,10,12], who apply this technique to images instead of time series data. Instead of returning only the last time step output, the bLSTM layer now passes on its complete output over all time steps. This was avoided in MarineNet, because the dense layer would have needed significantly more weights (number of neurons times exPAA parts). Since the conv1 kernel is not tied to the length of the input series, the computational cost did not increase substantially with the complete bLSTM output. Further, the output from this conv1 layer offers insight into which parts are most important, as only averaging and linear combinations are employed afterwards.

Because of the change to the bLSTM output, it is now possible to add more residual connections [7]. We create compatibility between the outputs by applying exPAA to acquire the same time resolution and a conv1 layer to adjust for differences in neuron count. More residual connections are added inside the fire-modules, after the single conv1 layers. Another change is that each residual connection also uses all compatible residual connections before them. ThTese kind of *dense* residuals are introduced by Zhang *et al.* [18] and Huang *et al.* [9].

Through changes to the number of neurons and layer compositions, our UMarineNet requires 3.04 times less weights, which amounts to 376188 compared to previously 1145072 weights. We increased the number of neurons for the first conv1 layer in fire modules from 48 to 64. In the bLSTM layer, now 192 instead of 512 neurons are employed. The conv1 layer that replaces the dense layer keeps its 512 neurons, but the weight matrix shrinks because of the smaller input from the bLSTM layer. All normal dropout layers utilize a 50% keep chance.

3.2   Automatic Training of Accurate Uncertainty Predictions

The loss function in Eq. 2 employs two counteracting mechanisms to learn the model noise: scaling the original error, which minimizes for small values and the negative logarithm of this noise that minimizes for large values. Depending on the scaling of the target variable and underlying processes, the negative logarithm can be a poor choice to train the noise. The trade-off parameter α partly mitigates this effect, but needs to be tuned separately. We are not optimizing directly for the uncertainty, since it would require the MC prediction during training, which is computationally costly at training time with the complete network.

We propose to completely remove this hyper-parameter α by altering the training process to directly learn the accurate noise function. In the beginning, we ignore the dynamic noise function g and train UMarineNet to create accurate point predictions f by minimizing MSE loss. Thereafter, the optimizer is not allowed to change the weights of the network anymore, it is *frozen*. Only the linear layer of the noise function is not frozen. This layer is then minimizing the following loss function:

$$
\begin{aligned}
L_{unc} := \quad & 2 \cdot \max\left(\Lambda(\tfrac{51}{100}) \cdot \left(\tfrac{51}{100} - \mathrm{acc}(\tfrac{51}{100})\right)^2, 0 \right) \\
& + \sum_{i=52}^{98} \left| \Lambda(\tfrac{i}{100}) \cdot \left(\tfrac{i}{100} - \mathrm{acc}(\tfrac{i}{100})\right)^2 \right|, \\
& + 2 \cdot \max\left(-\Lambda(\tfrac{99}{100}) \cdot \left(\tfrac{99}{100} - \mathrm{acc}(\tfrac{99}{100})\right)^2, 0 \right)
\end{aligned}
\tag{3}
$$

with actual accuracy $\mathrm{acc}(j)$ and $\Lambda(j)$ being the difference between the absolute prediction error and the uncertainty interval at percent accuracy j:

$$
\Lambda(j) := \frac{1}{\hat{n}} \sum_{t=1}^{\hat{n}} \left(|\mathbb{E}[\boldsymbol{y}_t] - \boldsymbol{y}_t| - \sqrt{\widetilde{\mathrm{Var}}[\boldsymbol{y}_t]} \cdot \sqrt{2} \cdot \mathrm{erf}^{-1}(j) \right),
\tag{4}
$$

with predictive mean $\mathbb{E}[\boldsymbol{y}]$, predictive variance $\widetilde{\mathrm{Var}}[\boldsymbol{y}]$, batch size $\hat{n}$, and inverse Gauss error function erf^{-1}. This actual accuracy at the desired accuracy $j \in (0, 1)$ over $\hat{n}$ samples is calculated by:

$$\text{acc}(j) = \frac{1}{\hat{n}} \sum_{t=1}^{\hat{n}} \left(|\boldsymbol{y}_t - \mathbb{E}[\boldsymbol{y}_t]| \leq \sqrt{\widetilde{\text{Var}}[\boldsymbol{y}_t]} \cdot \sqrt{2} \cdot \text{erf}^{-1}(j) \right), \qquad (5)$$

with the logical operator $\leq$ returning 0 for false and 1 for true. This loss function requires multiple MC forward passes through the network during one iteration to acquire the predictive mean $\mathbb{E}[\boldsymbol{y}]$ and variance $\widetilde{\text{Var}}[\boldsymbol{y}]$, but due to the frozen layers, only the gradient for the noise layer has to be computed. We only update the weights to optimize for the noise g in only one of the MC runs. This avoids too much change to the weights in one iteration and saves on computing resources by calculating the gradient only once.

By utilizing multiple Λ-function calls, we train the noise function g to converge between these desired accuracy levels between 51% and 99%. The scaling of these Λ calls by the difference between the desired and the actual accuracy, helps the convergence of the noise model. Ideally, one would only optimize for this difference, but because the logical operator $\leq$ is not differentiable. Consequently, this term only acts as a fixed value.

We define the first and third row of Eq. 3 as outer bounds. They only increase their loss value if they fall below or exceed their desired accuracy of either 51% or 99%. Since these bounds are critical for our uncertainty prediction, they are doubled. Further, the second row of Eq. 3 can be seen as support points for the actual accuracy to reach the desired accuracy.

The separation of learning prediction and noise can also be seen as a network for noise on top of a prediction network, enabling already trained networks to acquire reliable noise observations afterwards. Also, more complex layer structures could be employed if the noise seems to be a non-linear process.

4   Experimental Evaluation

The following experiments verify that the changes to the architecture can give insight to the importance of individual parts of the input and that the direct learning of the noise function is at least as good as tuning the trade-off parameter α beforehand. We compare the results of the original MarineNet and the UMarineNet with and without direct training of the observation noise.

4.1   Combined TSS and BEFmate Dataset

The training set cover the time from 2014-09-18 15:00 to 2015-03-31 22:40:00 in a 10-minute resolution, which amounts to 49867 time steps of 57 different sensors by the TSS and BEFmate project [14,15]. Since the target sensor mostly measured at high tide, when the sensor is in the water, only 11633 target sensor time steps are available for the same time frame. We employ a 60–40% training/testing split. For training, 6979 steps of the target sensors and 24922 steps of the surrounding sensors are available. To utilize the surplus time steps from the surrounding sensor, we append up to 24 h (144 steps) of data to each target input step. We optimize the hyper-parameters by dividing the training set into a 70/30%-split for training/validation. The complete training set is used after the hyper-parameter optimization. Table 1 shows the hyper-parameter settings for exPAA's original steps δ, reduced parts δ', and exponent e as well as qDrop's exponent ε value of UMarineNet. The remaining 40%, 4654 target sensor steps and 19946 surrounding sensor steps of the dataset represent the test set. Just as the original MarineNet, we create a model for each of the five target sensors, which are: *Speed*, *Temp*, *Conductivity*, *Pressure*, and *Direction*.

Table 1. Choice of optimized hyper-parameter settings for the UMarineNet.

sensor	#steps δ	#parts δ'	exponent e	quality exp.ε
Speed	72	4	2.0	0.25000
Temp	36	4	2.0	0.06250
Conductivity	18	8	2.0	0.03125
Pressure	36	8	1.5	0.25000
Direction	72	8	1.5	0.25000

4.2 Methodology

We measure the performance with three metrics. First, we employ the root mean squared error (RMSE) for the point prediction performance:

$$\text{RMSE} := \sqrt{\frac{1}{n}\sum_{t=1}^{n}(\boldsymbol{y}_t - \mathbb{E}[\boldsymbol{y}_t]))^2}, \tag{6}$$

with predictive mean $\mathbb{E}[\boldsymbol{y}_t]$, true target value $\boldsymbol{y}_t$, and number of samples n. Second, we calculate the mean standard uncertainty interval (SUI):

$$\text{SUI} := \frac{1}{n}\sum_{t=1}^{n}\sqrt{\widetilde{\text{Var}}[\boldsymbol{y}_t]}, \tag{7}$$

with the predictive variance $\widetilde{\text{Var}}[\boldsymbol{y}_t]$ from Eq. 1. Since the SUI has no meaning w.r.t. the actual achieved accuracy of the uncertainty prediction, we use the Brier score:

$$\text{Brier score} := \frac{1}{|\boldsymbol{i}|}\sum_{i\in\boldsymbol{i}}(\text{acc}(i) - i)^2, \tag{8}$$

with the actual mean accuracy $\text{acc}(j)$ from Eq. 5, which defines the percentage of values that should fall within the Gauss distribution of errors (actual against desired accuracy). The examined desired accuracy percentages are: $\boldsymbol{i} = (.55, .6, .65, .7, .75, .8, .85, .9, .95, .999)$. Only accuracies over 50% are relevant to us. A 100% accuracy of predictive uncertainty would be meaningless since a large or infinite interval always includes the true target. All metrics indicate a better performance when they are lower, although a smaller SUI but greater Brier score would indicate a too small SUI that does not fit the desired uncertainty accuracy.

We employ the one-sided Mann–Whitney U statistical test. If it returns a p-value below 0.05 and the U value is below or equal the critical value, we call the difference *significant*. The critical U value is 800 for 40 runs of MarineNet and UMarineNet.

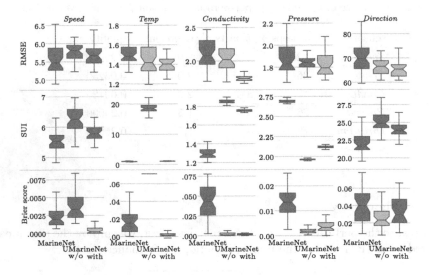

Fig. 2. Comparing performance of MarineNet and UMarineNet without (w/o) and with direct observation noise training through box plots. The columns show the target sensors and the rows different quality measurements. A red box stands for a significantly lower value in comparison to the MarineNet. (Color figure online)

4.3 Results

Figure 2 shows box plots that compare the best runs of MarineNet to UMarineNet with and without direct observation noise training. Rows depict the performance metrics and columns the target sensors. The RMSE improves for all target sensors, except *Speed* for UMarineNet with direct noise training. The architecture change alone only improved results for *Conductivity*, *Pressure*, and *Direction*. UMarineNet with direct noise training performs significantly better regarding the Brier score for *Speed*, *Temp*, *Conductivity*, and *Pressure*, but there is no distinctable difference for *Direction*. Without direct noise training, UMarineNet improves the Brier score for *Conductivity*, *Pressure*, and *Direction*, but is worse for *Speed* and *Temp*. A notable SUI change is seen for *Pressure*, where the interval is smaller, although the uncertainty accuracy is better. In summary, the performance of the target sensor models improved in most cases with UMarineNet, especially when direct noise training is applied.

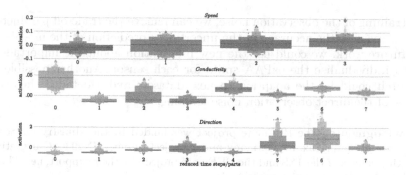

Fig. 3. Impact of exPAA parts for *Speed*, *Conductivity*, and *Direction*. The x-axis contains the part, while the y-axis shows the mean activation output.

We demonstrate the new interpretability of the exPAA parts in the letter value plots in Fig. 3. The plot depicts the exemplary distribution of outputs from the last conv1 layer for the target sensors *Speed*, *Conductivity*, and *Direction*. *Temp* and *Pressure* are not displayed for brevity, as their plots are similar to *Speed* and *Conductivity*, respectively. A single entry to the distribution is composed of the average output from the 512 filters per part. The samples are randomly chosen from the training and test set. Each box defines an observed quantile area, where the widest box encompasses the quartiles from 25% to 75%. Since exPAA creates parts with different amounts of time steps, we have less time steps with higher part number. We associate higher weights with a higher importance of that part, because it contributes to higher magnitude to the next output. The activation output for *Speed* increases with later parts, whereby four parts cover three hours of information (18 time steps). Further, for the *Conductivity* models, which reduce three hours to eight parts, the last four parts as well as the first part have high influence. Interestingly, the first part has a highly variable intensity. We observe for the twelve hour frame (72 time steps) with eight parts of the *Direction* model that the activation output is high for later parts, but the last part is less important than the previous two. Generally, the last parts contribute the most to the prediction, but earlier parts are also used.

5 Conclusion

In this paper, we propose UMarineNet, an upgrade to the MarineNet architecture for increased interpretability and a unique process to directly train for accurate observation noise. These changes are evaluated on the marine virtual sensor task of the combined dataset of BEFmate and TSS, where five sensors are modeled with the information of the surrounding sensors.

Through the architectural changes, we are able to analyze the impact of individual parts of the time series for the prediction. The point-prediction performance is also increased, whereby the highest improvement in RMSE is accomplished for the *Conductivity* target with a ~17% lower error. Because of our direct training of the observation noise, we can remove the trade-off parameter α and even increase the accuracy of the uncertainty prediction of the models.

In future work, we could use the new information about the importance of parts to individualize the exPAA splits for each sensor. Another possible line of research could be the adaption to new datasets and a detailed theoretical analyzes of the direct observation noise training.

Acknowledgments. The BEFmate project was funded by the Ministry for Science and Culture of Lower Saxony, Germany under project number ZN2930. Our gratitude goes to the experts of the TSS and the BEFmate project for their support, i.e., Thomas Badewien, Axel Braun, and Daniela Meier.

References

1. Badewien, T.H., Zimmer, E., Bartholomä, A., Reuter, R.: Towards continuous long-term measurements of suspended particulate matter (SPM) in turbid coastal waters. Ocean Dyn. **59**(2), 227–238 (2009)
2. Balke, T., et al.: Experimental salt marsh islands: a model system for novel meta-community experiments. Estuar. Coast. Shelf Sci. **198**(Part A), 288–298 (2017)
3. Gal, Y.: Uncertainty in deep learning. Ph.D. thesis, University of Cambridge (2016)
4. Gal, Y., Ghahramani, Z.: Dropout as a Bayesian approximation: representing model uncertainty in deep learning. In: International Conference on Machine Learning (ICML), pp. 1050–1059 (2016)
5. Gal, Y., Ghahramani, Z.: A theoretically grounded application of dropout in recurrent NNs. In: Advances in Neural Information Processing Systems: Annual Conference on Neural Information Processing Systems (NIPS), pp. 1019–1027 (2016)
6. Graves, A., Fernández, S., Schmidhuber, J.: Bidirectional LSTM networks for improved phoneme classification and recognition. In: Duch, W., Kacprzyk, J., Oja, E., Zadrożny, S. (eds.) ICANN 2005. LNCS, vol. 3697, pp. 799–804. Springer, Heidelberg (2005). https://doi.org/10.1007/11550907_126
7. He, K., Zhang, X., Ren, S., Sun, J.: Deep residual learning for image recognition. In: Conference on Computer Vision and Pattern Recognition (CVPR), pp. 770–778. IEEE (2016)
8. Hochreiter, S., Schmidhuber, J.: Long short-term memory. Neural Comput. **9**(8), 1735–1780 (1997)
9. Huang, G., Liu, Z., van der Maaten, L., Weinberger, K.Q.: Densely connected convolutional networks. In: Conference on Computer Vision and Pattern Recognition (CVPR), pp. 2261–2269. IEEE (2017)
10. Iandola, F.N., Han, S., Moskewicz, M.W., Ashraf, K., Dally, W.J., Keutzer, K.: Squeezenet: Alexnet-level accuracy with 50x fewer parameters and 0.5mb model size. CoRR abs/1602.07360 (2016)
11. Ioffe, S., Szegedy, C.: Batch normalization: accelerating deep network training by reducing internal covariate shift. In: International Conference on Machine Learning (ICML), pp. 448–456. International Machine Learning Society (2015)
12. Lin, M., Chen, Q., Yan, S.: Network in network. CoRR abs/1312.4400 (2013)
13. Murata, S., Masuda, W., Tomioka, S., Ogata, T., Sugano, S.: Mixing actual and predicted sensory states based on uncertainty estimation for flexible and robust robot behavior. In: International Conference on Artificial NNs - (ICANN), pp. 11–18 (2017)

14. Oehmcke, S., Zielinski, O., Kramer, O.: Input quality aware convolutional LSTM networks for virtual marine sensors. Neurocomputing **275**, 2603–2615 (2017)
15. Oehmcke, S., Zielinski, O., Kramer, O.: Rnns and exponential PAA for virtual marine sensors. In: International Joint Conference on NNs (IJCNN), pp. 4459–4466. IEEE (2017)
16. Romeu, P., Zamora-Martínez, F., Botella-Rocamora, P., Pardo, J.: Time-series forecasting of indoor temperature using pre-trained deep neural networks. In: Mladenov, V., Koprinkova-Hristova, P., Palm, G., Villa, A.E.P., Appollini, B., Kasabov, N. (eds.) ICANN 2013. LNCS, vol. 8131, pp. 451–458. Springer, Heidelberg (2013). https://doi.org/10.1007/978-3-642-40728-4_57
17. Srivastava, N., Hinton, G.E., Krizhevsky, A., Sutskever, I., Salakhutdinov, R.: Dropout: A simple way to prevent nns from overfitting. J. Mach. Learn. Res. (JLMR) **15**(1), 1929–1958 (2014)
18. Zhang, K., Sun, M., Han, T.X., Yuan, X., Guo, L., Liu, T.: Residual networks of residual networks: multilevel residual networks. IEEE Trans. Circuits Syst. Video Technol. **28**(6), 1303–1314 (2018). https://doi.org/10.1109/TCSVT.2017.2654543

Convolutional Soft Decision Trees

Alper Ahmetoğlu[1]([✉]), Ozan İrsoy[2], and Ethem Alpaydın[1]

[1] Department of Computer Engineering, Boğaziçi University,
Bebek, 34730 İstanbul, Turkey
{alper.ahmetoglu,alpaydin}@boun.edu.tr
[2] Bloomberg LP, 731 Lexington Ave, New York, NY 10022, USA
oirsoy@bloomberg.net

Abstract. Soft decision trees, aka hierarchical mixture of experts, are composed of soft multivariate decision nodes and output-predicting leaves. Previously, they have been shown to work successfully in supervised classification and regression tasks, as well as in training unsupervised autoencoders. This work has two contributions: First, we show that dropout and dropconnect on input units, previously proposed for deep multi-layer neural networks, can also be used with soft decision trees for regularization. Second, we propose a convolutional extension of the soft decision tree with local feature detectors in successive layers that are trained together with the other parameters of the soft decision tree. Our experiments on four image data sets, MNIST, Fashion-MNIST, CIFAR-10 and Imagenet32, indicate improvements due to both contributions.

Keywords: Soft decision trees · Convolutional neural networks

1 Introduction

Decision trees are hierarchical models that are composed of decision nodes and leaves. Decision nodes select among children nodes using a gating function that splits the input space, and the leaves contain output predictions, i.e., output labels in classification or real values in regression. In a hard decision tree, the decision nodes choose one of the children; with a soft decision tree, originally proposed as hierarchical mixture of experts [1], all the children are chosen but with different probabilities. In a hard tree, we follow a single path from the root to one leaf; in a soft tree, we traverse all the paths and reach all the leaves and we take a convex combination of leaves weighted by the probabilities on each path. This leads to a smoother fit and better generalization [2]. The parameters of the decision nodes and the leaves can be trained together by minimizing empirical error using gradient-descent.

Convolutional neural networks are shown to be successful in many applications, especially in computer vision [3]. The convolutional units have local receptive fields and learn basic primitives, which in successive layers are combined to learn more abstract features. The success of such networks imply that such a representation leads to better generalization. Building on this idea, we

© Springer Nature Switzerland AG 2018
V. Kůrková et al. (Eds.): ICANN 2018, LNCS 11139, pp. 134–141, 2018.
https://doi.org/10.1007/978-3-030-01418-6_14

incorporate convolutional layers to soft decision trees, so that the tree works not in the original input space but in the space learned by these convolutional layers. We show that as in deep neural networks, the convolutional layers can be trained together with the soft decision tree, leading to higher accuracy on four image recognition data sets, MNIST, Fashion-MNIST, CIFAR-10 and Imagenet32.

This paper is organized as follows. In Sect. 2, we review the soft decision tree architecture. In Sect. 3 we show how convolutional layers can be combined with a soft decision tree. We discuss the effect of input dropout on soft decision trees in Sect. 4. Our experimental results are given in Sect. 5; we conclude and discuss future work in Sect. 6.

2   Soft Decision Trees

Assume we have a K-class classification problem with d-dimensional input $\boldsymbol{x}$. The response of a binary decision tree node m is defined recursively as follows:

$$\boldsymbol{y}_m(\boldsymbol{x}) = \begin{cases} \boldsymbol{\rho}_m & \text{if } m \text{ is a leaf} \\ \boldsymbol{y}_m^L(\boldsymbol{x}) g_m(\boldsymbol{x}) + \boldsymbol{y}_m^R(\boldsymbol{x})(1 - g_m(\boldsymbol{x})) & \text{otherwise} \end{cases} \tag{1}$$

where $\boldsymbol{\rho}_m$ is a K-dimensional vector of predictions, $\boldsymbol{y}_m^L(\boldsymbol{x})$ and $\boldsymbol{y}_m^R(\boldsymbol{x})$ are responses of the left and the right children of node m respectively. In a hard decision node, the gating function $g_m(\boldsymbol{x})$ returns 0 or 1, and we choose either the left or the right subtree. In a soft decision tree, $g_m(\boldsymbol{x}) \in [0, 1]$, implements a soft split:

$$g_m(\boldsymbol{x}) = \frac{1}{1 + \exp[-(\boldsymbol{w}_m^T \boldsymbol{x} + b_m)]} \tag{2}$$

If we consider a decision node with two leaves, this tree of depth one is equivalent to a *mixture of experts* with two experts [4]. If we replace both leaves with two such trees of depth one each, we get a tree of depth two, which is a *hierarchical mixture of experts* [1]. Because of the continuity due to the sigmoid gating function, the gating parameters, $(\boldsymbol{w}_m^T, b_m)$ over the whole tree and the leaf values $(\boldsymbol{\rho}_m)$ can be trained in a coupled manner using stochastic gradient-descent by back-propagating the empirical error from the root to leaves through chain rule. Each decision node effectively takes a convex combination of its left and right subtree children.

Note that $g_m(\boldsymbol{x})$ uses all d features of the input; that is we have a multi-variate tree, as opposed to univariate trees that use one feature in each split. A multivariate node defines a split of arbitrary orientation whereas a univariate split is orthogonal to one of the axes. $\boldsymbol{\rho}_m$ stored at leaf m is a K-dimensional vector of values: For each class, we traverse the tree using the same gating values but the corresponding element of $\boldsymbol{\rho}_m$, we then softmax these to get posterior probabilities, and then minimize the cross-entropy during training. With constant leaves, we get a (smoothed) piecewise constant approximation. To get a (smoothed) piecewise linear approximation, we can have a linear model in each leaf, $\boldsymbol{\rho}_m = V_m \boldsymbol{x}$, where V_m is $K \times d$. In this setting, we learn V_m by adding one more term, $\partial \rho / \partial V_m$, to the chain rule when we back-propagate. Previously, we have shown that soft decision trees can be used successfully in regression and classification tasks [2], as well as for training unsupervised autoencoders [5].

3 Convolutional Soft Decision Trees

The performance of any learning algorithm directly depends on the quality of the input representation, and as such, any feature extraction step that returns better features helps accuracy. In applications where there is locality, having early layers with units that learn local convolutions lead to better generalization [3]. Indeed, all successful vision applications of deep learning use a number of convolution layers that start from the raw image and learn incrementally more abstract features in later layers. Once, we get to a representation that is abstract enough and is independent of location, dense fully-connected layers are used to learn to generate the correct output from that representation.

Using this same idea, one can incorporate convolutional layers to a soft decision tree too, where we learn the convolutional layers from scratch while also training the soft decision tree. This implies that all the gating models will include those convolutional layers and we back-propagate to update the parameters of these layers too. If our soft decision tree has linear leaves, those also have the convolution layers incorporated. In our implementation, we use weight sharing where all the gating models and the leaves share the same convolution layers. That is we back-propagate separately and then average them when we update.

4 Regularizing Soft Decision Trees

A full decision tree with depth P has $(2^P - 1) \cdot d$ parameters in the gating nodes and $2^P \cdot K$ parameters in constant leaves, or $2^P \cdot K \cdot d$ parameters if the leaves are linear. This makes a lot of parameters when P and/or d is high, and as with neural networks, L^2 or L^1 regularization can be used. In L^2 regularization, we add a penalty term $\alpha \|w\|^2$ to the error function where w is the set of gating parameters of the model and α is a hyper-parameter to adjust the relaxation. This penalty term is $\alpha \|w\|$ in L^1 regularization. Applying L^2 and L^1 regularization on soft decision trees are discussed in [6] and L^2 regularization is reported to work slightly better.

Another possibility is to use input dropout [7] where we set the elements of w_m to zero with some non-zero probability p, and scale w_m by $1/p$ for each gating function g_m. In doing this, there are two possibilities: We can do the dropout once and use the same non-dropped features in all gating models, or, we can do it independently in each, which corresponds to dropconnect [8]. Later in our experiments, we refer to the first one as input dropout and the second one as input dropconnect.

5   Experiments

5.1   Data Sets and Training Details

We have experimented on four datasets: MNIST, Fashion-MNIST, CIFAR-10 and Imagenet32. MNIST dataset contains handwritten digits by different writers where a sample is a 28×28 gray-scale image with pixel intensity in the range $[0, 255]$. There are 60,000 training and 10,000 test samples. Fashion-MNIST is a recently constructed dataset of fashion products with image sizes and the number of classes equal to those of MNIST. CIFAR-10 contains 60,000 32×32 colored images (RGB intensities) belonging to ten different classes. Downsampled Imagenet is developed as a more difficult replacement for CIFAR-10. It contains 1,281,167 32×32 colored images belonging to 1,000 different classes. There are 50,000 validation images which we used as the test set. In training, we made the training/validation split as 55K/5K for MNIST and Fashion-MNIST, 45K/5K for CIFAR-10. Imagenet is a very large data set on which we do a single run with recommended hyperparameters (as is frequently done) and thus did not need a validation set.

On all datasets, we divide the pixel intensity values by 255. We did not apply data augmentation for MNIST and Fashion-MNIST. For CIFAR-10 and Imagenet32, we subtracted the mean of the training set for each sample. We made random horizontal flips and shifted the image horizontal and/or vertical up to four pixels randomly. We use stochastic gradient-descent with a momentum factor of 0.9 in all our experiments. For MNIST and Fashion-MNIST, the learning rate is set to 0.01. For CIFAR-10, the initial learning rate is set to 0.1 and is divided by 10 at 32k and 48k iterations as in [9]. For Imagenet32, the initial learning rate is set to 0.01 and is divided by 5 at every 10 epochs. The batch size is 256 for MNIST and Fashion-MNIST, 128 for CIFAR-10 and Imagenet32. A weight decay of 0.0001 is used in CIFAR-10 training.

5.2   Regularization Experiments

We employ input dropout, dropconnect, and L^2 regularization with different coefficients for different models. On three data sets, we used trees with depths of one to five, and for each, we do five runs and report the average and standard deviation of test errors in Tables 1, 2 and 3—we could not do these experiments on Imagenet32 which is very large. Here, we only regularize the parameters of the gating functions. We see that dropout and dropconnect give better results than L^2 regularization. While the results of dropout and dropconnect are not significantly different, dropconnect seems to work slightly better with increasing tree depth. This makes sense because we drop weights of gatings independently of each other and we average over subtrees that use slightly different feature subsets (as in a random forest). Based on these results, we adopted input dropconnect with a keep probability of 0.5 as a regularizer in our later experiments.

Table 1. Effect of dropout for different keep probabilities.

Tree depth	0.25	0.4	0.5	0.6	0.75
MNIST					
1	5.04 ± 0.07	$\mathbf{4.89 \pm 0.15}$	4.93 ± 0.14	4.93 ± 0.06	4.93 ± 0.16
2	3.58 ± 0.09	3.58 ± 0.16	3.42 ± 0.09	3.48 ± 0.18	$\mathbf{3.41 \pm 0.18}$
3	3.15 ± 0.18	2.88 ± 0.17	$\mathbf{2.87 \pm 0.08}$	2.91 ± 0.16	2.94 ± 0.11
4	2.68 ± 0.07	2.67 ± 0.20	$\mathbf{2.48 \pm 0.15}$	2.64 ± 0.26	2.70 ± 0.06
5	2.55 ± 0.14	$\mathbf{2.44 \pm 0.26}$	2.47 ± 0.12	2.51 ± 0.25	2.57 ± 0.12
Fashion-MNIST					
1	13.78 ± 0.10	13.59 ± 0.13	13.58 ± 0.11	$\mathbf{13.42 \pm 0.09}$	13.48 ± 0.06
2	12.66 ± 0.07	12.55 ± 0.26	12.49 ± 0.12	12.56 ± 0.24	$\mathbf{12.47 \pm 0.23}$
3	12.21 ± 0.10	12.09 ± 0.06	$\mathbf{12.01 \pm 0.27}$	12.03 ± 0.32	12.10 ± 0.09
4	12.05 ± 0.27	11.87 ± 0.14	11.95 ± 0.16	$\mathbf{11.73 \pm 0.16}$	11.86 ± 0.23
5	11.96 ± 0.23	11.72 ± 0.21	11.65 ± 0.17	$\mathbf{11.49 \pm 0.10}$	11.55 ± 0.25
CIFAR-10					
1	59.10 ± 0.34	57.16 ± 0.57	57.47 ± 0.84	57.14 ± 0.60	$\mathbf{56.96 \pm 0.30}$
2	56.28 ± 0.79	54.96 ± 0.35	54.39 ± 0.79	54.20 ± 0.38	$\mathbf{53.51 \pm 0.57}$
3	53.69 ± 0.40	52.67 ± 0.75	51.78 ± 0.92	52.29 ± 0.37	$\mathbf{51.26 \pm 0.40}$
4	52.55 ± 0.47	51.05 ± 0.49	49.83 ± 0.48	50.98 ± 0.22	$\mathbf{49.76 \pm 0.47}$
5	51.02 ± 0.53	50.16 ± 0.35	$\mathbf{48.77 \pm 0.39}$	50.09 ± 0.87	48.84 ± 0.38

5.3 Convolutional Tree Experiments

On MNIST and Fashion-MNIST, the convolutional network structure we used consists of two blocks, each of which has two consecutive convolutional layers followed by a max-pooling layer. The number of filters are 8, 16 and 16, 32 for the two blocks. Filter sizes are 3×3 with a stride of 1 for all convolutional layers, and 2×2 with a stride of 2 for max pooling layers. After the second max pooling layer, the data is projected onto a z-dimensional space by a fully-connected layer where z is the hyper-parameter we finetune; it is the dimensionality of the input fed to the tree for classification. For CIFAR-10 and Imagenet32, we use the wide residual network (WRN) architecture previously successfully used on these data sets [9,10]. The WRN architecture we use consists of 4 residual blocks each of which has 6 convolutional layers. There is an additional convolutional layer between residual blocks, which leads to a total of 28 convolutional layers. In WRN-28-1, the number of filters are 16, 32 and 64 for residual blocks, and in WRN-28-2 these numbers are doubled. We add another fully-connected layer to the WRN to map to a specific z dimension which is the input to the tree.

We compare three different models. SDT-k is a convolutional soft decision tree of depth k that takes the output of the convolutional network as its input. SDT-Lk, is the same as the first model except that the leaves contain linear

Table 2. Effect of dropconnnect for different keep probabilities.

Tree depth	0.25	0.4	0.5	0.6	0.75
MNIST					
1	4.93 ± 0.06	4.93 ± 0.17	4.92 ± 0.08	$\mathbf{4.83 \pm 0.02}$	4.84 ± 0.06
2	3.74 ± 0.10	3.43 ± 0.07	$\mathbf{3.42 \pm 0.17}$	3.45 ± 0.17	3.43 ± 0.13
3	2.87 ± 0.14	$\mathbf{2.67 \pm 0.15}$	2.74 ± 0.10	2.77 ± 0.11	2.95 ± 0.37
4	2.43 ± 0.12	$\mathbf{2.41 \pm 0.09}$	2.55 ± 0.15	2.60 ± 0.08	2.58 ± 0.09
5	2.33 ± 0.17	$\mathbf{2.24 \pm 0.11}$	2.31 ± 0.11	2.48 ± 0.12	2.44 ± 0.17
Fashion-MNIST					
1	13.74 ± 0.09	13.71 ± 0.09	13.61 ± 0.17	13.62 ± 0.13	$\mathbf{13.53 \pm 0.15}$
2	12.70 ± 0.05	12.71 ± 0.23	12.60 ± 0.17	12.55 ± 0.16	$\mathbf{12.46 \pm 0.28}$
3	12.08 ± 0.20	11.98 ± 0.21	12.06 ± 0.18	$\mathbf{11.84 \pm 0.20}$	11.94 ± 0.21
4	11.83 ± 0.18	11.65 ± 0.22	$\mathbf{11.53 \pm 0.20}$	11.82 ± 0.19	11.59 ± 0.32
5	11.59 ± 0.12	11.64 ± 0.25	$\mathbf{11.46 \pm 0.19}$	11.54 ± 0.17	11.54 ± 0.25
CIFAR-10					
1	57.33 ± 0.22	57.24 ± 0.51	56.97 ± 0.40	57.49 ± 0.34	$\mathbf{56.88 + 0.38}$
2	55.50 ± 0.78	55.23 ± 0.34	54.48 ± 0.23	$\mathbf{54.33 \pm 0.43}$	54.71 ± 0.29
3	53.60 ± 0.29	53.05 ± 0.35	52.84 ± 0.46	52.70 ± 0.45	$\mathbf{52.49 \pm 0.51}$
4	51.42 ± 0.59	51.12 ± 0.67	$50.89 + 0.44$	$51.09 + 0.41$	$\mathbf{50.67 \pm 0.71}$
5	50.01 ± 0.27	50.26 ± 0.33	49.96 ± 0.31	50.18 ± 0.60	$\mathbf{49.77 \pm 0.53}$

projectors instead of constant vectors. In MLP-k we follow the convolution layers with a hidden layer of k units and then a layer of softmax units; both layers are fully connected and all are trained together, and we take k to be comparable with the number of gating units on SDT.

In Table 4, results are given on MNIST, Fashion-MNIST and CIFAR-10. For MNIST and Fashion-MNIST, we also give results where we use the original input without any convolutional layers—we did not do this for CIFAR-10 and Imagenet32 because one cannot get any decent accuracy on them without any convolutional layers. First we see that convolutional layers help significantly, both with SDT and MLP. We also see that SDT-L works generally better than SDT. On MNIST, Fashion-MNIST and CIFAR-10, we see that SDT-L is almost as accurate as MLP with an equivalent number of hidden units; sometimes it is slightly better, sometimes it is slightly worse.

On Imagenet32 where we could not run many models, we compare SDT-L and the base model which is an MLP variant, and we see in Table 5 that again SDT is almost as accurate. These experiments also indicate that deep convolutional layers can be trained with the error signal that is back-propagated through the soft decision tree without any problem.

Table 3. Effect of L^2 regularization for different α coefficients.

Tree depth	$\alpha = 1 \times 10^{-4}$	$\alpha = 5 \times 10^{-5}$	$\alpha = 1 \times 10^{-5}$
MNIST			
1	$\mathbf{5.00 \pm 0.03}$	5.07 ± 0.17	5.13 ± 0.11
2	4.15 ± 0.30	3.84 ± 0.22	$\mathbf{3.74 \pm 0.24}$
3	3.60 ± 0.18	3.52 ± 0.20	$\mathbf{3.22 \pm 0.17}$
4	3.55 ± 0.13	3.19 ± 0.15	$\mathbf{3.06 \pm 0.24}$
5	3.53 ± 0.19	3.28 ± 0.17	$\mathbf{3.03 \pm 0.12}$
Fashion-MNIST			
1	13.81 ± 0.12	$\mathbf{13.78 \pm 0.14}$	13.79 ± 0.15
2	13.19 ± 0.26	12.92 ± 0.15	$\mathbf{12.88 \pm 0.13}$
3	12.74 ± 0.20	12.70 ± 0.24	$\mathbf{12.41 \pm 0.22}$
4	12.71 ± 0.16	12.38 ± 0.22	$\mathbf{12.07 \pm 0.17}$
5	12.65 ± 0.12	12.48 ± 0.06	$\mathbf{11.84 \pm 0.12}$
CIFAR-10			
1	60.77 ± 0.28	$\mathbf{57.51 \pm 0.31}$	61.13 ± 0.77
2	57.45 ± 0.43	$\mathbf{54.64 \pm 0.47}$	57.36 ± 0.43
3	54.04 ± 0.73	$\mathbf{51.84 \pm 0.77}$	54.15 ± 0.23
4	52.29 ± 0.46	$\mathbf{50.64 \pm 0.33}$	51.99 ± 0.40
5	50.90 ± 0.28	$\mathbf{50.09 \pm 0.30}$	50.43 ± 0.23

Table 4. Error percentages on the test sets.

$dim(z)$	SDT-3	SDT-4	SDT-5	SDT-L3	SDT-L4	SDT-L5	MLP-8	MLP-16	MLP-32
MNIST									
Orig. x	11.96	7.99	7.51	2.67	2.57	**2.30**	7.76	4.74	3.16
50	1.37	1.08	0.76	0.72	0.71	0.63	0.56	0.54	**0.52**
100	1.02	0.96	0.98	0.66	0.67	0.74	**0.59**	0.61	0.59
200	1.11	0.84	0.95	0.76	0.76	0.62	0.68	**0.55**	0.57
Fashion-MNIST									
Orig. x	20.95	29.80	20.83	11.94	11.50	**11.35**	16.66	14.50	13.47
50	10.46	10.24	10.56	7.36	**7.28**	8.08	8.02	7.55	7.73
100	10.12	10.40	9.76	7.89	**7.36**	8.05	8.16	7.67	7.56
200	12.28	9.14	10.37	7.55	7.18	**7.08**	7.59	7.51	7.81
CIFAR-10									
50	9.38	9.52	9.18	8.85	8.76	**8.64**	8.94	8.66	8.99
100	9.71	9.27	9.67	8.83	8.72	8.96	9.02	**8.69**	9.07
200	11.83	10.90	9.95	8.91	9.60	9.75	9.16	9.01	**8.85**

Table 5. Error percentages on Imagenet32 validation set.

	Top-1 error		Top-5 error	
	Base	SDT-L5	Base	SDT-L5
WRN-28-1	67.10	**66.86**	42.33	**41.91**
WRN-28-2	56.40	**56.33**	**31.14**	31.34

6   Conclusions

We show that input dropout and dropconnect can be used with soft decision trees as alternatives to L^2 regularization; of the two, input dropout seems the more interesting. On four image data sets, we see that convolutional layers can be incorporated into a decision tree and the whole can be trained in a coupled manner. The resulting architecture is as accurate as a deep MLP with the added advantage of interpretability. The depth of a tree has a different interpretation than in an MLP: In the former it corresponds to levels of granularity or resolution, whereas in the latter it corresponds to levels of abstraction.

Acknowledgements. The numerical calculations are performed at TUBITAK ULAKBIM, High Performance and Grid Computing Center (TRUBA resources).

References

1. Jordan, M.I., Jacobs, R.A.: Hierarchical mixtures of experts and the EM algorithm. Neural Comput. **6**(2), 181–214 (1994)
2. İrsoy, O., Yıldız, O.T., Alpaydın E.: Soft decision trees. In: Proceedings of the International Conference on Pattern Recognition, Tsukuba, Japan, pp. 1819–1822 (2012)
3. LeCun, Y., et al.: Handwritten digit recognition with a back-propagation network. In: Advances in Neural Information Processing Systems, vol. 2, pp. 396–404 (1990)
4. Jacobs, R.A., Jordan, M.I., Nowlan, S.J., Hinton, G.E.: Adaptive mixtures of local experts. Neural Comput. **3**(1), 79–87 (1991)
5. İrsoy, O., Alpaydın E.: Autoencoder trees. In: Asian Conference on Machine Learning, Hong Kong, China, pp. 378–390 (2015)
6. Yıldız, O.T., Alpaydın E.: Regularizing soft decision trees. In: International Symposium on Computer and Information Sciences, Paris, France (2013)
7. Srivastava, N., Hinton, G., Krizhevsky, A., Sutskever, I., Salakhutdinov, R.: Dropout: a simple way to prevent neural networks from overfitting. J. Mach. Learn. Res. **15**, 1929–1958 (2014)
8. Wan, L., Zeiler, M., Zhang, S., LeCun, Y., Fergus, R.: Regularization of neural networks using DropConnect. In: International Conference on Machine Learning, Atlanta, GA, pp. 1058–1066 (2013)
9. He, K., Zhang, X., Ren, S., Sun, J.: Deep residual learning for image recognition. https://arxiv.org/abs/1512.03385 (2015)
10. Zagoruyko, S., Komodakis, N.: Wide residual networks. https://arxiv.org/abs/1605.07146 (2016)

A Multi-level Attention Model for Text Matching

Qiang Sun$^{(\boxtimes)}$ and Yue Wu

Department of Computer Engineering and Science, Shanghai University,
Shanghai, China
{sun1,ywu}@shu.edu.cn

Abstract. Text matching based on deep learning models often suffer from the limitation of query term coverage problems. Inspired by the success of attention based models in machine translation, which the models can automatically search for parts of a sentence that are relevant to a target word, we propose a multi-level attention model with maximum matching matrix rank to simulate what human does when finding a good answer for a query question. Firstly, we apply a multi-attention mechanism to choose the high effect document words for every query words. Then an approach we called reciprocal relative standard deviation (RRSD) will calculate the matching coverage score for all query words. Experiments on both question-answer task and learning to rank task have achieved state-of-the-art results compared to traditional statistical methods and deep neural network methods.

Keywords: Text matching · Multi-level attention
Reciprocal relative standard deviation

1 Introduction

Deep Neural Network models are extremely powerful that can achieve excellent performance on many hard problems, such as question answering(QA) [1] and Machine Translation(MT) [2]. A striking example of DNN's power is its ability to map input sequences to a fixed-sized vector while their lengths are unknown. Furthermore, DNN models can be trained with a large number of parameters which can contain rich information about the source text data. Thus, if there exists a well labeled training set, back propagation will find the appropriate parameters to solve the problems [3].

Matching two texts is central to many natural language applications, such as machine translation, question and answering, paraphrase identification and document retrieval [6]. Recently, researchers have been studying deep learning approaches to automatically learn semantic match between the two texts. Such methods are built on the top of neural network models such as convolutional neural networks (CNNs) and Long Short-Term Memory Models (LSTMs). The

© Springer Nature Switzerland AG 2018
V. Kůrková et al. (Eds.): ICANN 2018, LNCS 11139, pp. 142–153, 2018.
https://doi.org/10.1007/978-3-030-01418-6_15

proposed models have the benefit of not requiring hand-crafted linguistic features and external resources [16].

Despite their power and flexibility, current DNN text matching models only consider the similarity of query words and doc words. It's a significant limitation, since it's more important to make query words to find their matching doc words, rather than just one query word has many matching doc words and other query words just match nothing. For example, given the following three texts (Fig. 1):

Q: *How old was sue lyon when she made Lolita.*

D_{right}: *The actress who played Lolita, Sue Lyon, was fourteen at the time of filming.*

D_{wrong}: *Sue lyon is old old old old old old old old old old.*

The first two sentences are query text and right matching text, they all come from dataset WikiQA, the third one is a fake and obviously wrong matching sentence we created (In real world QA tasks, people may repeat one word many times because of the input device's malfunction or other reasons). The main difference between D_{right} and D_{wrong} is that the right one have covered all the words in the preprocessed query sentence, while the wrong one only covers three of them although it has more matching words. It is clear that a query coverage concerned method would be necessary.

Fig. 1. The query term coverage problem. Given a query sentence Q and two document sentences D_{wrong} and D_{right}, the D_{wrong} sentence only matches Three key words in query sentence Q which means it cannot answer what the query owner really wants, while the D_{right} matches all key words in Q.

The query term coverage problem [4] poses a challenge for current DNN text matching models, because we need to focus on the number of how many query words have been matched rather than how many document words are similar to some query words. In this paper, we introduce a multi-level attention model with reciprocal relative standard deviation(RRSD) [5] to solve the problem. The idea's purpose is to take different scale factors on softmax weights to obtain different attention matrixes, and then use a reciprocal relative standard deviation(RRSD) approach to calculate the matching coverage of all the query words.

The main result of this work is below. On the popular benchmark WikiQA data, we obtained a MAP score of 0.655. This is by far the best score in the dataset. For comparison, the MAP score of a statistical based baseline method BM25 on this dataset is 0.550. On another MQ2007 information rank task, we obtained a MAP score of 0.648 which is also higher than the most deep models.

In short, the major contributions of this paper include:

1. We apply a multi-level attention mechanism which will exact different levels matching signals and approximately find out the strongest one.
2. We point out a reciprocal relative standard deviation (RRSD) technique for calculating the matching coverage of all the query words.

2   The Model

This section we first discuss about what a right matching query-document pair looks like and try to figure out how to make the matching process clearly by just using a small example matching matrix. Then we implement the idea by our model. Throughout we will use a running example to illustrate it.

2.1   Matching Matrix Analysis

In the field of text matching, specially for deep models, it's very common to make a shared similarity matrix which we called matching matrix for further modeling. Given a query sequence $q : \{q_1, q_2, \ldots, q_m\}$ and a document sequence $d : \{d_1, d_2, \ldots, d_n\}$, both q_i and d_j represent a word. Firstly, mapping every word into a fixed-length vector $v_q : \{v_{q_1}, v_{q_2}, \ldots, v_{q_m}\}$ and $v_d : \{v_{d_1}, v_{d_2}, \ldots, v_{d_n}\}$, then calculating the similarity between word v_{q_i} and v_{d_j}. Generally we use $M_{i,j} = v_{q_i}^T \cdot v_{d_j}$ as the similarity. It's easy to treat the matching matrix M as a 2D pixel grid image and dig more interaction information from it [6]. But this method is too rough to find out delicate parts of text matching. A successful matching document text in a query-document pair should grab all the key matching signals in the query text.

That is to say, the more query words that a answer document can hit, the more likely the document is the right one. The heat map of the two matching pairs further explains this phenomenon which is shown in Fig. 2. The heat map also shows that a small number of grids have distinctive heat than others in rows. Past researches also affirmed only a few words in a document contribute to the

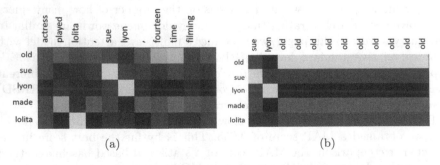

Fig. 2. The heat map of right matching pair (a) and wrong matching pair (b).

final matching score for a query word [18], we call these interactions of them effective matches. For those words which contribute little to the final matching score we call the interactions of them ineffective matches.

Generally, we assume two 4 × 4 matching matrixes as A and B (Fig. 3), and the dim of row represents the number of query words, while the dim of column represents the number of document words. We only focus on the number of effective matches, specifically we use yellow circle with value 1 represents an effective match, and use white circle with value 0 represents an inefficient match.

As Fig. 3 shows, for the first word of A's query sentence we can find two similar words in A's document sentences, the rest can be done in the same manner. We can assume that A's query words have effective matches count as (2,1,1,1) and the B's query words have effective matches count as (3,0,0,3). It seems that the second one has a better performance by just counting their match numbers. But the truth is that the matrix A has a rank of 4, and the matrix B has a rank of 2, which means more query words in A find their effective matching objects. So the matrix A has a more proper representation of the real matching pattern.

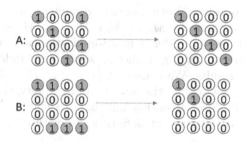

Fig. 3. A general example as the matching matrix analysis, The rank of matrix A is 4 while matrix B's rank is 2, which means A's query words have a better matching result compare to B.

2.2 Model Architecture

According to previous analysis, we conclude two important steps for successful matching: 1. Finding out the effective matches for a matching matrix. 2. Calculating the rank for a query-document matching matrix in a differentiable way.

Multi-level Attention. The model MA-RRSD uses multi-level attention to obtain effective matches, for choosing the high similarity documents words for a specific query word. As stated before, given a query q and a document d, MA-RRSD embed their words by a word embedding layer as $v_q : \{v_{q_1}, v_{q_2}, \ldots, v_{q_m}\}$ and $v_d : \{v_{d_1}, v_{d_2}, \ldots, v_{d_n}\}$. The translation layer constructs a translation matrix M. Each element in M represents the embedding similarity between a query word and a document word:

$$M_{i,j} = v_{q_i}^T U v_{d_j} \tag{1}$$

We then add a vector U to participate in computing similarity for a better result. In this way, we can calculate every pair-wise matching score between each document and query word, forming a matrix $M \in \mathbb{R}^{|Q|*|D|}$, where the value of i-th row and j-th column is filled by $M_{i,j}$. Our motivation is to find out the effective matches for the matching matrix. However, most of the previous works only computed a total single score for a query word with a document sentence, that is, the single score contains much noise information that come from ineffective matches.

To solve this problem, we introduce the attention mechanism firstly. The attention layer applies a row-wise softmax function to get probability distributions in each row, where each row is an individual document-level attention when considering a single query word. We denote $P_i \in \mathbb{R}^{|D|}$ as the document-level attention regarding i-th query word, which can be seen as a *query-to-document* attention [5]:

$$P_i = \{softmax(M_{i,1}^T), \ldots, softmax(M_{i,|D|}^T)\} \tag{2}$$

So far, we have obtained both *query-to-document* attention P_i, and the similarity vector of i-th row as $M_i = M_{i,1}, M_{i,2}, \ldots, M_{i,|D|}$. Instead of multiplying them directly, we consider a multi-level attention layer to produce a set of attention matrixes, as Fig. 4 shows, which have different attention P to get more heuristic results. We construct $(P^{t_{-n}}, \ldots, P^{t_{-1}}, P^{t_0}, \ldots, P^{t_n})$ with $t_{-n} < t_{-n+1} < \ldots < t_n$ for scaling the attention probability, then multiply by M to obtain a set of multi-level attention matrix $\{M \cdot P^t | t \in T\}$. For each query word, the attention matching vector defined as K_i^t with $t \in (t_{-n}, t_n)$:

$$K_i^t = \sum_{j \in |D|} M_{i,j} \cdot P_{i,j}^t \tag{3}$$

After that, we approximatively find out the effective matches for the i-th query word by applying K_i^t, because to some extent we have $max\{M_i\} \approx K_i^t$, which means a few words contribute to the final matching score.

Reciprocal Relative Standard Deviation. Then we need to count how many query feature words get the effective matches, we also call it matching matrix rank at matching matrix analysis. However we cannot calculate the rank for a query-document matching matrix directly by counting how many K_i^t bigger than some value, because it's not differentiable. A approach comes from statistics named reciprocal relative standard deviation (RRSD) will help to implement it. The relative standard deviation (RSD), also known as coefficient of variation (CV), is a standardized measure of dispersion of a probability distribution or frequency distribution in probability theory and statistics. Firstly we average all the K_i^t to get an average matching score K_u^t for a query sentence and a document sentence. According to the obtained K_u^t, we can calculate the standard deviation of K_i^t:

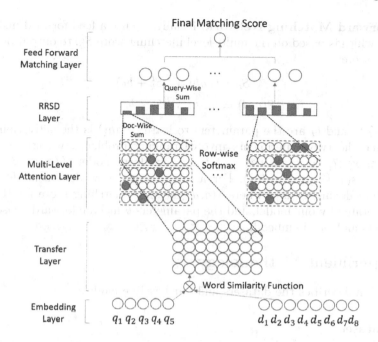

Fig. 4. The architecture of MA-RRSD. Given an input query sentence and a document sentence, the embedding layer maps them into distributed representations, the transfer layer constructs matching matrix by calculating word-word similarity. The multi-level layer picks out how many query words have been matched, and the RRSD layer counts the matched query words in a differentiable way. Finally, a feed forward matching layer produces the final ranking score.

$$K_u^t = 1/m \sum_{i=1}^{m} K_i^t \tag{4}$$

$$K_\sigma^t = 1/m \sqrt{\sum_{i=1}^{m}(K_i^t - K_u^t)^2} \tag{5}$$

After that, we use the quotient as the "rank" for a query-document matching matrix:

$$S_k^t = \frac{K_u^t}{(K_\sigma^t)^k} \tag{6}$$

Here, we use an index formed of denominator for the same reason at the last part. It's clear to know that $K_u^t \propto S_k$, it indicates that the more effective matches, the higher matching score for the matching pair. While the $1/K_\sigma^t \propto S_k$, it indicates that the more ineffective matches, the lower matching score for the matching pair, it prevents the situation that a matching pair has high matching score but only a few query words have been matched.

Feed Forward Matching Network. Finally, we use a feed forward matching network, which is based on the multi-level matching score S_k^t, to output our final matching score:

$$S_t = tanh(W_k^T S_k^t + b_k) \tag{7}$$

$$S(q,d) = tanh(W_t^T S_t + b_t) \tag{8}$$

W_k, W_t, b_k and b_t are the parameters to learn. $tanh()$ is the activation function. Since the two experiments involve ranking problems, we use the pairwise learning [7] to rank loss and train our deep model: $L(q, d+, d-, \theta) = max(0, 1 - s(q, d^+) + s(q, d^-))$. For a query sentence q, document $d+$ ranks higher than document $d-$, where $s(q, d)$ means a matching score for the pair (q, d) generated by our model, and the parameters θ include forward dense layer parameters and word embedding.

3   Experiment Methodology

This section describes the datasets and our baseline models.

3.1   Dataset

As we mentioned before, text matching is the basic part of many natural language applications. Our experiments use two datasets, which differ in data size, to evaluate our model in different natural language processing tasks.

WikiQA. The WikiQA [8] corpus is collected and annotated for researches on open-domain question answering. Each question comes from Bing query log and links to a Wikipedia page that potentially has a answer and it uses the summary section sentence as the candidate answers. With the help of crowdsourcing, it includes 3,047 questions and 29,258 sentences, where 1,473 sentences were labeled as answer sentences to their corresponding questions.

MQ2007. LETOR4.0 [9] dataset contains two separate data sampled from the .GOV2 corpus using the TREC 2007 and TREC 2008 Million query track queries, denoted as MQ2007 and MQ2008, respectively. MQ2007 is a bit larger, which contains 1692 queries and 65,323 documents (Table 1).

Table 1. Training and testing dataset characteristics.

Fields	WikiQA		MQ2007	
	Training	Testing	Training	Testing
	Question answering		Learning to rank	
Queries	2,118	236	1,455	336
Query average length	3.7	3.2	4.7	4.8
Docs per query	9.6	9.9	38.6	39.6
Document average length	15.7	15.5	1951.2	2063.9
Vocabulary size	18243	7623	189107	140713

3.2   Baseline Methods

We adopt statistical baseline BM25 and deep model baseline including K-NRM et al. for comparison.

BM25: The BM25 [10] is a ranking function used by search engines based on the probabilistic retrieval framework.

CDSSM: CDSSM [12] is the convolutional version of DSSM [11] based on a convolutional neural network (CNN) to learn lowdimensional semantic vectors for searching queries and Web documents.

ARC-I, ARC-II: ARC-I [13] is a general representation-focused deep matching model that finds the representation of each sentence, and then compares the representation of the two sentences with a multi-layer perceptron. ARC-II [13] is proposed to fix the drawbacks of the model ARC-I, it focuses on learning hierarchical matching patterns from local interactions using a CNN.

MatchPyramid: MatchPyramid [6] is another state-of-the-art interaction-focused deep matching model that uses convolutional neural network to capture rich matching patterns in a layer-by-layer way.

DRMM: DRMM [4] performs histogram pooling on the embedding based translation matrix and uses the binned soft-TF as the input to a ranking neural network.

KNRM: KNRM [14] is a kernel based neural model for document ranking. It uses a new kernel-pooling technique to softly count word matches at different similarity levels and provides soft-TF ranking features.

MVLSTM: MVLSTM [15] matches two sentences with multiple positional sentence representations and each positional sentence representation is generated by a bidirectional long short term memory (Bi-LSTM).

4   Experiments Details

4.1   Training Details

We found that the pre-trained word embeddings will help to reduce the training time and improve performance almost every time. After some comparison we choose Glove as the final pre-trained embedding to initialize our word representation. In the translation layer, we apply a parameter matrix U with uniform distribution to obtain better similarity matrixes. We give up to use any CNNs or LSTMs to demonstrate our model, because it will cause a heavy burden when training a large dataset. Earlier studies [16, 17] show that BM25 is also a strong baseline on these datasets, which is even better than some deep models such as DSSM and CDSSM. So we choose it as the compare baseline of the experiments. The complete training details are given below:

- We choose the max query length as 10 and the max doc length as 40 at dataset WikiQA. Since MQ2007 is much larger than WikiQA, we set max query length 15 and max doc length 2000 in MQ2007.
- We use GloVe as pre-trained word embedding to embed the query and document sentences with the embedding size of 300 and the vocab size of 18678.
- We then apply attention softmax operation for every query row-wise of the matching matrix, with scale index range as $(2^{-10}, 2^{-8}, ..., 0, ...2^{10})$. In the RRSD layer, we use another scale index range as $(2^{-5}, 2^{-3}, ..., 0, ...2^{5})$. These two types of scale are set as hyper-parameters here.
- Then we use a feed forward matching network to output the final score with the parameters initialized and the uniform distribution between -0.08 and 0.08.

4.2   Experiment Results

Table 2 shows the ranking performance of MA-RRSD and our baselines over two datasets. The results show that MA-RRSD outperformes the statistical baseline and almostly all the DNN based baselines on the both datasets. The closest baseline on WikiQA is DRMM, another interaction based models built upon the embedding translation matrix. MA-RRSD performed better in larger ranking positions: its NDCG@5 score has achieved three point promotion compared to the DRMM's. Although its NDCG@1 is lower than DRMM and MVLSTM on WikiQA, it reaches a significant score at MQ2007. Its NDCG@1 is almost doubled DRMM on dataset MQ2007. The most exciting thing is that our MA-RRSD outperform all the other models at MAP on both datasets. It reflects our model applies not only small datasets like WikiQA but also more practical large datasets like MQ2007.

5   Analysis of MA-RRSD

5.1   Attention Scale Factor Size and Embed Size

One of the most attractive features in our model is the usage of attention scale factors which we propose to construct a multi-level attention layer. Figure 5(a) visualizes the impact of different attention scale factor sizes which reflect how many levels of attention we applied. It seems that our model prefers large datasets because it reaches best performance at scale factor size of 3 in MQ2007 while at scale factor size of 6 in WikiQA. It also explains the best scale factor size exists at a proper number which is related to the dataset size. The Fig. 5(b) clearly shows that our model prefers larger embed size, it might contribute to higher quality similarity matrix that is calculated by a larger embed size pre-trained word-embedding.

Table 2. Ranking performances of MA-RRSD and baseline models. Relative performances compared with BM25 are in percentages. Significant improvement or degradation with respect to BM25 is indicated $(+/-)(p\text{-}value\text{<}=0.05)$.

(a) Performance Comparisons on WikiQA.

Method	NDCG@1		NDCG@3		NDCG@5		NDCG@10		MAP	
BM25	0.376	–	0.522	–	0.608	–	0.643	–	0.550	–
CDSSM	0.198	−47%	0.356	−32%	0.445	−27%	0.515	−20%	0.401	−27%
ARCII	0.367	−2%	0.547	−5%	0.602	−1%	0.649	+1%	0.555	+1%
K-NRM	0.412	+10%	0.557	+7%	0.624	+3%	0.669	+4%	0.577	+5%
ARCI	0.439	+17%	0.571	+9%	0.637	+5%	0.676	+5%	0.593	+8%
MATCHPYRAMID	0.426	+13%	0.604	+16%	0.663	+9%	0.695	+8%	0.607	+10%
MVLSTM	**0.502**	+34%	0.612	+17%	0.669	+10%	0.716	+11%	0.633	+15%
DRMM	0.485	+29%	0.643	+23%	0.681	+12%	**0.724**	+13%	0.647	+18%
MA-RRSD	0.447	+19%	**0.650**	+25%	**0.699**	+15%	0.710	+10%	**0.655**	+19%

(b) Performance Comparisons on MQ2007.

Method	NDCG@1		NDCG@3		NDCG@5		NDCG@10		MAP	
BM25	0.417	–	0.424	–	0.432	–	0.461	–	0.481	–
MVLSTM	0.288	−31%	0.317	−25%	0.325	−25%	0.363	−21%	0.401	−17%
ARCII	0.279	−33%	0.315	−26%	0.345	−20%	0.382	−17%	0.416	−14%
DRMM	0.342	−18%	0.347	−18%	0.364	−16%	0.392	−15%	0.418	−13%
ARCI	0.318	−24%	0.339	−20%	0.352	−19%	0.390	−15%	0.420	−13%
CDSSM	0.329	−21%	0.354	−17%	0.365	−16%	0.404	−12%	0.430	−11%
MATCHPYRAMID	0.536	+29%	0.561	+32%	0.574	+33%	0.612	+33%	0.604	+26%
K-NRM	0.642	+54%	**0.643**	+52%	**0.647**	+50%	0.648	+41%	0.643	+34%
MA-RRSD	**0.643**	+54%	0.640	+51%	0.646	+50%	**0.649**	+41%	**0.648**	+35%

5.2 A Comparison of Convergence Rate

Unlike other DNN models, we don't apply CNNs or LSTMs approach at all. We replace them with multi-level attention layer and reciprocal relative standard

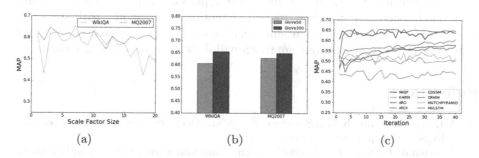

(a)   (b)   (c)

Fig. 5. (a) shows the best scale factor size for WikiQA and MQ2007. (b) tells us that the more dimensions the model takes, the better performance the result gets. From (c) we can see the convergence rate of our model and other baseline models at WikiQA. Our model achieve MAP 0.6 at iteration 3 while other models perform poor except DRMM.

deviation technique to catch global and local matching information. So it becomes faster than those models which are based on CNNs and LSTMs. As Fig. 5(c) shows, our model achieves MAP 0.60 on WikiQA at iteration 3 while other models almost achieve half of it at the beginning steps. The another model dropped CNNs or LSTMs is DRMM, it also shows a significant performance in convergence rate.

6   Related Work

There have been some related works to address the query term coverage problem with neural network. Our approach is inspired by Chenyan Xiong [14] et al. who used kernels to extract multi-level soft match features. Pang [4] introduced a novel deep relevance matching model which employs a deep architecture at the query term level for relevance matching. Wan [15] used another way to match two sentences with multiple positional sentence representations.

7   Conclusion

This paper presents MA-RRSD, a multi-level attention based model with reciprocal relative standard deviation technique for text matching. The model uses pre-trained embeddings to calculate word-level interactions on query and document text, and ranks documents using a feed forward matching network. The key of our model is the multi-level attention which uses different attention scale factors to grab the most effective matching word in the document for a specific query word. Then we count the final matching score for all the query words by reciprocal relative standard deviation technique(RRSD), which is guided by the concept of matching matrix rank that we introduce in Sect. 2.

Our experiments on WikiQA question answer task and MQ2007 learning to rank task demonstrated the advantage of multi-level attention layer. It achieved on both small and large datasets. It also can converge faster than almost all of the DNN which is based models due to the replacement of CNNs and LSTMs.

Most importantly, we show that an attention based model with statistical intuitions can outperform traditional DNN model on position-indepenent task. These results suggest that our approach will do well on other similar tasks.

References

1. Yu, L., Hermann, K.M., Blunsom, P., et al.: Deep learning for answer sentence selection. Comput. Sci. (2014)
2. Bahdanau, D., Cho, K., Bengio, Y.: Neural machine translation by jointly learning to align and translate. Comput. Sci. (2014)
3. Sutskever, I., Vinyals, O., Le, Q.V.: Sequence to sequence learning with neural networks, **4**, 3104–3112 (2014)

4. Guo J, Fan Y, Ai Q, et al.: A deep relevance matching model for Ad-hoc retrieval. In: ACM International on Conference on Information and Knowledge Management, pp. 55–64. ACM (2016)

5. Reed, G.F., Lynn, F., Meade, B.D.: Use of coefficient of variation in assessing variability of quantitative assays. Clin. Diagn. Lab. Immunol. **9**(6), 1235–1239 (2002)

6. Pang, L., Lan, Y., Guo, J., et al.: Text matching as image recognition (2016)

7. Liu, T.Y.: Learning to rank for information retrieval. Acm Sigir. Forum **41**(2), 904 (2010)

8. Yang, Y., Yih, W.T., Meek, C.: WikiQA: a challenge dataset for open-domain question answering. In: Conference on Empirical Methods in Natural Language Processing, pp. 2013–2018 (2015)

9. Qin, T., Liu, T.Y.: Introducing LETOR 4.0 datasets. Comput. Sci. (2013)

10. Zhai, C., Lafferty, J.: A study of smoothing methods for language models applied to Ad Hoc information retrieval. In: International ACM SIGIR Conference on Research and Development in Information Retrieval, pp. 334–342. ACM (2001)

11. Huang, P.S., He, X., Gao, J., et al.: Learning deep structured semantic models for web search using clickthrough data. In: ACM International Conference on Conference on Information & Knowledge Management, pp. 2333–2338. ACM (2013)

12. Shen, Y., He, X., Gao, J., et al.: Learning semantic representations using convolutional neural networks for web search. In: International Conference on World Wide Web, pp. 373–374. ACM (2014)

13. Hu, B., Lu, Z., Li, H., et al.: Convolutional neural network architectures for matching natural language sentences. In: International Conference on Neural Information Processing Systems. MIT Press, pp. 2042–2050 (2014)

14. Xiong, C., Dai, Z., Callan, J., et al.: End-to-end neural Ad-hoc ranking with Kernel pooling, pp. 55–64 (2017)

15. Wan, S., Lan, Y., Guo, J., et al.: A deep architecture for semantic matching with multiple positional sentence representations, pp. 2835–2841 (2015)

16. Yang, L., Ai, Q., Guo, J., et al.: aNMM: ranking short answer texts with attention-based neural matching model. In: ACM International on Conference on Information and Knowledge Management, pp. 287–296. ACM (2016)

17. Pang, L., Lan, Y., Guo, J., et al.: DeepRank: a new deep architecture for relevance ranking in information retrieval (2017)

18. Pang, L., Lan, Y., Guo, J., et al.: A deep investigation of deep IR models (2017)

Attention Enhanced Chinese Word Embeddings

Xingzhang Ren[1,2], Leilei Zhang[1,2], Wei Ye[2(✉)], Hang Hua[1,2],
and Shikun Zhang[2]

[1] School of Software and Microelectronics, Peking University, Beijing, China
[2] National Engineering Research Center for Software Engineering,
Peking University, Beijing, China
{xzhren,leilei_zhang,wye,huahang,zhangsk}@pku.edu.cn

Abstract. We introduce a new Chinese word embeddings method called
AWE by utilizing attention mechanism to enhance Mikolov's CBOW.
Considering the shortcomings of existing word representation methods,
we improve CBOW in two aspects. Above all, the context vector in
CBOW is obtained by simply averaging the representation of the surrounding words while our AWE model aligns the surrounding words with
the central word by global attention mechanism and self attention mechanism. Moreover, CBOW is a bag-of-word model which ignores the order
of surrounding words, and this paper uses the position encoding to further enhance AWE and proposes P&AWE. We design both qualitative
and quantitative experiments to analyze the effectiveness of the models.
Results indicate that the AWE models far exceed the CBOW model, and
achieve state-of-the-art performances on the task of word similarity. Last
but not least, we also further verify the AWE models through attention
visualization and case analysis.

Keywords: Word embedding · Attention mechanism
Representation learning · Natural language processing

1 Introduction

The task of word representation is of paramount importance in many natural
language processing (NLP) systems and techniques, because the word is the basic
unit of linguistic structure. In recent years, word representation approaches were
investigated quite intensively. Among them, one-hot encoding is the simplest and
most commonly used method. However, it cannot meet the needs of practical
applications for its high dimensions and limited ability to express semantics.
Hinton proposed distributed representation [6] in 1986, which can not only solve
the problem of dimensional disaster but also establish the concept of "distance"
between words. Afterwards, growing studies were conducted based on the principle and applied in word representation field called word embeddings. Representative models include CBOW, Skipgram [11,12] and GloVe [13]. They have

V. Kůrková et al. (Eds.): ICANN 2018, LNCS 11139, pp. 154–165, 2018.
https://doi.org/10.1007/978-3-030-01418-6_16

been widely used in various tasks such as part-of-speech tagging [3,16], sentence classification [7,9], text summarization [20] and question answering [4,8,10,15], which are common tasks in NLP.

Different from English, Chinese as a hieroglyphic has typical characteristics of character meaning and shape expression. Therefore, a multitude of research teams have made unique improvements on Chinese word embeddings. CWE [2] thought the semantic meaning of a word is related to the meanings of its composing characters for Chinese. Meanwhile, in view of the issues of character ambiguity and non-compositional words, it proposes multiple prototype character embeddings and an effective word selection method to joint learning character and word embeddings. After CWE, there are MGE [18], JWE [19], GWE [14] and cw2vec [1] exploiting the radicals, character pixel information, character substructure information, character stroke information to enhance the Chinese word embeddings. Owing to the good structure and scalability of word2vec[1], most works on Chinese word embedding are based on CBOW or Skipgram.

In fact, the size of sliding window in word2vec is usually small. It is not that the larger window size will increase computation load, actually, the size of the window has no effect on the calculation of the CBOW model, but the larger window size will make unfavorable effect to the model performance which will be detailed discussed in Sect. 2.1. Small sliding window cannot precisely gather semantic information, which will make the words similar to its antonym with the same surrounding words. As an example, for sentences "I love you" and "I hate you", when using word2vec, the central word "love" and "hate" are learned by the same surrounding words "I" and "you", so the word vectors of "love" and "hate" will be closer together in the vector space. Such word embedding is nearly irrelevant to semantic information. Indeed, similar to "love" should be "like" while similar to "hate" should be "disgust".

This paper examines a new measure of utilizing attention mechanism to enhance Chinese word embeddings based on existing word embedding methods called AWE. We propose a model uniting the attention mechanism to CBOW which can fit larger sliding window and thus allow word embedding to accommodate rich semantics. It is because the attention mechanism can emphasize useful surrounding words for the central word and avoid the influence of useless environmental words. The larger sliding window allows the central word to obtain more comprehensive semantic representation by capturing more information of surrounding words. We perform extensive experiments and both qualitative and quantitative analysis, which manifests that our model is able to learn better Chinese word representations than other state-of-the-art approaches.

2 Model

2.1 Motivation

The original CBOW model consists of an input layer, a projection layer, and an output layer as Fig. 1 shows. The inputs, one-hot vectors of the surrounding

---

[1] https://code.google.com/archive/p/word2vec/.

words, are mapped to the projection layer with embedding size neurons through a fully connected network. So, in the projection layer, we can obtain context vectors by averaging the embedding value of these surrounding vectors. The order of the words in the sentence has no effect on the result, it is why the model is called continuous bag-of-words model. Finally, the context vector of the projection layer is fully connected to the output layer with vocabulary size neurons. Because the dimension of the vocabulary in the output layer is extremely large, in practical applications, negative sampling or hierarchical softmax are used for optimization [5,12].

We divide the training process of CBOW into two parts. The first part is a full-connection neural network from the input layer to the projection layer, which mainly obtains the context vector by averaging the surrounding words vectors, and the second part is the full-connection neural network of the projection layer and the output layer, which mainly calculates the output probability of each word in vocabulary as target word. The bag-of-words model averages the vectors of the surrounding words as the context vector, which does not fit well with human language understanding behavior. Three major problems have yet to be addressed. Firstly, the degree of contribution of each context vector can not be same, but related to its importance. Context words such as "is","a" which do not have much substantive meaning should have smaller weight. Secondly, the order of context words should be concerned. For instance, "A love B" is exceedingly different from"B love A". Finally, the contribution of words to context may be related to the central word. As an example, in sentence "good rather than bad","rather" is important to predict "than", while"bad" is important to predict "good".

Attention mechanism was first proposed in computer visual area. In NLP field, it is often used to align the original text and the translation text in machine translation task. This paper tries to use the attention mechanism to improve the process of establishing the context vector of the surrounding word, thus generates more precise word vectors by enhanced context vector.

2.2   CBOW

As Fig. 1 shows, the word embeddings matrix was represented as $W \in \mathbb{R}^{d \times |V|}$ where d is the embedding dimension and $|V|$ is the size of vocabulary $V = \{v_1, v_2, .., v_{|V|}\}$. The output embeddings matrix was $W' \in \mathbb{R}^{|V| \times d}$. x_i or y_i is one-hot encoding of the word v_i, and w_i is the word embedding of the word v_i, thus $Wx_i = w_i$. The CBOW model predicts the central word w_t when given word distributed representations of the surrounding words in a sliding window $H = \{w_{t-b}, \ldots, w_{t-1}, w_{t+1}, \ldots, w_{t+b}\}$, where b is a hyper-parameter defining the sliding window size. The CBOW model calculates the average of the input words as a context vector, which is shown as

$$c_t = \frac{1}{2b} \sum_{i \in [t-b, t+b] - \{t\}} w_i \qquad (1)$$

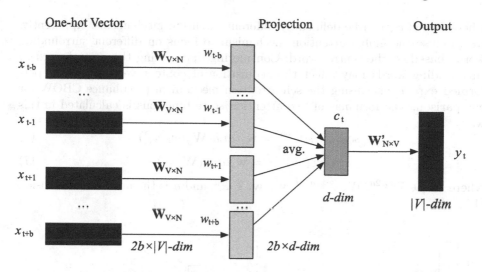

One-hot Vector   Projection   Output

Fig. 1. In Mikolov's CBOW model, the projection layer's w_i is the vector representation of the surrounding word x_i in the current sliding window, and the content vector c_t is calculated as the average of surrounding words representations. The CBOW model is to make the condition probability of the central word $p(y_t|w_{[t-b,t+b]-\{t\}})$ maximum.

and the objection is to maximum the Log-likelihood function L as follows.

$$p(y_t|w_{[t-b,t+b]-\{t\}}) = \frac{\exp y_t^\top W' c_t}{\sum_{x \in V} \exp x^\top W' c_t} \qquad (2)$$

$$L = \sum_{y_t \in V} \log p(y_t|w_{[t-b,t+b]-\{t\}}) \qquad (3)$$

2.3 Attention Enhanced CBOW (AWE)

In this paper, we proposed Attention Enhanced Chinese Word Embeddings (AWE) that aims to use attention mechanism to obtain more meaningful context vector. General attention mechanism is applied in encoder-decoder architecture by plugging a context vector into the gap between encoder and decoder. In AWE model, we calculate the context vector $c_t^{attention}$ as

$$c_t^{attention} = \sum_{i \in [t-b,t+b]-\{t\}} a(w_i) w_i \qquad (4)$$

where $a(w_i)$ represents a function that calculate attention of word w_i, which is a scalar. Then we define function $a(w_i)$ as

$$a(w_i) = \frac{\exp score(w_i)}{\sum_{w \in H} \exp score(w)} \qquad (5)$$

where $score(w_i)$ can be defined by different attention mechanisms. Apparently, we can use the global attention mechanism to focus on different surrounding words based on the central word. Considering that adding the central word to surrounding words may affect the acquisition of context vector, we also performed experiments using the self-attention mechanism to enhance CBOW for comparison. The formulas of two attention score functions is calculated in this way

$$score(w_i)^{global} = \mathbf{w}_g tanh(\mathbf{W}_g[w_i, w_t]) \tag{6}$$

$$score(w_i)^{self} = \mathbf{w}_s tanh(\mathbf{W}_s w_i) \tag{7}$$

where $\mathbf{W}_g \in \mathbb{R}^{a \times 2d}$, $\mathbf{W}_s \in \mathbb{R}^{a \times d}$, $\mathbf{w}_g, \mathbf{w}_s \in \mathbb{R}^a$, and a is the attention dimension (Fig. 2).

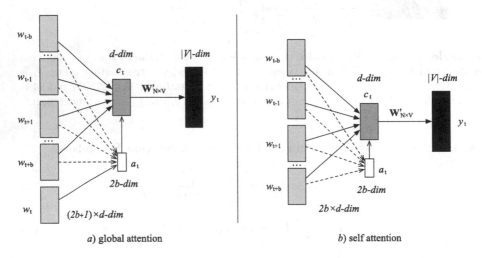

a) global attention   b) self attention

Fig. 2. In the AWE model, the context vector c_t is calculated by aligning the attention vector a_t to each surrounding word w_i. (a) In the global attention mechanism, the attention vector a_t is simultaneously related to the central word w_t and environmental words w_i. (b) In the self attention mechanism, the attention vector a_t does not rely on the central word w_t and only depends on the surrounding words w_i.

2.4 Position & Attention Enhanced CBOW (P&AWE)

Since the bag-of-words model dispense with recurrence and convolutions entirely, we must add some extra information about the relative or absolute position of the words in the sequence so that the model can utilize the order of the words. To this end, we added position encoding to the original surrounding word embeddings to get new surrounding word embeddings with position information and proposed the model called P&AWE. The positional encoding has the same dimension d as the word embeddings, thus we can make addition operation here. The formula of context vector $c_t^{position}$ of P&AWE is computed as follows, adding positional encoding $PE_{(i,j)}$ to raw word embedding where i is the position and j is the dimension.

$$c_t^{position} = \sum_{i \in [t-b, t+b] - \{t\}} a(w_i^p) w_i, \qquad w_i^p = w_i + PE_{(i,j)} \qquad (8)$$

Following [17] work, we used sine and cosine functions of different frequencies to define the positional encoding $PE_{(i,j)}$:

$$PE_{(i,2j)} = \sin(i/10000^{2j/d}) \qquad (9)$$

$$PE_{(i,2j+1)} = \cos(i/10000^{2j/d}) \qquad (10)$$

3 Experimental Setup

3.1 Preprocessing

We downloaded Chinese Wikipedia dump[2] on May 1, 2018, which consists of 405w lines of Chinese Wikipedia articles. We treated all articles as a sentence, and slid the context window from the beginning of an article to its end. We use a script in the gensim[3] toolkit to convert data from XML into text format. Based on our observation, the corpus consists of both simplified and traditional Chinese characters. Hence, we utilize the opencc[4] toolkit to normalize all characters as simplified Chinese. Word segmentation was performed using open source python package jieba[5]. All English words, numerical words were encoded as "W" and "D". Furthermore, In all 222,822,535 segmented words, we removed words whose frequency $<= 5$, leaving 507,260 unique words as the vocabulary set.

3.2 Baseline Algorithms

CBOW & Skipgram [11,12] are two models to produce a distributed representation of words. CBOW is used to predict the central word from a window of surrounding words, and skip-gram uses the central word to predict the surrounding words in a window.

CWE [2] is a character-based model aiming at learning Chinese word embeddings that exploits character level information by jointly learning character and word embeddings.

GWE [14] leverages pixel-level information, which exploits character features from font images by convolutional autoencoders.

---

[2] https://dumps.wikimedia.org/zhwiki/.
[3] https://radimrehurek.com/gensim/corpora/wikicorpus.html.
[4] https://github.com/BYVoid/OpenCC.
[5] https://github.com/fxsjy/jieba.

JWE [19] is a model for Chinese word embedding, which reduces Chinese words into components of characters, as the superset of radicals. Besides, it uses three likelihoods to evaluate whether the context words, characters, and components can predict the current target word.

cw2vec [1] captures semantic and morphological level information of Chinese words by using stroke n-grams, which is crucial for improving the learning of Chinese word embeddings.

3.3   Training Details of Word Representations

We used CWE code[6] to implement both CBOW and Skipgram, along with the CWE, and it was modified to produce cw2vec representations. We used GWE code[7] and JWE code[8] to implement both GWE and JWE, and GloVe code[9] was used to train the baseline GloVe vectors. Last but not least, we conducted four AWE models. AWE-global used global attention mechanism as enhancement. AWE-self exploited self attention mechanism as enhancement. P&AWE-global made full use of global attention mechanism and positional encoding as enhancement; P&AWE-self took advantage of self attention mechanism and positional encoding as enhancement.

For all models, we used the following hyper-parameters. The word embeddings size d was set to 100. Sliding window size b was set to 5. We used 10 negative samples, and threshold t of subsampling was set to 10^{-3}. The initial learning rate was 0.01. We used negative sampling policy to optimize the training process. The other parameters were set as default.

4   Evaluation

4.1   Word Similarity

A word similarity test has been widely used as a proxy for intrinsic evaluation of word vectors in NLP community. Word similarity evaluation correlates the distance between vectors and human annotated similarity scores of word pairs. Word representations are considered superior if the calculated similarity and human annotated scores have a strong correlation. We computed the Spearman's correlation between human annotated scores and cosine similarity of word representations to evaluate the outcome.

We used WordSim-240 (w/s-240) and WordSim-296 (w/s-296) datasets provided by [2], When calculating similarities, word pairs containing OOVs were removed. In Table 1, there are only 239 and 278 word pairs left in WordSim-240 and WordSim-296, respectively. The results are presented in Table 1.

---

[6] https://github.com/Leonard-Xu/CWE.
[7] https://github.com/ray1007/GWE.
[8] https://github.com/HKUST-KnowComp/JWE.
[9] https://github.com/stanfordnlp/GloVe.

Table 1. The second and third columns of the table show Spearman's correlation ($\rho \times 100$) between human annotated scores and cosine similarity of word representations on two datasets: WordSim-240 (w/s-240) and WordSim-296 (w/s-296). Higher values mean better results. And the fourth to seventh columns of the table represent accuracy (%) of analogy inference for capitals of countries, (China) states/provinces of cities and family relations dataset. The higher the values, the better the results.

Model	Word similarity		Word analogy			
	w/s-240	w/s-296	Total	Capital	State	Family
Skip-gram	44.21	48.34	59.75	62.16	74.69	44.17
GloVe	45.26	44.31	60.52	63.28	75.27	45.87
CWE	49.72	50.98	62.46	65.11	77.63	46.12
GWE	49.36	50.14	61.11	64.31	74.77	44.62
JWE	48.67	52.01	70.18	73.92	79.52	54.88
cw2vec	50.16	52.37	70.04	73.21	79.69	55.96
CBOW	47.11	50.02	55.93	58.03	71.01	41.04
AWE-global	47.13	**59.70**	59.79	61.45	75.43	45.59
AWE-self	**52.67**	59.42	62.81	66.77	74.29	45.59
P&AWE-global	46.21	57.38	64.59	68.24	79.43	45.96
P&AWE-self	47.20	58.06	**65.21**	**68.83**	**80.57**	**46.32**

As we can see in Table 1, the experimental result on word similarity demonstrates that our four models have excellent performances. On the w/s-240 dataset, AWE-self model makes a 5.56×10^{-2} improvement in contrast with the baseline CBOW model, and achieves the best performance until now. As for the w/s-296 dataset, all the models we proposed have achieved start-of-the-art results. Furthermore, AWE-global model makes a 7.33×10^{-2} improvement compared with the best result of cw2vec.

4.2 Word Analogy

An analogy problem has the following form: *"king":"queen" = "man":"?"*, and *"woman"* is answer to *"?"*. The model is considered to be able to express semantic relationships when correctly answering the questions. Furthermore, the analogy relation could be expressed by vector arithmetic of word representations as shown in [12]. The "?" word is inferred by searching for the word whose representation is the nearest to $w_{queen} - w_{king} + w_{man}$. For the above problem, we conclude that the word w_i can be acquired by $w_i = \arg\max_{w} cos(\boldsymbol{w}, \boldsymbol{w}_{queen} - \boldsymbol{w}_{king} + \boldsymbol{w}_{man})$.

The dataset in [2] contains three groups of analogy problems: capitals of countries, (China) states/provinces of cities, and family relations. The results are shown in Table 1.

The results shown in Table 1 indicate that adding attention mechanism enhancements to the baseline model can achieve better performance, and our four models have a considerable range of improvement over the CBOW model, especially the P&AWE-self model (total 9.28%). Compared to the existing state-of-the-art Chinese word embedding learning methods, our model did not achieve the best results because that most of these models added other source information such as characters, radicals, etc.

4.3 Attention Visualization

In order to show the effectiveness of the attention mechanism more clearly, we visualized the attention value of words in the sliding windows. The original sentence is "数学是利用符号语言研究数量、结构、变化以及空间等概念的一门学科。". In some sliding window, we set the central word is "等(etc.)" and windows size is 5, so the surrounding words are "结构(structure)", "、(,)", "变化(change)", "以及(and)", "空间(space)" and "概念(concept)", "的('s)", "一门(a)", "学科(subject)", "。(.)". The result is shown in Fig. 3. As we can see from Fig. 3, what AWE-global focused on is as same as our human being. However, P&AWE-global only focused on the preceding text, but not focused on the following text, which is similar to our intuition. While AWE-self even focused on the words which directly related to the central word, such as "、(,)","以及(and)".

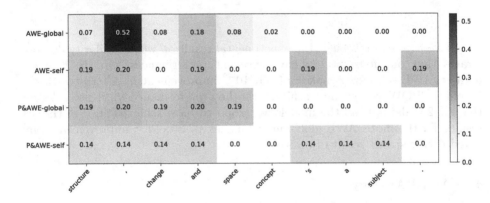

Fig. 3. Attention visualization of four AWE models when predicting the word "etc.", where the horizontal axis indicates the surrounding words in some sliding window and the vertical axis represents different models.

4.4 Qualitative Analysis

We chose some words related to the word "热 (heat)", including "烤炉(oven)", "烈日(sun)", "夏天(summer)". At the sametime, we have also selected a word "冬天(winter)" that is not related to the word "heat". By calculating the similarity between these word pairs, we can judge whether the model is good or bad. We believe that good word embeddings should have a higher degree of similarity to semantically similar words, while semantically opposite words have a lower similarity. We performed experiments on CBOW and our AWE models. The experimental results are shown in the Table 2. Experiments show that in the latter two columns, the CBOW model has even stronger correlation in the opposite semantic word, while three of the AWE models avoid this error. All in all, the AWE models can better capture semantic associations.

Table 2. Case study of word cosine similarity on word pairs about "heat". The word pairs in the first three columns are semantically related. Therefore, the higher the values, the better the results. The semantics of the word pairs in the last column are opposite. Therefore, the lower the values, the better the results.

Models	烤炉 (oven) & 热 (heat)	烈日 (sun) & 热 (heat)	夏天 (summer) & 热 (heat)	冬天 (winter) & 热 (heat)
CBOW	0.1776	0.1230	0.2255	0.3219
AWE-global	0.1913	0.1310	0.2371	0.3342
AWE-self	0.2372	0.1003	0.3556	**0.3143**
P&AWE-global	**0.3056**	**0.2368**	**0.4690**	0.3840
P&AWE-self	0.2900	0.2012	0.3939	0.3402

5   Conclusions

In this paper, we proposed four models on learning Chinese word representations. First, we used the global attention mechanism as enhancement to semantic information named AWE-global. Next, the AWE-self model which combines self attention mechanism was presented. Furthermore, we added position encoding based on the global attention mechanism and proposed P&AWE-global. Finally, the P&AWE-self model that uses self attention mechanism and positional encoding also was stated. We showed experimental studies for verifying the proposed model, results reveal that the AWE method outperformed CBOW model and achieved state-of-the-art results on the task of word similarity. We also verified the effectiveness of the AWE models through attention visualization and case analysis.

Results manifest attention mechanism could serve as an enhancement, and we will further examine the effect of attention mechanism on other tasks, such as word segmentation, POS tagging, dependency parsing, or downstream tasks such as text classification, document retrieval.

References

1. Cao, S., Lu, W., Zhou, J., Li, X.: cw2vec: learning Chinese word embeddings with stroke n-gram information (2018)
2. Chen, X., Xu, L., Liu, Z., Sun, M., Luan, H.B.: Joint learning of character and word embeddings. In: IJCAI, pp. 1236–1242 (2015)
3. Collobert, R., Weston, J., Bottou, L., Karlen, M., Kavukcuoglu, K., Kuksa, P.: Natural language processing (almost) from scratch. J. Mach. Learn. Res. 12(Aug), 2493–2537 (2011)
4. Devlin, J., Zbib, R., Huang, Z., Lamar, T., Schwartz, R., Makhoul, J.: Fast and robust neural network joint models for statistical machine translation. In: Proceedings of the 52nd Annual Meeting of the Association for Computational Linguistics, Long Papers, vol. 1, pp. 1370–1380 (2014)
5. Goldberg, Y., Levy, O.: word2vec explained: Deriving mikolov et al.'s negative-sampling word-embedding method. arXiv preprint arXiv:1402.3722 (2014)
6. Hinton, G.E., McClelland, J.L., Rumelhart, D.E.: Distributed representations. Parallel Distrib. Process.: Explor. Microstruct. Cogn. 1(3), 77–109 (1986)
7. Joulin, A., Grave, E., Bojanowski, P., Mikolov, T.: Bag of tricks for efficient text classification. arXiv preprint arXiv:1607.01759 (2016)
8. Kalchbrenner, N., Blunsom, P.: Recurrent continuous translation models. In: Proceedings of the 2013 Conference on Empirical Methods in Natural Language Processing, pp. 1700–1709 (2013)
9. Kim, Y.: Convolutional neural networks for sentence classification. arXiv preprint arXiv:1408.5882 (2014)
10. Liu, S., Yang, N., Li, M., Zhou, M.: A recursive recurrent neural network for statistical machine translation. In: Proceedings of the 52nd Annual Meeting of the Association for Computational Linguistics, Long Papers, vol. 1, pp. 1491–1500 (2014)
11. Mikolov, T., Chen, K., Corrado, G., Dean, J.: Efficient estimation of word representations in vector space. arXiv preprint arXiv:1301.3781 (2013)
12. Mikolov, T., Sutskever, I., Chen, K., Corrado, G.S., Dean, J.: Distributed representations of words and phrases and their compositionality. In: Advances in Neural Information Processing Systems, pp. 3111–3119 (2013)
13. Pennington, J., Socher, R., Manning, C.: Glove: global vectors for word representation. In: Proceedings of the 2014 conference on empirical methods in natural language processing (EMNLP), pp. 1532–1543 (2014)
14. Su, T.R., Lee, H.Y.: Learning Chinese word representations from glyphs of characters. arXiv preprint arXiv:1708.04755 (2017)
15. Sutskever, I., Vinyals, O., Le, Q.V.: Sequence to sequence learning with neural networks. In: Advances in neural information processing systems, pp. 3104–3112 (2014)
16. Turian, J., Ratinov, L., Bengio, Y.: Word representations: a simple and general method for semi-supervised learning. In: Proceedings of the 48th Annual Meeting of the Association For Computational Linguistics, pp. 384–394. Association for Computational Linguistics (2010)
17. Vaswani, A., et al.: Attention is all you need. In: Advances in Neural Information Processing Systems, pp. 6000–6010 (2017)
18. Yin, R., Wang, Q., Li, P., Li, R., Wang, B.: Multi-granularity Chinese word embedding. In: Proceedings of the 2016 Conference on Empirical Methods in Natural Language Processing, pp. 981–986 (2016)

19. Yu, J., Jian, X., Xin, H., Song, Y.: Joint embeddings of Chinese words, characters, and fine-grained subcharacter components. In: Proceedings of the 2017 Conference on Empirical Methods in Natural Language Processing, pp. 286–291 (2017)
20. Zhou, G., He, T., Zhao, J., Hu, P.: Learning continuous word embedding with metadata for question retrieval in community question answering. In: Proceedings of the 53rd Annual Meeting of the Association for Computational Linguistics and the 7th International Joint Conference on Natural Language Processing, Long Papers, vol. 1, pp. 250–259 (2015)

Balancing Convolutional Neural Networks Pipeline in FPGAs

Mark Cappello Ferreira de Sousa[1(✉)],
Miguel Angelo de Abreu de Sousa[2],
and Emilio Del-Moral-Hernandez[1]

[1] Department of Electronic Systems Engineering, School of Engineering,
University of São Paulo, São Paulo, Brazil
markfsousa@gmail.com, emilio@lsi.usp.br
[2] Electrical Department, Federal Institute of Education,
Science and Technology – IFSP, São Paulo, Brazil
angelo@ifsp.edu.br

Abstract. Convolutional Neural Networks (CNNs) have achieved excellent performance in image classification, being successfully applied in a wide range of domains. However, their processing power demand offers a challenge to their implementation in embedded real-time applications. To tackle this problem, we focused in this work on the FPGA acceleration of the convolutional layers, since they account for about 90% of the overall computational load. We implemented buffers to reduce the storage of feature maps and consequently, facilitating the allocation of the whole kernel weights in Block-RAMs (BRAMs). Moreover, we used 8-bits kernel weights, rounded from an already trained CNN, to further reduce the need for memory, storing them in multiple BRAMs to aid kernel loading throughput. To balance the pipeline of convolutions through the convolutional layers we manipulated the amount of parallel computation in the convolutional step in each convolutional layer. We adopted the AlexNet CNN architecture to run our experiments and compare the results. We were able to run the inference of the convolutional layers in 3.9 ms with maximum operation frequency of 76.9 MHz.

Keywords: CNN · FPGA · Object recognition

1 Introduction

The adoption of embedded image recognition has grown in popularity with emerging applications such as autonomous car, unmanned aerial vehicle (UAV), smart glasses, Internet of Things and Smart Cities. One powerful tool for image recognition is Convolutional Neural Networks (CNNs), whose computational power demand poses a big challenge for embedded systems using real time image recognition. This scenario represents an opportunity for specialized hardware, such as FPGAs, to accelerate CNNs with low power consumption.

CNNs are composed of a sequence of convolutional (Conv) layers followed by a sequence of Fully Connected (FC) layers. The Conv layers work as feature extractors

© Springer Nature Switzerland AG 2018
V. Kůrková et al. (Eds.): ICANN 2018, LNCS 11139, pp. 166–175, 2018.
https://doi.org/10.1007/978-3-030-01418-6_17

of the input image and the following FC layers work as classifier based on the features extracted by the Conv Layers. The Conv layers are responsible for 90% of total network computational load [1] and approximately 5% of total network parameters layers [2]. This matches the FPGAs parallel processing power and memory constraints, making them especially suitable for the execution of Conv layers.

Due to these parallel processing power and memory considerations, a System on Chip (SoC) with a FPGA device XC7Z100 and a Dual-Core ARM Cortex A9 conjugated in a single silicon substrate is used to run our experiments. The ARM processor can be used to run the FC layers while the FPGA device is used to run the convolutional layers. The FPGA components were designed using Very High Speed Integrated Circuits Hardware Description Language (VHDL). Considering the computational load related to the Conv layers, in this work we focused on the acceleration of Conv layers. As other works, we used 8-bits-rounded fixed-point kernel weights [3], obtained from an already trained CNN, instead of the traditionally 32-bit floating point used in implementations on general-purpose processors, such as CPUs and GPGPUs. With this reduction we manage to store all the kernel weights in FPGA on-chip memory, eliminating the need to access external memories.

To verify the suitability of the SoC for CNN acceleration, we adopted the AlexNet [4] as CNN architecture. This aimed to illustrate a methodology that identifies the opportunities for optimizing intermediate data storage, increasing weights memory loading throughput and executing parallel computation on convolutional layers.

By exploring the parallelism in the convolutional step computation and balancing the pipeline parallelism through Conv layers to avoid resource exhaustion, we were able to run the inference of the Conv layers in FPGA XC7Z100 in 3.9 ms, with 76.9 MHz maximum frequency operation.

2 Related Work

Other works already explored the parallel processing power of FPGAs to accelerate CNNs. The authors in [5] also worked with already trained network and used row- and partial column-based storage to cache and reuse data. They used processing elements to processes rows and columns in parallel, computing more than one convolutional step in different columns and rows at same time. As our focus is on the parallelization of single convolutional step computation, only the row-based buffer is required. They used High Level Synthesis (HLS) implementation, which generates less optimized circuits than VHDL. They also used external memory to store the parameters, proposing a memory hierarchy to reduce the memory bottleneck. Nevertheless, there is no memory bottleneck in our research, since we store all the parameters in on-chip memory. In work [6] the acceleration is performed by an ensemble of processing elements (PE) that execute matrix multiplication in parallel and the individuals PE have their own buffer to prefetch data. These PE are used to accelerate matrix multiplications in both Conv and FC layers. They use 32-bits floating, which consumes more FPGAs resources than 8-bits fixed point, providing similar classification accuracy [7–9].

3 Convolutional Neural Networks in FPGAs

A typical CNN is composed of chained convolutional layers followed by chained FC layers. Except for the first Conv layer, which receives data from input, each Conv layer receives data generated from previous layers, extracts features by convolving the data with kernels and propagates these extracted features as feature maps to the next layer. The arrangement of the feature map preserves the relative location where each feature was extracted from. These feature maps can be reduced by subsampling operation after certain layers. The feature map from the last convolutional layer is used as input to the first FC layer. The input image is composed by the RGB channels describing the features of a pixel. Thus, in this work we will generalize the input image as feature map to make the first layer discussion equivalent to the other layers.

The construction of the feature maps is the result of the repeatedly convolutional step operation, which can be described as:

$$y[i,j,k] = b[k] + \sum_{m=0}^{D-1}\sum_{n=0}^{D-1}\sum_{c=0}^{F-1} x[S \cdot i + m, S \cdot j + n, c] \cdot w_k[m,n,c] \qquad (1)$$

where $y[i,j,k]$ is one output word located in i,j in the extracted feature k plane, $b[k]$ is the bias related to the feature k, D is the kernel dimension, F is the number of features in the input feature map, x is the input feature map, S is the stride, $x[S \cdot i + m, S \cdot j + n, c]$ is the receptive field and w_k is the weights from kernel used to extract the feature k.

The three summations in Eq. (1) are opportunities for parallelism. This opportunity is the most explored by the experiments performed in this work. In such operation (1) the need for memory in FPGAs is directly linked to the kernel and feature map sizes. In Fig. 1 the region marked as buffered data reflects the amount of memory required for buffering the feature map. Two points of view are depicted (A and B). Both show the feature map from the first AlexNet Conv layer, but in A the feature planes are hidden.

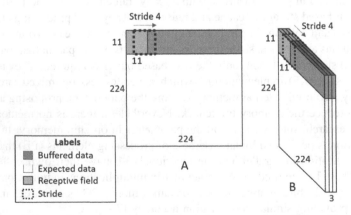

Fig. 1. Illustration of basic concepts in CNNs from two points of view (A and B).

The stride has a substantial impact in the reduction of data volume generated by a convolutional layer. This is due to a greater shift of the receptive field resulting in less data being generated in the output feature map.

Apart from convolution operation, local response normalization (LRN) is also used in AlexNet. While the volume of data generated in a CNN is not affect, it is expected to aid generalization [4]. In AlexNet error rates were reduced about 1.2%. Considering the removal of LRN in the following work from the same author [2] and the relatively small error reduction reported, the normalization will not be implemented in this work in exchange for logic reduction in FPGA as done in the work [10].

ReLu the **activation function** applied in AlexNet, instead of the traditional non-linear activation functions such as tanh and sigmoid, as this non-saturating nonlinearity is faster to train with gradient descent [4]. The adoption of ReLu is convenient for FPGA implementation, since the ReLu computation $f(x) = \max(0, x)$ is less complex than $f(x) = \tanh(x)$ or $f(x) = (1 + e^{-x})^{-1}$. ReLu is applied to the outputs of Conv layers as well as FC layers.

4 CNNs Parallelism Exploited in FPGA Implementation

In our experiments we applied the loop unrolling technique in the three summations given in Eq. (1) to accelerate the computation of convolutional steps. Depending on the unrolling factor adopted, the whole convolutional step can be executed in a single clock cycle, computing all the multiplications and additions in parallel in the FPGA. The definition of the unrolling factor must consider that more operations executed in parallel result in more FPGA resources being consumed.

Another parallelization opportunity explored in this work is the pipeline formed by the chaining of Conv layers. This pipeline was balanced by changing the unrolling factor to control the throughput in each layer. To determine the unrolling factor, we analyzed the number of convolutional steps executed in each layer, described in Table 1. The first layer is shown to be the one that demands the greater number of convolutional steps, followed by the second layer. With the execution of one convo-lutional step per clock cycle, the first convolutional layer will dictate the overall throughput of Conv Layers. In addition, it will be the reference balancing the pipeline. Table 1 also shows that Conv layers 3 and 4 execute less than 25% of the total convolutional steps executed by Conv layer 1. As that these layers depend on data from Conv layers 1 and 2, executing each convolutional step in one clock cycle would make them recurrently idle while waiting for data. To spare FPGA resources, we reduced the unrolling factor in these layers, raising the number of clock cycles per convolutional step to 4 in layers 3 and 4. There was no overall throughput degradation because fewer convolutional steps were executed in these layers. Similar consideration was made to reduce the unrolling factor in layer 5, raising to 6 the number of clock cycles per convolutional step. This same approach is not applicable to the second layer because a reduction of the unrolling factor in this layer would result in more than one clock cycle per convolutional. This change would result in more clock cycles needed to execute the second layer compared with the first one, reducing the overall throughput of the pipeline.

Table 1. Convolutional steps in each convolutional layer and the clock cycles required for each convolutional step.

	CL1	CL2	CL3	CL4	CL5
Convolutional steps per kernel	3025	729	169	169	169
Kernels	96	256	384	384	256
Total convolutional steps	290400	186624	64896	64896	43264
Clock cycles per convolutional step	1	1	4	4	6
Theoretical clock cycles per layer	290400	186624	259584	259584	259584

More than one convolutional step per clock cycle would be required to increase the overall throughput in layer 1. However, the experiments in this work indicate this increase in parallelization would require more resources than the available in the FPGA device used in this work.

5 Data Buffering Strategy

To reduce the memory required for implementation, we adopted buffers to partially store and reuse data between convolutions and pooling operations. Although the kernels account for most of memory utilization, the feature maps generated between layers also have a significative impact on memory usage. The total feature map data can reach up to 20% [1, 2] of total kernel data if we consider the intermediate data generated by pooling layers. Reducing the memory requirement for intermediate data enabled to store intermediate data in FPGAs Look Up Tables (LUTs). Compared with Block-RAMs (BRAMs), LUTs are handier when designing components with high data reading and writing throughput. Using LUTs to store the intermediate data also frees more BRAMs for kernel storage. As we stored all kernels using 8-bit precision in BRAMs, kernel weights resulted in about 19 MB of data. Thus, it is possible to store all kernels in BRAMs of some currently available mid-range FPGA devices.

The buffer used in our experiments stores data as it is generated from 2D convolutions. These are executed horizontally from left to right and then top to bottom, feeding each buffer row, column by column. Once the data received completes a receptive field, its corresponding addresses are read from LUTs and sent to the convolutional engine. The convolutional engine reuses the receptive field to compute the convolutional steps with all the corresponding kernels. After the last kernel is applied, the same operation is repeated with the next receptive field, until the last receptive field is received.

After a receptive field is used in a convolutional step, its overlapped region in contiguous receptive fields is held in buffer for the following convolutional steps. In addition, the non-overlapping region is reused to store new data. Figure 2 illustrates a Tubular Buffer with a 9 × 9 feature map, 3 × 3 kernel and stride of 2, using a 3 × 9 size buffer: (A) feature map, (B) 4 different states of Tubular buffer, and (C) 16 readings from buffer forming 16 different receptive fields. The first state on top of B shows the first three rows from feature map stored in the buffer. The second state shows the third, fourth, and fifth rows of feature map. The third state shows the fifth, sixth, and seventh and so on. In each state, one of the buffer rows is reused to keep data from the non-overlapped receptive field region. With this approach the number of rows the buffer needs to store is equals to the number of rows in the receptive field and the number of columns is equal to the feature map width. This is directly related to the memory reduction obtained by the adoption of these buffers.

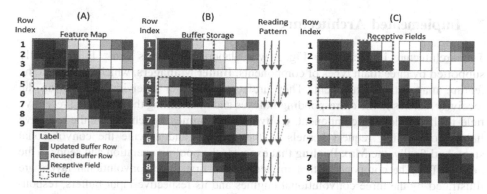

Fig. 2. Tubular buffer illustration. (A) Feature map, (B) 4 different states of Tubular buffer and (C) 16 different receptive fields.

Table 2 shows the memory usage reduction in each Conv and pooling layer due to the buffer utilization. The proportion between feature map width, receptive field height and the number of features in the feature map is shown to be related to the memory reduction, since these three values determine the buffer dimensions. Larger feature map dimensions associated with smaller receptive fields result in less memory required. The overall memory reduction obtained with this strategy is 88%.

Table 2. Memory reduction in each Conv and pooling layer by buffering and reusing feature map data

	CL1	P1	CL2	P2	CL3	CL4	CL5	P5
Feature map size	224	55	27	27	13	13	13	13
Receptive field size	11	3	5	3	3	3	3	3
Features	3	96	96	256	256	384	384	256
Total words	150528	290400	69984	186624	21632	64896	64896	43264
Maximum words stored	7392	15840	12960	20736	9984	14976	14976	9984
Memory reduction	95.1%	94.5%	81.5%	88.9%	53.9%	76.9%	76.9%	76.9%

6   Augmenting Kernel Loading Throughput

The continuous computation of complete convolutional steps in one clock cycle requires a kernel loading rate of one kernel per clock cycle. Meeting this requirement requires to store the kernels in BRAMs arranged to provide the necessary kernel loading throughput, considering the throughput limitation of each individual BRAM.

To address this issue, the kernels were segmented and stored in multiple BRAMs. This segmentation allows the whole kernel to be read in one clock cycle by reading its segments in parallel from multiples BRAMs. The contiguous addresses in the BRAM are used to store segments from different kernels, while the same address in different BRAMs are used to store different segments from the same kernels.

7 Implemented Architecture

The architecture illustrated by Fig. 3 was elaborated for this work. It is basically supported by three main types of components. **Buffer Managers**, which implement the feature map data management. They are responsible for receiving and storing the received features in the corresponding indexes and transmitting the completed receptive field to their following component. **Convolution Engines**, which receive the receptive fields from buffer, request kernels to the memory and execute the convolutional step. And finally, the **Max Pooling** that executes the pooling operation and sends to the next buffer. The components that implement the first three convolutional layers are illustrated by the three convolutional engines and its respective input buffers, responsible for feature storage.

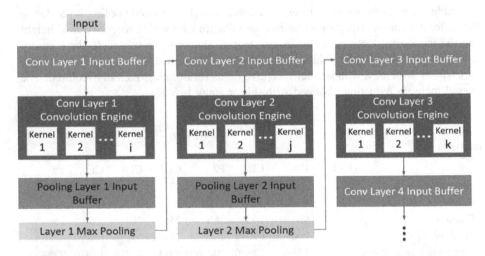

Fig. 3. Main components designed to accelerate the AlexNet convolutional layers.

8 Data Precision

Almost 62 million model parameters are involved in AlexNet CNN, which won the 2012 ImageNet [11] competition. Although other subsequent winner networks have even more parameters, the implementation of AlexNet still represent a challenge in currently available FPGAs. To store all these parameters using 32-bits floating point would require more than 240 MB of memory, which is not possible in any currently commercial FPGA. From the 62 million parameters, about 59 million are from FC layers, while 2.3 million are from convolutional layers. It is not possible to store all the FC layers parameters in currently available FPGAs. On the other hand, the use of 8-bits representation enables to store such convolutional parameters.

Related works reported that the use of low numerical precision for training deep neural networks (DNNs) is possible. Different approaches were reported with bit-widths ranging from 8 to 20 bits [12–16].

Although training the deep neural networks requires higher numerical precision due to the small changes accumulated when the parameters are updated by backpropagation [13], an already trained DNN can be used with less numerical precision for inference. In [1] a DNN trained with 32-bits floating point was scaled to 16-bits fixed point. [17] used 16-bits fixed point. Other work [18] used offline training and rounded the 32-bits floating point to 8-bits fixed point, compromising 1.41% in top-1 accuracy and less than 1% in top-5 accuracy. In this work the quantization is the same as [3], which used 8-bit fixed point and linear quantization to store the weights, with maximum magnitude normalized ranging from -128 to 127.

9   Experimental Results and Discussion

The implementation described in this work enabled to achieve up to 76.9 MHz operation frequency, with inference time of 3.94 ms (Table 3).

Table 3. Comparison with previous AlexNet implementations.

	[7]	[18]	[19]	This work
Convolution time	21.61 ms	19.86 ms	9.92 ms	3.94 ms
Operation frequency	100 MHz	193.6 MHz	100 MHz	76.9 MHz
FPGA	Virtex-7 VX485T	Stratix-V GXA7	Stratix-V GXA7	Zynq XC7Z100

We can use the Table 1 to validate this result. Multiplying the theoretical clock cycles of 290,400 for Conv Layer 1 by 13 ms, which is the clock period equivalent to the maximum frequency, results in an inference time estimation of 3.78 ms. While this value is compatible with our empirical results, it is underestimated. This occurs because it does not include the number of cycles to load the buffer until the first receptive field is completed. The theoretical clock cycles also do not include the number of cycles needed to finish the execution of the pipeline after the last convolutional step is executed in the first layer.

Considering that the Conv layer 1 is the one that limits the overall throughput, we can see that the number of theoretical clock cycles needed to execute all the convolutional steps in this layer is indeed compatible with the results from the experiments.

In conclusion, we can see that the parallelism, and hence the overall throughput, is limited by FPGA resources availability for multiplications and additions needed to compute the convolutional step operation. Moreover, it is important to spare FPGA parallel processing power in layers executing less convolutional steps and direct this processing power to the ones executing more convolutional steps.

Acknowledgments. Mark Cappello Ferreira de Sousa gratefully acknowledges the National Council for Scientific and Technological Development (CNPq) for partially supporting this research. Mark also acknowledges Stelvio Henrique Ignacio Barboza, Anelise Scotti Scherer and Academic Literacy Laboratory for valuable comments. Miguel Angelo de Abreu de Sousa acknowledges the support from the Federal Institute of Education, Science and Technology of São Paulo (IFSP).

References

1. Farabet, C., Martini, B., Akselrod, P., Talay, S., LeCun, Y., Culurciello, E.: Hardware accelerated convolutional neural networks for synthetic vision systems. In: Proceedings of the 2010 IEEE International Symposium Circuits System, pp. 257–260 (2010)
2. Krizhevsky, A.: One weird trick for parallelizing convolutional neural networks. Preprint (2014)
3. Vanhoucke, V., Senior, A., Mao, M.: Improving the speed of neural networks on CPUs. In: Proceedings of the Deep Learning Unsupervised Feature Learning Work, NIPS 2011, pp. 1–8 (2011)
4. Krizhevsky, A., Sutskever, I., Geoffrey, E.H.: ImageNet classification with deep convolutional neural networks. Adv. Neural. Inf. Process. Syst. **25**, 1–9 (2012)
5. Peemen, M., Setio, A.A.A., Mesman, B., Corporaal, H.: Memory-centric accelerator design for convolutional neural networks. In: 2013 IEEE 31st International Conference on Computer Design (ICCD), pp. 13–19 (2013)
6. Qiao, Y., Shen, J., Xiao, T., Yang, Q., Wen, M., Zhang, C.: FPGA-accelerated deep convolutional neural networks for high throughput and energy efficiency. Concurr. Comput. Pract. Exp. **22**, 685–701 (2016)
7. Zhang, C., Li, P., Sun, G., Guan, Y., Xiao, B., Cong, J.: Optimizing FPGA-based accelerator design for deep convolutional neural networks. In: Proceedings of the 2015 ACM/SIGDA International Symposium on Field-Programmable Gate Arrays - FPGA 2015, pp. 161–170. ACM (2015)
8. Rawat, W., Wang, Z.: Deep convolutional neural networks for image classification: a comprehensive review. Neural Comput. **29**, 2352–2449 (2017)
9. Lin, D.D., Talathi, S.S., Annapureddy, V.S.: Fixed point quantization of deep convolutional networks, vol. 48 (2015)
10. Simonyan, K., Zisserman, A.: Very deep convolutional networks for large-scale Image recognition. In: 2014 International Conference on Learning Representation, pp. 1–14 (2015)
11. Russakovsky, O., et al.: ImageNet large scale visual recognition challenge. Int. J. Comput. Vis. **115**, 211–252 (2015)
12. Dettmers, T.: 8-Bit approximations for parallelism in deep learning, pp. 1–14 (2015)
13. Courbariaux, M., Bengio, Y., David, J.-P.: Training deep neural networks with low precision multiplications, pp. 1–10 (2014)
14. Gupta, S., Agrawal, A., Gopalakrishnan, K., Narayanan, P.: Deep learning with limited numerical precision, vol. 37 (2015)
15. Han, S., Pool, J., Tran, J., Dally, W.J.: Learning both weights and connections for efficient neural networks, pp. 1–9 (2015)

16. Savich, A.W., Moussa, M., Areibi, S.: The impact of arithmetic representation on implementing MLP-BP on FPGAs: A study. IEEE Trans. Neural Netw. **18**, 240–252 (2007)
17. Gokhale, V., Jin, J., Dundar, A., Martini, B., Culurciello, E.: A 240 G-ops/s mobile coprocessor for deep neural networks. Presented at the June 2014
18. Suda, N., et al.: Throughput-optimized OpenCL-based FPGA accelerator for large-scale convolutional neural networks. In: Proceedings of the 2016 ACM/SIGDA International Symposium Field-Programmable Gate Arrays - FPGA 2016, pp. 16–25 (2016)
19. Ma, Y., Suda, N., Cao, Y., Seo, J.S., Vrudhula, S.: Scalable and modularized RTL compilation of convolutional neural networks onto FPGA. In: FPL 2016 - 26th International Conference on Field-Programmable Logic Applications (2016)

Generating Diverse and Meaningful Captions

Unsupervised Specificity Optimization for Image Captioning

Annika Lindh[1,2(✉)] , Robert J. Ross[1,2] , Abhijit Mahalunkar[2] ,
Giancarlo Salton[1,2] , and John D. Kelleher[1,2]

[1] ADAPT Centre, Dublin, Ireland
[2] Dublin Institute of Technology (DIT), Dublin, Ireland
{annika.lindh,robert.ross,abhijit.mahalunkar,
giancarlo.salton,john.d.kelleher}@dit.ie

Abstract. Image Captioning is a task that requires models to acquire a multi-modal understanding of the world and to express this understanding in natural language text. While the state-of-the-art for this task has rapidly improved in terms of n-gram metrics, these models tend to output the same generic captions for similar images. In this work, we address this limitation and train a model that generates more diverse and specific captions through an unsupervised training approach that incorporates a learning signal from an Image Retrieval model. We summarize previous results and improve the state-of-the-art on caption diversity and novelty. We make our source code publicly available online (https://github.com/AnnikaLindh/Diverse_and_Specific_Image_Captioning).

Keywords: Image Captioning · Diversity · Specificity
Natural Language Generation · Image Retrieval · Computer Vision
Natural Language Processing · Multimodal Training · Neural Networks
Deep Learning · Machine Learning · Contrastive Learning · MS COCO

1 Introduction

Image Captioning is a task that requires models to acquire a multimodal understanding of the world and to express this understanding in natural language text, making it relevant to a variety of fields from human-machine interaction to data management. The practical goal is to automatically generate a natural language caption that describes the most relevant aspects of an image. Most state-of-the-art neural models are built on an encoder-decoder architecture where a Convolutional Neural Network (CNN) acts as the encoder for the image features that are fed to a Recurrent Neural Network (RNN) which generates a caption by acting as a decoder. It is also common to include one or more attention layers to focus the captions on the most salient parts of an image. The standard way of training is through Maximum Likelihood Estimation (MLE) by using a cross-entropy loss to replicate ground-truth human-written captions for corresponding images. Recent Image Captioning models of this kind [1, 11, 12, 28] have shown impressive results, much thanks to the powerful language modelling capabilities

© Springer Nature Switzerland AG 2018
V. Kůrková et al. (Eds.): ICANN 2018, LNCS 11139, pp. 176–187, 2018.
https://doi.org/10.1007/978-3-030-01418-6_18

of Long Short-Term Memory (LSTM) [15] RNNs. However, although MLE training enables models to confidently generate captions that have a high likelihood in the training set, it limits their capacity to generate novel descriptions. Their output exhibits a disproportionate replication of common n-grams and full captions seen in the training set [9, 11, 26].

Contributing to this problem is a combination of biased datasets and insufficient quality metrics. While the main benchmarking dataset for Image Captioning, MS COCO, makes available over 120k images with 5 human-annotated captions each [6], the selection process for the images suggests a lack of diversity in both content and composition [11, 20]. Furthermore, the standard benchmarking metrics, based on n-gram level overlap between generated captions and ground-truth captions, reward models with a bias towards common n-grams. This leads to the (indirect and unwanted) consequence of incentivizing models that output generic captions that are likely to fit a range of similar images, despite missing the goal of describing the relevant aspects specific to each image.

In this paper, we propose a model that produces more *diverse and specific* captions by integrating a Natural Language Understanding (NLU) component in our training which optimizes the *specificity* of our Natural Language Generation (NLG) component. Our main contribution is an *unsupervised specificity-guided training approach* that improves the *diversity* and semantic accuracy of the generated captions. This approach can be applied to neural models of any multimodal NLG task (e.g. Image Captioning) where a corresponding NLU component can be made available.

We begin with an analysis of metrics for measuring caption quality in Sect. 2, where we define what we believe to be an informative set of metrics for our target. Following this, in Sect. 3 we describe our novel training approach along with the technical details of the NLG (our Image Captioning model) and NLU components for our experiments. In Sect. 4 we outline the experiments we undertook to evaluate our approach, followed by a discussion of our quantitative and qualitative results in Sect. 5. We review related work in Sect. 6 before presenting our conclusions and suggestions for future work in Sect. 7.

2 Measuring Caption Quality

The subjectivity in what defines a *good* caption, has made it difficult to identify a single metric for the overall quality of Image Captioning models [5, 26]. Benchmarking methods from Machine Translation [3, 19, 23] have been appropriated, while other somewhat similar methods such as CIDEr [27] have been proposed specifically for assessing the quality of image captions. All these approaches unfortunately have a strong focus on replicating common n-grams from the ground-truth captions [5] and do not take into account the richness and diversity of human expression [9, 26]. Moreover, it has been found that this class of metrics suffers from poor correlations with human evaluation, with CIDEr and METEOR having the highest correlations among them [5].

With the recognition of these limitations, there has been a growing interest in developing metrics that measure other desirable qualities in captions. SPICE [2] is a recent addition which measures the overlap of content by comparing automatically generated scene-graphs from the ground-truth and generated captions. While being a relevant addition, it does not solve the problem of generic captions. Rare occurrences and more detailed descriptions are more likely to incur a penalty than common concepts; e.g. correctly specifying *a purple flower* where the ground-truth text omits its color would register a false positive for the color. This, again, encourages the "safe" generic captions that we want to move away from.

2.1   Diversity Metrics

In an effort to measure the amount of generic captions produced by various Image Captioning models, [11] explores the concept of *caption diversity*. More recently, this concept has been employed as the focus for training and evaluation [26, 29], and it has been proposed that improving caption diversity leads to more human-like captions [26]. This research direction is still new and lacks clear benchmarks and standardized metrics. We propose the following set of metrics to evaluate the diversity of a model:

- *novelty* - percentage of generated captions where exact duplicates are not found in the training set [11, 26, 29]
- *diversity* - percentage of distinct captions (where duplicates count as a single distinct caption) out of the total number of generated captions [11]
- *vocabulary size* - number of unique words used in generated captions [26].

2.2   Meaningful Diversity Through Specificity

The diversity metrics alone do not tell us if a diverse model is more meaningful or if it simply introduced more noise. We argue that improving the *specificity* of the captions is essential to producing a meaningful increase in diversity. Our hypothesis is that by directly increasing the specificity, we will also achieve a higher diversity since diversity is a necessity for specificity. By improving both the specificity and diversity, we expect to generate qualitatively better captions that are less generic.

For this purpose, we propose a training architecture where a specificity loss is inferred by a separately trained Image Retrieval model. Specificity is measured by two standard Image Retrieval metrics:

- *recall at k* - percentage of generated captions resulting in the original image being found in the top k candidates retrieved by the Image Retrieval model
- *mean rank* - mean rank given by the Image Retriever to the correct image based on its generated caption.

3 Optimizing for Specificity

To train a model that produces more diverse and meaningful captions, we propose to use an Image Retrieval model to improve the caption specificity of an Image Captioning model. In Image Retrieval tasks, a given query must be specific enough to retrieve the correct image among other, possibly similar, images. In this paper, we investigate whether the error signal from an Image Retrieval model can improve caption specificity in an Image Captioning model, and whether these more specific captions are also more diverse.

The training process is inspired by [22] where the task is to generate Referring Expressions that unambiguously refer to a region of an image; their solution is to introduce a Region Discriminator that measures the quality of their generated expressions. Their method is in turn inspired by Generative Adversarial Networks (GANs) in which a Generator and a Discriminator are in constant competition - the Discriminator aims to distinguish between real and generated data, while the Generator aims to generate data that the Discriminator cannot tell apart from the real data [13]. In [22], the training is cooperative rather than competitive; both systems adjust to the other to provide the best joint results.

We take a slightly different approach from both the joint training in [22] and recent applications of GAN training in Image Captioning [9, 26]. Instead of allowing both systems to learn from each other, we freeze the NLU side and allow only the NLG to learn from the NLU; the NLU model is pre-trained on ground-truth captions, without any input from the NLG. Consequently, we avoid one of the problems observed in [22] where both systems adapt to each other and develop their own protocol of communication which gradually degrades the resemblance to human language. We also avoid the instability in training and difficulty in loss monitoring commonly seen in GANs.

3.1 Model Architecture

To demonstrate our training approach, we practically apply it to a neural Image Captioning model proposed in [1] which uses an encoder-decoder architecture with region-based attention. For our experiments, we use a publicly available re-implementation [21]. To leverage the fluency gained from MLE training, the model is pre-trained to minimize the cross-entropy loss L_{XE} for each ground truth sequence $y_{1:T}$ when conditioned on an image I and the attended image features $i_{1:T}$:

$$L_{XE}(\theta) = -\sum_{t=1}^{T} log(p\theta(y_t|y_{1:t-1}, i_t, I)). \qquad (1)$$

The pre-trained model also provides a strong baseline to compare to. The model architecture, illustrated in Fig. 1, consists of a ResNet-101 [14] CNN pre-trained on the ImageNet [25] dataset, followed by an LSTM for attention modelling, and a second LSTM that generates the captions. (Unlike [1], the attention-regions are 14×14 regions over the final convolutional layer instead of using a region proposal network.) During our specificity training, the CNN layers remain frozen while we update the weights of the two LSTMs.

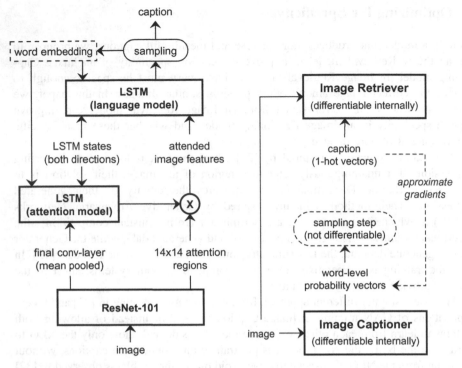

Fig. 1. Our Image Captioning model architecture.

Fig. 2. Interactions between the Image Captioning and Image Retrieval models during training.

For our NLU component, we use the neural Image Retrieval model from the Sent-Eval toolkit [8]; the NLU is pre-trained on ground-truth data and remains frozen during our specificity training. Given an image-caption pair, it produces the loss and gradients for our Image Captioning model by projecting the image and caption into the same space to estimate their similarity. The image embeddings are acquired by a ResNet-101 trained on ImageNet, and the captions are embedded using InferSent [7] with GloVe [24] word embeddings.

3.2 Specificity Loss Functions

We define four different loss functions to be calculated by our NLU component, each used in one of the model variations. The first two improve the individual similarity of a caption to its corresponding image, while the latter two implement contrastive pairwise versions of the first two.

Let c be the projected caption embedding and let i be the projected image embedding, both acquired by passing the generated caption C and its original corresponding image I_o through the Image Retrieval model. For the contrastive loss functions, let I_c be a contrastive image chosen at random from the top 1% most similar images to I_o based on its activations from the final convolutional layer of the encoder

CNN. We can now define the dot product similarity loss L_{DP}, the cosine similarity loss L_{Cos}, the contrastive dot product loss L_{CDP} and the contrastive cosine loss L_{CCos}. Equations 2, 3, 4 and 5 define the loss functions in terms of a single example; the final loss is the mean loss over all examples.

$$L_{DP}(C, I_o) = -(c \cdot i), \tag{2}$$

$$L_{Cos}(C, I_o) = -\frac{c \cdot i}{||c|| \cdot ||i||}, \tag{3}$$

$$L_{CDP}(C, I_o, I_c) = max(0, c \cdot i_c - c \cdot i_o), \tag{4}$$

$$L_{CCos}(C, I_o, I_c) = max\left(0, \frac{c \cdot i_c}{||c|| \cdot ||i_c||} - \frac{c \cdot i_o}{||c|| \cdot ||i_o||}\right). \tag{5}$$

3.3 Training

The interactions between the NLU and NLG components are illustrated in Fig. 2. At each iteration, the Image Captioning model generates a full caption for a given image (or a set of captions for a batch of images). This involves a non-differentiable sampling step to convert the word-level probabilities into a sequence of discrete words represented by 1-hot encoded vectors. The caption is then fed to the Image Retriever along with its corresponding image, where both are passed through the embedding and projection steps.

The Image Retriever calculates one of the specificity losses defined in Sect. 3.2. To minimize this loss, we need to backpropagate the gradients through the Image Retrieval model's (frozen) layers and then back through the Image Captioning model's layers that we wish to update. This is not trivial since our forward pass includes a non-differentiable sampling step. To overcome this, we apply the Straight-Through method [4] and use the gradients with respect to the 1-hot encoding as an approximation for the gradients with respect to the probabilities before sampling. We empirically validate this approach by observing that our loss decreases smoothly. We also experimented with the similar Gumbel Straight-Through method [16] but observed no empirical benefit.

4 Experiment Design

All experiments are conducted in PyTorch[1]. Our implementation extends the code of the baseline Image Captioning model by replacing the MLE training with our specificity training. The Image Retrieval code is modified to calculate our specificity losses defined in Sect. 3.2. We use the Adam [18] optimizer with an initial learning rate of 1×10^{-6} for the contrastive models and 1×10^{-7} for the other two models. Early stopping is used based on the lowest mean rank on the validation set. The contrastive

---

[1] https://pytorch.org/

models trained for about 190k iterations on the randomly shuffled training set, while the non-contrastive models trained for about 250k iterations, all using a batch-size of 2. When sampling from the final models on the test set, any tokens that are duplicates of the immediately previous token are automatically removed since such duplicates were an issue in our non-contrastive models; we do the same for all our models, including the baseline, for a fair comparison.

4.1 Dataset

We use the MS COCO dataset [20] with the Karpathy 5k splits [17], containing 113k images for training and 5k each for validation and test, with 5 captions for each image. The same splits were used for both the NLG and the NLU, including pre-training, ensuring that we have no overlap between training, validation and test data and that our improvements do not come from bridging a gap between different datasets. Note that the specificity training does not require any extra data in addition to that used during pre-training. Furthermore, since the labels are not used during our specificity training, one could also make use of unlabeled data. All splits were pre-processed by lower-casing all words and removing punctuation. Any words appearing less than 5 times in the training set were replaced by the UNK token, resulting in a vocabulary size of 9487 (including the UNK token).

Table 1. Diversity and specificity. Our models are named after the loss functions defined in Sect. 3.2. All metrics are percentages except Vocab Size and Mean Rank which are absolute numbers. Higher is better except for mean rank where lower is better. Results for a as reported in [11].

Diversity and Specificity							
	Diversity	Novelty	Vocab Size	R@1	R@5	R@10	Mean Rank
D-ME+DMSM [12][a]	47.0[a]	70.0[a]	-				
Adv-samp [26]	-	73.9	**1616**				
Ours DP	79.12	76.66	1029	10.38	31.38	44.48	33.70
Ours Cos	79.16	76.66	1034	10.04	30.66	43.54	35.25
Ours CDP	**84.48**	**77.49**	1064	**12.80**	36.16	49.67	32.79
Ours CCos	84.37	77.29	1052	12.53	**36.19**	**50.00**	**32.30**
Baseline	76.26	69.08	812	10.82	30.42	43.32	39.25

5 Results and Discussion

The models we compare to are the best models in terms of diversity from [11, 26], using the single best caption after re-ranking for the latter. We also report the specificity metrics used for our training goals. The results for specificity would not be directly comparable to models using other external systems, but they are relevant when assessing our own models and verifying that our increase in diversity follows from an increase in specificity. Results from our contrastive models are averaged over 3 runs each. The non-contrastive models are based on single runs.

As can be seen in Table 1, our models demonstrate increased diversity and novelty, outperforming previously reported results. The vocabulary size also increases but is lower than in [26]. When it comes to the specificity metrics, our contrastive models have the advantage over our non-contrastive ones. They all improve the overall mean rank, but the latter do not show the increase in smaller k recalls that the contrastive models do. This is not surprising since the contrastive models specifically minimize their loss in comparison to similar images, while the non-contrastive ones increase their semantic similarity in isolation. The higher specificity of the contrastive models is also accompanied by higher values in diversity and novelty.

Table 2. Novelty and diversity per image with up to 10 candidates; novelty and diversity was not reported for the single-best-caption output.

Diversity metrics for multi-candidate models		
	Diversity within candidates	Novelty within candidates
CVAE [29]	11.8	**82.0**
GMM-CVAE [29]	59.4	80.9
AG-CVAE [29]	**76.4**	79.5

For completeness, we include the best models from [29] in Table 2; however, they only report diversity results on multiple (up to 10) candidates per image (where duplicates of a novel caption are counted as multiple novel captions), so they are not directly comparable to the single-best-caption models. Note that [12, 29] use different data splits, while our models and [26] use the Karpathy 5k splits [17].

Table 3. Standard text metric results for single-best-caption models. All metrics are n-gram based except for SPICE which is based on scene graphs automatically inferred from the captions.

Standard text metrics B-n = BLEU-n R-L = ROUGE-L M = METEOR C = CIDEr S = SPICE								
	B-1	B-2	B-3	B-4	R-L	M	C	S
D-ME+DMSM [12]	-	-	-	0.257	-	0.236	-	-
Adv-samp [26]	-	-	-	-	-	0.236	-	0.166
CVAE [29]	0.698	0.521	0.372	0.265	0.506	0.225	0.834	0.158
GMM-CVAE [29]	0.718	0.538	0.388	0.278	0.516	0.238	0.932	0.170
AG-CVAE [29]	0.716	0.537	0.391	0.286	0.517	0.239	0.953	0.172
Ours DP	0.725	0.556	0.409	0.297	0.527	0.247	0.953	0.184
Ours Cos	0.725	0.556	0.409	0.297	0.527	0.247	0.953	0.184
Ours CDP	0.736	0.564	0.417	0.306	0.533	0.251	0.977	0.188
Ours CCos	0.737	0.565	0.419	0.307	0.533	0.253	0.980	0.188
Baseline	**0.746**	**0.579**	**0.432**	**0.320**	**0.545**	**0.262**	**1.036**	**0.197**

In Table 3, we report results on the standard text metrics. As expected, we see a slight decrease in these metrics when moving away from safer generic captions. They are, however, still in line with our state-of-the-art baseline and slightly stronger than previous diversity-focused models.

5.1 Qualitative Analysis

Our contrastive models tend to generate more specific (and accurate) captions while the baseline model prefers common patterns from the training data. Two examples of this can be seen in the leftmost images in Fig. 3. The rightmost image shows a failure case where our contrastive models focus on the wooden structure (which is more unique in this context) while omitting the skateboard (which is more common, but also more relevant). The improvement in diversity and specificity is not achieved by simply producing longer captions; the average caption length for our baseline, contrastive and non-contrastive models were 9.6, 9.4 and 8.9 words respectively.

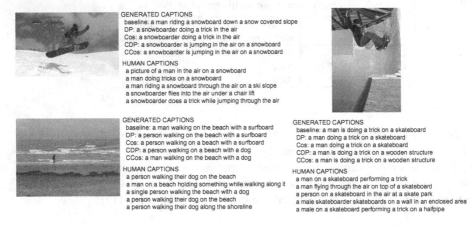

Fig. 3. Examples of generated captions and human annotations. The rightmost image shows a failure case where specificity took precedence over relevance.

6   Related Work

While Image Captioning has received a lot of attention, the focus has mainly been on n-gram metric results. [11] provides some insight into the problems that follow from the standard training and metrics, noting the lack of *diversity* observed in captions from state-of-the-art neural models. More recently, this has led to some initial attempts at improving caption diversity.

In [9], a GAN model conditioned on the image is proposed. The authors do not report any quantitative results for diversity, but they show qualitative examples after manually adjusting the variance of the input to the GAN. This demonstrates the ability of LSTMs to produce fluent captions under noisy conditions, leading to some variation in the output. We observed a similar effect in experiments with noise-based gradients. However, such methods are not constrained to produce *meaningful diversity* (as discussed in Sect. 3) and the level of noise that is appropriate for one caption might be too high for another.

Another example of GAN training is [26] where the Discriminator classifies whether a multi-sample set of captions are human-written or generated. In contrast, our evaluator only requires a single caption and uses a much simpler loss function. Furthermore, we let the NLU remain frozen during training, making the training stable and producing more informative learning curves.

A similar approach can be found in [10] where Contrastive Learning is used in a GAN-like setting. In contrast to our approach which is unsupervised after pre-training, theirs require image-caption pairs both during and after pre-training. Similar to our work, they are motivated by a specificity goal; unfortunately, they do not report results on any diversity metrics.

7 Conclusion

With this work, we have highlighted an important limitation in current Image Captioning research. We provided a discussion on the limitations of current evaluation metrics and proposed a set of metrics related to *diversity* while emphasizing the importance of *meaningful* diversity. Our work summarizes previously reported results and contributes a new state-of-the-art in this area in terms of diversity and novelty. The code for our model and training approach is made publicly available online to encourage further research.

To conclude, we believe that the standard MLE training has both benefits and drawbacks for Image Captioning and that much can be gained by combining it with additional optimization terms. By including an Image Retrieval learning signal, we introduced an additional dimension to our model's training by including text-to-image understanding in addition to its original image-to-text target.

We suggest further research into training approaches that incentivizes multimodal models to build a more complete, bi-directional understanding of its modalities. Additionally, we encourage further exploration of evaluation methods that assess additional desirable qualities in automatically generated captions.

Acknowledgments. This research was supported by the ADAPT Centre for Digital Content Technology which is funded under the SFI Research Centres Programme (Grant 13/RC/2106) and is co-funded under the European Regional Development Fund.

References

1. Anderson, P., et al.: Bottom-up and top-down attention for image captioning and visual question answering. In: The IEEE Conference on Computer Vision and Pattern Recognition (CVPR) (2018)
2. Anderson, P., Fernando, B., Johnson, M., Gould, S.: SPICE: semantic propositional image caption evaluation. In: Leibe, B., Matas, J., Sebe, N., Welling, M. (eds.) ECCV 2016. LNCS, vol. 9909, pp. 382–398. Springer, Cham (2016). https://doi.org/10.1007/978-3-319-46454-1_24

3. Banerjee, S., Lavie, A.: METEOR: an automatic metric for MT evaluation with improved correlation with human judgments. In: Proceedings of the ACL Workshop on Intrinsic and Extrinsic Evaluation Measures for Machine Translation and/or Summarization, pp. 65–72 (2005)
4. Bengio, Y., et al.: Estimating or propagating gradients through stochastic neurons for conditional computation. arXiv:1308.3432 [cs] (2013)
5. Bernardi, R., et al.: Automatic description generation from images: a survey of models, datasets, and evaluation measures. J. Artif. Intell. Res. **55**(1), 409–442 (2016)
6. Chen, X., et al.: Microsoft COCO captions: data collection and evaluation server. arXiv: 1504.00325 [cs] (2015)
7. Conneau, A., et al.: Supervised learning of universal sentence representations from natural language inference data. In: Proceedings of the 2017 Conference on Empirical Methods in Natural Language Processing, pp. 670–680 (2017)
8. Conneau, A., Kiela, D.: SentEval: an evaluation toolkit for universal sentence representations. In: Chair, N.C. et al. (eds.) Proceedings of the Eleventh International Conference on Language Resources and Evaluation (LREC 2018). European Language Resources Association (ELRA), Miyazaki, Japan (2018)
9. Dai, B., et al.: Towards diverse and natural image descriptions via a conditional GAN. In: 2017 IEEE International Conference on Computer Vision (ICCV), pp. 2989–2998 (2017)
10. Dai, B., Lin, D.: Contrastive learning for image captioning. In: Guyon, I., et al. (eds.) Advances in Neural Information Processing Systems 30, pp. 898–907. Curran Associates, Inc. (2017)
11. Devlin, J., et al.: Language models for image captioning: the quirks and what works. In: Proceedings of the 53rd Annual Meeting of the Association for Computational Linguistics and the 7th International Joint Conference on Natural Language Processing, Short Papers, vol. 2, pp. 100–105 (2015)
12. Fang, H., et al.: From captions to visual concepts and back. In: 2015 IEEE Conference on Computer Vision and Pattern Recognition (CVPR), pp. 1473–1482 (2015)
13. Goodfellow, I., et al.: Generative adversarial nets. Adv. Neural. Inf. Process. Syst. **27**, 2672–2680 (2014)
14. He, K., et al.: Deep residual learning for image recognition. In: 2016 IEEE Conference on Computer Vision and Pattern Recognition (CVPR), pp. 770–778 (2016)
15. Hochreiter, S., Schmidhuber, J.: Long short-term memory. Neural Comput. **9**(8), 1735–1780 (1997)
16. Jang, E., et al.: Categorical reparameterization with gumbel-softmax. In: Proceedings of the International Conference on Learning Representations (ICLR) (2017)
17. Karpathy, A., Fei-Fei, L.: Deep visual-semantic alignments for generating image descriptions. IEEE Trans. Pattern Anal. Mach. Intell. **39**(4), 664–676 (2017)
18. Kingma, D.P., Ba, J.: Adam: a method for stochastic optimization. In: International Conference on Learning Representations (ICLR) (2015)
19. Lin, C.-Y., Och, F.J.: Automatic evaluation of machine translation quality using longest common subsequence and skip-bigram statistics. In: Proceedings of the 42nd Annual Meeting on Association for Computational Linguistics. Association for Computational Linguistics, Stroudsburg, PA, USA (2004)
20. Lin, T.-Y., et al.: Microsoft COCO: common objects in context. arXiv:1405.0312 [cs] (2014)
21. Luo, R.: An Image Captioning codebase in PyTorch. GitHub repository. https://github.com/ruotianluo/ImageCaptioning.pytorch (2017)
22. Luo, R., Shakhnarovich, G.: Comprehension-guided referring expressions. In: 2017 IEEE Conference on Computer Vision and Pattern Recognition (CVPR), pp. 3125–3134 (2017)

23. Papineni, K., et al.: BLEU: a method for automatic evaluation of machine translation. In: Proceedings of the 40th Annual Meeting on Association for Computational Linguistics, pp. 311–318. Association for Computational Linguistics, Philadelphia (2002)
24. Pennington, J., et al.: Glove: global vectors for word representation. In: Proceedings of the 2014 Conference on Empirical Methods in Natural Language Processing (EMNLP), pp. 1532–1543 (2014)
25. Russakovsky, O., et al.: ImageNet large scale visual recognition challenge. Int. J. Comput. Vis. **115**(3), 211–252 (2015)
26. Shetty, R., et al.: Speaking the same language: matching machine to human captions by adversarial training. In: 2017 IEEE International Conference on Computer Vision (ICCV), pp. 4155–4164 (2017)
27. Vedantam, R., et al.: CIDEr: Consensus-based image description evaluation. In: 2015 IEEE Conference on Computer Vision and Pattern Recognition (CVPR), pp. 4566–4575 (2015)
28. Vinyals, O., et al.: Show and tell: lessons learned from the 2015 MSCOCO image captioning challenge. IEEE Trans. Pattern Anal. Mach. Intell. **39**(4), 652–663 (2017)
29. Wang, L., et al.: Diverse and accurate image description using a variational auto-encoder with an additive gaussian encoding space. In: Guyon, I., et al. (eds.) Advances in Neural Information Processing Systems 30. pp. 5758–5768. Curran Associates, Inc. (2017)

Assessing Image Analysis Filters as Augmented Input to Convolutional Neural Networks for Image Classification

K. Delibasis[1], Ilias Maglogiannis[2(✉)], S. Georgakopoulos[1],
K. Kottari[1], and V. Plagianakos[1]

[1] Department of Computer Science and Biomedical Informatics,
University of Thessaly, Volos, Greece
kdelibasis@gmail.com, spirosgeorg@dib.uth.gr,
kottarikonstantina@gmail.com, vpp@uth.gr
[2] Department of Digital Systems, University of Piraeus, Piraeus, Greece
imaglo@unipi.gr

Abstract. Convolutional Neural Networks (CNNs) have been proven very effective in image classification and object recognition tasks, often exceeding the performance of traditional image analysis techniques. However, training a CNN requires very extensive datasets, as well as very high computational burden. In this work, we test the hypothesis that if the input includes the responses of established image analysis filters that detect salient image structures, the CNN should be able to perform better than an identical CNN fed with the plain RGB images only. Thus, we employ a number of families of image analysis filter banks and use their responses to compile a small number of filtered responses for each original RGB image. We perform a large number of CNN training/testing repetitions for a 40-class building recognition problem, on a publicly available image database, using the original images, as well as the original images augmented by the compiled filter responses. Results show that the accuracy achieved by the CNN with the augmented input is consistently higher than that of the RGB image input, both in terms of different repetitions of the execution, as well as throughout the iterations of each repetition.

Keywords: Deep learning · Convolutional neural networks · Augmented input
Image analysis filter banks

1 Introduction

Convolutional neural networks (CNNs) are used frequently in several computer vision applications. CNNs' success relies on their inner capability to exploit an assumption of two statistical properties of image data, "local stationarity" and "compositional structure" [1]. In image processing, scale space is detected using filter banks of normalized Laplacian of Gaussian [2] with different values of the scale parameter and is used to extract scale invariant features. It is utilized by the CNNs' pooling operator, as well as the convolution operator using stride. These image properties are exploited by the CNNs to extract appropriate local features from the images and produce high

© Springer Nature Switzerland AG 2018
V. Kůrková et al. (Eds.): ICANN 2018, LNCS 11139, pp. 188–196, 2018.
https://doi.org/10.1007/978-3-030-01418-6_19

classification results. CNNs craft the proper local features to distinguish between different image classes, avoiding the exhaustive search of the image feature space. Although, in many cases, these CNN-crafted features have proven superior to hand-crafted ones, designed by experts for specific problems, the CNN approach is not always optimal. In cases with domain expertise/knowledge or image acquisition with special image formation models or with insufficient training set, hand-crafted image features can outperform CNNs or enhance their performance when embedded into them. For instance, it was shown in [3] that in the special case of pose recognition on fisheye images, the Zernike moment descriptors that were redefined using the image formation model, after camera calibration, were more successful than the application of CNNs, with or without transfer learning.

In this work we investigate the value of including mid-level computer vision filter responses as input to CNNs, along with the traditional input of the original RGB pixel values. Image analysis and computer vision theory have established the mathematical properties of such image operators. Our team has performed initial work on this issue in the context of dermoscopy feature classification at a superpixel level [4]. In this work, we test a range of image filters and apply the augmented input to a 40-class, entire image classification task, of different buildings. An attempt to include similar filter responses in traditional classifiers has been reported very recently (26 Jan 2018) in [5]. Our work is independent from [5], uses a different set of filters, specifically developed in Matlab from scratch. We evaluate the impact of augmenting the input of a traditional CNN architecture with the responses of these filters, to the classification performance for the problem of building recognition. In Sect. 2 the dataset is described, the image analysis filters and the compilation of image responses are defined in detail in Sect. 3 and results are presented in Sect. 4.

2 Dataset

In this work we utilized the Sheffield Building Image Dataset [6, 7] that consists of over 3,000 low-resolution images of forty different buildings – typically between 70 and 120 images per building. The images are taken from different viewpoints under widely different lighting conditions, obtained by hand-held mobile devices. Typical images are presented in Fig. 1.

Fig. 1. Sample of Sheffield building image dataset

3 Definition of Image Filters

In this section we describe the definition of image analysis filters that are applied to the original images in order to augment the input of the CNNs. For every available image, we calculated the following pixel-wise quantities that result in real-valued arrays of equal dimensions with the original image:

- The maximum of the response of the scale-normalized Laplacian of Gaussian (*LoG*) operator, over different values of the scale-defining parameter σ.
- The determinant and the eigenvalues of the Hessian matrix, over different scales.
- The maximum of the response of steerable Gabor filter bank and 2nd order partial derivative of a Gaussian filter bank, over a range of different orientations and image scales.

Details about the definition, response normalization, and parameterization of the aforementioned filters are provided in the following paragraphs. The input images are first converted to gray-scale and subsequently normalized to zero mean value ($\mu_I = 0$) and a standard deviation σ_I equal to 1.

3.1 Laplacian of Gaussian (LoG) Filters

The first set of filters is the scale-normalized *Laplacian of Gaussian* n*LoG*, for different values of standard deviation σ, which is frequently employed to detect a characteristic scale locally in images [2]. Let us denote the response of the image with the normalized *LoG* as $I_{LG,\sigma} = I * \sigma^2 LoG_\sigma$, where the "*" symbol stands for linear convolution. The n*LoG* filter bank calculates the image response for multiple increasing values of σ and constructs a single image that, for each pixel, collects the values of the responses over different σ with the maximum absolute value:

$$\sigma_0 = \arg\max\left(\left|I_{LG,\sigma}\right|\right), \sigma = 1, 2, 3, 4$$
$$I_{LG}(i,j) = I_{LG,\sigma_0}(i,j) \tag{1}$$

3.2 Image Features Based on the Hessian Matrix

Another family of filter response is based on the (pixelwise) image Hessian matrix, which has been used extensively for image feature extraction [8, 9]. At each image pixel, the 2×2 Hessian **H** is calculated using partial derivatives of the Gaussian kernel g, parameterized by its variance σ^2, (e.g.: $I_{xx}(x, y) = \sigma^2 I(x, y) * g_{xx}$, subscripts denote partial derivatives).

Filtered images L_{max}, I_{max}, based on the calculation of eigenvalues of **H**, have been used for image analysis (e.g. [16, 17]) and are also utilized in this work as following. Let λ_1, λ_2 be the real eigenvalues of **H** with a specified value of σ, at each location (x, y) of the image, which can be calculated in closed form

$$\lambda_1 = \frac{q}{a}, \lambda_2 = \frac{D}{q}, q = -\frac{1}{2}(b + \text{sgn}(D))\sqrt{Tr^2 - 4D} \tag{2}$$

where $\alpha = 1$, Tr is the trace and D the determinant of **H**. Let λ_{max} and λ_{min} be the eigenvalue with the maximum and minimum absolute value, respectively. The local structure of the image at each pixel can be determined by the relation of the λ_{max} and λ_{min}. In this work, we calculate the $\lambda_{min,\sigma}$ and $\lambda_{min,\sigma}$ for values of σ between 1 and σ_{max}, where the value of σ_{max} depends on the partial resolution of the image. The pixel-wise maximum of λ_{max} and λ_{min} is obtained as:

$$L_{max} = \lambda_{max,\sigma_0} \tag{3}$$

where $\sigma_0 = \operatorname{argmax}(|\lambda_{max,\sigma}|)$, $\sigma = 1, 2, \ldots, \sigma_{max}$

$$l_{max} = \lambda_{min,\sigma_0} \tag{4}$$

where $\sigma_0 = \operatorname{argmax}(|\lambda_{min,\sigma}|)$, $\sigma = 1, 2, \ldots, \sigma_{max}$.

Normalization is applied to L_{max}, l_{max} before they are input into the CNN:

$$L_{max} \leftarrow \frac{L_{max}}{\max(|L_{max}|, |l_{max}|)}, \; l_{max} \leftarrow \frac{l_{max}}{\max(|L_{max}|, |l_{max}|)} \tag{5}$$

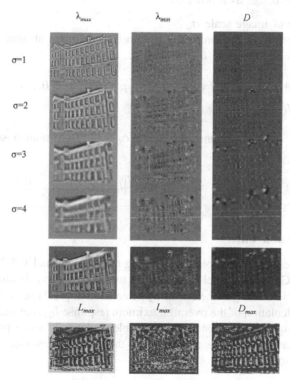

Values of σ for maximum absolute value response

Fig. 2. The Hessian-based images for the 1st image of the data set, for each one of the 4 different values of σ, the compiled Hessian-based images (5th line) and the corresponding values of σ (last line).

The determinant D_{max} of **H**, compiled as described above is also included in the image features. (The trace of **H** has already been used, as it is equal to the LoG).

The schematic representation of the calculation of L_{max}, l_{max} and D_{max} is shown in Fig. 2 for the 1st image of the dataset.

3.3   Gabor Filter Bank

Another well-known family of filters are the Gabor filters, defined as a complex sinusoid of wavelength λ, propagating parallel to an axis of angle θ with the X-axis, with its amplitude modulated by a Gaussian of standard deviation σ. Gabor filters possess interesting spectral properties, as well as analogies with certain mammalian cellular structures that perform early processing of visual stimuli [10]. Gabor filters have been used in many previous works such as in [11, 12].

In this work we parameterized the Gabor filter as following: $\lambda = 3\sigma$, $\theta = 0°$, $20°$, $40°$, ..., $160°$, $\sigma = 2, 3, 4$, and utilize the real part (cosine term only) in order to detect dark or light non-flat image linear structures, in any orientation and up to a few pixels in diameter. The responses of the Gabor filter bank (all combinations of θ, σ), are reduced to a single image as following:

1. For each value of image scale σ_0
   a. For all pixels (i, j), determine the θ with the maximum absolute value of $I_{Gb,\theta}$ and compile the response $I_{Gb,\sigma0}$:

$$\theta = \arg\max\left(\left|I * \mathrm{Re}\left(gb_{\lambda,\sigma,\theta}\right)\right|\right), \sigma = \sigma_0, \theta = \theta_1, \theta_2, \ldots, \theta_n$$
$$I_{Gb,\sigma_0}(i,j) = I_{Gb,\theta,\sigma_0}(i,j) \tag{6}$$

2. For all pixels (i, j), determine the scale σ_0 with maximum absolute value of $I_{Gb,\sigma}(i, j)$

$$I_{Gb}(i,j) = I_{Gb,\sigma_0}(i,j), \sigma_0 = \arg\max\left(\left|I_{Gb,\sigma}(i, j)\right|\right), \sigma = 1, 2, \ldots, \sigma_{max} \tag{7}$$

3.4   Other Steerable Filters

Finally, a similar class of steerable filters, using the scale-normalized 2nd order partial derivative of the Gaussian kernel with respect to x, $G_{xx,\sigma,\theta}(x,y)$, is also employed as input to CNN is this work, parameterized by orientation angle θ and scale parameter σ, with range and calculation of the overall maximum response I_{Gxx} identical to that of the Gabor filter (see Fig. 3). We consider the steerable, scalable 2nd order partial derivative of the Gaussian an advantageous alternative to the Gabor filters, since the later filters cannot be easily normalized.

3.5   Construction of Augmented Input to CNN

The augmented input for each RGB image consists of the original RGB color channels, as well as the aforementioned compiled filter responses. An example of the compiled

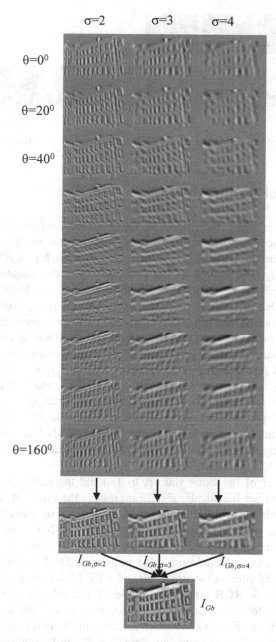

Fig. 3. The image responses using the streerable – scalable Gxx kernel for the 1st image of the data set, the compiled responses for each one of the three values of σ (5th line) and the final compiled response (last image).

filter responses, used as augmented input is shown in the 2nd line of Fig. 4, for the 1st image of the data set. The three-color channels of the original image are also shown (first line of Fig. 4).

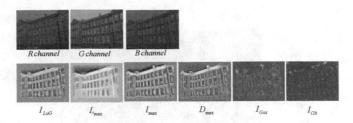

Fig. 4. An example of the traditional CNN input (RGB channels – 1st line) and the augmented CNN input (2nd line).

4   Experimental Results

In this section we examine the impact of the proposed augmented input on image classification accuracy. We evaluate this input data augmentation scheme on the dataset Sheffield Building Image Dataset against the classic approach of CNN with the RGB images as input only. Because of the small dimension of the images, we choose the architecture as specified in Caffe [13] for the problem of CIFAR-10 [14]. More specifically the architecture consists of 3 convolutional layers, each followed by a ReLU activation function and a pooling layer, and one fully connected layer, with an output layer of two neurons. The kernel size of the convolutional layers is 5×5, while the first two convolutional layer comprised of 32 feature maps and the third convolutional layer of 64 feature maps. The dataset is randomly split as 80% of each class images for training and the rest for testing, 3359 training and 819 test images. The training images are resized to 40×40 and during the training phase are randomly cropped to 32×32 pixels. The testing images are resized to 32×32. Because of the small size of the dataset and memory availability, the CNN has been trained by the Gradient Descent Algorithm with the whole training set in each iteration (epoch), using the NVIDIA Titan X Pascal GPU card.

The total number of iterations was set to 180 and the learning rate was fixed at 0.001. In order to extract statistically significant results, the experiments of training and testing the CNN with and without the augmented input, are repeated 50 times. Table 1 presents statistics of the best accuracy achieved by the CNN for both input schemes, calculated over 50 repetitions: mean accuracy (Mean), standard deviation (Standard Dev.), minimum (Min.) and maximum (Max.) accuracy. The CNN with the augmented input of the proposed filter responses achieved 3.7% higher mean accuracy, in comparison with the classic RGB input only, while significantly reducing inter-repetition variation from 4.4% to 1.2%. The minimum accuracy was drastically increased from 71.9% to 87.5%. Figure 5 shows the mean accuracy of the two input schemes at each iteration (epoch), as well as the standard deviation. It can be observed that almost in every iteration, the mean accuracy of the augmented CNN was consistently higher.

In order to validate the significance of the classification performance differences, the two-sided Wilcoxon rank sum test [15] was performed. The null hypothesis (i.e., that the samples are independent and derived by identical continuous distributions with equal medians) was rejected, justifying that there exist statistical differences between the accuracy of the two methods at the 5% significance level (p-values <0.05).

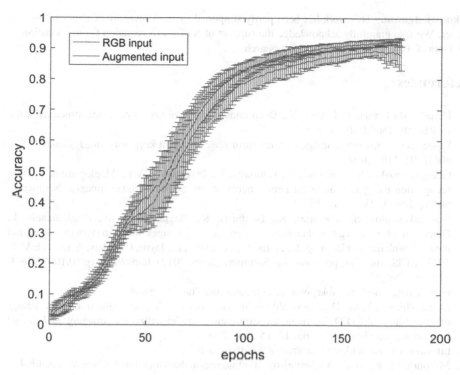

Fig. 5. Mean accuracy score (test set) of the augmented input CNN and the CNN with the RGB images only, with the corresponding error bars, calculated over 50 repetitions.

Table 1. Statistical measures of the achieved accuracy (%), calculated for 50 repetitions.

	Classification accuracy (%)			
	Mean	Standard dev.	Min.	Max.
CNN augmented input	92.0	1.2	87.5	92.9
CNN RGB input	88.3	4.4	71.9	91.6

5   Conclusion

A number of image analysis filter banks were selected, appropriately parameterized and their output compiled to generate few filter responses for each original RGB image. These filter responses were used to augment the input to a CNN. Experimental results in a 40-class image classification task show that the proposed input increased the achieved accuracy of the CNN, consistently with respect to repetition of executions, as well as throughout the iterations in each repetition. Statistical analysis showed the significance of the achieved classification improvement. As a future work we intend to exploit additional filter banks and prioritize them in terms of the effect they have on the classification accuracy.

Acknowledgment. This work has been partly supported by the University of Piraeus Research Center. We also gratefully acknowledge the support of NVDIA Corporation for the donation of the Titan X Pascal GPU used for this research.

References

1. Henaff, M., Bruna, J., LeCun, Y.: Deep convolutional networks on graph-structured data. CoRR, abs/1506.05163 (2015)
2. Lowe, D.G.: Distinctive image features from scale-invariant keypoints. Int. J. Comput. Vis. **60**(2), 91–110 (2004)
3. Georgakopoulos, S.V., Kottari, K., Delibasis, K., Plagianakos, V.P., Maglogiannis, I.: Pose recognition using convolutional neural networks on omni-directional images. Neurocomputing **280**(6), 23–31 (2018)
4. Georgakopoulos, S.V., Kottari, K., Delibasis, K., Plagianakos, V.P., Maglogiannis, I.: Detection of malignant melanomas in dermoscopic images using convolutional neural network with transfer learning. In: Boracchi, G., Iliadis, L., Jayne, C., Likas, A. (eds.) EANN 2017. CCIS, vol. 744, pp. 404–414. Springer, Cham (2017). https://doi.org/10.1007/978-3-319-65172-9_34
5. https://imagej.net/Trainable_Weka_Segmentation\#Training_panel
6. Li, J., Allinson, N.M.: Dimensionality reduction-based building recognition. In: Proceedings of the Ninth IASTED International Conference on Visualization, Imaging and Image Processing, Cambridge UK, pp. 13–15, July 2009
7. https://www.sheffield.ac.uk/eee/research/iel/research
8. Mikolajczyk, K., et al.: A comparison of affine region detectors. Int. J. Comput. Vis. **65**(43), 43–72 (2005)
9. Tuytelaars, T., Mikolajczy, K.: Local invariant feature detectors: a survey. Comput. Graph. Vis. **3**(3), 177–280 (2007)
10. Daugman, J.G.: Uncertainty relation for resolution in space, spatial frequency, and orientation optimized by two-dimensional visual cortical filters. Opt. Soc. Am. J. Opt. Image Sci. **2**(7), 1160–1169 (1985)
11. Weldon, T.P., Higgins, W.E., Dunn, D.F.: Efficient gabor filter design for texture segmentation. Pattern Recogn. **29**(12), 2005–2015 (1996)
12. Li, M., Staunton, R.C.: Optimum gabor filter design and local binary patterns for texture segmentation. Pattern Recogn. Lett. **29**(5), 664–672 (2008)
13. Jia Y., et al.: Caffe: convolutional architecture for fast feature embedding. arXiv preprint arXiv:1408.5093 (2014)
14. Torralba, A., Fergus, R., Freeman, W.T.: 80 million tiny images: a large dataset for nonparametric object and scene recognition. IEEE Trans. Pattern Anal. Mach. Intell. **30**(11), 1958–1970 (2008)
15. Wilcoxon, F.: Individual comparisons by ranking methods. Biometr. Bull. **1**(6), 80–83 (1945)
16. Frangi, A.F., Niessen, W.J., Vincken, K.L., Viergever, M.A.: Multiscale vessel enhancement filtering. In: Wells, W.M., Colchester, A., Delp, S. (eds.) MICCAI 1998. LNCS, vol. 1496, pp. 130–137. Springer, Heidelberg (1998). https://doi.org/10.1007/BFb0056195
17. Krissian, K., Malandain, G., Ayache, N., Vaillant, R., Trousset, Y.: Model based detection of tubular structures in 3D images. Comput. Vis. Image Underst. **80**(2), 130–171 (2000)

Spiking

Balanced Cortical Microcircuitry-Based Network for Working Memory

Hui Wei[1,2(✉)], Zihao Su[1,2], and Dawei Dai[1,2]

[1] Laboratory of Cognitive Model and Algorithm,
Department of Computer Science, Fudan University,
No. 825 Zhangheng Road, Shanghai 201203, China
{weihui, zhsu16}@fudan.edu.cn
[2] Shanghai Key Laboratory of Data Science,
No. 220 Handan Road, Shanghai 200433, China

Abstract. Working memory (WM) is an important part of cognitive activity. The WM system maintains information temporarily to be used in learning and decision-making. Recent studies of WM focused on positive feedback, but positive feedback models require fine tuning of the strength of the feedback and are sensitive to common perturbations. However, different people have different strength of the feedback and it is impossible to let every people have same network parameter. In this research, we proposed a new approach to understanding WM based on the theory that positive and negative feedback are closely balanced in neocortical circuits. Our experimental results demonstrated that the model does not need fine tuning parameter and can achieve the memory storage, memory association, memory updating and memory forgetting. Our proposed negative-derivative feedback model was shown to be more robust to common perturbations than previous models based on positive feedback alone.

Keywords: Working memory · Spiking neuron network · Balanced network
Computational model

1 Introduction

Working memory (WM) provides the ability to hold information "online" during cognitive processing, forming the essential foundation of cognitive activity. The inner neural circuits that explore higher brain functions are an important research hotspot in neuroscience [1–3]. Jacobsen found a close link between the prefrontal cortex (PFC) of monkeys and WM [4]. Fuster and Kubota found persistent neural activity in the dorsolateral prefrontal cortex during the performance of WM tasks [5, 6]. Since the presentation of that work, persistent neural activity in PFC neurons has been correlated with WM. Within the PFC, relatively isolated stripe-like patches of neurons have been observed, each of which exhibits dense within-stripe interconnectivity and sparse (largely inhibitory) between-stripe connectivity [7, 8]. Furthermore, these stripes project to distinct regions within the BG which, in turn, project back to different stripes within the PFC [9]. This anatomy and physiology can support a system of control in which association signals from the BG regulate when some stripe within the PFC are chose [10].

V. Kůrková et al. (Eds.): ICANN 2018, LNCS 11139, pp. 199–210, 2018.
https://doi.org/10.1007/978-3-030-01418-6_20

The recurrent network model was created to maintaining the persistent neural activity associated with WM. A "ring" model was proposed and achieved notable success in simulating persistent activity related to visuospatial WM (vsWM) [11]. However, little attention was paid to the heterogeneities in network topology and long-range connections. Edmund T. Rolls et al. proposed a model that can hold multiple items in memory and they emphasized the importance of inhibitory synaptic [12]. But their model's parameters need perfect tuning and cannot remember the order of memory and they did not address how to update WM. Trenton Kriete et al. proposed a variable binding model which saved a pattern's encoding and its' location in different part of the PFC. They used the variable binding mechanism to increase the flexibility of the network [10]. However, they did not describe how the pattern and location bound together and how to update memory when the WM is full. In addition, they neglected that WM can maintain memory for few second and the capacity of WM is limited. They trained their models with a lot of training data and used it to predict a lot of new data. But how can WM store the training data for so long? Therefore, their models are more like long-term memory than WM.

There were models about componential representations, and the researchers presenting some of these models have explicitly argued that long lasting statistical associations in prefrontal cortex would be disruptive. The associations will cause perturbations that disrupt their fine tuning. In contrast, in negative derivative feedback model, the perturbations caused by weak associations led to offsetting changes and would not break the balance.

Recent studies suggested an alternative mechanism for WM based on negative-derivate feedback that might play a critical part in maintaining persistent neural activity [13]. Our research follows on this work, using an attractor network model of the cortex that exhibits basic cortical operations, such as storage of stimuli, associative memory, and rivalry. The model can update and forget memories as well. Our proposed negative-derivate feedback model proved capable of maintaining persistent activity robustly across common perturbations. Furthermore, experimental results showed that the model duplicated successfully the results of Funahashi et al.'s oculomotor delayed-response task experiment using monkeys [14] and Inoue and Matsuzawa's limited-hold memory task experiment using Chimpanzees [15].

The remainder of this paper details our work as follows. The theory of negative-derivative feedback is given in Sect. 2. Section 3 describes our negative-derivative feedback model. In Sect. 4, we compare the results of our computational method with behavioral data from prior research, and our conclusions are given in Sect. 5.

2 Negative-Derivative Feedback Mechanism

The negative-derivative feedback model depends on two primary observations. First, cortical neurons receive massive amounts of excitation and inhibition [16]. Second, the pathways from one pyramidal cell to another pyramidal cell have slower kinetics than the pathways from pyramidal cells to interneurons [17]. These observations naturally lead to a negative-derivative feedback mechanism [13]. Compared with common previous positive feedback models, a negative-derivative feedback model is more robust against common perturbations (Fig. 1).

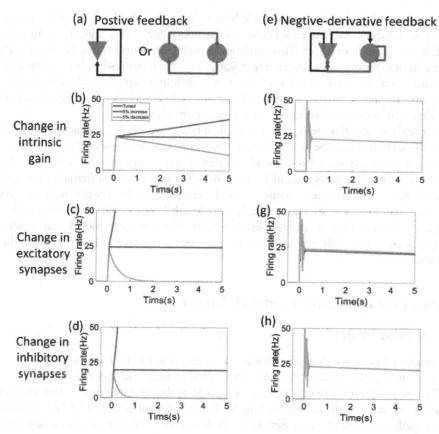

Fig. 1. Robustness to common perturbations in memory networks with different feedback models [13]. (a–d) Non-robustness positive-feedback model. (a) Positive-feedback models. (b–d) Firing rate of pyramidal cell population in perfect tuned network (blue) and following 5% deviations from perfect tuning (orange and yellow) of intrinsic gain (b) or synaptic connection strengths (c–d). (e–h) Robust persistent firing in negative-derivative feedback model. (e) negative-derivative feedback model. (f–h) Firing rate of pyramidal cell population in perfect tuned network and following 5% deviations from perfect tuning of intrinsic gain (f) or synaptic connection strengths (g–h). (Color figure online)

Lim proved that balance can be kept if Eqs. 1 and 2 are satisfied.

$$\frac{J_{EE}J_{II}}{J_{EI}J_{IE}} \sim 1 \quad \text{for large } J \text{ value} \tag{1}$$

$$\tau_+ = (\tau_{EE} + \tau_{II}) > (\tau_{EI} + \tau_{IE}) = \tau_- \tag{2}$$

Where J_{ij} represents the synaptic connection strength from population i to population j. τ_{ij} represents the time constant of activity decay from population i to population j. E represents pyramidal cell population and I represents interneuron population.

In real world, people can maintain WM for a few seconds. But previous negative-derivative feedback mechanisms could hold memory for a very long time. In other word, it was not able to forget. This condition is highly unnatural in real life, is contrary to the common wisdom of research psychology, and consumes resources unnecessarily. To address this issue, we added a flexible weak inhibition signal which value depends on reward magnitude to give the network the ability to forget like a real individual. In turn, this trait frees up more resources for new memories.

In previous negative-derivative feedback models, we needed to factitious assign where the stimuli should be stored. In real life, no one can do this for others. Therefore, we designed the assistant sub-network so that it could find out where to store the stimuli and which memory should be refresh by the new one. Furthermore, previous negative-derivative feedback models could remember only simple features. We expanded the structure so that multiple simple attributes could be combined into complex features. Our proposed negative-derivative feedback model can process multiple items, and different features in each item may correlate or depress other features.

3   Negative-Derivative Feedback Model

3.1   Network Model

Our proposed negative-derivative feedback model consists of two parts. One is the memory storage sub-network and the other is the assistant sub-network.

The assistant sub-network achieves the WM updating mechanism. The assistant sub-network can assign the new stimuli to the right neuron sets and let BG associate them together to express a new item (Fig. 2). When we want to remember a new item, several external stimuli come into our brain. Our brain forms a control signal for each stimulus to express its kind such as color, shape, position and so on. The assistant sub-network checks the control signal and send it to the corresponding selector circuit. For the individual without special training, there are 4 different sets in the selector circuit so that individuals can remember at most 4 items once. The pyramidal cells in the selector circuit but not in the set share the interneuron pool so that when a new signal comes, only 1 pyramidal cell activated and at most 1 set is chosen. The set will inhibit the activity of its corresponding pyramidal cell so that the set stores nothing will be chosen first and the next is the set that has the longest time to store stimulus because with the inhibition signal, the set that stores newer stimulus always has higher frequency than the set that stores older stimulus. After that BG cuts off the chosen set's old linkages and establishes new linkages between them so that they can be associated together to express an item.

The memory storage sub-network consists of neuron sets used to record external stimuli. For this paper, we used 400 neuron sets. Every neuron set contains several components that distinguish the features of stimuli. We used nine components for the current research. Each component is composed of two elements: E and I (Fig. 3). Element E contains several pyramidal cells, and element I contains several interneurons. There are 400 neuron sets in a global resource pool. For WM tasks of different

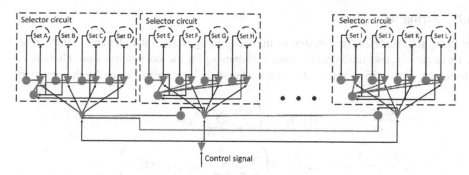

Fig. 2. Structure of the assistant sub-network. First, the assistant sub-network chooses one selector circuit by the frequency of control signal. Second, it chooses a suitable set to store the stimulus. (Color figure online)

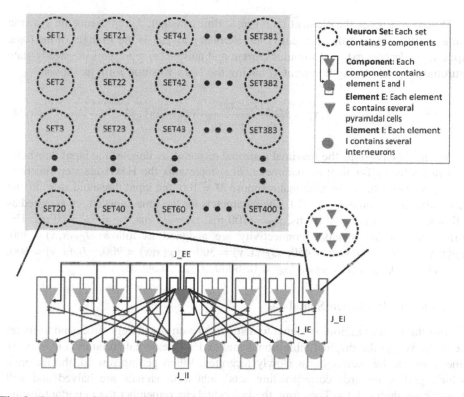

Fig. 3. Structure of memory storage sub-network. The memory storage sub-network consists of a neuron-set array of 20 * 20. Each set contains nine components.

complexity, various amounts of resources are required. According to Cowan's finding [18], the WM capacity is about 3–5 items. In our model, the memory storage sub-network can save 4 stimuli at most for each kind of external stimuli by the assistant of the assistant sub-network.

3.2   Firing Rate Model

In firing rate model, r_E and r_I denote the mean firing rates of the element E and element I, respectively, and the synaptic state variables s_{ij} for the connection from element i to element j. These firing rate and synaptic state variables are governed by the equations:

$$\tau_E \frac{dr_E(x, t)}{dt} = -r_E(x, t) + f\left(\sum_{i=E,I} \sum_{x'=1}^{9} J_{iE}(x, y)s_{iE}(y, t) + i_E(t)\right)$$

$$\tau_I \frac{dr_I(x, t)}{dt} = -r_I(x, t) + f\left(\sum_{i=E,I} \sum_{x'=1}^{9} J_{iI}(x, y)s_{iI}(y, t)\right) \qquad (3)$$

$$\tau_{ij} \frac{ds_{ij}(x, t)}{dt} = -s_{ij}(x, t) + r_i(x, t) \text{ for } i, j = E \text{ or } I$$

$$i_E(t) = J_{OE}I(t) + J_{E, tonic}$$

Where τ_i denotes the element i's intrinsic time constant, J_{ij} represents the synaptic connectivity strength from element i onto element j. $J_{E, tonic}$ is the strength of the tonic input. $i_E(t)$ denotes external stimulus current and noise. $f(x)$ represents the steady-state neuronal response to input current x, having the Naka-Rushton form as shown:

$$f(x) = M \frac{(x - x_\theta)^2}{x_0 + (x - x_\theta)^2} h(x - x_\theta) \qquad (4)$$

Where M represents the maximal neuronal response, x_θ denotes the input threshold, x_0 denotes the half-activation parameter, $h(x)$ represents the Heaviside step function. Throughout our study, the maximal response $M = 100$, the input threshold $x_\theta = 30$, the half-activation parameter $x_0 = 30$. The parameters for the time constant are assigned as follows: $\tau_E = 20$ ms, $\tau_I = 10$ ms, $\tau_{EE} = 100$ ms, $\tau_{EI} = 25$ ms, $\tau_{IE} = \tau_{II} = 10$ ms. The parameters for the synaptic connectivity are assigned as follow: $J_{EE}(x, x) = 300$, $J_{EE}(x, y) = 150$, $J_{EI}(x, x) = 450$, $J_{EI}(x, y) = 300$, $J_{IE}(x, x) = 900$, $J_{IE}(x, y) = 600$, $J_{II}(x, x) = 900$, $J_{II}(x, y) = 600$, $J_{OE} = 0{-}6000$, $J_{E, tonic} = 3000\$$.

3.3   Flexible Inhibition Signal

We use the flexible inhibition signal to distinguish memory storage times and to forget memory. We set the original inhibition signal as 1% of external stimulus (Fig. 4a). As time goes on, the memory was slowly forgotten. When getting reward, the feature's (which getting reward) corresponding sets' inhibition signals are halved and will slowly reset during 10 s. Therefore, the individual can remember the important feature longer (Fig. 4b). The flexible inhibition signal helps the assistant sub-network figuring out the right set and it give the model the ability to forget.

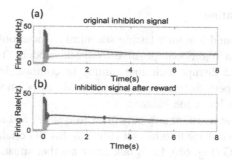

Fig. 4. Flexible inhibition signal. (a) The original inhibition signal in neuron set. It is about 1% of external stimulus. (b) The inhibition signal after reward. The inhibition signal is halved and slowly reset during 10 s.

3.4 Memory Updating

The negative-derivative feedback model can remember multi-features. For example, it can remember an apple that contains many features such as color, shape, and location. Each feature can be set to several values. For instance, color can be set to red or green. Now we wanted our model to remember a yellow stimulus applied at 2001–2100 ms. There were two possible situations. One of the situations is that set A stores a stimulus applied at 1–100 ms and set B stores a stimulus applied at 101–200 ms and set C and set D store nothing. Because set C and set D store nothing, the assistant sub-network chooses set D and sent the new stimulus to set D (Fig. 5a). So now set A, set B, set D saved stimulus. The other is that set A stores a stimulus applied at 1–100 ms and set B stores a stimulus applied at 101–200 ms. Set C stores a stimulus applied at 151 ms–250 ms and set D stores a stimulus appeared at 301–400 ms. Because set A, set B, set C and set D all stored stimulus and set A's frequency is the lowest, the assistant sub-network chooses set A and send the new stimulus to set A and the original memory stored in set A is refreshed (Fig. 5b).

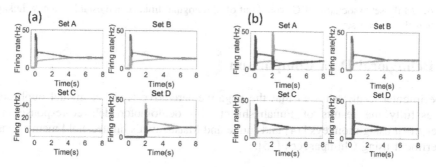

Fig. 5. Memory updating. (a) The assistant sub-network chose set D that saved nothing to store the new stimulus. (b) The assistant sub-network chose set A that had the lowest frequency to store the new stimulus.

3.5   Memory Association

Previous researchers found that long lasting statistical associations in prefrontal cortex would be disruptive in traditional positive-feedback models. The associations will cause perturbations that disrupt their fine tuning. In contrast, in negative derivative feedback model, the perturbations caused by weak associations led to offsetting changes and would not break the balance.

We assumed that the assistant sub-network chose set A and set G for a new item. Set A and set G had no linkage to other set (Fig. 6a). So BG established a new linkage between set A and set G (Fig. 6b). Let's talk about another situation. We assumed that the space choice chose set A and set G for item 1. Set G had a linkage with set C to express item 2 (Fig. 6c). So BG cut off the linkage between set C and set G and established a new linkage between set A and set G to express item 1 (Fig. 6d). Therefore, the item 2 lost a part of its expression and the memory about item 2 became more unclear than before. That is why people can remember things that happened recently clearly and for the things happened for a long time, people's memory is unclear.

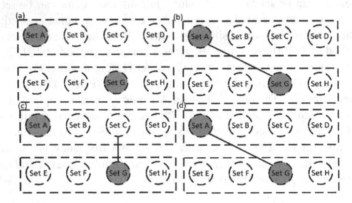

Fig. 6. Multi-set association. BG would cut off the original linkage and establish a new linkage between the chosen sets.

4   Behavioral Data Comparison

Experimental results showed that the negative-derivative feedback model duplicated successfully the results of Funahashi et al.'s oculomotor delayed-response task experiment using monkeys [14] and Inoue and Matsuzawa's limited-hold memory task experiment using Chimpanzees [15].

4.1   Experimental Study A

First, we compared the performance of our negative-derivative feedback model to the monkey's responses in Funahashi et al.'s WM study [14]. The results are shown in

Fig. 7. For the proposed model, the distribution of the firing rates of different components was largest during the response period. As time progressed, the firing rates between different components became more and more closed. These results demonstrated that the performance of the negative-derivative feedback model closely simulated the performance of the monkeys in Funahashi's study.

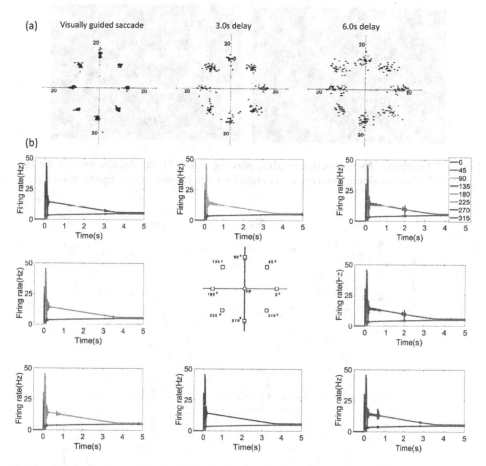

Fig. 7. (a) Monkey's oculomotor delayed-response task experiment [14] and (b) our model's stimulation results.

4.2 Experimental Study B

In this portion of our work, we compared the results generated by our negative-derivative feedback model to the findings of Inoue and Matsuzawa's WM study [15]. In that work, Matsuzawa and Inoue developed a new test called the "limited-hold memory task" to compare the WM of chimpanzees and humans. The numbers 1–9 were displayed on a touch-screen monitor for a limited time. The arrangement of numbers is shown in Fig. 8 [15]. The experiment used three different durations (hold times) for the display. When the display time was done, the numbers were covered by white squares. They trained a chimpanzee named Ayumu which performs well in the task. Subjects were required to touch the white squares in the original numerical order and Ayumu's performance was better than humans'.

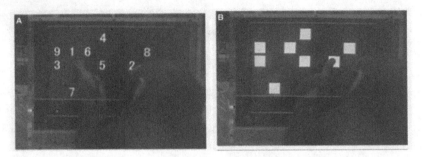

Fig. 8. Chimpanzee Ayumu performing the masking task [15]. (a) Ayumu touches the first number. (b) The remaining numbers are covered by white squares. (Color figure online)

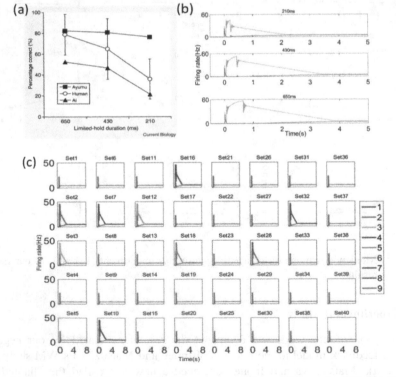

Fig. 9. (a) The results of Matsuzawa's chimpanzees on the masking tasks [15]. (b) Different mean firing rates of a component and memory maintenance times for different hold durations in the simulation. (c) The negative-derivative feedback model's stimulation during the 210 ms hold time.

Because of special trains, Ayumu broke throw the limit of WM capacity and could use more set to help accomplishing the "limited-hold memory task". For this task, Ayumu used forty neuron sets to encode the position, and nine components in each neuron set to encode the numbers. Figure 9a shows the experimental conditions. Figure 9b shows the mean firing rates of a component for different hold durations in the simulation. Figure 9c shows the mean firing rates of forty neuron sets during a 210 ms hold time. From the data, we can see that the memory of Ayumu was very clear at the beginning. As time went on, the memory became more and more confused and the accuracy declined. These results demonstrated that the performance of the negative-derivative feedback model closely simulated the performance of the Ayumu in Inoue and Matsuzawa's study.

5 Conclusion

In this paper, we suggested a new approach to studying the neural circuitry of WM based on a negative-derivative feedback mechanism. In our experiments, the computational negative-derivate feedback model duplicated the findings of Funahashi et al. [14] and Matsuzawa and Inouc [15] successfully, demonstrating that our proposed approach closely matched many characteristics of WM.

Our results showed that the memory storage sub-network can maintain memory and forget memory. The assistant sun-network can update memory and associate memory with the help of BG. In addition, our negative-derivative feedback model proved to be more robust to common parameter perturbations than previous models based on positive feedback alone. Our work provides a new approach to research WM.

Acknowledgments. This work was supported by the NSFC Project (Project Nos. 61771146 and 61375122), (in part) by Shanghai Science and Technology Development Funds (Project Nos. 13dz2260200, 13511504300).

References

1. Wei, H., Dai, D., Bu, Y.: A plausible neural circuit for decision making and its formation based on reinforcement learning. Cogn. Neurodyn. **11**(3), 259–281 (2017)
2. Wei, H., Bu, Y., Dai, D.: A decision-making model based on a spiking neural circuit and synaptic plasticity. Cogn. Neurodyn. **11**(5), 415–431 (2017)
3. Wang, Y., Wang, R., Zhu, Y.: Optimal path-finding through mental exploration based on neural energy field gradients. Cogn. Neurodyn. **11**(1), 99–111 (2017)
4. Jacobsen, C.F., Nissen, H.W.: Studies of cerebral function in primates. IV. The effects of frontal lobe lesions on the delayed alternation habit in monkeys. J. Comp. Psychol. **23**(1), 101 (1937)
5. Fuster, J.M., Alexander, G.E.: Neuron activity related to short-term memory. Science **173** (3997), 652–654 (1971)
6. Kubota, K., Niki, H.: Prefrontal cortical unit activity and delayed alternation performance in monkeys. J. Neurophysiol. **34**(3), 337–347 (1971)

7. Levitt, J.B., Lewis, D.A., Yoshioka, T., Lund, J.S.: Topography of pyramidal neuron intrinsic connections in macaque monkey prefrontal cortex (areas 9 and 46). J. Comp. Neurol. **338**(3), 360–376 (1993)
8. Pucak, M.L., Levitt, J.B., Lund, J.S., Lewis, D.A.: Patterns of intrinsic and associational circuitry in monkey prefrontal cortex. J. Comp. Neurol. **376**(4), 614–630 (1996)
9. Alexander, G.E., DeLong, M.R., Strick, P.L.: Parallel organization of functionally segregated circuits linking basal ganglia and cortex. Annu. Rev. Neurosci. **9**(1), 357–381 (1986)
10. Kriete, T., Noelle, D.C., Cohen, J.D., O'Reilly, R.C.: Indirection and symbol-like processing in the prefrontal cortex and basal ganglia. Proc. Nat. Acad. Sci. **110**(41), 16390–16395 (2013)
11. Compte, A., Brunel, N., Goldman-Rakic, P.S., Wang, X.J.: Synaptic mechanisms and network dynamics underlying spatial working memory in a cortical network model. Cereb. Cortex **10**(9), 910–923 (2000)
12. Rolls, E.T., Dempere-Marco, L., Deco, G.: Holding multiple items in short term memory: a neural mechanism. PLoS ONE **8**(4), e61078 (2013)
13. Lim, S., Goldman, M.S.: Balanced cortical microcircuitry for maintaining information in working memory. Nat. Neurosci. **16**(9), 1306 (2013)
14. Funahashi, S., Bruce, C.J., Goldman-Rakic, P.S.: Mnemonic coding of visual space in the monkey's dorsolateral prefrontal cortex. J. Neurophysiol. **61**(2), 331–349 (1989)
15. Inoue, S., Matsuzawa, T.: Working memory of numerals in chimpanzees. Curr. Biol. **17**(23), R1004–R1005 (2007)
16. Haider, B., McCormick, D.A.: Rapid neocortical dynamics: cellular and network mechanisms. Neuron **62**(2), 171–189 (2009)
17. Rotaru, D.C., Yoshino, H., Lewis, D.A., Ermentrout, G.B., Gonzalez-Burgos, G.: Glutamate receptor subtypes mediating synaptic activation of prefrontal cortex neurons: relevance for schizophrenia. J. Neurosci. **31**(1), 142–156 (2011)
18. Cowan, N.: Metatheory of storage capacity limits. Behav. Brain Sci. **24**(1), 154–176 (2001)

Learning Continuous Muscle Control for a Multi-joint Arm by Extending Proximal Policy Optimization with a Liquid State Machine

Juan Camilo Vasquez Tieck[1]([✉]), Marin Vlastelica Pogančić[1], Jacques Kaiser[1], Arne Roennau[1], Marc-Oliver Gewaltig[2], and Rüdiger Dillmann[1]

[1] FZI Research Center for Information Technology, 76131 Karlsruhe, Germany
tieck@fzi.de
[2] EPFL École polytechnique fédérale de Lausanne, BBP/HBP, Genève, Switzerland

Abstract. There have been many advances in the field of reinforcement learning in continuous control problems. Usually, these approaches use deep learning with artificial neural networks for approximation of policies and value functions. In addition, there have been interesting advances in spiking neural networks, towards a more biologically plausible model of the neurons and the learning mechanisms. We present an approach to learn continuous muscle control of a multi joint arm. We use reinforcement learning for a target reaching task, which can be modeled as partially observable markov decision processes. We extend proximal policy optimization with a liquid state machine (LSM) for state representation to achieve better performance in the target reaching task. The results show that we are able to learn to control the arm after training the readout of the LSM with reinforcement learning. The input current encoding used for encoding the state is enough to have a good projection into a higher dimensional space of the LSM. The results also show that we are able to learn a linear readout, which is equivalent to a one-layer neural network to learn to control the arm. We show that there are clear benefits of training the readouts of a LSM with reinforcement learning. These results can lead to demonstrate the benefits of using a LSM as a drop-in state transformation in general.

Keywords: Muscle control · Reinforcement learning
Reservoir computing · Neurorobotics · Spiking networks

1 Introduction

There have been many advances in the field of reinforcement learning in continuous control problems. Normally, these approaches use deep learning in artificial neural networks for approximation of policies and value functions [10,19]. Also,

© Springer Nature Switzerland AG 2018
V. Kůrková et al. (Eds.): ICANN 2018, LNCS 11139, pp. 211–221, 2018.
https://doi.org/10.1007/978-3-030-01418-6_21

in the biologically plausible counterpart there have been successes in using an actor-critic architecture with spiking neural networks on a toy-task [6] and discrete state-action spaces [15] where the actor and critic assume the role of the ventral and dorsal striatum, respectively.

The problem of reinforcement learning becomes more difficult when modeling partially observable Markov decision processes, where the state in which the process in is unknown, only partial information is given to the observer. This property motivates the use of stateful function approximators.

Liquid state machines [12] have been proven to be efficient in learning temporally correlated data in a supervised manner, where the internal connections are fixed [9] or trained [7], but there were no attempts that we know of to apply them to a reinforcement learning context. Furthermore, spiking neural network models [11] have an intrinsic memory property because of their activation function which is modeled by a first-order differential equation and therefore, they render themselves naturally to modeling temporally correlated data. The LSTMs are the go-to method for recurrent networks currently because they alleviate the vanishing gradient problem [8]. The problem is that one needs to train them by rolling out sequences and they are a purely engineered approach which doesnt have grounding in biology.

In this work we propose reinforcement learning on the readout as a method to alleviate the challenges of learning partially observable Markov decision processes. This work is based on [14], where a learning rule was proposed to adjust the readout in a reinforcement learning setting through a global reinforcement signal, but because of its online manner has shown instability in high-dimensional continuous control tasks on POMDPs. We make use of a well-known method of reducing the variance in the policy gradient [16] and show that we can even learn the readout of the LSM in the case of a pure linear approximation. We apply our findings to the task of continuous motor control on a musculo-skeletal model of the arm.

2   Methods

We present an approach to learn continuous muscle control for a multi-joint arm. The task consist in how to activate the muscles to move the arm to a given target and stay there. We understand the task as a partially observable markov decision process. Our approach combines three main components as illustrated in Fig. 1: the simulation of the musculoskeletal arm, an actor critic network, and a liquid state machine (LSM) [13].

The proprioception of the arm represents the state or observation. The LSM is used to create a temporal projection in a higher-dimensional space of the proprioceptive feedback.

To learn the correct stimuli for the muscles we use a variant of proximal policy optimization. This method allowed us to get a clear learning signal with a pessimistic estimate of the policy gradients lower-bound through likelihood ratio clipping. Essentially, for the policy we use a multivariate normal distribution

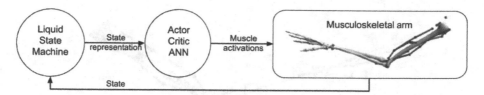

Fig. 1. General concept. An arm is simulated and controlled by six muscles. The state is described by the position, speed and acceleration of the joints. The state is transformed to a higher dimensional space with LSM. The output of the LSM is used to feed an actor critic ANN that generates the muscle activations.

$\mathcal{N}(\boldsymbol{\mu}, \sigma)$, where the vector $\boldsymbol{\mu}$ is estimated by a function approximator. In our case, we used an artificial neural network on top of a liquid state machine as a function approximator. To prevent high variance in the policy gradient, we used the surrogate objective function

$$\hat{E}[\min(r_t(\theta_\pi)\hat{A}_t, \text{clip}(1 - \epsilon, 1 + \epsilon, r_t(\theta_\pi)\hat{A}_t))] \tag{1}$$

as introduced in [16], which is effectively a pessimistic lower bound on the actual policy gradient. The ratio $r_t(\theta_\pi)$ is defined as

$$r_t(\theta_\pi) = \frac{\log \pi_\theta(a_t|s_t)}{\log \pi_{\theta_{\text{old}}}(a_t|s_t)}, \tag{2}$$

intuitively we can understand this as controlling the amount of change in the policy and increasing the objective for high likelihood actions. As proposed in the work of [16], we used the advantage function to control the bias of the critic with the parameter λ. The generalized advantage estimator is formulated as

$$\hat{A}_t = \sum_{l=0}^{\infty}(\gamma\lambda)^l \delta_{t+l}^V, \tag{3}$$

where $\delta_t^V = r_t + \gamma V(s_{t+1}) - V(s_t)$ is the TD residual for the state-value function. Generally we formulate the advantage as $\mathbb{E}[Q(s_t, a_t) - V(s_t)]$, what essentially signifies how the specific action is better that the average decision at state s_t. In our case we calculate the estimate $\hat{A}_t$ empirically after observing the proprioceptive feedback based on the consecutive stimuli and the value function estimate $\hat{V}$ by an estimator augmented with a liquid state machine.

2.1   Arm Model Description and Interface to the Muscles

The musculoskeletal arm is presented in Fig. 2 consists of a set of six muscles and a skeleton with two joints — the shoulder and the elbow. The network has to activate the muscles continuously to reach and maintain an specific target. The output and input interfaces to the arm are a state vector and the muscle activations. The feedback as observations from the arm model are the positions

Fig. 2. Musculoskeletal model of the arm. It has two degrees of freedom—shoulder and elbow—and six muscles controlling them. The simulation is made in OpenSim.

θ_i, angular velocities $\dot{\theta}_i$ and accelerations $\ddot{\theta}_i$ of the two joints, and the six muscle activations a_j.

$$state = [\theta_s, \theta_e, \dot{\theta}_s, \dot{\theta}_e, \ddot{\theta}_s, \ddot{\theta}_e, a_0, ..., a_5,] \qquad (4)$$

In our approach we normalized the arm state vector between -1 and 1, this was done by calculating the running mean and standard deviation of the observations. Neural stimuli between 0 and 1 are the inputs to the muscles.

The arm is simulated in OpenSim [4]. The model of the muscle used to move the arm is the Thelen model [17], which contains nonlinear dynamics for the tendons and activations. Concretely, the muscle activations are modeled by a first order differential equation. This results in temporally correlated observations from the arm model and therefore yields it self nicely to our use-case. We used the OpenAI gym [3] interface to connect to the OpenSim simulator based on the implementation of osim-rl[1].

2.2   ANN for Proximal Policy Optimization on the Readout

An actor critic ANN is used to learn the distribution parameters of the muscle activations. By training an actor-critic network on top of the liquid state machine we can approximate a multivariate gaussian distribution to model the policy for controlling the musculoskeletal arm [20].

Learning a multivariate gaussian process for muscle control appears to be hard with pure linear regression over the LSM, since the task is much harder than pure supervised learning. The network, presented in Fig. 3, is divided in two sub-networks one for the actor or the policy network and one for the critic or the value function. We use the LSM as a drop-in state transformation and the normalized firing rates of the LSM readout go as input for both sub-networks. This way we extend proximal policy optimization with a reservoir (the LSM).

The two networks consist of 3 layers each — $64 \times 64 \times 6$ neurons for the policy network and $64 \times 64 \times 1$ neurons for the value function network (see Fig. 3). All neurons have *tanh* activation functions, except for the output of the value function network which does not have an activation function but it is just a linear combination of the second layer. The standard deviation controls the exploration. It is a separate variable and is the same for every muscle in each

---

[1] https://github.com/stanfordnmbl/osim-rl/.

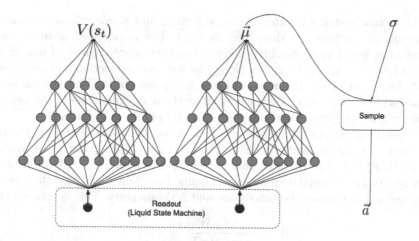

Fig. 3. The architecture of the ANN. There are two sub-networks, one for the policy and one for value function. The normalized output of the LSM is used as state representation for the ANN. The muscle activation is defined with the mean and the standard deviation.

timestep, it gets reduced based on the policy gradient, if the policy advances towards better rewards. The ANN is implemented in pytorch to perform the optimization of the read-out from the LSM. The LSM is wrapped as a module and integrated as a component.

2.3   LSM for State Representation

We use the LSM [13] as a drop-in state transformation. We modelled the LSM with an ensemble of leaky integrate-and-fire neurons. The LSM is in the end a temporal projection of the input states, so it is basically a feature extractor for the environment. Then the readout of the LSM is learned with proximal policy optimization i.e. the actor and the critic networks (see Fig. 4). The input of the

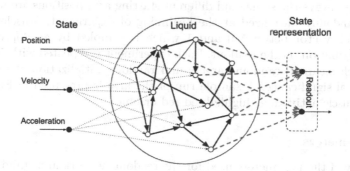

Fig. 4. The architecture of the LSM. The state is feed — dropped in — to different neurons in the liquid. Two readouts of the LSM are projected to the policy and value function networks (see Fig. 3).

LSM is a state vector with the angles, velocities and accelerations and muscle activations of the joints as described in Eq. 4. The normalized state vector is sent into the liquid state machine using a constant input current of magnitude between $[-1, 1]$, this is achieved in Nengo by a direct connection and setting the bias of the neurons to 0. The readout is the firing rates of the lsm neurons and is normalized between $[-1, 1]$. Because we draw the max firing rates of the neurons uniformly between $[min, max]$, the normalization is straight forward.

We used the Nengo [2] simulator which is based on the neural engineering framework [5] to implement the LSM. The LSM has 300 leaky integrate and fire neurons (LIF), using the default parameters from Nengo. The LSM is initialized with a spectral radius of 0.9 for all experiments. Based on [1] we used the spectral radius defined to control the echo state and LSM memory. This is achieved by

$$W = \frac{|eig(W)|}{max(|eig(W)|)} * sr, \tag{5}$$

where sr is the target spectral radius.

The connections are randomly initialized and inhibitory probability of 0.6, zero probability 0.07 and excitatory connection probability 0.33. With this probability setup, the activity can be kept from exploding and the activity from inhibitory connections are prevalent, preserving the echo state property [12,13]. Additionally, the dynamics of the LIF cannot be represented as simple matrix multiplication that setting the spectral radius alone is not enough to guarantee stability. The input weights are sampled from a uniform distribution between 0 and 5. We applied a noise current to the reservoir connections with mean 0 and standard deviation 1. The synapses withing the LSM are modelled as LTI filters. After sampling we divide weight matrix (inner connections) by the maximum absolute eigenvalue and multiply it by target radius.

3   Results

Given an initial position, the arm has to reach a target. For each experiment, the target is always the same, and different starting arm positions are used. The target is randomly initialized at the beginning of experiment. Muscles receive an activation vector between 0 and 1 which is sampled by an approximated normal distribution on the readout. Each experiment is repeated with 5 random seeds, which means 5 random targets and random initialization of the model for statistical significance. A sample run of the arm is presented in Fig. 5 with different muscle activations highlighted red or blue.

3.1   Parameters

A summary of the parameters used for the readout network are: standard deviation separate variable, policy = $[64 \times 64 \times 6]$, value = $[64 \times 64 \times 1]$, tanh activation functions to squash the output between -1 and 1, then output is fitted between 0 and 1.

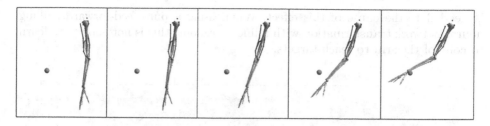

Fig. 5. Frame sequence of the arm movement with different muscle activations. After training, the network can activate the muscles to reach a target — the green ball — and maintain the activation to stay there. (Color figure online)

A summary of the parameters used for the proximal policy optimization algorithm are: $\lambda = 0.95$, $\gamma = 0.99$, epsilon (likelihood ratio clipping) 0.2, advantage estimation rollout 1024 steps, number of horizon steps 500 (seed from the graphs), the standard deviation is initialized to 1 at the beginning of training, we estimate the advantage for timestep t only based on the state transitions from within the same episode, if the length of the rollout is greater than the length of the episode, then to calculate the advantage for, state s_t, we take into consideration only the transitions that happened within the same episode for this, specific advantage calculation.

A summary of the parameters used for the LSM are: $synapse\_tau = 15e^{-4}$, $p_{inh} = 0.6$, $p_{zero} = 0.07$, $p_{exc} = 0.33$, $spectral\_radius = 0.0$, $reservoir\_neurons = 300$, for one osim simulation step $time\_step = 10e^{-3}$ and $simulation\_step\_size = 2e^{-3}$, max firing rate of neurons sampled between $[100, 500]$. Since the simulation time for the LSM for one step is equal to 10e-3 seconds and the episode length for the reaching task is equal to 200 steps, then in simulation time that means that the arm has 2 seconds to execute the reaching.

We ran experiments initialized with five different random seeds for each model. We sampled the target positions uniformly based on the random seeds. Sampling code for the targets:

```
theta = random.uniform(math.pi*9/8, math.pi*12/8)
radius = random.uniform(0.5, 0.65)
self.target_x = math.cos(theta) * radius
self.target_y = math.sin(theta) * radius
```

3.2 Average Reward and Policy Entropy

From Fig. 6 we can see that the approach of using a linear model for the policy under performs in comparison to even a random uniform policy, which effectively holds the arm at one position. Faster convergence to the solution is achieved with using less parameters on the readout and is comparable to the performance when using a multi-layer artificial neural network. The policy learned on the linear readout also shows less variance during fitting, but more investigation is needed to the cause of this effect. When using a pure feed-forward spiking neural network transformation with a linear readout, this is not enough to learn to control the arm to reach targets.

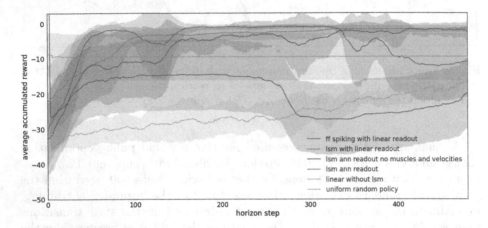

Fig. 6. Average reward. The figure shows the moving average over the last 100 episodes of the accumulated reward during the episode. A horizon step consists of doing an environment rollout with the policy for advantage estimation, we used the 1024 steps for advantage estimation. Each episode has a 200 step length for the reaching task. It can be seen that the linear readout performs comparably to the multilayer ANN readout, and favorably to not using the LSM, or using a feed-forward spiking net.

The policy entropy decreases because the policy advances towards better rewards, this is true for all cases except for the case of the feed-forward spiking transformation with linear readout (see Fig. 7). The projection in this case is not good enough to learn with a linear readout layer, therefore the policy remains in a constant state of exploration — yellow line in the figure - remains horizontal. Also the entropy decreases faster for higher capacity models on the readout - this one I am not sure how to explain correctly, probably because the solution space is bigger because of the increased capacity of the models, but the multilayer ann model is also more sensitive to small perturbations, which is why there is high variance in the end of the avg reward figure (the purple line).

3.3   Muscle Activations and Spike Activity

In Fig. 8 we highlight the relation between muscle activations and the LSM spike activity. We show the activity of three of the muscles together with the spike output of the 300 neurons in the LSM.

From Fig. 8 we can see that muscle stimuli to control the arm mostly vary between no stimuli and high stimuli, and some of the muscles receive stimuli more often than others. This learned behavior can be attributed to the temporally correlated nature of muscle activations.

We also noticed that in the development of the readout weights there is redundancy in the LSM neurons associated to one muscle. This implicates that a further parameter reduction could be done on the readout of the LSM. The training process could be simplified by learning the same problem with less neurons.

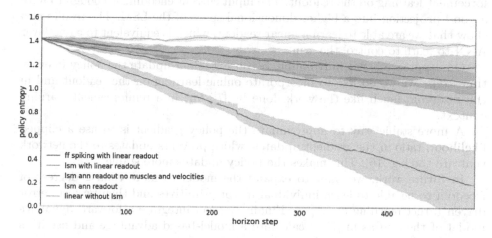

Fig. 7. Policy entropy. It is clear that the entropy decreases monotonically. This is in all of the cases accept feed-forward spiking with linear readout, you can see that the entropy remains high because there is no clear learning signal, i.e. high variance in the policy gradient (Color figure online)

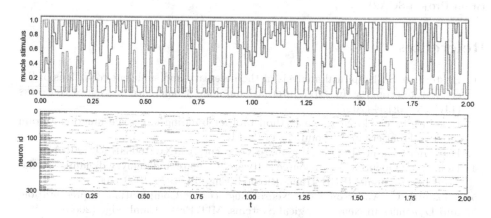

Fig. 8. (A) Muscle activation during the target reaching motion. (B) Neural activity in the 300 neurons in the LSM during the target reaching motion.

4 Discussion

The main contribution of this work is reinforcement learning of partially observable markov decision processes on the readout layer of the liquid state machine.

We extend proximal policy optimization with a reservoir (the LSM) to achieve better results in the target reaching task. We showed that there are clear benefits of reinforcement learning on the readout of a LSM. We currently work towards proving the benefits as using LSM as a drop-in state transformation in general.

The results show that we are able to learn to control the arm through reinforcement learning on the readout. The input current encoding is enough to have a good projection into a higher dimensional space of the LSM. The results also show that we are able to learn a linear readout, which is equivalent to a one-layer ANN to learn to control the arm.

Our approach is not fully online, because we dont update the policy in every time step. We would like to incorporate online learning on the readout and in the reservoir, much like the work done by [7], but in a reinforcement learning context.

A more stable way to approximate the policy gradient is to use a clipped likelihood ratio in the gradient updates, which prevents updates to the network that are too big [16]. This makes the policy updates more stable.

In future work, we want to expand the model to more than 2 degrees of freedom to be able to learn individual motor primitives and then perform error driven target reaching as in [18]. Finally, we can integrate a forward dynamics model of the arm as in [7] to calculate a model-based advantage and use it as bias to guide the policy gradient.

Acknowledgments. This research has received funding from the European Union's Horizon 2020 Framework Programme for Research and Innovation under the Specific Grant Agreement No. 720270 (Human Brain Project SGA1) and No. 785907 (Human Brain Project SGA2).

References

1. Basterrech, S.: Empirical analysis of the necessary and sufficient conditions of the echo state property. In: 2017 International Joint Conference on Neural Networks (IJCNN). IEEE (2017)
2. Bekolay, T., et al.: Nengo: a Python tool for building largescale functional brain models. Frontiers in Neuroinf. **7**, 48 (2014)
3. Brockman, G., et al.: Openai gym. arXiv preprint arXiv:1606.01540 (2016)
4. Delp, S.L.: OpenSim: open-source software to create and analyze dynamic simulations of movement. IEEE Trans. Biomed. Eng. **54**, 1940–1950 (2007)
5. Eliasmith, C., Anderson, C.H.: Neural Engineering: Computation, Representation, and Dynamics in Neurobiological Systems. MIT Press, Cambridge (2003)
6. Frémaux, N., Sprekeler, H., Gerstner, W.: Reinforcement learning using a continuous time actor-critic framework with spiking neurons. PLoS Comput. Biol. **9**, c1003024 (2013)
7. Gilra, A., Gerstner, W.: Predicting non-linear dynamics by stable local learning in a recurrent spiking neural network. Elife **6**, e28295 (2017)
8. Hochreiter, S., Schmidhuber, J.: Long short-term memory. Neural Comput. **9**(8), 1735–1780 (1997)

9. Kaiser, J., Stal, R., Subramoney, A., Roennau, A., Dillmann, R.: Scaling up liquid state machines to predict over address events from dynamic vision sensors. Bioinspir. Biomimet. **12**, 055001 (2017)
10. Lillicrap, T.P., et al.: Continuous control with deep reinforcement learning. arXiv preprint arXiv:1509.02971 (2015)
11. Maass, W.: Networks of spiking neurons: the third generation of neural network models. Neural Netw. **10**, 1659–1671 (1997)
12. Maass, W., Markram, H.: On the computational power of circuits of spiking neurons. J. Comput. Syst. Sci. **69**, 593–616 (2004)
13. Maass, W., Natschläger, T., Markram, H.: Real-time computing without stable states: a new framework for neural computation based on perturbations. Neural Comput. **14**, 2531–2560 (2002)
14. Pogančić, M.V.: Learning multi-joint continuous control with spiking neural networks. Master's thesis, KIT Department of Computer Science Institute for Anthropomatics and FZI Research Center for Information Technology, July 2017
15. Potjans, W., Morrison, A., Diesmann, M.: A spiking neural network model of an actor-critic learning agent. Neural Comput. **21**, 301–339 (2009)
16. Schulman, J., Wolski, F., Dhariwal, P., Radford, A., Klimov, O.: Proximal policy optimization algorithms. arXiv preprint arXiv:1707.06347 (2017)
17. Thelen, D.G.: Adjustment of muscle mechanics model parameters to simulate dynamic contractions in older adults. J. Biomech. Eng. **125**(1), 70–77 (2003)
18. Tieck, J.C.V., Steffen, L., Kaiser, J., Roennau, A., Dillmann, R.: Controlling a robot arm for target reaching without planning combining motor primitives with spiking neurons. In: ICCI*CC (2018, accepted)
19. Wang, Z., et al.: Sample efficient actor-critic with experience replay. arXiv preprint arXiv:1611.01224 (2016)
20. Williams, R.J.: Simple statistical gradient-following algorithms for connectionist reinforcement learning. Reinf. Learn. **8**, 229–256 (1992)

A Supervised Multi-spike Learning Algorithm for Recurrent Spiking Neural Networks

Xianghong Lin[✉] and Guoyong Shi

College of Computer Science and Engineering, Northwest Normal University,
Lanzhou 730070, China
linxh@nwnu.edu.cn

Abstract. The recurrent spiking neural networks include complex structures and implicit nonlinear mechanisms, the formulation of efficient supervised learning algorithm is difficult and remains an important problem in the research area. This paper proposes a new supervised multi-spike learning algorithm for recurrent spiking neural networks, which can implement the complex spatiotemporal pattern learning of spike trains. Using information encoded in precisely timed spike trains and their inner product operators, the error function is firstly constructed. Furthermore, the proposed algorithm defines the learning rules of synaptic weights based on inner product of spike trains. The algorithm is successfully applied to learn spike train patterns, and the high learning accuracy and efficiency are shown by the experimental results. In addition, the network structure parameters are analyzed, such as the neuron number and connectivity degree in the recurrent layer of spiking neural networks.

Keywords: Recurrent spiking neural networks · Supervised learning
Spike train inner product · Connectivity degree

1 Introduction

Spiking neural networks (SNNs) are the third generation artificial neural networks, which are biologically-inspired computational models and more efficient for spatiotemporal information processing than the traditional neural networks [1, 2]. In the networks of spiking neurons, the neural information is represented by the precisely timed spike trains, the purpose of supervised learning of SNNs is to make the neurons emit desired spike trains in response to given synaptic inputs. At present, researchers have proposed many supervised learning algorithms for SNNs, but many problems remain unsolved [3]. Recurrent spiking neural networks (RSNNs) have feedback loop structures, and can be used to solve a variety of difficult problems, such as robot control [4], olfactory pattern recognition [5], character recognition [6] and so on. However, due to the complex recurrent structures and intricately discontinuous, it is difficult to analyze and construct an efficient learning algorithm for RSNNs.

There are two classical supervised learning algorithms of traditional artificial recurrent neural networks, namely, real-time recurrent learning (RTRL) algorithm [7] and back propagation through time (BPTT) algorithm [8]. The characteristics of the

V. Kůrková et al. (Eds.): ICANN 2018, LNCS 11139, pp. 222–234, 2018.
https://doi.org/10.1007/978-3-030-01418-6_22

RTRL and BPTT algorithms are recurrent computation of error gradient for analog outputs. For RSNNs, the neural inputs and outputs are represented by the spike trains, so the internal state variables of neurons and the error function no longer satisfy the properties of continuous differentiability. Consequently, the supervised learning algorithms, such as RTRL and BPTT, cannot be used directly for RSNNs.

In earlier research, the researchers put forward the learning method based on the sensitivity equations, and realize the learning of synaptic weights for the recurrent networks with integrate-and-fire type spiking neurons [9, 10]. Tiňo and Mills extend the gradient-based SpikeProp algorithm for training feedforward spiking neuron networks, and proposed the learning algorithm for recurrent spiking network topologies [11]. In addition, the recent researches on RSNNs algorithm innovation and performance optimization have also made some breakthroughs and achievements [12–15]. Diehl et al. [14] presented a train-and-constrain method to enable the mapping of machine learned recurrent neural networks on a substrate of spiking neurons. Gilra and Gerstner [15] presented a supervised learning scheme for the feedforward and recurrent SNNs of heterogeneous spiking neurons. However, these methods above are lack of in-depth analysis for spike train coding of neural information and internal feedback mechanism of neural networks, so it is need to develop the general framework of supervised learning for RSNNs.

For RSNNs, input and output information is encoded through precisely timed spike trains, not only through the neural firing rate. In this paper, using a novel error function of spike trains and the feedback mechanism, a supervised multi-spike learning algorithm for RSNNs is presented based on inner product operators of spike trains, which can improve the capability for solving complex spatio-temporal pattern learning problems. The rest of this paper is organized as follows. In Sect. 2 we introduce the structure of RSNNs, spike train inner product definition and its transformation relation. In Sect. 3 we deduce the learning rules of synaptic weights in different layers based on the error function. In Sect. 4 we mainly carry out the experiments of spike train learning and analyze the experimental results. The conclusions are presented in Sect. 5.

2   Network Structure and Spike Train Transformation

2.1   The Structure of RSNNs

The multi-layer spiking neural network with recurrent structure is used in this paper, the network is structured in three layers, consisting of N_I input neurons, N_R hidden neurons (or recurrent neurons) and N_O output neurons, respectively. The connectivity structure of RSNNs is shown in Fig. 1. There is a feedforward full connectivity between the input layer and the hidden layer (or recurrent layer), the same is true for the connectivity between the hidden layer and the output layer. In addition, the neurons in the hidden layer are recurrently connected. A connectivity degree (C_d) is applied in the hidden layer and the recurrent connection is represented by the dotted line in Fig. 1.

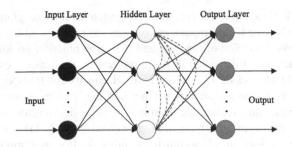

Fig. 1. The structure of RSNNs

The RSNNs structure, as described above, it is hard to construct the supervised learning algorithm. For convenience of description, the recurrent layer is copied to form the context layer, which is introduced to convert the RSNN to an equivalent feedforward structure, as shown in Fig. 2.

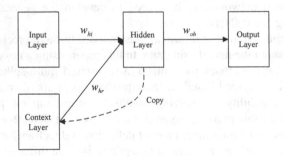

Fig. 2. The converted RSNNs with context layer

2.2 Spike Train Transformation Relationship

The discrete spikes are used to form a spike train. Therefore, it is assumed that the discrete spikes are generated by a spiking neuron in the time interval $\Gamma = [0, T]$, and then spike train $s = \{t^f \in \Gamma, f = 1, \ldots, F\}$ can be formally represented as:

$$s(t) = \sum_{f=1}^{F} \delta(t - t^f) \tag{1}$$

where F is the number of spikes, $\delta(\cdot)$ represents the Dirac delta function, $\delta(t) = 1$ if $t = 0$ and $\delta(t) = 0$ otherwise.

In order to facilitate calculation, it is necessary to transform discrete spike train into a continuous function. We can choose a specific smoothing function h, the convolution of spike train s is represented as:

$$f_s(t) = s * h = \sum_{f=1}^{F} h(t - t^f) \tag{2}$$

Through the convolution calculation, the spike train can be interpreted as a specific neural physiological signal, such as neuronal postsynaptic potential or spike firing intensity function. Using Eq. (2), we can define the inner product of spike trains s_i and s_j on the $L_2(\Gamma)$ space as follows [16]:

$$F(s_i, s_j) = \langle f_{s_i}, f_{s_j} \rangle_{L_2(\Gamma)} = \sum_{m=1}^{F_i} \sum_{n=1}^{F_j} \int_{\Gamma} h(t - t_i^m) \, h(t - t_j^n) \, dt = \sum_{m=1}^{F_i} \sum_{n=1}^{F_j} \kappa(t_i^m, t_j^n) \tag{3}$$

where kernel function κ is the autocorrelation of the smoothing function h, $k(t^m, t^n) = \int_{\Gamma} h(t - t^m) h(t - t^n) \, dt$.

A single neuron outputs a spike train s_o in response to its presynaptic input spike trains s_i. In order to establish the relationship between the input and output spike trains, we start from the linear Poisson neuron model in continuous time. The instantaneous spike firing intensity of a neuron o is determined by the instantaneous spike firing intensity of its presynaptic neurons i:

$$f_{s_o}(t) - \sum_{i=1}^{N} w_{oi} f_{s_i}(t) \tag{4}$$

where N is the number of presynaptic neurons, w_{oi} represents the synaptic weight between the presynaptic neuron i and the postsynaptic neuron o. The simplified linear summation of smoothed spike trains will be used for the derivation of the corresponding learning rule, in accordance with the preliminary results reported in [17, 18].

3   Supervised Multi-spike Learning Algorithm

Supervised learning in RSNNs involves a mechanism of providing the desired output spike trains with a given set of multiple input spike trains. And then errors are calculated to control the synaptic weight adjustment.

Supposed that s_o^a is the spike train of actual output and s_o^d is the desired one. The instantaneous network error is formally defined in terms of the square difference between the corresponding continuous functions $f_{s_o^a}(t)$ and $f_{s_o^d}(t)$ at time t for all output neurons. It can be represented as:

$$E(t) = \frac{1}{2} \sum_{o=1}^{N_o} \left[f_{s_o^a}(t) - f_{s_o^d}(t) \right]^2 \tag{5}$$

From Eqs. (3) and (5), the total error of the network in the time interval Γ is:

$$E = \int_\Gamma E(t)dt = \frac{1}{2}\sum_{o=1}^{N_o}\int_\Gamma \left[f_{s_o^a}(t) - f_{s_o^d}(t)\right]^2 dt = \frac{1}{2}\sum_{o=1}^{N_o}\left\langle f_{s_o^a}(t) - f_{s_o^d}(t), f_{s_o^a}(t) - f_{s_o^d}(t)\right\rangle$$

$$= \frac{1}{2}\sum_{o=1}^{N_o}\left[F(s_o^a, s_o^a) - 2F(s_o^a, s_o^d) + F(s_o^d, s_o^d)\right] \qquad (6)$$

Thus, the error function of output spiking neurons can be transformed into the inner products of spike trains.

Using error backpropagation for adjusting synaptic weights, the generalized delta update rule is employed to backpropagate the network error and modify the synaptic weights. The synaptic weight w from the presynaptic neuron to the postsynaptic neuron is computed as follows:

$$\Delta w = -\eta \nabla E \qquad (7)$$

where η is the learning rate, and ∇E is the gradient of the error function to synaptic weight w. The gradient computation is:

$$\nabla E = \int_\Gamma \frac{\partial E(t)}{\partial w} dt \qquad (8)$$

According to the structure of RSNNs, synaptic weight learning rules can be divided into the output layer, context layer and input layer.

3.1 Learning Rule of Synaptic Weights in Output Layer

From Eq. (8), the error gradient is represented by ∇E_{oh} between the output layer and the hidden layer, and it can expressed formally as:

$$\nabla E_{oh} = \int_\Gamma \frac{\partial E(t)}{\partial w_{oh}} dt \qquad (9)$$

where $\partial E(t)/\partial w_{oh}$ can be computed by chain rule:

$$\frac{\partial E(t)}{\partial w_{oh}} = \frac{\partial E(t)}{\partial f_{s_o^a}(t)} \frac{\partial f_{s_o^a}(t)}{\partial w_{oh}} \qquad (10)$$

Then, we compute the first term of the right-hand part of the Eq. (10):

$$\frac{\partial E(t)}{\partial f_{s_o^a}(t)} = f_{s_o^a}(t) - f_{s_o^d}(t) \qquad (11)$$

The second partial derivative term of the right-hand part of Eq. (10) is computed from Eq. (4):

$$\frac{\partial f_{s_o^a}(t)}{\partial w_{oh}} = f_{s_h}(t) \tag{12}$$

From Eqs. (11) and (12), the derivative of the error function $E(t)$ at time t to the hidden neurons becomes:

$$\nabla E_{oh} = \int_{\Gamma} f_{s_h}(t) \left[f_{s_o^a}(t) - f_{s_o^d}(t) \right] dt = \left\langle f_{s_o^a}(t), f_{s_h}(t) \right\rangle - \left\langle f_{s_o^d}(t), f_{s_h}(t) \right\rangle \tag{13}$$
$$= F(s_o^a, s_h) - F(s_o^d, s_h)$$

Therefore, the new learning rule based on the inner products of spike trains is obtained. The adjustment rule of synaptic weight between a neuron o in the output layer and a neuron h in the hidden layer is:

$$\Delta w_{oh} = -\eta \left[F(s_o^a, s_h) - F(s_o^d, s_h) \right] = \eta \left[\sum_{m=1}^{F_o^d} \sum_{n=1}^{F_h} \kappa(t_d^m, t_h^n) - \sum_{m=1}^{F_o^a} \sum_{n=1}^{F_h} \kappa(t_a^m, t_h^n) \right] \tag{14}$$

where F_o^a and F_o^d represent the number of spikes in the actual spike train and the number of spikes in the desired spike train respectively.

3.2 Learning Rule of Synaptic Weights in Context Layer

As shown by structure of RSNNs, the spike trains entered into the hidden layer comes from the input layer and the context layer, which can be obtained according to Eq. (4):

$$f_{s_h}(t) = \sum_{i=1}^{N_I} f_{s_i}(t) w_{hi} + \sum_{r=1}^{N_R} f_{s_r}(t) w_{hr} \tag{15}$$

where N_I and N_R represent the numbers of neurons in the input layer and the context layer, respectively.

The error gradient is represented by $\nabla E_{hr} = \int_{\Gamma} \partial E(t)/\partial w_{hr} dt$ between the hidden layer and the context layer, and then its computation is analogous to ∇E_{oh}. Using the chain rule we can obtain:

$$\frac{\partial E(t)}{\partial w_{hr}} = \frac{\partial E(t)}{\partial f_{s_h}(t)} \frac{\partial f_{s_h}(t)}{\partial w_{hr}} \tag{16}$$

Thus, the first term $\partial E(t)/\partial f_{s_h}(t)$ of the right-hand part of Eq. (16) is computed as:

$$\frac{\partial E(t)}{\partial f_{s_h}(t)} = \sum_{o=1}^{N_o} \frac{\partial E(t)}{\partial f_{s_o^a}(t)} \frac{\partial f_{s_o^a}(t)}{\partial f_{s_h}(t)} \tag{17}$$

Considering the recurrent connectivity of recurrent layer, $\partial f_{s_o^a}(t)/\partial f_{s_h}(t)$ is be computed as:

$$\frac{\partial f_{s_o^a}(t)}{\partial f_{s_h}(t)} = w_{oh} + \sum_{r=1}^{N_R} w_{hr} w_{or} \tag{18}$$

By combining Eqs. (11) and (18), Eq. (17) is rewritten as:

$$\frac{\partial E(t)}{\partial f_{s_h}(t)} = \sum_{o=1}^{N_o} \left[f_{s_o^a}(t) - f_{s_o^d}(t) \right] \left(w_{oh} + \sum_{r=1}^{N_R} w_{hr} w_{or} \right) \tag{19}$$

The second partial derivative term $\partial f_{s_h}(t)/\partial w_{hr}$ of the right-hand part of Eq. (16) is computed from Eq. (15):

$$\frac{\partial f_{s_h}(t)}{\partial w_{hr}} = f_{s_r}(t) \tag{20}$$

From Eqs. (19) and (20), the derivative of the error function $E(t)$ at time t to the hidden weight becomes:

$$\nabla E_{hr} = \int_\Gamma \frac{\partial E(t)}{\partial f_{s_h}(t)} \frac{\partial f_{s_h}(t)}{\partial w_{hr}} dt = \sum_{o=1}^{N_o} \int_\Gamma \left[f_{s_o^a}(t) - f_{s_o^d}(t) \right] \left(w_{oh} + \sum_{r=1}^{N_R} w_{hr} w_{or} \right) f_{s_r}(t) \, dt \tag{21}$$

The adjustment rule of synaptic weight between a neuron h in the hidden layer and a neuron r in the context layer is:

$$\Delta w_{hr} = -\eta \sum_{o=1}^{N_o} \left[F(s_o^a, s_r) - F(s_o^d, s_r) \right] \left(w_{oh} + \sum_{r=1}^{N_R} w_{hr} w_{or} \right)$$

$$= \eta \sum_{o=1}^{N_o} \left[\sum_{m=1}^{F_o^d} \sum_{n=1}^{F_r} \kappa(t_d^m, t_r^n) - \sum_{m=1}^{F_o^a} \sum_{n=1}^{F_r} \kappa(t_a^m, t_r^n) \right] \left(w_{oh} + \sum_{r=1}^{N_R} w_{hr} w_{or} \right) \tag{22}$$

3.3   Learning Rule of Synaptic Weights in Input Layer

The error gradient is represented by ∇E_{hi} between the hidden layer and the input layer, and its solution is analogous to ∇E_{hr}. Thus, the partial derivative term $\partial f_{s_h}(t)/\partial w_{hi}$ is computed from Eq. (15):

$$\frac{\partial f_{s_h}(t)}{\partial w_{hi}} = f_{s_i}(t) \tag{23}$$

From Eqs. (19) and (23), the derivative of the error function $E(t)$ at time t to the input weight becomes:

$$\nabla E_{hi} = \int_{\Gamma} \frac{\partial E(t)}{\partial f_{s_h}(t)} \frac{\partial f_{s_h}(t)}{\partial w_{hi}} \, dt = \sum_{o=1}^{N_o} \int_{\Gamma} \left[f_{s_o^a}(t) - f_{s_o^d}(t) \right] \left(w_{oh} + \sum_{r=1}^{N_R} w_{hr} w_{or} \right) f_{s_i}(t) \, dt$$

(24)

The adjustment rule of synaptic weight between a neuron h in the hidden layer and a neuron i in the input layer is:

$$\Delta w_{hi} = -\eta \sum_{o=1}^{N_o} \left[F(s_o^a, s_i) - F(s_o^d, s_i) \right] \left(w_{oh} + \sum_{r=1}^{N_R} w_{hr} w_{or} \right)$$

$$= \eta \sum_{o=1}^{N_o} \left[\sum_{m=1}^{F_o^d} \sum_{n=1}^{F_i} \kappa(t_d^m, t_i^n) - \sum_{m=1}^{F_o^a} \sum_{n=1}^{F_i} \kappa(t_a^m, t_i^n) \right] \left(w_{oh} + \sum_{r=1}^{N_R} w_{hr} w_{or} \right)$$

(25)

To sum up, the learning rules of synaptic weights in each layer are given. Specifically, the output layer is shown by Eq. (14), besides, the context layer and the input layer are respectively represented by Eqs. (22) and (25).

4 Experiments and Results

In this section, we demonstrate the learning ability of the proposed supervised multi-spike learning algorithm for RSNNs. At first, the algorithm is applied to test the learning performance of spike trains, by using its own initial parameters and analyzing the parameters which include the length and frequency of the desired output spike trains. Furthermore, we analyze the neuron number and connectivity degree in the recurrent layer of network structure. At the same time, when one parameter is analyzed, all other parameters remain unchanged.

4.1 Neuron Model and Parameter Settings

In this experiment, the short-term memory spike response model (SRM) [19] is used as a neuron model and the parameters are: the constant of time decay for spike response function is 7 ms, the time decay constant of refractoriness function is 80 ms, while the absolute refractory period is 1 ms and the neuron threshold is 1.0. The initial parameter settings in network structure for RSNNs are: the number of input neurons, hidden neurons are the same, which is $N_I = N_R = 100$, and number of output neurons $N_O = 1$. Initially, the weights of neuron synapses are uniformly distributed in the interval (0, 0.2). In addition, the connectivity degree $C_d = 0.5$ in the hidden layer.

The spike trains which include the actual inputs and desired outputs are generated by the Poisson process, each with a rate of $r_i = 20$ Hz and $r_d = 50$ Hz in the time interval of [0, T], and we set $T = 100$ ms here. Furthermore, the Gaussian kernel

$\kappa(x, y) = \exp(-|x - y|^2/2\sigma^2)$ is applied in inner product computation of spike trains. The learning rate is 0.001 and the time step is 0.1. At last, the results are averaged over 50 trials, and on each testing trail the learning algorithm is applied for a maximum of 200 learning epochs or until the network error $E = 0$.

4.2 Spike Train Learning Performance

Figure 3 shows the learning process of the supervised multi-spike learning algorithm. Figure 3(a) shows the complete learning process, which includes the initial output spike train, the desired output spike train and the actual output spike trains. From the result, we can know that it is to derive the desired output spike train from the initial output spike train by supervised learning about 100 epochs. The evolution process of the total network error in the time interval T is represented in Fig. 3(b). The error function value decreases rapidly at the beginning of the learning process, and it is reduced to 0 after 100 learning epochs. In other words, the actual output spike train is equals to desired spike train.

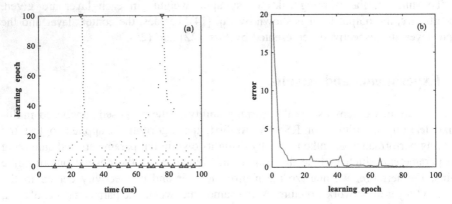

Fig. 3. The learning process of supervised multi-spike learning algorithm for RSNNs. (a) The complete learning process. Δ, initial actual output spike train; ∇, desired output spike train; $\cdot$, actual output spike train at some learning epochs. (b) The evolution of the network error.

Figure 4 shows the learning results with different lengths of desired output spike trains. Figure 4(a) illustrates that the algorithm can learn with high accuracy when the length of the desired output spike trains is 100 ms, and the error shows a significant increasing trend when the length of spike train increases. From Fig. 4(b) we can see that the learning epoch number of the algorithm are about 100 epochs on average. This is because when the length of desired output spike trains increases, the learning accuracy of the algorithm decreases.

Figure 5 shows the learning results with different frequencies of desired output spike trains. Figure 5(a) illustrates that the algorithm can learn with high accuracy when the frequency of the desired output spike trains is 50 Hz, and the error shows a

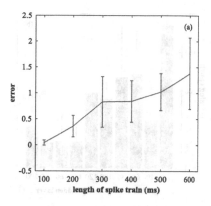
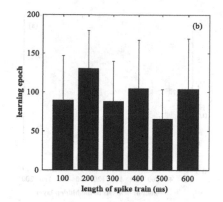

Fig. 4. The learning results with different lengths of desired output spike trains after 200 learning epochs. (a) The network error. (b) The learning epochs when the error reaches the minimum error.

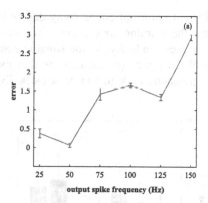
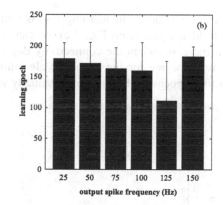

Fig. 5. The learning results with different frequencies of desired output spike trains after 200 learning epochs. (a) The network error. (b) The learning epochs when the error reaches the minimum error.

significant increasing trend when the desired output spike frequency increases. From Fig. 5(b) we can see that the learning epochs of the algorithm are relatively stable.

4.3 Network Structure Change and Analysis

In this section, the learning performance of spike trains is analyzed by changing the network structure, which includes the neuron number and connectivity degree in the recurrent layer (or hidden layer) of RSNNs.

Figure 6 shows the learning results with different numbers of neurons in the hidden layer. Figure 6(a) shows that the learning error tends to decrease firstly and then increase gradually with the increase of the number of neurons. From Fig. 6(b) we can see that the learning epochs of the algorithm tend to decrease gradually with the increase of the neuron numbers.

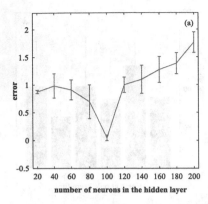 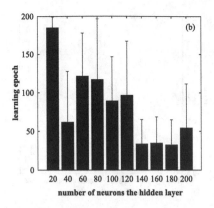

Fig. 6. The learning results with different numbers of neurons in the hidden layer after 200 learning epochs. (a) The network error. (b) The learning epochs when the error reaches the minimum error.

Figure 7 shows the learning results with different values of connectivity degree in the hidden layer. From Fig. 7(a) we can see that the learning error decreases at first, then increases when the connectivity degree increases gradually, so the suitable connectivity degree for the proposed algorithm is 0.5. Figure 7(b) we can see that the learning epochs tend to increase gradually when connectivity degree increases steadily.

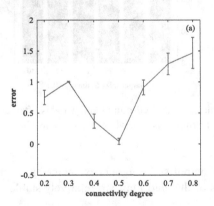 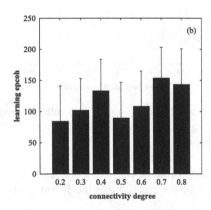

Fig. 7. The learning results with different values of connectivity degree in the hidden layer after 200 learning epochs. (a) The network error. (b) The learning epochs when the error reaches the minimum error.

5 Conclusions

In this paper, we present a new supervised multi-spike learning algorithm based on spike train inner product operators for RSNNs. The inner product of spike trains is used to construct the error function and deduce the learning rules for different layers of recurrent networks. The algorithm is tested on different learning processes, such as the learning performance of spike trains and the analysis of network structure change which includes the neuron number and connectivity degree in the recurrent layer. The experimental results show that the proposed algorithm has the high accuracy and efficiency for learning spike train patterns. In addition, the synaptic weight learning rule is based on the difference of inner products of spike trains, which can be applied to any neuron model, and neurons firing multiple spikes in all layers.

Acknowledgment. The research is supported by the National Natural Science Foundation of China under Grants nos. 61762080, and the Medium and Small Scale Enterprises Technology Innovation Foundation of Gansu Province under Grant no. 17CX2JA038.

References

1. Ghosh-Dastidar, S., Adeli, H.: Spiking neural networks. Int. J. Neural Syst. **19**(4), 295–308 (2009)
2. Adnanshiltagh, N.: Recurrent spiking neural networks the third generation in identification of systems. Int. J. Comput. Appl. **88**(1), 40–43 (2014)
3. Lin, X., Wang, X., Zhang, N., et al.: Supervised learning algorithms for spiking neural networks: a review. Acta Electron. Sin. **43**(3), 577–586 (2015)
4. Woo, J., Botzheim, J., Kubota, N.: Emotional empathy model for robot partners using recurrent spiking neural network model with Hebbian-LMS learning. Malays. J. Comput. Sci. **30**(4), 258–285 (2017)
5. Allen, J.N., Abdel-Aty-Zohdy, H.S., Ewing, R.L.: Plasticity recurrent spiking neural networks for olfactory pattern recognition. In: Midwest Symposium on Circuits and Systems, pp. 1741–1744. IEEE (2005)
6. Shen, J., Lin, K., Wang, Y., et al.: Character recognition from trajectory by recurrent spiking neural networks. In: The 39th Annual International Conference of the IEEE Engineering in Medicine and Biology Society, pp. 2900–2903. IEEE (2017)
7. Smith, A.W., Zipser, D.: Learning sequential structure with the real-time recurrent learning algorithm. Int. J. Neural Syst. **1**(2), 125–131 (2011)
8. Werbos, P.J.: Backpropagation through time: what it does and how to do it. Proc. IEEE **78** (10), 1550–1560 (1990)
9. Selvaratnam, K., Kuroe, Y., Mori, T.: Learning methods of recurrent spiking neural networks-transient and oscillatory spike trains. Trans. Inst. Syst. Control Inf. Eng. **13**(3), 95–104 (2000)
10. Kuroe Y., Ueyama T.: Learning methods of recurrent spiking neural networks based on adjoint equations approach. In: International Joint Conference on Neural Networks, pp. 1–8. IEEE (2010)
11. Tiňo, P., Mills, A.J.S.: Learning beyond finite memory in recurrent networks of spiking neurons. Neural Comput. **18**(3), 591–613 (2006)
12. Brodeur, S., Rouat, J.: Regulation toward self-organized criticality in a recurrent spiking neural reservoir. In: Villa, A.E.P., Duch, W., Érdi, P., Masulli, F., Palm, G. (eds.) ICANN 2012. LNCS, vol. 7552, pp. 547–554. Springer, Heidelberg (2012). https://doi.org/10.1007/978-3-642-33269-2_69
13. Bourdoukan, R., Deneve, S.: Enforcing balance allows local supervised learning in spiking recurrent networks. In: International Conference on Neural Information Processing Systems, pp. 982–990. MIT Press (2015)

14. Diehl, P.U., Zarrella, G., Cassidy, A., et al.: Conversion of artificial recurrent neural networks to spiking neural networks for low-power neuromorphic hardware. In: IEEE International Conference on Rebooting Computing, pp. 1–8. IEEE (2016)
15. Gilra, A., Gerstner, W.: Predicting non-linear dynamics by stable local learning in a recurrent spiking neural network. Elife **6**, e28295 (2017)
16. Paiva, A.R., Park, I., Príncipe, J.C.: A reproducing kernel Hilbert space framework for spike train signal processing. Neural Comput. **21**(2), 424–449 (2009)
17. Carnell, A., Richardson, D.: Linear algebra for time series of spikes. In: Proceedings of European Symposium on Artificial Neural Networks, pp. 363–368. DBLP (2005)
18. Sporea, I., Grüning, A.: Supervised learning in multilayer spiking neural networks. Neural Comput. **25**(2), 473–509 (2013)
19. Gerstner, W., Kistler, W.M.: Spiking Neuron Models: Single Neurons, Populations, Plasticity. Cambridge University Press, Cambridge (2002)

Artwork Retrieval Based on Similarity of Touch Using Convolutional Neural Network

Takayuki Fujita and Yuko Osana$^{(\boxtimes)}$

Tokyo University of Technology,
1404-1, Katakura, Hachioji, Tokyo 192-0982, Japan
osana@stf.teu.ac.jp

Abstract. In this paper, we propose an artwork retrieval based on similarity of touch using convolutional neural network. In the proposed system, a convolutional neural network is learned so that images can be classified into a group based on a touch, with saturation and value and the histogram of saturation and value as input data, and the trained network is used to realize the retrieval. Using the learned convolution neural network, feature vectors are generated for all images used for learning. The output of the full-connected layer before the soft-max layer when each image is input is obtained and normalized so that the magnitude becomes 1.0 is used as the feature vector. Then, the image and the normalized feature vector corresponding to the image are associated and stored in the database. A retrieval is realized by inputting an image as a retrieval key to the input layer, generating a feature vector, and comparing it with feature vectors in the database. We carried out a series of computer experiments and confirmed that the proposed system can realize artwork retrieval based on similarity of touch with higher accuracy than the conventional system.

Keywords: Image retrieval · Similarity of touch
Convolutional neural network

1 Introduction

Artwork (Illustrations) have various touch styles, but there is a desire to use a unified illustration of touch when using illustrations when preparing materials. In the illustration collection, there is little that is divided for each touch of illustration, so it is difficult to find illustrations of similar touch that is the content of the image that you want. Most of the current image retrieval systems use keywords to search, but it is difficult to properly specify the illustrations of touch that you want in these systems. So, if you do not know the name representing touch, or if it does not exist, you need a system to search the image using the image as a key.

© Springer Nature Switzerland AG 2018
V. Kůrková et al. (Eds.): ICANN 2018, LNCS 11139, pp. 235–243, 2018.
https://doi.org/10.1007/978-3-030-01418-6_23

As a system that can realize illustration search based on the similarity of touch, a retrieval system using a self-organizing feature map with refractriness [1] has been proposed [2]. In this system, image retrieval considering similar of touch is realized by inputting features of contour lines, texture features expressed by Local Binary Pattern (LBP)[3], histograms of saturation and value and so on.

On the other hand, many methods on image recognition using convolutional neural network [4] have been proposed. The convolutional neural network is a typical method of deep learning, and it is known that it has better performance than the conventional method in image recognition, speech recognition and so on. In the convolutional neural network, unlike the conventional image recognition method, it is not necessary to extract features beforehand, and features such as color and shape are automatically extracted by learning from the input learning data. However, in retrieval considering touch, we do not want to extract features of colors and shapes, but want to extract features such as trend of saturation, value, thickness of contour line. Therefore, to use convolutional neural network for illustration retrieval considering touch, it is necessary to extract features such as saturation and value without extracting features of color and shape.

In this paper, we propose an artwork retrieval based on similarity of touch using convolutional neural network. In the proposed system, a convolutional neural network is learned so that images can be classified into a group based on a touch, with saturation and value and the histogram of saturation and value as input data, and the trained network is used to realize the retrieval.

2   Artwork Retrieval Based on Similarity of Touch Using Convolutional Neural Network

In general, when image retrieval or image recognition is performed using a convolution neural network, an image or an image converted into a grayscale image is input, and features of colors and shapes are automatically extracted. On the other hand, in the proposed system, we do not want to search for images with similar shapes and color features. In the proposed system, we want to realize retrieval of images whose trends are similar, such as saturation, lightness, and contour line thickness.

Therefore, in the proposed system, the RGB image converted into the HSV value is used as a feature. Here, H is hue, S is saturation, and V is value (brightness)). However, in the proposed system, since the image as shown in Fig. 1 is handled as a similar image of the touch, the hues need not be similar. So, attention is focused only on saturation and value.

In addition, if the saturation and value information of each pixel is used as input, it is highly likely that features of shape information will be extracted, and it is considered difficult to extract features of the distribution of saturation and value. For this reason, the proposed system uses histograms of saturation and value as input data. In order to obtain information such as the thickness of the

(a)   (b)   (c)

Fig. 1. Examples of images belonging to same group

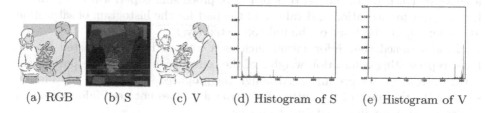

(a) RGB   (b) S   (c) V   (d) Histogram of S   (e) Histogram of V

Fig. 2. Images and corresponding features (1)

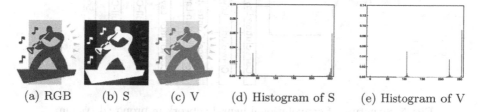

(a) RGB   (b) S   (c) V   (d) Histogram of S   (e) Hist-gram of V

Fig. 3. Images and corresponding features (2)

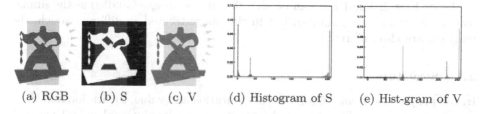

(a) RGB   (b) S   (c) V   (d) Histogram of S   (e) Histogram of V

Fig. 4. Images and corresponding features (3)

contour line, it is also necessary to input the state keeping the shape information. Therefore, saturation and value with pixel coordinates are used as input.

Figure 2 shows an image and a corresponding features. The features for the RGB image as shown in Fig. 2(a) are as shown in Fig. 2(b)–(e). In this figure, S represents saturation and V represents Value. Figure 3 shows another image treated as the similar touch as in Fig. 2 and its features. Figure 4 shows an image handled as a different touch from Fig. 2 and its features.

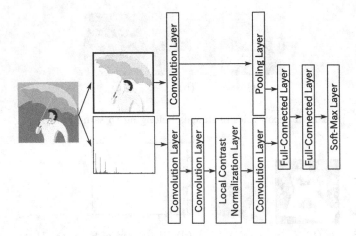

Fig. 5. Structure of convolutional neural network in proposed system.

From Figs. 2, 3 and 4, it can be seen that in the images handled as the similar touch, the features are similar, but in the image treated as different touch, the features are also different.

2.1 Structure

In the proposed system, histograms of saturation and value, saturation and value are used as inputs. The proposed system uses a convolutional neural network with a structure shown in Fig. 5 instead of a convolutional neural network with a general structure. In the network of Fig. 5, processing is performed separately for the part to saturation and value and the part for the histogram of saturation and value up to the front of the full-connected layer.

It is assumed that information such as a contour line is extracted by the filter representing connection weights of the convolution layer in the part where saturation and value are input. Although the proposed system uses information such as the thickness of the outline for retrieval, it does not need information on where the contour line exists in the image.

The output of the convolution layer has plural channels corresponding to each filter. In the pooling layer, average pooling is performed using the entire channel as a receptive field, and characteristics such as what kind of contour line is included at what proportion are extracted.

In a general convolution neural network, feature extracted in advance can not be used as input. However, as shown in Sect. 3.2, when retrieval considering similarity of touch is realized by using a convolution neural network with images as input, search accuracy for unlearned data is low. Therefore, in the proposed system, a histogram of saturation and value is extracted beforehand and used as features.

The outputs of both the part for the saturation and value and the part for the histogram of saturation and value are combined in the full-connected layer

1. Finally, the probability that the input belongs to each class in the soft-max layer is output.

2.2 Learning Process

In the proposed system, learning is performed as a classification problem so that the saturation and value, histograms of saturation and value of the image to be stored are input and the probability that the image belongs to each class is output. Here, it is assumed that images drawn with similar touch are handled as one class, and one image belongs to only one class.

2.3 Generation of Feature Vector

Using the learned convolution neural network, feature vectors are generated for all images used for learning. The output of the full-connected layer before the soft-max layer when each image is input is obtained and normalized so that the magnitude becomes 1.0 is used as the feature vector. Then, the image and the normalized feature vector corresponding to the image are associated and stored in the database.

2.4 Image Retrieval Process

In the image retrieval by the proposed system, first, an image to be the retrieval key is input to the learned convolutional neural network, and the output of the full-connected layer before the soft-max layer is normalized to generate a feature vector of the retrieval key. Then, the Euclidean distance between the feature vector of the search key and the feature vector in the database is calculated and images corresponding to the feature vector whose Euclidean distance is less than the threshold are output as the search result.

3 Computer Experiment Result

3.1 Retrieval Results

Figure 6 show example of retrieval results in the proposed system.

3.2 Search Accuracy

Experiments were conducted to examine the search accuracy in the proposed system, the conventional system [2], and the system using a general convolution neural network. As an index of retrieval accuracy, precision, recall, F value and MAP (Mean Average Precision)[6] were used.

The Table 1 shows the search accuracy when all data are learned as learning data and the same data are used as evaluation data. The Table 1 also shows the results of the conventional system and the system using a general convolutional

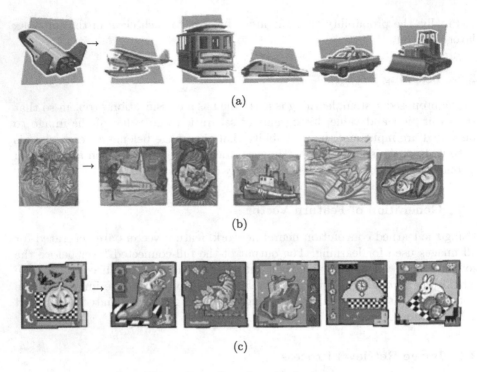

(a)

(b)

(c)

Fig. 6. Examples of retrieval results.

neural network (expressed as CNN in the table). For the system using the proposed system and general convolutional neural network, classification accuracy for learning data is also shown. This is the accuracy when classified based on the output of the soft-max layer of the convolutional neural network, not when operating as a search system. From Table 1, we can see that the proposed system can search with higher accuracy than the conventional system.

Table 1. Search accuracy (for trained data)

	Recall	Precision	F Value	Accuracy
Proposed system	0.932200	0.909641	0.920782	1.000000
Conventional system	0.443387	0.454866	0.449053	—
CNN	0.936400	0.925662	0.931000	0.981245

Table 2 shows the search accuracy when data different from the learning data are used for evaluation. For the proposed system, the value of MAP when $N^R = 15$ is also shown. Although F value is lower than when using all data as learning shown in the Table 1, it can be see that higher accuracy is obtained in the proposed system than in the conventional system. Moreover, it can be seen that the proposed system has higher accuracy than the system using the general convolutional neural network.

Table 2. Search accuracy (for evaluation data)

	Recall	Precision	F-value	MAP
Proposed system	0.585222	0.545125	0.564462	0.657010
CNN	0.551333	0.329679	0.412623	—

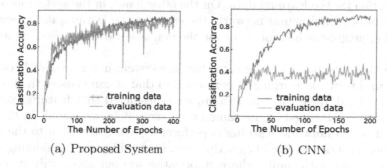

(a) Proposed System   (b) CNN

Fig. 7. Transition of classification accuracy

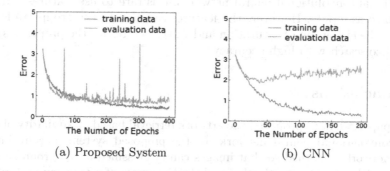

(a) Proposed System   (b) CNN

Fig. 8. Transition of error function

3.3 Transition of Classification Accuracy and Error Function

Here, we examined how the classification accuracy and error function for learning data and evaluation data changes in the learning process of the proposed system and the system using a general convolutional neural network.

The transition of classification accuracy for learning data and evaluation data in each system is shown in Fig. 7. In Fig. 7, it can be seen that in the proposed system, the classification accuracy for the evaluation data varies almost in same way as the classification accuracy for the learning data. On the other hand, in the system using the general convolutional neural network, the classification accuracy for the learning data increases as learning progresses, but the classification accuracy for the evaluation data becomes almost flat after 28 epochs. From this result, it can be see that there is no generalization ability in the network after learning in the system using the general convolutional neural network.

The transition of error function for learning data and evaluation data in each system is shown in Fig. 8. In Fig. 8, it can be seen that in the proposed system, the error function for the evaluation data varies almost in same way as the error function for the learning data. On the other hand, in the system using the general convolutional neural network, the error for the learning data decreases as learning progresses but the error for the evaluation data increases gradually after 29.

From these results, it can be seen that in a system using a general convolutional neural network, learning is performed so that it can classify the learning data correctly. However, in this system, it is considered that features common to images to be classified in the same group can not be extracted. In the convolutional neural network, learning is performed paying attention to the shape information included in the image. However, in classification considering touch similarity, images with similar shape information are not necessarily treated as the same group. Therefore, it can be considered that it could not be classified correctly for unlearned data. On the other hand, the proposed system uses not only saturation and value but also histogram of saturation and value as input. In the conventional convolutional neural networks, it is rare to use features extracted in advance as inputs. However, the features common to the group are learned by using the histogram of saturation and value, as a result, the proposed system can realize search with high accuracy.

4   Conclusions

In this paper, we have proposed the artwork retrieval based on similarity of touch using convolutional neural network. In the proposed system, a convolutional neural network is learned so that images can be classified into a group based on a touch, with saturation and value and the histogram of saturation and value as input data, and the trained network is used to realize the retrieval. We carried out a series of computer experiments and confirmed that the proposed system can realize artwork retrieval based on similarity of touch with higher accuracy than the conventional system.

References

1. Mogami, H., Otake, M., Kouno, N., Osana, Y.: Self-organizing map with refractoriness and its application to image retrieval. In: Proceedings of IEEE and INNS International Joint Conference on Neural Networks, Vancouver (2006)
2. Kawai, H., Osana, Y.: Search accuracy improvement in artwork retrieval based on similarity of touch. In: Proceedings of International Conference, Como (2015)
3. Ojala, T., Pietiäinen, M., Harwood, D.: A comparative study of texture measures with classification based on distributions. Pattern Recogn. **29**(1), 51–59 (1996)
4. LeCun, Y., Bottou, L., Bengio, Y., Haffner, P.: Gradient-based learning applied to document recognition. Proc. IEEE **86**(11), 2278–2324 (1998)
5. Krizhevsky, A., Sutskever, I., Hinton, G.E.: ImageNet classification with deep convolutional neural networks. In: Advances in NIPS, pp. 1097–1105 (2012)
6. Buckley, C., Voorhees, E.M.: Evaluating evaluation measure stability. In: Proceedings of the 23rd Annual International ACM SIGIR Conference on Research and Development in Information Retrieval, pp. 33–40 (2000)

Microsaccades for Neuromorphic Stereo Vision

Jacques Kaiser, Jakob Weinland, Philip Keller, Lea Steffen,
J. Camilo Vasquez Tieck[✉], Daniel Reichard, Arne Roennau, Jörg Conradt,
and Rüdiger Dillmann

FZI Research Center for Information Technology, 76131 Karlsruhe, Germany
{jkaiser,weinland,keller,steffen,tieck,daniel.reichard,roennau,
dillmann}@fzi.de, conradt@tum.de
https://www.fzi.de

Abstract. Depth perception through stereo vision is an important feature of biological and artificial vision systems. While biological systems can compute disparities effortlessly, it requires intensive processing for artificial vision systems. The computing complexity resides in solving the correspondence problem – finding matching pairs of points in the two eyes. Inspired by the retina, event-based vision sensors allow a new constraint to solve the correspondence problem: time. Relying on precise spike-time, spiking neural networks can take advantage of this constraint. However, disparities can only be computed from dynamic environments since event-based vision sensors only report local changes in light intensity. In this paper, we show how microsaccadic eye movements can be used to compute disparities from static environments. To this end, we built a robotic head supporting two Dynamic Vision Sensors (DVS) capable of independent panning and simultaneous tilting. We evaluate the method on both static and dynamic scenes perceived through microsaccades. This paper demonstrates the complementarity of event-based vision sensors and active perception leading to more biologically inspired robots.

Keywords: Spiking neural networks · Event-based stereo vision
Eye movements

1 Introduction

Depth perception is an essential feature of biological and artificial vision systems. Stereopsis (or stereo vision) refers to the process of extracting depth information from both eyes. The human eyes are shifted laterally, that is why each eye forms a slightly different image from the world. The brain is capable of matching a point in one image with its corresponding point in the other image, measuring its relative distance on the retina and using this value to estimate the distance of the object to the viewer. The relative difference of the projections of the same object on the two retinas is called disparity.

V. Kůrková et al. (Eds.): ICANN 2018, LNCS 11139, pp. 244–252, 2018.
https://doi.org/10.1007/978-3-030-01418-6_24

While stereo vision is realised unconsciously and effortlessly in biology, it requires intensive processing for artificial vision systems. The core problem of stereo vision systems is the well-known correspondence problem: finding matches between visual information perceived by the two sensors. A matched pair of pixels enables the precise calculation of the depth using the geometry of the camera setup and the disparity of the pixels on the epipolar line [1]. As the complexity of the scenery increases and noise is added to the images, the computational expense of common machine vision system increases significantly, affecting the speed, size, and efficiency of the used hardware [19].

Advances in neuromorphic engineering enable new approaches for stereo vision systems. The use of a Dynamic Vision Sensor (DVS, or silicon retina) [11] adds another constraint to the already existing spatial constraints for matching: time. Unlike conventional cameras which operate with frame-based images, a DVS emits independent pixel events at precise time on local light intensity changes. This leads to a continuous stream of events, well suited for processing with spiking neural networks. Spiking neural networks are referred to as the third generation of artificial networks [12]. Unlike their non-spiking counterpart, neurons are defined with dynamical systems in continuous time and not on a discrete time basis. Communication in spiking neural networks is asynchronous and is based on instantaneous spikes. While the form of the spike does not hold any specific information, it is the number and timing of spikes that matter [7]. Even though it is possible to simulate spiking networks on conventional computers, their real potential with respect to speed and efficiency is unveiled when processed on neuromorphic hardware [5, 19].

Recently, approaches have been proposed for disparity computation on event streams with spiking neural networks [3, 19], both based on groundwork in [13]. These approaches are discussed in Sect. 2. They consist of a three-dimensional spiking network where output neurons describe one unique point in the observed 3D-space (see Fig. 1). In other words, an output neuron emits a spike when location in 3D-space becomes occupied or unoccupied. In this paper, we show how the method can be used to perceive depth from motionless static scenes through microsaccadic eye movements. To this end, we built a robotic head for the humanoid robot HoLLiE [9] supporting two DVS capable of independent panning and simultaneous tilting, see Fig. 1a. Our results suggest that synchronous microsaccadic eye movements in both eyes could be used in biology for stereopsis. While the role of fixational eye movements is not fully understood, their importance in perception was already suggested in [10, 16, 21]. Additionally, our network is implemented in PyNN [2] and can run both on SpiNNaker [6] or classical CPU with the NEST simulator [8].

2   Related Work

In this Section, we present Poggio and Marr's cooperative algorithm for stereo matching, which was published in 1982 [13] and forms the foundation for further work in the field. The method has recently been improved in [3] with the introduction of small computational units, so-called micro-ensembles.

According to [14], three steps are involved in measuring stereo disparity. In the first step (S1) a point of interest is selected from a surface in one image. In step two (S2) the same point has to be identified in the other image. Step three (S3) measures the disparity between the two corresponding image points, which can be used to calculate the distance of the object to the viewer. However, false targets make it difficult to find a matching pair of points. Physical properties of rigid bodies are used to minimize the number of false matches. One of these properties is that a point on the surface of an object has a unique position at a given point in time (P1). The second physical restraint that can be used is the fact that surfaces of objects are perceived as smooth from the perspective of the observer. Small changes in topology such as roughness or protrusions are of minor importance for the estimation of distance (P2) [13]. To minimize the possibility of a mismatch, the physical constraints P1 and P2 can be rewritten into matching constraints (C). These matching constraints implement rules of communication between disparity-sensitive neurons (see Fig. 1b). Derived from P1, the *uniqueness constraint* (C1) states, that for every given point seen by one area of one eye, at a specific time, there can be at most one corresponding match in the other. Therefore C1 inhibits communication in horizontal and vertical directions between the disparity-sensitive neurons. The physical restraint P2 results in the *continuity constraint* (C2), which is based on the assumption that physical matter is cohesive and generally has a smooth surface. It encourages communications along the diagonal lines of constant disparity. The *compatibility constraint* (C3) states that "black dots can only match black dots" [14]. Recently, this method was improved in [3] with the addition of micro-ensembles. The structure of a micro-ensemble consists of two blocker neurons and one collector neuron (see Fig. 1c). Micro-ensembles prevent a high frequency stimulation of a single DVS pixel to trigger false matches by exceeding the collector's threshold value, if a corresponding pixel in the other DVS is not active. The micro-ensemble, therefore, emulates an AND-Gate behavior to ensure that only signals received by both sensors can trigger a match [3].

The structure of our spiking network computing disparity from stereo event-based vision sensors is based on [3,19]. The network consists of a three dimensional grid of disparity-sensitive neurons (see Fig. 1a). Each of these disparity-sensitive neurons describe one unique point in the observed 3D-space, relative to the common fixation point of the cameras [20]. For each disparity neuron, a micro-ensemble ensures hetero-lateral matching. If the timing of the events projected by the retinal pixels into the neural ensemble is temporally congruent, the signal reaches the disparity-sensitive neuron. However, if the temporal offset of the incoming signals between the left and right pixels is too large, the blockers prevent the activation of the disparity-sensitive neuron. The C3 constraint (*compatibility constraint*) could be implemented by separating ON and OFF events in two separate pathways. As this would double the number of neurons, the C3 constraint is often ignored so that ON and OFF events can match each other.

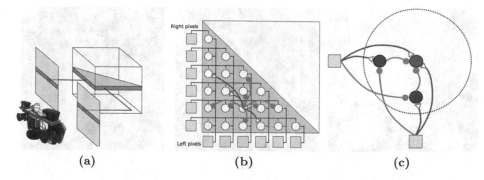

Fig. 1. Structure of the stereo network for detecting all possible positive disparities (schemas inspired from [3]). Triangular red edges denote excitatory synapses, rounded green edges denote inhibitory synapses. (a): Three-dimensional structure of the stereo network. Address events from the two DVS belonging to the same epipolar plane are fed to the corresponding epipolar layer in the network. (b): Organization of micro-ensembles within an epipolar layer. Each pixel connects to micro-ensembles defining a line of sight. The micro-ensembles are connected to each other with respect to the constraints mentioned in Sect. 2. For clarity, only the outgoing connections of a single micro-ensemble are drawn. The number of micro-ensembles can be reduced by bounding the minimum and maximum detectable disparities. (c): Schematic representation of a neural micro-ensemble. The two blue neurons on the left and bottom of the micro-ensemble are the blockers, while the red neuron in the middle is the disparity-sensitive collector neuron. Micro-ensembles are connected to each other by their collector neurons. (Color figure online)

3   Evaluation

In this paper, we rely on the spiking network structure presented in [3], see Sect. 2. The contribution of this paper is to enable the method to extract disparities from static scenes through microsaccadic eye movements by mounting the sensors on a robotic head. In this Section, we evaluate our approach on real world scenes with the built robotic head. Experiments are realized both on static scenes perceived with microsaccadic eye movements and dynamic scenes. The scenes are recorded with the two DVS with ROS using the driver from [17].

3.1   Micro-saccades on the Robotics Head

Pan-tilt units have already been used to convert image datasets to event-based datasets through microsaccadic eye movements [18]. In this paper, we present our robotic head platform for the humanoid robot HoLLiE [9], reproducing stereo eye movements. The head consists of three degrees of freedom: tilting both eyes simultaneously with a Dynamixel MX-64 servo, and panning the two eyes independently with two Dynamixel MX-28. The rotations are centered around the focal point the of the two DVS. The robotic head has a total width of 253 mm

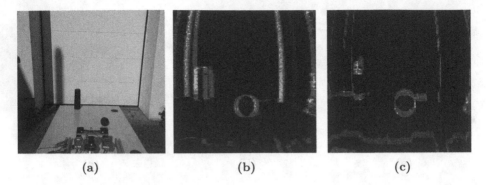

Fig. 2. Experiment setup for disparity computation on a static scene perceived with microsaccades. (a): Overview of the setup. The DVS head is laid on a table outdoors with two objects (a ball and a thermos flask) and both DVS look parallel towards them. (b): Accumulated events in the right DVS after an horizontal microsaccade (panning). Vertical edges have a high response. (c): Accumulated events in the right DVS after a vertical microsaccade (tilting). Horizontal edges have a high response.

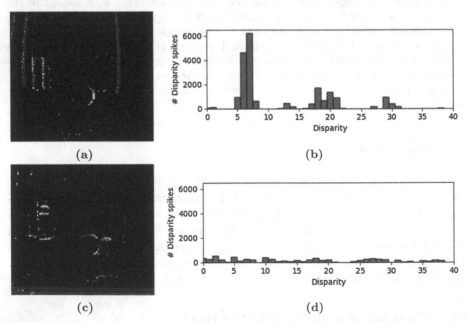

Fig. 3. Output of the stereo network for the static scene experiment perceived through microsaccades. (a): Rendering of the computed disparities during panning. (b): Histogram of the computed disparities during panning. Note the peaks around disparity 7 corresponding to the vertical garage door, around 20 for the thermos flask and around 29 for the ball (see Fig. 2a). (c): Rendering of the computed disparities during tilting. (d): Histogram of the computed disparities during tilting. Less events have been generated compared to horizontal microsaccades because of the verticality of the scene, leading to fewer disparity detections (see Fig. 2c).

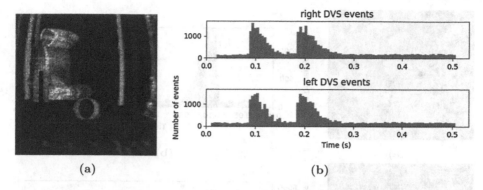

Fig. 4. Experiment data for disparity computation on a dynamic scene perceived with microsaccades. The same scene as in the first experiment (Fig. 2a) is used, with the addition of a person walking in the back. (a): Accumulated events in the right DVS for the whole duration of the experiment (1.4 s). Only a horizontal microsaccade is performed, while a person walks in the back. (b): Corresponding event histograms for the left and right DVS. The two peaks denote the positive and negative panning (go and return to position). The constant activity reflects the person walking in the back.

and an interpupillary distance of 188 mm (IPD). The average IPD of a human is around 63 mm [4]. Microsaccades are effectuated by slight panning or tilting motion with both DVS at very high speed. The robotic head is depicted in Fig. 1a.

3.2 Static Scenes Perceived Through Microsaccades

In this experiment, the robotic head is laid on a table outdoors and observes two objects (a ball and a thermos flask) at different depths, see Fig. 2a. The head performs an horizontal microsaccade followed by a vertical microsaccade of around 2.8°.

The network manages to compute the disparity of the different objects in the scene with an horizontal microsaccade (Fig. 3b), including the garage door in the background. Because most contrast lines in the scene are vertical, the tilting microsaccade does not trigger many events, leading to few disparity detections (Fig. 3d). Additionally, extracting disparity of horizontal edges is harder for the network, because many events will share the same epipolar layer (see Fig. 1b).

3.3 Dynamic Scenes Perceived Through Microsaccades

In this experiment, we evaluate whether the method can extract disparities of dynamic objects and static objects simultaneously with microsaccades. We rely on the same setup as for the previous experiment (Fig. 2a), with an additional person walking in the back of the scene. The generated address events are visualized in Fig. 4.

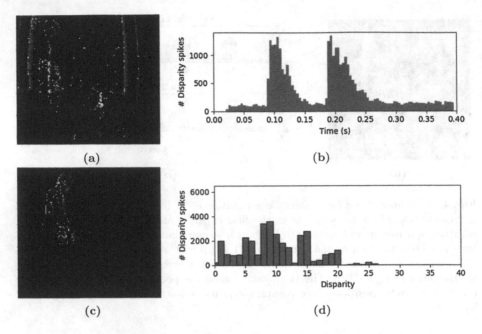

(a)   (b)

(c)   (d)

Fig. 5. Output of the stereo network for the dynamic scene experiment perceived through microsaccades. (a): Rendering of the computed disparities at $t = 0.1$ s during panning while a person walks in the back. (b): Histogram showing the number of detected disparities with respect to time. As expected, the number of detections correlates with the number of address events – see Fig. 4b. (c): Rendering of the computed disparities at $t = 0.3$ s when no microsaccades are performed. (d): Histogram of the computed disparities for the whole sequence. The events corresponding to the walking person have a disparity around 10, between the garage door and the thermos flask. Compared to the purely static scene, less events were generated for the garage door as it is occluded by the human, see Fig. 3b.

As can be seen in Fig. 5, the network manages to compute the disparity of the different objects in the scene as well as of the walking person.

4   Conclusion

Depth perception through stereo vision is an important feature for many biological and artificial systems. While biological systems can compute disparities effortlessly, it requires intensive processing for artificial vision systems. Recently, spiking network models were introduced in [3,19], both based on groundwork in [13]. Relying on event-based vision sensors, these models take advantage of a new constraint to solve the correspondence problem: time.

Since event-based vision sensors such as the DVS only report changes in light intensity, these methods could only extract disparities from dynamic scenes. In this paper, we show how synchronous microsaccadic eye movements enable such network to extract disparities out of static scenes. To this end, a robotic head platform for the humanoid robot HoLLiE [9] capable of simultaneous tilting and independent panning was built. As the retina also adapts rapidly to non-changing stimulus [15,21], it is likely that biology also relies on fixational eye movements to perceive depth in static scenes.

For future work, the robotic head could implement other types of eye movements such as saccades and smooth pursuit. Additionally, one could reduce greatly the number of required neurons with hard bounds on minimum and maximum detectable disparities. In this setup, active vision could be used to squint the eyes to the relevant baseline depth.

Acknowledgments. This research has received funding from the European Union's Horizon 2020 Framework Programme for Research and Innovation under the Specific Grant Agreement No. 720270 (Human Brain Project SGA1) and No. 785907 (Human Brain Project SGA2).

References

1. Davies, E.R.: Computer and Machine Vision: Theory, Algorithms, Practicalities. Academic Press, Cambridge (2012)
2. Davison, A.P.: PyNN: a common interface for neuronal network simulators. Front. Neuroinform. **2**, 11 (2008)
3. Dikov, G., Mohsen, F., Röhrbein, F., Conradt, J., Richter, C.: Spiking cooperative stereo-matching at 2 ms latency with neuromorphic hardware. Front. Neurosci. (2017)
4. Dodgson, N.A.: Variation and extrema of human interpupillary distance. Proc. Soc. Photo-Opt. Instrum. Eng. **12**(8), 36–46 (2004)
5. Furber, S., Temple, S., Brown, A.: On-chip and inter-chip networks for modelling large-scare neural systems, pp. 6–9 (2006)
6. Furber, S.B., Galluppi, F., Temple, S., Plana, L.A.: The spinnaker project. Proc. IEEE **102**(5), 652–665 (2014)
7. Gerstner, W., Kistler, W.M.: Spiking Neuron Models: Single Neurons, Populations. Plasticity. Cambridge University Press, Cambridge (2002)
8. Gewaltig, M.O., Diesmann, M.: Nest (neural simulation tool). Scholarpedia **2**(4), 1430 (2007)
9. Hermann, A., et al.: Hardware and software architecture of the bimanual mobile manipulation robot HoLLiE and its actuated upper body. In: 2013 IEEE/ASME International Conference on Advanced Intelligent Mechatronics: Mechatronics for Human Wellbeing, AIM 2013, pp. 286–292, July 2013
10. Kaiser, J., et al.: Benchmarking microsaccades for feature extraction with spiking neural networks on continuous event streams. In: International Conference on Development and Learning and Epigenetic Robotics (ICDL-EpiRob) (2018, submitted)
11. Lichtsteiner, P., Posch, C., Delbruck, T.: A 128 × 128 120 db 15 μs latency asynchronous temporal contrast vision sensor. IEEE J. Solid-State Circuits **43**(2), 566–576 (2008)
12. Maass, W.: Networks of spiking neurons: the third generation of neural network models. Neural Netw. **10**(9), 1659–1671 (1997)

13. Marr, D.: Vision: a computational investigation into the human representation and processing of visual information. W.H. Freeman and Company, San Francisco (1982)
14. Marr, D., Poggio, T.: A theory of human stereo vision. Proc. Roy. Soc. Lond. B Biol. Sci. **204**, 301–328 (1977)
15. Martinez-Conde, S., Macknik, S.L., Hubel, D.H.: The role of fixational eye movements in visual perception. Nat. Rev. Neurosci. **5**(3), 229–240 (2004)
16. Masquelier, T., Portelli, G., Kornprobst, P.: Microsaccades enable efficient synchrony-based coding in the retina: a simulation study. Sci. Rep. **6**, 24086 (2016)
17. Mueggler, E., Huber, B., Scaramuzza, D.: Event-based, 6-DOF pose tracking for high-speed maneuvers. In: International Conference on Intelligent Robots and Systems. IEEE (2014)
18. Orchard, G., Jayawant, A., Cohen, G., Thakor, N.: Converting static image datasets to spiking neuromorphic datasets using saccades. arXiv preprint arXiv:1507.07629 (2015)
19. Osswald, M., Ieng, S.H., Benosman, R., Indiveri, G.: A Spiking Neural Network Model of 3D Perception For Event-Based Neuromorphic Stereo Vision Systems, pp. 1–11. Nature Publishing Group, London (2017)
20. Osswald, M., Ieng, S.H., Benosman, R., Indiveri, G.: Supplementary Material: A Spiking Neural Network Model of 3D Perception for Event-Based Neuromorphic Stereo Vision Systems, pp. 1–14 (2017)
21. Rucci, M., Victor, J.D.: The unsteady eye: an information-processing stage, not a bug. Trends Neurosci. **38**(4), 195–206 (2015)

A Neural Spiking Approach Compared to Deep Feedforward Networks on Stepwise Pixel Erasement

René Larisch[(✉)], Michael Teichmann, and Fred H. Hamker

Department of Computer Science, Chemnitz University of Technology,
Str. der Nationen 62, 09111 Chemnitz, Germany
{rene.larisch,michael.teichmann,fred.hamker}@informatik.tu-chemnitz.de

Abstract. In real world scenarios, objects are often partially occluded. This requires a robustness for object recognition against these perturbations. Convolutional networks have shown good performances in classification tasks. The learned convolutional filters seem similar to receptive fields of simple cells found in the primary visual cortex. Alternatively, spiking neural networks are more biological plausible. We developed a two layer spiking network, trained on natural scenes with a biologically plausible learning rule. It is compared to two deep convolutional neural networks using a classification task of stepwise pixel erasement on MNIST. In comparison to these networks the spiking approach achieves good accuracy and robustness.

Keywords: STDP · Unsupervised learning
Deep convolutional networks

1 Introduction

Deep convolutional neural networks (DCNN) have shown outstanding performances on different object recognition tasks [10,11,19], like handwritten digits (MNIST [5]) or the ImageNet challenge [18]. Previous studies show that filters of a DCNN, trained on images, are similar to receptive fields of simple cells in the primary visual cortex of primates [21,24] and thus have been suggested, to a certain degree, as a model of human vision, despite the fact that back-propagation algorithm, does not seem to be biological plausible [14,16]. Alternatively, many models have been published in the field of computational neuroscience, whose unsupervised learning is based on occurrence of pre- and postsynaptic spikes. A previous work [16] presented a model using spike-timing-dependent plasticity (STDP) rule to recognize digits of the MNIST dataset. We propose a STDP network with biologically motivated STDP learning rules for excitatory and inhibitory synapses to better mirror the structure in the visual cortex. We use a voltage based learning rule from Clopath et al. [7] for excitatory synapses and a symmetric inhibitory learning rule from Vogels et al. [9]

© Springer Nature Switzerland AG 2018
V. Kůrková et al. (Eds.): ICANN 2018, LNCS 11139, pp. 253–262, 2018.
https://doi.org/10.1007/978-3-030-01418-6_25

for inhibitory synapses. During learning, we present natural scenes to our network [4]. The thereby emerging receptive fields [7] are similar to those of simple cells in the primary visual cortex [1,2]. After learning, we present digits of the MNIST data set to the network and measure the activity of the excitatory population. The activity vectors on the training set are used to train a support vector machine (SVM) with a linear kernel to be used on the test set to estimate the accuracy of our neural network.

We previously evaluated robustness of classification by a gradual erasement of pixels in the MNIST data set. Our evaluation showed, that inhibition can improve robustness by reducing redundant activities in the network [17]. To evaluate our spiking network, we apply this task by placing white pixels in 5% steps in all images of the MNIST test set and by measuring accuracy on these degraded digits. We compare our spiking network with two DCNNs. The first DCNN is the well known LeNet 5 network from LeCun et al. [5]. The second one is based on the VGG16 network from Simonyan and Zisserman [19]. Both deep networks are trained on the MNIST data set and accuracy is measured on the test set with different levels of pixel erasement.

We here follow the idea, that a biologically motivated model trained by Hebbian Learning on natural scene should discover a codebook of features that can be used for a large set of classification tasks. Thus, we train our spiking model on small segments of natural scenes. As these image patches contain different spatial orientations and frequencies, we obtain receptive fields which are selective for simple features. With this generalized coding, we archived a recognition accuracy of 98.08%. Further, our spiking network shows a good robustness against pixel erasement, even with only one layer of excitatory and inhibitory neurons.

2   Methods

Both deep convolutional networks are implemented in Keras v.2.0.6 [15] with tensorflow v.1.2.1 and Python 3.6. Our spiking network is implemented in Python 2.7 with the neuronal simulator ANNarchy (v.4.6) [20]. To classify activity vectors of our network, we used a support vector machine with a linear kernel, using the *LinearSVC* package from the sklearn library v.0.19.1.

2.1   Spiking Model

Populations. The architecture of our spiking network (Fig. 1A) is inspired by the primary visual cortex and consists of spiking neurons in two layers. The input size is 18×18 pixels. We used randomly chosen patches out of a set of whitened natural scenes [4] to train our network. To avoid negative firing rates, positive values of a patch are separated in an On-part and negative values in an Off-part. Therefore, the first layer consists of 648 neurons in a $18 \times 18 \times 2$ grid. Every pixel corresponds to one neuron in the layer. The neurons fire according to a Poisson distribution, whose firing rate is determined by the corresponding pixel values. The presented pixels are normalized with the absolute maximum value

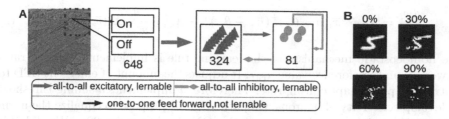

Fig. 1. A: Schematic diagram of our spiking network. The input layer consists of 648 neurons. The second layer consists of 324 excitatory and 81 inhibitory neurons. B: Example for the image distortion from the original digit to 90% pixel erasement.

of the original image and multiplied with a maximum firing rate of 125 Hz. Each patch was presented for 125 ms. Learning was stopped after 400.000 patches. The presented patch was flipped around vertical or horizontal axis with a probability of 50% to avoid an orientation bias [7].

The neurons in the first layer are all-to-all connected to the neurons in the second layer. The second layer consists of a population of 324 excitatory and 81 inhibitory neurons to achieve the 4:1 ratio between number of excitatory and inhibitory neurons as found in the visual cortex [3,13]. All neurons gather information from the whole presented input. Both populations consist of adaptive exponential integrate-and-fire neurons (AdEx) [7]. The description of the membrane potential u is presented in Eq. 1. The slope factor is δ_T, C is the membrane capacitance, E_L is the resting potential and g_L is the leaking conductance. The depolarizing after potential is described by z and w_{ad} is the hyperpolarizing adaption current. The input is denoted by I_{exc} for excitatory and I_{inh} for inhibitory current. Input currents are incremented by sum of the presynaptic spikes of the previous time step, multiplied with the synaptic weight.

$$C\frac{du}{dt} = -g_L(u - E_L) + g_L \Delta_T e^{\frac{u-V_T}{\Delta_T}} - w_{ad} + z + I_{exc} - I_{inh} \tag{1}$$

A spike is emitted, when the membrane potential exceeds the adaptive spiking threshold V_T. After a spike, the membrane potential is set to 29 mV for 2 ms, and then it is set back to E_L.

Excitatory Plasticity. The plasticity of excitatory connections from the first to the second layer, as well as connections from the excitatory to the inhibitory population within the second layer, follows the voltage-based STDP rule [7]. The development of the weight between a presynaptic neuron i and a postsynaptic neuron depends on the presynaptic spike event X_i and the presynaptic spike trace $\bar{x}_i$ as well as on the postsynaptic membrane potential u and two averages of the membrane potential $\bar{u}_+$ and $\bar{u}_-$. The parameters A_{LTP} and A_{LTD} are the learning rates for long-term potentiation (LTP) and long-term depression (LTD). Both parameters θ_+ and θ_- are thresholds, which must be exceeded by the membrane potential or its long time averages.

$$\frac{dw_i}{dt} = A_{LTP} \; \overline{x}_i (u - \theta_+)^+ (\overline{u}_+ - \theta_-)^+ - A_{LTD} \frac{\overline{\overline{u}}}{u_{ref}} X_i (\overline{u}_- - \theta_-)^+ \qquad (2)$$

The homoeostatic mechanism of the learning rule is implemented by the ratio between $\overline{\overline{u}}$ and a reference value u_{ref}. It adjusts the amount of emergent LTD to control the postsynaptic firing rate. Therefore, $\overline{\overline{u}}$ implements a sliding threshold to develop selectivity of neurons. Clopath et al. [7] propose to equalize the norm of the OFF weights to the norm of the ON weights every 20 s. We did this for the excitatory weights from the input layer to excitatory and the inhibitory population, per neuron. The weights are limited by an upper and lower bound.

Inhibitory Plasticity. The connections from the inhibitory to the excitatory population and the lateral connections between the inhibitory neurons develop with the inhibitory learning rule from Vogels et al. [9] (see Eq. 3).

$$\Delta w_{ij} = \eta(\overline{x}_j - \rho) \text{ , for pre-synaptic spike} \qquad (3)$$
$$\Delta w_{ij} = \eta(\overline{x}_i) \qquad \text{, for post-synaptic spike}$$

The pre-synaptic spike trace is $\overline{x}_i$ and the spike trace for the post-synaptic neuron is $\overline{x}_j$. When the particular neuron spikes, the spike trace increases with one, otherwise it decays with τ_i or τ_j to zero. The inhibitory weight changes on a pre- or postsynaptic spike with the learning rate η.

The constant value ρ specifies the strength of inhibition to suppress the postsynaptic activity until LTD can occur. The inhibitory weights are limited by a lower and upper bound.

2.2   Deep Convolutional Networks

To assess the performance of our network approach on MNIST recognition, we compared it to two deep convolutional neural networks (DCNN). The first network is the well known LeNet 5, introduced from LeCun et al. [5]. It is hierarchically structured with two pairs of 2D-convolutional and max-pooling layers, followed by two fully connected one-dimensional layers. The last layer is the classification layer with a *"softmax"* classifier. The first convolutional layer has a kernel size of 3×3 pixels and 32 feature maps. The kernel size of the second convolutional layer is 3×3 too, but consists of 64 feature maps. For the second max-pooling layer, a dropout regularisation with a dropout ratio of 0.5 is used. Both max-pooling layers have a 2×2 pooling size. The architecture of the second model is based on the VGG16 network proposed by Simonyan and Zisserman [19]. As a consequence of the small input size, we have to remove the last three 2D convolutional and the 2D max-pooling layer. Further, no dropout regularisation was done. This shortened model is further called *VGG*13. Both networks are learned for 50 epochs on the MNIST training set [5]. The validation accuracy is measured on 10% of the training set. The remaining 90% are used for learning. The adadelta optimizer [12] with $\rho = 0.95$ is used for both networks.

2.3   Measurement of Accuracy

The MNIST images have a resolution of 28 × 28 pixels. Because of the input size of the spiking network with 18 × 18 pixels, we divided each image of the MNIST set into four patches with each 18 × 18 pixel size. The first patch was cut out at the upper left corner and a horizontal and vertical pixel shift of 10 pixels was done to cut out the other three patches. We presented every patch for 125 ms, without learning, and measured the number of spikes per neuron. We repeated every patch presentation ten times to calculate a mean activity per neuron on every patch. For every digit, a final activity vector consists of $324 \times 4 = 1296$ values. We fitted a support vector machine (SVM) with the merged activity vectors of the training set. Before the fitting, we normed the activity vectors between zero and one. The SVM had a linear kernel, the squared hinge loss and the L2 penalty with a C-parameter of one. To measure accuracy, we used the merged activity vectors of the test set as input to fitted SVM and compared the known labels with the predictions of the SVM. Finally, we measured the accuracy of five separately learned networks and will present the average accuracy here.

We measured the accuracy of both DCNNs by presenting the MNIST test set and comparing their prediction with the known labels. As for the spiking network, we measured the accuracy of five separately learned networks and present the average accuracy here.

We calculated the f-score for all models and levels of pixel erasements as well. Because there is no difference to the accuracy noticeable, it is not shown here.

2.4   Robustness Against Pixel Erasement

In a previous study Kermani et al. demonstrated, that networks with biologically motivated learning rules in combination with inhibitory synapses are more robust against a loss of information in the input. They measured the classification accuracy of their network for different levels of pixel erasement in the MNIST dataset [17]. Following this approach, we erased pixels of all digits in the MNIST test sets in 5% steps, erasing only pixels with a value above zero (see Fig. 1B). We created one data set per erasement level and showed each model the same dataset. For each level of pixel erasement we measured the number of correct classifications as mentioned above. Independently from number of erased pixels, the SVM has always been fitted with the activity vectors measured on the original training set.

3   Results

Our network achieved on the original MNIST test data set an average accuracy of 98.08% over five runs. If inhibition is removed, 96.81% accuracy is archived. The LeNet 5 implementation achieved 99.24% and the VGG13 network 99.41%, averaged over five runs (Table 1). Our results show, that at 25% erased pixels the spiking network achieves higher accuracy values than the LeNet 5 network,

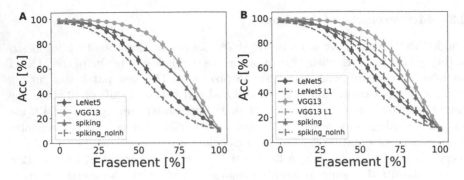

Fig. 2. Classification accuracy as a function of level of pixel erasement. A, Robustness of our spiking network (blue line) is between LeNet 5 (green line) and VGG13 (red line) network. Deactivation of inhibition leads to a less robust spiking network (dashed blue line). B, First layer of LeNet 5 (dashed green line) is more robust than complete LeNet 5. Whereas the first layer of the VGG13 is less robust (dashed red line). (Color figure online)

but lower values than the VGG13 network. We deactivated inhibition and measured again accuracy on the different levels of pixel erasement. As mentioned by Kermani et al., the accuracy decreases without inhibition stronger than with it (see Fig. 2A) [17].

Our spiking network only consists of one layer of excitatory neurons. Because of that, we measured accuracy of the LeNet 5 and VGG13 only with the activity of the first convolutional layer. Therefore, the output of the first layer was connected to a classification layer with 10 units and a softmax activation function. Only the weights from convolutional to classification layer were trained on the MNIST training set. The classification on the pixel erased dataset was done as for the other deep networks. With an accuracy of 98.1% from the first layer of LeNet 5 and 97.29% of the first layer of the VGG13, the first convolutional layer alone achieved a lower accuracy on the original MNIST test set than the complete network (Table 1). By stepwise pixel erasement, the first layer of the LeNet 5 is slightly robuster than the complete network. In contrast the first layer of the VGG13 model is less robust than the complete model. The course of the curve is similar to our spiking network (Fig. 2B). The size of the receptive fields in our spiking model does not correspond to the size of the convolutional kernel in the DCNNs. Further, every feature map in the convolutional layer shares the same convolutional kernel. Our spiking network learns 324 different receptive fields. That would be equivalent to 324 different feature maps in a DCNN. To accommodate these differences between the spiking approach and the DCNNs, we changed the number of feature maps in the first convolutional layer and the kernel size in the LeNet 5 and the VGG13 network to 9×9 and 18×18. To avoid unnecessary computational load and possibility of over fitting we increased the number of feature maps only to 64 and 96. The increased kernel size in the LeNet 5 implementation leads to a significant improvement (see Fig. 3A). However, for the VGG13 model, it does not lead to a significant change (see Fig. 3B). An increased number of feature maps in both DCNNs seems to have no effect on robustness.

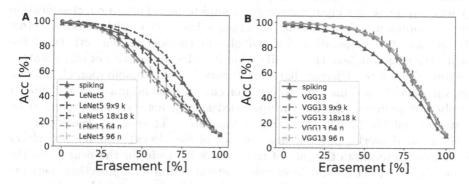

Fig. 3. Classification accuracy for different configurations of the DCNNs. A LeNet 5 with different numbers of feature maps (brighter lines) and larger kernel sizes (darker lines). B VGG13 with different numbers of feature maps (brighter lines) and larger kernel sizes (darker lines). More feature maps shows no change or slightly less robustness against pixel erasement. Larger kernel sizes lead to an improvement in LeNet5.

Table 1. Accuracy values on deep convolutional networks LeNet 5 and VGG13, with different number of features and sizes for the kernel filter. Measured on original MNIST test set. Averaged over five runs per model.

Architecture	Normal	First layer only	64 features	96 features	9×9 kernel	18×18 kernel
LeNet 5	99.24%	98.10%	99.38%	99.42%	99.03%	98.77%
VGG13	99.41%	97.29%	99.44%	99.43%	99.41%	99.32%

4   Discussion

Our proposed two layer spiking neural network (SNN) archived an accuracy of 98.08% on the original MNIST data set. Previous unsupervised learned SNN have shown slightly weaker results on the MNIST data set [16,22]. Diehl and Cook [16] presented a two layer SNN with a similar architecture to the here proposed one. They achieved an accuracy of 95.0% with 6400 excitatory neurons and an accuracy of 87.0% with 400 excitatory neurons. In contrast to our spiking network, the excitatory population in their network is one-to-one connected to the inhibitory one to implement a lateral inhibitory effect between the excitatory neurons. Second, each neuron was connected to the full input of the MNIST data set and thus learned complete digits as receptive fields. After learning, they assigned every neuron a class, referred to the class with the highest activity on the training set [16]. The class of the most active neuron defined the prediction of the network on the test set. Our network is learned on natural scene input [4] instead of images of the MNIST data set. Because presenting each neuron a small segment of different spatial orientations and spatial frequencies, our network learns Gabor-like receptive fields [7]. These feature detectors are selective for only a part of the presented input instead of a complete digit. Further on, classification for our approach is done by training a simple linear SVM with activity vectors of the excitatory population. Instead of only considering the activity of the most active neuron, here the classification includes the activity of all excitatory neurons. Therefore, different digits are decoded by the combination of different neuronal activities. This leads to a better classification accuracy with a smaller number of neurons. Another unsupervised spiking network was presented by Tavanaei and Maida [23], consisting of four layers. Their input consists of 5 × 5 pixels sized overlapping patches, cut out of the MNIST training set. Every pixel value determines the rate of the input spike train for the neurons in the second layer. In the second layer exists lateral inhibitory connections between the neurons. This lead to Gabor-like receptive fields in the second layer. The next layer was a max-pooling layer, followed by a so called 'feature discovery' layer. After learning in the second layer was finished, they learned the fourth layer. The output of the fourth layer was used to train a SVM for the classification. They used four SVMs with different kernels and averaged them. With 32 neurons in the second and 128 neurons in the last layer they archived an accuracy of 98.36% on the MNIST test.

A deeper unsupervised spiking approach was presented by Kheradpisheh et al. [22]. They presented a deep spiking network to mimic convolutional and max-pooling layers by using a temporal coding STDP learning algorithm. This means, that the first firing neuron learned most, while later firing neurons learned less or nothing. Their network consists of three pairs of a convolutional and a max-pooling layer. For classification, they used a linear SVM on the output of the last pooling layer. On the MNIST data set, they achieved an accuracy of 98.4% [22]. Their temporal coding implements a "winner takes it all" mechanism, what is less biologically plausible than the used learning rules in our approach. Nonetheless, the complex structure of the network from Tavanaei and Maida [23] and of the Kheradpisheh et al. [22] network is an evidence for possibility of unsupervised STDP learning rules in a multi-layer network.

A comparison with two deep convolutional networks on stepwise pixel erasement showed, that our LeNet 5 implementation is less robust and the VGG13 model is more robust than the here proposed spiking network (Fig. 2A). In case of accuracy is only been measured on the activity of the first layer, the LeNet 5 first layer is more robust than the complete model. For VGG13, the first layer is less robust. The first convolutional layer of both models has a same kernel size (3 × 3) and number of features (32), but the robustness of both layers is different (Fig. 2B). Both deep convolutional neural networks (DCNNs) have different numbers of layers and a different order of convolutional and max-pooling layers. This suggests, that the structure of the network influences learning result in the first convolutional layer, especially how the error between output and input is back propagated. In contrast to an increase of the number of features, an increase of the convolutional kernel size leads to an improvement of robustness (Fig. 3), but to a decrease in the accuracy on the original data set by the LeNet 5 model (Table 1). An increase of the number of features or the convolutional kernel size does not lead to a significant change for the VGG13 model. With a larger filter kernel, the erasement of a fixed number of pixels in the input has a lower influence on activity of the neurons. With a 3×3 kernel three erased pixels in the input cause a loss of 33.33% of the incoming activity and with a 9×9 kernel is the loss only 3.7%.

As mentioned in previous works [17], our results show that learned lateral inhibition leads to an improvement of classification robustness against pixel erasement in unsupervised neural networks. On one side, neurons loose sharpening of their selectivity without inhibition [6,8]. On the other side, the correlation between the neuron activities increases. This leads to less distinct input encoding, that in turn decreases the robustness against pixel erasement [17]. The robustness in DCNNs is influenced by the learned feature maps as a result of the back propagation mechanism and the network architecture. Further, a larger size of the kernel filter improves the robustness. Whereas the number of feature maps are not that relevant. The absence of inhibition in DCNNs suggest, that not only the influence of inhibition on the neuronal activity improves robustness. Rather, filter size and structure of the learned filters are important for a robust behaviour.

Acknowledgement. This work was supported by the European Social Fund (ESF) and the Freistaat Sachsen.

References

1. Hubel, D.H., Wiesel, T.N.: Receptive fields, binocular interaction and functional architecture in the cat's visual cortex. J. Physiol. **160**, 106–154 (1962)
2. Jones, J.P., Palmer, L.A.: The two-dimensional spatial structure of simple receptive fields in cat striate cortex. J. Neurophysiol. **85**, 187–211 (1987)
3. Beaulieu, C., Kisvarday, Z., Somogyi, P., Cynaer, M., Cowey, A.: Quantitative distribution of GABA-immunopositive and - immunonegative neurons and synapses in the monkey striate cortex (Area 17). Cereb. Cortex **2**, 295–309 (1992)
4. Olshausen, B.A., Field, D.J.: Emergence of simple-cell receptive field properties by learning a sparse code for natural images. Nature **381**, 607–609 (1996)
5. LeCun, Y., Bottou, L., Haffner, P.: Gradient-based learning applied to document recognition. Proc. IEEE **86**(11), 2278–2324 (1998)
6. Priebe, N.J., Ferster, D.: Inhibition, Spike Threshold, and Stimulus Selectivity in Primary Visual Cortex. Neuron **4**, 482–497 (2008)
7. Clopath, C., Büsing, L., Vasilaki, E., Gerstner, W.: Connectivity reflects coding: a model of voltage-based STDP with homeostasis. Nat. Neurosci. **13**, 344–352 (2010)
8. Katzner, S., Busse, L., Carandini, M.: GABAA inhibition controls response gain in visual cortex. J. Neurosci. **31**, 5931–5941 (2011)
9. Vogels, T.P., Sprekeler, H., Zenke, F., Clopath, C., Gerstner, W.: Inhibitory plasticity balances excitation and inhibition in sensory pathways and memory networks. Science **334**, 1569–1573 (2011)

10. Cireşan, D., Meier, U., Schmidhuber, J.: Multi-column deep neural networks for image classification. arXiv:1202.2745 (2012)
11. Krizhevsky, A., Sutskever, I., Hinton, G.E.: ImageNet classification with deep convolutional neural networks. Adv. Neural Inf. Process. Syst. **25**, 1097–1105 (2012)
12. Zeiler, M.D.: ADADELTA: an adaptive learning rate method arXiv:1212.5701v1 (2012)
13. Potjans, T.C., Diesmann, M.: The cell-type specific cortical microcircuit: relating structure and activity in a full-scale spiking network model. Cereb. Cortex **24**, 785–806 (2014)
14. Bengio, Y., Lee, D.H., Bornschein, J., Lin, Z.: Towards biologically plausible deep learning. arXiv:1703.08245 (2015)
15. Chollet, F., et al.: Keras (2015). https://keras.io. Accessed 23 Apr 2018
16. Diehl, P.U., Cook, M.: Unsupervised learning of digit recognition using spike-timing-dependent plasticity. Front. Comput. Neurosci. **9**, 99 (2015)
17. Kermani Kolankeh, A., Teichmann, M., Hamker, F.H.: Competition improves robustness against loss of information. Front. Comput. Neurosci. **9**, 35 (2015)
18. Russakovsky, O., Denk, J., Su, H., Krause, J., Satheesh, S., Ma, S., Huang, Z., Karpathy, A., Khosla, A., Bernstein, M., Berg, A.C., Fei-Fei, L.: ImageNet large scale visual recognition challenge. Int. J. Comput. Vis. **115**, 211–252 (2015)
19. Simonyan, K., Zisserman, A.: Very deep convolutional networks for large-scale image recognition. CoRR abs/1409.1556 (2015)
20. Vitay, J., Dinkelbach, H.Ü., Hamker, F.H.: ANNarchy: a code generation approach to neural simulations on parallel hardware. Front. Neuroinformatics **9**, 19 (2015). https://doi.org/10.3389/fninf.2015.00019
21. Cichy, R.M., Khosla, A., Pantazis, D., Torralba, A., Oliva, A.: Comparison of deep neural networks to spatio-temporal cortical dynamics of human visual object recognition reveals hierarchical correspondence. Sci. Rep. **6**, 27755 (2016)
22. Kheradpisheh, S.R., Ganjtabesh, M., Thorpe, S.J., Masquelier, T.: STDP-based spiking deep convolutional neural networks for object recognition. arXiv:1611.01421 (2017)
23. Tavanaei, A., Maida, A.S.: Multi-layer unsupervised learning in a spiking convolutional neural network. In: 2017 International Joint Conference on Neural Networks (IJCNN), pp. 2023–2030 (2017)
24. Wen, H., Shi, J., Zhang, Y., Lu, K., Cao, J., Liu, Z.: Neural encoding and decoding with deep learning for dynamic natural vision. Cereb. Cortex, 1–25 (2017)

Sparsity Enables Data and Energy Efficient Spiking Convolutional Neural Networks

Varun Bhatt[✉] and Udayan Ganguly

Department of Electrical Engineering, Indian Institute of Technology Bombay,
Mumbai, India
varun.bhatt@iitb.ac.in, udayan@ee.iitb.ac.in

Abstract. In recent days, deep learning has surpassed human performance in image recognition tasks. A major issue with deep learning systems is their reliance on large datasets for optimal performance. When presented with a new task, generalizing from low amounts of data becomes highly attractive. Research has shown that human visual cortex might employ sparse coding to extract features from the images that we see, leading to efficient usage of available data. To ensure good generalization and energy efficiency, we create a multi-layer spiking convolutional neural network which performs layer-wise sparse coding for unsupervised feature extraction. It is applied on MNIST dataset where it achieves 92.3% accuracy with just 500 data samples, which is 4× less than what vanilla CNNs need for similar values, while reaching 98.1% accuracy with full dataset. Only around 7000 spikes are used per image (6× reduction in transferred bits per forward pass compared to CNNs) implying high sparsity. Thus, we show that our algorithm ensures better sparsity, leading to improved data and energy efficiency in learning, which is essential for some real-world applications.

Keywords: Sparse coding · Unsupervised learning
Feature extraction · Spiking neural networks · Training data efficiency

1 Introduction

Deep learning [1] has been successfully used in recent times for computer vision, speech recognition, natural language processing, and other similar tasks. Availability of large amounts of data and the processing power of GPUs are vital in training a deep neural network (DNN). The need for high processing power to enable performance has led to research on specialized hardware for deep learning and algorithms that can make use of those hardware. Spiking neural networks (SNNs) [2] are brain inspired networks which promise energy efficiency and higher computational power compared to artificial neural networks. Information is communicated using spikes and learning is done using local learning rules.

© Springer Nature Switzerland AG 2018
V. Kůrková et al. (Eds.): ICANN 2018, LNCS 11139, pp. 263–272, 2018.
https://doi.org/10.1007/978-3-030-01418-6_26

In some real world applications like recognizing a new language, exploring new environment, etc., large datasets are initially unavailable. Extracting useful information with the little available data becomes a major metric when comparing algorithms for these tasks. Without enough data, DNNs fail to generalize, and hence, their performance on unseen data is bad. Gathering large amounts of data is a difficult task and training using it puts a high penalty on energy consumption. Attempts towards human-like learning, which is mostly unsupervised and can generalize with a few examples are being made [3] to solve the data availability issue. On the other hand, when large amount of data is available as part of a standard dataset, performance of SNNs are not on par with state of the art DNNs. Thus, a critical goal is to learn in an energy efficient manner with small data while getting comparable results with larger datasets.

To achieve this goal, we use an improved sparse coding algorithm to train a multi-layer SNN layer-wise, in an unsupervised manner. Motivated by visual cortex of animals, sparse coding [4] can lead to efficient feature extraction as shown in Fig. 1. When patches of input image is given as input, basis vectors are learnt which can reconstruct the input. The learnt features are then passed to a layer trained in a supervised fashion for classification, which allows quantification of the quality of features extracted in terms of the accuracy obtained.

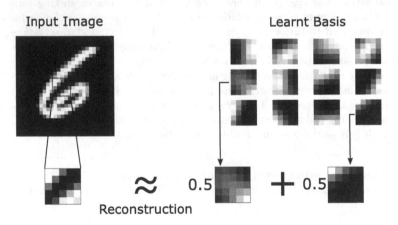

Fig. 1. Overview of sparse coding. A basis was learnt to efficiently reconstruct all patches of the input image. An example of how a patch is sparsely reconstructed using basis filters is shown.

In this paper, learning rules used to train the network are inspired by SAILnet [5], which is shown to perform sparse coding in SNNs. We modify the SAILnet learning rules to improve the quality of features extracted and promote higher sparsity which, in turn, is seen to improve the prediction accuracy. We then show that our network learns better than a vanilla CNN when small amount of data is given, while using local learning rules and being more efficient in terms of energy required for a forward pass. Such a performance is extremely relevant in applications like Internet of Things (IoT) or autonomous and mobile systems where large, labeled datasets are unavailable and energy is limited.

2   Background and Related Work

Spiking neural networks are becoming popular due to their energy efficiency, but they have not reached the accuracy levels given by DNNs. A possible reason for this is the lack of a general learning rule similar to backpropagation. Spike-timing-dependent plasticity (STDP) [6], training a DNN using backpropagation and transferring the weights to a SNN, sparse coding [4] are a few methods that have been tried to train SNNs.

Olshausen and Field [4] showed that sparse coding with an overcomplete basis leads to learning of filters which are similar to those found in the visual cortex of animals. Given a basis (dictionary), a class of algorithms called locally competitive algorithms (LCA) can be used to find the optimal sparse coefficients [7]. Further, it was proved in [8] that a SNN with lateral inhibition solves constrained LASSO problem and learns the optimal sparse coefficients. An algorithm to learn the dictionary in SNNs, called Sparse And Independent Local network (SAILnet) was proposed in [5]. Filters learnt using this algorithm were similar in shape to those found in biology. SAILnet is used to train one layer of convolutional filters in [9], which is extended to multiple layers in our work.

In comparison to our approach which involves rate coding, i.e., information is coded as rate of spiking, there exists various other examples of sparse coding using STDP - which is essentially temporal coding, i.e., information is coded in the exact time of spiking. STDP with hard lateral inhibition is used in [10] for unsupervised layer-wise training of a spiking CNN, followed by a SVM for classification. A similar architecture, with simplified STDP rule and a winner-takes-all (WTA) mechanism, is used in [11] to train the CNN. A multi-layer perceptron is used for classification. A fully unsupervised learning approach using SNNs is given in [12] where training is done using STDP and accuracy is calculated based on response of neurons. A non-local, gradient descent type learning rule is used in [13] to train individual layers of a multi-layer SNN similar to auto-encoders.

All the above examples use temporal coding, while our approach has been to use rate based learning rules to enable rate coding. Rate coding is easier to implement in hardware and robust to noise since the exact temporal structure of spiking is not relevant and only the rate of spiking matters. Certain sensory and motor neurons are found to use rate coding, giving it a biological validation.

3   Network Architecture and Learning Rules

Our network architecture consists of multiple convolutional layers, each followed by a max pooling layer. The last max pooling layer is followed by a fully connected layer for classification. Each convolutional layer consists of spiking neurons performing sparse coding as explained in Sect. 3.1. Figure 2 shows the architecture of our network for MNIST dataset which is chosen based on best accuracy obtained during experiments. We use two convolutional layers, one with 12 filters of size 5×5 and other with 64 filters of size 5×5, both with stride of 1. Max pooling filters following both the layers are of size 2×2. Fully connected layer is a single layer artificial neural network.

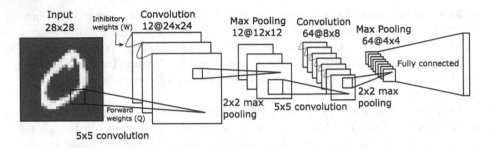

Fig. 2. Network architecture.

3.1 Spiking Neural Network

Our network uses spiking neurons in each convolutional layer. Since in a CNN, weights are shared between receptive fields, consider a single patch of image as the input and the SNN to be fully connected with number of outputs equal to the number of convolutional filters for the purpose of this discussion. For the first layer, current proportional to the intensity of input image is multiplied by the forward weights $(\mathbf{Q}^{(1)})$ and passed as input to the neurons. For subsequent layers, current proportional to the firing rate of neurons of previous layer is multiplied by the corresponding forward weights $(\mathbf{Q}^{(1)})$ and passed as input to next layer. The neurons integrate the current and fire a spike on reaching a threshold (θ). When a neuron spikes, other output neurons are inhibited through a negative current proportional to the inhibitory weights $(\mathbf{W}^{(1)})$.

Mathematically, each neuron is leaky integrate and fire, maintaining an internal variable $V_i^{(l)}$, which is updated as

$$V_i^{(l)}(t+1) \leftarrow (1-\eta)V_i^{(l)}(t) + \eta(\sum_k x_k^{(l)} Q_{ki}^{(l)} - \sum_j a_j^{(l)} W_{ij}^{(l)}), \qquad (1)$$

where $\mathbf{X}^{(l)}$ is the input to l^{th} layer, $a_j^{(l)}$ indicates whether neuron j spiked in the previous time step, and η (set to 0.1 in our experiments) is a parameter controlling the rate of decay of the internal variable. For each presentation of the input, SNN is simulated for 50 time steps and the rate of spiking $(n_i^{(l)})$ is given by number of spikes divided by 50.

3.2 Convolution and Max Pooling

To perform the convolution operation, we divide the input into patches which are to be passed through convolutional filters. Each patch is then passed as input to the SNN. Simulation of SNN is done and the firing rates are obtained which are used as inputs to the next layer. SNN simulation corresponding to individual patches can be performed in parallel since they are independent of each other.

Max pooling layer simply picks the neuron with highest firing rate in its receptive field.

3.3 Training

Training is done layer-wise, i.e., a layer is fully trained and its weights are frozen before training the next layer. While our algorithm allows training all layers together, we found that the quality of features extracted was worse compared to layer-wise training

For training a layer, a SNN corresponding to that layer is first initialized and convolution operation is performed. Based on the firing rates of the output neurons, weights in SNN are updated according to the rules given in the next subsection. The new weights are used while simulating SNN for future inputs. This cycle of simulating SNN and updating weights is repeated for given number of input presentations. Once enough images are presented, SNN weights are frozen and firing rates corresponding to each patch of images are used as input to the next layer.

When all convolutional layers are trained, the output of final max pooling layer is used as input to a fully connected artificial neural network which is trained to classify the dataset.

3.4 Learning Rules

The learning rules used to update weights of SNN are inspired by SAILnet [5] and LCA [8] and lead to solving the sparse coding problem.

Sparse coding tries to represent given input using a set of overcomplete basis vectors such that the components of the input in this new basis are sparse (as close to zero as possible). Mathematically, it involves solving the following optimization problem:

$$\min_{n_i^{(j)}, \mathbf{Q_i}} \sum_{j=1}^{m} \left[||\mathbf{x}^{(j)} - \sum_i n_i^{(j)} \mathbf{Q_i}||^2 + \lambda \sum_i S(n_i^{(j)}) \right], \qquad (2)$$

where $\mathbf{x}^{(j)}$ represents the jth input sample, $\mathbf{Q_i}$ are the basis vectors and $n_i^{(j)}$ are the coefficients corresponding to j^{th} input sample which can be used to reconstruct the input as $\mathbf{x}^{(j)} = \sum_i n_i^{(j)} \mathbf{Q_i}$. In our work, we have taken the sparsity penalty $S(.)$ to be the L1 norm.

Original SAILnet implementation updates the weights $(\mathbf{Q}, \mathbf{W})$ as well as the firing threshold of neurons (θ) to solve the sparse coding problem. It uses a hyperparameter p, which is kept equal to a low value, to represent the target firing rate. We modify the SAILnet learning rules in our implementation as given in Table 1.

We keep θ constant similar to LCA as opposed to updating it as given in SAILnet. This allows simpler neurons without varying thresholds to be used in the network. With θ constant, $-p^2$ term in update for $\mathbf{W}$ does not make sense and empirically, we found that our modified rules gave an improvement in final accuracy given by the network.

Table 1. Comparison of SAILnet learning rules and our modification.

Original SAILnet	Our modification
$\Delta Q_{ki} = \beta n_i(x_k - n_i Q_{ki})$	No modification
$\Delta W_{ij} = \alpha(n_i n_j - p^2)$	$\Delta W_{ij} = \alpha n_i n_j$
$\Delta \theta_i = \gamma(n_i - p)$	θ is constant

Updating $\mathbf{Q}$ ensures correct reconstruction of input while updating $\mathbf{W}$ ensures that firing rates of neurons are independent. Due to lateral inhibition in the architecture, $\mathbf{W}$ also leads to sparsity.

Gradient of the cost function with respect to Q_{ki} is $n_i(x_k - \sum_j n_j Q_{kj})$ but it is shown in [5] that this gradient can be approximated as above to make the learning rule local, without much loss in reconstruction error.

4   Experiments

This section describes the experimental setup, training method and the results obtained. We use MNIST dataset to evaluate our network. MNIST dataset consists of 60,000 training images and 10,000 test images of handwritten digits from 0 to 9. All images are grayscale and 28×28 in size.

4.1   Comparison of Learning Rules Using Fully Connected SNN

First, we check if the modifications done to the SAILnet learning rule lead to better performance of the network. To compare the quality of features extracted with our learning rule and the SAILnet baseline, we created a SNN which took whole MNIST images as the input and performed sparse coding using 25 output neurons. A fully-connected SNN is used since the difference between convolutional filters is hard to see visually.

Figures 3a and b show the filters learnt. Ideally, the filters should look like different digits since they are used to reconstruct MNIST images. But in the SAILnet case, there are many filters which are a mixture of digits and all digits are not represented. With our modified learning rule, such mixed digits are significantly reduced and the diversity of shapes in the filters is increased. We believe it is because SAILnet updates θ such that the firing rates are equal to a low value p, instead of ideally being close to zero, which drove some filters to learn redundant features for simple datasets like MNIST. Sparsity also improved with our modification, with an average of 65 spikes needed per image compared to 85 spikes when trained with original SAILnet rules.

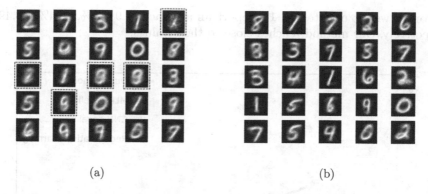

(a)   (b)

Fig. 3. Filters learnt by using (a) SAILnet rules and (b) our modification (Sect. 4.1). All 10 digits are represented when using our modification as compared to 8 digits with SAILnet. The marked filters are redundant since they are a mixture of multiple digits.

4.2   Comparing Learning with Varying Data Size

A random subset of data of size varying from 500 to 50000 is taken for training and validation. 75% of it is used for training and the rest is kept for validation. Both training and validation data are used to learn SNN weights in unsupervised manner. Training data is further used to train the supervised layer while the validation data is used to adjust the hyperparameters of the network. Accuracy is reported on an unseen subset of size 10000 and compared against two baselines. First baseline is randomly initializing the SNN, freezing the weights and training only the supervised layer (MLP baseline). This baseline shows the usefulness of features extracted by the convolutional layers. Second baseline is a vanilla CNN with same architecture but trained using backpropagation (CNN baseline). In all cases, no pre-processing or data augmentation is done.

For training data of size 500, $\alpha = 10$, $\beta = 0.1$ are used for SNN weight updates and $\theta = 0.005$ is taken as the firing threshold of neurons. Batch size of 100 is used and training is done for 1000 epochs. Number of epochs is scaled to keep the effective amount of updates same as the data size increases. Supervised layer and CNN baseline use Adam optimizer with learning rate 0.001 for backpropagation with same batch size and epochs.

Accuracy. Figure 4 shows classification error as a function of training data size. Our method reaches 92.3% accuracy with 500 samples, increasing to 95.6% with 3000 and 97.7% with 30000 samples respectively. With full dataset, the obtained accuracy is 98.1%. It can be seen from the figure that our method performs significantly better than baselines with small data while only becoming slightly worse than CNN baseline as the data size increases.

Regenerative learning [13] outperforms CNN baseline but is worse compared to our method below 10000 data samples. It also has an additional disadvantage of needing a non-local learning rule and requiring the internal variable of the neuron in weight updates. [9–11] report an accuracy of 98.36%, 98.4%, 98.49% respectively. Our method reaches close to those values.

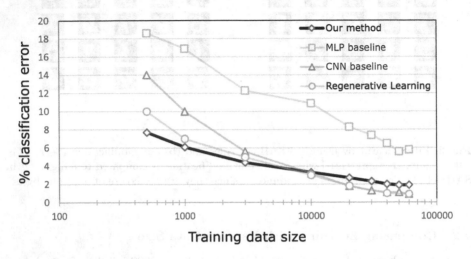

Fig. 4. Classification error vs data size for MNIST data set. SNN is not trained for MLP baseline. Backpropagation is used to train CNN in CNN baseline.

Sparsity. The learnt SNN weights promote sparsity and independence in the firing rate of neurons. Neurons in all layers combined, spike only 7000 number of times per image on an average. Lower number of spikes denotes efficient information transfer and also low energy usage if this is implemented in hardware. Figure 5a shows the distribution of firing rates of neurons. It can be observed that most neurons fire less than twice during a SNN simulation. Figures 5b and c show the average correlation between firing rates of neurons for first and second layer respectively. Near zero values of off-diagonal elements show that firing rates are almost independent. The mean reconstruction error in the first layer is 2.5 compared to 75.6 before training SNN weights.

We hypothesize that sparsity plays a major role in being able to generalize with little data. Since inhibitory weights are indirectly controlling the amount of sparsity and α controls the amount of increase in inhibitory weights, reducing α reduces sparsity. With 500 data samples, the network is trained with various values of α, keeping everything else constant. Figure 6 shows accuracy and average spikes per image as a function of α and it can be observed that lower sparsity indeed reduces the accuracy of the network.

To perform a rough estimate of the advantage of spiking architecture and sparsity for energy efficiency, we consider the number of bits that are needed to during forward pass of an image. Since a spike can be represented using 1 bit, our network uses an average of 7000 bits per image. Vanilla CNN baseline that we use needs to transmit around 1300 non-zero floating point numbers per image,

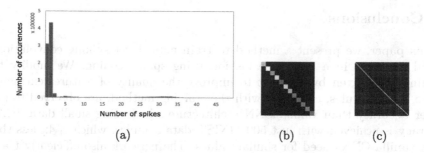

(a)   (b)   (c)

Fig. 5. (a) Distribution of firing rates corresponding to all images. Most of the neurons spike at most once per image presentation. (b), (c) Average correlation between firing rates of neurons for first and second layer respectively. Off-diagonal elements are close to zero showing independence in firing rates.

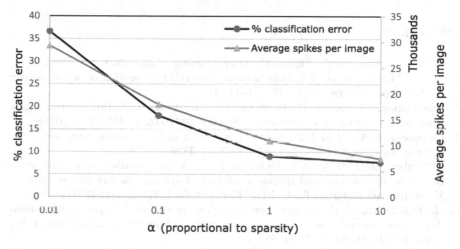

Fig. 6. Classification error and average spikes per image vs α. Lower α implies lower inhibition and hence, lower sparsity which is leading to more errors in classification.

translating to nearly 42000 bits which is 6 times worse than the performance of our network.

5   Discussions

Data and spike efficiency of our algorithm directly translates to energy efficiency when implemented in hardware. Examples of custom hardware for training SNNs are available in literature. Implementation of energy efficient algorithms in such custom SNN hardware is a promising approach to mobile, autonomous systems and IoT applications. Training and inference in such systems can be further optimized if the classification layer is also spiking based and implemented in similar hardware.

6   Conclusions

In this paper, we present a method to train multi-layer spiking convolutional neural networks in a layer-wise fashion using sparse coding. We modify the learning rules given by SAILnet to improve the quality of features extracted. These learning rules, combined with the training method, are observed to give better accuracy than vanilla CNN architecture when using small data. 92.3% accuracy is achieved with just 500 MNIST data samples, which is 4x less than what vanilla CNNs need for similar values. The network also efficiently transfers information between layers, using only 7000 spikes on average to represent a MNIST image, a 6x reduction in number of bits compared to CNN baseline. Such data and spike efficient algorithm will enable energy efficiency for mobile, autonomous systems and IoT applications.

References

1. LeCun, Y., Bengio, Y., Hinton, G.: Deep learning. Nature **521**, 436 (2015)
2. Maass, W.: Networks of spiking neurons: the third generation of neural network models. Neural Netw. **10**(9), 1659–1671 (1997)
3. Tenenbaum, J.B., Kemp, C., Griffiths, T.L., Goodman, N.D.: How to grow a mind: statistics, structure, and abstraction. Science **331**(6022), 1279–1285 (2011)
4. Olshausen, B.A., Field, D.J.: Sparse coding with an overcomplete basis set: a strategy employed by V1? Vis. Res. **37**(23), 3311–3325 (1997)
5. Zylberberg, J., Murphy, J.T., DeWeese, M.R.: A sparse coding model with synaptically local plasticity and spiking neurons can account for the diverse shapes of V1 simple cell receptive fields. PLoS Comput. Biol. **7**(10), 1–12 (2011)
6. Bi, G.Q., Poo, M.M.: Synaptic modifications in cultured hippocampal neurons: dependence on spike timing, synaptic strength, and postsynaptic cell type. J. Neurosci. **18**(24), 10464–10472 (1998)
7. Rozell, C., Johnson, D., Baraniuk, R., Olshausen, B.: Locally competitive algorithms for sparse approximation. In: 2007 IEEE International Conference on Image Processing, vol. 4, pp. IV-169–IV-172 (2007)
8. Tang, P.T.P., Lin, T., Davies, M.: Sparse coding by spiking neural networks: convergence theory and computational results. CoRR abs/1705.05475 (2017)
9. Tavanaei, A., Maida, A.S.: Multi-layer unsupervised learning in a spiking convolutional neural network. In: 2017 International Joint Conference on Neural Networks (IJCNN), pp. 2023–2030 (2017)
10. Kheradpisheh, S.R., Ganjtabesh, M., Thorpe, S.J., Masquelier, T.: STDP-based spiking deep neural networks for object recognition. CoRR abs/1611.01421 (2016)
11. Ferré, P., Mamalet, F., Thorpe, S.J.: Unsupervised feature learning with winner-takes-all based STDP. Front. Comput. Neurosci. **12**, 24 (2018)
12. Diehl, P., Cook, M.: Unsupervised learning of digit recognition using spike-timing-dependent plasticity. Front. Comput. Neurosci. **9**, 99 (2015)
13. Panda, P., Roy, K.: Unsupervised regenerative learning of hierarchical features in spiking deep networks for object recognition. CoRR abs/1602.01510 (2016)

Design of Spiking Rate Coded Logic Gates for C. elegans Inspired Contour Tracking

Shashwat Shukla$^{(\boxtimes)}$, Sangya Dutta, and Udayan Ganguly

Indian Institute of Technology Bombay, Mumbai, India
shashwat.shukla@iitb.ac.in

Abstract. Bio-inspired energy efficient control is a frontier for autonomous navigation and robotics. *Binary* input output neuronal logic gates are demonstrated in literature – while *analog* input-output logic gates are needed for continuous analog real-world control. In this paper, we design logic gates such as AND, OR and XOR using networks of Leaky Integrate-and-Fire neurons with *analog* rate (frequency) coded inputs and output, where refractory period is shown to be a critical knob for neuronal design. To demonstrate our design method, we present contour tracking inspired by the chemotaxis network of the worm *C. elegans* and demonstrate for the first time an end-to-end Spiking Neural Network (SNN) solution. First, we demonstrate contour tracking with an average deviation equal to literature with non-neuronal logic gates. Second, 2x improvement in tracking accuracy is enabled by implementing latency reduction leading to state of the art performance with an average deviation of 0.55% from the set-point. Third, a new feature of local extrema escape is demonstrated with an *analog* XOR gate, which uses only 5 neurons – better than *binary* logic neuronal circuits. The XOR gate demonstrates the universality of our logic scheme. Finally, we demonstrate the hardware feasibility of our network based on experimental results on 32 nm Silicon-on-Insulator (SOI) based artificial neurons with tunable refractory periods. Thus, we present a general framework of analog neuronal control logic along with the feasibility of their implementation in mature SOI technology platform for autonomous SNN navigation controller hardware.

Keywords: Spiking Neural Network · Motor control
Neuromorphic computing

1 Introduction

Spiking Neural Networks (**SNNs**) are third generation Artificial Neural Networks that attempt to model neurons as computing units with underlying temporal dynamics that resembles the spiking nature of biological neurons. While SNNs have been used to solve a variety of problems in classification and regression, an equally intriguing aspect is the implementation of control in a natural setting that could serve the dual purpose of (i) demystifying complex biological behavior and (ii) inspiring efficient robotics applications. Chemotaxis in *Caenorhabditis elegans* (C. *elegans*) is an example of such a biological behaviour which requires control. C. *elegans* is a free living nematode,

© Springer Nature Switzerland AG 2018
V. Kůrková et al. (Eds.): ICANN 2018, LNCS 11139, pp. 273–283, 2018.
https://doi.org/10.1007/978-3-030-01418-6_27

which can sense a large number of chemicals including NaCl. This ability allows these worms to find and subsequently move along a set point in the chemical concentration space so as to locate food sources. Typically, the sensory neurons ASEL and ASER provide chemical gradient information [4], and this information is used by interneurons in the worm to decide the direction to subsequently move along to reach the chemical set-point. The output of this computation is fed to motor neurons, which actuate their motion. Santurkar et al. [3] proposed a SNN model for chemical contour tracking inspired by C. *elegans*. They demonstrate the superiority of spiking architectures over non-spiking models and their tolerance to noise using the biologically realistic model of sensory neurons proposed in [4]. However, the inter-neuronal operations required to drive motor neurons were computed without using neural circuits. Instead, an artificial mathematical computation was used. Hence the SNN is not performing integrated, end-to-end control of all three stages of computation i.e. (i) sensory neuron (ii) interneuron (iii) motor neuron levels. Such external control is neither biologically realistic nor energy-area efficient. Further, more sophisticated/realistic behaviour, such as escaping a local extrema, without which the worm fails to reach the desired concentration over arbitrary concentration landscapes, has not been demonstrated in neuronal circuits.

Existing SNN based logic gates [11–14] encode binary logic values using fixed spiking frequencies (low/high). But, the output spiking frequency of the gate should vary proportionately to one or more input spiking frequencies so that the worm turns in proportion to the urgency of sensory signals. This motivates the design of *analog* rate coded logic gates.

In this paper, first, we implement *analog* rate-coded logic *gates* (AND, OR, XOR) by designing neuronal responses using *refractory periods*. Second, we integrate AND and OR with the sensory and motor neurons to demonstrate end-to-end control in the chemotaxis network. Third, we incorporate an additional sub-network using the XOR gate to escape a local extrema. The XOR, being a universal gate, also enables random logic circuit implementation. Our design enables a reduced number of neurons for logic gates which leads to lower response latency (measured between sensory input and motor neuron output), critical for many control applications. Fourth, we modify the response of sensory neurons proposed in [3] to reduce response latency to enable significantly improved tracking compared to state-of-the-art. Finally, a hardware neuron with configurable refractory period is demonstrated on a highly matured 32 nm silicon-on-insulator CMOS technology.

2 Network Architecture

Figure 1 shows the proposed SNN architecture for chemotaxis in C. *elegans*. All the neurons in our network are Leaky Integrate and Fire neurons. The following sections will discuss the functional role of all the neurons used in this network.

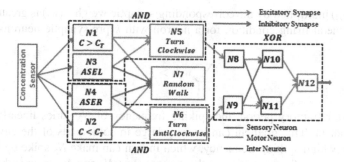

Fig. 1. Block diagram of the proposed SNN for contour tracking. N_1, N_2, N_3 and N_4 are sensory neurons, receiving input from the concentration sensor. N_5, N_6, N_7, N_{12} are motor neurons. N_8, N_9, N_{10}, N_{11} are the interneurons used to implement the XOR sub-network. The spiking frequency of N_{12} is the XOR of the spiking frequencies of N_5 and N_6.

2.1 Turning Left and Right: The AND Sub-network

2.1.1 Sensory Neurons

As shown in Fig. 1, the neurons N_1 and N_2 are threshold detectors. N_1 fires when the current concentration (C) is greater than the set-point C_T i.e. $C > C_T$, while N_2 fires when $C < C_T$. A hard-threshold (ideally a step-function) is compared to a soft-threshold based N_1 in Fig. 2. N_3 and N_4 are gradient (dC/dt) detectors, firing respectively for positive ($dC/dt > 0$) and negative ($dC/dt < 0$) changes in concentration. The input to all four sensory neurons, at each time step (t), is the concentration at the current location of the worm. The equations for the ionic currents that implement the required responses have been delegated to the appendix.

2.1.2 Motor Neurons

The target for the worm is to reach the desired concentration set-point C_T. If at a particular time instant, the worm detects $dC/dt > 0$ (i.e. N_3 spikes) and $C > C_T$ (i.e. N_1 spikes), the worm infers that it is moving away from C_T and hence tries to turn around. In this case the worm turns right by $3°$ and moves forward at a velocity of 0.01 mm/s with the rate of turning being proportional to dC/dt. The motor neuron N_5 encodes this command. Hence, the spiking frequency of N_5 has to be the output of an AND operation over the spiking frequencies of N_1 and N_3. i.e. $N_5 = \textbf{AND}(N_1, N_3)$. The bold face is used to denote spiking frequency of the corresponding neuron. Similarly, the motor neuron N_6 spikes if $dC/dt < 0$ (i.e. N_4 spikes) and $C < C_T$ (i.e. N_2 spikes). In this case, the worm turns left by $3°$ at a velocity of 0.01 mm/s and the motor neuron N_6 encodes this command i.e. $N_6 = \textbf{AND}(N_2, N_4)$. When $dC/dt > 0$ and $C < C_T$ or $dC/dt < 0$ and $C > C_T$, the worm infers that it is moving towards C_T and hence keeps moving forward at a constant velocity without turning.

2.1.3 Design Principles for the AND Sub-network

Under the rate-coded approximation (which implies that injected current is assumed to be proportional to the spiking frequency), a neuron fires if the sum of the input spiking frequencies (f_i) multiplied by the corresponding synaptic weights (w_i) is greater than f_{th}. Hence the general firing condition for a neuron with k pre-synaptic neurons is:

$$\sum_{i=1}^{k} w_i f_i > f_{th} \tag{1}$$

Without a refractory period, the spiking frequency of N_3 varies linearly with the observed gradient. This gradient can be very large in some parts of the environment, leading to very high spiking frequency, which in turn can make N_5 spike by itself even if N_1 is not spiking. The saturation in the responses of N_1 and N_3 ensures that N_5 only fires when *both* N_1 and N_3 fire and hence acts as an AND gate. We choose w_1 and w_3 such that: $w_1 f_{1,\max} = w_3 f_{3,\max} = f_{th}^-$, where $f_{1,\max}, f_{3,\max}$ are respectively the maximum spiking frequencies of N_1 and N_3, and f_{th}^- is some value close to, but *smaller than* f_{th} We choose f_{th}^- to be close to f_{th} so that even a small value of f_3 will lead to N_5 spiking, hence ensuring the control circuit's sensitivity to very small gradients as well.

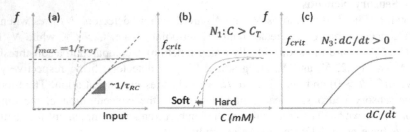

Fig. 2. (a) A typical LIF neuron (blue dashed line) has almost a rectified linear unit (ReLU) behaviour where the slope decreases with the membrane time constant τ_{RC} of the LIF neuron. Adding a refractory period (τ_{ref}) limits maximum frequency (f_{max}) to $1/\tau_{ref}$. (b) N_1 neuron $f(C)$ behaviour where it fires when C exceeds C_T. Softer threshold initiates spiking before the hard-threshold. (c) N_3 neuron has $f(dC/dt)$ behaviour which has a spike frequency proportional to the $dC/dt > 0$; Both N_1 and N_3 have an $f_{max} < f_{crit}$ such that neither can individually cause N_5 to spike but they need to fire together to cause N_5 to fire to enable the analog AND operation where N_5 fires proportionally to N_3 only if N_1 also fires. Otherwise, N_5 does not fire. (Color figure online)

The responses of the threshold detectors (N_1 and N_2) were taken as step functions in [3] with the transition at the desired set-point. This discontinuous response is softened to a sigmoid (as shown in Fig. 2(b)) by introducing a refractory period (chosen using the same logic as for N_3). The onset of the sigmoidal response is chosen to be *before* the set-point, allowing the worm to turn a little before it has reached the set-point. This enables latency reduction and closer tracking of the set-point. Identical reasoning holds for the N_2, N_4 and N_6 sub-network.

2.2 Random Walk

When the worm is on flat terrain and hence no gradient is detected ($dC/dt \sim 0$), the worm explores its surroundings randomly. This random search is initiated by motor neuron N_7. The spiking of N_7 causes the worm to move at an increased velocity of 0.3 mm/s and to randomly turn by an angle uniformly distributed in $[-22.5°, 22.5°]$. This strategy allows for rapid exploration of a local space, with N_7 continuing to fire until a gradient is detected.

2.3 Escaping Local Extrema: The XOR Sub-network

When the worm has found, and is tracking the set-point, N_5 and N_6 fire alternately as the worm keeps swerving left and right. However if only N_5 or only N_6 fires *exclusively*, then the worm is only turning left or right and hence going around in circles. Such a scenario is described in Fig. 3. If the worm starts anywhere in the valley, it will not be able to get out, as every time it moves up towards the rim of the valley (i.e. $dC/dt > 0$), N_3 fires with continuous firing of N_1 as $C > C_T$ at every point. As a consequence, N_5 will fire, making the worm turn back towards the basin. The worm then moves straight and now climbs up the other side and this process repeats. A second case where the worm would again be stuck is the scenario obtained when Fig. 3 is inverted on its head i.e. a small peak surrounded by a valley.

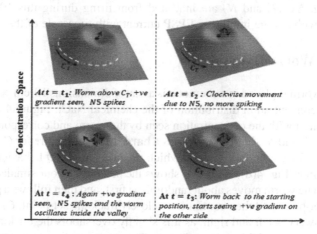

At $t = t_1$: Worm above C_T, +ve gradient seen, N5 spikes

At $t = t_2$: Clockwise movement due to N5, no more spiking

At $t = t_4$: Again +ve gradient seen, N5 spikes and the worm oscillates inside the valley

At $t = t_3$: Worm back to the starting position, starts seeing +ve gradient on the other side

Fig. 3. Panels depicting the worm stuck in a valley at four consecutive time steps, in the absence of the XOR subnetwork.

Hence to solve this problem of getting stuck close to a local extrema, the XOR sub network is developed whose output is N_{12}. N_{12} is supposed to fire, if only N_5 or only N_6 is found to spike over some time period, i.e. $N_{12} = \mathbf{XOR}(N_5, N_6)$. When N_{12} fires, the worm moves straight for 10 s, without turning, at a velocity of 0.5 mm/s and then resumes normal operation, having escaped the area where it was stuck. Such behavior has been observed in biology as well [5].

2.3.1   Design Principles for the XOR Sub-network

To enable XOR function, only the spiking events at N_5 or N_6 need to be detected. For such operation, we introduce a large refractory period of 10 s in the interneurons N_8 and N_9 and also set a very low voltage threshold for both these neurons, such that a single spike from N_5 is enough to make N_8 fire. Once N_8 fires, it will remain unresponsive for 10 s due to the refractory period. N_8 hence acts as a timed event detector. The same description holds for N_6 and N_9.

If we consider a long enough time period (~ 10 s) for our control problem, and N_8 fires once before and once after this period, without any spike from N_9, we infer that only N_5 has been firing for a significant amount of time. Hence, the worm needs to escape from this region. Similarly, if N_9 fired once before and once after a period of 10 s with N_8 not firing in between, the worm must escape this area.

We design N_{10} such that it fires once for every *two times* that N_8 fires. Note that if N_9 fires intermittently in the refractory period of N_8, then N_{10} will not fire due to the inhibitory connection linking N_9 to N_{10}. Interchanging the roles of N_8 and N_9 yields the behavior of N_{11}.

It is important to note that the current injected into N_{10} and N_{11} by N_8 and N_9 decay at a time scale much faster than the refractory period. Thus we chose very small values for the membrane conductance of N_8 and N_9 i.e. these two neurons are not very leaky and effectively function as integrators over this time-scale. Finally, N_{12} has a low spiking threshold, and functions as an OR gate. It fires when either N_{10} or N_{11} fires, i.e. $N_{12} = \text{OR}(N_{10}, N_{11})$. The firing of N_{12} causes the worm to move straight for 10 s, without turning. N_5, N_6 and N_7 are inhibited from firing during this 10 s period by injecting them with a large inhibitory EPSP current with timescale of the order of 10 s.

3   Results: Worm Dynamics

Our simulated worm is placed in a chemotaxis assay of dimensions 10 cm × 10 cm, with some arbitrary concentration distribution of the chemical NaCl. Figure 4 demonstrates the AND operation with the concentration seen by the worm and corresponding spiking patterns for N_1, N_3 and N_5. In Fig. 4, N_1 uses a **hard threshold** to fire for $C > C_T$ (Fig. 4 (b)) and N_3 fires for $C > C_T$ (Fig. 4(c)) which produces an AND behaviour at N_5 **with significant latency** (Fig. 4(d)). Figure 5 shows the behavior of our simulated worm for $C_T = 54$ mM. The worm moves about randomly at first, and then follows a gradient until it reaches the set-point and then continues to closely track the set-point, C_T. We observe that the worm swerves left and right, as it is slightly overshoots the tracking concentration, corrects it course and this process repeats. The corresponding concentration seen by the worm, shown in Fig. 6 shows an average 0.82% (absolute) deviation from set-point (as a fraction of the range of concentration in this space).

In Fig. 7, N_1 uses a pre-emptive soft threshold to fire earlier for $C > C_T$ (Fig. 7(b)) and N_3 fires for $C > C_T$ (Fig. 7c)). This produces an AND behaviour at N_5 with **reduced latency** (Fig. 7(d)). Figure 9 shows the concentration seen by the worm as it traced the trajectory in Fig. 8 to show 0.55% tracking accuracy, which is a 1.5× improvement over that in Fig. 6 due to the pre-emptive soft threshold. Figure 10 shows a simulated scenario where the worm gets stuck in a local minimum and is unable to escape. With the XOR sub-network added to our SNN, it can be seen that the worm can successfully come out of the concentration valley and starts tracking the set point as shown in Fig. 11.

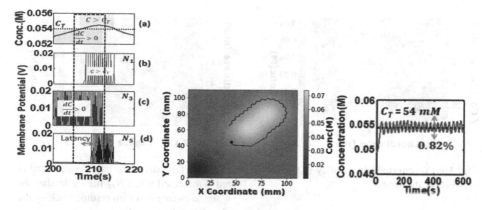

Fig. 4. (a) Concentration vs time (b) Response of N_1 for $C > C_T$ with **hard threshold** and (c) N_3 for dC/dt > 0 which produces (d) an AND function response at N_5 with a significant latency (red arrow). (Color figure online)

Fig. 5. Contour tracking with hard thresholding, $C_T = 54$ mM.

Fig. 6. Concentration tracking shows 0.82% deviation about set point due to hard-thresholding response of N_1.

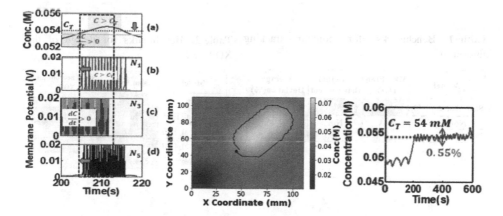

Fig. 7. (a) Concentration vs time (b) Response of N_1 with **soft threshold** f o r $C > C_T$ and (c) N_3 for dC/dt > 0 which produces (d) an AND function response at N_5 with a reduced latency (red arrow). (Color figure online)

Fig. 8. Improved contour tracking with soft thresholding, $C_T = 54$ mM.

Fig. 9. Concentration tracking shows 0.55% deviation which is a 1.5X improvement due to softened response of N_1.

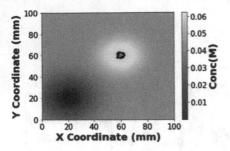
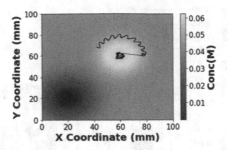

Fig. 10. Worm stuck in a valley (XOR sub-network is disabled).

Fig. 11. The part of the trajectory marked in red is traversed when N_{12} fires, allowing the worm to escape and then resume tracking the C_T. (Color figure online)

4 Benchmarking

Table 1 benchmarks our network with previously reported contour tracking algorithms. We achieve state-of-the-art performance, with lower spiking frequencies, making our network more energy efficient. Table 2 shows the efficiency of our XOR gate implementation in terms of number of neurons used. It also works in an analog fashion unlike other reported SNN based gates, which is essential for our network.

Table 1. Benchmarks for contour tracking algorithm

Model	Max Freq (Hz)	External Bias Current	Average Deviation(%)
Santurkar et al. [3]	10	Yes	1± 0.13
Non-SNN	N.A	N.A	10± 2.9
This Work	5	No	0.55 ± 0.16

Table 2. Benchmarks for design of the XOR gate

Model	Input Values	No. of neurons for XOR
Delaney et al. [11]	Binary	6
Wade et al. [14]	Binary	12
Berger et al. [12]	Binary	7
Ferrari et al. [13]	Binary	23
This Work	Continuous	5

5 Hardware Feasibility

Hardware realization of such a SNN calls for both the feasibility as well as designability of the neuronal response. Recently our group has proposed and experimentally demonstrated a SOI MOSFET based LIF neuron [2]. The neuronal functionality has been achieved by using the SOI transistor's intrinsic carrier dynamics. The response of the SOI neuron shows high sensitivity with MHz order frequency range.

Figure 12a shows the TEM image of the fabricated SOI neuron. Figure 12b shows the response curves of such SOI neuron for different refractory periods (t_{ref}).

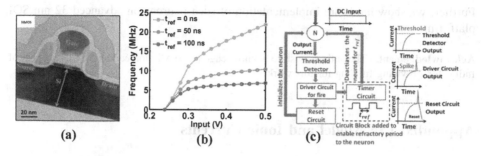

Fig. 12. (a) TEM image of the PD SOI MOSFET fabricated using 32 nm SOI technology [2]. (b) Experimental frequency vs input curve. Without t_{ref}, the response increases sharply with input, whereas adding t_{ref} limits the frequency range. (c) Block diagram demonstrating the implementation of refractory period in SOI neuron. The neuron generates current output which is fed to the threshold detector. At threshold, the driver circuit elicits a spike enabling the timer circuit. The timer circuit deactivates the neuron during the refractory period. The reset circuit initializes the neuron. The expected transient output is shown at the output of three circuit block.

Without any refractory period, the response keeps increasing with input stimuli. Addition of t_{ref} limits the firing rate and the frequency saturates at a particular value like biological neurons. Such a tunable response provides freedom in SNN design for various applications and also aids the scope of hardware implementation. Figure 12c shows the block diagram for the implementation of refractory period in SOI neuron. The proposed electronic neuron is highly energy (35 pJ/spike) efficient and consumes lesser area (~ 1700 F^2 at 32 nm technology node) compared to state of the art CMOS neurons.

6 Conclusions

A complete end-to-end SNN based control circuit is proposed for chemotaxis in *C. elegans*. To implement this, analog rate-coded AND, OR, and XOR logic gates based inter-neuronal circuits are proposed. We implemented these gates using a small number of neurons, allowing for energy and area efficiency as well as reduced network latency, which is crucial for many robotics applications. The network latency was further reduced by modifying the response of the threshold detecting sensory neurons. We ensure correct operation of the network over arbitrary concentration ranges and choose parameters of the network using an analytic approach designed using the rate-coded approximation. The neuronal behaviors required to implement the neural logic gates are achieved by LIF neurons with configurable refractory periods. State-of-the-art accuracy of tracking is demonstrated (<0.6% deviation from set-point). To address the problem of being stuck around a local extrema en route to a set-point, we designed a novel XOR based sub-network that presents a biologically relevant solution. As XOR is a universal gate, this enables the implementation of any arbitrary logical functions in SNN.

Further, we show hardware implementation of such neurons on advanced 32 nm SOI platform.

Acknowledgement. The authors wish to acknowledge Nano Mission & MeitY, Government of India, for providing funding for this work.

Appendix: LIF Model and Ionic Currents

All the neurons used in our model are LIF neurons with refractory periods [17]. N_1, N_2, N_3 and N_4 have ionic channels that inject input current $I_e(t)$. The specific nature of $I_e(t)$ is what allows them to functions as threshold and gradient detectors. The ionic currents injected into N_1 and N_2 respectively are $I_{e1}(t)$ and $I_{e2}(t)$, given as:

$$I_{e,1}(t) = I_{e,0}\max(0,\ C - C_T - \delta);\ I_{e,2}(t) = I_{e,0}\max(0,\ C_T + \delta - C) \qquad (2)$$

The δ governs the degree of preemptive response of the threshold detectors. A set of equations that define $I_{e3}(t)$ and $I_{e4}(t)$ was proposed in [4] and used in [3]. We also use the same equations for the gradient detectors N_3 and N_4. These equations along with a detailed explanation can be found in Sect. II of [3].

References

1. Maas, W.: Networks of spiking neurons: the third generation of neural network models. Neural Netw. **10**(9), 1659–1671 (1997)
2. Dutta, S., et al.: Leaky integrate and fire neuron by charge-discharge dynamics in floating-body MOSFET. Sci. Rep. **7**, 8257 (2017)
3. Santurkar, S., Rajendran, B.: C. elegans chemotaxis inspired neuromorphic circuit for contour tracking and obstacle avoidance. In: Neural Networks, IJCNN (2015)
4. Appleby, P.A.: A model of chemotaxis and associative learning in C. elegans. Biol. Cybern. **106**(6–7), 373–387 (2012)
5. Gray, J.M., Hill, J.J., Bargmann, C.I.: A circuit for navigation in Caenorhabditis elegans. Proc. Natl. Acad. Sci. U. S. A. **102**(9), 3184–3191 (2005)
6. Galarreta, M., Hestrin, S.: Fast spiking cells and the balance of excitation and inhibition in the neocortex. In: Hensch, T.K., Fagiolini, M. (eds.) Excitatory-Inhibitory Balance. Springer, Boston (2003). https://doi.org/10.1007/978-1-4615-0039-1_11
7. Kato, S., et al.: Temporal responses of C. elegans chemosensory neurons are preserved in behavioral dynamics. Neuron **81**(3), 616–628 (2014)
8. Liu, Q., Hollopeter, G., Jorgensen, E.M.: Graded synaptic transmission at the Caenorhabditis elegans neuromuscular junction. Proc. Natl. Acad. Sci. U. S. A. **106**, 10823–10828 (2009)
9. Goldental, A., et al.: A computational paradigm for dynamic logic-gates in neuronal activity. Front. Comput. Neurosci. **8**, 52 (2014)
10. Yang, J., Yang, W., Wu, W.: A novel spiking perceptron that can solve XOR problem. ICS AS CR (2011)
11. Reljan-Delaney, M., Wall, J.: Solving the linearly inseparable XOR problem with spiking neural networks. https://doi.org/10.1109/sai.2017.8252173

12. Berger, D.L., de Arcangelis, L., Herrmann, H.J.: Learning by localized plastic adaptation in recurrent neural networks (2016)
13. Ferrari, S., et al.: Biologically realizable reward-modulated Hebbian training for spiking neural networks. In: Neural Networks, IJCNN (2008)
14. Wade, J., et al.: A biologically inspired training algorithm for spiking neural networks. Dissertation. University of Ulster (2010)
15. Kunitomo, H., et al.: Concentration memory-dependent synaptic plasticity of a taste circuit regulates salt concentration chemotaxis in Caenorhabditis elegans. Nat. Commun. **4**, 2210 (2013)
16. Suzuki, H., et al.: Functional asymmetry in Caenorhabditis elegans taste neurons and its computational role in chemotaxis. Nature **454**(7200), 114 (2008)
17. Naud, R., Gerstner, W.: The performance (and limits) of simple neuron models: generalizations of the leaky integrate-and-fire model. In: Le Novère, N. (ed.) Computational Systems Neurobiology. Springer, Dordrecht (2012). https://doi.org/10.1007/978-94-007-3858-4_6

Gating Sensory Noise in a Spiking Subtractive LSTM

Isabella Pozzi[✉], Roeland Nusselder, Davide Zambrano, and Sander Bohté

Centrum Wiskunde & Informatica, Amsterdam, The Netherlands
isabella.pozzi@cwi.nl

Abstract. Spiking neural networks are being investigated both as biologically plausible models of neural computation and also as a potentially more efficient type of neural network. Recurrent neural networks in the form of networks of gating memory cells have been central in state-of-the-art solutions in problem domains that involve sequence recognition or generation. Here, we design an analog Long Short-Term Memory (LSTM) cell where its neurons can be substituted with efficient spiking neurons, where we use subtractive gating (following the subLSTM in [1]) instead of multiplicative gating. Subtractive gating allows for a less sensitive gating mechanism, critical when using spiking neurons. By using fast adapting spiking neurons with a smoothed Rectified Linear Unit (ReLU)-like effective activation function, we show that then an accurate conversion from an analog subLSTM to a continuous-time spiking subLSTM is possible. This architecture results in memory networks that compute very efficiently, with low average firing rates comparable to those in biological neurons, while operating in continuous time.

Keywords: Spiking neurons · LSTM · Recurrent neural networks
Supervised learning · Reinforcement learning

1 Introduction

With the manifold success of biologically inspired deep neural networks, networks of spiking neurons are being investigated as potential models for computational and energy efficiency. Spiking neural networks mimic the pulse-based communication in biological neurons: in brains, neurons spike only sparingly – on average 1–5 spikes per second [2]. A number of successful convolutional neural networks based on spiking neurons have been reported [3–7], with varying degrees of biological plausibility and efficiency. Still, while spiking neural networks have thus been applied successfully to solve image-recognition tasks, many deep learning algorithms use recurrent neural networks (RNNs), especially variants of Long Short-Term Memory (LSTM) layers [8] to implement dynamic kinds of memory. Compared to convolutional neural networks, LSTMs use memory cells to store select information and various gates to direct the flow of information in and out of the memory cells. The state-changes in such networks are iterative and lack an

© Springer Nature Switzerland AG 2018
V. Kůrková et al. (Eds.): ICANN 2018, LNCS 11139, pp. 284–293, 2018.
https://doi.org/10.1007/978-3-030-01418-6_28

intrinsic notion of continuous time. To translate LSTMs-like networks into networks, such a notion of time has to be included. At present, the only spike-based version of LSTM has been realized for the IBM TrueNorth platform [9]: this work proposes an approximate LSTM specifically for TrueNorth's constrains by using a store-and-release mechanism synchronized across its modules, effectively still iterative and synchronized model of computation; Intel recently introduced the first semi-commercial spike-based hardware [10], obviating the need for efficient and effective spiking neural network algorithms. Here, we propose a biologically plausible spiking LSTM network based on an asynchronous approach. While a continuous time model in LSTMs can be implemented by taking small, finite time-steps, a key problem in *spiking* LSTM models is the multiplicative nature of the gating mechanism: such gating requires a graded response from spiking neurons to create a gradient for learning the proper degree of gating. We found that multiplicative gating also needs to be precise, in that noisy gating signal disturbed the learning of memory tasks. We exploit subtractive gating, the "sub-LSTM" [1], to use spiking neurons that effectively compute a fast ReLU function, enabling a spiking subLSTM network to operate in continuous time. We construct a spiking subLSTM network and successfully demonstrate the efficacy of this approach on two standard machine learning tasks: we show that it is indeed possible to use standard analog neurons for the training phase of the modified subLSTM and accurately convert the networks into spiking versions, such that during inference phase spike-based computation is sparse (comparable to active biological neurons) and efficient.

2   Model

To construct a spiking subLSTM network, we first describe the Adaptive Spiking Neurons we aim to use, and we show how we can approximate their effective corresponding activation function. We then show how an LSTM network comprised of a spiking memory cell and a spike-driven input-gate can be constructed and we discuss how analog versions of this subLSTM network are trained and converted to spiking networks.

Adaptive Spiking Neuron. The requirements of the network architectures guide us in the demands put on spiking neuron models. Here, we use Adaptive Spiking Neurons (ASNs) as described in [11]. ASNs are a variant of an adapting Leaky Integrate & Fire (LIF) neuron model that includes fast adaptation to the dynamic range of input signals. The behavior of the ASN is determined by the following equations:

incoming postsynaptic current: $$I(t) = \sum_i \sum_{t_s^i} w_i \vartheta(t_s^i) \exp\left(\frac{t_s^i - t}{\tau_\beta}\right), \qquad (1)$$

input signal: $$S(t) = (\phi * I)(t), \qquad (2)$$

threshold:
$$\vartheta(t) = \vartheta_0 + \sum_{t_s} m_f \vartheta(t_s) \exp\left(\frac{t_s - t}{\tau_\gamma}\right), \quad (3)$$

internal state:
$$\hat{S}(t) = \sum_{t_s} \vartheta(t_s) \exp\left(\frac{t_s - t}{\tau_\eta}\right), \quad (4)$$

where w_i is the weight (synaptic strength) of the neuron's incoming connection; $t_s^i < t$ denote the spike times of neuron i, and $t_s < t$ denote the spike times of the neuron itself; $\phi(t)$ is an exponential smoothing filter with a short time constant τ_ϕ; ϑ_0 is the resting threshold; m_f is a variable controlling the speed of spike-rate adaptation; $\tau_\beta, \tau_\gamma, \tau_\eta$ are the time constants that determine the rate of decay of $I(t), \vartheta(t)$ and $\hat{S}(t)$ respectively. The ASN emits spikes following a firing condition defined as $S(t) - \hat{S}(t) > \frac{\vartheta(t)}{2}$, and, instead of sending binary spikes, the ASNs here communicate with "analog" spikes of which the height is equal to the value of the threshold at the time of firing; note that this model speculatively implies a tight coupling between spike-triggered adaptation and short-term synaptic plasticity (see [12] and [11] for more details).

Activation Function of the Adaptive Analog Neuron. In order to create a network of ASNs that performs correctly on typical LSTM tasks, our approach is to train a network of Adaptive Analog Neurons (AANs) and then convert the resulting analog network into a spiking one, similar to [5,6,11]. We define the activation function of the AANs as the function that maps the input signal S to the average PSC I that is perceived by the *next* (receiving) ASN. We then fit the normalized spiking activation function with a softplus-shaped function as:

$$\text{AAN}(S) = a \cdot \log\left(1 + b \cdot \exp(c \cdot S)\right), \quad (5)$$

with derivative:
$$\frac{\text{dAAN}(S)}{\text{d}S} = \frac{a \cdot b \cdot c \cdot \exp(c \cdot S)}{1 + b \cdot \exp(c \cdot S)}, \quad (6)$$

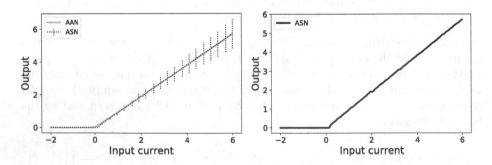

Fig. 1. Left panel: average output signal of the ASN as a function of its incoming PSC I, where the error bars indicate the standard deviation of the spiking simulation, and the corresponding AAN curve. The shape of the ASN curve is well described by the AAN activation function, Eq. 5; right panel: the output signal of the ASN alone.

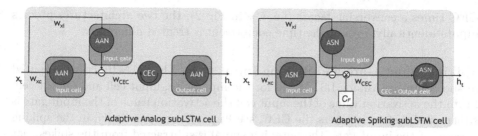

Fig. 2. Overview of the construction of an Adaptive Analog subLSTM and an Adaptive Spiking subLSTM cell. This compares to a subLSTM with only an input gate.

where, for the neuronal parameters used, we find $a = 0.04023$, $b = 1.636$ and $c = 23.54$. Using this mapping from the AAN to the ASN (see Fig. 1), the activation function can be used during training of the network with analog AANs: thereafter, the ASNs are used as "drop in" replacements for the AANs. The ASNs use $\tau_\eta = \tau_\beta = \tau_\gamma = 10\,\mathrm{ms}$, and ϑ_0 and m_f are set to 0.3 and 0.18 for all neurons.

Adaptive Spiking subLSTM. An LSTM cell usually consists of an input and output gate, an input and output cell and a CEC [8]. Deviating from the original formulation and more recent versions where forget gates and peepholes were added [13], the LSTM architecture as we present it here only consists of a (subtractive) input gate, input and output cells, and a CEC. Moreover, the original formulation, an LSTM unit uses a sigmoidal activation function in the input gate and input cell. However, when using spiking neurons, this causes inaccuracies between the analog and spiking network, as, due to the variance in the spike-based approximation, the gates are never completely closed nor completely open. In a recently proposed variation from the original LSTM architecture, called subLSTM [1], the typical multiplicative gating mechanism is substituted with a subtractive one, not requiring thus for the gates to output values exclusively in the range [0, 1]. This allows us to use neurons characterized by a smoothed ReLU as activation function. Mathematically, the difference between the integration in the CEC in the LSTM and subLSTM is given as:

$$\text{LSTM:} \quad c_t = c_{t-1} + \mathbf{z}_t \odot \mathbf{i}_t, \qquad | \qquad \text{subLSTM:} \quad c_t = c_{t-1} + \mathbf{z}_t - \mathbf{i}_t, \quad (7)$$

with c_t value of the memory cell at time t, $\mathbf{z}_t$ and $\mathbf{i}_t$ represent the signal coming from the input cell and the input gate, respectively.

As noted, to obtain a working Adaptive Spiking subLSTM, we first train its analog equivalent, the Adaptive Analog subLSTM. Figure 2 shows the schematic of the Adaptive Analog subLSTM and its spiking analogue: we aim for a one-on-one mapping from the Adaptive Analog subLSTM to the Adaptive Spiking subLSTM. This means that while we train the Adaptive Analog subLSTM network with the standard time step representation, the conversion to the continuous-time spiking domain is achieved by presenting each input for a time window of size Δt, which is determined by the neuronal parameters and by the size of the network. We find that by simply multiplying the signal incoming to the spiking

CEC times a conversion factor (i.e. C_F in Fig. 2), the two architectures process inputs identically, even if the time component is treated differently.

Spiking Input Gate and Spiking Input Cell. The AAN functions are used in the Adaptive Analog LSTM cell for the input gate, input cell and output cell. From the activation value of the input cell the activation value of the input gate is subtracted, before it enters the CEC, see Fig. 2. Correspondingly, in the spiking version of the input gate, the outgoing signal is subtracted from the spikes that move from the ASN of the input cell to the ASN of the output cell. This leads to a direct mapping from the Adaptive Analog subLSTM to the Adaptive Spiking subLSTM.

Spiking Constant Error Carousel (CEC) and Spiking Output Cell. The Constant Error Carousel (CEC) is the central part of the LSTM cell and avoids the vanishing gradient problem [8]. In the Adaptive Spiking subLSTM, we merge the CEC and the output cell to one ASN with an internal state that does not decay – in the brain could be implemented by slowly decaying (seconds) neurons [14]. The value of the CEC in the Adaptive Analog LSTM corresponds with state I of the ASN output cell in the Adaptive Spiking LSTM. In the Adaptive Spiking subLSTM, we set τ_β in Eq. 1 to a very large value for the CEC cell to obtain the integrating behavior of a CEC. Since no forget gate is implemented this results in a spiking CEC neuron that fully integrates its input. When τ_β is set to ∞, every incoming spike is added to a non-decaying PSC I. So if the state of the sending neuron (ASN_{in} in Fig. 3) has a stable inter-spike interval (ISI), then I of the receiving neuron (ASN_{out}) is increased with incoming spike height h every ISI, so $\frac{h}{\text{ISI}}$ per time step. The same integrating behavior needs to be translated to the analog CEC. Since the CEC cell of the Adaptive Spiking subLSTM integrates its input S every time step by $\frac{S}{\tau_\eta}$, we can map this to the CEC of the Adaptive Analog subLSTM. The CEC of a traditional LSTM without a forget gate is updated every time step by $\text{CEC}(t) = \text{CEC}(t-1) + S$, with S its input value (i.e. $\mathbf{z}_t - \mathbf{i}_t$ for a subtractive LSTM). The CEC of the Adaptive Analog subLSTM is updated every time step by $\text{CEC}(t) = \text{CEC}(t-1) + \frac{S}{\tau_\eta}$. This is depicted in Fig. 2 via a weight after the input gate with value $\frac{1}{\tau_\eta}$. To allow a correct continuous-time representation after the spike-coding conversion, we divide the incoming connection weight to the CEC, W_{CEC}, by the time window Δt. In our approach then, we train the Adaptive Analog subLSTM as for the traditional LSTM (without the τ_η factor), which effectively corresponds to set a continuous-time time window $\Delta t = \tau_\eta$. Thus, to select a different Δt, in the spiking version W_{CEC} has to be set to $W_{\text{CEC}} = \tau_\eta / \Delta t$. The middle plot in Fig. 3 shows that setting τ_β to ∞ for ASN_{out} in a spiking network results in the same behavior as using an analog CEC that integrates with $\text{CEC}(t) = \text{CEC}(t-1) + S$, since the slope of the analog CEC is indeed the same as the slope of the spiking CEC. Here, every time step in the analog experiment corresponds to $\Delta t = 40\,\text{ms}$.

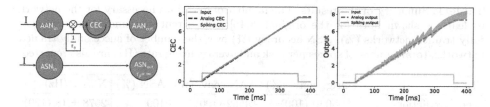

Fig. 3. A simulation to illustrate how the analog CEC integrates its input signal with the same speed as an ASN with $\tau_\beta = \infty$ provided that the input signal does not change and that 1 analog time step corresponds to $\Delta t = 40\,\mathrm{ms}$ (middle). In the right panel, the spiking output signal approximates the analog output.

Learning Rule. To train the analog subLSTMs on the supervised tasks, a customized truncated version of real-time recurrent learning (RTRL) was used. This is the same algorithm used in [13], where the partial derivatives w.r.t. the weights W_{xc} and W_{xi} (see Fig. 2) are truncated. For the reinforcement learning (RL) tasks we used RL-LSTM [15], which uses the same customized, truncated version of RTRL that was used for the supervised tasks. RL-LSTM also incorporates eligibility traces to improve training and Advantage Learning [16]. All regular neurons in the network are trained with traditional backpropagation.

3   Experiments

Since the presented Adaptive Analog subLSTM only has an input gate and no output or forget gate, we present four classical tasks from the LSTM literature that do not rely on these additional gates.

Sequence Prediction with Long Time Lags. The main concept of LSTM, the ability of a CEC to maintain information over long stretches of time, was demonstrated in [8] in a Sequence Prediction task: the network has to predict the next input of a sequence of $p + 1$ possible input symbols denoted as $a_1, \ldots, a_{p-1}, a_p = x, a_{p+1} = y$. In the *noise free* version of this task, every symbol is represented by the $p + 1$ input units with the i-th unit set to 1 and all the others to 0. At every time step a new input of the sequence is presented. As in the original formulation, we train the network with two possible sequences, $(x, a_1, a_2, \ldots, a_{p-1}, x)$ and $(y, a_1, a_2, \ldots, a_{p-1}, y)$, chosen with equal probability. For both sequences the network has to store a representation of the first element in the memory cell for the entire length of the sequence (p). We train 50 networks on this task for a total of $200k$ trials, with $p = 100$, on an architecture with $p + 1$ input units and $p + 1$ output units. The input units are fully connected to the output units without a hidden layer. The same sequential network construction method from the original paper was used to prevent the "abuse problem": the Adaptive Analog subLSTM cell is only included in the network after the error stops decreasing [8]. In the *noisy* version of the sequence prediction task, the network still has to predict the next input of the sequence, but the symbols from a_1 to a_{p-1} are presented in random order and the same symbol can occur

Table 1. Summary of the results. The number of iterations necessary for the network to learn is shown both for the original [8,15] and current implementation. Successfully trained networks (%), ASN accuracy (%) over the number of successfully trained networks, total number of spikes per task and average firing rate (Hz) are also reported.

Task	Orig. conv. (%)	AAN conv. (%)	ASN (%)	N_{spikes} (Hz)
Seq. prediction	5040 (100)	4562 (100)	100	2578 ± 18 (129)
Noisy seq. prediction	5680 (100)	64428 (100)	100	2241 ± 22 (112)
T-Maze	$1M$ (100)	15633 (86)	97	1901 ± 249 (77)
noisy T-Maze	$1.75M$ (100)	20440 (94)	92	1604 ± 216 (65)

multiple times. Therefore, only the final symbols a_p and a_{p+1} can be correctly predicted. This version of the sequence prediction task avoids the possibility that the network learns local regularities in the input stream. We train 50 networks with the same architecture and parameters of the previous task, for $200k$ trials.

T-Maze Task. In order to demonstrate the generality of our approach, we trained a network with Adaptive Analog subLSTM cells on a Reinforcement Learning task, originally introduced in [15]. In the T-Maze task, an agent has to move inside a maze to reach a target position in order to be rewarded while maintaining information during the trial. The maze is composed of a long corridor with a T-junction at the end, where the agent has to make a choice based on information presented at the start of the task. The agent receives a reward of 4 if it reaches the target position and -0.2 if it moves against the wall. If it moves to the wrong direction at the T-junction it also receives a reward of -0.2 and the system is reset. The agent has 3 inputs and 4 outputs corresponding to the 4 possible directions it can move to. At the beginning of the task the input can be either 011 or 110 (which indicates on which side of the T-junction the reward is placed). Here, we chose the corridor length $N = 20$. A noiseless and a noisy version of the task were defined: in the noiseless version the corridor is represented as 101, and at the T-junction 010; in a noisy version the input in the corridor is represented as $a0b$ where a and b are two uniformly distributed random variables in a range of $[0, 1]$. While the noiseless version can be learned by LSTM-like networks without input gating [17], the noisy version requires the use of such gates. The network consists of a fully connected hidden layer with 12 AAN units and 3 Adaptive Analog subLSTMs. The same training parameters are used as in [15]; we train 50 networks for each task and all networks have the same architecture. As a convergence criteria we checked whenever the network reached on average a total reward greater than 3.5 in the last 100 trials.

4   Results

As shown in Table 1, for the noise-free and noisy Sequence Prediction tasks all of the networks were both successfully trained and could be converted into spiking

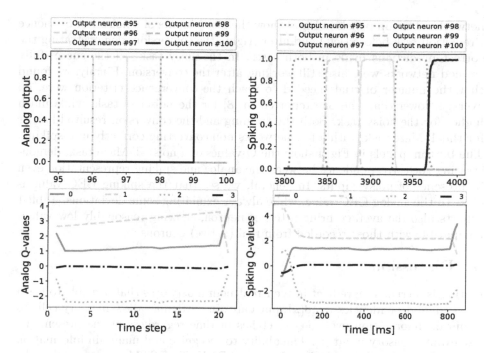

Fig. 4. Top panels: output values of the analog (left) and spiking (right) network for the noise-free sequence prediction task. Only the last 5 input symbols of the series are shown. The last symbol y (black) is correctly predicted both in the last time step (analog) and in the last 40 ms (spiking). Bottom panels: Q-values of the analog (left) and spiking (right) network for the noisy T-Maze task. At the last time step/40 ms it correctly selects the right action (solid gray line).

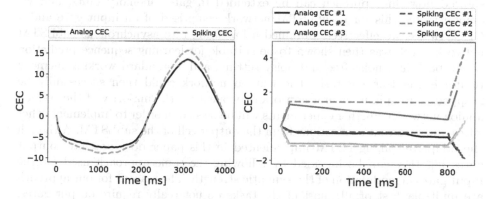

Fig. 5. The values of the analog CECs and spiking CECs for the noise-free sequence prediction (left panel) and noisy T-Maze (right panel) tasks. The spiking CEC is the internal state $\hat{S}$ of the output cell of the Adaptive Spiking LSTM.

networks. The top panels in Fig. 4 show the last 5 inputs of a noise-free Sequence Prediction task before (left) and after (right) the conversion, demonstrating the correct predictions made in both cases. In the noisy task, all the successfully trained networks were also still working after the conversion. Finally, we found that the number of trials needed to reach the convergence criterion were, on average, lower than the one reported in [8] for the noiseless task, while much higher for the noisy task. Both the training and the conversion resulted harder for the T-Maze task, with a few networks non converting correctly into spiking. The bottom panels in Fig. 4 show the Q-values of a noisy T-Maze task, demonstrating the correspondence between the analog and spiking representation even in presence of noisy inputs. In general, we see that the spiking CEC value is close to the analog CEC value, while always exhibiting some deviations. Table 1 reports also the average firing rate per neuron, showing reasonably low values compatible with those recorded from real (active) neurons.

5   Discussion

Gating is a crucial ingredient in recurrent neural networks that are able to learn long-range dependencies [8,18]. Input gates in particular allow memory cells to maintain information over long stretches of time regardless of the presented - irrelevant - sensory input [8]. The ability to recognize and maintain information for later use is also that which makes gated RNNs like LSTM so successful in the great many sequence-related problems, ranging from natural language processing to learning cognitive tasks [15]. To transfer deep neural networks to networks of spiking neurons, a highly effective method has been to map the transfer function of spiking neurons to analog counterparts and then, once the network has been trained, substitute the analog neurons with spiking neurons [5,6,11]. Here, we showed how this approach can be extended to gated memory units, and we demonstrated this for a subLSTM network comprised of an input gate and a CEC. Hence, we effectively obtained a low-firing rate asynchronous subLSTM network which was then shown to be suitable for learning sequence prediction tasks, both in a noise-free and noisy setting, and a standard working memory reinforcement learning task. The learned network could then successfully be mapped to its spiking neural network equivalent for the majority of the trained analog networks. Further experiments will be needed in order to implement other gates and recurrent connections from the output cell of the subLSTM. Although the adaptive spiking LSTM implemented in this paper does not have output gates [8], they can be included by following the same approach used for the input gates: a modulation of the synaptic strength. The reasons for our approach are multiple: first of all, most of the tasks do not really require output gates; moreover, modulating each output synapse independently is less intuitive and biologically plausible than for the input gates. A similar argument can be made for the forget gates, which were not included in the original LSTM formulation: here, the solution consists in modulating the decaying factor of the CEC. It must be mentioned that which gates are really needed in an LSTM network is still an open question, with answers depending on the kind of task to be solved [19,20].

Acknowledgments. DZ is supported by NWO NAI project 656.000.005.

References

1. Costa, R., Assael, I.A., Shillingford, B., de Freitas, N., Vogels, T.: Cortical micro-circuits as gated-recurrent neural networks. In: Advances in Neural Information Processing Systems, pp. 272–283 (2017)
2. Attwell, D., Laughlin, S.: An energy budget for signaling in the grey matter of the brain. J. Cereb. Blood Flow Metab. **21**(10), 1133–1145 (2001)
3. Esser, S., et al.: Convolutional networks for fast, energy-efficient neuromorphic computing. In: PNAS, p. 201604850, September 2016
4. Neil, D., Pfeiffer, M., Liu, S.C.: Learning to be efficient: algorithms for training low-latency, low-compute deep spiking neural networks (2016)
5. Diehl, P., Neil, D., Binas, J., Cook, M., Liu, S.C., Pfeiffer, M.: Fast-classifying, high-accuracy spiking deep networks through weight and threshold balancing. In: IEEE IJCNN, pp. 1–8, July 2015
6. O'Connor, P., Neil, D., Liu, S.C., Delbruck, T., Pfeiffer, M.: Real-time classification and sensor fusion with a spiking deep belief network. Front. Neurosci. **7**, 178 (2013)
7. Hunsberger, E., Eliasmith, C.: Spiking deep networks with LIF neurons. arXiv preprint arXiv:1510.08829 (2015)
8. Hochreiter, S., Schmidhuber, J.: Long short-term memory. Neural Comput, **9**(8), 1735–1780 (1997)
9. Shrestha, A., et al.: A spike-based long short-term memory on a neurosynaptic processor (2017)
10. Davies, M., Srinivasa, N., Lin, T.H., Chinya, G., Cao, Y., Choday, S.H., Dimou, G., Joshi, P., Imam, N., Jain, S.: Loihi: a neuromorphic manycore processor with on-chip learning. IEEE Micro **38**(1), 82–99 (2018)
11. Zambrano, D., Bohte, S.: Fast and efficient asynchronous neural computation with adapting spiking neural networks. arXiv preprint arXiv:1609.02053 (2016)
12. Bohte, S.: Efficient spike-coding with multiplicative adaptation in a spike response model. In: NIPS, vol. 25, pp. 1844–1852 (2012)
13. Gers, F.A., Schraudolph, N.N., Schmidhuber, J.: Learning precise timing with LSTM recurrent networks. J. Mach. Learn. Res. **3**(Aug), 115–143 (2002)
14. Denève, S., Machens, C.K.: Efficient codes and balanced networks. Nature Neurosci. **19**(3), 375–382 (2016)
15. Bakker, B.: Reinforcement learning with long short-term memory. In: NIPS, vol. 14, pp. 1475–1482 (2002)
16. Harmon, M., Baird III, L.: Multi-player residual advantage learning with general function approximation. Wright Laboratory, 45433–7308 (1996)
17. Rombouts, J., Bohte, S., Roelfsema, P.: Neurally plausible reinforcement learning of working memory tasks. In: NIPS, vol. 25, pp. 1871–1879 (2012)
18. Cho, K., et al.: Learning phrase representations using RNN encoder-decoder for statistical machine translation. arXiv preprint arXiv:1406.1078 (2014)
19. Greff, K., Srivastava, R.K., Koutník, J., Steunebrink, B.R., Schmidhuber, J.: LSTM: a search space odyssey. IEEE Trans. Neural Netw. Learn. Syst. **28**(10), 2222–2232 (2017)
20. Jozefowicz, R., Zaremba, W., Sutskever, I.: An empirical exploration of recurrent network architectures. In: International Conference on Machine Learning, pp. 2342–2350 (2015)

Spiking Signals in FOC Control Drive

L. M. Grzesiak[(✉)] [iD] and V. Meganck[(✉)] [iD]

Institute of Control and Industrial Electronics, Warsaw University of Technology,
Warsaw, Poland
{Lech.Grzesiak,Vincent.Meganck}@ee.pw.edu.pl

Abstract. This paper proposes to apply spiking signals to the control
of an AC motor drive at variable speed in real-time experimentation.
Innovative theoretical concepts of spiking signal processing (SSP, [1])
is introduced using the $I_{Na,p} + I_K$ neuron model [7]. Based on SSP
concepts, we designed a spiking speed controller inspired by the human
movement control. The spiking speed controller is then integrated in
the field oriented control (FOC, [13]) topology in order to control an
induction drive at various mechanical speed. Experimental results are
presented and discussed. This paper demonstrates that spiking signals
can be straightforwardly used for electrical engineering applications in
real time experimentation based on robust SSP theory.

Keywords: Spiking neuron · Firing rate · Spiking signal processing
FOC · AC drive

1 Spiking Signal Processing

1.1 Spiking Transformation

In previous paper [1], we assumed that a continuous signal $x(t)$ (black curve
in Fig. 1) could be mathematically transformed by a single neuron into a series
of spikes $\iota(t - t_n)$ (greek letter *iota*) called $x_\iota(t)$ (blue spikes in Fig. 1) and
representing the exact image of the original continuous signal x(t).

$$x_\iota(t) = \sum_{n=0}^{n=+\infty} \iota(t - t_n) \tag{1}$$

$$x(t) \approx x_\iota(t) \tag{2}$$

To ensure equivalence between both signals in (2), we have to set the firing
frequency $\nu_x(t)$ (greek letter *nu*) of the neuron as the image of the continuous
signal $x(t)$.

$$\nu_x(t) \approx x(t) \tag{3}$$

The firing rate or firing frequency $\nu[n]$ is defined as the frequency between
two consecutive spikes fired at t_n and t_{n-1} with $\Delta t[n]$ being the elapsed time

© Springer Nature Switzerland AG 2018
V. Kůrková et al. (Eds.): ICANN 2018, LNCS 11139, pp. 294–303, 2018.
https://doi.org/10.1007/978-3-030-01418-6_29

(Fig. 1). The Eq. (4) represents the firing rate in a discrete form since a fired spike can be identified by its position t_n. The next upcoming firing rate is represented in a continuous form (5) since time runs until the next potential upcoming spike.

$$\nu_x[n] = 1/\Delta t_x[n] = 1/(t_n - t_{n-1}) \tag{4}$$

$$\nu_x(t) = 1/\Delta t_x(t) = 1/(t - t_{n-1}) \tag{5}$$

By (4) and (5), we can express the series x_ι (1) according to its spiking elapsed time Δt (7) or firing frequency ν (8). The equations below are different ways to express the same spiking series x_ι (blue spikes in Fig. 1).

$$x_\iota(t) = \sum_{n=0}^{n=+\infty} \iota(t - (t_{n-1} + \Delta t_x[n])) \tag{6}$$

$$= \sum_{n=0}^{n=+\infty} \iota(\Delta t_x(t) - \Delta t_x[n]) \tag{7}$$

$$= \sum_{n=0}^{n=+\infty} \iota(\nu_x(t) - \nu_x[n]) \tag{8}$$

Taking into account the assumption (3), we can express the spiking series $x_\iota(t)$ as

$$x_\iota(t) = \sum_{n=0}^{n=+\infty} \iota(x(t) - 1/\Delta t_x(t)) \tag{9}$$

$$= \sum_{n=0}^{n=+\infty} \iota(x(t) - \nu_x(t)) \tag{10}$$

Despite their different aspects, we will see in real time experimentation that the spiking signal $x_\iota(t)$ (blue spikes in Fig. 1) is the approximation of the original continuous signal $x(t)$ (black curve in Fig. 1).

1.2   Accuracy

In Fig. 1, we see that the firing rate decomposition $\nu_x(t)$ of the spiking series $x_\iota(t)$ (blue spikes in Fig. 1) better approximates the signal $x(t)$ at higher signal amplitude. Low amplitude of $x(t)$ induces a low firing rate $\nu_x(t)$ and a long $\Delta t_x(t)$ sampling step with a poor approximation accuracy. In order to increase the accuracy, we set the constant a in (12) to artificially increase the firing frequency $\nu_x(t)$. We call a the *sensitivity* of the neuron. When the parameter a increases, the accuracy increases.

In order to conserve the energy equality between signals $x(t)$ and $x_\iota(t)$, it is necessary to decrease the energy of the spike by the same factor a (red spikes in Fig. 1). The spiking series ultimately equals:

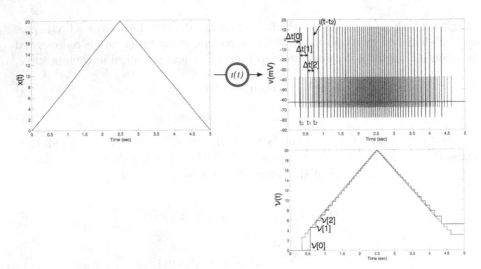

Fig. 1. Spiking sampling of $x(t)$ with $a = 1$ (in blue) and $a = 3$ (in red). (Color figure online)

$$x_\iota(t) = \frac{1}{a} \sum_{n=0}^{n=+\infty} \iota(x(t) - 1/a\Delta t_x(t)) \tag{11}$$

$$= \frac{1}{a} \sum_{n=0}^{n=+\infty} \iota(x(t) - \nu_x(t)/a) \tag{12}$$

Figure 1 shows the firing rate ν accuracy with a sensitivity parameter $a = 1$ (in blue) and $a = 3$ (in red). The accuracy of the red curve is enhanced compared to the blue one.

The accuracy principle is equivalent to the movement control principle found in the human body. Small and fast accurate movement requires fast muscle fibers excited by moto-neurons with small spike amplitude, while high amplitude movement requires slow muscle fibers exited by other types of neurons giving less accuracy in the movement. This movement control principle will be applied in the next chapter in real-time experimentation.

2   Spiking Signals in FOC Control Drive Experimentation

In this chapter, we apply SSP theoretical basis to design a spiking speed controller on real time AC control drive experimentation. After presenting the FOC (Field Oriented Control, [8–13]) control strategy and the experimental setup, the classical PI speed controller is replaced by a spiking speed controller inspired by the human movement control. Experimental results are presented and discussed for different control parameters.

2.1   Space Vector Modulation (SVM) - Field Oriented Control (FOC)

The principle of the FOC strategy is to allow a decoupling in the control of flux and electromagnetic torque such as DC machine does but without the drawbacks of high cost of maintenance concerning the usury of commutators and brushes. A coordinate frame (d, q) aligned and fixed to the rotor flux allow such decoupled torque and magnetization control.

Figure 2 presents the FOC control structure:

- the 3-phase stator current measurements (i_{sa}, i_{sb}, i_{sc}) are transformed in (d, q) components (i_{sd}, i_{sq}) through Clarke's and Park's transformations
  the reference rotor flux component $(i_{sd,ref})$ is kept constant and the reference electromagnetic torque component $(i_{sq,ref})$ is generated by a PI Speed controller
- the (d, q) stator current components (i_{sd}, i_{sq}) are controlled through PI current controllers generating the adequate (d, q) stator voltage (u_{sd}, u_{sq}) to apply
- after Park's inverse matrix transformation, the stator voltage components $(u_{s\alpha}, u_{s\beta})$ produce the stator voltage vector to apply to the motor.

SVM uses a 6 vectors rosace in ordre to rebuild the stator voltage vector. The two adjacent rosace vectors are time weighted in a sample period to produce the desired output voltage. In conclusion, the input for the SVM is the reference stator voltage vector and the outputs are the times to apply each of the IGBT transistors of the inverter. The stator voltage vector is electrically produced by SVM control technique and supply to the AC motor with the desired phase voltages.

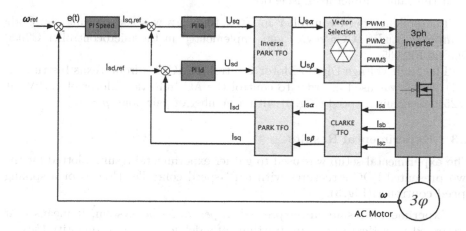

Fig. 2. PI speed controller in FOC AC drive.

2.2   Spiking Speed Controller in FOC

In order to test spiking signals in real-time experimentation, the classical PI speed controller [2–6] has been replaced by a spiking speed controller in FOC structure (Fig. 3 and [8–13]). The controller receives speed error $e(t)$ as input and generates a spiking time series as reference stator current $i_{\iota sq,ref}$ equivalent to a spiking reference electromagnetic torque. The topology of the spiking speed controller is inspired by the human movement control [1]. The main characteristics and parameters are detailed hereunder.

- The controller uses the reciprocity principle transforming negative speed error signal $e(t)$ into positive spiking series $e_\iota(t)$ by different reciprocal group of neuron (such as reciprocal muscles in the human arm).
- The main proportional action loop has an accuracy increasing with the neuron sensitivity parameter a.
- The controller uses a secondary loop called the tremor found in the human body. The tremor reflex loop innervates permanently the muscle in order to keep the arm bend in a steady state target position. The neurons fire permanently and react to any small drift of the reference arm position. The neuron has a high sensitivity parameter b which induces fast firing rate of small spikes increasing the controllability and the reactivity of the neuron. Moreover, an offset has been added in order to permanently fire a spiking control signal at steady state speed increasing the motor speed controllability.
- In the human body, motoneurons innervate low pass filter muscles in order to create a continuous action signal. In the control topology of Fig. 3, we use the current control loop and the AC drive as final low pass filter organ smoothing and integrating spike series. The resulting spiking action signal defines the spiking reference current $i_{\iota sq,ref}$. Spikes are transformed into continuous speed $\omega(t)$ and electric current $i_{\iota sq}$ signals through the FOC drive topology in the same manner as muscle does.

The spiking speed controller in FOC topology was coded using the Code Composer Studio (CCS rev.5) and implemented in the microcontroller C2000 Delfino F28035.

The High Voltage Digital Motor Control (DMC) kit from Texas Instrument (TI) [8–12] was used in order to control the AC Induction Motor of 1.5 kW at 1725 rpm nominal speed (Fig. 3) with a number of pair poles $p = 2$.

2.3   Experimental Results

The experimental setup was used to gather experimental results plotted for the two presented FOC structures with a PI speed controller (Fig. 2) or a spiking speed controller (Fig. 3).

Experimental results are expressed in *per-unit* (*pu*) system. It means that presented numerical values are fractions of a defined base unit quantity (*base*).

Figures 4 (speed) and 5 (electric q-current) present experimental results for the PI speed controller of Fig. 2. The PI speed controller has the following control parameters:

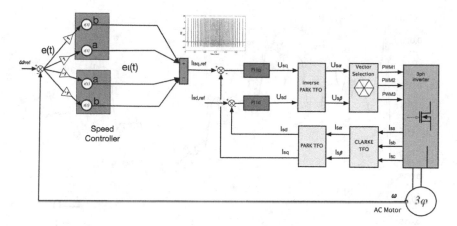

Fig. 3. Spiking speed controller in FOC AC drive.

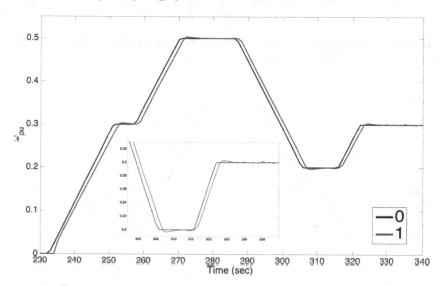

Fig. 4. PI speed controller in FOC AC drive. Reference speed (black line 0); speed (red line 1) (Color figure online)

- proportional gain $K_p = 1$
- integral gain $K_I = 0.04s^{-1}$.

Figures 6 (speed) and 7 (electric q-current) present experimental results for the spiking speed controller of Fig. 3. Spiking speed controller has the following control parameters:

- proportional action loop parameter $a = 10^4$
- tremor action loop parameter $b = 10^5$

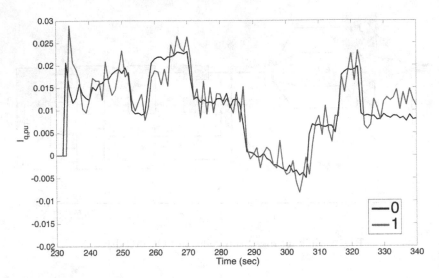

Fig. 5. PI speed controller in FOC AC drive. Reference q-current (black line 0); q-current (red line 1). (Color figure online)

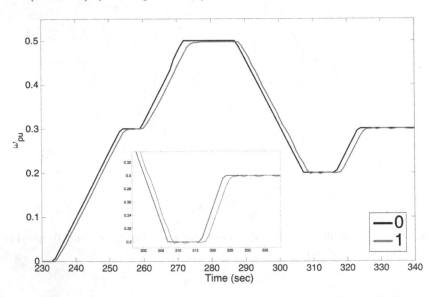

Fig. 6. Spiking speed controller ($a = 10^4$, $b = 10^5$) in FOC AC drive. Reference speed (black line 0); speed (blue line 1). (Color figure online)

Figure 7 depicts the spiking reference stator current $i_{Lsq,ref}$ composed of its proportional (black line 0) and tremor spiking series (grey line 1). The firing frequency decomposition of the spiking reference stator current is given in Fig. 8. It has to be emphasized that, despite the different reference stator current shapes

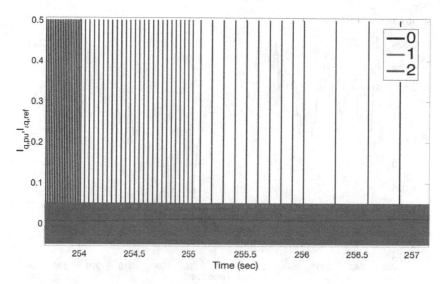

Fig. 7. Spiking speed controller ($a = 10^4$, $b = 10^5$) in FOC AC drive. Spiking reference stator current $i_{l,sq,ref}$ composed of proportional loop spikes (black line 0) and tremor loop spikes (grey line 1). q-current (blue line 2). (Color figure online)

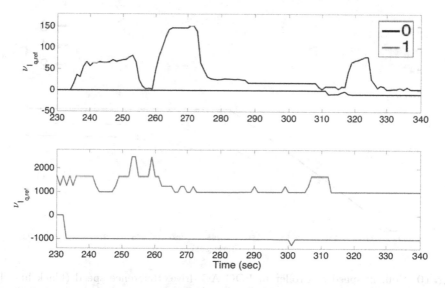

Fig. 8. Spiking speed controller ($a = 10^4$, $b = 10^5$) in FOC AC drive. Firing frequency decomposition of the spiking reference stator current $i_{l,sq,ref}$ with proportional loop (black line 0) and tremor loop (grey line 1).

of the PI solution (Fig. 5) and the spiking solution (Fig. 7), similar speed control performances (Figs. 4 and 6) and stator current shapes (Fig. 9) are observed. Different stator current shapes in the FOC control structure will give different stator

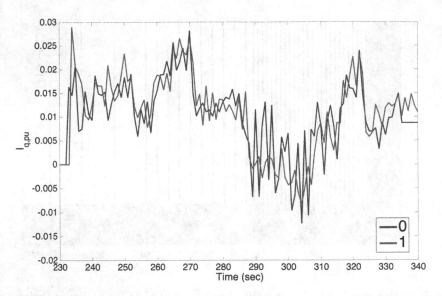

Fig. 9. q-current from spiking speed controller (blue line 0) and from PI controller (red line 1) (Color figure online)

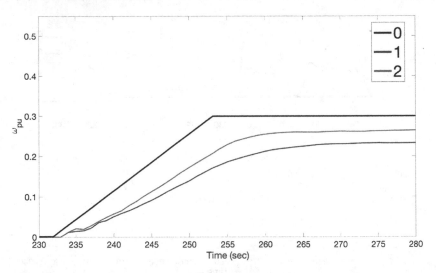

Fig. 10. Spiking speed controller in FOC AC drive. Reference speed (black line 0); Spiking controller with $a = 0.5 * 10^4$, $b = 0$ (blue line 1); $a = 10^4$, $b = 0$ (red line 2) (Color figure online)

voltage shape applies to the motor by SVM technique. However, performances remain equivalent no matter we use continuous signal (PI speed controller) or spiking signal (Spiking speed controller). Those results confirm the signal equivalence between $x(t)$ and $x_\iota(t)$ expressed in (2).

Figure 10 (speeds) compares the control performances of the spiking speed controller for different parameters:

- 1 (blue line) - Spiking speed controller with $a = 0.5 * 10^4$, $b = 0$
- 2 (red line) - Spiking speed controller with $a = 10^4$, $b = 0$

Figure 10 shows that, even by increasing the parameter a, a spiking controller without tremor action b does not reach a zero steady-state error. However, in Fig. 6, after adding a tremor action, the speed quickly reaches the reference speed.

3 Conclusion

This paper applies and demonstrates in real-time experimentation the robustness of spiking signal processing principle and formulas. Thanks to SSP theory, clear and simple description of spiking controller topology and parameters has been realized. Experimental results show that spiking signals are able to achieve comparable control performances than classical continuous signals. Researches are now open to apply firing rate decomposition of continuous signal for controller design and system identification.

References

1. Grzesiak, L.M., Meganck, V.: Spiking signal processing - principle and applications in control system. Neurocomputing **308**, 31–48 (2018). https://doi.org/10.1016/j.neucom.2018.03.054
2. Smith, S.W.: The Scientist and Engineer's Guide to Digital Signal Processing, 2nd edn. California Technical Publishing, San Diego (1999)
3. Ogata, K.: Discrete Time Control System, 2nd edn. Prentice-Hall International, Upper Saddle River (1995)
4. Tymerski, R.: Control Systems Design II. Portland State University (1994–2015). http://web.cecs.pdx.edu/tymerski/ece452/Chapter3.pdf
5. Arnould, B.: Automatique, Haute Ecole Leonard de Vinci ECAM (2003)
6. Maret, L.: Regulation Automatique, Presse polytechnique romanes (1987)
7. Izhikevich, E.M.: Dynamical Systems in Neuroscience: The Geometry of Excitability and Bursting. Springer, Heidelberg (2004)
8. Texas Instruments: High Voltage Motor Control and PFC Kit Hardware Reference Guide, Texas Instruments, October 2010
9. Texas Instruments: HVMotorCtrl+PFC (R1.1) Kit How to Run Guide, Texas Instruments (2010)
10. Akin, B., Bhardwaj, M.: Sensored field oriented control of 3-phase induction motors, Texas Instruments, July 2013
11. Texas Instruments: IQmath Library A Virtual Floating Point Engine Module User's Guide C28x Foundation Software, Texas Instruments, June 2012
12. Wikipedia: TMS320C2000 Motor Control Primer, February (2005). http://processors.wiki.ti.com/index.php/TMS320C2000_Motor_Control_Primer
13. Zelechowski, M.: Space vector modulated - direct torque controlled (DTC - SVM) inverter - fed induction motor drive, Ph.D. Thesis, Warsaw University of Technology (2005)

Spiking Neural Network Controllers Evolved for Animat Foraging Based on Temporal Pattern Recognition in the Presence of Noise on Input

Chama Bensmail[1], Volker Steuber[2], Neil Davey[2], and Borys Wróbel[1,3($\boxtimes$)]

[1] Evolving Systems Laboratory, Adam Mickiewicz University in Poznan,
Poznan, Poland
{chamabens,wrobel}@evosys.org
[2] Center for Computer Science and Informatics Research,
University of Hertfordshire, Hertfordshire, UK
[3] IOPAN, Sopot, Poland

Abstract. We evolved spiking neural network controllers for simple animats, allowing for these networks to change topologies and weights during evolution. The animats' task was to discern one correct pattern (emitted from target objects) amongst other different wrong patterns (emitted from distractor objects), by navigating towards targets and avoiding distractors in a 2D world. Patterns were emitted with variable silences between signals of the same pattern in the attempt of creating a state memory. We analyse the network that is able to accomplish the task perfectly for patterns consisting of two signals, with 4 interneurons, maintaining its state (although not infinitely) thanks to the recurrent connections.

Keywords: Spiking neural networks · Temporal pattern recognition
Animat · Adaptive exponential integrate and fire

1 Introduction

Brains process information through generating and recognizing temporal activity patterns of neurons [1,3,5,7,8,11,14]. Neuronal spike trains carry information about the environment received through different modalities, including audition [10], olfaction [9], and vision [20]. Neurons perform temporal pattern recognition of sensory neuron activity in order to decode this information [3,6], which in turn requires temporal storage of stimuli or maintenance of an internal state [12,16–19].

Several evolutionary neural-driven robotic models have attempted to reproduce insect phonotaxis, that is, movement based on the temporal recognition of sound [4,13,15,21]. The abstract task explored in this and our previous paper [2] was inspired by phonotaxis in the sense that animats had to navigate towards

© Springer Nature Switzerland AG 2018
V. Kůrková et al. (Eds.): ICANN 2018, LNCS 11139, pp. 304–313, 2018.
https://doi.org/10.1007/978-3-030-01418-6_30

target objects emitting one simple temporal pattern of signals (which could represent sounds, scents, or flashes of light) and avoid distractor objects, which emitted other patterns. In contrast to the previous work [2], here we allowed the silences between letters of the same pattern to vary, hoping for the emergence of a state maintenance mechanism in evolution. We allowed all types of connections between interneurons and an unlimited size of the network (although a relatively small number of generations during artificial evolution did not allow the networks to grow very much).

Our long-term goal is to understand how small networks can accomplish non-trivial computational tasks (here, control of foraging that depends on temporal pattern recognition) with robustness against noise (on input and/or state variables) and damage (variation of the parameters of the environment, the animat, and/or neurons).

2   The Model

We used the platform GReaNs [22] to evolve networks of adaptive exponential integrate and fire neurons with tonic spiking, as we did previously [2]. In contrast with our previous work [2], in the experiments described here, during both evolution and testing, (i) the objects did not reappear after collection, (ii) they were placed at a random position as before, but imposing a minimum and maximum distance (10 and 45 times, respectively, the radius of the animat) from the starting point of the animat, (iii) the world was open (not toroidal as previously during evolution), (iv) the duration of silences between the signals of the same pattern was drawn from a Poisson distribution with $\lambda = 30$ ms (the length of a signal (letter) remained fixed, at 10 ms; the silences between the patterns also remained fixed, at 150 ms), (v) the intensity of signals remained constant for both signals of the pattern (this makes the task more difficult—as the distance, measured considering the position of the animat at the start of the pattern, changes as the animat moves—but simplifies the analysis of how the network solves the assigned task). As previously, the intensity of the signals encoded the direction to the source of the pattern, as $\frac{1}{1+e^{-10(S_R-S_L)}}$, where S_R (S_L) is the distance between the source a point on the right (left) side of the animat; thus if the source is on the left, the value is above 0.5, and if it is on the right, it is below 0.5. Also as previously, the patterns consisted of two signals; we will refer to patterns sent by the target as **AB**, while the distractor sends (wrong) patterns (ba, aa, bb).

We carried out 200 independent runs (population size 300, size-2 tournament selection, no elitism), aiming to minimise the fitness function:

$$f_{fitness} = 1 - (\frac{T - 2D}{N} + c\frac{\alpha}{\beta}), \qquad (1)$$

where T is the number of targets collected; D is the number of distractors collected; N is the total number of targets that can be collected if the animat moves at maximum speed (which was 1 target during evolution); c is 0 for the first 100 generations and 0.5 for remaining generations; α is the length of a straight line connecting the start position of the animat to the position of the target and β is the length of the path made by the animat from the start position to the target (if it is collected) or to the last position of the animat during simulation. This reward term promotes directional movement toward target rather than circular motion at top speed often seen when this term was omitted (such circular motion allows to hit the target without directional movement). Since only one target and one distractor was present during evolution, the lowest (best) possible value for this fitness function was -0.5 and the highest (worst) was 3.

The mutation parameters used here are the same as in [2], but with a difference in the rate of duplication (0.002 per genome instead of 0.001 in our previous work) and the rate of deletion (0.001, instead of previously 0.0001). Although the duplication rate was twice the deletion rate, the networks did not grow large even though (in contrast to [2]) we allowed for an unlimited number of nodes in the network.

Each evolutionary run had 2500 generations, if an animat with fitness below -0.15 was detected, the run was stopped after additional 50 generations. In each generation, we evaluated first over 15 random worlds (worlds with different positions of objects and orientation of the animat) and 200 patterns for each world. Each target emitted pattern **AB**, and each distractor emitted a mixture of the other (wrong) patterns (with equal probability): aa, ba, and bb. The percentage of the correct pattern occurrence for these 15 evaluations (per_{AB}) was 30%. Then the animat was evaluated over additional 3 worlds, with $per_{AB} = 50\%$, but this time with the distractor emitting always a *specific* wrong pattern (for example, only aa). Finally, the 18 values of the fitness function obtained for 18 maps were averaged.

3   Results and Discussion

3.1   The Efficiency to Discern Correct Pattern

Out of 200 runs, 20 ended with $f_{fitness} < -0.25$. The 20 champions were ranked by their ability to collect targets and avoid distractors. The best champion out of the 20 (the winner) was a perfect recogniser such that $T = 1000$ in 1000 maps while $D = 0$. The winner had 4 interneurons, and showed a directional walk without circling (Fig. 1), which made it amenable to analysis. The networks' sizes of the remaining 19 champions ranged from 3 to 12 interneurons. In the rest of the paper, we will focus on the winner and analyse its performance and the underlying mechanism.

When the winner was tested for various frequencies of the correct pattern, we kept the number of occurrences of **AB**s constant, at 60. Even at 1% frequency of the correct pattern, the winner collected the target in 700 worlds out of 1000, while it could collect between 960 and 1000 for percentages greater than 10%. Thus, even for large numbers of wrong patterns, the task could still be achieved with high precision.

The winner was also tested for a wide range of durations of silent interval between letters (Fig. 2; in these tests, unlike during evolution, the duration of

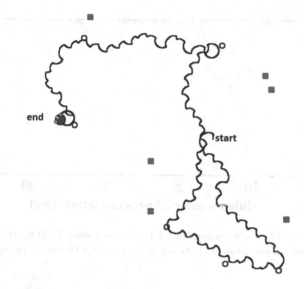

Fig. 1. Visualisation of the performance of the winner. The test world has 6 targets (black circles) and 6 distractors (red squares), the black swiping line is the movement trajectory of the animat. (Color figure online)

the interval was kept constant). When this interval was between 17 and 37 (close to the mean of the Poisson distribution that was used during evolution, 30 ms), the animat behaved almost perfectly. Longer duration of silences between letters led to an abrupt drop in performance, and no targets were collected for silences 45 ms and above. The loss of performance for values smaller than 17 ms was mainly due to whether or not a spike coming from neuron N0 coincided with another spike from neuron N1 (see Fig. 3 and Sect. 3.3), for a target on the left. Such a spike coincidence is necessary to trigger neuron N2 to spike, which in turn makes the animat turn left and thus to forage in a swiping fashion: going left-right-left-..., but keeping an overall direction towards the target (Fig. 1). On the other hand, when there was no silence at all between letters of the same pattern, the spike coincidence allowed the animat to still collect 346 targets.

Furthermore, long silences between patterns did not affect the performance of the animat. Even when they were 1000 ms long, the animat still collected much more targets than distractors (the ratio between the average number of targets T and distractors D hit over 1000 maps, T/D, was above 50). However, the number of collected targets decreased for silences below 40 ms—yet no distractor was hit during this test. Any decrease in the length of a stimulus (less than 10 ms) let to a circling movement around the starting point or to no movement at all. On the other hand, an increase to up to 13 ms allowed for a fair recognition ($T/D = 997/128 = 7.79$).

3.2 Robustness of the Winner

When we increased the number of objects equally for targets and distractors (up to 10 each), T/D remained within the range 12–18. In order to test the

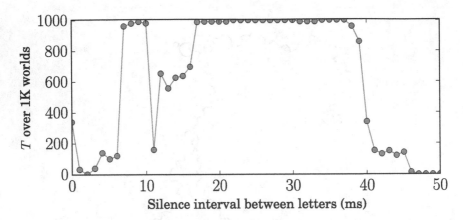

Fig. 2. The number of targets collected by the winner over 1000 random worlds, for various duration of silence interval between letters within the same pattern.

efficiency of the animat in foraging one target while avoiding a large number of distractors, we set the number of targets to 1 and distractors to 20 and evaluated the animat's performance with 700 patterns (140 s simulation time) on 1000 worlds. The animat collected 999 targets out of a total of 1000, and only 170 distractors out of a total of 20000.

We then investigated the robustness of the behavior to changes in the parameters of the animat. The winner showed robustness to changes in actuator forces; a two-fold increase of both actuator forces resulted in $T/D = 1000/44 = 22.73$. Surprisingly, even when we increased the forces 33 times, the animat could still maintain its discrimination ability $(T/D = 889/85 = 10.46)$.

Furthermore, we investigated the ability of the animat to recognise patterns with a larger number of signals in a pattern. We tested AAB being sent from the target, inter-spaced with wrong patterns (ba, aa, bb). This gave $T/D < 1$. In contrast, for all patterns that started with **A**, followed by any number of **B**s, the animat showed the ability to perform pattern recognition such that T/D was between 6 and 19. This could be explained by the way the network of the winner solves this task (Sect. 3.3).

Next, we perturbed the inhibitory gain of synapses, and obtained $T/D = 1000/77 = 12.99$ for a gain value of 0.5 nS (6 times less than the default value, 3 nS), whereas for 6 nS (2-fold increase) the quotient was 9.9 $(T = 1000, D = 101)$. However, any slight change in the excitatory synaptic gain resulted in $T/D \leqslant 1$.

The controller of the winner was not robust to any change of neuronal parameters apart from the change of V_r. When the V_r (reset voltage) was changed to a value 3 mV less/more then the default value (from -58 mV to -55 mV or -61 mV) for all neurons in the network, the winner showed a small but observable preference for correct patterns over wrong patterns by collecting more than twice as many targets as distractors $(T/D = 2.65)$.

3.3   Analysis of the Network

The key mechanism that causes the animat to adapt the direction towards the target while navigating is the sustained activation of interneuron N2 (see Fig. 3). The network holds a state that indicates **A** was received by sustained (thanks to a self-loop) firing of N0. When the network in such a state receives **B** from the left (the input is at a high level), first N1 spikes once, which together with the activity of N0 causes sustained (again, thanks to a self-loop) spiking of N2. AL can only spike thanks to the sustained spiking of N0 and a spike from N3. This N3 spike is triggered by SB (the input to the network that presents the signal B). The animat turns left only in this situation, because AR receives an excitatory connection only from N2. AR is the output (motor) neuron that controls the right actuator, so if its spikes outnumber AL spikes, the animat turns left. On the other hand, when the pattern is received from the right (the level of both inputs is low), N2 remains quiescent, and so does AR. N2 does not spike in this case—it does not receive any spike from N1, because the input is too low to cause N1 to spike.

To sum up, when the animat receives the pattern **AB** from the left side, it keeps turning left until the position of the animat changes enough for it to be in a location where the pattern is received from the right side, then it turns right, until again the signals in the correct pattern are received from the left. The alternation of these two movements results in an overall navigation towards the target, while ignoring all wrong patterns. Though the network can be in the state indicating **A** *was received, wait for* **B**, it does not produce a different action when more than one **B** is received after **A** (this scenario was not encountered during evolution).

The response of the network to the wrong stimuli (Fig. 3) agrees with the explanation above. Motor neurons are active only for one wrong pattern, aa. N0 starts sustained spiking when a is received (SA active), making AL spike and thus the animat turns right. N2 is silent because of the absence of activity in SB, therefore AR does not spike. So whether the distractor is placed on the left or on the right, the animat turns in a clockwise circle.

For ba, N2 does not spike, despite sustained spiking of N0, and—in the case of high stimulation from inputs, i.e. the source is on the left—N1 and N2 spiking once each. The reason is that when SB activation precedes SA activation, N1 spikes before N0, and thus N2 cannot spike. When the source is on the right, N1 cannot spike due to low stimulation from SB, and the final output behavior is similar to when the source is on the left. For bb, the absence of SA activity causes N0 to be quiescent, thus none of the two actuators can spike.

We then investigated the network responses to the target stimulus **AB** when presented with different sensory input levels. For a very low input level, there is no activity of interneurons and output neurons. The animat turns right only for input levels $\leqslant 0.5$ (that is, when the target is on the right). Greater values result in a larger number of spikes in AR than in AL, thus causing a left turn of the animat. The activity of interneurons for different input level values is similar to the activity showed in Fig. 3. N0 is the only interneuron that starts firing after

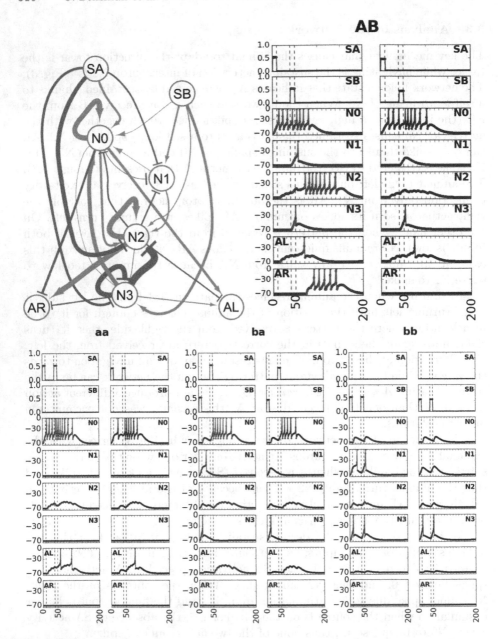

Fig. 3. The network topology of the winner and spike trains of the four patterns for two-level sensory inputs. Excitatory links are shown with arrow heads (orange), inhibitory are bar-headed (cyan). The voltage traces (vertical axes: voltage in mV, horizontal axes: time in ms) in green are the responses for signals coming from the right, red traces for signals coming from the left. (Color figure online)

receiving an activation from SA for higher values, and sustains activity until **B** is received. This is followed by the activity of neuron N3, right after receiving **B**, and only then AL spikes. N2 is triggered after a high rate spiking activity of N0, and does not require—for high values of input—any longer the coincidence of N0 and N1 spikes shown in Fig. 3 (Fig. 4). N2 starts spiking before N1 due to the stimulation from SB. As long as N2 spikes, AR spikes as well, at a higher rate for higher input values, hence outnumbering the number of spikes fired by AL and pushing the animat to turn left when the source is placed on the left.

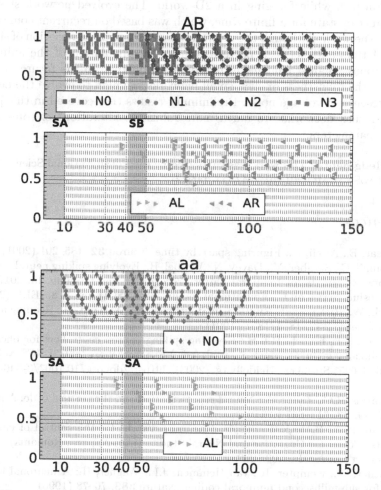

Fig. 4. The response of the network to the correct pattern (**AB**) and to one wrong pattern (**aa**). The raster plots are presented separately for interneurons and outputs. The sensory nodes are active during the time slots shaded in gray, at a constant level over a full range (vertical axis: gray horizontal lines are at the level 0.45 and 0.55, red line at 0.5; horizontal axis: simulation time covering all spikes of one stimulus) (Color figure online)

For the other wrong stimuli, similar output activities as in Fig. 3 can be observed for a wider spectrum of input levels, for example aa results in only one actuator (AL) being active, regardless of source location (Fig. 4).

4   Conclusions and Future Work

We have evolved a simple simulated robot governed by a very small neural network, which is capable of achieving a simple yet non-trivial temporal pattern recognition task while foraging in a 2D world. The evolved network showed a maintenance of state for a finite time, which was based on recurrent connections within the network. Although the network was robust against variation of silences between letters and between patterns during the simulation of the animat, it was not robust against changes in neuronal parameters. In the future, in order to explore the robustness of such small networks, we plan to evolve the network in the presence of voltage noise. Preliminary results (not covered in this paper) show that such networks are much more robust to alterations of some of the neuronal parameters.

Acknowledgments. This work was supported by the Polish National Science Center (project EvoSN, UMO-2013/08/M/ST6/00922).

References

1. Ahissar, E., Arieli, A.: Figuring space by time. Neuron **32**, 185–201 (2001)
2. Bensmail, C., Steuber, V., Davey, N., Wróbel, B.: Evolving spiking neural networks to control animats for temporal pattern recognition and foraging. In: 2017 IEEE Symposium Series on Computational Intelligence (SSCI), pp. 1–8. IEEE (2017)
3. Bialek, W., Rieke, F., de Ruyter van Steveninck, R., Warland, D.: Reading a neural code. Science **252**, 1854–1857 (1991)
4. Damper, R.I., French, R.L.B.: Evolving spiking neuron controllers for phototaxis and phonotaxis. In: Cagnoni, S., et al. (eds.) EvoWorkshops 2003. LNCS, vol. 2611, pp. 616–625. Springer, Heidelberg (2003). https://doi.org/10.1007/3-540-36605-9_56
5. Decharms, R.C., Zador, A.: Neural representation and the cortical code. Ann. Rev. Neurosci. **23**, 613–647 (2000)
6. Florian, R.V.: Biologically inspired neural networks for the control of embodied agents. Center for Cognitive and Neural Studies (Cluj-Napoca, Romania), Technical report Coneural-03-03 (2003)
7. Gerstner, W., Kempter, R., van Hemmen, J.L., Wagner, H.: A neuronal learning rule for sub-millisecond temporal coding. Nature **383**, 76–78 (1996)
8. Huxter, J., Burgess, N., O'Keefe, J.: Independent rate and temporal coding in hippocampal pyramidal cells. Nature **425**, 828–832 (2003)
9. Isaacson, J.S.: Odor representations in mammalian cortical circuits. Curr. Opin. Neurobiol. **20**, 328–331 (2010)
10. Joris, P., Yin, T.C.: A matter of time: internal delays in binaural processing. Trends Neurosci. **30**, 70–78 (2007)

11. Laurent, G.: Dynamical representation of odors by oscillating and evolving neural assemblies. Trends in Neurosci. **19**, 489–496 (1996)
12. Maex, R., Steuber, V.: The first second: models of short-term memory traces in the brain. Neural Netw. **22**, 1105–1112 (2009)
13. Reeve, R., Webb, B., Horchler, A., Indiveri, G., Quinn, R.: New technologies for testing a model of cricket phonotaxis on an outdoor robot. Rob. Auton. Syst. **51**, 41–54 (2005)
14. Rieke, F.: Spikes: Exploring the Neural Code. MIT Press, Cambridge (1999)
15. Rost, T., Ramachandran, H., Nawrot, M.P., Chicca, E.: A neuromorphic approach to auditory pattern recognition in cricket phonotaxis. In: European Conference on Circuit Theory and Design (ECCTD), pp. 1–4. IEEE (2013)
16. Steuber, V., De Schutter, E.: Rank order decoding of temporal parallel fibre input patterns in a complex Purkinje cell model. Neurocomputing **44**, 183–188 (2002)
17. Steuber, V., Willshaw, D.: A biophysical model of synaptic delay learning and temporal pattern recognition in a cerebellar Purkinje cell. J. Comput. Neurosci. **17**, 149–164 (2004)
18. Steuber, V., Willshaw, D., Van Ooyen, A.: Generation of time delays: simplified models of intracellular signalling in cerebellar Purkinje cells. Netw.: Comput. Neural Syst. **17**, 173–191 (2006)
19. Steuber, V., Willshaw, D.J.: Adaptive leaky integrator models of cerebellar Purkinje cells can learn the clustering of temporal patterns. Neurocomputing **26**, 271–276 (1999)
20. Thorpe, S., Fize, D., Marlot, C.: Speed of processing in the human visual system. Nature **381**, 520 (1996)
21. Webb, B.: Using robots to model animals: a cricket test. Rob. Auton. Syst. **16**, 117–134 (1995)
22. Wróbel, B., Abdelmotaleb, A., Joachimczak, M.: Evolving networks processing signals with a mixed paradigm, inspired by gene regulatory networks and spiking neurons. In: Di Caro, G.A., Theraulaz, G. (eds.) BIONETICS 2012. LNICST, vol. 134, pp. 135–149. Springer, Cham (2014). https://doi.org/10.1007/978-3-319-06944-9_10

Spiking Neural Networks Evolved to Perform Multiplicative Operations

Muhammad Aamir Khan[1], Volker Steuber[2], Neil Davey[2],
and Borys Wróbel[1,3(✉)]

[1] Evolving Systems Laboratory, Adam Mickiewicz University in Poznan,
Poznan, Poland
{aamir,wrobel}@evosys.org
[2] Center for Computer Science and Informatics Research,
University of Hertfordshire, Hertfordshire, UK
[3] IOPAN, Sopot, Poland

Abstract. Multiplicative or divisive changes in tuning curves of individual neurons to one stimulus ("input") as another stimulus ("modulation") is applied, called gain modulation, play an important role in perception and decision making. Since the presence of modulatory synaptic stimulation results in a multiplicative operation by proportionally changing the neuronal input-output relationship, such a change affects the sensitivity of the neuron but not its selectivity. Multiplicative gain modulation has commonly been studied at the level of single neurons. Much less is known about arithmetic operations at the network level. In this work we have evolved small networks of spiking neurons in which the output neurons respond to input with non-linear tuning curves that exhibit gain modulation—the best network showed an over 3-fold multiplicative response to modulation. Interestingly, we have also obtained a network with only 2 interneurons showing an over 2-fold response.

Keywords: Gain modulation · Multiplicative operation
Spiking neural network · Artificial evolution
Adaptive exponential integrate and fire

1 Introduction

Multiplicative or divisive changes in a tuning curve of individual neurons to one stimulus (here, *input*) as another stimulus (here, *modulation*) is applied, called gain modulation, are thought to play an important role in neural computation [6,7,10,12]. Gain modulation has been observed in the neurons responsible for keeping stable course during flight in domestic flies [4], and in the auditory system of owls [9] and crickets [5]. In the mammalian brain, neurons in cortical and subcortical regions vary their output response in a multiplicative fashion relative to a background modulatory synaptic input [7,10]. In this scenario, information is aggregated from different stimuli and the output response is modulated so

© Springer Nature Switzerland AG 2018
V. Kůrková et al. (Eds.): ICANN 2018, LNCS 11139, pp. 314–321, 2018.
https://doi.org/10.1007/978-3-030-01418-6_31

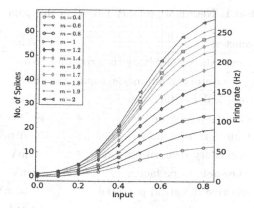

Fig. 1. Target tuning curves. The curves, generated with Eq. 5, show the expected number of spikes of the output neuron for different levels of *input* and different levels of *modulation*, which correspond to different multiplier, *m*.

that a change in the slope of input-output firing rate is produced. The control of the movement of the eyes and hands, the perception of visual information, and motor memory are other examples where gain modulation was observed [11].

Since gain modulation is an operation observed in single biological neurons, previous studies on modeling such multiplicative operations focused on models of single neurons (e.g., [1,3]). Here, we take a different approach—we evolve a *network* of simple neurons (adaptive exponential integrate and fire neurons [2]) to perform multiplicative operations inspired by the operations performed by single neurons—the fitness function in artificial evolution rewarded the networks that had a non-linear response (firing rate of the output neuron) to *input*, varying proportionally to different levels of *modulation* (and therefore matching the tuning curves in Fig. 1).

2   The Model

The adaptive exponential integrate and fire [2] neuronal model has four state variables and a number of parameters (Table 1; the parameters we used result in tonic spiking for constant input [8]):

$$C\frac{dV}{dt} = g_I(E_I - V) + g_E(E_E - V)$$

$$+ g_L(E_L - V) + g_L \Delta_T e^{(\frac{V - V_T}{\Delta_T})} - w \tag{1}$$

$$\tau_w \frac{dw}{dt} = a(V - E_L) - w \tag{2}$$

$$\frac{dg_E}{dt} = \frac{-g_E}{\tau_E} \tag{3}$$

$$\frac{dg_I}{dt} = \frac{-g_I}{\tau_I}. \tag{4}$$

Table 1. Neuronal parameters used in this paper

Parameter	Value
$\tau_{E/I}$ excitatory/inhibitory time constant	5 ms
$G_{E/I}$ excitatory/inhibitory synaptic gain	3 nS
g_L total leak conductance	10 nS
E_L effective rest potential	−70 mV
E_I inhibitory reversal potential	−70 mV
E_E excitatory reversal potential	0 mV
Δ_T threshold slope factor	2 mV
V_T effective threshold potential	−50 mV
C total capacitance	0.2 nF
a adaptation conductance	2 nS
b spike-triggered adaptation	0 pA
τ_w adaptation time constant	30 ms
V_r reset voltage	−58 mV
V_{th} spike detection threshold	0 mV

A spike is generated when the voltage (V) crosses a threshold $(V > V_{th})$; when this happens V takes a value V_r, and the adaptation (w) takes a value $w + b$. When a neuron receives a spike from a neuron that connects to it (a presynaptic neuron), the excitatory (inhibitory) conductance is increased by an excitatory (inhibitory) gain multiplied by the synaptic weight. In this paper, we use Euler integration with 1 ms time steps.

Each network, in addition to interneurons and the output neuron (all neurons had the same parameters), has two nodes: input and modulation nodes, which can be connected to interneurons but not to the output neuron. If an interneuron receives an excitatory (inhibitory) connection from the input or modulation node, at each time step the interneuron's excitatory (inhibitory) conductance is increased by the value of the *input* or *modulation* (a value between 0 and 1) multiplied by the excitatory (inhibitory) synaptic gain and the weight of the connection. In other words, each interneuron can receive stimulation (excitatory or inhibitory) from other interneurons (or, indeed, itself), and input or modulation nodes. But whereas each spike from a neuron in the network results in an increase of the excitatory or inhibitory conductance by a value proportional to the synaptic weight, the increase in the case of the stimulation from input or modulation nodes is also proportional to *input* or *modulation*.

Both the *input* and *modulation* are presented for 240 ms, and the network response (the spikes of the output neuron) is measured at the same time. In order to avoid that the response to one pair (*input, modulation*) would affect a response to another pair, all the neurons in the network are reset to their initial state $(V = E_L, w = 0, g_E = 0, g_I = 0)$ after each pair is presented to the network.

We used the platform GReaNs [13,14] to evolve the networks. In GReaNs, networks are encoded in linear genomes (Fig. 2); the encoding is inspired by the way biological genetic networks are encoded in biological genomes [14]. In principle, the number of interneurons encoded in the network and the number of links between them is unlimited (here, for reasons of computational efficiency, we limited the number of interneurons to 10; in practice, the networks did not grow during evolution beyond 7 interneurons). Each interneuron is encoded by a series of *cis* and *trans* genetic elements; input, modulation, and output nodes are encoded by a genetic element each. Each genetic element has an associated point in an abstract 2-dimensional affinity space. To determine the connectivity of the network, first the Euclidean distance between each ordered pair of points (*trans*, *cis*), (input, *cis*), (modulation, *cis*), and (*trans*, output) is obtained. This distance translates to a contribution to the weight of the connection between nodes in the network. Since each interneuron can be encoded by several *cis* and *trans* elements, the weight contributions are summed. If the distance is above a certain threshold, the contribution is zero. Otherwise, the contribution is an inverse exponential function of the distance. The sign of the contribution (positive or negative) is determined by the sign associated with each genetic element—if both signs are the same, the contribution is positive, otherwise it is negative. A positive (negative) sum of contributions results in an excitatory (inhibitory) link in the network.

Each independent run of artificial evolution was limited to 2000 generations, with a constant population (300 individuals), elitism (10), and size 2 tournament selection. The initial population consisted of random genomes created as described previously [15], and the genetic operators were exactly the same as in this previous work [15].

The fitness function rewarded the correct number of spikes of the output neuron in response to a given pair of *input* and *modulation*. In other words, the networks were evolved so to match target tuning curves (Fig. 1), which were generated using the equation

$$T(I, m) = m * (\frac{35}{1 + (exp(-8I + 4)}),\qquad(5)$$

where I is *input* and m is the multiplier, expected to be twice the *modulation* during evolution (for example, *modulation* of 0.2 is expected to produce the output corresponding to $m = 0.4$). The constant parameters in Eq. 5 were selected by

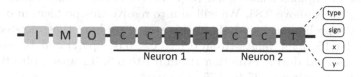

Fig. 2. The encoding of network in linear genome. Genetic elements I and M code for the nodes that allow for presenting the stimulation by *input* and *modulation*, O encodes the output neuron. See text for further details.

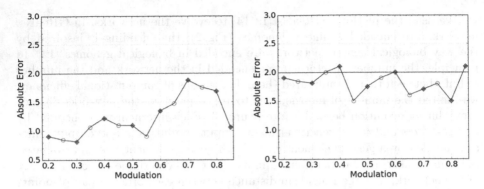

Fig. 3. Absolute error of the evolved networks. Both the network with six interneurons (champion 1, left) and two (champion 2, right) show the absolute error at most about 2 when compared to the best-fit tuning curves across 8 *modulation* levels experienced during evolution (filled symbols) and 6 intermediate values (empty symbols) used only in testing.

hand to give a clearly non-linear response (similar to the tuning curves observed in [3]) with biologically realistic firing rates, and so that the network with a perfect response would show a 5-fold multiplicative response (this is the ratio of the highest multiplier divided by the lowest).

The fitness function minimises the sum of absolute differences between the target and observed responses (absolute error), averaged over all np pairs of *input* and multiplier:

$$f_{fitness} = \frac{1}{np} \sum_{k=1}^{n} \sum_{l=1}^{p} |T(I_k, m_l) - O(I_k, m_l)| \tag{6}$$

During evolution we presented 209 pairs of *input* and *modulation*, $n = 19$ levels of *input*, from 0.1 to 1.0, 0.05 apart, times $p = 11$ levels of *modulation*, from 0.2 to 0.8, 0.1 apart, and from 0.85 to 1, 0.05 apart.

3   Results and Discussion

We have run 100 independent runs of artificial evolution, and then analysed the responses of the champion networks. During this analysis, we have noticed that none of the champions shows good responses for *input* values above 0.8, and modulation levels above 0.85. We will aim to resolve this problem in our future work. For the preliminary analysis in this paper, we have thus retested all the champions for 15 *input* values (from 0.1 to 0.8, 0.05 apart) and 14 *modulation* values, 8 presented during evolution (from 0.2 to 0.8, 0.1 apart, plus 0.85) and additional 6 values from 0.25 to 0.75, 0.1 apart.

Since we are interested in evolving networks for multiplicative operations in general, not networks whose responses match a particular set of tuning curves, we fitted (using least squares as the goodness-of-fit measure) the parameter m in Eq. 5 to the actual responses for these 14 levels of *modulation*, each over these 15 levels of *input*. Only two networks out of 100 had an absolute error (averaged for all *input* levels for a given *modulation* level) of around 2 (Fig. 3) for all 14 *modulation* levels—at most about 2 spikes difference from the best-fit tuning curve. One of this networks (champion 1) had six interneurons, the other (champion 2) had two—the genome coded for three, but one of the neurons did not spike for any (*input, modulation*) pair and thus could be removed.

The ratio of the highest to the lowest m value (m_{max}/m_{min}) fitted as described above for each network gives the maximum number by which the network actually multiplies its response to the *input* as the *modulation* varies. This ratio was 3.4 for champion 1 (the fitted value of m was $m_{min} = 0.54$ for *modulation* = 0.2 and $m_{max} = 1.82$ for *modulation* = 0.8) and 2.3 for champion 2 ($m_{min} = 0.74$, $m_{max} = 1.71$). Thus the larger network showed a larger multiplicative response to *modulation* (Fig. 4). Since in 100 runs we obtained only two networks with small absolute errors, we cannot judge yet if in general larger networks thus obtained will show larger multiplicative responses. We plan to investigate this in our future work.

The networks of both champion 1 and 2 had only excitatory connections. Perhaps if we reformulated the task so that the networks were not reset after each (*input, modulation*) pair, also inhibitory connections would be necessary. This is another issue we plan to investigate in our future work.

The preliminary analysis of the activity in the smaller network (Fig. 5) shows that while the firing rate of interneuron $N1$ is well above 100 Hz, the firing rate of $N0$ is lower, around 30 Hz, and $N0$ does not respond to low *modulation* and *input* levels. The activity of $N1$ is very similar to the activity of the output; the most noticeable exceptions are in the response to high levels of *input*, which in $N1$, unlike in output, does not change much with the varying *modulation*.

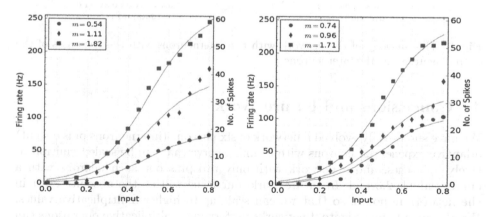

Fig. 4. The best-fit tuning curves of the evolved networks for three levels of *modulation*. The tuning curves correspond to the best fit of m (see text of details), for the *modulation* at the lowest (0.2), intermediate (0.6) and the highest level (0.8). The network with six interneurons (champion 1, left) shows a 3.4-fold multiplicative response, the network with two interneurons (champion 2, right) shows a 2.3-fold response.

We can speculate that the connection from $N0$ to $N1$ together with a self-connection of $N1$ is what allows the varied response to high *input* as the *modulation* varies.

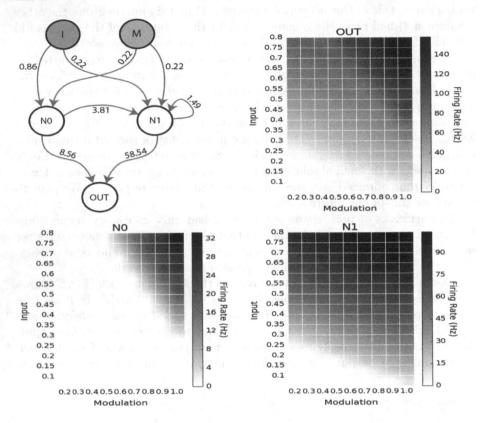

Fig. 5. The topology of the network with two interneurons with the responses of the output neuron and the interneurons.

4   Conclusions and Future Work

We have successfully evolved a network of six plus one (interneurons plus output) adaptive exponential neurons with a tuning curve that can be scaled multiplicatively 3.4 times, and a network with only two plus one such neurons with a curve scalable 2.3-fold. In future work, our focus will be the absolute error in the network response, so that we can scale up to higher multiplicative values. We also plan to investigate if networks performing multiplicative operations can be evolved in the presence of noise on the *input* and *modulation* and on the state variables of the neurons. We would like to test the hypothesis if larger networks will allow for better matching of tuning curves and higher multiplicative responses. We would also like to reformulate our model so not only the firing rates of the neurons in the network are kept within the biologically realistic values, but also the currents resulting from the stimulation—this was not the case here, as the synaptic weights in the evolved networks reached very high values; we plan to limit them by introducing an additional sigmoidal transformation in the encoding of synaptic weights in our model.

Acknowledgements. This work was supported by the Polish National Science Center (project EvoSN, UMO-2013/08/M/ST6/00922). MAK acknowledges the support of the PhD program of the KNOW RNA Research Center in Poznan (No. 01/KNOW2/2014).

References

1. Ayaz, A., Chance, F.S.: Gain modulation of neuronal responses by subtractive and divisive mechanisms of inhibition. J. Neurophysiol. **101**, 958–968 (2009)
2. Brette, R., Gerstner, W.: Adaptive exponential integrate-and-fire model as an effective description of neuronal activity. J. Neurophysiol. **94**, 3637–3642 (2005)
3. Chance, F.S., Abbott, L.F., Reyes, A.D.: Gain modulation from background synaptic input. Neuron **35**, 773–782 (2002)
4. Götz, K.G.: The optomotor equilibrium of the Drosophila navigation system. J. Comp. Physiol. **99**, 187–210 (1975)
5. Hildebrandt, K.J., Benda, J., Hennig, R.M.: Multiple arithmetic operations in a single neuron: the recruitment of adaptation processes in the cricket auditory pathway depends on sensory context. J. Neurosci. **31**, 14142–14150 (2011)
6. Koch, C., Poggio, T.: Multiplying with synapses and neurons. In: Single Neuron Computation, pp. 315–345. Elsevier (1992)
7. Murphy, B.K., Miller, K.D.: Multiplicative gain changes are induced by excitation or inhibition alone. J. Neurosci. **23**, 10040–10051 (2003)
8. Naud, R., Marcille, N., Clopath, C., Gerstner, W.: Firing patterns in the adaptive exponential integrate-and-fire model. Biol. Cybern. **99**, 335–347 (2008)
9. Peña, J.L., Konishi, M.: Robustness of multiplicative processes in auditory spatial tuning. J. Neurosci. **24**, 8907–8910 (2004)
10. Salinas, E., Abbott, L.: Coordinate transformations in the visual system: how to generate gain fields and what to compute with them. Progress Brain Res. **130**, 175–190 (2001)
11. Salinas, E., Sejnowski, T.J.: Gain modulation in the central nervous system: where behavior, neurophysiology, and computation meet. Neuroscientist **7**, 430–440 (2001)
12. Schnupp, J.W., King, A.J.: Neural processing: the logic of multiplication in single neurons. Curr. Biol. **11**, 640–642 (2001)
13. Wróbel, B., Abdelmotaleb, A., Joachimczak, M.: Evolving networks processing signals with a mixed paradigm, inspired by gene regulatory networks and spiking neurons. In: Di Caro, G.A., Theraulaz, G. (eds.) BIONETICS 2012. LNICST, vol. 134, pp. 135–149. Springer, Cham (2014). https://doi.org/10.1007/978-3-319-06944-9_10
14. Wróbel, B., Joachimczak, M.: Using the genetic regulatory evolving artificial networks (GReaNs) platform for signal processing, animat control, and artificial multicellular development. In: Kowaliw, T., Bredeche, N., Doursat, R. (eds.) Growing Adaptive Machines. SCI, vol. 557, pp. 187–200. Springer, Heidelberg (2014). https://doi.org/10.1007/978-3-642-55337-0_6
15. Yaqoob, M., Wróbel, B.: Robust very small spiking neural networks evolved with noise to recognize temporal patterns. In: Proceedings of the 2018 Conference on Artificial Life, ALIFE 2018, pp. 665–672. MIT Press (2018)

Very Small Spiking Neural Networks Evolved for Temporal Pattern Recognition and Robust to Perturbed Neuronal Parameters

Muhammad Yaqoob[1] and Borys Wróbel[1,2(✉)]

[1] Evolving Systems Laboratory, Adam Mickiewicz University in Poznan,
Poznan, Poland
{yaqoob,wrobel}@evosys.org
[2] IOPAN, Sopot, Poland

Abstract. We evolve both topology and synaptic weights of recurrent very small spiking neural networks in the presence of noise on the membrane potential. The noise is at a level similar to the level observed in biological neurons. The task of the networks is to recognise three signals in a particular order (a pattern ABC) in a continuous input stream in which each signal occurs with the same probability. The networks consist of adaptive exponential integrate and fire neurons and are limited to either three or four interneurons and one output neuron, with recurrent and self-connections allowed only for interneurons. Our results show that spiking neural networks evolved in the presence of noise are robust to the change of neuronal parameters. We propose a procedure to approximate the range, specific for every neuronal parameter, from which the parameters can be sampled to preserve, at least for some networks, high true positive rate and low false discovery rate. After assigning the state of neurons to states of the network corresponding to states in a finite state transducer, we show that this simple but not trivial computational task of temporal pattern recognition can be accomplished in a variety of ways.

Keywords: Temporal pattern recognition · Spiking neural networks
Artificial evolution · Minimal cognition · Complex networks
Genetic algorithm · Finite state automaton · Finite state machine

1 Introduction

Information in biological neuronal systems is represented temporally by *precise* timing of voltage spikes [1,3,5,6,12,13,15]. Thus noise poses a fundamental problem for informational processing in biological systems [9] (and also artificial systems inspired by them). On the other hand, noise has been postulated to play a computational role [14]. For example, neuronal noise enables the phenomenon of stochastic resonance in neural networks—a process in which a weak signal

© Springer Nature Switzerland AG 2018
V. Kůrková et al. (Eds.): ICANN 2018, LNCS 11139, pp. 322–331, 2018.
https://doi.org/10.1007/978-3-030-01418-6_32

gets amplified to reach a threshold, or a strong signal is prevented from spiking [7,20,21]. Moreover, neural networks formed in the presence of background noisy synaptic activity can be expected to be robust to disturbances [11].

In this work, we analyse very small spiking neural networks (SNNs) evolved to perform a simple temporal pattern recognition task in the presence of noise. We will show that networks evolved with noise maintain functionality even when the parameters of the neuronal model are changed. In contrast to our previous work [23] in which just one neuronal parameter was varied at any given time (while all the other parameters were kept at the default value), here we investigate the robustness against varying *all* the parameters simultaneously. Although the model for evolving the topology and weights in the SNNs we use here does not in principle limit the number of neurons, we limited this number to either three or four interneurons and one output neuron.

It has been observed before that the same computational task can be accomplished by networks with different structures [16,19]. Our long-term goal is to understand how various solutions—obtained by evolving networks numerous times, independently—can accomplish simple, but not trivial computational tasks.

2 The Model

The networks in this work consist of adaptive exponential integrate and fire neurons [17] with the default values of the parameters that result in tonic spiking for constant input. The four state variables of each neuron, membrane potential V, adaptation w, excitatory and inhibitory conductance g_E and g_I, are governed by the equations

$$\frac{dV}{dt} = \frac{1}{C}(g_E(E_E - V) + g_I(E_I - V) - w)$$
$$+ \frac{1}{\tau_m}(E_L - V + \Delta_T e^{(\frac{V-V_T}{\Delta_T})}) \quad (1)$$

$$\tau_w \frac{dw}{dt} = a(V - E_L) - w \quad (2)$$

$$\frac{dg_E}{dt} = \frac{-g_E}{\tau_E} \quad (3)$$

$$\frac{dg_I}{dt} = \frac{-g_I}{\tau_I} \quad (4)$$

with 13 parameters in total; the default values of parameters are presented in Table 1 [23,24]. We used Euler integration with 1 ms time step, and added a random value drawn from the normal distribution centered at 0 with standard deviation 2 mV to V at each step; this level of noise is similar to that observed in biological neurons [2,8,10,18].

When V of a neuron is above 0 mV, V is reduced to V_r, while w changes to $w + b$, and each neuron to which this neuron connects receives a spike. If

Table 1. The ranges of robustness for champions with 3 and 4 interneurons that were most robust (3/3 and 1/4, respectively) overall and for the most robust from the champions maintaining state (8/3 and 7/4).

Parameter	Default value	3/3	8/3	1/4	7/4
E_L	$-70\,\mathrm{mV}$	$[-72, -67]$	$[-72, -66]$	$[-72, -67]$	$[-74, -68]$
V_r	$-58\,\mathrm{mV}$	$[-59, -55]$	$[-60, -54]$	$[-60, -55]$	$[-59, -55]$
V_T	$-50\,\mathrm{mV}$	$[-51, -48]$	$[-51, -48]$	$[-52, -49]$	$[-51, -48]$
Δ_T	$2\,\mathrm{mV}$	$[1.6, 2.4]$	$[1.8, 2.3]$	$[1.8, 2.1]$	$[1.9, 2.2]$
C	$0.2\,\mathrm{nF}$	$[0.19, 0.22]$	$[0.17, 0.23]$	$[0.17, 0.21]$	$[0.17, 0.22]$
a	$2\,\mathrm{nS}$	$[-2, 4]$	$[1, 6]$	$[0, 3]$	$[1, 4]$
b	$0\,\mathrm{pA}$	$[0, 3]$	$[0, 4]$	$[0, 3]$	$[0, 2]$
τ_m	$20\,\mathrm{ms}$	$[19, 22]$	$[18, 23]$	$[17, 21]$	$[17, 23]$
τ_w	$30\,\mathrm{ms}$	$[29, 32]$	$[29, 33]$	$[27, 31]$	$[27, 31]$
τ_E	$5\,\mathrm{ms}$	$[4.8, 5.2]$	$[4.9, 5.3]$	$[4.7, 5.1]$	$[4.9, 5.3]$
τ_I	$5\,\mathrm{ms}$	$[4.9, 5.2]$	$[4.9, 5.3]$	$[4.6, 5.1]$	$[4.9, 5.3]$
E_E	$0\,\mathrm{mV}$	$[-2, 2]$	$[-2, 4]$	$[-3, 1]$	$[-1, 2]$
E_I	$-70\,\mathrm{mV}$	$[-71, -67]$	$[-73, -68]$	$[-72, -67]$	$[-71, 68]$
$gain_E$	$7\,\mathrm{nS}$	$[6.9, 7.3]$	$[6.9, 7.3]$	$[6.8, 7.3]$	$[6.7, 7.2]$
$gain_I$	$7\,\mathrm{nS}$	$[6.8, 7.3]$	$[6.8, 7.4]$	$[6.8, 7.3]$	$[6.7, 7.2]$

the connection is excitatory (inhibitory), g_E (g_I) in such a postsynaptic neuron is increased by the weight of the connection multiplied by the synaptic gain. Encoding of SNNs in our model has been described previously [22–24]. In order to recognise a subsequence of three signals in a random input stream, the network has three input nodes (one for each signal), either three or four interneurons, and a single output neuron. Dale rule [4] is not kept—a neuron can be both excitatory and inhibitory at the same time. Furthermore, input nodes cannot connect to the output neuron directly. Only interneurons can have self-loops. The settings for the artificial evolution in this work are as in our previous work [23], with three modifications: (i) the size of duplication of genetic elements was drawn from a geometric distribution with mean 6 (it was 11 previously), (ii) the elements coding for input and output were excluded both from duplications/deletions and crossover (they were allowed to undergo crossover in [23]), (iii) finally and most importantly, we modified slightly the way the fitness function is calculated, resulting in the procedure as follows.

During evolution, each individual was evaluated on six input streams with 500 signals, each signal 6 ms in duration and followed by 16 ms silence (each input stream thus lasted for 11 s). In four input streams, all signals (A, B and C) occurred with equal probability; two input streams were constructed by concatenating four triplets (with equal probability of occurrence): ABC and ABA, ABB, BBC (three triplets that our preliminary work showed the most problematic to distinguish from the pattern to be recognised, ABC). To calculate the fitness function, we calculated R (for reward), the number of 22 ms intervals (signal plus silence) of the last C of each ABC in the input sequence during which the output neuron actually spiked, correctly, at least once, divided by the total number of intervals in the input stream for which it should spike. In other words, R is the true positive rate (TPR) of the network. We also calculated P (for penalty), the number of other 22 ms intervals (signal plus silence) with spikes on output (wrongly), divided by the total number of 22 ms intervals in the input stream in which spikes should not occur. In contrast, false discovery rate (FDR) of the network has the same numerator as P, but the denominator is all the 22 ms intervals in which the spikes of the output neuron were observed. The fitness function we used,

$$f_{fitness} = 1 - R + 4P \tag{5}$$

penalises strongly spikes that do not follow the target pattern. The constant 4 in the penalty term was chosen by the preliminary exploration of values with the objective to find a value that gave the highest yield of successful evolutionary runs. We define a successful run as one that ends with a champion that is a perfect recogniser. A perfect recogniser evolved without noise is a network that spikes only after the correct pattern. For networks evolved with noise, we consider an SNN a perfect recogniser if it has TPR > 0.99 and FDR < 0.01).

The slight modifications of the settings of the artificial evolution (from the ones used in [23]) had a quite pronounced effect on the yield of perfect recognisers when no noise was present (for three interneurons, 81% of runs versus 33% for the settings in [23]). However, the effect on the evolvability in the presence of noise was less pronounced.

For each champion, we obtained the ranges of parameters for which it was robust using the following algorithm. We repeatedly extended the ranges of all parameters around their default values, by a small value (specific for each parameter), at first in both directions. We then drew 100 random sets of parameters using such extended ranges, gave the same parameters to all neurons in the network, and checked if at least 90 among these 100 SNNs had TPR > 0.90 and FDR < 0.10 (each network was tested for one random, and thus different, input stream with 50000 signals, with equal probability of occurrence for A, B, and C). If so, the extended ranges were kept. If not, the ranges were shrunk back to the previous sizes and the problematic parameter was identified (by excluding one by one the parameters from extension, in one of the two directions, in the set of parameters for which the ranges can be extended, and checking if this allowed to extend the range keeping TPR > 0.90 and FDF < 0.10). The algorithm stopped when the set of parameters for which the range could be extended became empty.

The size of the ranges (maximum minus the minimum value) were compared for the networks evolved with the limit of three versus four interneurons using the James test implemented in the package Rfast of the R project (https://cran.r-project.org/). Proportions were compared using function prop.test in R.

3   Results and Discussion

In 100 independent runs for 3000 generations each, when we allowed for three interneurons, 13 runs ended with perfect recognisers. When we allowed for four interneurons, 19 runs out of 100 resulted in perfect recognisers. Our previous work [23] suggested that at least three interneurons are needed to obtain perfect recognisers in the presence of noise; here also we were unable to evolve with noise when less than three interneurons were allowed, and none of the runs when the limit was set to three resulted in a champion with less. In contrast, two champions out of 19 obtained when the limit was set to four interneurons ended up having three interneurons.

The size of the ranges of robustness for 13 networks evolved with the limit of three versus 17 networks with four interneurons was not significantly different. We then tested how robust were the networks when each neuron in the network was given a different set of parameters drawn from the obtained range (during the range expansion algorithm, all neurons always had the same parameters drawn from the range; in this test, as during expansion, we made 100 evaluations, each on a different random input stream with 50000 signals). None of the networks remained perfect recognisers, but some—noticeably champion 3 evolved with three interneurons (champion 3/3)—were quite robust to such a disruption (Table 2), and so were champions 8/3 and 5/3; and for the networks with 4 interneurons, champions 1/4 and 12/4.

We have previously proposed a way to map the network activity to the states of finite state transducers (FST) [23,24]. Before we did such a mapping for the networks obtained here, we first analysed which networks could maintain their state for a very long time (in practice, noise may prevent a given network from maintaining the states infinitely). Nine out of 13 networks evolved with three interneurons sustained elongation of intervals between signals from 16 ms to at least 100 ms (Table 2; we assume that if the silence can be extended to 100 ms, the network maintains its state). Only four out of 17 with four interneurons did so (Table 2). Thus the fraction of perfect recognisers maintaining their state is

Table 2. Robustness of 13 networks evolved limiting the number of interneurons to three (top) and 19 networks evolved limiting the number of interneurons to four (bottom; champions with labels in bold evolved to have 3 interneurons), when sampling the neuronal parameters from the ranges of robustness specific for each champion, and their robustness to increased interval of silence between signals.

	0/3	1/3	2/3	3/3	4/3	5/3	6/3	7/3	8/3	9/3	10/3	11/3	12/3
TPR>0.99 & FDR<0.01	37	37	27	80	19	53	47	52	67	14	24	16	8
TPR>0.95 & FDR<0.05	71	79	75	97	68	99	93	98	93	80	50	51	79
TPR>0.90 & FDR<0.10	84	86	86	100	85	99	97	99	99	91	71	65	93
Maximum interval of silence	⩾100	35	⩾100	28	⩾100	⩾100	48	⩾100	⩾100	⩾100	⩾100	⩾100	19

	0/4	1/4	2/4	3/4	4/4	5/4	**6/4**	7/4	**8/4**	9/4	10/4	11/4	12/4	13/4	14/4	15/4	16/4	17/4	18/4
TPR>0.99 & FDR<0.01	5	66	1	39	39	18	58	39	11	34	17	38	64	17	5	24	29	7	48
TPR>0.95 & FDR<0.05	64	88	70	69	75	75	90	86	58	89	67	74	92	76	47	65	70	72	96
TPR>0.90 & FDR<0.10	90	94	92	85	86	91	93	98	83	95	86	83	98	93	73	81	82	90	98
Maximum interval of silence	17	20	24	21	36	⩾100	⩾100	⩾100	19	27	18	18	29	⩾100	23	50	18	⩾100	28

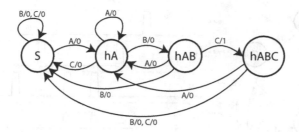

Fig. 1. Minimal FST for recognizing ABC. The nodes represent the states and edges represent the transitions from one state to another state on receiving an input symbol {A, B, C} and producing an output {0: no spike(s), 1: spike(s) of the output neuron}.

significantly larger for networks with three interneurons ($p = 0.017$; one-sided test). The reason for this might be that in networks with four interneurons the additional neuron acts as one more source of noise disrupting the memory maintained as self-sustained high-frequency spiking (see below).

We considered the network most robust if it had the highest number of sets of parameter values among 100 sets independently sampled from the robustness ranges (such as shown in Table 1) that gave TPR > 0.99 and FDR < 0.01. Interestingly, the most robust networks (3/3 and 1/4) failed to maintain their state. For mapping the network states on to the states of an FST, we have chosen therefore networks 8/3 and 7/4—the most robust of networks maintaining memory (Figs. 2 and 3).

There are four states in a minimal-size FST that recognises a pattern that consists of three different signals in a specific order in a stream of three signals (Fig. 1). In both networks (8/3 and 7/4) the state of the network after they receive ABC (state hABC, for *had ABC*) is reached after a transition from a state in which all interneurons have zero or zero/low activity (neural states Z or L, respectively; Tables 3 and 4). The same was the case for all the other perfect recognisers obtained in this work (not shown). This means that the output in each network will spike if the input stream consists of a single signal, C. Since we are interested here in recognition in a continuous stream of signals, we do not consider it a serious issue. Perhaps, however, introducing a strong penalty for output spikes after the initial C would allow us to obtain networks with different structure and activity; we plan to investigate this in our future work.

The interneurons of 8/3 are fully connected (Fig. 2), and all the interneurons have excitatory self-loops. However, it is not the case that full connectivity with self-loops for interneurons in networks evolved for three interneurons is a sufficient and necessary condition for state maintenance (for example, 6/3 and 12/3 have such a topology, but do not maintain the state, while 11/3 does so without full connectivity).

Going back to 8/3; both interneurons N1 and N2 self-excite themselves strongly—high-frequency spiking (H state) of N1 and N2 is observed in all states but hAB (which is maintained trivially—all neurons are inactive). When signal

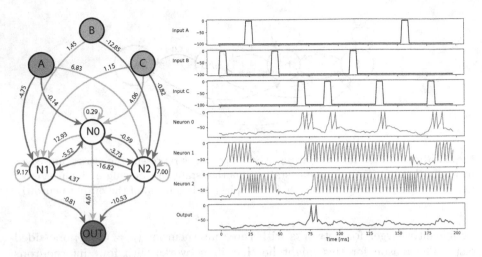

Fig. 2. The topology and activity of network 8/3.

Table 3. States of the neurons in network 8/3 in network states mapped on the states of the minimal FST. Z: zero, L: (zero or) low, H: high-spiking activity. See text for further details.

	S	hA	hAB	hABC
Neuron 0	L: 0, 2, 3 spikes	Z	Z	L: 3 spikes
Neuron 1	H: $332 \pm 1\,$Hz	L: 0, 1, 2 spikes	Z	H: $331 \pm 1\,$Hz
Neuron 2	H: 333 Hz	H: $334 \pm 1\,$Hz	L: 1, 2 spikes	H: 329 Hz
Output	Z	Z	Z	L: 1, 2 spikes

A is received, strong connection of input A to N2 puts N2 in the H state, and because of a strongly inhibitory connection both from input A and N2 to N1, N1 is in an L state in the network state hA. The activity of input B strongly inhibits N2; this is why the transition from network state hA to hAB corresponds to L or Z states of all interneurons. When a network in such a state receives a C, the excitatory connection from input C to N0 and N0's weak self-excitation combine to make N0 spike exactly three times, which is necessary for the output to spike once or twice (output can be excited only by N0); connections from N0 to N1 and from N1 to N2 are mainly responsible for putting both N1 and N2 in an H state. When, however, C is received in any other state, either N2 (state hA) or both N1 and N2 (states S and hABC) are in state H; their strong inhibitory connections to output prevent output from spiking (Fig. 2).

Limitations of space prohibit us from providing a similar analysis for 7/4. We do, however, provide the data (Fig. 3, Table 4) sufficient for making it.

Our preliminary analysis of the variability of the ways in which computation in this task is accomplished in networks that show state maintenance indicates that networks evolved with three interneurons belong to four distinct classes

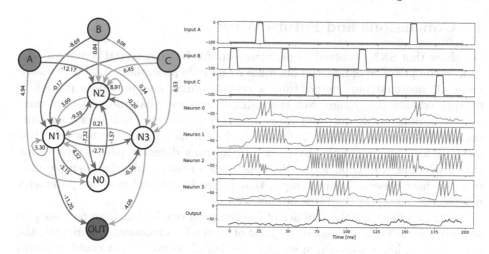

Fig. 3. The topology and activity of network 7/4.

Table 4. States of the neurons in network 7/4 in network states mapped on the states of the minimal FST. Z: zero, L: (zero or) low, H: high-spiking activity. See text for further details.

	S	hA	hAB	hABC
Neuron 0	Z	L: 2, 3 spikes	Z	Z
Neuron 1	H: 330 ± 3 Hz	H: 280 ± 3 Hz	L: 1 spike	H: 330 Hz
Neuron 2	H: 332 ± 2 Hz	L: 0, 1, 3 spikes	Z	H: 333 Hz
Neuron 3	L: 0, 4 spikes	Z	Z	L: 4 spikes
Output	Z	Z	Z	L: 1, 2 spikes

based on the assignment of neural states to network states. For network 8/3 we can encode this assignment as (S, hA, hAB, hABC) = (LHH, ZLH, ZZL, LHH), where Z means zero activity, L means zero or low activity (a few spikes at most), and H means high-frequency spiking. The order of symbols in each triplet assigned to a state follows the order of interneurons' labels (Table 3). Three other networks belong to this class, 0/3, 9/3, and 11/3 (such matching requires, of course, appropriate ordering of interneurons in each network). The other three possible classes are: (i) 4/3 and 7/3 have (ZHH, ZHL, ZLZ, LHH), (ii) 2/3 and 5/3 have (HHH, HLZ, LZZ, HHH), and (iii) 10/3 has (HHH, LHH, ZLL, HHH). The four networks that show state maintenance with four interneurons all belong to different classes based on such an assignment: whereas (i) 7/4 has (ZHHL, LHLZ, ZLZZ, ZHHL) (Table 4), (ii) 5/4 has (HZHH, HZHZ, LZHZ, HLHH), (iii) 13/4 has (HHHH, HLLH, LZZL, HHHH), and (iv) 17/4 has (HLLH, LZZH, ZZZL, HLLH). In our future work, we plan to further analyse the relationship between these classes and the network topologies, considering the signs and weights of the connections.

4   Conclusions and Future Work

We show that SNNs evolved to perform a simple but not trivial computational task in the presence of noise on neuronal membrane potential are robust to sampling all neuronal parameters from a certain range, and provide a procedure to approximate this range. Not surprisingly, we show that the range for varying all parameters is narrower than for varying a single parameter each time (as we did previously [23]). In future work, we plan to further fine tune this methodology—for example, by giving all neurons different parameters during this procedure, and considering the dependence relationships between parameters (we have observed, for example, that increasing the value of one parameter may allow increasing the value of another).

Setting a limit for the number of interneurons one higher than necessary to accomplish the tasks increased the yield of successful evolutionary runs (i.e., the evolvability), but resulted in a smaller fraction of networks that could maintain their state in the successful runs. Furthermore, there was no significant impact on the range of robustness to changes of parameters between slightly smaller and larger networks. In future work, we plan to investigate if larger networks will allow obtaining solutions in the presence of higher levels of noise. We would also like to see if other models of noise (such as an Ornstein-Uhlenbeck process, commonly used in computational neuroscience) impact evolvability and robustness. Another possible direction for future work is to investigate the evolution of recognition of longer patterns in the presence of noise.

In this work, we performed a preliminary analysis of how the networks accomplish the temporal pattern recognition with state maintenance by assigning neural states in network states corresponding to the state of an FST. We show that the solutions belong to different classes, and thus different topologies can allow solving this task. In future work, we will analyse in more detail the variety of solutions obtained in independent runs. We would also like to see if changing the spiking behavior of neurons during evolution (e.g., to bursting) or the model itself (e.g., to leaky integrate and fire) leads to other classes of solutions.

Acknowledgements. This work was supported by the Polish National Science Center (project EvoSN, UMO-2013/08/M/ST6/00922). MY acknowledges the support of the KNOW RNA Research Center in Poznan (No. 01/KNOW2/2014). We are grateful to Volker Steuber and Neil Davey for discussions and suggestions.

References

1. Ahissar, E., Arieli, A.: Figuring space by time. Neuron **32**, 185–201 (2001)
2. Anderson, J.S., Lampl, I., Gillespie, D.C., Ferster, D.: The contribution of noise to contrast invariance of orientation tuning in cat visual cortex. Science **290**, 1968–1972 (2000)
3. Bialek, W., Rieke, F., de Ruyter van Steveninck, R.R., Warland, D., et al.: Reading a neural code. In: Neural Information Processing Systems, pp. 36–43 (1989)
4. Burnstock, G.: Autonomic neurotransmission: 60 years since sir henry dale. Ann. Rev. Pharmacol. Toxicol. **49**, 1–30 (2009)

5. Buzsáki, G., Chrobak, J.J.: Temporal structure in spatially organized neuronal ensembles: a role for interneuronal networks. Curr. Opin. Neurobiol. **5**, 504–510 (1995)
6. Decharms, R.C., Zador, A.: Neural representation and the cortical code. Ann. Rev. Neurosci. **23**, 613–647 (2000)
7. Destexhe, A., Rudolph, M., Fellous, J.M., Sejnowski, T.: Fluctuating synaptic conductances recreate in vivo-like activity in neocortical neurons. Neuroscience **107**, 13–24 (2001)
8. Destexhe, A., Paré, D.: Impact of network activity on the integrative properties of neocortical pyramidal neurons in vivo. J. Neurophysiol. **81**, 1531–1547 (1999)
9. Faisal, A.A., Selen, L.P., Wolpert, D.M.: Noise in the nervous system. Nat. Rev. Neurosci. **9**, 292–303 (2008)
10. Finn, I.M., Priebe, N.J., Ferster, D.: The emergence of contrast-invariant orientation tuning in simple cells of cat visual cortex. Neuron **54**, 137–152 (2007)
11. Florian, R.V.: Biologically inspired neural networks for the control of embodied agents. Center for Cognitive and Neural Studies (Cluj-Napoca, Romania), Technical report Coneural-03-03 (2003)
12. Gerstner, W., Kempter, R., van Hemmen, J.L., Wagner, H.: A neuronal learning rule for sub-millisecond temporal coding. Nature **383**, 76–78 (1996)
13. Huxter, J., Burgess, N., O'keefe, J.: Independent rate and temporal coding in hippocampal pyramidal cells. Nature **425**, 828–832 (2003)
14. Jacobson, G., et al.: Subthreshold voltage noise of rat neocortical pyramidal neurones. J. Physiol. **564**, 145–160 (2005)
15. Laurent, G.: Dynamical representation of odors by oscillating and evolving neural assemblies. Trends Neurosci. **19**, 489–496 (1996)
16. Marder, E.: Variability, compensation, and modulation in neurons and circuits. Proc. Natl. Acad. Sci. USA **108**(Suppl. 3), 15542–15548 (2011)
17. Naud, R., Marcille, N., Clopath, C., Gerstner, W.: Firing patterns in the adaptive exponential integrate-and-fire model. Biol. Cybern. **99**, 335–347 (2008)
18. Paré, D., Shink, E., Gaudreau, H., Destexhe, A., Lang, E.J.: Impact of spontaneous synaptic activity on the resting properties of cat neocortical pyramidal neurons in vivo. J. Neurophysiol. **79**, 1450–1460 (1998)
19. Prinz, A.A., Bucher, D., Marder, E.: Similar network activity from disparate circuit parameters. Nat. Neurosci. **7**, 1345–1352 (2004)
20. Stacey, W., Durand, D.: Stochastic resonance improves signal detection in hippocampal neurons. J. Neurophysiol. **83**, 1394–402 (2000)
21. Wiesenfeld, K., Moss, F.: Stochastic resonance and the benefits of noise: from ice ages to crayfish and squids. Nature **373**, 33–36 (1995)
22. Wróbel, B., Abdelmotaleb, A., Joachimczak, M.: Evolving networks processing signals with a mixed paradigm, inspired by gene regulatory networks and spiking neurons. In: Di Caro, G.A., Theraulaz, G. (eds.) BIONETICS 2012. LNICST, vol. 134, pp. 135–149. Springer, Cham (2014). https://doi.org/10.1007/978-3-319-06944-9_10
23. Yaqoob, M., Wróbel, B.: Robust very small spiking neural networks evolved with noise to recognize temporal patterns. In: ALIFE 2018: Proceedings of the 2018 Conference on Artificial Life, pp. 665–672. MIT Press (2018)
24. Yaqoob, M., Wróbel, B.: Very small spiking neural networks evolved to recognize a pattern in a continuous input stream. In: 2017 IEEE Symposium Series on Computational Intelligence (SSCI), pp. 3496–3503. IEEE (2017)

Machine Learning/Autoencoders

Machine Learning to Predict Toxicity
of Compounds

Ingrid Grenet[1]([✉]), Yonghua Yin[2], Jean-Paul Comet[1], and Erol Gelenbe[1,2]

[1] University Côte d'Azur, I3S Laboratory, UMR CNRS 7271, CS 40121,
06903 Sophia Antipolis Cedex, France
grenet@i3s.unice.fr
[2] Intelligent Systems and Networks Group, Department of Electrical and Electronic
Engineering, Imperial College, London, UK

Abstract. Toxicology studies are subject to several concerns, and they raise the importance of an early detection of the potential for toxicity of chemical compounds which is currently evaluated through *in vitro* assays assessing their bioactivity, or using costly and ethically questionable *in vivo* tests on animals. Thus we investigate the prediction of the bioactivity of chemical compounds from their physico-chemical structure, and propose that it be automated using machine learning (ML) techniques based on data from *in vitro* assessment of several hundred chemical compounds. We provide the results of tests with this approach using several ML techniques, using both a restricted dataset and a larger one. Since the available empirical data is unbalanced, we also use data augmentation techniques to improve the classification accuracy, and present the resulting improvements.

Keywords: Machine learning · Toxicity · QSAR · Data augmentation

1 Introduction

Highly regulated toxicology studies are mandatory for the marketing of chemical compounds to ensure their safety for living organisms and the environment. The most important studies are performed *in vivo* in laboratory animals during different times of exposure (from some days to the whole life-time of the animal). Also, in order to rapidly get some indication of a compound's effects, *in vitro* assays are performed using biological cell lines or molecules, to obtain hints about the bioactivity of chemicals, meaning their ability to affect biological processes. However, all of these studies raise ethical, economical and time concerns; indeed it would be ideal if the toxicity of chemical compounds could be assessed directly through physical, mathematical, computational and chemical means and processes.

Therefore, in order to predict as early as possible the potential toxic effect of a chemical compound, we propose to use machine learning (ML) methods. The ambitious objective is to predict long term effects that will be observed in *in vivo*

© Springer Nature Switzerland AG 2018
V. Kůrková et al. (Eds.): ICANN 2018, LNCS 11139, pp. 335–345, 2018.
https://doi.org/10.1007/978-3-030-01418-6_33

studies, directly from chemical structure. Nonetheless, this long term prediction seems to be difficult [24] because of the high level of biological variability and because toxicity can result from a long chain of causality. Therefore, in this paper we investigate whether taking into consideration the *in vitro* data, can improve the quality of the prediction. In such a case the global objective of the long term toxicity prediction could be split into two parts: (i) first the prediction of *in vitro* bioactivity from chemical structure [27], and (ii) secondly the prediction of long term *in vivo* effects from *in vitro* bioactivity [23].

Here we focus on the first part (i) using ML approaches to determine a "quantitative structure-activity relationship" (QSAR) [17]. QSAR models aim at predicting any kind of compounds activity based on their physico-chemical properties and structural descriptors. Our purpose is to predict using an ML approach, whether a compound's physico-chemical properties, can be used to determine whether the compound will be biologically active during *in vitro* assays. If ML could be shown to be effective in this respect, then it would serve to screen compounds and prioritize them for further *in vivo* studies. Then, *in vivo* toxicity studies would only be pursued with the smaller set of compounds that ML has indicated as being less bioactive, and which must then be certified via *in vivo* assessment. Thereby a significant step forward would be achieved, since animal experimentation could be reduced significantly with the help of a relevant ML based computational approach.

This paper is organized as follows. Section 2 details the data, algorithms and performance metrics used in this work. Section 3 presents the first results obtained on a subset of data. Section 4 shows the performance of an algorithm on the global dataset. Finally, we conclude in Sect. 5.

2 Learning Procedure

In this section we first describe the data used, then the ML algorithms that are tested and finally the metrics used to evaluate performances of the models.

2.1 Data Description

Since the long term objective aims at predicting *in vivo* toxicity, we need publicly available data for both *in vivo* and *in vitro* experimental results. The US Environmental Protection Agency (EPA) released this type of data in two different databases: (i) ToxCast database contains bioactivity data obtained for around 10,000 of compounds tested in more than several hundreds *in vitro* assays [7], (ii) the Toxicity Reference database (ToxRefDB) gathers results from several types of *in vivo* toxicity studies performed for several hundreds of chemicals [20]. It is important to notice that not all the compounds have been tested in all the assays from ToxCast and in each type of *in vivo* studies present in ToxRefDB.

Still guided by the long term objective, we consider a subset of these data including compounds for which both *in vitro* and *in vivo* results were available.

The subset selection follows three steps. First, we look for the overlap of compounds present both in ToxCast and ToxRefDB and having results for *in vivo* studies performed in rats during two years. We obtain a matrix with 418 compounds and 821 assays, with a lot of missing values. Secondly, we look for a large complete sub-matrix and we obtain a matrix of 404 compounds and 60 *in vitro* assays. Finally, in order to be sure to get a minimum of active compounds in the datasets, i.e. compounds for which an AC50 (half maximal activity concentration), could be measured, we remove assays with less than 5% of them and obtain a final matrix of 404 compounds and 37 assays.

For each of the 37 assays, we build a QSAR classification model to predict the bioactivity of a compound. These models use structural descriptors computed from the compound's structure described in Structured Data Files. Two types of descriptors are used: (i) 74 physico-chemical properties (*e.g.* molecular weight, logP, *etc.*) which are continuous and normalized variables and (ii) 4870 fingerprints which are binary vectors representing the presence or absence of a chemical sub-structure in a compound [21]. Fingerprints being present in less than 5% of compounds are removed, leading to a final set of 731 fingerprints. Therefore, the obtained dataset is composed of 805 structural descriptors for the 404 compounds.

The property that we wish to predict, is the activity in each *in vitro* assay in a binarised form. It is generally measured as a AC50 value which is the dose of compound required to obtain 50% of activity in the assay. In the following, we consider that the binary version of the activity is 0 if AC50 value equals 0 and 1 otherwise.

2.2 Learning Algorithms

- **The Random Neural Network (RNN)** is a mathematical model of the spiking (impulse-like) probabilistic behaviour of biological neural systems [9, 11] and it has been shown to be a universal approximator for continuous and bounded functions [10]. It has a compact computationally efficient "product form solution", so that in steady-state the joint probability distribution of the states of the neurons in the network can be expressed as the product of the marginal probabilities for each neuron. The probability that any cell is excited satisfies a non-linear continuous function of the states of the other cells, and it depends on the firing rates of the other cells and the synaptic weights between cells. The RNN has been applied to many pattern analysis and classification tasks [6]. Gradient descent learning is often used for the RNN, but in this work we determine weights of the RNN using the cross-validation approach in [28].
- **The Multi Layer RNN (MLRNN)** uses the original simpler structure of the RNN and investigates the power of single cells for deep learning [25]. It achieves comparable or better classification at much lower computation cost than conventional deep learning methods in some applications. A cross-validation approach is used to determine the structure and the weights and

20 trials are conducted to average the results. The structure of the MLRNN used here is fixed as having 20 inputs and 100 intermediate nodes.

– **The Convolutional Neural Network (CNN)** is a deep-learning tool [18] widely used in computer vision. Its weight-sharing procedure improves training speed with the stochastic gradient descent algorithm recently applied to various types of data [15,26]. In this work, we use it with the following layers: "input-convolutional-convolutional-pooling-fully*connected-output" [5].

– **Boosted Trees** (called XGBoost in the sequel) is a popular tree ensemble method (such as Random Forest). The open-source software library XGBoost [4] provides an easy-to-use tool for implementing boosted trees with gradient boosting [8] and regression trees.

2.3 Classification Settings and Performance Metrics

For each of the 37 assays, we randomly subdivide the corresponding dataset D into a training set D_T and a testing set D_t. From D we randomly create 50 instances of D_T and its complementary test set D_t so that for each instance, $D = D_T \cup D_t$. Each of the ML techniques listed above are first trained on each D_T and then tested on D_t. The results we present below are therefore averages over the 50 randomly selected training and testing sets. Since the output of the datasets is either 0 or 1, this is a binary classification problem.

Let TP, FP, TN and FN denote the number of true positives, false positives, true negatives and false negatives, respectively. Then the performance metrics that we use to evaluate the results are the *Sensitivity* $(TP/(TP + FN))$, the *Specificity* $(TN/(TN + FP))$ and the *BalancedAccuracy*, denoted for short BA $((Sensitivity + Specificity)/2)$.

3 Classification Results

In the 37 datasets corresponding to the 37 assays, the ratio between positive and negative compounds varies between 5% and 30% with a mean around 12%. This highlights the unbalanced property of the data in the favor of negative compounds. Here we test the ML algorithms on these unbalanced data and after balancing using data augmentation.

3.1 Results on Unbalanced Datasets

The MLRNN, RNN, CNN and XGBoost algorithms are exploited to classify the 50×37 pairs of training and testing datasets and results are summarized into Fig. 1. Since these are unbalanced datasets, the BA may be a better metric to demonstrate the classification accuracy. In addition, the situation of misclassifying positive as negative may be less desirable than that of misclassifying negative as positive. Therefore, the metric of *Sensitivity* is also important.

When looking at the BA obtained on the training data set (Fig. 1(a)), we observe that the RNN method is not good at learning from these unbalanced datasets, while the CNN, MLRNN and XGBoost techniques learn much better.

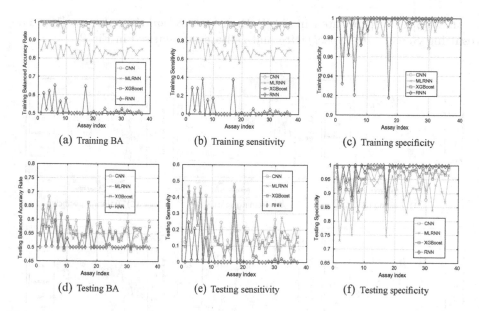

Fig. 1. Training and testing mean-value results (Y-axis) versus different assays (X-axis) when the CNN, MLRNN, XGBoost, RNN are used for classification.

Compared to the training accuracy, the performance on the testing dataset is more important since it demonstrates whether the model generalises accurately with regard to classifying previously unseen chemical compounds. The testing results are presented in Figs. 1(d) to (f). Here, we see that RNN performs the worst in identifying true positives (*Sensitivity*) and tends to classify most unseen chemical compounds as inactive, except for some assays. It can be explained by the overall number of inactive compounds much larger than the number of active compounds in the training dataset. The CNN, MLRNN and XGBoost perform a bit better in identifying the TPs, and the MLRNN performs the best. But *Sensitivity* is still low and really depends on the assays and probably on the balance between active and inactive compounds in the corresponding datasets.

Among all assays, the highest testing *BA* achieved by these classification tools is 68.50% attained by the CNN for assay number 4, with the corresponding *Sensitivity* being 47.10%. Among all assays, the highest testing *Sensitivity* is 47.75% (MLRNN for assay 17) with a corresponding *BA* of 60.80%.

3.2   Results on Balanced Datasets

From the previous results, it appears that most of the classification techniques used are not good at learning unbalanced datasets. Therefore, we try balancing the 50×37 training datasets with data augmentation, while the corresponding testing datasets remain unchanged.

Here, the CNN, MLRNN, RNN and XGBoost are used to learn from the 50×37 datasets which are augmented for balanced training using the SMOTE method [3] as implemented in the Python toolbox *unbalanced_learn* [19]. The resulting *Sensitivity*, *Specificity* and *BA* are summarised in Fig. 2.

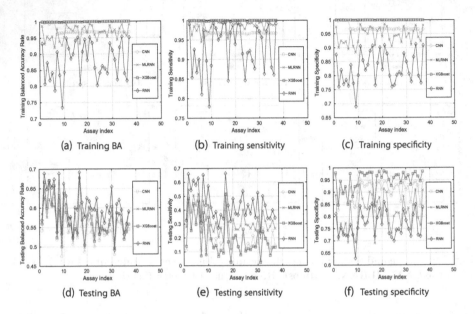

Fig. 2. Training and testing mean-value results (Y-axis) versus different assays (X-axis) on balanced datasets.

Compared to the training balanced accuracies given in Figs. 1(a) and 2(a) shows that it is now evident that all the classification techniques we have discussed are capable of learning the training datasets after data augmentation. The training *BA* of the RNN method is still the lowest, but its testing *BA* is the highest for most of the assays.

Among all assays, the highest testing *BA* is 68.88% which is obtained with the RNN for the assay 17, with the corresponding testing *Sensitivity* being 66% and which is also the highest testing *Sensitivity* observed. Note that these values are higher than those reported in Fig. 1.

Finally, for a better illustration, Fig. 3 compares the highest testing results obtained among all classification tools for classifying the datasets before and after data augmentation. This figure highlights the clear improvement of *Sensitivity* for all assays, which also leads to a better *BA* for most of them. Not surprisingly, *Specificity* is decreased after data augmentation since the proportion of negatives in the balanced training sets is much lower compared to the original ones. Therefore, the models do not predict almost everything as negative as they did before data augmentation.

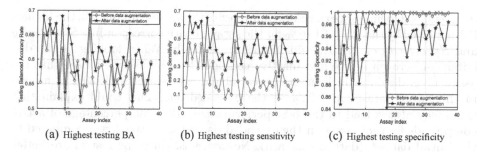

(a) Highest testing BA   (b) Highest testing sensitivity   (c) Highest testing specificity

Fig. 3. Comparison between the highest testing results (Y-axis) versus different assay index (X-axis) on both unbalanced and balanced datasets.

4   Classification Results on Extended Datasets

4.1   New Datasets and Learning Procedure

In this section we use a bigger dataset of 8318 compounds to classify the same 37 assays. This 8318×37 matrix is not complete since not all the compounds were tested in all the assays. Thus, for each of the 37 assays, we build a classification model based on the compounds which were actually tested in the assay, leading to different datasets for each assay. Note that, as previously, the instance numbers of the two classes are very unbalanced.

Compared to the previous datasets, all the generated fingerprints are included in the global dataset which corresponds to 4870 fingerprints in total (added to the 74 molecular descriptors previously described). Nonetheless, for each of the 37 assays and before the learning, a descriptor selection is performed based on two steps: (i) descriptors having a variance close to 0 (in such case, they are not sufficiently informative) are removed, (ii) Fisher test is computed between each descriptor and the output assay and descriptors are ranked according to the obtained p-value; we keep the 20% best descriptors.

Random Forest (RF) classifier, an ensemble technique that combines many decision trees built using random subsets of training examples and features [2], is used for the learning because is has the advantage to deal with a large number of features without overfitting. A 10-fold cross-validation is performed 10 times and the average $Sensistivity$, $Specificity$ and BA are computed to evaluate the internal performance of the classifiers. As previously, we test the RF classifier on both unbalanced and balanced datasets.

4.2   Results on Unbalanced Datasets

Figure 4 presents the results obtained with the method described above applied to the datasets used in Sect. 3 as well as to the extended ones described in Sect. 4.1. We observe that, for both ensembles of datasets, the RF method is not good at identifying TPs ($Sensitivity < 50\%$) and is predicting almost all compounds as negatives ($Specificity > 90\%$). However, we see that the extended datasets lead to higher performance for most of the assays. Among all, the highest BA achieved by the RF is 71.08% for the assay 17 with corresponding *Sensitivity* and *Specificity* of 47.10% and 95.05% respectively. When looking at the distribution between active and inactive compounds in all assays, we see that the assay 17 is the one which has the less unbalanced dataset with 30% of actives in the initial dataset and 22% in the extended one. This could explain that this assay always lead to the best performances. Also, the percentage of active compounds for each assay in the extended dataset is always lower compared to the initial dataset (data not shown). Nevertheless, since the results are better with the extended dataset, it seems that the total number of observations has an impact on the results and not only the ratio between actives and inactives.

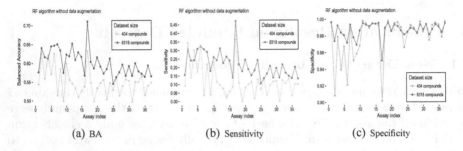

(a) BA   (b) Sensitivity   (c) Specificity

Fig. 4. Results of RF algorithm (Y-axis) versus different assays (X-axis).

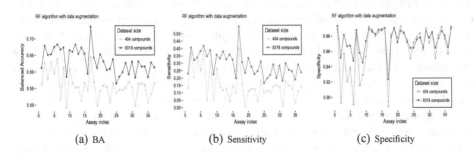

(a) BA   (b) Sensitivity   (c) Specificity

Fig. 5. Results of the RF algorithm (Y-axis) versus different assays (X-axis) on balanced datasets.

4.3   Results on Balanced Datasets

Figure 5 presents the results obtained with the same protocol but with the data augmentation method SMOTE applied to each training dataset of the cross-validation. As in Sect. 3, we observe that for extended datasets, all the results are improved after data augmentation (*Sensitivity* is increased by 8% in average and BA by 3%). But still, the *Sensivity* is low compared to the *Specificity*. Among all assays, the highest *BA* achieved by the RF on the extended dataset is

73.64% with corresponding *Sensitivity* and *Specificity* of 54.93% and 92.36% respectively, still for the assay 17. These results highlight that both the total number of compounds in the dataset and the ratio between active and inactive compounds have an impact on the performance of the models. Indeed, having a bigger dataset which is balanced allows increasing performances.

5 Conclusion and Perspectives

From the results presented here, we can draw several conclusions. First, the methods we have proposed can correctly predict bioactivity from the physico-chemical descriptors of compounds. However, some methods appear to be significantly better than others. Also, this appears to depend strongly on the assays themselves and their corresponding datasets. Moreover, we showed that the use of a larger dataset improves the classification performance, even if the data is unbalanced. Furthermore, we see that data augmentation techniques can play an important role in classification performance for the unbalanced datasets.

This work on ML applied to toxicology data raises further interesting issues. Since there is no absolute winner among the classification techniques that we have used, we may need to test other methods such as Support Vector Machines (SVM) [1] or Dense Random Neural Networks (DenseRNN) [14]. Also, it would be interesting to apply the algorithms used on the small dataset to the extended one and compare against the RF method. We may also test other data augmentation techniques to seek the most appropriate ones [16]. Furthermore, in order to assess the prediction accuracy of bioactivity for a new compound, it is important to know if this compound has a chemical structure that is similar to the ones used in the training set. For this, we could use the "applicability domain" approach [22] as a tool to define the chemical space of a ML model. Finally, if we refer to the long term objective of this work which is to link the molecular structure to *in vivo* toxicity, we could think about using the approach we have used as an intermediate step, and also train ML techniques to go from *in vitro* data to the prediction of *in vivo* effects. However, some preliminary tests that we have carried out (and not yet reported), reveal a poor correlation between *in vitro* and *in vivo* results, so that other data that is more directly correlated to toxicity, could be considered in future ML predictive models of toxicity. In addition, we could consider combining the results obtained with several ML methods, similar to a Genetic Algorithm based combination [12,13], to enhance the prediction accuracy.

References

1. Akbani, R., Kwek, S., Japkowicz, N.: Applying support vector machines to imbalanced datasets. In: Boulicaut, J.-F., Esposito, F., Giannotti, F., Pedreschi, D. (eds.) ECML 2004. LNCS (LNAI), vol. 3201, pp. 39–50. Springer, Heidelberg (2004). https://doi.org/10.1007/978-3-540-30115-8_7
2. Breiman, L.: Random Forests. Mach. Learn. **45**, 5–32 (2001)

3. Chawla, N.V., Bowyer, K.W., Hall, L.O., Kegelmeyer, W.P.: SMOTE: synthetic minority over-sampling technique. J. Artif. Intell. Res. **16**, 321–357 (2002)
4. Chen, T., Guestrin, C.: XGBoost: a scalable tree boosting system. In: Proceedings of the 22nd ACM SIGKDD International Conference on Knowledge Discovery and Data Mining, pp. 785–794. ACM (2016)
5. Chollet, F., et al.: Keras (2015). https://github.com/fchollet/keras
6. Cramer, C.E., Gelenbe, E.: Video quality and traffic QoS in learning-based sub-sampled and receiver-interpolated video sequences. IEEE J. Sel. Areas Commun. **18**(2), 150–167 (2000)
7. Dix, D.J., Houck, K.A., Martin, M.T., Richard, A.M., Setzer, R.W., Kavlock, R.J.: The ToxCast program for prioritizing toxicity testing of environmental chemicals. Toxicol. Sci. **95**(1), 5–12 (2007)
8. Friedman, J.H.: Greedy function approximation: a gradient boosting machine. Ann. Stat. **29**(5), 1189–1232 (2001). https://doi.org/10.1214/aos/1013203451
9. Gelenbe, E.: Learning in the recurrent random neural network. Neural Comput. **5**(1), 154–164 (1993)
10. Gelenbe, E., Mao, Z.H., Li, Y.D.: Function approximation with spiked random networks. IEEE Trans. Neural Netw. **10**(1), 3–9 (1999)
11. Gelenbe, E.: Réseaux neuronaux aléatoires stables. Comptes rendus de l'Académie des Sciences. Série 2, Mécanique, Physique, Chimie, Sciences de l'Univers, Sciences de la Terre **310**(3), 177–180 (1990)
12. Gelenbe, E.: A class of genetic algorithms with analytical solution. Rob. Auton. Syst. **22**, 59–64 (1997)
13. Gelenbe, E.: Learning in genetic algorithms. In: Sipper, M., Mange, D., Pérez-Uribe, A. (eds.) ICES 1998. LNCS, vol. 1478, pp. 268–279. Springer, Heidelberg (1998). https://doi.org/10.1007/BFb0057628
14. Gelenbe, E., Yin, Y.: Deep learning with dense random neural networks. In: Gruca, A., Czachórski, T., Harezlak, K., Kozielski, S., Piotrowska, A. (eds.) ICMMI 2017. AISC, vol. 659, pp. 3–18. Springer, Cham (2018). https://doi.org/10.1007/978-3-319-67792-7_1
15. Goh, G.B., Hodas, N.O., Vishnu, A.: Deep learning for computational chemistry. J. Comput. Chem. **38**(16), 1291–1307 (2017)
16. He, H., Garcia, E.: Learning from imbalanced data. IEEE Trans. Knowl. Data Eng. **21**(9), 1263–1284 (2009)
17. Hansch, C.: Quantitative structure-activity relationships and the unnamed science. Acc. Chem. Res. **26**(4), 147–153 (1993)
18. LeCun, Y., Bengio, Y., Hinton, G.: Deep learning. Nature **521**(7553), 436–444 (2015)
19. Lemaître, G., Nogueira, F., Aridas, C.K.: Imbalanced-learn: a python toolbox to tackle the curse of imbalanced datasets in machine learning. J. Mach. Learn. Res. **18**(17), 1–5 (2017)
20. Martin, M.T., Judson, R.S., Reif, D.M., Kavlock, R.J., Dix, D.J.: Profiling chemicals based on chronic toxicity results from the U.S. EPA ToxRef database. Environ. Health Perspect. **117**(3), 392–399 (2009)
21. Rogers, D., Hahn, M.: Extended-connectivity fingerprints. J. Chem. Inf. Model. **50**(5), 742–754 (2010)
22. Schultz, T.W., Hewitt, M., Netzeva, T.I., Cronin, M.T.D.: Assessing applicability domains of toxicological QSARs: definition, confidence in predicted values, and the role of mechanisms of action. QSAR Comb. Sci. **26**(2), 238–254 (2007)
23. Sipes, N.S., et al.: Predictive models of prenatal developmental toxicity from Tox-Cast high-throughput screening data. Toxicol. Sci. **124**(1), 109–127 (2011)

24. Thomas, R.S., et al.: A comprehensive statistical analysis of predicting in vivo hazard using high-throughput in vitro screening. Toxicol. Sci. **128**(2), 398–417 (2012)
25. Yin, Y., Gelenbe, E.: Single-cell based random neural network for deep learning. In: 2017 International Joint Conference on Neural Networks (IJCNN), pp. 86–93 (2017)
26. Yin, Y., Wang, L., Gelenbe, E.: Multi-layer neural networks for quality of service oriented server-state classification in cloud servers. In: 2017 International Joint Conference on Neural Networks (IJCNN), pp. 1623–1627 (2017)
27. Zang, Q., Rotroff, D.M., Judson, R.S.: Binary classification of a large collection of environmental chemicals from estrogen receptor assays by quantitative structure-activity relationship and machine learning methods. J. Chem. Inf. Model. **53**(12), 3244–3261 (2013)
28. Zhang, Y., Yin, Y., Guo, D., Yu, X., Xiao, L.: Cross-validation based weights and structure determination of chebyshev-polynomial neural networks for pattern classification. Pattern Recogn. **47**(10), 3414–3428 (2014)

Energy-Based Clustering for Pruning Heterogeneous Ensembles

Javier Cela[✉] and Alberto Suárez

Computer Science Department, Universidad Autónoma de Madrid,
C/ Francisco Tomás y Valiente, 11, 28049 Madrid, Spain
javiercela1007@gmail.com, alberto.suarez@uam.es

Abstract. In this work, an energy-based clustering method is used to prune heterogeneous ensembles. Specifically, the classifiers are grouped according to their predictions in a set of validation instances that are independent from the ones used to build the ensemble. In the empirical evaluation carried out, the cluster that minimizes the error in the validations set, besides reducing computational costs for storage and the prediction times, is almost as accurate as the complete ensemble. Furthermore, it outperforms subensembles that summarize the complete ensemble by including representatives from each of the identified clusters.

Keywords: Machine learning · Clustering analysis · Classifier ensembles
Bagging · Random forests

1 Introduction

In ensemble learning, the outputs of a collection of diverse predictors are combined to yield a global prediction that is expected to be more accurate than the individual ones. The key to obtaining accuracy improvements is that the predictors be complementary. This means that their errors should be independent, so that the mislabeling of an instance by a given classifier can be compensated in the combination process by correct predictions from other classifiers. A homogeneous ensemble is composed of predictors of the same type. Since the ensemble classifiers are trained on the same set of labeled data, diversification mechanisms are needed to generate predictors that are actually different (Dietterich 2000). To this end, instabilities of the learning algorithm that is used to build the individual ensemble members can be exploited. Heterogeneous ensembles are composed of classifiers of different types. In practical applications they have proven to be very effective: The aggregation of the predictions of classifiers of different types can be used to compensate their individual biases, which should be distinct. In spite of their practical advantages, heterogeneous ensembles have not been analyzed as extensively as their homogeneous counterparts. This analysis is the major novelty of this work. One reason for this gap in the literature is the difficulty of analyzing their aggregated prediction. Specifically, it is no longer possible to assume that the predictions of the classifiers on an individual instance are independent identically distributed random variables (Lobato et al. 2012).

The main drawback of ensemble methods is their high computational costs in terms of space and time: All the predictors need to be stored in memory. Furthermore, one

© Springer Nature Switzerland AG 2018
V. Kůrková et al. (Eds.): ICANN 2018, LNCS 11139, pp. 346–351, 2018.
https://doi.org/10.1007/978-3-030-01418-6_34

needs to query every ensemble member to compute the final, aggregated prediction. In homogeneous ensembles, pruning techniques have been designed to identify subsets of classifiers whose predictive accuracy is equivalent, or, in some cases, better than the complete ensemble (Suárez et al. 2009). In this manner, both memory costs and prediction times are reduced, which could be a key advantage in real-time applications. In this work, we propose to analyze the problem of pruning heterogeneous ensembles using a novel perspective based on clustering techniques. Previously, clustering has been used to identify representatives that can be used to effectively summarize a complete ensemble (Bakker and Heskes 2003). For homogeneous ensembles, clustering can be made on the basis of the parameters of the models or based on the models' outputs on a dataset, typically a validation or a test set independent of the data used for training. Given the disparate nature of the ensemble classifiers, in heterogeneous ensembles only the latter ensemble clustering technique can be applied. For the sake of completeness, we describe the energy-based clustering algorithm described in (Bakker and Heskes 2003) in the following section.

2 Ensemble Clustering Based on Model Outputs

Let $D_{train} = \left\{ \left(\mathbf{x}_n^{train}, y_n^{train} \right) \right\}_{n=1}^{N_{train}}$ be a set of labeled instances used to build the ensemble. The components of the vector $\mathbf{x}_n^{train} \in X$ are the attributes of the nth instance in the training set. The value $y_n^{train} \in Y$ is the corresponding class label. An ensemble $H = \{h_c\}_{c=1}^{C}$ is composed of C predictors. The cth predictor in the ensemble is a function $h_c : X \to Y$ that takes attribute vectors as inputs and yields a class label. Specifically, $h_c(\mathbf{x})$ is the prediction of the cth ensemble member on the instance characterized by the vector of attributes $\mathbf{x} \in X$. The global ensemble prediction for this instance is given an aggregation of the individual prediction $(\mathbf{x}) = A\left[\{h_c\}_{c=1}^{C}\right]$. In this work, the individual outputs of the ensemble predictors are aggregated using (unweighted) majority voting.

The goal of clustering is to making groupings based on similarities among the outputs of the members of the ensemble on an set of validation instances $\mathbf{h}_c^{val} = \left\{ h_c\left(\mathbf{x}_n^{val}\right) \right\}_{n=1}^{N_{val}} \in Y^{N_{val}}$. To avoid biases, the validation set should be independent of the training set. Since the class labels are not needed for clustering, the test set, if available in the training phase, can be used for clustering. The clusters are characterized by their centroids $\{\mathbf{m}_k \in Y^{N_{val}}; k = 1, \ldots, K\}$. To identify the clusters one could use some standard algorithm, such as K-means or its fuzzy version (Bezdek et al. 1984) (MacQueen 1967). However, from our empirical investigation, the energy-based clustering method introduced in (Bakker and Heskes 2003) is more effective. In this procedure, one minimizes the free energy, which is the difference between an enthalpic and an entropic term

$$(\mathbf{P}^*, \mathbf{M}^*) = \arg \min_{(\mathbf{P},\mathbf{M})} F(\mathbf{P}, \mathbf{M}) = \arg \min_{(\mathbf{P},\mathbf{M})} [H(\mathbf{P}, \mathbf{M}) - TS(\mathbf{P})]. \tag{1}$$

The free energy depends on the $C \times K$ matrices $\mathbf{M} = \{\mathbf{m}_k\}_{k=1}^{K}$ and $\mathbf{P} = \{\mathbf{p}_k\}_{k=1}^{K}$ where $\mathbf{p}_k = \{\mathbf{p}_{ck}\}_{c=1}^{C}$ and $\mathbf{p}_{ck}$ is the probability that the classifier h_c belongs to cluster k. By normalization, $\sum_{k=1}^{K} \mathbf{p}_{ck} = 1$. The enthalpy is the average distance of the classifiers to the cluster centroids

$$H(\mathbf{P}, \mathbf{M}) = \sum_{c=1}^{C} \sum_{k=1}^{K} p_{ck} D(\mathbf{h}_c, \mathbf{m}_k), \tag{2}$$

where $D(\mathbf{h}_c, \mathbf{m}_k)$ is the distance between the cth classifier in the ensemble and centroid k. In principle, any distance function, such as the mean-square error, or the cross-entropy error can be used. The minimum of (2) is achieved when all the ensemble members are assigned to the nearest cluster; that is, predictor h_c is assigned to cluster

$$k^* = \underset{k \in \{1,\dots,K\}}{\arg \min} D(h_c, m_k). \tag{3}$$

The entropy is a measure of how sharply the clusters are defined

$$S(\mathbf{P}) = -\sum_{c=1}^{C} \sum_{k=1}^{K} p_{ck} \log p_{ck}. \tag{4}$$

The term proportional to the entropy is included in the objective function to avoid that the clustering algorithm gets trapped in a local minimum. At the beginning of the search, in the absence of knowledge of the structure of the clusters, the temperature parameter takes a high value to favor exploration. As the algorithm proceeds, T is decreased according to a deterministic annealing schedule (Rose 1998). At a fixed temperature $T > 0$, and for fixed values of the cluster centroids $\{m_k\}_{k=1}^{K}$, the solution of the optimization problem (1) is of the softmax form

$$p_{ck}^* = \frac{e^{-\beta D(\mathbf{h}_c, \mathbf{m}_k)}}{\sum_{l=1}^{K} e^{-\beta D(\mathbf{h}_c, \mathbf{m}_l)}}, \quad k = 1, \dots, K, \tag{5}$$

where $\beta = \frac{1}{T}$ is the inverse temperature (Rose 1990; Buhmann and Kühnel 1993; Bakker and Heskes 2003). In the infinite temperature limit $\beta \to \infty$, a given ensemble member is assigned to all clusters with equal probability. At low temperatures, only configurations around the minimum of (2) are explored. In the limit of zero temperature $\beta \to 0$, the clusters become sharply defined according to (3). For each annealing epoch, the value of the temperature is fixed. The expectation-maximization algorithm is then used to find the optimum of the free energy. If the mean-squared error or the cross-entropy error are used as distance function, starting from an initial configuration of the probabilities $p_k^{[0]}$, the update rule is

$$\mathbf{m}_k^{[i]} \leftarrow \arg\max_{\mathbf{m}_k} \sum_{c=1}^{C} p_{ck}^{[i-1]} D(\mathbf{h}_c, \mathbf{m}_k) = \frac{\sum_{c=1}^{C} p_{ck}^{[i-1]} \mathbf{h}_c}{\sum_{c=1}^{C} p_{ck}^{[i-1]}}; \ k = 1, \dots, K \qquad (6)$$

$$\mathbf{p}_k^{[i]} \leftarrow \frac{e^{-\beta D\left(\mathbf{h}_c, \mathbf{m}_k^{[i]}\right)}}{\sum_{l=1}^{K} e^{-\beta D\left(\mathbf{h}_c, \mathbf{m}_l^{[i]}\right)}}, k = 1, \dots, K \qquad (7)$$

Iterative updates of the maximization and the expectation steps, given by Eqs. (6) and (7), respectively are made until convergence. While the cluster centroids and the probabilities have not converged, the inverse temperature is incremented according to the annealing schedule. Following the prescription given in (Bakker and Heskes 2003), initially $\beta = 1$. This value is incremented by 1 at each annealing epoch until the clusters become sufficiently sharp (the centroids have reached convergence and the clusters remain practically unalterable).

3   Empirical Evaluation

The goal of ensemble pruning is to reduce the costs of storage and the time for the predictions without a significant loss (in some cases, with improvements) of accuracy. Clustering can be used to carry out this selection in different ways. For instance, the ensemble can be replaced by representatives from each of the identified clusters, as in (Bakker and Heskes 2003). In this work, we take a different approach and attempt to identify the most accurate cluster. To this end, we select the cluster that has the lowest error in a validation set $k^* = \arg\min_{k \in \{1,\dots,K\}} E_{val}(H_k)$, where H_k is the subset of predictors assigned to cluster k. The accuracy of this subensemble is then evaluated on a test set that is independent of both the training and the validation set.

The experiments have been carried out in 10 different classification problems from the UCI repository (Bache and Lichman 2017). For each classification problem, 1/3 of the labeled instances are set aside for testing. From the remaining 2/3, 80% are used for training and 20% for validation. Using the training data, 100 multilayer percetrons (MLP) and 100 random trees (RT) are built using the Scikit-learn Python package [10]. Each of the classifiers in this heterogeneous ensemble is built on a bootstrap sample of the same size as the original training set, as in bagging (Breiman 1996). The random trees are built as in random forest (Breiman 2001), using the following settings: Random subsets whose size is the square root of the total number of attributes are considered for the splits at the inner nodes of the random trees. The split that minimizes the Gini impurity is selected. Splits are made until either the node is pure or it has only 2 instances. Five different clusters are identified on the basis of the predictions of the ensemble classifiers on the validation instances using the algorithm described in the previous section. Similar accuracies (but different pruning rates) are obtained fixing the number of clusters to 2, 3 or 7. The best cluster is selected using also the validation set, which is independent from the one used for training. The results of the empirical evaluation performed are summarized in Table 1. The values displayed in the columns labeled E_{test} are the test error rate averaged over 30 independent train/test partitions followed by the standard deviation after the $\pm$ symbol. The errors reported in second column correspond to the homogenous bagging ensemble composed of the 100 MLPs that have been built. The second column corresponds to a random forest composed of the 100 random trees generated. The third column corresponds to the heterogeneous ensemble that includes both the 100 MLPs and the 100 RFs. Finally, the composition of the optimal cluster (k^*) and the corresponding test error are displayed in the fourth and fifth columns, respectively. The size of the optimal cluster is C_{k^*}. The number of MLP's in this cluster is $C_{k^*}^{[MLP]}$. The number of RT's is $C_{k^*}^{[MLP]}$.

Table 1. Summary of the results of the empirical evaluation

Ensemble	MLP	RF	MLP + RF	Best cluster k^*	
	E_{test}	E_{test}	E_{test}	$C_{k^*}\left(C_{k^*}^{[MLP]}+C_{k^*}^{[MLP]}\right)$	E_{test}
Blood	0.246 ± 0.026	0.263 ± 0.024	0.252 ± 0.018	42 (42 + 0)	**0.243 ± 0.026**
Breast cancer Wisconsin	0.046 ± 0.011	0.062 ± 0.011	0.068 ± 0.011	43 (42 + 1)	**0.045 ± 0.009**
Cars	0.123 ± 0.024	0.103 ± 0.015	0.118 ± 0.016	51 (7 + 44)	0.118 ± 0.016
Chess	**0.021 ± 0.006**	0.025 ± 0.004	0.023 ± 0.005	45 (30 + 15)	**0.021 ± 0.005**
Diabetes (Pima)	**0.239 ± 0.022**	0.246 ± 0.013	0.239 ± 0.009	35 (32 + 3)	**0.239 ± 0.021**
German	0.275 ± 0.021	0.285 ± 0.017	0.269 ± 0.015	46 (42 + 4)	0.271 ± 0.019
Heart disease	0.472 ± 0.045	0.466 ± 0.040	0.450 ± 0.033	47 (2 + 45)	0.452 ± 0.035
Liver	0.391 ± 0.043	**0.382 ± 0.075**	0.454 ± 0.062	37 (1 + 36)	0.387 ± 0.077
SPECT heart	0.350 ± 0.044	0.350 ± 0.031	0.336 ± 0.029	43 (34 + 9)	0.350 ± 0.039
Tic-tac-toe	0.203 ± 0.028	**0.118 ± 0.024**	0.132 ± 0.019	44 (3 + 2)	**0.118 ± 0.023**

From these results it is apparent that, in most of the problems analyzed, the accuracy of the selected cluster is comparable to the best among the three complete ensembles. Furthermore, one achieves a pruning rate of $\approx 20\%$, which directly translates into a five-fold reduction of storage needs and prediction times. These optimal clusters are fairly homogeneous: In six of the problems analyzed, it is composed mostly of MLPs; in the remaining four, random trees form a majority.

An interesting question is whether these pure ensembles are more accurate that ensembles that retain a single representative per cluster as in (Bakker and Heskes 2003). To provide a more fair comparison, we consider also the possibility of summarizing the ensemble by retaining multiple representatives per cluster so that the final subensemble has the same size as the selected cluster. The results of this comparison, which are presented in Table 2 show that, in fact, the increased diversity of the ensembles of representatives, is detrimental and increases the test error.

In summary, we have applied an energy-based clustering method to identify a subensemble whose accuracy is comparable to the complete heterogeneous ensemble, which is composed of random trees and multilayer perceptrons. The selected

Table 2. Test error rates for clustering-based pruned ensembles

Ensemble	Single representatives	Multiple representatives	Best cluster k^*
Blood	0.251 ± 0.023	0.253 ± 0.023	**0.243 ± 0.026**
Breast cancer Wisconsin	0.055 ± 0.015	0.056 ± 0.015	**0.045 ± 0.009**
Cars	0.123 ± 0.024	0.123 ± 0.024	**0.118 ± 0.016**
Chess	0.023 ± 0.004	0.023 ± 0.004	**0.021 ± 0.005**
Diabetes (Pima)	0.0246 ± 0.017	0.249 ± 0.015	**0.239 ± 0.021**
German	0.277 ± 0.020	0.277 ± 0.020	**0.271 ± 0.019**
Heart disease	0.472 ± 0.045	0.479 ± 0.044	**0.452 ± 0.035**
Liver	0.392 ± 0.059	0.394 ± 0.060	**0.387 ± 0.077**
SPECT heart	0.347 ± 0.044	**0.345 ± 0.038**	0.350 ± 0.039
Tic-tac-toe	0.162 ± 0.046	0.159 ± 0.048	**0.118 ± 0.023**

subensemble is fairly homogeneous: it is either composed mainly of MLPs or mainly of RTs. Contrary to what could be expected, in this particular setting the reduction of diversity leads to improvements of accuracy.

Acknowledgements. The authors acknowledge financial support from the Spanish Ministry of Economy, Industry and Competitiveness, project TIN2016-76406-P.

References

Bache, K., Lichman, M.: UCI Machine Learning Repository (2017). http://archive.ics.uci.edu/ml

Bakker, B., Heskes, T.: Clustering ensembles of neural network models. Neural Netw. **16**, 261–269 (2003)

Bezdek, J., Elrich, R., Full, W.: The fuzzy C-means clustering algorithm. Comput. Geosci. **10**, 191–203 (1984)

Breiman, L.: Bagging predictors. Mach. Learn. **24**, 123–140 (1996)

Breiman, L.: Random forests. Mach. Learn. **45**, 5–32 (2001)

Buhmann, J., Kühnel, H.: Vector quantization with complexity costs. IEEE Trans. Inf. Theory **39**, 1133–1145 (1993)

Dietterich, T.G.: Ensemble methods in machine learning. In: Proceedings of Multiple Classifier Systems: First International Workshop, MCs 2000, Cagliari, Italy, 21–23 June 2000, pp. 1–15 (2000)

Lobato, D.H., Muñoz, G.M., Suárez, A.: On the independence of the individual predictions in parallel randomized Ensembles. In: 20th European Symposium on Artificial Neural Networks, Bruges (2012)

MacQueen, J.: Some methods for classification and analysis of multivariate observations. In: Proceedings of the Fifth Berkeley Symposium on Mathematical Statistics and Probability, pp. 281–297 (1967)

Rose, K.: Statistical mechanics of phase transition in clustering. Phys. Rev. Lett. **65**, 945–948 (1990)

Rose, K.: Deterministic annealing for clustering, compression, classification, regression and related optimization problems. In: Proceedings for the IEEE, pp. 2210–2239 (1998)

Suárez, A., Hernández-Lobato, D., Martínez-Muñoz, G.: An analysis of ensemble pruning techniques based on ordered aggregation. IEEE Trans. Pattern Anal. Mach. Intell. **31**, 245–259 (2009)

Real-Time Hand Gesture Recognition Based on Electromyographic Signals and Artificial Neural Networks

Cristhian Motoche[(✉)] and Marco E. Benalcázar[(✉)]

Departamento de Informática y Ciencias de la Computación,
Escuela Politécnica Nacional, Quito, Ecuador
{cristhian.motoche,marco.benalcazar}@epn.edu.ec

Abstract. In this paper, we propose a hand gesture recognition model based on superficial electromyographic signals. The model responds in approximately 29.38 ms (real time) with a recognition accuracy of 90.7%. We apply a sliding window approach using a main window and a sub-window. The sub-window is used to observe a segment of the signal seen through the main window. The model is composed of five blocks: data acquisition, preprocessing, feature extraction, classification and postprocessing. For data acquisition, we use the Myo Armband to measure the electromyographic signals. For preprocessing, we rectify, filter, and detect the muscle activity. For feature extraction, we generate a feature vector using the preprocessed signals values and the results from a bag of functions. For classification, we use a feedforward neural network to label every sub-window observation. Finally, for postprocessing we apply a simple majority voting to label the main window observation.

Keywords: Artificial Neural Networks · Electromyography
Hand gesture recognition · Machine learning · Signal processing

1 Introduction

Hand gesture recognition consists of identifying the instant and the class associated with a movement of the hand [1]. Hand gesture recognition has many applications in the scientific and technological fields, for example: human computer interfaces (HCI), active prosthesis, and interaction with virtual environments [2]. A model that is suitable for these types of applications requires high recognition accuracy and usually has to respond in real time (i.e., in less than 300 ms) [3]. Additionally, some applications (e.g., HCI) require a recognition model to run on a computer with limited resources of RAM memory and processing. Hand gesture recognition models commonly use sensors like instrumented gloves, color cameras, depth cameras, and electromyographic sensors to acquire the input data for the model [4–6]. In this work, we use electromyographic (EMG) sensors because they are not affected by the variations of light, position and orientation

© Springer Nature Switzerland AG 2018
V. Kůrková et al. (Eds.): ICANN 2018, LNCS 11139, pp. 352–361, 2018.
https://doi.org/10.1007/978-3-030-01418-6_35

of the hand. According to the scientific literature, the state-of-the-art recognition accuracy is about 85% for the models that use electromyographic sensors for hand gesture recognition [7]. For this reason, in this work our goal is to develop a model that achieves a recognition accuracy higher than 85% and responds in real time with limited resources of memory and processing.

Machine learning is a framework that can be used to solve the problem of hand gesture recognition based on superficial electromyographic (sEMG) signals. The most common classifiers for hand gesture recognition include: Support Vector Machines [8], Artificial Neural Networks [9,10], Deep Convolutional Neural Networks [11], and k-Nearest Neighbors [12,13]. The conventional features used for hand gesture recognition are defined in the following domains: time (e.g., Mean Absolute Value and Zero Crossing), frequency (e.g., Mean Frequency and Frequency Histograms) and time-frequency (e.g., Wavelets). Models based on these classifiers and feature domains present high recognition accuracy and respond in real time. However, they also have some disadvantages, for instance: small number of predicted classes [7], too many repetitions for training the model [14], and demand for high computational resources [11]. Therefore, hand gesture recognition is still an open problem for new research.

In this paper, we develop a hand gesture recognition model based on sEMG signals that responds in real time, achieves a recognition accuracy over the state-of-the-art, and works in a computer with limited resources of RAM memory and processing. The proposed model follows a sliding window approach using a main window and a sub-window. The model is composed of the following blocks: data acquisition, preprocessing, feature extraction, classification, and postprocessing. For data acquisition, we measure the sEMG signals using the Myo Armband. For preprocessing, we rectify, filter and detect the muscle activity in the main window observation. For feature extraction, we generate a feature vector by concatenating the values of the preprocessed signal with the results of applying a bag of functions. For classification, we use a feedforward neural network to label every sub-window observation. Finally, for postprocessing we apply a simple majority voting, based on the labels from the sub-window classification, to label the main window observation with the corresponding gesture. The source code and the data used in this work are publicly available in the following link: https://drive. google.com/drive/folders/1rNgBFC38WXfruBocWmJnWNrR0iuA0HQw.

Following this introduction, this paper is organized in three sections. In Sect. 2, we describe the materials and methods used in this work. In Sect. 3, we present the results obtained. Finally, in Sect. 4, we present the conclusions and outline future work.

2   Materials and Methods

2.1   Materials

Myo Armband. In this work, we use the Thalmic's Myo Armband illustrated in Fig. 1(a) because it provides an open software development kit, has low cost, can be expanded from 19 to 34 cm, and weighs only 93 g. [15]. The Myo includes the following components: 8 superficial electromyographic sensors (Fig. 1(b)), a Bluetooth 4.0, and a 9-axes inertial measurement unit. The Myo streams data at 200 Hz and represents every measured value with 8 bits [16]. The Myo is also equipped with a *proprietary software* (black box model) that recognizes five gestures: *Fist, Wave In, Wave Out, Fingers Spread,* and *Double Tap* (Fig. 1(c)).

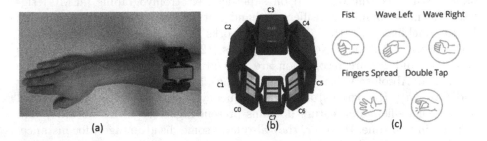

(a)   (b)   (c)

Fig. 1. (a) Myo Armband and (b) its channels. (c) Gestures detected by the Myo.

Dataset. In this paper, we use the data of 10 healthy volunteers used previously in [12,13] for training, validation and testing. We used this dataset to compare the proposed model with the previous models presented in [12,13]. This dataset contains a set for training and another set for testing. The training set consists of five repetitions of the five gestures indicated in Fig. 1(c) recorded during two seconds. Additionally, the training set includes five sEMG measurements recorded during two seconds with the arm in the relax position. This set was used for training and validation. The testing set consists of 30 repetitions recorded during five seconds of only the five gestures in Fig. 1(c). For every repetition, the volunteer started with his arm relaxed, then performs the gesture (around the middle of the recording), and then returns the arm to the relaxed position until the end of the recording.

2.2   Methods

Notation. In this paper, we denote the matrices with bold uppercase letters (e.g., $\mathbf{A}$). The vectors are denoted with bold lowercase letters (e.g., $\mathbf{x}$). Constants are denoted with uppercase letters (e.g., N) and indices are denoted with italic lowercase letters (e.g., i).

Data Acquisition. For this block, we apply a sliding window approach using a main window of length N. We represent the sEMG signals acquired with the Myo Armband and seen trough the main window as a matrix $\mathbf{A}$ of size N × 8, where 8 is the number of sensors of the Myo Armband. The value $\mathbf{A}_{i,j}$ represents the measure in the instant of time i and from the sensor j, where $i = 1, 2, \ldots, N$ and $j = 1, 2, \ldots, 8$, respectively. Each element of the matrix $\mathbf{A}$ is in the range

$[-1,1]$. To generate the feature vectors for training the model, we use a main window MW_{train} of length $N_{train} = 400$ for every repetition in the training set. To validate and test the model, we use a main window MW_{test} of length $N_{test} = 200$ with a stride of 20 points between two consecutive windows.

Preprocessing. The sEMG signals can be modeled by a non-stationary stochastic process [13]. This means that the probability distribution of the sEMG changes with time. However, we can reduce the non-stationarity of the sEMG by smoothing out its values. The idea of this process is to reduce the changes of the probability distribution of the sEMG over the time assuming that the smoothed sEMG is locally stationary [17]. In this work, for smoothing out the sEMG signals we apply rectification and filtering. The preprocessing starts with the signal rectification using the *absolute value* function. Then, a *Butterworth low-pass filter* ψ of fourth order and cutoff frequency of 5 Hz is applied to **A**.

Additionally, we apply a muscle activity detection function Φ to the main window observation, which is described in [13]. The function Φ returns the initial and final indices that contain the muscle activity within MW_{train}. This function is used to *remove* the head and tail that refer to the relaxed position of the hand for every repetition in the training set. In addition, we apply a muscle activity verification function Ω to the main window observation in the testing set. The function Ω is described in Eq. (1), where **C** is the observation of the signal rectified and $\tau_{preprocessing}$ is a threshold. If $\Omega(\mathbf{C})$ is true, then the recognition process continues, otherwise the response is *No Gesture* for the main window.

$$\Omega(\mathbf{C}) = \sum_{i=1}^{N} \sum_{j=1}^{8} \mathbf{C}_{ij} > \tau_{preprocessing} \tag{1}$$

We apply Φ only to the training set because Φ returns the boundaries of the muscle activity. In contrast, Ω only verifies if there is or not activity within the main window observation. Additionaly, Φ increases the time of preprocessing compared to Ω. We tested different thresholds and $\tau_{preprocessing} = 0.39$ gave us the best results in the validation set.

Feature Extraction. For this block, we use a sub-window SW to observe a segment of the signal seen trough the main window (Fig. 2(a)). The segment of the signal seen through the sub-window SW is represented by a matrix **E** of size M × 8; meanwhile, the signals observed through the main window MW are represented as a matrix **A** of size N × 8, where N > M. We use a stride of one point for two consecutive sub-windows (Fig. 2(b)).

The features for our classifier came from two different sources: the values of the preprocessed signals and the results of applying a bag of functions to the raw signals. We only use functions from the time domain because using functions from the frequency and the time-frequency domains increases the computational cost of this block. We apply the following steps to extract feature vectors, where the index i represents the ith instant of the sEMG signal seen through MW:

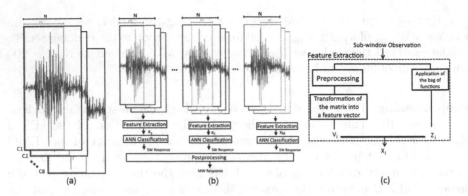

Fig. 2. (a) Signals seen through both the main and the sub windows. (b) Movement of the sub-windows over the main window for feature extraction, classification, and postprocessing. (c) Process to generate a feature vector from a sub-window observation.

1. Align the first point of the sub-window SW with the point $i = 1$ of the sEMG signal seen through the main window MW.
2. Preprocess the sub-window observation $\mathbf{E}$ to get $\mathbf{F} = \psi(abs(\mathbf{E}))$. Convert the matrix $\mathbf{F}$ into a feature vector $\mathbf{v}_i$ by concatenating its rows.
3. Apply a bag of functions to the raw values of $\mathbf{E}$ to get the feature vector $\mathbf{z}_i$.
4. Concatenate $\mathbf{v}_i$ with $\mathbf{z}_i$ horizontally to get the vector $\mathbf{x}_i$.
5. Move the first point of the sub-window SW to the instant $i := i + 1$ and repeat the steps from (2) to (5) until $i = \mathrm{N} - \mathrm{M} + 1$.

The process for feature extraction is illustrated in Fig. 2(c). Every $\mathbf{x}_i$ is of length $|\mathbf{v}_i| + |\mathbf{z}_i|$ (where $|\mathbf{x}|$ denotes the length of vector $\mathbf{x}$) and is associated with a label $\mathbf{y}_i$ that corresponds to the gesture of the repetition from which $\mathbf{x}_i$ comes from. Empirically, we found that a sub-window length of $\mathrm{M} = 75$ gave us the highest recognition accuracy in the validation set. The length of $\mathbf{v}$ is equal to $\mathrm{M} * 8$ so there is $|\mathbf{v}| = 75 * 8 = 600$ features. The bag of functions is composed of the Mean Absolute Value, Slope Sign Changes, Waveform Length, Root Mean Square, and the Hjorth parameters [18]. The application of these functions creates a vector $\mathbf{z}$ of 56 features. The final length of the feature vector $\mathbf{x}$ is equal to $|\mathbf{x}| = 600 + 56 = 656$ features. The number of training vectors obtained from the sub-window observation along the main window is $\mathrm{N} - \mathrm{M} + 1$ per gesture repetition. Therefore, the total number of vectors is $(\mathrm{N} - \mathrm{M} + 1) *$ NumberOfGestures $*$ RepetitionsPerGesture $= (\mathrm{N} - \mathrm{M} + 1) * 5 * 5$. The number of vectors for training is different per user (between 2995 and 5606) because the length of the muscle activity varies from one repetition to the others.

We used the *t-Distributed Stochastic Neighbor Embedding (t-SNE)* to visualize how the training feature vectors from each user and from each class (gesture) are clustered in the feature space. The results from the t-SNE applied to a single user are displayed in Fig. 3. We can note that when the length of the sub-window increases, the projected feature vectors of each class get closer to each other. However, if the length of the sub-window increases, then the amount of feature vectors from a repetition is reduced and the length of the feature vector increases. This effect causes that the recognition model tends to overfitting.

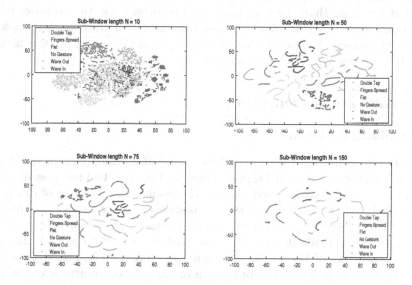

Fig. 3. t-SNE results from different sub-window lengths.

Classification. In this work, we use artificial neural networks (ANN) for classification because this family of functions are universal approximators [19]: a feedforward neural network with only three layers (input, hidden and output), with a sigmoid transfer functions and an appropriate number of nodes in the hidden layer is able to approximate any function. For our model, we implemented an ANN with three layers and trained this network using full batch gradient descent, with a cross entropy cost function and 75 epochs. The input layer of the network has 656 nodes, which corresponds to the length of the feature vectors. After experimenting with different number of nodes in the hidden layer, we obtained the best recognition results in the validation set using 328 nodes, which is half of nodes in the input layer. The output layer has only 6 nodes, which corresponds to the number of predicted gestures. We tested the following transfer functions for the hidden layer: *logsig*, *relu*, *softplus*, *elu* and *tanh*. We obtained the best results in the validation set using the *tanh* transfer function. For training the network, we applied regularization using weight decay with a factor $\lambda = 750/(N - M + 1) * 5 * 5$. Additionally, we applied feature scaling using $\mathbf{x}' = (\mathbf{x}_i - \bar{\mathbf{x}})./\sigma$, where $\bar{\mathbf{x}}$ is a vector with the mean values, and σ is also a vector with the standard deviation values for each feature of the vector $\mathbf{x}_i$, and ./ represents the element wise division between two vectors.

Postprocessing. For each observation of the sEMG using the main window, we obtain a vector of labels, where each label corresponds to the feature vector of a sub-window observation. We define a threshold $\tau_{postprocessing}$ and apply a simply majority voting to assign a label to the main window observation. We assign the label that has more than the $\tau_{postprocessing}$ of occurrences in the vector of labels of the main window. Otherwise, we assign the label *No Gesture*. After testing different thresholds, we found that $\tau_{postprocessing} = 70\%$ gave us the highest recognition accuracy in the validation set.

3   Results and Discussion

3.1   Evaluation Method

In addition to evaluating the proposed model, we also evaluated a model that is based only on the preprocessed signal values (rectification and low pass filtering) and another model that is based only on the results from the bag of functions. Lets remember that the proposed model combines these two types of features.

To evaluate the recognition accuracy, we trained a model for each volunteer using his/her own training set. Then, we used the model to predict the label of every repetition of the testing set using a window of length $N_{test} = 200$ with a stride of 20 points. The application of our method returns a vector with $(1000 - 20)/200 = 40$ labels for each repetition of the testing set. Lets remember that the length of every repetition of the testing set is around 1000 points. A recognition was considered successful when all the labels different from the class *No Gesture* match with the actual class of the repetition. Otherwise, the recognition was considered wrong and the label returned from the repetition was the first label of the vector different from *No Gesture* [12]. To measure the response time of the tested models, we used a desktop computer with an Intel Core i7-3770S processor and 4GB of RAM. The average time reported in this paper is the mean of all the times of classifying each window observation in the testing set.

3.2   Results

The confusion matrix for the proposed model is illustrated in Fig. 4. This confusion matrix shows an overall recognition accuracy of 90.7%. The gesture *Fist* was the one with the highest sensitivity (98.3%) and *Double tap* was the one with the lowest (85.3%). Regarding precision, the gesture *Wave Out* had the highest result (99.6%) and the gesture *Fist* the lowest (86.8%). Therefore, the best predictions of the proposed model are for the gesture *Wave Out*. On the other hand, the proposed model is more likely to predict the gesture *Fist* incorrectly. Additionally, some repetitions are predicted as *No Gesture* because they did not pass the thresholds for preprocessing or postprocessing.

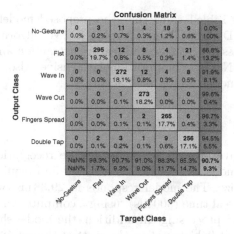

Fig. 4. Confusion matrix for the proposed model.

3.3   Discussion

Table 1 shows that the proposed model, which uses both types of features (the preprocessed signal values and the results from the bag of functions), has the best accuracy compared to the other models. The model that uses only the preprocessed signal values responds quickly and its recognition accuracy is higher than the model that uses only the results from the bag of functions. However, the model that uses only the bag of functions has the lowest training time because its architecture is less complex. Table 1 also shows that the proposed model responds in 29.38 ms that is much lower than the real time limit (300 ms).

Table 1. Summary and comparative table.

Model	Accuracy (%)	Response (ms)	Training (s)
Evaluated models:			
- Model using both approaches	90.7	29.38	34.78
- Model using only the preprocessed signals values	88.3	2.59	29.71
- Model only using only the results from the bag of functions	86.1	26.52	2.08
Other models:			
- Private Myo Armband model [12,13]	83.1	–	–
- Model using k-NN and DTW [12]	86.0	245.50	–
- Model using k-NN and DTW with muscle activity detection [13]	89.5	193.10	–

The results from Table 1 show that the proposed model is faster than the models that use the Dynamic Time Warping (DTW) algorithm with k-Nearest Neighbor (k-NN) classifier because the feature extraction and the classification performed by the ANN is less computational expensive. Also, the proposed model overcome the other models in terms of accuracy.

4   Conclusions

In this paper, we have presented a hand gesture recognition model based on sEMG signals. The model is trained for each user and requires 5 repetitions for each class to recognize. The model responds in 29.38 ms, which is lower than the limit defined for real time (300 ms), using a computer with limited resources of RAM memory and processing. In addition, the model showed a recognition accuracy of 90.7% that is higher than the state-of-the-art (85%).

For this model, we applied a sliding window approach using a main window and a sub-window. The sub-window allowed us to observe a segment of the signal seen through the main window. The model is composed of five blocks: data acquisition, preprocessing, feature extraction, classification, and postprocessing. For data acquisition, we used the Myo Armband to acquire the sEMG signals. For preprocessing, we rectified, filtered and detected the muscle activity in the main window observation. For feature extraction, we used two sets of features: the preprocessed signal values and the results from a bag of functions. For classification, we used an ANN of three layers to classify every sub-window observation. Finally, for postprocessing we applied a simple majority voting on the results of the ANN to decide the final gesture within the main window.

We found that the recognition accuracy of the proposed model improves when we combine the values of the preprocessed signal with the results of applying a bag of functions. Future work includes defining a generalized model for all the users with high accuracy, that works in real time, and uses limited computational resources of RAM and processing.

Acknowledgment. The authors gratefully acknowledge the financial support provided by Escuela Politécnica Nacional for the development of the research project PIJ-16-13 'Clasificación de señales electromiográficas del brazo humano usando técnicas de reconocimiento de patrones y machine learning'.

References

1. Konar, A., Saha, S.: Gesture Recognition: Principles, Techniques and Applications. SCI, vol. 724, pp. 1–29. Springer, Cham (2018). https://doi.org/10.1007/978-3-319-62212-5
2. Xu, Y., Dai, Y.: Review of hand gesture recognition study and application. Contemp. Eng. Sci. **10**, 375–384 (2017)
3. Mizuno, H., Tsujiuchi, N., Koizumi, T.: Forearm motion discrimination technique using real-time EMG signals. In: 2011 Annual International Conference of the IEEE, Engineering in Medicine and Biology Society, EMBC, pp. 4435–4438 (2011)

4. Chen, L., Wang, F., Deng, H., Ji, K.: A survey on hand gesture recognition. In: 2013 International Conference on Computer Sciences and Applications (2013)
5. Khan, R.Z., Ibraheem, N.A.: Survey on various gesture recognition technologies. Int. J. Comput. Appl. **50**(7), 38–44 (2012)
6. Pradipa, R., Kavitha, S.: Hand gesture recognition analysis of various techniques, methods and their algorithm. Int. J. Innov. Res. Sci. Eng. Technol. **3**(3), 2003–2010 (2014)
7. Benatti, S., et al.: A sub-10 mW real-time implementation for EMG hand gesture recognition based on a multi-core biomedical SoC. In: 2017 7th IEEE International Workshop on Advances in Sensors and Interfaces (IWASI), Vieste, Italy (2017)
8. Mesa, I., Rubio, A., Diaz, J., Legarda, J., Segado, B.: Reducing the number of channels and signal-features for an accurate classification in an EMG pattern recognition task. In: Proceedings of the International Conference on Bio-inspired Systems and Signal Processing, San Sebastian, Spain, pp. 38–48 (2012)
9. Ahsan, R., Ibn Ibrahimy, M., Khalifa, O.: Electromygraphy (EMG) signal based hand gesture recognition using Artificial Neural Network (ANN). In: 4th International Conference on Mechatronics (ICOM) (2011)
10. Chowdhury, R., Reaz, M., Mohd, A., Bakar, A., Kalaivani, C., Chang, T.: Surface electromyography signal processing and classification techniques. Sensors **13**(12), 12431–12466 (2013)
11. Geng, W., Du, Y., Jin, W., Wei, W., Hu, Y., Li, J.: Gesture recognition by instantaneous surface EMG images. Sci. Rep. **6**(1), 1–8 (2016)
12. Benalczar, M., Jaramillo, A.G., Zea, J.A., Paez, A., Andaluz, V.H.: Hand gesture recognition using machine learning and the Myo armband. In: 2017 25th European Signal Processing Conference (EUSIPCO) (2017)
13. Benalczar, M., et al.: Real-time hand gesture recognition using the myo armband and muscle activity detection. In: 2017 IEEE Second Ecuador Technical Chapters Meeting (ETCM) (2017)
14. Xu, Z., Xiang, C., Lantz, V., Kong-qiao, W., Wen-hui, W., Ji-hai, Y.: Hand gesture recognition and virtual game control based on 3D accelerometer and EMG sensors. In: Proceedings of the 13th International Conference on Intelligent User Interfaces - IUI 2009, pp. 401–405 (2009)
15. Myo Thalmic Labs Inc. https://www.myo.com/techspecs
16. Myo Support Thalmic Labs Inc. https://support.getmyo.com/hc/en-us/articles/202536726-How-do-I-access-the-raw-EMG-data-from-the-Myo-armband
17. Peter, K.: The ABC of EMG. A Practical Introduction to Kinesiological Electromyography. Noraxon U.S.A. Inc., Scottsdale (2006)
18. Ct-Allard, U., et al.: Deep Learning for Electromyographic Hand Gesture Signal Classification by Leveraging Transfer Learning (2018)
19. Farago, A., Lugosi, G.: Strong universal consistency of neural network classifiers. IEEE Trans. Inf. Theory, San Antonio **39**, 1146–1151 (1993)

Fast Communication Structure
for Asynchronous Distributed ADMM Under
Unbalance Process Arrival Pattern

Shuqing Wang and Yongmei Lei[(✉)]

School of Computer Engineering and Science,
Shanghai University, Shanghai 200444, China
lei@shu.edu.cn

Abstract. The alternating direction method of multipliers (ADMM) is an algorithm for solving large-scale data optimization problems in machine learning. In order to reduce the communication delay in a distributed environment, asynchronous distributed ADMM (AD-ADMM) was proposed. However, due to the unbalance process arrival pattern existing in the multiprocessor cluster, the communication of the star structure used in AD-ADMM is inefficient. Moreover, the load in the entire cluster is unbalanced, resulting in a decrease of the data processing capacity. This paper proposes a hierarchical parameter server communication structure (HPS) and an asynchronous distributed ADMM (HAD-ADMM). The algorithm mitigates the unbalanced arrival problem through process grouping and scattered updating global variable, which basically achieves load balancing. Experiments show that the HAD-ADMM is highly efficient in a large-scale distributed environment and has no significant impact on convergence.

Keywords: Consensus optimization · ADMM · Asynchronous
Hierarchical communication structure

1 Introduction

With the rapid growth of Internet data, the performance and efficiency of a single computer cannot meet current computing needs. Therefore, how to solve machine learning problems in cluster is increasingly important.

The alternating direction method of multipliers (ADMM) decomposes the original problem into sub-problems for parallel iterations. It can solve a variety of machine learning problems, such as SVM [1] and the optimization of neural networks [2]. The ADMM was first proposed by [3] and [4]. Then, [5] proved that the ADMM is suitable for distributed optimization problems. [6] have applied the ADMM to the global consensus optimization problem. [7] solves the decentralized consensus optimization problem by ADMM.

However, in the global consensus problem, the ADMM needs to synchronize variables at each iteration. So network delay become the bottleneck of algorithm efficiency. [8] proposed an asynchronous ADMM algorithm (AD-ADMM) for the global consensus optimization problem. [9] and [10] added a penalty term based on [8]

© Springer Nature Switzerland AG 2018
V. Kůrková et al. (Eds.): ICANN 2018, LNCS 11139, pp. 362–371, 2018.
https://doi.org/10.1007/978-3-030-01418-6_36

to improve the convergence efficiency of non-convex problems. However, the AD-ADMM was implemented in master-slave model, whose communication efficiency is low in multiprocessor cluster.

On the one hand, for the distributed environment, such as MPI, intra-node and inter-node communication is different greatly. This is called unbalanced arrival problem [11, 12]. For this issue, [13] proposes RDMA-based process arrival model to optimizes aggregate communication, [14] uses remote shared memory to improve the communication speed, [15] overlaps inter-node communications with intra-node communications through a pipelined method. On the other hand, all slaves need to communicate with the master. The large load of the master can be reduced through the parameter server. The concept of parameter server derives from [16], which uses distributed Memcached as a storage parameter. There are already many frameworks for parameter server, such as Petuum [17] and ps-lite [18], which divide the nodes into several masters and workers. The worker updates local parameters, and the master updates global variables.

In this paper, in order to increase communication efficiency and achieve load balancing, a hierarchical parameter server structure (HPS) is designed. Besides, an asynchronous ADMM based on HPS (HAD-ADMM) and AD-ADMM is proposed. In addition, a number of simulation experiments verify that HAD-ADMM basically has no great impact on convergence and performs well in a large multiprocessor distributed environment.

2 Distributed ADMM

In general, many distributed machine learning problems can be expressed as the following global consensus optimization problem:

$$\min f(x) = \sum_{i=1}^{N} f_i(x_i), \text{ s.t. } x_i - z = 0, \ i = 1, \dots, N \quad (1)$$

where $x \in R^n, f_i : R^n \to R \cup \{+\infty\}$, z is the consensus variable. The local variables x_i should be equal to each other. (1) divides the objective function $f(x)$ into N parts, so this problem can be solved with N processes. Solving (1) through the ADMM is:

$$x_i^{k+1} = \underset{x_i}{\mathrm{argmin}} \left(f_i(x_i) + y_i^{kT}(x_i - z^k) + \frac{\rho}{2} \left\| x_i - z^k \right\|_2^2 \right) \quad (2a)$$

$$z^{k+1} = \underset{z}{\mathrm{argmin}} \left(f_i(x_i^{k+1}) + y_i^{kT}(x_i^{k+1} - z) + \frac{\rho}{2} \left\| x_i - z^k \right\|_2^2 \right) \quad (2b)$$

$$y_i^{k+1} = y_i^k + \rho \left(x_i^{k+1} - z^{k+1} \right) \quad (2c)$$

where y_i is the Lagrangian multipliers, $\rho > 0$ is the penalty parameter.

According to (2a), (2b), (2c), x and y can update independently across N processes, while z needs to aggregate all the local variables in cluster. So the network delay is high. Therefore, the AD-ADMM [8] is proposed to reduce the time overhead by partial barrier and bounded delay.

2.1 Asynchronous Distributed ADMM

The AD-ADMM divides processes into one master and N workers. The master does not have to wait for all workers, but receives parameters from A workers, $0 < A < N$, i.e. partial barrier. In order to guarantee convergence, the AD-ADMM constrains the staleness to a certain range, i.e. bounded delay. The AD-ADMM sets a clock k for each process, and the clock increases after each iteration. Master should wait workers whose clock is greater than $\tau > 0$. The AD-ADMM is given in Table 1.

Table 1. Asynchronous distributed ADMM (AD-ADMM).

Algorithm 1: AD-ADMM
Master:
1:    **initialize:** z, $k = 0$, $d_1 = d_2 = \cdots = d_N = 0$.
2:    **broadcast** z to all Workers.
3:    **repeat**
4:        **wait** until receiving $\{\hat{x}_i, \hat{y}_i\}$ from Workers i, $i \in A_k$ such that $|A_k| \geq A$ and $\forall i \in A_k^c, d_i < \tau$.
5:        **update**

$$x_i^{k+1} = \begin{cases} \hat{x}_i, i \in A_k \\ x_i^k, i \in A_k^c \end{cases}, y_i^{k+1} = \begin{cases} \hat{y}_i, i \in A_k \\ y_i^k, i \in A_k^c \end{cases}, d_i = \begin{cases} 1, i \in A_k \\ d_i + 1, i \in A_k^c \end{cases},$$

$$z^{k+1} = \underset{z}{\arg\min} \left(f_i(x_i^{k+1}) + y_i^{(k+1)T}(x_i^{k+1} - z) + \frac{\rho}{2} \|x_i^{k+1} - z\|_2^2 \right).$$

6:        **broadcast** z^{k+1} to the Workers i, $i \in A_k$.
7:        **set** $k \leftarrow k + 1$.
8:    **until** the stopping criterion is satisfied.
9:    **output** z^k.

the ith Worker:
1:    **initialize:** x_i, y_i, $k_i = 0$.
2:    **repeat**
3:        **wait** until receiving $\hat{z}$ from Master.
4:        **update**

$$x_i^{k_i+1} = \underset{x_i}{\arg\min} \left(f_i(x_i) + y_i^{k_i T}(x_i - \hat{z}) + \frac{\rho}{2} \|x_i - \hat{z}\|_2^2 \right),$$

$$y_i^{k_i+1} = y_i^{k_i} + \rho(x_i^{k_i+1} - \hat{z}).$$

5:        **send** $\{x_i^{k_i+1}, y_i^{k_i+1}\}$ to Master.
6:        **set** $k_i \leftarrow k_i + 1$.
7:    **until** the stopping criterion is satisfied.

---

where $\{d_1, d_2 \ldots d_N\}$ records the clock of N workers' last arrival. A_k is the set of workers which is reached in the clock k. A_k^c is the complement of A_k.

2.2 Star Communication Topology

The AD-ADMM is based on the master-slave model, which adopts a star structure. This section analyzes the problems in the star structure. We start with some definitions:

Definition 1. *In a cluster with N_n nodes, each node has $M_i > 0$ workers, $i \in 1, 2, \ldots N_n$. There is only one master in the entire cluster on the ξth node. There are N workers in the cluster, i.e. $\sum_1^{N_n} M_i = N$.*

Because of the process arrival pattern in MPI, the M_ξ workers in the ξth node must wait for other workers. In addition, the master must communicate with the N workers, causing network congestion. Finally, the master needs to store N worker parameters, which is a big challenge. For these issues, this paper proposes the HPS structure.

3 Asynchronous Distributed ADMM Based on Hierarchical Parameter Server

3.1 Hierarchical Parameter Server

This paper expands the parameter server into HPS through process grouping. Similar to [15], the communication of intra-node and inter-node is distinguished.

Processing Grouping. HPS associates processes with the node, and sets a master in each node called submaster. And a master is set up to communicate with each submaster. The workers only communicate with their own submasters. The submaster only communicates with the master and the workers. Therefore, except the communication between submasters and master, the rest is the intra-node communication. When the node size is large, HPS can effectively reduce the times of inter-node communication.

Update Strategy. Every submaster store variables from workers on the same node, and uses these parameters to update z. The master storages and aggregates parameters from submasters. This strategy greatly reduces the load of the master. The HPS topology and the star topology is shown in Fig. 1:

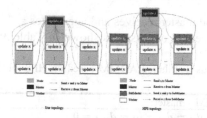

Fig. 1. The star and HPS topology.

3.2 Asynchronous Distributed ADMM Based on HPS

HAD-ADMM is similar to AD-ADMM, but provides a new update strategy based on HPS. The clock of submaster is equal to workers belong to it.

Updating x_{ij} and y_{ij} by Worker. HAD-ADMM updates y first, updates x secondly, and finally transfers variables to the submaster. Otherwise, the dual variable y sent by the worker is the result of the kth iteration. The worker procedure only changed the update order compared to AD-ADMM. And the subscript of x and y means the jth Worker in ith SubMaster.

Aggregation x_{ij} and y_{ij} by SubMaster. From (2b), we have that

$$z^{k+1} = \frac{1}{N} \sum_{i=1}^{N} \left(x_i^{k+1} + \frac{1}{\rho} y_i^k \right) \tag{3}$$

(3) is separable. The submaster updates the global variable z dispersed, and then sends $z_i^{k_i+1}$ to master. The procedure of submaster is shown in Table 2.

Table 2. Asynchronous distributed ADMM based on HPS (HAD-ADMM) – submaster

Algorithm 3 HAD-ADMM - the ith SubMaster:
1:　**initialize:** $x_i, y_i, P_i, k_i = 0$.
2:　**repeat**
3:　　**wait** $\hat{z}$ from Master.
4:　　**broadcast** $\hat{z}$ to the Worker $j, j \in P_i$.
5:　　**wait** $\left\{ \{ \widehat{x_{i1}}, \widehat{y_{i1}} \}, \{ \widehat{x_{i2}}, \widehat{y_{i2}} \}, \ldots, \{ \widehat{x_{iM_i}}, \widehat{y_{iM_i}} \} \right\}$ from all Workers in P_i.
6:　　**compute:**
$z_i^{k_i+1} = \frac{1}{N} \sum_{j=1}^{M_i} \left(x_{ij}^{k_i+1} + \frac{1}{\rho} y_{ij}^{k_i+1} \right)$.
7:　　**send** $z_i^{k_i+1}$ to Master.
8:　　**set** $k_i \leftarrow k_i + 1$.
9:　**until** the stopping criterion is satisfied.

where P_i is the set of workers in ith node.

Update z by Master. The master receives and aggregates $z_i^{k_i+1}$. And finally sends z to each submaster. The procedure of master is shown in Table 3:

Table 3. Asynchronous distributed ADMM based on HPS (HAD-ADMM) – master

Algorithm 4 HAD-ADMM - master:
1:　**initialize:** $z, k = 0, d_{1'} = d_{2'} = \cdots = d_{N_n'} = 0$.
2:　**broadcast** z to all SubMasters.
3:　**repeat**
4:　　**wait** until receiving $\left\{ \widehat{z_1}, \ldots, \widehat{z_{N_n}} \right\}$ from SubMaster $i, i \in A'_k$ such that $|A'_k| \geq A_n$ and $\forall i \in A'^c_k, d_{i'} < \tau$.
5:　　**update**
$z_i^{k+1} = \begin{cases} \widehat{z_i}, i \in A'_k \\ z_i^k, i \in A'^c_k \end{cases}$,
$d_i = \begin{cases} 1, i \in A'_k \\ d_i + 1, i \in A'^c_k \end{cases}$,
$z^{k+1} = \sum_{i=1}^{N_n} z_i^{k+1}$.
6:　　**broadcast** z^{k+1} to the SubMaster $i, i \in A'_k$.
7:　　**set** $k \leftarrow k + 1$.
8:　**until** the stopping criterion is satisfied.
9:　**output** z^k.

where A'_k is the set of submaster arrived when the clock is k, $A_n \leq |A'_k| \leq N_n$.

The algorithm procedure of HAD-ADMM is shown in Fig. 2, the processes in the same color in the figure are on the same node.

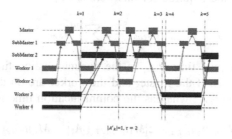

Fig. 2. Asynchronous distributed ADMM based on HPS (HAD-ADMM) (Color figure online)

4 Convergence and Performance Analysis

4.1 Convergence Analysis

First, a definition of the relevant variables is given in the following paragraph.

Definition 2. *Assume that the clock k has run for T iterations, and T_i is the number of iterations when the clock of the lth worker is k_i. $z_i^{k_i}$ is the z received by ith worker at its k_ith iteration. $\bar{x}_i$ is the average of x_i throughout its T_i iterations. Similarly, $\bar{z}$ is the average of z through T iterations.*

[8] proves that Theorem 1 is practical under Assumption 1.

Assumption 1 [8]. *At any master iteration k, updates of the N workers have the same probability of arriving at the master.*

Theorem 1 [8]. *Let (x^*, z^*) be the optimal solution of problem (1), and y_i^* is the optimal dual variable in ith worker. Then*

$$\mathbb{E}\left[\sum\nolimits_{i=1}^{N} f_i(\bar{x}_i) - f_i(x^*) + \left\langle y_i^*, \bar{x}_i - \bar{z}\right\rangle\right] \leq \frac{N\tau}{2TA}\left\{\sum\nolimits_{i=1}^{N} \rho\left\|z_i^0 - z^*\right\|^2 + \frac{1}{\rho}\left\|y_i^0 - y_i^*\right\|^2\right\}$$

(4)

where z_i^0 and y_i^0 are the initial values of z_i and y_i.

In other words, the convergence rate of AD-ADMM is $O\left(\frac{N\tau}{TA}\right)$. HAD-ADMM only changes A into $\sum_{i=1}^{A_n} M_i$, $i \in A_k'$. Therefore, under Assumption 2, the convergence rate of HAD-ADMM is basically the same as AD-ADMM.

Assumption 2. *At any master iteration, when $A = \sum_{i=1}^{A_n} M_i, i \in A_k'$, $\sum_{i=1}^{|A_k'|} M_i \geq |A_k|$.*

4.2   Performance Analysis

In order to simplify the analysis, assume that the master in the cluster is on the first node.

Star Topology. The time required for one iteration T_{star} is:

$$T_{star} = t_{calcs} + 2 \sum_{i=1}^{|A_k|} t_{wm_i} \tag{5}$$

where t_{calcs} is the compute time. t_{wm_i} is the communication time of master and ith worker, $i = 1, 2, \ldots, |A_k|$. If the master and the worker are on the same node, let the communication time be t_{intra}, whereas the communication time is t_{inter}. Therefore,

$$T_{star} \approx t_{calcs} + 2[M_1 t_{intra} + (|A_k| - M_1)t_{inter}] \tag{6}$$

HPS Topology. The time T_{HPS} required by one iteration is:

$$T_{HPS} = t_{calch} + 2 \left(\sum_{i=1}^{|A_k'|} t_{sm_i} + \sum_{i=1}^{|A_k'|} \sum_{j=1}^{M_i} t_{w_{ij}s_1} \right) \tag{7}$$

where $t_{w_{ij}s_1}$ is the communication time between the worker and the ith submaster, t_{sm_i} is the communication time between ith submaster and master. Similarly, if the master and the submaster are on the same node, let the communication time be t_{intra}', otherwise the communication time is t_{inter}'. In addition, let the communication time between the submaster and the worker be t_{intra}''. Thus

$$T_{HPS} \approx t_{calch} + 2 \left[(|A_k'| - 1)t_{inter}' + t_{intra}' + \sum_{i=1}^{|A_k'|} \sum_{j=1}^{M_i} t_{intra}'' \right] \tag{8}$$

where $i \in A_k'$. In the same cluster, $t_{calcs} \approx t_{calcl}$, $t_{intra}'' \approx t_{intra}$, Make $T_{star} - T_{HPS}$, so

$$\Delta T = 2(|A_k'| - 1)(M t_{inter} - t_{inter}') + 2[(M - M|A_k'|)t_{intra} - t_{intra}'] \tag{9}$$

Since the submaster in the HAD-ADMM only sends one variable to the master, and workers in the AD-ADMM needs to send two variables to the master. So, $t_{inter}' < t_{inter}$. Similarly, $t_{intra}' < t_{intra}$. Let $\Delta T > 0$, then

$$t_{inter} - t_{intra} > \frac{1}{M(|A_k'| - 1)}(t_{inter}' + t_{intra}') = \mu(t_{inter}' + t_{intra}') \tag{10}$$

If $|A_k'| = 1$, $\Delta T < 0$. When $|A_k'| > 1$, $\mu \leq 1$. Therefore, when μ is small enough, $\Delta T > 0$.

5 Experiment

In order to test the convergence and performance of HAD-ADMM, a simulation experiment was carried.

The data is set as $T = \{(\alpha_1, \beta_1), (\alpha_2, \beta_2), \ldots, (\alpha_S, \beta_S)\}$, where $\alpha_i \in R^S$ is feature vector, $\beta_i \in \{0, 1\}$ is label, T is evenly distributed over N nodes. So the global consensus optimization problem of LR problem is:

$$\min_{w_i} \sum_{i=1}^{N} L(w_i) = \sum_{i=1}^{N} \sum_{j=1}^{S} \left[\beta_j (w_i \cdot \alpha_j) - \log(1 + exp(w_i \cdot \alpha_j)) \right] \tag{11a}$$

$$\text{s.t. } w_i - z = 0, \ i = 1, \ldots, N \tag{11b}$$

In this paper, two clusters are used. One cluster has 8 compute nodes with fast Ethernet. The other has 16 nodes with Gigabit Ethernet. There are 4 cores and 8 GB memory in each node. In addition, the data set is a sparse set with dimension $s = 10000000$ and size $S = 43264$. The algorithm is implemented in C++ and MPICH v3.2. For each worker, L-BFGS is chosen to solve (2a). The penalty parameter $\rho = 1$. The stopping criterion is that the residual r^k and s^k [5] satisfy:

$$\|r^k\|_2 \leq 10^{-2}\sqrt{S} + 10^{-4}\max\left\{\|w^k\|_2, \|z^k\|_2\right\}, \ \|s^k\|_2 \leq 10^{-2}\sqrt{S} + 10^{-4}\|y^k\|_2 \tag{12}$$

where

$$\|r^k\|_2^2 = \sum_{i=1}^{N} \|w_i^k - z^k\|_2^2, \ \|s^k\|_2^2 = N\rho^2\|z^k - z^{k-1}\|_2^2 \tag{13}$$

5.1 Convergence Test

Figure 3 shows the dual residual variation with the number of iteration. Assumption 1 [8] and Assumption 2 are established in the experiment. In some cases, it was found that workers that reached the master process on each iteration of the HAD-ADMM were basically the same as the AD-ADMM. Even under different conditions, the convergence of the two algorithms is similar. This is consistent with the analysis in Sect. 4.1. Therefore, the performance of HAD-ADMM is mainly related to μ from Eq. 10.

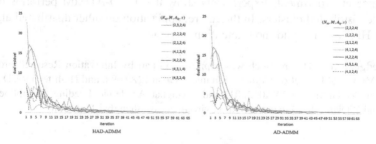

Fig. 3. The convergence of HAD-ADMM and AD-ADMM.

5.2 Performance Test

It can be seen from Fig. 4(a) that the value of τ has a great influence on the running time. There is a big difference of $\tau = 4$ and $\tau = 8$, which is the characteristic of the asynchronous algorithm. When $N_n = 2$ and $N_n = 4$, the effect of the μ on run time is consistent with the analysis in Sect. 4.2. In the cluster used in this paper, the HAD-ADMM has a shorter running time if $\mu \leq 1/3$. When $N_n = 8$, μ has little effect. Under this condition, the algorithm runtime of HAD-ADMM is much shorter than AD-ADMM. The reason may be when the number of nodes is large, the communication load of the Master in the AD-ADMM has greater influence.

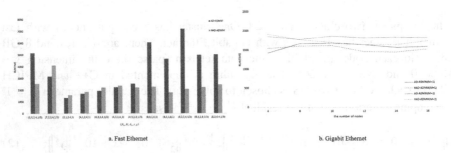

a. Fast Ethernet   b. Gigabit Ethernet

Fig. 4. The runtime of HAD-ADMM and AD-ADMM.

Figure 4(b) shows experiments on Gigabit Ethernet, which $\tau = 4$ and $A_k = 0.5M$. It can be seen that HAD-ADMM is better than AD-ADMM obviously when $\mu \leq 1/5$. Because of the smaller $t_{inter} - t_{intra}$ on Gigabit Ethernet, smaller μ is needed to maintain $\Delta T < 0$.

6 Conclusion

Aiming at AD-ADMM and MPI, this paper proposes HPS structure based on the parameter server, which reduces the inter-node communication through processing grouping and balance the load through scattered update. In addition, this paper proposes the HAD-ADMM based on AD-ADMM, and analyzes the convergence and performance in experiment. Experiments show that HAD-ADMM performs better in large-scale distributed clusters. In the future, application on other distributed algorithm based on HPS will be paid more attention.

Acknowledgements. This research was supported in part by Innovation Research program of Shanghai Municipal Education Commission under Grant 12ZZ094, and High-tech R&D Program of China under Grant 2009AA012201, and Shanghai Academic Leading Discipline Project J50103, and ZiQiang 4000 experimental environment of Shanghai University.

References

1. Chen, Q., Cao, F.: Distributed support vector machine in master–slave mode. Neural Netw. Off. J. Int. Neural Netw. Soc. **101**, 94 (2018)
2. Taylor, G., Burmeister, R., Xu, Z., et al.: Training neural networks without gradients: a scalable ADMM approach. In: International Conference on International Conference on Machine Learning, pp. 2722–2731. JMLR.org (2016)
3. Glowinski, R., Marrocco, A.: On the solution of a class of non linear Dirichlet problems by a penalty-duality method and finite elements of order one. In: Marchuk, G.I. (ed.) Optimization Techniques IFIP Technical Conference. LNCS. Springer, Heidelberg (1975). https://doi.org/10.1007/978-3-662-38527-2_45
4. Gabay, D., Mercier, B.: A dual algorithm for the solution of nonlinear variational problems via finite element approximation. Comput. Math Appl. **2**(1), 17–40 (1976)
5. Boyd, S., Parikh, N., Chu, E., et al.: Distributed optimization and statistical learning via the alternating direction method of multipliers. Found. Trends Mach. Learn. **3**(1), 1–122 (2010)
6. Lin, T., Ma, S., Zhang, S.: On the global linear convergence of the ADMM with multi-block variables. SIAM J. Optim. **25**(3), 1478–1497 (2014)
7. Wang, Y., Yin, W., Zeng, J.: Global convergence of ADMM in nonconvex nonsmooth optimization. J. Sci. Comput., 1–35 (2018)
8. Zhang, R., Kwok, J.T.: Asynchronous distributed ADMM for consensus optimization. In: International Conference on Machine Learning, pp. II-1701. JMLR.org (2014)
9. Chang, T.H., Hong, M., Liao, W.C., et al.: Asynchronous distributed alternating direction method of multipliers: algorithm and convergence analysis. In: IEEE International Conference on Acoustics, Speech and Signal Processing, pp. 4781–4785. IEEE (2016)
10. Chang, T.H., Liao, W.C., Hong, M., et al.: Asynchronous distributed ADMM for large-scale optimization—Part II: linear convergence analysis and numerical performance. IEEE Trans. Signal Process. **64**(12), 3131–3144 (2016)
11. Faraj, A., Patarasuk, P., Yuan, X.: A study of process arrival patterns for MPI collective operations. In: International Conference on Supercomputing, pp. 168–179. ACM (2007)
12. Patarasuk, P., Yuan, X.: Efficient MPI Bcast across different process arrival patterns. In: IEEE International Symposium on Parallel and Distributed Processing, pp. 1–11. IEEE (2009)
13. Qian, Y., Afsahi, A.: Process arrival pattern aware alltoall and allgather on InfiniBand clusters. Int. J. Parallel Program. **39**(4), 473–493 (2011)
14. Tipparaju, V., Nieplocha, J., Panda, D.: Fast collective operations using shared and remote memory access protocols on clusters. In: International Parallel & Distributed Processing Symposium, p. 84a (2003)
15. Liu, Z.Q., Song, J.Q., Lu, F.S., et al.: Optimizing method for improving the performance of MPI broadcast under unbalanced process arrival patterns. J. Softw. **22**(10), 2509–2522 (2011)
16. Smola, A., Narayanamurthy, S.: An architecture for parallel topic models. VLDB Endow. **3**, 703–710 (2010)
17. Xing, E.P., Ho, Q., Dai, W., et al.: Petuum: a new platform for distributed machine learning on big data. In: ACM SIGKDD International Conference on Knowledge Discovery & Data Mining, pp. 1335–1344. IEEE (2015)
18. Li, M., Zhou, L., Yang, Z., Li, A., Xia, F.: Parameter server for distributed machine learning. In: Big Learning Workshop, pp. 1–10 (2013)

Improved Personalized Rankings Using Implicit Feedback

Josef Feigl[(✉)] and Martin Bogdan

Department of Computer Engineering, University of Leipzig,
Augustusplatz 10, 04109 Leipzig, Germany
{feigl,bogdan}@informatik.uni-leipzig.de

Abstract. Most users give feedback through a mixture of implicit and explicit information when interacting with websites. Recommender systems should use both sources of information to improve personalized recommendations. In this paper, it is shown how to integrate implicit feedback information in form of pairwise item rankings into a neural network model to improve personalized item recommendations. The proposed two-sided approach allows the model to be trained even for users where no explicit feedback is available. This is especially useful to alleviate a form of the new user cold-start problem. The experiments indicate an improved predictive performance especially for the task of personalized ranking.

Keywords: Personalized ranking · Neural networks
Collaborative filtering · Implicit feedback

1 Introduction

Personalized feedback about user preferences is mostly limited to clicks, purchases or other forms of implicit information. It is rather uncommon that users give explicit feedback, for example in form of ratings. Recommender systems for both types of information are well covered in the collaborative filtering literature [7,10]. However, a more realistic problem is given when dealing with a mixture of both sources of information. This is especially interesting when information about most users is limited to implicit feedback.

This paper builds on the results of [4] and [5] aiming to make use of both sources of information to improve the predictions of explicit user preferences. Therefore, our proposed neural network model integrates implicit feedback by learning additional user-specific pairwise item preferences, similar to the popular Bayesian Personalized Ranking criterion (BPR) [14]. Aside from the increased predictive performance of this approach, the model can thus also be trained for users where no explicit information is present. This is useful to ease a form of the common cold-start problem for new users.

Therefore, the main contributions of this paper are (i) to show a novel way of integrating implicit feedback in a recommender system using pairwise rankings,

© Springer Nature Switzerland AG 2018
V. Kůrková et al. (Eds.): ICANN 2018, LNCS 11139, pp. 372–381, 2018.
https://doi.org/10.1007/978-3-030-01418-6_37

(ii) to introduce mixed feedback dataset and show how to deal with them and (iii) to evaluate the impact of implicit feedback for personalized ranking. This paper is structured as followed: A brief description of the general problem is given in Sect. 2. Afterwards in Sect. 3, we give an overview of the proposed neural network architecture. In Sect. 4, we detail how to train the model. The proposed model is evaluated in Sect. 5. We summarize our findings in Sect. 6.

2   Preliminaries

Let $U = \{1, \ldots, N\}$ be a set of users and $I = \{1, \ldots, M\}$ a set of items with $N, M \in \mathbb{N}$. The set of all ratings is given by $R = \{-1, 0, 1\}$, where the value 1 is given if a user liked the item and vice versa for 0. The value -1 highlights that no explicit information is available for this user-item tuple.

We have a dataset of observed interactions S with

$$S := S^{expl} \cup S^{impl}, \tag{1}$$

where

$$S^{expl} := \{(u, i, r) \mid u \in U, i \in I, r \in R\} \tag{2}$$

defines the set of all explicit feedback information and

$$S^{impl} := \{(u, i, -1) \mid u \in U, i \in I\} \tag{3}$$

defines the set of all implicit information. For each sample of S^{impl}, the user interacted with an item in some way but did not explicitly assign it a rating. Both datasets can easily be visualized by a table with three columns (see Table 1).

We are calling an item i *positive* for user u if this user had some kind of interaction with the item. Let I_u^+ be the set of all positive items of user u. It is defined as:

$$I_u^+ := \{i \mid (u, i, r) \in S\} \tag{4}$$

Therefore, all interactions with an explicit rating, even if the rating was negative, are also considered as positive feedback. Analogous to the definition above, we use I_u^- for the set of all *negative* items, e.g. all items, user u had no interaction with [5].

Table 1. Training data (left): The rating value of -1 highlights that no explicit information was available. User 1 has explicit as well as implicit information in his training data. User 2 has only implicit data. Test data (right): Explicit ratings have to be predicted for both users.

User	Item	Rating
1	1	0
1	2	1
1	3	-1
2	1	-1
2	4	-1

User	Item	Rating
1	4	0
2	2	1
2	3	0

3 Model

3.1 Main Idea

Common matrix factorization models learn a set of latent user and latent item factors to predict a target. Our model learns an additional set of item factors: one for the explicit and one for the implicit information in the dataset. The final target prediction of our model is a weighted average of two separate predictions: one using the user factors in combination with the explicit item factors and one using the user factors in combination with the implicit item factors.

Therefore, our model consists of one part to train the explicit item factors and one part to train the implicit item factors. However, both parts share the same user factors. Each part will update their relevant item factors, but both parts will use and update the same user factors.

While the explicit item factors are updated using all available explicit feedback information (similar to most matrix factorization models), the implicit item factors are trained to rank positive and negative items. This is similar to a matrix factorization model using the BPR criterion ($BPRMF$) [14]. Therefore, our model is a combination of a biased regularized matrix factorization model ($BRMF$) [4] and a $BPRMF$ model.

3.2 Model Overview

Our proposed network consists of two parts: one part to process the explicit feedback and one for the implicit feedback (see Fig. 1). The network is a concatenation of five specific layers L: An user layer L^1 with N units. This layer has as many units as there are users and is responsible for learning the user representations. The next layer is the hidden layer L^2 with K units, which determines the size of all learned representations. The following item layer L^3 holds the explicit and implicit item representations. It has $2 \cdot M$ units. The second to last layer is the bias layer L^4, which is responsible for dealing with user, item and global biases. The last layer L^5 is a combination layer, which merges the outputs of the explicit as well as the implicit part of the network.

3.3 Notation

The following short notations are used in this paper: let $\mathbf{U}$ be the set of weights connecting the user layer to the hidden layer. It can be represented as a weight matrix $\mathbf{U} \in \mathbb{R}^{N \times K}$. A single representation of user u is given by the weights connecting unit u of the user layer with all units of the hidden layer. We use the notation $\mathbf{U}_u$ for this single user representation [4].

Let $\mathbf{I}^{expl} \in \mathbb{R}^{K \times M}$ be the set of weights connecting the hidden layer to the explicit item layer. Analogous to the user layer, we use $\mathbf{I}_i^{expl}$ to define the explicit representation for the item i. Similar notations are used for the implicit item weights $\mathbf{I}^{impl} \in \mathbb{R}^{K \times M}$. Additionally, $\mathbf{a}^l$ defines the activation of layer l [5].

User Layer   Hidden Layer   Item Layer   Bias Layer   Combination Layer

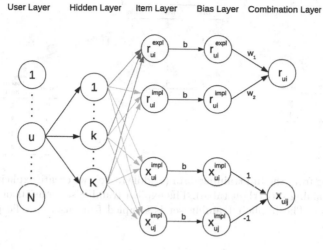

Fig. 1. The upper part of the network leading to r_{ui} handles the prediction of explicit ratings. The final prediction of this part is a weighted average of one prediction using the implicit item factors (green) and one using the explicit item factors (red). The lower part leading to x_{uij} updates the implicit item factors by learning to rank user-specific positive and negative items. The letter b symbolizes the addition of biases to the activation of the item layer. (Color figure online)

We use r_{ui} as a short notation for the rating r given by user u for item i. The prediction $\hat{r}_{ui}$ for this rating is made by the explicit part of our model. The implicit part of the network measures the difference between the preferences of a positive and a negative item of user u. We use x_{ui} as the measure of preference to determine how much user u likes item i. Therefore, user u prefers item i over item j if $x_{ui} > x_{uj}$. The output of the implicit part of the network x_{uij} is given by the probability that user u prefers item i over item j [5].

4   Training

We use a two-sided approach to train the network. All explicit samples are used to train the explicit part of the network. The implicit part of the network is trained by learning to rank positive and negative items. To do this, we need two separate training sets.

4.1   Preparation of Training Sets

To train the network, we need training samples for the explicit as well as the implicit part of the model (see Fig. 2). All samples for the explicit part are given in S^{expl}. For consistency, we use the notation $T^{expl} := S^{expl}$ for this set.

The training samples for the implicit part T^{impl} are created using the following process: to create a set of p training samples, we choose a uniformly

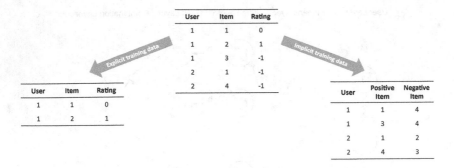

Fig. 2. Starting from the full training data (middle table), we create explicit (left table) and implicit training sets (right table). The explicit training set consists of all available explicit samples. The implicit training set is sampled from user-specific positive and negative items.

randomly selected set of p users $u \in U$ (with replacement). For each user, one of his positive items $i \in I_u^+$ and one of his negative items $j \in I_u^-$ is randomly selected (uniformly distributed with replacement):

$$T^{impl} \subseteq \left\{ (u,i,j) \mid u \in U, i \in I_u^+, j \in I_u^- \right\}. \tag{5}$$

A model should therefore learn to rank x_{ui} above x_{uj} for each training triple $(u,i,j) \in T^{impl}$.

4.2   Explicit Part

Let $(u,i,r) \in T^{expl}$ be a single training triple for the explicit part of the network, where $u \in U$ is a user, $i \in I$ is an item and $r \in \{0,1\}$ is a rating.

A binarized version $\mathbf{a}^1 = 1_u \in \{0,1\}^N$ of u is used as the input for the network. It is defined as the indicator vector $1_u := (z_0, z_1, \cdots, z_N)$ with $z_j = 1$ if $j = u$ and $z_j = 0$ otherwise. Using 1_u as input for the network implies that only the weights $\mathbf{U}_u$ contribute anything to the input of the hidden layer [4]. The output $\mathbf{a}^2 \in \mathbb{R}^K$ is therefore given by:

$$\begin{aligned} \mathbf{a}^2 &= \mathbf{U} \cdot \mathbf{a}^1 \\ &= \mathbf{U}_u. \end{aligned} \tag{6}$$

We select the implicit and explicit weights for item i to compute the output of the item layer $\mathbf{a}^3$:

$$\mathbf{a}_0^3 = \mathbf{a}^2 \cdot \mathbf{I}_i^{expl} \tag{7}$$

$$\mathbf{a}_1^3 = \mathbf{a}^2 \cdot \mathbf{I}_i^{impl} \tag{8}$$

In our evaluation, we found no benefit from using anything other than identity activation functions for the hidden and item layer. We are therefore omitting the notation of activation functions for these two layers.

The following bias layer is responsible for adding a user bias, an explicit item bias and a global bias to the previous output. The output of the explicit part of our network $\hat{r}_{ui}$ is therefore given by:

$$\hat{r}_{ui} = \sigma(w_1 \cdot \hat{r}_{ui}^{expl} + w_2 \cdot \hat{r}_{ui}^{impl}) \tag{9}$$

with

$$\hat{r}_{ui}^{expl} = f(\mathbf{a}_0^3 + b_u + b_i^{expl} + b_g), \tag{10}$$
$$\hat{r}_{ui}^{impl} = f(\mathbf{a}_1^3 + b_u + b_i^{impl} + b_g). \tag{11}$$

The function $f : \mathbb{R} \rightarrow \mathbb{R}$ is the activation function of the bias layer. For the combination layer, we use the logistic sigmoid activation function σ to get the probability estimate that user u likes item i.

After forward-propagating, we compare the prediction $\hat{r}_{ui}$ with the target r_{ui} and back-propagate the loss $r_{ui} - \hat{r}_{ui}$ using the common cross entropy cost function [2,15]. We are updating all weights except the implicit item weights and the implicit item bias, which get updated during the training of the implicit part of the network.

We achieved our best results using the weights $w_1 = 0.5$ and $w_2 = 0.5$ instead of letting the network learn them. This way the network is forced to use both parts of the network equally. Using $w_1 = 1$ and $w_2 = 0$ disables the implicit part and reduces our model to a $BRMF$ model [4,17].

4.3 Implicit Part

Let $(u, i, j) \in T^{impl}$ be a single training triple for the implicit part, where $u \in U$ is a user, $i \in I_u^+$ is a positive item and $j \in I_u^-$ is a negative item for this user. Similarly to the training of the explicit part of our network, feed-forwarding this sample through the implicit part of the network yields:

$$\hat{x}_{uij} = \sigma(\hat{x}_{ui}^{impl} - \hat{x}_{uj}^{impl}) \tag{12}$$

with

$$\hat{x}_{ui}^{impl} = f(\mathbf{U}_u \cdot \mathbf{I}_i^{impl} + b_u + b_i^{impl} + b_g), \tag{13}$$
$$\hat{x}_{uj}^{impl} = f(\mathbf{U}_u \cdot \mathbf{I}_j^{impl} + b_u + b_j^{impl} + b_g). \tag{14}$$

Again, we use the logistic sigmoid activation function σ to get the probability estimate that user u prefers item i over item j.

The training samples T^{impl} are missing target values y in the classical machine learning sense, but our training set is constructed in such a way that $x_{ui}^{impl} > x_{uj}^{impl}$ for each sample (Subsect. 4.1). This means that, the measure of preference of a positive item is always greater than this measure for a negative item. Learning to maximize the probability $\hat{x}_{uij}$ is sufficient to achieve this goal and we can therefore set $y = 1$ for every training sample (also see [5]). Again, using the cross entropy cost function, we back-propagate the loss $1 - \hat{x}_{uij}$ and update the user weights, the implicit item weights and the implicit item bias.

The constant weights of the combination layer force the implicit part of our network to learn pairwise item rankings. This part of the model is therefore equivalent to a $BPRMF$ model [5,14].

4.4   Mini-Batch-Processing

For each training epoch, we have a set of $|T^{expl}|$ samples for the explicit part and a set of $|T^{impl}|$ samples for the implicit part of our model. Instead of processing a single sample at a time, we split each set into mini-batches of P samples. During each training epoch, we process all available mini-batches in a random order, which helps to improve convergence of both parts of the network. An epoch is finished once all mini-batches were processed. We create a new set of training samples T^{impl} for each training epoch.

Using the set of negative items I_u^- to create T^{impl} can be memory-consuming and computationally slow. Since most users interact only with a small percentage of all items, we found it to be sufficient to sample item from all possible items instead of using I_u^-. We found no significant loss of predictive performance using this approximate approach.

5   Experiments and Results

5.1   Setting

The MovieLens 1M dataset [6] and the Netflix Prize dataset [1] are used to evaluate our model. Since both datasets contain explicit movie ratings in the range $[1, 5]$, we convert these ratings to binary targets by checking if the rating is above or equal to 3.

To simulate the situation where users have only provided few or even no explicit feedback information, we create multiple mixed variants of these two datasets. The following process was used to create all benchmark datasets: at first, a given percentage s of all explicit ratings are dropped. Afterwards, all explicit ratings of t percent of all users are dropped. This way, t percent of all users have only implicit information left and the remaining users lose about s percent of their provided explicit information. We use the short notation $ML(s, t)$ and $Netflix(s, t)$ to denote all benchmark datasets, which were created using the explained process on the Movielens 1M and Netflix Prize dataset, respectively. Using this notation, $ML(0, 0)$ and $Netflix(0, 0)$ simply refer to the full datasets.

For the Movielens 1M dataset, we used a 5-fold cross-validation. The Netflix Prize dataset comes with a predefined probe dataset, which we use as test set to validate all predictions. To speed up computation, we randomly selected 10 000 out of 480 189 users of the Netflix Prize dataset in each run. The process to create the benchmark datasets was applied on the training data of each run. The test data was left untouched since we want to benchmark our model predicting explicit ratings even if there was no explicit information in the training data of a user. We did a total of five runs for each dataset and averaged the results.

Our model is compared against two popular baseline models:

BRMF. A biased regularized matrix factorization model, which is implemented using the explicit part of our model (see 4.2). This model is especially useful as a fair comparison with our full network to directly evaluate the impact of the integration of implicit information.

FM. A factorization machine was used as the second baseline model [12]. The results for this model were computed using the open-source library *libFM* [13].

We are using three metrics to evaluate the model performance: The Area Under the Receiver Operating Characteristic Curve (AUC) to measure the ranking quality [3], logistic loss ($LogLoss$) and $Accuracy$ to measure the general predictive performance.

5.2   Network Initialization Details

The user weights and the explicit and implicit item weights are initialized with uniformly distributed random numbers from the range $[-0.01, 0.01]$. We are using a $SELU$ activation function in the bias layer [9] and two $Adam$ optimizer [8]: one for the explicit and one for the implicit part of the network. To regularize the network, we use $L2$ [11] and max-norm regularization [16] for all weights.

5.3   Results

The evaluation results of all models for the movielens 1M datasets can be found in Table 2 and for the Netflix Prize datasets in Table 3.

Our model achieves a significantly improved predictive performance compared to the $BRMF$ model on all metrics and on all datasets. This is especially

Table 2. Evaluation results for the Movielens 1M dataset

Metric	Model	ML (0, 0)	ML (0.5, 0.25)	ML (0.5, 0.5)	ML (0.5, 0.75)
AUC	$BRMF$	0.8216	0.7830	0.7633	0.7382
	FM	0.8248	0.7877	0.7668	0.7410
	Our Model	**0.8249**	**0.7901**	**0.7709**	**0.7455**
$LogLoss$	$BRMF$	0.5196	0.5574	0.5737	0.5929
	FM	**0.5032**	**0.5438**	0.5642	0.5885
	Our Model	0.5119	0.5466	**0.5635**	**0.5860**
$Accuracy$	$BRMF$	0.7470	0.7173	0.7032	0.6855
	FM	0.7504	0.7217	0.7067	0.6890
	Our Model	**0.7512**	**0.7233**	**0.7089**	**0.6918**

Table 3. Evaluation results for the netflix prize dataset

Metric	Model	Netflix (0, 0)	Netflix (0.5, 0.25)	Netflix (0.5, 0.5)	Netflix (0.5, 0.75)
AUC	BRMF	0.7844	0.7446	0.7181	0.6868
	FM	**0.7879**	0.7482	0.7211	0.6889
	Our Model	0.7871	**0.7486**	**0.7237**	**0.6969**
LogLoss	BRMF	0.5443	0.5812	0.6001	0.6194
	FM	**0.5373**	**0.5751**	**0.5955**	0.6171
	Our Model	0.5416	0.5784	0.5975	**0.6151**
Accuracy	BRMF	0.7221	0.6906	0.6733	0.6513
	FM	**0.7279**	0.6942	0.6733	0.6521
	Our Model	0.7255	**0.6950**	**0.6756**	**0.6583**

interesting since both models share many similarities, with the only difference being the integration of implicit feedback using pairwise item rankings.

It can also be seen, that the FM model performs significantly better than the $BRMF$ model. This is no surprise, since the FM model can easily mimic most matrix factorization models [12].

Our model performs consistently better or at least equally good than the FM model on the AUC and $Accuracy$ metrics. The difference between both models also gets larger the more of the explicit information is dropped from the dataset. This is to be expected, because our model can still use the remaining implicit information. It can also be seen, that integrating implicit information in form of pairwise item rankings is especially beneficial for the AUC metric. This is due to the fact that the implicit part of our model is basically a matrix factorization model using the BPR criterion, which is well suited to optimize AUC [12].

The FM model performs especially better than our model regarding the $LogLoss$ metric on both full datasets. Nevertheless, integrating the implicit information helps to close this gap and enables our model to perform even stronger than the FM model regarding the $LogLoss$ metric on the sparser mixed datasets.

6   Summary

In this paper, we have proposed a neural network recommender system to solve collaborative filtering problems where users give feedback through a mixture of implicit and explicit information and in particular the case where all information about most users is limited to implicit feedback. Our model integrates implicit information by additionally learning personalized item rankings using the Bayesian Personalized Ranking criterion. These features are further used to influence the processing of the explicit information. This two-sided approach enables the model to be trained for users that never gave any explicit feedback, which is useful to improve recommendations and alleviate the cold start problem for new users. It was shown that integrating implicit feedback using our proposed approach leads to an increase of predictive performance especially for the task of personalized ranking.

References

1. Bennett, J., Lanning, S., Netflix, N.: The Netflix Prize. In: KDD Cup and Workshop in Conjunction with KDD (2007)
2. Bishop, C.M.: Pattern Recognition and Machine Learning (Information Science and Statistics). Springer, New York Inc., Heidelberg, New York (2006)
3. Bradley, A.P.: The use of the area under the ROC curve in the evaluation of machine learning algorithms. Pattern Recogn. **30**(7), 1145–1159 (1997)
4. Feigl, J., Bogdan, M.: Collaborative filtering with neural networks. In: ESANN 2017, 25th European Symposium on Artificial Neural Networks, Computational Intelligence and Machine Learning, pp. 441–446 (2017)
5. Feigl, J., Bogdan, M.: Neural networks for implicit feedback datasets. In: ESANN 2018, 26th European Symposium on Artificial Neural Networks, Computational Intelligence and Machine Learning, pp. 255–260 (2018)
6. Harper, F.M., Konstan, J.A.: The movielens datasets: history and context. ACM Trans. Interact. Intell. Syst. **5**(4), 19:1–19:19 (2015)
7. Hu, Y., Koren, Y., Volinsky, C.: Collaborative filtering for implicit feedback datasets. In: Proceedings of the 2008 Eighth IEEE International Conference on Data Mining, ICDM 2008, pp. 263–272 (2008)
8. Kingma, D.P., Ba, J.: ADAM: a method for stochastic optimization. CoRR abs/1412.6980 (2014)
9. Klambauer, G., Unterthiner, T., Mayr, A., Hochreiter, S.: Self-normalizing neural networks. CoRR abs/1706.02515 (2017)
10. Koren, Y., Bell, R., Volinsky, C.: Matrix factorization techniques for recommender systems. Computer **42**(8), 30–37 (2009)
11. Krogh, A., Hertz, J.A.: A simple weight decay can improve generalization. In: Advances in Neural Information Processing Systems, vol. 4, pp. 950–957. Morgan Kaufmann (1992)
12. Rendle, S.: Factorization machines. In: Proceedings of the 2010 IEEE International Conference on Data Mining, ICDM 2010, pp. 995–1000. IEEE Computer Society, Washington (2010). https://doi.org/10.1109/ICDM.2010.127
13. Rendle, S.: Factorization machines with LIBFM. ACM Trans. Intell. Syst. Technol. **3**(3), 57:1–57:22 (2012)
14. Rendle, S., Freudenthaler, C., Gantner, Z., Schmidt-Thieme, L.: BPR: Bayesian personalized ranking from implicit feedback. In: Proceedings of the Twenty-Fifth Conference on Uncertainty in Artificial Intelligence, UAI 2009, pp. 452–461. AUAI Press, Arlington (2009)
15. Rumelhart, D.E., Hinton, G.E., Williams, R.J.: Neurocomputing: foundations of research. In: Learning Representations by Back-propagating Errors, pp. 696–699. MIT Press, Cambridge (1988)
16. Srebro, N., Rennie, J.D.M., Jaakkola, T.S.: Maximum-margin matrix factorization. In: Proceedings of the 17th International Conference on Neural Information Processing Systems, NIPS 2004, pp. 1329–1336. MIT Press, Cambridge (2004). http://dl.acm.org/citation.cfm?id=2976040.2976207
17. Takács, G., Pilászy, I., Németh, B., Tikk, D.: Scalable collaborative filtering approaches for large recommender systems. J. Mach. Learn. Res. **10**, 623–656 (2009)

Cosine Normalization: Using Cosine Similarity Instead of Dot Product in Neural Networks

Chunjie Luo[1,2], Jianfeng Zhan[1,2(✉)], Xiaohe Xue[1], Lei Wang[1],
Rui Ren[1], and Qiang Yang[3]

[1] State Key Laboratory of Computer Architecture,
Institute of Computing Technology, Chinese Academy of Sciences,
Beijing, China
zhanjianfeng@ict.ac.cn
[2] University of Chinese Academy of Sciences, Beijing, China
[3] Beijing Academy of Frontier Science and Technology, Beijing, China

Abstract. Traditionally, multi-layer neural networks use dot product between the output vector of previous layer and the incoming weight vector as the input to activation function. The result of dot product is unbounded, thus increases the risk of large variance. Large variance of neuron makes the model sensitive to the change of input distribution, thus results in poor generalization, and aggravates the internal covariate shift which slows down the training. To bound dot product and decrease the variance, we propose to use cosine similarity or centered cosine similarity (Pearson Correlation Coefficient) instead of dot product in neural networks, which we call cosine normalization. We compare cosine normalization with batch, weight and layer normalization in fully-connected neural networks, convolutional networks on the data sets of MNIST, 20NEWS GROUP, CIFAR-10/100, SVHN. Experiments show that cosine normalization achieves better performance than other normalization techniques.

Keywords: Neural networks · Cosine similarity · Cosine normalization

1 Introduction

Deep neural networks have received great success in recent years in many areas. Training deep neural networks is nontrivial task. Gradient descent is commonly used to train neural networks. However, due to gradient vanishing problem [1], it works badly when directly applying to deep networks.

In previous work, multi-layer neural networks use dot product (also called inner product) between the output vector of previous layer and the incoming weight vector as the input to activation function.

$$net = w \bullet x \tag{1}$$

where net is the input to activation function (pre-activation), w is the incoming weight vector, and x is the input vector which is also the output vector of previous layer, • indicates dot product. Equation 1 can be rewritten as Eq. 2, where $\cos \theta$ is the cosine of angle between w and x, $\|$ is the Euclidean norm of vector.

© Springer Nature Switzerland AG 2018
V. Kůrková et al. (Eds.): ICANN 2018, LNCS 11139, pp. 382–391, 2018.
https://doi.org/10.1007/978-3-030-01418-6_38

$$net = |w||x| \cos \theta \tag{2}$$

The result of dot product is unbounded, thus increases the risk of large variance. Large variance of neuron makes the model sensitive to the change of input distribution, thus results in poor generalization. Large variance could also aggravate the internal covariate shift which slows down the training [2]. Using small weights can alleviate this problem. Weight decay (L2-norm) [3] and max normalization (max-norm) [4, 5] are methods that could decrease the weights. Batch normalization [2] uses statistics calculated from mini-batch training examples to normalize the result of dot product, while layer normalization [6] uses statistics from the same layer on a single training case. The variance can be constrained within certain range using batch or layer normalization. Weight normalization [7] re-parameterizes the weight vector by dividing its norm, thus partially bounds the result of dot product.

To thoroughly bound dot product, a straight-forward idea is to use cosine similarity. Similarity (or distance) based methods are widely used in data mining and machine learning [8]. Particularly, cosine similarity is most commonly used in high dimensional spaces. For example, in information retrieval and text mining, cosine similarity gives a useful measure of how similar two documents are [9].

In this paper, we combine cosine similarity with neural networks. We use cosine similarity instead of dot product when computing the pre-activation. That can be seen as a normalization procedure, which we call cosine normalization. Equation 3 shows the cosine normalization.

$$net_{norm} = \cos \theta = \frac{w \bullet x}{|w||x|} \tag{3}$$

To extend, we can use the centered cosine similarity, Pearson Correlation Coefficient (PCC), instead of dot product. By dividing the magnitude of w and x, the input to activation function is bounded between -1 and 1. Higher learning rate could be used for training without the risk of large variance. Moreover, network with cosine normalization can be trained by both batch gradient descent and stochastic gradient descent, since it does not depend on any statistics on batch or mini-batch examples.

We compare our cosine normalization with batch, weight and layer normalization in fully-connected neural networks on the MNIST and 20NEWS GROUP data sets. Additionally, convolutional networks with different normalization techniques are evaluated on the CIFAR-10/100 and SVHN data sets. Experiments show that cosine normalization and centered cosine normalization (PCC) achieve better performance than other normalization techniques.

2 Background and Motivation

Large variance of neuron in neural network makes the model sensitive to the change of input distribution, thus results in poor generalization. Moreover, variance could be amplified as information moves forward along layers, especially in deep network. Large variance could also aggravate the internal covariate shift, which refers the change of distribution of each layer during training, as the parameters of previous layers change [2].

Internal covariate shift slows down the training because the layers need to continuously adapt to the new distribution. Traditionally, neural networks use dot product to compute the pre-activation of neuron. The result of dot product is unbounded. That is to say, the result could be any value in the whole real space, thus increases the risk of large variance.

Using small weights can alleviate this problem, since the pre-activation net in Eq. 2 will be decreased when $|w|$ is small. Weight decay [3] and max normalization [4, 5] are methods that try to make the weights to be small. Weight decay adds an extra term to the cost function that penalizes the squared value of each weight separately. Max normalization puts a constraint on the maximum squared length of the incoming weight vector of each neuron. If update violates this constraint, max normalization scales down the vector of incoming weights to the allowed length. The objective (or direction to objective) of original optimization problem is changed when using weight decay (or max normalization). Moreover, they bring additional hyper parameters that should be carefully preset.

Batch normalization [2] uses statistics calculated from mini-batch training examples to normalize the pre-activation. The normalized value is re-scaled and re-shifted using additional parameters. Since batch normalization uses the statistics on mini-batch examples, its effect is dependent on the mini-batch size. To overcome this problem, normalization propagation [10] uses a data-independent parametric estimate of mean and standard deviation, while layer normalization [6] computes the mean and standard deviation from the layer on a single training case. Weight normalization [7] re-parameterizes the incoming weight vector by dividing its norm. It decouples the length of weight vector from its direction, thus partially bounds the result of dot product. But it does not consider the length of input vector. These methods all bring additional parameters to be learned, thus make the model more complex.

An important source of inspiration for our work is cosine similarity, which is widely used in data mining and machine learning [8, 9]. To thoroughly bound dot product, a straight-forward idea is to use cosine similarity. We combine cosine similarity with neural network, and the details will be described in the next section.

3   Methods

3.1   Cosine Normalization

To decrease the variance of neuron, we propose a new method, called cosine normalization, which simply uses cosine similarity instead of dot product in neural network. Cosine normalization bounds the pre-activation between -1 and 1. The result could be even smaller when the dimension is high. As a result, the variance can be controlled within a very narrow range. A simple multi-layer neural network is shown in Fig. 1. Using cosine normalization, the output of hidden unit is computed by Eq. 4, where net_{norm} is the normalized pre-activation, w is the incoming weight vector and x is the input vector, f is nonlinear activation function.

$$o = f(net_{norm}) = f(\cos \theta) = f\left(\frac{w \bullet x}{|w||x|}\right) \tag{4}$$

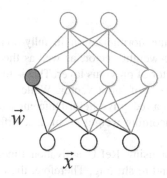

Fig. 1. A simple neural network with cosine normalization. The output of hidden unit is the nonlinear transform of cosine similarity between input vector and incoming weight vector.

We use gradient descent (back propagation) to train the neural network with cosine normalization. Comparing to batch normalization, cosine normalization does not depend on any statistics on batch or mini-batch examples, so the model can be trained by both batch gradient descent and stochastic gradient descent. The procedure of back propagation in neural network with cosine normalization is the same as ordinary neural network except the derivative of net_{norm} with respect to w or x.

To show the derivative conveniently, the cosine normalization can be rewritten as Eq. 5. Then, the derivative of net_{norm} with respect to w_i or x_i can be calculated by Eq. 6 or Eq. 7.

$$net_{norm} = \cos\theta = \frac{\sum_i (w_i x_i)}{\sqrt{\sum_i w_i^2}\sqrt{\sum_i x_i^2}} \tag{5}$$

$$\frac{\partial net_{norm}}{\partial w_i} = \frac{x_i}{\sqrt{\sum_i w_i^2}\sqrt{\sum_i x_i^2}} - \frac{w_i \sum_i (w_i x_i)}{\left(\sum_i w_i^2\right)^3 \sum_i x_i^2} \tag{6}$$

$$\frac{\partial net_{norm}}{\partial x_i} = \frac{w_i}{\sqrt{\sum_i w_i^2}\sqrt{\sum_i x_i^2}} - \frac{x_i \sum_i (w_i x_i)}{\left(\sum_i x_i^2\right)^3 \sum_i w_i^2} \tag{7}$$

As pointed in [11], centering the inputs of units can help the training of neural networks. Batch or layer normalization centers the data by subtracting the mean of batch or layer, while mean-only batch normalization can enhance the performance of weight normalization [7]. We can use Pearson Correlation Coefficient (PCC), which is centered cosine similarity as shown Eq. 8, to extend cosine normalization, where μ_w is the mean of w and μ_x is the mean of x.

$$net_{norm} = \frac{(w - \mu_w) \bullet (x - \mu_x)}{|w - \mu_w||x - \mu_x|} \tag{8}$$

3.2   Implementation

When implementing of cosine normalization in fully-connected nets, we just need divide the norm of incoming weight vector, as well as the norm of input vector. The input vector is the output vector of previous layer. That is to say, the hidden units in the same layer have the same norm of input vector. While in the convolutional nets, the input vector is constrained in a receptive field. Different receptive fields have different input norms, but the same incoming weight norm since different receptive fields share the same weight.

Empirically, we find that using ReLU activation function, the result of normalization needs no re-scaling and re-shifting. Therefore, there is no additional parameter to be learned or hyper-parameter to be preset. However, when using other activation functions, like Sigmoid, Tanh, or Softmax, the result of normalization should be re-scaled and re-shifted to fully utilize the non-linear regime of the functions.

One thing should be noticed is that cosine similarity can only measure the similarity between two non-zero vectors, since denominator can not be zero. Non-zero bias can be added to avoid the situation of vector of zero. Let $w = [w_1, w_2, \ldots, w_i]$, and $x = [x_1, x_2, \ldots, x_i]$. After adding bias, then w becomes $[w_0, w_1, w_2, \ldots, w_i]$, and x becomes $[x_0, x_1, x_2, \ldots, x_i]$, where w_0 and x_0 should be non-zero.

As mentioned above, cosine normalization makes the pre-activation within a very narrow range. As a result, when using non ReLU activation functions, e.g. Sigmoid, Tanh, or Softmax, the result of normalization should use larger re-scaling coefficient to fully utilize the non-linear regime of the functions. Besides, as shown in Eqs. 6 and 7, the magnitudes of derivatives are much smaller since they are also divided by the length of w and x. Therefore, we need larger learning rate to train the network with ReLU activation when the result of normalization do not re-scale and re-shift.

4   Experiments

In this section, we compare our cosine normalization and centered cosine normalization (PCC) with batch, weight and layer normalization in fully-connected neural networks on the MNIST and 20NEWS GROUP data sets. Additionally, convolutional networks with different normalization are evaluated on the CIFAR-10, CIFAR-100 and SVHN data sets.

4.1   Fully-Connected Networks

There are two data sets used in this section. (1) MNIST. The MNIST [12] data set consists of 28×28 pixel handwritten digit black and white images. The task is to classify the images into 10 digit classes. There are 60, 000 training images and 10, 000 test images in the MNIST data set. We scale the pixel values to the [0, 1] range before inputting to our models. (2) 20NEWS GROUP. The original training set contains 11269 text documents, and the test set contains 7505 text documents. Each document is classified into one topic out of 20. For convenience of using mini-batch gradient descent, 69 examples in training set and 5 examples in test set are randomly dropped.

As a result, there are 11200 training examples and 7500 test examples in our experiments. The words, of which document frequency is larger than 5, are used as the input features. There are 21567 feature dimensions finally. Then, the model of Term Frequency-Inverse Document Frequency (TF-IDF) is used to transform the text documents into vectors. After that, each feature is re-scaled to the range of [0, 1].

A fully-connected neural network which has two hidden layers is used in experiments of MNIST and 20NEWS GROUP. Each hidden layer has 1000 units. The last layer is the Softmax classification layer with 10-class for MNIST, and 20-class for 20NEWS GROUP. ReLU activation function is used in the hidden layers. All weights are randomly initialized by truncated normal distribution with 0 mean and 0.1 variance. Mini-batch gradient descent is used to train the networks. The batch size is 100. In our experiments, we use no re-scaling and re-shifting after normalization for hidden layers which use ReLU activation. However, for the last layer, we re-scale the normalized values before inputting to Softmax. The learning rate of the cosine normalization, centered cosine normalization (PCC), batch normalization, weight normalization, layer normalization is 10, 10, 1, 1, 1, respectively in our experiments. No any regularization, dropout, or dynamic learning rate is used. We train the fully-connected nets with 200 epochs since the performances are not improved anymore.

The results of test error for MNIST are shown in Fig. 2. As we can see, the converging speeds for different normalization techniques are close. That observation is also true for other data sets we will present next. That is to say, cosine normalization can accelerate the training of networks as well as other normalization. We can also observe that centered cosine normalization (Pearson Correlation Coefficient) and cosine normalization achieve similar test errors, and which are slightly better than layer normalization. Centered cosine normalization achieves the lowest mean of test error 1.39%, while cosine and layer normalization achieve 1.40%, 1.43% respectively. Weight normalization has the highest test error 1.65 comparing to other normalization. Although batch normalization gets lowest test error at some point, it causes large

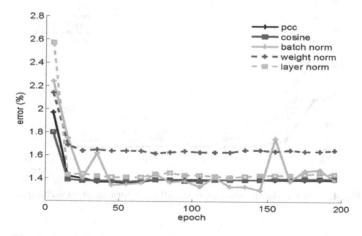

Fig. 2. The MNIST test errors of different normalization techniques.

variance of test error as training continues. Large fluctuation of batch normalization is caused by the change of statistics on different mini-batch examples.

The results for 20NEWS GROUP are shown in Fig. 3. Centered cosine normalization achieves the lowest test error 29.37%, and cosine normalization achieves the second lowest test error 31.73%. The batch normalization performs poorly in this task of high dimensional text classification. It only achieves 43.94% test error. Weight normalization (33.55%) and layer normalization (33.29%) achieve close performances. Both batch and weight normalization have larger variances of test error than other normalization.

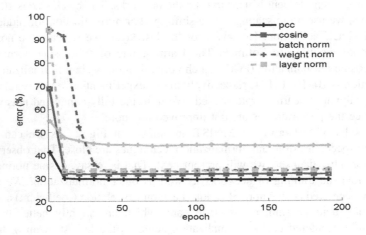

Fig. 3. The 20NEWS test errors of different normalization techniques

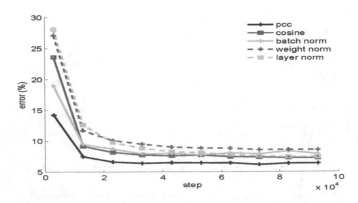

Fig. 4. The CIFAR-10 test errors of different normalization techniques.

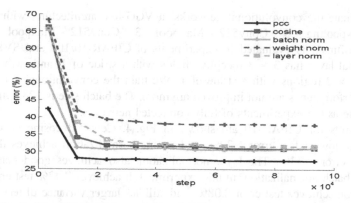

Fig. 5. The CIFAR-100 test errors of different normalization techniques.

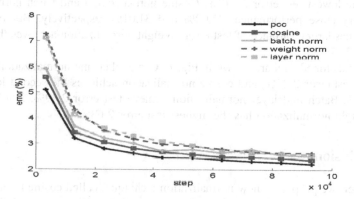

Fig. 6. The SVHN test errors of different normalization techniques.

4.2 Convolutional Networks

In this section, convolutional networks with different normalization are evaluated on the CIFAR-10, CIFAR-100 and SVHN data sets. (1) CIFAR-10/100. CIFAR-10 [13] is a data set of natural 32×32 RGB images in 10-classes with 50,000 images for training and 10,000 for testing. CIFAR-100 is similar with CIFAR-10 but with 100 classes. To augment data, the images are cropped to 24×24 pixels, centrally for evaluation or randomly for training. Then, a series of random distortions are applied: (a) randomly flip the image from left to right, (b) randomly distort the image brightness, (c) randomly distort the image contrast. The procedure of augmentation is the same as CIFAR-10 example in Tensorflow [14]. (2) SVHN. The Street View House Numbers (SVHN) [15] dataset includes 604,388 images (both training set and extra set) and 26,032 testing images. Similar to MNIST, the goal is to classify the digit centered in each 32×32 RGB image. We augment the data using the same procedure as CIFAR-10/100 mentioned above.

To evaluate the convolutional networks, a VGG-like architecture, with 3 * Conv512 - Maxpooling - 3 * Conv512 - Maxpool - 3 * Conv512 - Maxpool - 2 * Fully1000 - Softmax, is evaluated in experiments of CIFAR-10/100 and SVHN. Each convolutional layer has 3×3 receptive fields with a stride of 1, and each max pool layer has 2×2 regions with a stride of 1. We train the convolutional nets 105 step since the performances are not improved anymore. The batch size is 128. Other setups are the same as the experiments of fully-connected networks.

The results for CIFAR-10 are shown in Fig. 4. Centered cosine normalization achieves the lowest test error 6.39%, and cosine normalization achieves the second lowest test error 7.33%. The layer normalization also achieves good performance, better than batch normalization, in this experiment. It achieves 7.42% test error. Batch normalization achieves test error 8.08%, and still has larger variance of test error than other normalization. Weight normalization achieves the highest test error 8.55%.

The results for CIFAR-100 are shown in Fig. 5. Centered cosine normalization achieves the lowest test error 27.49%. Cosine normalization and batch normalization achieve very close performance, 31.02% and 31.01% respectively. But batch normalization has larger variance of test error. Weight normalization achieves the highest test error 37.87%.

The results for SVHN are shown in Fig. 6. Centered cosine normalization achieves the lowest test error 2.22%, and cosine normalization achieves the second lowest test error 2.34%. Batch and layer normalization achieve test error 2.49%, 2.58% respectively. Weight normalization has the highest test error 2.63%.

5   Conclusions

In this paper, we propose a new normalization technique, called cosine normalization, which uses cosine similarity or centered cosine similarity, Pearson correlation coefficient, instead of dot product in neural networks. Cosine normalization bounds the preactivation of neuron within a narrower range, thus makes lower variance of neurons. Moreover, cosine normalization makes the model more robust for different input magnitude. Networks with cosine normalization can be trained using back propagation. It does not depend on any statistics on batch or mini-batch examples, and performs the same computation in forward propagation at training and inference times. We evaluate cosine normalization on the fully-connected networks, convolutional networks and recurrent networks on various data sets. Experiments show that cosine normalization and centered cosine normalization (PCC) achieve better performance than other normalization techniques.

References

1. Hochreiter, S., Bengio, Y., Frasconi, P., Schmidhuber, J.: Gradient flow in recurrent nets: the difficulty of learning long-term dependencies (2001)
2. Ioffe, S., Szegedy, C.: Batch normalization: accelerating deep network training by reducing internal covariate shift. In: Proceedings of the 32nd International Conference on Machine Learning, pp. 448–456 (2015)

3. Krogh, A., Hertz, J.A.: A simple weight decay can improve generalization. In: NIPS, vol. 4, pp. 950–957 (1991)
4. Srebro, N., Shraibman, A.: Rank, trace-norm and max-norm. In: Auer, P., Meir, R. (eds.) COLT 2005. LNCS (LNAI), vol. 3559, pp. 545–560. Springer, Heidelberg (2005). https:// doi.org/10.1007/11503415_37
5. Srivastava, N., Hinton, G.E., Krizhevsky, A., Sutskever, I., Salakhutdinov, R.: Dropout: a simple way to prevent neural networks from overfitting. J. Mach. Learn. Res. **15**(1), 1929–1958 (2014)
6. Ba, J.L., Kiros, J.R., Hinton, G.E.: Layer normalization. arXiv preprint arXiv:1607.06450 (2016)
7. Salimans, T., Kingma, D.P.: Weight normalization: a simple reparameterization to accelerate training of deep neural networks. In: Advances in Neural Information Processing Systems, p. 901 (2016)
8. Tan, P.N., et al.: Introduction to Data Mining. Pearson Education India, London (2006)
9. Singhal, A.: Modern information retrieval: a brief overview. IEEE Data Eng. Bull. **24**(4), 35–43 (2001)
10. Arpit, D., Zhou, Y., Kota, B.U., Govindaraju, V.: Normalization propagation: a parametric technique for removing internal covariate shift in deep networks. arXiv preprint arXiv:1603. 01431 (2016)
11. LeCun, Y.A., Bottou, L., Orr, G.B., Müller, K.-R.: Efficient BackProp. In: Montavon, G., Orr, G.B., Müller, K.-R. (eds.) Neural Networks: Tricks of the Trade. LNCS, vol. 7700, pp. 9–48. Springer, Heidelberg (2012). https://doi.org/10.1007/978-3-642-35289-8_3
12. LeCun, Y., Bottou, L., Bengio, Y., Haffner, P.: Gradient-based learning applied to document recognition. Proc. IEEE **86**(11), 2278–2324 (1998)
13. Krizhevsky, A., Hinton, G.: Learning multiple layers of features from tiny images (2009)
14. Abadi, M., et al.: Tensorflow: large-scale machine learning on heterogeneous distributed systems. arXiv preprint arXiv:1603.04467 (2016)
15. Netzer, Y., Wang, T., Coates, A., Bissacco, A., Wu, B., Ng, A.Y.: Reading digits in natural images with unsupervised feature learning. In: NIPS Workshop on Deep Learning and Unsupervised Feature Learning, vol. 2011, p. 5 (2011)

Discovering Thermoelectric Materials Using Machine Learning: Insights and Challenges

Mandar V. Tabib[1]([✉]), Ole Martin Løvvik[2]([✉]), Kjetil Johannessen[1],
Adil Rasheed[1], Espen Sagvolden[2], and Anne Marthine Rustad[1]

[1] SINTEF Digital, Mathematics and Cybernetics, Trondheim, Norway
Mandar.Tabib@sintef.no
[2] SINTEF Industry, Sustainable Energy Technology, Oslo, Norway
OleMartin.Lovvik@sintef.no

Abstract. This work involves the use of combined forces of data-driven machine learning models and high fidelity density functional theory for the identification of new potential thermoelectric materials. The traditional method of thermoelectric material discovery from an almost limitless search space of chemical compounds involves expensive and time consuming experiments. In the current work, the density functional theory (DFT) simulations are used to compute the descriptors (features) and thermoelectric characteristics (labels) of a set of compounds. The DFT simulations are computationally very expensive and hence the database is not very exhaustive. With an anticipation that the important features can be learned by machine learning (ML) from the limited database and the knowledge could be used to predict the behavior of any new compound, the current work adds knowledge related to (a) understanding the impact of selection of influence of training/test data, (b) influence of complexity of ML algorithms, and (c) computational efficiency of combined DFT-ML methodology.

Keywords: Machine learning · Density functional theory
Thermoelectric · Material screening · Discovery

1 Introduction

Thermoelectric (TE) materials are receiving wide attention due to their potential role in mitigating global greenhouse effects as they enable conversion of waste heat energy directly to electrical energy. Currently, the three approaches to find better thermoelectric material involve: (a) traditional experimental approach, (b) physics based computational approach like Density Functional Theory (DFT), and (c) recent machine learning (ML) based data-driven approach. Amongst these, the machine learning approach has shown some success in finding new chemistries (that are capable of being thermoelectric) but it is a nascent application area with limited published work. There are certain limitations with

© Springer Nature Switzerland AG 2018
V. Kůrková et al. (Eds.): ICANN 2018, LNCS 11139, pp. 392–401, 2018.
https://doi.org/10.1007/978-3-030-01418-6_39

all the approaches, like: (a) The traditional experimental approaches are not efficient way of exploring new unknown chemistries and they focus mostly on modifying known material compounds by doping and nano-structuring to make these known thermoelectric materials better, while, (b) high fidelity physics based models like DFT are computationally prohibitive to use, and (c) for ML, obtaining bountiful data is an expensive process. ML models need to be able to generalize well, and learn patterns well enough from a small pool of available training data to be able to search for new potential materials in the vast expense of search-space of unknown materials. The current work aims to contribute to the field of machine learning and material screening by understanding influence of limited dataset, and whether it can be mitigated by studying: (a) influence of training-test split in model development, (b) influence of model selection and (c) by applying a framework combining data-driven machine learning models with physics-based density functional theory (DFT) to identify potential thermoelectric materials using a metric called 'figure of merit'. DFT enables generation of training data for ML, and a trained ML is expected to save time in finding potential material in the vast material search-space. The main objectives of this work can be enumerated as:

1. In the limited dataset scenario: understand the influence of training/test compound selection on ML predictions.
2. Combine data-driven models with physics-driven models to mitigate limited dataset scenarios, and understanding efficiency of this approach in identifying potential thermoelectric materials.
3. Compare the performance of the two ML algorithms: Random Forest (RF) and Deep Neural Network (DNN) for the limited dataset scenario.

2   Methodology and Data

This is treated as a regression problem, where the ML model learns to predict the figure of merit (ZT) values of a given compound at a given temperature and at a given chemical potential state. The performance of a material as a thermoelectric material is evaluated using this ZT. A material with a high ZT is supposed to be a good thermoelectric material. The ZT is a function of Seebeck coefficient, temperature, electrical conductivity, the electronic thermal conductivity, and lattice thermal conductivity. Previous research on thermoelectric materials involving machine learning did not use ZT as a characteristics, instead, it used the key properties in a stand-alone way (i.e. band gap, Seebeck coefficient, etc.). The three key components needed for developing the methodology are described next: (a) Data: data for model development (cross-validation/training data), for model testing (hidden test data) and for model application (search-space data to look for potential materials), (b) Descriptors (features), and (c) Choice of ML algorithms. These three components are discussed next:

2.1 Descriptors

Descriptors (known as features in ML community) are the characteristics of materials (e.g., crystal structure, chemical formula, etc.) that might correlate with material's properties of interest (ZT). Here, we use 50 features (descriptors or independent variables) for a given data-point. The features involve both numerical variables and categorical variables (crystal shape). The list of 50 features used are: temperature, chemical potential - eV, elements in cell, mean and variance of atomic mass, atomic radius, electronegativity, valence electrons, a set of features related to periodic table (group numbers, row numbers,electronic configurations), 6 one-hot encoded features for crystal shape ('tetragonal', 'trigonal', 'orthorhombic', 'cubic', 'monoclinic', 'triclinic', 'hexagonal').

2.2 Data

Limited Data Scenario: The dataset is deemed limited in this work because based on the available training dataset of just 115 compounds (having about 87,975 instances/data points with known ZT values), the trained ML model has to learn to predict potential compounds (i.e. ZT values) in a vast chemical search-space of 4800 compound (having 2,40,312 data-points). The compounds in training dataset will be different than the compounds in the chemical search-space.

Data Generation and DFT: It is time-consuming to generate dataset using experiments. Here, the database is generated using high-fidelity physics-driven DFT followed by semi-classical Boltzmann theory. The DFT is a computational quantum mechanical modeling method used to investigate the electronic structure (principally the ground state) of many-body systems, in particular atoms, molecules, and the condensed phases. Using this theory, the properties of a system can be determined by using functionals, i.e. functions of the spatially dependent electron density. Boltzmann theory helps to estimate the Boltzmann transport properties of candidate materials (like, Seebeck Coefficient, thermal conductivity, electrical conductivity) based on DFT-predicted band structures. The ZT for each compound is then computed using these transport properties. The ZT values of about 115 materials (compounds) have been generated. A database of about 87,975 instances (datapoints) comprising of 115 compounds materials has been created, as each compound material is studied over 15 temperature levels and over 51 chemical potential states. Thus, the number of datapoints are $115 \times 51 \times 15 = 87,975$. Each instance (or data-point) has 50 features associated with it. Thus, the input data matrix for building ML model is $87,975 \times 50$ - which is to be divided into training data (training and validation sets) and test data set.

Uniqueness in Splitting the Training and Test Dataset: We do not randomly split the 87,975 datapoints into training and test dataset. The dataset is split so that ML model is trained on certain compounds and the model is tested on unseen compounds. About 85% of data-set (about 98 compounds - a dataset of $74,970 \times 50$) is used for model building through both training and validation sets, and 15% of dataset (about 17 compounds - a dataset of $13,005 \times 50$) is to test the model. Since, the purpose is to test the generalization ability of the ML model to discover new chemical species - so, we looked at whether the ML model trained on 98 compounds can help to predict the ZT values of the unseen 17 compounds. Hence, sensitivity of selection of compounds into training and test data needs to be checked. This is checked by creating 3 cases of train/test split data:

1. Case 1. Test/train split. Randomly selecting 17 compounds in test (corresponding to 13,005 datapoints) and 98 compounds in train (corresponding to 74,970 datapoints) (with random seed 0.2).
2. Case 2. Test/train split. Randomly selecting 17 compounds in test and 98 compounds in train (with random seed 0.4). A different random selection gives different sets of compounds in train/test than case 1.
3. Case 3. Deterministically selecting Test and train compound. Out of the 115 compound database, a chunk of 17 compounds lying in the middle have been selected as test data. These 17 compounds in the middle do not possess extreme characteristics (like either being too simple compound or too complex compound, which are represented in the values of features associated with the compound), while the training data encompasses all types of compound. Here, by *complex compounds*, we refer to compounds with more than 3 elements.

Search-Space Data: For screening and discovering potential thermoelectric materials, the trained machine learning model has been applied on database of silicides (silica based compounds). This database is extracted from the material science project, and is called chemical search-space data set in this work. The search-space data-matrix size is: 2,40,312 data instance $\times$ 50 features.

2.3 Choice of Algorithms

Here, two different algorithms have been tested: Random Forest [1] and a more complex Deep Neural Network [2]. This work is intended to understand whether with the limited dataset, a complex model can perform well or not.

2.4 Model Selection - Cross Validation and Learning Curve

The two machine learning models have been compared using the cross-validation (CV) method. CV is a model validation technique for assessing the generalization ability of a machine learning algorithm to an independent data set. In our work, we split the original dataset into the 'training' and the 'test' dataset. Here, we have selected a *3-fold CV* procedure, where the 'training set' is split further into

3 different smaller sets. The model prediction is learned using 2 of these 3 folds at a time, and the 3rd fold that is left out is used for validation (called validation set). The average R2 (coefficient of determination) score from 3-fold CV is used as performance measure accuracy. Best possible R2 score is 1.0 suggesting a model with high accuracy and the score can be negative if the model performs badly. The learning curve helps to obtain the best parameter sets for the two models using the above CV process. In Fig. 1, we use CV procedure to obtain a learning curve. The curve shows the variation of average R2 score with training data and validation data (for RF) and variation of average R2 score with increasing epochs (iteration) for DNN. These curves help in understanding the bias-variance tradeoff. The learning curve (in Fig. 1) is shown for only case (case 3), and for only the best parameter sets of case 3 (for brevity). For case 3, the best parameter sets are: *RF*: Maximum number of trees - 30. The maximum depth of the tree is 20. *DNN*: The network used in this work comprises of an input layer (with 50 neurons representing the 50 input feature), an output layer and six hidden layers (comprising of following number of units in each successive layer: 43; 20; 20; 15; 10; 5 respectively). A combination of ReLU and Tanh activation functions are used in this work.

The learning curve (in Fig. 1) suggests some over-fitting for both the models; which is more dominant in the case of DNN compared to the RF model. This could be attributed to the need for larger data needed by DNN models. The R2 score on training data for both RF and DNN are in the range of 0.95–1, while, for the validation data (called test in DNN figure here), the R2 scores fall drastically in case of DNN to R2 = 0.45, while, the R2 scores falls slightly to 0.985 for RF. The overfitting (variance errors) is seen in other cases too (case 1 and case 2, but these learning curves are not shown here for brevity). The influence of 3 different train-test split on the performance of two ML models is considered next. It needs to be seen whether proper selection of training compound-test compound split can mitigate the overfitting and improve generalization ability of ML models.

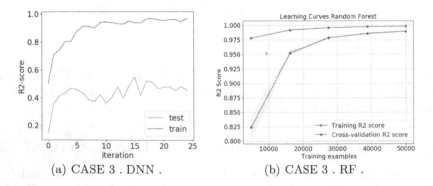

(a) CASE 3 . DNN .   (b) CASE 3 . RF .

Fig. 1. Judging bias (underfitting) vs variance (overfitting) errors for RF and complex DNN models for the two cases

3   Results and Discussion

Material screening is challenging in the sense that using the available limited database of known chemistry, the trained ML model should have learned the ability to find new potential material characteristics in new unseen chemistry in the vast material search-space. It is important to understand whether the way to split the limited material database into training dataset (training and validation dataset) and testing dataset (of unseen compounds) will influence the performance of the two machine learning models (simple RF or complex DNN).

3.1   Sensitivity Study: Influence of Training and Testing Dataset Selection

Figure 2 shows the influence of splitting the training/test data on the performance of models for the three cases. For each case, the Fig. 2 shows the predicted ZT values vis-a-vis the actual ZT values for the compounds in training and test data by the two models (RF and DNN). Results for the 3 cases show:

Case 1 and Case 2 (Comparing R2 Scores on Train and Test Data by the Two Models): Both cases have randomly generated but different sets of 98 compounds for training and 18 compounds in test.

DNN Performance: R2 score for case 1 drops to 0.2; while, the corresponding case 1 train R2 score is 0.97. Similarly, case 2 test R2 score drops to −0.14; while, the corresponding case 2 train R2 score is 0.97. The large drop in R2 scores for test indicates poorer generalization ability for DNN.

RF Performance: In case of RF too, R2 scores drop for the two test dataset, but its performance is much better than the DNN. For RF, the Case 1 test R2 score is 0.82; while the corresponding case 1 train R2 score is 0.99. Similarly, Case 2 test R2 score drops to 0.23; while the corresponding case 2 train R2 score of 0.99.

Thus, for both RF and DNN, as the split of train/test varies, the generalization ability is influenced (despite selecting the best parameter set of the respective model for that database during CV). The reason for lower R2 scores in case 2 test dataset (for both the models) as compared to their case 1 test scores is that the 98 randomly selected compounds in case 2 training dataset with their features (a dataset of $74,970 \times 50$) do not provide similar pattern characteristics (i.e. variation of ZT with features) as in the 17 compound case2-test dataset (a dataset of $13,004 \times 50$).

Case 3 (Comparing R2 Scores on Train and Test Data): Case 3 involves 98 training compounds that encompasses both simple and extreme compounds, and hence the models trained on it are able to capture the pattern to enable determination of ZT values of data-points pertaining to the 17 unseen test compounds. That is why we see improved predictions by the DNN and RF model on the case 3-test dataset: *DNN* shows a case 3-test R2 score of 0.45; while corresponding case 3 train R2 score is 0.96.

RF shows a case 3 test R2 score of 0.76; while corresponding case 3 train R2 score of 0.99.

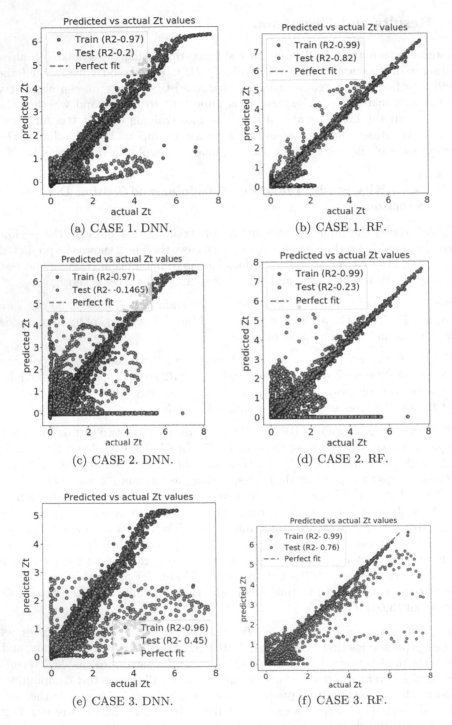

Fig. 2. Predicted vs actual ZT (with R2-score) for DNN and RF on training and unseen test data for the three cases.

Next, we check whether the improvements in generalization ability (better test R2 scores) brought about by balanced training-test split leads to better predictions of material in both models?.

3.2   Comparison of RF vs. DNN Models: Material Screening and Efficiency

Searching for Potential Thermoelectric in New Search-Space: Figure 3 shows the best two thermoelectric materials identified in a new chemical search-space of silicide materials of 4800 compounds for the 3 cases. For brevity, only top two are shown in Fig. 3 but the results explained are beyond the best two predicted. This chemical search-space has not been exposed to the ML models during their training/validation/testing phase. In all the figures, the predicted *figure of merit* (ZT) is plotted against one of the most influential features (chemical potential - eV). These six compounds below have the highest predicted ZT values as obtained by DNN and RF.

The RF is mostly predicting comparatively simpler compounds than the DNN with maximum value of ZT in the range of 3–3.6. RF has predicted only simple compounds (such as Li2MgSi, SrMgSi, BeSilr2, SiP2O7, VSiPt) as potential thermoelectric silicides in its top two predictions. While, DNN is predicting complex compounds (with more than 3 elements) in about 66% of the top two predictions (with compounds such as Sr2AI3Si3HO13 in case 1, LiCoSiO4 in case 2, and Na3CaAI3Si3SO16 and Na3VSiBO7 in case 3) with higher maximum value of ZT in range 4–5. Both DNN and RF have identified a common thermoelectric silicide (BeSilr2) as potential candidate but predict a different maximum ZT value (RF predicts ZT of 3.5, while DNN predicts around $ZT = 4.5$).

DNN is learning complex patterns than RF and predicting higher ZT values due to overfitting (higher variance error) as observed in previous fits in Fig. 2. Further, DNN is predicting erroneous profile of Zt as a function of chemical potential (Fig. 3(c) left, and (e) both) as they are not physically realistic. Thus, the split in training data is not benefitting DNN. The solution for overfitting in DNN is to either build artificial neural network (ANN) models with simpler architecture or to generate a larger training dataset.

Since the intention of this paper was to gain knowledge about possible behavior of DNN in current material screening applications (where most have limited dataset), so simpler ANN models were not shown in this work. DNN despite being the most popular model today does not work when dataset is limited.

Validation of Selecting Training/Test Dataset and Model Selection: In the literature, currently the materials of the form Mg2LiSi are under investigation [3]. Li2MgSi is the closest form that has been predicted by RF in the balanced Case 3 training/test dataset. This work shows the importance of balancing training/test dataset when the dataset is limited and when, the trained model has to have good generalization ability so as to find materials in new chemical space. Most of the complex compounds predicted by DNN are not possible to test experimentally in lab, but the overfitting seen in DNN performance

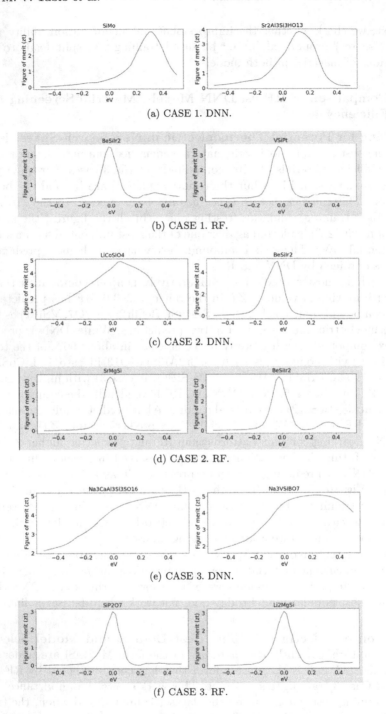

(a) CASE 1. DNN.

(b) CASE 1. RF.

(c) CASE 2. DNN.

(d) CASE 2. RF.

(e) CASE 3. DNN.

(f) CASE 3. RF.

Fig. 3. DNN vs RF (shaded) predicted best two thermoelectric materials for the three cases. eV refers to chemical potential on the horizontal axis. DNN suggests more complex compounds as compared to the Random Forest.

suggests that it is better not to pursue those complex models (as the results may not be reliable).

Computational Efficiency: For DFT alone, the CPU consumption is between 25 and 1500 h to evaluate Z_T value of a composition (compound), and the average CPU time per compound is 85 h for finding Zt of material. It would take around 4,08,000 CPU hrs for discovering the material with best ZT amongst the 4800 compound chemical search-space. For ML step alone, the computation cost for obtaining Zt values of about 4800 compounds, after getting trained on dataset of 115 compounds is: 132 s for DNN and 80 s for RF. The cost of preparing training base for these 115 compounds from DFT could be around = 85 h per compound × 115 compounds =9775 h. Thus, we can neglect the 132 s from DNN and 80 s of RF with respect to the 9775 h required to generate the training database. Thus, the total cost for evaluating Zt using ML approach for 4800 compounds is **just 2% of time** needed by the DFT-alone method.

4   Conclusions

1. In limited dataset scenario: RF has lesser variance error than DNN and is seen to predict potentially simpler compounds from the search-space data than the DNN model. DNN predicts complex compounds from search-space data (that are difficult to make in lab and verify). Further, DNN sometimes shows physically unrealistic Zt profile prediction due to overfitting and the solution to this is that only more data can make the DNN better.
2. Significant influence of training-test split on the model is seen despite using CV procedure to select the best model parameters for generalization. Hence, when dataset is limited - this aspect should be checked. Amongst the three cases (two random and one deterministic train-test split), the variances error lowered for the case where training data could encompass compounds with extreme features. The RF model also provided the 'verifiable' predicted potential thermochemical in search-space (Li2MgSi) from this balanced deterministic train-test dataset, but this strategy did not benefit DNN.
3. Combined DFT and machine learning approach with RF is computationally efficient than an approach involving DFT alone.

Acknowledgment. We would like to thank SINTEF Foundation for the internal SEP funding for enabling the methodology development.

References

1. Breiman, L.: Random forests. Mach. Learn. **45**(1), 5–32 (2001)
2. Lecun, Y., Bengio, Y., Hinton, G.: Deep learning. Nature **521**(7553), 436–444 (2015)
3. Nieroda, P., Kolezynski, A., Oszajca, M., Milczarek, J., Wojciechowski, T.: Structural and thermoelectric properties of polycrystalline p-type Mg2-x LixSi. J. Electron. Mater. **45**, 3418 (2016)

Auto-tuning Neural Network Quantization Framework for Collaborative Inference Between the Cloud and Edge

Guangli Li[1,2], Lei Liu[1]($\boxtimes$), Xueying Wang[1,2], Xiao Dong[1,2], Peng Zhao[1,2], and Xiaobing Feng[1]

[1] State Key Laboratory of Computer Architecture,
Institute of Computing Technology, Chinese Academy of Sciences, Beijing, China
{liguangli,liulei,wangxueying,dongxiao,zhaopeng,fxb}@ict.ac.cn
[2] University of Chinese Academy of Sciences, Beijing, China

Abstract. Recently, deep neural networks (DNNs) have been widely applied in mobile intelligent applications. The inference for the DNNs is usually performed in the cloud. However, it leads to a large overhead of transmitting data via wireless network. In this paper, we demonstrate the advantages of the cloud-edge collaborative inference with quantization. By analyzing the characteristics of layers in DNNs, an auto-tuning neural network quantization framework for collaborative inference is proposed. We study the effectiveness of mixed-precision collaborative inference of state-of-the-art DNNs by using ImageNet dataset. The experimental results show that our framework can generate reasonable network partitions and reduce the storage on mobile devices with trivial loss of accuracy.

Keywords: Neural network quantization · Auto-tuning framework
Edge computing · Collaborative inference

1 Introduction

In recent years, deep neural networks (DNNs) [14] are widely used and show impressive performance in various fields including computer vision [12], speech recongnition [9], natural language processing [15], etc. As the neural network architectures become more complex and deeper—from LeNet [13] (5 layers) to ResNet [8] (152 layers), the storage and computation of the model is increasing. In other words, it leads to more resource requirements for network training and inference. The large size of DNN models limits the applicability of the network inference on mobile edge devices. Therefore, most of artificial intelligence (AI) applications on mobile devices send input data of DNN to cloud servers, and the procedure of network inference is executed in the cloud only. However, the cloud-only inference has some assignable weaknesses: (1) transmission overhead:

© Springer Nature Switzerland AG 2018
V. Kůrková et al. (Eds.): ICANN 2018, LNCS 11139, pp. 402–411, 2018.
https://doi.org/10.1007/978-3-030-01418-6_40

it leads to a large overhead of uploading data especially when the mobile edge devices are in the low-bandwidth wireless environments. (2) privacy disclosure: sometimes, personal data, e.g. one's photos and videos, are not allowed to send to the cloud servers directly.

Today's mobile devices, such as Apple's iPhone and NVIDIA's Jetson TX2, have more powerful computability and larger memory. In addition, many neural network quantization methods [3,4,7,18,19] have been proposed for reducing the resource consumption of DNNs. By using quantization, the data of a network can be represented by low-precision values, e.g. INT8 (8-bit integer). On the one hand, low-precision data reduces storage of DNNs and enables network models to be stored on the mobile edge device with limited resources. On the other hand, with the use of high-performance libraries for low-precision computing [1,2], the speed of the network inference will be improved. This makes it possible to perform some or all parts of neural network inference on mobile devices and leads to a new inference mode: cloud-edge collaborative inference.

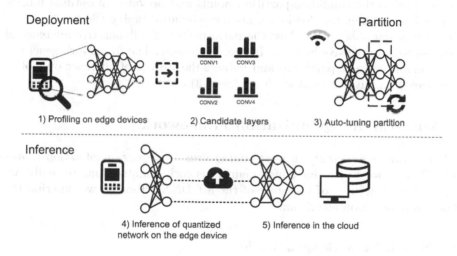

Fig. 1. Overview of auto-tuning framework

In this paper, we propose an auto-tuning neural network quantization framework as shown in Fig. 1. During deployment, the framework profiles the operators of DNNs on edge devices and generates the candidate layers as partition points. When the neural network is ready to be used, the framework starts auto-tuning for network partition. In the time of inference, the first part of the network is quantized and executed on the edge devices, and the second part of the network is executed in the cloud servers. On the edge, we use quantized neural network to reduce storage and computation. In the cloud, we use original full-precision network to achieve high accuracy.

In the collaborative inference, quantized neural networks can reduce the storage of models. Intermediate results of quantized networks are also low-precision data, which can reduce data communication between cloud and edge. So user's mobile device could transmit less data when using AI applications. Additionally, transmitting intermediate result data, rather than the original input data, can protect personal information. In realistic scenarios, the process of analysis and testing is tedious and time-consuming. It's unfriendly for a program developer to test and decide how to partition the network. Our automatic tuning framework will help developers find the most reasonable partition of a DNN. The contributions of this paper are summarized as follows:

- *Analysis of DNN partition points* – We analyze the structures of deep neural networks and show which layers are reasonable partition points. Based on the analysis, we could generate candidate layers as partition points of a specific neural network (Sect. 2.2)
- *Auto-tuning quantization framework for collaborative inference* – We develop an auto-tuning neural network quantization framework for collaborative inference between cloud and edge. The framework quantizes neural networks according to the candidate partition points and provides an optimal mixed-precision partition for cloud-edge inference by auto-tuning (Sect. 2.3).
- *Experimental study* – We show the performance of collaborative inference of state-of-the-art DNNs by using ImageNet dataset. The framework generates reasonable network partitions and reduces the storage of inference on mobile devices with trivial loss of accuracy (Sect. 3).

2   Auto-tuning Quantization Framework

In this section, we present our auto-tuning neural network quantization framework. Firstly, we briefly introduce neural network quantization. Secondly, we analyze the structures of the state-of-the-art DNNs. Finally, we describe the auto-tuning partition algorithm.

2.1   Neural Network Quantization

In order to accelerate inference and compress the size of DNN models, many network quantization methods are proposed. Some studies focus on scalar and vector quantization [4,7], while others center on fixed-point quantization [18,19]. In this paper, we are mainly interested in scalar quantization of INT8, which is supported by many advanced computing libraries such as Google's gemmlowp [1] and NVIDIA's cuDNN [2]. In general, an operator computation of scalar quantized neural networks can be summarized as follows:

- Off-line Quantization
  Step 1. Find quantization thresholds (T_{min} and T_{max}) for calculating scale factors of *Input*, *Weights* and *Output*;

Step 2. Quantize *Input* and *Weights* according to the following formula:

$$Data_Q(x) = \begin{cases} \dfrac{Data(x) - T_{min}}{|T_{max} - T_{min}|} \times Range_{LP} & x \in (T_{min}, T_{max}) \\ \|V_{low-precision}\|_\infty & x \geq T_{max} \\ \|V_{low-precision}\|_{-\infty} & x \leq T_{min} \end{cases} \tag{1}$$

where: $Range_{LP}$ is the range of low-precision values (e.g. 255 for INT8), $V_{low-precision}$ is the set of low-precision values, $Data(x)$ is the original value, $Data_Q(x)$ is the quantized value.

- On-device Computation

Step 1. $Output_Q = \text{Operator}(Input_Q, Weights_Q)$;

Step 2. Dequantize $Output_Q$ according to the following formula:

$$Output = \frac{|T_{max} - T_{min}|}{Range_{LP}} \times Output_Q(x) + T_{min} \tag{2}$$

Step 3. $Output = \text{ActivationFunction}(Output)$;

Step 4. Quantize *Output* as $Input_{Next}$ according to Formula 1.

2.2 Candidate Network Partition Points

In general, a deep neural network contains many kinds of layers such as convolution layers, fully-connected layers and activation layers. We analyze the characteristics of different network layers and decide how to select candidate layers as reasonable partition points. The set of candidate layers, $Rule = \{L_1, L_2, \ldots, L_n\}$, is based on the results of the following analysis.

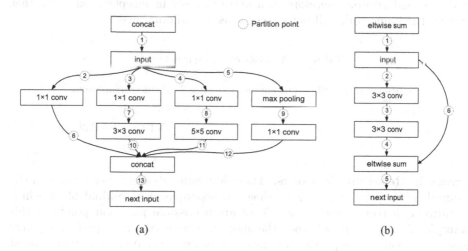

(a) (b)

Fig. 2. Partition points of DNNs

Table 1. Analysis of inception

Partition points	Brother branch exists?	Inference mode of the brother branch	Data transmission
1, 13	No	/	INT8 × 1
2, 3, 4, 5 7, 8, 9 6, 10, 11, 12	Yes	Mobile edge	INT8 × 4
2, 3, 4, 5 7, 8, 9 6, 10, 11, 12	Yes	Cloud	INT8 × 1 + FP32 × 1

Layers in Inception Networks. Inception is a structure that contains branches, and these branches are executed in parallel and their results are merged into a network layer (e.g. concat layer). Figure 2(a) is an example of inception from GoogLeNet [17]. As shown, the inception contains 13 possible partition points. If we try all the partition points, it will take a lot of time. We divide these partition points into two groups according to whether they have at least a brother branch (separate from the same layer and merge in the same layer). The results of the analysis are shown in Table 1. When a partition point has no brother branch (e.g. 1 and 13), the output of the sub-network on edge devices contains only 1 × INT8 Blob (4D array for storing data). When a partition point has a brother branch, there are two cases: (1) its brother branch runs on the edge devices, and the sub-network output contains 4 × INT8 Blobs; (2) its brother branch runs in the cloud, and the sub-network output contains 1 × INT8 Blob and 1 × FP32 Blob. The transmission data in first group is smaller than it is in the second group. Therefore, if a network layer in inception has a brother branch, the framework will not choose it as a candidate layer.

Table 2. Analysis of residual network

Partition points	Shortcut connection exists?	Data transmission
1, 5	No	INT8 × 1
2, 3, 4, 6	Yes	INT8 × 1 + FP32 × 1

Layers in Residual Networks. There are many shortcut connections in the residual network [8]. Figure 2(b) shows an example of a residual block which contains a shortcut connection. There are 6 possible partition points in this example. According to whether the shortcut connection of a partition points exists, we divide these partition points into two groups. When a partition point has no shortcut connection (e.g. 1 and 5), the output of the sub-network on edge devices contains only 1 × INT8 Blob. Otherwise, the output of the sub-network contains $1 \times$ INT8 Blob and $1 \times$ FP32 Blob. Table 2 shows the analysis result. Therefore, the network layers with shortcut connections are not reasonable candidate layers.

Non-parametric Layers. Non-parametric layers, such as ReLU and pooling, have no parameters, so they require almost no memory storage. In addition, the computation of the non-parametric layers accounts for a very small proportion of the total network computation. Therefore, our framework merges the non-parametric layers into the nearest previous parametric layers, i.e. these non-parametric layers will not be used as candidate layers.

2.3   Auto-Tuning Partition

According to the candidate rule *Rule*, the framework performs auto-tuning partition for cloud-edge collaborative inference, as described in Algorithm 1. The input of the algorithm contains candidate layer rules and a neural network. Firstly, candidate rules are used to select candidate partition points in the neural network (lines 1–2). Secondly, all candidate partition networks are tested, and the information of performance is recorded in P (lines 3–9). The function of *PredictPerformance* can predict the performance of collaborative inference based on the results of off-line profiling. Finally, we find the best partition point in P for collaborative inference of mixed-precision neural network (lines 10–14).

Algorithm 1. Auto-Tuning Partition

Input: candidate rules *Rule*, neural network $Net = \{L_1, L_2, \dots, L_n\}$
Output: optimize partition p_{best}

1 $P \leftarrow \Phi$; $p_{best} \leftarrow null$;
2 $Candidate \leftarrow \{L_i | L_i \in Rule\}$;
3 **for** L_i in $Candidate$ **do**
4 $\quad$ $Net_{edge} \leftarrow Net.Split(First, L_i)$;
5 $\quad$ $Net_{Cloud} \leftarrow Net.Split(L_i + 1, Last)$;
6 $\quad$ $Engine_{Edge} \leftarrow Net_{Edge}(DataType_{<INT8>})$;
7 $\quad$ $Engine_{Cloud} \leftarrow Net_{Cloud}(DataType_{<FP32>})$;
8 $\quad$ $(L_i, info) \leftarrow PredictPerformance(Engine_{Edge}, Engine_{Cloud})$;
9 $\quad$ $P \leftarrow P \cup (L_i, info)$;
10 $Env = GetEnvironment(Device_{Edge})$;
11 **for** p_i in P **do**
12 $\quad$ **if** $Env(p_i)$ is better than $Env(p_{best})$ **then**
13 $\quad\quad$ $p_{best} \leftarrow p_i$;
14 return p_{best};

---

3   Experiments

In this section, we use ImageNet [6] dataset to test the collaborative inference of DNNs [8,12,16,17] and show results of our auto-tuning framework. We illustrate the most reasonable partition for each neural network. The inference of the edge performs on a mobile platform – NVIDIA Jetson TX2 (NVIDIA's latest mobile SoC) – with 4 × ARM Cortex-A57 CPUs and 2 × Denver CPUs, 8G of RAM. The inference of the cloud performs on a server with Intel Core-i7 CPU, NVIDIA TITAN Xp GPU, 16G of RAM. We use Caffe [10] with cuDNN (version 7.0.5) on the GPU of cloud servers. We use gemmlowp's [1] implementation on the CPU of the edge devices.

3.1   Experimental Results

Table 3 summarizes the results of our framework. We tested AlexNet, VGG16, ResNet-18 and GoogLeNet in different wireless network environments. For each neural network, the framework gives the best partition point and the fastest partition point. According to the inference time and the speed-up in the table, we can see that sometimes the speed of collaborative inference is faster than that of the cloud inference only. This is due to the large transmission overhead in the low-bandwidth wireless environments. In collaborative inference, we only need to download the parameters required by the edge inference, which can significantly reduce the size of download data. If users need to achieve the fastest inference speed, the fastest partition point should be selected. If users need to avoid privacy disclosure, the best partition point should be selected. In addition, quantized neural networks do not lead to a significant drop in accuracy (usually less than 1%).

Table 3. Experimental results of our framework

Neural network	AlexNet	VGG16	ResNet-18	GoogLeNet
Wireless upload (KB/s)	250	240	70	180
Best partition point	conv5	conv1_2	res4a	conv2
Inference time (s)	0.36	5.65	1.86	1.16
Speed-up	1.7×	<1×	1.13×	<1×
Model download (KB)	2278	38	1569	121
Model storage reduction	96.17%	99.97%	85.63%	98.22%
TOP-1 accuracy↓	−0.09%	0.00%	−0.19%	−0.10%

Figure 3 shows the collaborative inference time of each candidate layer in the wireless network environments. We take AlexNet as an example. Each bar represents a network partition, which consists of three parts: edge inference, data upload and cloud inference. After auto-tuning of framework, conv5 layer is

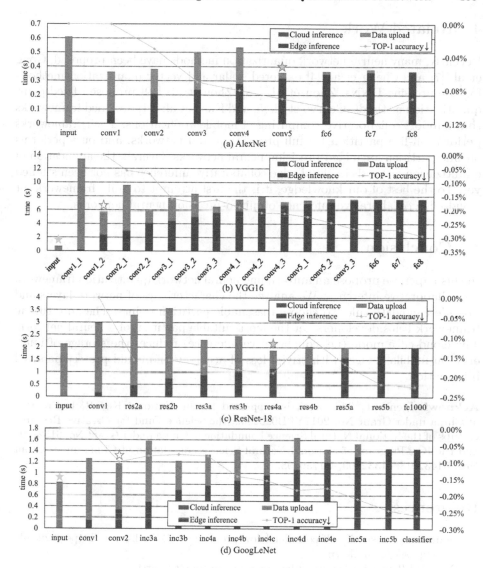

Fig. 3. Performance of each DNN partition

selected as the best partition point (marked with a hollow pentagram) and the fastest partition point (marked with a filled pentagram). On edge devices, we feed input data to the neural network and perform inference of layers from conv1 to conv5. The output data of conv5 (pool and relu are merged) is uploaded to the cloud, and then the inference of layers from fc6 to fc8 is executed in the cloud. The approach of collaborative inference achieves 1.7× speed-up. It can be seen that the accuracy drop of the network is trivial, and the largest accuracy loss in all partitions is only −0.11%.

4   Related Work

Recently, many neural network quantization methods have been proposed. Gong et al. [7] and Cheng et al. [4] explored scalar and vector quantization methods for compressing DNNs. Zhou et al. [18], Zhou et al. [19] proposed fixed-point quantization methods. Cuervo et al. [5] and Kang et al. [11] designed frameworks that support collaborative computing of mobile applications. Their frameworks perform off-line partition for full-precision neural networks, and ours performs on-line partition for mixed-precision neural networks. Overall, the application of quantization methods in cloud-edge collaborative inference has not been studied yet. To the best of our knowledge, it is the first attempt to build framework for cloud-edge collaborative inference of mixed-precision neural networks.

5   Conclusion

In this paper, we propose an auto-tuning neural network quantization framework for collaborative inference. We analyze the characteristics of network layers and provide candidate rules to choose reasonable partition points. The auto-tuning framework helps developers get the most suitable partition of a neural network. The cloud-edge mode (i.e. collaborative inference) reduces the storage of inference on mobile devices with trivial loss of accuracy and could protect personal information.

Acknowledgement. This work is supported by the National Key R&D Program of China under Grant No. 2017YFB0202002, the Science Fund for Creative Research Groups of the National Natural Science Foundation of China under Grant No. 61521092 and the Key Program of National Natural Science Foundation of China under Grant Nos. 61432018, 61332009, U1736208.

References

1. gemmlowp: a small self-contained low-precision GEMM library. https://github.com/google/gemmlowp
2. NVIDIA TensorRT. https://developer.nvidia.com/tensorrt
3. Cheng, J., Wang, P., Li, G., Hu, Q., Lu, H.: Recent advances in efficient computation of deep convolutional neural networks. CoRR abs/1802.00939, pp. 1–12 (2018). http://arxiv.org/abs/1802.00939
4. Cheng, J., Wu, J., Leng, C., Wang, Y., Hu, Q.: Quantized CNN: a unified approach to accelerate and compress convolutional networks. IEEE Trans. Neural Netw. Learn. Syst. **99**, 1–14 (2017)
5. Cuervo, E., et al.: MAUI: making smartphones last longer with code offload. In: International Conference on Mobile Systems, Applications, and Services, pp. 49–62 (2010)
6. Deng, J., et al.: ImageNet: a large-scale hierarchical image database. In: Computer Vision and Pattern Recognition, pp. 248–255. IEEE Computer Society (2009)

7. Gong, Y., Liu, L., Yang, M., Bourdev, L.D.: Compressing deep convolutional networks using vector quantization. CoRR abs/1412.6115, pp. 1–10 (2014). http://arxiv.org/abs/1412.6115
8. He, K., Zhang, X., Ren, S., Sun, J.: Deep residual learning for image recognition. In: Computer Vision and Pattern Recognition, pp. 770–778 (2015)
9. Hinton, G., et al.: Deep neural networks for acoustic modeling in speech recognition: the shared views of four research groups. IEEE Signal Process. Mag. **29**(6), 82–97 (2012)
10. Jia, Y., et al.: Caffe: convolutional architecture for fast feature embedding. In: ACM International Conference on Multimedia, pp. 675–678 (2014)
11. Kang, Y., Hauswald, J., Gao, C., Rovinski, A., Mudge, T., Mars, J., Tang, L.: Neurosurgeon: collaborative intelligence between the cloud and mobile edge. ACM Sigplan Not. **52**(4), 615–629 (2017)
12. Krizhevsky, A., Sutskever, I., Hinton, G.E.: ImageNet classification with deep convolutional neural networks. In: Advances in Neural Information Processing Systems, pp. 1097–1105 (2012)
13. Lecun, Y., Bottou, L., Bengio, Y., Haffner, P.: Gradient-based learning applied to document recognition. Proc. IEEE **86**(11), 2278–2324 (1998)
14. Lecun, Y., Bengio, Y., Hinton, G.: Deep learning. Nature **521**(7553), 436–444 (2015)
15. Mikolov, T., Sutskever, I., Chen, K., Corrado, G.S., Dean, J.: Distributed representations of words and phrases and their compositionality. In: Advances in Neural Information Processing Systems, pp. 3111–3119 (2013)
16. Simonyan, K., Zisserman, A.: Very deep convolutional networks for large-scale image recognition. CoRR abs/1409.1556, pp. 1–14 (2014). http://arxiv.org/abs/1409.1556
17. Szegedy, C., et al.: Going deeper with convolutions. In: Computer Vision and Pattern Recognition, pp. 1–9 (2015)
18. Zhou, A., Yao, A., Guo, Y., Xu, L., Chen, Y.: Incremental network quantization: towards lossless CNNs with low-precision weights. CoRR abs/1702.03044, pp. 1–14 (2017). http://arxiv.org/abs/1702.03044
19. Zhou, S., Ni, Z., Zhou, X., Wen, H., Wu, Y., Zou, Y.: DoReFa-Net: training low bitwidth convolutional neural networks with low bitwidth gradients. CoRR abs/1606.06160, pp. 1–13 (2016). http://arxiv.org/abs/1606.06160

GraphVAE: Towards Generation of Small Graphs Using Variational Autoencoders

Martin Simonovsky[(✉)] and Nikos Komodakis

Imagine & LIGM, Université Paris Est & École des Ponts,
Champs sur Marne, France
{martin.simonovsky,nikos.komodakis}@enpc.fr

Abstract. Deep learning on graphs has become a popular research topic with many applications. However, past work has concentrated on learning graph embedding tasks, which is in contrast with advances in generative models for images and text. Is it possible to transfer this progress to the domain of graphs? We propose to sidestep hurdles associated with linearization of such discrete structures by having a decoder output a probabilistic fully-connected graph of a predefined maximum size directly at once. Our method is formulated as a variational autoencoder. We evaluate on the challenging task of molecule generation.

1 Introduction

Deep learning on graphs has very recently become a popular research topic [3]. Past work has concentrated on learning graph embedding tasks so far, *i.e.* encoding an input graph into a vector representation. This is in stark contrast with fast-paced advances in generative models for images and text, which have seen massive rise in quality of generated samples. Hence, it is an intriguing question how one can transfer this progress to the domain of graphs, *i.e.* their decoding from a vector representation. Moreover, the desire for such a method has been mentioned in the past [5].

However, learning to generate graphs is a difficult problem, as graphs are discrete non-linear structures. In this work, we propose a variational autoencoder [9] for probabilistic graphs of a predefined maximum size. In a probabilistic graph, the existence of nodes and edges, as well as their attributes, are modeled as independent random variables.

We demonstrate our method, coined GraphVAE, in cheminformatics on the task of molecule generation. Molecular datasets are a challenging but convenient testbed for generative models, as they easily allow for both qualitative and quantitative tests of decoded samples. While our method is applicable for generating smaller graphs only and its performance leaves space for improvement, we believe our work is an important initial step towards powerful and efficient graph decoders.

© Springer Nature Switzerland AG 2018
V. Kůrková et al. (Eds.): ICANN 2018, LNCS 11139, pp. 412–422, 2018.
https://doi.org/10.1007/978-3-030-01418-6_41

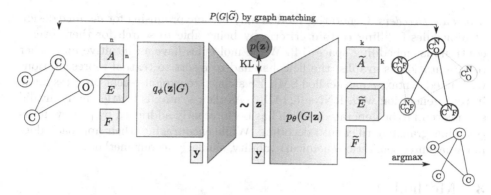

Fig. 1. Illustration of the proposed variational graph autoencoder. Starting from a discrete attributed graph $G = (A, E, F)$ on n nodes (*e.g.* a representation of propylene oxide with 3 carbons and 1 oxygen), stochastic graph encoder $q_\phi(\mathbf{z}|G)$ embeds the graph into continuous representation $\mathbf{z}$. Given a point in the latent space, our novel graph decoder $p_\theta(G|\mathbf{z})$ outputs a probabilistic fully-connected graph $\widetilde{G} = (\widetilde{A}, \widetilde{E}, \widetilde{F})$ on predefined $k \geq n$ nodes, from which discrete samples may be drawn. The process can be conditioned on label $\mathbf{y}$ for controlled sampling at test time. Reconstruction ability of the autoencoder is facilitated by approximate graph matching for aligning G with $\widetilde{G}$.

2   Related Work

Graph Decoders in Deep Learning. Graph generation has been largely unexplored in deep learning. The closest work to ours is by Johnson [8], who incrementally constructs a probabilistic (multi)graph as a world representation according to a sequence of input sentences to answer a query. While our model also outputs a probabilistic graph, we do not assume having a prescribed order of construction transformations available and we formulate the learning problem as an autoencoder.

Xu *et al.* [23] learns to produce a scene graph from an input image. They construct a graph from a set of object proposals, provide initial embeddings to each node and edge, and use message passing to obtain a consistent prediction. In contrast, our method is a generative model which produces a probabilistic graph from a single opaque vector, without specifying the number of nodes or the structure explicitly.

Discrete Data Decoders. Text is the most common discrete representation. Generative models there are usually trained in a maximum likelihood fashion by teacher forcing [22], which avoids the need to backpropagate through output discretization but may lead to expose bias [1]. Recently, efforts have been made to overcome this problem by using Gumbel distribution [10] or reinforcement learning [24]. Our work also circumvents the non-differentiability problem, namely by formulating the loss on a probabilistic graph.

Molecule Decoders. Generative models may become promising for *de novo* design of molecules fulfilling certain criteria by being able to search for them over a continuous embedding space [14]. While molecules have an intuitive and richer representation as graphs, the field has had to resort to textual representations with fixed syntax, *e.g.* so-called SMILES strings, to exploit recent progress made in text generation with RNNs [5, 14, 16]. As their syntax is brittle, many invalid strings tend to be generated, which has been recently addressed by [11] by incorporating grammar rules into decoding. While encouraging, their approach does not guarantee semantic (chemical) validity, similarly as our method.

3   Method

Our method is formulated in the framework of variational autoencoders (VAE) [9]. The main idea is to output a probabilistic fully-connected graph and use a graph matching algorithm to align it to the ground truth. We briefly recapitulate VAE below and continue with introducing our novel graph decoder together with an appropriate objective.

3.1   Variational Autoencoder

Let $G = (A, E, F)$ be a graph specified with its adjacency matrix A, edge attribute tensor E, and node attribute matrix F. We wish to learn an encoder and a decoder to map between the space of graphs G and their continuous embedding $\mathbf{z} \in \mathbb{R}^c$, see Fig. 1. In the probabilistic setting of a VAE, the encoder is defined by a variational posterior $q_\phi(\mathbf{z}|G)$ and the decoder by a generative distribution $p_\theta(G|\mathbf{z})$, where ϕ and θ are learned parameters. Furthermore, there is a prior distribution $p(\mathbf{z})$ imposed on the latent code representation as a regularization; we use a simplistic isotropic Gaussian prior $p(\mathbf{z}) = N(0, I)$. The whole model is trained by minimizing the upper bound on negative log-likelihood $-\log p_\theta(G)$ [9]:

$$\mathcal{L}(\phi, \theta; G) = \mathbb{E}_{q_\phi(\mathbf{z}|G)}[-\log p_\theta(G|\mathbf{z})] + \mathrm{KL}[q_\phi(\mathbf{z}|G)||p(\mathbf{z})] \tag{1}$$

The first term of $\mathcal{L}$, the reconstruction loss, enforces high similarity of sampled generated graphs to the input graph G. The second term, KL-divergence, regularizes the code space to allow for sampling of $\mathbf{z}$ directly from $p(\mathbf{z})$ instead from $q_\phi(\mathbf{z}|G)$ later. While the regularization is independent on the input space, the reconstruction loss must be specifically designed for each input modality.

3.2   Probabilistic Graph Decoder

In a related task of text sequence generation, the currently dominant approach is character-wise or word-wise prediction [2]. However, graphs can have arbitrary connectivity and there is no clear way how to linearize their construction in a sequence of steps: Vinyals *et al.* [21] empirically found out that the linearization order matters when learning on sets. On the other hand, iterative construction of discrete structures during training without step-wise supervision involves discrete decisions, which are not differentiable and therefore problematic for back-propagation.

Fortunately, the task can become much simpler if we restrict the domain to the set of all graphs on maximum k nodes, where k is fairly small (in practice up to the order of tens). Under this assumption, handling dense graph representations is still computationally tractable. We propose to make the decoder output a probabilistic fully-connected graph $\widetilde{G} = (\widetilde{A}, \widetilde{E}, \widetilde{F})$ on k nodes at once. This effectively sidesteps both problems mentioned above.

In probabilistic graphs, the existence of nodes and edges is modeled as Bernoulli variables, whereas node and edge attributes are multinomial variables. While not discussed in this work, continuous attributes could be easily modeled as Gaussian variables represented by their mean and variance. We assume all variables to be independent.

Each tensor of the representation of $\widetilde{G}$ has thus a probabilistic interpretation. Specifically, the predicted adjacency matrix $\widetilde{A} \in [0,1]^{k \times k}$ contains both node probabilities $\widetilde{A}_{a,a}$ and edge probabilities $\widetilde{A}_{a,b}$ for nodes $a \neq b$. The edge attribute tensor $\widetilde{E} \in \mathbb{R}^{k \times k \times d_e}$ indicates class probabilities for edges and, similarly, the node attribute matrix $\widetilde{F} \in \mathbb{R}^{k \times d_n}$ contains class probabilities for nodes.

The decoder itself is deterministic. Its architecture is a simple multi-layer perceptron (MLP) with three outputs in its last layer. Sigmoid activation function is used to compute $\widetilde{A}$, whereas edge- and node-wise softmax is applied to obtain $\widetilde{E}$ and $\widetilde{F}$, respectively. At test time, we are often interested in a (discrete) point estimate of $\widetilde{G}$, which can be obtained by taking edge- and node-wise argmax in $\widetilde{A}, \widetilde{E}$, and $\widetilde{F}$. Note that this can result in a discrete graph on less than k nodes.

3.3 Reconstruction Loss

Given a particular instance of a discrete input graph G on $n \leq k$ nodes and its probabilistic reconstruction $\widetilde{G}$ on k nodes, evaluation of Eq. 1 requires computation of likelihood $p_\theta(G|\mathbf{z}) = P(G|\widetilde{G})$.

Since no particular ordering of nodes is imposed in either $\widetilde{G}$ or G and matrix representation of graphs is not invariant to permutations of nodes, comparison of two graphs is hard. However, approximate graph matching described further in Subsect. 3.4 can obtain a binary assignment matrix $X \in \{0,1\}^{k \times n}$, where $X_{a,i} = 1$ only if node $a \in \widetilde{G}$ is assigned to $i \in G$ and $X_{a,i} = 0$ otherwise.

Knowledge of X allows to map information between both graphs. Specifically, input adjacency matrix is mapped to the predicted graph as $A' = XAX^T$, whereas the predicted node attribute matrix and slices of edge attribute matrix are transferred to the input graph as $\widetilde{F}' = X^T \widetilde{F}$ and $\widetilde{E}'_{\cdot,\cdot,l} = X^T \widetilde{E}_{\cdot,\cdot,l} X$. The maximum likelihood estimates, *i.e.* cross-entropy, of respective variables are as follows:

$$\log p(A'|\mathbf{z}) = 1/k \sum_a A'_{a,a} \log \widetilde{A}_{a,a} + (1 - A'_{a,a}) \log(1 - \widetilde{A}_{a,a}) +$$

$$+ 1/k(k-1) \sum_{a \neq b} A'_{a,b} \log \widetilde{A}_{a,b} + (1 - A'_{a,b}) \log(1 - \widetilde{A}_{a,b})$$

$$\log p(F|\mathbf{z}) = 1/n \sum_i \log F_{i,\cdot}^T \widetilde{F}'_{i,\cdot}. \tag{2}$$

$$\log p(E|\mathbf{z}) = 1/(\||A\||_1 - n) \sum_{i \neq j} \log E_{i,j,\cdot}^T \widetilde{E}'_{i,j,\cdot}.$$

where we assumed that F and E are encoded in one-hot notation. The formulation considers existence of both matched and unmatched nodes and edges but attributes of only the matched ones. Furthermore, averaging over nodes and edges separately has shown beneficial in training as otherwise the edges dominate the likelihood. The overall reconstruction loss is a weighed sum of the previous terms:

$$- \log p(G|\mathbf{z}) = -\lambda_A \log p(A'|\mathbf{z}) - \lambda_F \log p(F|\mathbf{z}) - \lambda_E \log p(E|\mathbf{z}) \tag{3}$$

3.4   Graph Matching

The goal of (second-order) graph matching is to find correspondences $X \in \{0,1\}^{k \times n}$ between nodes of graphs G and $\widetilde{G}$ based on the similarities of their node pairs $S : (i,j) \times (a,b) \rightarrow \mathbb{R}^+$ for $i,j \in G$ and $a,b \in \widetilde{G}$. It can be expressed as integer quadratic programming problem of similarity maximization over X and is typically approximated by relaxation of X into continuous domain: $X^* \in [0,1]^{k \times n}$ [4]. For our use case, the similarity function is defined as follows:

$$S((i,j),(a,b)) = (E_{i,j,\cdot}^T \widetilde{E}_{a,b,\cdot}) A_{i,j} \widetilde{A}_{a,b} \widetilde{A}_{a,a} \widetilde{A}_{b,b}[i \neq j \wedge a \neq b] +$$

$$+ (F_{i,\cdot}^T \widetilde{F}_{a,\cdot}) \widetilde{A}_{a,a}[i = j \wedge a = b] \tag{4}$$

The first term evaluates similarity between edge pairs and the second term between node pairs, $[\cdot]$ being the Iverson bracket. Note that the scores consider both feature compatibility ($\widetilde{F}$ and $\widetilde{E}$) and existential compatibility ($\widetilde{A}$), which has empirically led to more stable assignments during training. To summarize the motivation behind both Eqs. 3 and 4, our method aims to find the best graph matching and then further improve on it by gradient descent on the loss. Given the stochastic way of training deep networks, we argue that solving the matching step only approximately is sufficient. This is conceptually similar to the approach for learning to output unordered sets [21], where the closest ordering of the training data is sought.

   In practice, we are looking for a graph matching algorithm robust to noisy correspondences which can be easily implemented on GPU in batch mode. Max-pooling matching (MPM) by [4] is a simple but effective algorithm following the iterative scheme of power methods. It can be used in batch mode if similarity tensors are zero-padded, *i.e.* $S((i, j), (a, b)) = 0$ for $n < i, j \leq k$, and the amount of iterations is fixed.

Max-pooling matching outputs continuous assignment matrix X^*. Unfortunately, attempts to directly use X^* instead of X in Eq. 3 performed badly, as did experiments with direct maximization of X^* or soft discretization with softmax or straight-through Gumbel softmax [7]. We therefore discretize X^* to X using Hungarian algorithm to obtain a strict one-on-one mapping. While this operation is non-differentiable, gradient can still flow to the decoder directly through the loss function and training convergence proceeds without problems. Note that this approach is often taken in works on object detection, *e.g.* [19], where a set of detections need to be matched to a set of ground truth bounding boxes and treated as fixed before computing a differentiable loss.

3.5 Further Details

Encoder. A feed forward network with edge-conditioned graph convolutions (ECC) [17] is used as encoder, although any other graph embedding method is applicable. As our edge attributes are categorical, a single linear layer for the filter generating network in ECC is sufficient. As usual in VAE, we formulate the encoder as probabilistic and enforce Gaussian distribution of $q_\phi(\mathbf{z}|G)$ by having the last encoder layer outputs $2c$ features interpreted as mean and variance, allowing to sample $\mathbf{z}_l \sim N(\mu_l(G), \sigma_l(G))$ for $l \in 1, .., c$ using the reparameterization trick [9].

Disentangled Embedding. In practice, rather than random drawing of graphs, one often desires more control over generated graphs. In such case, we follow [18] and condition both encoder and decoder on label vector $\mathbf{y}$ associated with each input graph G. Decoder $p_\theta(G|\mathbf{z}, \mathbf{y})$ is fed a concatenation of $\mathbf{z}$ and $\mathbf{y}$, while in encoder $q_\phi(\mathbf{z}|G, \mathbf{y})$, $\mathbf{y}$ is concatenated to every node's features just before the graph pooling layer. If the size of latent space c is small, the decoder is encouraged to exploit information in the label.

Limitations. The proposed model is expected to be useful only for generating small graphs. This is due to growth of GPU memory requirements and number of parameters ($O(k^2)$) as well as matching complexity ($O(k^4)$), with small decrease in quality for high values of k. In Sect. 4 we demonstrate results for up to $k = 38$. Nevertheless, for many applications even generation of small graphs is still very useful.

4   Evaluation

We demonstrate our method for the task of molecule generation by evaluating on two large public datasets of organic molecules, QM9 and ZINC.

4.1   Application in Cheminformatics

Quantitative evaluation of generative models of images and texts has been troublesome [20], as it very difficult to measure realness of generated samples in an automated and objective way. Thus, researchers frequently resort there to qualitative evaluation and embedding plots. However, qualitative evaluation of graphs can be very unintuitive for humans to judge unless the graphs are planar and fairly simple.

Fortunately, we found graph representation of molecules, as undirected graphs with atoms as nodes and bonds as edges, to be a convenient testbed for generative models. On one hand, generated graphs can be easily visualized in standardized structural diagrams. On the other hand, chemical validity of graphs, as well as many further properties a molecule can fulfill, can be checked using software packages (`SanitizeMol` in RDKit [12]) or simulations. This makes both qualitative and quantitative tests possible.

Chemical constraints on compatible types of bonds and atom valences make the space of valid graphs complicated and molecule generation challenging. In fact, a single addition or removal of edge or change in atom or bond type can make a molecule chemically invalid. Comparably, flipping a single pixel in MNIST-like number generation problem is of no issue.

To help the network in this application, we introduce three remedies. First, we make the decoder output symmetric $\widetilde{A}$ and $\widetilde{E}$ by predicting their (upper) triangular parts only, as undirected graphs are sufficient representation for molecules. Second, we use prior knowledge that molecules are connected and, at test time only, construct maximum spanning tree on the set of probable nodes $\{a : \widetilde{A}_{a,a} \geq 0.5\}$ in order to include its edges (a, b) in the discrete pointwise estimate of the graph even if $\widetilde{A}_{a,b} < 0.5$ originally. Third, we do not generate Hydrogen explicitly and let it be added as "padding" during chemical validity check.

4.2   QM9 Dataset

QM9 dataset [15] contains about 134k organic molecules of up to 9 heavy (non Hydrogen) atoms with 4 distinct atomic numbers and 4 bond types, we set $k = 9$, $d_e = 4$ and $d_n = 4$. We set aside 10k samples for testing and 10k for validation (model selection).

We compare our unconditional model to the character-based generator of Gómez-Bombarelli et al. [5] (CVAE) and the grammar-based generator of Kusner et al. [11] (GVAE). We used the code and architecture in [11] for both baselines, adapting the maximum input length to the smallest possible. In addition, we demonstrate a conditional generative model for an artificial task of generating molecules given a histogram of heavy atoms as 4-dimensional label $\mathbf{y}$, the success of which can be easily validated.

Setup. The encoder has two graph convolutional layers (32 and 64 channels) with identity connection, batchnorm, and ReLU; followed by the graph-level output

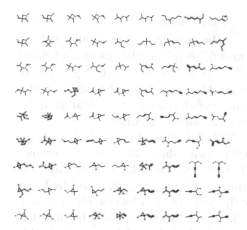

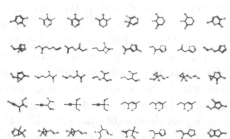

Fig. 2. Decodings over a random plane in z-space. Chemically invalid graphs in red. (Color figure online)

Fig. 3. Linear interpolation between row-wise pairs of randomly chosen molecules in z-space in a conditional model. Color highlight legend: encoder inputs (green), chemically invalid graphs (red), valid graphs with wrong label (blue). (Color figure online)

formulation in Eq. 7 in [13] with auxiliary networks being a single fully connected layer (FCL) with 128 output channels; finalized by a FCL outputting (μ, σ). The decoder has 3 FCLs (128, 256, and 512 channels) with batchnorm and ReLU; followed by parallel triplet of FCLs to output graph tensors. We set $c = 40$, $\lambda_A = \lambda_F = \lambda_E = 1$, batch size 32, 75 MPM iterations and train for 25 epochs with Adam with learning rate 1e-3 and $\beta_1 = 0.5$.

Embedding Visualization. To visually judge the quality and smoothness of the learned embedding z of our model, we may traverse it in two ways: along a slice and along a line. For the former, we randomly choose two c-dimensional orthonormal vectors and sample z in regular grid pattern over the induced 2D plane. Figure 2 shows a varied and fairly smooth mix of molecules (for unconditional model with $c = 40$ and within 5 units from the origin). For the latter, we randomly choose two molecules $G^{(1)}, G^{(2)}$ of the same label from test set and interpolate between their embeddings $\mu(G^{(1)}), \mu(G^{(2)})$. This also evaluates the encoder, and therefore benefits from low reconstruction error. In Fig. 3 we can find both meaningful (1st, 2nd and 4th row) and less meaningful transitions, though many samples on the lines do not form chemically valid compounds.

Decoder Quality Metrics. The quality of a conditional decoder can be evaluated by the validity and variety of generated graphs. For a given label $\mathbf{y}^{(l)}$, we draw $n_s = 10^4$ samples $\mathbf{z}^{(l,s)} \sim p(\mathbf{z})$ and compute the discrete point estimate of their decodings $\hat{G}^{(l,s)} = \arg\max p_\theta(G|\mathbf{z}^{(l,s)}, \mathbf{y}^{(l)})$.

Let $V^{(l)}$ be the list of chemically valid molecules from $\hat{G}^{(l,s)}$ and $C^{(l)}$ be the list of chemically valid molecules with atom histograms equal to $\mathbf{y}^{(l)}$. We are interested in ratios $\text{Valid}^{(l)} = |V^{(l)}|/n_s$ and $\text{Accurate}^{(l)} = |C^{(l)}|/n_s$. Furthermore, let $\text{Unique}^{(l)} = |\text{set}(C^{(l)})|/|C^{(l)}|$ be the fraction of unique correct graphs and $\text{Novel}^{(l)} = 1 - |\text{set}(C^{(l)}) \cap \text{QM9}|/|\text{set}(C^{(l)})|$ the fraction of novel out-of-dataset graphs; we define $\text{Unique}^{(l)} = 0$ and $\text{Novel}^{(l)} = 0$ if $|C^{(l)}| = 0$. Finally, the introduced metrics are aggregated by frequencies of labels in QM9, *e.g.* $\text{Valid} = \sum_l \text{Valid}^{(l)}\text{freq}(\mathbf{y}^{(l)})$. Unconditional decoders are evaluated by assuming there is just a single label, therefore $\text{Valid} = \text{Accurate}$.

In Table 1, we can see that on average 50% of generated molecules are chemically valid and, in the case of conditional models, about 40% have the correct label which the decoder was conditioned on. Larger embedding sizes c are less regularized, demonstrated by a higher number of Unique samples and by lower accuracy of the conditional model, as the decoder is forced less to rely on actual labels. The ratio of Valid samples shows less clear behavior, likely because the discrete performance is not directly optimized for. For all models, it is remarkable that about 60% of generated molecules are out of the dataset, *i.e.* the network has never seen them during training.

Looking at the baselines, CVAE can output only very few valid samples as expected, while GVAE generates the highest number of valid samples (60%) but of very low variance (less than 10%). Additionally, we investigate the importance of graph matching by using identity assignment X instead and thus learning to reproduce particular node permutations in the training set, which correspond to the canonical ordering of SMILES strings from RDKit. This ablated model (denoted as NoGM in Table 1) produces many valid samples of lower variety and, surprisingly, outperforms GVAE in this regard. In comparison, our model can achieve good performance in both metrics at the same time.

Likelihood. Besides the application-specific metric introduced above, we also report evidence lower bound (ELBO) commonly used in VAE literature, which corresponds to $-\mathcal{L}(\phi, \theta; G)$ in our notation. In Table 1, we state mean bounds over test set, using a single $\mathbf{z}$ sample per graph. We observe both reconstruction loss and KL-divergence decrease due to larger c providing more freedom. However, there seems to be no strong correlation between ELBO and Valid, which makes model selection somewhat difficult.

4.3   ZINC Dataset

ZINC dataset [6] contains about 250k drug-like organic molecules of up to 38 heavy atoms with 9 distinct atomic numbers and 4 bond types, we set $k = 38$, $d_e = 4$ and $d_n = 9$ and use the same split strategy as with QM9. We investigate the degree of scalability of an unconditional generative model. The setup is equivalent as for QM9 but with a wider encoder (64, 128, 256 channels).

Our best model with $c = 40$ has archived $\text{Valid} = 0.135$, which is clearly worse than for QM9. For comparison, CVAE failed to generated any valid sample, while GVAE achieved $\text{Valid} = 0.357$ (models provided by [11], $c = 56$). We attribute such a low performance to a generally much higher chance of producing

Table 1. Performance on conditional and unconditional QM9 models evaluated by mean test-time reconstruction log-likelihood ($\log p_\theta(G|\mathbf{z})$), mean test-time evidence lower bound (ELBO), and decoding quality metrics (Sect. 4.2). Baselines CVAE [5] and GVAE [11] are listed only for the embedding size with the highest Valid.

		$\log p_\theta(G|\mathbf{z})$	ELBO	Valid	Accurate	Unique	Novel
Cond.	Ours $c = 20$	-0.578	-0.722	0.565	0.467	0.314	0.598
	Ours $c = 40$	-0.504	-0.617	0.511	0.416	0.484	0.635
	Ours $c = 60$	-0.492	-0.585	0.520	0.406	0.583	0.613
	Ours $c = 80$	-0.475	-0.557	0.458	0.353	0.666	0.661
Unconditional	Ours $c = 20$	-0.660	-0.916	0.485	0.485	0.457	0.575
	Ours $c = 40$	-0.537	-0.744	0.542	0.542	0.618	0.617
	Ours $c = 60$	-0.486	-0.656	0.517	0.517	0.695	0.570
	Ours $c = 80$	-0.482	-0.628	0.557	0.557	0.760	0.616
	NoGM $c = 80$	-2.388	-2.553	0.810	0.810	0.241	0.610
	CVAE $c = 60$	–	–	0.103	0.103	0.675	0.900
	GVAE $c = 20$	–	–	0.602	0.602	0.093	0.809

a chemically-relevant inconsistency (number of possible edges growing quadratically). To confirm the relationship between performance and graph size k, we kept only graphs not larger than $k = 20$ nodes, corresponding to 21% of ZINC, and obtained Valid = 0.341 (and Valid = 0.185 for $k = 30$ nodes, 92% of ZINC).

5   Conclusion

In this work we addressed the problem of generating graphs from a continuous embedding in the context of variational autoencoders. We evaluated our method on two molecular datasets of different maximum graph size. While we achieved to learn embedding of reasonable quality on small molecules, our decoder had a hard time capturing complex chemical interactions for larger molecules. Nevertheless, we believe our method is an important initial step towards more powerful decoders and will spark interest in the community.

Acknowledgments. We thank Shell Xu Hu for discussions on variational methods, Shinjae Yoo for project motivation, and anonymous reviewers for their comments.

References

1. Bengio, S., Vinyals, O., Jaitly, N., Shazeer, N.: Scheduled sampling for sequence prediction with recurrent neural networks. In: NIPS, pp. 1171–1179 (2015)
2. Bowman, S.R., Vilnis, L., Vinyals, O., Dai, A.M., Józefowicz, R., Bengio, S.: Generating sentences from a continuous space. In: CoNLL, pp. 10–21 (2016)
3. Bronstein, M.M., Bruna, J., LeCun, Y., Szlam, A., Vandergheynst, P.: Geometric deep learning: going beyond Euclidean data. IEEE Signal Process. Mag. **34**(4), 18–42 (2017)

4. Cho, M., Sun, J., Duchenne, O., Ponce, J.: Finding matches in a haystack: a max-pooling strategy for graph matching in the presence of outliers. In: CVPR, pp. 2091–2098 (2014)
5. Gómez-Bombarelli, R., et al.: Automatic chemical design using a data-driven continuous representation of molecules. CoRR abs/1610.02415 (2016)
6. Irwin, J.J., Sterling, T., Mysinger, M.M., Bolstad, E.S., Coleman, R.G.: ZINC: a free tool to discover chemistry for biology. J. Chem. Inf. Model. **52**(7), 1757–1768 (2012)
7. Jang, E., Gu, S., Poole, B.: Categorical reparameterization with Gumbel-Softmax. CoRR abs/1611.01144 (2016)
8. Johnson, D.D.: Learning graphical state transitions. In: ICLR (2017)
9. Kingma, D.P., Welling, M.: Auto-encoding variational Bayes. CoRR abs/1312.6114 (2013)
10. Kusner, M.J., Hernández-Lobato, J.M.: GANS for sequences of discrete elements with the Gumbel-Softmax distribution. CoRR abs/1611.04051 (2016)
11. Kusner, M.J., Paige, B., Hernández-Lobato, J.M.: Grammar variational autoencoder. In: ICML, pp. 1945–1954 (2017)
12. Landrum, G.: RDKit: Open-source cheminformatics. http://www.rdkit.org
13. Li, Y., Tarlow, D., Brockschmidt, M., Zemel, R.S.: Gated graph sequence neural networks. CoRR abs/1511.05493 (2015)
14. Olivecrona, M., Blaschke, T., Engkvist, O., Chen, H.: Molecular de novo design through deep reinforcement learning. CoRR abs/1704.07555 (2017)
15. Ramakrishnan, R., Dral, P.O., Rupp, M., von Lilienfeld, O.A.: Quantum chemistry structures and properties of 134 kilo molecules. Sci. Data **1**, 140022 (2014)
16. Segler, M.H.S., Kogej, T., Tyrchan, C., Waller, M.P.: Generating focussed molecule libraries for drug discovery with recurrent neural networks. CoRR abs/1701.01329 (2017)
17. Simonovsky, M., Komodakis, N.: Dynamic edge-conditioned filters in convolutional neural networks on graphs. In: CVPR (2017)
18. Sohn, K., Lee, H., Yan, X.: Learning structured output representation using deep conditional generative models. In: NIPS, pp. 3483–3491 (2015)
19. Stewart, R., Andriluka, M., Ng, A.Y.: End-to-end people detection in crowded scenes. In: CVPR, pp. 2325–2333 (2016)
20. Theis, L., van den Oord, A., Bethge, M.: A note on the evaluation of generative models. CoRR abs/1511.01844 (2015)
21. Vinyals, O., Bengio, S., Kudlur, M.: Order matters: sequence to sequence for sets. arXiv preprint arXiv:1511.06391 (2015)
22. Williams, R.J., Zipser, D.: A learning algorithm for continually running fully recurrent neural networks. Neural Comput. **1**(2), 270–280 (1989)
23. Xu, D., Zhu, Y., Choy, C.B., Fei-Fei, L.: Scene graph generation by iterative message passing. In: CVPR (2017)
24. Yu, L., Zhang, W., Wang, J., Yu, Y.: SeqGAN: sequence generative adversarial nets with policy gradient. In: AAAI (2017)

Generation of Reference Trajectories for Safe Trajectory Planning

Amit Chaulwar[1], Michael Botsch[1(✉)], and Wolfgang Utschick[2]

[1] Faculty of Electrical Engineering, Ingolstadt University of Applied Sciences,
Ingolstadt, Germany
{amit.chaulwar,michael.botsch}@thi.de
[2] Department of Electrical Engineering, Technical University of Munich,
Munich, Germany
utschick@tum.de

Abstract. Many variants of a sampling-based motion planning algorithm, namely Rapidly-exploring Random Tree, use biased-sampling for faster convergence. One of such recently proposed variant, the Hybrid-Augmented CL-RRT+, uses a predicted predefined template trajectory with a machine learning algorithm as a reference for the biased sampling. Because of the finite number of template trajectories, the convergence time is short only in scenarios where the final trajectory is close to predicted template trajectory. Therefore, a generative model using variational autoencoder for generating many reference trajectories and a 3D-ConvNet regressor for predicting those reference trajectories for critical vehicle traffic-scenarios is proposed in this work. Using this framework, two different safe trajectory planning algorithms, namely GATE and GATE-ARRT+, are presented in this paper. Finally, the simulation results demonstrate the effectiveness of these algorithms for the trajectory planning task in different types of critical vehicle traffic-scenarios.

Keywords: Safe trajectory planning · Hybrid machine learning
Variational autoencoder

1 Introduction

Autonomous driving is one of the area extensively being researched, in both academia and industry, because of its expected immense social and economic impacts. In order to realize a fully autonomous driving, the vehicle must be able to plan a trajectory with simultaneous intervention in the lateral and longitudinal dynamics of the vehicle for the collision avoidance/mitigation in critical, dynamic traffic-scenarios as well as for smooth and comfortable traveling.

Many motion planning algorithms have been proposed in the literature summarized in [1]. A probabilistic sampling algorithm 'Rapidly-exploring Random Tree' (RRT) [2] is most popular because of its fast runtimes and ability to plan the path with dynamic constraints without discretizing the state-space. Many

© Springer Nature Switzerland AG 2018
V. Kůrková et al. (Eds.): ICANN 2018, LNCS 11139, pp. 423–434, 2018.
https://doi.org/10.1007/978-3-030-01418-6_42

variants of this algorithm have been developed for different applications, as summarized in [3]. Only few of these variants [4,5] claim to run in real time with dynamic constraints. However, they either require precomputation of many safe states or high performance computers.

RRT is a probabilistically complete algorithm, i.e., it always finds a solution, if it exists, given infinite time. Therefore, many approaches define rule-based heuristics for biased-sampling [7–12] to increase the convergence rate. Nevertheless, all of these methods require an initial approximate solution for biased-sampling.

Machine learning algorithms can be used to find solutions for complex problems with short inference time. Since they are purely data-based methods they are seen as black-box methods. Therefore, they are not used in safety critical applications like vehicle trajectory planning. A learned Gaussian Mixture Models distribution is used for the biased-sampling in learned free spaces in [13] to decrease the number of collision checks drastically for the trajectory planning with the RRT algorithm. In another approach [15], a conditional variational autoencoder is used to generate biased samples in space from a learned sampling distribution to increase the convergence rate of the RRT algorithm. However, both approaches perform biased-sampling in space only.

The use of hybrid machine learning algorithms, a combination of machine learning algorithms and model-based search algorithms, opens a new way of using machine learning algorithms in safety critical applications. AlphaGo [16] and ExIT [17] are two examples of guided tree search algorithms with neural networks for the board games Go and Hex, respectively. But, these algorithms are limited to discrete state-spaces and action-spaces. The Hybrid Augmented CL-RRT (HARRT) [14] and the Hybrid Augmented CL-RRT+ (HARRT+) [18] are examples of hybrid machine learning algorithms for safe trajectory planning in complex, critical traffic scenarios which use 3D convolutional neural networks (3D-ConvNets)[19], in combination with RRT variants the Augmented CL-RRT (ARRT) [6] and the Augmented CL-RRT+ (ARRT+) [18], respectively. The HARRT+ algorithm is described briefly in Sect. 3 along with its drawbacks.

Other approaches of developing generative models for trajectories have been proposed for different applications such as handwriting generation [21] and predicting basketball trajectories [22]. In this work, a methodology for generating better reference trajectories with two machine learning algorithms is proposed. First one is a generative model for trajectory generation using a variational autoencoder (VAE) [23] and second is a 3D-ConvNet regressor for predicting those reference trajectories for critical traffic-scenario. Two different motion planning algorithms are also presented by combining this machine learning framework with an optimization procedure and the ARRT+ algorithm to decrease the convergence time further.

The paper is organised as follows: Sect. 2 briefly explains VAEs. Section 3 describes HARRT+ motion planning algorithm with its drawbacks. Two machine learning algorithms, a generative model for trajectories and 3D-ConvNet regressor, are presented in Sect. 4. Based on this framework, two new vehicle motion planning algorithms namely, GATE and GATE-ARRT+, are proposed in Sect. 5 followed by results and a conclusion.

Throughout this paper, upper case bold letters denote matrices and lower case bold letters denote vectors.

2 Variational Autoencoder

This Section briefly reviews Variational autoencoder (VAE) [23] that is a key mechanism used for developing a generative model for vehicle trajectories. It tries to minimize the difference between model distribution $P_\theta(X)$ with parameters θ and data distribution $P_{data}(X)$, given a data-set $X = \{x_i\}_{i=1}^N$ of N identical and independent samples of some discrete or continuous random variable x. It assumes that this data-set is generated with a two-step random process using a latent variable z. First, a realization of z is sampled from a prior distribution $P_\theta(z)$. Then, X is generated from a conditional distribution $P_\theta(X|z)$. The goal is to maximize the probability of observing realizations X according to

$$P_\theta(X) = \int P_\theta(X|z)P_\theta(z)dz. \tag{1}$$

The problem with above equation is that it is intractable as it is impossible to find $P_\theta(X)$ for every z. Also, the posterior distribution $P_\theta(z|X)$ is also intractable. VAE proposes a solution for this by defining an encoder model $Q_\phi(z|X)$ that approximates $P_\theta(z|X)$. As X is fixed and $P_\theta(X)$ is not dependent on $Q_\phi(z|X)$, the log likelihood of the data can be found by taking the expectation with respect to z using an encoder network $Q_\phi(z|X)$ such that

$$\log P_\theta(X) = E_{z \sim Q_\phi(z|X)}\left[\log P_\theta(X)\right], \tag{2}$$

Applying Bayes' Rule to Eq. 2, the equation becomes

$$\log P_\theta(X) = E_{z|X}\left[\log \frac{P_\theta(X|z)P_\theta(z)}{P_\theta(z|X)}\right], \tag{3}$$

where $E_{z \sim Q_\phi(z|X)}$ is replaced by $E_{z|X}$ to avoid the clutter. Multiplying and dividing by $Q_\phi(z|X)$ and applying logarithmic rules, we get

$$\log P_\theta(X) = E_{z|X}\left[\log P_\theta(X|z)\right] - E_{z|X}\left[\log \frac{Q_\phi(z|X)}{P_\theta(z)}\right] + E_{z|X}\left[\log \frac{Q_\phi(z|X)}{P_\theta(z|X)}\right]. \tag{4}$$

Writing above equation with KL-terms, log data likelihood becomes

$$\log P_\theta(X) = \underbrace{E_{z|X}\left[\log P_\theta(X|z)\right] - D_{KL}(Q_\phi(z|X)\|P_\theta(z))}_{\mathcal{L}(X,\theta,\phi)} +$$

$$\underbrace{D_{KL}(Q_\phi(z|X)\|P_\theta(z|X))}_{\geq 0}. \tag{5}$$

The estimate of the first term on right hand side of the Eq. 5 can be computed by the decoder network through sampling. This non-continuous sampling procedure is made differentiable through reparameterization technique [23] required for backpropagation. Generally, cross-entropy or root mean square error criteria is considered for calculating the reconstruction loss. The second term in Eq. 5 of KL divergence between approximate posterior and the prior distribution is possible to compute. This is because the approximate posterior $Q_\phi(z|X)$ is often chosen as a multivariate Gaussian with diagonal covariance matrix whose distribution parameters are learnt from the data while the prior $P_\theta(z)$ is commonly chosen as isotropic multivariate Gaussian. The third term in Eq. 5 is intractable as $P_\theta(z|X)$ is intractable. But as per the definition of KL-Divergence it is always equal to or greater than 0. The first two terms together are termed as variational lower bound $\mathcal{L}(X, \theta, \phi)$ and the goal becomes to maximize the lower bound to find the optimal θ^* and ϕ^* such that

$$\theta^*, \phi^* = \arg\max_{\theta, \phi} \mathcal{L}(X, \theta, \phi). \tag{6}$$

3   HARRT+ Algorithm

The ARRT+ algorithm considers vehicle nonlinear dynamics for trajectory planning in the form

$$\dot{s}(t) = f(s(t), u(t)), \tag{7}$$

where $u(t) \in \mathbb{R}^m$ is the control input and $s(t)$ is the area occupied by the EGO vehicle at time t which is the subspace in $\mathbb{R}^2$. In an iterative process, this algorithms construct a tree $\mathcal{T}$ with multiple safe states $s(t)$. Throughout this paper, the term *safe* used in context of states and trajectories means either collision-free or with a predicted nonsevere collision. In every iteration, a random point s_{rand} is sampled with some bias towards a goal region S_{goal}. The state $s_{nearest}(t)$ which are previously stored in the tree $\mathcal{T}$ nearest to s_{rand} is found. The tree is extended by an incremental motion towards s_{rand} from $s_{nearest}(t)$. The incremental extension is performed for the time interval Δt using differential constraints f as in Eq. (7) to get the new state $s_{new}(t + \Delta t)$. The new state $s_{new}(t + \Delta t)$ is added to the tree $\mathcal{T}$, if the trajectory from $s_{nearest}(t)$ to $s_{new}(t + \Delta t)$ is collision-free or it encounters a collision with predicted low severity. A two-track model [20] is used as a constraint f while extending the tree.

A traffic-scenario is converted into a sequence of predicted occupancy grids $\mathbf{M} = \{\mathcal{G}_{t_0}, \ldots, \mathcal{G}_{t_0+\tau_1}\}$ for the prediction interval $[t_0, t_0+\tau_1]$ with each occupancy grid $\mathcal{G}_t$ representing the occupancies of road objects at time t. The cells in the predicted occupancy grid $\mathcal{G}_t$ which lie outside of the road or occupied by other vehicle at time t are assigned a value 1. Rest of the grids are assigned a value 0 indicating they are free. A scenario described by $\{\mathbf{M}, \boldsymbol{\eta}\}$, where $\boldsymbol{\eta}$ are EGO vehicle physical parameters like velocity, yaw-rate, etc. Due to the 3D structure of the input $\mathbf{M}$, the 3D-ConvNet is used as a machine learning algorithm. In a simulation environment developed in Matlab, many critical traffic-scenarios are simulated and best trajectories π^* are found by the ARRT+ algorithm. The steering wheel angle profile and longitudinal acceleration profile are extracted from the found trajectories and their clusters are formed using hierarchical clustering based on Euclidean criteria. The combination of these clusters in which the acceleration profile and steering wheel angle profile of the best trajectory for a scenario lies is considered as a label for that scenario. The HARRT+ algorithm uses the mean vectors of the predicted acceleration and steering wheel angle clusters to generate a reference trajectory that is used for the biased-sampling to increase the convergence speed of the algorithm. Basically, HARRT+ algorithm predicts a template trajectory $\hat{\pi}_t$ from total T template trajectories formed by combination of mean vectors of all acceleration and steering wheel angle profile clusters. The reference acceleration profile $\hat{a}_x$ and waypoints $\hat{W}$ are extracted from this template trajectory for simultaneous biased sampling in the lateral and longitudinal dynamics. Figure 1 explains the procedure for finding π^* with HARRT+ algorithm.

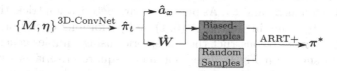

Fig. 1. HARRT+ algorithm

HARRT+ algorithm uses combination of biased and random sampling algorithm. Therefore, it still have the property of probabilistic completeness even with wrong prediction of template trajectory $\hat{\pi}_t$. However, the computation time for finding a safe trajectory is high when a wrong cluster is predicted because of the wrong bias generation. Even if a right template trajectory is predicted, the final safe trajectory may not always lie near it (as it can lie on the boundary of clusters) or the final safe trajectory has very different shape compared to $\hat{\pi}_t$. In such situations as well, it is observed that HARRT+ algorithm converges slowly.

4 Generation of Reference Trajectories

From the explanation of the drawbacks of HARRT+ algorithm, it is clear that the final computation time required for trajectory planning with HARRT+ algorithm strongly depends on the quality of the predicted reference trajectory, i.e., closer the predicted reference trajectory $\hat{\pi}_t$ in distance and shape to π^* lesser the computation time will require to find π^*. This will not be possible in all scenarios with finite number of template trajectories. Therefore, a generative model for trajectory generation using VAE is proposed with which many reference trajectories can be generated. This trained VAE is further used in the label generation and inference procedure of the other machine learning algorithm, i.e., 3D-ConvNet regressor, which maps the traffic-scenarios to the reference trajectories. This section describes training procedure for both machine learning algorithms and its usage for predicting reference trajectories for vehicle critical traffic-scenarios.

4.1 Generative Model for Trajectories π

In order to train VAE for trajectories, 60000 different trajectories for time τ_1 (=2 s) are generated using the two-track vehicle dynamic model [20] with different initial velocities, lateral and longitudinal dynamic intervention over entire trajectory with actuator and stable profile constraints as mentioned in [18]. These trajectories are provided as input to the VAE in the form

$$\pi = \{r_{x_{t_0}}, r_{x_{t_0+\Delta t}} \cdots, r_{x_{\tau_1}}, r_{y_{t_0}}, r_{y_{t_0+\Delta t}}, \ldots, r_{y_{\tau_1}}\}, \tag{8}$$

where $r_{x_{t_i}}$ and $r_{y_{t_0}}$ are the coordinates of the center of gravity of the vehicle at time t_i. The encoder $Q_\phi(z|\pi)$ maps trajectories to latent space mean vector $z_\mu|\pi$ and standard deviation vector $z_\sigma|\pi$ each of dimension 2. To avoid clutter, they are simply written as z_μ and z_σ. As per the reparameterization trick, the samples z are obtained by sampling ϵ from $\mathcal{N}(0,1)$ and performing operation $z_\mu + \epsilon z_\sigma$. The decoder $P_\theta(\pi|z)$ reconstruct the trajectories using samples generated from z_μ and z_σ as shown in Fig. 2. The root mean square criteria is used for the reconstruction loss. Also, the trajectories are normalized before first layer in the encoder and the final trajectories $\bar{\pi}$ are obtained by denormalization and smoothing with moving average filter. The activation function used in each layer of the encoder and decoder is hyperbolic tan.

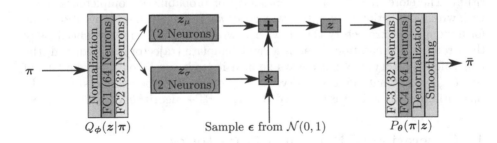

Fig. 2. VAE for trajectories

4.2 3D-ConvNet Regressor

The task of 3D-ConvNet here is to predict the value of continuous variable z_μ instead of predicting only finite class labels as in HARRT+ algorithm. Therefore, the 3D-ConvNet is used as regressor with the input $\{M, \eta\}$ and corresponding target values z_μ. The architecture of 3D-ConvNet used is same as in the HARRT+ algorithm except the loss function calculation criteria changed from the cross-entropy to the root mean square error.

The label generation procedure for the 3D-ConvNet regressor is explained in Fig. 3. For each traffic-scenario $\{M, \eta\}$, the best trajectory π^* is found with the ARRT+ algorithm in the Matlab simulation environment. This trajectory is fed to the encoder $Q_\phi(z|\pi)$ of trained VAE to find corresponding z_μ which is assigned as a label for that scenario. In total 44692 curved road critical traffic-scenarios with different radius of curvatures, number and type of objects are used.

$$\{M, \eta\} \xrightarrow{\text{ARRT+}} \pi^* \xrightarrow{Q_\phi(z|\pi)} z_\mu$$

Fig. 3. Label generation using VAE

The inference procedure for 3D-ConvNet is defined in Fig. 4. When a traffic-scenario $\{M, \eta\}$ is encountered, the trained 3D-ConvNet is used to predict $\hat{z}_\mu$ which is directly fed to the decoder network $P_\theta(\pi|z)$, eliminating reparameterization trick to get value of sample z as in VAE, to get the predicted reference trajectory $\hat{\pi}$.

$$\{M, \eta\} \xrightarrow{\text{3D-ConvNet}} \hat{z}_\mu \xrightarrow{P_\theta(\pi|z)} \hat{\pi}$$

Fig. 4. Inference using VAE

5 Vehicle Motion Planning Algorithms

5.1 Generative Algorithm for Trajectory Exploration (GATE)

Because of the probabilistic nature of VAE, the latent space generated in VAE is continuous unlike in simple autoencoders where deterministic mapping is used. An optimization procedure can be carried out to find the optimal latent variable values z^*, which generate the best trajectory π^* using decoder $P_\theta(\pi|z)$, from the randomly initialized z. The cost function J can be defined as per the application based on criterias such as safety, comfort, etc. As the goal is to find trajectories for the collision avoidance, the area occupied by the EGO vehicle during the whole trajectory should not intersect with non-free area, i.e., area occupied by other road participants and area outside of the road. Simultaneously, the criteria of keeping as large as possible distance from other road participants is added so that a small variation in other road participants prediction does not lead to a collision. Therefore, the optimal z^* is found such that

$$z^* = \arg\min_z [J]$$

$$= \arg\min_z \left[\sum_t (S_{nf}(t) \cap s_{\pi \sim P_\theta(\pi|z)}(t)) - d_{\pi \sim P_\theta(\pi|z)} \right], \tag{9}$$

where $S_{nf}(t)$ is the non-free area of the road at time t, i.e., area outside of the road and area within the road occupied by other road participants at time t, $s_{\pi \sim P_\theta(\pi|z)}(t)$ is the area occupied by the EGO vehicle at time t along the trajectory π obtained by feeding z to decoder $P_\theta(\pi|z)$ and d_{min} is the shortest distance between the $s_{\pi \sim P_\theta(\pi|z)}(t)$ and $S_{nf}(t)$ over the whole trajectory π in time interval $t = [t_0, t_0 + \tau_1]$. The first term on the right hand side of Eq. 9, is the summation of intersection of non-free area of the road with EGO vehicle along the trajectory π. The goal is to make this term zero and increase d_{min}. The optimization solver used is a Matlab function for Nelder-Mead Simplex method [24].

The final trajectory obtained by this procedure is highly dependent on the initialization of the latent variable values. With wrong initialization, it may get trapped in a local minima leading to suboptimal values which could generate a trajectory with severe collision. Therefore, the trained 3D-ConvNet is used to predict the initial values of the latent variables $\hat{z}$ which should already very close to z^*. This whole procedure is shown in Fig. 5 and this algorithm is named as *Generative Algorithm for Trajectory Exploration* (GATE).

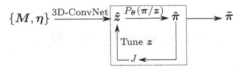

Fig. 5. GATE algorithm

5.2   GATE-ARRT+

Although GATE provides an opportunity to sample trajectories directly, it is still not a probabilistic complete algorithm like RRT algorithm. This is because VAE only learns the approximate training data distribution and not true data distribution. Therefore, its capacity of generating trajectories is dependent on the training data. But, the reference trajectory generated by GATE can be used to bias the sampling of the ARRT+ algorithm to increase its convergence rate. This combination is named as the GATE-ARRT+ algorithm. As reference trajectories generated by the GATE algorithm are closer to best trajectories for that traffic-scenario compared to the reference trajectories predicted in the

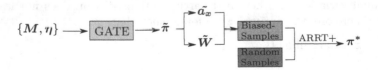

Fig. 6. GATE-ARRT+ algorithm

HARRT+ algorithm, the GATE-ARRT+ algorithm converges even more rapidly. The procedure for finding best trajectories with the GATE-ARRT+ algorithm is shown in Fig. 6.

6   Results

In order to validate the effectiveness of the proposed vehicle motion planning algorithms, many different curved-road traffic-scenarios with different number of objects having different initial velocities, positions are simulated in Matlab simulation environment and safe trajectories with different motion planning algorithms such as ARRT+, HARRT+, GATE and GATE-ARRT+ are found. The search of collision-free trajectory is stopped when a collision-free trajectory is found or the maximum number of samples used. The maximum number of samples N used for ARRT+ algorithm is 2100 as it uses pure random sampling while for the HARRT+ and GATE-HARRT+ 300 samples used. The number of iterations I for optimization procedure is limited to 10 and 2 with the GATE and GATE-ARRT+ algorithm, respectively. Note that this optimization procedure is optional in the GATE-ARRT+ algorithm. The results are summarized in the Table 1. The results show that the scenarios with less number of object (1–2 objects), the GATE algorithm is able to find a collision-free trajectory in the highest number of traffic-scenarios with shortest computation time because of lots of free space available. As the number of objects increases, the free space available decreases, and therefore the GATE algorithm converges in lesser number of traffic-scenarios. In such cases, the GATE-ARRT+ algorithm is proven to be more effective. The more efficiency of the GATE-ARRT+ algorithm compared to the HARRT+ algorithm is because of better reference trajectory provided by the VAE.

Figures 7, 8 and 9 shows the safe trajectory planned with algorithms GATE-ARRT+, HARRT+ and GATE algorithm in a traffic-scenario where a collision with pedestrian crossing the street is predicted. From figures it is clear that the HARRT+ algorithm required more number of samples compared to the GATE-ARRT+ algorithm. Also, the final trajectory (longest black trajectory) found

Table 1. Comparison of Vehicle Motion Planning Algorithms

		ARRT+ ($N = 2100$)	HARRT+ ($N = 300$)	GATE ($I = 10$)	GATE-ARRT+ ($N = 300, I = 2$)
1–2 objects (834 scenarios)	Time (Sec.)	3.33	0.81	0.31	0.45
	% Conv.	97.52	96.04	98.92	97.24
3–4 objects (1728 scenarios)	Time (Sec.)	3.62	1.08	0.83	0.68
	% Conv.	92.99	91.14	72.22	93.17
5–6 objects (3625 scenarios)	Time (Sec.)	4.34	1.32	1.15	0.87
	% Conv.	89.02	86	57.98	88.02

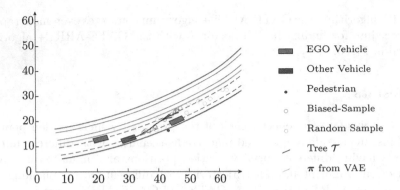

Fig. 7. Simulation result with GATE-ARRT+ algorithm

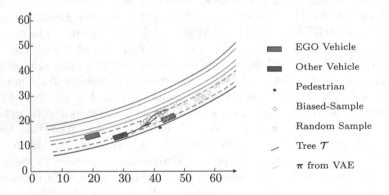

Fig. 8. Simulation result with HARRT+ algorithm

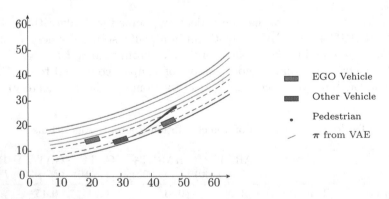

Fig. 9. Simulation result with GATE algorithm

by GATE-ARRT+ algorithm has smoother shape compared to ones found by HARRT+ and GATE algorithm. This example shows indeed a better reference trajectory will lead to better final trajectory found by the ARRT+ algorithm.

7   Conclusion

This paper presents a methodology of using variational autoencoder for generating many template trajectories which can be used for biased-sampling with a sampling-based motion planning algorithm. Two different motion planning algorithms, namely GATE and GATE-ARRT+, are proposed using the framework of generating trajectories with variational autoencoder. The simulation results not only demonstrate increase in the convergence speed compared to previously proposed sampling-based motion planning algorithms but also exemplarily show improvement in the quality of the final trajectory produced.

References

1. Mohanan M., Salgoankar A.: A survey of robotic motion planning in dynamic environments Robotics and Autonomous Systems (2017). https://doi.org/10.1016/j.robot.2017.10.011
2. Kuffner, J., LaValle, S.: RRT-connect: an efficient approach to single-query path planning. In: IEEE International Conference on Robotics and Automation (2000)
3. Elbanhawi, M., Simic, M.: Sampling-based robot motion planning: a review. IEEE Access **2**, 56–77 (2014)
4. Otte, M., Frazzoli, E.: RRT-X: real-time motion planning/replanning for environments with unpredictable obstacles. In: International Workshop on the Algorithmic Foundations of Robotics (2014)
5. Kuwata, Y., et al.: Real-time motion planning with applications to autonomous urban driving. IEEE Trans. Control Syst. Tech. **17**, 1105–1118 (2009)
6. Chaulwar, A., et al.: Planning of safe trajectories in dynamic multi-object traffic-scenarios. J. Traffic Logist. Eng. (2016)
7. Urmson, C., Simmons, R.: Approaches for heuristically biasing RRT growth. In: IEEE International Conference on Intelligent Robots and Systems, vol. 2 (2003)
8. Kiesel, S., Burns, E., Ruml, W.: Abstraction-guided sampling for motion planning. In: SoCS (2012)
9. Karaman, S., et al.: Anytime motion planning using the RRT*. In: IEEE International Conference on Robotics and Automation (2011)
10. Akgun, B., Stilman, M.: Sampling heuristics for optimal motion planning in high dimensions. In: IROS (2011)
11. Kim, D., Lee, J., Yoon, S.: Cloud RRT*. In: IEEE International Conference on Robotics and Automation (2014)
12. Gammell, J., Srinivasa, S., Barfoot, T.: Batch Informed Trees (BIT*): sampling-based optimal planning via the heuristically guided search of implicit random geometric graphs. In: IEEE International Conference on Robotics and Automation (2015)
13. Huh, J., Lee, D.: Learning high-dimensional mixture models for fast collision detection in rapidly-exploring random trees. In: IEEE International Conference on Robotics and Automation (2016)
14. Chaulwar, A., Botsch, M., Utschick, W.: A hybrid machine learning approach for planning safe trajectories in complex traffic-scenarios. In: International Conference on Machine Learning and Applications (2016)
15. Ichter, B., Harrison, J., Pavone, M.: Learning sampling distributions for robot motion planning. In: International Conference on Robotics and Automation (2018)

16. Silver, D., et al.: Mastering the game of Go with deep neural networks and tree search. Nature **529**(7587), 484–489 (2016)
17. Anthony, T., Tian, Z., Barber, D.: Thinking fast and slow with deep learning and tree search. arXiv:1705.08439 (2017)
18. Chaulwar, A., Botsch, M., Utschick W.: A machine learning based biased-sampling approach for planning safe trajectories in complex traffic-scenarios. In: IEEE Intelligent Vehicles Symposium (2017)
19. Ji, S., Xu, W., Yang, M., Yu, K.: 3D convolutional neural networks for human action recognition. IEEE TPAMI **35**, 221–231 (2013)
20. Jazar, R.: Vehicle Dynamics Theory and Application. Vehicle Planar Dynamics, 2nd edn. Springer, Heidelberg (2014). https://doi.org/10.1007/978-0-387-74244-1. Chapter 10
21. Graves, A.: Generating sequences with recurrent neural networks. arXiv preprint arXiv:1308.0850 (2013)
22. Shah, R., Romijnders, R.: Applying deep learning to basketball trajectories. arXiv preprint arXiv:1608.03793 (2016)
23. Kingma, D.P., Welling, M.: Auto-encoding variational Bayes. In: International Conference on Learning Representations (ICLR) (2013)
24. Lagarias, J.C., Reeds, J.A., Wright, M.H., Wright, P.E.: Convergence properties of the Nelder-Mead simplex method in low dimensions. SIAM J. Optim. **9**(1), 112–147 (1998)

Joint Application of Group Determination of Parameters and of Training with Noise Addition to Improve the Resilience of the Neural Network Solution of the Inverse Problem in Spectroscopy to Noise in Data

Igor Isaev[1,2]($\boxtimes$), Sergey Burikov[1,2], Tatiana Dolenko[1,2],
Kirill Laptinskiy[1,2], Alexey Vervald[2], and Sergey Dolenko[1]

[1] D. V. Skobeltsyn Institute of Nuclear Physics,
M. V. Lomonosov Moscow State University, Moscow 119991, Russia
isaev_igor@mail.ru, dolenko@sinp.msu.ru
[2] Physical Department, M. V. Lomonosov Moscow State University,
Moscow 119991, Russia

Abstract. In most cases, inverse problems are ill-posed or ill-conditioned, which is the reason for high sensitivity of their solution to noise in the input data. Despite the fact that neural networks have the ability to work with noisy data, in the case of inverse problems, this is not enough, because the incorrectness of the problem "outweighs" the ability of the neural network. In previous studies, the authors have shown that separate use of methods of group determination of parameters and of noise addition during training of neural networks can improve the resilience of the solution to noise in the input data. This study is devoted to the investigation of joint application of these methods. The study is performed at the example of an inverse problem in laser Raman spectroscopy - determination of concentrations of ions in a solution of inorganic salts by Raman spectrum of the solution.

Keywords: Artificial neural networks · Perceptron
Multi-parameter inverse problems · Noise resilience
Group determination of parameters

1 Introduction

Inverse problems (IPs) represent a very important class of problems. Almost any problem of indirect measurements belongs to this class. IPs include many problems from the areas of geophysics [1], spectroscopy [2], various types of tomography [3], and many others.

This study has been performed at the expense of the grant of Russian Science Foundation (project no. 14-11-00579).

© Springer Nature Switzerland AG 2018
V. Kůrková et al. (Eds.): ICANN 2018, LNCS 11139, pp. 435–444, 2018.
https://doi.org/10.1007/978-3-030-01418-6_43

Practical IPs have a number of features that significantly complicate their solution. As a rule, they are nonlinear and often have high input dimension and high output dimension (they are multi-parameter problems). In general, the IPs have no analytical solution, so in most cases they are solved numerically.

Traditional methods for solving IPs are matrix methods using Tikhonov regularization [4], as well as optimization methods based on multiple solutions of the direct problem and minimization of the discrepancy in the space of the observed values [5].

However, traditional methods have a number of disadvantages. For methods based on regularization, the main difficulty is the choice of the regularization parameter. In addition, matrix methods are linear methods, so in order to use them to solve nonlinear problems, it is necessary to perform nonlinear data preprocessing.

Optimization methods are characterized by high computational cost and require a good first approximation (in some cases obtained by alternative measurement methods). The main disadvantage of optimization methods is the need to have a correct model of solving the direct problem, in the absence of which this method is not applicable. In addition, due to the incorrectness of IPs, a small discrepancy in the space of the observed values does not guarantee a small error in the space of the determined parameters [6].

Therefore, in this paper we consider artificial neural networks as an alternative that is free from the shortcomings inherent in traditional methods of solving IPs.

In most cases, IPs are ill-posed or ill-conditioned, which is the reason for the high sensitivity of their solutions to noise in the input data, both for traditional methods and for neural networks. At the same time, the IP solutions will almost always deal with noisy data, because any measurements are characterized by some measurement error. As a result, the development of some approaches to improve the resilience of the IP solution to noise in the input data is an urgent task.

Despite the fact that neural networks have the ability to work with noisy data, in the case of IPs, this is not enough, because the incorrectness of the problem often "outweighs" the ability of the neural network.

This study, as well as a number of previous works of the authors [7–10], is devoted to the development of approaches to improve the resilience of neural network solutions of multi-parameter inverse problems to noise in the input data.

In [7, 8] it has been demonstrated that simultaneous determination of a group of parameters in some cases allows increasing the resilience of the neural network solution to noise in the input data. In this case, as a rule, the higher is the noise level, the more pronounced is the effect of using this approach.

Adding noise during perceptron type neural network training showed itself as a useful method to improve the trained network in various respects. The basis for use of this method was founded in [9, 10], where it was demonstrated that it can improve the generalizing capabilities of the network. In [11] it was shown that use of this method is equivalent to Tikhonov regularization. In addition, it can be used to prevent network overtraining [12–14], as well as to speed up learning [15]. The method is also used in the training of deep neural networks [16]. In [17, 18], the authors used adding noise during training to increase noise resilience of trained perceptron type neural networks to noise in the input data, where it showed its effectiveness.

In this paper, the efficiency of the two named methods was compared at the data of a high-dimensional multi-parameter non-linear inverse problem in laser Raman spectroscopy, and their combined use was investigated.

2 Problem Statement

The problem considered in this paper was to determine the concentrations of 10 ions (Cl^-, F^-, HCO_3^-, K^+, Li^+, Mg^{2+}, Na^+, NH_4^+, NO_3^-, SO_4^{2-}) contained in multi-component solutions of 10 inorganic salts ($MgSO_4$, $Mg(NO_3)_2$, $LiCl$, $LiNO_3$, NH_4F, $(NH_4)_2SO_4$, KF, $KHCO_3$, $NaHCO_3$, $NaCl$) by their Raman scattering spectra (Fig. 1). The investigated solutions contained 1 to all 10 of the salts in the concentration range 0–1.5 M (mole/liter) with an increment of 0.15–0.25 M. The excitation of the spectra was performed with an argon laser with the wavelength of 488 nm. Spectrum registration was carried out by a multi-channel detector based on a CCD matrix. For each solution, the spectrum was registered in 1824 channels in the range of Raman frequencies of 565...4000 cm^{-1}. The initial data set on which this study was performed contained 4445 patterns.

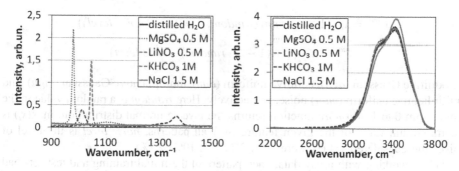

Fig. 1. Sample Raman spectra of multi-component solutions.

The principle possibility of using Raman spectra to determine ion concentrations in a solution is due to the high sensitivity of the spectrum to the type and concentration of substances dissolved in water. Many complex ions (sulfides, sulfates, nitrates, phosphates etc.) have their proper Raman bands in the region of 300–2000 cm^{-1} (Fig. 1, left) [19, 20]. The position of these lines strictly corresponds to the frequency of oscillations of molecular groups of these ions, and the intensity of the lines depends on their concentration in water. For the solution of several salts, the dependence of the line intensity on the concentration is non-linear. Monoatomic (simple) ions (e.g. Na^+, Cl^-, K^+ etc.) have no proper Raman lines; however, they have an effect on the Raman valence band of the water itself (Fig. 1, right) [21–24]. At present, no adequate mathematical models describing such types of interactions are available; therefore, practically the only way to solve the problem under consideration is to use machine learning methods based on experimental data.

3   Description of the Noise

For the considered problem, experimental data may contain the following types of data distortions:

a. Inaccuracies in salt concentration values;
b. Random noise in determining the intensity of the spectrum in various channels;
c. Distortions arising from factors influencing the entire spectrum: excessive illumination of the sample, change in laser power, channel shifting of the spectrum due to small changes of alignment etc.

In this paper, we consider case b – Random noise in determining the intensity of the spectrum in various channels.

Two types of noise were considered: additive and multiplicative, and two kinds of statistics: uniform noise (uniform noise distribution) and Gaussian noise (normal distribution). The value of each observed feature was transformed as follows:

$$x_i^{agn} = x_i + norminv(random, \mu = 0, \sigma = noise\ level) \cdot \max(x_i)$$

$$x_i^{aun} = x_i + (1 - 2 \cdot random) \cdot noise\ level \cdot \max(x_i)$$

$$x_i^{mgn} = x_i \cdot (1 + norminv(random, \mu = 0, \sigma = noise\ level))$$

$$x_i^{mun} = x_i \cdot (1 + (1 - 2 \cdot random) \cdot noise\ level)$$

for additive Gaussian (*agn*), additive uniform (*aun*), multiplicative Gaussian (*mgn*), and multiplicative uniform (*mun*) noise, respectively. Here *random* is a random value in the range from 0 to 1, *norminv* function returns the inverse normal distribution, max(x_i) is the maximum value of the given feature over all patterns, *noise level* is the level of noise (the considered values were: 1%, 3%, 5%, 10%, 20%).

When working with noisy data, each pattern of the initial training and test sets had 10 implementations with noise. Each set contained noise of certain level, type and statistics. Including a set without noise, there were total 21 out-of-sample (examination) data sets: 5 noise levels × 2 noise types × 2 kinds of statistics + 1 = 21.

4   Solving the Problem

4.1   Use of Neural Networks

To solve the problem, one of the most widespread neural network architectures was used – a multilayer perceptron (MLP). We used neural networks containing three hidden layers with 64, 32 and 16 neurons in the 1st, 2nd and 3rd hidden layers, respectively. The activation function in the hidden layers was logistic, in the output layer it was linear. Training was carried out by the method of stochastic gradient descent. Each network was trained 5 times with various weights initializations. Statistics of application of these 5 networks were averaged.

To prevent overtraining of neural networks, the method of early stop of the training was used. The initial data set was randomly divided into training, validation and test sets. Training was performed on the training data set; training was stopped by the minimum of the mean squared error on the validation set (after 1000 epochs without improving the result). Independent evaluation of the results was performed on the test (out-of-sample) set along with additional test sets with noise described in Sect. 3.

In the case of data without noise, the number of patterns in the training, validation and test sets was 70, 20, 10% of the number of patterns in the original set. So, the training data set contained 3112 patterns, validation set – 889 patterns, test set – 444 patterns.

In the case of data containing noise, each patterns of these sets was presented in 10 noise implementations. So, the size of the sets was: training – 31120 patterns, test – 4440 patterns each. The validation set was left unchanged (see Sect. 4.4).

When using training with noise, neural networks trained with noise were applied to test sets with the same noise type and noise statistics. In the case of noise-free training, neural networks were applied to all test sets.

4.2 Selection of Input Features

To reduce the input dimension of the problem, a priori knowledge about the object was used. The input of the neural network was fed with the features representing the spectrum intensities in the channels lying in the intervals 960–1143, 1312–1690, 3014–3601 cm^{-1}, which correspond to the most informative parts of the spectrum: the valence band of water and the characteristic lines of complex ions. Thus, the input dimension of the problem was reduced almost three-fold and amounted to 664 features.

4.3 Method of Group Determination of Parameters

The following ways of parameter determination were considered:

- *Autonomous determination* – for each ion, a separate single-output MLP was trained.
- *Simultaneous determination* – with a single neural network with 10 outputs.
- *Group determination* – using the following grouping principles: simple ions, complex ions, cations, anions. So, from 4 to 6 parameters were determined simultaneously using a neural network with the corresponding number of outputs.

Each of the listed methods of parameter determination was presented both independently and in conjunction with the method of training with noise.

4.4 Method of Training with Noise

This method was implemented by using training data sets containing a certain level of noise. In this case it is possible to abandon the validation data set, because the addition of noise is in itself a method of preventing overtraining [12–14]. In the case where the validation set is used, it must contain noise with the same noise type and noise statistics and with the same noise level as in the training set. It is possible to use a validation set that does not contain noise. In [17] it was shown that the optimal method of training was when training was performed on a training set, which contained noise, and the training was stopped on a validation set without noise. With this method, the quality of the solution was higher, and the training time was lower.

This method was the one used in the present study.

5   Results

Figure 2 shows the dependence of the solution quality (mean absolute error, MAE) for the original solution, separately for the method of training with noise and for the method of group determination of parameters, on the noise level in the test set. It can be seen that the resilience of the solution to noise in the data is higher for multiplicative noise than for additive noise and higher for uniform noise than for Gaussian noise.

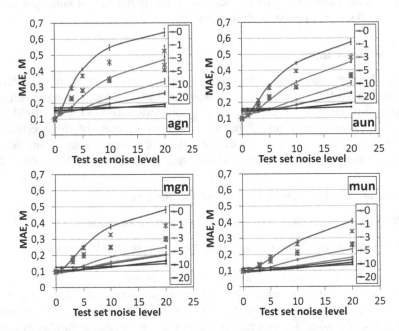

Fig. 2. The dependence of the quality of the solution (MAE) for the Cl⁻ ion on the noise level in the test set for different noise types and noise statistics. Red lines represent the original solution (no noise and no grouping), other line colors represent the method of adding noise to the training patterns; markers show the results of group determination. (Color figure online)

For the method of adding noise during training, it can be seen that the higher is the noise level in the training data set, the worse the network performs on data without noise, but the slower it degrades with increasing noise level. For other ions under consideration, the nature of the dependencies is completely similar.

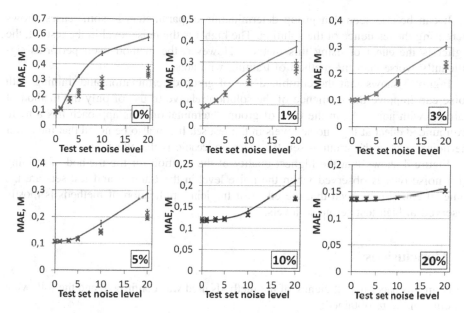

Fig. 3. The dependence of the solution quality (MAE) on the noise level in the test set for the K^+ ion for additive Gaussian noise. Lines – only method of adding noise during training, markers – joint use of both methods. Various graphs correspond to various noise levels added to the training set.

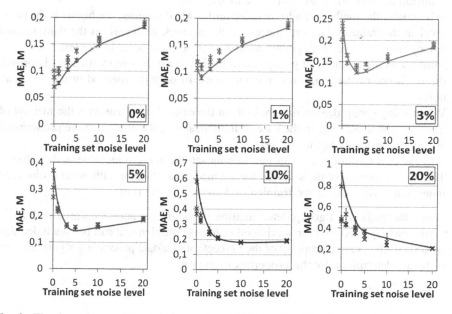

Fig. 4. The dependence of the solution quality (MAE) on the noise level in the training set for the NH_4^+ ion for additive uniform noise. Lines – only method of adding noise during training, markers – joint use of both methods. Various graphs correspond to various noise levels contained in the test sets.

I. Isaev et al.

It can be also seen that group determination of parameters in some cases allows increasing the resilience of the solution. The higher is the noise level in the test set, the higher is the effect of using this method. However, the method itself performs significantly worse than the method of training with noise.

Figure 3 shows that the combined use of group determination and training with noise can improve the resilience of the solution relative to use of only the method of training with noise. As in the case of group determination, this approach has a more pronounced effect at high noise levels in the test set. It can also be noted that the lower the noise level in the training set, the more noticeable is the effect.

Figure 4 shows that the highest quality of the solution for the method of training with noise only is observed when the noise level in the training and test sets are the same. It can also be seen that the effect of the joint application of methods is mostly observed at high test set noise levels.

6 Conclusions

Thus, in this paper the efficiency of the methods used was confirmed, and the following conclusions were obtained:

- For the inverse problem of Raman spectroscopy for all the approaches used, the resilience of the solution to the noise in the input data is higher for the multiplicative noise type than for the additive noise type, and higher for the uniform noise distribution than for the Gaussian noise distribution.
- When using the method of adding noise during MLP training, the higher is the noise level in the training data set, the worse the network performs on the data without noise, but the slower it degrades with increasing noise level in the test set.
- Joint use of the methods of group determination and of training with noise improves the resilience of the solution compared to use of only the method of training with noise.
- When using group determination, both in the case of joint use with the method of training with noise, and in the case of individual use, the effect is more pronounced at high noise levels in the test set.
- The lower is the noise level in the training set, the more noticeable is the effect.
- The highest quality of the solution for the method of training with noise is observed when the noise level in the training and test sets is the same.

Since the methods of group determination of parameters and of training with noise were successfully used also for solving other inverse problems, it can be concluded that the observed effects are a property of the perceptron as a data processing algorithm, and they are not determined by the properties of the data.

References

1. Zhdanov, M.: Inverse Theory and Applications in Geophysics, 2nd edn. Elsevier, Amsterdam (2015)
2. Yagola, A., Kochikov, I., Kuramshina, G.: Inverse Problems of Vibrational Spectroscopy. De Gruyter, Berlin (1999)
3. Mohammad-Djafari, A. (ed.): Inverse Problems in Vision and 3D Tomography. Wiley, Hoboken (2010)
4. Zhdanov, M.S.: Geophysical Electromagnetic Theory and Methods. Methods in Geochemistry and Geophysics, vol. 43. Elsevier, Amsterdam (2009)
5. Spichak, V.V. (ed.): Electromagnetic Sounding of the Earth's Interior. Methods in Geochemistry and Geophysics, vol. 40. Elsevier, Amsterdam (2006)
6. Isaev, I., Dolenko, S.: Comparative analysis of residual minimization and artificial neural networks as methods of solving inverse problems: test on model data. In: Samsonovich, A., Klimov, V., Rybina, G. (eds.) Biologically Inspired Cognitive Architectures (BICA) for Young Scientists. Advances in Intelligent Systems and Computing, vol. 449, pp. 289–295. Springer, Cham (2016). https://doi.org/10.1007/978-3-319-32554-5_37
7. Isaev, I., Obornev, E., Obornev, I., Shimelevich, M., Dolenko, S.: Increase of the resistance to noise in data for neural network solution of the inverse problem of magnetotellurics with group determination of parameters. In: Villa, A., Masulli, P., Pons Rivero, A. (eds.) ICANN 2016, LNCS, vol. 9886, pp. 502–509. Springer, Cham (2016). https://doi.org/10.1007/978-3-319-44778-0_59
8. Isaev, I., Vervald, E., Sarmanova, O., Dolenko, S.: Neural network solution of an inverse problem in Raman spectroscopy of multi-component solutions of inorganic salts: group determination as a method to increase noise resilience of the solution. Procedia Comput. Sci. **123**, 177–182 (2018)
9. Holmstrom, L., Koistinen, P.: Using additive noise in back-propagation training. IEEE Trans. Neural Netw. **3**(1), 24–38 (1992)
10. Matsuoka, K.: Noise injection into inputs in back-propagation learning. IEEE Trans. Syst. Man Cybern. **22**(3), 436–440 (1992)
11. Bishop, C.M.: Training with noise is equivalent to Tikhonov regularization. Neural Comput. **7**(1), 108–116 (1995)
12. An, G.: The effects of adding noise during back propagation training on a generalization performance. Neural Comput. **8**(3), 643–674 (1996)
13. Zur, R.M., Jiang, Y., Pesce, L.L., Drukker, K.: Noise injection for training artificial neural networks: a comparison with weight decay and early stopping. Med. Phys. **36**(10), 4810–4818 (2009)
14. Piotrowski, A.P., Napiorkowski, J.J.: A comparison of methods to avoid overfitting in neural networks training in the case of catchment runoff modeling. J. Hydrol. **476**, 97–111 (2013)
15. Wang, C., Principe, J.C.: Training neural networks with additive noise in the desired signal. IEEE Trans. Neural Netw. **10**(6), 1511–1517 (1999)
16. Yin, S., et al.: Noisy training for deep neural networks in speech recognition. EURASIP J. Audio Speech Music. Process. **2015**(2), 1–14 (2015)
17. Isaev, I.V., Dolenko, S.A.: Training with noise as a method to increase noise resilience of neural network solution of inverse problems. Opt. Mem. Neural Netw. (Inf. Opt.) **25**(3), 142–148 (2016)

18. Isaev, I.V., Dolenko, S.A.: Adding noise during training as a method to increase resilience of neural network solution of inverse problems: test on the data of magnetotelluric sounding problem. In: Kryzhanovsky, B., Dunin-Barkowski, W., Redko, V. (eds.) Neuroinformatics 2017. Studies in Computational Intelligence, vol. 736, pp. 9–16. Springer, Cham (2018). https://doi.org/10.1007/978-3-319-66604-4_2
19. Baldwin, S.F., Brown, C.W.: Detection of ionic water pollutants by laser excited Raman spectroscopy. Water Res. **6**, 1601–1604 (1972)
20. Rudolph, W.W., Irmer, G.: Raman and infrared spectroscopic investigation on aqueous alkali metal phosphate solutions and density functional theory calculations of phosphate-water clusters. Appl. Spectrosc. **61**(12), 274A–292A (2007)
21. Furic, K., Ciglenecki, I., Cosovic, B.: Raman spectroscopic study of sodium chloride water solutions. J. Mol. Struct. **6**, 225–234 (2000)
22. Dolenko, T.A., Churina, I.V., Fadeev, V.V., Glushkov, S.M.: Valence band of liquid water Raman scattering: some peculiarities and applications in the diagnostics of water media. J. Raman Spectrosc. **31**(8–9), 863–870 (2000)
23. Rull, F., De Saja, J.A.: Effect of electrolyte concentration on the Raman spectra of water in aqueous solutions. J. Raman Spectrosc. **17**(2), 167–172 (1986)
24. Gogolinskaia, T.A., Patsaeva, S.V., Fadeev, V.V.: The regularities of change of the 3100–3700 cm^{-1} band of water Raman scattering in salt aqueous solutions. Dokl. Akad. Nauk SSSR **290**(5), 1099–1103 (1986)

Learning

Generating Natural Answers
on Knowledge Bases and Text
by Sequence-to-Sequence Learning

Zhihao Ye[✉], Ruichu Cai, Zhaohui Liao, Zhifeng Hao, and Jinfen Li

School of Computer Science and Technology, Guangdong University of Technology,
Guangzhou, China
zhihaoye.chn@qq.com

Abstract. Generative question answering systems aim at generating more contentful responses and more natural answers. Existing generative question answering systems applied to knowledge grounded conversation generate natural answers either with a knowledge base or with raw text. Nevertheless, performance of their methods is often affected by the incompleteness of the KB or text facts. In this paper, we propose an end-to-end generative question answering model. We make use of unstructured text and structured KBs to establish an universal schema as a large external facts library. Each words of a natural answer are dynamically predicted from the common vocabulary and retrieved from the corresponding external facts. And our model can generate natural answer containing arbitrary number of knowledge entities through selecting from multiple relevant external facts by the dynamic knowledge enquirer. Finally, empirical study shows that our model is efficient and outperforms baseline methods significantly in terms of automatic evaluation and human evaluation.

Keywords: Natural answers · Universal schema
Sequence-to-sequence learning

1 Introduction

Recent neural models of dialogue generation such as sequence to sequence model can be trained in an end-to-end and completely data-driven fashion. However, these fully data-driven models tend to generate safe responses that are boring and carry little information. In other words, these models can not have access to any external knowledge, which makes it difficult to respond substantively. From another perspective, we can consider generative question answering as a special case of knowledge grounded conversation. As the examples shown in Table 1, daily conversations generally depends on individual's knowledge. Recently, some researchers proposed neural conversation model that can generate natural answers and knowledge-grounded responses either with knowledge base or with raw text.

© Springer Nature Switzerland AG 2018
V. Kůrková et al. (Eds.): ICANN 2018, LNCS 11139, pp. 447–455, 2018.
https://doi.org/10.1007/978-3-030-01418-6_44

Table 1. Examples of training instances for our model. The natural answer containing mutil-number of knowledge entities is generated based on both Knowledge Bases and Text.

KB fact	(Peking University, President,Yan Fu)
text fact	Yan Fu is the first President of Peking University.
UserA: Who was the first President of Peking University? **UserB:** The first President is Yan Fu	
KB fact	(The Journey to the West, author, Wu Chenen) (The Journey to the West, written time,Ming dynasty)
text fact	Wu Chenen who is the author of The Journey to the West was an outstanding novelist of the Ming dynasty.
UserA: Who is the author of "journey to the west". **UserB:** It was wu chengen in the Ming dynasty.	

In order to generate more contentful responses, more and more generative question answering systems and knowledge-grounded conversation model are proposed. On one hand, Ghazvininejad et al. [4] utilized external textual information as the unstructured knowledge. They found that unstructured knowledge can make a response more contentful. On the other hand, Yin et al. [18], He et al. [6] and Zhu et al. [20] have proposed generative question answering (QA) model that can generate natural answers by entities retrieved from the KB and seq2seq model [15]. But, the performance of model above are often affected by the incompleteness of the KB or text. How to generate more contentful resposes or natural answer by exploiting KB and text together is necessary to study.

In this paper, we propose our neural generative dialogue model, which can generate responses based on input message and external facts. For the first time, we propose our approach that combined text and KB library as our external facts by building the universal schema [10] to generate natural answer. In each time step of generating the natural answer, the possible word may come from common word vocabulary or knowledge entity vocabulary and the natural answer that contains the relevant arbitrary number of entities can be generated. Finally we conduct experiments on real-world datasets. Experimental results demonstrate that combining unstructured knowledge with structured knowledge is effective for generating natural answer, and our model is more efficient than the existing end-to-end QA/Dialogue model.

2   Related Work

Recently, sequence-to-sequence [7, 15] learning, which can predict target sequence given source sequence, has been widely applied in dialogue systems. Shang et al. [14] first utilized the encoder and decoder framework to generate responses on micro-blogging websites. And after that, more and more dialogue system [12,13,16] on the basis of seq2seq framework were proposed. In our work, our model is also based on seq2seq framework and we try to combine the external facts composed of KB and text to generate more contentful responses.

Many researchers propose open domain dialogue system which can incorporate external knowledge to enhance reply generation. Han et al. [5] proposed a rule-based dialogue system by filling the response templates with retrieved KB. Ghazvininejad et al. [4] utilized external textual information as the unstructured knowledge. As demonstrated, the external textual information can convey more relevant information to responses. Some recent work used external structured knowledge graph to build end-to-end question answering systems. Yin et al. [18] proposed a seq2seq-based model where answers were generated in two ways, where one was based on a language model and the other was by some entities retrieved from the KB. He et al. [6] and [20] further studied the cases where questions require multiple facts and out-of-vocabulary entities.

In older to improve the performance of knowledge base QA model. Das et al. [3] extend universal schema to natural language question answering, employing memory networks to attend to the large amount of facts in the combination of text and KB. Inspired by them, we also have built the universal schema to combine KB and text and tried to employ a key-value MemNN model as our knowledge enquirer. But different from them, our model can generate more natural answer, rather than a single entity. Other work such as [17,19], also put forward some models to exploit KB and the text together, but their formulations are totally different from ours.

3 Our Framework

3.1 Framework Overview

In real-world environments, people prefer to reply one's question with a more natural way. Jsut like the example shown in Table 1, When user A asks "Who is the first President of Peking University?", user B should answer: "The first President is Yan Fu" rather than only one entity or an answer that is not relevant to the question. For the above natural language question-answering scenario, in our work,the problem can be defined as: given an input message $Q = (x_1, x_2, ..., x_L)$, the problem is to generate an appropriate response $Y = (y_1, y_2, ..., y_L)$ based all possible facts form text and KB. And in order to try to solve the above problems, we propose an end-to-end generative question answering system, which is illustrated in Fig. 1.

3.2 Candidate Facts Retriever

The candidate facts retriever identifies facts that are related to the input message. In our work, the model retrieve the relevant text facts by firstly finding the

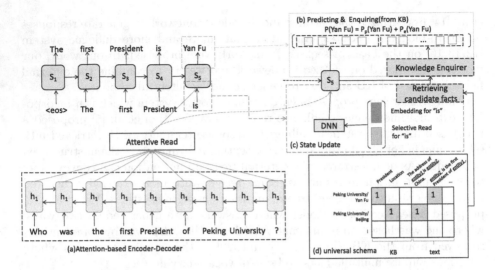

Fig. 1. The overview of our model. Our model consists of message encoder, candidate facts retriever, reply decoder, and universal schema containing external facts. When the user inputs a question, the knowledge retrieval module is firstly employed to retrieve related facts. And then message encoder encode the problem into hidden states. Finally, hidden state from message encoder are feed to reply decoder for generating natural answer.

relevant KB triples (subject-property-object) from the universal schema. Specifically, We denote the entities of Q by $E = (e_1, e_2, ..., e_m)$. E can be identified by keyword matching, or detected by more advanced methods such as entity linking or named entity recognition. Based on detected triples, we can retrieve the relevant facts from universal schema. Usually, question contains the information used to match the subject and property parts in a fact triple, and answer incorporates the object part information.

3.3 Question Encoder

In older to catch the user's intent and get hidden representations of input message. We employ a bidirectional GRU [2,11] to transform the message $Q = (x_1, x_2, ..., x_L)$ into a sequence of concatenated hidden states with two independent GRU. Once a message is encoded by message encoder, the forward and backward GRU respectively obtain the hidden state$\{\overrightarrow{h_1}, \overrightarrow{h_1}, ..., \overrightarrow{h_L}\}$ and $\{\overleftarrow{h_L}, ..., \overleftarrow{h_2}, \overleftarrow{h_1}\}$, where L is the maximum length of the message. The context memory of input message can be obtained by concatenated hidden state list $H_Q = \{h_1, ..., ht, ..., h_L\}$, where h_t is equal to $[\overrightarrow{h}_t, \overleftarrow{h}_{(L-t+1)}]$. Besides, the last hidden state h_t is used to represent the entire message.

3.4 Reply Decoder

The reply decoder generates the final response Y based on the hidden representations of input message H_Q and candidate facts F_Q that come from the universal schema. There are two categories of possible words, the common words and knowledge words, in the generated response. Specifically, the probability of generating the answer:

$$p(y_1, y_2, ..., y_{L_Y}|H_Q, F_Q; \theta) =$$

$$p(y_1|H_Q, F_Q; \theta) \prod_{t=2}^{L_Y} p(y_t|y_1, y_2, ..., y_{t-1}, H_Q, F_Q; \theta) \quad (1)$$

where θ represents the parameters in the model. The generation probability of y_t is specified by

$$p(y_t|y_1, y_2, ..., y_{L_Y}, H_Q, F_Q; \theta) = p(y_t|y_{t-1}, z_t, s_t, H_Q, F_Q; \theta) \quad (2)$$

where s_t is the hidden state of the decoder model and $z_t \in \{0,1\}$ is the value predicted by a binary classifier. In generating the tth word y_t in the answer, the probability is given by the following mixture model.

$$p(y_t|y_1, y_2, ..., y_{L_Y}, H_Q, F_Q; \theta) = p_c(y_t|z = 0)p(z = 0|y_{t-1}, s_t, H_Q, F_Q; \theta)$$
$$+ p_e(y_t|z = 1)p(z = 1|y_{t-1}, s_t, H_Q, F_Q; \theta) \quad (3)$$

Response Words Prediction Classifier. In order to generate the final response containing common words and knowledge words, we apply a MLP as a binary classifier and at each time step, feeding a time step s_{t-1}, y_{t-1}, the MLP classifier outputs a predicted value $z_t \in \{0,1\}$. If $z_t = 0$, it means that the next generation word is from the entity vocabulary and in our work, the entity vocabulary contains all the "object" of the KB triples. And conversely, if $z_t = 1$, the next generation word is generated from common vocabulary. In summary, the y_t is generated as:

$$p(yt|y_{t-1}, z_t, s_t, H_Q, F_Q; \theta) = p_c(y_t)p(z = 0|y_{t-1}, s_t, H_Q, F_Q; \theta)$$
$$+ p_e(y_t)p(z = 1|y_{t-1}, s_t, H_Q, F_Q; \theta) \quad (4)$$

Universal Schema. To make full use of external facts from structured KBs and unstructured text, our external knowledge M comprise of both KB and text. And Inspired by Das et al. [3], we applied universal schema to integrate KB and text. Each cell of universal schema is in the form of key-value pair. Specifically, let $(s, r, o) \in K$ represent a KB triple, the key $\mathbf{k}$ is represented by concatenating the embeddings $\mathbf{s}$ and $\mathbf{r}$ and the object entity $\mathbf{o}$ is treated as it's value $\mathbf{v}$. For text, Let $(s, [w_1, ..., entity_1, ..., entity_2, w_n], o) \in T$ represent a textual fact, where $entity_1$ and $entity_2$ correspond to the positions of the entities subject and object. We represent the key as the sequence formed by replacing $entity_1$ with subject and $entity_2$ with a special 'blank' token, i.e., $k = [w_1, ..., s, ..., blank, w_n]$, which is converd to a distributed representation using a bidirectional GRU, and value as just the entity object $\mathbf{o}$.

Knowledge Enquirer. We have chosen two implementations that have similar effect in our experiment as knowledge enquirer to calculate the matching scores between question and candidate facts. The first model is a two-layer MLP. The fact representation f is then defined as the concatenation of key and value. The list of all related facts' representations, $\{f\} = \{f_1, f_2, ..., f_{L_F}\}$ (L_F denotes the maximum of candidate facts), is considered to be a short-term memory of the large body external knowledge memory M. We define the matching scores function between question and facts as function is $S(q, s_t, f_j) = DNN1(q, s_t, f_j)$ where s_t is the hidden state of decoder at time t and DNN1 is the two-layer MLP. In addition, we also adopt the key-value MemNN proposeed by Miller et al. [8] where each memory slot consists of a key and value. It is worth noting that, excepting for question and related facts, We also need to use state s_t of decoding process as the input of the key-value MemNN because the matching results also depend on the state of decoding process at different times.

Common Word Generator. To generate richer content and more matching answers to user questions, we applied a GRU model and attention mechanism to generate common words. Firstly, we calculate a message context vector c_t by using the attention mechanism [1] on the message hidden vectors H with the current generator hidden state s_{t-1}. And then, the word of the next time step s_t is obtained as $s_t = f(y_{t-1}, s_{t-1}, c_t)$. Finally, the predicted target word y_t at time t is performed by a softmax classifier over a settled vocabulary (e.g. 40,000 words) through function g:$p(yt|y_{<t}, X) = g(y_{t-1}, s_t, c_t)$.

State Update. In the generic decoding process, each hidden state s_t is updated with the previous state s_{t-1}, the word embedding of previous predicted symbol y_{t-1}, and an optional context vector c_t (with attention mechanism). However, y_{t-1} may not come from entity vocabulary and not owns a word vector. Therefore, we modify the state update process. More specifically, y_{t-1} will be represented as $[e(y_{t-1}), \zeta_{k_{t-1}}]$, where $e(y_{t-1})$ is the word embedding associated with y_{t-1} and $\zeta_{k_{t-1}}$ are the weighted sum of hidden states in M_F corresponding to y_{t-1}.

$$\zeta_{kb_t} = \sum_{j=1}^{L_F} \delta_{tj} f_i \quad \delta_{tj} = \begin{cases} \frac{1}{K} P_e(f_j|\cdot) & object(f_j) = y_t \\ 0 & otherwise \end{cases} \quad (5)$$

where $object(f)$ indicate the "object" part of fact f, and K are the normalization terms which equal $\sum_{j':object(f'_j)} P_e(f'_j|\cdot)$, which can consider the multiple positions matching y_t in external facts.

4 Experiments

4.1 Dataset

For our experimental data, we used the data set provided by He et al. [6]. In addition, we have crawled the corresponding text facts from Baidu baike (a Chinese encyclopedia website). In our work, all "subject" entities and "object" entities of triples are used as encyclopedic items, and we crawl all article related to these encyclopedic items. The texts in Chinese in the data are converted into sequences of words using the Jieba Chinese word segmentor, then all related text facts were extracted through Keyword matching with KB triples. After extracting all the relevant facts from the article, we used the facts from text and KB to establish the universal schema.

4.2 Model

Firstly, we use seq2seq model with attention (seq2seq+atten) as one of our baselines, which is widely used in chit-chat dialogues system. And then, we also use generative QA model (GenQA [18] and COREQA [6]) as our baselines, which can be applied in knowledge grounded conversation. Finally, We apply our model, and compared three types of external knowledge source which respectively comprise of only KB, only textual and universal schema containing both text and KB.

4.3 Evaluation Metrics

We have compared our model with baselines by both automatic evaluation and human evaluation.

Automatic Evaluation. Following the existing works, we employ the BLEU [9] automatic evaluation, which reflects the words occurrence between the ground truth and the generated response. And to measure the information correctness, we evaluate the performance of the models in terms of accuracy. Meanwhile (same as COREQA [6]) we separately present the results according to the number of the facts which a question needs in knowledge base, including just one single fact (marked as Single), multiple facts (marked as Multi) and all (marked as Mixed). In our work, we randomly selected 5120 samples from data set as our test set, and the result is shown in Table 2.

Human Evaluation. We also recruit human annotators to judge the quality of the generated responses with aspects of Fluency, Correctness and grammar. All scores range from 1 to 5. Higher score represents better performance in terms of the above three metrics. In older to provide human evaluation, we randomly selected 300 samples from our test set, and the result is shown in Table 3.

4.4 Results

Table 2 shows the accuracies of the models on the test set. We can clearly observe that our model significantly outperforms all other baseline models and our model can generate correct answer that need single fact or multiple facts. This also proves that using KB and text as an external knowledge is helpful for generating more accurate natural answers and generating contentful responses.

Table 2. The result of automatic evaluation on test data.

Models	BLEU	Single	Multi	Mixed
seq2seq+atten	0.39	20.1	3.5	19.4
GenQA	0.38	47.2	28.9	45.1
COREQA	-	58.4	42.7	56.6
Our model$_{kb}$	0.42	56.2	45.9	54.7
Our model$_{text}$	**0.45**	47.2	42.9	45.9
Our model$_{text\&kb}$	0.43	**65.4**	**52.7**	**63.6**

Table 3. The result of human evaluation on test data.

Models	Fluency	Correctness	Grammar
seq2seq+atten	3.67	2.34	3.93
GenQA	3.56	3.39	3.73
Our model$_{text\&kb}$	**4.12**	**4.42**	**4.19**

As illustrated in Table 3, the results show that our framework outperforms other baseline models. The most significant improvement is from correctness, indicating that our model can generate more accurate answer.

5   Conclusion and Future Work

In this paper, we propose an end-to-end generative question answering system to generate natural answers containing arbitrary number of knowledge entities. We establish an universal schema as large external fact library using unstructured text and structured KB. The experimental results show that our model can generate more natural and fluent answers and universal schema is a promising knowledge source for generating natural answer than using KB or text alone. However, after extracting related text facts from raw text through keyword matching with KB triples, a lot of useful text data also were discarded. In the future, we plan to explore ways to more effectively combine structured and unstructured knowledge with a fuller use of text.

References

1. Bahdanau, D., Cho, K., Bengio, Y.: Neural machine translation by jointly learning to align and translate. Comput. Sci. (2014)
2. Chung, J., Gulcehre, C., Cho, K.H., Bengio, Y.: Empirical evaluation of gated recurrent neural networks on sequence modeling. Eprint Arxiv (2014)
3. Das, R., Zaheer, M., Reddy, S., Mccallum, A.: Question answering on knowledge bases and text using universal schema and memory networks, pp. 358–365 (2017)
4. Ghazvininejad, M., et al.: A knowledge-grounded neural conversation model (2017)

5. Han, S., Bang, J., Ryu, S., Lee, G.G.: Exploiting knowledge base to generate responses for natural language dialog listening agents. In: Meeting of the Special Interest Group on Discourse and Dialogue, pp. 129–133 (2015)
6. He, S., et al.: Generating natural answers by incorporating copying and retrieving mechanisms in sequence-to-sequence learning. In: Meeting of the Association for Computational Linguistics, pp. 199–208 (2017)
7. Hochreiter, S., Schmidhuber, J.: Long short-term memory. Neural Comput. **9**(8), 1735–1780 (1997)
8. Miller, A., Fisch, A., Dodge, J., Karimi, A.H., Bordes, A., Weston, J.: Key-value memory networks for directly reading documents, pp. 1400–1409 (2016)
9. Papineni, S.: Blue: a method for automatic evaluation of machine translation. In: Meeting of the Association for Computational Linguistics (2002)
10. Riedel, S., Yao, L., Mccallum, A., Marlin, B.M.: Relation extraction with matrix factorization and universal schemas. In: NAACL-HLT, pp. xxi–xxii (2013)
11. Schuster, M., Paliwal, K.K.: Bidirectional recurrent neural networks. IEEE Press (1997)
12. Serban, I.V., Sordoni, A., Bengio, Y., Courville, A., Pineau, J.: Building end-to-end dialogue systems using generative hierarchical neural network models. In: Thirtieth AAAI Conference on Artificial Intelligence, pp. 3776–3783 (2016)
13. Serban, I.V., et al.: A hierarchical latent variable encoder-decoder model for generating dialogues (2016)
14. Shang, L., Lu, Z., Li, H.: Neural responding machine for short-text conversation, pp. 52–58 (2015)
15. Sutskever, I., Vinyals, O., Le, Q.V.: Sequence to sequence learning with neural networks, vol. 4, pp. 3104–3112 (2014)
16. Yao, K., Zweig, G., Peng, B.: Attention with intention for a neural network conversation model. Comput. Sci. (2015)
17. Yao, L., Riedel, S., Mccallum, A.: Collective cross-document relation extraction without labelled data. University of Massachusetts, Amherst (2010)
18. Yin, J., Jiang, X., Lu, Z., Shang, L., Li, H., Li, X.: Neural generative question answering, vol. 27, pp. 2972–2978 (2015)
19. Zeng, D., Liu, K., Chen, Y., Zhao, J.: Distant supervision for relation extraction via piecewise convolutional neural networks. In: Conference on Empirical Methods in Natural Language Processing, pp. 1753–1762 (2015)
20. Zhu, W., Mo, K., Zhang, Y., Zhu, Z., Peng, X., Yang, Q.: Flexible end-to-end dialogue system for knowledge grounded conversation (2017)

Mitigating Concept Drift via Rejection

Jan Philip Göpfert[1,2]([✉]) [iD], Barbara Hammer[1], and Heiko Wersing[2]

[1] Bielefeld University, Research Institute for Cognition and Robotics,
Universitätsstraße 25, 33615 Bielefeld, Germany
jgoepfert@techfak.uni-bielefeld.de
[2] Honda Research Institute Europe GmbH,
Carl-Legien-Straße 30, 63065 Offenbach, Germany

Abstract. Learning in non-stationary environments is challenging, because under such conditions the common assumption of independent and identically distributed data does not hold; when concept drift is present it necessitates continuous system updates. In recent years, several powerful approaches have been proposed. However, these models typically classify any input, regardless of their confidence in the classification – a strategy, which is not optimal, particularly in safety-critical environments where alternatives to a (possibly unclear) decision exist, such as additional tests or a short delay of the decision. Formally speaking, this alternative corresponds to classification with rejection, a strategy which seems particularly promising in the context of concept drift, i.e. the occurrence of situations where the current model is wrong due to a concept change. In this contribution, we propose to extend learning under concept drift with rejection. Specifically, we extend two recent learning architectures for drift, the self-adjusting memory architecture (SAM-kNN) and adaptive random forests (ARF), to incorporate a reject option, resulting in highly competitive state-of-the-art technologies. We evaluate their performance in learning scenarios with different types of drift.

Keywords: Rejection · Reject option
Learning in non-stationary environments · Concept drift

1 Introduction

Machine learning (ML) increasingly permeates our daily lives in the form of intelligent household devices, robot companions, autonomous driving, intelligent decision support systems, fraud prevention, etc. Although ML models are getting ever more reliable – in particular due to increasing data volumes for training – they do not achieve 100% accuracy since they rely on statistical inference. Usually, there exist situations where ML models fail and provide invalid results.

This work was supported by Honda Research Institute Europe GmbH, Offenbach am Main, Germany.

V. Kůrková et al. (Eds.): ICANN 2018, LNCS 11139, pp. 456–467, 2018.
https://doi.org/10.1007/978-3-030-01418-6_45

Because users of a model struggle to interpret its abilities and limitations correctly [1], such failures have a measurable impact on the user's trust [2] – hence, failures should be avoided not only in safety critical environments where failures could be fatal, but also in everyday applications in order to improve user acceptance. In the case of agent models (e.g. robots), failures can often be observed easily from the agent's state (e.g. a robot not reaching its prescribed goal), and the challenge is how to communicate the cause of failure [3]. In stark contrast, failures can remain unobserved for classification models since most classifiers do not provide an explicit notion of their domain of validity. Hence the challenge arises how to enhance classifiers with an explicit notion when to reject a classification.

The notion of classification with a reject option explicitly takes into account the possibility to reject a classification in unclear cases. Pioneered by Chow [4], who derived optimal reject rules if true class probabilities are known, a number of extensions of learning with reject options have been proposed for batch learning scenarios, such as plugin rules for class probabilities [5], efficient surrogate losses [6,7], or optimal combination schemes of local rejection [8]. These approaches deal with the classical setting of batch training based on i.i.d. data. A minor extension is offered by so-called *conformal prediction*, a framework which allows to assign probabilities to classification decisions for single inputs, and, consequently, to reject classification based on those values [9]. Here, the weaker condition of exchangeability is posed, opening the floor to online learning scenarios, but not yet to concept drift [10].

A number of approaches have been proposed for learning in non-stationary environments in the presence of concept drift, whereby several recent technologies are also suited for heterogeneous types of drift [10–14]. Generally speaking, concept drift is present whenever the underlying input distribution or class posterior changes, which is the case when sensors are subject to fatigue, novel and previously unseen data is observed over time, class concepts such as opinions develop over time, settings are subject to seasonal changes, etc. When learning with drift, it is almost inevitable to encounter domains of uncertain classification – otherwise, it would not be necessary to further adapt the classification mapping, contradicting the idea of drift. Nevertheless, most learning models for non-stationary environments do not incorporate reject options. The only notable exception is the Droplets algorithm [15], which assigns some inputs explicitly to the class "reject"; size and shape of this class depend on (fixed) model metaparameters for training. A scalable reject threshold based on the required level of certainty or user acceptance is not induced by this model.

In this contribution, we aim for an enhancement of models for learning with drift by a reject option which is based on a classifier-specific certainty measure of the classification. To the best of our knowledge, this contribution constitutes the first attempt to extend learning with drift to include rejection in such a way. The overall design implies that a suitable reject threshold can be chosen in applications. We investigate rejection for an online perceptron learning algorithm, demonstrating the complexity of the task. Afterwards, we propose a reject option for two techniques, the self-adjusting memory model and adaptive random forests, achieving convincing results. We demonstrate the benefit of learning with rejection in a couple of benchmarks which incorporate different types of drift.

2 Learning with a Reject Option

A given classifier provides a mapping $f: \mathbb{R}^n \to \{1, \dots, N\}$ of real-valued data to N classes. Classification with reject option extends such functionality by a special output class ϱ, which indicates that the classifier abstains from making a decision. This option is beneficial whenever the probability of a misclassification is higher than the costs for a reject. In practice, many classifiers are equipped with a certainty measure $c: \mathbb{R}^n \to \mathbb{R}$ which indicates the certainty of the classification, e.g. the (signed) distance to the decision boundary. In such cases, a reject strategy is often based on a simple threshold θ, i.e. the classification is of the form

$$f_\theta(x) = \begin{cases} f(x) & \text{if } c(x) \geq \theta, \\ \varrho & \text{otherwise.} \end{cases} \tag{1}$$

Provided $c(x)$ is the class probability of the output class $f(x)$, this strategy is optimal [4]. For many popular classification methods, certainty measures c exist which empirically lead to excellent results [8].

2.1 Classifiers

In addition to a linear model as an initial baseline, we address an ensemble of k-NN classifiers and random forests, respectively – more complex machine learning technologies that yield state-of-the-art results. For these algorithms, the following certainty measures have been proposed:

Linear Classifier: One of the first models which has been enhanced with a reject option is the classical linear classifier. For two classes (0 and 1), a linear classifier provides the classification $f(x) = H(w^\top x - \theta)$ with the Heaviside function H, an adjustable weight vector $w \in \mathbb{R}^n$ and bias θ. A typical confidence measure is offered by $c(x) = \mathrm{sgd}(w^\top x - \theta)$ with the sigmoidal $\mathrm{sgd}(t) = 1/(1 + \exp(-t))$ for class 1 and $1 - \mathrm{sgd}(w^\top x - \theta)$ for class 0. This measure correlates to the distance of the data point x to the decision boundary. It has been demonstrated by Platt [16] that this form usually yields reasonable confidence measures, where – typically – slope and offset of the sigmoidal function are optimized based on the given data to enable an optimum match of its range to true confidence values.

k-NN classifier: Assume a point x is given with its k nearest neighbors $x_1, \dots, x_k$ and corresponding labels $y_1, \dots, y_k$. For the simple k-NN we could rely on the fraction of points of the same label within the k nearest neighbors [17]. However, this measure has the drawback that it provides $k + 1$ discrete values only.

A continuous extension can be based on formal grounds such as Dempster-Shafer theory [18], but this would require the tuning of several meta-parameters, rendering this measure unsuitable for online learning. Here, we rely on weighted k-NN classification instead:

$$f(x) = \text{argmax}_j \left\{ \sum_{i=1}^{k} \frac{\mathbb{I}(y_i, j)}{d(x, x_i)} \,\bigg|\, j = 1, \dots, N \right\} \tag{2}$$

where $d(x, x_i)$ is the (euclidean) distance[1] between x and x_i, and

$$\mathbb{I}(y_i, j) = \begin{cases} 1, & y_i = j, \\ 0, & y_i \neq j. \end{cases} \tag{3}$$

Delany et al. [19] investigate several certainty measures and propose an accumulation of several criteria that take into account distances to closest neighbors of the same class and different classes, respectively. We approximate this value by an efficient surrogate function which can be directly derived from the weighted k-NN classification rule, the normalized average distance with values in $[0, 1]$:

$$c(x) = \left(\sum_{j=1}^{N} \sum_{i=1}^{k} \frac{\mathbb{I}(y_i, j)}{d(x, x_i)} \right)^{-1} \cdot \sum_{i=1}^{k} \frac{\mathbb{I}(y_i, \hat{y})}{d(x, x_i)}. \tag{4}$$

Random forests: Random forests as introduced by Breiman [20] constitute one of the current state-of-the-art classifiers [21], offering a classification as an ensemble of decision trees. Typically, decision trees are grown iteratively from the training data (or bootstrap samples thereof in the case of random forests), and every leaf is assigned a class probability distribution in terms of the relative frequency of the labels of the training samples assigned to this leaf. This probability can directly be interpreted as a certainty measure, but it is subject to large variance for single trees. This is greatly diminished when averaging over a bootstrap sample, as present in random forests. It has been investigated experimentally by Niculescu-Mizil and Caruana [22] that the resulting values strongly correlate to the true underlying class probabilities, hence we will use this certainty measure in the case of random forests. Its values lie within the range $[0, 1]$.

2.2   Evaluation Measure

Based on the underlying class probabilities, one could obtain optimal reject strategies, but they are not known in practical applications. Good certainty measures typically strongly correlate with said probabilities, although their precise values differ [22]. An optimal choice of the threshold is often problem-dependent, reflecting the desired balance of the number of rejected data points versus the accuracy for the remaining data. As such, it is common practice to compare

---

[1] We subsitute a small $\epsilon > 0$ for $d(x, x_i)$ if $d(x, x_i) < \epsilon$.

the efficiency of classification with a reject option by a comparison of the so-called *accuracy-reject curve*: Sampling certainty thresholds $\theta \in [0,1]$, we report the accuracy of the classification method for all points that are not rejected (i.e. accepted) using this threshold, together with the ratio of points that are accepted [23].

3   Learning with Concept Drift and Its Extension to Rejection

In online learning, a potentially infinite stream $(\ldots, (x_t, y_t), (x_{t+1}, y_{t+1}), \ldots)$ of training data is given, where t denotes the current time, and each sample (x_t, y_t) is generated from an unknown probability distribution p_t. The presence of drift refers to the fact that $p_t(x, y)$ changes over time, i.e. at least two time points t_1 and t_2 exist such that $p_{t_1}(x, y) \neq p_{t_2}(x, y)$. If the posterior class probabilities change, $p_{t_1}(y|x) \neq p_{t_2}(y|x)$, we call this *real concept drift*; if only the input distribution changes, $p_{t_1}(x) \neq p_{t_2}(x)$, this is referred to as *virtual concept drift* or *covariate shift*. In particular for real concept drift, a static classifier is often suboptimal, and the goal is to evolve a classification mapping h_t over time, which adjusts to the current class posterior distribution, whereby h_{t+1} is inferred from h_t and the current sample (x_t, y_t) only. The objective is to minimize the average misclassification over time as measured, for example, by the so-called *interleaved test-train error* for a time period T

$$E = \sum_{t=1}^{T} \frac{\mathbb{I}(f_t(x_t), y_t)}{T}. \tag{5}$$

This setting can be extended to online learning with rejection as soon as the classification mapping f_t is accompanied by a certainty measure c_t. In this case, given a threshold θ, classification at time point t is rejected if, and only if, $c_t(x) < \theta$. Evaluation takes place by reporting the modified interleaved test-train error

$$E_\theta = \sum_{t \leq T \,:\, c_t(x_t) \geq \theta} \frac{\mathbb{I}(f_t(x_t), y_t)}{|\{t \leq T \,:\, c_t(x_t) \geq \theta\}|} \tag{6}$$

and the ratio of classified data points

$$\frac{|t \leq T \,:\, c_t(x_t) \geq \theta|}{T}. \tag{7}$$

A number of learning models have been proposed which are capable of dealing with drift [10–14]. We address two recent models (SAM and ARF) which are suited for heterogeneous drift and which can be naturally extended to include a reject option. For comparison, we look at a linear classifier (perceptron) that can adapt to drift but where useful reject strategies are problematic, as well as two sliding windows to serve as a baseline.

Online perceptron: One simple – yet popular – method, which is also available in stream mining suites such as the massive online analysis toolbox for data streams, is online perceptron learning [24]. Essentially, this consists of an online gradient descent of the squared error of the perceptron activation function $\text{sgd}(w^\top x - \theta)$ based on given data with fixed step size. This model is naturally restricted to linear settings, yet it yields surprisingly accurate behavior in an initial demonstration scenario as we will show in an experiment, a behavior which has also been substantiated analytically [25]. Yet, for online settings, it is not possible to adjust the sigmoidal rescaling of the perceptron output as proposed by [16], hence we will directly rely on the measure $c(x)$ for rejection as introduced above.

SAM-kNN: The Self-Adjusting Memory (SAM) architecture [26] keeps two complementary memories – short-term and long-term. The former contains the most recent samples of a data stream, whereby the length of this window is adjusted based on the classification performance, while the latter stores and continuously refines a compacted representation of previous samples as long as these are consistent with the short term memory. Depending on how the data stream changes, SAM makes flexible use of its two memories and a weighted k-nearest neighbors classifier to accurately classify even when drift is present. We extend the output of the classifier by the certainty measure as introduced above as the basis for a reject option.

ARF: Adaptive random forests (ARF) [14] constitute a state-of-the-art ensemble method for learning with drift. Random forests grow very fast decision trees (Hoeffding trees) online based on Poisson sampling to mimic bootstrapping effects. ARF wraps this technology into an active drift detection loop, which assigns suitable weights to an ensemble of trees, replaces unsuitable trees if drift is observed, and grows trees in the background that can serve as an intelligent initialization of such replacements when drift is expected. We can use the certainty measure as introduced for random forests above and extend it to weighted averages over the ensemble of trees as a basis for rejection.

Sliding window: Techniques which use a classifier based on a sliding window of the data stream can serve as a baseline. We will consider a weighted k-NN classifier with a sliding window of fixed size (referred to as *fixed window*) as well as a window whose size is adapted based on the optimum classification error such as the short term memory in SAM (referred to as *adaptive window*).

4   Experiments

4.1   Linear Setting

Initially, we investigate how a perceptron's certainty responds to concept drift and demonstrate that it is not easily augmented with a reject option. To that

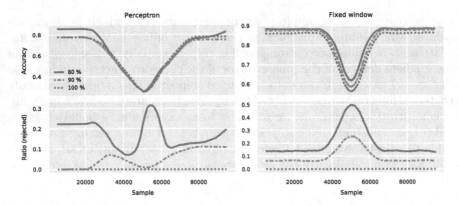

Fig. 1. Accuracy and reject ratio over time according to different reject thresholds for the perceptron and the fixed window. Thresholds are chosen such that 100%, 90% and 80% of points are accepted. Accuracy and ratio are calculated over a sliding window that contains 10% of the dataset's total number of samples. Between samples 37 500 to 62 500 the data-generating rectangles move through one another, making the classification more difficult.

end, we create a 2-dimensional dataset with two classes. Points are sampled uniformly from two rectangles (which determine the class label) that move towards, through, and apart from one another over time. The two classes are initially linearly separable, then become indistinguishable, and eventually become linearly separable again – albeit with a flipped separating hyperplane. To add noise, we flip the class label of every 7th sample.

For comparison, the data is used to evaluate a fixed window[2] as well as the perceptron. The results are presented in Fig. 1, with different certainty thresholds that correspond to 100% 90% and 80% of accepted (classified) points. It is apparent that the simple online perceptron is surprisingly accurate for this data set, despite its rather simple learning rule. As expected, an increasing classification difficulty is reflected in a decrease in accuracy. When the rectangles move apart (and the classes become linearly separable again), both algorithms recover. However, it is apparent that the perceptron hardly benefits from a reject option, whereas the fixed window clearly does, rejecting more points the more difficult the problem is and in such a way that the accuracy increases. Hence, it is a nontrivial task to identify effective rejection for learning with drift.

4.2   General Setting

We evaluate the efficiency of classification with rejection on a number of benchmark datasets with nonlinear characteristics. Here, model meta-paramaters are

---

[2] The fixed window serves as a straight-forward example. Results for the adaptive window, SAM, and ARF are comparable – the largest difference in accuracy between all four is below 2%.

chosen in the same way as reported in Losing et al. [26] and Gomes et al. [14]. We determine accuracy reject curves by dividing the range of observed certainties into equally sized intervals and deriving the respective pareto-optimal accuracy-reject pairs. For reporting, we focus on the practically interesting range of 100% to 50%. We consider the benchmark datasets as described in Losing et al. [12,26], since they cover a wide variety of different data and drift characteristics. See Table 1 for an overview over the datasets.

Table 1. Datasets considered for our experiments. Real-world datasets are followed by artificial datasets – other than that, they are presented in no particular order. Drift properties are given according to Losing et al. [12].

	# Samples	# Features	# Classes	Drift
Outdoor objects	4000	21	40	Virtual
Rialto bridge	82250	27	10	Virtual
Poker hand	829201	10	10	Virtual
Electricity	45312	6	2	Real
Weather	18159	8	2	Virtual
Transient chessboard	200000	2	8	Virtual
Rotating hyperplane	200000	10	2	Real
Interchanging RBF	200000	2	15	Real
Mixed drift	600000	2	15	Real
Moving RBF	200000	10	5	Real
Moving squares	200000	2	4	Real
SEA concepts	50000	3	2	Real

Effectiveness of Reject. The resulting accuracy-recject curves with respect to different certainty thresholds for all twelve datasets and all four classifiers are presented in Fig. 2. As reported by Losing et al. [26] and Gomes et al. [14], it is apparent that the methods SAM and ARF are robust classifiers capable of dealing with drift, with SAM performing consistently well across all datasets considered, while ARF shows excellent results in most, but not all (in particular *Outdoor Objects*, *Moving RBF*, and *Moving Squares*). Surprisingly, also the baselines yield acceptable results for certain datasets. We observe that rejection increases the classifiers' accuracy consistently for all datasets, and influence all methods similarly: Averaged over all datasets and all four classifiers, rejecting 10% or 20% of all samples leads to an increase in accuracy by 3.19% or 5.64%, respectively. The smallest increase is 1.06% or 1.17%, the highest increase is 5.43% or 10.07%.

At present, we have used certainty measures that are intuitive and fast to compute in all cases. The curves indicate one possible weakness of these measures: in particular for k-NN classifiers (including SAM), the accuracy does not

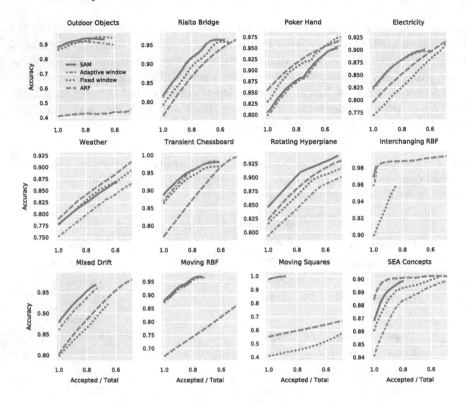

Fig. 2. Accuracy-reject curves for all datasets considered. Note the different vertical axes. The nearest neighbor based classifiers classify many samples with maximal certainty, which explains why the respective curves often terminate early.

reach 100% – rather, the curves end prematurely. This is due to the fact that k-NN assigns a certainty of 100% to a great number of points since their k-neighborhoods are uniformly labeled. More elaborate certainty measures such as a reject option based on absolute distances, that respects outliers, or an extension of the method to ensembles and according averaged certainties, could enable a "subtler" assessment of certainty. Hence, we see room for further improvement beyond the already satisfactory results.

Temporal Behavior. As expected, accuracy varies over time in the presence of non-homogeneous drift in real-life datasets. For *Outdoor Objects* and *Rialto Bridge* we show this together with how accuracy is affected by rejection, and how the rejection ratio varies over time, when SAM with a reject option is used to classify (Fig. 3). Interestingly, the sharp drop in accuracy at samples 1700 to 2200 from *Outdoor Objects* is mirrored in the ratio of rejected points as a pronounced peak in rejected points. In this case, increasing the number of rejected points allows the classifier to improve so much that no notable drop in accuracy remains.

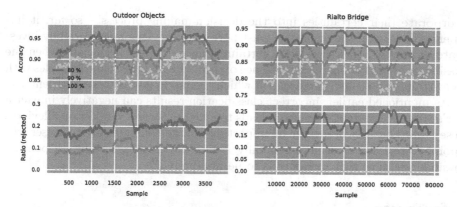

Fig. 3. Accuracy and reject ratio over time according to different reject thresholds for SAM, shown for the datasets *Outdoor Objects* and *Rialto Bridge*. Thresholds are chosen such that 100%, 90% and 80% of points are accepted. Accuracy and ratio are calculated over a sliding window that contains 10% of the respective dataset's total number of samples. Note the abrupt, temporary drop in accuracy for *Outdoor Objects* and the corresponding increase in the number of rejected points for samples 1700 to 2200.

A similar – albeit less pronounced – behavior can be observed for *Rialto Bridge*. Here the overall variation in accuracy becomes much narrower. For samples 30 000 to 40 000 the abrupt loss in accuracy is compensated by more rejected points.

5 Discussion

We have introduced and evaluated diverse online learning classifiers with reject options in the presence of concept drift. Across all datasets and classifiers, we see a notable increase in accuracy when using a reject option for k-NN classifiers and ensembles of random forests. In stark contrast, rejection as presented for the perceptron do not seem easily extendable to the setting of concept drift; within an initial linear setting, rejection did not show any benefits. As expected, also for the real life non-linear data sets, no classifier achieves 100% accuracy in the presence of drift. Interestingly, although techniques such SAM-kNN are consistently good for all settings, there is not one clear winner among the classifiers as they perform differently on various datasets. This is in line with the findings of Losing et al. [26].

Rejecting with respect to a fixed certainty threshold does not merely increase the accuracy overall but can specifically alleviate low accuracy that stems from low certainty, as seen in Fig. 3. It remains to be seen how more sophisticated, time- and drift-dependent strategies for dynamically choosing certainty thresholds can improve performance even further.

Considering the particular structure of SAM, where classification depends on a choice between long- and short-term memory, it might prove beneficial to incorporate their certainties into the decision-making process – so far, it has depended solely on the memories' past performances. One must carefully investigate, however, how a classifier's certainty can be trusted, especially when the classifier performs badly in the presence of drift. On the other hand, samples with low certainty could indicate areas in which the model needs to be augmented.

As mentioned earlier, incorrect classification results can negatively impact a user's trust in a system. Because it leads to a higher accuracy, rejection alleviates these issues, but it will further be important how to communicate to a user *why* a point is rejected or – more generally – with how high a certainty a point is classified and how that certainty is to be interpreted.

References

1. Cha, E., Dragan, A.D., Srinivasa, S.S.: Perceived robot capability. In: 24th IEEE International Symposium on Robot and Human Interactive Communication, RO-MAN 2015, Kobe, Japan, August 31–September 4 2015, pp. 541–548 (2015)
2. Desai, M., et al.: Impact of robot failures and feedback on real-time trust. In: HRI. IEEE/ACM, pp. 251–258 (2013)
3. Kwon, M., Huang, S.H., Dragan, A.D.: Expressing robot incapability. In: Proceedings of the 2018 ACM/IEEE International Conference on Human-Robot Interaction, HRI 2018, Chicago, IL, USA, 05–08 March 2018, pp. 87–95 (2018)
4. Chow, C.: On optimum recognition error and reject tradeoff. IEEE Trans. Inf. Theor. **16**(1), 41–46 (2006). ISSN 0018-9448
5. Herbei, R., Wegkamp, M.H.: Classification with reject option. Can. J. Stat. **34**(4), 709–721 (2006)
6. Bartlett, P.L., Wegkamp, M.H.: Classification with a reject option using a hinge loss. J. Mach. Learn. Res. **9**, 1823–1840 (2008). ISSN 1532-4435
7. Villmann, T., et al.: Self-adjusting reject options in prototype based classification. In: Merényi, E., Mendenhall, M.J., O'Driscoll, P. (eds.) Advances in Self-organizing Maps and Learning Vector Quantization. AISC, vol. 428, pp. 269–279. Springer, Cham (2016). https://doi.org/10.1007/978-3-319-28518-4_24
8. Fischer, L., Hammer, B., Wersing, H.: Optimal local rejection for classifiers. Neurocomputing **214**, 445–457 (2016)
9. Vovk, V., Gammerman, A., Shafer, G.: Algorithmic Learning in a Random World. Springer, New York (2005). https://doi.org/10.1007/b106715. ISBN 0387001522
10. Ditzler, G.: Learning in nonstationary environments: a survey. IEEE Comput. Intell. Mag. **10**(4), 12–25 (2015). ISSN 1556-603X
11. Gomes, H.M.: A survey on ensemble learning for data stream classification. ACM Comput. Surv. **50**(2), 23:1–23:36 (2017)
12. Losing, V., Hammer, B., Wersing, H.: Tackling heterogeneous concept drift with the Self-Adjusting Memory (SAM). Knowl. Inf. Syst. **54**(1), 171–201 (2018)
13. Loeffel, P.-X., Bifet, A., Marsala, C., Detyniecki, M.: Droplet ensemble learning on drifting data streams. In: Adams, N., Tucker, A., Weston, D. (eds.) IDA 2017. LNCS, vol. 10584, pp. 210–222. Springer, Cham (2017). https://doi.org/10.1007/978-3-319-68765-0_18
14. Gomes, H.M., et al.: Adaptive random forests for evolving data stream classification. Mach. Learn. **106**, 1469–1495 (2017)

15. Loeffel, P.X., Marsala, C., Detyniecki, M.: Classification with a reject option under concept drift: the droplets algorithm. In: 2015 IEEE International Conference on Data Science and Advanced Analytics (DSAA), pp. 1–9, October 2015
16. Platt, J.C.: Probabilistic outputs for support vector machines and comparisons to regularized likelihood methods. In: Advances in Large Margin Classifiers, pp. 61–74. MIT Press (1999)
17. Hellman, M.E.: The nearest neighbor classification rule with a reject option. IEEE Trans. Syst. Sci. Cybern. **6**(3), 179–185 (1970). ISSN 0536–1567
18. Denoeux, T.: A k-nearest neighbor classification rule based on Dempster-Shafer theory. IEEE Trans. Syst. Man Cybern. **25**(5), 804–813 (1995)
19. Delany, S.J., Cunningham, P., Doyle, D., Zamolotskikh, A.: Generating estimates of classification confidence for a case-based spam filter. In: Muñoz-Ávila, H., Ricci, F. (eds.) ICCBR 2005. LNCS (LNAI), vol. 3620, pp. 177–190. Springer, Heidelberg (2005). https://doi.org/10.1007/11536406_16
20. Breiman, L.: Random forests. Mach. Learn. **45**(1), 5–32 (2001). ISSN 0885–6125
21. Fernández-Delgado, M.: Do we need hundreds of classifiers to solve real world classification problems? J. Mach. Learn. Res. **15**, 3133–3181 (2014)
22. Niculescu-Mizil, A., Caruana, R.: Predicting good probabilities with supervised learning. In: Proceedings of the 22nd International Conference on Machine Learning, ICML 2005, pp. 625–632. ACM, Bonn (2005). ISBN 1-59593-180-5
23. Nadeem, M.S.A., Zucker., Hanczar, B.: Accuracy-rejection curves (ARCs) for comparing classification methods with a reject option. In: Džeroski, S., Guerts, P., Rousu, J. (eds.) Proceedings of the Third International Workshop on Machine Learning in Systems Biology, Proceedings of Machine Learning Research, vol. 8, pp. 65–81. PMLR, Ljubljana (May 2009)
24. Bifet, A.: MOA: massive online analysis. J. Mach. Learn. Res. **11**, 1601–1604 (2010). ISSN 1532–4435
25. Timothy, L.H., Watkin, A.R., Biehl, M.: The statistical mechanics of learning a rule. Rev. Mod. Phys. **65**, 499–556 (1993)
26. Losing, V., Hammer, B., Wersing, H.: KNN classifier with self adjusting memory for heterogeneous concept drift. In: 2016 IEEE 16th International Conference on Data Mining (ICDM), pp. 291–300. IEEE, Barcelona (2016)

Strategies to Enhance Pattern Recognition in Neural Networks Based on the Insect Olfactory System

Jessica Lopez-Hazas[(✉)], Aaron Montero, and Francisco B. Rodriguez

Grupo de Neurocomputación Biológica, Dpto. de Ingeniería Informática Escuela Politécnica Superior, Universidad Autónoma de Madrid, Madrid 28049, Spain
jessicalopezhazas@gmail.com, aaron.montero.m@gmail.com, f.rodriguez@uam.es

Abstract. Some strategies used by the insect olfactory system to enhace its discrimination capability are an heterogeneous neural threshold distribution, gain control and sparse activity. To test the influence of these mechanisms on the performance for a classification task, we propose a neural network based on the insect olfactory system. In this model, we introduce a regulation term to control de activity of neurons and a structured connectivity between antennal lobe and mushroom body based on recent findings in Drosophila that differs from the classical stochastic approach. Results show that the model achieves better results for high sparseness and low connectivity between Kenyon cells and projection neurons. For this configuration, the use of gain control further improves performance. The structured connectivity model proposed is able to achieve the same discrimination capacity without using gain control or activiy regulation techniques, which opens up interesting possibilities.

Keywords: Neural computation · Pattern recognition
Bio-inspired neural networks · Neural threshold · Sparse coding
Olfactory system

1 Introduction

In this paper, we are going to focus on different strategies that are used in the olfactory system of insects for stimuli recognition and how they can be applied to improve the performance of artificial neural networks. Insect olfactory system is one of the most studied biological neural networks since it is less complex than the vertebrates olfactory system, so a lot of details about its structure and the function of different neural populations are known [7]. The insect olfactory system is organized in layers as follows: olfactory receptor neurons (ORNs) expressing different receptors capture the information of odorants and pass it to the projection neurons (PNs) in the antennal lobe (AL). PNs encode odorant information through oscillations and activity sequences which are then sent to the Kenyon cells (KCs) in the mushroom body (MB). It is in the MB where

© Springer Nature Switzerland AG 2018
V. Kůrková et al. (Eds.): ICANN 2018, LNCS 11139, pp. 468–475, 2018.
https://doi.org/10.1007/978-3-030-01418-6_46

stimuli identification and learning take place. KCs make use of sparse coding to improve the separability of patterns, showing little activity and no spike response for most of odorants [5,11]. Finally, the output from KCs goes to the MB output neurons (MBONs), responsible for the final identification of odorants. To achieve such a great discrimination capability between stimuli, some strategies that the biological system uses and that our model includes are the following:

i. Heterogeneous threshold distribution in KCs: it has been found that an heterogeneous neural thresholds among KCs enhances pattern classification compared to the same model using an homogeneous distribution [8–10].
ii. Gain control: a mechanism for gain control at the AL level is crucial to provide a standard representation of the stimuli regardless of its concentration, even when it is extremely high [14].
iii. Sparse coding in the MB: as stated before, KCs show low activity since each one of them only responds to a little set of stimuli [11]. This sparse activity in combination with the fan-out phase between the AL and MB assures an internal representation of patterns that prevents the occurrence of overlaps and, therefore, enhances pattern recognition while also assures energetic efficiency [3].

Although insect olfactory system has been extensively studied, there is still controversy about the value that some basic parameters of the PN-KC connectivity may take and about the topology that these connections follow. One of these parameters is the connection probability p_c between PNs and KCs. For example, in the case of locust, some authors have suggested that $p_c = 0.5$ [6], while others argue that it would be $p_c = 0.1$ [11] or even lower than that [3].

Regarding connection topology, as the PN-KC connections are not learned and cannot be reproduced across individuals, they are usually modeled using a stochastic matrix, since this is sufficient to assure information transmission, low energy cost [3] and is also used in artificial neural networks [13]. However, recent findings on the olfactory system of *Drosophila* points toward a more structured connectivity pattern where certain subsets of KCs receive a different number of connections from PNs [2].

In this work, using a simple model of the olfactory system based on neural networks and supervised learning [4,5,8,10], we aim to test the effects of the three strategies presented above and the new connectivity proposed, checking whether they improve the discrimination capacity of the network.

2   Methods

2.1   Model of the Insect Olfactory System

The model we proposed is based on a single hidden layer neural network and supervised learning and includes the three mechanisms to enhance pattern discrimination presented in the Sect. 1.

A graphic representation of the model and all the details are shown in Fig. 1. Basically, the input layer of the neural network X represent the PNs, while the

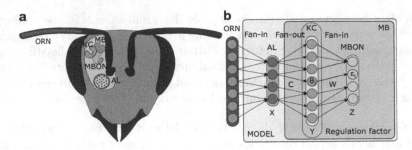

Fig. 1. (a) Structure of the biological olfactory system of insects. The ORNs capture the information of odorants and send it to AL and from there to the MB, where KCs use sparse coding to represent it. The MBONs are responsible for the final identification of stimuli. (b) Computational model used to explore the strategies to improve pattern recognition. It is a SLFN that uses supervised learning to determine the weights of the matrix W and the neural thresholds of KCs (θ) in the hidden layer Y and MBONs (ϵ) in the output layer (Z). AL is the input (X) to the network and is connected to the KCs by a binary matrix C. No learning takes place at this layer.

hidden layer Y represents the KCs, and should show sparse activity. The output layer, Z, represents the MBONs.

Gain control is introduced through the renormalization of patterns in the input layer so that the activation of the neurons is uniform for all patterns [4]. To achieve an heterogeneous neural threshold distribution in the KCs, the learning algorithm of the network is capable of adjusting the thresholds of each KC (θ) and MBON (ϵ) to the values that best fit the classification problem. Apart from that, the weights W of the connections between KCs and MBONs are also adjusted, since it is known that associative learning happens in this layer.

To enable sparse coding in the KC layer, we introduce an activity regulation term (ART) in the learning rule that allows us to 2control the level of activity of the neurons:

$$ART(Y) = \frac{1}{2} \left(\frac{1}{N_{KC}} \sum_{i=1}^{N_{KC}} y_i - s \right)^2 , \tag{1}$$

where the parameter N_{KC} is the number of KCs, $s \in [0.0, 1.0]$ allows to control the level of activity in the KCs layer from no activity when s $= 0$ to maximum activity when s $= 1$, and y_i is the activation of each KC in the network.

Another mechanism to enable sparse coding is the PN-KC ratio, which has been set to 1:50 [3,11], same as in the olfactory system of locust, to assure the fan-out phase between these layers and allow the representation of the stimuli without overlapping between them [3].

Given all the above, the objective function the network has to minimize in order to resolve the classification task is the following:

$$E(Z, T, Y) = H(Z, T) + ART(Y), \tag{2}$$

where Z is the output of the model, Y the activation of KCs, T the objective data labels for each pattern, $H(Z,T)$ is the cross-entropy function and ART the activity regulation term for the KC layer. Further details on the derivation of the learning rule for neural thresholds will be provided on later publications.

2.2 PN-KC Connectivity

To implement PN-KC connectivity, we follow the approach used in most insect olfactory system models, using a stochastic binary matrix C where each connection between a KC and a PN exists with a probability p_c that can be set to different values from $p_c = 0.0$ to $p_c = 1.0$ [3,5].

Conversely, taking into account the recent finding in *Droshophila*, we test a different PN-KC connectivity based on what is described in [2]. KCs are divided into different subsets depending on how many PNs they are connected to. Hence, there is a population of one-claw KCs that are just connected to a single PN, two-claw KCs, up to six-claw KC, the maximum observed in the biological system [2]. So, in this model, the connection probability p_c will depend entirely on the proportions of each type of KC.

2.3 Input Patterns

To test the performance of the model in a pattern classification problem, we use a reduced version of the well known MNIST dataset for hand-written digit recognition [1] that consists of 940 patterns, 209 attributes and 10 different classes. Some samples of these patterns are shown in Fig. 2 panel (c). We choose these patters because they are presented to the network as a one dimensional array with different activity regions similar to the complexity of the odorant patterns the biological system encounters in nature [12].

3 Results

For simulations, we use the locust olfactory system as reference, where PN-KC ratio is 1:50. The size of the neural network is $210 \times 10451 \times 10$. We use 5-fold cross validation and execute 10 simulations of each trial to compute the average of the classification error, that we use as the measure of system performance.

3.1 Level of Sparseness and PN-KC Connection Probability

We compared the performance of the model including the ART with different values of s to control the level of activity on KCs with the performance of the model without ART. The PN-KC connectivity is implemented using the stochastic matrix approach for values of p_c biologically plausible, between 0.01 and 0.5. Results are shown in Fig. 2. A model including the activity regulation term outperforms one that lacks it for most of the combinations of s and p_c values. The model achieves the best results when the sparseness level in KC layer

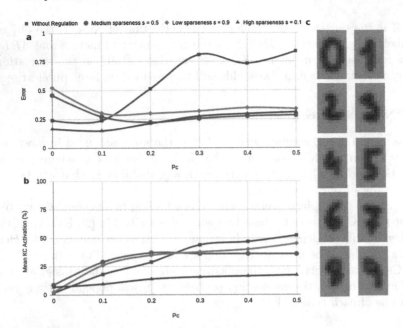

Fig. 2. (a) Classification error for the handwritten digits dataset for different values of p_c and low, medium and high sparseness level. (b) Mean activation level for KCs. High sparseness values correspond to lower activation in KCs and assures energetic efficiency. (c) A sample of the patterns used for classification.

is high, which is consistent with what is observed in the biological system [3,11]. Also, for this sparseness level, the lowest error rates happen when the connection probability between AL and MB neurons is low, in the interval [0.01–0.3]. The result we obtained is within the range of values considered possible and it is also consistent with energetic efficiency, but it is still lower than the more generally accepted value, $p_c = 0.5$ [3,6,11]. In the mean KC activation plot for different values of s and p_c, it can be seen that when sparseness is high, the KCs show a level of activation between 10% and 20%. This result is also consistent with the biological facts, since the level of activity for KCs is very low due to the sparse coding they used, according to [11].

Therefore, for high sparseness levels and low PN-KC probability connections the network is able to reach an optimal codification, maximizing the transference of information and minimizing the energy costs.

3.2   Gain Control

In order to test the influence of the gain control mechanism in the performance of the model, we carry out simulations with high sparseness level with and without gain control for different p_c values. Results are shown in Fig. 3. When the model works without gain control, its behavior is more stable and its performance is independent of p_c value. But the minimum classification error can only be achieved when gain control is enabled. It seems that only in the cases where p_c is very low, in the range [0.01–0.2], gain control has a positive effect, reducing the error by 5%, while for greater values of p_c, it is counterproductive. This behavior can be explained by the nature of the patters used for classification, as handwritten digits can be classified by the level of activity they cause in neurons. When p_c is low and a little number of connections between PNs and KCs are available, gain control helps to maximize the transmission of information, while in the case of bigger p_c, when almost all the information is available and transmitted, it makes the level of activity uniform and therefore it elimates some important information for discrimination. Also, it should be noticed that our mechanism for gain control is fairly limited, so these results should be further tested with more realistic gain control models.

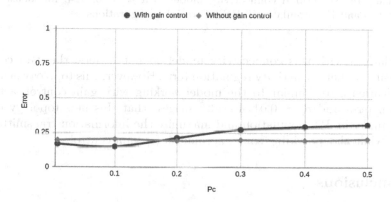

Fig. 3. Classification error for high sparseness level and different p_c values with and without gain control. Gain control only has a positive effect for low values of p_c, improving the performance by 5%. When $p_c > 0.2$, gain control worsens the performance achieved by 5–10%, although this effect can be explained by the structure of the problem patterns.

3.3 Structured PN-KN Connectivity Model

We introduce the structured connectivity model explained in Sect. 2.2, where KCs are divided into different sets, each of them receiving connections from a certain number of PCs. There can be six different types of KCs in the system, from single-claw KCs to six-claw KCs, the maximum observed in the biological system. The proportions of each type are the same found in [2]. Results in [2] show that the new connectivity minimizes redundancy and optimizes stimuli discrimination. We wonder how this connectivity pattern could affect the behavior of our neural network, so we extrapolate this connectivity model to the locust, where the size of the network is bigger, by just maintaining the proportions mentioned before. The value of p_c that corresponds to this connectivity pattern is $p_c = 0.0124$ (Fig. 4).

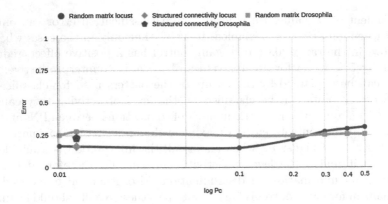

Fig. 4. Classification error using the stochastic matrix connectivity model for different p_c and using the structured connectivity model with $p_c = 0.0124$, for locust (1:50 PN-KC ratio) and Drosophila (1:10 PN-KC ratio) configurations.

Simulations with this connectivity model do not include the gain control mechanism, neither the activity regulation term. However, this topology achieves a classification error similar to the model working with gain control, activity regulation term and $p_c = 0.01$. Results suggest that this new topology could better sample the PN population and maximize the information transmitted to the KCs while also providing some mechanism for gain control.

4   Conclusions

In this paper we have introduced an insect olfactory system model based on neural networks and supervised learning that includes three strategies to improve the pattern recognition capability of the system. These mechanisms are gain control, sparse coding and an heterogeneous threshold distribution in KCs. Apart from adjusting the weights of the connections between KCs and MBONs, the model is also able to get the distribution of thresholds that best fit a certain classification problem for KCs and MBONs. To control the level of activity in the KC layer and allow sparse coding, we introduce a new regulation term that allows us to choose the activity level.

We carry out simulations for different parameters of the model to study how these mechanisms influence the performance of the system in a classification task. We have shown that the system achieves the minimum error when the sparseness level in the KC layer is high (activity level of 10%) and the PN-KC connection probability low. Also, gain control has a positive impact on the performance of the system, but only for low p_c, due to the structure of the patterns used for the classification task. However, our mechanism for gain control is not much realistic, so further investigation must be carried out on this particular point.

We also tested a new PN-KC connectivity topology proposed in [2] with a different structure to the classic stochastic matrix approach and found that this connectivity can reach the minimum error without making use of gain control or the activity regulation term. Hence, the behavior and properties that this new connectivity may introduce could be helpful to understand the processing of information in the olfactory system and to end controversies about the value of certain of its parameters. The potential properties of this new connectivity will be further explored in the future.

Acknowledgments. We thank Ramon Huerta for his useful discussions. We acknowledge support from MINECO/FEDER TIN2014-54580-R and TIN2017-84452-R (http://www.mineco.gob.es/).

References

1. MNIST handwritten digit database. http://yann.lecun.com/exdb/mnist/
2. Eichler, K., et al.: The complete connectome of a learning and memory centre in an insect brain. Nature **548**(7666), 175–182 (2017)
3. García-Sanchez, M., Huerta, R.: Design parameters of the fan-out phase of sensory systems. J. Comput. Neurosci. **15**(1), 5–17 (2003)
4. Huerta, R., Nowotny, T.: Fast and robust learning by reinforcement signals: explorations in the insect brain. Neural Comput. **21**(8), 2123–2151 (2009)
5. Huerta, R., Nowotny, T., García-Sanchez, M., Abarbanel, H.D.I., Rabinovich, M.I.: Learning classification in the olfactory system of insects. Neural Comput. **16**(8), 1601–1640 (2004)
6. Jortner, R.A., Farivar, S.S., Laurent, G.: A simple connectivity scheme for sparse coding in an olfactory system. J. Neurosci. **27**(7), 1659–1669 (2007)
7. Kaupp, U.B.: Olfactory signalling in vertebrates and insects: differences and commonalities. Nature Rev. Neurosci. **11**(3), 188 200 (2010)
8. Montero, A., Huerta, R., Rodríguez, F.B.: Neuron threshold variability in an olfactory model improves odorant discrimination. In: Ferrández Vicente, J.M., Álvarez Sánchez, J.R., de la Paz López, F., Toledo Moreo, F.J. (eds.) IWINAC 2013. LNCS, vol. 7930, pp. 16–25. Springer, Heidelberg (2013). https://doi.org/10.1007/978-3-642-38637-4_3
9. Montero, A., Huerta, R., Rodríguez, F.B.: Regulation of specialists and generalists by neural variability improves pattern recognition performance. Neurocomputing **151**(Part 1), 69–77 (2015)
10. Montero, A., Huerta, R., Rodríguez, F.B.: Stimulus space complexity determines the ratio of specialist and generalist neurons during pattern recognition. J. Frankl. Inst. **355**, 2951–2977 (2018)
11. Perez-Orive, J., Mazor, O., Turner, G.C., Cassenaer, S., Wilson, R.I., Laurent, G.: Oscillations and sparsening of odor representations in the mushroom body. Science **297**(5580), 359–365 (2002)
12. Rubin, B.D., Katz, L.C.: Optical imaging of odorant representations in the mammalian olfactory bulb. Neuron **23**(3), 499–511 (1999)
13. Scardapane, S., Wang, D.: Randomness in neural networks: an overview. Wiley Interdiscip. Rev.: Data Min. Knowl. Discov. **7**(2), e1200 (2017)
14. Serrano, E., Nowotny, T., Levi, R., Smith, B.H., Huerta, R.: Gain control network conditions in early sensory coding. Plos Comput. Biol. **9**(7), e1003133 (2013)

HyperNets and Their Application to Learning Spatial Transformations

Alexey Potapov[1,2(✉)], Oleg Shcherbakov[1,2], Innokentii Zhdanov[1,2], Sergey Rodionov[1,3], and Nikolai Skorobogatko[1,3]

[1] SingularityNET Foundation, Amsterdam, The Netherlands
pas.aicv@gmail.com, astroseger@gmail.com
[2] ITMO University, St. Petersburg, Russia
{scherbakovolegdk, avenger15}@yandex.ru
[3] Novamente LLC, Rockville, USA
nicksk@mail.ru

Abstract. In this paper we propose a conceptual framework for higher-order artificial neural networks. The idea of higher-order networks arises naturally when a model is required to learn some group of transformations, every element of which is well-approximated by a traditional feedforward network. Thus the group as a whole can be represented as a hyper network. One of typical examples of such groups is spatial transformations. We show that the proposed framework, which we call HyperNets, is able to deal with at least two basic spatial transformations of images: rotation and affine transformation. We show that Hyper-Nets are able not only to generalize rotation and affine transformation, but also to compensate the rotation of images bringing them into canonical forms.

Keywords: Artificial neural networks · Higher-order models
Affine transformation · Rotation compensation · Currying neural networks
HyperNets

1 Introduction

Generalization properties of different neural networks architectures have been of interest since the invention of these type of models. Theoretical and empirical studies of models' generalization properties remain relevant till present [1]. In addition, this problem has a very special place in the field of computer vision: it is crucial for a general-purposed computer vision system to learn the invariant representations of sensor inputs [2]. Classic feedforward discriminative architectures even for deep models have been studied decently, and it seems like their generalization properties are quite restricted since such models cannot directly transfer the results of previous learning to very new domains [3]. Moreover, even whilst working in the same domain but with great variability in data, these models still give very poor results. A very instructive example is the inability of multilayered perceptron to effectively recognize rotated versions of handwritten digits while being trained on canonical ones [4]. Convolutional neural networks partially address the problem of invariant features by making assumptions of locality and shared parameters. However, these assumptions are yet not enough to force different types of ConvNets learn to distinguish between rotated

© Springer Nature Switzerland AG 2018
V. Kůrková et al. (Eds.): ICANN 2018, LNCS 11139, pp. 476–486, 2018.
https://doi.org/10.1007/978-3-030-01418-6_47

digits without training on rotated examples [5, 6]. Recently, new models named capsule networks have been proposed [7], which are aimed to treat the invariance problem in a very specific way. Capsules are intended to store additional pieces of information in a basic neuron structure that could result in learning of non-trivial spatial relationships between the elements of sensor input on different levels of abstraction. However, training methods for CapsNets are still not as efficient as traditional version of gradient descent due to intensive process of dynamic routing.

It is also interesting that generalization properties of traditional models, which have been trained to reconstruct the original or canonical representations of modified inputs in autoencoder style, are also weak, especially if data domain has changed [8, 9].

Nonetheless, one of the most successful techniques to address the problem of geometric transform compensation for input images is the usage of spatial transforming layers [10]. Usually such layer consists of three main parts: localization net, grid generator and sampler. Such architecture allows for explicit spatial manipulation with data within a network for a wide family of parameterized spatial transformations. It has been shown that models with spatial transforming layers generally have increased classification accuracy. However, the concept of ST-layer has several drawbacks: the necessity to choose only differentiable sampling kernels (*e.g.*, the bilinear), explicit representation of parameterized family of transformations, dependency on grid generation and some domain specificity.

As an alternative, we present a technique, which we call hyper-neural networks or simply HyperNets. This is a method for manipulating model parameters by another model. Herewith, one deep neural network can represent both models. Let us consider the HyperNets in more detail.

2 Main Idea

Consider a network that accepts an image as input and produces its transformed version. The network with dense connections between input and output can easily learn to apply any (but fixed) spatial transformation to an arbitrary image. E.g. it can learn to rotate an image by $45°$, or flip an image vertically, etc., but the weights of connections will be different for each individual transformation.

Imagine we want the network to learn how to rotate an image by arbitrary angle provided as an input without hard-coding a special (non-neural) procedure for spatially transforming images. If we add traditional neurons accepting the parameters of transformation as input in addition to image, the network will just mix the image content with these parameters. Even making the network deeper and appending its latent code with the transformation parameters does not help the network to learn how to transform images independently of their content as we shall see later.

Thus, if we have an input image $x \in X$ and transform parameters $\varphi \in \Phi$, it is convenient to represent transformation process as mapping $X \times \Phi \rightarrow X$:

$$\mathbf{x}' = f(\mathbf{x}|\boldsymbol{\varphi}),\tag{1}$$

where x′ denotes the transformed image. Given a labeled training set, a traditional model tries to learn an approximation g to the function f:

$$f(\mathbf{x}|\boldsymbol{\varphi}) \approx g_\theta(\mathbf{x}, \boldsymbol{\varphi}), \tag{2}$$

where θ denotes adjustable parameters of the model. In such approach φ is usually treated as an additional vector of input values that could be connected to an arbitrary layer of the model presented by a deep network (Fig. 1). As we shall see later in this case the model will not have enough generalization properties.

Instead we can do some form of currying for the function g. As a result we obtain a new function curry(g):

$$\mathbf{curry}(g) = h_\omega(\varphi) = (\varphi \mapsto g_\theta(\mathbf{x}, \boldsymbol{\varphi})), \tag{3}$$

which should also have trainable parameters ω. So now we can directly search for the mapping $h: \Phi \rightarrow (X \rightarrow X)$.

Since it is easy for networks to learn how to transform images by an individual transformation, but their trained weights depend on the parameters of this transformation, it seems quite natural to introduce control neurons, which take these parameters as input and modulate the connection weights of the controlled network through higher-order connections.

The core idea behind HyperNets is representation of neural networks as higher-order functions, which implies a very special network architecture where function $h_\omega(\varphi)$ is a neural network too (Fig. 2). This means that parameters θ of the network g are described as outputs of the network $h_\omega(\varphi)$: $\theta(\varphi) = h_\omega(\varphi)$. Thus, we try to approximate the target function f by the following model:

$$f(\mathbf{x}|\varphi) \approx g_{h_\omega(\varphi)}(\mathbf{x}). \tag{4}$$

In case of complex models g, especially some deep ones, not all of the parameters θ could depend on transformation parameters φ. Hence, we can rewrite our expression for a higher-order model using a slightly redundant notation:

$$f(\mathbf{x}|\boldsymbol{\varphi}) \approx g_{h_\omega(\boldsymbol{\varphi}), \theta'}(\mathbf{x}), \tag{5}$$

where θ' denotes the parameters of the model g that are not affected by higher-order terms, i.e. $\theta = \{h_\omega(\varphi), \theta'\}$. Again, having the training set D comprised by m pairs of canonical and transformed images along with respective transformation parameters: $D = \{\mathbf{x}_i, \mathbf{x}'_i, \boldsymbol{\varphi}_i\}_{i=1}^{m}$, the goal of the model is to learn the transformation concept $h_\omega(\varphi)$ and its properties by minimizing some error/loss function and, thus, finding optimal values for θ' and ω:

$$\omega^*, \theta'^* = \mathrm{argmin}_{\omega, \theta'} \left(\sum_{i=1}^{m} L\left(\mathbf{x}'_i, \mathbf{z}_i = g_{h_\omega(\boldsymbol{\varphi}_i), \theta'}(\mathbf{x}_i)\right) \right), \tag{6}$$

where L(x, z) is the corresponding loss function between the model's output and the target image.

The name 'hyper network' comes from the analogy between the higher-order functions represented by neural nets and hypergraphs, which could be considered as an extension of traditional computational graph approach.

In this work we have considered relatively simple HyperNet architectures. The interaction between parameters of the higher-order part and the 'core' part of the model presented in Fig. 2 can be described as follows:

$$\mathbf{W}_{hi-ord} = \text{softmax}(\mathbf{a}(\boldsymbol{\varphi})) \tag{7}$$

$$\mathbf{z} = (\mathbf{W}_{hi-ord}\mathbf{W})\mathbf{x}, \tag{8}$$

where $\mathbf{a}$ is an activation of the last layer of the higher-order part of the network, $\mathbf{W}$ denotes the parameters (weights) of the 'core' part of the model and $\otimes$ denotes element-wise product between matrices.

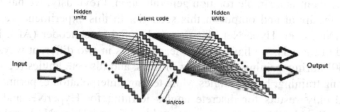

Fig. 1. Regular autoencoder with control (sin and cos of desired angle)

It can be seen that the model, whilst being structurally complex, remains differentiable, which allows to directly apply standard optimization techniques under various computational graph frameworks and to simultaneously train both higher-order and 'core' parts of the network. It is also worth saying that transformation parameters φ could be represented in numerous ways. For example, in case of planar image rotation

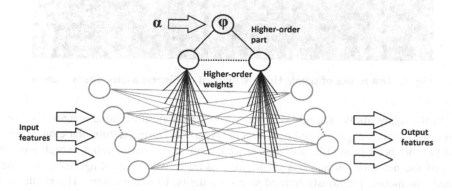

Fig. 2. Simple higher-order model architecture

φ might be parameterized by one angle α with activation constrains for the next hidden layer of the network or by two values representing $\sin(\alpha)$ and $\cos(\alpha)$. So the input to higher-order part of the network will be the transformation parameter, and the input for the 'core' part of the network will be the image. For example, if you want to train a model to rotate an image, you may use cos and sin of an angle as parameters and the unrotated image as an input. The rotated image will be the desired output. Thus, the model is trained in supervised style.

3   Experiments and Results

We have performed several types of experiments using a developed HyperNet. Also we have tried many architecture modifications, such as adding more dense layers to 'core' network, using convolutional layers, etc.

3.1   Rotation Experiment

The first experiment is a simple rotation generalization. Previously, we have discussed what will be the input and output in this scenario. In this experiment we have used simple HyperNet, deep HyperNet, deep convolutional autoencoder (AE). Besides of different kind of models, we have tried to learn angles in two different ways: using all angles [0, 360] during training and testing process, and discrete angles (0, 45, 90, 135 … 360°) during training, but all angles while testing (interpolation experiment). Below we presented only results for discrete angles learning for HyperNet and all angles learning for AE. Also, both experiments (with AE and HyperNet) included some extrapolation part for 4 and 9 digits. For these two digits the angles were taken not from [0, 360], but from [0, 90] range of degrees while training. The results of these experiments are shown in Fig. 3.

Fig. 3. Test results of simple HyperNet trained on discrete angles. Digits 1 and 4

In the figure above, the odd columns contain groundtruth rotated images, the even columns contain images rotated by a simple HyperNet. During testing phase only digits that had not been present in training set were used. Again, as an input to higher-order part of the network sin and cos of the desired angle were used. Moreover, we have tested our model, previously trained solely on digits, to rotate letters. The results are shown in Fig. 4 (left). As can be seen, after adding the higher-order weights, a simple model with just one input and output could be trained to generalize rotation. However, there are some artifacts present on the images, especially if you take a look at digit 1. Hence, a simple model was unable to interpolate rotation on discrete angles learning.

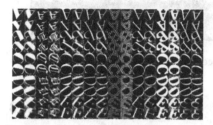 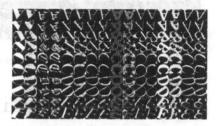

Fig. 4. Test results of simple (left) and deep convolutional (right) HyperNet applied to letters. Letters have not been used for training

A slightly deeper model with two convolutional, two dense and two deconvolutional layers (higher-order weights are applied to weights between two dense layers) could return better results, as you can see in Fig. 5. These results were obtained from training on discrete angles and it can be seen that deep higher-order network could already interpolate rotation. At the right part of Fig. 4 the results of testing by deep HyperNet on letters are presented.

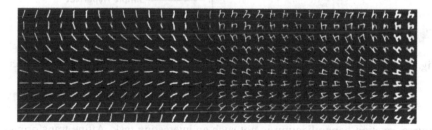

Fig. 5. Test results of deep HyperNet trained on discrete angles. Digits 1 and 4

We have also compared reconstruction loss between HyperNet and baseline convolutional autoencoder (AE), which had been designed to learn the rotation transform using information about sin and cos of desired angle added to latent code (see Fig. 7). Ten graphs mean ten digits. Also, in Fig. 6 the results of AE rotation generalization are presented. It is worth saying though, that AE was trained on all angles, not only discrete. It also has to be mentioned, that HyperNet was able to extrapolate rotation representation for 4 and 9 while regular AE with control could not do this.

Fig. 6. Test results of AE model trained on all angles. Digits 1 and 4

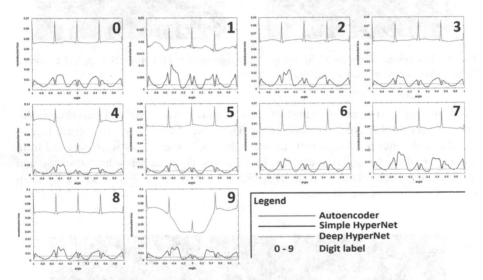

Fig. 7. Reconstruction loss comparison of HyperNet models with baseline autoencoder

3.2 Affine Transformation Experiment

Of course, rotation generalization is not such an interesting task. Affine transformation generalization is more challenging. In this case, we have used six affine transformation parameters as a higher-order input, and the canonical image as an input for the core part of the network. The transformed image was used as the desired output. It is worth saying though, that affine transformation parameters were limited in their range to ensure that the digit is still present on the 28×28 image and is recognizable for human. In Fig. 8 you can see the results. In this experiment we are presenting only deep model (with convolutional layers), since simple model shows worse results (though still decent).

As you can see, the convolutional HyperNet was able to learn almost random affine transformation and to apply it to digits that had not been contained in the training set. Though a simple model still can generalize affine transformation thanks to the higher-order part network, deeper network shows much smoother results. The ability of the AE model to learn affine transformation was also tested and the results are shown in Fig. 9.

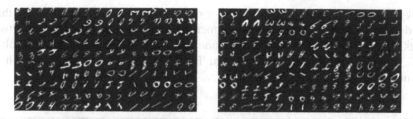

Fig. 8. Results of deep HyperNet on the training set (left) and test set (right)

Fig. 9. Results of AE model for the training set (left) and test set (right)

The AE model shows decent results, however some blurring and artifacts are present at these pictures. The comparison between AE and HyperNet for the affine transformation generalization experiment is presented in Table 1.

Table 1. Comparison between AE and higher-order model

	Simple HyperNet	Deep HyperNet	Autoencoder
Reconstruction loss	0.049395	0.0138223	0.0606265

3.3 Rotation Compensation Experiment

In previous experiments we have tried to learn a model to transform or to simply rotate an input image using control parameters and higher-order architecture. In this last part we were interested in compensating rotation without any knowledge of the angle. This means that control parameters in this scenario will be not sin and cos, since this would be an inverse problem, not so interesting and challenging. But what could be used as an input to the HyperNet then? We have tried to use the rotated image as an input to the core network AND as an input to the higher-order network. And, of course, the canonical image as the desired output. The idea is that the higher-order part of network could possibly extract parameters of the transformation from the rotated image by itself. In this case the dynamics of the higher-order part of network can be described as follows:

$$\mathbf{W}_{hi-ord} = \mathrm{softmax}(\mathbf{a}(\mathbf{x})). \tag{9}$$

But we had to slightly deepen the higher-order part of the network to ensure that it could do such a thing. So, in this experiment, the higher-order part of the network consists of two convolutional layers and one dense layer. Let us see some results in Fig. 10. Only the results of convolutional HyperNet are shown again since it has performed better in previous experiments.

Fig. 10. Results of rotation compensation using deep HyperNet. Test set. Digits 6, 1 and 9

In the figures above, the odd columns are the rotated input images and the even columns are the canonical images, which were received from the network. Most interesting results are 6 and 9 digits, since when rotated 180 degrees, 6 actually becomes 9. So, the one could expect that 6 and 9 would be mistaken by the network. However, the HyperNet was able to somehow correctly compensate rotated digits, including 6 and 9. There are some artifacts at the images, but overall the quality is good. Figure 12 presents the results of AE rotation compensation experiment, and Fig. 11 shows the comparison graphs between these two models. Just to remind, models were trained on digits 4 and 9 that had been rotated only in [0, 90] range of degrees. That explains the difference in graphs for these two digits for the AE model.

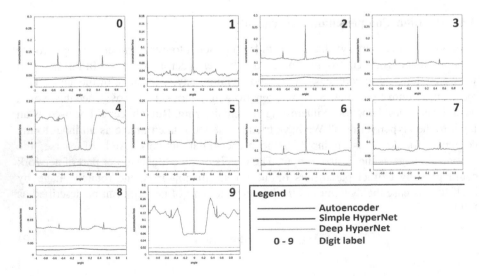

Fig. 11. Comparison of HyperNet and autoencoder applied for rotation compensation

Fig. 12. Rotation compensation results using AE model. Test set. Digits 6, 1 and 9

4 Conclusion

In this article we have proposed a new approach to artificial neural networks based on generating networks' parameters by higher-order modules that constitute other networks themselves. In other words, the output of the higher-order part acts as a weight matrix for the core part of the network. It has been shown that even a simple HyperNet with just one input layer and one output layer in its core part can generalize rotation and affine transformation. The addition of convolution layers allows to receive smoother results. Moreover, deep HyperNet allows to compensate rotation without any information about the angle. In future work it is possible to use such approach to compensate other types of transformations or to extrapolate such approach on generative models.

Our code is available on github https://github.com/singnet/semantic-vision/tree/master/experiments/invariance/hypernets.

References

1. On the importance of single directions for generalization. https://arxiv.org/abs/1803.06959v4. Accessed 23 May 2018
2. Goodfellow, I., Le, Q., Saxe, A., Lee, H., Ng, A.: Measuring invariances in deep networks. In: Proceedings of the 22nd International Conference on Neural Information Processing Systems, NIPS 2009, Vancouver, British Columbia, Canada, pp. 646–654 (2009)
3. Tan, B., Zhang, Y., Pan, S., Yang, Q.: Distant domain transfer learning. In: AAAI, pp. 2604–2610 (2017)
4. Yoon, Y., Lee, L.-K., Oh, S.-Y.: Semi-rotation invariant feature descriptors using Zernike moments for MLP classifier. In: Proceedings of 2016 International Joint Conference on Neural Networks, IJCNN 2016, pp. 3990–3994. IEEE, Vancouver (2016)
5. Malashin, R., Kadykov, A.: Investigation of the generalizing capabilities of convolutional neural networks in forming rotation-invariant attributes. J. Opt. Technol. **82**(8), 509–515 (2015)
6. Khasanova, R., Frossard, P.: Graph-based isometry invariant representation learning. In: ICML, pp. 1847–1856 (2017)
7. Sabour, S., Frosst, N., Hinton, G.: Dynamic routing between capsules. In: Proceedings of 2017 Advances in Neural Information Processing Systems, pp. 3859–3869 (2017)
8. Matsuo, T., Fukuhara, H., Shimada, N.: Transform invariant auto-encoder. In: proceedings of 2017 IEEE/RSJ International Conference on Intelligent Robots and Systems (IROS), Vancouver, BC, Canada, pp. 2359–2364 (2017)

9. Hinton, G.E., Krizhevsky, A., Wang, S.D.: Transforming auto-encoders. In: Honkela, T., Duch, W., Girolami, M., Kaski, S. (eds.) ICANN 2011. LNCS, vol. 6791, pp. 44–51. Springer, Heidelberg (2011). https://doi.org/10.1007/978-3-642-21735-7_6
10. Jaderberg, M., Simonyan, K., Zisserman, A., Kavukcuoglu, K.: Spatial transformer networks. In: Proceedings of 2015 Advances in Neural Information Processing Systems, vol. 28, pp. 2017–2025 (2015)

Catastrophic Forgetting: Still a Problem for DNNs

B. Pfülb[(✉)], A. Gepperth[(✉)], S. Abdullah[(✉)], and A. Kilian[(✉)]

Fulda University of Applied Sciences, Leipzigerstr. 123, 36037 Fulda, Germany
{benedikt.pfuelb,alexander.gepperth,saad.abdullah,
andre.kilian}@cs.hs-fulda.de
https://www.hs-fulda.de

Abstract. We investigate the performance of DNNs when trained on class-incremental visual problems consisting of initial training, followed by retraining with added visual classes. Catastrophic forgetting (CF) behavior is measured using a new evaluation procedure that aims at an application-oriented view of incremental learning. In particular, it imposes that model selection must be performed on the initial dataset alone, as well as demanding that retraining control be performed only using the retraining dataset, as initial dataset is usually too large to be kept. Experiments are conducted on class-incremental problems derived from MNIST, using a variety of different DNN models, some of them recently proposed to avoid catastrophic forgetting. When comparing our new evaluation procedure to previous approaches for assessing CF, we find their findings are completely negated, and that none of the tested methods can avoid CF in all experiments. This stresses the importance of a realistic empirical measurement procedure for catastrophic forgetting, and the need for further research in incremental learning for DNNs.

Keywords: DNN · Catastrophic forgetting · Incremental learning

1 Introduction

The context of this article is the susceptibility of DNN to an effect usually termed "catastrophic forgetting" or "catastrophic interference" [2]. When training a DNN incrementally, that is, first training it on a sub-task D_1 and subsequently retraining on another sub-task D_2 whose statistics differ (see Fig. 1), CF implies an abrupt and virtually complete loss of knowledge about D_1 during retraining. In various forms, knowledge of this effect dates back to very early works on neural networks [2], of which modern DNNs are a special case. Nevertheless, known solutions seem difficult to apply to modern DNNs trained in a purely gradient-based fashion. Recently, several approaches have been published with the explicit goal of resolving the CF issue for DNNs in incremental learning tasks, illustrated in [3,5,10]. On the other hand, there are "shallow" machine learning methods explicitly constructed to avoid CF (reviewed in, e.g., [9]), although

© Springer Nature Switzerland AG 2018
V. Kůrková et al. (Eds.): ICANN 2018, LNCS 11139, pp. 487–497, 2018.
https://doi.org/10.1007/978-3-030-01418-6_48

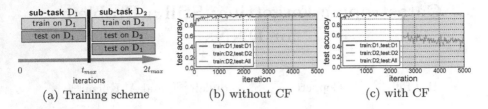

(a) Training scheme   (b) without CF   (c) with CF

Fig. 1. Scheme of incremental training experiments (see (a)) and representative outcomes without and with CF (see (b) and (c)). Initial training with sub-task D_1 for t_{max} iterations is followed by retraining on sub-task D_2 for another t_{max} iterations. During training (white background) and retraining (grey background), test performance is measured on D_1 (blue curves), D_2 (green curves) and $D_1 \cup D_2$ (red curves). The red curves allow to determine the presence of CF by simple visual inspection: if there is significant degradation w.r.t. the blue curves, then CF has occurred. (Color figure online)

this ability seems to be achieved at the cost of significantly reduced learning capacity. In this article, we test the recently proposed solutions for DNNs using a variety of class-incremental visual problems constructed from the well-known MNIST benchmark [6]. In particular, we propose a new experimental protocol to measure CF which avoids commonly made [3,5,7,10] implicit assumptions that are incompatible with incremental learning in applied scenarios.

1.1 Application Relevance of Catastrophic Forgetting

When DNNs are trained on a single (sub-)task D_1 only, catastrophic forgetting is not an issue. When retraining is necessary with a new sub-task D_2, one often recurs to retraining the DNN with all samples from D_1 and D_2 together. This heuristic works in many situations, especially when the cardinality of D_1 is moderate. When D_1 becomes very large, however, or many slight additions $D_{(1+n)}$ are required, this strategy becomes unfeasible, and an incremental training scheme (see Fig. 1a) must be used. Thus, the issue of catastrophic forgetting becomes critically important, which is why we wish to assess, once and for all, where DNNs stand with respect to CF.

1.2 Approach of the Article

In all experiments, we consider class-incremental learning scenarios divided into two training steps on disjunct sub-tasks D_1 and D_2, as outlined in Sect. 1 and visualized in Fig. 1. Both training steps are conducted for a fixed number of iterations, with the understanding that in practice retraining would have to be stopped at some point by an appropriate criterion before forgetting of D_1 is complete. The occurrence of forgetting is quantified using classification performance on all test samples from $D_1 \cup D_2$ at the time retraining is stopped (see Fig. 1 for a visual impression). In contrast to previous works, our experiments take into account how (class-)incremental learning works in practice:

Table 1. Overview over 6 DNN models used in this study. They are obtained by combining the concept of Dropout (D) with the basic DNN models: fully-connected (fc), convolutional (conv), LWTA and EWC.

Concept	Model			
	fc	conv	LWTA	EWC
With Dropout	D-fc	D-conv	✗	D-EWC (EWC)
Without Dropout	fc	conv	LWTA-fc (LWTA)	✗

- D_2 is not available at initial training
- D_1 is not available at retraining time as it might be very large.

This training paradigm (which we term "realistic") has profound consequences, most importantly that initial model selection has to be performed using D_1 alone, which is in contrast to previous works on CF in DNNs [3,5,10], where $D_1 \cup D_2$ is used for model selection purposes. Another consequence is that the decision on when to stop retraining has to be taken based on D_2 alone.

In order to reproduce earlier results, we introduce another training paradigm which we term "prescient", where both D_1 and D_2 are known at all times, and which aligns well with evaluation methods in recent works. As classifiers, we use typical DNN models like fully-connected- (fc), convolutional- (conv), LWTA-based- (fc-LWTA) and DNNs based on the EWC model (EWC). Most of these can be combined with the concepts of Dropout (D, [4]). An overview of possible combinations is given in Table 1.

For all models, hyperparameter optimization is conducted in order to ensure that our results are not simply accidental.

1.3 Related Work on CF in DNNs

In addition to early works on CF in connectionist models [2], new approaches specific to DNNs have recently been unveiled, some with the explicit goal of preventing catastrophic forgetting [3,5,7,10]. The work presented in [3] advocates the popular Dropout method as a means to reduce or eliminate CF, validating their claims on tasks derived a randomly shuffled version of MNIST [6] and a Sentiment Analysis problem. In [10], a new kind of competitive transfer function is presented which is termed LWTA (Local Winner Takes All). In a very recent article [5], the authors advocate determining the hidden layer weights that are most "relevant" to a DNNs performance, and punishing the change of those weights more heavily during retraining by an additional term in the energy functional. Experiments are conducted on random data, randomly shuffled MNIST data as in [3,10], and on a task derived from Deep Q-learning in Atari Games [8]. Even more recently, authors in [7] propose the so-called incremental moment matching (IMM) technique which suggests an alignment of statistical properties of the DNN between D_1 and D_2 which is not included here, because it inherently requires knowledge of D_1 at re-training time to select the best regularization parameter(s).

2   Methods

The principal dataset this investigation is based on is MNIST [6]. Despite being a very old benchmark, and a very simple one, it is still widely used, in particular in recent works on incremental learning in DNNs [3,5,7,10]. It is used here because we wish to reproduce these results, and also because we care about performance in class-incremental settings, not offline performance on the whole dataset. As we will see, MNIST-derived problems are more than a sufficient challenge for the tested algorithms, so it is really unnecessary to add more complex ones (but see Sect. 4 for a more in-depth discussion of this issue).

2.1   Learning Tasks

As outlined in Sect. 1.2, incremental learning performance of a given model is evaluated on several datasets constructed from the MNIST dataset. The model is trained successively on two sub-tasks (D_1 and D_2) from the chosen dataset and it is recorded to what extend knowledge about previous sub-tasks is retained. The precise way the sub-tasks of all datasets are constructed from the MNIST dataset shall be described below.

Exclusion: D5-5. These datasets are obtained by randomly choosing 5 MNIST classes for D_1, and the remaining 5 for D_2. To verify that results do not depend on a particular choice of classes, we create a total of 8 datasets where the partitioning of classes is different (see Table 2).

Exclusion: D9-1. We construct these datasets in a similar way as D5-5, selecting 9 MNIST classes for D_1 and the remaining class for D_2. In order to make sure that no artifacts are introduced, we create three datasets (D9-1a, D9-1b and D9-1c) with different choices for D_1 and D_2, see Table 2.

Permutation: DP10-10. This is the dataset used to evaluate incremental retraining in [3,5,10], so results can directly be compared. It contains two sub-tasks, each of which is obtained by permuting each 28×28 image in a random fashion that is different between, but identical within, sub-tasks. Since both sub-tasks contain 10 MNIST classes, we denote this dataset by DP10-10, the "P" indicating permutation, see Table 2.

2.2   Models

We use TensorFlow/Python to implement or re-create all models used in this article. The source code for all experiments is available at https://gitlab.informatik.hs-fulda.de/ML-Projects/CF_in_DNNs.

Table 2. MNIST-derived datasets (DS) used in this article. All partitions of MNIST into D_1 and D_2 are non-overlapping. For the DP10-10 dataset, the classes are identical for D_1 and D_2 but pixels are permuted in D_2 as described in the text.

Part.	DS											
	D5-5								D9-1			DP10-10
	D5-5a	D5-5b	D5-5c	D5-5d	D5-5e	D5-5f	D5-5g	D5-h	D9-1a	D9-1b	D9-1c	
D_1 classes	0–4	02468	34689	02567	01345	03489	05678	02368	0–8	1–9	0, 2–9	0–9
D_2 classes	5–9	13579	01257	13489	26789	12567	12349	14579	9	0	1	0–9

Fully Connected Deep Network. Here, we consider a "normal" fully-connected (FC) feed-forward MLP with two hidden layers, a softmax (SM) read-out layer trained using cross-entropy, and the (optional) application of Dropout (D) and ReLU operations after each hidden layer. Its structure can thus be summarized as In-FC1-D-ReLU-FC2-D-ReLU-FC3-SM. In case more hidden layers are added, their structure is analogous.

ConvNet. A convolutional network inspired by [1] is used here, with two hidden layers and the application of Dropout (D), max-pooling (MP) and ReLU after each layer, as well as a softmax (SM) readout layer trained using cross-entropy. It structure can thus be stated as In-C1-MP-D-ReLU-C2-MP-D-ReLU-FC3-SM.

EWC. The Elastic Weight Consolidation (EWC) model has been recently proposed in [5] to address the issue of CF in incremental learning tasks. We use a TensorFlow-implementation provided by the authors that we integrate into our own experimental setup; the corresponding code is available for download as described. The basic network structure is analogous to that of fc models.

LWTA. Deep learning with a fully-connected Locally-Winner-Takes-All (LWTA) transfer function has been proposed in [10], where it is also suggested that deep LWTA networks have a significant robustness when trained incrementally with several tasks. We use a self-coded TensorFlow implementation of the model proposed in [10]. Following [10], the number of LWTA blocks is always set to 2. The basic network structure is analogous to that of fully-connected models.

Dropout. Dropout, introduced in [4] and widely used in recent research on DNNs, is a special transfer function that sets a random subset of activities in each layer to 0 during training. It can, in principle, be applied to any DNN and thus can be combined with all previously listed models except EWC (already incorporated) and LWTA (unclear whether this would be sensible as LWTA is already a kind of transfer function).

2.3 Experimental Procedure

The procedure we employ for all experiments is essentially the one given in Sect. 1.2, where all models listed in Sect. 2.2 and Table 1 are applied to a subset of class-incremental learning tasks described in Sect. 2.1. For each experiment, characterized by a pair of model and task, we conduct a search in model parameter space for the best model configuration, leading to multiple runs per experiment, each run corresponding to a particular set of parameters for a given model and a given task.

Each run lasts for $2t_{max}$ iterations and is structured as shown in Fig. 1, initially training the chosen model first on sub-task D_1 and subsequently on sub-task D_2, each time for t_{max} iterations. Classification accuracy, measured at iteration t, on a test set $\mathcal{B}$ while training on a train set $\mathcal{A}$, is denoted $\chi(\mathcal{A}, \mathcal{B}, t)$. For a thorough evaluation, we record the quantities $\chi(D_1, D_1, t < t_{max})$, $\chi(D_2, D_2, t \geq t_{max})$ and $\chi(D_2, D_1 \cup D_2, t \geq t_{max})$. Finally, the best-suited parameterized model must be chosen among all the runs of an experiment. We investigate two strategies for doing this, corresponding to different levels of knowledge at training and retraining time during a single run. As detailed in Sect. 1.2, these are the strategies which we term "prescient" and "realistic". The "prescient" evaluation strategy (see Algorithm 1) corresponds to an a priori knowledge of sub-task D_2 at initial training time, as well as to a knowledge about D_1 at retraining time. Both assumptions are difficult to reconcile with incremental training in applied scenarios, as detailed in Sect. 1.2. We use this strategy here to compare our results to previous works in the field [3,5,10]. In contrast, the "realistic" evaluation strategy (see Algorithm 2) assumes no knowledge about future sub-tasks (D_2) and furthermore supposes that D_1 is unavailable at retraining time due to its size (see Sect. 1.2 for the reasoning). It is this strategy which we propose for future investigations concerning incremental learning.

2.4   Hyperparameters and Model Selection

For runs from all experiments, not involving CNNs, the parameters that are varied are: number of hidden layers $L \in \{2, 3\}$, layer sizes $S \in \{200, 400, 800\}$, learning rate during initial training $\epsilon_{D_1} \in \{0.01, 0.001\}$, and learning rate during retraining $\epsilon_{D_2} \in \{0.001, 0.0001, 0.00001\}$. Based on the parameter set $\mathcal{P} \subseteq L \times S \times \epsilon_{D_1} \times \epsilon_{D_2}$, all models are evaluated, respectively are model-specific hyperparameters used or supplanted. For experiments using CNNs, we fix the topology to a form known to achieve good performances on MNIST as an exhaustive optimization of all relevant parameters would prove too time-consuming in this case, and vary only the ϵ_{D_1} and ϵ_{D_2} as detailed before. For EWC experiments, the importance parameter λ of the retraining run is fixed at $1/\epsilon_{D_2}$, this choice is nowhere to be found in [5] but is used in the provided code, which is why we adopt it. For LWTA experiments, the number of LWTA blocks is fixed to 2 in all experiments, corresponding to the values used in [10]. Dropout rates, if applied, are set to 0.2 (input layer) and 0.5 (hidden layers), consistent with the choices made in [3]. For CNNs, only a single Dropout rate of 0.5 is applied for input and hidden layers alike. The length t_{max} of training/retraining period is empirically fixed to 2500 iterations, each iteration using a batch size of 100 (batch$_{size}$). The Momentum optimizer provided by TensorFlow is used for performing training, with a momentum parameter $\mu = 0.99$.

2.5   Reproduction of Previous Results by Prescient Evaluation

In this experiment, we wish to determine whether it is possible to find a parameterization for a given DNN model and task when there is a perfect knowledge about and availability of the initial and future sub-tasks. Applying the models listed in Sect. 2.2 to the tasks described in Sect. 2.1, and using the experimental procedure detailed in Sect. 2.3, we obtain the results summarized in Table 3 (applying the "prescient" evaluation of Algorithm 1). We can state the following insights: first of all, we can reproduce the basic results from [3] using the fc model on DP10-10, which avoids catastrophic forgetting (contrarily to the conclusions drawn in this paper: these authors consider the very modest decrease in performance to be catastrophic forgetting). This is however very specific to this particular task, and in fact all models except EWC exhibit blatant catastrophic forgetting behavior particularly on the D5-5 type tasks, while performing adequately if not perfectly on the D9-1 tasks. EWC performs well on these tasks as well, so we can state that EWC is the only tested algorithm that avoids CF for all tasks when using prescient evaluation. Another observation is that the use of Dropout, as suggested in [3], does not seem to significantly improve matters. The LWTA method performs a little better than fc, D-fc, conv and D-conv but is surpassed by EWC by a very large margin.

2.6   Realistic Evaluation

This experiment imposes the much more restrictive/realistic evaluation, detailed in Sect. 2.3 and Algorithm 2, essentially performing initial training and model selection only on D_1 and retraining only using D_2. It is this or related schemes that would have to be used in typical application scenarios, and thus represents the principal subject of this article. The performances of all tested DNN models on all of the tasks from Sect. 2.1 are summarized in Table 4. Plots of experimental results over time for the D-fc and EWC models are given in Figs. 2, 3, 4 and 5. The results show a rather bleak picture where only the EWC model achieves significant success for the D9-1 type tasks while failing for the D5-5 tasks. All other models do not even achieve this partial success and exhibit strong CF for all tasks. We can therefore observe that a different choice of evaluation procedure strongly impacts results and the conclusions which are drawn concerning CF in DNNs. For the realistic evaluation condition, which in our view is much more relevant than the prescient one used in nearly all of the related work on the subject, CF occurs for all DNN models we tested, and partly even for the EWC model. As to the question why EWC performs well for all of the D9-1 type task in contrast to the D5-5 type tasks, one might speculate that the addition of five new classes, as opposed to one, might exceed EWC's capabilities of protecting the weights most relevant to D_1. Various different values of the constant λ governing the contribution of Fisher information in EWC were tested but with very similar results.

3   Discussion of Results and Principal Conclusions

From our experiments, we draw the following principal conclusions:

- CF should be investigated using the appropriate evaluation paradigms that reflect application conditions. At the very least, using future data for model selection is inappropriate, which leads to conclusions that are radically different from most related experimental work, see Sect. 1.3.
- using a realistic evaluation paradigm, we find that CF is still very much a problem for all investigated methods.
- in particular: Dropout is not effective against CF; neither is LWTA.
- the permuted MNIST task can be solved by almost any DNN model in almost any topology. So all conclusions drawn from using this task should be revisited.
- EWC seems to be partly effective but fails for all of the D5-5 tasks, indicating that it is not the last word in this matter.

Data: model m, sub-tasks D_1 & D_2, parameter set $\mathcal{P}$
Result: quality of best model $q^*_{m_p}$
initialize $q^*_{m_p} \leftarrow -1$
foreach *parameters* $p \in \mathcal{P}$ **do**
    initial training of m_p on D_1 for $t_{\max}$ iterations
    for $t \leftarrow 0$ **to** t_{max} *iterations* **do**   // *retraining of* m_p *on* D_2
        update m_p on D_2 using batch$_{\text{size}}$
        $q_{m_p,t} \leftarrow \chi(D_2, D_1 \cup D_2, t)$
        if $q_{m_p,t} > q^*_{m_p}$ **then** $q^*_{m_p} \leftarrow q_{m_p,t}$
return $q^*_{m_p}$

Algorithm 1. The *prescient evaluation* strategy.

We write that EWC "seems to be partly effective", meaning it solves some incremental tasks well while it fails for others. So we observe that there is no guarantee that can be obtained from a purely empirical validation approach such as ours; yet another type of incremental learning task might be solved perfectly or not at all. This points to the principal conceptual problem that we see when investigating CF in DNNs: there is no theory that might offer any guarantees. Such guarantees could be very useful in practice, the most interesting one being how to determine a lower bound on performance loss on $D_1 \cup D_2$, without having access to D_1, only to the network state and D_2. Other guarantees could provide upper bounds on retraining time before performance on $D_1 \cup D_2$ degrades.

Table 3. Results for **prescient evaluation**. Please note that the performance level of complete catastrophic forgetting (i.e., chance-level classification after retraining with D_2) depends on the dataset considered: for the D5-5 dataset it is at 0.5, whereas it is at 0.1 for the D9-1 datasets. The rightmost column indicates the DP10-10 task which is solved near-perfectly by all models.

Model	Dataset											
	D5-5								D9-1			DP10-10
	D5-5a	D5-5b	D5-5c	D5-5d	D5-5e	D5-5f	D5-5g	D5-5h	D9-1a	D9-1b	D9-1c	
EWC	0.92	0.92	0.91	0.93	0.94	0.94	0.89	0.93	1.00	1.00	1.00	1.00
fc	0.69	0.63	0.58	0.65	0.61	0.58	0.61	0.69	0.87	0.87	0.86	0.97
D-fc	0.58	0.60	0.61	0.66	0.61	0.54	0.63	0.64	0.87	0.87	0.85	0.96
conv	0.51	0.50	0.50	0.50	0.50	0.50	0.51	0.49	0.89	0.89	0.87	0.95
D-conv	0.51	0.50	0.50	0.50	0.50	0.50	0.50	0.49	0.81	0.84	0.87	0.96
LWTA	0.66	0.68	0.64	0.73	0.71	0.62	0.68	0.71	0.88	0.91	0.91	0.97

Data: model m, sub-tasks D_1 & D_2, parameter set $\mathcal{P}$
Result: quality of best model $q^*_{m_p}$
initialize $q^*_T \leftarrow -1$
forall the *parameters* $p \in \mathcal{P}$ **do**   *//determine best model parameter training D_1*
    for $t \leftarrow 0$ **to** t_{max} *iterations* **do**
        update of m_p on D_1 using batch$_{size}$; $q_{m_p,t} \leftarrow \chi(D_1, D_1, t)$
        if $q_{m_p,t} > q^*_T$ **then** $q^*_T \leftarrow q_{m_p,t}$; $m^*_p \leftarrow m_p$
initialize $q^*_{m_p} \leftarrow -1$
forall the *retraining learning rates* $\epsilon \in \epsilon_{D_2}$ **do**
    initialize $q^*_R \leftarrow -1$
    for $t \leftarrow 0$ **to** t_{max} *iterations* **do**   *//retraining of m^*_p on D_2*
        update m^*_p on D_2 with learning rate ϵ; $q_{m_p,t} \leftarrow \chi(D_2, D_2, t)$
        if $q_{m_p,t} > q^*_R$ **then** $q^*_R \leftarrow q_{m_p,t}$
    $t_E \leftarrow \arg\min_t(q_{m_p,t} > 0.99 \cdot q^*_R)$; $q_{m_p} \leftarrow \chi(D_2, D_1 \cup D_2, t_E)$
    if $q_{m_p} > q^*_{m_p}$ **then** $q^*_{m_p} \leftarrow q_{m_p}$
return $q^*_{m_p}$

Algorithm 2. The *realistic evaluation* strategy.

Table 4. Results for **realistic evaluation**. Please note that the performance level of total catastrophic forgetting (i.e., chance-level classification after retraining with D_2) depends on the dataset: for the D5-5 dataset it is at 0.5, whereas it is at 0.1 for the D9-1 datasets. The rightmost column indicates the DP10-10 task ("permuted MNIST") which is again solved near-perfectly by all models.

Model	Dataset											
	D5-5								D9-1			DP10-10
	D5-5a	D5-5b	D5-5c	D5-5d	D5-5e	D5-5f	D5-5g	D5-5h	D9-1a	D9-1b	D9-1c	
EWC	0.48	0.56	0.62	0.52	0.58	0.58	0.55	0.53	0.82	0.91	0.97	0.99
fc	0.47	0.49	0.50	0.50	0.48	0.49	0.50	0.49	0.15	0.10	0.23	0.97
D-fc	0.47	0.50	0.50	0.50	0.49	0.49	0.50	0.49	0.52	0.10	0.16	0.96
conv	0.48	0.50	0.50	0.50	0.49	0.50	0.51	0.49	0.29	0.33	0.11	0.95
D-conv	0.48	0.50	0.50	0.50	0.45	0.50	0.50	0.49	0.24	0.22	0.14	0.96
LWTA	0.47	0.50	0.50	0.50	0.49	0.49	0.51	0.49	0.48	0.29	0.66	0.97

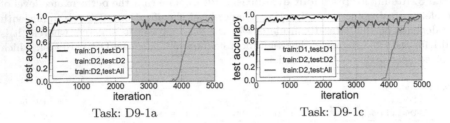

Fig. 2. Best EWC runs on D9-1 datasets in the **realistic evaluation** condition.

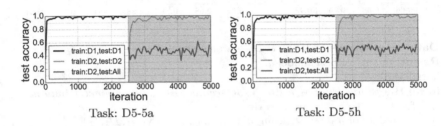

Fig. 3. Best EWC runs on D5-5 datasets in the **realistic evaluation** condition.

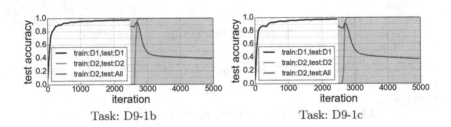

Fig. 4. Best D-fc runs on D9-1 datasets in the **realistic evaluation** condition.

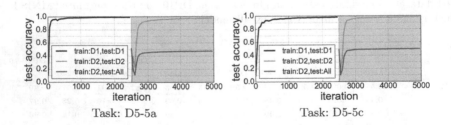

Fig. 5. Best D-fc runs on D5-5 datasets in the **realistic evaluation** condition.

4   Future Work

The issue of CF is a complex one, and correspondingly our article and our experimental procedures are complex as well. There are several points where we made rather arbitrary choices, e.g., when choosing the constant $\mu = 0.99$ in the realistic evaluation Algorithm 2. The results are affected by this choice although we verified that the trend is unchanged. Another weak point is our model selection procedure: a much larger combinatorial set of model hyper-parameters should be sampled, including Dropout rates, convolution filter kernels, number and size of layers. This might conceivably allow to identify model hyperparameters avoiding CF for some or all tested models, although we consider this unlikely. Lastly, the use of MNIST might be criticized as being too simple: this is correct, and we are currently doing experiments with more complex classification tasks (e.g., SVHN and CIFAR-10). However, as our conclusion is that none of the currently proposed DNN models can avoid CF, this is not very likely to change when using an even more challenging classification task (rather the reverse, in fact).

References

1. Ciresan, D.C., Meier, U., Masci, J., Maria Gambardella, L., Schmidhuber, J.: Flexible, high performance convolutional neural networks for image classification. In: IJCAI Proceedings of International Joint Conference on Artificial Intelligence, Barcelona, Spain, vol. 22, p. 1237 (2011)
2. French, R.: Catastrophic forgetting in connectionist networks. Trends Cogn. Sci. (4) (1999)
3. Goodfellow, I.J., Mirza, M., Xiao, D., Courville, A., Bengio, Y.: An empirical investigation of catastrophic forgetting in gradient-based neural networks. arXiv preprint arXiv:1312.6211 (2013)
4. Hinton, G.E., Srivastava, N., Krizhevsky, A., Sutskever, I., Salakhutdinov, R.R.: Improving neural networks by preventing co-adaptation of feature detectors. arXiv preprint arXiv:1207.0580 (2012)
5. Kirkpatrick, J., et al.: Overcoming catastrophic forgetting in neural networks. Proc. Natl. Acad. Sci. **114**, 3521–3526 (2017). https://doi.org/10.1073/pnas.1611835114
6. LeCun, Y., Bottou, L., Bengio, Y., Haffner, P.: Gradient-based learning applied to document recognition. In: Intelligent Signal Processing. IEEE Press (2001)
7. Lee, S.W., Kim, J.H., Jun, J., Ha, J.W., Zhang, B.T.: Overcoming catastrophic forgetting by incremental moment matching. In: Advances in Neural Information Processing Systems, pp. 4655–4665 (2017)
8. Mnih, V., et al.: Human-level control through deep reinforcement learning. Nature **7540**, 529–533 (2015)
9. Sigaud, O., Salaün, C., Padois, V.: On-line regression algorithms for learning mechanical models of robots: a survey. Rob. Auton. Syst. **12**, 1115–1129 (2011)
10. Srivastava, R.K., Masci, J., Kazerounian, S., Gomez, F., Schmidhuber, J.: Compete to compute. In: Advances in Neural Information Processing Systems (2013)

Queue-Based Resampling for Online Class Imbalance Learning

Kleanthis Malialis[(✉)], Christos Panayiotou, and Marios M. Polycarpou

KIOS Research and Innovation Center of Excellence,
Department of Electrical and Computer Engineering,
University of Cyprus, Nicosia, Cyprus
{malialis.kleanthis,christosp,mpolycar}@ucy.ac.cy

Abstract. Online class imbalance learning constitutes a new problem and an emerging research topic that focusses on the challenges of online learning under class imbalance and concept drift. Class imbalance deals with data streams that have very skewed distributions while concept drift deals with changes in the class imbalance status. Little work exists that addresses these challenges and in this paper we introduce queue-based resampling, a novel algorithm that successfully addresses the co-existence of class imbalance and concept drift. The central idea of the proposed resampling algorithm is to selectively include in the training set a subset of the examples that appeared in the past. Results on two popular benchmark datasets demonstrate the effectiveness of queue-based resampling over state-of-the-art methods in terms of learning speed and quality.

Keywords: Online learning · Class imbalance · Concept drift
Resampling · Neural networks · Data streams

1 Introduction

In the area of monitoring and security of critical infrastructures which include large-scale, complex systems such as power and energy systems, water, transportation and telecommunication networks, the challenge of the state being normal or healthy for a sustained period of time until an abnormal event occurs is typically encountered [10]. Such abnormal events or faults can lead to serious degradation in performance or, even worse, to cascading overall system failure and breakdown. The consequences are tremendous and may have a huge impact on everyday life and well-being. Examples include real-time prediction of hazardous events in environment monitoring systems and intrusion detection in computer networks. In critical infrastructure systems the system is at a healthy state the majority of the time and failures are low probability events, therefore, class imbalance is a major challenge encountered in this area.

Class imbalance occurs when at least one data class is under-represented compared to others, thus constituting a minority class. It is a difficult problem as the skewed distribution makes a traditional learning algorithm ineffective,

V. Kůrková et al. (Eds.): ICANN 2018, LNCS 11139, pp. 498–507, 2018.
https://doi.org/10.1007/978-3-030-01418-6_49

specifically, its prediction power is typically low for the minority class examples and its generalisation ability is poor [16]. The problem becomes significantly harder when class imbalance co-exists with concept drift. There exists only a handful of work on online class imbalance learning. Focussing on binary classification problems, we introduce a novel algorithm, queue-based resampling, where its central idea is to selectively include in the training set a subset of the negative and positive examples by maintaining a separate queue for each class. Our study examines two popular benchmark datasets under various class imbalance rates with and without the presence of drift. Queue-based resampling outperforms state-of-the-art methods in terms of learning speed and quality.

2   Background and Related Work

2.1   Online Learning

In **online learning** [1], a data generating process provides at each time step t a sequence of examples (x^t, y^t) from an unknown probability distribution $p^t(x, y)$, where $x^t \in \mathbb{R}^d$ is an d-dimensional input vector belonging to input space X and $y^t \in Y$ is the class label where $Y = \{c_1, \ldots, c_N\}$ and N is the number of classes. An online classifier is built that receives a new example x^t at time step t and makes a prediction $\hat{y}^t$. Specifically, assume a concept $h : X \to Y$ such that $\hat{y}^t = h(x^t)$. The classifier after some time receives the true label y^t, its performance is evaluated using a loss function $J = l(y^t, \hat{y}^t)$ and is then trained i.e. its parameters are updated accordingly based on the loss J incurred. The example is discarded to enable learning in high-speed data streaming applications. This process is repeated at each time step. Depending on the application, new examples do not necessarily arrive at regular and pre-defined intervals.

We distinguish **chunk-based learning** [1] from online learning where at each time step t we receive a chunk of $M > 1$ examples $C^t = \{(x_i^t, y_i^t)\}_{i=1}^M$. Both approaches build a model incrementally, however, the design of chunk-based algorithms differs significantly and, therefore, the majority is typically not suitable for online learning tasks [16]. This work focuses on online learning.

2.2   Class Imbalance and Concept Drift

Class imbalance [6] constitutes a major challenge in learning and occurs when at least one data class is under-represented compared to others, thus constituting a minority class. Considering, for example, a binary classification problem, class 1 (positive) and 0 (negative) constitutes the minority and majority class respectively if $p(y = 1) \ll p(y = 0)$. Class imbalance has been extensively studied in offline learning and techniques addressing the problem are typically split into two categories, these are, data-level and algorithm-level techniques.

Data-level techniques consist of resampling techniques that alter the training set to deal with the skewed data distribution, specifically, oversampling techniques "grow" the minority class while undersampling techniques "shrink" the majority class. The simplest and most popular resampling techniques are random oversampling (or undersampling) where data examples are randomly added (or removed) respectively [16,17]. More sophisticated resampling techniques exist, for example, the use of Tomek links discards borderline examples while the SMOTE algorithm generates new minority class examples based on the similarities to the original ones. Interestingly, sophisticated techniques do not always outperform the simpler ones [16]. Furthermore, since their mechanism relies on identifying relations between training data, it is difficult to be applied in online learning tasks, although some initial effort has been recently made [13].

Algorithm-level techniques modify the classification algorithm directly to deal with the imbalance problem. Cost-sensitive learning is widely adopted and assigns a different cost to each data class [17]. Alternatives are threshold-moving [17] methods where the classifier's threshold is modified such that it becomes harder to misclassify minority class examples. Contrary to resampling methods that are algorithm-agnostic, algorithm-level methods are not as widely used [16].

A challenge in online learning is that of **concept drift** [1] where the data generating process is evolving over time. Formally, a drift corresponds to a change in the joint probability $p(x, y)$. Despite that drift can manifest itself in other forms, this work focuses on $p(y)$ drift (i.e. a change in the prior probability) because such a change can lead to class imbalance. Note that the *true* decision boundary remains unaffected when $p(y)$ drift occurs, however, the classifier's *learnt* boundary may drift away from the true one.

2.3   Online Class Imbalance Learning

The majority of existing work addresses class imbalance in offline learning, while some others require chunk-based data processing [8,16]. Little work deals with class imbalance in online learning and this section discusses the state-of-the-art.

The authors in [14] propose the cost-sensitive online gradient descent ($CSODG$) method that uses the following loss function:

$$J = (I_{y^t=0} + I_{y^t=1}\frac{w_p}{w_n})\, l(y^t, \hat{y}^t) \tag{1}$$

where $I_{condition}$ is the indicator function that returns 1 if *condition* is satisfied and 0 otherwise, $0 \le w_p, w_n \le 1$ and $w_p + w_n = 1$ are the costs for positive and negative classes respectively. The authors use the perceptron classifier and stochastic gradient descent, and apply the cost-sensitive modification to the hinge loss function achieving excellent results. The downside of this method is that the costs need to be pre-defined, however, the extent of the class imbalance problem may not be known in advance. In addition, it cannot cope with concept drift as the pre-defined costs remain static. In [5], the authors introduce $RLSACP$ which is a cost-sensitive perceptron-based classifier with an adaptive cost strategy.

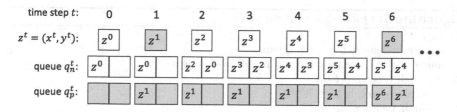

Fig. 1. Example of $Queue_2$ resampling (Color figure online)

A time decayed class size metric is defined in [15] where for each class c_k, its size s_k is updated at each time step t according to the following equation:

$$s_k^t = \theta s_k^{t-1} + I_{y^t = c_k}(1 - \theta) \qquad (2)$$

where $0 < \theta < 1$ is a pre-defined time decay factor that gives less emphasis on older data. This metric is used to determine the imbalance rate at any given time. For instance, for a binary classification problem where the positive class constitutes the minority, the imbalance rate at any given time t is given by s_p^t / s_n^t.

Oversampling-based online bagging (OOB) is an ensemble method that adjusts the learning bias from the majority to the minority class adaptively through resampling by utilising the time decayed class size metric [15]. An undersampling version called UOB had also been proposed but was demonstrated to be unstable. OOB with 50 neural networks has been shown to have superior performance. To determine the effectiveness of resampling solely, the authors examine the special case where there exists only a single classifier denoted by OOB_{sg}. Compared against the aforementioned $RLSACP$ and others, OOB_{sg} has been shown to outperform the rest in the majority of the cases, thus concluding that resampling is the main reason behind the effectiveness of the ensemble [15].

Another approach to address drift is the use of sliding windows [8]. It can be viewed as adding a memory component to the online learner; given a window of size W, it keeps in the memory the most recent W examples. Despite being able to address concept drift, it is difficult to determine a priori the window size as a larger window is better suited for a slow drift, while a smaller window is suitable for a rapid drift. More sophisticated algorithms have been proposed, such as, a window of adaptable size or the use of multiple windows of different size [11]. The drawback of this approach is that it cannot handle class imbalance.

3 Queue-Based Resampling

Online class imbalance learning is an emerging research topic and this work proposes queue-based resampling, a novel algorithm that addresses this problem. Focussing on binary classification, the central idea of the proposed resampling algorithm is to selectively include in the training set a subset of the positive and negative examples that appeared so far. Work closer to us is [4] where the authors apply an analogous idea but in the context of chunk-based learning.

Algorithm 1. Queue-based Resampling

1: **Input:**
    maximum length L of each queue
    queues (q_p^t, q_n^t) for positive and negative examples
2: **for** each time step t **do**
3:     receive example $x^t \in \mathbb{R}^d$
4:     predict class $\hat{y}^t \in \{0, 1\}$
5:     receive true label $y^t \in \{0, 1\}$
6:     let $z^t = (x^t, y^t)$
7:     **if** $y^t == 0$ **then**
8:         $q_n^t = q_n^{t-1}.append(z^t)$
9:     **else**
10:        $q_p^t = q_p^{t-1}.append(z^t)$
11:     **end if**
12:     let $q^t = q_p^t \cup q_n^t$ be the training set
13:     calculate cost on q^t using Eq. 3
14:     update classifier
15: **end for**

The selection of the examples is achieved by maintaining at any given time t two separate queues of equal length $L \in \mathbb{Z}^+$, $q_n^t = \{(x_i, y_i)\}_{i=1}^L$ and $q_p^t = \{(x_i, y_i)\}_{i=1}^L$ that contain the negative and positive examples respectively. Let $z_i = (x_i, y_i)$, for any two $z_i, z_j \in q_n^t$ or (q_p^t) such that $j > i$, z_j arrived more recently in time. Queue-based resampling stores the most recent example plus $2L-1$ old ones. We will refer to the proposed algorithm as $Queue_L$. Of particular interest is the special case $Queue_1$ where the length of each queue is $L = 1$, as it has the major advantage of requiring just a single data point from the past.

An example demonstrating how $Queue_L$ works when $L = 2$ is shown in Fig. 1. The upper part shows the examples that arrive at each time step e.g. z^0 and z^6 arrive at $t = 0$ and $t = 6$ respectively. Positive examples are shown in green. The bottom part shows the contents of each queue at each time step. Focussing on $t = 5$, we can see that the queue q_n^5 contains the two most recent negative examples i.e. z^4 and z^5, and the queue q_p^5 contains the most recent positive example i.e. z^1 which is carried over since $t = 1$.

The union of the two queues is then taken $q^t = q_p^t \cup q_n^t = \{(x_i, y_i)\}_{i=1}^{2L}$ to form the new training set for the classifier. The cost function is given in Eq. 3:

$$J = \frac{1}{|q^t|} \sum_{i=1}^{|q^t|} l(y_i, h(x_i)) \tag{3}$$

where $|q^t| \leq 2L$ and $(x_i, y_i) \in q^t$. At each time step the classifier is updated once according to the cost J incurred i.e. a single update of the classifier's weights is performed. The pseudocode of our algorithm is shown in Algorithm 1.

The effectiveness of queue-based resampling is attributed to a few important characteristics. Maintaining separate queues for each class helps to address the class imbalance problem. Including positive examples from the past in the most

Table 1. Compared methods

Method	Class imbalance	Concept drift	Access to old data
Baseline	No	No	No
Cost sensitive	Yes	No	No
Sliding window	No	Yes	Yes $(W-1)$
OOB_{sg}	Yes	Yes	No
$Queue_1$	Yes	Yes	Yes (1)
$Queue_L$	Yes	Yes	Yes $(2L-1)$

recent training set can be viewed as a form of oversampling. The fact that examples are propagated and carried over a series of time steps allows the classifier to 'remember' old concepts. Additionally, to address the challenge of concept drift, the classifier needs to also be able to 'forget' old concepts. This is achieved by bounding the length of queues to L, therefore, the queues are essentially behaving like sliding windows as well. Therefore, the proposed queue-based resampling method can cope with both class imbalance and concept drift.

4   Experimental Setup

Our experimental study is based on two popular synthetic datasets from the literature [2] where in both cases a classifier attempts to learn a non-linear decision boundary. These are, the Sine and Circle datasets and are described below.

Sine. It consists of two attributes x and y uniformly distributed in $[0, 2\pi]$ and $[-1, 1]$ respectively. The classification function is $y = sin(x)$. Instances below the curve are classified as positive and above the curve as negative. Feature rescaling has been performed so that x and y are in $[0, 1]$.

Circle. It has two attributes x and y that are uniformly distributed in $[0, 1]$. The circle function is given by $(x - x_c)^2 + (y - y_c)^2 = r_c^2$ where (x_c, y_c) is its centre and r_c its radius. The circle with $(x_c, y_c) = (0.4, 0.5)$ and $r_c = 0.2$ is created. Instances inside the circle are classified as positive and outside as negative.

Our baseline classifier is a neural network consisting of one hidden layer with eight neurons. Its configuration is as follows: He [7] weight initialisation, backpropagation and the $ADAM$ [9] optimisation algorithms, learning rate of 0.01, $LeakyReLU$ [12] as the activation function of the hidden neurons, sigmoid activation for the output neuron, and the binary cross-entropy loss function.

For our study we implemented a series of state-of-the-art methods as described in Sect. 2.3. We implemented a cost sensitive version of the baseline which we will refer to as CS; the cost of the positive class is set to $\frac{w_p}{w_n} = \frac{0.95}{0.05} = 19$ as in [14]. Furthermore, the sliding window method has been implemented with

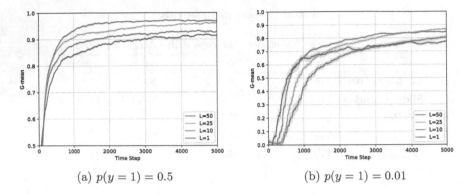

(a) $p(y = 1) = 0.5$ (b) $p(y = 1) = 0.01$

Fig. 2. Effect of queue length on the Sine dataset

a window size of W. Moreover, the OOB_{sg} has been implemented with the time decay factor set to $\theta = 0.99$ for calculating the class size at any given time.

For the proposed resampling method we will use the special case $Queue_1$ and another case $Queue_L$ where $L > 1$. Section 5.1 performs an analysis of $Queue_L$ by examining how the queue length L affects the behaviour and performance of queue-based resampling. For a fair comparison with the sliding window method, we will set the window size to $W = 2L$ i.e. both methods will have access to the same amount of old data examples. A summary of the compared methods is shown in Table 1 indicating which methods are suitable for addressing class imbalance and concept drift. It also indicates whether methods require access to old data and, if yes, it includes the maximum number in the brackets.

A popular and suitable metric for evaluating algorithms under class imbalance is the geometric mean as it is not sensitive to the class distribution [16]. It is defined as the geometric mean of recall and specificity. Recall is defined as the true positive rate ($R = \frac{TP}{P}$) and specificity is defined as the true negative rate ($S = \frac{TN}{N}$), where TP and P is the number of true positives and positives respectively, and similarly, TN and N for the true negatives and negatives. The geometric mean is then calculated using $G\text{-}mean = \sqrt{R \times S}$. To calculate the recall and specificity online, we use the prequential evaluation using fading factors as proposed in [3] and set the fading factor to $\alpha = 0.99$. In all graphs we plot the prequential $G\text{-}mean$ in every time step averaged over 30 runs, including the error bars showing the standard error around the mean.

5 Experimental Results

5.1 Analysis of Queue-Based Resampling

In this section we investigate the behaviour of $Queue_L$ resampling under various queue lengths ($L \in [1, 10, 25, 50]$) and examine how these affect its performance. Furthermore, we consider a balanced scenario (i.e. $p(y = 1) = 0.5$) and a scenario with a severe class imbalance of 1% (i.e. $p(y = 1) = 0.01$).

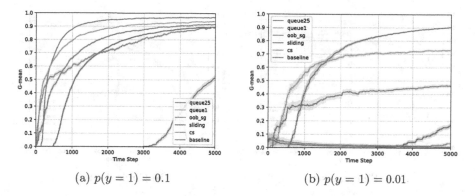

(a) $p(y = 1) = 0.1$ (b) $p(y = 1) = 0.01$

Fig. 3. Class imbalance on the Circle dataset

Figures 2a and b depict the behaviour of the proposed method on the balanced and severely imbalanced scenario respectively for the Sine dataset. It can be observed from Fig. 2a that the larger the queue length the better the performance, specifically, the best performance is achieved when $L = 50$. It can be observed from Fig. 2b that the smaller the queue length the faster the learning speed. $Queue_1$ dominates in the first 500 time steps, however, its end performance is inferior to the rest. The method with $L = 10$ dominates for over 3000 steps. Given additional learning time the method with $L = 25$ achieves the best performance. The method with $L = 50$ is unable to outperform the one with $L = 10$ after 5000 steps, in fact, it performs similarly to $Queue_1$.

It is important to emphasise that contrary to offline learning where the end performance is of particular concern, in online learning both the end performance and learning time are of high importance. For this reason, we have decided to focus on $Queue_{25}$ as it constitutes a reasonable trade-off between learning speed and performance. As already mentioned, we will also focus on $Queue_1$ as it has the advantage of requiring only one data example from the past.

5.2 Comparative Study

Figure 3a depicts a comparative study of all the methods in the scenario involving 10% class imbalance for the Circle dataset. The baseline method, as expected, does not perform well and only starts learning after about 3000 time steps. The proposed $Queue_{25}$ has the best performance at the expense of a late start. $Queue_1$ also outperforms the rest although towards the end other methods like OOB_{sg} close the gap. Similar results are obtained for the Sine dataset but are not presented here due to space constraints.

Figure 3a shows how each method compares to each other in the 1% class imbalance scenario. Both the proposed methods outperform the state-of-the-art OOB_{sg}. Despite the fact that $Queue_{25}$ performs considerably better than $Queue_1$, it requires about 1500 time steps to surpass it. Additionally, we stress out that $Queue_1$ only requires access to a single old example.

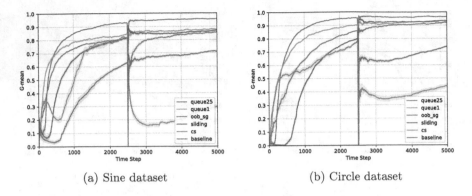

(a) Sine dataset   (b) Circle dataset

Fig. 4. Class imbalance and concept drift

We now examine the behaviour of all methods in the presence of both class imbalance and drift. Figures 4a and b show the performance of all methods for the Sine and Circle datasets respectively. Initially, class imbalance is $p(y = 1) = 0.1$ but at time step $t = 2500$ an abrupt drift occurs and this becomes $p(y = 1) = 0.9$. At the time of drift we reset the prequential $G\text{-}mean$ to zero, thus ensuring the performance observed remains unaffected by the performance prior the drift [15]. Similar results are observed for both datasets. $Queue_{25}$ outperforms the rest at the expense of a late start. $Queue_1$ starts learning fast, initially it outperforms other methods but their end performance is close. OOB_{sg} is affected more by the drift in the Sine dataset but recovers soon. The baseline method outperforms its cost sensitive version after the drift because the pre-defined costs of method CS are no longer suitable in the new situation.

6   Conclusion

Online class imbalance learning constitutes a new problem and an emerging research topic. We propose a novel algorithm, queue-based resamping, to address this problem. Focussing on binary classification problems, the central idea behind queue-based resampling is to selectively include in the training set a subset of the negative and positive examples by maintaining at any given time a separate queue for each class. It has been shown to outperform state-of-the-art methods, particularly, in scenarios with severe class imbalance. It has also been demonstrated to work well when abrupt concept drift occurs. Future work will examine the behaviour of queue-based resampling in various other types of concept drift (e.g. gradual). A challenge faced in the area of monitoring of critical infrastructures is that the true label of examples can be noisy or even not available. We plan to address this challenge in the future.

Acknowledgements. This work has been supported by the European Union's Horizon 2020 research and innovation programme under grant agreement No 739551 (KIOS CoE) and from the Republic of Cyprus through the Directorate General for European Programmes, Coordination and Development.

References

1. Ditzler, G., Roveri, M., Alippi, C., Polikar, R.: Learning in nonstationary environments: a survey. IEEE Comput. Intell. Mag. **10**(4), 12–25 (2015)
2. Gama, J., Medas, P., Castillo, G., Rodrigues, P.: Learning with drift detection. In: Bazzan, A.L.C., Labidi, S. (eds.) SBIA 2004. LNCS (LNAI), vol. 3171, pp. 286–295. Springer, Heidelberg (2004). https://doi.org/10.1007/978-3-540-28645-5_29
3. Gama, J., Sebastião, R., Rodrigues, P.P.: On evaluating stream learning algorithms. Mach. Learn. **90**(3), 317–346 (2013)
4. Gao, J., Ding, B., Fan, W., Han, J., Philip, S.Y.: Classifying data streams with skewed class distributions and concept drifts. IEEE Internet Comput. **12**(6), 37–49 (2008)
5. Ghazikhani, A., Monsefi, R., Yazdi, H.S.: Recursive least square perceptron model for non-stationary and imbalanced data stream classification. Evol. Syst. **4**(2), 119 131 (2013)
6. He, H., Garcia, E.A.: Learning from imbalanced data. IEEE Trans. Knowl. Data Eng. **9**, 1263–1284 (2008)
7. He, K., Zhang, X., Ren, S., Sun, J.: Delving deep into rectifiers: Surpassing human-level performance on ImageNet classification. In: Proceedings of the IEEE International Conference on Computer Vision, pp. 1026–1034 (2015)
8. Hoens, T.R., Polikar, R., Chawla, N.V.: Learning from streaming data with concept drift and imbalance: an overview. Progress Artif. Intell. **1**(1), 89–101 (2012)
9. Kingma, D.P., Ba, J.: Adam: a method for stochastic optimization. arXiv preprint arXiv:1412.6980 (2014)
10. Kyriakides, E., Polycarpou, M.: Intelligent Monitoring, Control, and Security of Critical Infrastructure Systems, vol. 565. Springer, Heidelberg (2014). https://doi.org/10.1007/978-3-662-44160-2
11. Lazarescu, M.M., Venkatesh, S., Bui, H.H.: Using multiple windows to track concept drift. Intell. Data Anal. **8**(1), 29–59 (2004)
12. Maas, A.L., Hannun, A.Y., Ng, A.Y.: Rectifier nonlinearities improve neural network acoustic models. In: Proceedings of ICML, vol. 30, p. 3 (2013)
13. Mao, W., Wang, J., Wang, L.: Online sequential classification of imbalanced data by combining extreme learning machine and improved smote algorithm. In: 2015 International Joint Conference on Neural Networks (IJCNN), pp. 1–8. IEEE (2015)
14. Wang, J., Zhao, P., Hoi, S.C.: Cost-sensitive online classification. IEEE Trans. Knowl. Data Eng. **26**(10), 2425–2438 (2014)
15. Wang, S., Minku, L.L., Yao, X.: Resampling-based ensemble methods for online class imbalance learning. IEEE Trans. Knowl. Data Eng. **27**(5), 1356–1368 (2015)
16. Wang, S., Minku, L.L., Yao, X.: A systematic study of online class imbalance learning with concept drift. IEEE Trans. Neural Netw. Learn. Syst. (2018). https://doi.org/10.1109/TNNLS.2017.2771290
17. Zhou, Z.H., Liu, X.Y.: Training cost-sensitive neural networks with methods addressing the class imbalance problem. IEEE Trans. Knowl. Data Eng. **18**(1), 63–77 (2006)

Learning Simplified Decision Boundaries from Trapezoidal Data Streams

Ege Beyazit$^{(\boxtimes)}$, Matin Hosseini$^{(\boxtimes)}$, Anthony Maida$^{(\boxtimes)}$, and Xindong Wu$^{(\boxtimes)}$

University of Louisiana at Lafayette, Lafayette, LA 70503, USA
{exb6143,mxh0212,maida,xwu}@louisiana.edu

Abstract. We present a novel adaptive feedforward neural network for online learning from doubly-streaming data, where both the data volume and feature space grow simultaneously. Traditional online learning and feature selection algorithms can't handle this problem because they assume that the feature space of the data stream remains unchanged. We propose a Single Hidden Layer Feedforward Neural Network with Shortcut Connections (SLFN-S) that learns if a data stream needs to be mapped using a non-linear transformation or not, to speed up the learning convergence. We employ a growing strategy to adjust the model complexity to the continuously changing feature space. Finally, we use a weight-based pruning procedure to keep the run time complexity of the proposed model linear in the size of the input feature space, for efficient learning from data streams. Experiments with trapezoidal data streams on 8 UCI datasets were conducted to examine the performance of the proposed model. We show that SLFN-S outperforms the state of the art learning algorithm from trapezoidal data streams [16].

Keywords: Online learning · Trapezoidal data streams
Feedforward Neural Networks · Shortcut connections

1 Introduction

Online learning makes it possible to learn in applications where the complete data is initially not available or the data is too large to fit into memory. Online learning algorithms can learn from continuously growing data, where new patterns are introduced over time. A wide range of online learning algorithms are available, and can be grouped into first-order and second-order methods. First-order methods such as [1] use first-order derivatives to minimize a loss function. Second-order methods such as [2] exploit the second-order information to improve the convergence. However, second-order methods are more prone to be stuck at local minima and tend to be computationally costly while working with high-dimensional data. Traditional online learning algorithms assume that the feature space of the input data remains constant, and try to fit a model of constant complexity to it. However in many applications, feature spaces can grow over time. New features can be introduced, and combinations of new and existing

© Springer Nature Switzerland AG 2018
V. Kůrková et al. (Eds.): ICANN 2018, LNCS 11139, pp. 508–517, 2018.
https://doi.org/10.1007/978-3-030-01418-6_50

features can form meaningful higher order concepts. For example in social networks, sets of attributes provided by each user can grow over time. In an infinite vocabulary topic model [15], the number of documents and the text vocabulary can simultaneously increase over time. In high resolution video streams, both the number of frames and the feature space formed by the extracted features can grow over time.

Data streams where the numbers of instances and features grow simultaneously are referred to as trapezoidal data streams [16]. Learning from trapezoidal data streams is more challenging than other online learning problems, because of their doubly-streaming nature. While learning from trapezoidal data streams, the model should be able to:

- Learn from sequentially presented instances on a single pass,
- Have low running time and memory complexity,
- Adapt to increasing complexity of the feature space, and
- Do feature selection to bound the number of features used in the model.

Zhang et al. proposed OL_{SF} algorithms [16] to learn a classifier from trapezoidal data streams by using a passive-aggressive update rule for the existing features and a structural risk minimization principle for the newly introduced features. Also, OL_{SF} algorithms contain projection and truncation steps to promote sparsity and do feature selection. They do not however consider the increasing complexity of the feature space, which can be caused by various feature interactions. Additionally, OL_{SF} algorithms are limited to learn linear decision boundaries, which are likely to perform poorly on nonlinearly separable data. Finally unless an additional method such as One vs. One or One vs. Rest is employed, OL_{SF} algorithms can only work under binary classification settings.

Fully connected neural networks consider complex unknown nonlinear mappings of the input features and form decision regions of arbitrary shapes to make predictions [4]. A features value at any layer affects the values of all features at the next layer. Therefore, feature interactions are naturally considered. There are also a wide range of studies for online learning with neural networks [9]. Constructive methods such as Resource Allocating Networks (RAN) [8] can adapt the network architecture based on the *novelty* of the received data in a sequential manner, and by adding hidden layer nodes to approximate the complexity of the underlying function. Minimal Resource Allocating Networks (M-RAN) [14] combine the growth criterion of the RAN's with a pruning strategy. Their pruning strategy removes hidden units that consistently make little contribution, to learn a more compact network compared to RAN. Single Hidden Layer Feedforward Neural Networks (SLFN) [5] can form decision boundaries in arbitrary shapes with any bounded continuous nonconstant activation function or any arbitrary bounded activation function with unequal limits at infinities.

Encouraged by the capabilities of the neural networks mentioned above, we propose SLFN-S, an Adaptive Single Hidden Layer Feedforward Neural Network with Shortcut Connections. Our proposed model provides growing and pruning capabilities to learn from trapezoidal data streams. The model learns if a linear mapping is enough to correctly classify the current instance, to speed up the learning convergence. Unlike the existing neural network based models, SLFN-S is able to learn simplified linear and nonlinear decision boundaries to converge on a single pass, and adapt itself to the increasing complexity of the trapezoidal data streams.

2   Methodology

We consider the classification problem on trapezoidal data streams where (x_t, y_t) is the input training data, class label pair received at time t. $x_t \in \mathbb{R}^{d_t}$ is a d_t dimensional vector where $d_t \leq d_{t+1}$. Let the numbers of input and hidden layer nodes of the network at time t be d_t^i and d_t^h respectively. Note that d_t^i, d_t^h and d_t^o represent the sizes of the feature spaces that the network operates in for the input, hidden and output layers. When the network receives an input (x_t, y_t), if $d_t = d_t^i$, the feedforward pass calculates a mixture of linear and nonlinear mapping for the input and makes a prediction $\hat{y}_t$. If $d_t > d_t^i$, then $d_t - d_t^i$ new nodes for the input and hidden layers are allocated and $(d_t - d_t^i) \cdot (d_t^i + d_t^h)$ fully connected weights are initialized. Note that after this operation d_t is equal to d_t^i, therefore the network can make a prediction and update its weights. Finally, the network is pruned to bound the number of connections. Steps for training the proposed model are given in Algorithm 1.

2.1   Network Architecture

We propose a single hidden layer feedforward neural network with shortcut connections shown in Fig. 1. x_t^1 to x_t^D represent the set of features provided by the instance x_t. The input layer is connected to the hidden layer and the mixing layer with weights W_{in} and $W_{identity}$ respectively. In an unpruned network, the input and the hidden layers are fully connected. The hidden layer uses ReLu activation and is also connected to the mixing layer with $W_{identity}$. The mixing layer receives the output values from the input and hidden layers, then passes the element-wise summation of its two inputs to the next layer. The mixing layer is fully connected to the output layer with weights W_o, which acts as a linear classifier. The output layer uses Softmax activation. The prediction $\hat{y}_t$ of the network for the instance x_t can be expressed as:

$$\hat{y}_t = \sigma(W_o(g(W_{in}x_t) + x_t)) \tag{1}$$

Note that if the ideal mapping of the input x_t is $H(x_t)$, the network tries to approximate this mapping by learning the residual $H(x_t) - x_t = g(W_{in}x_t)$ in the hidden layer.

As the loss function, we use the Kullback-Leibler divergence between the prediction $\hat{y}_t$ and the true label y_t. We regularize the loss function using the norm of the network weights. The loss for the prediction-true label pair $(\hat{y}_t, y_t)$ is calculated by:

$$L_t = -\sum_{d \in d_t^o} \hat{y}_t^d \log \frac{y_t^d}{\hat{y}_t^d} + \lambda(\|W_{in}\|_F^2 + \|W_o\|_F^2), \tag{2}$$

Algorithm 1. Network training.

Input:
        ϵ: Learning rate
        ϕ: Pruning strength parameter
        λ: Regularization parameter

1 **for** $t = 1,\dots T$ **do**
2   Receive instance $x_t \in \mathbb{R}^{d_t}$.
3   Receive label y_t.
4   **if** $t==1$ **then**
5 | Initialize network with d_t input and hidden layer nodes.
6   **end**
7   Let d_t^i be the input feature space of the network.
8   **if** $d_t^i < d_t$ **then**
9   Allocate $d_t - d_t^i$ input layer nodes.
10   Allocate $d_t - d_t^i$ hidden layer nodes.
11   Randomly initialize new $(d_t - d_t^i) \cdot (d_t^i + d_t^h)$ weights to fully connect new and existing nodes.
12   **end**
13   Predict the class label $\hat{y}_t = \sigma(W_o(g(W_{in}x_t) + x_t))$
14   Calculate loss $L_t = -\sum_{d \in d_t^o} \hat{y}_t^d \log \frac{y_t^d}{\hat{y}_t^d} + \lambda(\|W_{in}\|_F^2 + \|W_o\|_F^2)$.
15   Do a single epoch back propagation and weight update using L_t and ϵ.
16   Prune the network to keep the largest ϕd_t weights.
17 **end**

---

where d_t^o is the number of the output neurons and λ is the parameter that controls the regularization strength and y_t^d is the dth element of the vector y.

2.2 Shortcut Connections

Shortcut connections have been used in neural networks for various reasons. [10] uses shortcut connections to model linear dependencies and separate the learning of linear and non-linear parts of the mapping. [13] uses shortcut connections to decompose the network into biased and centered subnets, and train them simultaneously. [11] uses shortcut connections to center the input, hidden layer activations and error signals to improve the learning speed. [12] address vanishing and exploding gradients with shortcut connections. Finally, [3] uses shortcut connections to ensure that deeper layers do not make worse mappings than their shallower counterparts.

While learning from data streams, because there is no bound to the number of instances received, the learner can only do a single pass over each instance. Therefore, the model complexity should be low enough to converge in a single pass, and high enough to extract useful patterns of various complexity from the data. For a classification problem, these constraints can be associated with the complexity of the decision boundary. We use shortcut connections to condition the network to learn linear decision boundaries, unless a nonlinear mapping is

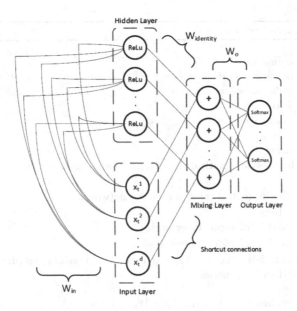

Fig. 1. The network architecture.

necessary. At each feedforward pass, the mixing layer outputs the summation of input x_t and the nonlinear mapping $g(W_{in}x_t)$. Then, the output layer uses this summation to make a linear classification. If a linear decision boundary is enough for the instance x_t, output of the hidden layer $g(W_{in}x_t)$ will be equal to zero. As a result, the input itself will be passed to the linear output layer for prediction. Else, a mixture of the input and its nonlinear mapping will be used. This mechanism helps the network to use simpler decision boundaries by forcing the hidden layer to learn a residual mapping on top of the input features, instead of learning a completely new mapping.

2.3   Growing and Pruning

While learning from data streams, the data volume continuously grows without an upper bound. Therefore, the learning process must be fast and memory efficient. Also because the learning is incremental, the actual complexity of the decision boundary is unknown. A network with too few trainable parameters will not be able to capture the underlying function from which data is being generated. On the other hand, a network with too many trainable parameters will overfit [6]. While learning from trapezoidal data streams the task is more challenging, because the feature space and the data volume grow simultaneously. As the feature space grows, interactions of existing and new features generate new higher order features that can be useful for classification. Therefore, the interaction of new and existing features need to be considered. Also, the new features introduced in the data stream can be irrelevant or redundant. If the network keeps growing without any feature selection mechanism, it will most likely overfit and have a poor generalization ability. Moreover, the running time complexity of the model will be high.

To address these issues, we introduce growing and pruning mechanisms to the proposed model. When a training instance x_t with a higher dimension d_t arrives, the network allocates $d_t - d_t^i$ input and hidden layer nodes and randomly initializes $(d_t - d_t^i) \cdot (d_t^i + d_t^h)$ weights in a fully connected manner. Allocation of the new input nodes ensures that the network can use the new features and consider their combinations with the existing features. Moreover, the allocation of the new hidden layer nodes increases the learning capacity of the model. Therefore, it helps the network to adjust itself to the increasing classification complexity by the growing feature space of trapezoidal data streams.

The network is trained using Kullback-Leibler divergence loss with weight penalty, shown in Eq. 2. This forces the network to learn small weights for less important connections. After each growing and weight update step, the network is pruned to keep only the largest $O(d_t)$ connections. The number of connections to be preserved is calculated by ϕd_t, where $0 \leq \phi \leq 1$ is a parameter that controls the pruning strength. This aggressive pruning strategy ensures that the number of trainable parameters in the network is linearly bounded by the size of the input feature space.

3   Experiments and Results

We empirically evaluate the performance of the proposed method SLFN-S on trapezoidal data streams. We first compare the accuracy of SLFN-S with a single hidden layer neural network without shortcut connections, which will be referred to as SLFN, to show that the shortcut connections help to simplify the decision boundary and improve the convergence. Note that SLFN has the same growing and pruning capabilities as SLFN-S for the sake of fairness. Then, we compare the accuracy of SLFN-S with the state of the art learning algorithm for trapezoidal data streams OL_{SF} [16]. We use 8 UCI datasets from [16] and simulate trapezoidal data streams by splitting each dataset into 10 chunks such that the number of features included by each chunk increases. For example, the instances in the first chunk have the first 10% of features, instances in the second chunk have the first 20% of features and so on. The numbers of instances, features and the parameter setting used for each dataset are listed in Table 1. We use 20-fold cross validation on random permutations of the datasets and measure the average error rate. Parameters are chosen with cross validation. We use ADAM [7] to update the network weights.

Figure 2 shows the mean number of incorrect predictions made by SLFN-S, SLFN and OL_{SF} over 20 folds for each dataset, with standard error. Several observations can be drawn. First, SLFN-S has lower error rates than SLFN in all 8 UCI datasets, because SLFN needs more iterations over the data to converge. This is because SLFN-S tends to learn simpler decision boundaries and use non-linear mappings only when needed. Second, SLFN-S significantly outperforms

Table 1. Number of samples, features and parameters used for each UCI dataset.

Dataset	#Samples	#Features	ϵ	ϕ	λ
wbc	699	10	0.75	1	0.2
wpbc	198	34	0.85	0.8	0.1
wdbc	569	31	0.05	1	0.01
german	1,000	24	0.05	1	0.1
ionosphere	351	35	0.15	1	0.05
svmguide3	1,234	21	0.1	1	0.1
magic04	19,020	10	0.02	1	0.1
a8a	32,561	123	0.05	0.5	0.1

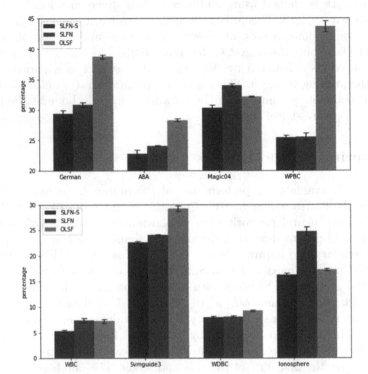

Fig. 2. Mean number of incorrect predictions for SLFN, SLFN-S and OL_{SF} algorithms.

SLFN in 6 of the 8 UCI datasets. For WDBC and WPBC, SLFN-S has fewer errors than SLFN but the difference is not significant. WPBC is nonlinearly separable, which can also be observed from the performance difference between the linear OL_{SF} and nonlinear neural network based models. Therefore, simplification of the decision boundary made by SLFN-S did not significantly improve the convergence of SLFN. On the other hand WDBC is highly linearly separa-

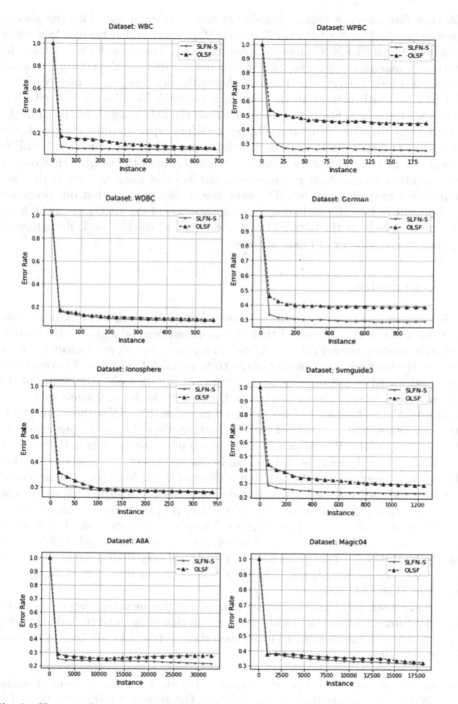

Fig. 3. Change of error rates of SLFN-S and OL_{SF} algorithms in trapezoidal data streams.

516   E. Beyazit et al.

ble, therefore does not require learning of nonlinear mappings. This can also be observed in the Fig. 3, where SLFN-S and OL_{SF} show similar trends. As a result both SLFN and SLFN-S achieve similar accuracy. These results verify that the shortcut connections improve the convergence by allowing the network to learn simpler decision boundaries. Figure 3 shows the changing error rate of OL_{SF} and SLFN-S with respect to the instances received. We observe that SLFN-S converges faster and has higher accuracy than the OL_{SF} algorithm in all of the 8 UCI datasets. This is because OL_{SF} considers input features independently and does not take feature combinations into account. On the other hand, SLFN-S explores new useful feature combinations and prunes the weights that do not have significant contribution. Moreover, SLFN-S can learn non-linear decision boundaries when it is needed. The experiment results show that our proposed method SLFN-S significantly outperforms the state of the art OL_{SF} algorithms. The running time of the both SLFN-S and OL_{SF} algorithms scale linearly with respect to the number of input features.

4   Conclusion

This paper proposed a Single Hidden Layer Neural Network with Shortcut Connections (SLFN-S) and showed that the proposed method significantly outperforms the state of the art OL_{SF}. SLFN-S provides a growing mechanism to adapt itself to the increasing complexity of the trapezoidal data streams. Moreover, the proposed model uses a pruning mechanism to ensure that the complexity of the network linearly scales with respect to the size of the input feature space. We compared the performance of the proposed model with SLFN without any shortcut connection, and the state of the art learning algorithm for trapezoidal data streams OL_{SF} [16]. We showed that the shortcut connections help the network to learn simpler decision boundaries and converge faster. We also showed that the proposed method significantly outperforms OL_{SF}. Note that unlike OL_{SF}, SLFN-S does not have an active feature selection mechanism. OL_{SF} uses one weight for each input feature. At each iteration, it projects its weights and truncates a portion of the smallest weights. Therefore, it stops using the features that are associated with the truncated weights. On the other hand, SLFN-S uses multiple weights per feature. A feature is removed only if all weights associated with that feature are pruned. Therefore, OL_{SF} is capable of learning sparser solutions than SLFN-S.

Future work includes conducting extensive experiments on larger datasets. Another future direction is to add a feature selection policy, and trainable weights for the shortcut connections to learn the ratios of mixtures for linear and non-linear mappings.

Acknowledgments. This research is supported by the US National Science Foundation (NSF) under grants 1652107 and 1763620. The authors would like to thank Dr. Amirhossein Tavanaei for constructive criticism of the manuscript.

References

1. Blondel, M., Kubo, Y., Naonori, U.: Online passive-aggressive algorithms for non-negative matrix factorization and completion. In: Artificial Intelligence and Statistics, pp. 96–104 (2014)
2. Crammer, K., Kulesza, A., Dredze, M.: Adaptive regularization of weight vectors. Mach. Learn. **91**(2), 155–187 (2013)
3. He, K., Zhang, X., Ren, S., Sun, J.: Deep residual learning for image recognition. In: Proceedings of the IEEE Conference on Computer Vision and Pattern Recognition, pp. 770–778 (2016)
4. Huang, G.B.: Learning capability and storage capacity of two-hidden-layer feedforward networks. IEEE Trans. Neural Netw. **14**(2), 274–281 (2003)
5. Huang, G.B., Chen, Y.Q., Babri, H.A.: Classification ability of single hidden layer feedforward neural networks. IEEE Trans. Neural Netw. **11**(3), 799–801 (2000)
6. Huang, G.B., Zhu, Q.Y., Siew, C.K.: Real-time learning capability of neural networks. IEEE Trans. Neural Netw. **17**(4), 863–878 (2006)
7. Kingma, D.P., Ba, J.: Adam: a method for stochastic optimization. arXiv preprint arXiv:1412.6980 (2014)
8. Lee, K.M., Street, W.N.: An adaptive resource-allocating network for automated detection, segmentation, and classification of breast cancer nuclei topic area: image processing and recognition. IEEE Trans. Neural Netw. **14**(3), 680–687 (2003)
9. Liang, N.Y., Huang, G.B., Saratchandran, P., Sundararajan, N.: A fast and accurate online sequential learning algorithm for feedforward networks. IEEE Trans. Neural Netw. **17**(6), 1411–1423 (2006)
10. Raiko, T., Valpola, H., LeCun, Y.: Deep learning made easier by linear transformations in perceptrons. In: Artificial Intelligence and Statistics, pp. 924–932 (2012)
11. Schraudolph, N.N.: Centering neural network gradient factors. In: Montavon, G., Orr, G.B., Müller, K.-R. (eds.) Neural Networks: Tricks of the Trade. LNCS, vol. 7700, pp. 205–223. Springer, Heidelberg (2012). https://doi.org/10.1007/978-3-642-35289-8_14
12. Szegedy, C., et al.: Going deeper with convolutions. In: CVPR (2015)
13. Vatanen, T., Raiko, T., Valpola, H., LeCun, Y.: Pushing stochastic gradient towards second-order methods – backpropagation learning with transformations in nonlinearities. In: Lee, M., Hirose, A., Hou, Z.-G., Kil, R.M. (eds.) ICONIP 2013. LNCS, vol. 8226, pp. 442–449. Springer, Heidelberg (2013). https://doi.org/10.1007/978-3-642-42054-2_55
14. Yingwei, L., Sundararajan, N., Saratchandran, P.: A sequential learning scheme for function approximation using minimal radial basis function neural networks. Neural Comput. **9**(2), 461–478 (1997)
15. Zhai, K., Boyd-Graber, J.: Online latent dirichlet allocation with infinite vocabulary. In: International Conference on Machine Learning, pp. 561–569 (2013)
16. Zhang, Q., Zhang, P., Long, G., Ding, W., Zhang, C., Wu, X.: Online learning from trapezoidal data streams. IEEE Trans. Knowl. Data Eng. **28**(10), 2709–2723 (2016)

Improving Active Learning by Avoiding Ambiguous Samples

Christian Limberg[1,2(✉)], Heiko Wersing[2], and Helge Ritter[1]

[1] CoR-Lab, Bielefeld University, Universitätsstraße 25, 33615 Bielefeld, Germany
{climberg,helge}@techfak.uni-bielefeld.de
[2] HONDA Research Institute Europe GmbH,
Carl-Legien-Straße 30, 63073 Offenbach, Germany
heiko.wersing@honda-ri.de

Abstract. If label information in a classification task is expensive, it can be beneficial to use active learning to get the most informative samples to label by a human. However, there can be samples which are meaningless to the human or recorded wrongly. If these samples are near the classifier's decision boundary, they are queried repeatedly for labeling. This is inefficient for training because the human can not label these samples correctly and this may lower human acceptance. We introduce an approach to compensate the problem of ambiguous samples by excluding clustered samples from labeling. We compare this approach to other state-of-the-art methods. We further show that we can improve the accuracy in active learning and reduce the number of ambiguous samples queried while training.

Keywords: Active learning · Ambiguous samples · Certainty Rejection · Clustering

1 Motivation

User-adaptable learning systems, who are post-trained by the user have the advantage, that they can adjust to new circumstances or improve towards a user-specific environment. In a classification system the samples can be trained incrementally and labeled by the user. Active learning [10] is an efficient training technique, where the samples which are predicted to deliver the highest improvement for the classifier are chosen for labeling by a human.

Whenever the user is involved, the system has to make sure that interaction and training is efficient. A user often feels bored with labeling tasks, therefore the learning system should limit the number of actions and they should be solvable for the human to not annoy him and instead make him feel comfortable and meaningful in his role as interaction partner. To know the time when the learning system needs advice, it is necessary to predict the competence of the learning system, which we demonstrated in our recent contribution [6] with respect to a classifier's accuracy in pool-based incremental active learning. However, on the

© Springer Nature Switzerland AG 2018
V. Kůrková et al. (Eds.): ICANN 2018, LNCS 11139, pp. 518–527, 2018.
https://doi.org/10.1007/978-3-030-01418-6_51

other side the human teacher can also have limited competence to fulfill his task in an oracle role.

In most active learning approaches the oracle is expected to have perfect domain knowledge [11]. But in many real world applications a perfect oracle is not realistic because there can be samples resulting from noisy recordings like a dirty camera or bad light conditions. Also a specific oracle might not know the labels for specific samples because it can not identify them.

Our goal in this contribution is, that the learning system should adapt to the human weaknesses and adapt its strategy of interacting as a good cooperation partner. Related to active learning that means, rather than forcing the human to give uncertain answers, we want to give him the opportunity to reject the samples he is uncertain about.

There are diverse approaches in the literature for handling uncertainty in labeling. Much research was done on active learning with noisy labels or with labels from multiple oracles [15]. However in our task setting the robot is intended to have access to only one oracle. Käding et al. [5] proposed an approach for their Expected Model Output Change (EMOC) model that adds uncertain samples in one error class. However, their method only works with EMOC and is directly integrated into the classifier. A similar approach was done by Fang et al. [3]. They train a classifier that should distinguish certain and uncertain objects. However, in their evaluation they have clustered the data in three clusters and define two of them as ambiguous, which is too simplistic and does not model a real world task. The problem with classifier-based solutions for finding and rejecting ambiguous samples is that they, according to our experiments, can not generalize well in highly complex scenarios like the one we are facing. In our application scenario, a service robot acts in a garden environment [7], mows the lawn and records the garden and occurring objects by a camera. However, because occurring objects are diverse, there is no clear concept between recognizable and ambiguous samples in the feature space, making it hard to train i.e. a secondary classifier to separate them, as is shown in the experiment section.

We show that a more local method is better able to adapt to this distributed ambiguous samples and therefore we introduce Density-Based Querying Exclusion (DBQE), a lightweight clustering-based approach which finds ambiguous clusters and excludes them from querying in active learning. Our approach does not inhibit exploration of unknown classes, and can be stacked up to any existing active learning model and every querying technique. We evaluate it using a challenging outdoor data set (Fig. 1).

2   Active Learning

In pool-based active learning there is a labeled set $\mathcal{L}$ and an unlabeled set $\mathcal{U}$. The active training of a classifier C starts with an empty or small $\mathcal{L}$. The learner C can choose which samples from $\mathcal{U}$ should be labeled by a so-called oracle (which is often a human) and added to $\mathcal{L}$. This is called querying and there are a variety of approaches to find the best samples to query [11]. An often used querying technique is uncertainty sampling [1] which queries the samples with the least certainty for labeling. Other strategies select samples based on the expected model output change [5], or they consider a committee of different classifiers [12] for choosing the samples to be queried. C is then trained in an incremental fashion or again from scratch on $\mathcal{L}$.

Fig. 1. Images from the outdoor object recognition benchmark [7,8]: The upper row images are labeled as recognizable and the bottom row as ambiguous. Objects like the basketball or the leaves are recognizable from every angle. The car is recorded in its canonical view, opposed to the blue duck which is ambiguous from this perspective. There are also views of different objects which are hardly distinguishable, like an apple (bottom center) and a tomato (bottom right).

3   Density-Based Querying Exclusion

We introduce Density-Based Querying Exclusion (DBQE) which clusters ambiguous samples and prevents them from querying by excluding them from $\mathcal{U}$. Our assumption is that ambiguous samples are located in clusters which can occur in a variety of places in the feature space. Density-based clustering approaches showed to be versatile and deliver good performance while at the same time are robust with handling outliers [2]. Another advantage is that the number of clusters does not have to be known in advance. This is important in particular because in our case we want to find only one cluster at a time, while there can be any number of clusters in the data set.

The training procedure of an active learning classifier using DBQE is illustrated in Algorithm 1.

Algorithm 1. Active learning with Density-Based Querying Exclusion (DBQE)

Require: $maxPts$ ▷ do clustering on $maxPts$ points nearby x_e
Require: $minPts$ ▷ minimum number of neighbors to be a core sample
Require: ϵ ▷ distance range describing a sample's neighborhood
 1: $\mathcal{U} \leftarrow load\_data()$ ▷ unlabeled data
 2: $\mathcal{L} \leftarrow \{\}$ ▷ labeled Set is empty
 3: $C \leftarrow initialize\_classifier()$ ▷ initialize active classifier
 4: **while** not $C.is\_trained()$ **do**
 5:      $s \leftarrow C.query\_next\_sample(\mathcal{U})$ ▷ querying using uncertainty sampling
 6:      $l \leftarrow ask\_for\_label(s)$ ▷ ask oracle for supervision
 7:      **if** $l.is\_ambiguous()$ **then**   ▷ oracle labeled s as ambiguous
 8:          $c \leftarrow DBQE(s, minPts, maxPts, \epsilon)$ ▷ DBQE clustering is applied
 9:          $\mathcal{U} \leftarrow \mathcal{U} \setminus c$ ▷ found cluster c is excluded from $\mathcal{U}$
10:      **else**   ▷ s is not ambiguous and oracle labeled it
11:          $C.train(s, l)$ ▷ classifier C is trained with new sample s and label l
12:      **end if**
13: **end while**
14:
15: **function** DBQE($x_e, minPts, maxPts, \epsilon$)
16:      $v \leftarrow \{\}$ ▷ visited samples
17:      $c \leftarrow \{x_e\}$ ▷ samples considered to be in cluster
18:      $t \leftarrow \{x_e\}$ ▷ samples to be processed
19:      $\mathcal{R} \leftarrow get\_samples\_nearby(\mathcal{U}, x_e, maxPts)$ ▷ get $maxPts$ nearest samples to x_e
20:      **for** $a \in t$ **do**
21:          **if** not $a \in v$ **then**   ▷ if a was not visited before
22:              $v \leftarrow v \cup a$ ▷ mark a as visited
23:              $n \leftarrow region\_query(a, \epsilon)$ ▷ find neighborhood points
24:              **if** $n.size() > minPts$ **then**   ▷ if a is a core sample
25:                  $c \leftarrow c \cup a$ ▷ add a to cluster set c
26:                  $t \leftarrow t \cup n$ ▷ add n to t
27:              **end if**
28:          **end if**
29:          $t \leftarrow t \setminus a$ ▷ remove a from queue t
30:      **end for**
31:      **return** c ▷ return ambiguous cluster c
32: **end function**
33:
34: **function** $region\_query(s, \epsilon)$ ▷ returns samples from $\mathcal{R}$ within range ϵ to s
35:      $n \leftarrow \{\}$
36:      **for** $i \in \mathcal{R}$ **do**
37:          **if** $|i - s| < \epsilon$ **then**   ▷ sample i is within ϵ range
38:              $n \leftarrow n \cup i$ ▷ i is added to set n
39:          **end if**
40:      **end for**
41:      **return** n ▷ samples in neighborhood are returned
42: **end function**

The active learning is applied as usual: First the query strategy selects a sample and the oracle is asked for a label. If it can provide it, the classifier is trained, otherwise our DBQE approach is applied which does a region growing to find the cluster containing the queried ambiguous sample, which we call x_e. In the clustering function we select a subset of samples $\mathcal{R} \subseteq \mathcal{U}$ which are the nearest samples to x_e for speed improvements and to limit the maximum number of excluded samples, denoting $maxPts$ as the number of points in $\mathcal{R}$. The region growing is applied similar to DBSCAN [2], also illustrated in Fig. 2. DBSCAN iteratively applies this region growing until the whole data set is clustered. There are two parameters involved: ϵ is a distance range describing an arbitrary sample's neighborhood points. The other parameter to choose is $minPts$ which is the minimum number of samples in a sample's neighborhood for the sample to be a so-called core sample, otherwise it is an outlier. The main idea is to expand a cluster c around the ambiguous sample x_e. The cluster samples in c are excluded from $\mathcal{U}$.

If there is no cluster containing x_e (so x_e itself is an outlier) DBQE is only excluding x_e from $\mathcal{U}$.

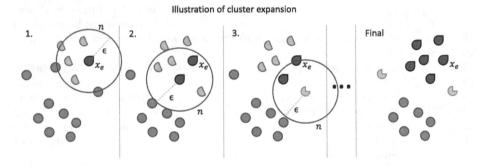

Fig. 2. Illustration of DBQE: the points represent samples from the unlabeled subset $\mathcal{R} \subseteq \mathcal{U}$ with the number of samples $maxPts = 14$. Blue points (circles) are samples not visited, visited points in v are displayed orange (half circles) and points determined as part of the ambiguous cluster c are in red (peaked circles), outliers in gray (pacman shape). The progress of the region growing is displayed with the minimum neighborhood size $minPts = 3$. The oracle defines x_e as ambiguous and in the first step x_e is determined as a core sample. The cluster is expanded, finding the second core sample in step 2. In step 3, an outlier is found, which is not included into the cluster. The final clustering result is displayed on the right. (Color figure online)

4   Evaluation

We evaluated our method together with some baseline methods on our outdoor data set [7] because it provides a real application benchmark of high difficulty [6–8]. The data set is an image data set consisting of 50 object classes. The objects are laying on the lawn and were recorded by a mobile robot in a way that the robot approaches the object and makes ten consecutive pictures each approach. In total each object has ten approaches with ten images each, summing up a total of 5000 images. Some objects can be hard to distinguish due to unfavorable viewing angle. Also there are some objects that look rather similar like an apple, onion, tomato, orange and ball or e.g. several rubber ducks. A feature representation of each image is extracted with the VGG16 deep convolutional net [13] trained on images from the imagenet competition. We removed the last softmax layer and using the outputs of the penultimate layer as a 4096 dimensional feature vector. There can be approaches or partial approaches of an object, from which the object images can be ambiguous for a human. We annotated this ambiguity property for our data set (compare to Fig. 1). In total we annotated 24% of the images as ambiguous, a selection of recognizable and ambiguous images can be seen in Fig. 1. For evaluation a 50/50 train-test split was done. The data was split by approaches, so that the images of a single approach are either completely in the train or in the test set. We repeated the experiment 15 times to average our results. As a classifier we chose Generalized Learning Vector Quantization (GLVQ). GLVQ has proved to be an accurate classifier in incremental learning [8] and is also suitable for active learning with uncertainty sampling [6].

DBQE needs the parameters $minPts$ and ϵ to be set to a suitable value. To have a better idea how the data is clustered, a look at unsupervised statistics related to the distances to neighboring samples can help. We achieved good results with many parameter combinations but we also applied a grid search where we defined ranges of $minPts$ and ϵ values and tested all combinations of those. There we found out $\epsilon = 35$, $minPts = 3$ and $maxPts = 20$ give best results for our evaluation on the outdoor data set. For training and evaluating an active learning classifier we developed the framework ALeFra[1] in context of this paper. By using it any offline and incremental classifier can be converted to an active classifier. There are also basic querying techniques implemented and the user can visualize the progress of the training with a few lines of code. There is a visualization of the feature space which uses a dimensional reduction like t-SNE [9] or MDS [14] and if the data consists of images, they are visualized in a collage which is created after each batch while training.

We investigate three approaches and compare them to simple baselines:

- **Classifier:** The problem can be represented as a binary classification task, predicting whether samples are recognizable or not [3]. The classifier is trained with all yet queried recognizable and ambiguous samples. We evaluated the classifiers GLVQ, kNN, logistic regression and SVM, where the kNN outperformed the others. This may occur because a local model like kNN can better adapt to the ambiguous samples, who may be diverse in feature space. Also we have observed, that if using classifier's confidence information of predicted samples can improve performance and exploring new classes in $\mathcal{U}$. Therefore we make use of a certainty value of the kNN-classifier, which uses distance information of the winning and loosing classes defined in [6]. Only samples

---
[1] https://github.com/limchr/ALeFra.

who are classified as ambiguous with a certainty value greater than a predefined threshold are avoided in querying. We tuned this threshold to the best performance for our evaluation on the outdoor data set.

- **Rejection:** The problem can be represented as a rejection task, where some samples are rejected from querying. Therefore we implemented a local rejection approach [4] for the GLVQ-classifier. Here every prototype has a rejection threshold which is set to zero at beginning. If an ambiguous sample is queried, the winning prototype's threshold is adjusted to $d*\alpha$, where d is the certainty of the ambiguous sample and α is a parameter that can be tuned. Only those samples are considered for querying, for which the distance d to their winning prototype is higher than the threshold of that particular prototype.

- **Clustering:** The problem can be represented as a clustering task. DBQE is using density-based clustering to represent ambiguous samples. We also tried to apply silhouette analysis, but density-based clustering results in higher accuracy in finding the ambiguous clusters and additionally it is very fast to expand a cluster and it can also detect outliers.

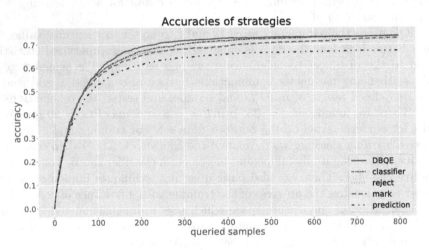

Fig. 3. Evaluation on the outdoor data set: test-accuracies (y-axis) of all approaches vs. number of queried samples (x-axis).

We also implemented the following two baseline strategies for comparison:

- **Mark:** If an ambiguous sample is queried, it is marked as ambiguous and is not considered in future queryings. This baseline strategy can be seen as a naive approach for handling ambiguous samples.

- **Prediction:** If an ambiguous sample is queried, the classifier predicts its label and uses this for training. With this baseline we want to determine if the classifier itself is able to classify the samples that the human rejected as ambiguous.

Figure 3 shows the test-accuracies of the strategies for active training. DBQE and *classifier* are the two strategies with the highest accuracy where DBQE is better in the middle stage of the training. *Reject* is slightly better than *mark*, where at the end of training, both are converging to DBQE and *classifier*. *Prediction* is significantly worse than the other approaches, indicating that the classifier is not accurate at predicting those labels that the human can not provide.

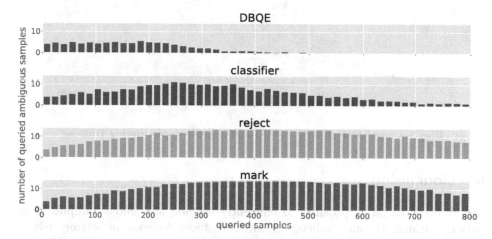

Fig. 4. Number of queried ambiguous samples during training. Each bin of the histograms represents the number of ambiguous samples queried, pooled in bins of 16 queryings giving a total of 50 bins. The number of ambiguous samples is displayed on the y-axis and the number of queries on the x-axis. Please note that the baseline strategy *prediction* is not represented here because it is using ambiguous samples for training.

DBQE is slightly better than *classifier* in terms of accuracy while training. However, another important objective was to minimize human frustration and to make him feel comfortable in his role. Therefore we visualized the number of ambiguous queried samples while training. In Fig. 4 it can be seen that significantly fewer samples are queried using DBQE. After 400 trained samples, ambiguous samples are queried only occasionally. The querying of ambiguous samples using *classifier* only drops slowly and especially in the earlier stage of training is significantly higher than DBQE. *Mark* is querying the most ambiguous samples compared to DBQE and *classifier*. To better visualize the total number of ambiguous queried samples, we plotted the cumulative sum of ambiguous queried samples in Fig. 5. DBQE is capable of querying approximately three times less ambiguous samples than *classifier* and five times less than *reject* and *mark*.

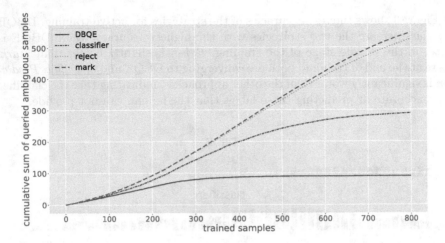

Fig. 5. Cumulative sum of queried ambiguous samples during training.

5 Conclusion

We showed that it is possible to efficiently exclude ambiguous samples from active learning. In our challenging outdoor object recognition setting, where ambiguous samples were distributed over the whole feature space, DBQE is able to improve the accuracy in active learning and further reduces the amount of meaningless queries significantly. We implemented and evaluated a variety of other approaches in depth and compared them to DBQE in a realistic setting.

We think that DBQE can be used to model human capabilities and significantly improve robot acceptance as a cooperation partner. To prove this as a next step we want to integrate DBQE in a robotic application and investigate a larger number of benchmarks.

References

1. Constantinopoulos, C., Likas, A.: Active learning with the probabilistic RBF classifier. In: International Conference on Artificial Neural Networks (ICANN), pp. 357–366 (2006)
2. Ester, M., Kriegel, H., Sander, J., Xu, X.: A density-based algorithm for discovering clusters in large spatial databases with noise. In: Proceedings of the Second International Conference on Knowledge Discovery and Data Mining (KDD 1996), pp. 226–231 (1996)
3. Fang, M., Zhu, X.: I don't know the label: active learning with blind knowledge. In: Proceedings of the 21st International Conference on Pattern Recognition (ICPR), pp. 2238–2241 (2012)
4. Fischer, L., Hammer, B., Wersing, H.: Optimal local rejection for classifiers. Neurocomputing **214**, 445–457 (2016)

5. Käding, C., Freytag, A., Rodner, E., Bodesheim, P., Denzler, J.: Active learning and discovery of object categories in the presence of unnameable instances. In: Conference on Computer Vision and Pattern Recognition (CVPR), pp. 4343–4352 (2015)
6. Limberg, C., Wersing, H., Ritter, H.: Efficient accuracy estimation for instance-based incremental active learning. In: European Symposium on Artificial Neural Networks (ESANN), pp. 171–176 (2018)
7. Losing, V., Hammer, B., Wersing, H.: Interactive online learning for obstacle classification on a mobile robot. In: International Joint Conference on Neural Networks (IJCNN), pp. 1–8 (2015)
8. Losing, V., Hammer, B., Wersing, H.: Incremental on-line learning: a review and comparison of state of the art algorithms. Neurocomputing 275, 1261–1274 (2018)
9. van der Maaten, L., Hinton, G.: Visualizing data using t-SNE. J. Mach. Learn. Res. 9, 2579–2605 (2008)
10. Ramirez-Loaiza, M.E., Sharma, M., Kumar, G., Bilgic, M.: Active learning: an empirical study of common baselines. Data Min. Knowl. Discov. 31(2), 287–313 (2017)
11. Settles, B., Craven, M.: An analysis of active learning strategies for sequence labeling tasks. In: Conference on Empirical Methods in Natural Language Processing (EMNLP), pp. 1070–1079 (2008)
12. Seung, H.S., Opper, M., Sompolinsky, H.: Query by committee. In: Conference on Computational Learning Theory (COLT), pp. 287–294 (1992)
13. Simonyan, K., Zisserman, A.: Very deep convolutional networks for large-scale image recognition. CoRR abs/1409.1556 (2014)
14. Strickert, M., Teichmann, S., Sreenivasulu, N., Seiffert, U.: High-throughput multidimensional scaling (HiT-MDS) for cDNA-array expression data. In: Duch, W., Kacprzyk, J., Oja, E., Zadrożny, S. (eds.) ICANN 2005. LNCS, vol. 3696, pp. 625–633. Springer, Heidelberg (2005). https://doi.org/10.1007/11550822_97
15. Zhang, J., Wu, X., Sheng, V.S.: Learning from crowdsourced labeled data: a survey. Artif. Intell. Rev. 46(4), 543–576 (2016)

Solar Power Forecasting Using Dynamic Meta-Learning Ensemble of Neural Networks

Zheng Wang and Irena Koprinska[(⊠)]

School of Information Technologies, University of Sydney, Sydney, Australia
{zheng.wang, irena.koprinska}@sydney.edu.au

Abstract. We consider the task of predicting the solar power output for the next day from previous solar power data. We propose EN-meta, a meta-learning ensemble of neural networks where the meta-learners are trained to predict the errors of the ensemble members for the new day, and these errors are used to dynamically weight the contribution of the ensemble members in the final prediction. We evaluate the performance of EN-meta on Australian solar data for two years and compare its accuracy with state-of-the-art single models, classical ensemble methods and EN-meta versions without the meta-learning component. The results showed that EN-meta was the most accurate method and thus highlight the potential benefit of using meta-learning for solar power forecasting.

Keywords: Solar power · Dynamic ensembles · Neural networks
Meta-learning

1 Introduction

Solar energy is a clean and renewable source of electricity. Its use is rapidly growing due to the improved efficiency and reliability of PhotoVoltaic (PV) solar panels and their reduced cost. However, the generated solar power is highly variable as it depends on the solar irradiance and other meteorological factors, which makes its large-scale integration in the power grid more difficult. This motivates the need for accurate prediction of the produced solar power, in order to ensure reliable electricity supply.

In this paper we consider the task of predicting the PV power output for the next day at half-hourly intervals using only previous PV data. The other commonly used data source is weather information, however reliable weather measurements and forecasts are not always available for the PV site. Recent studies [1, 2] investigating the use of previous PV data only have shown promising results and in this paper we also consider univariate prediction. Specifically, given a time series of PV power outputs up to the day d: $[P^1, \ldots, P^d]$, where P^i is a vector of half-hourly power outputs for day i, our goal is to forecast P^{d+1}, the half-hourly power output for day $d + 1$.

Different approaches for PV power forecasting have been proposed, e.g. using statistical methods such as linear regression and autoregressive moving average [1], or machine learning methods such as Neural Networks (NN) [1, 3, 4], Support Vector Regression [5] and k-Nearest Neighbor (kNN) based methods [1, 3, 6]. Ensembles

V. Kůrková et al. (Eds.): ICANN 2018, LNCS 11139, pp. 528–537, 2018.
https://doi.org/10.1007/978-3-030-01418-6_52

combining the predictions of several models have also been investigated for solar power and other time series forecasting tasks and shown to be very competitive [7–9].

In [8] we developed an ensemble of NNs for PV power forecasting that tracks the error of the ensemble members on previous data and uses this error to determine the weights of the ensemble members for the prediction for the new day. In this paper, motivated by [9], we investigate a different approach that uses meta-learning to predict the error of the ensemble members for the new day and calculate their weights based on their predicted error, rather than on their errors on previous days. Thus, the idea is to adapt the ensemble to the characteristics of the new day by selecting and combining the most appropriate ensemble members, the ones with the most suitable expertise, estimated based on their predicted error. In summary, the contributions of this paper are:

1. We propose EN-meta, a new dynamic ensemble combining NNs. It uses meta-learners to predict the error of each ensemble member for the new example, and based on it to determine the contribution of the ensemble member in the final prediction.
2. We investigate four strategies for determining the weights of the ensemble members based on their predicted errors and consider two different types of meta-learners.
3. We conduct an evaluation using Australian PV data for two years and compare the performance of EN-meta with a single NN, SVR, kNN and persistence baseline, classic ensembles (bagging, boosting and random forest) and two EN-meta versions without the meta-learning component. The results demonstrate the effectiveness of EN-meta and the potential of meta-learning methods for solar power forecasting.

2 Data and Experimental Setup

Data. We used PV power data for two years, from 1 January 2015 to 31 December 2016, for 10 h during the daylight period: from 7am to 5 pm. The data comes from a rooftop PV plant located at the University of Queensland in Brisbane, Australia, and is available from http://www.uq.edu.au/solarenergy/.

The original PV power data was recorded at 1-min intervals. As our task is to predict the PV power at 30-min intervals, the raw 1-min data was aggregated to 30-min data by averaging the values in the 30-min intervals. The data was also normalized to [0, 1]. The small number of missing values (0.02%) were replaced before the aggregation using a nearest neighbor method as in [8]. Hence, our dataset contains 14,620 values in total (= (365 + 366) days × 20 values).

Data Sets. The PV data was split into three subsets: (1) training - 70% of the 2015 data, used for model training; (2) validation - the remaining 30% of the 2015 data, used for parameter selection and (3) testing - the 2016 data, used to evaluate the accuracy.

Evaluation Measures. We used two performance measures: Mean Absolute Error (MAE) and Root Mean Squared Error (RMSE):

$$\mathrm{MAE} = \frac{1}{N \times n} \sum_{i=1}^{n} |P^i - \hat{P}i|, \mathrm{RMSE} = \sqrt{\frac{\sum_{i=1}^{n} \left(P^i - \hat{P}i\right)^2}{N \times n}}$$

where P^i and $\hat{P}^i$ are the vectors of actual and predicted half-hourly PV power outputs for day i, N is the number of days in the testing set and n is the number of predicted power outputs for a day ($n = 20$).

3   Dynamic Meta-Learning Ensemble

There are three main steps in creating the dynamic meta-learning ensemble EN-meta as shown in Fig. 1: (i) training ensemble members, (ii) training meta-learners and (iii) calculating the weights of the ensemble members for the prediction of the new example.

We train the ensemble members to predict the PV power for the next day and their corresponding meta-learners (one for each ensemble member) to predict the error of this prediction. Thus, each meta-learner learns to predict how accurate the prediction of the ensemble member will be for the new day based on the characteristics of the day. The predicted errors are converted into weights (higher weights for the more accurate ensemble members and lower for the less accurate) and the final prediction is given by the weighted average of the individual predictions.

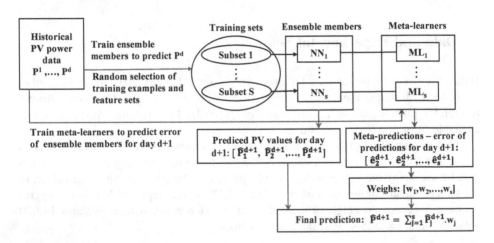

Fig. 1. Structure of EN-meta

3.1   Training Ensemble Members

Figure 2 illustrates the training of the ensemble members. The ensemble consists of S NNs. Effective ensembles include diverse ensemble members [10]. We generate diversity using two strategies - random example sampling and random feature sampling, using the method from [8] which was shown to perform well.

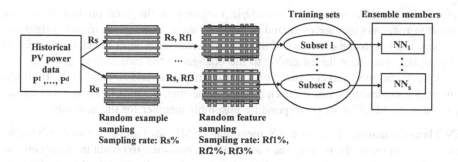

Fig. 2. Training ensemble members

Random Example Sampling: We create S bootstrap samples, one for each NN, using random sampling with replacement and a pre-defined example sampling rate Rs. Each sample contains only $Rs\%$ of the d examples for the first year, which is the whole data used for training and validation. These examples are then randomly divided into training set (70%, used for training of the NN) and validation set (30%, used for selecting the NN parameters). Thus, the training set for a single NN will contain a smaller number of examples than the original training set and will have the same number of features. The best Rs was selected by experimenting with different values and evaluating the performance on the validation set (Rs best = 25%).

Random Feature Sampling: The S training sets from the previous step are filtered by retaining only some of their features and discarding the rest. This is done by using feature sampling with replacement with a pre-defined sampling rate Rf. We split the S training sets into three parts and applied $Rf1 = 25\%$, $Rf2 = 50\%$ and $Rf3 = 75\%$ for each third.

A single ensemble member is a NN with f input neurons ($f < 20$), corresponding to the sampled features (PV power of the previous day), and 20 outputs, corresponding to all 20 PV values of the next day. It had one hidden layer where the number of neurons was set to the average of the input and output neurons, and was trained using the Levenberg-Marquardt version of backpropagation algorithm. We combined $S = 30$ NNs.

3.2 Training Meta-Learners

Every ensemble member NN_i has an associated meta-learner ML_i, which is trained to predict the error of NN_i for the new day. Thus, ML_i, takes as an input the PV data for day d and predicts the forecasting error of NN_i for day $d + 1$. This error is then converted into a weight for NN_i and used in the weighted average vote combining the predictions of all ensemble members.

The motivation behind using dynamic ensembles is that the different ensemble members have different areas of expertise, with their performance changing as the time series evolves over time. We can learn to predict the error of an ensemble member for the next day based on its prior performance. Then we can use these predicted errors to weight the contributions of the ensemble members in the final prediction, so that ensemble members that are predicted to be more accurate are given higher weights. In this way we match the expertise of the ensemble members with the characteristics of the new day and adapt the ensemble to the changes in the time series.

We implemented and compared two sets of meta-learners: NN and kNN. Both sets contain S meta-learners, one for each ensemble member. Each meta-learner was trained to predict the MAE of its corresponding ensemble member for the next day.

NN Meta-Learners. To train a NN meta-learner ML_i for ensemble member NN_i, we firstly need to create the training data for it, and in particular to obtain the target output. Using the trained ensemble member NN_i, we obtain its prediction for all examples from the training set; the input is P^d, the PV power vector of the previous day d but containing only the f sampled features, and the output is P^{d+1}, the PV power vector for the next day $d + 1$ containing all 20 values. We then calculate MAE^{d+1}, the error for day $d + 1$. A training example for ML_i will have the form: $[P^d, MAE^{d+1}]$, where P^d is the input vector (containing the same f features as NN_i) and MAE^{d+1} is the target output. Thus, the NN meta-learner has f input and 1 output neurons. We again used 1 hidden layer and the same rule for the number of hidden neurons as for the ensemble members.

kNN Meta-Learners. In contrast to the NN meta-learners, there is no need to pre-train the kNN meta-learners as the computation is delayed till the arrival of the new day. Specifically, to build a kNN meta-learner for ensemble member NN_i for the new day $d + 1$, the PV data of the previous day d is collected and processed by selecting the same subset of features f as for NN_i. Then, the training set is searched to find the k most similar days to day d in terms of the f features. The errors (MAE) of the NN_i for the days immediately *following* the neighbors are calculated and averaged to calculate MAE^{d+1}, the predicted error of ensemble member NN_i for day $d + 1$. To select the value of k, we experimented with k from 5 to 15, evaluating the performance on the validation set; the best k was 10 and it was used in this study.

3.3   Weight Calculation and Combination Methods

The predicted errors of the corresponding meta-learners for each ensemble member need to be converted into weights for the ensemble members. We investigated two strategies for calculating the weights: linear and nonlinear.

Linear. The weight of ensemble member NN_i for predicting day $d + 1$ is calculated as:

$$w_i^{d+1} = \frac{1 - e_i^{norm}}{\sum_{j=1}^{S} \left(1 - e_j^{norm}\right)}$$

where e_i^{norm} is the predicted error for NN_i for day $d + 1$ by its corresponding meta-learner ML_i, normalised between 0 and 1, and j is over all S ensemble members.

It is necessary to use $1 - e_i^{norm}$ and not e_i^{norm} as lower errors should be associated with higher weights and vice versa. The denominator ensures that the weights of all ensemble members sum to 1.

Non-linear. The weight of ensemble member NN_i for predicting day $d + 1$ is calculated as a softmax function of the negative of its predicted error e_i for day $d + 1$:

$$w_i^{d+1} = \frac{exp(-e_i)}{\sum_{j=1}^{S} exp(-e_j)}$$

where e_i is the predicted error for NN_i by its corresponding meta-learner ML_i, j is over all S ensemble members and exp denotes the exponential function.

Ensemble Member Combination. The final prediction of *EN-meta* is calculated by the weighted average of the predictions of the individual ensemble members: $\hat{P}^{d+1} = \sum_{j=1}^{S} \hat{P}_j^{d+1} \cdot w_j^{d+1}$.

In addition to combining the predictions of all ensemble members, we also considered combining only the M best ensemble members, based on their predicted error. To select the best M, we experimented with $M - 1/3$, $1/2$ and $2/3$ of all ensemble members (30 in our study), evaluating the performance on the validation set.

Hence, there are four strategies for combining the individual predictions – linear vs non-linear weight calculation and combining all vs only the best M ensemble members.

4 Methods Used for Comparison

We compared EN-meta with three groups of methods. (i) single methods: NN, SVR, k-NN and a persistence model; (ii) classical ensembles: bagging, boosting and random forest; and (iii) static and dynamic versions of EN-meta without meta-learners.

4.1 Single Models

NN. An NN with one hidden layer of m nodes, where m was the average of the input and output nodes. It takes as an input the 20 half-hourly PV power data of the previous day d and predicts the 20 half-hourly PV data for day $d + 1$.

SVR. The SVR model is similar to the NN model, except that we train 20 SVRs, each predicting one of the 20 half-hourly value for the next day $d + 1$. All SVRs take as an input the 20 half-hourly PV values of the previous day d.

kNN. To forecast the PV power data of day $d + 1$, kNN firstly finds the k nearest neighbors of day d - the days from the training set with the most similar PV power using the Euclidean distance. To compute the predicted PV power output for day $d + 1$, it then finds the days immediately following the neighbors and averages their PV power.

Persistence (P). As a baseline, we developed a persistence model which uses the PV power output of day d as the forecast for day $d + 1$.

4.2 Classical Ensembles

We also implemented the regression tree based ensembles **Bagging (Bagg)**, **Boosting (Boost)** and **Random Forest (RF)**. For consistency with the proposed ensemble, the number of trees in Bagg, Boost and RF was set to 30. As regression trees cannot predict all 20 values for the next day simultaneously, a separate ensemble is created for each half-hourly value, as in the SVR model. Thus, we create 20 ensembles of each type.

4.3 Static and Dynamic Ensembles Without Meta-Learners

To assess the contribution of the meta-learning component, we also compare EN-meta with two versions of this ensemble without meta-learning: static and dynamic.

The static ensemble is EN-meta without the meta-learning component and using the average of the individual predictions to form the final prediction. We refer to this ensemble as *EN-static*.

The dynamic ensemble is an extension of EN-static; it uses weighed average for combining the individual predictions. The weighs of the ensemble members are calculated based on their *previous* performance (error) in the last D days. We used the total MAE error, over the previous 7 days. The errors of the ensemble members are converted into weights using the same four methods as in the EN-meta ensemble.

We evaluated the different versions using validation set testing; the best result were achieved for the version using a linear transformation and combining the best M ensemble members with $M = 15$; we refer to this ensemble as *EN-dynamic*.

5 Results and Discussion

5.1 Performance of EN-Meta

Table 1 shows the accuracy results of EN-meta for the two different types of meta-learners and four weight calculation methods. The graph in Fig. 3 presents the MAE results in sorted order for visual comparison. We also conducted a pair-wise comparison for statistical significance of the differences in accuracy using the Wilcoxon rank-sum test with $p \leq 0.05$. The results can be summarized as follows:

- *Overall performance:* The most accurate version of EN-meta is kNN-bestM-lin, which uses kNN meta-leaners, combines the predictions of only the best M ensemble members and uses linear transformation to convert the predicted errors into weights. It is followed by kNN-bestM-softmax, which differs only in the weight calculation function –softmax instead of linear, and then by NN-bestM-softmax.
- The pair-wise differences in accuracy between these three best models are not statistically significant but all other differences between the best model (kNN-bestM-lin) and the other models are statistically significant.
- *All vs best M ensemble members:* The EN-meta versions combining only the predictions of the best M ensemble members are more accurate than their corresponding

versions which combine the predictions of all ensemble members and these differences are statistically significant.

- *Linear vs softmax weight calculation:* The EN-meta versions using linear weight calculations outperform their corresponding versions using the softmax weight calculation in 3/4 cases but the differences are not statistically significant.
- *NN vs kNN meta-learners:* The EN-meta versions using kNN meta-learners are more accurate than their corresponding versions using NN meta-learners in all 4 cases but these differences are not statistically significant.

Based on these results we selected the best version (EN-meta-kNN-bestM-lin) for further investigation. We will refer to it as EN-meta.

Table 1. Accuracy of EN-meta versions

EN-meta	MAE [kW]	RMSE [kW]
with NN meta-learners		
NN-lin	88.40	115.35
NN-softmax	89.63	116.13
NN-bestM-lin	87.75	115.55
NN-bestM-softmax	87.68	115.29
with kNN meta-learners		
kNN-lin	88.10	114.89
kNN-softmax	89.61	116.11
kNN-bestM-lin	86.77	114.57
kNN-bestM-softmax	87.34	115.00

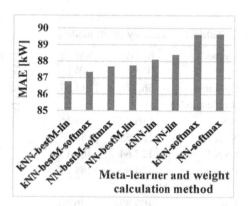

Fig. 3. MAE comparison

5.2 Comparison with Other Methods

Table 2 compares the accuracy of EN-meta with the single models, classical ensembles and the two EN versions without meta-learners (static and dynamic). Figure 4 graphically presents the MAE results in sorted order for visual comparison. The main results can be summarized as follows:

- The proposed EN-meta is the most accurate method. It considerable outperforms all other methods and all differences are statistically significant (Wilcoxon sun-rank test, $p \leq 0.05$).
- The next best performing methods are EN-dynamic and EN-static, the EN-meta versions without meta-learners. This shows that the use of meta-learners was beneficial.
- EN-dynamic is more accurate than EN-static and the difference is statistically significant. This shows the advantage of tracking the error of the ensemble members

on recent data and correspondingly weighting their contribution in the weighed vote.

- By comparing the two dynamic ensembles, EN-meta and EN-dynamic, we can see that the use of meta-learners and the more proactive approach of EN-meta for assessing the ensemble members - based on predicted error for the new day rather than error on previous days, gives better results.
- Bagg is the most accurate classical ensemble, followed by RF and Boost. All classical ensemble models outperform the single models, except for Boost which performed slightly worse than the single NN.
- From the single prediction models, NN is the best, followed by SVR, P and kNN. All forecasting models except kNN outperform the baseline P model.

Table 2. Accuracy of all models

Method	MAE [kW]	RMSE [kW]
EN-meta	86.77	114.57
Single models		
NN	116.64	154.16
SVR	121.58	158.63
kNN	127.64	166.15
Persistence	124.80	184.29
Classic ensembles		
Bagg	109.87	146.40
Boost	118.08	158.80
RF	110.29	146.25
EN-meta without meta learners		
EN-static	102.50	134.25
EN-dynamic	100.46	130.61

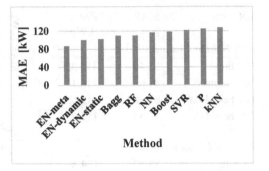

Fig. 4. Comparison of all models (MAE)

6 Conclusion

We considered the task of forecasting the PV power output for the next day at half-hourly intervals from previous PV power data. We proposed EN-meta - a meta-learning ensemble of NNs. The key idea is to pair each ensemble member with a meta-learner and train the meta-learner to predict the error for the next day of its corresponding ensemble member. The errors are then converted into weights and the final prediction is formed using weighed average of the individual predictions. EN-meta is a dynamic ensemble as the combination of predictions is adapted to the characteristics of the new day based on the expected error.

We investigated four strategies for converting the predicted error into weights and two types of meta-learners (kNN and NN). We also compared the performance of EN-meta with three state-of-the-art ensembles (bagging, boosting and random forest), four single models (NN, SVM, kNN and persistence) and two versions of EN-meta without meta-learners. The evaluation was conducted using Australian data for two years. Our results showed that EN-meta was the most accurate model, considerably and statistically significantly outperforming all other methods. The kNN meta-learners were slightly more accurate than the NN meta-learners, and the most effective strategy was combining only the best M ensemble members and using linear transformation to calculate the weights. The use of meta-learners to directly predict the error for the new day, instead of estimating it based on the error for the previous days, was beneficial.

Hence, we conclude that dynamic meta-learning ensembles are promising methods for solar power forecasting.

References

1. Pedro, H.T.C., Coimbra, C.F.M.: Assessment of forecasting techniques for solar power production with no exogenous inputs. Sol. Energy **86**, 2017–2028 (2012)
2. Rana, M., Koprinska, I., Agelidis, V.: Univariate and multivariate methods for very short-term solar photovoltaic power forecasting. Energy Convers. Manag. **121**, 380–390 (2016)
3. Chu, Y., Urquhart, B., Gohari, S.M.I., Pedro, H.T.C., Kleissl, J., Coimbra, C.F.M.: Short-term reforecasting of power output from a 48 MWe solar PV plant. Sol. Energy **112**, 68–77 (2015)
4. Chen, C., Duan, S., Cai, T., Liu, B.: Online 24-h solar power forecasting based on weather type classification using artificial neural networks. Sol. Energy **85**, 2856–2870 (2011)
5. Rana, M., Koprinska, I., Agelidis, V.G.: 2D-interval forecasts for solar power production. Sol. Energy **122**, 191–203 (2015)
6. Wang, Z., Koprinska, I.: Solar power prediction with data source weighted nearest neighbours. In: International Joint Conference on Neural Networks (IJCNN) (2017)
7. Oliveira, M., Torgo, L.: Ensembles for time series forecasting. In: Sixth Asian Conference on Machine Learning, pp. 360–370 (2015)
8. Wang, Z., Koprinska, I., Troncoso, A., Martinez-Alvarez, F.: Static and dynamic ensembles of neural networks for solar power forecasting. In: International Joint Conference on Neural Networks (IJCNN) (2018)
9. Cerqueira, V., Torgo, L., Pinto, F., Soares, C.: Arbitrated ensemble for time series forecasting. In: Ceci, M., Hollmén, J., Todorovski, L., Vens, C., Džeroski, S. (eds.) ECML PKDD 2017. LNCS (LNAI), vol. 10535, pp. 478–494. Springer, Cham (2017). https://doi.org/10.1007/978-3-319-71246-8_29
10. Kuncheva, L.: Combining Pattern Classifiers: Methods and Algorithms. Wiley, Hoboken (2014)

Using Bag-of-Little Bootstraps
for Efficient Ensemble Learning

Pablo de Viña and Gonzalo Martínez-Muñoz[✉]

Escuela Politécnica Superior, Universidad Autónoma de Madrid, Madrid, Spain
pablo.vinna@estudiante.uam.es, gonzalo.martinez@uam.es

Abstract. The technique bag-of-little bootstrap provides statistical estimates equivalent to the ones of bootstrap in a tiny fraction of the time required by bootstrap. In this work, we propose to combine bag-of-little bootstrap into an ensemble of classifiers composed of random trees. We show that using this bootstrapping procedure, instead of standard bootstrap samples, as the ones used in random forest, can dramatically reduce the training time of ensembles of classifiers. In addition, the experiments carried out illustrate that, for a wide range of training times, the proposed ensemble method achieves a generalization error smaller than that achieved by random forest.

1 Introduction

One of the most successful paradigms of machine intelligence is ensemble learning [3,5,7]. Ensembles build a set of diverse predictors by applying different randommization and/or optimization techniques. One of the first optimization based ensembles is adaboost [8]. In adaboost, the base predictors of the ensemble are trained sequentially. To train each single model, adaboost modifies the training set in order to increase the importance of the examples incorrectly classified by the previous models. This can be seen as an optimization problem solved by gradient descent in functional space [13]. On the other hand, diversity in the base classifiers could be generated by introducing some randomization into the generation process of the base classifiers. The randomization can be applied at different levels (e.g. into the training dataset, into the learning algorithm, etc.). Randomization is especially effective when unstable base learning are used. For instance, random forest uses random trees as the base learners of the ensemble. Such trees are unstable by construction as the splits of the tree are computed from a reduced random subset of the input attributes [3]. In addition, random forest trains each base classifier on a random bootstrap sample, where a bootstrap sample consists in extracting n instances at random with replacement from the original training data of size n.

The bootstrap technique was first proposed as a statistical technique to assess the quality of estimates [6] and was later applied to the generation of classifiers in ensemble learning [2]. An important drawback of this technique, however, is its high computational complexity. There are several alternatives to bootstrap that

© Springer Nature Switzerland AG 2018
V. Kůrková et al. (Eds.): ICANN 2018, LNCS 11139, pp. 538–545, 2018.
https://doi.org/10.1007/978-3-030-01418-6_53

are computational more efficient, such as subsampling (i.e. small samples without replacement) or m-out-n bootstrap (with $m < n$). In fact, several theoretical and empirical studies have shown that the accuracy of bagging can increase significantly when smaller samples are used [9,12,14]. Notwithstanding, in [10] it is shown that m-out-of-n and subsampling require statistical corrections when used as a technique to assess the quality of estimates. In [10], and in a previous study of the same authors [11], bag-of-little bootstrap (BLB) is proposed as an alternative to bootstrap, which is computationally more efficient and that has the same statistical properties (consistency and correctness) of bootstrap. The study provides a theoretical analysis of the method and several experiments in synthetic and real data that show the good statistical properties of BLB. However, no real application to classification or regression is performed.

In this article we analyze the use of bag-of-little bootstrap as a mean to accelerate the construction of random forest ensembles. The generalization performance of this modified version of random forest is compared to standard random forest. The experiments carried out show that the proposed ensemble clearly outperforms standard random forest achieving, for a wide range of allowed training time budgets, a lower generalization error. In the actual context of large datasets, this benefit can be a fundamental advantage to be able to produce a classification model in reasonable time.

The article is organized as following: Sect. 2 describes bag-of-little bootstrap technique and its combination with random forest; Sect. 3 shows a experimental comparison of random forest using standard bootstrap and bag-of-little bootstraps; Finally, in Sect. 4, the conclusions of the present study are presented.

2   Proposed Method

The method bag-of-little bootstrap (BLB) [11], samples the data in two steps. First, a small number of instances is sampled without replacement from the original dataset. The size of this small sample is set to $b = n^\gamma$, with $\gamma \in [0.5, 1]$ and where n is the size of the dataset. A number of s small samples are extracted from the original dataset. We will call these samples primary samples, $\mathcal{D}_{primary}$. Then, r secondary samples of size n are extracted with replacement from each of the primary samples, $\mathcal{D}_{primary}$. Finally, from each of the secondary samples, an estimate of the desired quantity is obtained. It is important to note that the secondary samples can contain at most b instances, which is the size of $\mathcal{D}_{primary}$. Hence, instead of actually sampling from $\mathcal{D}_{primary}$, it is sufficient to weight the instances using a vector containing the number of times each instance is sampled. This vector of counts can be obtained by drawing n-trials from a uniform multinomial distribution of b elements. Note that the value of b is expected to be much smaller than n ($b << n$). This is the key implementation feature that allows bag-of-little bootstrap to achieve computational efficient estimates. The focus of [11] is on the statistical properties of BLB and not as a tool to create ensembles of classifiers.

In this article, we propose to use bag-of-little bootstrap in combination with random trees. The procedure is shown in Algorithm 1. The algorithm has as input the training dataset, $\mathcal{D}_{train}$, composed of n instances, and three parameters: the size of the primary samples, b, the number of primary samples, s, and the number of secondary samples, r. The secondary samples are weighted with a vector of counts drawn from a n-trial uniform multinomial distribution of size b. Finally, this weighted dataset is used to train a random tree classifier.

Algorithm 1. BLB-RF

Data:
    $\mathcal{D}_{train} = \{(\mathbf{x}_i, y_i)\}_{i=1}^n$
    $b = n^\gamma$ size of the primary samples
    s, number of primary iterations
    r, number of secondary iterations
Result: $\{h_i\}_{i=1}^{s \times r}$

1 **for** $i \leftarrow 1$ **to** s **do**
2     $\mathcal{D}_{primary} = $ sample_without_replacement$(\mathcal{D}_{train}, b)$
3   **for** $j \leftarrow 1$ **to** r **do**
4   counts $=$ uniform_multinomial(n, b)
5         $h_{(i-1)r+j} = $ train_random_tree$(\mathcal{D}_{primary}, $counts$)$
6   **end**
7 **end**

---

3   Experiments

Several experiments have been carried out in order to analyze the validity of the technique bag-of-little-bootstraps (BLB) applied to ensembles of classifiers. To this end, BLB was implemented as the random sampling mechanism to build an ensemble composed of random trees, i.e. the decision tree algorithm used in random forest. The efficiency of the proposed ensemble, in the following BLB-RF, is compared with standard random forest (RF) under several experimental conditions. The base classifier used in both ensembles is random trees, which is a modified CART tree [4] in which no pruning is applied and in which at each node a random subset of attributes is selected to find the best split. The default parameter value was used for the number of attributes to be selected at each node (i.e. sqrt(#attribs)) for both random forest and BLB-RF. The two algorithms were trained using two fairly large datasets in order to assess the lower computational complexity of BLB-RF with respect to RF. The datasets used are: *Magic04* [1], that has 19020 instances and ten numeric attributes, and *Waveform* [4], a synthetic dataset with 21 numeric attributes. *Waveform* was used in the experiments since it is possible to generate as many instances as needed. Two dataset sizes were considered in the experiments with *Waveform*: $20,000$ and $1,000,000$ instances.

In a first batch of experiments, the performance of BLB-RF was analyzed for mid-sized datasets ($n \approx 20000$ instances) for different values of: s, the number of subsamples taken from the original training set; γ, that determines the size of the samples as n^γ; and, r, the number of secondary bootstrap samples extracted from the s primary random samples. The range of values used in this experiments are: $s \in [1, 20]$, $\gamma = \{0.5, 0.6, 0.7, 0.8, 0.9, 0.95\}$ and $r \in [1, 40]$ for *Magic04*. For *Waveform* with 20000 instances the same values for *gamma* were used but s and r were expanded to $s \in [1, 25]$ and $r \in [1, 60]$. The size of random forest with standard bootstrap sampling is set to 500 trees. Ten times 10-fold cross-validation was used as the validation procedure. The reported values are averages over the 100 train-test realizations. In addition, for each realization and given value of γ, a single execution of BLB-RF is carried out using the maximum value of s and r. Once this ensemble is trained, results for intermediate values of s and r can be readily obtained by discarding the corresponding decision trees. The reason for this experimental design decision is twofold. First, to reduce the total computational burden of the experiments and second, and more importantly, to reduce the variability of the results that would be obtained with independent executions.

Figure 1 shows the average results for some representative values of γ for *Magic04* (*left column*) and *Waveform* (*right column*). Each plot in the figure shows, for the given γ value, the average error of the ensembles with respect to the average CPU time needed to train each single ensemble, in log scale. Each point in the plots represents a complete ensemble for a pair of s and r values. To facilitate the interpretation of the plots, executions sharing the same value of s but different values of r are linked with solid lines. For instance, the first point of the yellow line ($s = 5$) corresponds to an ensemble with $s = 5$ primary samples each of which is used $r = 1$ time to generate secondary bootstrap samples. This corresponds to an ensemble of 5 trees. The second point on the same line is the ensemble trained using $s = 5$ and $r = 2$, which has 10 trees, and so on. As another example, for *Magic04*, the last point of all BLB curves corresponds to $r = 40$, which means that the larger ensembles for each curve are of size $1 \times 40 = 40$ for the red line, 200 for the yellow, 400 for the blue and $20 \times 40 = 800$ for the purple line. In the case of *Waveform*, in which we used an expanded grid up to $r = 60$, the purple curve gets to $25 \times 60 = 1500$ decision trees.

From Fig. 1 several interesting aspects of BLB-RF can be identified. First, for small values of γ (plots in the first row), BLB-RF is able to output a decision at a fraction of the time needed by random forest. The first random forest tree is build after almost 1 s for both *Magic04* and *Waveform* datasets. BLB-RF is able to obtain the first tree is less than 0.002 s and in consequence is able to produce a first classification over 500 times faster than random forest. In fact, for *Magic04* the ensemble with s_{max} and r_{max} (composed of $20 \times 40 = 800$ trees) is trained in approximately the same time as the first tree of random forest. In addition, this ensemble obtains a classification error significantly better than the one obtained by the first tree of random forest. In *Waveform*, the training time to build BLB-RF with $s = 25$ and $r = 60$ is roughly the same as the time needed to build two trees of random forest with a noticeable difference in generalization performance. BLB-RF with $s = 25$ and $r = 60$ achieves an average generalization error of $\approx 15\%$, and two random trees of random forest achieves $\approx 25\%$.

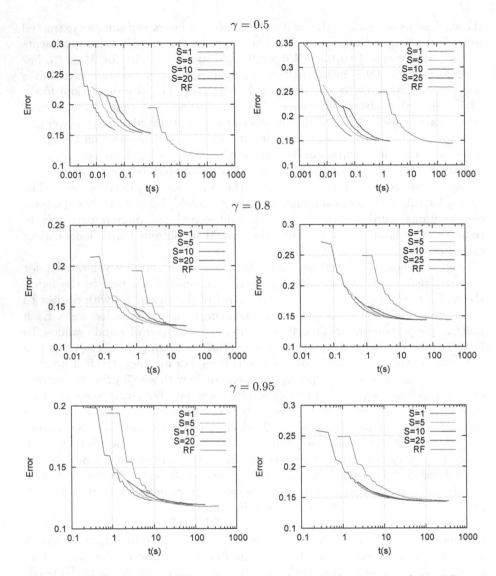

Fig. 1. Results for *Magic04* (*left column*) and *Waveform* (*right column*) for different values of γ

As the value of γ increases, the curves corresponding to BLB-RF tend to be closer to the curve of random forest. As it can be observed from the figures of *Magic04* and *Waveform*, in general the performance of BLB-RF is better than that of random forest except in *Magic04* for $\gamma = 0.95$ in some configurations of s and r. For these last cases, the generalization error of BLB-RF is slightly worse than random forest for the same computational time.

In order better visualize this aspect, we have computed the best and worst performance in terms of the generalization error with respect to the computational time of the executions. That is, for a given computational budget, t, the best and worst results are extracted from all the combinations of s, γ and r that could be trained in less than or equal to t seconds. The result is plotted in Fig. 2. From this plot it is clear that for both analyzed dataset, the performance of BLB-RF is generally better than random forest for all possible time budgets.

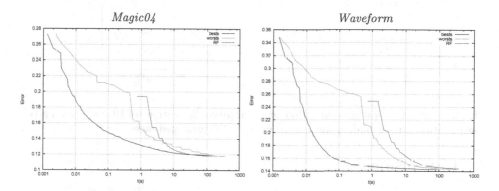

Fig. 2. Best and worst generalization error for all configurations of BLB-RF with respect to the computational time budget for *Magic04* (*left*) and *Waveform* of 20000 instances (*right*)

To validate the performance of BLB-RF in a larger dataset, we have conducted a second experiment on the *Waveform* dataset generating 10^6 instances. For this experiment one 10-fold cross-validation was used to validate the performance of the algorithms. Hence, the training times are based on training datasets composed of 900000 instances. For computational limitations, the size of random forest is reduced to 50 random trees. Similarly the range of parameter values for BLB-RF is reduced to $s = \in [1, 10]$ and $r \in [1, 20]$. The values for γ are kept the same, that is $\{0.5, 0.6, 0.7, 0.9, 0.95\}$. The results for this experiment are shown in Fig. 3. Similarly to Fig. 2, this figure shows the average generalization error of the best and worst configurations of BLB-RF with respect to the training computational budget, t. Random forest is also plotted.

From Fig. 3, we can observe that the performance of BLB-RF in significantly better than the one of random forest for all possible time budgets. The differences between both methods have clearly increased with respect to the use of the smaller *Waveform* set (see right plot on Fig. 2). BLB-RF produces the first classification result in less than 0.05 s while random forest needs ≈500 s, which is over 10000 times slower. In fact, in this setting, BLB-RF is able to achieve a generalization error lower than the one of random forest before the first tree of random forest is trained. BLB-RF achieves the final error of random forest (14.3) after 20 s and random forest needs over 24,000 s.

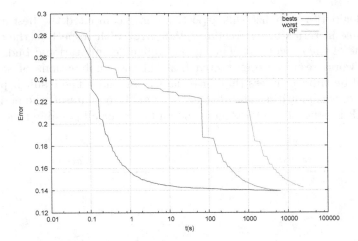

Fig. 3. Best and worst generalization error for all configurations of BLB-RF for a given computational time budget for waveform with 10^6 total instances

4   Conclusions

In this article we propose the use of the technique of bag-of-little bootstraps together with an ensemble of random trees. This technique produces statistical estimates equivalent to bootstrap using a fraction of the time. The techniques proceeds in two steps. First, small random samples from the data are extracted without replacement. From each of these small samples, r bootstrap samples with replacement are generated with the size of the original dataset. For this second sampling, the instances are weighted using a vector of counts drawn from a uniform multinomial distribution. Finally, a random tree is trained on each of the weighted samples to compose the ensemble.

We have shown that the proposed ensemble is computationally much more effective than random forest. On the one hand, we have shown that for relatively large datasets, the proposed method is able to train an ensemble in a time that is orders of magnitude smaller that the time required to build the first tree of random forest. On the other hand, for a large range of given time budgets, the proposed ensemble is able to achieve a generalization error lower than that of random forest.

Acknowledgments. The research has been supported by the Spanish *Ministry of Economy, Industry, and Competitiveness* project TIN2016-76406-P, and *Comunidad de Madrid*, project CASI-CAM-CM (S2013/ICE-2845).

References

1. Bache, K., Lichman, M.: UCI machine learning repository (2013). http://archive.ics.uci.edu/ml
2. Breiman, L.: Bagging predictors. Mach. Learn. **26**, 123–140 (1996)

3. Breiman, L.: Random forests. Mach. Learn. **45**(1), 5–32 (2001)
4. Breiman, L., Friedman, J.H., Olshen, R.A., Stone, C.J.: Classification and Regression Trees. Chapman & Hall, New York (1984)
5. Chen, T., Guestrin, C.: XGBoost: a scalable tree boosting system. In: Proceedings of the 22Nd ACM SIGKDD International Conference on Knowledge Discovery and Data Mining, KDD 2016, pp. 785–794. ACM, New York (2016)
6. Efron, B.: Bootstrap methods: another look at the jackknife. Ann. Stat. **7**(1), 1–26 (1979)
7. Fernández-Delgado, M., Cernadas, E., Barro, S., Amorim, D.: Do we need hundreds of classifiers to solve real world classification problems? J. Mach. Learn. Res. **15**, 3133–3181 (2014)
8. Freund, Y., Schapire, R.E.: A decision-theoretic generalization of on-line learning and an application to boosting. J. Comput. Syst. Sci. **55**(1), 119–139 (1997)
9. Hall, P., Samworth, R.J.: Properties of bagged nearest neighbour classifiers. J. Roy. Stat. Soc. Ser. B **67**(3), 363–379 (2005)
10. Kleiner, A., Talwalkar, A., Sarkar, P., Jordan, M.: A scalable bootstrap for massive data. J. Roy. Stat. Soc. Ser. B **76**, 795–816 (2014)
11. Kleiner A., Talwalkar A., Sarkar, P., Jordan, M.: The big data bootstrap. In: ICML (2012)
12. Martínez-Muñoz, G., Suárez, A.: Out-of-bag estimation of the optimal sample size in bagging. Pattern Recognit. **43**(1), 143–152 (2010)
13. Mason, L., Baxter, J., Bartlett, P., Frean, M.: Boosting algorithms as gradient descent. In: Advances in Neural Information Processing Systems, vol. 12, pp. 512–518. MIT Press (2000)
14. Zaman, F., Hirose, H.: Effect of subsampling rate on subbagging and related ensembles of stable classifiers. In: Chaudhury, S., Mitra, S., Murthy, C.A., Sastry, P.S., Pal, S.K. (eds.) PReMI 2009. LNCS, vol. 5909, pp. 44–49. Springer, Heidelberg (2009). https://doi.org/10.1007/978-3-642-11164-8_8

Learning Preferences for Large Scale Multi-label Problems

Ivano Lauriola[1,2]($\boxtimes$), Mirko Polato[1], Alberto Lavelli[2], Fabio Rinaldi[2,3], and Fabio Aiolli[1]

[1] Department of Mathematics, University of Padova,
Via Trieste, 63, 35121 Padova, Italy
ivano.lauriola@phd.unipd.it
[2] Fondazione Bruno Kessler, Via Sommarive, 18, 38123 Trento, Italy
[3] Institute of Computational Linguistics, University of Zurich,
Andreasstrasse 15, 8050 Zurich, Switzerland

Abstract. Despite that the majority of machine learning approaches aim to solve binary classification problems, several real-world applications require specialized algorithms able to handle many different classes, as in the case of single-label multi-class and multi-label classification problems. The Label Ranking framework is a generalization of the above mentioned settings, which aims to map instances from the input space to a total order over the set of possible labels. However, generally these algorithms are more complex than binary ones, and their application on large-scale datasets could be untractable.

The main contribution of this work is the proposal of a novel general on-line preference-based label ranking framework. The proposed framework is able to solve binary, multi-class, multi-label and ranking problems. A comparison with other baselines has been performed, showing effectiveness and efficiency in a real-world large-scale multi-label task.

Keywords: Preference Learning Machine · Multi-class · Multi-label Big data · Large-scale

1 Introduction

Nowadays, the majority of Machine Learning techniques are able to solve binary classification problems, where the algorithms try to determine if a pattern belongs to either a positive $(+1)$ or a negative (-1) class. Despite that the binary classification setting is the most known, studied and used, there are several problems and real-world applications in which this approach is not suitable, as is the case of multi-class and multi-label models.

In the literature several mechanisms exist to extend the binary classification setting. The simplest approach is based on decomposition methods, such as the one-against-one and one-against-all [8] approaches. Basically, these methods decompose the original multi-class problem in several binary tasks. Then, these

© Springer Nature Switzerland AG 2018
V. Kůrková et al. (Eds.): ICANN 2018, LNCS 11139, pp. 546–555, 2018.
https://doi.org/10.1007/978-3-030-01418-6_54

binary problems are solved using binary classifiers and predictions are combined with a voting procedure. More complex approaches try to model a single multi-class/multi-label problem, as in the case of the Label Ranking framework based on preferences [15], which aims to learn a total order on the set of possible labels. However, these methods usually suffer from scalability issues with respect to the number of classes, making the original problem untractable when this number is large. Besides, due to the constant growth of the available data, a challenging goal of these algorithms is to solve these problems efficiently in terms of computational cost, and required resources.

Inspired by these motivations, this paper presents an extension of the Preference Learning Machine (PLM) [2], a general label ranking framework to learn preferences in binary, multi-class and multi-label setting. The proposed extension mainly includes an efficient and scalable learning procedure, based on the Voted Perceptron algorithm [7], and online learning capability.

The proposed approach has been compared with Neural Networks on a real-world multi-label application. The multi-label task consists of a large-scale semantic indexing of PubMed documents, based on the Medical Subject Headings (MeSH) thesaurus.

2   Notation and Background

In the (single-label) multi-class classification problem, the unique label associated to each pattern x from the input space $\mathcal{X} \subseteq \mathbb{R}^d$, is selected from a predefined set of labels $\Omega = \{\omega_1, \ldots, \omega_m\}$, where m is the number of possible labels $m = |\Omega|$. A common example of multi-class problem is the digit recognition, where the goal is to find the true digit corresponding to a handwritten input [9].

Let us now consider the problem of associating keywords from a given set Ω to a textual document [3]. Differently from the previous case, the number of associated labels (keywords) can be more than 1, and each document might have a different number of keywords. Hence, the task is to learn a mapping from a document to a set of labels. These kinds of problems are referred to multi-label classification problems.

It is easy to see that the single-label multi-class problem is a generalization of the binary setting, where $m = 2$ and, in turn, the multi-label is a generalization of the single-label multi-class problem.

In all of these settings, the label set $y \in \mathcal{Y} \subseteq \{+1, -1\}^m$ associated to each pattern $x \in \mathcal{X}$ can be coded as a binary m-dimensional vector, where each element y_i is active $(+1)$ if and only if the label ω_i is assigned to the pattern x.

Based on this code, training examples can be kept into two matrices. Let $X \in \mathbb{R}^{l \times d}$ be the training matrix, where d-dimensional vectors are arranged in l rows, and let $Y \in \{+1, -1\}^{l \times m}$ be the corresponding label matrix, where rows contain the code of the training patterns. The notation x_i is also used to identify the i-th pattern.

Besides the concept of multi-label classification, the more general *multi-label ranking* has been introduced [4]. The multi-label ranking approach aims to predict the ranking of all labels instead of predicting only the set of relevant ones.

2.1 Related Work

Motivated by the increasing number of new applications, such as automatic annotations of video, images and textual documents, the problem of learning from multi-label data is affecting a large part of the modern research. Recently, several different approaches have been developed aiming to solve multi-label problems [6,12,14]. It is possible to divide these methods into two categories [13]: adaption methods and problem transformation methods.

Adaption methods extend specific machine learning algorithms to handle multi-label data, as in the case of Neural Networks which use an extended back-propagation algorithm with dedicated error functions (see [11] for a detailed explanation).

Problem transformation methods, instead, are those algorithms which map the multi-label classification problem into one or more binary tasks. The most known problem transformation approach is the one-against-all decomposition method [8]. This method generates an ensemble of $m = |\Omega|$ binary classifiers. The i-th classifier is trained with all the examples of the i-th class as positive labels, and all the other examples as negative labels. When models are trained, there are m decision functions. In a ranking multi-label setting, these decision functions define the score for each label. Furthermore, in a single-label multi-class problem the predicted label is the one which achieves the highest score.

See [1,15,16] for detailed surveys of multi-label problems.

3 Working with Preferences

Several algorithms able to solve Label Ranking problems exist in the literature. Some of them are based on the concept of *preferences*, which define an ordering relation on labels and examples. Methods based on preferences try to find a ranking hypothesis $f_\Theta : \mathcal{X} \times \Omega \to \mathbb{R}$ with parameters Θ, which assigns for each label $\omega_i \in \Omega$ a score to a fixed pattern $x \in \mathcal{X}$, $f_\Theta(x, \omega_i)$.

These algorithms can be restricted to two particular cases: *learning instance preference* and *learning label preference* [5].

In the instance preference scenario, a preference relations is defined as a bipartite graph $g = (N, A)$, where $N \subseteq \mathcal{X} \times \Omega$ is the set of nodes and $A \subseteq N \times N$ is the set of arcs.

A node $n = (x_i, \omega_j) \in N$ is a pair composed by an example and a label, and it is a positive node iff the label ω_j is positive for the example x_i, otherwise n is a negative node.

An arc $a = (n_s, n_e) \in A$ connects a starting (positive) node $n_s = (x_i, \omega_j)$ to its ending (negative) node $n_e = (x_k, \omega_q)$. The direction of the arc indicates that the starting node must be *preferred* over the ending node.

The margin of an arc $a = (n_s, n_e)$ is the difference between the application of the ranking function f_Θ on the starting and ending nodes,

$$\rho_A(a, \Theta) = f_\Theta(n_s) - f_\Theta(n_e) = f_\Theta(x_i, \omega_j) - f_\Theta(x_k, \omega_q).$$

An arc $a = (n_s, n_e)$ is consistent with the hypothesis f_Θ iff the assigned score to the node n_s is greater than the score assigned to the node n_e, $f_\Theta(n_s) > f_\Theta(n_e)$, thus the margin $\rho_A(a, \Theta) > 0$. The margin of a graph $g = (N, A)$ is the minimum margin of its arcs $\rho_G(g, \Theta) = \min_{a \in A} \rho_A(a, \Theta)$. Then, a graph is consistent with the hypothesis f_Θ iff its arcs are consistent, $\rho_G(g, \Theta) > 0$.

In the instance preference task instead, preferences are defined by considering a single example at a time. In this scenario, an arc $a \in A$ considers nodes with the same example, $a = (n_s, n_e)$, with $n_s = (\boldsymbol{x}_i, \omega_j)$ and $n_e = (\boldsymbol{x}_i, \omega_q)$

It is easy to see that the label preference scenario tries to separate simultaneously the whole set of examples with their positive nodes and the set of negative nodes. Thus, it is suitable for solving classification tasks. In the instance preference approach instead the algorithms try to optimize the inner ordering for each example.

Some examples of instance preference graphs for a 2-label classification problem are shown in Fig. 1, where for each example: (a) there is only one fully connected graph which connects all positive labels to all negative ones; (b) for each example there are two graphs which connect each positive label to all of the negatives; (c) there is a graph for each pair of labels, the first positive and the second negative. The architecture of these graphs is a hyperparameter selected a priori. Note that for each graph structure, the number of total arcs is the same.

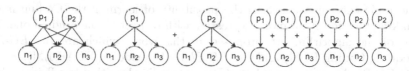

Fig. 1. Examples of preferences for 2-label classification. p_i are the positive labels and n_j the negative ones.

The last ingredient of a preference algorithm is a loss function $\mathcal{L}$ which penalizes the non-consistent preferences. A label ranking algorithm based on preferences tries to find the hypothesis $\hat{f}$ from the hypothesis space $\mathcal{F}$ which minimizes $\mathcal{L}$. Loss functions considered in this work are based on the margin of graphs:

$$\hat{f} = \arg \min_{f_\Theta \in \mathcal{F}} \sum_{g \in \mathcal{V}} \mathcal{L}(\rho_G(g, \Theta))$$

where $\mathcal{V}$ is the set of preference graphs.

3.1   Preference Learning Machine

The Preference Learning Machine (PLM) [2] belongs to the label preference setting. It is a general kernelized framework for solving multi-class and label ranking problems, by learning a function to map each example to a total order on the set of possible labels.

The PLM framework consists of a multivariate embedding $h : \mathcal{X} \rightarrow \mathbb{R}^s$ parametrized by a set of s vectors $W_k \in \mathbb{R}^d$, $k \in \{1, \ldots, s\}$ arranged in the matrix $W \in \mathbb{R}^{s \times d}$. Thus, $h(x) = [h_1(x), \ldots, h_s(x)] = [\langle W_1, x \rangle, \ldots, \langle W_s, x \rangle]$. Furthermore, let $M \in \mathbb{R}^{m \times s}$ be the matrix containing the s-dimensional code for each label $\omega_i \in \Omega$.

The scoring function for a given example x and a given label ω_r can be computed as the dot product between the embedding and the code vector of ω_r, that is

$$f(x, \omega_r) = \langle h(x), M_r \rangle = \sum_{k=1}^{s} M_{rk} \langle W_k, x \rangle.$$

The original PLM [2] considers a fixed m-dimensional orthogonal coding M, defined as the $m \times m$ identity matrix. Authors also formulated the problem of learning the embedding W as a kernelized optimization problem.

4   The Proposed Extension

In the proposed setting, preferences consist of graphs with two nodes connected by a single arc. The first node is represented by an example with one of its positive labels, whereas the latter node is an (potentially different) example with one of its negative labels.

The main extension concerns the possibility of learning the Coding matrix M, making the algorithm more expressive with respect to the original one. Two version of the algorithm are proposed in this work, which are the *EC-PLM* (Embedding-Coding PLM) and the *EP-PLM* (Embedding-PCA PLM).

The EC-PLM uses a pair of Voted Perceptron [7] algorithm to efficiently learn both, the Embedding W and the coding M. Broadly speaking, the EC-PLM performs an alternate optimization procedure to learn its parameters. During each epoch, the algorithm fixes the Coding and optimizes the Embedding by means of a Voted Perceptron. Then, it fixes the Embedding while optimizes the Coding by using the same procedure. After each optimization, the Embedding W and the Coding M are rescaled with their Frobenius norm, $W \leftarrow \frac{W}{\sum_{ij} W_{ij}}$, $M \leftarrow \frac{M}{\sum_{ij} M_{ij}}$.

The training set used to learn the Embedding is composed by preferences. Let a be the arc of a preference graph which connect the starting node (x_i, ω_j) with the ending node (x_k, ω_q). The preference uses the same representation of the PLM, which consists of a $s \times d$ dimensional vector $z = (M_{\omega_j} \otimes x_i) - (M_{\omega_q} \otimes x_k)$, where $\otimes$ denotes the *kron* product between vectors and M_{ω_j}, M_{ω_q} are the codes of ω_j and ω_q. The dimensionality s of codes is a hyperparameter.

When the latter perceptron learns the coding matrix, preferences are defined as $z = (y_s \otimes \langle W, x_i \rangle) - (y_e \otimes \langle W, x_j \rangle)$, where y_j is a 0 m-dimensional vector with an 1 at the j-th element. However, the algorithm requires an initialized code matrix at the first epoch, to learn the first embedding. The initial coding M contains random values.

Furthermore, a faster version of the PLM has been considered, dubbed *EP-PLM*, in which the coding M is computed by means of a Principal Component Analysis (PCA) procedure. Thus, the algorithm requires a single Voted Perceptron procedure.

Let K_T be the linear kernel between labels $K_T = YY^\top$, which counts the number of common examples for each pair of labels. The kernel matrix is then decomposed as $U\Lambda U^\top$, where U is the matrix contains the eigenvectors, and Λ the diagonal matrix containing the eigenvalues. The Coding M is defined as $U_s\Lambda_s$, where U_s is the matrix contains the s eigenvectors associated to the top s eigenvalues. Note that the complexity of this approach mainly depends on the number of labels, and it can be applied on very large scale datasets.

The pseudo-code of the EC-PLM algorithm is shown in the Algorithm 1.

Algorithm 1. The Embedding-Coding Preference Learning Machine

Input:
    s: the dimensionality of codes
    t: the number of epochs
    X: the training matrix
    Y: the label matrix
Output:
    W: the embedding function
    M: the coding function
1 $W^{(0)} \leftarrow \{0\}^{s \times d}$
2 $M^{(0)} \leftarrow$ random $m \times s$ code matrix
3 **for** $i \in 1 \dots t$ **do**
4     $W^{(i)} \leftarrow Voted\_Perceptron(M^{(i-1)})$
5     $M^{(i)} \leftarrow Voted\_Perceptron(W^{(i)})$
6 **end**
7 **return** $W^{(t)}, M^{(t)}$

Due to the characteristics of the Voted Perceptron algorithm and its capability to work with one preference at a time, the EC-PLM can be easily used to work with on-line streams of examples and preferences.

On the other hand, the EP-PLM is able to learn the coding with millions of examples efficiently. Furthermore, on each epoch it uses a single Voted Perceptron to learn the Embedding. The complete procedure is very fast, especially if the input examples use a sparse representation.

5 Experimental Assessment

In order to empirically evaluate the proposed method, it has been tested on a complex multi-label task, which consists of a large-scale online biomedical semantic indexing of PubMed documents based on the Medical Subject Headings (MeSH) [10]. The MeSH thesaurus is a controlled vocabulary produced by the National Library of Medicine (NLM), used for indexing and cataloging the biomedical literature in MEDLINE, that is the NLM bibliographic database containing 24 million journal articles.

The MeSH vocabulary consists of a hierarchy of tags. This work focused on the bottom layer of this hierarchy, which includes 28 333 descriptors or heading tags, that represent main topics or concepts in the biomedical literature.

In this setting, heading tags represent the set of all possible classes or labels, and the task is to find for each example a total order in this set.

5.1 Baselines

The proposed methods have been compared against a Multiple Layer Perceptron (MLP) which represents the same architecture used in the PLM. Let us consider a fully connected MLP with a d-dimensional input layer, which maps the input into a hidden s-dimensional layer by means of a dense $d \times s$ linear connection. Then, the hidden layer maps information on a $m = |\Omega|$ dimensional output layer by using a dense $s \times c$ linear connection. With this perspective, it is easy to show that the two mappings between layers correspond to the Embedding W and Coding M used in the PLM setting.

However, although the PLM can be mapped into a MLP and vice versa, the learning mechanisms used are quite different. The MLP uses a back-propagation procedure whereas the PLM tries to optimize each input preference.

Other baselines have been initially considered. These are the Support Vector Machine (SVM) with one-against-all multi-class strategy, and the original PLM. Anyhow, due to the dimensionality of the considered problem and the complexity of these methods, only the MLP has been used.

5.2 Empirical Evaluation

A wide experimental setting has been used to compare the two versions of the algorithm, in terms of AUC score, computational cost and required resources.

At first, 20 000 abstracts have been randomly selected from the PubMed repository with their respective MeSH tags. Abstracts have been tokenized by considering spaces and punctuation, and stop-words have been removed. The stop-list is the one defined by the scikit-learn library. The global dictionary has been computed by considering only unigrams.

Then, the resulting dictionary has been reduced, by considering only the 100 000 most frequent terms. Finally, the Bag-Of-Words (BOW) feature vector has been computed on each input document. A test set has been preprocessed using the same pipeline, and it also includes 20 000 abstracts. To compute the coding matrix M used in the EP-PLM version, a PCA over 10 million of PubMed documents has been used. The dimension s of codes has been fixed to 50. On each epoch, the Voted Perceptron procedure optimizes 2000 preferences randomly selected. Finally, the training subsampling covers 17071 different MeSH tags.

In order to understand properly the behavior and the empirical convergence of the two algorithms, a preliminary analysis has been performed, showing the micro and macro AUC measures while increasing the number of training epochs. Results are shown in the Fig. 2.

It is self-evident from the picture that the EP-PLM outperforms empirically the EC-PLM, even if it uses a fixed code matrix instead of learning dynamically it from data. Probably, this improvement is due to the fact that the EP-PLM uses 10 million of examples to learn the coding instead of 20 000 as is the case of EC-PLM. In terms of computational cost, the EC-PLM requires on average 132 s to complete a single epoch, whereas the EP-PLM required 95 min to compute the PCA, and 19 s per epoch. The experiments were carried out on an Intel(R) Xeon(R) CPU E5-2650 v3 @ 2.30 GHz.

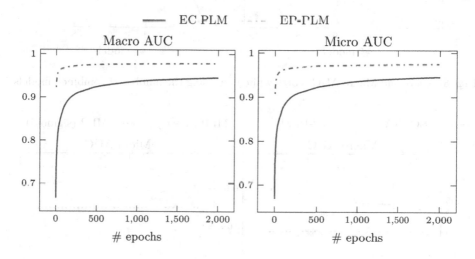

Fig. 2. Empirical convergence of the proposed algorithm.

Subsequently, the combination of several EC/EP-PLM models have been analyzed exploiting a bagging procedure, aiming to facilitate the application of these algorithms on large-scale problems. 10 different datasets have been extracted from the PubMed repository following the procedure mentioned at the beginning of this section, each with 20 000 training examples. Figure 3 shows the empirical effectiveness of the algorithm while increasing the number of models in the case of EC-PLM and EP-PLM. Not surprisingly, the bagging procedure has a strong impact on the EC-PLM setting, in which each model uses only 20 000 examples for both the Embedding and the Coding. The EP-PLM also increases the AUC scores while the number of models increases.

Finally, a comparison against the Multiple Layer Perceptron has been performed. Figure 4 shows Micro and Macro AUC scores of the EC-PLM and EP-PLM against the MLP with linear and sigmoid activation functions, while increasing the dimension $s \in \{25, 50, 100, 200\}$ of the codes and the hidden layer. This experiment shows that the proposed methodologies outperform a MLP with the same inner structure of the PLM. Moreover, the value of s affects significantly the EC/EP-PLM and the linear MLP in particular.

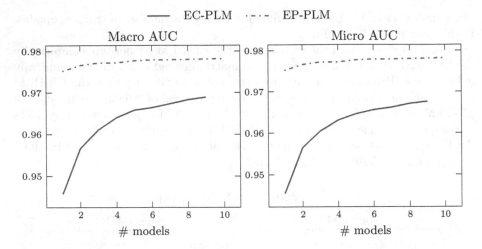

Fig. 3. Micro and Macro AUC scores while increasing the number of combined models.

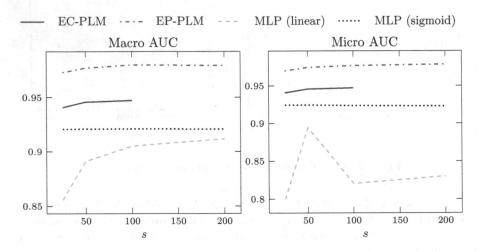

Fig. 4. Micro and Macro AUC scores of EC/EP-PLM and the MLP while increasing the dimension s of the middle space.

6   Conclusion

We have proposed a general framework for on-line preference-based label ranking that can be applied to binary, multi-class, multi-label and ranking problems. Two different versions of the algorithm have been discussed and analyzed. The first focuses on the efficiency whereas the latter is an effective on-line learner. A comparison with some baselines has shown its effectiveness and efficiency in a real-world large-scale multi-label task.

References

1. Aiolli, F.: Large margin multiclass learning: models and algorithms. Ph.D. thesis, Department of Computer Science, University of Pisa (2004)
2. Aiolli, F., Sperduti, A.: Learning preferences for multiclass problems. In: Advances in Neural Information Processing Systems, pp. 17–24 (2005)
3. Allan, J.: Topic Detection and Tracking: Event-Based Information Organization, vol. 12. Springer, Heidelberg (2012)
4. Brinker, K., Fürnkranz, J., Hüllermeier, E.: A unified model for multilabel classification and ranking. In: Proceedings of the 2006 conference on ECAI 2006: 17th European Conference on Artificial Intelligence, 29 August - 1 September 2006, Riva del Garda, Italy, pp. 489–493. IOS Press (2006)
5. Chu, W., Ghahramani, Z.: Preference learning with gaussian processes. In: Proceedings of the 22nd International Conference On Machine learning, pp. 137–144. ACM (2005)
6. Dembczynski, K., Cheng, W., Hüllermeier, E.: Bayes optimal multilabel classification via probabilistic classifier chains. In: ICML, vol. 10, pp. 279–286 (2010)
7. Freund, Y., Schapire, R.E.: Large margin classification using the perceptron algorithm. Mach. Learn. **37**(3), 277–296 (1999)
8. Hsu, C.W., Lin, C.J.: A comparison of methods for multiclass support vector machines. IEEE Trans. Neural Netw. **13**(2), 415–425 (2002)
9. Meier, U., Ciresan, D.C., Gambardella, L.M., Schmidhuber, J.: Better digit recognition with a committee of simple neural nets. In: 2011 International Conference on Document Analysis and Recognition (ICDAR), pp. 1250–1254. IEEE (2011)
10. Nentidis, A., Bougiatiotis, K., Krithara, A., Paliouras, G., Kakadiaris, I.: Results of the fifth edition of the BioASQ challenge. In: BioNLP 2017, pp. 48–57. Association for Computational Linguistics, Vancouver, August 2017
11. Ou, G., Murphey, Y.L.: Multi-class pattern classification using neural networks. Pattern Recognit. **40**(1), 4–18 (2007)
12. Read, J., Pfahringer, B., Holmes, G., Frank, E.: Classifier chains for multi-label classification. Mach. Learn. **85**(3), 333 (2011)
13. Tsoumakas, G., Katakis, I.: Multi-label classification: an overview. Int. J. Data Warehous. Min. **3**(3), 1–13 (2006)
14. Tsoumakas, G., Vlahavas, I.: Random k-labelsets: an ensemble method for multilabel classification. In: Kok, J.N., Koronacki, J., Mantaras, R.L., Matwin, S., Mladenič, D., Skowron, A. (eds.) ECML 2007. LNCS (LNAI), vol. 4701, pp. 406–417. Springer, Heidelberg (2007). https://doi.org/10.1007/978-3-540-74958-5_38
15. Vembu, S., Gärtner, T.: Label ranking algorithms: a survey. In: Fürnkranz, J., Hüllermeier, E. (eds.) Preference Learning, pp. 45–64. Springer, Heidelberg (2010). https://doi.org/10.1007/978-3-642-14125-6_3
16. Zhang, M.L., Zhou, Z.H.: A review on multi-label learning algorithms. IEEE Trans. Knowl. Data Eng. **26**(8), 1819–1837 (2014)

Affinity Propagation Based Closed-Form Semi-supervised Metric Learning Framework

Ujjal Kr Dutta$^{(\boxtimes)}$ and C. Chandra Sekhar

Department of Computer Science and Engineering,
Indian Institute of Technology Madras, Chennai, India
ukd@cse.iitm.ac.in

Abstract. Recent state-of-the-art deep metric learning approaches require large number of labeled examples for their success. They cannot directly exploit unlabeled data. When labeled data is scarce, it is very essential to be able to make use of additionally available unlabeled data to learn a distance metric in a *semi-supervised* manner. Despite the presence of a few traditional, non-deep semi-supervised metric learning approaches, they mostly rely on the *min-max principle* to encode the pairwise constraints, although there are a number of other ways as offered by traditional *weakly-supervised* metric learning approaches. Moreover, there is no flow of information from the available pairwise constraints to the unlabeled data, which could be beneficial. This paper proposes to learn a new metric by constraining it to be close to a prior metric while propagating the affinities among pairwise constraints to the unlabeled data via a closed-form solution. The choice of a different prior metric thus enables encoding of the pairwise constraints by following formulations other than the *min-max principle*.

Keywords: Mahalanobis distance · Affinity propagation
Metric learning · Image retrieval · Person re-identification
Graph-based learning · Semi-supervised learning · Classification
Fine-grained visual categorization

1 Introduction

Distance Metric Learning (DML) aims at learning the distance between a pair of examples with the objective of bringing similar examples together while pushing away dissimilar examples. Deep neural networks have demonstrated remarkable success in machine learning tasks such as classification, clustering, verification and retrieval. DML is a pivotal step in such tasks. As such, deep DML has gained much popularity lately. Popular deep DML approaches [8,18,20,22,25] aim at learning distance metrics in an end-to-end fashion with a pretrained network, such as GoogLeNet [23]. Their success depends on a number of factors: (i) Availability of large number of labeled examples, (ii) Formulation of an

© Springer Nature Switzerland AG 2018
V. Kůrková et al. (Eds.): ICANN 2018, LNCS 11139, pp. 556–565, 2018.
https://doi.org/10.1007/978-3-030-01418-6_55

appropriate loss function (which mainly involves the last layer) and (iii) Mining informative constraints. [20–22] discuss a few mining strategies. However, the ability to learn from unlabeled data has not been exploited by the deep DML approaches. Recently, [15] employed a random walk process to mine constraints for deep DML by considering the manifold similarity in an unsupervised manner. But the random walk process therein cannot exploit already available pairwise similarity/ dissimilarity constraints and hence cannot be directly extended to a *Semi-Supervised* DML (SS-DML) setting. Another important observation is that apart from a few approaches like [18,25], very few alternative loss functions have been explored in deep DML. On the other hand, conventional DML approaches like [6,11,16,28] offer a plethora of ways to formulate a DML loss function. In fact, the recent work in [9] represented the last layer as a Symmetric Positive Definite (SPD) matrix following a conventional metric learning approach. This SPD matrix is jointly learned with a PCA projection matrix following a Riemannian optimization framework, along with the parameters of the network. These factors motivate us to revisit traditional SS-DML approaches utilizing different criteria to formulate the DML loss function. Once such a parametric matrix is found, it can be easily incorporated within a deep framework as in [9].

Traditional DML is referred to as the problem of learning a Mahalanobis-like distance: $d_\mathbf{A}(\mathbf{x}, \mathbf{y}) = (\mathbf{x} - \mathbf{y})^T \mathbf{A}\mathbf{A}^T (\mathbf{x} - \mathbf{y}) = (\mathbf{x} - \mathbf{y})^T \mathbf{M}(\mathbf{x} - \mathbf{y}) = d_\mathbf{M}(\mathbf{x}, \mathbf{y})$ for a pair of examples represented as feature vectors $\mathbf{x}, \mathbf{y} \in \mathbb{R}^d$ (which may have been obtained using a convolutional neural network). Here, $\mathbf{A}^T \colon \mathbb{R}^d \to \mathbb{R}^l$ is a linear mapping such that $\mathbf{M} = \mathbf{A}\mathbf{A}^T$ and $\mathbf{M} \succeq 0$, is a symmetric Positive Semi-Definite (PSD) parametric matrix to be learned. Equivalently we can learn $\mathbf{A}$. Any SS-DML approach can be formulated as the following general optimization problem:

$$\min_{\mathbf{M} \succeq 0} f_1(\mathbf{M}, \mathcal{S}, \mathcal{D}) + f_2(\mathbf{M}, \mathcal{X}) \tag{1}$$

$\mathcal{S}$ and $\mathcal{D}$ are the sets of must-link (similarity) and cannot-link (dissimilarity) constraints respectively. They provide prior side-information (*weak-supervision*). f_1 is a function of the *weak-supervision*, and f_2 is a function of the given dataset $\mathcal{X}$ which also includes the unlabeled data $\mathcal{X}_U$. A majority of the SS-DML approaches like [2,14,17,27] use the unlabeled data by expressing f_2 as the *Laplacian regularizer* [13], which aims at preserving the topology of the data via a graph constructed using the neighborhood relationships among the examples. However, an important observation is that in most of these approaches, f_1 is always a variation of the *min-max principle*: minimizing (maximizing) the distances between the data points with must-link (cannot-link) constraints. By considering different criteria to choose f_1, we can achieve our goal of formulating an alternative DML loss function as discussed above.

This paper addresses the problem of formulating SS-DML approaches by expressing f_1 in terms of prior metrics learned using different criteria, apart from the *min-max principle*. Another important aspect with the existing SS-DML approaches like [2,14,27] is that the *Laplacian regularizer* is computed using an affinity matrix based on neighborhood relationships among the data alone, without considering the pairwise constraints, which could provide further information. This paper attempts to overcome these limitations. The major contributions of this paper are as follows: (i) To make use of the pairwise constraints in the *Laplacian regularizer* as well, we follow the affinity propagation principle [17] and propose a general, topology-preserving SS-DML framework; (ii) The framework enables a closed-form solution to learn a new metric by constraining it to be close to a prior metric in a simple way; (iii) Different choices for the prior metric have been discussed to facilitate the formulation of new SS-DML approaches by expressing f_1 with alternatives to the *min-max principle*.

2 Proposed Semi-supervised DML Framework

Let $X = [\mathbf{x}_1 \ldots \mathbf{x}_N] \in \mathbb{R}^{d \times N}$ denote the matrix containing N examples of a dataset $\mathcal{X}$ as its columns. Let the two sets of pairwise constraints be: $\mathcal{S} = \{(\mathbf{x}_i, \mathbf{x}_j): \mathbf{x}_i \text{ and } \mathbf{x}_j \text{ are similar}\}$ and $\mathcal{D} = \{(\mathbf{x}_i, \mathbf{x}_j): \mathbf{x}_i \text{ and } \mathbf{x}_j \text{ are dissimilar}\}$. Let $\mathbf{y}_i = \mathbf{A}^T \mathbf{x}_i$. The goal is to find $\mathbf{M} \in \mathbb{R}^{d \times d}$ (or $\mathbf{A} \in \mathbb{R}^{d \times l}$), $\mathbf{M} \succeq 0$ using the information provided in $\mathcal{S}$ and $\mathcal{D}$, such that $d_{\mathbf{M}}(\mathbf{x}_i, \mathbf{x}_j) = d_{\mathbf{A}}(\mathbf{x}_i, \mathbf{x}_j) = \|\mathbf{y}_i - \mathbf{y}_j\|_2^2$. Our proposed framework can be expressed as:

$$\min_{\mathbf{M} \succeq 0} \|\mathbf{M} - \mathbf{M}_0\|_F^2 + \beta tr(\mathbf{M} X L X^T) \tag{2}$$

where $\beta > 0$ is a trade-off parameter and $\|Q\|_F^2 = \sum_{ij} Q_{ij}^2 = tr(QQ^T)$ is the squared Frobenius norm of a matrix Q. The first term in (2) can be any function $f_1(\mathbf{M}, \mathcal{S}, \mathcal{D})$ of the *weak-supervision*. The main advantage of using this expression is that it enables us to arrive at a closed-form solution to the SS-DML problem. The goal is to learn the required metric $\mathbf{M} \in \mathbb{R}^{d \times d}$ in such a way that it is close to a prior metric $\mathbf{M}_0$ (defined apriori or precomputed using $\mathcal{S}$ and $\mathcal{D}$). One may argue to set f_1 using log-determinant divergence as: $f_1(\mathbf{M}, \mathcal{S}, \mathcal{D}) = D_{ld}(\mathbf{M}, \mathbf{M}_0) = tr(\mathbf{M}\mathbf{M}_0^{-1}) - log |\mathbf{M}\mathbf{M}_0^{-1}| - d$. Although it leads to a convex formulation, the solution is non-trivial, and would require a method like Bregman projection [6]. Furthermore, the computation of $\mathbf{M}^{-1}$ required in computing the gradient of $D_{ld}(\mathbf{M}, \mathbf{M}_0)$ is hard. Another reason is that while in theory the log-det term ensures that the optimum is within the PSD cone $\mathbb{S}_+^d$, the intermediate iterates are not necessarily confined to the cone in practice [1].

The second term in (2) represents the *Laplacian regularizer* for representing the manifold structure of the data by a graph [13] constructed using the relationships among the data in an Euclidean space, and is defined as:

$$tr(\mathbf{M} X L X^T) = tr(\mathbf{A}^T X L X^T \mathbf{A}) = \frac{1}{2} \sum_{i,j=1}^N \|\mathbf{y}_i - \mathbf{y}_j\|_2^2 W_{ij} \tag{3}$$

where $L = D - W$ is the *graph Laplacian* and D is a diagonal matrix with $D_{ii} = \sum_{j=1}^N W_{ij}$, denoting the degree of a node in the neighborhood graph. The affinity/weight W_{ij} represents a measure of similarity between two nodes i and j in the graph representing examples $\mathbf{x}_i$ and $\mathbf{x}_j$ respectively. One may use the heat kernel [13] to set $W_{ij} = e^{-\|\mathbf{x}_i - \mathbf{x}_j\|_2^2 / t}$, if $\mathbf{x}_i \in \mathcal{N}_j$ or $\mathbf{x}_j \in \mathcal{N}_i$, and

$W_{ij} = 0$ otherwise. Here t is a scale parameter and $\mathcal{N}_i$ is the set of k nearest neighbors of $\mathbf{x}_i$, computed using pairwise Euclidean distances for constructing the graph. However, such an assignment of affinity does not make use of the pairwise constraints in $\mathcal{S}$ and $\mathcal{D}$, which can provide further information about the proximity of *unlabeled examples* (an example not associated with any pairwise constraint). It is desirable to have a mechanism for flow of information from the sets $\mathcal{S}$ and $\mathcal{D}$ to an unlabeled example. For this purpose, an adaptation of the Affinity Propagation (AP) procedure [17] is considered. Define an initial affinity matrix $W^0 \in \mathbb{R}^{N \times N}$. Assign $W_{ij}^0 = +1$ if $i \neq j$ and either $(\mathbf{x}_i, \mathbf{x}_j) \in \mathcal{S}$ or $(\mathbf{x}_j, \mathbf{x}_i) \in \mathcal{S}$ or both. Assign $W_{ij}^0 = -1$ if $i \neq j$ and either $(\mathbf{x}_i, \mathbf{x}_j) \in \mathcal{D}$ or $(\mathbf{x}_j, \mathbf{x}_i) \in \mathcal{D}$ or both. Note that the symmetry in affinities is intuitive, and useful in practice as well. Assign $W_{ii}^0 = +1$, and $W_{ij}^0 = 0$ for $(\mathbf{x}_i, \mathbf{x}_j) \notin \mathcal{S}$ and $(\mathbf{x}_i, \mathbf{x}_j) \notin \mathcal{D}$. Define a neighborhood indicator matrix $P \in \mathbb{R}^{N \times N}$ as follows: Assign $P_{ij} = 1/k$ if $\mathbf{x}_j \in \mathcal{N}_i$, and $P_{ij} = 0$ otherwise. k is the number of nearest neighbors under consideration. Note that P is asymmetric. Now, the goal is to propagate the affinities from entries corresponding to the sets $\mathcal{S}$ and $\mathcal{D}$, to the 0-entries of W^0 using the neighborhood structure information provided by the matrix P. It can be achieved by following a Markov random walk as: $W^{t+1} = (1 - \alpha)W^0 + \alpha P W^t$, where α is a trade-off parameter. As $0 < \alpha < 1$ and eigenvalues of P are in [-1,1], the limit $W^* = \lim_{t \to \infty} W^t$ exists [17], and can be expressed as:

$$W^* = (1 - \alpha)(I - \alpha P)^{-1} W^0 \tag{4}$$

The matrix $I - \alpha P$ is usually sparse in practice. (4) can also be solved as a linear system using the conjugate gradient method. For large scale computations, the k-NN graph can be efficiently approximated by the method in [7], which is orders of magnitudes faster without any effect on performance. The final symmetric affinity matrix is obtained as follows: $W_{ij} = (W_{ij}^* + W_{ji}^*)/2$, and used in (3).

Directly optimizing (2) in terms of $\mathbf{M}$ requires maintaining the PSD constraint, which involves computationally expensive projection onto the PSD cone $\mathbb{S}_+^d$ after every gradient step. Therefore, we consider the following optimization problem:

$$\min_{\mathbf{A}} \|\mathbf{A} - \mathbf{A}_0\|_F^2 + \beta tr(\mathbf{A}^T X L X^T \mathbf{A}) \tag{5}$$

where $\mathbf{M}_0 = \mathbf{A}_0 \mathbf{A}_0^T$. Though we drop the convexity in (5), recent studies [3,4] show that non-convex problems like this indeed work very well in practice and facilitate scalability. The advantage of using the formulation in (5) is two-fold: (1) It eliminates the need for maintaining the PSD constraint, as the final matrix $\mathbf{M} = \mathbf{A}\mathbf{A}^T$ will be PSD by virtue of construction. (2) It can be solved using a simple closed-form solution. Setting the gradient of the objective function in (5) to zero, leads to the following closed-form solution for $\mathbf{A}$:

$$\boxed{\mathbf{A} = [I_d + \beta X L X^T]^{-1} \mathbf{A}_0} \tag{6}$$

where I_d is the $d \times d$ identity matrix. We refer to this proposed general framework as Affinity Propagation based Semi-Supervised Metric Learning (APSSML).

3   Choices for the Prior Metric

Based on the choice of the prior metric, we can define a family of related SS-DML approaches:

(i) **Log-likelihood ratio based prior metric:** The prior metric M_0 is computed based on a statistical inference perspective obtained using the Keep It Simple and Straightforward MEtric (KISSME) learning approach [16]. It considers the space of pairwise differences and computes a log-likelihood ratio between two multivariate Gaussians to learn the metric. The SS-DML approach using this prior metric is called as Affinity Propagation and Log-Likelihood Ratio (APLLR) based SS-DML. The motivation behind choosing the prior metric following [16] is its effectiveness and simplicity while being orders of magnitudes faster than other DML approaches.

(ii) **Identity matrix as prior metric:** A naive way of defining M_0 is to set it to the identity matrix I_d, which avoids the need to compute a prior metric using a learning method. This can be done in applications where time is a constraint. The resulting approach is called as Affinity Propagation and IDentity matrix (APID) based SS-DML. Despite its naiveness, the APID approach performs decently as observed later.

(iii) **Information-theoretic prior metric:** The prior metric can also be obtained from the Information-Theoretic Metric Learning (ITML) [6] approach that aims at minimizing the Kullback-Leibler (KL) divergence between an initial Gaussian distribution and the distribution parameterized by the learned metric. The resulting approach is called as Affinity Propagation and Information-Theoretic (APIT) SS-DML.

4   Experimental Studies

The proposed approaches APLLR, APID and APIT are compared with the following baselines: the recently proposed state-of-the-art Geometric Mean Metric Learning (GMML) [28], two SS-DML approaches: Laplacian Regularized Metric Learning (LRML) [14] and SEmi-supervised metRic leArning Paradigm with Hyper-sparsity (SERAPH) [19]. SERAPH follows entropy regularization instead of preserving the topological structure. Hyperparameters of the baseline approaches have been tuned to yield the best performance. For the proposed approaches, number of neighbors for computing the *graph Laplacian* is set between 6 to 20. α is mostly kept as 0.5 or 0.6, as the performance is mostly insensitive to its value. However, we do set it to 0.9 or 0.1 occasionally. All other parameters related to the APSSML framework are empirically tuned in the range $\{10^{-7}, ..., 10^2\}$.

Using both hand-crafted as well as deep features, experiments have been conducted on a variety of machine learning tasks: (i) Classification on benchmark **UCI datasets** (iris, wine, balance, diabetes and breast cancer), (ii) Handwritten digit recognition on the **USPS dataset**, (iii) Fine-grained visual categorization on the **Caltech-UCSD Birds-200-2011 dataset (CUB)** [24], (iv) Person re-identification on the **VIPeR dataset** [10], and (v) Image retrieval on the **NUS-WIDE dataset** [5]. The UCI datasets are split into 70%-15%-15% ratio for training-validation-testing with data normalization. Only 10% of the training data is considered as labeled for both UCI and USPS datasets. For the CUB dataset, the ResNet [12] features given in [26] have been used. The *train-val* classes as given in [26] have been used for learning the parametric matrix. Only 30% of the data from each of 150 training classes is considered as labeled. Performance on the *test-seen* data has been reported here. The approaches under consideration have been compared using the classification accuracy based on 1-NN classifier (in %) for the UCI, USPS and CUB datasets.

For the VIPeR dataset, the experimental protocol followed and features used are the same as in [16], while revealing (dis)similarity information of only 20% random pairs. The matching rate at rank 1 (in %) is used as the performance measure. A subset of 11 concepts have been chosen from the NUS-WIDE dataset and represented by the normalized CM55 features [5]. The data has been organized in 10 different disjoint folds, such that for each fold a subset of 2200 images is selected in such a way that each concept has 200 relevant images and 200 irrelevant images from each of the other 10 concepts. Out of this subset 10% examples have been chosen to generate the pair-wise constraints. Testing is done on a subset of the dataset with 500 images for each concept that have not been seen during training. Mean Average Precision (AP) across all concepts based on top 10 retrieved images (in %) is used as the performance measure.

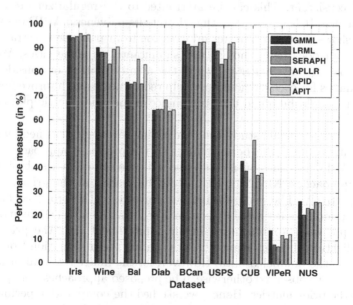

Fig. 1. Performance measures (in %, higher the better) obtained using distance metrics learned by different approaches across different tasks.

Table 1. Average ranks (lower the better) along with standard deviation of the compared approaches across all the tasks as shown in Fig. 1

	Baseline approaches			Proposed semi-supervised approaches		
	State-of-the-art	Semi-supervised approaches				
	GMML	LRML	SERAPH	APLLR	APID	APIT
Avg. Rank±std	2.33 ± 1.58	4.44 ± 1.42	4.77 ± 1.20	3.22 ± 2.27	3.77 ± 1.30	2.44 ± 1.01

The appropriate performance measures (as discussed) for all the studied tasks, obtained using distance metrics learned by different approaches have been collectively shown in Fig. 1. The average ranks along with the standard deviation of the compared approaches, based on their performance across all the tasks/datasets have been shown in Table 1. As seen in Table 1, the proposed SS-DML approaches APLLR, APID and APIT outperform the baseline SS-DML approaches LRML and SERAPH. This highlights the importance of considering an alternative formulation to encode the *weak-supervision* by following criteria other than the *min-max principle* alone. The proposed approaches also perform competitive to the state-of-the-art GMML approach.

In fact, the proposed APLLR obtains the best performance in the following datasets: iris, balance, diabetes and CUB. However, the APLLR approach is less stable as well. This is because of the underlying prior metric obtained using KISSME approach. It is not surprising because despite its success, KISSME requires careful preprocessing and denoising. The invertibility of the scatter matrix of the similar pairs involved in KISSME also plays a crucial role, which is obviously dataset dependent. On the other hand, the APIT approach is much stable and consistent. This can be attributed to the regularizer present in the ITML approach. It is noteworthy that despite its naiveness, APID does perform well. This shows that propagating information from pairwise constraints to the unlabeled data does help, though not significantly in some cases. We believe that thresholding out smaller values in the affinity matrix, or considering only the top affinities for each element may help reduce noise and improve further performance. It should be noted that the choice of the prior metric plays a pivotal role.

In order to specifically study the relative improvement obtained by the affinity propagation alone, the performances of the proposed approaches APLLR, APID and APIT have also been compared with the prior metrics obtained by the following approaches: KISSME, EUC (Identity matrix as the prior metric) and ITML respectively. The comparative performance of the proposed approaches with their prior metrics can be seen in Fig. 2(a), (c) and (e). In most of the cases, the proposed approaches gain an improvement over the prior metrics, again highlighting the importance of propagating the information from pairwise constraints to the unlabeled data. However, for the image retrieval task in NUS-WIDE dataset we observed otherwise. The proposed approaches were performing inferior to the prior metrics. Hence, we studied the comparative performance of the proposed approaches and the prior metrics on individual concepts of the NUS-WIDE dataset. Performances (AP, in %) in five of the eleven concepts are

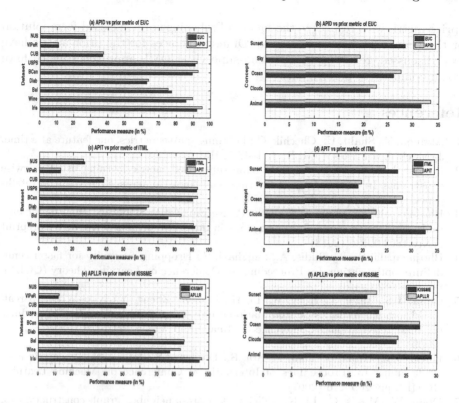

Fig. 2. Comparison of performance measures (in %, higher the better) obtained for the proposed approaches with that of the prior metrics.

shown in Fig. 2(b), (d) and (f). It has been observed that although the proposed approaches performed better for 4 concepts (sky, ocean, clouds and animal), except APLLR the remaining performed inferior on the sunset concept. Even for the remaining concepts (buildings, grass, lake, person, plants and reflection) we did not observe any improvement. We suspect that adding unlabeled data for these concepts was not beneficial. In such cases it is advisable to simply apply an approach like ITML or GMML. It may have happened due to the multi-concept nature of the dataset and the incapability of the SS-DML approaches to unravel the manifold structure of data of some of the concepts, thus lowering the average performance in the NUS-WIDE dataset.

It should be noted that, as an alternative to the two-stage nature of APSSML framework, jointly learning the prior metric $\mathbf{M}_0$ and the current metric $\mathbf{M}$ using an Alternating Optimization scheme could be looked at as a future work.

5   Conclusions

A general affinity propagation based topology-preserving semi-supervised DML framework has been proposed. By constraining the metric to learn to be closer to a prior metric with respect to the squared Frobenius norm, a closed-form solution for the framework has been derived. Different choices for the prior metric have been discussed, resulting in new semi-supervised DML approaches which have shown competitive performance.

References

1. Atzmon, Y., Shalit, U., Chechik, G.: Learning sparse metrics, one feature at a time. J. Mach. Learn. Res. (JMLR) **1**, 1–48 (2015)
2. Baghshah, M.S., Shouraki, S.B.: Semi-supervised metric learning using pairwise constraints. In: Proceedings of International Joint Conference on Artificial Intelligence (IJCAI), pp. 1217–1222 (2009)
3. Bhojanapalli, S., Boumal, N., Jain, P., Netrapalli, P.: Smoothed analysis for low-rank solutions to semidefinite programs in quadratic penalty form. arXiv preprint arXiv:1803.00186 (2018)
4. Bhojanapalli, S., Kyrillidis, A., Sanghavi, S.: Dropping convexity for faster semi-definite optimization. In: Proceedings of Conference on Learning Theory (COLT), pp. 530–582 (2016)
5. Chua, T.S., Tang, J., Hong, R., Li, H., Luo, Z., Zheng, Y.: NUS-WIDE: a real-world web image database from national university of Singapore. In: Proceedings of ACM International Conference on Image and Video Retrieval (CIVR), p. 48 (2009)
6. Davis, J.V., Kulis, B., Jain, P., Sra, S., Dhillon, I.S.: Information-theoretic metric learning. In: Proceedings of International Conference on Machine Learning (ICML), pp. 209–216 (2007)
7. Dong, W., Moses, C., Li, K.: Efficient k-nearest neighbor graph construction for generic similarity measures. In: Proceedings of International Conference on World Wide Web (WWW), pp. 577–586. ACM (2011)
8. Duan, Y., Zheng, W., Lin, X., Lu, J., Zhou, J.: Deep adversarial metric learning. In: Proceedings of IEEE Conference on Computer Vision and Pattern Recognition (CVPR), pp. 2780–2789 (2018)
9. Faraki, M., Harandi, M.T., Porikli, F.: Large-scale metric learning: a voyage from shallow to deep. IEEE Trans. Neural Netw. Learn. Syst. **29**(9), 4339–4346 (2018)
10. Gray, D., Brennan, S., Tao, H.: Evaluating appearance models for recognition, reacquisition, and tracking. In: IEEE International Workshop on Performance Evaluation for Tracking and Surveillance (PETS), vol. 3 (2007)
11. Harandi, M., Salzmann, M., Hartley, R.: Joint dimensionality reduction and metric learning: a geometric take. In: Proceedings of International Conference on Machine Learning (ICML) (2017)
12. He, K., Zhang, X., Ren, S., Sun, J.: Deep residual learning for image recognition. In: Proceedings of IEEE Conference on Computer Vision and Pattern Recognition (CVPR), pp. 770–778 (2016)
13. He, X., Niyogi, P.: Locality preserving projections. In: Proceedings of Neural Information Processing Systems (NIPS), pp. 153–160 (2003)
14. Hoi, S.C., Liu, W., Chang, S.F.: Semi-supervised distance metric learning for collaborative image retrieval and clustering. ACM Trans. Multimed. Comput. Commun. Appl. **6**(3), 18 (2010)
15. Iscen, A., Tolias, G., Avrithis, Y., Chum, O.: Mining on manifolds: metric learning without labels. In: Proceedings of IEEE Conference on Computer Vision and Pattern Recognition (CVPR) (2018)

16. Koestinger, M., Hirzer, M., Wohlhart, P., Roth, P.M., Bischof, H.: Large scale metric learning from equivalence constraints. In: Proceedings of IEEE Conference on Computer Vision and Pattern Recognition (CVPR), pp. 2288–2295 (2012)
17. Liu, W., Ma, S., Tao, D., Liu, J., Liu, P.: Semi-supervised sparse metric learning using alternating linearization optimization. In: Proc. of ACM International Conference on Special Interest Group on Knowledge Discovery and Data Mining (SIGKDD), pp. 1139–1148 (2010)
18. Movshovitz-Attias, Y., Toshev, A., Leung, T.K., Ioffe, S., Singh, S.: No fuss distance metric learning using proxies. In: Proceedings of IEEE International Conference on Computer Vision (ICCV) (2017)
19. Niu, G., Dai, B., Yamada, M., Sugiyama, M.: Information-theoretic semi-supervised metric learning via entropy regularization. Neural Comput. 26(8), 1717–1762 (2014)
20. Oh Song, H., Xiang, Y., Jegelka, S., Savarese, S.: Deep metric learning via lifted structured feature embedding. In: Proceedings of IEEE Conference on Computer Vision and Pattern Recognition (CVPR), pp. 4004–4012 (2016)
21. Schroff, F., Kalenichenko, D., Philbin, J.: FaceNet: a unified embedding for face recognition and clustering. In: Proceedings of IEEE Conference on Computer Vision and Pattern Recognition (CVPR), pp. 815–823 (2015)
22. Sohn, K.: Improved deep metric learning with multi-class n-pair loss objective. In: Proceedings of Neural Information Processing Systems (NIPS), pp. 1857–1865 (2016)
23. Szegedy, C., et al.: Going deeper with convolutions. In: Proceedings of IEEE Conference on Computer Vision and Pattern Recognition (CVPR), pp. 1–9 (2015)
24. Wah, C., Branson, S., Welinder, P., Perona, P., Belongie, S.: The Caltech-UCSD Birds-200-2011 Dataset. Technical report (2011)
25. Wang, J., Zhou, F., Wen, S., Liu, X., Lin, Y.: Deep metric learning with angular loss. In: Proceedings of IEEE International Conference on Computer Vision (ICCV) (2017)
26. Xian, Y., Lampert, C.H., Schiele, B., Akata, Z.: Zero-shot learning-a comprehensive evaluation of the good, the bad and the ugly. arXiv preprint arXiv:1707.00600 (2017)
27. Ying, S., Wen, Z., Shi, J., Peng, Y., Peng, J., Qiao, H.: Manifold preserving: an intrinsic approach for semisupervised distance metric learning. IEEE Trans. Neural Netw. Learn. Syst. (2017)
28. Zadeh, P., Hosseini, R., Sra, S.: Geometric mean metric learning. In: Proceedings of International Conference on Machine Learning (ICML), pp. 2464–2471 (2016)

Online Approximation of Prediction Intervals Using Artificial Neural Networks

Myrianthi Hadjicharalambous(✉), Marios M. Polycarpou,
and Christos G. Panayiotou

KIOS Research and Innovation Center of Excellence,
Department of Electrical and Computer Engineering,
University of Cyprus, Nicosia, Cyprus
{hadjicharalambous.myrianthi,mpolycar,christosp}@ucy.ac.cy

Abstract. Prediction intervals offer a means of assessing the uncertainty of artificial neural networks' point predictions. In this work, we propose a hybrid approach for constructing prediction intervals, combining the Bootstrap method with a direct approximation of lower and upper error bounds. The main objective is to construct high-quality prediction intervals – combining high coverage probability for future observations with small and thus informative interval widths – even when sparse data is available. The approach is extended to adaptive approximation, whereby an online learning scheme is proposed to iteratively update prediction intervals based on recent measurements, requiring a reduced computational cost compared to offline approximation. Our results suggest the potential of the hybrid approach to construct high-coverage prediction intervals, in batch and online approximation, even when data quantity and density are limited. Furthermore, they highlight the need for cautious use and evaluation of the training data to be used for estimating prediction intervals.

Keywords: Prediction intervals · Lower and upper error bounds
Online learning · Adaptive approximation

1 Introduction

The use of Artificial Neural Networks (ANN) in approximating unknown functions has attracted significant research interest over the last decades [1,2], motivated by the universal approximator properties of ANN [2]. However, in practical scenarios where the function to be approximated is unknown, ANN's accuracy relies on the quality and quantity of the available measurements. Noise-corrupted measurements, multi-valued targets along with data uncertainty stemming from variabilities of the physical system, significantly impact ANN's point predictions. The reliability of point predictions is further deteriorated in online approximation scenarios, whereby the training data might be sparse – especially at initial training stages – or might not representatively cover the entire region of interest.

© Springer Nature Switzerland AG 2018
V. Kůrková et al. (Eds.): ICANN 2018, LNCS 11139, pp. 566–576, 2018.
https://doi.org/10.1007/978-3-030-01418-6_56

Such issues will likely force the ANN to extrapolate, limiting its generalisation ability along with the practical utility of point predictions. As an alternative to point predictions, Prediction Intervals (PIs) have been proposed [3–5] which provide lower and upper bounds for a future observation, with a prescribed probability. From a practical point of view, PIs could be preferable to point predictions as they provide an indication of the reliability of the ANN as well as enable practitioners to consider best- and worst-case scenarios. For example, PIs could be particularly useful in control engineering and fault detection applications [6], where uncertainty bounds could help distinguish the healthy operation of the system from faulty behaviour.

A range of methods have been proposed in the literature for constructing PIs and assessing the reliability of ANN. Amongst them, the delta technique [3], the mean variance estimation method and Bootstrap approaches [4] have been used extensively to evaluate PIs on real and synthetic problems. These traditional approaches first generate the point predictions and subsequently compute the PIs following assumptions on error or data distributions, which might be invalid in real world applications. Additionally, as the resulting PIs are not constructed to optimise PI quality, they might suffer from low coverage of the training/test set or might result in wide, over-conservative error bounds.

An alternative approach (Lower Upper Bound Estimation (LUBE)) has been proposed by Khosravi et al., focusing on directly estimating high-quality PIs, while avoiding restrictive assumptions on error distributions [5]. Instead of quantifying the error of point predictions, LUBE uses ANN to directly approximate lower and upper error bounds, by optimising model coefficients to achieve maximum coverage of available measurements, with the minimum PI width [5,7]. Although LUBE has demonstrated significant potential against traditional approaches in terms of accuracy, interval width and computational cost [8,9], it is less reliable when limited or non-uniformly distributed training data are available [10]. In fact, Bootstrap and delta methods produce wider PIs in regions with sparse data, signifying the larger level of uncertainty in ANN approximation; capturing model uncertainty is an important feature of PIs [9,11], lacking in the LUBE approach which mainly accounts for noise variance.

In this work, we propose a combination of the Bootstrap and LUBE methods, which exploits good characteristics from both techniques. The proposed Bootstrap-LUBE Method (BLM) enhances the reliability of the LUBE approach when data is sparse or limited, by augmenting the training set with pseudo-measurements stemming from Bootstrap replications. The pseudo-measurements will present larger variability in regions with sparse data, forcing BLM to produce a wider local PI and thus capture the larger uncertainty in approximation. Following LUBE, BLM constructs PIs by optimising their coverage and width, while at the same time avoiding any assumptions on data/error distributions.

Another important contribution of this work is to extend the proposed hybrid approach to adaptively approximate the PIs during the online operation of the system. In cases where data becomes continuously available in a sequential way, use of the either LUBE or BLM on the entire current dataset would become infeasible as it would incur a continuously increasing computational cost. At the same time, offline estimation of PIs based on past data would likely be unsuitable as it would be unable to accommodate dynamic changes in data patterns. We propose an online learning scheme for estimating PIs, in which the lower and upper bounds are iteratively updated to also account for recent measurements. At each iteration only recent data are used in PI-optimisation, thus significantly reducing the computational cost and further enhancing the efficiency of BLM.

2 Methods

Throughout this section, we assume that we want to construct a PI for the approximation of an unknown function $f(x)$, $x \in D$, where the region of interest D is a compact subset of $\mathbb{R}$. Available measurements are denoted by (x_i, Y_i), $i = 1, \cdots, N$, which are assumed to be corrupted by noise ϵ ($Y_i = f(x_i) + \epsilon_i$). A PI of a predetermined confidence level $(1-a)$ for a future observation Y_{N+1} consists of a lower $L(x_{N+1})$ and upper bound $U(x_{N+1})$, denoting that the future observation will lie within the interval with a probability $1 - a$:

$$P(Y_{N+1} \in [L(x_{N+1}),\ U(x_{N+1})]) = 1 - a. \tag{1}$$

For the Bootstrap method, let us assume that we want to approximate the unknown function $f(x)$ with $\hat{f}(x; w, c, \sigma)$, using a Radial Basis Function (RBF) network:

$$\hat{f}(x; w, c, \sigma) = \sum_{h=1}^{H} w_h \phi_h(x; c_h, \sigma_h), \quad \phi_h(x; c_h, \sigma_h) = \exp(\frac{-(x - c_h)^2}{\sigma_h^2}). \tag{2}$$

Here H denotes the number of ANN neurons ($H = 20$ for the tests considered) and w_h are weighting coefficients scaling the RBF ϕ_h. The centres c_h are evenly distributed over the region of interest and the widths σ_h are evaluated using a nearest-neighbour heuristic, leading to a linear-in-parameter approximator $\hat{f}(x; w)$. The weight vector w can then be estimated by minimising the error function $\sum_{i=1}^{N}[Y_i - \hat{f}(x_i; w)]^2$ using least squares estimation.

2.1 Prediction Interval Estimation Methods

Bootstrap Residual Method. Bootstrap methods rely on multiple pseudo-replications of the training set to approximate unbiased estimates of prediction errors. Here we concentrate on the Bootstrap residual method, whereby model residuals are randomly resampled with replacement. The Bootstrap residual method algorithm described in [4] can be summarised as follows:

- Get an initial estimate $\hat{w}$ from available measurements, compute residuals $r_i = Y_i - \hat{f}(x_i; \hat{w})$ and then compute variance-corrected residuals s_i [4].
- Generate B samples of size N drawn with replacement from residuals $s_1, \cdots, s_N$, denoted by $s_1^b, \cdots, s_N^b$ for the bth sample. For the bth replication:

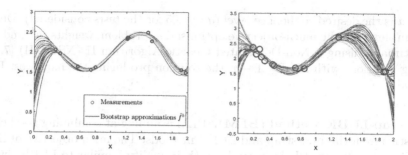

Fig. 1. Function approximations $\hat{f}^b$ at 50 Bootstrap replications (*grey shaded lines*). The variability among approximations from different replications is significantly larger in regions where measurements used for training (*red circles*) are limited. (Color figure online)

- Generate b^{th} replication's "measurements" $Y_i^b = \hat{f}(x_i; \hat{\boldsymbol{w}}) + s_i^b$.
- Estimate $\boldsymbol{w}_b$ by minimising the error $\sum_{i=1}^{N}[Y_i^b - \hat{f}(x_i; \boldsymbol{w})]^2$ and calculate the Bootstrap approximation $\hat{f}^b(x; \boldsymbol{w}_b)$.
- Calculate the current estimate for the approximation error ϵ_{N+1}^b.
- Construct PI using percentiles of the error ϵ_{N+1}.

LUBE Method. LUBE's cornerstone is the direct approximation of PIs using ANNs. Instead of the unknown function $f(x)$, LUBE approximates the lower $L(x)$ and upper $U(x)$ bounds using RBFs: $\hat{L}(x; \boldsymbol{w}^L) = \sum_{h=1}^{H} w_h^L \phi_h(x)$, $\hat{U}(x; \boldsymbol{w}^U) = \sum_{h=1}^{H} w_h^U \phi_h(x)$. The main goal is to produce high-quality PIs, where quality is assessed using two indices: (a) PI Coverage Probability (PICP) and (b) Normalised Mean Prediction Interval Width (NMPIW). In particular, PICP is given by:

$$PICP(\boldsymbol{w}^L, \boldsymbol{w}^U) = \frac{1}{N} \sum_{i=1}^{N} C_i, \tag{3}$$

with $C_i = 1$ if $Y_i \in [\hat{L}(x_i; \boldsymbol{w}^L), \quad \hat{U}(x_i; \boldsymbol{w}^U)]$ and $C_i = 0$ otherwise. Similarly, for R denoting the range of observations, NMPIW is given by:

$$NMPIW(\boldsymbol{w}^L, \boldsymbol{w}^U) = \frac{1}{N} \sum_{i=1}^{N} [\hat{U}(x_i; \boldsymbol{w}^U) - \hat{L}(x_i; \boldsymbol{w}^L)]/R. \tag{4}$$

From a practical point of view it is useful to have narrow PIs (small NMPIW) which offer high coverage of the measurements (large PICP), leading to the following optimisation problem [5,7]:

$$Minimise \quad NMPIW(\boldsymbol{w}^L, \boldsymbol{w}^U) \tag{5}$$

$$1 - PICP(\boldsymbol{w}^L, \boldsymbol{w}^U) \tag{6}$$

$$Subject\ to \quad NMPIW(\boldsymbol{w}^L, \boldsymbol{w}^U) > 0, \tag{7}$$

$$1 - PICP(\boldsymbol{w}^L, \boldsymbol{w}^U) \le a, \tag{8}$$

where a is the desired confidence level ($a = 0.05$ for the tests considered). Due to the complexity of the mutli-objective optimisation problem, weights $\boldsymbol{w}^L$ and $\boldsymbol{w}^U$ are estimated using a Non-Dominated Genetic Algorithm II (NSGA-II) [7,12]. Among solutions with PICP$\geq 1 - a$, the solution producing the narrowest PI is selected.

Bootstrap-LUBE Method (BLM). BLM is aiming at combining good characteristics from the Bootstrap and LUBE methods. The main objective of BLM is to directly estimate PIs by optimising their quality (similar to LUBE), while at the same time accounting for model uncertainty (similar to Bootstrap).

In fact, Bootstrap produces wider bounds in regions with sparse data, capturing the larger model uncertainty while the LUBE approach which mainly accounts for noise variance lacks this feature (Figs. 1, 2 and 3). Looking closer into Bootstrap (Fig. 1), there is significant variability between the Bootstrap approximations $\hat{f}^b$ from different replications in regions with sparse data, most likely due to extrapolation. In such regions the error at each replication will be large leading to large regional error variance and wide regional error bounds.

The main idea of BLM is to enrich the N available measurements with pseudo-measurements originating from the Bootstrap approximations ($\hat{f}^b$), to force BLM to account for data density. We first define an auxiliary set of points (x_j^*, $j = 1, \cdots, N_{aux}$) evenly distributed in the region of interest. We then compute the Bootstrap approximation of each replication for all of the x^* points ($\hat{f}^b(x_j^*)$, $b = 1, \cdots, B$, $j = 1, \cdots, N_{aux}$) which will lead to $B \cdot N_{aux}$ pseudo-measurements (light blue dots in Figs. 2 and 3). The multi-objective optimisation problem of LUBE is now augmented to finding $\boldsymbol{w}^L$ and $\boldsymbol{w}^U$ which:

$$Minimise \quad NMPIW(\boldsymbol{w}^L, \boldsymbol{w}^U) + NMPIW_{pseudo}(\boldsymbol{w}^L, \boldsymbol{w}^U) \tag{9}$$

$$1 - PICP(\boldsymbol{w}^L, \boldsymbol{w}^U) \tag{10}$$

$$Subject\ to \quad NMPIW(\boldsymbol{w}^L, \boldsymbol{w}^U) > 0, \tag{11}$$

$$1 - PICP(\boldsymbol{w}^L, \boldsymbol{w}^U) \leq a, \tag{12}$$

$$1 - PICP_{pseudo}(\boldsymbol{w}^L, \boldsymbol{w}^U) \leq 0.01, \tag{13}$$

where PICP and NMPIW are computed over the N actual measurements, and PICP$_{pseudo}$ and NMPIW$_{pseudo}$ are computed on the pseudo-measurements. With the BLM formulation the PIs will be forced to be wider in regions with sparse data (where pseudo-measurements will present substantial variations), indicating larger model uncertainty. At the same time, regions with dense data will not be affected, as the variation in pseudo-measurements will be small (the Bootstrap approximation in those regions is similar throughout replications (Fig. 1)).

2.2 Online Estimation of Prediction Intervals

During the online operation of a system where data becomes available in a sequential manner, use of either LUBE or BLM on the entire current dataset would become infeasible. To this end, we propose an online approximation scheme which takes into account past and current data, in a computationally efficient way. Based on a weighted sliding window learning scheme, the lower and upper bounds are iteratively updated at specific time instances.

In particular, the lower and upper bounds' weights (condensed into vector w) are first trained on the N_i initial measurements, leading to estimate w_i. Assuming a continual and uniform in time inflow of measurements, the bounds are updated at the first sliding window when $N_i + N_w$ measurements are available ($N_w \leq N_i$):

$$w(N_i + N_w) = w_i \frac{N_i}{N_i + N_w} + w_w \frac{N_w}{N_i + N_w}. \tag{14}$$

Here w_w denote the weights of the lower and upper bounds estimated with multi-objective optimisation based only on the most recent N_w measurements of the current window. The contribution of the recent measurements in the current weights' evaluation is determined by the ratio of measurements in the current window (N_w) to the total number of available measurements ($N_i + N_w$). Similarly, for the kth window, the weights will be iteratively updated to account for past and current measurements with equal contributions:

$$w(N_i + kN_w) = w(N_i + (k-1)N_w)\frac{N_i + (k-1)N_w}{N_i + kN_w} + w_w \frac{N_w}{N_i + kN_w}. \tag{15}$$

For each window only N_w measurements are used in the optimisation, significantly reducing the computational cost of the optimisation problem. Note that when BLM is used, the weights are estimated using the measurements of the current window as well as the auxiliary Bootstrap-based measurements.

3   Results and Discussion

3.1   Comparison of Prediction Interval Estimation Methods

The methods for constructing PIs described in Sect. 2.1 are tested and compared on synthetic tests. Of interest in this work is the quality of the PIs when non-uniformly distributed or sparse data are available. Accordingly, as we are investigating extreme scenarios, the training data are generated from random uniformly distributed data under specific restrictions. In particular, we are replicating two scenarios: (a) the training data do not representatively cover the entire domain, but only regions of it (Fig. 2), (b) very few training data are available over the entire domain (Fig. 3). For both scenarios the test data are uniformly covering the entire domain, to enable reliable assessment of PI accuracy.

Two functions to be approximated are considered ($f_1(x) = 0.5\sin(1.5\pi x + \pi/2) + 2$, $f_2(x) = 5\sin(\pi x + \pi/2) + \exp(x)$). Training and test data are generated based on these functions and white Gaussian noise of 10% of the mean function value is added. For both functions we consider the two training scenarios, leading to the following tests: Test1: PI for regional data generated from f_1, Test2: PI for regional data generated from f_2, Test3: PI for sparse data generated from f_1, Test4: PI for sparse data generated from f_2. For Test1 and Test2, we consider 100 training points, while 15 training points are considered for Test3 and Test4. Every test is repeated 10 times with different randomly generated training data, to enable a more reliable comparison of the methods. Table 1 presents PI quality indices for all methods, averaged over the 10 replications of each test. Representative PIs are demonstrated in Fig. 2 for scenario (a) and Fig. 3 for scenario (b).

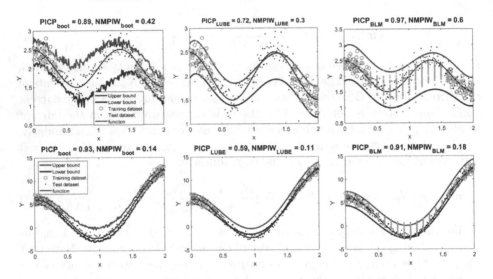

Fig. 2. PIs constructed using the Bootstrap (*left column*), LUBE (*middle column*) and BLM (*right column*) approaches. Data limited to certain regions of the domain following scenario (a), originate from f_1 (Test1, *top row*) and f_2 (Test2, *bottom row*). *Light blue dots* indicate Bootstrap pseudo-measurements used by BLM. PICP and NMPIW are evaluated on the test dataset, uniformly covering the entire domain. (Color figure online)

Across the tests considered BLM clearly outperforms LUBE method in terms of coverage, with an average increase of 15–30% in PICP. By considering Bootstrap pseudo-measurements, BLM is able to produce larger bounds in regions with fewer data, providing an indication of the uncertainty in the estimation. Additionally, due to BLM's optimisation of PI quality, BLM produces a better coverage compared to Bootstrap in the majority of tests. Increased PICP comes at the cost of wider PIs, nevertheless, the fundamental requirement for a PI to reliably include future observations is clearly prioritised over narrow – yet invalid – PIs.

Finally, it is worth noting that BLM is performed on a larger number of training measurements compared to LUBE, without significantly impacting the computational cost. The increased cost in computing PICP and NMPIW over the pseudo-measurements is not substantial (note that B and N_{aux} do not need

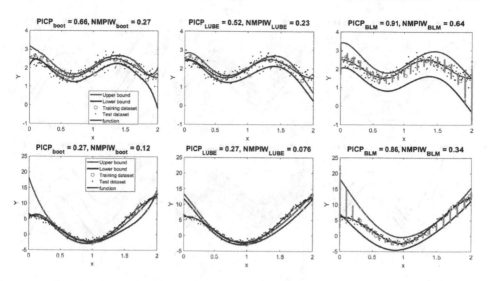

Fig. 3. PIs constructed using the Bootstrap (*left column*), LUBE (*middle column*) and BLM (*right column*) approaches. Sparse data originate from f_1 (Test3, *top row*) and f_2 (Test4, *bottom row*) following scenario (b). *Light blue dots* indicate Bootstrap pseudo-measurements used by BLM. PICP and NMPIW are evaluated on the test dataset, uniformly covering the entire domain. (Color figure online)

to be very large to enable BLM to account for data density), while the dimensions of the parameters ($\boldsymbol{w}^L$ and $\boldsymbol{w}^U$) to be estimated remain the same.

Table 1. Average characteristics of the PIs constructed for four synthetic tests, using the Bootstrap, LUBE and BLM approaches. PICP and NMPIW are evaluated on the test dataset, uniformly covering the entire domain.

Tests	Bootstrap		LUBE		BLM	
	PICP(%)	NMPIW(%)	PICP(%)	NMPIW(%)	PICP(%)	NMPIW(%)
Test1	83.23	43.54	74.33	37.68	89.75	57.63
Test2	65.06	20.74	62.47	18.61	91.76	41.00
Test3	65.27	33.56	66.67	29.72	94.68	62.68
Test4	65.72	10.77	64.97	9.23	90.30	24.93

3.2   Online Estimation of Prediction Intervals with LUBE and BLM

The proposed online learning scheme (Eq. 15) is compared against batch (offline) estimation using both the LUBE and BLM approaches. Initially, LUBE is used with $N_i = 100$ initial training points and $N_w = 10$, subsequently with $N_i = 1000$ and $N_w = 100$ and finally BLM is used with $N_i = 100$ and $N_w = 10$. In all tests $k = 10$ sliding windows are considered, and each of the three cases is repeated

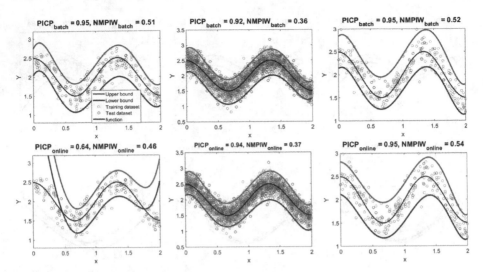

Fig. 4. PIs constructed using batch (*top row*) and online (*bottom row*) estimation. Online PI estimation is tested using LUBE on $N_i = 100$ and $N_w = 10$ training points (*left column*), using LUBE on $N_i = 1000$ and $N_w = 100$ training points (*middle column*) and using BLM on $N_i = 100$ and $N_w = 10$ training points (*right column*).

Table 2. Average characteristics of the PIs constructed using the LUBE and BLM methods, based on batch or online approximation.

	LUBE ($N_w = 10$)		LUBE ($N_w = 100$)		BLM ($N_w = 10$)	
Estimation	PICP(%)	NMPIW(%)	PICP(%)	NMPIW(%)	PICP(%)	NMPIW(%)
Batch	94.95	54.80	94.84	42.64	92.50	46.60
Online	76.14	64.41	95.95	43.94	89.57	43.93

10 times. For batch approximation all $N_i + kN_w$ training points are used for PI optimisation. Representative results are presented in Fig. 4 and average PI indices in Table 2.

When LUBE is used with only $N_w = 10$ training points, online results are suboptimal compared to batch approximation. This is due to the fact that LUBE's accuracy suffers when only sparse data is available (as demonstrated in Fig. 3 and Table 1). This issue can be alleviated by increasing the number of training points ($N_w = 100$), in which case online estimation with LUBE is able to provide very similar PIs to batch estimation, and in a much more efficient way. Alternatively, BLM is able to provide very similar PIs through online and batch estimation without increasing the number of training points as it is designed to provide reliable bounds even when trained on sparse data.

It is worth noting that the proposed learning scheme can easily be adjusted to accommodate the needs of the specific application. For example, the relative contribution of the current sliding window could be increased in cases where recent measurements are considered more critical than past measurements.

4   Conclusions

Combining Bootstrap with LUBE method enables BLM to present improved characteristics in terms of coverage, compared to both Bootstrap and LUBE approaches. In particular, BLM can provide high-coverage PIs even when limited data are available, clearly outperforming the LUBE approach. The results highlight the fact that even commonly used methods such as Bootstrap might provide unreliable PIs when the bounds are based on limited or sparse data, an issue that should be carefully considered by ANN practitioners. Finally, extending BLM to online approximation constitutes a significant improvement, as it enables the efficient and reliable construction of PIs even when approximating dynamically changing processes.

Acknowledgements. This work has been supported by the European Union's Horizon 2020 Research and Innovation Programme under grant agreement No 739551 (KIOS CoE) and from the Republic of Cyprus through the Directorate General for European Programmes, Coordination and Development.

References

1. Bishop, C.M.: Pattern Recognition and Machine Learning. Springer, Heidelberg (2006)
2. Hastie, T., Tibshirani, R., Friedman, J.: The Elements of Statistical Learning: Data Mining, Inference, and Prediction, 2nd edn. Springer, New York (2009). https://doi.org/10.1007/978-0-387-84858-7
3. Hwang, J.T.G., Ding, A.A.: Prediction intervals for artificial neural networks. J. Am. Stat. Assoc. **92**, 748–757 (1997)
4. Davidson, A.C., Hinkley, D.V.: Bootstrap Methods and Their Application. Cambridge University Press, Cambridge (2013)
5. Khosravi, A., Nahavandi, S., Creighton, D., Atiya, A.F.: Lower upper bound estimation method for construction of neural network-based prediction intervals. IEEE Trans. Neural Netw. **22**, 337–346 (2011)
6. Reppa, V., Polycarpou, M.M., Panayiotou, C.G.: Adaptive approximation for multiple sensor fault detection and isolation of nonlinear uncertain systems. IEEE Trans. Neural Netw. Learn. Syst. **25**, 137–153 (2014)
7. Zhang, C., Wei, H., Xie, L., Shen, Y., Zhang, K.: Direct interval forecasting of wind speed using radial basis function neural networks in a multi-objective optimization framework. Neurocomputing **205**, 53–63 (2016)
8. Ye, L., Zhou, J., Gupta, H.V., Zhang, H., Zeng, X., Chen, L.: Efficient estimation of flood forecast prediction intervals via single and multi-objective versions of the LUBE method. Hydrol Process. **30**, 2703–2716 (2016)
9. Pearce, T., Zaki, M., Brintrup, A., Neely, A.: High-quality prediction intervals for deep learning: a distribution-free, ensembled approach. In: 35th International Conference on Machine Learning. arXiv:1802.07167v3 (2018)
10. Khosravi, A., Nahavandi, S., Creighton, D.: Prediction intervals for short-term wind farm power generation forecasts. IEEE Trans. Sustain. Energy **4**, 602–610 (2013)

11. Lakshminarayanan, B., Pritzel, A., Blundell, C.: Simple and scalable predictive uncertainty estimation using deep ensembles. In: 31st Conference on Neural Information Processing Systems (2017)
12. Deb, K., Pratap, A., Agarwal, S., Meyarivan, T.: A fast and elitist multiobjective genetic algorithm: NSGA-II. IEEE Trans. Evol. Comput. **6**, 182–197 (2002)

Classification

Estimation of Microphysical Parameters of Atmospheric Pollution Using Machine Learning

C. Llerena[1(✉)], D. Müller[2], R. Adams[3], N. Davey[1,2,3], and Y. Sun[1,2,3]

[1] Polytechnic School, University of Alcalá, Alcalá de Henares, Spain
cosme.llerag@gmail.com
[2] School of Physics, Astronomy and Mathematics,
University of Hertfordshire, Hertfordshire, UK
{d.mueller,n.davey,y.2.sun}@herts.ac.uk
[3] Centre for Computer Science and Informatics Research,
University of Hertfordshire, Hertfordshire AL10 9AB, UK
r.g.adams@herts.ac.uk

Abstract. The estimation of microphysical parameters of pollution (effective radius and complex refractive index) from optical aerosol parameters entails a complex problem. In previous work based on machine learning techniques, Artificial Neural Networks have been used to solve this problem. In this paper, the use of a classification and regression solution based on the k-Nearest Neighbor algorithm is proposed. Results show that this contribution achieves better results in terms of accuracy than the previous work.

Keywords: LIDAR · Particle extinction coefficient · Particle backscatter
Effective radius · Complex refractive index · K-Nearest Neighbor

1 Introduction

One of the main important factors that drive climate change is particulate pollution [1]. To understand atmospheric temperatures changes that cause climate change, it is necessary to study and characterize the optical, chemical and microphysical properties of these particles in the atmosphere. Some technologies like radiometers or Light Detection and Ranging (LIDAR) make possible the observation of aerosols. LIDAR has become a key tool for the characterization of atmospheric pollution in the atmosphere. LIDAR is the only remote sensing technique used in research on atmospheric pollution that allows for vertically-resolved observations of particulate pollution, for example, [2]. Using LIDAR, optical aerosol parameters can be extracted [3] but more information about particles is required to understand the impact of pollution on climate change.

Microphysical particle parameters are also of key interest to determine pollution effects. In [4–8], inversion algorithms are used to estimate microphysical information (particle size or complex refractive index) from optical data. Their estimation is a very complex task because many factors such as ambient atmospheric humidity, the

© Springer Nature Switzerland AG 2018
V. Kůrková et al. (Eds.): ICANN 2018, LNCS 11139, pp. 579–588, 2018.
https://doi.org/10.1007/978-3-030-01418-6_57

condensation of gases on existing particles or the mixing of particles of different chemical properties modify the values of the optical data [9]. Due to these difficulties, inversion algorithms are very complex and require an extensive mathematical background as we are dealing with ill-posed inverse problems [10].

Therefore, less complex solutions must be proposed as we need techniques that (a) allow for fast data processing in view of current and up-coming LIDAR space missions; (b) offer autonomous data retrieval in view of serious lack of experts in this research field; and (c) provide us with ways of exploiting the information content of these highly complex data sets in an optimum way. Using synthetic optical data, authors in [9] have developed a computational model using Artificial Neural Networks (ANNs) [11] to estimate the effective radius of particles (r_{eff}) and the complex refractive index from combinations of extinction (α) and backscatter (β) coefficients. Specifically, these authors use values of α and β at different wavelengths ($\lambda = 355$, 532 and 1064 nm). These wavelengths are currently used by most of the LIDAR system in the world for the investigation of particulate pollution in the atmosphere. Most notably and in view of advantages not further detailed in this contribution, there has been a push for emitting all three wavelengths simultaneously in the past 20 years. Five combinations of α and β were tested, resulting in finding the most suitable one which uses the values of α at $\lambda = 355$ and 532 nm (α_{355} and α_{532}) and the values of β at $\lambda = 355$, 532 and 1064 nm (β_{355}, β_{532} and β_{1064}). For technical reasons the measurement of α at 1064 nm has become possible just recently. The quality of these data, however, still needs to be improved before tests with this extended set of $\beta + \alpha$ data can be carried out. Moreover, ANNs were evaluated for three different size ranges of effective radii, that is, particles with r_{eff} between 10–100 nm, 110–250 nm and 260–500 nm, respectively. This separation was performed by hand due to two reasons: (a) to limit the computation time and (b) to separate particles according to their nature. Without going into further details particles in these three different size ranges have different effect on climate change and human health.

The aim of this work is to investigate whether we can develop a computational method based on ML techniques which can first classify particles in to the three categories, then, can estimate particle properties within each category, or not. In addition, we look for a model with less computational cost than the one proposed in [9].

2   Data Description

The dataset is the synthetic one used in [9], which was generated using a Mie scattering algorithm [12]. It contains 1,665,343 particles. According to the three ranges of r_{eff}, there are 330,480 particles with a radius between 10 nm and 100 nm, 503,155 samples with a radius between 110 nm and 250 nm and 831,708 particles with a radius between 260 nm and 500 nm.

The following information for each *particle size distribution* can be found:

- Extinction and backscatter coefficients at different wavelengths (355, 532 and 1064 nm). As in [9], the best combination of α and β will be used (α_{355}, α_{532}, β_{355}, β_{532} and β_{1064}).

- Mode width, from 1.4 to 2.5 in step of 0.1. The mode width is the geometrical standard deviation of the theoretical model that describes in an approximate manner the shape (number concentration versus particle size) of naturally occurring atmospheric size distributions. This shape, referred to as logarithmic-normal can be described as a Gauss distribution if particle radius is plotted on a logarithmic scale. More details can be found in e.g. [13]. The total number of particles in the atmosphere can be modeled by a sum of sets (distributions) according to the radius. Particle size distributions in the atmosphere can be described by 5–6 different modes. Each mode has its own mean radius (or alternatively we can also use mode radius) which is the value where the size distribution reaches its maximum value) and the mode width. In the present case we simplified our simulations in the sense that we did not use combinations of these modes in order to cover the vast size range of particles from a few nanometers to several tens of micrometers. In this first set of studies we mimicked these naturally-occurring multimodal size distributions by the use of single-mode logarithmic-normal (log-normal) distributions which not only cover the relevant particle radius range but result in sufficiently realistic optical properties as well. Furthermore, effective radius is a commonly used number in climate modeling. It reduced the complexity of size distribution information from *mean radius and mode width* (in each mode) to a single number. Alternatively effective radius can also be used for each individual mode. Optical properties of particle size distributions described in terms of effective radius are sufficiently close to optical properties of the underlying size distribution when used in modeling.
- Mean radius (nm), from 10 nm to 500 nm in step size of 10.
- Real (from 1.2 to 2 in step size of 0.025) and imaginary part (from 0 to −0.1 in step size of $9.99 \cdot 10^{-6}$) of the complex refractive index. This index indicates the attenuation suffered by light when passing through a particle.

Figure 1 shows how α and β vary with respect to λ for a mode width equal to 1.4. Looking at this figure, the reader can note that α has quite similar values at the different wavelengths, while β decreases as the wavelength increases. It must be said that similar behavior is observed in the rest of the mode widths (from 1.5 to 2.5). It can be seen that the backscatter coefficient increases as the effective radius increases. Those variations are larger for higher mode widths. Similar observations can be found in the variations of α.

Furthermore, the variation of α and β across the particle effective radius in different width modes are also investigated. Figures 2 and 3 show the variation of β in two different width modes, 2.0 and 2.5, namely. It can be seen that the backscatter coefficient increases as the effective radius increases. These variations are larger when the value of the mode width is higher. Similar observations can also be found in the variations of α.

To determine which ML techniques can be applied to the classification and estimation stages, first Principal Component Analysis (PCA) has been applied. Figure 4 shows a PCA plot of the original synthetic data. It can be seen that the class of 110–250 nm overlaps with the class of 10–100 nm and the class of 260–500 nm, but the class of 10–100 nm and the class of 260–500 nm do not overlap between them.

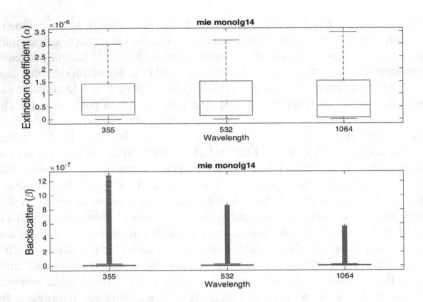

Fig. 1. Variation of α and β in mode width 1.4 at the different values of λ.

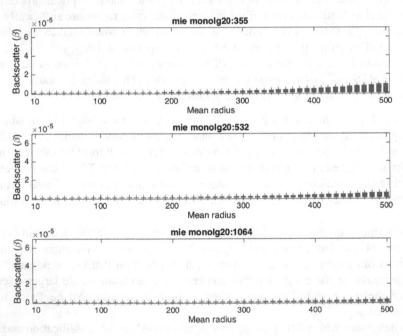

Fig. 2. Variation of β with respect to effective radius in mode width equal to 2.0.

According to Fig. 4, k-NN [14] can be considered as a solution because the three classes are not strongly overlapped. In addition, Extreme Learning Machine (ELM) [15] has been chosen to be a potential solution since this deep learning solution

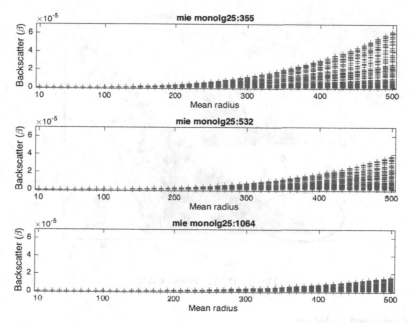

Fig. 3. Variation of β with respect to effective radius in mode width equal to 2.5.

uses a similar ANNs architecture to the one used in [9] and it can have a lower computational cost.

3 Retrieval of Microphysical Parameters

The estimation of microphysical parameters using ANNs was addressed in [9]. Due to the computational cost and the nature of particles, this estimation was performed in three different ranges of particle sizes separately. Taking this into account, we propose two solutions in this paper. The first one is a single regression solution, which uses an ML technique to estimate microphysical parameters for all the particles together. This technique must outperform ANNs in terms of accuracy. The second one includes two steps: (1) a classification that will separate particles into the three classes and then (2) a regression that will estimate microphysical parameters.

3.1 Single Regression Solution

In work [9], a Multi-Layer Perceptron (MLP) with one hidden layer was used to estimate microphysical parameters. Specifically, different configurations of MLPs (training algorithms, number of neurons in the hidden layer, activation functions) were tested. They concluded that the most suitable MLP contains five neurons in the hidden layer and uses the Levenberg Marquardt training algorithm. In this sense, we have implemented the same MLP to be compared with ELM and k-NN both in terms of accuracy and computational cost.

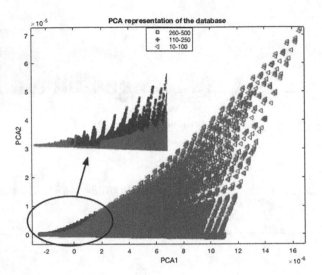

Fig. 4. PCA2 versus PCA1.

3.2   Combined Solution

Figure 5 shows a flow diagram of this combined solution. It can be seen that five-feature vectors are classified into three classes according to r_{eff} first. Then one single regression estimation model is trained within each class. In both classification and estimation stages, the suitability of using ELM and K-NN will be evaluated. The detailed solution is given as follows:

1. The whole dataset has been split into training (75%) and test (25%) sets.
2. Training a classification model using the training set.
3. The test set has been split into the three classes.
4. Within each class, a regression model is trained.
5. Finally, the regression models in step 4 were used to estimate microphysical parameters on the test set.

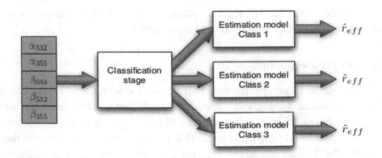

Fig. 5. Scheme of the full solution combining classification and regression estimation.

4   Experiments

In this section the results of both solutions are provided. To evaluate the classification solution, precision, recall and F1-score [16] are calculated for each class since the three classes are imbalanced. To test the suitability of each microphysical parameter estimation solution, the Root Mean Square Error (RMSE) has been used. The computational cost of each technique is evaluated with CPU time.

4.1   Single Regression Solution

In Table 1, ELM and k-NN are compared with the MLP configuration in the previous work, when all the particles are analyzed together. For the MLP, the whole dataset has been split into training (65%), validation (15%) (where the validation set is used to control overfitting) and test (25%) sets while for k-NN and ELM, the dataset has been split into training (75%) and test (25%). Note that the results for the different classes are also extracted from the total results and shown in the table.

Due to the space limit, only the results for the best configuration of each method are presented in the table. For instance, the methodology based on k-NN has been tested for different number of neighbours (1, 3, 4, 5, 7, 11, 15, 19, 29 and 39), resulting in k = 1 being the best choice. In the case of ELM, different activation functions (sigmoid, sine or hard limit) and number of neurons in the hidden layer (N = 2, 3, 4, 5, 7, 10, 20, 30, 50, 75, 100, 150, 200 and 300) have been tested. Sigmoid function and N = 300 achieve the best results.

Looking at Table 1, it is clear that k-NN produces the best results (the lowest values of RMSE) for all the parameters and across all class of particles.

Table 1. RMSE obtained by MLP [9], ELM and k-NN based solutions when r_{eff}, real and imaginary part of the complex index are estimated.

Param.	Method	Whole data	10–100 nm	110–250 nm	260–500 nm
r_{eff}	*MLP [9]*	43.40	14.51	37.97	53.03
	kNN (k = 1)	**31.18**	**6.17**	**27.80**	**38.24**
	ELM (N = 300)	44.37	15.29	39.82	53.74
Real part	*MLP [9]*	0.15	0.19	0.14	0.14
	kNN (k = 1)	**0.08**	**0.13**	**0.07**	**0.07**
	ELM (N = 300)	0.19	0.23	0.17	0.18
Imag. part	*MLP [9]*	0.18	0.25	0.16	0.15
	kNN (k = 1)	**0.08**	**0.10**	**0.09**	**0.06**
	ELM (N = 300)	0.26	0.29	0.27	0.26

Another aspect to be considered is the computational cost associated with each solution. In some applications, study of the atmospheric pollution must be in real-time and so, it is important to have fast algorithms. Bearing this in mind, Table 2 shows the mean values of CPU times of each solution for training and test. These experiments have been carried out on a computer with a 2.8 GHz Intel Core i7 processor and 8 Gb RAM.

Table 2. Mean values of CPU time (s) associated with MLP [9], ELM and k-NN based solutions.

	MLP [9]	k-NN	ELM
Training	753.86	7.25	181.79
Test	0.44	3.00	5.29

It is clear that the solution based on k-NNs is less expensive in terms of CPU time when training. In test, the MLP needs less time but it is less accurate obtaining parameters. In the case of ELM, larger values of CPU time are required and it achieves worst RMSE values. For these reasons, larger number of neurons have not been studied with ELM.

4.2   Combined Solution

As it is shown in Fig. 5, the combined solution allows us to split particles into the three classes (10–100 nm, 110–250 nm, 260–500 nm) before estimating parameters. At the classification stage, MLP, k-NN and ELM based classifiers have been studied with k-NN giving the highest accuracy (96.09%) when k = 3. Since classes are unbalanced, precision, recall and F1-scores are also provided for each class in Table 3.

Table 3. Precision, recall and F1-scores obtained by the solution based on k-NNs (k = 3) for each particle class.

Class	Precision (%)	Recall (%)	F1-score
Class 1 (10–100 nm)	98.76	97.69	0.98
Class 2 (110–250 nm)	93.63	93.43	0.94
Class 3 (260–500 nm)	96.52	97.07	0.97

Very good results are achieved, the worst being for class 2, what makes sense, since it overlaps with the rest of the classes (Fig. 5).

Once particles in the test set have been separated using k-NN, the estimation models must be applied. Obtained RMSE scores are presented in Table 4.

It can be seen from this table, the combined solution based on k-NN achieves the best results for all the classes and microphysical parameters. If we compare these results with those in Table 1, we can see that in general the combined method performs better or similar to the single regression solution when the classification stage has been applied previously. Moreover, it shows ELM performs much better after classification is done first, that is, it performs better within each class. As for the computational cost, similar conclusions as those from Table 2 can be made.

Table 4. RMSE obtained by MLP [9], ELM and k-NN based solutions when r_{eff}, real and imaginary part of the complex index are estimated for combined solution.

Param.	Method	10–100 nm	110–250 nm	260–500 nm
r_{eff}	MLP [9]	10.56	30.29	51.17
	kNN (k = 1)	**5.86**	**27.83**	**37.82**
	ELM (N = 300)	11.01	32.38	50.79
Real Part	MLP [9]	0.22	0.16	0.17
	kNN (k = 1)	**0.09**	**0.07**	**0.07**
	ELM (N = 300)	0.21	0.15	0.17
Imag. Part	MLP [9]	0.27	0.27	0.15
	kNN (k = 1)	**0.06**	**0.08**	**0.07**
	ELM (N = 300)	0.24	0.25	0.23

5   Discussion and Conclusions

Estimating microphysical parameters from optical data can be done using ML techniques. [9] is a very interesting paper and from it, two objectives have been met in our work. Firstly, we provide a solution that produces lower RMSE and computational cost when estimating microphysical parameters. Secondly, a new combined solution, which produces high accuracy at the classification stage, has been implemented.

References

1. Stocker, T.F., et al.: Climate change 2013: the physical science basis. Intergovernmental panel on climate change, working group I contribution to the IPCC fifth assessment report (AR5), Cambridge, UK and New York, NY, USA, p. 1535 (2013)
2. Ansmann, A., Müller, D.: Lidar and atmospheric aerosol particles. In: Weitkamp, C. (ed.) Lidar, pp. 105–141. Springer, New York (2005). https://doi.org/10.1007/0-387-25101-4_4
3. Ansmann, A., Riebesell, M., Weitkamp, C.: Measurement of atmospheric aerosol extinction profiles with a Raman lidar. Opt. Lett. **15**, 746–748 (1990)
4. Veselovskii, I., Kolgotin, A., Griaznov, V., Müller, D., Wandinger, U., Whiteman, N.D.: Inversion with regularization for the retrieval of tropospheric aerosol parameters from multiwavelength lidar sounding. Appl. Opt. **41**(18), 3685–3699 (2002)
5. Müller, D., Wandinger, U., Ansmann, A.: Microphysical particle parameters from extinction and backscatter lidar data by inversion with regularization: simulation. Appl. Opt. **38**, 2358–2368 (1999)
6. Böckmann, C., Mironova, I., Müller, D., Schneidenbach, L., Nessler, R.: Microphysical aerosol parameters from multiwavelength lidar. J. Opt. Soc. Am. A **22**, 518–528 (2005)
7. Kolgotin, A., Müller, D.: Theory of inversion with two-dimensional regularization: profiles of microphysical particle properties derived from multiwavelength lidar measurements. Appl. Opt. **47**, 4472–4490 (2008)
8. Müller, D., Kolgotin, A., Mattis, I., Petzold, A., Stohl, A.: Vertical profiles of microphysical particle properties derived from inversion with two-dimensional regularization of multi-wavelength Raman lidar data: experiment. Appl. Opt. **50**, 2069–2079 (2011)

9. Mamun, M.M., Müller, D.: Retrieval of Intensive aerosol microphysical parameters from multiwavelength Raman/HSRL lidar: feasibility study with artificial neural networks. Neural Netw. Atmos. Meas. Tech. Discuss. 7 (2016)
10. Hadamard, J.: Bull. Univ. Princeton **13**, 49 (1902)
11. Schalkoff, R.J.: Artificial Neural Networks, vol. 1. McGraw-Hill, New York (1997)
12. Bohren, C., Huffman, D.: Absorption and Scattering of Light by Small Particles. Wiley, Hoboken (1998). Wiley science paperback series
13. Hinds, C.W.: Aerosol Technology: Properties, Behavior, and Measurement of Airborne Particles, 2nd edn., p. 504, January 1999. ISBN 978-0-471-19410-1
14. Peterson, L.E.: K-nearest neighbor. Scholarpedia **4**(2), 1883 (2009)
15. Huang, G.-B., Zhu, Q.-Y., Siew, C.-K.: Extreme learning machine: theory and applications. Neurocomputing **70**(1–3), 489–501 (2006)
16. Goutte, C., Gaussier, E.: A probabilistic interpretation of precision, recall and F-score, with implication for evaluation. In: Losada, David E., Fernández-Luna, Juan M. (eds.) ECIR 2005. LNCS, vol. 3408, pp. 345–359. Springer, Heidelberg (2005). https://doi.org/10.1007/978-3-540-31865-1_25

Communication Style - An Analysis from the Perspective of Automated Learning

Adriana Mihaela Coroiu[✉], Alina Delia Călin, and Maria Nuțu

Department of Computer Science, Faculty of Mathematics and Computer
Science, Babeş-Bolyai University, 400084 Cluj-Napoca, Romania
{adrianac, alinacalin, maria.nutu}@cs.ubbcluj.ro

Abstract. This paper is intended to bring added value in the interdisciplinary
domains of computer science and psychology, more precisely and in particular,
automated learning and applied psychology. We present automated learning
techniques for classification of new instances, new observations of a patient,
taking into account the particularities of the attributes describing each of these
observations. Specifically, information collected by applying a questionnaire for
communication style (non-assertive style, manipulative style, aggressive style
and assertive style) was analyzed.

Through these experiments, we have tried to determine which of the classification models are best suited to be applied in specific situations and, given the
type of attributes that make up the instances of the dataset, what kind of preprocessing methods can be applied to get the most qualitative results using the
selected classification models: Decision Tree Based Model, Support Vector
Machine, Random Forest, Classification based on instances (k-NN), and
Logistic Regression. Standard metrics were used to evaluate the performance of
each of the analyzed classification patterns: accuracy, sensitivity, precision, and
specificity.

Keywords: Multi-classification model · Prediction · Communication style

1 Introduction

The use of the techniques offered by the Artificial Intelligence field becomes a
necessity every day. One of the reasons that support this need may be that intelligent
techniques can bring added value, even help in people's work. Lately, the number of
areas of applicability of these techniques has increased.

Classification is an automated learning technique, particularly supervised learning
that requires labeled training data to generate rules. This is a two-stage process [14].
The first stage is the learning stage in which the training set is analyzed and new
classification rules are generated, and the second step is the classification itself, in
which the testing set is split into appropriate classes based on the rules established in
the previous step.

Within this classification process, the classes are defined based on the attribute
values of the instances in the datasets. In view of these considerations, the classification

V. Kůrková et al. (Eds.): ICANN 2018, LNCS 11139, pp. 589–597, 2018.
https://doi.org/10.1007/978-3-030-01418-6_58

process can be of several types: binary classification, multi-class classification, multi-label classification and multi-task classification [3, 14].

In this article, we will consider studying the multiple classification (or multi-classification). Multi-classification assumes that each instance belongs to only one labeled class of a total of n labeled classes (with $n > 2$).

The classification models analyzed in our experiments are: Decision Tree Based Modeling Model, Support Vector Machine (SVM) based classification model, Random forest classification based on a Random forest, Classification based on instances (k-NN), the logistic regression classification model.

Measures that quantify the performance of each of the analyzed classification patterns are some of the standard metrics to evaluate the quality of a model: accuracy, precision, sensitivity, and specificity.

The analyzed data set is a set of data in the phycology domain, consisting of 220 instances and 63 mixed attributes. The set contains information on how people communicate. The target variable of this dataset is the communication style appropriate to each of the individuals analyzed, based on the given responses.

2 State of the Art

Moving beyond the initial focus of psychology of studying and explaining human behaviors, many researchers emphasize the need to advance further into predicting future behaviors. In this regard machine learning can be a very accurate tool, proving these concepts and helping answer important research questions from psychology [18].

In what concerns communication styles, it is of a great social impact to predict accurately its impact in diverse socio-economic fields. For example, charity fundraising is influenced by the interaction of both helper and receiver, especially if the receiver is considered agreeable [19].

A research study examining the feasibility of using machine learning for predicting psychological wellbeing indices [20] has obtained promising results using Support Vector Regression (0.76), Generalized Regression Neural Network (0.80), and k Nearest Neighbor Regression (0.70), but poor results with Multi-layer Perceptron, Given the impact of stress on human behavior, Pandey et al. [22] use machine learning to predict stress based on heart rate and age using Logistic Regression, Support Vector Machine (SVM), VF -15 and Naïve Bayes, with results up to 68% for SVM.

3 Methods and Experiments

All experiments follow next stages:
Stage 1:   Data preparation;
Stage 2:   Training the classification model;
Stage 3:   Evaluating the classification model.

3.1   Dataset Descriptions

A. Psychological Perspective Over Dataset Characteristics

The data analyzed in this experiment were obtained by applying the Questionnaire for the Communication Style (QCS) analysis [16] to a group of 220 people. The group is homogeneous, from the perspective of age and the living environment, all the persons questioned belonging to the urban environment.

The questionnaire for communication style analysis consists of a set of 60 questions, whose answers can be yes/no (or true/false) [16].

The participants of this study were informed and they agreed to the fact of using, in research purposes, the results of the presented questionnaire.

Each of the 60 questions is part of a category of communication style as follows: 1, 7, 15, 16, 17, 25, 26, 35, 36, 37, 50, 51, 52, 59, 60 for the non-assertive style; in the category of aggressive style we have the questions 4, 6, 10, 11, 20, 21, 28, 29, 30, 39, 40, 48, 49, 55, 56 and in the category of manipulative style are questions 3, 5, 9, 12, 13, 19, 22, 31, 32, 41, 42, 46, 47, 54, 57, and finally in the assertive style category we have the following questions: 2, 8, 14, 18, 23, 24, 27, 33, 34, 38, 43, 44, 45, 53, 58.

As a result, this questionnaire highlights four different styles of communication: non-assertive style, manipulating style, aggressive style and assertive style.

Besides the answers that make up the questionnaire, the people involved also quantified their stress level, referring to three possible degrees: low, medium, high.

This stress-related information attempts to highlight whether there is a link between the level of stress and the style of communication of a particular person. The applied questionnaire was proposed by Marcus [21].

B. Computer science perspective over dataset characteristics

Taking into consideration all of the above informative aspects, translating them into a form conducive to computer-based analysis, we have:

- We have a set of data that contains 220 instances (observations) with the following characteristics: a discrete attribute of the nominal type (gender of the person), a numerical attribute (age), a discrete type of ordinal type (the level of stress) and the 60 binary attributes (true/false) corresponding to the questionnaire.
- Each of the 220 instances of the dataset belongs to one of the four possible classes (non-assertive style class, manipulator style class, aggressive style class, and assertive style class).
- Consequently, we have a mixed data set divided into four existing classes.

With all this information, our goal in this research is first and foremost to determine whether there is a link between the attribute level of stress and the style of communication of a particular person, and secondly to determine in a way more precisely the classification of a new data instance. The 4 classes corresponding to the four styles of communication (non-assertive style, manipulative style, aggressive style and assertive style) lead to the idea of multi-classification.

4   Classification Methods Used

The purpose is to determine a classification model that finds the relationship between the attribute associated with the class, in our case the communication style, and the other existing attributes. This constructed model must be able to determine subsequently the class to which a new instance belongs.

The used models in our experiments are:

- Decision tree-based classification model (DT) [5]
- Support Vector Machine based classification model (SVM) [9, 10]
- Random forest classification model (RF) [12]
- The instance-based classification model (kNN) [4, 8]
- The Bayesian-based classification model (NB) [7, 13]
- The logistic regression classification model (mLR) reproduces the relationship between a set of independent variables x_i (categorical, continuous) and a dependent variable (nominal, binary) Y.

The multinomial logistic regression model (also known as multinomial logistic regression - or discrete choice model) is a generalization of the logistic model, accepting that the dependent variable Y has more than two values. Assuming that the variable Y has as possible values the elements of the unordered set $\{1, ..., g\}$. The multinomial logistic model assumes that the probability of Y to be equal to s in the observation i depends on the values of the variables $x_{i1}, ..., x_{ip}$ by [6, 11]:

$$P(Y_i = s) = \frac{e^{\eta_{is}}}{\sum_{t=1}^{g} e^{\eta_{it}}} \tag{1}$$

5   Data Preprocessing

The dataset analyzed in this article contains mixed types of data, therefore we have considered some preprocessing operations, detailed below.

First, for the age attribute, we considered the preprocessing operation called standardization to eliminate the influence of different scales relative to the other attributes.

Second, it was important to consider how to calculate distances (for dissimilarity/similarity measures), considering that we had different types of attributes, as follows:

- *For nominal attributes*, the distance between the values of an attribute is considered 0 if the values are equal and 1 if they are different. There are no other relationships between attribute values and there are no intermediate distances between 0 and 1.
- *For ordinal attributes*, we may consider equally distributed values between 0 and 1. For example, in the case of the three stress levels {Low, Medium, High}, we used the transformation: *Low = 0, Medium = 0.5,* and *High = 1.* Therefore, the calculation of the distances is the absolute value of the difference between these numerical values, such as: *d (Low, High) = 1, d (Low, Medium) = d (Medium, High) = 0.5.*

- *For numerical attributes*, the distance is the absolute value of the difference between the normalized values of the attributes.

In the case of some missing attributes, we've replaced those attributes with the average of the existing attributes, and in terms of attribute hierarchy, we did not apply any prioritization methods for these experiments.

Another preprocessing step, the method of dividing the data into subsets, was done taking into account cross-validation, a method which involves the division of the data k times ($k-1$ sub-sets for training and 1 sub-set for validation). In this context, the size of a sub-set is equal to the size of the set divided by k and the performance is given by the average of the k executions [15].

6   Evaluation of the Classification Models

The quality of a classifier from the perspective of the correct identification of a class is measured using information in the confusion matrix containing [1, 4]:

- The number of data correctly classified as belonging to the interest class: True positive cases (TP)
- The number of data correctly classified as not belonging to the class of interest: True negative cases (TN)
- The number of data incorrectly classified as belonging to the interest class: False positive cases (FP)
- The number of data incorrectly classified as not belonging to the interest class: False negative cases (FN)

6.1   Metrics Used for Evaluation

The metrics that measure the quality of the evaluation used in this article are described blow.

Classification accuracy is determined by the ratio of the number of correctly classified instances to the total number of classified instances [2].

$$Accuracy = \frac{TP + TN}{TP + TN + FP + FN} \tag{2}$$

The sensitivity metric is given by the ratio between the number of correctly classified data as belonging to the class of interest and the sum of the number of data correctly classified as belonging to the interest class and the number of data incorrectly classified as not belonging to the class of interest.

$$Sensitivity = \frac{TP}{TP + FN} \tag{3}$$

The metric of specificity is given by the ratio of the number of data correctly classified as not belonging to the interest class and the sum of the number of correctly classified data as not belonging to the interest class and the number of data incorrectly classified as belonging to the class of interest.

$$Specificity = \frac{TN}{TN + FP} \qquad (4)$$

The precision metric is given by the ratio between the number of data correctly classified as belonging to the class of interest and the sum of the number of data correctly classified as belonging to the interest class and the number of data incorrectly classified as belonging to the class of interest [17]:

$$Precision = \frac{TP}{TP + FP} \qquad (5)$$

6.2   Results and Discussion

The value of the accuracy metric for each of the classification models analyzed in our experiments are shown in Fig. 1.

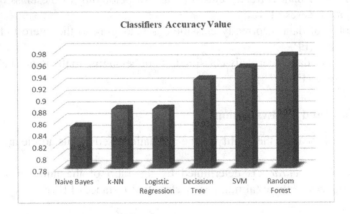

Fig. 1. Accuracy values for the analysed models

Both the Random Forest and Support Vector based algorithms are non-parametric models (their complexity increases as the number of instances used for training increases) [15]. That being said, the training of a non-parametric model is costlier, from a computational perspective, compared to a generalized linear model (k-NN, Naive-Bayes, in our case). However, the added benefit of the two non-parametric models used is the fact that they allow working with several classes immediately.

A disadvantage of the algorithm based on the Support Vectors is that the results are sometimes more difficult to interpret, but in our case the evaluation metric is the accuracy, which helps us overcome this shortcoming.

In contrast, Decision Trees allow an interpretation of the results in a much simpler and faster way, and it is additionally a fact that it is one of the classification models that behave best when it comes to ordinal and/or mixed attributes, as in the dataset analyzed in our experiments.

The Logistic Regression (multinomial logistic regression in our case) is another well-known and used classification model. In order to better outline the results, we also used it, but the accuracy obtained was not as good as the other classification models used: a value of 0.88. One of the reasons that led to such a result is that the attributes of the instances should be linearly separable, which was not true in our case. This shortcoming is, however, overcome in the case of the Support Vector based classification, which yielded an accuracy of 0.95.

The different values obtained for each of the analyzed classification models fall within the standard ranges accepted in the research literature. They also come to confirm what determines our accuracy metric; namely that for the type of data analyzed by us (mixed) with such dimensions, the best classification models are Random Forest and Support Vector Machine.

The value of the other metrics whose value was calculated is highlighted in Table 1:

Table 1. Results achieved

Metrics\classifier models	Naive Bayes	k-NN	Logistic regression	Decision tree	SVM	Random forest
Sensitivity	0.75	0.73	**0.77**	**0.78**	0.74	0.77
Specificity	0.68	**0.72**	0.62	0.63	0.62	0.63
Precision	0.81	0.79	0.81	0.78	**0.82**	**0.81**

7   Conclusions and Future Directions

In this paper, we approached an interdisciplinary topic between psychology and computer science, more particular applied cognitive psychology and machine learning.

We investigated the behavior of 6 learning classification models for a data set gathered based on QCS. We applied these models for a training data set and then we used the results achieved within testing data set in order to select the best of the learning models. Once we have established model with the best accuracy value, we can apply this model to new instances of data, to a new item unclassified yet.

This work provides us a baseline to other future constructions related to this domain. We treated here the classification task, an approach useful to psychology area, and as far as we know, an innovative one in analysis of communication style from machine learning perspective.

As new development directions, we propose to apply other classification methods that increase the value of accuracy metrics, to be more robust in relation to the data type (regardless of preprocessing methods applied) and obviously, increase the sample size of people questioned for a better generalization of results.

References

1. Amiri, A., Rafe, V.: Hybrid algorithm for detecting diabetes. Int. Res. J. Appl. Basic Sci. **8** (12), 2347–2353 (2014)
2. Bansal, A., Agarwal, R., Sharma, R.: Determining diabetes using iris recognition system. Int. J. Diabetes Dev. Countries **35**(4), 432–438 (2015)
3. Ding, S., Zhao, H., Zhang, Y., Xu, X., Nie, R.: Extreme learning machine: algorithm, theory and applications. Artif. Intell. Rev. **44**(1), 103–115 (2015)
4. Dwivedi, A.K.: Performance evaluation of different machine learning techniques for prediction of heart disease. Neural Comput. Appl. **29**, 1–9 (2016)
5. Dwivedi A.K., Chouhan, U.: On support vector machine ensembles for classification of recombination breakpoint regions in Saccharomyces cerevisiae. Int. J. Comput. Appl. **108** (13) (2014)
6. Dwivedi, A.K., Chouhan, U.: Genome-scale classification of recombinant and non-recombinant HIV-1 sequences using artificial neural network ensembles. Curr. Sci. **111** (5), 853 (2016)
7. Farran, B., Channanath, A.M., Behbehani, K., Thanaraj, T.A.: Predictive models to assess risk of type 2 diabetes, hypertension and comorbidity: machine-learning algorithms and validation using national health data from Kuwait—a cohort study. BMJ Open **3**(5), e002457 (2013)
8. Gadodiya, S., Chandak, M.B.: Combined approach for improving accuracy of prototype selection for k-NN classifier. Compusoft **3**(5), 808 (2014)
9. Goswami, S.K., et al.: Antioxidant potential and ability of phloroglucinol to decrease formation of advanced glycation. Sex Med. **4**(2), e104–e112 (2016)
10. Goswami, S.K., Vishwanath, M., Gangadarappa, S.K., Razdan, R., Inamdar, M.N.: Efficacy of ellagic acid and sildenafil in diabetes-induced sexual dysfunction. Pharmacogn. Mag. **10** (39), 581 (2014)
11. Hajmeer, M., Basheer, I.: Comparison of logistic regression and neural network-based classifiers for bacterial growth. Food Microbiol. **20**(1), 43–55 (2003)
12. Heydari, M., Teimouri, M., Heshmati, Z., Alavinia, S.M.: Comparison of various classification algorithms in the diagnosis of type 2 diabetes in Iran. Int. J. Diabet. Dev. Countries **36**, 1–7 (2015)
13. Maldonado, H., Leija, L., Vera, A.: Selecting a computational classifier to develop a clinical decision support system (CDSS). In: 2015 12th International Conference on Electrical Engineering, Computing Science and Automatic Control (CCE), pp. 1–3. IEEE (2015)
14. Nikam, S.S.: A comparative study of classification techniques in data mining algorithms. Orient. J. Comput. Sci. Technol. **8**(1), 13–19 (2015)
15. Rodriguez-Galiano, V., Sanchez-Castillo, M., Chica-Olmo, M., Chica-Rivas, M.: Machine learning predictive models for mineral prospectivity: an evaluation of neural networks, random forest, regression trees and support vector machines. Ore Geol. Rev. **71**, 804–818 (2015)
16. Ailincăi, A., Cleminte, A., Cluci, A., et al.: Analysis of the working style of supervisors (Analiza stilului de lucru al supervizorului). Seminary Sandu, A. Group supervision in social services (Supervizare de grup în asistența social) (2010)
17. Vapnik, V.N., Vapnik, V.: Statistical Learning Theory, vol. 2. Wiley, New York (1998)
18. Yarkoni, T., Westfall, J.: Choosing prediction over explanation in psychology: lessons from machine learning. Perspect. Psychol. Sci. **12**(6), 1100–1122 (2017)

19. Yarkoni, T., Ashar, Y.K., Wager, T.D.: Interactions between donor agreeableness and recipient characteristics in predicting charitable donation and positive social evaluation. PeerJ **3**, e1089 (2015). https://doi.org/10.7717/peerj.1089
20. Park, J., Kim, K., Kwon, O.: Comparison of machine learning algorithms to predict psychological wellness indices for ubiquitous healthcare system design. In: Innovative Design and Manufacturing (ICIDM), pp. 263–269 (2014). https://doi.org/10.1109/idam.2014.6912705
21. Marcus, S.: Empathy and the Teacher-Student Relationship (Empatia şi relaţia profesor-elev). Academia R.S.R. Publishing House, Bucharest (1987)
22. Pandey, P.S.: Machine learning and IoT for prediction and detection of stress. In: Computational Science and Its Applications (ICCSA), pp. 1–5. IEEE (2017). https://doi.org/10.1109/iccsa.2017. 8000018

Directional Data Analysis for Shape Classification

Adrián Muñoz[✉] and Alberto Suárez

Computer Science Department, Universidad Autónoma de Madrid,
C. Francisco Tomás y Valiente 11, 28049 Madrid, Spain
adrian.munnozp@estudiante.uam.es, alberto.suarez@uam.es
http://www.eps.uam.es/~gaa

Abstract. In this work we address the problem of learning from images to perform grouping and classification of shapes. The key idea is to encode the instances available for learning in the form of directional data. In two dimensions, the figure to be categorized is characterized by the distribution of the directions of the normal unit vectors along the contour of the object. This directional characterization is used to extract characteristics based on metrics defined in the space of circular distributions. These characteristics can then be used to categorize the encoded shapes. The usefulness of the representation proposed is illustrated in the problem of clustering and classification of otolith shapes.

Keywords: Directional data · Shape representation
Shape clustering · Shape classification

1 Introduction

Automatic induction from complex data that are characterized by functions, graphs, distributions or shapes is one of the important open problems in Machine Learning. In this work we address the task of grouping or classifying objects according to their shapes. A system that automatically discriminates among shapes is useful in numerous domains of application, such as archeology, paleontology, biology, geology, or medicine [10,12,15]. Shape can be defined as an equivalence class that is invariant under a family of transformations, such as translations, scaling, rotations, and small deformations [8].

One of the difficulties of this task is to provide an appropriate characterization of shape that is tractable yet preserves sufficient amounts of information to allow grouping and discrimination. Previous approaches to this problem are representations based on landmarks [11], medial representations [16,20], and others such as probability density functions [14]. In this work we will adopt a functional approach [17] and characterize the shape by the distribution of the normal vectors to the curve (in 2 dimensions) or surface (in 3 dimensions) that delimits

The authors acknowledge financial support from the Spanish Ministry of Economy, Industry and Competitiveness, project TIN2016-76406-P.

V. Kůrková et al. (Eds.): ICANN 2018, LNCS 11139, pp. 598–607, 2018.
https://doi.org/10.1007/978-3-030-01418-6_59

the figure [7]. Alternative functional encodings have been considered in recent investigations [1, 13]. These representations are based on encoding shape the distribution of distances between points within [1] or at the boundary of the object [13]. The focus of this work is on two-dimensional (planar) representations of objects. Nevertheless, the method proposed can be readily extended to higher dimensions using the tools of directional statistics [11]. To encode the distribution of the directions of the normal vectors in two dimensions it is sufficient to store the angles of such vectors at each location on the boundary. These values can be viewed as samples from a random variable defined in $[-\pi, \pi]$. This random variable is characterized by a probability distribution function defined on the circle. Examples of such probability density estimates are depicted in Fig. 1. To build an empirical estimates of these distributions we consider a set of N points sampled at regular intervals along the contour of the figure. At each of these points we compute the direction of the normal to the contour and store the corresponding angles $\{\theta_n\}_{n=1}^{N}$. An empirical estimate of the probability density is given by the histogram of the data using N_{bins} equally spaced bins in $[-\pi, \pi]$. The histogram is scaled so that the area under it is one. Alternatively, a kernel estimator is used to provide a smooth approximation of the density

$$f_{KDE}(\theta; \nu) = \frac{1}{N} \sum_{n=1}^{N} K(\theta - \theta_n; \nu), \tag{1}$$

where $K(\theta; \nu)$ is a periodic normalized kernel (i.e. its integral in $\theta \in [-\pi, \pi]$ is 1), whose characteristic width is $h = 1/\nu$. In this work, the von Mises kernel is used

$$K(\theta; \nu) = \frac{1}{2\pi I_0(\nu)} e^{\nu \cos(\theta)}, \tag{2}$$

where I_0 is the modified Bessel function of the first kind of order 0. For higher dimensions the von Mises-Fisher distribution can be used [4]. The quality of the kernel density estimate depends strongly on the value of this parameter [2, 3, 5, 18]: On the one hand, if the kernel is too narrow, the density estimate will lack stability and exhibit large variance. If, on the other hand, the width is too large, relevant features of the probability density will be smoothed out. In the experimental evaluation performed, $h = \frac{2\pi}{64}$ provides a good compromise between stability and smoothness. Correspondingly, for the histogram density estimate,

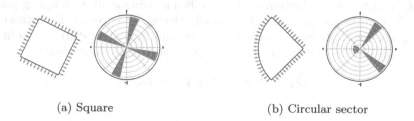

(a) Square   (b) Circular sector

Fig. 1. Empirical probability density for the directional variables in simple figures.

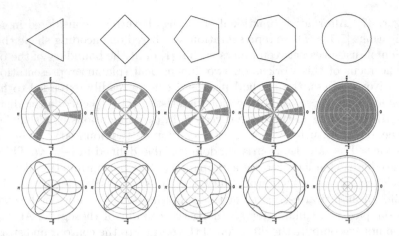

Fig. 2. Characterization of planar geometrical figures (top row) using a scaled histogram (middle row) and kernel density (bottom row) empirical estimates of the probability density of the direction of the normal vectors along the contour of the figure.

$N_{bins} = 64$ bins have been used. Figure 2 displays examples of these estimates for simple geometrical figures. Once the object representations have been characterized by the corresponding probability density estimates, their shapes can be compared using different metrics. To define these metrics, the discretized version of the probability densities $f(\theta)$ and $g(\theta)$ in the circle ($\theta \in [-\pi, \pi]$), at the sampling points $\{\theta_n\}_{n=1}^{N}$ are considered; namely, $\mathbf{f} = \{f_n\}_{n=1}^{N}$, and $\mathbf{g} = \{g_n\}_{n=1}^{N}$, with $f_n \equiv f(\theta_n)$ and $g_n \equiv g(\theta_n)$, respectively. In terms of these discretized versions of the densities, the metrics in Table 1 have been considered. Let F and G be two figures, characterized by $\mathbf{f}$ and $\mathbf{g}$, respectively. The relative orientations of F and G could be different. Therefore, a distance between these figures can be defined as the minimum value of the metric between a rotation of the first density and the second density

$$\hat{D}(F,G) = \min_{n=1,2,\ldots,N} D\left(\mathbf{f}^{[n]}, \mathbf{g}\right) \tag{3}$$

where D is one of the metrics considered and $\mathbf{f}^{[n]} = \{f_n, f_{n+1}, \ldots, f_N, f_1, \ldots, f_{n-1}\}$ is a rotation of the density $\mathbf{f}$. The distance function given by Eq. (3) requires the evaluation of the specified metric for all N sampling points, which is a costly computation. A more effective way to account for rotations is to measure distances with respect to C, the uniform circular distribution in two dimensions (or the uniform distribution on a sphere in 3 dimensions):

$$\tilde{D}(F,G) = |D(F,C) - D(G,C)|. \tag{4}$$

As will be illustrated in the section on empirical evaluation this measure retains sufficient information to provide a reasonably good characterization of shape at a reduced computational cost.

Table 1. Distance functions between the discretized distributions $\mathbf{f} = \{f_n\}_{n=1}^N$, and $\mathbf{g} = \{g_n\}_{n=1}^N$.

Distance	Expression
Manhattan	$L_1(\mathbf{f}, \mathbf{g}) = \sum_{n=1}^N \lvert f_n - g_n \rvert$
Euclidean	$L_2(\mathbf{f}, \mathbf{g}) = \sqrt{\sum_{n=1}^N \lvert f_n - g_n \rvert^2}$
Total variation	$L_\infty(\mathbf{f}, \mathbf{g}) = \max_{n=1,2,\dots,N} \lvert f_n - g_n \rvert$
χ^2	$\chi^2(\mathbf{f}, \mathbf{g}) = \sum_{n=1}^N \frac{\lvert f_n - g_n \rvert^2}{f_n + g_n}$
Hellinger	$H(\mathbf{f}, \mathbf{g}) = \frac{1}{\sqrt{2}} \sqrt{\sum_{n=1}^N \left(\sqrt{f_n} - \sqrt{g_n}\right)^2}$
Earth Mover's	$EMD(\mathbf{f}, \mathbf{g}) = \inf \mathbb{E}\left[\lvert \theta - \theta' \rvert\right]$ where the infimum is taken over all possible joint distributions θ and θ', random variables whose marginals are $\mathbf{f}$ and $\mathbf{g}$, respectively

2   Clustering and Classification of Otoliths

In this section we consider the categorization of otoliths for grouping and identification of fish species. Otoliths are concretions of calcium carbonate and other inorganic salts that are formed by aggregation on a protein matrix in the inner ear of vertebrates [6]. The dataset studied consists of 240 high-contrast images of otoliths for three different families of fish: *labridae* (125 images), *soleidae* (70 images), and *scombridae* (45 images). The images are centered and oriented so the to the frontal part of the otolith appears to the right of the image. This set has been retrieved from the AFORO database (http://www.icm.csic.es/aforo/), which is a an extensive open online repository of data for different fish species. Otoliths in *labridae* family are cuneiform, oval, bullet-shaped, or rectangular. They present a cleavage in the frontal zone, which, in general, is more prominent than in the other fish families. *Soleidae* otoliths are mainly discoidal and elliptic. Their shapes are in general more regular and smooth than in other two families. Finally, otoliths of the *scombridae* family have serrate contours and generally are more elongated [19]. Examples of these otoliths are displayed in Fig. 3. *Labridae* and *soleidae* otoliths present higher shape variability than *scombridae* otoliths, which are typically more regular. In each of the images, the contour of the otolith is retrieved using the *marching squares* algorithm [9] and later rectified so that all figures have the same number of vertices. In the experiments, a number of 64 vertices is considered. This quantization of the contour reduces the variability in the representation and allows to preserve a sufficient amount of detail for an accurate characterization of the shape of the object. The figure is then characterized by sampling a total of $N_{sample} = 1000$ points at regularly spaced intervals along the contour. For each of these sampling points the direction of the normal unitary vector is computed to obtain a sample of the directional variable. For planar figures, it can be represented as the angle that specifies the direction of this normal vector. The probability density of these direction values is then approximated using either a scaled histogram with 64 bins or a KDE estimate that utilizes von Mises kernels of width $h = \frac{2\pi}{64}$. In both cases, the probability density estimates are discretized at $N = 64$ points located at the center of the histogram bins. From the probability density estimates, two different characterizations will be used. In a first characterization, the figures are aligned at the maximum of the corresponding density estimates. The vector of attributes in this *aligned* representation consists in the $N = 64$ values of the corresponding histogram or KDE. A second characterization (labeled *distances*) is by a vector composed of the 6 distances between the corresponding density estimation and the uniform distribution, according to Eq. (4). Both unsupervised (clustering) and supervised (classification) learning tasks are considered. In a first set of experiments, the K-means algorithm is used to group the otoliths into $K = 3$ clusters. The results of this unsupervised learning task are displayed in Table 2. Several conclusions can be drawn from these results. The first one is that the clusters identified when the characterization based on distances to the uniform circular distribution are rather impure. The results are significantly better when the representation based on alignment is used, especially when the kernel density estimates (KDE) are employed. The reason why alignment is useful in these data is because otoliths typically have an oblong shape, with clearly defined axis. In a second set of experiments various k-nearest neighbors (k-NN) models are used to predict the shape of the figure based on different characterizations proposed. First rotationally invariant distance between shapes given by Eq. (3) is employed in the nearest-neighbors algorithm. The distances are computed using one of the six different metrics described in the previous section. The number of neighbors is determined using 3-fold cross-validation within the training data. The range of values explored is $k = 3, 5, \ldots, 13$. In most cases the values selected are either $k = 3$ or $k = 5$. The results are not particularly sensitive to the choice of this parameter. The generalization error is estimated using 10-fold cross-validation over the complete data set. The results of these experiments are summarized in Table 3. In all cases, the predictions are very accurate for all metrics, specially when the smoother kernel density estimation is used. However, because of the minimization step required in computing the distances Eq. (3), the computational cost of this algorithm is high.

In a last set of experiments, as a solution with reduced computational cost, the *aligned* and *distances* representations are employed. For the *distances* representation, neighboring instances are identified using the Euclidean distance of the corresponding vector of attributes. Aligned version will be used to approximate rotationally invariant metrics aligning discretizations according to its maximum value. The generalization error and the optimal number of neighbors are selected by cross validation as in previous experiment. The confusion matrices and cross-validation error estimates for these experiments are displayed in

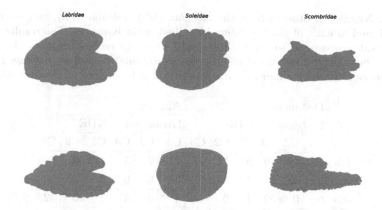

Fig. 3. Examples of *labridae*, *soleidae*, and *scombridae* otoliths. The frontal part of the otolith, which corresponds to the head of the fish, appears on the right of the image.

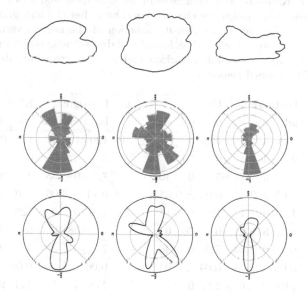

Fig. 4. In the top row of this figure the contours of otoliths of different fish families are shown: *labridae* (left), *soleidae* (middle), and *scombridae* (right). The histogram and kernel density estimates of the directional variables for these figures are displayed in the middle and bottom rows, respectively.

Table 4 for aligned representation and in Table 5. As in the clustering experiment, the accuracy is better when aligned representations are used. The best overall accuracy is obtained when kernel density estimates are used, also when instances are characterized by *distances* representation. As in the previous experiments, the *scombridae* and *soleidae* otoliths are well separated. It is apparent from Fig. 4, that the shapes of *soleidae* and *scombridae* otoliths are markedly different from each other. As a result, the discrimination between items from

Table 2. Number of otoliths from the *labridae* (lab), *soleidae* (sol), and *scombridae* (sco) assigned to each of the 3 clusters identified using K-means. The results on the left-hand side correspond to the 6-dimensional *distances* representations. The results obtained when the 64-dimensional *aligned* representations are used are displayed on the right-hand side. The error indicates the proportion of incorrectly grouped instances.

	Distances						Aligned					
	Histogram			KDE			Histogram			KDE		
	C1	C2	C3	C1	C2	C3	C1	C2	C3	C1	C2	C3
lab	86	20	19	93	11	21	113	7	5	113	6	6
sol	7	63	0	4	66	0	3	67	0	0	70	0
sco	6	0	39	4	0	41	4	0	41	3	0	42
Err	0.22			0.17			0.08			0.06		

Table 3. 10-fold cross-validation estimates of the confusion matrices for otolith classification. The instances, which are characterized by either the histogram or a kernel estimate (KDE) of the probability density function of the normal vectors along the contour of the figure, are categorized as *labridae* (**lab**), *soleidae* (**sol**), and *scombridae* (**sco**) using k-NN with rotationally invariant metrics. The error indicates the proportion of incorrectly grouped instances.

		Histogram			KDE				Histogram			KDE		
		lab	sol	sco	lab	sol	sco		lab	sol	sco	lab	sol	sco
lab	L_1	119	0	6	123	0	2	EMD	120	1	4	124	0	1
sol		2	68	0	0	70	0		3	67	0	0	70	0
sco		8	0	37	5	0	40		7	0	38	4	0	41
Err		0.05 ± 0.04			0.05 ± 0.04				0.11 ± 0.06			0.10 ± 0.06		
lab	L_2	121	0	4	124	0	1	H	119	0	6	123	1	1
sol		3	67	0	0	70	0		2	68	0	0	70	0
sco		9	0	36	5	0	40		7	0	38	5	0	40
Err		0.05 ± 0.04			0.04 ± 0.04				0.06 ± 0.05			0.06 ± 0.05		
lab	L_∞	119	0	6	123	0	2	χ^2	118	1	6	121	2	2
sol		2	68	0	0	70	0		2	68	0	0	70	0
sco		6	0	39	5	0	40		7	0	38	6	0	39
Err		0.05 ± 0.04			0.05 ± 0.04				0.06 ± 0.04			0.06 ± 0.04		

these classes is fairly easy. If fact, they are well separated in all the representations considered. This is not the case for the *labridae* otoliths. Some otoliths from this class present elongated shapes, which are more characteristic of *scombridae*. Others present a circular, more regular shapes, and can be mistaken for instances from the *soleidae* class.

Table 4. 10-fold cross-validation estimates of the confusion matrices for otolith classification. The instances, which are characterized by aligned representations of either the histogram or a kernel estimate (KDE) of the probability density function of the normal vectors along the contour of the figure, are categorized as *labridae* (**lab**), *soleidae* (**sol**), and *scombridae* (**sco**) using K-NN. The error indicates the proportion of incorrectly grouped instances.

		Histogram			KDE				Histogram			KDE		
		lab	sol	sco	lab	sol	sco		lab	sol	sco	lab	sol	sco
lab	L₁	116	7	2	121	4	0	EMD	113	10	2	122	3	0
sol		7	62	1	2	68	0		9	61	0	3	67	0
sco		7	0	38	8	0	37		6	0	39	8	0	37
Err		0.10 ± 0.04			0.06 ± 0.05				0.11 ± 0.06			0.06 ± 0.03		
lab	L₂	117	6	2	122	3	0	H	116	6	3	120	5	0
sol		10	59	1	4	66	0		10	60	0	2	68	0
sco		10	0	35	7	0	38		9	0	36	7	0	38
Err		0.12 ± 0.06			0.06 ± 0.04				0.12 ± 0.06			0.06 ± 0.07		
lab	L∞	116	7	2	121	3	1	χ²	114	8	3	120	5	0
sol		8	62	0	3	67	0		10	59	1	3	67	0
sco		11	0	34	7	0	38		10	0	35	8	0	37
Err		0.12 ± 0.05			0.06 ± 0.05				0.13 ± 0.06			0.07 ± 0.04		

Table 5. Confusion matrices and 10-fold cross-validation errors for the classification of *labridae* (lab), *soleidae* (sol), and *scombridae* (sco) otoliths using a characterization based on distances to the uniform circular distribution (*distances*). The error indicates the proportion of incorrectly grouped instances.

	Histogram			KDE		
	lab	sol	sco	lab	sol	sco
lab	98	5	22	110	7	8
sol	18	52	0	10	60	0
sco	11	0	34	15	0	30
Err	0.27 ± 0.06			0.15 ± 0.06		

3 Conclusions

In this work we propose a characterization of shapes of objects based on directional data. The ultimate goal is to categorize these objects according to their shapes. Intuitively, shape can be defined as the geometrical property shared by different objects that is invariant to a loosely-defined family of transformations, which includes translations, scaling, rotations, and small deformations. In our method, shape is encoded by the distribution of unit vectors along the normal direction at the boundaries of the object. In this manner, information on scale and absolute distances is eliminated while preserving directional information, which is expected to encode shape. This representation is obtained by first locating these boundaries with standard image processing algorithms. Then, normal unit vectors are computed at a set of points located on this boundary. These vectors can be seen as realizations of a directional random variable. This random variable can be characterized by its distribution. In two dimensions, the boundary is a curve, so the distribution of normal vectors is defined on the circle. Empirical estimates of the probability density function can be computed using a scaled histogram, or a smoother kernel density estimation using, for instance, von Mises kernels. In this work both options are explored. For three-dimensional representations, the boundary of the object is a surface. The distribution of three-dimensional unit normal vectors are defined on a sphere. In this case von Mises-Fisher kernels can be used [4]. Since the representation is functional (and therefore, infinite dimensional), further reductions of information are needed so that it can be used in practice. In particular, for two-dimensional data, the probability densities are discretized at regularly $N = 64$ spaced points along the circle. Since shape should be invariant with respect to rotations, computationally expensive shape-alignment operations are needed when this representations are used for clustering or classification. A further dimensionality reduction, which is rotationally invariant, can be made using as features the distances of the discretized densities and the uniform circular distribution. The usefulness of these representations for clustering and classification of images of objects according to their shapes is illustrated with otolith data. Techniques based on exhaustive minimization, while being computationally costly, are very accurate and provide the best overall results, especially when kernel estimates of the density of directional variables are used. From these experiments we conclude that *distances* representation provides a significant reduction on the computational cost while reducing the quality of the results. The *aligned* representation provides a good balance between performance and computational cost. This empirical investigation illustrates the effectiveness of the directional data representation proposed to encode shapes.

References

1. Berrendero, J.R., Cuevas, A., Pateiro-Lpez, B.: Shape classification based on inter-point distance distributions. J. Multivariate Anal. **146**, 237–247 (2016). Special Issue on Statistical Models and Methods for High or Infinite Dimensional Spaces
2. Chaubey, Y.P.: Smooth kernel estimation of a circular density function: a connection to orthogonal polynomials on the unit circle. J. Probab. Stat. **2018**, 4 p. (2018). https://doi.org/10.1155/2018/5372803. Article ID 5372803
3. Di Marzio, M., Panzera, A., Taylor, C.: A note on density estimation for circular data (2012)
4. Fisher, R.: Dispersion on a sphere. Proc. Roy. Soc. Lond. Ser. A: Math. Phys. Sci. **217**(1130), 295–305 (1953)
5. García-Portugués, E.: Exact risk improvement of bandwidth selectors for kernel density estimation with directional data. Electron. J. Statist. **7**, 1655–1685 (2013). https://doi.org/10.1214/13-EJS821

6. Giménez, J., Manjabacas, A., Tuset, V.M., Lombarte, A.: Relationships between otolith and fish size from Mediterranean and Northeastern Atlantic species to be used in predator-prey studies. J. Fish Biol. **89**(4), 2195–2202 (2016)
7. Grogan, M., Dahyot, R.: Shape registration with directional data. Pattern Recogn. **79**, 452–466 (2018)
8. Kendall, D.G.: A survey of the statistical theory of shape. Statist. Sci. **4**(2), 87–99 (1989). https://doi.org/10.1214/ss/1177012582
9. Lorensen, W.E., Cline, H.E.: Marching cubes: a high resolution 3D surface construction algorithm. Comput. Graph. **21**(4), 163–169 (1987)
10. MacLeod, N.: Geometric morphometrics and geological shape-classification systems. Earth-Sci. Rev. **59**(1), 27–47 (2002)
11. Mardia, K.V., Jupp, P.: Directional Statistics. Wiley Series in Probability and Statistics. Wiley, New York (2009)
12. Gavrielides, M.A., Kallergi, M., Clarke, L.P.: Automatic shape analysis and classification of mammographic calcifications (1997). https://doi.org/10.1117/12.274175
13. Montero-Manso, P., Vilar, J.: Shape classification through functional data reparametrization and distribution-based comparison (2017)
14. Moyou, M., Ihou, K.E., Peter, A.M.: LBO-Shape densities: a unified framework for 2D and 3D shape classification on the hypersphere of wavelet densities. Comput. Vis. Image Underst. **152**, 142–154 (2016)
15. Mu, T., Nandi, A.K., Rangayyan, R.M.: Classification of breast masses using selected shape, edge-sharpness, and texture features with linear and kernel-based classifiers. J. Digit. Imaging **21**(2), 153–169 (2008)
16. Pizer, S.M., Thall, A.L., Chen, D.T.: M-Reps: a new object representation for graphics. Technical report, ACM Transactions on Graphics (2000)
17. Ramsay, J., Silverman, B.: Functional data analysis (1997)
18. Taylor, C.C.: Automatic bandwidth selection for circular density estimation. Comput. Stat. Data Anal. **52**(7), 3493–3500 (2008)
19. Tuset, V., Lombarte, A., Assis, C.: Otolith atlas for the Western Mediterranean, North and Central Eastern Atlantic. Scientia Marina **72**(Suppl. 1), 7–198 (2008)
20. Yushkevich, P., Pizer, S.M., Joshi, S., Marron, J.S.: Intuitive, localized analysis of shape variability. In: Insana, M.F., Leahy, R.M. (eds.) IPMI 2001. LNCS, vol. 2082, pp. 402–408. Springer, Heidelberg (2001). https://doi.org/10.1007/3-540-45729-1_41

Semantic Space Transformations for Cross-Lingual Document Classification

Jiří Martínek[1], Ladislav Lenc[2], and Pavel Král[1,2(✉)]

[1] Department of Computer Science and Engineering, Faculty of Applied Sciences, University of West Bohemia, Plzeň, Czech Republic
{jimar,pkral}@kiv.zcu.cz
[2] NTIS - New Technologies for the Information Society, Faculty of Applied Sciences, University of West Bohemia, Plzeň, Czech Republic
llenc@kiv.zcu.cz

Abstract. Cross-lingual document representation can be done by training monolingual semantic spaces and then to use bilingual dictionaries with some transform method to project word vectors into a unified space. The main goal of this paper consists in evaluation of three promising transform methods on cross-lingual document classification task. We also propose, evaluate and compare two cross-lingual document classification approaches. We use popular convolutional neural network (CNN) and compare its performance with a standard maximum entropy classifier. The proposed methods are evaluated on four languages, namely English, German, Spanish and Italian from the Reuters corpus. We demonstrate that the results of all transformation methods are close to each other, however the orthogonal transformation gives generally slightly better results when CNN with trained embeddings is used. The experimental results also show that convolutional network achieves better results than maximum entropy classifier. We further show that the proposed methods are competitive with the state of the art.

1 Introduction

The performance of many Natural Language Processing (NLP) systems is strongly dependent on the size and quality of annotated resources. Unfortunately, there is a lack of annotated data for particular languages/tasks and manual annotation of new corpora is a very expensive and time consuming task. Moreover, the linguistic experts from the target domain are often required. These issues can be solved by the usage of cross-lingual text representation methods. The classifiers are trained on resource-rich languages and the cross-linguality allows using the models with data in other languages with no available training data.

The text document representations are often created using multi-dimensional word vectors, often so called word embeddings (Levy and Goldberg [10]). One way of creating cross-lingual representations is to use transformed semantic spaces. Such approaches take a monolingual, independently trained, semantic space and project it into a unified space using some transformation method.

© Springer Nature Switzerland AG 2018
V. Kůrková et al. (Eds.): ICANN 2018, LNCS 11139, pp. 608–616, 2018.
https://doi.org/10.1007/978-3-030-01418-6_60

Several such transformation methods have been proposed. However, to the best of our knowledge, a comparative study of the role of different transformation methods/classifiers for the document classification across several languages is missing. Therefore, the main contribution of this paper consists in the thorough study of the impact of three promising transform methods, namely Least Squares Transformation (LST), Orthogonal Transformation (OT) and Canonical Correlation Analysis (CCA), for cross-lingual document classification. More information about linear transformations to build cross-lingual semantic spaces can be found in [2,3]. In this context, we propose, evaluate and compare two cross-lingual document classification approaches. The first one uses directly the transformed embeddings in different languages while the second one realizes a simple word translation by choosing the closest word using cosine similarity of the embedding vectors.

For classification, we use popular convolutional neural network (CNN) and compare its performance with a standard maximum entropy classifier. The proposed methods are evaluated on four languages, namely English, German, Spanish and Italian from the Reuters corpus.

2   Literature Review

Recent work in cross-lingual text representation field is usually based on word-level alignments. Klementiev et al. [7] train simultaneously two language models based on neural networks. The proposed method uses a regularization which ensures that pairs of frequently aligned words have similar word embeddings. Therefore, this approach needs parallel corpora to obtain the word-level alignment. Zou et al. [13] propose an alternative approach based on another neural network language models using different regularization.

Kočiský et al. [8] propose a bilingual word representation approach based on a probabilistic model. This method simultaneously learns alignments and distributed representations for bilingual data. Contrary to the prior work, which is based on parallel corpora or hard alignment, this method marginalizes out the alignments, thus captures a larger bilingual semantic context.

Chandar et al. [4] investigate an efficient approach based on autoencoders that uses word representations coherent between two languages. This method is able to obtain high-quality text representations by learning to reconstruct the bag-of-words of aligned sentences without any word alignments.

Coulmance et al. [5] introduce an efficient method for bilingual word representations called Trans-gram. This approach extends popular skip-gram model to multi-lingual scenario. This model jointly learns and aligns word embeddings for several languages, using only monolingual data and a small set of sentence-aligned documents.

3 Cross-Lingual Document Classification

3.1 Document Representation

We use three document representations in our experiments. The first one is the Bag-of-Words (BoW). The second approach called *averaged embeddings* utilizes word embeddings. It averages the word vectors for all words occurring in the document. Its length corresponds to the embeddings dimensionality. The last method uses the sequence of words in the document and transforms it to the 2D representation suitable for the CNN. The words are one-hot encoded and are translated using a look-up table by the corresponding embeddings. Further we describe the three ways how we achieve the cross-linguality in our classification methods.

Machine Translation. Machine translation (MT) is used as a strong baseline for comparison with the two other methods. The documents are translated using Google API. The translation is then used in the same way as if classifying documents in one language.

Transformed Embeddings. This approach relies on the transformed word embeddings. The representations of the training documents are created from the original word embeddings in the language, which was used for the training of the model. The documents in the testing dataset are then represented by the embeddings transformed to the language of the model. This method will be hereafter called *transformed (emb)eddings*.

Embedding Translation. This method is also based on the transformed embeddings. However, the embeddings are used for *per-word* translation of the documents instead of using it directly. It utilizes the non-transformed embedding in the target language and the transformed one from source to target language for similarity search. The most similar word in the target language is found for each word in the source language by *cosine similarity*. This method is in the following text referred as *(emb)edding translation* approach.

3.2 Classification Models

Maximum Entropy. The first classifier is the Maximum Entropy (ME) model Berger et al. [1]. It takes for each document an input with a fixed number of features, represented as a feature vector F, and outputs the probability distribution $P(Y = y|F)$ where $y \in C$ (set of all possible document classes). This model is popular in the natural language processing field, because it usually gives good classification scores.

Convolutional Neural Network. The second classifier is a popular Convolutional Neural Network (CNN). It also outputs normalized scores interpreted as a probability distribution $P(Y = y|F)$ over all possible labels. The network we use was proposed by Lenc and Král [9] and it was successfully used for multi-label classification of Czech documents. The architecture of the network is inspired by Kim [6]. The main difference from Kim's network is that this net uses different number and size of convolutional kernels.

We perform a basic preprocessing which detects all numbers and replaces them by one "NUMERIC" token. Then the document length is adjusted to a fixed value. Longer documents are shortened while shorter ones are padded so that they have fixed length L. A vocabulary of the most frequent words is prepared from the training data. The words are then represented by their indexes in the vocabulary. The words that are not in the vocabulary are assigned to a reserved index ("OOV") and the "PADDING" token has also a reserved index.

The input of the network is a vector of word indexes of the length L where L is the number of words used for document representation. The second layer is an embedding layer which represents each input word as a vector of a given length. The document is thus represented as a matrix with L rows and E columns where E is the embeddings dimensionality. The embedding layer can be initialized either randomly and trained during the network training process or use the pre-trained word embeddings as its weights. The third layer is the convolutional one. N convolutional kernels of the size $K \times 1$ are used which means that a 1D convolution over one position in the embedding vector over K input words is performed. The following layer performs max pooling over the length $L - K + 1$ resulting in N $1 \times E$ vectors. This layer is followed by a dropout layer Srivastava et al. [12] for regularization. The output of this layer is then flattened and connected with a fully connected layer with D neurons. After another dropout layer follows the output layer with C neurons which corresponds to the number of the document categories. The architecture of the network is depicted in Fig. 1.

4 Experiments

4.1 Reuters Corpus Volume I

We use four languages, namely English (en), German (de), Spanish (es) and Italian (it) from Reuters Corpus Volume I (RCV1-v2) Lewis et al. [11] with similar setup as used by Klementiev et al. [7]. The documents are classified into four following categories: *Corporate/industrial – CCAT, Economics – ECAT, Government/social – GCAT* and *Markets – MCAT*.

As the other studies we use the standard accuracy metric in our experiments. The confidence interval is $\pm 0.3\%$ at the confidence level of 0.95.

4.2 Baseline Approaches Results

Our first baseline method is a *majority class (MC)* classifier which determines the distribution of categories in the training dataset and chooses the most fre-

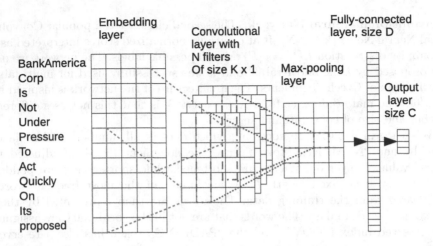

Fig. 1. Convolutional neural network architecture.

quent class. In testing phase, all test documents are classified into this most frequent class. The accuracy of this classifier is depicted in third column of Table 1. These results show that the corpus is unbalanced and that there are significant differences among different languages.

The second baseline is the *machine translation (MT)* approach. The results with the ME classifier are reported in Table 1, while the accuracy of the CNN is shown in Table 2 (column *MT*). Classification accuracies of this approach are very high and show that the translation results have a strong impact on document classification.

4.3 Proposed Approaches Results

The embedding translation approach needs repeatedly searching the target semantic space which is computationally demanding. In order to reduce the computational burden we set the vocabulary size $|V| = 20,000$. The vocabulary is constructed from the most frequent words in the training set. To increase efficiency of searching, we created vocabulary mapping dictionary between each pair of languages. There is a mapping onto target language vocabulary for each word in the source language. This dictionary is the centerpiece of the embedding translation. If the source word is not present in the vocabulary, the out of vocabulary token ("OOV") is used. Each proposed method is experimentally validated on two classification models.

Maximum Entropy Results. The last six columns in Table 1 show the results of the maximum entropy classifier with *transformed (emb)eddings* and *(emb)edding translation* methods. Three linear transformations are used.

Table 1. ME classifier results. Columns 3 and 4 represent the majority class (MC) and machine translation (MT) baselines. The rest of the table shows results for the proposed methods with different embedding transformations.

| Languages | | Baselines [%] | | Proposed approaches [%] | | | | | |
| | | MC | MT | Transformed emb | | | Emb translation | | |
Train	Test			LST	CCA	OT	LST	CCA	OT
en	de	30.4	91.9	54.4	62.0	52.2	75.6	75.8	76.3
en	es	14.7	81.5	52.9	39.0	49.9	57.2	48.8	49.8
en	it	36.0	71.2	48.4	42.2	56.0	58.1	51.0	51.5
de	en	23.9	76.7	59.9	60.4	57.4	66.6	69.0	70.2
do	cs	8.76	81.1	35.9	32.5	29.4	73.2	58.5	63.8
de	it	9.50	67.0	58.7	57.5	57.0	47.2	47.7	46.4
es	en	23.3	74.3	47.8	53.2	45.4	67.3	70.5	69.6
es	de	22.6	85.7	51.7	43.8	47.6	74.5	70.1	70.3
es	it	36.4	67.9	22.8	19.8	29.7	71.2	72.0	72.1
it	en	23.3	69.7	68.5	69.8	63.8	56.8	55.6	50.2
it	de	22.6	86.9	48.7	45.1	52.6	76.6	77.4	76.8
it	es	67.7	80.8	61.4	49.4	59.5	75.3	75.2	70.5

This table shows that the grammatically close languages (same family) give usually better results than the other ones. More concrete, en ↔ de and es ↔ it have generally better results than for instance en ↔ es (it) or de → es (it).

The results further show, that the three transformation are comparable in many cases. However, LST gives the best results in several other cases (e.g. en → es (it) or de → es (it)) and OT gives the significantly worst results for some cases (e.g. it → en). Based on this experiment we can propose generally to use LST with ME classifier and static word embeddings.

CNN Results. In all our experiments we use the vocabulary size $|V| = 20,000$. The document length L is set to 100 tokens and the embedding length E is 300 in all cases. We use $N = 40$ convolutional kernels of size 16×1 ($K = 16$). The dropout probability is set to 0.2. The size of the first fully connected layer is 256. The output layer has 4 neurons ($C = 4$) while we are classifying into 4 classes. All layers except the output one use *relu* activation function. The output layer uses the *softmax* activation function.

The direct usage of embedding vector is depicted in the leftmost columns of the Proposed Approaches part of Table 2. The results of this method are the worsts one among the other proposed approaches, however it is the simplest one.

The last six columns *emb translation* in Table 2 show the results of CNN on the *(emb)edding translation* method. In Table 2 there are two sets of results. The first one is the set of results, when embedding layer was excluded from learning (*stat*), while in the second case the embeddings layer are further fine-tuned by

Table 2. CNN results. Columns 3 and 4 represent the MT baseline. The rest of the table presents result of the proposed methods with different embedding transformations. Term *stat* means the static word embeddings while the term *rnd* means the using of randomly initialized embeddings with a subsequent training.

Languages		Baselines [%]		Proposed approaches [%]								
		MT		Transformed emb			Emb translation (stat)			Emb translation (rnd)		
Train	Test	rnd	stat	LST	CCA	OT	LST	CCA	OT	LST	CCA	OT
en	de	89.7	86.5	62.2	64.4	56.0	78.9	79.1	81.3	80.4	80.4	82.7
en	es	85.7	69.8	24.4	26.7	23.6	82.0	77.0	76.9	81.9	75.7	72.9
en	it	74.7	65.8	27.7	26.9	18.0	68.1	70.2	68.6	71.1	70.5	68.3
de	en	61.3	59.4	66.4	64.8	58.4	69.3	70.0	70.2	72.3	75.6	75.6
de	es	64.7	55.7	65.0	57.6	55.2	51.0	55.3	54.5	81.4	79.3	80.7
de	it	47.8	48.8	39.1	50.9	58.4	44.8	48.6	49.2	68.7	71.1	71.2
es	en	60.7	67.6	49.2	41.1	41.5	51.9	54.9	55.0	59.0	63.1	63.0
es	de	76.8	81.8	42.9	54.1	58.0	58.5	72.2	81.5	54.7	69.2	82.0
es	it	62.4	61.9	20.2	35.5	37.5	68.0	70.9	71.5	73.0	76.2	76.7
it	en	69.1	65.7	42.5	44.8	46.4	41.4	41.8	41.1	54.8	54.7	51.3
it	de	85.4	81.5	37.0	38.3	44.5	59.6	72.7	74.1	63.0	76.0	60.8
it	es	80.1	73.8	68.5	68.8	68.1	61.3	61.3	62.1	78.6	78.6	78.7

a training (*rnd*). In the table we can observe, that the embedding training has a positive impact for classification. Moreover, the impact of the transformation differ from the previous case (see Table 1). We can suggest to use OT as the best transformation method when CNN with trained embeddings are used.

4.4   Comparison with the State of the Art

In this experiment, we compare the results of our best approach with the state of the art (see Table 3). These results show that the state-of-the-art methods slightly outperform the proposed approaches, however we must emphasize that our main goal consists in the comparison of several different methods. Moreover, the proposed approaches are very simple.

Table 3. Comparison with the state of the art.

Method	en → de [%]	de → en [%]
Klementiev et al. [7]	77.6	71.1
Kočiský et al. [8]	83.1	76.0
Chandar et al. [4]	91.8	74.2
Coulmance et al. [5]	91.1	78.7
Best proposed configuration	82.7	75.6

5 Conclusions

This paper presented a thorough study of the impact of three promising transform methods, namely least squares transformation, orthogonal transformation and canonical correlation analysis, for cross-lingual document classification. In this context, we proposed and evaluated two cross-lingual document classification approaches. The first one uses directly the transformed embeddings in different languages without any modification while the second one realizes the simple word translation choosing the closest word using cosine similarity of the embeddings. We compared the performance of standard maximum entropy classifier with our architecture of convolutional neural network for this task.

We evaluated the proposed approaches on four languages including English, German, Spanish and Italian from Reuters corpus. We have shown that the results of all transformation methods are close to each other, however the orthogonal transformation gives generally slightly better results when CNN with trained embeddings is used. We have also demonstrated that convolutional neural network achieves significantly better results than maximum entropy classifier. We have further presented that the proposed methods are competitive with the state of the art.

Acknowledgements. This work has been partly supported by the project LO1506 of the Czech Ministry of Education, Youth and Sports and by Grant No. SGS-2016-018 Data and Software Engineering for Advanced Applications.

References

1. Berger, A.L., Pietra, V.J.D., Pietra, S.A.D.: A maximum entropy approach to natural language processing. Comput. Linguist. **22**(1), 39–71 (1996)
2. Brychcin, T.: Linear transformations for cross-lingual semantic textual similarity. CoRR abs/1807.04172 (2018). http://arxiv.org/abs/1807.04172
3. Brychcin, T., Taylor, S.E., Svoboda, L.: Cross-lingual word analogies using linear transformations between semantic spaces. CoRR abs/1807.04175 (2018). http://arxiv.org/abs/1807.04175
4. Sarath Chandar, A.P., et al.: An autoencoder approach to learning bilingual word representations. In: Ghahramani, Z., Welling, M., Cortes, C., Lawrence, N.D., Weinberger, K.Q. (eds.) Advances in Neural Information Processing Systems 27, pp. 1853–1861. Curran Associates, Inc. (2014)
5. Coulmance, J., Marty, J.M., Wenzek, G., Benhalloum, A.: Trans-gram, fast cross-lingual word-embeddings. arXiv preprint arXiv:1601.02502 (2016)
6. Kim, Y.: Convolutional neural networks for sentence classification. arXiv preprint arXiv:1408.5882 (2014)
7. Klementiev, A., Titov, I., Bhattarai, B.: Inducing crosslingual distributed representations of words. In: Proceedings of COLING 2012, pp. 1459–1474 (2012)
8. Kočiský, T., Hermann, K.M., Blunsom, P.: Learning bilingual word representations by marginalizing alignments. In: Proceedings of the 52nd Annual Meeting of the Association for Computational Linguistics (Volume 2: Short Papers), vol. 2, pp. 224–229 (2014)

9. Lenc, L., Král, P.: Deep neural networks for czech multi-label document classification. In: Gelbukh, A. (ed.) CICLing 2016. LNCS, vol. 9624, pp. 460–471. Springer, Cham (2018). https://doi.org/10.1007/978-3-319-75487-1_36

10. Levy, O., Goldberg, Y.: Dependency-based word embeddings. In: Proceedings of the 52nd Annual Meeting of the Association for Computational Linguistics (Volume 2: Short Papers), vol. 2, pp. 302–308 (2014)

11. Lewis, D.D., Yang, Y., Rose, T.G., Li, F.: Rcv1: A new benchmark collection for text categorization research. J. Mach. Learn. Res. 5(Apr), 361–397 (2004)

12. Srivastava, N., Hinton, G., Krizhevsky, A., Sutskever, I., Salakhutdinov, R.: Dropout: a simple way to prevent neural networks from overfitting. J. Mach. Learn. Res. 15(1), 1929–1958 (2014)

13. Zou, W.Y., Socher, R., Cer, D., Manning, C.D.: Bilingual word embeddings for phrase-based machine translation. In: Proceedings of the 2013 Conference on Empirical Methods in Natural Language Processing, pp. 1393–1398 (2013)

Automatic Treatment of Bird Audios by Means of String Compression Applied to Sound Clustering in Xeno-Canto Database

Guillermo Sarasa[1(⊠)], Ana Granados[2], and Francisco B. Rodriguez[1]

[1] Grupo de Neurocomputación Biológica, Escuela Politécnica Superior,
Universidad Autónoma de Madrid, Madrid, Spain
`guillermo.sarasa@predoc.uam.es, f.rodriguez@uam.es`
[2] CES Felipe II, Universidad Complutense de Madrid, Aranjuez, Madrid, Spain
`ana.granados@ajz.ucm.es`
`http://arantxa.ii.uam.es/~gnb/`

Abstract. Compression distances can be a very useful tool in automatic object clustering because of their parameter-free nature. However, when they are used to compare very different-sized objects with a high percentage of noise, their behaviour might be unpredictable. In order to address this drawback, we have develop an automatic object segmentation methodology prior to the string-compression-based object clustering. Our experimental results using the xeno-canto database show that this methodology can be successfully applied to automatic bird species identification from their sounds. These results show that applying our methodology significantly improves the clustering performance of bird sounds compared to the performance obtained without applying our automatic object segmentation methodology.

Keywords: Data mining · Normalized compression distance
Clustering · Dendrogram · Bird sound classification
Silhouette coefficient · Similarity · Object segmentation

1 Introduction

Automatic bird species classification from their sounds may be extremely useful in fields such as ecology, behavioral biology or conservation biology, among others. However, from a technical point of view, it can be a challenging task to perform due to aspects such as the high variety of existing species, song similarities between distinct species or background noises. The xeno-canto dataset [13] is a collection of bird sound recordings from birds all over the word that is available online. This data set has been used in several studies on bird songs classification in the literature [1,11,12]. In order to improve the classification performance, these works usually carry out an extensive previous analysis, which in

© Springer Nature Switzerland AG 2018
V. Kůrková et al. (Eds.): ICANN 2018, LNCS 11139, pp. 617–625, 2018.
https://doi.org/10.1007/978-3-030-01418-6_61

most cases comprises, at least, previous treatment of the samples (background noise), feature extraction (analysis and identification of the song components) and parameter selection (discrimination process). This strong dependence on parameter selection may not be the most appropriate for such a heterogeneous data set. Some examples of this heterogeneity are the variability in the duration of the data samples, the background noise, or even other bird songs that occasionally appear in audio recordings.

Compression distances can be a very convenient tool in the automatic bird song species identification because of their parameter-free nature, broad applicability and leading efficacy in many domains. Among others, audio [15], images [5,6], documents [7,8] or computer security [2] represent examples of the transversal application of this methodology. In a preliminary study, we utilized one of the most successfully applied compression distances, the Normalized Compression Distance (NCD) to bird song classification [15]. We showed that NCD can be applied as an alternative approach to identify bird species from audio samples. This work, however, does not address an issue that compression distances have when they are applied to compare two very different-sized objects. This problem resides in the fact that two objects can be considered to be significantly different by the NCD even though they are similar [3,9]. Although this might not be a problem in scenarios where there are significant differences in the size of the objects to be compared, it does not apply to this database. In this case, the high heterogeneity in the duration and noise of the data samples demands additional considerations.

Another issue that was not addressed either in [15] and typically appears in the xeno-canto data base, occurs in audios where the relevant information is surrounded by big amounts of noise. This is the case of some audios where the majority of the sample is composed of background noise such as microphone artifacts, human voices or even other bird species. Although compression distances have a high noise tolerance, they are based on size reduction relations between pairs of objects. This makes them robust against objects where the information is mixed with the noise, but very weak against data samples where the noise size overcomes the relevant-information size.

In this work, we address these issues reassembling each audio file from a selection of their fragments. Our aim was to segment the bird song recordings, analyze their NCD matrix and select only the fragments with relevant-information. Next, we use the "relevant" fragments to assemble new audios without noise and, thereby, to achieve a more accurate representation of their distances. The results presented in this paper show that applying our methodology significantly improves the clustering performance of bird sounds compared to the performance obtained without applying our automatic object segmentation methodology.

2   Normalized Compression Distance

The Normalized Compression Distance (NCD) is a metric that provides a measure of similarity between two objects based on the use of compression algorithms. The fundamental idea behind the NCD is that given two objects x and

y, when a compression algorithm encodes the concatenated xy, it searches for the information shared by x and y to reduces the redundancy of the whole sequence. This concept was studied by [3,10]. The NCD between two objects x and y is defined as:

$$NCD(x,y) = \frac{\max\{C(xy) - C(x), C(yx) - C(y)\}}{\max\{C(x), C(y)\}}, \tag{1}$$

where C is a compression algorithm and $C(x)$ and $C(xy)$ are the size of the C-compressed versions of x and the concatenation of x and y, respectively. Since compression algorithms can be applied to all types of digital data, the NCD has been applied in many areas (see Sect. 1). However, the application of the NCD involves some difficulties that depend on the context. The size differences between objects, the symbolization of the information or a high percentage of noise, are some examples of these difficulties. The first problem could be understand simply by looking at the Eq. 1. Initially, the NCD is based on the assumption that every object x, is reducible by a compressor. A typical case where this does not occur is when one or both objects have already been compressed. In the same fashion, if two similar and reducible objects x and y are not reduced proportionally by a compressor the NCD will be near 1.

2.1 Object Size Problem

If we consider the case where one of the objects is extremely big, and the other one is significantly small, the NCD between these objects will be closer to 1, regardless of the information contained in them. In Fig. 1, one can see that the resolution of the NCD domain decreases as the size difference increases. For instance, around 20 KB the average NCD is 0.998 while for 1 MB it increases to 0.9995. This means that the NCD metric loses resolution as the object size heterogeneity increases.

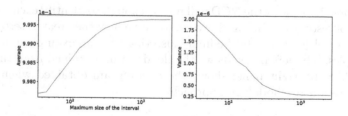

Fig. 1. Average NCD and variance, for different subsets of samples of the same bird species. Each subset is taken from a unique set limiting the size of the samples by an upper bound. In other words, for a Maximum size of 50 KB the objects' size used to measure the average NCD will be between 0 and 50 KB. Hence, while the maximum size increases, the NCD gets closer to 1. This is a problem because an NCD near to 1 implies dissimilarity. Simultaneously the variance falls near to 0. This, together with the average, reduces the resolution of the NCD domain, and thereby, the identification capabilities of this method.

As we mentioned in the introduction, another issue related with this database appears when the bird song appears in a small percentage of the audio sample. Following the Eq. 1, one can observe that as long as the compression algorithm correctly identifies the information between the objects x and y, the size of $C(xy)$ should be smaller than the size of $max\{C(x), C(y)\}$. For our case, one will assume that only when x and y belong to the same bird species, the NCD will be low. However, the noise can also be used to reduce the size of $C(xy)$. As an example, two audios can have the same background noise (other bird songs, microphone artifacts, crickets, etc.) and belong to different species.

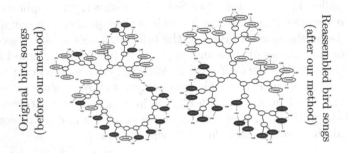

Fig. 2. Hierarchical clustering of different NCD matrix of the *Great Horned Owl* and the *Common Redshank* (the blue nodes correspond to the *Common Redshank*). The left panel shows the dendrogram obtained from the original samples (pre-processed to the same format), while the right panel shows the dendrogram obtained when applying our segmentation methodology, described in Sect. 3. The sizes of the objects of the left dendrogram are different, while in the right one each object has the same size. The Silhouette Coefficients for both panels are 0.081 and 0.291, respectively. It has to be pointed out that, the right dendrogram corresponds to the highest point of Fig. 3. (Color figure online)

Hence, for these cases the NCD will not be enough to identify each species due to the loss of resolution. In Fig. 2, we can observe how the great heterogeneity in the size of the objects affects the final clustering with an example of a subset of audio samples. The left panel shows the dendrogram obtained from the original objects, while the right panel shows the dendrogram obtained when applying our segmentation methodology approach.

3   Materials and Methods

We have used the audio data from the online database xeno-canto [13], which has a great heterogeneity among its audio files. This increases the difficulty of the problem but also makes it very interesting from the point of view of a free parameter identification technique. The clustering process has been performed by a MQTC based hierarchical clustering algorithm from Complearn software [4].

As described in Sect. 2, the size variety and significant percentage of noise (compared to the relevant information) in objects could harm the identification process considerably. For these reasons, we propose a simple methodology to use the NCD, as a parameter free technique, among sets of audio samples with big heterogeneity without further considerations.

In our previous work [15], we successfully identified different bird song samples between pairs of species, in similar-sized objects. In this case, we address the problem of size differences between objects and their noise, as an amplified version of the problem presented in [15]. In this fashion, our hypothesis is that finding the relevant segments among the audio samples is equivalent to solve the loss of resolution, metioned in Sect. 2.1.

In order to determine the relevant information of the audio samples, we have performed a segmentation process. Initially, we have parsed each sample to a standard format (for more details see Sect. 4) removing any metadata in the process. Next, we have split each audio sample into fragments of 1.2 s long (as a first approach) and we have measured the NCD between each pair of them. At this point, we have got a row of distances between each fragment and all the other fragments, which could be seen as a description of the information contained on a fragment.

Once the audios have been segmented into fragments, we have examined the NCD distribution (between each fragment and the rest of fragments) in order to sort and select the most relevant fragments. One fragment could include bird songs of one out of two species, or noise. Hence, one could assume that among the fragment distances with all the other fragments, those that belong to the fragments of the same class should be nearer than the ones that belong to other class. According to this assumption, we examined the NCD distribution for each fragment with all the other fragments, searching for a (at least) bimodal distribution. In this manner, one mode should belong to those fragments similar to the one used as reference (same bird species), while the other(s) mode(s) will correspond to the distances of the less similar fragments (noise, other specie, etc.).

The study of the distances' distribution of each fragment revealed that some fragments follow our previous assumption (multimodality) better than others. In this work, we have used this fact to score the relevant information of each fragment, and discriminate the fragments by their noise. Hence, we have assumed that the fragments with a bigger distance between their modes will contain a better quality than the fragments with smaller distance between their modes (in terms of species discrimination). Next, we have taken the distances between each pair of modes, for each fragment, and sort the fragments according to it. Finally, we have reconstructed the original audios taking the n best fragments of each audio sample (according to their modes distances).

From a technical point of view, we have made use of the zlib compression algorithm to calculate the NCD. This algorithm, together with the software to calculate the dendrogram, is provided by CompLearn Toolkit [4]. The audio samples have been processed with *ffmpeg* and *lame* linux packages, and optimized using GNU *Parallel* [16]. In Fig. 2, we show the dendrograms produced by the clustering of the original objects and the clustering obtained with our method from the fragments of the initial objects. In this figure, one can see that our method improves the clustering quality from a slight separability (SC = 0.081) to an almost classified clustering (SC = 0.291). It is important to point out that the low clustering reported by the first case is due to the big size variety among the audio samples.

4   Experimental Results

For our experiments, we have taken two different species: The *Great Horned Owl* and the *Common Redshank*, from the xeno-canto database. Taking into account that our purpose in this work is to deal with the variety of size and noise, we have limited the audio samples to specific types of bird songs for each experiment.

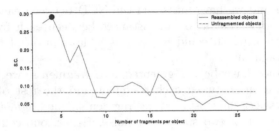

Fig. 3. Silhouette Coefficient for different objects' configurations over the number of fragments contained in each object. Each object was reconstructed from a subset of its fragments sorted by their distribution modes distance. The black dot corresponds to the configuration of the riZght dendrogram of Fig. 2. The dashed black line corresponds to SC value of the left dendrogram depicted in Fig. 2 before applying our method.

For each experiment, we have used the audios labeled as "song" (in xeno-canto), with no other type of bird call involved in the audio (for the selected species, the background bird songs can differ). The number of files has been reduced to only 14 per species. We have selected the audios randomly and equally balanced between species. In terms of format, we have used the *.mp3* raw format, removing the metadata and normalizing the audio properties from each one of them. The configuration used for each audio was: sampling rate and frequency 56 kbps and 22.05 KHz, respectively, and 8 bit width at a constant bit rate. It is important to point out that we have calculated the Silhouette Coefficient [14] for each experiment, in order to easily measure the separability of the clusters through their clustering quality.

As described in Sect. 2.1, we have re-assembled each object from its fragments according to their modes distance. Also, for each experiment, the number of fragments selected (X axis of Fig. 3) has been the same for each object (repeating them if necessary) in order to reduce the problems introduced by the size differences.

In our experiments, we have obtained good results compared with the SC obtained from the original objects. Looking closely to the Fig. 3, it can be observed that this method achieves an improvement over the base SC using 2–4 fragments per object. The SC, however, tends to fall for bigger configurations (more fragments per object) with some noise for the final configurations.

Finally, in order to test the capabilities of our method for a more hetero-geneous set of objects, we have performed an experiment over a bigger subset of audio samples. In this case, we have used 80 audio samples of the same two species, using 6 fragments to reassemble each object. The results obtained from this experiment (Fig. 4) show the impact of our method, improving the SC from 0.08 to 0.22.

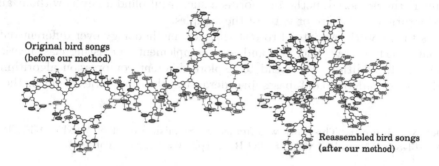

Fig. 4. Hierarchical clustering from the distances matrix of 80 audio samples, and their fragmented version, respectively. The blue nodes correspond to *Common Red-shank* species, while the black ones belong to the *Great Horned Owl* species. The left dendrogram is computed from the original distance matrix. The right dendrogram is obtained from the re-assemble of the audios from the fragments of the original objects. In this case, the best 2 fragments were selected from each object (according to their statistical mode distance). The Silhouette Coefficient for these dendrogram are 0.08 and 0.22 respectively. (Color figure online)

5   Conclusions

In this work, we have proposed a novel method to use the normalize compression distance in datasets with a great size heterogeneity and high percentage of noise inside objects. We have tested this methodology to improve the identification of bird species in the xeno-canto database. Throughout this study, we have used an automatic segmentation selection methodology to extract the relevant information and prevent the loss of resolution, maintaining the parameter free nature of the NCD.

Our hypothesis in this work is that finding the relevant intervals inside the audio samples and reassembling them in new equal-sized objects, is equivalent to solve the loss of resolution caused by the high percentage of noise and variety of object sizes. Hence, we have aimed to locate the best fragments (according to their clustering) by segmenting each object into fragments. First, we have measured the quality of each fragment using the distance between the modes of its NCD distribution. Then, we have selected the n best fragments in order to reassemble the audio. Finally, we have measured the NCD between these reassembled objects as a more accurate representation of the distances of the original audios.

The results presented in this paper show that applying our methodology has significantly improved clustering performance when compared to the results of the clustering without our methodology. As an example, Figs. 2 and 4 show the clustering differences between the clustering of the unprocessed and reassembled objects, respectively. With this approach, reasonable results of separability among species can be achieved without preprocessing the data. In the same manner, the proposed method performs a successful blind analysis without any consideration in the size or noise of the samples.

As future work, we intend to test this new methodology over different data formats, such as wav, flac, etc. and as a complement to existing classification methods. In addition, we intend to explore different compression algorithms, birds species and audio databases, in order to test the capabilities of our methodology.

Acknowledgment. This work was funded by Spanish project of MINECO/FEDER TIN2014-54580-R and TIN2017-84452-R, (http://www.mineco.gob.es/).

References

1. Albornoz, E.M., Vignolo, L.D., Sarquis, J.A., Leon, E.: Automatic classification of Furnariidae species from the Paranaense Littoral region using speech-related features and machine learning. Ecol. Inform. **38**, 39–49 (2017)
2. Borbely, R.S.: On normalized compression distance and large malware Towards a useful definition of normalized compression distance for the classification of large files. J. Comput. Virol. Hacking Tech. **12**(4), 235–242 (2016)
3. Cilibrasi, R., Vitanyi, P.M.B.: Clustering by compression. IEEE Trans. Inf. Theory **51**(4), 1523–1545 (2005)
4. Cilibrasi, R., Cruz, A.L., de Rooij, S., Keijzer, M.: CompLearn Home. CompLearn Toolkit. http://www.complearn.org/
5. Cohen, A., Bjornsson, C., Temple, S., Banker, G., Roysam, B.: Automatic summarization of changes in biological image sequences using algorithmic information theory. IEEE Trans. Pattern Anal. Mach. Intell. **31**(8), 1386–1403 (2009)
6. Cui, S., Datcu, M.: A comparison of Bag-of-Words method and normalized compression distance for satellite image retrieval. In: 2015 IEEE International Geoscience and Remote Sensing Symposium (IGARSS), pp. 4392–4395, July 2015
7. Granados, A., Cebrian, M., Camacho, D., de Borja Rodriguez, F.: Reducing the loss of information through annealing text distortion. IEEE Trans. Knowl. Data Eng. **23**(7), 1090–1102 (2011)
8. Granados, A., Koroutchev, K., de Borja Rodriguez, F.: Discovering data set nature through algorithmic clustering based on string compression. IEEE Trans. Knowl. Data Eng. **27**(3), 699–711 (2015)

9. Granados, A., Martnez, R., Camacho, D., de Borja Rodriguez, F.: Improving NCD accuracy by combining document segmentation and document distortion. Knowl. Inf. Syst. **41**(1), 223–245 (2014)
10. Li, M., Chen, X., Li, X., Ma, B., Vitanyi, P.: The similarity metric. IEEE Trans. Inf. Theory **50**(12), 3250–3264 (2004)
11. Livezey, K.: An approach to identifying bird songs: a key to more than 300 songs in the pipeline road area, Soberana National Park, Panama. Open Ornithol. J. **9**(1), 70–112 (2016)
12. Marini, A., Turatti, A.J., Britto, A.S., Koerich, A.L.: Visual and acoustic identification of bird species. In: 2015 IEEE International Conference on Acoustics, Speech and Signal Processing (ICASSP), pp. 2309–2313, April 2015
13. Planqué, B., Vellinga, W.-P.: Xeno-Canto: sharing bird sounds from around the world. http://www.xeno-canto.org/
14. Rousseeuw, P.J.: Silhouettes: a graphical aid to the interpretation and validation of cluster analysis. J. Comput. Appl. Math. **20**, 53–65 (1987)
15. Sarasa, G., Granados, A., Rodriguez, F.B.: An approach of algorithmic clustering based on string compression to identify bird songs species in Xeno-Canto database. In: 2017 3rd International Conference on Frontiers of Signal Processing (ICFSP), pp. 101–104, September 2017
16. Tange, O.: GNU parallel - the command-line power tool. USENIX Mag. **36**(1), 42–47 (2011). http://www.gnu.org/s/parallel

FROD: Fast and Robust Distance-Based Outlier Detection with Active-Inliers-Patterns in Data Streams

Zongren Li, Yijie Wang[(✉)], Guohong Zhao, Li Cheng, and Xingkong Ma

National Laboratory for Parallel and Distributed Processing,
College of Computer, National University of Defense Technology,
Changsha, Hunan 410073, People's Republic of China
{lizongren16,wangyijie,guohongzhao,licheng,
maxingkong}@nudt.edu.cn

Abstract. The detection of distance-based outliers from streaming data is critical for modern applications ranging from telecommunications to cybersecurity. However, existing works mainly concentrate on improving the responding speed, none of these proposals can perform well in streams with varying data distribution. In this paper, we propose a Fast and Robust Outlier Detection method (FROD in short) to solve this dilemma and achieve the promotion in both detection performance and processing throughput. Specifically, to adapt the changing distribution in data streams, we employ the Active-Inliers-Pattern which dynamically selects reserved objects for further outlier analysis. Moreover, an effective micro-cluster-based data storing structure is proposed to improve the detection efficiency, which is supported by our theoretical analysis on the complexity bounds. Moreover, we present a potential background updating optimization approach to hide the updating time. Experiments performed on real-world and synthetic datasets verify our theoretical study and demonstrate that our algorithm is not only faster than state-of-the-art methods, but also achieve a better detection performance when the outlier rate fluctuates.

Keywords: Outlier detection · Cybersecurity · Data streams
Distance-based outliers

1 Introduction

Detection of outliers in data streams [1] is an essential task in several cybersecurity applications. An object is considered as an outlier if it significantly deviates from the typical case. There are many definitions of the outlier [4]. One of the most widely used is based on distance [6]. The definition is provided as follows where an important concept neighbor is introduced first:

Definition 1 *(Neighbor). Given a distance threshold $R(R > 0)$, a data point o is a neighbor of data point o' if the distance between o and o' is not greater than R. A data point is not considered a neighbor of itself.*

© Springer Nature Switzerland AG 2018
V. Kůrková et al. (Eds.): ICANN 2018, LNCS 11139, pp. 626–636, 2018.
https://doi.org/10.1007/978-3-030-01418-6_62

Definition 2 *(Distance-based Outlier). Given a dataset D, a count threshold k(k > 0), a data object o_i will be regarded as a distance-based outlier, if o_i has less than k neighbors in D. In general when R is fixed, k will change with the size of D to get better performance.*

According to the definition of outliers, we can easily find distance-based outliers in static datasets. However, when it comes to the data stream scenario because the dataset size is potentially unbounded, this process is performed over a fixed amount of real-time data instead to ensure computational efficiency. The most common approach is based on a *sliding-window*, which always maintains W most recent objects. When new objects arrive, the window slides to incorporate S new objects in the stream. As a result, the oldest S data points will be discarded from the current window.

There are two goals for detecting distance-based outlier in data streams, (i) the accuracy of the data determination, (ii) and the responding speed of labeling the data objects. Unfortunately, these two goals are contradictory most of the times. For a data stream whose distribution changes dynamically, the window needs to be set large enough to resist the influence brought by the dynamic change of the data. However, if the window is set too large, the responding time will be greatly increased, so it will fail to satisfy the real-time performance.

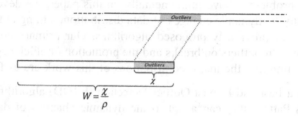

Fig. 1. The working scheme of the algorithms based on sliding-window

As mentioned before, the current distance-based outliers detection methods in data streams are based on sliding-window. These methods assume that the data distribution in the current window is similar to the global distribution, so they regard the outliers in current window as global outliers. Hence, they are prone to misjudgments in scenarios when the data distribution significantly changes such as a large-scale outbreak of outliers. For example, the DDoS attack is accomplished by making massive accesses in a short time to flood the targeted machine.

Figure 1 shows an example of what happens in a real network. Assume that on the given data set D, the distance-based outlier detection can exert good performance while the proportion of abnormal data in D is ρ. When the outliers arrive in a burst manner (For example, χ outliers occur continuously), the classic methods based on the sliding-window need to maintain a window of size $\frac{\chi}{\rho}$ to ensure good performance, which will increase the responding time dramatically.

In the model of the sliding window, the temporal cost is mainly focused on the updating of the model (the structure of the window) [8] in each sliding. On the original model without any optimization, the time complexity of each sliding is $O(W^2)$ (W refers to the size of the window). At present, many methods have been proposed to solve the problem. They adopt various methods to reduce the time complexity required for this step, such as using duplicate calculation information to simplify operations [2, 9], designing special storage structures [3, 7], etc.

We summarize the time complexity of some representative algorithm when the window slides each time and provide a side-by-side comparison in Table 1.

Table 1. The temporal cost of some representative algorithms.

Algorithm	Time complexity
Exact-storm [2]	$O(\text{W}\log k)$
AbstractC [9]	$O(W^2/S)$
DUE [7]	$O(W/\log W)$
Thresh LEAP [3]	$O(W^2 \log S/S)T$
MCOD [7]	$O((1-c)\text{W}\log(1-c)\text{W} + k\text{W}\log k)$

Although these algorithms increase the responding speed, they still do not solve the problem of dynamically adapting the data distribution in essence.

To solve the problems above fundamentally, in this paper, we developed a novel method to adapt to the dynamic changes of data distribution, aiming at the elimination of the limitations of previously proposed algorithms. Our primary concerns are the reliability to cope with outliers outbreaks and the promotion of efficiency and accuracy of detection. In summary, the major contributions of this work are as follows:

1. We proposed a Fast and Robust Outlier Detection (FROD) algorithm based on the Active-Inliers-Pattern that can adapt to the dynamic changes of data distribution without storing a lot of data (large window), which considerably improves the responding speed under the premise of detection accuracy assurance.
2. We adopt an effective structure based on micro-clusters for the proposed algorithm to maintain the Active-Inliers-Pattern. And corresponding updating strategies are given, which has been proved to have a better performance on real and synthetic datasets compared to the state-of-the-art techniques.
3. We present theoretical bounds for its superiority and a possible optimization approach is given.

The remaining of this paper is organized as follows. We present our methods in Sect. 2, whereas Sect. 3 contains the performance evaluation results based on real-life and synthetic data sets. Finally, Sect. 4 concludes the work and briefly discusses future work in the area.

2   Methods

Figure 2 shows the framework of FROD: when objects in the data streams arrive continuously, they are first stored in a *Buffer*. Once the trigger condition is satisfied, outlier detection will be performed in *Buffer* with the *Active-Inliers-Pattern*. *Active-*

Inliers-Pattern consists of selected inliers, which are maintained by a micro-cluster-based structure and these inliers dynamically updated by the detection results.

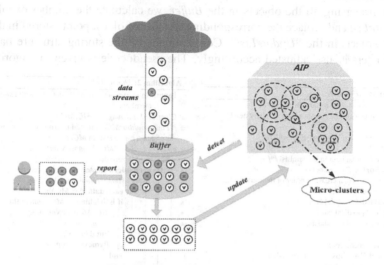

Fig. 2. The framework of FROD

In this section, the algorithm FROD is described in detail. We start by introducing the *Active-Inliers-Pattern* which is used to detect outliers. Then an efficient structure based on micro-clusters is proposed to maintain the *Active-Inliers-Pattern*. After that, we depict complete workflow of FROD and provide an optimization approach to accelerate. Moreover, we theoretically prove that FROD is more effective than other detection methods in data streams.

2.1 AIP for Outlier Detection

We employ the *Active-Inliers-Pattern* (AIP), which is similar to the window in methods based on the sliding-window, storing only selected inliers instead. And then we create a *Buffer* at fixed size $S(S \ll$(size of) AIP). Each newly incoming data will be stored in the *Buffer* if the *Buffer* has not been filled yet.

When the *Buffer* is full, we mark each object stored in the *Buffer* as inlier or outlier according to whether it has more than k neighbors in the AIP (this process is efficiently

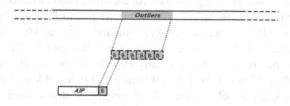

Fig. 3. The working scheme of FROD

implemented, shown in Sect. 2.3). And an *UpdateList* is preserved to keep all the objects newly marked as inliers. Meanwhile, objects considered to be outliers are directly removed.

After traversing all the objects in the *Buffer*, we calculate the number of inliers in the *UpdateList* and replace the corresponding number of oldest points stored in the AIP with the objects in the "*UpdateList*". Correspondingly, the storing structure based on micro-clusters is also adjusted accordingly. The pseudocode is given in Algorithm 1.

Algorithm 1: *AIP-Update*

Input : An old *Active-Inliers-Pattern AIP$_0$*
An UpdateList *l* contains some inliers newly arrived

Output: A new *Active-Inliers-Pattern AIP$_1$*

1 $AIP_1 = AIP_0$
2 $c = length(l)$/*total item in UpdateList *l*/
3 dataList=**Sort**(AIP_0.members)
4 /*Rank members in increasing order of their arrival time*/
5 **for** i:=1...c **do**
6 | **Remove** dataList[i-1] **from** dataList
7 | **Add** *l*[i-1] **to** dataList
8 | AIP_0.members ← dataList
9 **end**
10 **for** $d \in AIP_1$.members **do**
11 | **if CheckForAdjust**(data) is *ture* **then**
12 | **AdjustMicroCluster**(AIP_1)
13 | **end**
14 **end**
15 **return** AIP_1;

Algorithm 2: *SharingPoint*

Input: An incomplete micro-cluster MC_i with fewer than k members

1 Clusters=**Find _neighborMC**(MC_i);
2 /*Find_neighborMC() can find micro-clusters whose center is within a range R from MC_i.center*/
3 $count = \lfloor k * 1.1 - MC_i.MemberNum \rfloor$
4 **while** count ≠ zero **do**
5 | **for each micro-cluster** MC ∈ Clusters **do**
6 | **if** *MC.MemberNum* > $k * 1.1$ **then**
7 | **for each data** d *in* MC **do**
8 | **if isNeighbor**(d, MC_i.center) **then**
9 | MC_i.MemberNum + +;
10 | count − −;
11 | **Put** d in MC_i;
12 | **Remove** d from MC;
13 | **end**
14 | **end**
15 | **end**
16 | **end**
17 **end**

As mentioned before, traditional methods based on the *sliding-window* are difficult to adapt to dynamic changes in data streams. As shown in Fig. 1, when outliers occur on a large scale, the window can only be set large enough to prevent misjudging local outliers as global outliers. However, when large-scale outliers erupt in the AIP model, shown in Fig. 3, the outliers are first separated into *Buffers* with the size of S. Since only the data judged as inliers can be saved, the AIP will not be "contaminated" by outliers. Therefore, a fixed size AIP can robustly cope with the outliers outbreak scenario, and judge the data label quickly and accurately. This also applies to other scenarios where data distribution changes.

2.2 Micro-cluster-Based Storing Structure

In the algorithm proposed above, we maintain a structure based micro-clusters to store the data in the AIP to help the model update more promptly, and we design a corresponding effective algorithm to evaluate range queries for each new object to all other active inliers.

For each micro-cluster MC_i in AIP, We set the radius to $R/2$, which means that any object belonging to MC_i is in a range of $R/2$ from the center of MC_i, and the minimum size of a micro-cluster is $k + 1$. So each object o_i belonging to MC_i is definitely an inlier, because the maximum distance of any two objects in the MC_i cannot exceed R. Also, the size of the MC_i is at least $k + 1$, it means that o_i has at least k neighbors within distance R. In general, an object may have neighbors that belong to other micro-clusters.

In the example of Fig. 4, We show the distribution of some points in AIP. There are four micro-clusters and some isolated data points. For the objects of each kind of them, a different symbol has been used.

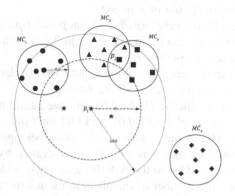

Fig. 4. The distribution of some points in AIP with k = 5.

Objects that do not belong to any micro-cluster are stored in a structure called a *Singular Queue* (SQ), which are depicted with the "star" symbol. Besides, for each point in SQ (e.g., p_1), we keep a list containing the identifiers of the micro-clusters, whose centers are less than $3R/2$ far away from this point. As shown in Fig. 4, p_1 can only find its neighbors in these micro-clusters, which can be easily proved. Consequently, when we calculate the number of p_1's neighbors, we only need to detect among members of these micro-clusters, which can accelerate considerably.

When the micro-clusters are thought of as spheres with radius $R/2$, they can be some overlap (e.g., MC_1, MC_4), although an object can only belong to a single micro-cluster at one time. For these points in the overlapping area, we have set up a unique *Sharing-Point* mechanism so that they can be dynamically adjusted. For example, when p_2 is eliminated, the members in MC_3 are less than 5, but we will not disperse this MC_1 in a hurry like other algorithms usually do. We set it as an *incomplete micro-clusters* instead. After all old points are eliminated, we check if these incomplete micro-clusters can "*share*" points from other micro-clusters to become normal micro-clusters. The pseudocode of these operations is given in Algorithm 2.

2.3 Workflow of FROD

The primary rationale behind our approach is to drastically reduce the number of micro-clusters that need to be reorganized when the AIP is updated and the complexity in finding neighbors for each data point when performing outlier detection. The detailed steps of the FROD algorithm are as follows:

Step 1: When the data arrives consecutively, we first determine whether an AIP already exists. If not, the initialization operation is performed. Else, proceed to the next step.

Step 2: The newly arrived data will be added to *Buffer*, and outlier detection is performed on the data in *Buffer*:

(2a) For each object p in Buffer, find the nearest micro-cluster MC_i from p and calculate the distance from p to MC_i, and if the distance is less than $R/2$, put p into *UpdateList*. Else, find neighbor of p in SQ;

(2b-i) If p has no less than k neighbors in SQ, put p into *UpdateList*. Otherwise, we find micro-clusters whose center point is less than $3R/2$ far away from p and look for neighbors in these micro-clusters;

(2b-ii) If p has more than k neighbors in total, put p into *UpdateList*. Otherwise, p is added to *OutlierList*, and the Buffer will be cleared.

Step 3: AIP is updated with the *UpdateList* generated from the previous step:

(3a) Calculate the length l of *UpdateList,* and find the l oldest points in AIP, then remove them from AIP, if the removed point once belonged to a micro-cluster, decrement the number of members of this micro-cluster by one. Similarly, the points in *UpdateList* are added to the AIP. If these newly added points belong to a certain micro-cluster, the number of members in the micro-cluster is increased by one.

(3b) If there are *incomplete micro-clusters* in the AIP, for each *incomplete micro-cluster*, we check if it can *share* some neighbors from its neighbor-clusters to make itself a normal cluster. And reconstruct the micro-cluster in AIP based on the result.

(3c) If there are still *incomplete micro-clusters*, these clusters will be dismantled, and their points will be added to the SQ.

Step 4: Report the outliers with *OutliersList*, then re-execute the step 2. And if outliers thrown by the algorithm is manually determined as inliers [5], these points will still be added to the *UpdateList* to prevent the occurrence of inliers that have never appeared.

2.4   Optimization and Analysis

In this section, we present an approach to optimize our algorithm, and then we analyze the temporal cost of the FROD, by comparing FROD with other popular outliers detection algorithm to illustrate its superiority.

Optimization. Since normal data is similar in FROD, we needn't update the AIP each time the *Buffer* cleared. Instead, the AIP update process (refer to step 3) can be executed in the background. When outlier detection is performed, we check whether the update module generates a new AIP first. If so, the new AIP will be used for detection, and the Update module will be triggered again with the newly generated *UpdateList*. Otherwise, the original AIP is kept for detection.

Analysis. Let $0 \leq c \leq 1$ denote the fraction of the window stored in micro-clusters then the number of data points in SQ is $(1 - c)W$, and the number of micro-clusters is approximately equal to $\log\left(\frac{cW}{k}\right)$. Because the model update module can be executed in the background, the temporal cost is mainly concentrated on step 2 with a time complexity of $O(S(\log\left(\frac{cW}{k}\right) + (1 - c)^2 W))$, and the value of c is proved to be very large (close to 1) in practical experiments, so it can be approximated as $O(S\log(w/k))$, which outperforms other popular algorithms.

Compared with the MCOD method proposed in [6], which is also based on the concept of micro-cluster, FROD can not only adapt to the dynamic change of data distribution in the data streams but also improve the response speed significantly.

In the phase of outlier detection, the time complexity of MCOD is $O((1-c)W\log((1-c)W) + kWlogk)$, which is much larger than FROD. Furthermore, FROD has set up an efficient sharing point mechanism that allows a micro-cluster can be incomplete temporarily. It helps the AIP update quickly and efficiently. However, the MCOD is to eliminate those clusters whose number of members is less than k while eliminating the points, which will exceedingly increase the number of operations required for updating, especially when S is large.

3 Experiments

3.1 Experimental Methodology

To evaluate the performance of the proposed algorithms, we compare FROD with four typical distance-based outlier detection methods in both responding time and detection accuracy. These methods are referred to as MCOD [7], Abstract-C [9], LUE [7], ExactStorm [2]. Our experiments were conducted on a macOSSierra machine with a 2.2 GHz processor and 15 GB Java heap space.

Datasets. We chose the following datasets for our evaluation. **FC (Forest Cover)** is available from the UCI KDD Archive, which is also used in [2], containing 581,012 records with 55 attributes. **TAO** is available at Tropical Atmosphere Ocean project, containing 575,648 records with 3 attributes. **STOCK** is available at UPenn Wharton Research Data Services, which is also used in [3] containing 1,048,575 transaction records with 1 attribute, **Gauss** is synthetically generated by mixing three Gaussian distributions and a random noise distribution, it contains 1 million records with 1 attribute.

Default Parameter Settings. There are four parameters to be determined: the size of the sliding-window or Active-Inliers-Pattern: W, the size of slide or Buffer: S, the distance threshold R, and the neighbor count threshold k.

W is the key parameters in influencing the responding speed which determine the volume of data streams, and we set it as 1k as default. For fairness of measurement, we set S to 5% of W, for all datasets. In general, when R is fixed, k should change with W to ensure that the data distribution in current window is approximately equivalent it in global. For all datasets, we maintain the outlier rate as 1%. In our experiment, we maintain the entire outlier rate as 1% for all datasets, and the default value of R is set to 525 for FC, 1.9 for TAO, 0.45 for Stock, and 0.028 for Gauss according to [8]. Based on this, the default value of k is set to $W/200$ for all datasets to ensure the accuracy.

3.2   Results

Responding Time. In this part, we measure the responding time of data labeling. To present the results clearly, we compare the sum of responding time for every 100k objects with varying W in the range [1 – 2k].

As shown in Fig. 5, when W increases, the CPU time for each algorithm increases as well, yet our best solution FROD consistently utilizes the least CPU time and exhibits the slowest increase in CPU consumption for all database. It's about 4 to 6 times faster in FC. Meanwhile, FROD can up to 1 – 2 orders of magnitude faster than the state-of-the-art in TAO and Stock.

Moreover, we can notice that MCOD which is also based on micro-cluster structure also shows good performance in most cases. However, when W is larger than 5k in the FC, the responding time grows rapidly, this is mainly because when W increases in FC, more and more outliers which do not participate in any micro-cluster will be added to the window, and many additional reorganizations will be performed. Both of them will greatly increase the processing speed, while FROD can exclude outliers from AIP and update AIP efficiently with the *"Sharing-Point"* mechanism.

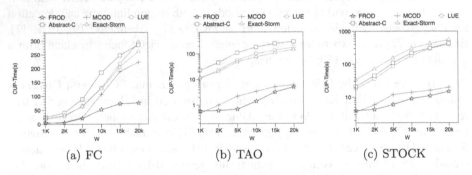

(a) FC   (b) TAO   (c) STOCK

Fig. 5. The comparative results of different algorithms running on three datasets

Accuracy. In this section, we analyze the robustness of the methods in facing the dynamic changes of data distribution, we first label all the data according to their distribution in the entire Gauss data set and then calculate the frequency of outliers occurrences in units of 1K. We have selected a piece of data with abnormal fluctuations to compare the performance of each algorithm under different data distributions. We use F1-score [10] to measure the accuracy of outlier detection.

As shown in Fig. 6, FROD maintains a high detection performance when the distribution of data in the stream fluctuates. In contrast, although other algorithms can perform well when the outlier rate fluctuates little, the accuracy of these methods will degrade significantly in the presence of outlier outbreaks because the windows they maintained are contaminated by the flocking outliers. So they may misjudge outliers and inliers, while the FROD that only retains normal points does not have this problem.

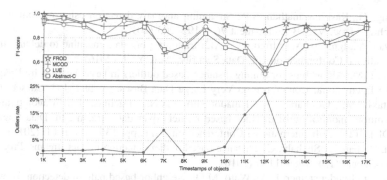

Fig. 6. The comparative results of different algorithms running on three datasets

4 Conclusion

Outlier detection for extracting abnormal phenomena from dynamic streaming data is a crucial yet difficult task. In this paper, we study the problem of continuous outlier detection over data streams by using an Active-Inliers Pattern. We employ the Active-Inliers-Pattern to adapt the distribution changing in data streams to ensure the accuracy and improve the responding speed by setting an effective structure based on the micro-cluster for objects storing. Besides, our experimental evaluation with both real and synthetic datasets shows that our approach can perform well even when the distribution of data is dynamically changing, and it is also faster than the state-of-the-art methods.

For future work, a meaningful direction is to design a distributed algorithm to implement the model update phase of FROD, aiming at the significant improvement of efficiency under the premise of detection accuracy assurance.

Acknowledgement. The authors would like to thank the anonymous reviewers for their valuable comments. This work was supported by the National Key Research and Development Program (Grant No. 2016YFB1000101), the National Natural Science Foundation of China (Grant No. 61379052), the Natural Science Foundation for Distinguished Young Scholars of Hunan Province (Grant No. 14JJ1026), Specialized Research Fund for the Doctoral Program of Higher Education (Grant No.20124307110015).

References

1. Aggarwal, C.C.: Outlier Analysis. Data Mining, pp. 237–263. Springer, Cham (2015). https://doi.org/10.1007/978-3-319-14142-8_8
2. Angiulli, F., Fassetti, F.: Detecting distance-based outliers in streams of data. In: Proceedings of the Sixteenth ACM Conference on Information and Knowledge Management, pp. 811–820. ACM (2007)
3. Cao, L., Yang, D., Wang, Q., Yu, Y., Wang, J., Rundensteiner, E.A.: Scalable distance-based outlier detection over high-volume data streams. In: Data Engineering (ICDE), IEEE 30th International Conference on 2014. pp. 76–87. IEEE (2014)

 4. Huang, H., Kasiviswanathan, S.P.: Streaming anomaly detection using randomized matrix sketching. Proc. VLDB Endowment **9**(3), 192–203 (2015)
 5. Kalyan, V., Ignacio, A., Alfredo, C.: AI2: training a big data machine to defend. In: IEEE International Conference on Big Data Security, New York (2016)
 6. Knox, E.M.: Algorithms for mining distance based outliers in large datasets. In: Proceedings of the International Conference on Very Large Data Bases, pp. 392–403. Citeseer (1998)
 7. Kontaki, M., Gounaris, A., Papadopoulos, A.N., Tsichlas, K., Manolopoulos, Y.: Continuous monitoring of distance-based outliers over data streams. In: Data Engineering (ICDE), IEEE 27th International Conference on 2011. pp. 135–146. IEEE (2011)
 8. Tran, L., Fan, L., Shahabi, C.: Distance-based outlier detection in data streams. Proc. VLDB Endowment **9**(12), 1089–1100 (2016)
 9. Yang, D., Rundensteiner, E.A., Ward, M.O.: Neighbor-based pattern detection for windows over streaming data. In: Proceedings of the 12th International Conference on Extending Database Technology: Advances in Database Technology, pp. 529–540. ACM (2009)
10. Yang, Y., Liu, X.: A re-examination of text categorization methods. In: Proceedings of the 22nd Annual International ACM SIGIR Conference on Research and Development in Information Retrieval, pp. 42–49. ACM (1999)

Unified Framework for Joint Attribute Classification and Person Re-identification

Chenxin Sun[1], Na Jiang[1], Lei Zhang[1], Yuehua Wang[2], Wei Wu[1], and Zhong Zhou[1($\boxtimes$)]

[1] State Key Laboratory of Virtual Reality Technology and Systems,
Beihang University, Beijing, China
zz@buaa.edu.cn
[2] Department of Computer Science,
Texas A&M University – Commerce, Texas, USA

Abstract. Person re-identification (re-id) is an essential task in video surveillance. Existing approaches mainly concentrate on extracting useful appearance features from deep convolutional neural networks. However, they don't utilize or only partially utilize semantic information such as attributes or person orientation. In this paper, we propose a novel deep neural network framework that greatly improves the accuracy of person re-id and also that of attribute classification. The proposed framework includes two branches, the identity one and the attribute one. The identity branch employs the refined triplet loss and exploits local cues from different regions of the pedestrian body. The attribute branch has an effective attribute predictor containing hierarchical attribute loss functions. After training the identification and attribute classifications, pedestrian representations are derived which contains hierarchical attribute information. The experimental results on DukeMTMC-reID and Matket-1501 datasets validate the effectiveness of the proposed framework in both person re-id and attribute classification. For person re-id, the Rank-1 accuracy is improved by 7.99% and 2.76%, and the mAP is improved by 14.72% and 5.45% on DukeMTMC-reID and Market-1501 datasets respectively. Specifically, it yields 90.95% in accuracy of attribute classification on DukeMTMC-reID, which outperforms the state-of-the-art attribute classification methods by 3.42%.

Keywords: Deep learning · Person re-identification · Attribute classification

1 Introduction

Person re-identification (re-id) aims at retrieving persons from non-overlapping cameras or different timetamps. Recently, person re-id has been drawing increasing attention from both academia and industry in that it has broad applications in surveillance systems for efficiently preventing and tracking crimes. However, the effects caused by factors like viewpoint variations, occlusion and illumination condition differences potentially make the person re-id an extremely challenging task.

As deep learning arises in the recent years, deep convolutional neural networks have been widely used in person re-id and yielded promising performance [1, 2]. However, when being applied to real scenarios, these methods tend to be less effective

© Springer Nature Switzerland AG 2018
V. Kůrková et al. (Eds.): ICANN 2018, LNCS 11139, pp. 637–647, 2018.
https://doi.org/10.1007/978-3-030-01418-6_63

due to the lack of detailed cues. In [3], person re-id model is proposed to utilize different parts of the image therefore it can extract regional features containing localized information. The feature maps of different regions of a person appear quite different, which makes the body region alignment of great importance for person re-id. In our re-id framework, we use accurate keypoint locations of a person through keypoint detection to extract desired body regions.

Another common used solution is to exploit person attributes with consideration that the attribute information may contain some domain cues which are identified as the powerful complementary information in the person re-id task [4–7]. Theoretically, attributes often represent a high level feature of a pedestrian which could be easily missed by approaches based on appearance features. As shown in Fig. 1, people with similar appearance can be easily distinguished by attribute information, which motivated us to study this problem. To solve it, we integrate attribute information into the CNN model for re-id task using our framework.

Fig. 1. Examples of pedestrians in similar appearance with different attribute labels. The attribute labels (e.g., bag vs. handbag, long sleeves vs. short sleeves, etc.) are denoted as discriminative information to distinguish the pedestrians.

The main contributions of this paper are as: (1) A deep neural network incorporating body parts and pose information is proposed. (2) A hierarchical loss guided structure is used to extract meaningful attribute features and consequently to combine the attribute representation with the appearance representation for better re-id. (3) Experiment results on DukeMTMC-reID and Market-1501 datasets demonstrate the effectiveness of the proposed framework. We outperform the state-of-the-art re-id methods in terms of mAP and Rank-1.

2 Related Work

Person re-identification is first introduced and studied by Zajdel et al. [8] in 2005. It is assumed that every individual is associated with unique hidden labels. They design a dynamic Bayesian network to encode the statistical relationships between the features and the labels of the same identity. Typical traditional person re-identification methods use color or hand-crafted features as feature descriptors. Liao et al. [9] design the Local Maximal Occurrence Representation together with a XQDA metric learning approach for person re-id.

Convolutional Neural Networks have first been used for person re-id by [2, 10]. [2] splits the input person images into three horizontal strips processed by several convolutional layers independently. Meanwhile, there are approaches [10, 11] which solve re-id problem from the aspect of directly minimizing the feature distance between image pairs or triplets. The Siamese model proposed by Li et al. [10] takes two images as input, directly ending with a same person /different person classification through a deep neural network. Cheng et al. [11] extend this idea and design a similar framework, which processes three images at a time and introduces the triplet loss for metric learning. There are also methods which extract more efficient person features from a tree-structured competitive neural network [3] or different levels of neural network representations [1].

Visual semantic attributes have been investigated in the studies [4–7, 12]. Zhang et al. [4] compute the appearance distances and the attribute distances from two separate models and fuse these two distances together to get the final ranking list. To train unified neural networks, a few methods [5–7] use identification and attribute classification loss at the same time to encourage the neural networks to capture both identification and attribute information. However, the information extracted from different domains are difficult to integrate using loss aiming to solve distinct problems. Su et al. [12] propose a weekly supervised multi-type attribute learning algorithm which only uses a limited number of labeled attribute data. In their work, Su et al. employ a three-stage fine-tune strategy to train the model either on attribute datasets or other datasets only labeled with person IDs. The work closest to this paper is [6], in which a combination of re-id and attribute classification losses is used to learn overall representations for person re-id.

3 Proposed Approach

We propose a novel deep neural network framework that jointly learns person re-identification and attribute classification, as shown in Fig. 2. Our approach includes an identity branch based on DenseNet-121 and an attribute branch based on ResNet-50 to learn identity and attribute classification respectively. In Fig. 2, the upper part of the framework is the identity branch while the lower part is the attribute branch. At inference time, given as input a person image, we combine identity feature vectors and attribute feature vectors extracted from identity and attribute branch respectively to get the final re-id feature vectors. We then rank the gallery images according to their feature distances to the final representations of the retrieving images. In the following part, we first describe the detail of identity learning framework in Sect. 3.1 and then the attribute classification structure in Sect. 3.2.

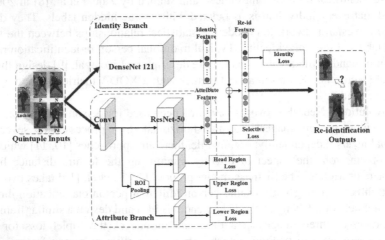

Fig. 2. Overview of our approach. Inputs are quintuples described in Sect. 3.1.

3.1 Identity Learning Framework

To mitigate occlusions and reduce misalignments, several person re-id studies combine global features with local features which are extracted from certain body parts. Compared with fixed mandatory horizontal strips, accurate body part segmentation can yield more representative local features and greatly eliminate the influence of background. Inspired by such observation, we use the PAFs model [13] to localize fourteen accurate body keypoints and pool three ROI (Region-of-Interest) areas, head, UpperBody and LowerBody, from the feature maps according to the locations of the keypoints. In each forward process, four feature vectors, extracted from the main full image branch and three body part branches, are concatenated to one identity vector which is used for model training, represented by colored rectangle in Fig. 3. Three images on the yellow shadow produce the Triplet loss while three images on the green shadow produce the Orientation loss. Then these two losses are added together to get the identity loss.

In the training process, we introduce a new orientation-based triplet loss based on the traditional triplet loss [14] in the proposed identity learning model. Concretely, The traditional triplet loss is trained on triplets $\{x_i^a, x_i^p, x_i^n\}$, where x_i^a and x_i^p denote two different images of the same person i, while x_i^n is the third image of a different person. The purpose of triplet loss is to train the network to pull x_i^a closer to x_i^p and push away x_i^n, as formulated as following:

$$Loss_{triplet} = \max\left(d\left(f\left(x_i^a\right), f\left(x_i^p\right)\right) - d\left(f\left(x_i^a\right), f\left(x_i^n\right)\right) + \alpha, 0\right) \tag{1}$$

where $f(x)$ is the feature of the image x, and $d(x, y)$ represents the distance between x and y. α represents the margin between positive pairs and negative pairs.

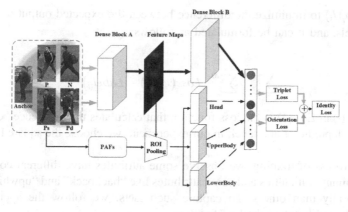

Fig. 3. Identity learning network. Inputs of the convolutional neural network are quintuples including the original image, the positive example, the negative example and two positive examples with same /different orientation, represented by Anchors, P, N, Ps, Pd respectively. (Color figure online)

In our identity learning framework, we argue that we further improve the performance of triplet loss with the pose information. Smaller feature distances between positive samples with the same orientation can be achieved according to the following loss:

$$Loss_{orientation} = \max\left(d\left(f(x_i^a), f(x_i^{ps})\right) - d\left(f(x_i^a), f\left(x_i^{pd}\right)\right) + \beta, 0 \right) \qquad (2)$$

where x_i^{ps} represents the positive sample having the same orientation with anchor sample x_i^a, while x_i^{pd} represents the positive sample having the different orientation. β represents the margin between the same orientation pairs and different orientation pairs. Other symbols in Eq. (2) are the same as the symbols in Eq. (1).

As for the accurate orientation of the images, we use the orientation classification results from the attribute classifier.

The overall loss function for identity learning is formulated as:

$$Loss_{identity} = Loss_{triplet} + \omega * Loss_{orientation} \qquad (3)$$

where ω is a weight balancing the two losses of different purposes.

3.2 Attribute Classification

Attributes classifiers are designed to effectively predict the attribute labels and provide meaningful feature vectors to the identity branch for offering complementary information. We dynamically tune training strategies for differentiated phases.

Phase 1. Person attribute classification is formulated as a multitask problem, which requires optimizing all attribute predictors. Suppose we have N training images I_i, $(i = 1, \ldots, N)$ labeled with M attributes $Label_{ij}$, $(j = 1, \ldots, M)$. We need to learn M predictors $\varphi_j(I_i)$ to minimize the difference between the expected output of predictors and the labels, and it can be formulated as follows:

$$\sum_{i=1}^{N} \sum_{j=1}^{M} Loss\big(\varphi_j(I_i) - Label_{ij}\big) \tag{4}$$

where Loss $(\cdot)$ in Eq. (4) is the loss function that calculates the difference between the output of each predictor and label; in our experiment, we choose the square loss as loss function.

In the process of training, we observe some attributes have different convergence rates and training difficulties and some attributes like "backpack" and "upwhite" appear more frequently than others. To capture such facts, we follow the approach [14] weighting the attributes in the loss function:

$$\sum_{i=1}^{N} \sum_{j=1}^{M} \lambda_j * Loss\big(\sigma_j(I_i) - Label_{ij}\big) \tag{5}$$

where λ_j is the scalar value to weight the importance of attribute j to overall loss function.

Instead of manually tuning the hyper-parameter λ_j using methods like cross validation, we propose an adaptive method to update λ_j every k iterations during training. In each batch, we separate the training images into two parts: the training part and the auxiliary part, all of which are passed through the neural network. We get two kinds of loss vectors from the output of the neural network. But only the loss vector obtained from the training part is used to update the neural network, while the loss vector obtained from the auxiliary part is stored in a data structure $Loss_{[\cdot]}$ used to update the weight vector λ. We formulate the weight update algorithm in Eqs. (6) and (7).

$$\lambda = \Big[\big[Loss_{[n-k:n]} - Loss_{[n-2k:n-k]}\big]_{norm} \cdot \big[Loss_{[n-k:n]}\big]_{norm}\Big]_{norm} \tag{6}$$

$$\big[\vec{v}\big]_{norm} = \frac{\vec{v} - v_{min}}{v_{max} - v_{min}} \tag{7}$$

where λ is a M-dim vector, $\cdot$ stands for dot product, $Loss_{[\cdot]}$ is a data structure storing the auxiliary loss vectors, n is the number of losses stored in $Loss_{[\cdot]}$, $Loss_{[b:a]}$ stands for an average loss whose every element is the mean value of the corresponding elements from $Loss_a$ to $Loss_b$, $[\cdot]_{norm}$ is the normalization function in Eq. (7), v_{min} and v_{max} refer to the minimum and the maximum values in vector $\vec{v}$ respectively, and k is set to 12 with experiential experience in our experiment.

In Eq. (6), the $\big[Loss_{[n-k:n]} - Loss_{[n-2k:n-k]}\big]_{norm}$ factor encourages weights of certain attributes to be larger ones whose current losses change drastically compared to previous losses, while the $\big[Loss_{[n-k:n]}\big]_{norm}$ factor encourages weights of the other kind of attributes to be larger which have not converged. To this end, we keep training our attribute classification network using the weighted loss until convergence, as shown in

Fig. 4(a). When we train the attribute classification network with our identity learning network, we use an adaptive strategy to assist the re-id task discussed in Phase 2.

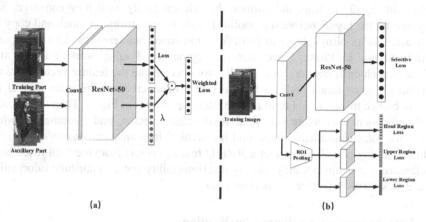

(a)   (b)

Fig. 4. A figure caption is always placed below the illustration. Short captions are centered, while long ones are justified. The macro button chooses the correct format automatically.

Phase 2. It is noted that attributes in datasets are generally classified into two groups according to whether they can be assigned to certain image regions. The attributes like the color of upper clothes, backpack, and the color of lower clothes, rely on small regions of images rather than the whole images. Based on this observation we design a multi-branch framework for efficient attribute classification which predicts region based attributes respectively, as shown in Fig. 4(b). We initialize the weights of our deep neural network gained by Phase 1 and use the locations of ROI regions in Sect. 3.1 to pool three regions from the first pooling layer.

Besides, according to the influence of attribute labels on the person re-id task, we choose several attribute labels to train the overall framework using Eq. (4), discarding the prediction layer trained in Phase 1. The selective attribute loss from the main branch together with three losses from region based branches constitute our hierarchical loss.

4 Experiments

4.1 Implementation Details

In our experiments, we choose DenseNet [15] model as our identity branch and ResNet [16] as the attribute classification branch. For the identity branch, it includes a backbone network and three body part subnetworks. They share the weights from the first convolutional layer to the first dense block. We add an ROI pooling layer behind the first dense block to pool three areas from the shared feature maps according to the output of PAFs keypoint estimator. The backbone network and three subnetworks all have four dense blocks with different growth rates. For the attribute branch, the network is designed similarly like the identity branch except that the attribute branch uses proposed hierarchical loss as the objective function.

In the training phase, we firstly use $Loss_{identity}$ in Eq. (3) to train the identity branch and loss in Eq. (5) to train the attribute branch separately until they converge. Secondly, we fix the layers before the pooling1 layer in our attribute branch and copy the layers after the pooling1 layer to from 3 region based subnetworks. Using proposed hierarchical loss in Phase 2, we train the region based subnetworks and the main attribute branch until convergence. Finally, we concatenate the feature vector extracted from the identity branch and the feature vector obtained from the main part of our attribute branch to get a final re-id feature vector as shown in Fig. 2. Then we calculate the classification loss using this final re-id feature vector, and finetune the whole framework using classification loss and hierarchical loss until convergence.

In the testing phase, we extract a 3048-D feature vectors from the final fused layer. This feature vector has not only identity discriminability but also attribute information. We use this 3048-D feature for person re-id.

4.2 Performance on Attribute Classification

To evaluate the effect of the attribute domain learning, we conduct the attribute classification on DukeMTMC-reID [17] and Market-1501 [18] datasets. In such a way, the identity and attribute labels are obtained for the designed framework.

Table 1. Attribute recognition accuracy on DukeMTMC-reID

Methods	Gender	Hat	Boots	Top	Backpack	Handbag	Bag	Shoes	Upcolor	Downcolor	Mean
SVM [20]	77.03	82.24	82.45	87.64	69.59	93.60	83.01	90.05	70.94	68.48	80.50
APR [10]	82.61	**86.94**	**86.15**	88.04	77.28	**93.75**	82.51	**90.19**	72.29	41.48	80.12
Baseline	83.12	81.09	80.52	89.91	76.05	90.06	81.08	81.92	75.54	70.55	80.98
Ours	**88.94**	82.97	80.13	**93.60**	**87.02**	89.60	**91.60**	83.65	**93.94**	**91.84**	**90.95**

Table 2. Attribute recognition accuracy on market-1501

Methods	Gender	Age	Hair	Up	Down	Clothes	Backpack	Handbag	Bag	Hat	Upcolor	Downcolor	Mean
APR [10]	86.45	**87.08**	**83.65**	**93.66**	**93.32**	**91.46**	82.79	**88.98**	75.07	**97.13**	73.40	69.91	85.33
Baseline	81.08	85.39	70.49	87.47	84.59	81.51	**86.22**	85.18	67.30	92.10	71.57	71.05	80.33
Ours	**88.94**	84.76	78.26	93.53	92.11	84.79	85.46	88.40	67.28	97.06	**87.50**	**87.21**	**86.98**

In Tables 1 and 2, we compare the attribute recognition accuracy of the proposed method with two state-of-the-art ones, Baseline and APR [5]. Baseline denotes the attribute branch trained by loss in Eq. 4 and Ours represents the attribute classifier finetuned by weighted attribute loss in Eq. 5. As shown in the tables, we have achieved competitive results in these two datasets and the proposed framework significantly outperforms the baseline. It is worth noting that the results in [14] are also very competitive with the mean average accuracy of 87.53% and 88.49% on the

DukeMTMC-reID and Market-1501 datasets. Our framework achieves 90.95% accuracy on DukeMTMC-reID, outperforming all state-of-the-art methods by 3.42%.

4.3 Performance on Person Re-Identification

In this section, we evaluate the performance of our method on the DukeMTMC-reID and Market-1501 datasets.

Table 3. Comparison with the state-of-the-art approaches.

DukeMTMC-reID	Rank-1	mAP	Market-1501	Rank-1	mAP
LOMO + XQDA [9]	30.8	17.0	LOMO + XQDA [9]	43.80	47.78
GAN [17]	67.68	47.13	GAN [17]	79.33	55.95
Loss Embedding [19]	68.90	49.30	Loss Embedding [19]	79.51	59.87
APR [6]	70.69	51.88	ACRN [7]	83.61	62.60
ACRN [7]	72.58	51.96	APR [6]	84.29	64.67
Baseline	67.58	47.46	Baseline	72.50	45.23
Baseline + Triplet	72.33	51.72	Baseline + Triplet	81.32	61.50
Baseline + Improved Triplet	75.72	56.20	Baseline + Improved Triplet	85.88	67.28
Ours	**80.57**	**66.68**	Ours	**87.05**	**70.12**

Table 3 shows the performances of the proposed method comparing to that of several state-of-the-art methods. Baseline represents our identity network without the triplet loss, Baseline + Triplet represents identity network with the original triplet in Eq. 1, Baseline + Improved Triplet represents identity network with proposed triplet loss in Eq. (3) and Ours represents the results of our overall framework in Fig. 2. As shown in Table 3, the Rank-1 accuracy is improved by 7.99% and 2.76%, while the mAP is improved by 14.72% and 5.45% on DukeMTMC-reID and Market-1501 datasets respectively in our overall framework. This result shows the effectiveness of proposed attribute information transferring. With the use of triplet loss and proposed attribute supplementary information, we can observe significant improvement in the final results.

5 Conclusion

In this paper, we have presented a deep convolutional neural framework employing hierarchical attribute information for person re-identification. With the joint learning of the identity and attribute supervision from the same dataset, we invoke information transferring from the attribute domain to the identity domain which is used as supplementary information. According to the evaluation results, the proposed framework shows highly accurate attribute and person re-id comparing to the state-of-the-art methods in the field on two datasets.

Acknowledgment. This work is supported by the Natural Science Foundation of China under Grant No. 61572061, 61472020, 61502020, and the China Postdoctoral Science Foundation under Grant No. 2013M540039.

References

1. Meng, X., Leng, B., Song, G.: A Multi-level Weighted Representation for Person Re-identification. In: Lintas, A., Rovetta, S., Verschure, P., Villa, A. (eds.) ICANN 2017. LNCS, vol. 10614, pp. 80–88. Springer, Cham (2017). https://doi.org/10.1007/978-3-319-68612-7_10
2. Yi, D., Lei, Z., Liao, S., Li, S. Z.: Deep metric learning for person re-identification. In: Pattern Recognition (ICPR), 22nd International Conference on 2014, pp. 34–39. IEEE (2014)
3. Zhao, H., et al.: Spindle net: person re-identification with human body region guided feature decomposition and fusion. In: Proceedings of the IEEE Conference on Computer Vision and Pattern Recognition, pp. 1077–1085 (2017)
4. Zhang, X., Pala, F., Bhanu, B.: Attributes co-occurrence pattern mining for video-based person re-identification. In: Advanced Video and Signal Based Surveillance (AVSS), (2017) 14th IEEE International Conference on 2017, pp. 1–6. IEEE (2017)
5. Matsukawa, T., Suzuki, E.: Person re-identification using CNN features learned from combination of attributes. In: Pattern Recognition (ICPR), 23rd International Conference on 2016 , pp. 2428–2433. IEEE (2016)
6. Lin, Y., Zheng, L., Zheng, Z., Wu, Y., Yang, Y.: Improving person re-identification by attribute and identity learning. arXiv preprint arXiv:1703.07220 (2017)
7. Schumann, A., Stiefelhagen, R.: Person re-identification by deep learning attribute-complementary information. In: Computer Vision and Pattern Recognition Work-shops (CVPRW), IEEE Conference on 2017, pp. 1435–1443. IEEE (2017)
8. Zajdel, W., Zivkovic, Z., Krose, B.: Keeping track of humans: have I seen this person before? In: Proceedings of the 2005 IEEE International Conference on 2005 Robotics and Automation, ICRA 2005, pp. 2081–2086. IEEE (2005)
9. Liao, S., Hu, Y., Zhu, X., Li, S.Z.: Person re-identification by local maximal occurrence representation and metric learning. In: Proceedings of the IEEE Conference on Computer Vision and Pattern Recognition, pp. 2197–2206 (2015)
10. Li, W., Zhao, R., Xiao, T., Wang, X.: Deepreid: deep filter pairing neural network for person re-identification. In: Proceedings of the IEEE Conference on Computer Vision and Pattern Recognition, pp. 152–159 (2014)
11. Cheng, D., Gong, Y., Zhou, S., Wang, J., Zheng, N.: Person re-identification by multi-channel parts-based CNN with improved triplet loss function. In: Proceedings of the IEEE Conference on Computer Vision and Pattern Recognition, pp. 1335–1344 (2016)
12. Su, C., Zhang, S., Xing, J., Gao, W., Tian, Q.: Multi-type attributes driven multi-camera person re-identification. Pattern Recogn. **75**, 77–89 (2018)
13. Cao, Z., Simon, T., Wei, S.E., Sheikh, Y.: Realtime multi-person 2D pose estimation using part affinity fields. In: CVPR, vol.1, p. 7 (2017)
14. He, K., Wang, Z., Fu, Y., Feng, R., Jiang, Y.G., Xue, X.: Adaptively weighted multi-task deep network for person attribute classification. In: Proceedings of the 2017 ACM on Multimedia Conference, pp. 1636–1644. ACM (2017)

15. Huang, G., Liu, Z., Weinberger, K.Q., van der Maaten, L.: Densely connected convolutional networks. In: Proceedings of the IEEE Conference on Computer Vision and Pattern Recognition, vol. 1, p. 3 (2017)
16. He, K., Zhang, X., Ren, S., Sun, J.: Deep residual learning for image recognition. In: Proceedings of the IEEE Conference on Computer Vision and Pattern Recognition, pp. 770–778 (2016)
17. Zheng, Z., Zheng, L., Yang, Y.: A discriminatively learned CNN embedding for person re-identification. ACM Trans. Multimedia Comput., Commun. Appl. (TOMM) **14**(1), 13 (2017)
18. Zheng, L., Shen, L., Tian, L., Wang, S., Wang, J., Tian, Q.: Scalable person re-identification: a benchmark. In: Proceedings of the IEEE International Conference on Computer Vision, pp. 1116–1124 (2015)
19. Zheng, Z., Zheng, L., Yang, Y.: Unlabeled samples generated by GAN improve the person re-identification baseline in vitro. arXiv preprint arXiv:1701.077173 (2017)
20. Kurnianggoro, L., Jo, K.H.: Identification of pedestrian attributes using deep network. In: IECON 2017 - Conference of the IEEE Industrial Electronics Society, pp. 8503–8507. IEEE (2017)

Associative Graph Data Structures Used for Acceleration of K Nearest Neighbor Classifiers

Adrian Horzyk$^{(\boxtimes)}$ ⓘ and Krzysztof Gołdon ⓘ

AGH University of Science and Technology, Krakow, Poland
horzyk@agh.edu.pl, krzysztofgoldon@gmail.com

Abstract. This paper introduces a new associative approach for significant acceleration of k Nearest Neighbor classifiers (kNN). The kNN classifier is a lazy method, i.e. it does not create a computational model, so it is inefficient during classification using big training data sets because it requires going through all training patterns when classifying each sample. In this paper, we propose to use Associative Graph Data Structures (AGDS) as an efficient model for storing training patterns and their relations, allowing for fast access to nearest neighbors during classification made by kNNs. Hence, the AGDS significantly accelerates the classification made by kNNs, especially for large and huge training datasets. In this paper, we introduce an Associative Acceleration Algorithm and demonstrate how it works on this associative structure sub-stantially reducing the number of checked patterns and quickly selecting k nearest neighbors for kNNs. The presented approach was compared to classic kNN approaches successfully.

Keywords: Classification · K nearest neighbors · Associative acceleration
Brain-inspired associative approach · Associative Graph Data Structures

1 Introduction

Today, in computer science, we need to face computational difficulties of Big Data [4, 18], and create new efficient models operating on Big Data producing intelligent systems for various uses [14]. The big problem of Big Data processing is not only about computational methods but also about the data structures which we use for representing data because they significantly influence the effectiveness of algorithms implemented to big amounts of data. Data stored in traditional data structures (usually tables and relational databases) is easy to read and interpret for humans. Such structures do not represent many important relations [7] that must be searched in many nested loops spoiling computational complexity and efficiency of data access [9]. We try to overcome a part of these inefficiencies using biologically inspired associative mecha-nisms [6, 7, 13]. We focus on a very popular k Nearest Neighbor classifier that is easy to use and supply users with satisfactory results without a big effort or time invested in designing and training more advanced computational intelligence models [4, 17].

K Nearest Neighbors (kNN) were already widely studied, extended and described in many papers, e.g. [1, 2, 5, 11, 16], where fuzzy-logic, genetic algorithms, rough sets,

V. Kůrková et al. (Eds.): ICANN 2018, LNCS 11139, pp. 648–658, 2018.
https://doi.org/10.1007/978-3-030-01418-6_64

various trees and other approaches were used to improve the efficiency of kNNs. An interesting approach presented in [20] is using a weighted voting method for kNN. In this approach, the neighbor which is closer to test object is weighted more heavily. Similar solution based on weighted voting approach was also shown in [21].

This paper describes Associative Graph Data Structures (AGDS) [6, 7], and a specially developed algorithm operating on these structures that allows finding k nearest neighbors very quickly, i.e. without looking through all training patterns, but checking only a limited subset of them using special features of the AGDS structures. They allow us to move to close or similar objects in constant time, so we can also compute the distance of the limited subset of close training patterns very quickly pointing out k nearest neighbors. This paper shows advantages of AGDS structures and their use for acceleration of kNN classifiers. The AGDS structures remove the inconvenience of classic tabular structures typically used by kNN classifiers [4]. The main contribution is the presentation of an Associative Acceleration Algorithm for kNN classifiers using AGDS structures and comparisons of its speed to the classic approaches.

2   Associative Graph Data Structures

Associative Graph Data Structures (AGDS) first introduced by Horzyk in [6] and accelerated by the use of AVB+trees in [7] were inspired by the associative processes that take place in real brains [12]. They are defined as graphs of nodes representing aggregated, counted, and sorted attribute values represented by value nodes and objects defined by the values and represented by object nodes. Value nodes represent unique attribute values and are connected to the object nodes defined by the values of the connected value nodes. Moreover, AGDS structures can contain additional nodes representing subsets or ranges of values, and various combinations of values or objects, defining clusters or classes, as well as various dependencies and relations between the nodes of such graphs, e.g. the sequence in time or the proximity or neighborhood in space. AGDS structures can directly represent a lot of useful features and relations between stored values and objects, e.g. neighborhood, similarity, proximity, order, defining, aggregations of the same value and objects, and numbers of aggregated value or objects. Therefore, they eliminate the necessity to search for various relations in loops, delivering results in a much faster time because such features and relations are always available in constant time. Thanks to the aggregations of duplicates made during the transformation of data stored in tables into AGDS structures which often compress the data losslessly. The possible compression factor depends on the number of duplicates in raw tabular data and the types of aggregated duplicates because each duplicate is replaced by an extra connection that also uses some memory. The compression is treated as a side product of this transformation, but it can have a certain value for Big Data collections. The aggregated, counted, and sorted values for all attributes simultaneously allow us to compute minima, maxima, sums, averages, medians faster in AGDS structures than using tables as described in [7, 8]. We can also quickly move to neighbor values for each attribute. This feature was a basis to define a new associative data model for kNN classifiers which allows to significantly limit the number of checked training patterns to lift the efficiency of kNN classifiers presented in this paper.

The above-described features make AGDS structures a universal model for data and relation storing that can be adapted to many computational tasks optimizing access to the stored data and decreasing computational complexities of various operations. In computer science, we used to talk about data structures, focusing on storing data and optimizing the access to them. The main disadvantage of this approach is that almost all data relations must be searched in single or nested loops. The AGDS structures remove this disadvantage making data and their relations available faster and often decreasing the computational complexity of many operations in the way that is not achievable in classic tabular structures.

Table 1. Sample data consisting of two attributes of the Iris training patterns of two classes from UCI ML Repository [19] used for the presentation of the introduced algorithm approach.

No	leaf length	leaf width	class	No	leaf length	leaf width	class	No	leaf length	leaf width	class	No	leaf length	leaf width	class
1	5.1	3.5	setosa	26	5	3	setosa	51	7	3.2	versicolor	76	6.6	3	versicolor
2	4.9	3	setosa	27	5	3.4	setosa	52	6.4	3.2	versicolor	77	6.8	2.8	versicolor
3	4.7	3.2	setosa	28	5.2	3.5	setosa	53	6.9	3.1	versicolor	78	6.7	3	versicolor
4	4.6	3.1	setosa	29	5.2	3.4	setosa	54	5.5	2.3	versicolor	79	6	2.9	versicolor
5	5	3.6	setosa	30	4.7	3.2	setosa	55	6.5	2.8	versicolor	80	5.7	2.6	versicolor
6	5.4	3.9	setosa	31	4.8	3.1	setosa	56	5.7	2.8	versicolor	81	5.5	2.4	versicolor
7	4.6	3.4	setosa	32	5.4	3.4	setosa	57	6.3	3.3	versicolor	82	5.5	2.4	versicolor
8	5	3.4	setosa	33	5.2	4.1	setosa	58	4.9	2.4	versicolor	83	5.8	2.7	versicolor
9	4.4	2.9	setosa	34	5.5	4.2	setosa	59	6.6	2.9	versicolor	84	6	2.7	versicolor
10	4.9	3.1	setosa	35	4.9	3.1	setosa	60	5.2	2.7	versicolor	85	5.4	3	versicolor
11	5.4	3.7	setosa	36	5	3.2	setosa	61	5	2	versicolor	86	6	3.4	versicolor
12	4.8	3.4	setosa	37	5.5	3.5	setosa	62	5.9	3	versicolor	87	6.7	3.1	versicolor
13	4.8	3	setosa	38	4.9	3.1	setosa	63	6	2.2	versicolor	88	6.3	2.3	versicolor
14	4.3	3	setosa	39	4.4	3	setosa	64	6.1	2.9	versicolor	89	5.6	3	versicolor
15	5.8	4	setosa	40	5.1	3.4	setosa	65	5.6	2.9	versicolor	90	5.5	2.5	versicolor
16	5.7	4.4	setosa	41	5	3.5	setosa	66	6.7	3.1	versicolor	91	5.5	2.6	versicolor
17	5.4	3.9	setosa	42	4.5	2.3	setosa	67	5.6	3	versicolor	92	6.1	3	versicolor
18	5.1	3.5	setosa	43	4.4	3.2	setosa	68	5.8	2.7	versicolor	93	5.8	2.6	versicolor
19	5.7	3.8	setosa	44	5	3.5	setosa	69	6.2	2.2	versicolor	94	5	2.3	versicolor
20	5.1	3.8	setosa	45	5.1	3.8	setosa	70	5.6	2.5	versicolor	95	5.6	2.7	versicolor
21	5.4	3.4	setosa	46	4.8	3	setosa	71	5.9	3.2	versicolor	96	5.7	3	versicolor
22	5.1	3.7	setosa	47	5.1	3.8	setosa	72	6.1	2.8	versicolor	97	5.7	2.9	versicolor
23	4.6	3.6	setosa	48	4.6	3.2	setosa	73	6.3	2.5	versicolor	98	6.2	2.9	versicolor
24	5.1	3.3	setosa	49	5.3	3.7	setosa	74	6.1	2.8	versicolor	99	5.1	2.5	versicolor
25	4.8	3.4	setosa	50	5	3.3	setosa	75	6.4	2.9	versicolor	100	5.7	2.8	versicolor

Sample data presented in Table 1 represent typical data from ML Repository [19] which include many duplicates. Training patterns are numbered, aggregated (when defined by the same combinations of attribute values), and presented as nodes in Fig. 1 at the intersections of the attribute values which define them. The data are sorted, and the duplicates are aggregated and represented by single representatives in the AGDS structure, where training patterns are represented by object nodes connected to value nodes. On this basis, it is possible to go along the axes to the nearest values and objects until k nearest neighbors are found. Fig. 1 presents an AGDS structure constructed for the sample data presented in Table 1. In this structure, horizontal nodes below

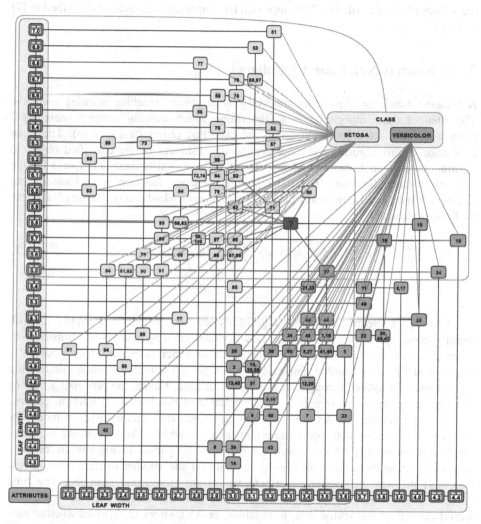

Fig. 1. Object proximity in the 2D space representing two attributes of the Iris data. The automatically widened sample areas (the red dotted lines) for a given classified object depicted by a question mark "?" are used by the AGDS structure and the introduced algorithm for searching for the nearest neighbors of this classified object. The IDs of the training patterns are displayed in the yellow and green vertices. (Color figure online)

represent leaf width attribute values, vertical nodes on the left represent leaf length attribute values, where all the same values from training data (from Table 1) where already aggregated and represented by the same value nodes. Training patterns are represented by green and yellow object nodes where the colors of nodes indicate the connected class labels that are also connected to the appropriate object nodes which define these classes. In the AGDS structure, class labels are treated in the same way as the values of other attributes. This approach has important significance described in [7] and [10].

3   K Nearest Neighbor Classifiers

K Nearest Neighbor algorithms are well-known among machine learning methods. The idea of these algorithms is to determine which training patterns (neighbors) from a training set are the closest to the classified object (test pattern). The main challenge of this algorithm is to determine the distances of the classified object to training patterns in order to find the closest ones (called nearest neighbors) for the defined distance function. The most popular distance function is undoubtedly an Euclidean distance (1), but many times, it is also used a Manhattan distance (2) that can be faster calculated:

$$d_e(x, y) = \sqrt{\sum_{i=1}^{n} (x_i - y_i)^2} \tag{1}$$

$$d_m(x, y) = \sum_{i=1}^{n} |x_i - y_i| \tag{2}$$

Although k Nearest Neighbor algorithms are very simple and supply us with usually good results, they can be very slow for large training datasets in comparison to other classifiers because the kNN is a lazy method which does not create a computational model for any training dataset. To find k nearest neighbors, the whole training dataset must be looked through, so it takes linear time. Hence, the processing time of classifying a single test sample is proportional to a number of all training patterns stored in the training dataset [15, 17]. This paper introduces an associative model for storing data together with some important relations which allows reducing the computational complexity of the search for k nearest neighbors to logarithmic or even constant computational complexity dependently on the number of duplicates in raw data and the way how unique attribute values are stored and searched. The final computational complexity depends on the way how the unique attribute values are stored (sorted tables, sorted lists, hash-tables, or AVB+trees [3, 7]) and whether new training patterns can be added to the AGDS structure, and how many duplicates of values are in raw training data. The way of organizing and storing attribute values determines the search algorithms that can be used to get fast access to the given value using a binary search algorithm, an approximation search algorithm, hash functions [3], or AVB+trees [7]. In this paper, lists and a modified binary search algorithm were used to represent attribute values.

4 Acceleration Associative Algorithm for kNN Classifiers

Classifiers are usually built for datasets which consist of training patterns collected in the past and stored in the tables. In this paper, we use AGDS structures instead of tables to store training patterns as well as their selected relations that are important from the kNN point of view. To accelerate kNN classifiers, we need to have fast access to nearest neighbors. AGDS structures automatically aggregate all attribute value duplicates and sort the nodes representing these aggregated values for all attributes simultaneously. Hence, we have fast access to all nodes representing objects (training patterns) which are defined by the same or close values. The nearest neighbors are always represented by the training patterns which are defined by the same or close attribute values to the values defining classified sample. Therefore, we need to create an AGDS structure for a given training dataset and use the features of the AGDS structures to move only to the nodes representing training patterns which are the closest from all attributes point of view in order to compute their distances from the depicted classified input sample.

The introduced Acceleration Associative Algorithm (AAA) operating on ADGS structures describes the way how to quickly move to the nodes representing the closest (most similar) training patterns to the given combination of input values (classified object), e.g. "?" in Fig. 1.

Assume that we have N training patterns $P_1, \ldots, P_N$ which are defined by J attributes, i.e. $P_n = \{p_n^1, \ldots, p_n^J\}$, where each attribute value p_n^j is a real number. During the construction process of the AGDS structure for the training patterns, all duplicated values of each attribute j are aggregated separately and represented by value nodes $V_1^j, \ldots, V_M^j$ that represent M_j unique attribute values $v_1^j, \ldots, v_M^j$. Moreover, each value node V_m^j contains the counter c_m^j that represents the number of aggregated duplicates of the values $p_{n_1}^j, \ldots, p_{n_{c_m^j}}^j$ that are equal to the value v_m^j represented by this node (Fig. 2). Training patterns are represented by the object nodes $O_1, \ldots, O_R$. Each object node O_r represents and counts up all duplicates of training patterns, where duplicates of training patterns mean the training patterns defined by the same attribute values. If there are no duplicated training patterns in the training dataset, then the number of the object nodes is equal to the number of training patterns $R = N$ else $R < N$.

Acceleration Associative Algorithm for kNN classifiers using AGDS:

Input: T: training data, x: classified sample, k: number of nearest neighbor
Output: winClass: classified label of x

BinSearchEqualOrLess(array, val) // It returns an index of the node which value
equals to val if such a node exists, else it returns the closest lower value if
there is such a value in the array, else the null value is returned.

```
   size = len(array); start = 0; end = size - 1; result = null;
   while(start <= end)
     middle = (start + end) / 2
     if (array[middle] <= x)
       start = middle + 1
       result = middle
     else end = mid - 1
return result
```

FindNextClosest(val)
```
if (valueNodeLessClosest == null) and (valueNodeGreaterClosest == null)
then
   valueNodeLessClosest = BinSearchEqualOrLess(val)
   if (valueNodeLessClosest == null)
   then valueNodeGreaterClosest = First
        return valueNodeGreaterClosest
   else if (valueNodeLessClosest.Val == val)
      then valueNodeGreaterClosest = valueNodeLessClosest
           return valueNodeGreaterClosest
      else if (valueNodeLessClosest.IsNotMax)
         then valueNodeGreaterClosest = valueNodeLessClosest.Next
              if (val-valueNodeLessClosest.Val  <  valueNodeGreaterClosest.Val-
              val)
                 then return valueNodeLessClosest
                 else return valueNodeGreaterClosest
            else valueNodeGreaterClosest = null
                 return valueNodeLessClosest
else if (val - valueNodeLessClosest.Val < valueNodeGreaterClosest.Val - val)
   then if (valueNodeLessClosest.IsNotMin)
        then valueNodeLessClosest = valueNodeLessClosest.Prev
        else if (valueNodeGreaterClosest.IsNotMax)
             then valueNodeGreaterClosest = valueNodeGreaterClosest.Next
             else return null
   else if (valueNodeGreaterClosest.IsNotMax)
        then valueNodeGreaterClosest = valueNodeGreaterClosest.Next
        else if (valueNodeLessClosest.IsNotMin)
             then valueNodeLessClosest = valueNodeLessClosest.Prev
             else return null
   if (val - valueNodeLessClosest.Val < valueNodeGreaterClosest.Val - val)
   then return valueNodeLessClosest
   else return valueNodeGreaterClosest
```

```
FindkNN(k, x)
valueNodeLessClosest = null
valueNodeGreaterClosest = null
create empty rankList of k object pointers and distances
// Create the rankList of k nearest objects to the classified sample x
do valueNode = AGDS.Attributes[0].FindNextClosest(x[0])
    foreach objectNode connected to valueNode
        d = calculateDistance(objectNode, x)
        if d < rankList.LastDistance then
            rankList.InsertInAscendingOrder(objectNode)
            if (rankList.Count > k) then
                while (rankList.LastDistance > rankList[k-1].Distance)
                    rankList.RemoveLast
while (x[0] - valueNodeLessClosest.Val <= rankList.LastDistance) and
        (valueNodeGreaterClosest.Val - val <= rankList.LastDistance)
// Determine the winning class for the classified sample
foreach objectNode in ranklist
    countLabels[objectNode.ClassLabel] += 1
    if (countLabels[objectNode.ClassLabel] > countMax)
    then countMax = countLabels[objectNode.ClassLabel]
        winClass = objectNode.ClassLabel
    else if (countLabels[objectNode.ClassLabel] == countMax) and
        (objectNode.ClassLabel != winClass) then winClass = null
return winClass
```

The AAA algorithm described above is run for each classified object to quickly determine its k nearest neighbors that are necessary for a used kNN method to classify this object. This algorithm can be combined and used with any variation of this method. Its role is to supply the selected kNN method with k nearest neighbors faster than looking through all training patterns. This new combination of AGDS structures with kNN classifiers was called a kNN+AGDS classifier.

5 Comparison of Results and Efficiencies

The results of the implemented AAA algorithm operating on AGDS structures together with the kNN classifiers on various training data are shown in Table 2 and Fig. 2. The classification times shown in Table 2 are means from one hundred of single classification time. The presented approach can successfully accelerate k Nearest Neighbor classifiers and work as an eager data-relation model for them.

In this paper, all datasets used in the described experiments came from the UCI Machine Learning Repository [19], and the results obtained for these datasets are presented in Table 2. For the experiments, we used datasets with various numbers of instances, various numbers of attributes, and various numbers of duplicates to objectively show differences between the average classification time of an input instance

Table 2. Comparison of classification time using kNN and kNN+AGDS.

Dataset	Number of instances	Number of attributes	kNN classification time [ms]	kNN+AGDS classification time [ms]	kNN+AGDS construction time [ms]
Iris	150	4	0.10	0.08	1
Banknote	1372	4	0.29	0.09	5
HTRU2	17898	8	3.14	0.09	134
Shuttle	43500	9	7.67	1.06	278
Credit Card	30000	23	8.69	1.07	499
Skin	245057	3	26.87	1.10	683
Drive	58509	48	46.15	1.24	2224
HEPMASS	1048576	28	362.32	1.41	31214

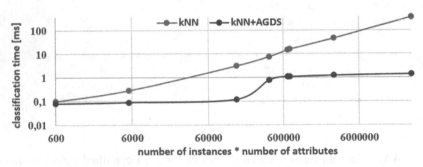

Fig. 2. Classification time as a function of the number of the instances multiplied by the number of attributes, i.e. the number of data stored in the training data tables.

processed by kNN and kNN+AGDS classifiers. The presented combination of AGDS structures with kNNs becomes to be an eager solution instead of a lazy one as for classic kNNs because this new classifier creates a model using an AGDS structure. Thus, the use of AGDS structures removed the main inconvenience of the classic kNN classifiers.

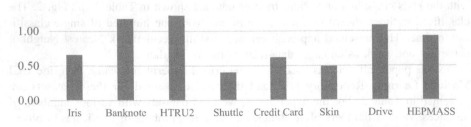

Fig. 3. Memory usage ratio of using AGDS structures to arrays for various training data.

The results shown in Fig. 3 confirm compression ability of AGDS for some training datasets. The most of the datasets used in this work using AGDS lead to the significantly shorter classification time and lower memory usage. The compression was not achieved for the three from eight datasets in Fig. 3 due to the small number of duplicated values in these datasets and the memory used for the representation of the connections. On the other hand, the small extra memory usage is compensated by the much higher speed of classification. For sorting purposes, the quicksort algorithm was used.

6   Conclusions and Final Remarks

This paper did not focus on improving classification results of kNN classifiers but on the efficiency of their use implementing a new Associative Acceleration Algorithm operating on Associative Graph Data Structures. The computational complexity of the presented algorithm is independent of the number of training patterns, so it always works in constant time (when k is much smaller than the number of all training patterns) for a given k of searched nearest neighbors using associations between attribute values defining training patterns. However, the number of computations depends on the density of training patterns in hyperspace that is close to the classified samples. Hence, the efficiency of the presented algorithm grows with the amount of training data. Therefore, it is convenient to use for classification for Big Data collections. It was shown that AGDS structures could be used as a data-relation model for kNN classifiers, and thanks to the use of this model we can accelerate classification of various k Nearest Neighbor algorithms. The efficiency of the presented algorithm and AGDS structures is significant for big training datasets especially when they contain many duplicated values that define training patterns. The construction of an AGDS structure for a training dataset can be treated as an adaptation process that develops a computational model for kNN classifiers because AGDS structures contain all training data enhanced by extra useful relations quickly available for kNN classifiers. In the future studies, we will consider further improvements of the introduced approach concerning the use of AVB+trees [7] to even more accelerate the access to attribute values when searching for the closest values of the classified samples. This work was supported by AGH 11.11.120.612.

References

1. Abidin, T., Perrizo, W.: A fast and scalable nearest neighbor based classifier for data mining. In: Proceedings of ACM SAC 2006, Dijon, France, pp. 536–540. ACM Press, New York (2006)
2. Agrawal, R.: Extensions of k-nearest neighbor algorithm. Res. J. Appl. Sci. Eng. Technol. 13 (1), 24–29 (2016)
3. Cormen, T., Leiserson, C., Rivest, R., Stein, C.: Introduction to Algorithms, 3rd edn. MIT Press, Cambridge (2009)
4. Goodfellow, I., Bengio, Y., Courville, A.: Deep Learning. MIT Press, Cambridge (2016)

5. Grana, M.: Advances in Knowledge-Based and Intelligent Information and Engineering Systems. IOS Press, Amsterdam (2012)
6. Horzyk, A.: Artificial Associative Systems and Associative Artificial Intelligence. EXIT, Warsaw (2013)
7. Horzyk, A.: Associative graph data structures with an efficient access via AVB+trees. In: 11th Conference on Human System Interaction (HSI 2018). IEEE Xplore (2018, in print)
8. Horzyk, A.: Neurons can sort data efficiently. In: Rutkowski, L., Korytkowski, M., Scherer, R., Tadeusiewicz, R., Zadeh, L.A., Zurada, J.M. (eds.) ICAISC 2017. LNCS (LNAI), vol. 10245, pp. 64–74. Springer, Cham (2017). https://doi.org/10.1007/978-3-319-59063-9_6
9. Horzyk, A.: Deep associative semantic neural graphs for knowledge representation and fast data exploration. In: Proceedings of KEOD 2017, pp. 67–79. Scitepress Digital Library (2017)
10. Horzyk, A., Starzyk, J.A.: Multi-class and multi-label classification using associative pulsing neural networks. In: 2018 IEEE WCCI IJCNN, pp. 427–434. IEEE Xplore (2018)
11. Jensen, R., Cornelis, C.: A new approach to fuzzy-rough nearest neighbour classification. In: Chan, C.-C., Grzymala-Busse, J.W., Ziarko, W.P. (eds.) RSCTC 2008. LNCS (LNAI), vol. 5306, pp. 310–319. Springer, Heidelberg (2008). https://doi.org/10.1007/978-3-540-88425-5_32
12. Kalat, J.W.: Biological Grounds of Psychology, 10th edn. Wadsworth Publishing, Belmont (2008)
13. Tadeusiewicz, R.: New trends in neurocybernetics. Comput. Methods Mater. Sci. 10, 1–7 (2010)
14. Tadeusiewicz, R.: Introduction to intelligent systems. In: Fault Diagnosis. Models, Artificial Intelligence, Applications, CRC Press, Boca Raton (2011)
15. Shalev-Shwartz, S., Ben-David, S.: Understanding Machine Learning: From Theory to Algorithms. Cambridge university Press, Cambridge (2014)
16. Vivencio, D.P., et al.: Feature-weighted k-nearest neighbor classifier. In: Proceedings of FOCI, pp. 481–486 (2007)
17. Witten, I.H., Frank, E.: Data Mining: Practical Machine Learning Tools and Techniques, 2nd edn. Morgan Kaufmann Publishers, Morgan Kaufmann Publishers (2005)
18. Wu, X., Zhu, X., Wu, G.Q., Ding, W.: Data mining with big data. Trans. Knowl. Data Eng. 26(1), 97–107 (2014)
19. UCI ML Repository. https://archive.ics.uci.edu/ml/index.php. Accessed 25 May 2018
20. Dudani, S.A.: The distance-weighted k-nearest neighbor rule. IEEE Trans. Syst. Man Cybern. 6, 325–327 (1976)
21. Gou, J., Lan, D., Zhang, Y., Xiong, T.: A new distance-weighted k-nearest neighbor classifier. J. Inf. Comput. Sci. 9(6), 1429–1436 (2012)

A Game-Theoretic Framework for Interpretable Preference and Feature Learning

Mirko Polato[✉] and Fabio Aiolli

Department of Mathematics, University of Padova,
Via Trieste, 63, 35121 Padova, Italy
{mpolato,aiolli}@math.unipd.it

Abstract. We are living in an era that we can call machine learning revolution. Started as a pure academic and research-oriented domain, we have seen widespread commercial adoption across diverse domains, such as retail, healthcare, finance, and many more. However, the usage of machine learning poses its own set of challenges when it comes to explain what is going on under the hood. The reason being models interpretability is very important for the business is to explain each and every decision being taken by the model. In order to take a step forward in this direction, we propose a principled algorithm inspired by both preference learning and game theory for classification. Particularly, the learning problem is posed as a two player zero-sum game which we show having theoretical guarantees about its convergence. Interestingly, feature selection can be straightforwardly plugged into such algorithm. As a consequence, the hypotheses space consists on a set of preference prototypes along with (possibly non-linear) features making the resulting models easy to interpret.

Keywords: Game theory · Margin maximization · Classification
Preference learning

1 Introduction

Machine learning and intelligent systems in general are becoming increasingly ubiquitous. However, after a first enthusiastic reaction to these seemingly unbounded technologies, nowadays some concerns start to rise regarding the *black box* nature of these methods. There are many examples of applications in which the explanation plays a key role, such as recommender systems, bioinformatical applications and support systems for physicians. The need of explanations is also theme of the Article 22.1 of the *General Data Protection Regulation* which states that: *"The data subject shall have the right not to be subject to a decision based solely on automated processing"*. Unfortunately, most of the state-of-the-art machine learning approaches are based on highly non-linear optimization problems which are not very suited for being interpreted. A glaring example

© Springer Nature Switzerland AG 2018
V. Kůrková et al. (Eds.): ICANN 2018, LNCS 11139, pp. 659–668, 2018.
https://doi.org/10.1007/978-3-030-01418-6_65

are deep neural networks (DNNs). Despite in many applications DNNs are one of the most successful approach, they represent a really hard challenge when dealing with model interpretation. Similar considerations can also be done for theoretical grounded methods such as Support Vector Machines.

In this work we present a principled algorithm inspired by game theory and preference learning for classification. Specifically the learning problem is seen as a zero-sum game between the nature and a learner. Interestingly, feature selection can be easily plugged into the same algorithm in a natural way. The hypotheses space consists on a set of preference prototypes attached with possibly non-linear features making the interpretation and visualization of the resulting models very easy.

2 Background

2.1 Preference Learning

Broadly speaking, a preference learning (PL) task consists of some set of items for which (some) preferences are known, and the task is to learn a function able to predict preferences for previously unseen items, or other preferences for the same set of items [5]. In the context of PL, three different ranking tasks can be defined, namely *label ranking*, *instance ranking*, and *object ranking*. In this work we focus on label ranking which can be defined as follows: given a set of input instances $\mathbf{x}_i \in \mathcal{X}$, $i \in [1, \ldots, n]$, and a finite set of labels $\mathcal{Y} \equiv \{y_1, y_2, \ldots, y_m\}$ the goal of a ranker is to learn a scoring function $f_\theta : \mathcal{X} \times \mathcal{Y} \to \mathbb{R}$ which assigns for each label y_i a score to a pattern $\mathbf{x}$. Hence, a label ranking task represents a generalization of a classification task, since f_θ implicitly defines a full ranking over $\mathcal{Y}$ for an instance $\mathbf{x}$. In PL, the training set usually consists of a set of pairwise preferences of the form $y_i \succ_{\mathbf{x}} y_j$, which means that, for the instance $\mathbf{x}$, y_i is preferred to y_j. In particular, in the case of classification, in which each pattern $\mathbf{x}$ is associated to a single label y_i, the following set of preferences are implicitly defined $\{y_i \succ_{\mathbf{x}} y_j \mid 1 \leq j \neq i \leq m\}$.

Formally, f_θ has the following form [1]: $f_\theta(\mathbf{x}, y) = \mathbf{w}^\mathsf{T} \psi(\mathbf{x}, y)$, where $\psi : \mathcal{X} \times \mathcal{Y} \to \mathbb{R}^{d \cdot m}$ is a joint representation of item-label pairs, $\mathcal{X} \equiv \mathbb{R}^d$, $\mathcal{Y} \equiv \{1, \ldots, m\}$, and $\mathbf{w}$ is a weight vector. Since f_θ has to properly rank the labels for each item, given a preference $y_i \succ_{\mathbf{x}} y_j$ then $f_\theta(\mathbf{x}, y_i) > f_\theta(\mathbf{x}, y_j)$ should hold, that is,

$$\mathbf{w}^\mathsf{T} \psi(\mathbf{x}, y_i) > \mathbf{w}^\mathsf{T} \psi(\mathbf{x}, y_j) \quad \Rightarrow \quad \mathbf{w}^\mathsf{T} (\psi(\mathbf{x}, y_i) - \psi(\mathbf{x}, y_j)) > 0,$$

which can be interpreted as the margin (or *confidence*) of the preference. Higher the confidence, higher the generalization capability of the obtained ranker. Thus, given a preference $y_i \succ_{\mathbf{x}} y_j$ we construct its corresponding representation by $\mathbf{z} = \psi(\mathbf{x}, y_i) - \psi(\mathbf{x}, y_j)$, with $\mathbf{z} \in \mathbb{R}^{d \cdot m}$.

We assume that the item-label joint representation is defined as

$$\psi(\mathbf{x}, y) = \mathbf{x} \otimes \mathbf{e}_y^m$$

$$= (\underset{\underset{1}{\uparrow}}{0}, \underset{\underset{2}{\uparrow}}{0}, \ldots, \underset{\underset{y}{\uparrow}}{x_1}, 0, \ldots, \underset{\underset{y+m}{\uparrow}}{x_2}, \ldots, \underset{\underset{y+(i-1)m}{\uparrow}}{x_i}, \ldots, \underset{\underset{y+(d-1)m}{\uparrow}}{x_d}, \ldots, 0),$$

where $\mathbf{e}_y^m$ is the y-*th* vector from the canonical basis of $\mathbb{R}^m$. We indiciate the f-th d-dimensional chunk of a preference $\mathbf{z}$ with

$$\mathbf{z}[f] = (z_{(f-1)m}, z_{(f-1)m+1}, \dots, z_{fm}) \in \mathbb{R}^m.$$

Similarly, we define $\mathbf{z}[y] = (z_y, z_{y+m}, \dots, z_{y+(d-1)m}) \in \mathbb{R}^d$.

At classification time, given a new example $\mathbf{x}$ the predicted class $\hat{y}$ is computed by selecting the label which mazimizes the value of the scoring function f_θ, that is, $\hat{y} = \arg\max_{y \in \mathcal{Y}} f_\theta(\mathbf{x}, y)$.

2.2   Game Theory

Game theory studies the problem of making strategic decisions in competitive environments. In this paper, we focus on two players zero-sum games. The strategic form of a two-player zero-sum game is defined by a matrix $\mathbf{M}$ (the game matrix). The two players, the row player P and the column player Q, play the game simultaneously. In particular, the row player selects a row and the column player selects a column of $\mathbf{M} \in \mathbb{R}^{P \times Q}$, where P and Q are the number of available strategies for P and Q respectively. Each entry $\mathbf{M}_{i,j}$ represents the loss of P, or equivalently the payoff of Q, when the strategies i and j are played by the two players. The player P aims at finding a strategy minimizing its expected loss (the value of the game) V, while the player Q aims at finding a strategy maximizing V, its payoff. The strategies of the players are typically randomized, meaning that the player P selects a row according to a distribution $\mathbf{p}$ over the rows, and the player Q selects a column according to a distribution $\mathbf{q}$ over the columns. These distributions are referred to as the mixed strategies of players P and Q, respectively. The vectors $\mathbf{p}$ and $\mathbf{q}$ can be thought of as stochastic vectors, that is $\mathbf{p} \in \mathscr{S}_P$ and $\mathbf{q} \in \mathscr{S}_Q$, where $\mathscr{S}_P = \{\mathbf{p} \in \mathbb{R}_+^P \mid \|\mathbf{p}\|_1 = 1\}$ and $\mathscr{S}_Q = \{\mathbf{q} \in \mathbb{R}_+^Q \mid \|\mathbf{q}\|_1 = 1\}$.

It is well known [11] that for any game matrix $\mathbf{M}$ there exists a saddle-point, that is a pair of optimal strategies $\mathbf{p}^*$ and $\mathbf{q}^*$ for the two players such that

$$V = \mathbf{p}^{*\mathsf{T}} \mathbf{M} \mathbf{q}^* = \min_{\mathbf{p}} \max_{\mathbf{q}} \mathbf{p}^\mathsf{T} \mathbf{M} \mathbf{q} = \max_{\mathbf{q}} \min_{\mathbf{p}} \mathbf{p}^\mathsf{T} \mathbf{M} \mathbf{q}$$

A saddle-point of this type can be computed by solving an appropriately defined linear program with a number of variables and constraints growing linearly with the number of (pure) strategies of the two players. It is clear that this computation becomes prohibitive for game matrices of high dimensionality. An alternative method called *adaptive multiplicative weights* (AMW) [3,4] has been proposed to compute approximate optimal saddle-point values and strategies. The *ficticious play* (FP) strategy, also called Brown-Robinson learning process, introduced by Brown in the 50's [2], is a simple algorithm to efficiently compute an approximation of the solution of a game. The FP method starts with an arbitrary initial pure strategy for P. Then, each player in turn chooses his next pure strategy as a best response assuming the other player chooses among his previous choices at random equally likely. In other words, at each step each player tries to infer the mixed strategy of the opponent from its previous choices. The pseudo-code of FP is reported in Algorithm 1.

Algorithm 1. FP: The Fictitious Play algorithm

Input:
    $\mathbf{M} \in \mathbb{R}^{P \times Q}$: matrix game
    T_e: number of iterations
Output:
    $\mathbf{p}, \mathbf{q}$: row/column player strategy
    V: the value of the game

1 $r \leftarrow randint[1, P]$
2 $\mathbf{s}_p, \mathbf{v}_p \leftarrow \mathbf{0}, \mathbf{0}$
3 $\mathbf{s}_q, \mathbf{v}_q \leftarrow \mathbf{M}_{r,:}, \mathbf{e}_r^P$
4 **for** $t \leftarrow 1$ **to** T_e **do**
5 | $\hat{q} \leftarrow \arg\max \mathbf{s}_q, \quad \mathbf{s}_p \leftarrow \mathbf{s}_p + \mathbf{M}_{:,\hat{q}}, \quad \mathbf{v}_q \leftarrow \mathbf{v}_q + \mathbf{e}_{\hat{q}}^Q$
6 | $\hat{p} \leftarrow \arg\max \mathbf{s}_p, \quad \mathbf{s}_q \leftarrow \mathbf{s}_q + \mathbf{M}_{\hat{p},:}, \quad \mathbf{v}_p \leftarrow \mathbf{v}_p + \mathbf{e}_{\hat{p}}^P$
7 **end**
8 $\mathbf{p} \leftarrow \mathbf{v}_p / \|\mathbf{v}_p\|_1, \quad \mathbf{q} \leftarrow \mathbf{v}_q / \|\mathbf{v}_q\|_1$
9 $V \leftarrow \mathbf{p}^\mathsf{T}\mathbf{M}\mathbf{q}$
10 **return** $\mathbf{p}, \mathbf{q}, V$

---

3   A Game Theoretic Perspective of Preference Learning

In this section we describe a new learning approach for label ranking based on game theory. Specifically, we assume to have a set of training preferences of the form $p_i \equiv (y_+ \succ_\mathbf{x} y_-)$ which can be converted in their vectorial representation $\mathbf{z}_i$ as described in Sect. 2.1. We consider an hypothesis space of linear functions, that is, $\mathcal{F} \equiv \{ f_\mathbf{w}(\mathbf{z}) : \mathbf{z} \mapsto \mathbf{w}^\mathsf{T}\mathbf{z} \mid \mathbf{w}, \mathbf{z} \in \mathbb{R}^{d \cdot m}, \|\mathbf{w}\|_2 = 1 \}$. Given any preference vector $\mathbf{z}$ then, for the preference to be satisfied, $\mathbf{w}^\mathsf{T}\mathbf{z} > 0$ should hold. The margin of the preference $\rho(\mathbf{z}) = \mathbf{w}^\mathsf{T}\mathbf{z}$ will represent the confidence of the current hypothesis over the preference $\mathbf{z}$. According to the maximum margin principle, our aim is to select the hypothesis ($\mathbf{w}$) that maximizes the minimum margin over the preferences of the training set.

From the Representer Theorem (see e.g. [7,9]) we know that $\mathbf{w}$ can be defined as a convex combination of a subset of the training preferences, that is $\mathbf{w} \propto \sum_j \alpha_j \mathbf{z}_j, \alpha \in \mathscr{S}_P$. Thus, the margin of a preference can be expressed as

$$\rho(\mathbf{z}) = \sum_j \alpha_j \mathbf{z}_j^\mathsf{T}\mathbf{z} = \sum_j \alpha_j \sum_f \mu_f \mathbf{z}_j[f]^\mathsf{T}\mathbf{z}[f], = \sum_{(j,f)} q_{(j,f)} \mathbf{z}_j[f]^\mathsf{T}\mathbf{z}[f]$$

where the dot product $\mathbf{z}_j^\mathsf{T}\mathbf{z}$ is generalized by giving different weights to the features according to a distribution μ over the features, and $\mathbf{q}$ such that $q_{(j,f)} = \alpha_j \mu_f$ is a new distribution over all the possible preference-feature pairs.

Now, let $\mathbf{p}$ be a distribution over the set of training preferences, the expected preference margin when the preferences are drawn according to $\mathbf{p}$ is:

$$\bar{\rho}(\mathbf{p}, \mathbf{q}) = \sum_i p_i \sum_{(j,f)} q_{(j,f)} \mathbf{z}_i[f]^\mathsf{T}\mathbf{z}_i[f] = \mathbf{p}^\mathsf{T}\mathbf{M}\mathbf{q} \tag{1}$$

where $\mathbf{M}_{i,(j,f)} = \mathbf{z}_i[f]^{\mathsf{T}}\mathbf{z}_j[f]$. This formulation highlights the relation between a preference learning problem and game theory. Consider a two-player zero-sum game in which the row player P (the nature) chooses a distribution over the whole set of training preferences as its mixed strategy aiming at minimizing the expected margin. Simultaneously, the column player Q (the learner) chooses a distribution over the set of hypothesis, or preference-feature pairs, as its mixed strategy aiming at maximizing the expected margin (its payoff). Then the value of the game, that is the maximal minimum margin solution will be:

$$V = \bar{\rho}(\mathbf{p}^*, \mathbf{q}^*) = \min_{\mathbf{p}} \max_{\mathbf{q}} \mathbf{p}^{\mathsf{T}}\mathbf{M}\mathbf{q}$$

4 Approximating the Optimal Strategies

The game matrix $\mathbf{M}$ has number of rows equal to the number of training preferences P, and number of columns equal to $Q = P \cdot F$ where F is the number of features. The number of preference-feature pairs can be huge, thus solving the game using standard off-the-shelf methods from game theory is impractical.

For this, in this section we propose a new method to solve the game incrementally. The pseudo-code of the algorithm is given in Algorithm 2. Specifically, given a game matrix $\mathbf{M}$ and the optimal solution $(\mathbf{p}^*, \mathbf{q}^*, V^*)$ for the game. At each iteration we only consider a subset of columns of the entire matrix, that is $\mathbf{M}_t - \mathbf{M}\boldsymbol{\Pi}_t$ where $\boldsymbol{\Pi}_t \subseteq \{0,1\}^{|Q| \times B}$ are left-stochastic $(0,1)$-matrices, i.e. matrices whose entries belong to the set $\{0,1\}$ and whose columns add up to one. Let $(\mathbf{p}_t^*, \mathbf{q}_t^*, V_t^*)$ be the solution for the matrix $\mathbf{M}_t$. The columns of $\mathbf{M}_t$ corresponding to null entries in $\mathbf{q}_t^*$ are replaced by new columns drawn randomly from $\mathbf{M}$. We show in the following that the value of the game obtained at each iteration increases monotonically and it is upper bounded by the optimal margin.

At the iteration $t+1$ a new left-stochastic $(0,1)$-matrix $\boldsymbol{\Pi}_{t+1}$ is considered which is $\boldsymbol{\Pi}_t$ where every column corresponding to null entries in $\mathbf{q}_t^*$ are substituted with a new random stochastic vector $\mathbf{e}_r^Q$ for a random pair r. Thus, it can be shown that

$$\begin{aligned}
V_t^* = \mathbf{p}_t^*\mathbf{M}_t\mathbf{q}_t^* &= \mathbf{p}_t^*\mathbf{M}\boldsymbol{\Pi}_t\mathbf{q}_t^* \\
&\leq \mathbf{p}_{t+1}^*\mathbf{M}\boldsymbol{\Pi}_t\mathbf{q}_t^* \\
&= \mathbf{p}_{t+1}^*\mathbf{M}\boldsymbol{\Pi}_{t+1}\mathbf{q}_t^* \\
&\leq \mathbf{p}_{t+1}^*\mathbf{M}_{t+1}\mathbf{q}_{t+1}^* = V_{t+1}^*
\end{aligned}$$

and $V_t^* \leq \mathbf{p}^*\mathbf{M}\underbrace{\boldsymbol{\Pi}_t\mathbf{q}_t^*}_{\hat{\mathbf{q}}_t} \leq \mathbf{p}^*\mathbf{M}\mathbf{q}^* = V^*$ for every t.

5 Evaluation

In this section we describe the experiments performed to assess the effectiveness of our proposal. We performed two different sets of experiments. The first set aims to assess the proposed algorithm in terms of interpretability. The second one is focused on the performance comparison between our method and a standard SVM.

Algorithm 2. Proposed algorithm

Input:
$\mathcal{P}$: set of training preferences
$genF$: random feature generator
B: size of the working set
T: number of epochs
T_e: number of iterations of *Fictitious Play* (FP)
Output:
$\mathcal{Q}$: working set of preference-feature pairs
$\mathbf{q}$: mixed strategy of preference-feature pairs in $\mathcal{Q}$

1 random initialization of the set $\mathcal{Q}$ such that $|\mathcal{Q}| = B$
2 compute the matrix game $\mathbf{M}$ on the basis of $\mathcal{P}$ (rows) and $\mathcal{Q}$ (cols)
3 **for** $t \leftarrow 1$ **to** T **do**
4    $\mathbf{p}, \mathbf{q}, v \leftarrow FP(\mathbf{M}, T_e)$
5   **if** $t < T$ **then**
6   **foreach** $(j, f) \mid \mathbf{q}_{(j,f)} = 0$ **do**
7        $(j', f') \leftarrow pick(\mathcal{P}), genF()$
8   update $\mathcal{Q}$: replace (j, f) with (j', f')
9   update columns of $\mathbf{M}$ w.r.t. $\mathcal{Q}$:
10   let k the position of (j', f') in $\mathcal{Q}$,
11   for all $i \in \mathcal{P}$, $\mathbf{M}_{i,k} = \mathbf{z}_i[f]^\mathsf{T} \mathbf{z}_{j'}[f]$
12   **end**
13   **end**
14 **end**
15 **return** $\mathbf{q}, \mathcal{Q}$

5.1   Model Interpretation

In the first set of experiments, we employed our algorithm to select the most relevant features in order to interpret the model. The aim is to use these features to explain the decision. We run the method on four benchmark datasets, three of which (namely, `tic-tac-toe`, `monks-1` and `monks-3`) have a specific logical rule that explains the positive class. The `tic-tac-toe` dataset has been converted into a binary-valued dataset through one-hot encoding. The remaining dataset, i.e., `mnist-49`, is composed with instances of the handwritten digit dataset `mnist` concerning only the classes 4 and 9. In this case, the extracted features are used as a visual aid in order to highlight the points of interest that the model uses to discriminate a 4 from a 9, and viceversa. The details of the datasets are reported in Table 1. Table 2, instead, shows the logical rules which explain the positive class. It is noteworthy that the difference between `monks-1` and `monks-3` is only the instance labelling. Even though both these datasets have been artificially created, their coverage w.r.t. the associated explanation rule is not complete. These experiments have been performed using the following procedure. We trained our model by using polynomial features of different degrees $[1, \ldots, 3]$. This choice depends on the fact that all the interested rules are expressed in terms of disjunctive normal form formulas with conjunctive

Table 1. Datasets information: name, number of instance, number of features, and class prior. All the dataset are freely available in the UCI repository [10].

Dataset	#Instances	#Features	Class prior
tic-tac-toe	958	27	65/35
monks-1	432	17	50/50
monks-3	432	17	53/47
mnist-49	13782	784	50/50

Table 2. Logical rules which explain the positive class of the datasets. The variable x_i indicates the i-th input feature of a vector in the corresponding dataset.

Dataset	Rule
tic-tac-toe	$(x_8 \wedge x_{14} \wedge x_{20}) \vee (x_5 \wedge x_{14} \wedge x_{23}) \vee (x_2 \wedge x_{14} \wedge x_{26}) \vee$ $(x_8 \wedge x_{17} \wedge x_{26}) \vee (x_{11} \wedge x_{14} \wedge x_{17}) \vee (x_2 \wedge x_{11} \wedge x_{20}) \vee$ $(x_{20} \wedge x_{23} \wedge x_{26}) \vee (x_2 \wedge x_5 \wedge x_8)$
monks-1	$(x_0 \wedge x_3) \vee (x_1 \wedge x_4) \vee (x_2 \wedge x_5)$
monks-3	$(x_{13} \wedge x_8) \vee (\neg x_5 \wedge \neg x_{14})$

clauses up to the arity 3. In the case of binary valued data, polynomial features correspond to conjunctions, and hence they are suited for our purposes. Since we have a-priori knowledge about the game tic-tac-toe, for this specific dataset we only used the polynomial of degree 3.

Table 3 shows the 10 most relevant features for each tested dataset for each polynomial. Features are sorted with respect to their corresponding weight in the solution. It is evident from the table that the retrieved best features are the ones involved in the explanation rules (Table 2). In tic-tac-toe the first 8 polynomial features correspond to the rule which describe the wins of the crosses. The remaining two features represent a single naught in the central and in the bottom right cell. These features are useful to discriminate a win for the naught, which is reasonable in particular for the central cell which is actually one of the most useful square to get a three-in-a-row. Despite the tic-tac-toe case in which the polynomial was suited for the specific set of rules, in the case of monks we tried all polynomials up to the degree 3. Nonetheless, in these cases the algorithm managed to retrieve the right features regardless of the used polynomial. For example, in monks-1 with $d = 3$ the first three features contain repeated variables, which means that the features are actually of degree 2 ($x = x^2$ if $x \in \{0, 1\}$). Same considerations can be done for monks-3. Moreover, in monks-3 the algorithm has also been able to correctly identify the polarity of the features. In fact, x_{14} and x_5 contribute to distinguish the negative class w.r.t. the positive which reflect the $\neg$ logical operator in the explanation rule.

The mnist-49 dataset has been used as a more realistic use case since there are not simple rules that govern the classification. The goal here is to use the most relevant features for interpreting, in a human fashion, which are the visual

Table 3. Logical rules which explain the positive class of the datasets. The variable x_i indicates the i-th input feature of a vector in the corresponding dataset. ($\cdot$) means that the feature discriminate the negative class from the positive one. The column **d** indicates the degree of the used polynomial.

Data	d	R1	R2	R3	R4	R5	R6	R7	R8	R9	R10
t-t-t	3	$x_8x_{17}x_{26}$	$x_2x_{11}x_{20}$	$x_2x_{14}x_{26}$	$x_8x_{14}x_{20}$	$x_{20}x_{23}x_{26}$	$x_{11}x_{14}x_{17}$	$x_2x_5x_8$	$x_5x_{14}x_{23}$	$x_{13}^3\cdot$	$x_{25}^3\cdot$
mks-1	1	$x_{14}\cdot$	$x_{13}\cdot$	$x_{12}\cdot$	x_5	x_1	x_3	x_8	x_0	x_{10}	x_4
mks-1	2	x_0x_3	x_1x_4	x_2x_5	x_{11}^2	$x_{14}^2\cdot$	$x_{12}^2\cdot$	$x_{13}^2\cdot$	$x_{16}^2\cdot$	$x_{15}^2\cdot$	$x_7^2\cdot$
mks-1	3	$x_0^2x_3$	$x_1^2x_4$	$x_2x_5^2$	$x_1x_3^2$	$x_{14}^3\cdot$	$x_{12}^3\cdot$	$x_{13}^3\cdot$	$x_6^3\cdot$	$x_7^3\cdot$	$x_{15}^3\cdot$
mks-3	1	$x_{14}\cdot$	$x_5\cdot$	x_{13}	x_8	x_3	x_4	x_2	x_1	x_0	x_{12}
mks-3	2	x_8x_{13}	$x_{14}^2\cdot$	$x_5^2\cdot$	x_4^2	x_3^2	x_{11}^2	x_{13}^2	x_{12}^2	x_1^2	x_2^2
mks-3	3	$x_8x_{13}^2$	$x_{14}^3\cdot$	$x_5^3\cdot$	x_4^3	x_3^3	x_{12}^3	x_{11}^3	x_{13}^3	x_{15}^3	$x_3x_6^2$

characteristics that are leveraged by the model to discriminate the two classes. Also for this dataset all polynomials up to the degree 3 have been considered. The best results in terms of accuracy have been achieved by the degree 2. For this reason and also for visualization purposes we used the degree 2 features to build Fig. 1. The figure shows the most relevant poly 2° features used by the model to distinguish a 4 from a 9 (left) and viceversa (right). The features are represented as segment between the two involved variables (i.e., pixels) in each monomial. In the background is depicted the average digits. From the figure it is clear that there are huge differences in how the two numbers are discriminated. In the 4 vs 9 case (left), the region of interests is the left (almost) vertical line of the 4. In particular, each pair of pixels involved in the features seems to follow the gradient of this line. Similarly, in the 9 vs 4 case (right), the region of interest

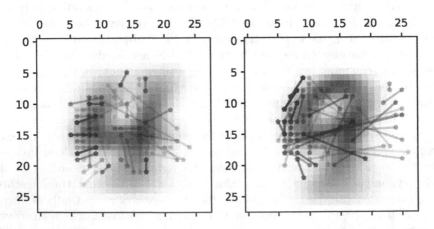

Fig. 1. Visualization of the most relevant polynomial features of degree 2. The polynomial features are visualized as segments limited by the involved input variables. The left hand side plot shows the features relevant to discriminate the 4 from the 9, viceversa in the right hand side plot. In the plots, the opacity of the visualized feature is exponentially related to its weight.

is represented by the left curvature of the circle of the 9. In this case, the pair of pixels seems to follow the border of such curvature. It is also interesting to notice that some of the relevant pixels are outside the grey region. This can be explained as a way to deal with outliers.

5.2   Feature Selection

This set of experiments aims to assess the effectiveness of the proposed algorithm on datasets with many noisy and redundant features. The chosen testbeds have been the datasets of the NIPS 2003 Feature selection challenge [6]. The details of these datasets are reported in Table 4. An important observation about the datasets is the huge number of features w.r.t. the number of training instances. In addition to the number of features of each datasets, Table 4 reports the actual number of real features. For more details about the datasets please refer to [6,8]. All datasets concern binary classification tasks.

Table 4. Datasets information: name, number of instance, number of features, number of relevant features (probes), and class prior. All the dataset are freely available at the NIPS 2003 Feature selection challenge site, http://clopinet.com/isabelle/Projects/NIPS2003/.

Dataset	#Instances	#Features	# Real feat.	Class prior
arcene	200	10000	7000	44/56
dexter	600	20000	9947	50/50
dorothea	1150	100000	50000	90/10
gisette	7000	5000	250	50/50
madelon	2600	500	20	50/50

We compared the proposed algorithm with a standard SVM. Given the huge number of features of the target datasets, the usage of higher degree polynomial kernels was not effective. For this reason, the reported results have been obtained using the linear kernel. The C parameter of the SVM has been validated in the set of values $\{10^{-4}, \ldots, 10^{5}\}$ using a 5-fold cross validation procedure. The reported results are the average over 10 runs of the experiments over different data splits. Table 5 summarizes the achieved results. The size B of the working set has been set to 2000.

As evident from the table, the proposed method is able to achieve comparable and sometimes better performances than SVM. It is worth to mention that, since the working set had size of 2000, generally the number of used features by our algorithm was order of magnitude less than the number of original features.

Table 5. Accuracy results achieved by SVM and the proposed algorithm. The last column indicate the number of support preference-feature pairs used by the proposed algorithm.

Dataset	SVM	Proposal	# Relevant feat.
arcene	90.00	88.33	125
dexter	92.78	91.11	260
dorothea	91.88	93.04	468
gisette	96.71	97.05	1056
madelon	60.10	60.10	1448

6   Conclusions and Future Work

We proposed a principled algorithm for classification inspired by preference learning and game theory. Empirical evaluations have shown the feasibility of efficiently making non linear feature selection. Moreover, we have shown how it is possible to leverage the selected (possibly) non linear features to interpret the resulting model. In the future we plan to adapt the proposed method to very large scale datasets.

References

1. Aiolli, F., Sperduti, A.: A preference optimization based unifying framework for supervised learning problems. In: Fürnkranz, J., Hüllermeier, E. (eds.) Preference Learning, pp. 19–42. Springer, Heidelberg (2010). https://doi.org/10.1007/978-3-642-14125-6_2
2. Brown, G.W.: Iterative solutions of games by fictitious play. In: Activity Analysis of Production and Allocation, pp. 374–376 (1951)
3. Freund, Y., Schapire, R.E.: Game theory, on-line prediction and boosting. In: COLT, pp. 325–332 (1996)
4. Freund, Y., Schapire, R.E.: Adaptive game playing using multiplicative weights. Games Econ. Behav. **29**(1–2), 79–103 (1999)
5. Fürnkranz, J., Hüllermeier, E.: Preference Learning, 1st edn. Springer, Heidelberg (2010). https://doi.org/10.1007/978-0-387-30164-8
6. Guyon, I., Gunn, S., Ben-Hur, A., Dror, G.: Result analysis of the nips 2003 feature selection challenge. In: Saul, L.K., Weiss, Y., Bottou, L. (eds.) Advances in Neural Information Processing Systems, vol. 17, pp. 545–552. MIT Press, Cambridge (2005)
7. Hofmann, T., Schlkopf, B., Smola, A.J.: Kernel methods in machine learning. The Ann. Stat. **36**(3), 1171–1220 (2008)
8. Johnson, N.: A study of the nips feature selection challenge (2009). https://web.stanford.edu/~hastie/ElemStatLearn/comp.pdf
9. Kimeldorf, G.S., Wahba, G.: Some results on Tchebycheffian spline functions. J. Math. Anal. Appl. **33**(1), 82–95 (1971)
10. Lichman, M.: UCI machine learning repository (2013). http://archive.ics.uci.edu/ml
11. von Neumann, J.: Zur theorie der gesellschaftsspiele. Math. Ann. **100**, 295–320 (1928)

A Dynamic Ensemble Learning Framework for Data Stream Analysis and Real-Time Threat Detection

Konstantinos Demertzis[1], Lazaros Iliadis[1],
and Vardis-Dimitris Anezakis[2]([⊠])

[1] School of Engineering, Department of Civil Engineering,
Democritus University of Thrace, University Campus, Kimmeria, Xanthi, Greece
kdemertz@fmenr.duth.gr, liliadis@civil.duth.gr
[2] Department of Forestry and Management of the Environment and Natural
Recourses, Democritus University of Thrace,
193 Pandazidou St., 68200 N Orestiada, Greece
danezaki@fmenr.duth.gr

Abstract. Security incident tracking systems receive a continuous, unlimited inflow of observations, where in the typical case the most recent ones are the most important. These data flows and characterized by high volatility. Their characteristics can change drastically over time in an unpredictable way, differentiating their typical normal behavior. In most cases it is not possible to store all of the historical samples, since their volume is unlimited. This fact requires the extraction of real-time knowledge over a subset of the flow, which contains a small but recent percentage of all observations. This creates serious objections to the accuracy and reliability of the employed classifiers. The research described herein, uses a Dynamic Ensemble Learning (DYENL) approach for Data Stream Analysis (DELDaStrA) which is employed in RealTime Threat Detection systems. More specifically, it proposes a DYENL model that uses the "Kappa" architecture to perform analysis of data flows. The DELDaStrA is based on the hybrid combination of k Nearest Neighbor (kNN) Classifiers, with Adaptive Random Forest (ARF) and Primal Estimated SubGradient Solver for Support Vector Machines (SVM) (SPegasos). In fact, it performs a dynamic extraction of the weighted average of the three results, to maximize the classification accuracy.

Keywords: Dynamic ensemble learning · Big data · Data streams analysis
"Kappa" architecture · Critical infrastructure · Real-time threat detection

1 Introduction

The data created by SCADA [31] and more generally by Industrial Control Systems (ICS) [20], has caused an exponential increase of the obtained information. This fact has led to the adoption of architectures which incorporate proper algorithms for real-time data stream processing. These algorithms are dynamically adjusted by new models or when the data are produced as a function of time [5]. The "Kappa" architecture uses a real-time engine and it is the most suitable approach for the analysis of data flows [25].

© Springer Nature Switzerland AG 2018
V. Kůrková et al. (Eds.): ICANN 2018, LNCS 11139, pp. 669–681, 2018.
https://doi.org/10.1007/978-3-030-01418-6_66

For each new sample, a small gradual update of the model takes place, which gradually improves as more data arrive. The error in the real-time engine is calculated at each iteration as data characteristics can change drastically and in an unpredictable way. This changes the typical, normal behavior, and an object that may have been considered extreme, can be included in the normal observations, due to rapid developments in the data stream (Fig. 1).

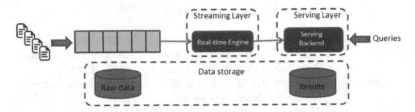

Fig. 1. Kappa architecture (https://www.oreilly.com/ideas/applying-the-kappa-architecture-in-the-telco-industry)

Due to the unlimited volume of data, data mining is performed on a subset of the flow, which is called a sliding window (SLWI). Clearly the SLIWI contains a small but recent percentage of the observations included in the global set. The goal of these data processing algorithms is to minimize the cumulative error for all iterations, which can be calculated by the following function (1) [2]:

$$I_n[w] = \sum_{j=1}^{n} V(\langle w, x_j \rangle, y_j) = \sum_{j=1}^{n} \left(x_j^T w - y_j \right)^2 \tag{1}$$

where $x_j \in R^d$, $w \in R^d$ and $y_j \in R$ supposing that $Xi \times d$ is a data matrix and $Yi \times 1$ is a target values vector, obtained after the arrival of the first i data points. If we accept that the covariance matrix $\Sigma i = X^T X$ is reversable, the optimal solution $f^*(x) = \langle w*, x \rangle$ is given by the following function (2):

$$w^* = \left(X^T X \right)^{-1} X^T \Upsilon = \Sigma_i^{-1} \sum_{j=1}^{i} x_j y_j \tag{2}$$

If we estimate the covariance matrix $\Sigma_i = \sum_{j=1}^{i} x_j x_j^T$ the time complexity (TC) changes from $O(id^2)(d \times d)$ and it becomes $O(d^3)$, whereas the rest of the multiplication requires TC equal to $O(d^2)$. Thus, the TC finally becomes equal to $O(id^2 + d^3)$. If n is the number of points in the dataset, it is necessary to recalculate the solution after the arrival of each new data point $i = 1, 2, \ldots, n$. So, the final time complexity is of the order $O(n^2 d^2 + n d^3)$ which would make the algorithm unsuitable for application in demanding fast changing environments such as the one under consideration [2, 24]. It is therefore important to note that in-stream processing is subject to time constraints, as applications require explanatory results in real time, and there are also significant memory requirements.

It is clear from the above, that a secure approach for data flow mining problems, requires robust systems characterized by reliability and high accuracy rates, without a demand for high resources availability. Good preparation and methodological determination of their operating parameters is needed, to avoid long-term convergence, or undesirable fluctuations in accuracy, which may be associated with frequent model updates and instability or loss of generalization, which may be due to corrupted and noisy data.

1.1 Literature Review

Soft computing techniques are capable to model and detect cyber security threats [6–14] and they also offer optimization mechanisms in order to produce reliable results. In many applications, learning algorithms have to act in dynamic environments where data are collected in the form of transient data streams. Krawczyk et al. [21] investigated 3 data stream classification as well as regression tasks. Besides presenting a comprehensive spectrum of ensemble approaches for data streams, authors also discussed advanced learning concepts such as imbalanced data streams. According to Liu et al. [26] a weight computation policy based on confidence was presented to deal with the problem in the sub-classifier's weight in dynamic data stream ensemble classification. The policy fully considers influence of the sample on the weight of the sub-classifier. Krawczyk and Cano [22] introduced a dynamic and self-adapting threshold that was able to adapt to changes in the data stream, by monitoring outputs of the ensemble to exploit underlying diversity in order to efficiently anticipate drifts.

Nowadays, the intrusion detection systems (IDS) have become one of the most important weapons against cyber-attacks. Chand et al. [4] performed a comparative analysis of SVM classifier's performance when it was stacked with other classifiers like BayesNet, AdaBoost and Random Forest. Ahmin and Ghoualmi-Zine [1] used two different classifiers iteratively, where each-iteration represented one level in the built model. To ensure the adaptation of their model, authors added a new level whenever the sum of new attacks and the rest of the training dataset reached the threshold.

Data mining in non-stationary data streams is gaining more attention recently, especially in the context of Internet of Things and Big Data. Losing et al. [27] proposed the Self Adjusting Memory (SAM) model for the k-Nearest Neighbor (k-NN) algorithm since k-NN constitutes a proven classifier within the streaming setting. SAM-kNN could deal with heterogeneous concept drift, i.e. different drift types and rates, using biologically inspired memory models and their coordination. Rani and Sumathy [28] used k-NN algorithm to determine the best optimal subset.

There are a few researches about Primal Estimated sub-Gradient Solver for SVM (Pegasos) algorithm. Shalev-Shwartz et al. [29] described and analyzed a simple and effective stochastic sub-gradient descent algorithm for solving the optimization problem cast by SVM. Their algorithm was particularly well suited for large text classification problems, where authors demonstrated an order-of-magnitude speedup over previous SVM methods. Farda [18] explored machine learning in Google Earth Engine and its accuracy for multi-temporal land used mapping of coastal wetland area.

1.2 Datasets

Appropriate datasets were chosen that closely simulate ICS communication and transaction data. They were used in the development and evaluation of the proposed model. The following preprocessed network transaction data, and preprocessed to strip lower layer transmission data, were used in this research (e.g. TCP, MAC) [15]:

- The water_tower_dataset includes 23 independent parameters and 236,179 instances, from which 172,415 are normal and 63,764 outliers. Totally 86,315 normal instances were used in the training phase (water_train_dataset) whereas the water_test_dataset comprised of 86,100 normal instances and 63,764 outliers.
- The gas_dataset includes 26 independent features and 97,019 instances, from which 61,156 normal and 35,863 outliers. Training of the algorithm was done with the gas_train_dataset that contains 30,499 normal instances, whereas the gas_test_dataset comprises of 30,657 normal instances and 35,863 outliers.
- Finally, the electric_dataset includes 128 independent variables with 146,519 instances, from which 90,856 normal and 55,663 outliers. The training was performed 4 based on the electric_train_dataset comprising of 45,402 normal instances, whereas the rest 45,454 normal and the 55,663 outliers, belong to the electric_test_dataset.

More details regarding the dataset and their choice can be found in [15].

2 Proposed Dynamic Weighted Average Methodology

This research proposes an intelligent and dynamic Ensemble Machine Learning system (EMLS) [32] aiming to develop a stable and accurate framework, which will have the ability to generalize. The EMLS employs an innovative version of the "Kappa" architecture that combines the ARF, SPegasos and k-NN SAM algorithms. DEL-DaStrA performs real time analysis and assessment of critical infrastructure data, in order to classify and identify undesirable digital security situations, related to cyber-attacks. The reason for using the ensemble approach, is the multivariance that usually appears in such multifactorial problems of high complexity, due to the heterogeneity of the data flows. This is a typical case of digital security and critical infrastructures.

The two most important advantages of the Ensemble Techniques focus on the fact that they offer better prediction and more stable models, as the overall behavior of a multiple model is less noisy than a corresponding single [23]. Also, an Ensemble method can lead to very stable prediction models, while offering generalization. Finally, these models can reduce the bias, the variance, and they can avoid overfitting [17] producing robust learning models.

Three classifiers were employed in the development of this model (Ensemble Size). The number of the classifiers was determined after considering the law of *diminishing returns in ensemble construction* in a trial and error approach. The applied algorithms were chosen based on their different decision-making philosophy and methodology to address the problem, in order to cover the number of possible cases associated with the tactic of attacks against critical infrastructure. In general, the choice was based on both static tests combined with the trial and error method, but also on the basic properties of these algorithms regarding the way they handle each situation.

More specifically, the following approaches were used: SVM non-parametric models due to the way they handle outliers. Random Forests which are using subsets of the training sets with bagging, and subsets of features that favor the reduction of the outliers' or extreme values' effect. The k-NN classifier is automatically non-linear, it can detect linear or non-linear distributed data and it tends to perform very well with a lot of data points. Also, the choice of the algorithms was based on the diversity of their operation and parameterization (Reliability of Ensemble) which is achieved with different architectures, hyper-parameter settings and training techniques. The weights' determination of the different models of the Ensemble, was based exclusively on static trial and error tests [16].

The DELDaStrA operation mode, includes the parallel analysis of the data flow by all three algorithms and the dynamic extraction of the weighted average of the three results. More specifically, each data flow is checked by each algorithm and the classification accuracy is obtained. Then the maximum accuracy isincreased by a weight equal to 0.6 whereas in the rest of the forecasts this weight is equal to 0.2 and the weighted average is calculated. This process is presented in the pseudocode of the following Algorithm 1.

Algorithm 1. Dynamic Weighted Average

Input: x_1, x_2, x_3 /* *classifier accuracy*

Step 1: *if* $((x_1 > x_2)$ && $(x_1 > x_3))$
    max = x_1; *else if* $(x_2 > x_3)$
    max = x_2; *else* max = x_3;

Step 2: Set w_{max}=0.6, w_1=0.2 and w_2=0.2

Step 3: Calculate $\bar{x} = \frac{x_1 w_1 + x_2 w_2 + x_{max} w_{max}}{w_1 + w_2 + w_{max}}$

Output: The dynamic weighted average of classification accuracy

---

The use of the weighted average potential significantly enhances the visualization of the trends in the estimated state, as it eliminates or at least minimizes the statistical noise of the data streams. This is one of the best ways to assess the strength of a trend and the likelihood of its reversal, as it places more weight on the classification with the highest accuracy. It provides real indications before the start of a new situation or event, thus allowing for a quick and optimal decision.

It is also important to note that this dynamic process ensures the adaptation of the system to new situations, by offering generalization which is one of the key issues in the field of machine learning. In this way we are implementing a robust framework capable of responding to high complexity problems. Also, this architecture greatly accelerates the process of making an optimal decision with the rapid convergence of the multiple model, which is less noisy and much more reliable than a single learning algorithm [23].

3 Ensemble Algorithms

3.1 Adaptive Random Forests

It is clear that data flow management and especially knowledge extraction procedures with Machine Learning algorithms applied on the flows, are unlikely to be performed with iterations over input data. Accordingly, the adaptation of the Random Forest algorithm depends on a suitable accumulation process that is partly achieved by bootstrap, and partly by limiting any decision to divide the sheets into a subset of attributes. This is achieved by modifying the base tree algorithm, by effectively reducing the set of features examined for further separation into random subsets of size m, όπου $m < M$ (M corresponds to the total number of characteristics examined per case) [19].

In non-streaming bagging, each of the n-base models is trained in a Z-size bootstrap sample, created by random samples being substituted by the original training kit. Each bootstrapped sample contains a prototype training snapshot K, where P (K = k) follows a binomial distribution. For large values of Z this binomial distribution adheres to a Poisson distribution with $\lambda = 1$. In contrast to the ARF method for streaming data, Poisson is used with $\lambda = 6$ instead of Poisson $\lambda = 1$. This "feedback" has the practical effect of increasing the possibility of assigning higher weights to instances during the training of the basic models.

ARF is an adaptation of the original Random Forest algorithm, which has been successfully applied to a multitude of machine learning tasks. In layman's terms the original Random Forest algorithm is an ensemble of decision trees, which are trained using bagging and where the node splits are limited to a random subset of the original set of features. The "Adaptive" part of ARF comes from its mechanisms to adapt to different kinds of concept drifts, given the same hyper-parameters.

The overall ARF pseudo-code is presented below [19].

Algorithm 2. Adaptive Random Forests

---

function ARF (m, n, δ_w, δ_d)
  $T \leftarrow CreateTrees(n)$
  $W \leftarrow InitWeits(n)$
  $B \leftarrow \emptyset$
  while HasNext(S) do
    $(x, y) \leftarrow next(S)$
    for all $t \in T$ do
      $\breve{y} \leftarrow predict (t, x)$
      $W_{(t)} \leftarrow P\big(W_{(t)}, \breve{y}, y\big)$
      $RFTreeTrain (m, t, x, y)$
      if $C (\delta_w, t, x, y)$ then
        $b \leftarrow CreateTrees()$
        $B(t) \leftarrow b$
      end if
    end for
    for all $b \in B$ do
      $RFTreeTrain (m, b, x, y)$
    end for
  end while
end function

Where m: the maximum features evaluated per split; n: the total number of trees (n = |T|); δ_w: the warning threshold; δ_d: the drift threshold; c(·): the change detection method; S: the data stream; B: the Set of background trees; W(t): the Tree t weight; P (·): the learning performance estimation function.

3.2 K-NN Classifier with Self Adjusting

The k-NN SAM algorithm is inspired by the Short-Term and Long-Term memory (STM & LTM) model [27]. The information arriving in STM, are accompanied by relevant knowledge from the LTM. The information that receives enough attention is transferred in the LTM in the form of the Synaptic Consolidation. The memories are assigned the following sets M_{ST}, M_{LT}, M_C which are subsets of the $R^n \times \{1, \ldots, c\}$. The STM is a dynamic sliding window that contains the most *recent m* examples of the data flow [27]:

$$M_{ST} = \{(x_i, y_i) \in R^n \times \{1, \ldots, c\} | i = t - m + 1, \ldots, t\} \tag{3}$$

The LTM retains all of the initial information and unlike the STM, it is not a continuous part of the data flow. It is a set of points p:

$$M_{LT} = \{(x_i, y_i) \in R^n \times \{1, \ldots, c\} | i = 1, \ldots, p\} \tag{4}$$

The combined memory C_M is the union of both memories with size m + p:

$$M_C = M_{ST} \cup M_{LT} \tag{5}$$

Each set includes the weighted k-NN classifier:

$$R^n \times \{1, \ldots, c\}, k - NN_{M_{ST}}, k - NN_{M_{LT}}, k - NN_{M_C} \tag{6}$$

The k-NN approach assigns a label to each data point x based on a set $Z = \{(x_i, y_i) \in R^n \times \{1, \ldots, c\} | i = 1, \ldots, n\}$:

$$k - NN_Z(x) = argmax\left\{ \sum_{x_i \in N_k(x,Z)|y_i = \hat{c}} \frac{1}{d(x_i, x)} | \hat{c} = 1, .., c \right\} \tag{7}$$

where $d(x_i, x)$ is the Euclidean distance between two points and $N_k(x, Z)$ returns the set comprising of the k nearest neighbors x in Z [27].

3.3 Primal Estimated Sub-Gradient Solver for SVM

The SPegasos is a simple and effective stochastic sub-gradient descent algorithm for solving the optimization problem by using SVM [29]. Initially, w_1 is defined. In the t iteration of the algorithm, we use a random training example (x_{i_t}, y_{i_t}) by choosing an index $i_t \in \{1, \ldots, m\}$. Then we use the following Eq. (8):

$$\min_{w} \frac{\lambda}{2} \|w\|^2 + \frac{1}{m} \sum_{x,y \in S} l(w; (x,y)) \tag{8}$$

where $l(w; (x,y)) = \max\{0, 1 - y\langle w, x\rangle\}$, with a sample (x_{i_t}, y_{i_t}), giving input to the following function:

$$f(w, i_t) = \frac{\lambda}{2} \|w\|^2 + l(w; (x_{i_t}, y_{i_t})) \tag{9}$$

where

$$\nabla_t = \lambda w_t - \mathbb{1}[y_{i_t}\langle w_t, x_{i_t}\rangle < 1] y_{i_t} x_{i_t} \tag{10}$$

and $\mathbb{1}[y_{i_t}\langle w_t, x_{i_t}\rangle < 1]$ is the index function, which takes the value 1 if the argument is true and it becomes equal to 0 in any other case. Then, we update the relation $w_{t+1} \leftarrow w_t - \eta_t \nabla_t$ by using weight step $\eta_t = \frac{1}{\lambda t}$. After T iterations, the last value of the weight is the w_{T+1} [29].

4   Results and Discussion

We have evaluated the performance of the proposed methods by measuring the average values for Kappa Statistic and Kappa Temporal Statistic. The results of all experiments are shown in the following Tables 1, 2 and 3.

The learning evaluation used 10,000 instances and the validation of the results was done by employing the Prequential Evaluation method [3]. The training window used 5,000 instances. Window based approaches were allowed to store 5,000 samples (for the sake of completeness, we also report the error rates of all window-based approaches with a window size of 1,000 samples) but never more than 10% of the whole dataset. This large amount gives the approaches a high degree of freedom and prevents the concealment of their qualities with a too restricted window.

Table 1. Results for the *water_tower_dataset*

Network traffic analysis				
Performance metrics				
Classifier	Window size 5000		Window size 1000	
	Kappa statistic	Kappa temporal statistic	Kappa statistic	Kappa temporal statistic
k-NN SAM	**74.56%**	**75.29%**	**79.22%**	**79.96%**
SPegasos	72.07%	72.94%	74.65%	76.51%
ARF	71.86%	72.47%	75.24%	77.72%
Ensemble averaging	**73.52%**	**74.26%**	**77.51%**	**78.82%**

Table 2. Results for the *gas_dataset*

Network traffic analysis

Performance metrics

Classifier	Window size 5000		Window size 1000	
	Kappa statistic	Kappa temporal statistic	Kappa statistic	Kappa temporal Statistic
k-NN SAM	**72.03%**	**72.73%**	**74.18%**	**75.41%**
SPegasos	72.02%	72.69%	73.94%	75.01%
ARF	71.83%	72.41%	73.87%	74.89%
Ensemble averaging	**71.99%**	**72.66%**	**74.07%**	**75.23%**

Table 3. Results for the *electric_dataset*

Network traffic analysis

Performance metrics

Classifier	Window size 5000		Window size 1000	
	Kappa statistic	Kappa temporal statistic	Kappa statistic	Kappa temporal statistic
k-NN SAM	**75.72%**	**76.33%**	**78.93%**	**79.56%**
SPegasos	75.63%	76.12%	77.95%	78.93%
ARF	74.47%	75.16%	76.18%	77.97%
Ensemble averaging	**75.45%**	**76.05%**	**78.19%**	**79.17%**

The assessment of the actual error of the data flow classifiers, is done in terms of the Accuracy Kappa statistic and the Kappa-Temporal statistic. The "true" label is presented right after the instance has been used for testing, where there is a delay between the time an instance is presented and the moment in which its "true" label becomes available [30]. The use of the dynamically estimated weighted average is the optimal approach, considering that is solves a real problem of information systems security, where it is rare for all data flows to have the same importance. The algorithm, which has achieved the highest accuracy for each data stream, is multiplied by the corresponding weighting factor of 0.6, reflecting its transient superiority and hence the relative importance of the model to the particular algorithm at that time.

Based on this technique, the model is led to a relatively smooth but high learning rate, which determines how quickly learning is converging. A high rate of learning can lead to faster convergence and oscillation around optimal weight values, while the low rate of learning results in slower convergence and can lead to trapping at local extremes. The high learning rate is confirmed by the high accuracy rates of the model, since very small size data flows are considered compared to the evaluation of a batch data set. According to this technique, the quality of the model's adaptation is interpreted as a "better forecasting" rate, due to the increased percentage of classification precision. More specifically, the temporal bias created to the dynamics of a model at a specific time, is reflected in the high precision percentages of Table 1.

An additional important interpretation, resulting from the high accuracy of the 9 learning algorithms and the mild "mutation", attributable to the dynamically determined weighted average, is to assist in discovering the local extremes that may be included in a data flow or in a learning window. This is expected, since new areas of the multidimensional solution space are examined.

On the contrary, if the "mutation" rate was too high, it could lead to a reduction in the exploitation of highly suitable areas of the solution space, and it could trap the system into solutions that do not generalize [30, 33]. An important comment also refers to the Kappa coefficient that links the level of observed agreement to the level of the random agreement. It estimates the variability in each observer rater variation that occurs when the same observer - evaluates differently in repeated evaluations of the same size. The maximum value of the Kappa index represents the full agreement between observers - markers, while the minimum value 0 is interpreted as there is only random agreement and thus no reliability between observers - markers.

As we can see, there is considerable reliability in all cases tested, which also strengthens the overall reliability and usability of the proposed model. Similarly, by attempting a comparison of the results between the algorithms, we see that the ARF method generally needs a larger number of cases to yield new data. In addition, ARF works by combining some loose linear boundaries on the decision surface, as opposed to SPegasos which can achieve max margin in non-linear boundaries. Therefore, given that sliding windows are characterized by a small amount of data, SPegasos yielded higher success rates than ARF. Regarding the comparison between SPegasos and k-NN SAM, an clear reason that k-NN SAM performed better, is because a particular problem is located in a high-dimensional space where this algorithm is more efficient. Also, the optimal combination of the two levels of memory, the different retention intervals between the memories and the transfer of knowledge, has been shown to minimize errors and to increase classification accuracy.

5   Conclusions

An innovative, reliable and highly effective cyberattack detection system, based on sophisticated computational intelligence, was presented in this paper. The DELDaStrA, is an innovative effort to analyze large-scale, reliable and accurate data flows in order to detect cyber-attacks in critical infrastructure networks. The implementation of DEL-DaStrA was based on the philosophy of the dynamic ensemble learning method, which ensures the adaptation of the system to new situations offering impartiality and generalization. It is a robust framework capable of responding to high complexity problems. The performance of the proposed system has been tested by using three multidimensional datasets of high complexity. These datasets were obtained after extensive research in the operation of ICS (SCADA, DCS, PLC). They realistically state the operating states of these devices under normal conditions and under situations of cyberattacks. The very high precision results that have emerged, reinforce the general   methodology   followed.   Proposals   for   the   development   and   future improvements of this system, should focus on further optimizing the algorithms used to achieve an even more efficient, accurate and faster classification process. Also, new approaches for further optimization should be considered, by employing self-improvement and adaptive learning, which will fully automate the cyber-detection process.

References

1. Ahmim, A., Ghoualmi-Zine, N.: A new adaptive intrusion detection system based on the intersection of two different classifiers. Int. J. Secur. Netw. **9**(3), 125–132 (2014)
2. Aretz, K., Bartram, S.M., Pope, P.F.: Asymmetric loss functions and the rationality of expected stock returns. Int. J. Forecast. **27**(2), 413–437 (2011)
3. Brzezinski, D., Stefanowski, J.: Prequential AUC for classifier evaluation and drift detection in evolving data streams. In: Appice, A., Ceci, M., Loglisci, C., Manco, G., Masciari, E., Ras, Z.W. (eds.) NFMCP 2014. LNCS (LNAI), vol. 8983, pp. 87–101. Springer, Cham (2015). https://doi.org/10.1007/978-3-319-17876-9_6
4. Chand, N., Mishra, P., Krishna, C.R., Pilli, E.S., Govil, M.C.: A comparative analysis of SVM and its stacking with other classification algorithm for intrusion detection. In: Proceedings - 2016 International Conference on Advances in Computing, Communication and Automation, ICACCA 2016, pp. 1–6 (2016)
5. Dedić, N., Stanier, C.: Towards differentiating business intelligence, big data, data analytics and knowledge discovery. In: Piazolo, F., Geist, V., Brehm, L., Schmidt, R. (eds.) ERP Future 2016. LNBIP, vol. 285, pp. 114–122. Springer, Cham (2017). https://doi.org/10.1007/978-3-319-58801-8_10
6. Demertzis, K., Iliadis, L.: A hybrid network anomaly and intrusion detection approach based on evolving spiking neural network classification. In: Sideridis, A.B., Kardasiadou, Z., Yialouris, C.P., Zorkadis, V. (eds.) E-Democracy 2013. CCIS, vol. 441, pp. 11–23. Springer, Cham (2014). https://doi.org/10.1007/978-3-319-11710-2_2
7. Demertzis, K., Iliadis, L.: Evolving computational intelligence system for malware detection. In: Iliadis, L., Papazoglou, M., Pohl, K. (eds.) CAiSE 2014. LNBIP, vol. 178, pp. 322–334. Springer, Cham (2014). https://doi.org/10.1007/978-3-319-07869-4_30
8. Demertzis, K., Iliadis, L.: Evolving smart URL filter in a zone-based policy firewall for detecting algorithmically generated malicious domains. In: Gammerman, A., Vovk, V., Papadopoulos, H. (eds.) SLDS 2015. LNCS (LNAI), vol. 9047, pp. 223–233. Springer, Cham (2015). https://doi.org/10.1007/978-3-319-17091-6_17
9. Demertzis, K., Iliadis, L.: A bio-inspired hybrid artificial intelligence framework for cyber security. In: Daras, N.J., Rassias, M.T. (eds.) Computation, Cryptography, and Network Security, pp. 161–193. Springer, Cham (2015). https://doi.org/10.1007/978-3-319-18275-9_7
10. Demertzis, K., Iliadis, L.: SAME: an intelligent anti-malware extension for android ART virtual machine. In: Núñez, M., Nguyen, N.T., Camacho, D., Trawiński, B. (eds.) ICCCI 2015. LNCS (LNAI), vol. 9330, pp. 235–245. Springer, Cham (2015). https://doi.org/10.1007/978-3-319-24306-1_23
11. Demertzis, K., Iliadis, L.: Bio-inspired hybrid intelligent method for detecting android malware. In: Kunifuji, S., Papadopoulos, G.A., Skulimowski, A.M.J., Kacprzyk, J. (eds.) Knowledge, Information and Creativity Support Systems. AISC, vol. 416, pp. 289–304. Springer, Cham (2016). https://doi.org/10.1007/978-3-319-27478-2_20
12. Demertzis, K., Iliadis, L.: Ladon: a cyber-threat bio-inspired intelligence management system. J. Appl. Math. Bioinf. **6**(3), 45–64 (2016)

13. Demertzis, K., Iliadis, L., Spartalis, S.: A spiking one-class anomaly detection framework for cyber-security on industrial control systems. In: Boracchi, G., Iliadis, L., Jayne, C., Likas, A. (eds.) EANN 2017. CCIS, vol. 744, pp. 122–134. Springer, Cham (2017). https://doi.org/10.1007/978-3-319-65172-9_11

14. Demertzis, K., Iliadis, L., Anezakis, V.-D.: An innovative soft computing system for smart energy grids cybersecurity. Adv. Build. Energy Res. **12**(1), 3–24 (2018)

15. Demertzis, K., Iliadis, L., Anezakis, V.D.: A deep spiking machine-hearing system for the case of invasive fish species. In: 2017 IEEE International Conference on Innovations in Intelligent Systems and Applications, pp. 23–28. IEEE (2017)

16. Demertzis, K., Iliadis, L., Anezakis, V.-D.: Commentary: Aedes albopictus and Aedes japonicus—two invasive mosquito species with different temperature niches in Europe. Front. Environ. Sci. **5**(DEC), 85 (2017)

17. Dietterich, Thomas G.: Ensemble methods in machine learning. In: Kittler, J., Roli, F. (eds.) MCS 2000. LNCS, vol. 1857, pp. 1–15. Springer, Heidelberg (2000). https://doi.org/10.1007/3-540-45014-9_1

18. Farda, N.M.: Multi-temporal land use mapping of coastal wetlands area using machine learning in Google earth engine. In: 5th Geoinformation Science Symposium 2017, vol. 98, no. 1, pp. 1–12 (2017)

19. Gomes, H.M., et al.: Adaptive random forests for evolving data stream classification. Mach. Learn. **106**(9–10), 1469–1495 (2017). https://doi.org/10.1007/s10994-017-5642-8

20. Hurst, W., Merabti, M., Fergus, P.: A survey of critical infrastructure security. In: Butts, J., Shenoi, S. (eds.) ICCIP 2014. IAICT, vol. 441, pp. 127–138. Springer, Heidelberg (2014). https://doi.org/10.1007/978-3-662-45355-1_9

21. Krawczyk, B., Minku, L.L., Gama, J., Stefanowski, J., Woźniak, M.: Ensemble learning for data stream analysis: a survey. Inf. Fus. **37**, 132–156 (2017)

22. Krawczyk, B., Cano, A.: Online ensemble learning with abstaining classifiers for drifting and noisy data streams. Appl. Soft Comput. **68**, 677–692 (2018)

23. Kuncheva, L.I.: Combining Pattern Classifiers: Methods and Algorithms, 1st edn. Wiley, Hoboken (2004). ISBN 0-471-21078-1

24. Kushner, H.J., Yin, G.G.: Stochastic Approximation and Recursive Algorithms and Applications. Stochastic Modeling and Applied Probability, vol. 35, 2nd edn. Springer, Heidelberg (2003). https://doi.org/10.1007/b97441

25. Lin, J.: The Lambda and the Kappa. IEEE Internet Comput. **21**(5), 60–66 (2017)

26. Liu, S.M., Liu, T., Wang, Z.Q., Xiu, Y., Liu, Y.X., Meng, C.: data stream ensemble classification based on classifier confidence. J. Appl. Sci. **35**(2), 226–232 (2017)

27. Losing, V., Hammer, B., Wersing, H.: KNN classifier with self-adjusting memory for heterogeneous concept drift. In: 16th IEEE International Conference on Data Mining, vol. 7837853, pp. 291–300. IEEE (2017)

28. Rani, M.S., Sumathy, S.: Analysis of KNN, C5.0 and one class SVM for intrusion detection system. Int. J. Pharm. Technol. **8**(4), 26251–26259 (2016)

29. Shalev-Shwartz, S., Singer, Y., Srebro, N., Cotter, A.: Pegasos: primal estimated sub-gradient solver for SVM. Math. Program. **127**(1), 3–30 (2011)

30. Vinagre, J., Jorge, A.M., Gama, J.: Evaluation of recommender systems in streaming environments. In: Workshop on Recommender Systems Evaluation: Dimensions and Design, SV, US, pp. 1–6 (2014)

31. Wang, C., Fang, L., Dai, Y.: A simulation environment for SCADA security analysis and assessment. In: Conference on Measuring Technology and Mechatronics Automation, vol. 1, pp. 342–347. IEEE (2010)

32. Zhou, Z.H.: Ensemble Methods: Foundations and Algorithms. Chapman & Hall/CRC Machine Learning & Pattern Recognition Series, 1st edn. CRC Press, T&F, New York (2012)
33. Žliobaitė, I., Bifet, A., Read, J., Pfahringer, B., Holmes, G.: Evaluation methods and decision theory for classification of streaming data with temporal dependence. Mach. Learn. **98**(3), 455–482 (2014)

Fuzzy/Feature Selection

Gaussian Kernel-Based Fuzzy Clustering with Automatic Bandwidth Computation

Francisco de A. T. de Carvalho[1]($\boxtimes$), Lucas V. C. Santana[1],
and Marcelo R. P. Ferreira[2]

[1] Centro de Informatica, Universidade Federal de Pernambuco,
Av. Jornalista Anibal Fernandes s/n - Cidade Universitaria,
Recife-PE 50740-560, Brazil
fatc@cin.ufpe.br
[2] Departamento de Estatistica, Centro de Ciencias Exatas e da Natureza,
Universidade Federal da Paraiba, João Pessoa-PB 58051-900, Brazil

Abstract. The conventional Gaussian kernel-based fuzzy c-means clustering algorithm has widely demonstrated its superiority to the conventional fuzzy c-means when the data sets are arbitrarily shaped, and not linearly separable. However, its performance is very dependent on the estimation of the bandwidth parameter of the Gaussian kernel function. Usually this parameter is estimated once and for all. This paper presents a Gaussian fuzzy c-means with kernelization of the metric which depends on a vector of bandwidth parameters, one for each variable, that are computed automatically. Experiments with data sets of the UCI machine learning repository corroborate the usefulness of the proposed algorithm.

1 Introduction

Clustering means the task of organizing a set of items into clusters such that items within a given cluster have a high degree of similarity, while items belonging to different clusters have a high degree of dissimilarity. Clustering has been successfully used in different fields, including bioinformatics, image processing, and information retrieval [14,21].

Hierarchy and Partition are the most popular cluster structures provided by clustering methods. Hierarchical methods yield a complete hierarchy, i.e., a nested sequence of partitions of the input data, whereas partitioning methods aims to obtain a single partition of the data into a fixed number of clusters, usually based on an iterative algorithm that optimizes an objective function.

Partitioning methods can be divided into crisp and fuzzy. Crisp clustering provides a crisp partition in which each object of the dataset belongs to one and only one cluster. Fuzzy clustering [1] generates a fuzzy partition that provides a membership degree for each object in a given cluster. This allows distinguish objects that belong to more than one cluster at the same time [15].

Fuzzy c-means partitioning algorithms often use the Euclidean distance to compute the dissimilarity between the objects and the cluster representatives.

© Springer Nature Switzerland AG 2018
V. Kůrková et al. (Eds.): ICANN 2018, LNCS 11139, pp. 685–694, 2018.
https://doi.org/10.1007/978-3-030-01418-6_67

However, when the data structure is complex (i.e., clusters with non-hyper-spherical shapes and/or linearly non-separable patterns), the conventional fuzzy c-means will not be able to provide effective results. Kernel-based clustering algorithms have been proposed to tackle these limitations [3,6,8,9].

There are two major variations of kernel-based clustering: one is the kernel-ization of the metric, where the cluster centroids are obtained in the original space and the distances between objects and cluster centroids are computed by means of kernels, while the other is the clustering in feature space, in which the cluster representatives are not in the original space and can only be obtained indirectly in the feature space [3,9].

In kernel-based clustering algorithms it is possible to compute Euclidean distances by using kernel functions and the so-called distance kernel trick [9]. This trick uses a kernel function to calculate the dot products of vectors implicitly in the higher dimensional space using the original space.

The most popular kernel function in applications is the Gaussian kernel. In general, this kernel function provides effective results and requires the tuning of a single parameter, that is, the bandwidth parameter [4]. This parameter is tuned once and for all, and it is the same for all variables. Thus, implicitly the conventional Gaussian kernel fuzzy c-means assumes that the variables are equally rescaled and, therefore, they have the same importance to the clustering task. However, it is well known that some variables have different degrees of relevance while others are irrelevant to the clustering task [7,11,17,20].

Recently, Ref. [5] proposed a Gaussian kernel c-means crisp clustering algorithm with kernelization of the metric, where each variable has its own hyper-parameter that is iteratively computed during the running of the algorithm.

The main contribution of this paper is to provide a Gaussian kernel c-means fuzzy clustering algorithms, with both kernelization of the metric and automated computation of the bandwidth parameters using an adaptive Gaussian kernel. In these kernel-based fuzzy clustering algorithm, the bandwidth parameters change at each algorithm iteration and differ from variable to variable. Thus, these algorithms are able to rescale the variables differently and thus select the relevant ones for the clustering task.

The paper is organized as follows. Section 2 first recalls the conventional kernel c-means fuzzy clustering algorithm with kernelization of the metric. Then presents the Gaussian c-Means fuzzy clustering algorithm with kernelization of the metric and with automatic computation of bandwidth parameters. In Sect. 3, experiments with data sets of the UCI machine learning repository corroborate the usefulness of the proposed algorithm. Section 4 provides the final remarks of the paper.

2   Kernel Fuzzy c-Means with Kernelization of the Metric

This section briefly recalls the basic concepts about kernel functions and the conventional kernel c-means algorithm with kernelization of the metric. Let $E =$

$\{e_1, \ldots, e_n\}$ be a set of n objects described by p real-valued variables. Let $\mathcal{D} = \{\mathbf{x}_1, \ldots, \mathbf{x}_n\}$ be a non-empty set where for $k = 1, \ldots, n$, the kth object e_k is represented by a vector $\mathbf{x}_k = (x_{k1}, \ldots, x_{kp}) \in \mathbb{R}^p$. A function $\mathcal{K} : \mathcal{D} \times \mathcal{D} \to \mathbb{R}$ is called a positive definite Kernel (or Mercer kernel) if, and only if $\mathcal{K}$ is symmetric (i.e., $\mathcal{K}(\mathbf{x}_k, \mathbf{x}_l) = \mathcal{K}(\mathbf{x}_l, \mathbf{x}_k)$) and if the following inequality holds [18]:

$$\sum_{l=1}^{n} \sum_{k=1}^{n} c_l c_k \mathcal{K}(\mathbf{x}_l, \mathbf{x}_k) \geq 0, \forall n \geq 2 \tag{1}$$

where $c_l, c_k \in \mathbb{R}(1 \leq l, k \leq n)$.

Let $\varPhi : \mathcal{D} \to \mathcal{F}$ be a nonlinear mapping from the input space $\mathcal{D}$ to a high dimensional feature space $\mathcal{F}$. By applying the mapping $\varPhi$, the inner product $\mathbf{x}_l^T \mathbf{x}_k$ in the input space is mapped to $\varPhi(\mathbf{x}_l)^T \varPhi(\mathbf{x}_k)$ in the feature space. The basic notion in the kernel approaches is that the non-linear mapping $\varPhi$ does not need to be explicitly specified because each Mercer kernel can be expressed as $\mathcal{K}(\mathbf{x}_l, \mathbf{x}_k) = \varPhi(\mathbf{x}_l)^T \varPhi(\mathbf{x}_k)$ [18].

One the most relevant implications is that it is possible to compute Euclidean distances in $\mathcal{F}$ without knowing explicitly $\varPhi$, by using the so-called distance kernel trick [9]:

$$\begin{aligned} \|\varPhi(\mathbf{x}_l) - \varPhi(\mathbf{x}_k)\| &= (\varPhi(\mathbf{x}_l) - \varPhi(\mathbf{x}_k))^T (\varPhi(\mathbf{x}_l) - \varPhi(\mathbf{x}_k)) \\ &= \varPhi(\mathbf{x}_l)^T \varPhi(\mathbf{x}_l) - 2\varPhi(\mathbf{x}_l)^T \varPhi(\mathbf{x}_k) + \varPhi(\mathbf{x}_k)^T \varPhi(\mathbf{x}_k) \\ &= \mathcal{K}(\mathbf{x}_l, \mathbf{x}_l) - 2\mathcal{K}(\mathbf{x}_l, \mathbf{x}_k) + \mathcal{K}(\mathbf{x}_k, \mathbf{x}_k). \end{aligned}$$

2.1 Kernel Fuzzy c-Means with Kernelization of the Metric

The kernel fuzzy c-means with kernelization of the metric (hereafter named KFCM-K) provides a fuzzy partition of E into c clusters, represented by a matrix of membership degrees $\mathbf{U} = (u_{ki}) (1 \leq k \leq n; 1 \leq i \leq c)$, and a matrix of cluster representatives (called hereafter matrix of prototypes) $\mathbf{G} = (\mathbf{g}_1, \ldots, \mathbf{g}_c)$ of the fuzzy clusters in the fuzzy partition $\mathbf{U}$. The prototype of cluster $i (i = 1, \ldots, c)$ is represented by the vector $\mathbf{g}_i = (g_{i1}, \ldots, g_{ip}) \in \mathbb{R}^p$.

From an initial solution, the matrix of prototypes $\mathbf{G}$ and the fuzzy partition $\mathbf{U}$ are obtained iteratively in two steps (representation and assignment) by the minimization of a suitable objective function, here-below denoted as J_{KFCM-K}, that gives the total heterogeneity of the fuzzy partition computed as the sum of the heterogeneity in each fuzzy cluster:

$$J_{KFCM-K}(\mathbf{G}, \mathbf{U}) = \sum_{i=1}^{c} \sum_{k=1}^{n} (u_{ki})^m \|\varPhi(\mathbf{x}_k) - \varPhi(\mathbf{g}_i)\|^2 \tag{2}$$

where $1 < m < \infty$ is the fuzziness parameter. Using the so-called distance kernel trick [9], we have $\|\varPhi(\mathbf{x}_k) - \varPhi(\mathbf{g}_i)\|^2 = \mathcal{K}(\mathbf{x}_k, \mathbf{x}_k) - 2\mathcal{K}(\mathbf{x}_k, \mathbf{g}_i) + \mathcal{K}(\mathbf{g}_i, \mathbf{g}_i)$.

Hereafter we consider the Gaussian kernel, the most commonly used in the literature: $\mathcal{K}(\mathbf{x}_l, \mathbf{x}_k) = \exp\left\{-\frac{\|\mathbf{x}_l - \mathbf{x}_k\|^2}{2\sigma^2}\right\} = \exp\left\{-\frac{1}{2} \sum_{j=1}^{p} \frac{1}{\sigma^2}(x_{lj} - x_{kj})^2\right\}$, where σ^2 is the bandwidth parameter of the Gaussian kernel.

Then, $\mathcal{K}(\mathbf{x}_k, \mathbf{x}_k) = 1, \forall k$, $\mathcal{K}(\mathbf{g}_i, \mathbf{g}_i) = 1, \forall i$, and $||\Phi(\mathbf{x}_k) - \Phi(\mathbf{g}_i)||^2 = 2 - 2\,\mathcal{K}(\mathbf{x}_k, \mathbf{g}_i)$ and thus, the objective function J_{KFMC-K} becomes:

$$J_{KFCM-K}(\mathbf{G}, \mathbf{U}) = 2 \sum_{i=1}^{c} \sum_{k=1}^{n} (u_{ki})^m \left(1 - \mathcal{K}(\mathbf{x}_k, \mathbf{g}_i)\right) \tag{3}$$

During the representation step, the fuzzy partition $\mathbf{U}$ is kept fixed. The objective function J_{KFMC-K} is optimized with respect to the prototypes. Thus, from $\frac{\partial J_{KFMC-K}}{\partial \mathbf{g}_i} = 0$ and after some algebra, the fuzzy cluster prototypes are obtained as follows:

$$\mathbf{g}_i = \frac{\sum_{k=1}^{n} (u_{ki})^m \, \mathcal{K}(\mathbf{x}_k, \mathbf{g}_i) \mathbf{x}_k}{\sum_{k=1}^{n} (u_{ki})^m \mathcal{K}(\mathbf{x}_k, \mathbf{g}_i)} \; (1 \leq i \leq c). \tag{4}$$

In the assignment step, the cluster prototypes are kept fixed. The components $u_{ki}\,(1 \leq k \leq n; 1 \leq i \leq c)$ of the matrix of membership degrees $\mathbf{U}$, that minimizes the clustering criterion given in Eq. (3), are computed as follows:

$$u_{ki} = \left[\sum_{h=1}^{c} \left(\frac{(1 - \mathcal{K}(\mathbf{x}_k, \mathbf{g}_i))}{(1 - \mathcal{K}(\mathbf{x}_k, \mathbf{g}_h))} \right)^{\frac{1}{m-1}} \right]^{-1}. \tag{5}$$

2.2   KFCM-K with Automatic Computation of Bandwidth Parameters

The kernel fuzzy c-means with kernelization of the metric and automatic computation of bandwidth parameters (hereafter named KFCM-K-H) provides a partition of E into c clusters, represented by a matrix of membership degrees $\mathbf{U} = (u_{ki})\,(1 \leq k \leq n; 1 \leq i \leq c)$, a vector of bandwidth parameters (one for each variable) $\mathbf{s} = (s_1^2, \ldots, s_p^2)$ and a matrix of prototypes $\mathbf{G} = (\mathbf{g}_1, \ldots, \mathbf{g}_c)$ of the fuzzy clusters in the fuzzy partition $\mathbf{U}$.

From an initial solution, the matrix of prototypes $\mathbf{G}$, the vector of bandwidth parameters $\mathbf{s}$ and the fuzzy partition $\mathbf{U}$ are obtained interactively in three steps (representation, computation of the bandwidth parameters and assignment) by the minimization of a suitable objective function, here-below denoted as $J_{KFCM-K-H}$, that gives the total heterogeneity of the fuzzy partition computed as the sum of the heterogeneity in each fuzzy cluster:

$$J_{KFCM-K-H}(\mathbf{G}, \mathbf{s}, \mathbf{U}) = \sum_{i=1}^{c} \sum_{k=1}^{n} (u_{ki})^m ||\Phi(\mathbf{x}_k) - \Phi(\mathbf{g}_i)||^2 \tag{6}$$

where

$$||\Phi(\mathbf{x}_k) - \Phi(\mathbf{g}_i)||^2 = \mathcal{K}^{(\mathbf{s})}(\mathbf{x}_k, \mathbf{x}_k) - 2\mathcal{K}^{(\mathbf{s})}(\mathbf{x}_k, \mathbf{g}_i) + \mathcal{K}^{(\mathbf{s})}(\mathbf{g}_i, \mathbf{g}_i) \tag{7}$$

with

$$\mathcal{K}^{(\mathbf{s})}(\mathbf{x}_l, \mathbf{x}_k) = \exp \left\{ -\frac{1}{2} \sum_{j=1}^{p} \frac{1}{s_j^2} (x_{lj} - x_{kj})^2 \right\}$$

Because $\mathcal{K}^{(\mathbf{s})}(\mathbf{x}_k, \mathbf{x}_k) = 1, \forall k$, $\mathcal{K}^{(\mathbf{s})}(\mathbf{g}_i, \mathbf{g}_i) = 1, \forall i$, and $||\Phi(\mathbf{x}_k) - \Phi(\mathbf{g}_i)||^2 = 2 - 2\,\mathcal{K}^{(\mathbf{s})}(\mathbf{x}_k, \mathbf{g}_i)$, the objective function $J_{KFMC-K-H}$ becomes:

$$J_{KFCM-K-H}(\mathbf{G}, \mathbf{s}, \mathbf{U}) = 2 \sum_{i=1}^{c} \sum_{k=1}^{n} (u_{ki})^m (1 - \mathcal{K}^{(\mathbf{s})}(\mathbf{x}_k, \mathbf{g}_i)) \tag{8}$$

During the representation step, the vector of bandwidth parameters $\mathbf{s}$ and the fuzzy partition $\mathbf{U}$ are kept fixed. The objective function $J_{KFMC-K-H}$ is optimized with respect to the prototypes. Thus, from $\frac{\partial J_{KFMC-K-H}}{\partial \mathbf{g}_i} = 0$ and after some algebra, the cluster prototypes are obtained as follows:

$$\mathbf{g}_i = \frac{\sum_{k=1}^{n} (u_{ki})^m \mathcal{K}^{(\mathbf{s})}(\mathbf{x}_k, \mathbf{g}_i) \mathbf{x}_k}{\sum_{k=1}^{n} (u_{ki})^m \mathcal{K}^{(\mathbf{s})}(\mathbf{x}_k, \mathbf{g}_i)} \quad (1 \le i \le c). \tag{9}$$

In the computation of the bandwidth parameters step, the matrix of prototypes $\mathbf{G}$ and the fuzzy partition $\mathbf{U}$ are kept fixed. First, we use the method of Lagrange multipliers with the restriction that $\prod_{j=1}^{p} \left(\frac{1}{s_j^2} \right) = \gamma$, where γ is a suitable parameter, and obtain

$$\mathcal{L}_{KFCM-K-H}^1(\mathbf{G}, \mathbf{s}, \mathbf{U}) = 2 \sum_{i=1}^{c} \sum_{k=1}^{n} (u_{ki})^m (1 - \mathcal{K}^{(\mathbf{s})}(\mathbf{x}_k, \mathbf{g}_i)) - \omega \left(\prod_{j=1}^{p} \frac{1}{s_j^2} - \gamma \right).$$
$$\tag{10}$$

Then, we compute the partial derivatives of $\mathcal{L}_{KFCM-K-H}^1$ w.r.t $\frac{1}{s_j^2}$ and ω, and by setting the partial derivatives to zero, and after some algebra we obtain

$$\frac{1}{s_j^2} = \frac{\gamma^{\frac{1}{p}} \left\{ \prod_{h=1}^{p} \left[\sum_{i=1}^{c} \sum_{k=1}^{n} (u_{ki})^m \mathcal{K}^{(\mathbf{s})}(\mathbf{x}_k, \mathbf{g}_i)(x_{kh} - g_{ih})^2 \right] \right\}}{\sum_{i=1}^{c} \sum_{k=1}^{n} (u_{ki})^m \mathcal{K}^{(\mathbf{s})}(\mathbf{x}_k, \mathbf{g}_i)(x_{kj} - g_{ij})^2} \quad (1 \le j \le p). \tag{11}$$

In the assignment step, the matrix of fuzzy cluster prototypes $\mathbf{G}$ and the vector of bandwidth parameters $\mathbf{s}$ are kept fixed. First, we use the method of Lagrange multipliers with the restriction that $\sum_{i=1}^{c} u_{ki} = 1$, and obtain

$$\mathcal{L}_{KFCM-K-H}^2(\mathbf{G}, \mathbf{s}, \mathbf{U}) = 2 \sum_{i=1}^{c} \sum_{k=1}^{n} (u_{ki})^m (1 - \mathcal{K}^{(\mathbf{s})}(\mathbf{x}_k, \mathbf{g}_i)) - \sum_{k=1}^{n} \omega_k \left(\sum_{i=1}^{c} u_{ki} - 1 \right).$$
$$\tag{12}$$

Then, we compute the partial derivatives of $\mathcal{L}_{KFCM-K-H}^2$ w.r.t u_{ki} and ω_k, and by setting the partial derivatives to zero, and after some algebra we obtain

$$u_{ki} = \left[\sum_{h=1}^{c} \left(\frac{(1 - \mathcal{K}^{(\mathbf{s})}(\mathbf{x}_k, \mathbf{g}_i))}{(1 - \mathcal{K}^{(\mathbf{s})}(\mathbf{x}_k, \mathbf{g}_h))} \right)^{\frac{1}{m-1}} \right]^{-1} \quad (1 \le k \le n; 1 \le i \le c). \tag{13}$$

Algorithm 1. KCM-K and KCM-K-H algorithms
***

1: **Iput**
2:     $\mathcal{D} = \{\mathbf{x}_1, \ldots, \mathbf{x}_n\}$ (the data set); c (the number of clusters); $\gamma > 0$ (a suitable parameter); T (maximum number of iterations); ϵ (threshold parameter);
3: **Output**
4:     KCM-K-GH and KCM-K-LH: the matrix of prototypes $\mathbf{G} = (\mathbf{g}_1, \ldots, \mathbf{g}_c)$;
5:     KCM-K-H: the vector of bandwidth parameters $\mathbf{s} = (s_1^2, \ldots, s_p^2)$;
6:     KCM-K-GH and KCM-K-LH: the matrix of membership degrees $\mathbf{U} = (u_{ki})$ $(1 \leq k \leq n; 1 \leq i \leq c)$.
7: **Initialization**
8:     $t = 0$;
9:     KCM-K and KCM-K-H: randomly select c distinct prototypes $\mathbf{g}_i^{(t)} \in \mathcal{D}$ $(1 \leq i \leq c)$;
10:    KCM-K-H: set $\frac{1}{(s_j^{(t)})^2} = (\gamma)^{\frac{1}{p}}$ $(1 \leq j \leq p)$;
11:    KCM-K: compute the components $u_{ki}^{(t)}$ $(1 \leq k \leq n; 1 \leq i \leq c)$ of the the matrix of membership degrees $\mathbf{U}^{(t)}$ according to Eq. (5);
12:    KCM-K-H: compute the components $u_{ki}^{(t)}$ $(1 \leq k \leq n; 1 \leq i \leq c)$ of the the matrix of membership degrees $\mathbf{U}^{(t)}$ according to Eq. (13);
13:    KCM-K: compute $J_{KFCM-K}(\mathbf{G}^{(t)}, \mathbf{U}^{(t)})$ according to Eq. (3);
14:    KCM-K-H: compute $J_{KFCM-K-H}(\mathbf{G}^{(t)}, \mathbf{s}^{(t)}, \mathbf{U}^{(t)})$ according to Eq. (8).
15: **repeat**
16:    $t = t + 1$;
17:    **Step 1: representation.**
18:       KCM-K: compute the cluster representatives $\mathbf{g}_1^{(t)}, \ldots, \mathbf{g}_c^{(t)}$ using Eq. (4);
19:       KCM-K-H: compute the cluster representatives $\mathbf{g}_1^{(t)}, \ldots, \mathbf{g}_c^{(t)}$ using Eq. (9).
20:    **Step 2: computation of the vector of bandwidth parameters**
21:       KCM-K: skip this step;
22:       KMC-K-H: compute the vector of bandwidth parameters $\mathbf{s}^{(t)}$ using Eq. (11);
23:    **Step 3: assignment**
24:       KCM-K: compute the components $u_{ki}^{(t)}$ $(1 \leq k \leq n; 1 \leq i \leq c)$ of the the matrix of membership degrees $\mathbf{U}^{(t)}$ according to Eq. (5).
25:       KCM-K-H: compute the components $u_{ki}^{(t)}$ $(1 \leq k \leq n; 1 \leq i \leq c)$ of the the matrix of membership degrees $\mathbf{U}^{(t)}$ according to Eq. (13).
26:    KCM-K: compute $J_{KFCM-K}(\mathbf{G}^{(t)}, \mathbf{U}^{(t)})$ according to Eq. (3).
27:    KCM-K-H: compute $J_{KFCM-K-H}(\mathbf{G}^{(t)}, \mathbf{s}^{(t)}, \mathbf{U}^{(t)})$ according to Eq. (8).
28: **until**
29:    KCM-K: $|J_{KFCM-K}(\mathbf{G}^{(t)}, \mathbf{U}^{(t)}) - J_{KFCM-K}(\mathbf{G}^{(t-1)}, \mathbf{U}^{(t-1)})| < \epsilon$ or $t > T$;
30:    KCM-K-H:
       $|J_{KFCM-K-H}(\mathbf{G}^{(t)}, \mathbf{s}^{(t)}, \mathbf{U}^{(t)}) - J_{KFCM-K-H}(\mathbf{G}^{(t-1)}, \mathbf{s}^{(t-1)}, \mathbf{U}^{(t-1)})| < \epsilon$ or $t > T$.
***

2.3   The Algorithms

The two steps of KFCM-K and the three steps of KFCM-K-H are repeated until the convergence. The Algorithm 1 summarizes these steps.

3   Empirical Results

This section discusses the performance and the usefulness of the proposed algorithm in comparison with the standard KFCM-K and FCM [1] algorithms.

Twelve datasets from the UCI Machine learning Repository [2], namely, Breast tissue, Ecoli, Image segmentation, Iris plants, Leaf, Libras Movement, Multiple features, Seeds, Thyroid gland, Urban land cover, Breast cancer wisconsin (diagnostic), and Wine, with different number of objects, variables and a priori classes, were considered in this study. Table 1 (in which n is the number of objects, p is the number of real-valued variables and K is the number of a priori classes) summarizes these data sets.

Table 1. Summary of the data sets

Data sets	n	p	K	Data sets	n	p	K
Breast tissue	106	9	6	Multiple features	2000	649	10
Ecoli	336	7	8	Seeds	210	7	3
Image segmentation	2100	19	7	Thyroid gland	215	5	3
Iris	150	4	3	Urban land cover	675	148	9
Leaf	310	14	36	Brest cancer winsconsin	569	30	2
Libras Movement	360	90	15	Wine	178	13	3

FCM, KFCM-K and KFCM-K-H were run on these data sets 100 times, with c (the number of clusters) equal to K (the number of a priori classes). The parameter *gamma* of the KFCM-K-H algorithm was set as $\gamma = (\sigma^2)^p$, where σ is the optimal width hyper-parameter used in the conventional KFCM-K algorithm that is estimated as the average of the 0.1 and 0.9 quantiles of $||\mathbf{x}_l - \mathbf{x}_k||^2$, $l \neq k$ [4]. The fuzziness parameter was set as $m = 1.6$ and $m = 2.0$.

To compare the quality of the fuzzy partitions provided by these algorithms, the Rand index for a fuzzy partition (Rand-F) [10], and the Hullemeyer index (HUL) [13] were considered. Rand-F and HUL indexes allow to compare the dataset a priori partition with the fuzzy partitions provided by the algorithms. They range between 0 and 1, where a value equal to one corresponds to total agreement between the partitions.

Table 2 shows the best results (according to the respective objective functions) of the FCM, KCM-K and KCM-K-H algorithms on the data sets of Table 1, according to the Rand-F and HUL indexes and for the fuzziness parameter set as $m = 1.6$ and $m = 2.0$.

It can be observed that whatever the considered indexes (Rand-F and HUL), FCM (for the great majority of the datasets), KFCM-K (for the great majority of the datasets) and KFCM-K-H (for the totality of the datasets) algorithms performed better with the $m = 1.6$. Moreover, whatever the considered indexes and fuzziness parameters, the KFCM-K-H algorithm performed better than the KFCM-K algorithm on the majority of the data sets of the Table 1. Besides, whatever the considered indexes and fuzziness parameters, the standard FCM algorithm outperformed both KFCM-K and KFCM-K-H algorithms on the majority of the datasets of the Table 1. This is not unexpected because

Table 2. Performance of the algorithms: fuzzy partition

Data sets	Rand-F						HUL					
	FCM		KFCM-K		KFCM-K-H		FCM		KFCM-K		KFCM-K-H	
	$m=1.6$	$m=2.0$	$m=1.6$	$m=2.0$	$m=1.6$	$m=2.0$	$m=1.6$	$m=2.0$	$m=1.6$	$m=2.0$	$m=1.6$	$m=2.0$
Breast tissue	0.6236	0.6296	0.7153	0.7280	0.7268	0.7095	0.6205	0.6143	0.6937	0.6183	0.7163	0.6505
Ecoli	0.7624	0.7239	0.7246	0.6969	0.7653	0.7211	0.7445	0.6470	0.6364	0.5263	0.7524	0.6448
Image segmentation	0.7796	0.7787	0.7571	0.7588	0.8671	0.8113	0.7171	0.5974	0.4155	0.3111	0.8404	0.7049
Iris	0.8620	0.8131	0.7723	0.6881	0.7999	0.7037	0.8641	0.8187	0.7661	0.6632	0.8004	0.6880
Leaf	0.9528	0.9450	0.9499	0.9452	0.9551	0.9462	0.9035	0.7416	0.8223	0.5798	0.8772	0.6414
Libras Movement	0.8887	0.8793	0.8813	0.8789	0.8815	0.8788	0.6543	0.2603	0.3998	0.2656	0.4039	0.2599
Multiple features	0.8689	0.8500	0.8284	0.8227	0.8291	0.8226	0.8336	0.7141	0.3915	0.2707	0.3967	0.2590
Seeds	0.8287	0.7608	0.6047	0.5798	0.7515	0.6675	0.8268	0.7543	0.5133	0.4547	0.7412	0.6339
Thyroid gland	0.7195	0.6070	0.4941	0.4913	0.5731	0.4985	0.7213	0.6175	0.4634	0.4647	0.5856	0.5257
Urban land cover	0.7320	0.7477	0.7836	0.7830	0.8039	0.7852	0.6371	0.5184	0.2960	0.2085	0.5442	0.2755
Brest cancer winsconsin	0.7317	0.7151	0.5000	0.5000	0.7531	0.6452	0.7346	0.7234	0.5046	0.5095	0.7731	0.6978
Wine	0.7015	0.6758	0.8198	0.6664	0.7683	0.6471	0.6987	0.6651	0.6934	0.6533	0.7792	0.6279

as pointed out by Ref. [19], kernelization may impose undesirable structures on the data, and hence, the clusters obtained in the kernel space may not exhibit the structure of the original data.

From the fuzzy partition **U** it is obtained a crisp partition $Q = (Q_1, \ldots, Q_c)$, where the cluster $Q_i (i = 1, \ldots, c)$ is defined as: $Q_i = \{e_k \in E : u_{ik} = \max\limits_{m=1}^{c} u_{mk}\}$. To compare the quality of the crisp partitions provided by KFCM-K and KFCM-K-H algorithms, the adjusted Rand index (ARI) [12], and the mutual normalized information (MNI) [16] were considered. ARI and MNI indexes allow to compare the dataset a priori partition with the crisp partitions obtained from the fuzzy partitions provided by the algorithms. ARI index takes its values on the interval $[-1, 1]$, in which the value 1 indicates perfect agreement between partitions. The NMI takes its values on the interval $[0, 1]$, in which the value 1 also indicates perfect agreement between partitions.

Table 3 shows the best results (according to the respective objective functions) of the KCM-K and KCM-K-H algorithms on the data sets of Table 1, according to the ARI and NMI indexes and for the fuzziness parameter set as $m = 1.6$ and $m = 2.0$.

Table 3. Performance of the algorithms: crisp partition

Data sets	ARI						NMI					
	FCM		KFCM-K		KFCM-K-H		FCM		KFCM-K		KFCM-K-H	
	$m=1.6$	$m=2.0$	$m=1.6$	$m=2.0$	$m=1.6$	$m=2.0$	$m=1.6$	$m=2.0$	$m=1.6$	$m=2.0$	$m=1.6$	$m=2.0$
Breast tissue	0.1101	0.1252	0.2065	0.1143	0.2944	0.2934	0.3083	0.3218	0.3428	0.2766	0.5515	0.5356
Ecoli	0.3880	0.3682	0.3230	0.3277	0.4182	0.4015	0.5721	0.5514	0.5232	0.5162	0.6075	0.5927
Image segmentation	0.3116	0.3045	0.2133	0.2832	0.5257	0.4429	0.4920	0.4670	0.2931	0.3885	0.6444	0.6234
Iris	0.7163	0.7294	0.8015	0.7859	0.8856	0.9037	0.7419	0.7496	0.7899	0.7773	0.8641	0.8801
Leaf	0.3145	0.2654	0.3096	0.2877	0.3566	0.3602	0.6652	0.6477	0.6738	0.6538	0.7061	0.6981
Libras Movement	0.3227	0.1667	0.2726	0.1515	0.2419	0.2070	0.5821	0.3767	0.5315	0.4399	0.5239	0.4970
Multiple features	0.4280	0.4206	0.4128	0.3615	0.5324	0.4073	0.5669	0.5612	0.6053	0.5693	0.6397	0.6303
Seeds	0.7166	0.7166	0.7034	0.7034	0.6975	0.6954	0.6949	0.6949	0.6737	0.6737	0.6804	0.6716
Thyroid gland	0.5698	0.4413	0.0588	0.0495	0.1538	0.1810	0.4088	0.3434	0.1500	0.1353	0.2793	0.3240
Urban land cover	0.0356	0.0373	0.0737	0.0491	0.4289	0.2626	0.1345	0.1272	0.1909	0.1383	0.5011	0.3640
Brest cancer winsconsin	0.4810	0.4914	0.0215	0.0176	0.7178	0.7182	0.4567	0.4647	0.0593	0.0561	0.6174	0.6045
Wine	0.3602	0.3539	0.3711	0.3749	0.8332	0.8482	0.4212	0.4167	0.4287	0.4315	0.8199	0.8329

It can be observed that also in this case whatever the considered indexes (ARI and NMI), for the majority of the datasets, FCM, KFCM-K and KFCM-K-H algorithms performed better with the $m = 1.6$. Moreover, whatever the considered indexes and fuzziness parameters, the KFCM-K-H algorithm outperformed both the KFCM-K and FCM algorithms on the majority of the data sets of the Table 1. Besides, for the ARI index and whatever the considered fuzziness parameters, the standard FCM algorithm performed better than the KFCM-K algorithm on the majority of the datasets of the Table 1.

4 Final Remarks and Conclusions

The clustering performance of the conventional KFCM-K, the gaussian kernel-based fuzzy clustering algorithm, is highly related to the estimation of the bandwidth parameter of the Gaussian kernel function, that is estimated once and for all. In this paper we proposed KFCM-K-H, a Gaussian fuzzy c-Means with kernelization of the metric and automatic computation of a vector of bandwidth parameters, one for each variable. In the proposed kernel-based fuzzy clustering algorithm, the bandwidth parameters change at each iteration of the algorithm and are different from variable to variable. Thus, the proposed algorithm is able to select the important variables for the clustering task.

Experiments with twelve data sets from UCI machine learning repository, with different number of objects, variables and a priori classes, showed the performance of the proposed algorithm. It was observed that, for the majority of these data sets, the proposed KFCM-K-H algorithm provided crisp and fuzzy partitions of better quality than those provided by the conventional KFCM-K algorithm. Moreover, the KFCM-K-H algorithm provided crisp partitions of better quality than those provided by the standard FCM algorithm. Besides, it was observed that the FCM algorithm outperformed both KFCM-K and KFCM-K-H algorithms on the majority of these data sets, concerning the quality of the fuzzy partitions. These later finds support the remark provided by Ref. [19], i.e, that the kernelization may impose undesirable structures on the data and the clusters obtained in the kernel space may not exhibit the structure of the original data.

Acknowledgments. The authors are grateful to the anonymous referees for their careful revision, and CNPq and FACEPE (Brazilian agencies) for their financial support.

References

1. Bezdek, J.: Pattern Recognition with Fuzzy Objective Function Algorithms. Plenum, New York (1981)
2. Blake, C.L., Merz, C.J.: UCI repository of machine learning databases. University of California, Department of Information and Computer Science, Irvine (1998). http://www.ics.uci.edu/mlearn/MLRepository.html
3. Camastra, F., Verri, A.: A novel kernel method for clustering. IEEE Trans. Neural Netw. **27**, 801–804 (2005)

4. Caputo, B., Sim, K., Furesjo, F., Smola, A.: Appearence-based object recognition using SVMs: which kernel should I use? In: Proceedings of NIPS Workshop on Statistical methods for Computational Experiments in Visual Processing and Computer Vision (2002)

5. de Carvalho, F.A.T., Ferreira, M.R.P., Simões, E.C.: A Gaussian kernel-based clustering algorithm with automatic hyper-parameters computation. In: Cheng, L., Liu, Q., Ronzhin, A. (eds.) ISNN 2016. LNCS, vol. 9719, pp. 393–400. Springer, Cham (2016). https://doi.org/10.1007/978-3-319-40663-3_45

6. Cleuziou, G., Moreno, J.: Kernel methods for point symmetry-based clustering. Pattern Recogn. **48**, 2812–2830 (2015)

7. Diday, E., Govaert, G.: Classification automatique avec distances adaptatives. R.A.I.R.O. Inform. Comput. Sci. **11**(4), 329–349 (1977)

8. Fauvel, M., Chanussot, J., Benediktsson, J.: Parsimonious mahalanobis kernel for the classification of high dimensional data. Pattern Recogn. **46**, 845–854 (2013)

9. Filippone, M., Camastra, F., Masulli, F., Rovetta, S.: A survey of kernel and spectral methods for clustering. Pattern Recogn. **41**, 176–190 (2008)

10. Frigui, H., Hwanga, C., Rhee, F.C.H.: Clustering and aggregation of relational data with applications to image database categorization. Pattern Recogn. **40**, 3053–3068 (2007)

11. Huang, J., Ng, M., Rong, H., Li, Z.: Automated variable weighting in k-means type clustering. IEEE Trans. Pattern Anal. Mach. Intell. **27**(5), 657–668 (2005)

12. Hubert, L., Arabie, P.: Comparing partitions. J. Classif. **2**(1), 193–218 (1985)

13. Huellermeier, E., Rifki, M., Henzgen, S., Senge, R.: Comparing fuzzy partitions: a generalization of the rand index and related measures. IEEE Trans. Fuzzy Syst. **20**, 546–556 (2012)

14. Jain, A.K.: Data clustering: 50 years beyond k-means. Pattern Recogn. Lett. **31**, 651–666 (2010)

15. Kaufman, L., Rousseeuw, P.: Finding Groups in Data: An Introduction to Cluster Analysis. Wiley, Hoboken (2005)

16. Manning, C., Raghavan, P., Schuetze, H.: Introduction to Information Retrieval. Cambridge University Press, Cambridge (2008)

17. Modha, D.S., Spangler, W.S.: Feature weighting in k-means clustering. Mach. Learn. **52**(3), 217–237 (2003)

18. Mueller, K.R., Mika, S., Raetsch, G., Tsuda, K., Schoelkopf, B.: An introduction to kernel-based learning algorithms. IEEE Trans. Neural Netw. **12**, 181–202 (2001)

19. Pal, N.R.: What and when can we gain from the kernel versions of c-means algorithm? IEEE Trans. Fuzzy Syst. **22**, 363–369 (2014)

20. Tsai, C., Chiu, C.: Developing a feature weight self-adjustment mechanism for a k-means clustering algorithm. Comput. Stat. Data Anal. **52**, 4658–4672 (2008)

21. Xu, R., Wunusch, D.I.I.: Survey of clustering algorithms. IEEE Trans. Neural Netw. **16**, 645–678 (2005)

Fuzzy Clustering Algorithm Based on Adaptive Euclidean Distance and Entropy Regularization for Interval-Valued Data

Sara Inés Rizo Rodríguez[✉] and Francisco de Assis Tenorio de Carvalho

Centro de Informática - CIn, Universidade Federal de Pernambuco, Recife, Brazil
{sirr,fatc}@cin.ufpe.br
http://www.cin.ufpe.br

Abstract. Symbolic Data Analysis provides suitable new types of variable that can take into account the variability present in the observed measurements. This paper proposes a partitioning fuzzy clustering algorithm for interval-valued data based on suitable adaptive Euclidean distance and entropy regularization. The proposed method optimizes an objective function by alternating three steps aiming to compute the fuzzy cluster representatives, the fuzzy partition, as well as relevance weights for the interval-valued variables. Experiments on synthetic and real datasets corroborate the usefulness of the proposed algorithm.

1 Introduction

Clustering methods seek to organize a set of items into clusters such that objects within a given group have a high degree of similarity, whereas elements belonging to different clusters have a high degree of dissimilarity [15]. Partition and hierarchy are the most popular cluster structures provided by clustering methods. Hierarchical methods yield a complete hierarchy, i.e., a nested sequence of partitions of the input data, whereas partitioning methods aims to obtain a single partition of the data into a fixed number of clusters, usually based on an iterative algorithm that optimizes an objective function.

Partitioning methods can be divided into hard and fuzzy clustering. Hard clustering methods restrict each point of the dataset to exactly one cluster. On the other hand, in fuzzy clustering, a pattern may belong to all clusters with a specific membership degree. Generally, in conventional clustering methods, all the variables participate with the same importance to the clustering process. However, in real situations, some variables could be more or less important or even irrelevant for this task. A better solution is to introduce the proper attribute weight into the clustering process [16].

Most clustering algorithms are defined to deal with data described by single-valued variables, i.e., variables that takes a single measurement or a category for an object. However, there are many other kinds of information that cannot be explained with single-valued variables. For example, to take into account

© Springer Nature Switzerland AG 2018
V. Kůrková et al. (Eds.): ICANN 2018, LNCS 11139, pp. 695–705, 2018.
https://doi.org/10.1007/978-3-030-01418-6_68

variability inherent to the data, variables must be multi-valued, assuming sets of categories or intervals, possibly even with frequencies or weights. These kinds of data have been mainly studied in *Symbolic Data Analysis (SDA)*, a domain related to multivariate analysis, pattern recognition and artificial intelligence. The *SDA* aim is to provide suitable methods for managing aggregated data described by multi-valued variables [2].

Hard and fuzzy clustering methods are already available for manage interval-valued data. For example, Ref. [17] introduced a fuzzy clustering algorithms for mixed features of symbolic and fuzzy data. In these fuzzy clustering algorithms, the membership degree is associated to the values of the features in the clusters for the cluster centers instead of being associated to the patterns in each group, as is the usual case. De Carvalho [4] presented a fuzzy C-means clustering algorithms based on suitable Euclidean distances for interval valued-data.

This paper presents a new fuzzy C-means type algorithm based on adaptive Euclidean distances with Entropy Regularization for interval-value data, where the adaptive distance takes into account lower and upper boundaries of the data. The improvement in comparison with Ref. [4] concerns a new automatic weighting scheme for the interval boundaries. The weights of the lower and upper boundaries in Ref. [4] are managed independently. In that case, even if a boundary plays a minor role concerning the others, the algorithm of Ref. [4] may assign a relevant contribution also if it is not relevant. Following Ref. [14], this paper proposes a solution to solve this side effect. The proposed fuzzy clustering algorithm alternates three steps: allocation, weighting and representation steps that computes the objects memberships to the clusters, the weights for each variable and/or each boundary and the clusters' prototypes respectively, until a stationary value of a homogeneity criterion is reached.

Section 2 presents the fuzzy clustering algorithm based on Adaptive Euclidean distance and entropy regularization. Section 3 provides several experiments with synthetic and real datasets that corroborate the usefulness of the proposed algorithm. Finally, conclusions are drawn in Sect. 4.

2   Fuzzy Clustering Algorithm Based on Adaptive Euclidean Distance and Entropy Regularization for Interval Data

This section describes the proposed fuzzy clustering algorithm based on Adaptive distance and Entropy Regularization for interval-valued data (hereafter referred as AIFCM-ER).

Let $E = \{e_1, \ldots, e_N\}$ be a set of N objects described by P interval-valued variables [2]. An interval-valued variable is a mapping that it is defined from the dataset E into the set $\mathfrak{I}$ of closed intervals of $\mathbb{R}$. In other words, for any $e \in E$ the value $y(e)$ is an interval of the form $[a, b]$ where a, b are some real numbers such that $a \leq b$. The i-th object e_i $(1 \leq i \leq N)$ is represented by a vector $\mathbf{x}_i = (x_{i1}, \ldots, x_{iP})$, where $x_{ij} = [a_{ij}, b_{ij}]$, with $a_{ij} \leq b_{ij}$, is the interval value taken by the j-th variable $(1 \leq j \leq P)$. Let $\mathcal{D} = \{\mathbf{x}_1, \ldots, \mathbf{x}_N\}$ be the interval-valued dataset. Each fuzzy cluster $\mathbf{P}_k(k = 1, ..., C)$ has a representative element, called hereafter a prototype. As the examined variables are interval-valued, each prototype $\mathbf{g}_k = (g_{k1}, ..., g_{kP})$ is a vector of P intervals with $g_{kj} = [\alpha_{kj}, \beta_{kj}]$ $(1 \leq j \leq P; 1 \leq k \leq C)$.

Conventional clustering models consider that all variables are equally important to the clustering task. However, in most applications some variables may be irrelevant and, among the relevant ones, some may be more or less relevant than others. Furthermore, the relevance of each variable to each cluster may be different, i.e., each cluster may have a different set of relevant variables [5,8]. In previous works, the boundary weights of the interval data were assigned independently. Therefore, it was not possible to compare the relevance of the lower boundaries concerning the upper boundaries. Furthermore, if the lower/upper boundary is not (or very few) relevant for the clustering process, a set of weights that are significantly greater than zero is always assigned. For overcome these drawbacks, is proposed to consider the jointly weighting of the lower and upper boundaries [14].

In this paper, we will denote as $\mathbf{V}_l = (\mathbf{v}_{l,1}, ..., \mathbf{v}_{l,k}, ..., \mathbf{v}_{l,C})$ and $\mathbf{V}_u = (\mathbf{v}_{u,1}, ..., \mathbf{v}_{u,k}, ..., \mathbf{v}_{u,C})$ the matrices of positive weights for the lower and upper boundaries respectively. The $\mathbf{v}_{l,k} = (v_{l,k1}, ..., v_{l,kP})$ and $\mathbf{v}_{u,k} = (v_{u,k1}, ..., v_{u,kP})$ are the P-dimensional vectors of relevance weights and each of these weights measuring the importance of each interval-valued variable on the i-th fuzzy cluster for lower and upper boundaries respectively.

The proposed algorithm provides a fuzzy partition represented by the matrix $\mathbf{U} = (\mathbf{u}_1, ..., \mathbf{u}_N) = (u_{ik})_{\substack{1 \leq i \leq N \\ 1 \leq k \leq C}}$, where u_{ik} is the membership degree of object e_i into the fuzzy cluster k and $\mathbf{u}_i = (u_{i1}, ..., u_{iC})$, a matrix of prototypes $\mathbf{G} = (\mathbf{g}_1, ..., \mathbf{g}_C)$ that represents the fuzzy clusters in the fuzzy partition, as well as the matrices of relevance weights of the variables $\mathbf{V}_l$ and $\mathbf{V}_u$.

The matrix of prototypes $\mathbf{G}$, the matrices of positive weights $\mathbf{V}_l, \mathbf{V}_u$ and the matrix of membership degrees $\mathbf{U}$ are obtained iteratively by the minimization of a suitable adequacy criterion, here-below denoted as $J_{AIFCM-ER}$, that gives the total homogeneity of the fuzzy partition computed as the sum of the homogeneity in each fuzzy cluster:

$$J_{AIFCM-ER} = \sum_{k=1}^{C} \sum_{i=1}^{N} (u_{ik}) d^2_{(\mathbf{v}_{l,k}, \mathbf{v}_{u,k})}(\mathbf{x}_i, \mathbf{g}_k) + T_u \sum_{k=1}^{C} \sum_{i=1}^{N} (u_{ik}) \ln(u_{ik}) \quad (1)$$

$$\text{subject to:} \quad \sum_{k=1}^{C} (u_{ik}) = 1 \text{ and } \prod_{j=1}^{P} (v_{l,kj} v_{u,kj}) = 1$$

$$\text{where} \quad d^2_{(\mathbf{v}_{l,k}, \mathbf{v}_{u,k})}(\mathbf{x}_i, \mathbf{g}_k) = \sum_{j=1}^{P} [v_{l,kj} (a_{ij} - \alpha_{kj})^2 + v_{u,kj} (b_{ij} - \beta_{kj})^2] \quad (2)$$

is a suitable adaptive dissimilarity between the vectors of intervals $\mathbf{x}_i$ and $\mathbf{g}_k$ parameterized by the vectors of relevance weights of the variables $\mathbf{v}_{l,k}$ and $\mathbf{v}_{u,k}$ on the fuzzy cluster k, for lower and upper boundaries respectively. The second term is the negative entropy and is used to control the membership degree u_{ik}. T_u is a positive regularizing parameter.

In the literature, two main types of constraints are proposed: a product-to-one constraint [5] and a sum-to-one constraint [10]. However, in this paper, we will not consider this last alternative because it depends on the setting of additional parameters. Thus, this dissimilarity function is parameterized by the vectors of relevance weights $\mathbf{v}_{l,k}$ and $\mathbf{v}_{u,k}$, in which $v_{l,kj} > 0$, $v_{u,kj} > 0$ and $\prod_{j=1}^{P} v_{l,kj} v_{u,kj} = 1$, and it is associated with the k-th fuzzy cluster $(k = 1, ..., C)$. Note that the vectors of weights $\mathbf{v}_{l,k} = (v_{l,k1}, ..., v_{l,kP})$ and $\mathbf{v}_{u,k} = (v_{u,k1}, ..., v_{u,kP})$ are estimated locally and change at each iteration, i.e., they are not determined absolutely, and are different from one cluster to another. Moreover, note also that the relevant variables in the groups have weights that are superior to 1.

2.1   The Optimization Steps of the AIFCM-ER Algorithm

This section provides the optimization algorithm aiming to compute the prototypes, the relevance weights of the variables and the fuzzy partition. For the AIFCM-ER algorithm, the minimization of $J_{AIFCM-ER}$ (Eq. 1) is performed iteratively in three steps (representation, weighting, and allocation).

The computation of the matrices $\mathbf{U}$, $\mathbf{V}_l$ and $\mathbf{V}_u$ can be obtained applying the Lagrange multipliers λ_i and γ_k to the constraints of Eq. 1 as:

$$\mathcal{L} = J_{AIFCM-ER} - \sum_{k=1}^{C} \gamma_k \left[\prod_{j=1}^{P} v_{l,kj} v_{u,kj} - 1 \right] - \sum_{i=1}^{N} \lambda_i \left[\sum_{k=1}^{C} u_{ik} - 1 \right] \quad (3)$$

Representation Step: This section provides the solution for the optimal computation of the prototype associated to each cluster. During this step, the matrix of membership degree $\mathbf{U}$ and the matrices of positive weights $\mathbf{V}_l$ and $\mathbf{V}_u$ are kept fixed. The prototype $\mathbf{g}_k = (g_{k1}, ..., g_{kP})$ of fuzzy cluster k which minimizes the clustering criterion (Eq. 1) has the bounds of the interval $g_{kj} = [\alpha_{kj}, \beta_{kj}]$ $(j = 1, ..., P)$ computed according to:

$$\alpha_{k,j} = \frac{\sum_{i=1}^{N} u_{ik} a_{ij}}{\sum_{i=1}^{N} u_{ik}} \text{ and } \beta_{k,j} = \frac{\sum_{i=1}^{N} u_{ik} a_{ij}}{\sum_{i=1}^{N} u_{ik}} \quad (4)$$

Weighting Step: This step provides the solutions for the computation of the matrices of relevance weights. During the weighting step, the vector $\mathbf{G}$ of prototypes, and the matrix of membership degrees $\mathbf{U}$ are kept fixed. The objective function (1) is optimized with respect to the relevance weights. After setting the partial derivatives of $\mathcal{L}$ w.r.t. $v_{l,kj}$, $v_{u,kj}$ and γ_k to zero and after some algebra, the relevance weights are computed as follows:

$$v_{l,kj} = \frac{\left\{ \prod_{h=1}^{P} \left[\sum_{i=1}^{N} u_{ik}(a_{ih} - \alpha_{k,h})^2 \right] \left[\sum_{i=1}^{N} u_{ik}(b_{ih} - \beta_{k,h})^2 \right] \right\}^{\frac{1}{2P}}}{\sum_{i=1}^{N} u_{ik}(a_{ij} - \alpha_{k,j})^2} \tag{5}$$

$$v_{u,kj} = \frac{\left\{ \prod_{h=1}^{P} \left[\sum_{i=1}^{N} u_{ik}(a_{ih} - \alpha_{k,h})^2 \right] \left[\sum_{i=1}^{N} u_{ik}(b_{ih} - \beta_{k,h})^2 \right] \right\}^{\frac{1}{2P}}}{\sum_{i=1}^{N} u_{ik}(b_{ij} - \beta_{k,j})^2} \tag{6}$$

Allocation Step: This step provides an optimal solution to the computation of the matrix of membership degrees of the objects into the fuzzy clusters. During the allocation step, the vector $\mathbf{G}$ of prototypes, the matrices $\mathbf{V}_l$ and $\mathbf{V}_u$ of relevance weights are kept fixed. The objective function 1 is optimized with respect to the membership degrees. After setting the partial derivatives of $\mathcal{L}$ w.r.t. u_{ik} and λ_i to zero and after some algebra, we obtain:

$$u_{ik} = \frac{\exp\left\{ -\frac{\sum_{j=1}^{P}[v_{l,kj}(a_{ij} - \alpha_{kj})^2 + v_{u,kj}(b_{ij} - \beta_{kj})^2]}{T_u} \right\}}{\sum_{h=1}^{C} \exp\left\{ -\frac{\sum_{j=1}^{P}[v_{l,hj}(a_{ij} - \alpha_{hj})^2 + v_{u,hj}(b_{ij} - \beta_{hj})^2]}{T_u} \right\}} \tag{7}$$

The Algorithm: The AIFCM-ER fuzzy clustering algorithm is summarized in Algorithm 1.

Algorithm 1. AIFCM-ER Algorithm

Input: The dataset $\mathcal{D} = \{\mathbf{x}_1, \ldots, \mathbf{x}_N\}$; the number C of clusters ($2 \leq C \leq N$) and the parameter $T_u > 0$; the parameter T (maximum number of iterations); the threshold $\varepsilon > 0$ and $\varepsilon \ll 1$.

Output: The vector of prototypes $\mathbf{G}$; the matrix of membership degrees $\mathbf{U}$; the relevance weight matrices $\mathbf{V}_l$ and $\mathbf{V}_u$.

1: **Initialization:** Set $t = 0$;
    Randomly select C distinct prototypes $\mathbf{g}_k^{(t)} \in \mathcal{D}$ ($k = 1, \ldots, C$) to obtain the vector of prototypes $\mathbf{G}^{(t)} = (\mathbf{g}_1^{(t)}, \ldots, \mathbf{g}_C^{(t)})$;
    Initialize the matrices of relevance weights $\mathbf{V}_l^{(t)} = (v_{l,kj}^{(t)})_{\substack{1 \leq k \leq C \\ 1 \leq j \leq P}}$ with $v_{l,kj}^{(t)} = 1$ and $\mathbf{V}_u^{(t)} = (v_{u,kj}^{(t)})_{\substack{1 \leq k \leq C \\ 1 \leq j \leq P}}$ with $v_{u,kj}^{(t)} = 1, \forall k, j$;

2: **repeat**
    Set $t = t + 1$

3:    **Representation step:** Compute $\mathbf{G}^{(t)}$ using Equation 4;

4:    **Weighting step:** Compute $\mathbf{V}_l^{(t)}$ and $\mathbf{V}_u^{(t)}$ using the Equations 5 and 6;

5:    **Allocation step:** Compute $\mathbf{U}^{(t)}$ using Equation 7;

6: **until** $|J_{AIFCM-ER}^{(t)} - J_{AIFCM-ER}^{(t-1)}| < \varepsilon$ or $t > T$

---

3   Experimental Results

This section aims to evaluate the performance and illustrates the usefulness of
the AIFCM-ER algorithm by applying it to suitable synthetic and real datasets.

3.1   Experimental Setting

The proposed algorithm performance will be compared with two previous fuzzy
clustering models: the fuzzy C-means for symbolic interval data ($IFCM$) and
the fuzzy C-means for symbolic interval data based on an Adaptive squared
Euclidean distance between intervals vectors ($IFCMADC$) [4].

To compare the clustering results furnished by the algorithms four measures
were used: Fuzzy Rand index (FRI) [7], The Hullermeier index (HUL) [12], the
Adjusted Rand index (ARI) [11] and the F-Measure [1]. From the fuzzy parti-
tion $\mathbf{U} = (\mathbf{u}_1, \ldots, \mathbf{u}_C)$ is obtained a hard partition $Q = (Q_1, \ldots, Q_C)$, where the
cluster $Q_k (k = 1, \ldots, C)$ is defined as: $Q_k = \{i \in \{1, \ldots, N\} : u_{ik} \geq u_{im}, \forall m \in$
$\{1, \ldots, C\}\}$. FRI and HUL indices compare the a priori partition of the synthetic datasets with the fuzzy partition provided by the algorithms and ARI and
F-Measure with the hard partition.

All the interval datasets (synthetic and real) were normalized as follows.
Let $\mathcal{D}_j = \{x_{1j}, \ldots, x_{Nj}\}$ be the set of observed intervals $x_{ij} = [a_{ij}, b_{ij}]$ on
variable $j (j = 1, \ldots, P)$. The dispersion of the j-th variable is defined as: $s_j^2 =$
$\sum_{i=1}^{N} d_j(x_{ij}, g_j) = \sum_{i=1}^{N} \left[(a_{ij} - \alpha_j)^2 + (b_{ij} - \beta_j)^2 \right]$ where $g_j = [\alpha_j, \beta_j]$ is the
"central" interval computed from $\mathcal{D}_j$ as: $\alpha_j = \frac{\sum_{i=1}^{N} a_{ij}}{N}$ and $\beta_j = \frac{\sum_{i=1}^{N} b_{ij}}{N}$. Each
observed interval x_{ij} is normalized as $\overline{x}_{ij} = [\overline{a}_{ij}, \overline{b}_{ij}]$, where $\overline{a}_{ij} = \frac{a_{ij} - \alpha_j}{\sqrt{s_j^2}}$ and
$\overline{b}_{ij} = \frac{b_{ij} - \beta_j}{\sqrt{s_j^2}}$, with $\overline{a}_{ij} \leq \overline{b}_{ij}$ for all i, j. Therefore $\overline{\mathcal{D}}_j = \{\overline{x}_{1j}, \ldots, \overline{x}_{Nj}\}$ and for this
dataset, one can show that $\overline{g}_j = [\overline{\alpha}_j, \overline{\beta}_j] = [0, 0]$ and that $s_j^2 = \sum_{i=1}^{N} d_j(\overline{x}_{ij}, \overline{g}_j) =$
$\sum_{i=1}^{N} \left[(\overline{a}_{ij} - \overline{\alpha}_j)^2 + (\overline{b}_{ij} - \overline{\beta}_j)^2 \right] = 1$.

The choice of the parameter T_u for the proposed algorithm was achieved
without supervision as follows. For each dataset, the value of T_u was varied
between 10^{-4} to 100 (with step 10^{-4}), and the threshold for T_u corresponds to
the value of the fuzzifier at which the minimum centroid distance falls under 0.1
for the first time. The parameter m for $IFCM$ and $IFCMADC$ algorithms was
set to 1.5 and 2.0. The parameter ε was set to 10^{-5}, the maximum number of
iterations T was 50, and for each dataset, the number of clusters was set equal
to the number of a priori classes.

3.2   Synthetic Interval-Valued Datasets

This section investigates with synthetic datasets, performance aspects of the
AIFCM-ER algorithm. First, two datasets of 150 points in $\mathbb{R}^2$ were constructed
to show the usefulness of the proposed method on interval datasets with linearly
non-separable classes of different shapes and sizes. In each dataset, the 150 points
are drawn from three bi-variate normal distributions of independent components.

There are three classes of unequal sizes and shapes: two classes with an ellipsoidal shape and size 50 and one class with a spherical shape and size 50. The first dataset shows well-separated classes and the second shows overlapping classes. The data points of each class in these datasets were acquired according to the parameters showed in Table 1.

Table 1. Mean (μ_1, μ_2) and standard deviation (σ_1, σ_2) vectors for every class in synthetic dataset 1 and 2.

Dataset 1				Dataset 2			
μ	Class 1	Class 2	Class 3	μ	Class 1	Class 2	Class 3
μ_1	28	60	46	μ_1	50	60	52
μ_2	22	30	38	μ_2	28	30	38
σ_1	100	9	9	σ_1	100	9	9
σ_2	9	144	9	σ_2	9	144	9

In order to build interval datasets from datasets 1 and 2, each point (z_1, z_2) of these datasets is considered as the 'seed' of a rectangle. Each rectangle is therefore a vector of two intervals defined by: $([z_1 - \frac{\delta_1}{2}, z_1 + \frac{\delta_1}{2}], [z_2 - \frac{\delta_2}{2}, z_2 + \frac{\delta_2}{2}])$. The parameters δ_1 and δ_2 are the width and the height of the rectangle. In our experiments, δ_1 and δ_2 are obtained randomly from $[1, 8]$.

Another synthetic dataset was created using lower and upper boundary configurations shown in Table 2. For the lower boundary, variables x_1 and x_2 are relevant for class 1 and class 2, and variables x_2 and x_3 are relevant for the class 3 and class 4. For the upper boundary, all variables are equally relevant for the class definition. The purpose of this dataset is to see what happens if the variable weight is heavily determined by just one boundary. In this case, the IFCMADC algorithm should fail in identifying a cluster structure.

Table 2. Mean (μ_1, μ_2, μ_3) and standard deviation $(\sigma_1, \sigma_2, \sigma_3)$ vectors for every class in synthetic dataset 3.

Lower boundary configuration				Upper boundary configuration			
μ	Class 1	Class 2	Class 3	Class 4	μ	Class 1	Class 2	Class 3	Class 4
μ_1	−0.5	0.5	0	0	μ_1	3.0	4.0	3.5	3.5
μ_2	−0.5	−0.5	0.5	0.5	μ_2	3.0	3.0	4.0	4.0
μ_3	0.0	0.0	−0.5	0.5	μ_3	3.5	3.5	3.5	3.5
σ_1	0.04	0.04	1.0	1.0	σ_1	1.0	1.0	1.0	1.0
σ_2	0.04	0.04	0.04	0.04	σ_2	1.0	1.0	1.0	1.0
σ_3	1.0	1.0	0.04	0.04	σ_3	1.0	1.0	1.0	1.0

In the framework of a Monte Carlo experiment, 100 replications of the previous process have been repeated for seeds taken from all datasets. In each replication, the algorithm was executed 50 times, and the cluster centers were randomly initialized at each time. The best result for each algorithm was selected according to their respective objective function. The average and standard deviation of the indexes were calculated based on the 100 Monte Carlo iterations.

Results: Table 3 gives the values of the indexes obtained with adaptive and non-adaptive distances for the synthetic interval-valued datasets.

Table 3. Performance of the algorithms on the synthetic interval-valued data.

Algorithms	FRI	HUL	ARI	F-Measure	FRI	HUL	ARI	F-Measure	FRI	HUL	ARI	F-Measure
Dataset 1					Dataset 2				Dataset 3			
m=1.5					m=1.5				m=1.5			
IFCM	0.7966	0.7966	0.5892	0.7331	0.6901	0.6846	0.3668	0.5868	0.6443	0.5153	0.1125	0.3333
(std)	(0.0207)	(0.0210)	(0.0461)	(0.0284)	(0.0180)	(0.0189)	(0.0504)	(0.0320)	(0.0039)	(0.0085)	(0.0263)	(0.0197)
m=2					m=2				m=2			
IFCM	0.7456	0.7404	0.6082	0.7442	0.6471	0.6186	0.3842	0.5965	0.6268	0.2904	0.1236	0.3897
(std)	(0.0179)	(0.0203)	(0.0522)	(0.0327)	(0.0126)	(0.0163)	(0.0485)	(0.0313)	(0.0006)	(0.0180)	(0.0265)	(0.0172)
m=1.5					m=1.5				m=1.5			
IFCMADC	0.9356	0.9382	0.9283	0.9519	0.7763	**0.7758**	0.5696	0.7139	0.6542	0.5496	0.1393	0.3537
(std)	(0.0135)	(0.0133)	(0.0389)	(0.0261)	(0.0231)	(0.0238)	(0.0680)	(0.0441)	(0.0057)	(0.0118)	(0.0280)	(0.0212)
m=2					m=2				m=2			
IFCMADC	0.8499	0.8600	0.9274	0.9513	0.7075	0.6972	0.5754	0.7175	0.6277	0.3106	0.1351	0.3883
(std)	(0.0115)	(0.0116)	(0.0390)	(0.0261)	(0.0156)	(0.0190)	(0.0652)	(0.0427)	(0.0011)	(0.0212)	(0.0281)	(0.0185)
AIFCM-ER	**0.9416**	**0.9453**	**0.9316**	**0.9541**	**0.7766**	0.7722	**0.5783**	**0.7194**	**0.9827**	**0.9827**	**0.9537**	**0.9652**
(std)	(0.0526)	(0.0471)	(0.0353)	(0.0236)	(0.0508)	(0.0570)	(0.0730)	(0.0476)	(0.0294)	(0.0294)	(0.0787)	(0.0591)

As expected, the average indexes are better for the adaptive distances algorithms. It is also noticed that whatever the index considered, the proposed algorithm presents the best average performance since in general, can identify clusters with different structure. Respect to the third dataset results, it is seen that the AIFCM-ER algorithm is able also to discover cluster structures also when this occurs for not all the boundaries of the interval variables, representing an advantage in comparison with previous results reported on the literature. To see how the learned metrics help to understand the data, Table 4 shows the matrices of relevance weights of the variables on the fuzzy clusters obtained by the IFCMADC algorithm for $m = 1.5$ and $m = 2$ and $\mathbf{V_l}$ and $\mathbf{V_u}$ for the proposed method both on the Dataset 3.

Table 4. Relevance weights for the IFCMADC and the AIFCM-ER algorithms for the Dataset 3.

	IFCMADC ($m = 1.5$)			IFCMADC ($m = 2$)			AIFCM-ER					
	Var. 1	Var. 2	Var. 3	Var. 1	Var. 2	Var. 3	Var. 1		Var. 2		Var. 3	
							v_{l1}	v_{u1}	v_{l2}	v_{u2}	v_{l3}	v_{u3}
Cluster 1	0.7832	1.5333	0.8328	0.9960	1.0991	0.9135	0.3595	0.3453	8.8843	0.2682	10.4799	0.3226
Cluster 2	0.4985	2.0149	0.9955	0.9940	1.0994	0.9150	7.2457	0.3581	10.0801	0.3162	0.3050	0.3964
Cluster 3	0.8471	1.7137	0.6889	0.7260	1.2295	1.1203	7.2740	0.3358	10.2935	0.3806	0.3283	0.3182
Cluster 4	0.9693	1.6952	0.6085	1.0910	1.0850	0.8448	0.3374	0.3743	9.5973	0.3193	8.6486	0.2988

We can observe in the Table 4 that the weights for the upper boundary are similar for each cluster for the proposed algorithm. For the lower boundary, variables x_2 and x_3 have higher values for cluster 1 and 4 and for cluster 2 and 3, variables x_1 and x_2. These results confirm that the selection of the more influent variables, and/or boundaries in the cluster partition improve the clustering performance.

3.3 Symbolic Interval Datasets

For the purpose of validating the proposed method, we have conducted several experiments on the following datasets of type interval: Car models [6] ($N = 33$, $P = 8$, $C = 4$), City temperature [9] ($N = 37$, $P = 12$, $C = 4$), Freshwater fish species [3] ($N = 12$, $P = 13$, $C = 4$), Horses ($N = 12$, $P = 7$, $C = 4$), Ichino [13] ($N = 8$, $P = 4$, $C = 4$) and Wine ($N = 23$, $P = 21$, $C = 4$) symbolic interval datasets (in which N represents the number of objects, P represents the number of interval-valued variables and C represents the number of a priori classes). For each dataset the algorithms were run 50 times and the best results were selected according to the minimum value of their objective function. Table 5 presents the results provided by the algorithms on the real interval-valued datasets.

Table 5. Performance of the algorithms on the interval-valued data.

Algorithms	FRI	HUL	ARI	F-Measure	Algorithms	FRI	HUL	ARI	F-Measure
Car models					City temperature				
IFCM (m=1.5)	0.8240	0.8178	0.5623	0.6667	IFCM (m=1.5)	0.7578	0.7592	0.5458	0.6051
IFCM (m=2)	0.7448	0.6871	0.5623	0.6667	IFCM (m=2)	0.6708	0.6801	0.5134	0.6710
IFCMADC (m=1.5)	0.8148	0.8109	0.4998	0.6190	IFCMADC (m=1.5)	0.7639	0.7674	0.5458	0.6951
IFCMADC (m=2)	0.7644	0.7203	0.5257	0.6371	IFCMADC (m=2)	0.6875	0.6978	0.5160	0.6710
AIFCM-ER	0.7936	0.7638	0.6312	0.7160	AIFCM-ER	0.7460	0.8103	0.5458	0.6951
Freshwater fish species					Horses				
IFCM (m=1.5)	0.6621	0.6257	0.2376	0.4324	IFCM (m=1.5)	0.6972	0.6868	0.0559	0.2667
IFCM (m=2)	0.6798	0.5539	0.0671	0.2041	IFCM (m=2)	0.0900	0.0279	0.0559	0.2667
IFCMADC (m=1.5)	0.7569	0.7569	0.2757	0.4286	IFCMADC (m=1.5)	0.7848	0.7824	0.3295	0.4615
IFCMADC (m=2)	0.7332	0.7149	0.2087	0.3704	IFCMADC (m=2)	0.7041	0.6604	0.1417	0.3333
AIFCM-ER	0.9242	0.9242	0.7534	0.8000	AIFCM-ER	0.8026	0.7984	0.4272	0.5517
Ichino					Wine				
IFCM (m=1.5)	0.8212	0.8213	0.4444	0.5455	IFCM (m=1.5)	0.5745	0.4320	0.0059	0.3026
IFCM (m=2)	0.8131	0.8090	0.4444	0.5455	IFCM (m=2)	0.5879	0.3241	-0.0183	0.3828
IFCMADC (m=1.5)	0.8250	0.8250	0.3396	0.4444	IFCMADC (m=1.5)	0.5854	0.5126	0.1092	0.4048
IFCMADC (m=2)	0.8301	0.8285	0.3396	0.4444	IFCMADC (m=2)	0.5879	0.3243	0.0341	0.4098
AIFCM-ER	0.9988	0.9988	1.0000	1.0000	AIFCM-ER	0.6050	0.5475	0.1306	0.3922

The obtained results (Table 5) show that the proposed method obtain the best result for almost all datasets according to FRI and HUL. Concerning to the comparison between the hard partitions and the a priori partition, the proposed method achieves the best results for all datasets. In general, the AIFCM-ER algorithm shown that the selection of the more influent variables, and/or boundaries in each fuzzy partition, helps to obtain better performance compared with previous methods.

4 Conclusion

This paper presented a fuzzy clustering algorithm for interval-valued data based on adaptive Euclidean distance and entropy regularization. In particular, the algorithm can discover cluster structures also when this occurs for not all the boundaries of the interval-valued variables. The algorithm starts from an initial fuzzy partition, and then it alternates over three steps (i.e., representation, weighting, and allocation) until it converges as the adequacy criterion reaches a stationary value. The paper provides a new objective function and updated rules are derived. The applications on synthetic and real data confirm the hypothesis that algorithms based on adaptive distances are useful to discover non-spherical clusters and to perform a selection of the more influent variables, and/or boundaries, in the cluster partition.

Acknowledgment. The authors would like to thank CNPq and FACEPE (Brazilian agencies) for their financial support and the anonymous referees for their helpful suggestions.

References

1. Baeza-Yates, R., Ribeiro-Neto, B.: Modern Information Retrieval, vol. 463. ACM press, New York (1999)
2. Bock, H.H., Diday, E.: Analysis of Symbolic Data: Exploratory Methods for Extracting Statistical Information from Complex Data. Springer, Heidelberg (2012). https://doi.org/10.1007/978-3-642-57155-8
3. Boudou, A., Ribeyre, F.: Mercury in the food web: accumulation and transfer mechanisms. Met. Ions Biol. Syst. **34**, 289–320 (1997)
4. de Carvalho, F.D.A.: Fuzzy c-means clustering methods for symbolic interval data. Pattern Recognit. Lett. **28**(4), 423–437 (2007)
5. Diday, E.: Classification automatique avec distances adaptatives. RAIRO Inform. Comput. Sci. **11**(4), 329–349 (1977)
6. Duarte Silva, P., Brito, P.: Model and analyse interval data. https://cran.r-project.org/web/packages/MAINT.Data/index.html. Accessed 27 Apr 2018
7. Frigui, H., Hwang, C., Rhee, F.C.H.: Clustering and aggregation of relational data with applications to image database categorization. Pattern Recognit. **40**(11), 3053–3068 (2007)
8. Frigui, H., Nasraoui, O.: Unsupervised learning of prototypes and attribute weights. Pattern Recognit. **37**(3), 567–581 (2004)
9. Guru, D., Kiranagi, B.B., Nagabhushan, P.: Multivalued type proximity measure and concept of mutual similarity value useful for clustering symbolic patterns. Pattern Recognit. Lett. **25**(10), 1203–1213 (2004)
10. Huang, J.Z., Ng, M.K., Rong, H., Li, Z.: Automated variable weighting in k-means type clustering. IEEE Trans. Pattern Anal. Mach. Intell. **27**(5), 657–668 (2005)
11. Hubert, L., Arabie, P.: Comparing partitions. J. Classif. **2**(1), 193–218 (1985)
12. Hullermeier, E., Rifqi, M.: A fuzzy variant of the rand index for comparing clustering structures. In: Joint 2009 International Fuzzy Systems Association World Congress and 2009 European Society of Fuzzy Logic and Technology Conference, IFSA-EUSFLAT 2009 (2009)
13. Ichino, M., Yaguchi, H.: Generalized Minkowski metrics for mixed feature-type data analysis. IEEE Trans. Syst. Man Cybern. **24**(4), 698–708 (1994)
14. Irpino, A., Verde, R., de Carvalho, F.A.T.: Fuzzy clustering of distributional data with automatic weighting of variable components. Inf. Sci. **406–407**, 248–268 (2017)

15. Jain, A.K.: Data clustering: 50 years beyond k-means. Pattern Recognit. Lett. **31**(8), 651–666 (2010)
16. Tsai, C., Chiu, C.: Developing a feature weight self-adjustment mechanism for a k-means clustering algorithm. Comput. Stat. Data Anal. **52**, 4658–4672 (2008)
17. Yang, M.S., Hwang, P.Y., Chen, D.H.: Fuzzy clustering algorithms for mixed feature variables. Fuzzy Sets Syst. **141**(2), 301–317 (2004)

Input-Dependably Feature-Map Pruning

Atalya Waissman$^{(\boxtimes)}$ and Aharon Bar-Hillel

Ben-Gurion University, Beer-Sheva, Israel
{ataliaw,barhille}@post.bgu.ac.il

Abstract. Deep neural networks are an accurate tool for solving, among other things, vision tasks. The computational cost of these networks is often high, preventing their adoption in many real time applications. Thus, there is a constant need for computational saving in this research domain. In this paper we suggest trading accuracy with computation using a gated version of Convolutional Neural Networks (CNN). The gated network selectively activates only a portion of its feature-maps, depending on the given example to be classified. The network's 'gates' imply which feature-maps are necessary for the task, and which are not. Specifically, full feature maps are considered for omission, to enable computational savings in a manner compliant with GPU hardware constraints. The network is trained using a combination of back-propagation for standard weights, minimizing an error-related loss, and reinforcement learning for the gates, minimizing a loss related to the number of feature maps used. We trained and evaluated a gated version of dense-net on the CIFAR-10 dataset [1]. Our results show that with slight impact on the network accuracy, a potential acceleration of up to ×3 might be obtained.

Keywords: Neural networks · Pruning · Acceleration
Conditional computation · Feature-map

1 Introduction

The variability and richness of natural visual data make it almost impossible to build accurate recognition systems manually. Thus, it is machine learning algorithms which dominate these problems today. Deep Neural Networks (DNN) are hierarchical machine learning algorithm which currently provide the best results at the fields of computer vision, speech processing and Natural Language Processing (NLP). Focusing on vision, CNN allow obtaining good solutions for difficult tasks such as image classification, object detection/localization, captioning, segmentation and image generation. The research regarding CNNs is constantly evolving and the industrial integration of these nets increases significantly.

CNNs are a cascade of convolution, sub-sampling and activation layers which are applied on the input. The computational cost of these networks is high, often preventing their usage in real time applications. The improvement in computer hardware and specifically GPUs allow the usage of deeper networks providing more accuracy but raises the need for computational saving even more.

In this paper we present a network that uses only some of its feature maps, chosen in an input-depended manner, to classify images. Using the assumption that each

© Springer Nature Switzerland AG 2018
V. Kůrková et al. (Eds.): ICANN 2018, LNCS 11139, pp. 706–713, 2018.
https://doi.org/10.1007/978-3-030-01418-6_69

feature map of the network allocates and extracts a certain feature from its input [2, 3] we assume that given a specific example, only the computation of some feature maps is indeed improving the network accuracy. We hence build decision mechanisms, termed 'gates', which decide for each feature map in every layer whether the map should be computed or not. Since these gates make sharp decisions, we optimize their parameters using a reinforcement learning framework. We experiment with a dense-net base architecture, which is one of the more accurate contemporary alternatives, on the Cifar-10 dataset. Our results indicate that speedups of up to $3\times$ are obtainable with less than 2% error reduction.

2 Related Work

Many studies considered saving deep neural networks' computational cost. Diverse approaches are suggested, including low rank decomposition for convolutional and global layers using separable filters [4, 5], tensor decomposition [6, 7], weights and activations quantization [8, 9] and implementation using FFT [10]. In this research we decrease CNN's computational cost using conditional computation, and we hence focus on this literature.

Combining conditional computation with networks is often non-trivial since it makes the training process difficult. Despite this, the usage of conditional computation during train and test time has been studied using several approaches. A CNN that deals with dynamic time budget was suggested in [11], allowing output estimation without completing the entire forward propagation process, using additional loss layers in earlier stages of the network. Although an early classification is obtained, the accuracy decreases significantly when having low time budget.

The model described in [12] suggests selection of a sub-networks combination located between stacked LSTMs, in an input-depended fashion. This model aims to increase its number of parameters using these sub-networks, thus allow handling tasks with many parameters, such as language modeling. This model does not save computation on tasks such as image classification considered in the present paper.

Another suggested model is a recurrent neural network which selectively processes only some regions of the input, using reinforcement learning methods [13]. Also in [14] reinforcement learning technique is used to train a fully connected neural network to drop neurons in an input-depended manner. These models use sparse tensors which are less compliant with hardware constrains, causing computational saving to be less efficient.

In our model we trained a CNN with bypass connections in an input depended manner, such that only the necessary feature-maps are computed. Our results show that using this approach allows computational saving with significant test time speedup. The method is orthogonal to many methods suggested above [4–7, 10], and hence can be combined with them to obtain further acceleration.

3   Baseline Network – 'DenseNet'

In traditional networks the layers are sequentially connected one after the other. Different studies [15, 16] have shown that networks containing shorter connections (bypasses) enable deeper architectures which are more accurate. One such recent architecture is our network's baseline – DenseNet [17]. While traditional CNNs' layers are serially connected, in DenseNet the layers are sorted in large blocks, each containing multiple convolutional layers. Within each block, convolutional layers (followed by ReLU and Batch Normalization (BN)) forward their output maps to all subsequent convolution layers within the same block. Transition layers (convolution and average-pooling) separate between blocks and decrease the feature map size. Deeper layer in the block hence get as input maps from all their predecessors in the block, so their input size (number of input maps) increases. To reduce the amount of input maps, the output size of all layers is limited to k maps.

Using the DenseNet architecture, each omitted feature map implies significant computation saving, as the map is used as input for all following layers in the block, and not only the one next following layer. Our architecture takes advantage of this insight to reduce computation amount during test time.

4   Model

4.1   Motivation

As part of the efforts to reduce the deep networks' computational cost, our model prunes feature maps input-dependably. A computation of a feature-map can have significant or negligible influence on the output accuracy for a given example, depending on its content. For example, classifying dogs and cats is considerably different from distinguishing trains from tracks, thus these two tasks depend on different feature maps. Motivated by this observation, we created an architecture selecting which maps to compute and which to omit while classifying a given input.

4.2   Architecture

The model is based on the architecture described in [17], and to identify the essential feature-maps of the networks, for a given input to be classified, input depended 'gates' are added. Each gate is associated with a feature-map and indicates if the feature-map computation is necessary or not. These gates are binary valued: '1' implies to the necessity of using the feature-map, '0' implies it is unnecessary. As shown in Fig. 1, to produce these gates we connected to each layer a 'gates branch' whose outputs are k gate values (one for each map). To keep the net's computation's efficiency, the computational cost of the gates branches is low. Average pooling with fixed 4×4 output size is applied on the input layers (all the L preceding layers in the block), diminishing the input size of the following fully-connected (FC) layer. The FC layer outputs k neurons, each associated with one output map (of the $L + 1$ layer). Following this, BN and sigmoid activation layers are applied, producing probability-like values for map computation. Following the sigmoid layer, a stochastic decision is made regarding map computation by a Bernoulli trail with the probability of '1' provided by the gate. At test time, only the maps whose gate output is '1' are computed.

At training, to apply the gate decision for information flows on the main branch, each output map of the convolutional layer is multiplied by its associated gate value. Therefore, a gate's decision of "not computing a map" causes multiplication of the corresponding output map by 0 and avoiding the unnecessary map, while a gate valued 1 keeps the information of the map unchanged.

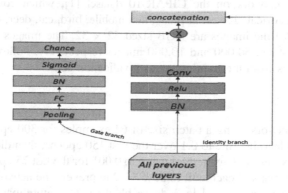

Fig. 1. The unit structure: The unit consists of 3 branches: the main branch, the bypass (identity) branch and the gate branch.

4.3   Optimization

The loss used for training is the standard softmax loss (the gates' actions and probabilities are implicit). During training the weights of the network's main branch (i.e. the DenseNet architecture) are adjusted using standard Stochastic Gradient Descent (SGD).

Since stochastic decisions are made in the gate branch, the introduced discontinuity and non-differentiability prevent optimization of the entire network using SGD. For optimization of the gate branches we use a reinforcement learning derivation as in [18] and minimize the expected loss while taking expectations also with respect to the stochastic decision made. For a single batch with B examples, the loss we minimize to encourage map pruning is

$$L_{Gate} = \frac{\lambda \sum_{l=1}^{L} \sum_{k=1}^{K} \sum_{i=1}^{B} \left(p_{ki}^{l} - t\right)^{Q} - |t|^{Q}}{K \cdot L \cdot B} \tag{1}$$

Where p_{ki}^{l} is the map computation probability of map k of layer l in example i. K is the number of maps in a layer and L is the number of gated layers of the network. λ, t and Q are scalar parameters. Raising the probabilities p_{ki}^{l} to the power $Q > 1$

encourages diversity of p_{ki}^l values. The parameter t is used to avoid the derivatives from obtaining very high values approaching $+\infty$, which may happen otherwise for $Q < 1$. This loss is added to the standard Softmax loss to provide the total loss minimized. λ is used to weight the pruning-related loss function and create a balance between accuracy and computational saving.

5   Experiments and Results

5.1   Dataset – CIFAR-10

We evaluate the network on the CIFAR-10 dataset [1], which consists of 60,000 images of 10 categorical classes: airplane, automobile, bird, cat, deer, dog, frog, horse, ship and truck. All the images are RGB sized 32×32. The images are divided to a train set and a test set: 50,000 and 10,000 images respectively. Followed by [17], we used 5,000 images from the training set as a validation set.

5.2   Training

We trained the network using a batch size of 64 examples for 300 epochs on a single GPU. We set the learning rate to 0.1 over the first 150 epochs, then diminish it to 0.01 for the next 75 epochs, and again diminish it to 0.001 for the last 75 epochs. We set the number of output maps of each unit to be $k = 12$ to prevent the network from growing too wide. The layers are sorted in 3 dense blocks with feature-map sized 32×32, 16×16 and 8×8, each block contains 12 BN-Relu-Conv units. Followed by [17], between the blocks we set a sequence of BN-Relu-Conv-Average-pooling with 2×2 pool size. The weight decay is set to 0.0001, the momentum is set to 0.9 and Q is set to 6. We initialize all the main branch weights to the final weights of a trained same-sized DenseNet. We removed the drop-out layers from the network, since the map-pruning produces significant training noise, and the additional drop-out noise disturbs the network optimization and convergence.

Gradual Learning
In some experiments we trained the network gradually, with each dense block trained separately at a time for 300 epochs, using the same parameters stated above. First, for 300 epochs, only the gate branches' parameters of the bottom dense block were adjusted. Then, for another 300 epochs, the gate branches' parameters of the second block as well as the first block were adjusted. Finally, the third block's gate branches were added to the process, and the entire network was trained simultaneously for 300 epochs.

5.3   Results

We evaluated the networks on the 10,000 remaining test set images. At test time, a pruning threshold was set to 0.5 and if the gate probability is above this threshold, the map is computed. To evaluate the computational saving potential of our gated version, note that the computation complexity of a convolutional layer with input size $W \times H \times d_{in}$, output size $W \times H \times K$ and filter size $F \times F$ is

$$O\left(W \times H \times d_{in} \times K \times F^2\right) \tag{2}$$

In our framework, the average probability of a map to be computed is $P = E_{l,i,k}\left[P_{ki}^l\right]$. If both the d_{in} input maps and the K output maps are not pruned with probability P, the complexity of convolutional layer computing is

$$O\left(W \times H \times Pd_{in} \times PK \times F^2\right) \tag{3}$$

And the speedup resulting from dividing (2) by (3) is $1/P^2$, i.e. quadratic in P. Assuming that the pruning probability is approximately invariant across layers, this provides a good estimation of the potential acceleration. We hence compute the expected acceleration as $1/P^2$ where P is estimated by averaging $P_{i,k}^l$ over all the maps and all test examples.

Our main results are shown in Table 1. For $\lambda = 0$, i.e. when the map pruning loss is not active, the network prefers to keep almost all its gates at '1', thus using almost all the maps. When λ is raised to 5 our input dependent version can provide significant potential accelerations of up to ×3, with small accuracy drops of up to 1.7%.

We compare the results of our input-dependent version with DenseNet networks containing less maps. In each row, we compare to a DenseNet with the number of maps reduced to get a computational cost comparable to the gated network. This is done by choosing $k_{DenseNet} = k \cdot P$ with P is the gate not-pruning probability. It can be seen that the input dependent versions provide an advantage over the simpler alternatives.

Table 1. Accuracy and potential speedup of gated networks using different train methods and parameters. Together with the initial convolutional layer and the transition layers, the networks depth is L = 40.

Training technique	λ	Bias	Error rate	Average P	Potential speedup	$k_{DensNet}$	Baseline error rate
Standard	0	4	7.2%	99.95%	×1	12	7.2%
Gradual	5	1	8%	83.82%	×1.42	10	8.18%
Standard	5	1	8.9%	57.73%	×3	7	9.34%

Another advantage of a gated network version is that one can further control the speed-accuracy trade-off by tuning the pruning threshold as test time. Hence the same network can provide a certain range of speed-accuracy working points, chosen at test time according to the application needs. This trade-off obtained by the network of row three from Table 1 is shown in Fig. 2.

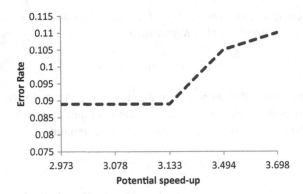

Fig. 2. The potential speed-up and the corresponding error rate using different test threshold values. The results are using a network that was trained with $\lambda = 5$ and bias = 1.

6 Conclusions and Further Work

We have presented an architecture with input dependent gates, enabling partial computation of feature maps in an input dependent manner. We showed that such a gated version provides convenient accuracy to speed trade off, which is slightly preferable to the trade-off obtained with plain DenseNet versions. Beyond that, the gated version allows additional accuracy-speed trade-off at run time, hence enabling further flexibility when computational constraints are present.

We currently work on optimizing the model during training using other techniques and extending the testing to more datasets.

References

1. Krizhevsky, A.: Learning multiple layers of features from tiny images. Technical report, Computer Science Department, University of Toronto, pp. 1–60 (2009)
2. Erhan, D., Bengio, Y., Courville, A., Vincent, P.: Visualizing higher-layer features of a deep network. Bernoulli **1341**, 1–13 (2009)
3. Yosinski, J., Clune, J., Nguyen, A., Fuchs, T., Lipson, H.: Understanding neural networks through deep visualization (2015)
4. Rigamonti, R., Sironi, A., Lepetit, V., Fua, P.: Learning separable filters. In: 2013 IEEE Conference on Computer Vision and Pattern Recognition, pp. 2754–2761 (2013)
5. Mamalet, F., Garcia, C.: Simplifying ConvNets for fast learning. In: Villa, A.E.P., Duch, W., Érdi, P., Masulli, F., Palm, G. (eds.) ICANN 2012. LNCS, vol. 7553, pp. 58–65. Springer, Heidelberg (2012). https://doi.org/10.1007/978-3-642-33266-1_8
6. Jaderberg, M., Vedaldi, A., Zisserman, A.: Speeding up convolutional neural networks with low rank expansions. arXiv Preprint. arXiv 1405.3866, p. 7 (2014)
7. Jin, J., Dundar, A., Culurciello, E.: Flattened convolutional neural network for feedforward acceleration. ICLR Work. **2014**, 1–11 (2015)

8. Rastegari, M., Ordonez, V., Redmon, J., Farhadi, A.: XNOR-Net: ImageNet classification using binary convolutional neural networks. In: Leibe, B., Matas, J., Sebe, N., Welling, M. (eds.) ECCV 2016. LNCS, vol. 9908, pp. 1–17. Springer, Cham (2016). https://doi.org/10.1007/978-3-319-46493-0_32

9. Vanhoucke, V., Senior, A., Mao, M.: Improving the speed of neural networks on CPUs. In: Proceedings of Deep Learning and Unsupervised Feature Learning NIPS, pp. 1–8 (2011)

10. Mathieu, M., Henaff, M., LeCun, Y.: Fast training of convolutional networks through FFTs. In: International Conference on Learning Representations, pp. 1–9 (2014)

11. Amthor, M., Rodner, E., Denzler, J.: Impatient DNNs - deep neural networks with dynamic time budgets, no. 2 (2016)

12. Shazeer, N., Mirhoseini, A., Maziarz, K., Davis, A., Le, Q., Dean, J.: Outrageously large neural networks : the sparsely-gated mixture-of-experts layer, pp. 1–15 (2017)

13. Mnih, V., Heess, N., Graves, A., Kavukcuoglu, K.: Recurrent models of visual attention. Adv. Neural. Inf. Process. Syst. **27**, 1–9 (2014)

14. Bengio, E., Bacon, P.-L., Pineau, J., Precup, D.: Conditional computation in neural networks for faster models, pp. 1–9 (2015)

15. He, K., Zhang, X., Ren, S., Sun, J.: Deep residual learning for image recognition. Arxiv.Org, vol. 7, no. 3, pp. 171–180 (2015)

16. He, K., Zhang, X., Ren, S., Sun, J.: Identity mappings in deep residual networks importance of identity skip connections usage of activation function analysis of pre-activation structure, no. 1, pp. 1–15 (2016)

17. Huang, G., Liu, Z., Weinberger, K.Q., van der Maaten, L.: Densely connected convolutional networks (2016)

18. Willia, R.J.: Simple statistical gradient-following algorithms for connectionist reinforcement learning. Mach. Learn. **8**(3), 229–256 (1992)

Thermal Comfort Index Estimation and Parameter Selection Using Fuzzy Convolutional Neural Network

Anirban Mitra, Arjun Sharma, Sumit Sharma, and Sudip Roy[✉]

CoDA Laboratory, Department of Computer Science and Engineering,
IIT Roorkee, Roorkee, India
anbanmta@gmail.com, arjunjamdagni@gmail.com, sumitsharma1825@gmail.com,
sudiproy.fcs@iitr.ac.in

Abstract. In order to monitor the comfort level of the city, which depends on several thermal metrics, in many indoor and outdoor applications it is required to estimate the comfort level of the city in real-time. Out of the many thermal comfort indices proposed so far, predicted mean voter (PMV) is one of the widely used measures for both indoor and outdoor ambiances. Due to the complexity of calculating PMV in real-time, many techniques have been proposed to estimate it without using all the required parameters. So far fuzzy networks have shown the best results for PMV estimation because of its rule generation capability. Convolutional neural network (CNN) is an deep learning based technique to classify, or to estimate particular parameter by shrinking them to significant data-collections. In this work, we fuzzified the system before applying CNN for regression to estimate the PMV values. Simulation results show that the proposed model outperforms the existing ANFIS model for PMV estimation with a lower root mean square error value.

Keywords: Convolutional neural network · Fuzzy neural network
Predicted mean vote · Thermal comfort index

1 Introduction

In various fields of everyday life such as traveling, going to work, even in indoor systems, prediction of comfort level is an important concern of the ambiance. A prediction comfort level of certain area or indoor system can have several applications such as prediction of travel suitability, prediction of thermal stress of residents and helping the workers to decide their working hours. Even in indoor one could tune ventilation or air-conditioning according to predictions. Thermal comfort is referred to as the condition of mind that expresses satisfaction of the thermal environment. It is not only associated with air-temperature, but also greatly associated with relative humidity, air velocity, mean radiant temperature, metabolic rate, clothing factor along with air-temperature [2]. As a choice of thermal comfort index, predicted mean vote (PMV) is a widely used one and

© Springer Nature Switzerland AG 2018
V. Kůrková et al. (Eds.): ICANN 2018, LNCS 11139, pp. 714–724, 2018.
https://doi.org/10.1007/978-3-030-01418-6_70

uses all the six parameters mentioned previously along with some synthesized variables. It is often very difficult to estimate PMV in real time because of the complexity, but from meteorological data, it is easy to retrieve only some of the parameters mentioned. Methods have been developed to estimate the PMV value from a few of the parameters. Fuzzy systems ([15], [16]) has been proved to work well in this scenario.

Convolutional neural network (CNN) has the ability to shrink large chunks of data into smaller data containing most key features, which can be used for both classification and regression. This work aims at solving the estimation (regression) problem with a novel architecture comprising of fuzzy system and deep neural network along with analysis of the system leveraging rule synthesizing ability of fuzzy systems and estimating ability of CNN. Moreover, the choice and inter-dependency of parameters are also demonstrated.

The remainder of the paper is organized as follows. Basic background is presented in Sects. 2 and 3 provides a literature survey. Motivation and problem statement are presented in Sect. 4. The proposed approach using fuzzy-CNN architecture is discussed in Sect. 5, whereas the input system description and functionality of the architecture are explained in Sect. 6. Simulation results and analysis are presented in Sect. 7. Finally, the paper is concluded in Sect. 8.

2 Basic Background

2.1 Predicted Mean Vote (PMV)

As defined by Fanger [9], predicted mean vote (PMV) is to scale human sensation of thermal comfort, which is backed by ASHRAE [2]. PMV is defined as a function of six parameters namely air-temperature (T_a in °C or degree Celsius), relative humidity (RH in %), mean radiant temperature (T_R in °C or degree Celsius), air-velocity (V_{air} in m/sec), human metabolic rate (Met in W/m^2) and clothing factor (Clo in Km^{2}W^{-1}). This quantification of thermal comfort of a group of persons is defined within a scale of -3 to $+3$ as shown in Table 1.

Table 1. Correspondence between PMV indices and PMV labels.

PMV index	−3	−2	−1	0	1	2	3
Label	Cold	Cool	Less cool	Neutral	Less warm	Warm	Hot

Equation 1 below presents the PMV as a function of different parameters, where W is the external work done (in W/m^2), P_a is the water vapour pressure in *Pascal*. T_{cl} is the surface temperature of clothing (in °C), h_c is the convective heat transfer coefficient (in °C) and f_{cl} is the ratio of clothed body surface area to naked body surface area.

$$PMV = (0.303e^{-0.036Met} + 0.028)[(Met - W) - 3.05 \times 10^{-5} \times [5733 - 6.99(Met - W)$$
$$- P_a] - 0.42[(Met - W) - 58.15] - 1.7 \times 10^{-5}Met(5867 - P_a) - 0.0014 \times Met(34$$
$$- T_a) - 3.96 \times 10 - 8f_c \times [(T_{cl} + 273)^4 - (T_R + 273)^4] - f_{cl}h_c(T_{cl} - T_a)] \tag{1}$$

2.2 ANFIS Model

The adaptive-network-based fuzzy inference system (ANFIS) model was developed by *Jang et al.* [13] using Takagi-Sugeno fuzzy model [20] to leverage fuzzy-rule strength and estimate outputs. For a rule i, the rule strength (w_i) is defined as $w_i = \mu_1^i(x_1) \times \mu_2^i(x_2)... \times \mu_p^i(x_p)$, where μ_j^i is the membership function for input x_j and the rule i. In ANFIS model, then the rule strengths are normalized $(\bar{w}_i)$ and put into linear combination with input values in order to get output y as given by Eq. 2, where a_j is called the consequent parameter.

$$y = \sum_i \bar{w}_i(a_0 + a_1x_1 + a_2x_2 + ... + a_nx_n) \tag{2}$$

2.3 Convolutional Neural Network (CNN)

A convolutional neural network (CNN) is similar to a generic feed-forward artificial neural network (ANN) except that they are specifically used to shrink or "convolve" the input data into a lower dimensional data-form for further use. The hidden layers of a CNN typically consists of three types of layers: convolutional layer, pooling layer and fully-connected (FC) layer. In the convolutional layer, a window of randomly initialized values is applied to convolve with the part of input data having identical dimension; while the window is slid by some predefined value. Pooling layer transforms the region of input into a singular value (stride), which is generally done by taking maximum (max-pool), minimum (min-pool) or average (average-pool). In a fully-connected (FC) layer, every neuron in previous layer is connected to every neuron in the next layer. This layer is generally applied after convolving and/or pooling in order to obtain the classification or regression value. The relative positioning and deciding number of layers are specific to a problem scenario.

3 Related Work

Various ways of estimating the thermal comfort levels proposed by researches include simple version of comfort index [6] and weight-based or weighted comfort index [19], predicted mean vote (PMV) [9], physiological equivalent temperature (PET) [12], standardized PMV (SPMV) [10]. Among all these, PMV is the widely used measure for thermal comfort index. Techniques like neural network, vector machine [14], fuzzy set, genetic algorithm, etc. have been used to enhance the accuracy of estimating the PMV value both in indoor and outdoor scenarios. *Ciglar et al.* [5] showed a model-predictive control framework. Another work presents how PMV zones in an outdoor environment of a district in Italy are analyzed [11]. Similarly, PMV is also used for analysis of an outdoor environment during urban planning [4].

Neural networks can learn the error in parameters in a converging manner, while fuzzy sets are able to distribute the parameters over intervals in order to express the result in a realistic manner. Combination of both have been leveraged in various works. *Li et al.* [15] proposed a type-2 fuzzy set based neural network to estimate the PMV value and also used back-propagation to adjust the membership function parameters. *Yifan et al.* [16] developed a simple fuzzy neural network model with the 6-parameter variation and 4-parameter variation (excluding metabolic rate, clothing factor) using multivariate regression for estimating PMV and obtained excellent results in term of accuracy of prediction. *Popko et al.* [18] used fuzzy logic module along with CNN for handwritten digits classification. *Moreno et al.* [17] combined CNN and a final fuzzy layer to achieve classification for object recognition. *Zhou et al.* [21] attempted regression using CNN to estimate the pain of certain facial expressions in video data.

4 Motivation and Problem Statement

4.1 Motivation

CNN is primarily used for classification using deep layer techniques, converting large data into to smaller and significant data-chunks. On the other hand, in order to extend the use of PMV value as comfort index in both indoor and outdoor environment, finding a different technique for better estimation of PMV is a challenge. *Li et al.* [15] and *Yifan et al.* [16] were able to achieve significant accuracy with root-mean-square-error (RMSE) values as 0.2 and 0.045, respectively, using fuzzy sets and neural networks. A know fact that the deep neural network architectures like CNN can also be used to perform regression-like tasks motivates us to leverage the advantages of both CNN as regression model and fuzzy-set for better estimation of the PMV value.

4.2 Problem Statement

Here the problem is to have an efficient and effective method to estimate the PMV value from a few known parameter values. In this paper, an attempt is made to use CNN for regression along with fuzzy sets for PMV estimation. This finding also incorporated selecting important parameters.

5 Proposed Approach: Fuzzy-CNN Architecture

We adopt the ANFIS model (without any prior knowledge of rules), while the estimation of consequent parameters (a_j as in Eq. 2) is left to the CNN layers. Regression using neural networks is a widely used practiced approach. In case of 5-parameter case, five parameters are considered to estimate the PMV value namely air-temperature (T_a), relative humidity (RH), air velocity (V_{air}), metabolic rate (Met) and clothing factor (Clo). Whereas, for 6-parameter case, mean radiant temperature (T_R) is included as the sixth parameter.

5.1 Pre-processing

Six parameters are distributed into multiple fuzzy sets using standard Gaussian distribution function (μ) that can be calculated as $\mu_i^j(x_i) = e^{\left[-\frac{(x_i - a_i^j)^2}{2(b_i^j)^2} \right]}$, where μ_i^j is membership function for input x_i and the corresponding rule j; while a and b are corresponding mean and standard deviation (s.d.) of the distribution, respectively, for x_i and j. Figure 1 depicts the initial fuzzy distributions step for air-temperature, relative humidity and air velocity. The initial pre-processing steps of all the six parameters are distributed into three fuzzy sets as follows. Air-temperature is distributed into three fuzzy sets: cold, normal (with higher s.d., i.e., flat/spread curve for the two extreme sets), hot as shown in Fig. 1(a). For relative humidity Gaussian functions are used to split into 3 sets: humid, normal, dry as shown in Fig. 1(b). Very low s.d. is applied to the two extreme sets while flat curve was maintained for normal one. For air velocity, again Gaussian distribution is used to divide into three sets: stormy, moderate air flow, almost still air (giving moderate s.d. in two extreme sets and high s.d. in the median set) as shown in Fig. 1(c). The mean radiant temperature T_R is distributed in same way as T_a. The metabolic rate is divided into three sets: slow, moderate, active giving moderate set with a high variance. Finally, the clothing factor is divided into three sets: heavily clothed, normal and minimal clothing. Heavily clothing is given low variance while moderately clothing set is given high variance.

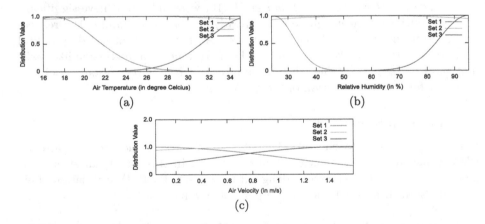

Fig. 1. Initial fuzzy distribution of (a) air-temperature, (b) relative humidity and (c) air velocity.

5.2 Layer Architecture

Initially, all the five parameters are divided into three fuzzy sets, i.e., a total of 15 fuzzy-sets are obtained. The proposed fuzzy-CNN architecture consists of five layers as depicted in Fig. 2 and discussed here layer-wise.

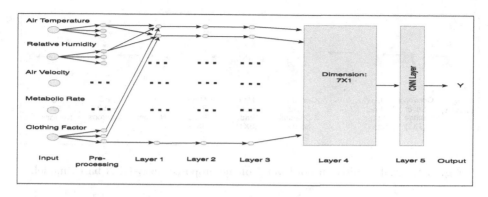

Fig. 2. Overall architecture of proposed fuzzy-CNN based model.

Layer 1: Using the pre-processed fuzzified values, the rule combinations are generated. Each rule is considered to be a tuple of five values for the 5-parameter case (six values for the 6-parameter case), where each value is corresponding to the particular fuzzy-set value of one parameter. Hence, a total of 243 (729) rules are generated for 5-parameter (6-parameter) case. One sample rule j is "if x_1 is $\mu_1^j(x_1)$, x_2 is $\mu_2^j(x_2)$, ..., x_p is $\mu_p^j(x_p)$, then output is y", where x_is are total p input parameters and μ_is are the corresponding membership functions. For 5-parameter case, combinations are generated as follows: if there are two sets $A = [a_1, a_2]$ and $B = [b_1, b_2]$, then their ordered combinations will be $[(a_1, b_1), (a_1, b_2), (a_2, b_1), (a_2, b_2)]$.

Layer 2: Each rule values are intra-multiplied in order to obtain the rule-strength (w_j) as discussed in Sect. 2.2.

Layer 3: Each rule strength value is normalized $(\bar{w}_j)$ as given by Eq. 3, where j ranges from 1 to 243 (729) for the 5-parameter (6-parameter) case.

$$\bar{w}_j = \frac{w_j}{\sum_j w_j} \tag{3}$$

Layer 4: The input data tuple (dimension 5×1) is transformed into a 7×1 sized tuple by appending the average of five parameters and numeric value integer 1. This appending can be regarded as bias term a_0 as mentioned in Eq. 2. Then, the output of layer 3, i.e., the normalized value of each rule (size 1×1) is multiplied with the transformed tuple to get the expanded rule value of 7×1.

Layer 5: In order to get the parameters or to estimate y of Eq. 2, deep networks are incorporated. First, generic 3 layer neural network with RMSProp optimizer [3] is used with a learning rate of around 0.0005 to find y from 1701 ($= 243 \times 7$) parameters for the 5-parameter case and 5832 ($= 729 \times 8$) for the 6-parameter case. Later on for the 5-parameter case, it is compared with the deep architecture consisting of a 7×1 (8×1 for the 6-parameter case) convolve layer with one channel and stride of 7 (8 for the 6-parameter case) units, followed

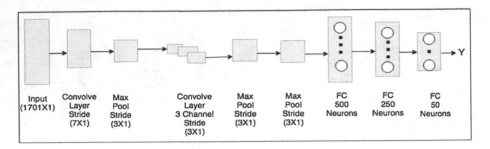

Fig. 3. Internal architecture of layer 5 of the proposed fuzzy-CNN based model.

by a 3 × 1 max-pool layer and stride of 3 units, which is again passed through a convolve layer of size 1 × 1, 3 channels and unit stride, followed by the max-pool layer same as the last one. This is followed by three fully-connected (FC) layers with 500, 250 and 50 neurons, respectively. This entire architecture of layer 5 for 5-parameter case is depicted in Fig. 3.

5.3   Choice of Parameters

The mean radiant temperature (MRT) is related to the air-temperature according to ISO 7726 standard [1]. Considering MRT as one of the input parameters would grow the number of rules to significantly large number (729 × 8 = 5832 for the 6-parameter case) of consequent parameters reached, which is a threefold increase in terms of parameter estimation. The metabolic rate and clothing factor were unavoidable as shown by *Yifan et al.* [16], whereas air-temperature, relative humidity and air-velocity are maintained as the key parameters.

5.4   Input System

For experimenting and analysis, RP-884 are used as reference, where the datasets for one NV building by *Dear et al.* [7] and 22 HVAC buildings by *Cena et al.* [8] are combined as the entire dataset. The former one was obtained from wet equatorial climate of Singapore, in the year 1991 and the latter one was from hot arid region of Kalgoorlie-Boulder, Australia for both winter and summer seasons in 1998. The Singapore and Australian winter and summer datasets has 584, 625 and 589 samples, respectively, totaling 1798 samples; out of which around 1400 samples were used for training and 400 for testing randomly at runtime. The parameters used in simulation are in the range as follows: air-temperature from 16.7 °C to 36.1 °C, relative humidity from 24.54 % to 97.82 %, air velocity from 0.043 m/s to 1.567 m/s, mean radiant temperature from 16.82 °C to 32.81 °C, metabolic rate from 0.772 Met to 2.58 Met (where 1 Met = 58 W/m^2), and the clothing factor from 0.045 to 1.57.

6 Deep Layer Functioning

As discussed in Sect. 2, convolutional layer performs dot product and hence results in downsampling of input. In the 5-parameter case, the input dimension is $1701 \times 1 \times 1 \times 1$ (height $\times$ width $\times$ depth $\times$ channels). This is obtained by expanding all 243 rules with 7×1 sized tuples as described earlier ($243 \times 7 = 1701$). After convolving with 7×1 sized filter with a stride of $7 \times 1 \times 1 \times 1$, expanded rule values are reduced to a singular value meaning, i.e., into 243 parameters for the 5-parameter case. Similarly, in the 6-parameter case the expanded rule values are reduced to 729 parameters. This value can be considered as related to the normalized rule strength from layer 3. This reduction is similar to layer 4 to 3 (backward), but in a different way. Max-pooling with window size $3 \times 1 \times 1 \times 1$ downsamples every 3 consecutive values into a singular one (maximum one). Before normalizing in layer 3, in layer 2 every 3 consecutive rule strengths differs only in terms of the values of clothing factor (Clo) as a membership function. Here, this pooling step is kept as the maximum (not an average) as it would be easier for optimization. Then it is reduced to 81 parameters for the 5-parameter case and 243 parameters for the 6-parameter case. The next convolve layer performs dot product with each value obtained in the last step, but adds 3 channels to it making it 81×3 sized data. Reshaping this data produces to 243×1 shape again. Furthermore, the max-pooling reduces it to 81 values for the 5-parameter case (243 values for the 6-parameter case), which imply getting rid of the effect of parameter clothing factor (Clo). One more layer of max-pooling of similar dimension and stride reduces it to 27 parameters, this can be considered as neutralizing the human metabolic rate (Met). Adding layers to it affects the results and time to train the model. The second convolve layer is added to make an increase in the number of parameters to optimize and pass different values to second pooling layer. A few fully-connected (FC) layers those are added to it start having neurons almost 20-fold of the number of parameters ($27 \times 19 \approx 500$). Weights and biases of these FC layers are initialized with the random normal values.

These rules basically boil down to a normalized value (Eq. 2). Those are first expanded (refer to layer 4 of Sect. 5.2) and then compressed through the CNN architecture in layer 5. The last max-pooling layer converts it from 243 to 27 for the 5-parameter case (from 729 to 81 for the 6-parameter case), which is a fairly scalable size that the Tensorflow fully-connected nets can handle. Compressing those many rules using the proposed CNN architecture is important step to tackle the combinatorial explosion of many fuzzy rules.

7 Simulation Results

The proposed method is implemented using Python 3.2 and Tensorflow and NumPy. Initially, 3 FC traditional neural network layers are appended to layer 4 of the ANFIS model, which results in best root mean-squared error (RMSE) value of around 0.8 on the test dataset. The proposed fuzzy-CNN model is fed with the train and test dataset as mentioned in Sect. 5.4. It provides a good RMSE value of around 0.018 for the 5-parameter case and around 0.08 the 5-parameter case, considering no prior knowledge were used in both the cases. The ANFIS model with prior knowledge for the 6-parameter case with multivariate regression reaches the best RMSE value of 0.04.

The error plot in Fig. 4(a) shows the variation of actual and predicted PMV values for the 5-parameter case for first 100 test samples. The shrinked size of most of the data points indicate closeness of predicted and actual PMV values. Figure 4(b) represents the amount of error in the predicted value for each sample for both the 5-parameter case and 6-parameter case of proposed model (i.e., F-CNN without MRT and F-CNN with MRT, respectively, where MRT is mean radiant temperature) and ANFIS model with prior knowledge for the 6-parameter case. The error in the 6-parameter case deviates the most from 0. Over 400 samples, the RMSE values are around 0.02 and 0.08 for the 5-parameter and the 6-parameter case, respectively, while for ANFIS model [16] with prior knowledge it is around 0.04. The consideration of MRT reduces the accuracy.

It is also observed that RMSProp is able to converge slowly but more efficiently (with global minima ≤ 0.019) for both the 5-parameter and 6-parameter

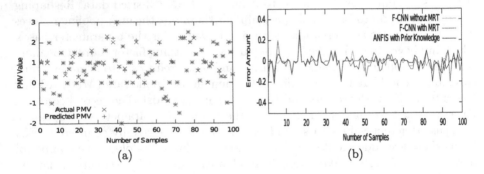

Fig. 4. Variation of (a) predicted and actual PMV values, and (b) relative error of three approaches with varying number of samples.

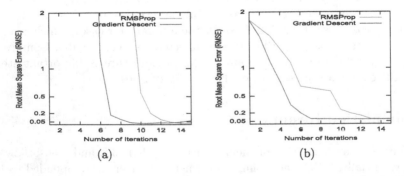

Fig. 5. Comparison between RMSProp and GD optimzer for (a) 5-parameter case and (b) 6-parameter case.

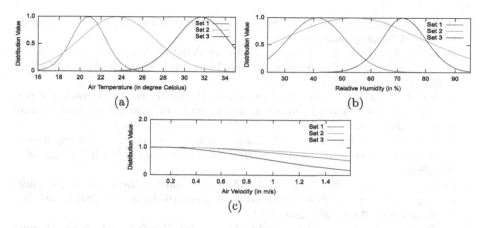

Fig. 6. Final fuzzy distribution of (a) air-temperature, (b) relative humidity and (c) air velocity.

cases, while the gradient descent (GD) optimizer converged quickly but with a higher global minima ≥ 0.021. Here, the learning rate is maintained as 0.0005 and batch size was maintained as 5. It is observed that increasing the batch size does not have significant effect on global minima except, it converged at slower rate. Figure 5(a) and (b) show how the RMSE converges against iterations for the 5-parameter and 6-parameter case, respectively, with both the optimizers.

Figure 6 shows the finally tuned fuzzy set values for the three parameters air-temperature, relative humidity and air-velocity, respectively.

8 Conclusions

Predicted mean voter (PMV) is a widely used thermal comfort index. In this paper, we have proposed a novel method based on fuzzy convolutional neural network (F-CNN) model to estimate the PMV values. This proposed model outperforms the existing model for PMV estimation with a lower root mean square error value. It is found that CNN can efficiently deduce the inter-dependencies of the parameters and their impact in estimating the final PMV values. In future, this work can be extended by incorporating selective networks like restricted Boltzmann machine or belief networks in order to obtain better accuracy in PMV value estimation.

References

1. Mean radiant temperature. https://en.wikipedia.org/wiki/Mean_radiant_temperature. Accessed July 2018
2. Thermal Comfort. https://en.wikipedia.org/wiki/Thermal_comfort. Accessed June 03 2018

3. RMSPropOptimizer   (2018).   https://www.tensorflow.org/api_docs/python/tf/train/RMSPropOptimizer
4. Barakat, A., Ayad, H., El-Sayed, Z.: Urban design in favor of human thermal comfort for hot arid climate using advanced simulation methods. Alexandria Eng. J. **56**(4), 533–543 (2017)
5. Cigler, J., Prívara, S., Vána, Z., Komarkova, D., Sebek, M.: Optimization of predicted mean vote thermal comfort index within model predictive control framework. In: Proceedings of the IEEE CDC, pp. 3056–3061 (2012)
6. Dai, M., et al.: A neural network short-term load forecasting considering human comfort index and its accumulative effect. In: Proceedings of the ICNC, pp. 262–266 (2013)
7. de Dear, R.J., Leow, K.G., Foo, S.C.: Thermal comfort in the humid tropics: field experiments in air-conditioned and naturally ventilated buildings in Singapore. Int. J. Biometeorol. **34**(4), 259–265 (1991)
8. de Dear, R., Cena, K.: Field Study of Occupant Comfort and Office Thermal Environments In a Hot-Arid Climate: Final Report on ASHRAE RP-921 (1998)
9. Fanger, P.O.: Thermal Comfort: Analysis and Applications in Environmental Engineering. McGraw-Hill, New York (1972)
10. Gagge, A., Fobelets, A., Berglund, L.: A standard predictive index of human response to the thermal environment. ASHRAE Trans. **92**(2B), 709–731 (1986)
11. Gaspari, J., Fabbri, K.: A study on the use of outdoor microclimate map to address design solutions for urban regeneration. Energy Procedia **111**, 500–509 (2017)
12. Höppe, P.: The physiological equivalent temperature - a universal index for the biometeorological assessment of the thermal environment. Int. J. Biometeorol. **43**(2), 71–75 (1999)
13. Jang, J.S.R.: ANFIS: adaptive-network-based fuzzy inference system. IEEE Trans. Syst. Man, Cybern. **23**(3), 665–685 (1993)
14. Kumar, M., Kar, I.: Non-linear HVAC computations using least square support vector machines. Energy Convers. Manag. **50**(6), 1411–1418 (2009)
15. Li, C., Yi, J., Wang, M., Zhang, G.: Prediction of thermal comfort index using type-2 fuzzy neural network. In: Zhang, H., Hussain, A., Liu, D., Wang, Z. (eds.) BICS 2012. LNCS (LNAI), vol. 7366, pp. 351–360. Springer, Heidelberg (2012). https://doi.org/10.1007/978-3-642-31561-9_40
16. Luo, Y., Li, N., Li, S.: ANFIS modeling of the PMV thermal comfort index based on prior knowledge. In: Proceedings of the IEEE ICIE, pp. 214–219 (2014)
17. Moreno, R.J., Sanchez, O.A., Ovalle, D.M.: RGB-D training for convolutional neural network with final fuzzy layer for depth weighting. Contemp. Eng. Sci. **10**(29), 1419–1429 (2017)
18. Popko, E., Weinstein, I.: Fuzzy logic module of convolutional neural network for handwritten digits recognition. J. Phys.: Conf. Ser. **738**(1), 012123 (2016)
19. Rawi, M.I.M., Al-Anbuky, A.: Development of intelligent wireless sensor networks for human comfort index measurement. In: Proceedings of the ANT, pp. 232–239 (2011)
20. Takagi, T., Sugeno, M.: Fuzzy identification of systems and its applications to modeling and control. IEEE Trans. Syst. Man and Cybern. SMC **15**(1), 116–132 (1985)
21. Zhou, J., Hong, X., Su, F., Zhao, G.: Recurrent convolutional neural network regression for continuous pain intensity estimation in video. In: Proceedings of the IEEE CVPRW, pp. 1535–1543 (2016)

Soft Computing Modeling of the Illegal Immigration Density in the Borders of Greece

Serafeim Koutsomplias[✉] and Lazaros Iliadis

School of Engineering, Department of Civil Engineering,
Lab of Mathematics and Informatics, University Campus,
Democritus University of Thrace, Xanthi, Greece
serafeim_sefis@windowslive.com, liliadis@civil.duth.gr

Abstract. It is a fact that due to the war in Syria and to instability/poverty in wide regions of the world, immigration flows to Europe have increased to a very significant extent. From the EU countries, Greece and Italy are accepting the heaviest load due to their geographical location. This research paper, proposes a flexible and rational Soft Computing approach, aiming to model and classify areas of the Greek (sea and land) borderline, based on the density and range of illegal immigration (ILIM). The proposed model employs Intuitionistic Fuzzy Sets (IFUS) and Fuzzy Similarity indices (FUSI). The application of this methodology can provide significant aid towards the assessment of the situation in each of the involved areas, depending on the extent of the flow they face.

Keywords: Illegal immigration · Intuitionistic fuzzy sets
Degrees of membership · Degrees of non-membership · Similarity indices
Classification

1 Introduction

To the best of our knowledge, this is the first and pioneer Soft Computing approaches employing Intuitionistic Fuzzy Sets, towards illegal immigration risk modeling for Greece. This was achieved by employing Fuzzy Algebraic approaches, offering the most flexible and effective solution for the representation and modeling of real world concepts (e.g. "high temperature", "small rain height", "high altitude"). From this point of view this research effort has a certain level of innovation.

Fuzzy Logic constitutes a part of Soft Computing, a branch of Artificial Intelligence that is used in many scientific applications, like control systems and Hybrid Decision Support systems. It is widely used in risk estimation. However, the most important innovative element of this research is the introduction of a new risk estimation approach, employing Intuitionist Fuzzy Sets in order to enhance flexibility. This is really important for totally unstructured problems like the one faced herein.

This research proposes several annual local ILIM risk models for a period of eight years (2010–2017). These models were compared to each other and analyzed thoroughly. The result was the estimation of cross checked indices, regarding annual illegal immigration risk (ANIIR) similarities and differences, among the areas of entry. The areas considered are the following: Greek - Albanian border, Greek - FYROM border,

© Springer Nature Switzerland AG 2018
V. Kůrková et al. (Eds.): ICANN 2018, LNCS 11139, pp. 725–735, 2018.
https://doi.org/10.1007/978-3-030-01418-6_71

Greek - Bulgarian border, river Evros (natural border between Greece and Turkey) the islands of Lesvos, Samos, Crete, the islands of Dodecanese and Cyclades and finally the rest of the country. The classification of all areas based on the produced metadata, was performed through an innovative and flexible algorithmic approach. More attention was given to the area of river Evros and to the island of Lesvos as they are the major entry points, carrying a major part of the illegal immigration flow.

2 Materials and Methods

2.1 Theoretical Background – Methodology (Hung and Yang 2004)

According to Athanassov (1999), an IFUS $\tilde{A}$ is defined as follows:

$$\tilde{A} = \{(x, \mu_{\tilde{A}}(x), v_{\tilde{A}}(x))| \ x \in X\} \tag{2.1}$$

where $\mu_{\tilde{A}}(x), v_{\tilde{A}}(x) \in [0,1]$ denote the degree of membership and the degree of non-membership of $x \in \tilde{A}$ respectively.

The following condition must be met:

$$0 \leq \mu_{\tilde{A}}(x) + v_{\tilde{A}}(x) \leq 1 \ \forall x \in X \tag{2.2}$$

For each IFUS $\tilde{A}$ in the universe of discourse X,

$$\pi_A(x) = 1 - \mu_A(x) - \frac{1 - \mu_A(x)}{1 + \lambda \mu_A(x)} \tag{2.3}$$

and

$$\pi_A(x) = 1 - \mu_A(x) - v_A(x) \tag{2.4}$$

is called the hesitancy degree of x to $\tilde{A}$ and it satisfies the inequality $0 \leq \pi_A(x) \leq 1 \ \forall x \in X$.

The following membership function has been used:

$$\mu(x) = 0.7 e^{\frac{-(x-b)^2}{2\sigma^2}} \tag{2.5}$$

A very important aspect of IFUS is the estimation of their degree of similarity (DESI). The DESI S between two IFUS $\tilde{A}$ *and* $\tilde{B}$ can be calculated with various functions such as:

- (Li and Cheng 2002):

$$S_d^p(\tilde{A}, \tilde{B}) = 1 - \frac{1}{\sqrt[p]{n}} \sqrt[p]{\sum_{i=1}^{n} |m_{\tilde{A}}(i) - m_{\tilde{B}}(i)|^p} \tag{2.6}$$

where

$$m_{\tilde{A}}(i) = (\mu_{\tilde{A}}(x_i) + 1 - v_{\tilde{A}}(x_i))/2, \ m_{\tilde{B}}(i) = (\mu_{\tilde{B}}(x_i) + 1 - v_{\tilde{B}}(x_i))/2 \qquad (2.7)$$

and $1 \leq p \leq \infty$.

- (Liang and Shi 2003):

$$S_d^p(\tilde{A}, \tilde{B}) = 1 - \frac{1}{\sqrt[p]{n}} \sqrt[p]{\sum_{i=1}^{n} (\Phi_{s\tilde{A}\tilde{B}}(i) + \Phi_{f\tilde{A}\tilde{B}}(i))^p} \qquad (2.8)$$

where

$$\Phi_{s\tilde{A}\tilde{B}}(i) = |\mu_{\tilde{A}}(x_i) - \mu_{\tilde{B}}(x_i)|/2 \qquad (2.9)$$

and

$$\Phi_{f\tilde{A}\tilde{B}}(i) = |(1 - v_{\tilde{A}}(x_i))/2 - (1 - v_{\tilde{B}}(x_i))/2| \qquad (2.10)$$

The degree of similarity S for all IFUS $\tilde{A}$, $\tilde{B}$ *and* $\tilde{C}$ satisfies the following properties:

$$0 \leq S(\tilde{A}, \tilde{B}) \leq 1 \qquad (2.11)$$

$$S(\tilde{A}, \tilde{B}) = 1 \ if \ \tilde{A} = \tilde{B} \qquad (2.12)$$

$$S(\tilde{A}, \tilde{B}) = S(\tilde{B}, \tilde{A}) \qquad (2.13)$$

$$S(\tilde{A}, \tilde{C}) \leq S(\tilde{A}, \tilde{B}) \ and \ S(\tilde{A}, \tilde{C}) \leq S(\tilde{B}, \tilde{C}) \qquad (2.14)$$

$$if \ \tilde{A} \subseteq \tilde{B} \subseteq \tilde{C}, \ \tilde{C} \in IFSs(X)$$

A new edition of property (2.12) is (2.15) (Mitchell 2003):

$$S(\tilde{A}, \tilde{B}) = 1 \ \ if \ and \ only \ if \ \tilde{A} = \tilde{B} \qquad (2.15)$$

2.2 Data

The data used in this research, were obtained from the official website of the Hellenic Police: http://www.astynomia.gr/newsite.php?&lang.

3 The Proposed Fuzzy Intuitionistic System

The proposed model estimates the degree of membership of each area to the Linguistics "Low Risk", "Moderate Risk", "High Risk" separately, based on the number of incidents. It is an indirect multiclass classification. Also the intuitionistic fuzzy sets (INFS) are used towards the estimation of the degree of similarities between the most risky areas.

Initially, the raw data were stored in MS Excel. The global range of the problem was found by obtaining the minimum and the maximum number of ILIM for the whole country and for every year.

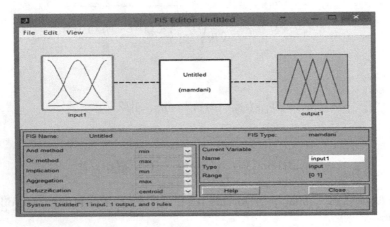

Screen 1.   Fuzzy toolbox of MATLAB

Then, the raw data were transferred in proper tables in MATLAB, and three Membership functions corresponding to the three fuzzy Linguistics mentioned above, have been defined automatically by the Fuzzy Toolbox of MATLAB after the input of the range (minimum and maximum values). For all three linguistics Gaussian membership functions were employed. Screens 1 and 2 are the graphical user interface of the Fuzzy toolbox of MATLAB.

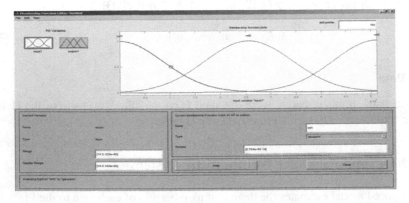

Screen 2.   Gaussian membership function

4 Results and Discussion

4.1 Comparison Between the River Evros Area and Island of Lesvos

The river Evros area has been chosen because it is the natural main land border between Greece and Turkey and the island of Lesvos is a characteristic destination that can be easily reached by sea from the Turkish coast, using small boats.

The following chart resulted after the Analysis of Fuzzy Sets and the usage of Intuitionistic Fuzzy Sets and it presents the degree of Similarity between the two areas.

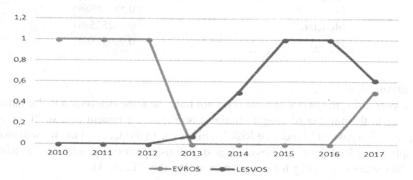

Graph 1. The characteristic categories of risk according to the number of illegal immigrants for Evros and Lesvos (2010–2017) (0 low risk, 0.5 moderate risk, 1 high risk)

As we have seen in 2016, the risk for Lesvos has started dropping (maybe because there is no place in the refugee camps of Lesvos any more, and the refugees have realized this). The same time the risk for Evros has started rising as the people were looking for a new entry to Greece that can lead to Athens or to western Europe. The very impressive in this case is the fast that the two lines almost met in 2017 and the two areas have the same DOS.

Comparison 1

According to the number of ILIM incidents, for the years 2010–2012, the two above areas do not have the same behavior and the same risk. Evros is a case of "High Risk" whereas Lesvos is a case of "Low Risk" for the above years. Their degree of similarity (DOS) is Moderate. All other degrees are almost equal to zero.

Table 1. Risk similarity for 2010–2012

Degrees of risk similarity (Lesvos-Evros)	2010	2011	2012
Low	0.017103	9.55E−05	0.024268
Moderate	0.977549	0.998743	0.971531
High	2.28E−07	2.03E−07	8.95E−07

As it can be seen in Table 1 the degree of similarity is not high.

Comparison 2

For the year 2013, the two above areas have almost the same behavior for all risk Linguistics as they have a very high degree of similarity and they are both "Low Risky". However, Evros is 7.7 times closer to the category of "Moderate Risk". We examine the year 2013 separately, because as we will see below 2013 is the start of a new era (Table 2).

Table 2. Risk similarities for the year 2013

Degrees of risk similarity (Lesvos-Evros)	2013
Low	0.583859885
Moderate	0.662525807
High	0.999935607

Comparison 3

For the year 2014, the two above areas do not have the same behavior and the same risk according to the number of illegal immigrants. Evros is a typical case of "Low Risk" and Lesvos is a case of "Moderate Risk". This is due to the fact that (as we will also see in Graph 1) the Risk level for Lesvos has started rising seriously, whereas the Risk for Evros has started dropping for some years in the row (Table 3).

Table 3. Risk similarities for the year 2014

Degrees of risk similarity	2014
Low	0.094242768
Moderate	0.373050006
High	0.763732614

Comparison 4

If we compare the two areas for 2015 and 2016, we see that they do not have the same behavior and the same risk according to the number of illegal immigrants. Evros is still a typical case of "Low Risk" and Lesvos is a characteristic case of "High Risk". The refuges keep preferring the seaway and they keep risking their lives by using small rotten boats to reach the islands, preferring mainly the island of Lesvos which is very close to the Turkish mainland and it is also a major one. The 12 km fence that has been built by Greece in the north land border with Turkey has plaid a significant role towards this situation (Table 4).

Table 4. Comparison of risk similarities for 2015–2016

Degrees of risk similarity	2015	2016
Low	0.000351104	0.009087607
Moderate	0.997457414	0.984788473
High	$1.04915E{-}07$	$2.75765E{-}07$

Comparison 5

For the year 2017, the two above areas have almost the same behavior for all risk Linguistics as they have a high degree of similarity and they are both "Moderate Risky". However, Lesvos is 1560 times closer to the category of "Moderate Risk" (Table 5).

Table 5. Comparison of risk similarities for the year 2017

Degrees of risk similarity	2017
Low	0.541804804
Moderate	0.678369381
High	0.823298925

5 Conclusion-Discussion

After analyzing the results, we see that the degree of risk of the two pilot areas (Lesvos and Evros) changes on an annual basis and it ranges from high to low, depending on the orientation of the immigrants' flow. It proves that the desperate immigrants who left their countries to escape from war, are sometimes motivated to use land borders and sometimes to cross the sea. This depends on the information they get and on the interests of the people who exploit this unfortunate situation in order to make profit. Another measure that motivated immigrants to cross the sea to the islands after 2013 is the construction of the fence in river Evros from the Greek side. The construction of this fence finished in 2014. In Fig. 4.1 we see that from 2013 (when the works for the fence had started) till 2016 the ILIM incidents from the land border (Evros) has dropped to an extremely Low level whereas the incidents in Lesvos have increased dramatically. In 2017 the tendency of the refugees was to use both diodes equally. The research has shown that the immigration of the refuges is not done randomly, but it is

Table 6. Comparison of degrees of immigration risk for Greece for 2010 and 2011

Areas	Years					
	2010			2011		
	L	M	H	L	M	H
Albanian	1E−04	**0.432**	0.25739	**0.4557**	0.24	2E−05
FYROM	**0.986**	0.021	7.8E−08	**0.9947**	0.0177	5E−08
Bulgarian	**0.996**	0.017	5E−08	**0.998**	0.0158	4E−08
Evros	3E−08	0.013	**1**	3E−08	0.0132	**1**
Lesvos	**0.974**	0.025	1.1E−07	**0.9999**	0.0138	3E−08
Samos	**0.991**	0.019	6.6E−08	**0.9996**	0.0143	4E−08
Chios	**1**	0.014	3.4E−08	**1**	0.0133	3E−08
Dodecanese	**0.988**	0.021	7.5E−08	**1**	0.0132	3E−08
Cyclades	**1**	0.013	3E−08	**0.9999**	0.0137	3E−08
Crete	**0.964**	0.028	1.4E−07	**0.9854**	0.0215	8E−08
Rest of Greece	2E−06	0.099	**0.73042**	0.0094	**0.9937**	0.0182

732 S. Koutsomplias and L. Iliadis

organized and the desperate ILIM are following specific roots that changes annually, depending on the policies of the involved countries.

The following Tables 6, 7, 8 and 9 present the fuzzy degrees of membership of all border areas of Greece to the Linguistics Low, Medium and High ILIM Risk.

Evros is a typical case of High Risk with a Degree of Membership (DOM) equal to 1 for both 2010 and 2011 whereas Lesvos is Low Risky with DOM practically equal to 1 (0.99). The other areas are all Low Risky compared to these two spots.

Table 7. Comparison of degrees of immigration risk for Greece for 2012 and 2013

Areas	Years					
	2012			2013		
	L	M	H	L	M	H
Albanian	0.108	**0.708**	0.0008	0.0009	**0.7191**	0.1028
FYROM	**0.975**	0.025	1.1E−07	**0.9447**	0.0336	2E−07
Bulgarian	**0.998**	0.016	4.4E−08	**0.99**	0.0198	7E−08
Evros	3E−08	0.013	**1**	**0.9349**	0.0363	2E−07
Lesvos	**0.964**	0.028	1.4E−07	**0.4069**	0.2774	3E−05
Samos	**0.979**	0.024	9.7E−08	**0.5241**	0.1959	1E−05
Chios	**1**	0.014	3.2E−08	**0.8705**	0.054	6E−07
Dodecanese	**0.98**	0.023	9.4E−08	**0.7049**	0.1088	3E−06
Cyclades	**1**	0.013	3E−08	**1**	0.0132	3E−08
Crete	**0.862**	0.057	6.4E−07	**0.6728**	0.1218	4E−06
Rest of Greece	7E−07	0.058	**0.85442**	3E−08	0.0131	**1**

Evros is still a High-risk area for 2012 and suddenly the risk drops to zero (Low Risk area with the maximum DOM) for the next year 2013 whereas Risk for Lesvos starts rising and the Rest of the country becomes High Risky with DOM equal to 1.

Table 8. Comparison of degrees of immigration risk for Greece for 2014 and 2015

Areas	Years					
	2014			2015		
	L	M	H	L	M	H
Albanian	0.013	**1**	0.0138	**0.9958**	0.0172	5E−08
FYROM	**0.952**	0.032	1.8E−07	**1**	0.0134	3E−08
Bulgarian	**0.986**	0.021	8E−08	**1**	0.0133	3E−08
Evros	**0.863**	0.056	6.3E−07	**0.9995**	0.0145	4E−08
Lesvos	5E−04	**0.627**	0.14156	3E−08	0.0132	**1**
Samos	0.054	**0.871**	0.00243	**0.4916**	0.2159	2E−05
Chios	0.122	**0.672**	0.00064	**0.3873**	0.2937	4E−05
Dodecanese	2E−06	0.083	**0.77688**	0.3233	**0.3545**	7E−05
Cyclades	**1**	0.013	3E−08	**1**	0.0132	3E−08
Crete	**0.65**	0.132	4.6E−06	**0.9997**	0.0142	3E−08
Rest of Greece	3E−08	0.013	**1**	**0.9616**	0.0289	2E−07

In 2014 the problem is in recession (no area is High risky) whereas in 2015 all of a sudden, only Lesvos is assigned DOM equal to 1 (extreme value) for the Linguistic High Risk.

It is remarkable that is 2016 only Lesvos still remains High risky with the maximum Dom equal to 1. Suddenly the situation changes completely in 2017, where many areas are assigned the Moderate Risk linguistic. These areas are: Lesvos, Samos, Chios, Evros and the surprise is the Greek Albanian border. It should be mentioned that Lesvos (though moderate risky is still the most risky one, followed by the Albanian borders and the island of Chios.

Table 9. Comparison of degrees of immigration risk for Greece for 2016 and 2017

Areas	Years					
	2016			2017		
	L	M	H	L	M	H
Albanian	**0.95**	0.032	1.9E−07	0.1284	**0.6568**	0.0006
FYROM	**1**	0.014	3.3E−08	**0.9996**	0.0142	4E−08
Bulgarian	**0.999**	0.015	4.1E−08	**0.9632**	0.0284	1E−07
Evros	**0.986**	0.021	7.8E−08	0.3269	**0.3506**	7E−05
Lesvos	3E−08	0.013	**1**	0.0009	**0.7246**	0.1012
Samos	**0.68**	0.119	3.6E−06	0.3183	**0.3597**	7E−05
Chios	0.053	**0.875**	0.00252	0.1974	**0.5211**	0.0002
Dodecanese	**0.506**	0.207	1.5E−05	**0.5321**	0.1909	1E−05
Cyclades	**1**	0.013	3E−08	**1**	0.0132	3E−08
Crete	**0.998**	0.016	4.5E−08	**0.9182**	0.0407	3E−07
Rest of Greece	**0.658**	0.128	4.3E−06	3E−08	0.0132	**1**

All of the above conclusions are very interesting, and they show the roots that the immigrants decide to follow every year. It is impressive that the vast majority of them are guided to follow specific roots that change depending on the situations. This data and results will be much more interesting to the people who have a clear view of the situation and they can explain the root changes on an annual basis. Of course, the life conditions of the immigrants must be improved.

Future research will focus on the estimation of similarities among all border areas of Greece.

References

Deshpande, A.W., Raje, D.V.: Fuzzy logic applications to environment management systems Case studies. In: Proceedings of IEEE on Industrial Informatics. IEEE Explore Digital Library (2003)

Atanassov, K.: Intuitionistic Fuzzy Sets. Springer, Heidelberg (1999). https://doi.org/10.1007/978-3-7908-1870-3

Bradshaw, L.S., et al.: The 1978 National Fire – Danger Rating System, Technical documentation (1978)

Booty, W.G.: Design and implementation of environmental decision support system (2001)

EC, European Commission: Forest Fires in Europe 2010, 92 p. EUR 24910 EN, ISBN 978-92-79-20919-2. Publications Office of the European Union, Luxembourg (2011)

Hájek, P., Olej, V.: Adaptive intuitionistic fuzzy inference systems of Takagi-Sugeno type for regression problems. In: Iliadis, L., Maglogiannis, I., Papadopoulos, H. (eds.) AIAI 2012. IAICT, vol. 381, pp. 206–216. Springer, Heidelberg (2012). https://doi.org/10.1007/978-3-642-33409-2_22

Iakovidis, D.K., Pelekis, N., Kotsifakos, E., Kopanakis, I.: Intuitionistic fuzzy clustering with applications in computer vision. In: Blanc-Talon, J., Bourennane, S., Philips, W., Popescu, D., Scheunders, P. (eds.) ACIVS 2008. LNCS, vol. 5259, pp. 764–774. Springer, Heidelberg (2008). https://doi.org/10.1007/978-3-540-88458-3_69

Iliadis, L., Vangeloudh, M., Spartalis, S.: An intelligent system employing an enhanced fuzzy c-means clustering model: application in the case of forest fires. Comput. Electron. Agric. **70**(2), 276–284 (2010)

Iliadis, L., Tsataltzinos, T.: Fuzzy adaptive clustering of the Greek forest terrain towards forest fire risk assessment (2008)

Iliadis, L.: A decision support system applying an integrated fuzzy model for long-term forest fire risk estimation. EMS Environ. Model. Softw. **20**(5), 613–621 (2005)

Iliadis, L., Spartalis, S.: Fundamental fuzzy relation concepts of a D.S.S. for the estimation of natural disasters risk (The case of a trapezoidal membership function). J. Math. Comput. Model. **42**, 747–758 (2005)

Iliadis, L., Papastavrou, A., Lefakis, P.: A computer-system that classifies the prefectures of Greece in forest fire risk zones using fuzzy sets. For. Policy Econ. **4**(1), 43–54 (2002a). ISSN: 1389-9341

Iliadis, L., Papastavrou, A., Lefakis, P.: A heuristic expert system for forest fire guidance in Greece. J. Environ. Manag. **65**(3), 327–336 (2002b)

Iliadis, L., Zigkrika, N.: Performing fuzzy multi-feature scenarios for the determination of forest fire risk. In: Proceedings of 3rd International Conference on Information and Communication Technologies in Agriculture, Food, Forestry and Environment (ITAFFE 2010), pp. 170–177 (2010)

Kecman, V.: Learning and Soft Computing. MIT Press, Cambridge (2001)

Chang, K.-H., Cheng, C.-H.: A risk assessment methodology using intuitionistic fuzzy set in FMEA. Int. J. Syst. Sci. **41**(12), 1457–1471 (2010)

Li, D., Cheng, C.: New similarity measures of intuitionistic fuzzy sets and application to pattern recognition (2002)

Liang, Z., Shi, P.: Similarity measures on intuitionistic fuzzy sets (2003)

Leondes, C.T.: Fuzzy Logic and Expert Systems Applications. Elsevier, New York (1998)

Mitchell, H.B.: On the Dengfeng – Chuntian similarity measure and its application to pattern recognition (2003)

Malek, M.R., Karimipour, F., Nadi, S.: Intuitionistic fuzzy spatial relationships in mobile GIS environment. In: Masulli, F., Mitra, S., Pasi, G. (eds.) WILF 2007. LNCS (LNAI), vol. 4578, pp. 313–320. Springer, Heidelberg (2007). https://doi.org/10.1007/978-3-540-73400-0_39

Sadiq, R., Tesfamarian, S.: Environmental Decision-making under uncertainty using intuitionistic fuzzy analytic hierarchy process. Environ. Res. Risk Assess. **23**, 75–91 (2009). https://doi.org/10.1007/s00477-007-0197-z

Sharma, A., Yadav, J., Mandlik, P., Ladkat, P.: Fuzzy logic applications in water supply system management: a case study. In: Proceedings of the Annual Meeting of the North American Fuzzy Information Processing Society (2012)

Sotirov, S., Vardeva, I., Krawczak, M.: Intuitionistic fuzzy multilayer perceptron as a part of integrated systems for early forest-fire detection. In: Proceedings of the 17th International Conference on Intuitionistic Fuzzy Sets. Notes on IFS, vol. 19, no. 3, pp. 81–89 (2013)

Sotirova, E., et al.: Hexagonal Game Method model of forest fire spread with intuitionistic fuzzy estimations. In: Proceedings of the 17th International Conference on Intuitionistic Fuzzy Sets. Notes on IFS, vol. 19, no. 3, pp. 73–80 (2013)

Szmidt, E., Kacprzyk, J.: Classification with nominal data using intuitionistic fuzzy sets. In: Melin, P., Castillo, O., Aguilar, L.T., Kacprzyk, J., Pedrycz, W. (eds.) IFSA 2007. LNCS (LNAI), vol. 4529, pp. 76–85. Springer, Heidelberg (2007). https://doi.org/10.1007/978-3-540-72950-1_8

Tsataltzinos, T., Iliadis, L., Spartalis, S.: A generalized fuzzy-rough set application for forest fire risk estimation feature reduction. In: Iliadis, L., Maglogiannis, I., Papadopoulos, H. (eds.) AIAI/EANN 2011. IAICT, vol. 364, pp. 332–341. Springer, Heidelberg (2011). https://doi.org/10.1007/978-3-642-23960-1_40

Tsataltzinos, T., Iliadis, L., Spartalis, S.: A fuzzy Inference rule-based System for the estimation of forest fire risk: the case of Greece. J. Eng. Intell. Syst. 18(1), 59–67 (2010)

Tsataltzinos, T., Iliadis, L., Spartalis, S.: An intelligent fuzzy inference system for risk estimation using matlab platform: the case of forest fires in Greece. In: Iliadis, L., Vlahavas, I., Bramer, M. (eds.) AIAI 2009. IFIP International Federation for Information Processing, vol. 296, pp. 303–311. Springer, Heidelberg (2009). https://doi.org/10.1007/978-1-4419-0221-4_36

Chaira, T.: Intuitionistic fuzzy set approach for colour region extraction (2010)

Tzionas, P., Ioannidou, I., Paraskevopoulos, S.: A Hierarchical Fuzzy Decision Support System for the Environmental Rehabilitation of Lake Koronia, Greece (2004)

Hung, W.L., Yang, M.S.: Similarity measures of intuitionistic fuzzy sets based on Hausdorff distance (2004)

Hung, W.L., Yang, M.S.: Similarity measures of intuitionistic fuzzy sets based on L_p metric (2004)

Deng, Y., Sadiq, R., Jiang, W., Tesfamariam, S.: Risk analysis in a linguistic environment: a fuzzy evidential reasoning-based approach. Expert. Syst. Appl. 38(12), 15438–15446 (2011)

Fuzzy Implications Generating from Fuzzy Negations

Georgios Souliotis and Basil Papadopoulos$^{(\boxtimes)}$

Department of Civil Engineering Section of Mathematics and Informatics,
Democritus University of Thrace, 67100 Kimeria, Greece
{gsouliot, papadob}@civil.duth.gr

Abstract. A basic building block in the foundation of fuzzy neural networks is the theory of fuzzy implications. Fuzzy implications play a crucial role in this topic. The aim of this paper is to find a new method of generating fuzzy implications. based on a given fuzzy negation. Specifically, we propose using a given fuzzy negation and a function so as to generate rules of fuzzy implications, that is rules which regulate decision making, thus adapting mathematics to human common sense. A great advantage of this construction is that the implications generated in this way fulfil many axioms and serious properties among the set of required ones.

Keywords: Fuzzy implication · Fuzzy negation · t-norm · t-conorm

1 Introduction

Everything starts from the well-known connection «if ...... then ....», which is s called implication in mathematic. In the above reasoning by filling the gaps with phrases, we have a hypothesis, which, in classical logic, t is true or false, so their values are 1 or 0, respectively. Fuzzy logic is not only to do with the values 0 and 1 but explores these implications when their values are between 0, 1.

Basically, a fuzzy system is in essence a system of linguistic rules of the form "if .... then ....", which match two fuzzy linguistic concepts A and B according to natural language and common sense, as in the following examples

- "If someone is tall, then (s) he is also heavy"

  or

- "If it snows heavily, then the road gets dangerous".

In other words, through implications and fuzzy operations, fuzzy systems enable 'engines' and mathematics to incorporate the way of expression of everyday language and common sense. Note here that both mathematics and engines function according to Boolean algebra.

In this paper our goal is to import a way of generating fuzzy implications through fuzzy negations as has been described in the literature.

A fuzzy implication is a generalization of the classical implication, in the same way that a t-norm and a t-conorm are generalizations of the classical conjunction and disjunction, respectively. In the rest of the paper we will import the most fundamental

V. Kůrková et al. (Eds.): ICANN 2018, LNCS 11139, pp. 736–744, 2018.
https://doi.org/10.1007/978-3-030-01418-6_72

properties of fuzzy conjunctions and examine the relations that connect negations and conjunctions in fuzzy logic theory.

To find out whether a fuzzy negation can generate fuzzy implications, the we need to ensure that effect of negation must be such that it will not alter the axioms of fuzzy implications. For this reason, it is necessary to briefly mention the basic axioms and properties of fuzzy implications [1].

2 Theoretical Background

In this paper as a definition of a fuzzy implication we will use the definition proposed by Kitainik [2], Foodor and Roubens [3].

2.1 Fuzzy Implication

Definition 1. A function $I : [0, 1] \times [0, 1] \rightarrow [0, 1]$ is called a fuzzy implication if for all $x, x_1, x_2, y, y_1, y_2 \in [0, 1]$ the following conditions are satisfied:

(I1) $x1 \leq x2$ then $I(x_1, y) \geq I(x_2, y)$, i.e., $I(\cdot, y)$ is decreasing,
(I2) $y1 \leq y2$ then $I(x, y_1) \leq I(x, y_2)$, i.e., $I(x, \cdot)$ is increasing,
(I3) $I(0, 0) = 1$
(I4) $I(1, 1) = 1$
(I5) $I(1, 0) = 0$

The set of all fuzzy implications will be denoted by $\mathcal{FI}$.
Examples for Fuzzy Implications are given in the Table 1 below:

Table 1. Examples for fuzzy implications.

Name	Formula implication
Lukasiewicz	$I_{LK}(x, y) = \min\{1, 1 - x + y\}$
Godel	$I_{GD}(x, y) = \begin{cases} 1 & \alpha v\ x \leq y \\ y & \alpha v\ x > y \end{cases}$
Reichenbach	$I_{RC}(x, y) = 1 - x + xy$
Kleene-Dienes	$I_{KD} = \max(1 - x, y)$

2.2 Basic Properties of Fuzzy Implications

Additional properties of fuzzy implications have been published in many works (see Trillas and Valverde [6], Dubois and Prade [7], Smets and Magrez [8], Fodor and Roubens [3], Gottwald [4]). The most important of them are presented below [1].

Definition 2. A fuzzy implication I is said to satisfy

– the left neutrality property, if

$$I(1, y) = y, \qquad y \in [0, 1] \qquad (NP)$$

– the exchange principle, if

$$I(x, I(y, z)) = I(y, I(x, z)), \quad x, y, z \in [0, 1] \quad (EP)$$

– the identity principle, if

$$I(x, x) = 1, \qquad x \in [0, 1] \qquad (IP)$$

– the ordering property, if

$$I(x, y) = 1 \Leftrightarrow x \leq y, \quad x, y \in [0, 1]. \quad (OP).$$

2.3 Fuzzy Negation

The fuzzy implication and fuzzy negation must be defined together.

A fuzzy negation N is a generalization of the classical complement or negation $\neg$. Fuzzy negation truth table consists of the two conditions: $\neg 1 \equiv 0$ *and* $\neg 0 \equiv 1$. The following definitions can be found in any introductory text book on Fuzzy logic (see, Fodor and Roubens [3], Klir and Yuan [4], Nguyen and Walker [5]).

Definition 3. A function $N: (0, 1) \rightarrow [0, 1]$ is called a Fuzzy negation if

$$N(0) = 1, \quad N(1) = 0 \tag{N1}$$

$$N \text{ is decreasing.} \tag{N2}$$

Definition 4

– A fuzzy negation N is called strict if, in addition,

$$N \text{ is strictly decreasing,} \tag{N3}$$

$$N \text{ is continious,} \tag{N4}$$

– A fuzzy negation N is called strong if the following property is met,

$$N(N(x)) = x, \qquad x \in [0, 1]. \tag{N5}$$

In this paper the strong negation will be denoted by

$$N_s(x) \qquad x \in [0, 1]$$

Examples for Fuzzy Negations are given in the Table 2 below:

Table 2. Examples of fuzzy negation with properties.

Formula	Properties
$N_K(x) = 1 - x^2$	N1 to N4 strict
$N_R(x) = 1 - \sqrt{x}$	N1 to N4 strict
Sugeno class $N^\lambda(x) = \frac{1-x}{1+\lambda x}$, $\lambda \in (-1, +\infty)$	N1 to N5 strong
Yager class $N^w(x) = (1 - x^w)^{\frac{1}{w}}$, $w \in (0, +\infty)$	N1 to N5 strong

2.4 Law of Contraposition

One of the most important tautologies in classical logic is the law of contraposition:

$$p \to q \equiv \neg q \to \neg p$$

$$\neg p \to q \equiv \neg q \to p$$

$$p \to \neg q \equiv q \to \neg p$$

Definition 5. Let $I \in \mathcal{FI}$ and N be a fuzzy negation. I is said to satisfy the

- law of contraposition with respect to N, if

$$I(x,y) = I(N(y), N(x)), \quad x, y \in [0, 1]. \qquad (CP)$$

- law of left contraposition with respect to N, if

$$I(N(x), y) = I(N(y), x), \quad x, y \in [0, 1] \qquad (L - CP)$$

- law of right contraposition with respect to N, if

$$I(x, N(y)) = I(y, N(x)), \quad x, y \in [0, 1] \qquad (R - CP)$$

If I satisfies the (left, right) law of contraposition with respect to N, then we denote this by $CP(N)$.

If I satisfies the left or right law of contraposition with respect to N, then we denote this by $L - CP(N)$ or $R - CP(N)$, respectively [1].

2.5 Natural Negations of Fuzzy Implications

Lemma 1. If a function $I : [0, 1]^2 \to [0, 1]$ satisfies $(I1), (I3)$ and $(I5)$, then the function $N_I : [0, 1] \to [0, 1]$ defined by

$$N_I(x) = I(x, 0), \quad x \in [0, 1] \qquad (1)$$

is a fuzzy negation. Proof [1].

Let $I \in \mathcal{FI}$. The function N_I defined by (1) is called the natural negation of I.

3 New Results

In this section, we will provide the definition of new generated implications and prove some propositions using definitions introduced in the previous sections.

3.1 Production of Fuzzy Implications Through Fuzzy Negations

Definition 7. Let $f : [0,1] \to [0,1]$ be a strictly decreasing and continuous function with $f(1) = 0, f(0) = 1$ and N a fuzzy negation. The function $I : [0,1]^2 \to [0,1]$ defined by

$$I(x,y) = f^{-1}(f(N(x)) \cdot f(y)), \ x,y \in [0,1] \tag{2}$$

is called an $f - generated$ implication and is denoted I_f.

Proposition 1. If f is an $f - generator$ and N is fuzzy negation, then $I_f \in \mathcal{FI}$.

Proof Firstly, since for every $x,y \in [0,1]$ we have $0 \le f(N(x)) \cdot f(y) \le 1$, we see that formula (3) is correctly defined.

- Since f is strictly decreasing, so is f^{-1} and for any $y \in [\mathbf{0,1}]$,

$$x_1 \le x_2 \Rightarrow N(x_1) \ge N(x_2) \Rightarrow f(N(x_1)) \le f(N(x_2)) \Rightarrow$$
$$f(N(x_1)) \cdot f(y) \le f(N(x_2)) \cdot f(y) \Rightarrow$$
$$f^{-1}(f(N(x_1)) \cdot f(y)) \ge f^{-1}(f(N(x_2)) \cdot f(y)) \Rightarrow$$
$$I(x_1,y) \ge I(x_2,y) \quad i.e., I_f \ satisfies \ (I1).$$

- Once again for any $x \in [\mathbf{0,1}]$, we have

$$y_1 \le y_2 \Rightarrow f(y_1) \ge f(y_2) \Rightarrow f(N(x)) \cdot f(y_1) \ge f(N(x)) \cdot f(y_2) \Rightarrow$$
$$f^{-1}(f(N(x)) \cdot f(y_1)) \le f^{-1}(f(N(x)) \cdot f(y_2)) \Rightarrow$$
$$I(x,y_1) \le I(x,y_2) \ i.e., \ I_f \ satisfies \ (I2).$$
$$I_f(0,0) = f^{-1}(f(N(0)) \cdot f(0)) =$$
$$= f^{-1}(f(1) \cdot 1) = f^{-1}(0) = 1 \ i.e., \ I_f \ satisfies \ (I3)..$$
$$I_f(1,1) = f^{-1}(f(N(1)) \cdot f(1)) = f^{-1}(f(0) \cdot 0) = f^{-1}(0) = 1 \ i.e., \ I_f \ satisfies \ (I1).$$
$$I_f(1,0) = f^{-1}(f(N(1)) \cdot f(0)) = f^{-1}(f(0) \cdot 1) = f^{-1}(1) = 0 \ i.e., \ I_f \ satisfies \ (I1).$$

3.2 Natural Negations and $f - generator$

Proposition 2. Let I_f be a fuzzy implication with respect to fuzzy negation N then the natural negation is N i.e., $N_{I_f} = N$.

Proof Actually

$$N_{I_f}(x) = I_f(x,0) = f^{-1}(f(N(x)) \cdot f(0)) = f^{-1}(f(N(x)) \cdot 1) =$$
$$f^{-1}(f(N(x))) = N(x).$$

3.3   Laws of Contraposition and I_f

Proposition 3. If N_s is the strong negation of I_f then I_f satisfies the law of contraposition with respect to N_s.

Proof

$$I_f(N_s(x), N_s(y)) = f^{-1}(f(N_s(N_s(x))) \cdot f(N_s(y))) = f^{-1}(f(x) \cdot f(N_s(y)))$$
$$= f^{-1}(f(N_s(y)) \cdot f(x)) = I_f(y,x).$$

Proposition 4. If N_s is the strong negation of I_f then I_f satisfies the law of left contraposition with respect to N_s.

Proof

$$I_f(N_s(x), y) = f^{-1}(f(N_s(N_s(x))) \cdot f(y)) = f^{-1}(f(x) \cdot f(y))$$
$$= f^{-1}(f(x) \cdot f(N_s(N_s(y)))) = f^{-1}(f(x) \cdot f(N_s(N_s(y))))$$
$$= f^{-1}(f(N_s(N_s(y))) \cdot f(x)) == I_f(N_s(y), x).$$

Proposition 5. If N_s is the strong negation of I_f then I_f satisfies the law of right contraposition with respect to N_s.

Proof

$$I_f(x, N_sN(y)) = f^{-1}(f(N_s(x))) \cdot f(N_s(y)) =$$
$$f^{-1}(f(N_s(y)) \cdot f(N_s(x))) = f^{-1}(f(N_s(y)) \cdot f(N_s(x))) =$$
$$= I_f(y, N_s(x)).$$

3.4   The Left Neutrality Property

Proposition 6. Let I_f be a fuzzy implication with respect to negation N, then the fuzzy implication I_f satisfies the left neutrality property.

Proof

$$I_f(1,y) = f^{-1}(f(N(1)) \cdot f(y)) = f^{-1}(f(0) \cdot f(y)) = f^{-1}(1 \cdot f(y)) =$$
$$I_f(1,1) = f^{-1}(f(y)) = y.$$

3.5 The Exchange Principle

Proposition 7. Let I_f be a fuzzy implication with respect to negation N, then a fuzzy implication I_f satisfies the exchange principle.

Proof

$$\begin{aligned}
I_f\left(x, I_f(y,z)\right) &= f^{-1}\left(f(N(x)) \cdot f\left(I_f(y,z)\right)\right) \\
&= f^{-1}(f(N(x)) \cdot f(f^{-1}(f(N(y)) \cdot f(z)) \\
&= f^{-1}(f(N(x)) \cdot f(N(y)) \cdot f(z)) \\
&= f^{-1}(f(N(y)) \cdot f(N(x)) \cdot f(z)).
\end{aligned}$$

Similarly

$$\begin{aligned}
I_f\left(y, I_f(x,z)\right) &= f^{-1}\left(f(N(y)) \cdot f\left(I_f(x,z)\right)\right) = f^{-1}(f(N(y)) \cdot f(f^{-1}(f(N(x)) \cdot f(z)) \\
&= f^{-1}(f(N(y)) \cdot f(N(x)) \cdot f(z))
\end{aligned}$$

Therefore

$$I_f\left(x, I_f(y,z)\right) = I_f\left(y, I_f(x,z)\right).$$

3.6 The Identity Principle

Proposition 8. Let I_f be a fuzzy implication with respect to negation N, then a fuzzy implication I_f satisfies the identity principle if and only if $x = 0$ or $x = 1$.

Proof

$$\begin{aligned}
I_f(x,x) = 1 &\Leftrightarrow f^{-1}(f(N(x)) \cdot f(x)) = 1 \\
&\Leftrightarrow f(N(x)) \cdot f(x) = f(1) \\
&\Leftrightarrow f(N(x)) \cdot f(x) = 0 \\
&\Leftrightarrow f(N(x)) = 0 \ or \ f(x) = 0 \\
&\Leftrightarrow N(x) = 1 \ or \ x = 1 \\
&\Leftrightarrow x = 0 \ or \ x = 1.
\end{aligned}$$

3.7 The Ordering Property

Proposition 9. Let I_f be a fuzzy implication with respect to negation N, then a fuzzy implication I_f satisfies the ordering property if and only if $x = 0$ or $x = 1$.

Proof

$$I_f(x, y) = 1 \Leftrightarrow f^{-1}(f(N(x)) \cdot f(y)) = 1$$
$$\Leftrightarrow f(N(x)) \cdot f(y) = f(1)$$
$$\Leftrightarrow f(N(x)) \cdot f(y) = 0$$
$$\Leftrightarrow f(N(x)) = 0 \ or \ f(y) = 0$$
$$\Leftrightarrow N(x) = 1 \ or \ y = 1$$
$$\Leftrightarrow x = 0 \ or \ y = 1.$$

i.e., $x = 0 \le y, \forall y \in [0, 1]$ or $x \le 1, \forall x \in [0, 1]$.

3.8   Example

Let $f(x) = 1 - x$ strictly decreasing

and fuzzy negation $N(x) = \begin{cases} 1, & if \ x = 0 \\ 0, & if \ x \in (0, 1] \end{cases}$ then

the implication of Definition 6 yields

$$I(x, y) = f^{-1}(f(N(x)) \cdot f(y))$$
$$if \ x = 1 \ then \ N(0) = 1 \ therefore$$

$$I(x, y) = f^{-1}(f(1) \cdot f(y)) \Leftrightarrow I(x, y) = f^{-1}(0 \cdot f(y)) \Leftrightarrow I(x, y) = f^{-1}(0) = 1$$
$$\Leftrightarrow I(x, y) = f^{-1}(0) = 1.$$

$$if \ x \in (0, 1] \ then \ N(x) = 0 \ therefore$$

$$I(x, y) = f^{-1}(f(0) \cdot f(y)) \Leftrightarrow I(x, y) = f^{-1}(1 \cdot f(y)) = f^{-1}(f(y)) = y$$

That is, we produce (implication)

$$I(x, y) = \begin{cases} 1, & if \ x = 0 \\ y, & if \ x \in (0, 1] \end{cases}.$$

4   Conclusion

The above procedure has enabled us to generate a new class of fuzzy implications. The importance of this relies on the fact that the reasoning process has improved, since we have the possibility, for a given application, to choose the most appropriate implication from a wider class. This methodology, to choose the most suitable fuzzy implication from a given class of implications, will be applied in a forthcoming study based on statistical data from previous research ([10–12]).

References

1. Baczynski, M., Balasubramaniam, J.: Fuzzy Implications. Springer, Heidelberg (2008). https://doi.org/10.1007/978-3-540-69082-5
2. Kitainik, L.: Fuzzy decision procedures with binary relations. Kluwer, Dordrecht (1993)
3. Fodor, J.C., Roubens, M.: Fuzzy preference modelling and multicriteria decision support. Kluwer, Dordrecht (1994)
4. Klir, G.J., Yuan, B.: Fuzzy sets and fuzzy logic. Theory and applications. Prentice Hall, New Jersey (1995)
5. Nguyen, H.T., Walker, E.A.: A first course in fuzzy logic, 2nd edn. CRC Press, BocaRaton (2000)
6. Trillas, E., Valverde, L.: On implication and indistinguishability in the setting of fuzzy logic. In: Kacprzyk, J., Yager, R.R. (eds.) Management Decision Support Systems Using Fuzzy Sets and Possibility Theory, pp. 198–212. TÜV-Rhineland, Cologne (1985)
7. Dubois, D., Prade, H.: Fuzzy sets in approximate reasoning. Part 1: Inference with possibility distributions. Fuzzy Sets Syst. **40**, 143–202 (1991). https://doi.org/10.1016/0165-0114(91)90050-Z
8. Smets, P., Magrez, P.: Implication in fuzzy logic. Internat. J. Approx. Reason. **1**, 327–347 (1987). https://doi.org/10.1016/0888-613X(87)90023-5
9. Gottwald, S.: A Treatise on Many-Valued Logics. Research Studies Press, Baldock (2001)
10. Ellina, G., Papaschinopoulos, G., Papadopoulos, B.K.: Fuzzy inference systems selection of the most appropriate fuzzy implication from available lake water quality statistical data. Environ. Process. **4**(4), 923–935 (2017). https://doi.org/10.1007/s40710-017-0266-3
11. Pagouropoulos, P., Tzimopoulos, Christos D., Papadopoulos, Basil K.: A method for the detection of the most suitable fuzzy implication for data applications. In: Boracchi, G., Iliadis, L., Jayne, C., Likas, A. (eds.) EANN 2017. CCIS, vol. 744, pp. 242–255. Springer, Cham (2017). https://doi.org/10.1007/978-3-319-65172-9_21
12. Botzoris, N.G., Papadopoulos, K., Papadopoulos, K.B.: A method for the evaluation and selection of an appropriate fuzzy implication by using statistical data. Fuzzy Econ. Rev. **20**(2), 19–29 (2015)

Facial/Emotion Recognition

Improving Ensemble Learning Performance with Complementary Neural Networks for Facial Expression Recognition

Xinmin Zhang and Yingdong Ma[✉]

The School of Computer Science, Inner Mongolia University, Hohhot, China
csmyd@imu.edu.cn

Abstract. Facial expression recognition has significant application value in fields such as human-computer interaction. Recently, Convolutional Neural Networks (CNNs) have been widely utilized for feature extraction and expression recognition. Network ensemble is an important step to improve recognition performance. To improve the inefficiency of existing ensemble strategy, we propose a new ensemble method to efficiently find networks with complementary capabilities. The proposed method is verified on two groups of CNNs with different depth (eight 5-layer shallow CNNs and twelve 11-layer deep VGGNet variants) trained on FER-2013 and RAF-DB, respectively. Experimental results demonstrate that the proposed method achieves the highest recognition accuracy of 74.14% and 85.46% on FER-2013 and RAF-DB database, respectively, to the best of our knowledge, outperforms state-of-the-art CNN-based facial expression recognition methods. In addition, our method also obtains a competitive result of the mean diagonal value in confusion matrix on RAF-DB test set.

Keywords: Convolutional Neural Networks · Ensemble learning Expression recognition

1 Introduction

Facial Expression Recognition (FER) analyzes the category (e.g., happiness, sadness) of human expression based on face recognition. FER has been widely studied as accurate recognition of human facial expression is a fundamental step for many computer vision applications, such as medical security and human-computer interaction. Significant progress has been made in the last decade [1–5]. However, FER is a difficult task due to various illumination conditions, head position and occlusion in different face images. If feature extraction is carried out directly using these raw data, it would increase feature extraction error and eventually reduce FER performance. As a result, before feature extraction, preprocessing of facial images is necessary, such as face recognition, facial landmarks detection, face registration, histogram equalization, etc.

Despite the continues research efforts, FER under uncontrolled environment is still a challenging problem [5]. So far, most top performance approaches tend to utilize shallow neural networks with ensemble learning methods [5–7]. Ensemble of networks

V. Kůrková et al. (Eds.): ICANN 2018, LNCS 11139, pp. 747–759, 2018.
https://doi.org/10.1007/978-3-030-01418-6_73

not only makes use of strong feature learning ability of neural networks, but also explores the ability of different networks to complement each other during ensemble learning. As a result, ensemble of multiple networks usually has better FER performance than single classifier based methods. However, these methods have three main limitations: (1) shallow networks need more training overhead than deep networks to reach the same training termination condition; (2) because of the weak fitting ability, shallow networks are often inferior to deep networks in terms of performance; (3) most ensemble learning methods utilize all trained networks to make final decisions. But according to our experiment, ensemble of all networks does not necessarily achieve optimal performance. To solve these problems, in this paper, we propose a new ensemble learning method which combines complementary CNNs to achieve high performance with less time consumption. The method framework is shown in Fig. 1. The main steps of this method are summarized as follows:

- Twenty CNNs (including twelve deep CNNs and eight shallow CNNs) are trained as the candidate network set.
- An optimal deep network is selected to form our baseline system according to recognition performance.
- Candidate networks are added to or removed from our system until the best performance is achieved.

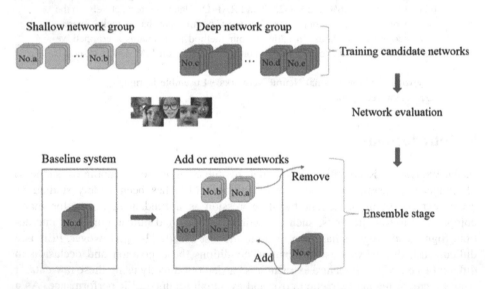

Fig. 1. Overview of our ensemble method.

The proposed method is evaluated on two real-world facial expression databases (FER-2013 [8] and RAF-DB [9]). To the best of our knowledge, our method outperforms state-of-the-art top performing works on FER-2013 and RAF-DB databases.

2 Related Works

2.1 Facial Landmarks Detection and Expression Recognition

Face images obtained under non-restrictive settings tend to have different degrees of occlusions and varied postures. To extract accurate facial features from these images, facial landmarks detection is usually required. Xiong and Torre proposed a Supervised Descent Method for minimizing a Non-linear Least Squares function. They also proposed a well-defined alignment error function which can be minimized using existing algorithms [10]. Sun et al. proposed an effective three-layer CNNs cascaded for facial landmarks detection [11]. Ren et al. learned a set of highly discriminative local binary features for each facial landmark independently [12]. These features are then used to jointly learn a linear regression to quickly locate facial landmarks. Zhu et al. proposed a 3D Dense Face Alignment and used cascaded CNNs to handle face alignment in the case of large pose variations and self-occlusions [13].

Kim et al. utilized alignable faces and non-alignable faces to improve FER performance [7]. They designed an alignment-mapping network to learn how to generate aligned faces from non-aligned faces. Rudovic et al. proposed a probabilistic method to implement facial expression recognition using head pose invariant [14]. The method performed head pose estimation, head pose normalization and facial expression recognition based on 39 facial landmarks.

2.2 Neural Networks

Krizhevsky et al. [15] proposed an eight-layer CNN in 2012 and made breakthrough progress in image classification. Because of their powerful feature representation ability, neural networks have been successfully applied to many computer vision applications, such as speech recognition [16] and semantic segmentation [17]. Recently, several FER methods utilized deep neural networks for improving performance. Liu et al. proposed a Boosted Deep Belief Network framework to carry out feature learning, feature selection and classifier construction iteratively [18]. Mollahosseini et al. proposed a deep neural architecture which applied the Inception layer [19] to address FER problem across multiple standard face databases [20]. In [21], Tang showed that significant gains can be obtained on several deep learning databases by simply replacing softmax with L2-SVMs. Meng et al. proposed an identity-aware convolutional neural network to alleviate high inter-subject variations [22]. They introduced an expression-sensitive contrastive loss and an identity-sensitive contrastive loss to show that learning features are not influenced by the variations of facial expression and different subjects. Vo et al. proposed CNN-based method to detect global and local facial expression features [23]. In their work, global features were computed to obtain possible candidate classification results for a face, and then, local features were utilized to reorder the previously obtained candidates to yield final recognition results.

2.3 Ensemble Learning

Ensemble learning builds a hypothesis set by training a series of learners [24]. It has been studied for a long time towards ensemble multiple neural networks in different visual fields [25–28]. As different neural networks provide complementary decision-making information, theoretically, the more diverse training networks are, the better performance they will be. Data preprocessing and different training configuration schemes can lead to network diversity (e.g., using different training sets, whether to adopt the dropout strategy [29]). In recent FER studies, combination of deep learning and ensemble learning has made remarkable progress. Yu and Zhang trained six 8-layer CNNs and automatically learned the ensemble weights among these networks by optimizing two loss functions [5]. Kim et al. constructed a hierarchical committee architecture with exponentially weighted decision fusion [6]. They combined nine 5-layer shallow CNNs with three 3-layer MLP classifiers (trained using features extracted from three alignment-mapping networks) in test stage [7]. Images in the training and test set were divided into alignable faces and non-alignable faces. The results on FER-2013 database showed that combination of alignable faces and non-alignable faces can improve FER performance.

3 Proposed Approach

3.1 Problem Analysis

Depth of Networks. In general, adding network layers leads to significant increasing of network parameters. As a result, it increases the training overhead in time and space. For this reason, many works have limited the training to shallow networks [5–7]. However, we observe counter-examples in our experiments. For example, when using "Xavier" [30] for parameter initialization and "ReLU" for activation to train FER-2013 database, shallow networks spend more training time than deep networks. Nevertheless, these networks do not get expected performance improvement. This fact shows that considering the time overhead and recognition accuracy, we should primarily train deep networks.

As some literatures have pointed out, the diversity of networks affects ensemble performance. However, to our best knowledge, most works did not explore the diversity of network depth. We believe that ensemble learning performance can be improved if shallow networks can also be trained to utilize network diversity.

Ensemble Strategy. Ensemble of all networks does not necessarily achieve optimal performance, which is mainly based on the following consideration: some networks do not provide complementary capabilities to other networks. In this case, addition of more networks might introduce negative effects for samples which had been predicted correctly.

3.2 Configurations of All Networks

Considering different data preprocessing, parameter initialization, activation function, training settings and network layer settings can lead to a variety of network models, we train eight 5-layer networks (shallow CNNs) and twelve 11-layer VGGNet [31] variants (deep CNNs) for ensemble stage.

The forward propagation process of 5-layer shallow CNNs is shown in Fig. 2. The architecture can be simplified as CPCPCPFDF (C, P, F, and D stands for Convolution, Pooling, Fully connected layer, and Dropout, respectively). The detailed configurations of 5-layer networks are summarized in Table 1. All of these networks use ReLU [32] as activation function.

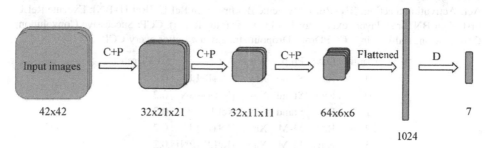

Fig. 2. The forward propagation process of 5-layer shallow CNNs.

Table 1. Configurations of eight 5-layer networks. Raw: Raw train data. Hist: Histogram equalization. Prep: Preprocessing methods. Stand: Standardization. M-M: Maximum-Minimum normalization. WIni: Weight Initialization. TruN: Truncation Normal distribution. Xav: Xavier initialization [30]. WRe: Weight Regularization. FCDrop: Dropout strategy used in Fully Connected layer (FC). FC_1: The first Fully Connected layer.

Config	Data	Prep	WIni	WRe	FCDrop
1	Raw	Stand	TruN	0.0001	$FC_1 = 0.5$
2	Raw	Stand	Xav	0.0001	$FC_1 = 0.5$
3	Raw	M-M	TruN	0.0001	$FC_1 = 0.5$
4	Raw	M-M	Xav	0.0001	$FC_1 = 0.5$
5	Hist	Stand	TruN	0.0001	$FC_1 = 0.5$
6	Hist	Stand	Xav	0.0001	$FC_1 = 0.5$
7	Hist	M-M	TruN	0.0001	$FC_1 = 0.5$
8	Hist	M-M	Xav	0.0001	$FC_1 = 0.5$

The forward propagation process of 11-layer VGGNet variants is shown in Fig. 3. Their architecture can be expressed as 4*(CCPD)FDFF (4* indicates repeat four times). The detailed configurations of 11-layer CNNs are summarized in Table 2. The activation process of 11-layer CNNs uses BN+ReLU, ReLU+BN, and ReLU, respectively.

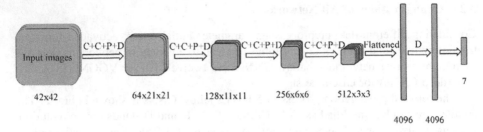

Fig. 3. The forward propagation process of 11-layer VGGNet variants.

Table 2. Configurations of twelve 11-layer VGGNet variants. BN: Batch Normalization [33]. Act: Activation function. BN+ReLU: Execute BN first, then ReLU. [ReLU+BN]: Execute ReLU first, then BN for all layers except for last FC layer (only ReLU). CCP: Successive Convolution, Convolution, and Pooling. CCPDrop: Dropout strategy used after every CCP.

Config	Data	Prep	WIni	Act	CCPDrop
9	Raw	Stand	Xav	BN+ReLU	0.2
10	Raw	Stand	Xav	[ReLU+BN]	0.2
11	Raw	Stand	Xav	ReLU	0.2
12	Raw	M-M	Xav	BN+ReLU	0.2
13	Raw	M-M	Xav	[ReLU+BN]	0.2
14	Raw	M-M	Xav	ReLU	0.2
15	Hist	Stand	Xav	BN+ReLU	0.2
16	Hist	Stand	Xav	[ReLU+BN]	0.2
17	Hist	Stand	Xav	ReLU	0.2
18	Hist	M-M	Xav	BN+ReLU	0.2
19	Hist	M-M	Xav	[ReLU+BN]	0.2
20	Hist	M-M	Xav	ReLU	0.2

In training stage, we use exponential decay learning to update a new learning rate. The learning rate of a network is updated as:

$$\eta = \eta_0 * (0.99)^N \tag{1}$$

where η_0 denotes the initial learning rate, η represents new learning rate, and N is the number of epochs. In order to fully learn the feature of training samples, a more severe termination condition must be satisfied to stop the training, that is, the training error of a batch does not exceed 10^{-6} for three consecutive times or the training reaches maximum number of iterations.

3.3   Ensemble Method

According to the above analysis, combination of complementary CNNs improves system performance. It can be achieved by gradually adding networks that improve recognition accuracy and removing networks which cause system performance degradation.

In general, the fitting ability of deep networks is better than that of shallow networks. Therefore, at the beginning, we select a network with the best accuracy from deep network group as our baseline system.

In the next step, candidate networks from all shallow and deep networks are added to or removed from baseline system step by step until the best performance is achieved. The system ensemble mode in this paper is majority vote. It is important to note that the evaluation scores of all networks on validation and test data have been calculated in advance, so we do not need to spend a long time in the process of ensemble selection. All we need to do is matrix addition.

4 Experiments on the FER-2013 Database

4.1 FER-2013

FER-2013 [8] is one of the largest facial expression databases so far. It has 28,709 images for training, 3,589 images for public test, and 3,589 images for private test. To reduce training errors, we remove 46 non-face images and 11 non-number filled images from original database.

We use IntraFace [10, 34] to detect facial landmarks. We label an image as Non-Alignable Faces (NAF) if its detection score is smaller than a given threshold, and otherwise, label it as Before Registered Alignable Faces (BRAF). The affine transformation principle is applied to adjust two eyes to horizontal position. We refer to the After Registered Alignable Faces as ARAF.

Data increment is implemented for training, validation and test set following the method introduced in [7]. Specifically, 10 times increment are used in this work (four 42 * 42 corners and a resize of original image, as well as their horizontal flip images).

4.2 Training and Evaluation

In training stage, the initial learning rate of shallow and deep network group is set to 0.05. The maximum number of iterations for shallow and deep network groups is 600000 and 200000, respectively.

During validation and testing stage, the score of each image is the mean of 10 corresponding incremental images. For Alignable Faces (AF), we evaluate Before Registered Alignable Faces (BRAF) and After Registered Alignable Faces (ARAF) respectively and average the two values. After evaluating Non-Alignable Faces (NAF), results of all validation (testing) samples are combined using the following formula:

$$acc = acc(AF) * \alpha + acc(NAF) * \beta \qquad (2)$$

where α is the proportion of alignable faces in validation (testing) set, and β is the proportion of non-alignable faces in validation (testing) set.

4.3   Ensemble and Analysis

For FER-2013, we conduct network ensemble experiments on validation set. After determining the optimal network combination, testing set is used as the final performance evaluation.

Baseline System. In deep network group, network No. 11 is selected as the baseline system as it has the highest validation accuracy (70.52%).

Ensemble Process. In this experiment, ensemble of all deep and shallow networks is utilized to explore the change of system performance. Candidate networks are selected from deep and shallow network groups. At the beginning, network No. 18 is selected as combination of No. 18 and baseline system set has top performance (71.79%). In the second step, network No. 13 is selected as combination of network No. 13 and new system has best performance (72.35%). This process continues until system performance is no longer growth. In the seventh step, after removing network No. 3, the highest performance (72.64%) is obtained. The ensemble process is summarized in Table 3. We observe performance reduction when more networks are added. For example, ensemble of all 20 networks yields 72.30% validation accuracy. Finally, the system achieves 74.14% test accuracy with an ensemble of five deep CNNs.

Table 3. Ensemble process on FER-2013.

Steps	System	Acc	Select	Candidate
1	11	70.52	18	1–20
2	11 18	71.79	13	1–20
3	11 18 13	72.35	9	1–20
4	11 18 13 9	72.42	12	1–20
5	11 18 13 9 12	72.64	3	1–20
6	11 18 13 9 12 3	72.62	–	1–20
7#	11 18 13 9 12	72.64	3	1–20

To prove the feasibility of our method, we list ensemble accuracy of the shallow network group, the deep network group, and all networks on the validation set in Table 4.

Table 4. Performance comparison of different combinations on FER-2013.

Networks	Accuracy
Shallow network group	70.52
Deep network group	72.16
All 20 networks	72.30

Result Analysis. Table 5 lists performance comparison of ours and state-of-the-art works on the FER-2013 database. The proposed method only combines five deep

CNNs (11-layer) to achieve 74.14% test accuracy. To our best knowledge, this method outperforms other state-of-the-art CNN-based FER methods. Moreover, the proposed method is efficient than other methods. The method is implemented on a personal computer with i7-7700k CPU, 16 GB memory and a GTX 1080Ti GPU. The average time to process a test image using a shallow network and a deep network is 12.3 ms and 14.1 ms, respectively. Ensemble of five deep networks consumes 72.7 ms. As a contrast, [5] and [7] spend 76.3 ms and 146.6 ms to process the same image on our personal computer.

Table 5. Performance comparison of the proposed method and state-of-the-art works on FER-2013.

	Methods	Accuracy	Average time (ms)
[21]	A DCN using L2-SVM Loss.	71.16%	–
	A DCN using cross-entropy Loss	70.1%	–
[5]	Ensemble of six 8-layer CNNs using learned weights	72%	76.3
[6]	Ensemble of 36 DCNs in a hierarchical committee	72.72%	–
[7]	Ensemble three MLP classifiers and nine 5-layer CNNs	73.73%	146.6
Ours	Five 11-layer CNNs	**74.14%**	**72.7**

5   Experiments on the RAF-DB Database

5.1   RAF-DB

RAF-DB [9] is also a real-world facial expression database that used the crowdsourcing technology for facial annotation. The database contains about 30000 images of basic 7 single-class expressions and 11 compound expressions. In our experiment, we use only 15339 registrated images of single-class expressions, including 12271 training images and 3068 test images. We tripled the training and test set, including an original image, and its horizontal mirror and vertical mirror.

5.2   Training and Evaluation

In training stage, the initial learning rate of shallow and deep network group is set to 0.01 and 0.05, respectively. The maximum number of iterations for shallow and deep network group is 200000 and 20000, respectively.

During testing stage, the score of each image is the mean of three corresponding incremental images.

5.3   Ensemble and Analysis

Baseline System. Similar to FER-2013, the best performing network No. 19 (83.41%) from deep network group is selected as baseline system.

Ensemble Process. Candidate networks are also selected from deep and shallow network groups. In the third step, the system performance increases to 85.46% when three networks are combined. Please see Table 6 for detail information. Since then, adding more networks leads to system performance reduction. For instance, adding network No. 19 reduces system performance from 85.46% to 85.23%. However, the highest ensemble performance can be observed after removing network No. 19 from system network set. Finally, the system achieves 85.46% accuracy with an ensemble of two deep CNNs and one shallow CNNs.

Table 6. Ensemble process on RAF-DB.

Steps	System	Acc	Select	Candidate
1	19	83.41	13	1–20
2	19 13	84.88	3	1–20
3	19 13 3	85.46	19	1–20
4	19 13 3 19	85.23	–	1–20
5#	19 13 3	85.46	19	1–20

In Table 7, we list the ensemble performance of shallow network group, deep network group, and all 20 networks on the RAF-DB database.

Table 7. Performance comparison of different combinations on RAF-DB.

Networks	Accuracy
Shallow network group	83.54
Deep network group	84.39
All 20 networks	84.42

Table 8. Our method is compared with the existing methods on two evaluation criteria: diagonal average of confusion matrix (Ave) and recognition accuracy (Acc). The results of center loss [35] + LDA, center loss + mSVM, DLP-CNN [9] + LDA and DLP-CNN + mSVM are tested in [9]. Seven numbers in the second line represent the number of samples of different expressions on original training set. Sur: Surprise, Fea: Fear, Dis: Disgust, Hap: Happy, Ang: Anger, Neu: Neutral.

Methods	Sur	Fea	Dis	Hap	Sad	Ang	Neu	Ave	Acc
	1290	281	717	4772	1982	705	2524		
Our	80.24	47.30	45	94.68	82.22	74.07	90.59	**73.44**	**85.46**
center loss + LDA	76.29	54.05	49.38	92.41	74.90	64.81	77.21	69.86	79.96
center loss + mSVM	79.63	54.05	53.13	93.08	78.45	68.52	83.24	72.87	82.86
DLP-CNN + LDA	74.07	52.50	55.41	90.21	73.64	77.51	73.53	70.98	78.81
DLP-CNN + mSVM	81.16	62.16	52.15	92.83	80.13	71.60	80.29	74.20	82.84

Result Analysis. The proposed ensemble method not only achieves the best recognition accuracy, but also have competitive results for the average accuracy of seven single-class expressions (the mean diagonal value of confusion matrix). After ensemble of three networks, the values of diagonal in the confusion matrix are shown in Table 8. As shown in the table, four existing methods are listed for comparison. All of them apply different loss functions to train neural networks, and then use feature vectors extracted to train LDA and SVM classifier. In contrast, our method only uses softmax loss for training, and directly uses neural networks to present competitive classification performance.

6 Conclusion

In this paper, we propose a new ensemble learning based method for improving facial expression recognition. Specifically, two groups of CNNs (eight 5-layer CNNs and twelve 11-layer CNNs) are trained with various configurations. On this basis, a new network ensemble method is proposed to combine complementary CNNs to improve FER performance. Extensive experiments on FER-2013 and RAF-DB show that the proposed method achieves excellent recognition accuracy with less time overhead. Performance comparison of the proposed method and state-of-the-art works demonstrates that our method reaches the best recognition accuracy (74.14%) on the FER-2013 database. On RAF-DB database, our ensemble method also achieves the highest recognition accuracy (85.46%) and competitive performance of diagonal mean value of confusion matrix (73.44%) without complicated training process.

References

1. Shan, C., Gong, S., McOwan, P.W.: Robust facial expression recognition using local binary patterns. In: IEEE International Conference on Image Processing, vol. 2, pp. II-370 (2005)
2. Liu, W., Wang, Z.: Facial expression recognition based on fusion of multiple Gabor features. In: 18th International Conference on Pattern Recognition, vol. 3, pp. 536–539 (2006)
3. Happy, S., Routray, A.: Automatic facial expression recognition using features of salient facial patches. IEEE Trans. Affect. Comput. 6(1), 1–12 (2015)
4. Jung, H., Lee, S., Yim, J., Park, S., Kim, J.: Joint fine-tuning in deep neural networks for facial expression recognition. In: Proceedings of the IEEE International Conference on Computer Vision, pp. 2983–2991 (2015)
5. Yu, Z., Zhang, C.: Image based static facial expression recognition with multiple deep network learning. In: Proceedings of the 2015 ACM on International Conference on Multimodal Interaction, pp. 435–442 (2015)
6. Kim, B.K., Roh, J., Dong, S.Y., Lee, S.Y.: Hierarchical committee of deep convolutional neural networks for robust facial expression recognition. J. Multimodal User Interfaces 10 (2), 173–189 (2016)
7. Kim, B.K., Dong, S.Y., Roh, J., Kim, G., Lee, S.Y.: Fusing aligned and non-aligned face information for automatic affect recognition in the wild: a deep learning approach. In: Proceedings of the IEEE Conference on Computer Vision and Pattern Recognition Workshops, pp. 48–57 (2016)

8. Goodfellow, I.J., et al.: Challenges in representation learning: a report on three machine learning contests. Neural Netw. **64**, 59–63 (2015)
9. Li, S., Deng, W., Du, J.P.: Reliable crowdsourcing and deep locality-preserving learning for expression recognition in the wild. In: IEEE Conference on Computer Vision and Pattern Recognition, pp. 2584–2593 (2017)
10. Xiong, X., De la Torre, F.: Supervised descent method and its applications to face alignment. In: Proceedings of the IEEE Conference on Computer Vision and Pattern Recognition, pp. 532–539 (2013)
11. Sun, Y., Wang, X., Tang, X.: Deep convolutional network cascade for facial point detection. In: Proceedings of the IEEE Conference on Computer Vision and Pattern Recognition, pp. 3476–3483 (2013)
12. Ren, S., Cao, X., Wei, Y., Sun, J.: Face alignment at 3000 fps via regressing local binary features. In: Proceedings of the IEEE Conference on Computer Vision and Pattern Recognition, pp. 1685–1692 (2014)
13. Zhu, X., Lei, Z., Liu, X., Shi, H., Li, S.Z.: Face alignment across large poses: A 3D solution. In: Proceedings of the IEEE Conference on Computer Vision and Pattern Recognition, pp. 146–155 (2016)
14. Rudovic, O., Pantic, M., Patras, I.: Coupled gaussian processes for pose-invariant facial expression recognition. IEEE Trans. Pattern Anal. Mach. Intell. **35**(6), 1357–1369 (2013)
15. Krizhevsky, A., Sutskever, I., Hinton, G.E.: ImageNet classification with deep convolutional neural networks. In: Advances in Neural Information Processing Systems, pp. 1097–1105 (2012)
16. Hinton, G., et al.: Deep neural networks for acoustic modeling in speech recognition: the shared views of four research groups. IEEE Sig. Process. Mag. **29**(6), 82–97 (2012)
17. Long, J., Shelhamer, E., Darrell, T.: Fully convolutional networks for semantic segmentation. In: Proceedings of the IEEE Conference on Computer Vision and Pattern Recognition, pp. 3431–3440 (2015)
18. Liu, P., Han, S., Meng, Z., Tong, Y.: Facial expression recognition via a boosted deep belief network. In: Proceedings of the IEEE Conference on Computer Vision and Pattern Recognition, pp. 1805–1812 (2014)
19. Szegedy, C., et al.: Going deeper with convolutions. In: Proceedings of the IEEE Conference on Computer Vision and Pattern Recognition, pp. 1–9 (2015)
20. Mollahosseini, A., Chan, D., Mahoor, M.H.: Going deeper in facial expression recognition using deep neural networks. In: IEEE Winter Conference on Applications of Computer Vision, pp. 1–10 (2016)
21. Tang, Y.: Deep learning using linear support vector machines. Comput. Sci. (2013)
22. Meng, Z., Liu, P., Cai, J., Han, S., Tong, Y.: Identity-aware convolutional neural network for facial expression recognition. In: IEEE International Conference on Automatic Face and Gesture Recognition, pp. 558–565 (2017)
23. Vo, D.M., Sugimoto, A., Le, T.H.: Facial expression recognition by re-ranking with global and local generic features. In: 23rd International Conference on Pattern Recognition, pp. 4118–4123 (2016)
24. Zhou, Z.H.: Ensemble learning. In: Li, S.Z. (ed.) Encyclopedia of Biometrics, vol. 1, pp. 270–273. Springer, Berlin (2009)
25. Hansen, L.K.: Neural network ensemble. IEEE Trans. Pattern Anal. Mach. Intell. **12**, 993–1001 (1990)
26. Guan, Y., Li, C.T., Roli, F.: On reducing the effect of covariate factors in gait recognition: a classifier ensemble method. IEEE Trans. Pattern Anal. Mach. Intell. **37**(7), 1521–1528 (2015)

27. Paisitkriangkrai, S., Shen, C., van den Hengel, A.: Pedestrian detection with spatially pooled features and structured ensemble learning. IEEE Trans. Pattern Anal. Mach. Intell. **38**(6), 1243–1257 (2016)
28. Ding, C., Tao, D.: Trunk-branch ensemble convolutional neural networks for video-based face recognition. IEEE Trans. Pattern Anal. Mach. Intell. **40**(4), 1002–1014 (2018)
29. Hinton, G.E., Srivastava, N., Krizhevsky, A., Sutskever, I., Salakhutdinov, R.R.: Improving neural networks by preventing co-adaptation of feature detectors. Comput. Sci. **3**(4), 212–223 (2012)
30. Glorot, X., Bengio, Y.: Understanding the difficulty of training deep feedforward neural networks. In: Proceedings of the Thirteenth International Conference on Artificial Intelligence and Statistics, pp. 249–256 (2010)
31. Simonyan, K., Zisserman, A.: Very deep convolutional networks for large-scale image recognition. Comput Sci. (2014)
32. Nair, V., Hinton, G.E.: Rectified linear units improve restricted Boltzmann machines. In: Proceedings of the 27th International Conference on Machine Learning, pp. 807–814 (2010)
33. Ioffe, S., Szegedy, C.: Batch normalization: accelerating deep network training by reducing internal covariate shift. In: International Conference on Machine Learning, pp. 448–456 (2015)
34. Fernando, D.L.T., Chu, W.S., Xiong, X., Vicente, F., Ding, X., Cohn, J.: Intraface. In: 11th IEEE International Conference and Workshops on Automatic Face and Gesture Recognition (FG), pp. 1–8 (2015)
35. Wen, Y., Zhang, K., Li, Z., Qiao, Y.: A discriminative feature learning approach for deep face recognition. In: Leibe, B., Matas, J., Sebe, N., Welling, M. (eds.) ECCV 2016. LNCS, vol. 9911, pp. 499–515. Springer, Cham (2016). https://doi.org/10.1007/978-3-319-46478-7_31

Automatic Beautification for Group-Photo Facial Expressions Using Novel Bayesian GANs

Ji Liu[1], Shuai Li[1,2(✉)], Wenfeng Song[1], Liang Liu[1], Hong Qin[3], and Aimin Hao[1]

[1] Beihang University, Beijing, China
{lishuai,ham}@buaa.edu.cn
[2] Qingdao Research Institute, Beihang University, Beijing, China
[3] Stony Brook University (SUNY at Stony Brook), Stony Brook, USA
qin@cs.stonybrook.edu

Abstract. Directly benefiting from the powerful generative adversarial networks (GANs) in recent years, various new image processing tasks pertinent to image generation and synthesis have gained more popularity with the growing success. One such application is individual portrait photo beautification based on facial expression detection and editing. Yet, automatically beautifying group photos without tedious and fragile human interventions still remains challenging. The difficulties inevitably arise from diverse facial expression evaluation, harmonious expression generation, and context-sensitive synthesis from single/multiple photos. To ameliorate, we devise a two-stage deep network for automatic group-photo evaluation and beautification by seamless integration of multi-label CNN with Bayesian network enhanced GANs. First, our multi-label CNN is designed to evaluate the quality of facial expressions. Second, our novel Bayesian GANs framework is proposed to automatically generate photo-realistic beautiful expressions. Third, to further enhance naturalness of beautified group photos, we embed Poisson fusion in the final layer of the GANs in order to synthesize all the beautified individual expressions. We conducted extensive experiments on various kinds of single-/multi-frame group photos to validate our novel network design. All the experiments confirm that, our novel method can uniformly accommodate diverse expression evaluation and generation/synthesis of group photos, and outperform the state-of-the-art methods in terms of effectiveness, versatility, and robustness.

Keywords: Beautification of group-photo facial expressions
Multi-label CNN · Bayesian networks
Generative adversarial networks · Poisson fusion

1 Introduction and Motivation

With the omnipresence of digital cameras in today's society, group photos are routinely captured to record wonderful moments shared by families, friends,

© Springer Nature Switzerland AG 2018
V. Kůrková et al. (Eds.): ICANN 2018, LNCS 11139, pp. 760–770, 2018.
https://doi.org/10.1007/978-3-030-01418-6_74

colleagues, etc. Hence, higher expectations are focused on the overall quality of group photos. In practice, it is almost impossible to capture satisfying facial expressions in a synchronous way for all involved people at any moment with various types of hand-held devices. Therefore, it urgently needs to develop smart group photo evaluation and beautification techniques. However, to achieve this goal, there are still several challenges yet to be overcome, including evaluation of the group-photo facial expression on an individual basis, simultaneous generation of satisfying expressions for all people involved, natural synthesis integration of individual facial expression into the final production of a group photo, etc. Obviously, evaluation and beautification of facial expressions in such unconstrained settings remain an ill-posed task due to various factors, such as non-frontal faces, varying lighting in different outdoor/indoor settings, and/or even the large variation in facial identities and appearances.

With a goal of tackling the aforementioned challenges, more research works began to endeavor great efforts in related techniques. For example, recent works have demonstrated generative adversarial networks (GANs) are extremely effective. This ranges from image translation [6,8,17,20], to face generation [2,13,15,16] and even image completion [4,7,12]. Nonetheless, most of the existing methods commonly employ the entire feature space to approximate the generative feature distribution, which could not well respect facial expression details for all individuals involved. In addition, most of the existing works concentrate on the attribute manipulation/transformation of single object, lacking a principled way to optimize group-photo facial expressions.

In this paper, our research efforts are devoted to pioneering a systematic approach for synthesizing a satisfying group photo by leveraging the synchronized power of CNNs and GANs. Specifically, we propose a two-stage deep network for automatic group-photo evaluation and beautification, which could greatly reduce the negative influences caused by the diversity of faces. Figure 1 highlights the framework of our novel method, which mainly consists of three major steps: (1) Facial expression recognition with multi-label CNN and our newly-proposed facial expression evaluation metric—the multi-label CNN recognizes two main beautification related expressions (e.g., mouth-smiling and eyes-opening) and predicts the softmax value of the expression for further evaluation; (2) Face beautification with our Bayesian GANs—it is guided by the subspace clustering based on attributes-aware priors, wherein we pre-distribute all the attributes' weights according to the specific face regions' impacts on the entire face appearances; (3) Multiple single-person faces' integration driven by ensemble Poisson fusion—we add a Poisson layer to naturally fuse single-person face into the original group photo with gradual gradient changes. The salient contributions of this paper can be summarized as follows:

- We pioneer a two-stage group-photo beautification framework by combining multi-label CNN with Bayesian network enhanced GANs, which could naturally and automatically perform evaluation and beautification on group photos in a uniform and elegant way.

- We propose novel Bayesian GANs to automatically generate beautiful expressions by embedding Bayesian prior network into the powerful CycleGANs, which has strong generalization ability for weakly-matched training datasets.
- We propose to embed the Poisson image clone technique in the final layer of our Bayesian GANs in order to synthesize all the to-be-beautified expressions on all individuals from single-/multi-frame continuous group photos, which would lead to meaningful and harmonious manipulation in any local region of a group photo.

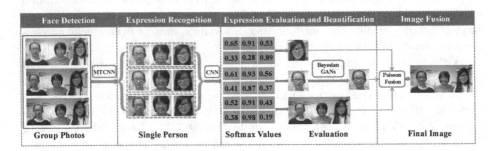

Fig. 1. The architecture of our framework. A group photo is converted into several single-person faces by using the MTCNN [19], which is a multi-task cascaded convolutional network to process the face detection tasks from coarse to fine.

2   Related Works

Facial Expression Recognition Methods. Facial expression recognition has been gaining growing momentum, with a wide range of applications. Specially, the expression recognition methods based on CNNs [1,18] and DBN [9] have achieved excellent results on facial datasets. For example, Burkert et al. [1] proposed a facial emotion recognition architecture based on CNNs. It consists of two parallel feature extraction blocks (FeatEx), which dramatically improves the performance on public datasets. Liu et al. [9] proposed a boosted deep belief network (BDBN) for feature learning, feature selection, and classification in a loopy framework. However, these methods are in some sense cumbersome due to high-dimensional varying features for each attribute, leading to inefficiency in recognition. Therefore, we apply multi-task learning to simultaneously optimize multiple objective functions.

Facial Expression Generation and Editing Methods. In recent years, many image generation approaches have been proposed. For example, Isola et al. proposed a pix2pix approach [5] and achieved amazing results on paired datasets. However, in many cases, paired data are not readily available. Therefore, the image conversion based on unpaired data is particularly important. Recently, Zhu et al. proposed the CycleGAN [20] method, which employed two

GANs and an additional cycle consistency loss to improve the quality of the generated images. Meanwhile, DualGAN and DiscoGAN [6,17] adopted the similar idea for image-to-image translation based on unpaired data. Particularly, many GAN-based methods have also been proposed for face generation. Perarnau et al. introduced ICGAN [13], which combined the encoder with cGAN to manipulate face images conditioned on arbitrary attributes. Shen et al. introduced a framework [15] to avoid learning redundant facial information by learning residual images, which only focused on the attribute-specific area of a face image. However, these works commonly have significant dependencies on the training dataset and are difficult to preserve more details on other images. Moreover, these methods are designed for single pre-processed face images instead of group photos. Therefore, we should solve this to achieve strong generalization ability for weakly-matched test datasets.

3   Facial Expression Evaluation and Beautification

3.1   Facial Expression Evaluation Based on Multi-label CNN

In order to synthesize group photo with perfect facial expressions, we need to first select the face images that will be manipulated after face detection. Considering the unbalanced distribution of samples in the training and testing phases for multi-label classification, we adopt a mixed objective optimization network [14] to recognize different facial attributes. We perform a joint optimization over all the face attributes on CelebA dataset [10]. In practice, we focus on two main beautification related attributes, including mouth-smiling and eyes-opening. Based on the two attributes, we further construct a multi-label CNN to recognize the two expressions at the same time, and this multi-task loss is defined as

$$L(x,y) = \sum_{i=1}^{2} p(i|y_i(x))\|f_i(x) - y_i(x)\|^2, \tag{1}$$

where $p(i|y_i(x))$ is the assigned probability for the attribute i, which can make the training set biased. $f_i(x)$ and $y_i(x)$ respectively represent the predicted value and the ground truth for attribute i. Meanwhile, we formulate a beautification

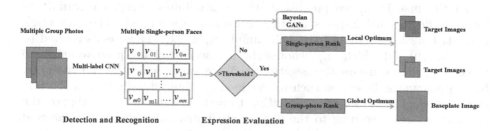

Fig. 2. Illustration of our facial expression evaluation pipeline.

evaluation metric for facial expressions, which facilitates beautifying group photos with lower cost. First, we count the number of individual faces with better expression in each group photo, so that we can choose the relatively better group photo to serve as our baseplate image. The metric used for measuring facial expression is the softmax value $V_i = e^{z_i}/\sum_{j=1}^{2} e^{z_j}$, which is obtained from the recognition network. As shown in Fig. 2, the softmax value v_{mn} means the n-th person of the m-th group photo. We can directly substitute the target image with the highest softmax value (the softmax value must be greater than 0.5) for the worse one (the softmax value is less than 0.5) in the baseplate image using our improved Poisson fusion. It should be noted that, if there is no satisfying facial image of certain person, we resort to our Bayesian GANs to generate a desirable image.

3.2   Facial Expression Beautification with Bayesian GANs

Considering the importance of diverse faces with various kinds of attributes, as shown in Fig. 3, we propose a three-layer Bayesian network to augment GAN models. Of which, the first layer of the Bayesian network relates to the attributes distribution prior, which is vital to cluster the semantics-similar images into one attributes-specific subspace. The second layer relates to the subspaces, which are clustered according to the attributes' influences on the targeted face regions. The third layer relates to the trained GANs, which are guided by the attributes-aware priors resulted from subspace clustering.

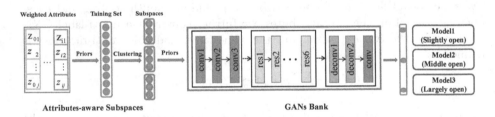

Fig. 3. Pipeline of our Bayesian GANs based on facial-attribute priors.

In the first layer, we pre-distribute the attributes' weights according to the specific regions' impacts on the entire face appearance. The j-th original attribute label value of the i-th sample $z_{ij} \in \{1, -1\}$ is re-distributed to $z_{ij} \in \{a_{ij}, 0\}$. Of which, a_{ij} denotes the new weight of the positive attribute value, and the '0' means the negative attribute value, which has no effects on face appearances. Based on such re-weighted attribute distribution in the first layer, we employ the k-means algorithm to perform subspace clustering on the training images according to the diverse attributes' influence on the targeted face regions. Here, we use the mean square errors of the attribute vectors to cluster all the samples into K subspaces,

$$E = \sum_{i=1}^{K} \sum_{z \in \mathcal{S}_i} \|z - u_i\|^2, \tag{2}$$

where $\mathcal{S}_i$ denotes the i-th subspace, and $\|z - u_i\|^2$ is the Euclidean distance between sample z and the subspace center u_i.

After attribute-aware subspace clustering, we further describe the image sample generating process from source domain X to target domain Y in details. Given two datasets X, Y: source domain $X = \{x_i | 1 \leqslant i \leqslant n_x\}$ and target domain $Y = \{y_i | 1 \leqslant i \leqslant n_y\}$, n_x, n_y respectively represent the numbers of dataset X and Y. We cluster the sample space into three subspaces $\mathcal{S}_i, i = 1, 2, 3$ based on the attributes with important impacts. With the mapping function $X \to Y$, we adopt a loss function as:

$$L_{X \to Y}^{\mathcal{S}_i} = \mathbb{E}_{y \sim p_{data}(y)}[(D_Y(y) - 1)^2] + \mathbb{E}_{x \sim p_{data}(x)}[(1 - D_Y(G(x)))^2], \tag{3}$$

where $X, Y \in \mathcal{S}_i$. Therefore, our Bayesian GANs have excellent generation ability, which can successfully transform images between two domains according to the attribute-specific subspaces. Considering a test image, we first predict its 40 facial attributes using a multi-label CNN model, and then calculate which subspace the test image belongs to, according to the prior knowledge and the Bayesian network.

For our generator, we use three convolution layers to extract features from input images, six residual blocks to preserve the features of the original image, and simultaneously transform feature vectors from source domain to target domain. Meanwhile, we use three deconvolution layers to restore low-level features from feature vectors. Residual blocks consist of two convolution layers, wherein part of the input data is directly added to the output, so that we can reduce the deviation of the corresponding output from the original input. Finally, we use four convolution layers for our discriminative network.

3.3 Poisson Fusion in Our GANs

To obtain a natural group photo, we need to conduct global fusion via local image editing [11]. Therefore, we embed a Poisson fusion layer in our GANs' final layer. In this layer, we naturally fuse all the generated facial expressions of different persons into the selected baseplate group photo. The key of Poisson fusion is to obtain the transformed pixel by solving the Poisson equation. Here, we construct the linear equation according to the method of Poisson image editing as: $\boldsymbol{A} \times \boldsymbol{x} = \boldsymbol{b}$. Please refer to [3] for the details about this equation.

If we solve the above Poisson equation with Gaussian elimination, it will exhibit a lot of time and memory cost. Considering the fusion region is a rectangle, some characteristics of matrix $\boldsymbol{A}$ can be leveraged: $\boldsymbol{A}$ is sparse, positive definite, and can be partitioned into smaller square matrices. According to these characteristics, we adopt the conjugate gradient method to solve the equation. And we do not need to store the matrix $\boldsymbol{A}$, because the conjugate gradient method only needs the value of $\boldsymbol{A} \times \boldsymbol{p}$, which can be easily obtained via the operation of block matrix. Thus, our method not only can embed larger region, but also can achieve more than 5000 times speedup (compared to the Gaussian elimination method) when both the height and width of the region are 100 pixels.

In practice, for ease of image synthesis, we need to store the facial coordinate information during face detection. By means of Poisson fusion method, the generated target images can be seamlessly fused into the selected baseplate group photo. Meanwhile, it can well keep the consistency of the color, texture, and illumination in the scene.

4   Experimental Results and Evaluations

Experimental Settings. We carefully design three types of experiments to evaluate the overall performance of our method: (1) single-person facial expression beautification of a group photo; (2) single-frame image based group photo beautification (the images are randomly-crawled from the internet); (3) multi-frame continuous images based group photo beautification (the images are captured by our hand-held device). CelebA is used as our training dataset, which includes 202,599 colored face images and 40-attribute binary vectors for each image. We use the aligned and cropped version and scale the images to the size of 128 × 128. In addition, the distribution of attribute labels are highly biased. In practice, for each attribute that needs to be edited, 1000 images from the attribute-positive class and 1000 images from the attribute-negative class are randomly chosen as our test set. We select all the rest images as our training dataset. Meanwhile, to demonstrate the superiorities of our method, we randomly search some facial images from the internet and take some photos casually, which also serve as our test dataset. Please refer to our supplemental document for more vivid results[1].

Fig. 4. Comparison of the mouth-smiling results produced by different methods on single-person faces of a group photo.

---

[1] https://drive.google.com/file/d/159my8s52wzL-Eq9vGtubKDegMQLfLfQq/view?usp=sharing.

Evaluations on Single-person Facial Expression Beautification of Group Photos. Considering the detailed wrinkles on elder faces, we respectively conduct experiments on the different-age faces of group photos. As shown in Fig. 4, we compare our results with those produced by some state-of-the-art methods, including ICGAN [13], learning residual images [15], and Cycle-GAN [20]. We observe that, the compared methods commonly have a significant dependence on the training dataset, thus, their results on other test images are not satisfactory. In sharp contrast, our results are more natural and can preserve more details. Moreover, when facing diversified and complicated expression manipulation tasks, our approach outperforms the state-of-the-art facial expression beautifying methods with respects to effectiveness, versatility, and robustness.

Evaluations on Single-frame Image Based Group Photo Beautification. In this kind of experiments, we use our generalization network to manipulate facial attributes and further synthesize a beautiful group photo. Our network can successfully synthesize semantically-meaningful and visually-plausible contents for the key face regions that need to be beautified. As shown in Fig. 5, our method can generate satisfying results with high perceptual quality, which shows a great promise for smart facial expression beautification during group photo capturing.

Fig. 5. The results of our method for single-frame image based group photo beatification.

Evaluations on Multi-frame Continuous Images Based Group Photo Beautification. Our method can also synthesize a new satisfying group photo from unsatisfying multi-frame continuous images. Considering diverse poses in multi-frame continuous group photos, we detect facial landmarks from the generated images and a group photo to locate a rectangle region of eyes/mouth for ease of fusing the manipulated regions. As shown in Fig. 6, we replace worse facial expressions with the beautified ones in the baseplate group photo based on our improved Poisson fusion strategy.

Quantitative Evaluations. To quantitatively evaluate the visual quality of the synthesized group photos, we carry out user study, wherein 20 people are asked to classify the randomly shuffled images as real or synthetic ones. Each person is shown a random selection of 50 real images and 50 synthesized images in a random order, and is asked to label the images as either real image or synthetic

Fig. 6. The results of our method for multi-frame continuous images based group photo beautification.

image. Table 1 shows the confusion matrix, which indicates that, people feel very hard to reliably distinguish real images from our synthetic ones.

Meanwhile, we conduct user study based on the survey from 20 participants, wherein participants are required to assess the visual realism, image quality, and individual detail preservation by asking them to label the best generated image from the randomly shuffled images generated by different methods. Table 2 documents the results. For the voting about the best performance on attributes manipulation, our method gains the majority of votes. It clearly shows that, our method can well accommodate photo-realistic facial expression beautification for highly-diverse group photos. In addition, as shown in Fig. 7, we further ask participants to grade our results between 0 and 5 according to the image quality and visual realism. It confirms that, our method outperforms other approaches on facial expression beautification.

Table 1. Visual Turing test results for distinguishing real/synthesized images. The average human classification accuracy is 57.25% (chance = 50%).

	Labeled as real	Labeled as synthetic
Real	557	443
Synthetic	412	588

Table 2. Visual Turing test results about different-methods' facial expression manipulations on group photos. The voting percentage sum of each column is equal to 100%.

Methods	Mouth-smiling beautification	Eyes-opening beautification
ICGAN	0.7%	–
Residual	2.1%	1.3%
CycleGAN	37.3%	45.4%
Ours	**59.9%**	**53.3%**

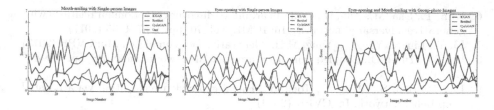

Fig. 7. The subjective evaluation on different methods.

5   Conclusion and Future Works

This paper detailed a two-stage first-evaluation-then-beautification framework with which we could synthesize satisfactory group photos from original single- or multi-frame group photos that are routinely-captured in our daily life. Benefiting from the novel integration of multi-label CNN and Bayesian prior embedded GANs, our novel framework could generate natural and realistic images, which helps improve the generalization ability of facial expression manipulation and synthesis. Various qualitative and quantitative experiments were carried out to evaluate the overall performance of our method, and all the experiments confirmed that, our method has apparent advantages over the existing techniques in terms of efficacy, effectiveness, versatility, and robustness. Despite many promising results in most cases, the obtained results are sometimes less ideal. For example, it remains difficult to generate and synthesize group photos when we only have images of low quality, or images involving facial occlusion and/or complex body pose. Such challenging cases deserve more research efforts. Besides, we plan to exploit more intrinsic temporal context priors and how such priors could further enhance group photo beautification in the near future.

Acknowledgments. This research is supported in part by National Natural Science Foundation of China (NO. 61672077 and 61532002), Applied Basic Research Program of Qingdao (NO. 161013xx), National Science Foundation of USA (NO. IIS-0949467, IIS-1047715, IIS-1715985, and IIS-1049448), National Key R&D Program of China (NO. 2017YFF0106407), and capital health research and development of special 2016-1-4011.

References

1. Burkert, P.E.A.: Dexpression: deep convolutional neural network for expression recognition. arXiv preprint arXiv:1509.05371 (2015)
2. Cole, F., Belanger, D., Krishnan, D., Sarna, A., Mosseri, I., Freeman, W.T.: Synthesizing normalized faces from facial identity features. In: CVPR (2017)
3. Gangnet, M., Blake, A.: Poisson image editing. In: SIGGRAPH, pp. 313–318 (2003)
4. Iizuka, S., Simo-Serra, E., Ishikawa, H.: Globally and locally consistent image completion. TOG **36**(4), 107:1–107:14 (2017)
5. Isola, P., Zhu, J.Y., Zhou, T., Efros, A.A.: Image-to-image translation with conditional adversarial networks. In: CVPR (2017)

6. Kim, T., Cha, M., Kim, H., et al.: Learning to discover cross-domain relations with generative adversarial networks. In: ICML, vol. 70, pp. 1857–1865 (2017)
7. Li, Y., Liu, S., Yang, J., Yang, M.H.: Generative face completion. In: CVPR (2017)
8. Liu, M., Tuzel, O.: Coupled generative adversarial networks. In: NIPS, pp. 469–477 (2016)
9. Liu, P., Han, S., Meng, Z., Tong, Y.: Facial expression recognition via a boosted deep belief network. In: CVPR (2014)
10. Liu, Z., Luo, P., Wang, X., Tang, X.: Deep learning face attributes in the wild. In: ICCV (2015)
11. Mccann, J., Pollard, N.S.: Real-time gradient-domain painting. SIGGRAPH **27**(3), 93 (2008)
12. Pathak, D., Krahenbuhl, P., Donahue, J., Darrell, T., Efros, A.A.: Context encoders: feature learning by inpainting. In: CVPR (2016)
13. Perarnau, G., van de Weijer, J., Raducanu, Bogdan, J.Y.: Invertible conditional GANs for image editing (2016)
14. Rudd, E.M., Günther, M., Boult, T.E.: MOON: a mixed objective optimization network for the recognition of facial attributes. In: Leibe, B., Matas, J., Sebe, N., Welling, M. (eds.) ECCV 2016. LNCS, vol. 9909, pp. 19–35. Springer, Cham (2016). https://doi.org/10.1007/978-3-319-46454-1_2
15. Shen, W., Liu, R.: Learning residual images for face attribute manipulation. In: CVPR (2017)
16. Shu, Z., Yumer, E., Hadap, S., Sunkavalli, K., Shechtman, E., Samaras, D.: Neural face editing with intrinsic image disentangling. In: CVPR (2017)
17. Yi, Z., Zhang, H., Tan, P., Gong, M.: DualGAN: unsupervised dual learning for image-to-image translation. In: ICCV (2017)
18. Yu, Z., Zhang, C.: Image based static facial expression recognition with multiple deep network learning. In: ICMI, pp. 435–442 (2015)
19. Zhang, K.E.A.: Joint face detection and alignment using multitask cascaded convolutional networks. IEEE Sig. Process. Lett. **23**(10), 1499–1503 (2016)
20. Zhu, J.Y., Park, T., Isola, P., Efros, A.A.: Unpaired image-to-image translation using cycle-consistent adversarial networks. In: ICCV (2017)

Fast and Accurate Affect Prediction Using a Hierarchy of Random Forests

Maxime Sazadaly[1]([⊠]), Pierre Pinchon[1], Arthur Fagot[1],
Lionel Prevost[1], and Myriam Maumy Bertrand[2]

[1] Learning, Data and Robotics Lab, ESIEA, Paris, France
sazadaly@et.esiea.fr, lionel.prevost@esiea.fr
[2] Centre National de la Recherche Scientifique, Institut de Recherche
Mathématique Avancé, Université de Strasbourg, Strasbourg, France

Abstract. Hierarchical systems are powerful tools to deal with non-linear data with a high variability. We show in this paper that regressing a bounded variable on such data is a challenging task. As an alternate, we propose here a two-step process. First, an ensemble of ordinal classifiers affect the observation to a given range of the variable to predict and a discrete estimate of the variable. Then, a regressor is trained locally on this range and its neighbors and provides a finer continuous estimate. Experiments on affect audio data from the AVEC'2014 and AV+EC'2015 challenges show that this cascading process can be compared favorably to the state of the art and challengers results.

Keywords: Affective computing · Ensemble of classifiers · Random forests

1 Introduction

Nowadays, vocal recognition of emotions has multiple applications in domains as diverse as medicine, telecommunications or transport. For example, in telecommunications, it would become possible to priorities the calls from individuals in imminent danger situations over less relevant ones. In general, emotion recognition enables the improvement of human/machine interfaces, which justifies the unexpected increase of research on this field, due to the progresses in artificial learning.

Human interactions rely on multiple sources: body language, facial expressions, etc. A vocal message carries a lot of information that we translate implicitly. This information can be expressed or perceived verbally, but also non-verbally, through the tone, the volume or the speed of the voice. The automatic analysis of such information gives insights on the speaker emotional state.

The conceptualization of emotions is still a hot topic in psychology. Opinions do not converge towards a unique model. In fact, we can mainly differentiate three approaches [8]: (1) the basic emotions like happiness, sadness, surprise, fear, anger, or disgust; described by Ekman, (2) the circumplex model of affect and (3) the appraisal theory. In the second model, the affective state is generally described, at least, by two dimensions: the valence which determines the positivity of the emotion and the arousal which determines the activity of the emotion [17]. These two values, bounded on $[-1, +1]$, describe much more precisely the emotional state of an individual than the basic

V. Kůrková et al. (Eds.): ICANN 2018, LNCS 11139, pp. 771–781, 2018.
https://doi.org/10.1007/978-3-030-01418-6_75

emotions. However, it has been shown that other dimensions were necessary to report more accurately this state during an interaction [7].

The choice of one model or the other restrains the kind of machine learning algorithms used to estimate the emotional state. In case of basic emotions, the variable to be predicted is qualitative and nominal. Classification methods must be used. On the contrary, affective dimensions are quantitative, continuous, and bounded variables. So, regression predictor will be needed. To take advantage of the best of both worlds, we propose in this study a method that combines classification and regression. To predict a continuous and bounded variable, we first quantize the affect variable into bounded ranges. For example, a 5 ranges valence quantization would give the following boundaries $\{-1, -0.5, -0.2, +0.2, +0.5, +1\}$. It could be interpreted as "very negative", "negative", "neutral", "positive" and "very positive". Then, we proceed into 3 steps:

- Train an ensemble of classifiers to estimate if the affect value associated to an observation is higher than a given boundary;;
- Combine the ensemble decisions to predict the optimal range;
- Regress locally the variable on this range.

The proposed method is therefore a cascade of ordinal classifiers and local regressors (COCLR). We will see in the following state of art that similar proposals have been made. But in this paper, we perform a thorough study on the key parameter of this method: the number of ranges to be separated by the ensemble of ordinal classifiers. We show experimentally that:

- On small and numerous ranges, ordinal classification performs correctly;
- On large ranges, the COCLR cascade performs better;
- On challenging databases (AVEC'2014 [20] and AV+EC'2015 [16], described in Sect. 4), the COCLR cascade can be compared favorably to challengers' and winner's proposals with an acceptable development and computational cost.

This paper is organized as follows. Section 2 focuses on the state of the art in affect prediction on audio data. In Sect. 3, we will present the COCLR flowchart. In Sect. 4, we will introduce the datasets used to train and evaluate our system and the different pre-processing realized. Then, in Sect. 5, we will expose and discuss our results. Finally, Sect. 6 offers some conclusions.

2 State of the Art

The Audio-Visual Emotion recognition Challenges (AVEC), that takes place every year since 2011, enables to assess the systems proposed on similar datasets. The main objective of these challenges is to ensure a fair comparison between research teams by using the same data. Particularly, the unlabeled test set is released to registered participants some days before the challenge deadline. Moreover, the organizers provide to the competitors a set of audio and video descriptors extracted by approved methods.

The prosodic features such as the height, the intensity, the speech rate, and the quality of the voice, are important to identify the different types of emotions. Low level acoustic descriptors like energy, spectrum, cepstral coefficients, formants, etc. enable an accurate description of the signal.

2.1 Emotion Classification and Prediction

The classification of emotion is done through classical methods like support vector machines (SVM) [1], Gaussian mixture models (GMM) [18] or random forests (RF) [14]. For regression task, numerous models have been proposed: support vector regressors (SVR) [4], deep belief networks (DBN) [12], bidirectional long-short term memory networks (BLSTM) [13], etc. As all these models having their own pros and cons, recent works focus on model combinations to improve overall accuracy. Thus, in [10], authors propose to associate BLSTM and SVR to benefit from the treatment of the past/present context of the BLSTM and the generalization ability of the SVR.

AV+EC'2015 challenge winners proposed in [11] a hierarchy of BLSTM. They deal with 4 information channels: audio, video (described by frame-by-frame geometric features and temporal appearance features), electrocardiogram and electro dermal activity. They combine the predictions of single-modal deep BLSTM with a multi-modal deep BLSTM that performs the final affect prediction.

2.2 Ordinal Classification and Hierarchical Prediction

The standard approach to ordinal classification converts the class value into a numeric quantity and applies a regression learner to the transformed data, translating the output back into a discrete class value in a post-processing step [6]. Here, we work directly on numerical values of affect variables but quantify them into several ranges. Recently, a discrete classification of continuous affective variables through generative adversarial networks (GAN) has been proposed [2]. Five ranges are considered.

The idea of a combining regressors and classifiers has already been applied to deal with age estimation from images. In [9], a first "global" regression is done with an SVR on all ages. Then, it is refined by locally adjusting the age regressed value by using an SVM. In [19] authors propose another hierarchy on the same issue. They define 3 age ranges (namely "child", "teen" an "adult"). An image is classified by combining the results of a pool of classifiers (SVC, FLD, PLS, NN and naïve Bayes) in a majority rule. Then, a second stage uses the appropriate relevant vector machine regression model (trained on one age range) to estimate the age.

The idea of such a hierarchy is not new, but its application to affect data, have not been proposed yet. Moreover, we show in the following experiments that the number of boundaries to be considered impacts the performance of the whole hierarchy.

3 Cascade of Ordinal Classifiers and Local Regressors

The cascade of ordinal classifiers and local regressors proposed here is a hybrid combination of classification and regression systems. Let us note X, the observation (feature vector), y the affective variable to be predicted (valence or arousal) and $\hat{y}$, the prediction. The variable y is continuous and defined on the bounded interval $[-1; +1]$. Therefore, it is possible to segment this interval into a set of n smaller sub-intervals called "ranges" in the following, bounded by the boundaries b_i and b_{i+1} with $i \in \{1, n+1\}$. For example, $n = 2$ define 2 ranges: $[-1;0[$ ("negative") and $[0; +1]$ ("positive") and 3 boundaries $b_i \in \{-1, 0, +1\}$. Each boundary b_i (except -1 and $+1$) may define a binary classification issue: given the observation X, the prediction $\hat{y}$ is lower (resp. higher) than b_i. By combining the outputs of the $(n-1)$ binary classifiers, we get an ordinal classification. Given the observation X, the prediction $\hat{y}$ is probably (necessarily in case of perfect classification) located within the range $[b_i, b_{i+1}]$. Once this range obtained, a local regression is run on it along to its direct neighbors to predict y. Figure 1 illustrate the full cascade. The structure of this system is modular and compatible with any kind of classification and regression algorithms. Moreover, it is generic and may be adapted to other subjects than affective dimension prediction.

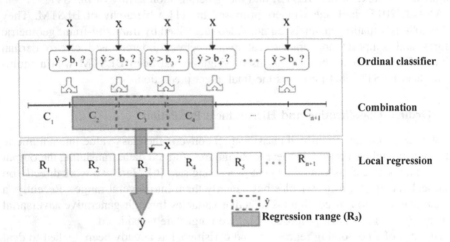

Fig. 1. COCLR: a two-stage cascade. The first stage is a combination of binary classifiers which aim is to estimate y's range. The observation X is handled by the corresponding local regressor which will evaluate the value of y on this range and its neighbors.

3.1 Ordinal Classification

The regression of an affect value y on an observation X can be bounded by the minimum and the maximum this value might take. If y is not originally bounded, we bound it by the minimal and maximal values of the studied dataset. The interval on which y is defined, $I = [min(y), max(y)]$, can be divided in n ranges.

The first stage of the cascade is an ensemble of $(n-1)$ binary classifiers. Each classifier decides if, given the observation X, the variable to be predicted is higher than the lower boundary b_i of a range or not. Training samples are labeled -1 if their y value is lower than b_i and $+1$ otherwise. Considering the sorted nature of the boundaries b_i, we build here an ensemble of ordinal classifiers [6].

We combine the decisions of these classifiers to compute the lower and upper bounds of the optimal range $[b_i, b_{i+1}]$. Consider an observation X with $y = 0.15$. Suppose the number of ranges $n = 6$ and linearly distributed boundaries b_i. The following ranges are defined: $[-1.0, -0.5, -0.25, 0, 0.25, 0.5, 1.0]$. In case of perfect classification, the output vector of the ensemble of classifiers will be: $\{1, 1, 1, 1, -1, -1\}$ where -1 means "y is lower than b_i" while $+1$ means "y is higher than b_i". Obviously, b_i is the bound associated to the "latest" classifier with a positive output and b_{i+1} the first classifier with a negative output. By combining the local decisions of these binary classifiers, we get the (optimal) range $[b_i, b_{i+1}]$. This range C_i will be used in the second stage to locally predict y. In the example, this range is $[0, 0.25]$. However, indecision between two classifiers can happen [15]. This indecision will be handled by the second stage of the cascade.

The performance measure of the ordinal classifiers, the accuracy, is directly linked to the definition of the ranges. The choice of the number of ranges n is a key parameter of our system and can be seen as a hyper-parameter. The n ranges and their corresponding boundaries b_i can be defined in several ways. If they are linearly distributed, they will define a kind of affective scale as in [2]. But the choice of the boundaries b_i could also prevent strong imbalances between classes. In case of highly imbalanced classes, the application of a data augmentation method is strongly recommended [3].

From now on, we can evaluate the accuracy (ranges detection rates) of the classifier combination. It can also be used to compute a discrete estimate of y, using for $\hat{y}$ the center of the predicted range. Finally, we can estimate the correlation of $\hat{y}$ to the ground truth y.

3.2 Local Regression

The aim of the second stage of the cascade is to compute the continuous value of y. Thus, each range i is associated to a regressor R_i that locally regresses y on $[b_i, b_{i+1}]$. So, each regressor is specialized in the regression on a specific range. However, as explained previously, indecisions between nearby classes throughout the ordinal

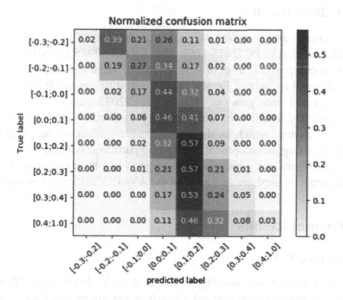

Fig. 2. Confusion matrix of the first stage of the cascade

classification may induce an improper prediction of the range. *De facto*, the wrong regressor can be activated, causing a drop of the correlation. The analysis of the first stage results, illustrated by the confusion matrix (Fig. 2), indicates that prediction mistakes are close enough or even connected to the optimal range which y belongs to. Thus, we can expand the regression range to $[b_{i-1}; b_{i+2}]$, if they exist.

Widening the local regression ranges helps to solve the indecision issue between the nearby boundaries. Moreover, it frees us from the obligation to strongly optimize the first stage. In fact, the use of a perfect classifier instead of a classifier that reaches an accuracy of 90% on the first stage won't modify deeply the result of the whole cascade. By the way, the second stage local regression produces a continuous estimate $\hat{y}$ of y and it is possible to compute a correlation between both variables.

4 Databases

4.1 AVEC'2014

The AVEC'2014 database is an ensemble of audio and video recordings of human/machine interaction [20]. This base is composed of 150 recordings, each of them containing the reactions of only one person, realized from 84 German subjects. In order to create this dataset, a part of the subjects has been recorded many times with a break of two weeks between each recording session. The distribution of the records is arranged as following: 18 subjects have been recorded three times, 31 of them have been recorded twice and the 34 lefts have been recorded only once. Then the recordings are split in 3 parts: learning set, validation set, and test set. We used generic audio features provided by the organizers [21].

4.2 AV+EC'2015/RECOLA

The second dataset we used to measure the performance of our system is the affect recognition challenge AV+EC'2015 [16]. The AV+EC'2015 relies on the RECOLA base. This one is composed of a set of 9.5 h of audio, video and physiologic recordings (ECG, EDA) from 46 records of French people with different origins (Italian, German, and French) and different genders. The AV+EC'2015 relies on a sub-set of 27 recordings completely labelled. In our case, we only used the audio records and only worked on the valence, which is the most complex affect to be predicted in this challenge. The learning, development and testing partitions contain 9 recordings each. The diversity of origins and genders of the subjects has been preserved in these. The different audio features used are available in the AV+EC'2015 presentation paper [16].

5 Experimental Results

5.1 Performance Metrics

The cascade performance are directly linked to those of both stages. Thus, the performances of the ensemble of ordinal classifiers are measured by the accuracy. It measures the ratio of examples for which the interval has been correctly predicted. We use the confusion matrix in order to analyze the behavior of this system in a more precise way.

The performance of the ensemble of local regressors are measured using Pearson's correlation (PC), gold standard metric of the challenge AVEC'2014 [20] on which we base our work. However, as these data are not normally distributed, we decided to measure the performance of our system with Spearman's correlation (SC) and the concordance correlation coefficient (CCC) as well.

The experimental results presented in the following are computed on the development/validation set of the different databases.

5.2   Used Systems and Baseline

The study of the valence on a bounded interval allows the identification of several intensity thresholds of the felt emotion. For example, we can qualify this as negative, neutral, positive, depending on this value. However, for the AVEC'2014 and the AV +EC'2015 bases, these intensity thresholds are no equally represented: more than 60% of the data belong to the range $[-0.1; 0.1]$ and 80% within the range $[-0.2; 0.2]$. Considering the fact that some systems poorly support strong class unbalances, we increased the volume of our using the Synthetic Minority Over-sampling Technique [3].

As previously stated, our architecture is modular and adapted to any kind of classification or regression method. Throughout our experimentations, we tried to use support vector machines (C-SVM with RBF kernels) and random forests (RF with 300 decision trees, attribute bagging on $\sqrt{nfeatures}$) as classifiers). Table 1 presents the ordinal classification rate obtained by these two systems on the development sets of AVEC'2014 and AV+EC'2015, for the prediction of valence. We choose this affect variable because it's known to be particularly hard to predict. By taking the center of the predicted intervals as values of y, we have been able to process the correlations of these two systems. These correlations enable to compare the performance of our classifier ensemble to those of a unique "global" random forest regressor dealing with the whole interval $[-1; +1]$.

Table 1. Valence prediction: comparison of different ordinal classifiers (SVM-OC and RF-OC) and one global random forest regressor (RF-GR) on a subset of the training set. The performance measure is the Pearson correlation coefficient.

	AVEC'2014	AV+EC'2015
Baseline	0.38	0.17
RF-GR	0.45	–
SVM-OC	0.61	0.56
RF-OC	**0.77**	**0.65**

The results obtained on both databases encouraged us to continue with random forests rather than the support vector machines. Indeed, the results returned by these are significantly sharper than the SVM ones, independently of the choice of the sub-intervals. For the same reasons, we have decided to use an ensemble of random forests to perform local regression.

5.3   Results on AVEC'2014

Table 2 compares the performance of the different systems presented on the development base of the AVEC'2014, while using several number of ranges n.

First, the interval I has been split here in 10 ranges: $[-1.0; -0.4; -0.3; -0.2; -0.1; 0.0; 0.1; 0.2; 0.3; 0.4; 1.0]$. The most performant system in term of correlation is here, without a doubt, the ordinal classifier ensemble, where the values are the centers of the predicted ranges. It is as well relevant to point out that, despite the very high correlation of the local regressors alone, the COCLR system does not seem efficient.

Then, the interval I has been split into 6 ranges: $[-1.0; -0.4; -0.2; 0.0; 0.2; 0.4; 1.0]$. The most performant system, as far as the correlation is concerned, is still the ordinal classifier ensemble. However, the performance gap between the COCLR and the ordinal classifier ensemble has tightened. It is also noteworthy that the accuracy of the classification system has risen and the correlation of the local regressors alone, has slightly dropped.

Finally, the interval I here has been split into $n = 4$ ranges, $[-1.0; 0.3; 0.0; 0.3; 1.0]$.previous conclusions on ordinal classifiers and local regressors remain checked. But this time, the COCLR cascade, turned out to be significantly the most efficient one. The correlation bound to this system is the highest obtained for every choice of intervals of any sort. These different results highlighted the importance of the choice of the number of ranges on which the COCLR system stands.

Table 2. Valence prediction: impact of the number of ranges on performance of global regressor (GR), ordinal classifier (OC), local regressors (LR) and cascade (COCLR). LR performance are computed considering the classification as "perfect" (Accuracy = 1).

n	Model	Accuracy	Pearson C	Spearman C	CCC
1	GR	–	0.45	0.47	0.27
10	OC	0.78	0.69	0.70	0.60
	LR	–	0.91	0.90	0.89
	COCLR	–	0.51	0.53	0.37
6	OC	0.83	0.63	0.66	0.54
	LR	–	0.85	0.85	0.76
	COCLR	–	0.54	0.53	0.39
4	OC	0.89	0.47	0.48	0.29
	LR	–	0.80	0.81	0.77
	COCLR	–	0.77	0.77	0.65

5.4   Results on AV+EC'2015/RECOLA

As we did previously, we measured the performance of our system according to the different sub-intervals. Affect value varies within $[-0.3; 1]$ so we discard classifier and regressors trained on [−1; −0.3]. The Table 3 presents a summary of these results. Throughout our tests, we used 3 groups of different sub-intervals. The biggest, composed of 8 ranges, is: [−0.3; −0.2; −0.1; 0.0; 0.1; 0.2; 0.3; 0.4; 1.0]. The second one, composed of 5 ranges, is: [−0.3; −0.1; 0.0; 0.1; 0.3; 1.0]. Finally, the last one, composed of 3 ranges, is: [−0.3; 0.0; 0.3; 1.0].

We can observe in Table 3 that the results on the RECOLA database are similar to the ones the AVEC'2014. In fact, the most performant system remains the COCLR, when we chose a small number of ranges. The correlation obtained by the cascade of ordinal classifiers and local regressors for the valence on the development base is worth 0.67. As previously, we have observed a decline of the correlation of the local regressors and a rise of the accuracy of the first stage of the cascade when the size of the sub-intervals increased. Comparisons with challenge winner's results [11] are encouraging. Though our cascade get lower results (0.675) than their multimodal system (0.725), it get better result than those obtained on the audio channel only (0.529). These latter are similar to those of the first stage ordinal classifier (0.521).

Last but not least, our proposal is fast to train (<10 mn for 3 ranges) and evaluate (<0.1 ms) on an Intelcore I7-8 cores-3.4 GHz and doesn't require too memory space (<1 Go for 3 ranges).

Table 3. Valence prediction: best obtained models for each number of ranges on AV+EC'2015 development set. Challenge results [11] on the audio channel (AC) and their multimodal system (MM). The performance measure is the Pearson correlation coefficient.

	Proposal			Baseline AC	Winner AC	Winner MM
N	1	5	3	–	–	–
Best model	GR	OC	COCLR	–	–	–
Pearson C	0.463	0.521	0.675	0.167	0.529	**0.725**

6 Conclusions

We propose in this article an original approach for the regression of a continuous, bounded variable, based on a cascade of ordinal classifiers and local regressors. We chose to applicate it to the estimation of affective variables such as the valence. The first stage allows us to predict a trend, depending to the chosen interval. Thus, taking into account, for example, four intervals, the emotional state of a person will be qualified as very negative, negative, positive or very positive. We have been able to observe that this trend is more accurately estimated while the number of interval is increasing. The second stage enable a sharper prediction of the variable by regressing locally, on its interval and its direct neighbors. It seems even more efficient when the number of considered interval is low. Indeed, it allows to reduce the influence of the first stage on the prediction. Finally, we showed that the performances of this cascade can be compared favorably to those of the winner of the challenge AV+EC'2015.

Despite these satisfying results, there are still room to improve it (others than applying it to the prediction of the *arousal* and the − running − assessment of the performances on the challenges test data). The COCLR is a cascade which first stage is an ensemble of classifiers. The decision here is sanctioned by the least performant classifier. A more adapted combination rule would impact advantageously the global performances. The outputs (binary or probabilistic) of the ordinal classifier might also enrich the descriptors used by the local regressors.

Acknowledgment. This work has been partially supported by the French National Agency (ANR) in the frame of its FRQC program (TEEC, project number ANR-16-FRQC-0009-03).

References

1. Bitouk, D., Verma, R., Nenkova, A.: Class-level spectral features for emotion recognition. Speech Commun. **52**(7), 613–625 (2010)
2. Chang, J., Scherer, S.: Learning representations of emotional speech with deep convolutional generative adversarial networks. In: ICASSP, pp. 2746–2750, 2017
3. Chawla, N.V., Bowyer, K.W., Hall, L.O., Kegelmeyer, P.W.: SMOTE: synthetic minority oversampling technique. J. Artif. Intell. Res. **16**, 321–357 (2002)
4. Drucker, H., Burges, C., Kaufman, L., Smola, A.J., Vapnik, V.: Support vector regression machines. In: Advances in Neural Information Processing Systems, pp. 155–161 (1997)
5. Ekman, P.: Basic emotions. In: Handbook of Cognition and Emotion, pp. 45–60. Wiley, New York (1999)
6. Frank, E., Hall, M.: A simple approach to ordinal classification. In: De Raedt, L., Flach, P. (eds.) ECML 2001. LNCS (LNAI), vol. 2167, pp. 145–156. Springer, Heidelberg (2001). https://doi.org/10.1007/3-540-44795-4_13
7. Fontaine, J.R., Scherer, K.R., Roesch, E.B., Ellsworth, P.C.: The world of emotions is not two-dimensional. Psychol. Sci. **18**(12), 1050–1057 (2007)
8. Grandjean, D., Sander, D., Scherer, K.R.: Conscious emotional experience emerges as a function of multilevel, appraisal-driven response synchronization. Conscious. Cogn. **17**(2), 484–495 (2008)
9. Guo, G., Fu, Y., Wang, T.S., Dyer, C.R.: Locally adjusted robust regression for human age estimation. In: WACV (2008)
10. Han, J., Zhang, Z., Ringeval, F., Schuller, B.: Prediction-based learning for continuous emotion recognition in speech. In: ICASSP, pp. 5005–5009 (2017)
11. He, L., Jiang, D., Yang, L., Pei, E., Hu, P., Sahli, H.: Multimodal affective dimension prediction using deep bidirectional long short-term memory recurrent neural networks. In: AVEC, pp. 73–80 (2015)
12. Hinton, G.E., Osindero, S., Teh, Y.: A fast learning algorithm for deep belief nets. Neural Comput. **18**(7), 1527–1554 (2006)
13. Nicolaou, M.A., Gunes, H., Pantic, M.: Continuous prediction of spontaneous affect from multiple cues and modalities in valence-arousal space. IEEE Trans. Affect. Comput. **2**(2), 92–105 (2011)
14. Noroozi, F., Sapinski, T., Kaminska, D., Anbarjafari, G.: Vocal-based emotion recognition using random forests and decision tree. Int. J. Speech Technol. **20**(2), 239–246 (2017)
15. Qiao, X.: Noncrossing ordinal classification. arXiv:1505.03442 (2015)
16. Ringeval, F., et al.: AV+EC 2015: the first affect recognition challenge bridging across audio, video, and physiological data. In: AVEC, pp. 3–8 (2015)
17. Russell, J.: A circumplex model of affect. J. Pers. Soc. Psychol. **39**(6), 1161–1178 (1980)

18. Sethu, V., Ambikairajah, E., Epps, J.: Empirical mode decomposition based weighted frequency feature for speech-based emotion classification. In: ICASSP, pp. 5017–5020 (2008)
19. Thukral, P., Mitra, K., Chellappa, R.: A hierarchical approach for human age estimation. In: ICASSP, pp. 1529–1532 (2012)
20. Valstar, M.F., et al.: AVEC 2014: 3D dimensional affect and depression recognition challenge. In: AVEC (2014)

Gender-Aware CNN-BLSTM for Speech Emotion Recognition

Linjuan Zhang[1], Longbiao Wang[1(✉)], Jianwu Dang[1,2(✉)], Lili Guo[1], and Qiang Yu[1]

[1] Tianjin Key Laboratory of Cognitive Computing and Application, Tianjin University, Tianjin, China
{linjuanzhang,longbiao_wang,liliguo,yuqiang}@tju.edu.cn
[2] Japan Advanced Institute of Science and Technology, Nomi, Ishikawa, Japan
jdang@jaist.ac.jp

Abstract. Gender information has been widely used to improve the performance of speech emotion recognition (SER) due to different expressing styles of men and women. However, conventional methods cannot adequately utilize gender information by simply representing gender characteristics with a fixed unique integer or one-hot encoding. In order to emphasize the gender factors for SER, we propose two types of features for our framework, namely distributed-gender feature and gender-driven feature. The distributed-gender feature is constructed in a way to represent the gender distribution as well as individual differences, while the gender-driven feature is extracted from acoustic signals through a deep neural network (DNN). These two proposed features are then augmented into the original spectrogram respectively to serve as the input for the following decision-making network, where we construct a hybrid one by combining convolutional neural network (CNN) and bi-directional long short-term memory (BLSTM). Compared with spectrogram only, adding the distributed-gender feature and gender-driven feature in gender-aware CNN-BLSTM improved unweighted accuracy by relative error reduction of 14.04% and 45.74%, respectively.

Keywords: Speech emotion recognition · Gender information · DNN
CNN · BLSTM

1 Introduction

It is believed that SER can significantly improve the quality of spoken dialogue systems. Although SER has been studied for many years, machines still have difficulties in recognizing speakers' emotions.

In many studies [1,2], gender differences are observed in emotional speech expression, suggesting that gender information will bring certain advantages in SER. Ways of incorporating gender information into SER can be summarized into two methods. The first is to create a separate emotion model for each gender,

© Springer Nature Switzerland AG 2018
V. Kůrková et al. (Eds.): ICANN 2018, LNCS 11139, pp. 782–790, 2018.
https://doi.org/10.1007/978-3-030-01418-6_76

which is referred to as Sep-System for the separate model [3]. The second is to take gender information as an augmented feature vector, which is referred to as Aug-System [4]. Both methods can utilize the gender information of speakers and thus improve the accuracy of SER.

In Sep-System, gender information need not to be represented and the problem can be decomposed into gender identification followed by emotion recognition. However, utterances of the corresponding genders can be used to train male and female emotion classifiers individually. Moreover, treating gender separately increases the error of gender recognition and needs longer time in emotion recognition. Regarding Aug-System, all the utterances in a training set are used to train the emotion classifier, which makes it difficult to represent gender information. Conventional methods of encoding gender employ a unique integer or one-hot encoding. The gender ID is assigned by a nominal value, using fixed and simple numerical values to encode gender may not make use of gender information adequately.

In this work, we present a novel approach to deal with these challenges. Aug-System is chosen to address the problem of insufficient training data. To represent gender information more properly, the distributed-gender feature is proposed to describe the distribution of male and female speakers. The distributed-gender feature is a set of random values, where male speakers are distributed between 0 and 0.5 and female speakers are distributed between 0.5 and 1. The distributed-gender feature is different in each utterance and reflects individual differences. In order to utilize acoustic information and real individual differences of humans, we propose the gender-driven feature, a gender-conscious bottleneck feature that is extracted from acoustic features using DNN. The gender-driven feature not only distinguishes between men and women, but also retains discriminative acoustic information. Then, the two features are augmented into original spectrogram individually. Finally, the gender-aware CNN-BLSTM model is used to extract hierarchical feature and distinguish emotions. To the best of our knowledge, our work is the first to make use of gender information, acoustic information and original spectrographic features simultaneously for SER.

The outline of this paper is as follows: related work is presented in Sect. 2. Our proposed gender-aware CNN-BLSTM is introduced in Sect. 3. Sections 4 and 5 cover the experiments, conclusion and future work.

2   Related Work

Gender information has been widely used for SER task. In [5], they used gender information to improve the accuracy of SER. They revealed that the combined gender and emotion recognition system performed better than gender-independent emotion recognition system.

In [6], additional speaker-related information such as speaker identity, gender and age were used on Sep-System and Aug-System. However, adding gender information resulted only in a slight improvement.

Methods for SER have great achievements using acoustic features provided by INTERSPEECH 2009 Emotion Challenge [7]. The 384-dimensional acoustic

Table 1. Acoustic features of INTERSPEECH emotion challenge 2009

LLDs (16 * 2)	Statistical values (12)
(Δ)ZCR (Δ)RMS energy	Mean; standard deviation; extremes: min/max value; range;
(Δ)F0 (Δ)HNR	Relative min/max position; kurtosis; skewness;
(Δ)MFCC(1–12)	Linear regression: offset; slope; MSE

features consist of 32-dimensional low-level descriptors (LLDs) and their statistical values, which are described in Table 1.

In recent years, deep networks based on spectrogram [8,9] improved the accuracy of speech recognition. In [10–12], they employed CNN-BLSTM to deal with spectrograms and showed significant enhancements on SER. In the present work, we follow the successful structure to perform emotion recognition.

3 Gender-Aware CNN-BLSTM

3.1 Distributed-Gender Feature

Although basic emotions are shared between cultures and nationalities [13], different speakers express their emotions in different ways. In order to reflect individual differences, random variables are added to a fixed male or female template. It means that even the same gender has a slight difference. Finally, the distributed-gender feature of males is set to change from 0 to 0.5, while that of females varies from 0.5 to 1.

3.2 Gender-Driven Feature

Acoustic information can be used to classify male and female speakers. However, acoustic features are interrelated having small inter-class distances [14]. In this study, a DNN is used to transfer high-dimensional acoustic features to gender-driven feature that is discriminative to represent gender information.

Visualization of Gender-Driven Feature. In this section, the gender-driven feature is described graphically. Figures 1 and 2 show the feature space of the acoustic features and gender-driven feature, respectively. We use the PCA to reduce the acoustic features and gender-driven feature to two dimensions individually. The abscissa and ordinate in these two figures represent the first and second components of PCA, respectively.

From the right panel of Fig. 2, the distribution of male and female data is clear using gender-driven feature. Moreover, the boundaries of different emotions in the gender-driven feature are sharper than those in the acoustic features. Compared with Figs. 1 and 2, the gender-driven feature not only reflects gender information, but also retains acoustic information that is useful for SER. Therefore, the gender-driven feature is conjectured more effective for SER, which will be supported by experiments described in Sect. 4.

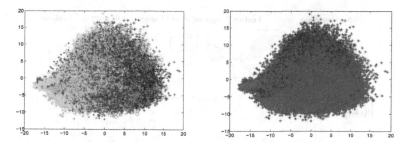

Fig. 1. Feature space of the acoustic features. The left panel shows the distribution of seven emotions. The right panel shows the distribution of male and female speakers.

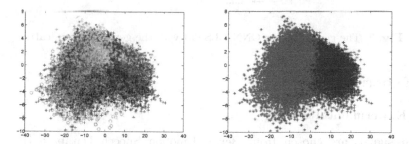

Fig. 2. Feature space of the gender-driven feature. The left panel shows the distribution of seven emotions. The right panel shows the distribution of male and female.

Gender-Driven Feature for SER. In this study, there are two reasons to add the gender-driven feature into spectrographic data. The first is that adding gender information can help improve the accuracy for SER. The gender-driven feature encodes male and female data better with variable values. The second reason is that wide-band spectrogram emphasizes formants but not F0, whereas F0 is the main vocal cue for emotion recognition [15]. Since the gender-driven feature is extracted from the acoustic features, it still retains some acoustic information (e.g. F0) that is complementary to spectrogram.

Figure 3 depicts the structure of our proposed method. In feature preparation and fusion stages, the DNN extracts 32-dimensional gender-driven feature from 384-dimensional acoustic features. Then, the spectrogram and gender-driven feature are combined as compositional feature (F). The compositional feature vectors of the j-th segment in the i-th utterance can be formulated as:

$$F_{ij} = [S_{ij}, GDF_{ij}], \tag{1}$$

where the S_{ij} and GDF_{ij} correspond to spectrogram vector and gender-driven feature vector of the j-th segment in the i-th utterance, respectively.

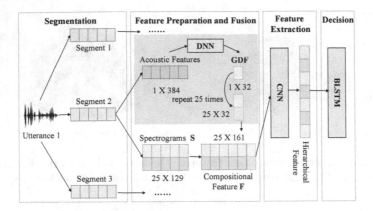

Fig. 3. The gender-aware CNN-BLSTM with the gender-driven feature

4   Experiments

4.1   Experimental Setup

Speech signals are chosen from Berlin Emotion Speech Database [16]. The database has seven categorical emotion types including disgust, sadness, fear, happiness, neutral, boredom and anger, where the numbers of utterances in each category are 46, 62, 69, 71, 79, 81 and 127, respectively. The dataset consists of 535 simulated emotional utterances in German. There are 233 male utterances and 302 female utterances.

Procedures in this study are as follows. All the trials are based on a CNN-BLSTM model. CNN is chosen first to extract hierarchical feature from original spectrogram, because it models temporal and spectral local correlations [17]. Adding BLSTM layers is to recognize sequential dynamics in consecutive utterances [18]. There are two convolutional layers and two max-pooling layers of CNN. The first convolutional layer has 32 filters with 5×5 size, and the second convolutional layer has 64 filters with 5×5 size. The size of two pooling layers is 2×2. After flatten layer, a fully connected layer is used with 1024 units. There are two hidden layers in BLSTM, each of which has 256 units. In our experiment, utterances are split into segments with a 265 ms window size and a 25 ms shift length. For the limited size of Berlin Emotion Database, 10-fold cross validations are used in following trials.

- Spectrogram: This is the baseline model, where only one emotion recognizer is created for speakers. Short-time Fourier transform (STFT) are used to transform segmental signals into amplitude spectrogram. When doing STFT, the FFT points are 256.
- Spectrogram (Sep-System): Compared with the above trial, we create male and female emotion classifiers separately.

- Spectrogram + one-hot gender feature: It is a straightforward way to add 2-dimensional gender information into spectrogram. Male is represented as "0 1", while female is "1 0".
- Spectrogram + fixed gender feature: The ground truth of gender information is encoded as fixed male template or female template. Then, spectrogram is augmented with fixed gender feature.
- **Spectrogram + distributed-gender feature (Proposed):** 32-dimensional distributed-gender feature has been described in Sect. 3.1.
- Spectrogram + LLDs: 32-dimentional LLDs described in Table 1 are added into spectrogram for SER.
- **Spectrogram + gender-driven feature (Proposed):** The detail of this method is shown in Fig. 3. The structure of DNN contains three layers. There are 32 units in the bottleneck layer and 1024 units in other hidden layers. The input of DNN is acoustic features, and teacher signal is gender labels.

4.2 Evaluation Results

Table 2 shows results from the trials shown in the previous section. From Table 2, we conclude: (1) The spectrogram (Sep-System) perform worse than the baseline. It may be because there is less training data to train male and female emotion classifiers separately. (2) Because the size of one-hot gender feature is small, adding the one-hot gender feature into spectrogram shows slight improvements than baseline. (3) Using the distributed-gender feature and gender-driven feature in the gender-aware CNN-BLSTM outperforms the baseline by 14.04% and 45.74% relative error reduction in UA, respectively. In addition, the use of the gender-driven feature performs better than that of the distributed-gender feature. The reason is that the gender-driven feature represents gender characteristics, real individual differences and acoustic information, while the distributed-gender feature only reflects gender information. (4) Using the distributed-gender feature or gender-driven feature performs better than that of the fixed values. The reason is that the variable features can handle gender information in a

Table 2. Weighted accuracy (WA) and unweighted accuracy (UA) of different features for SER. WA refers to the accuracy of all test utterances. UA is defined as average of per emotional category recall. F1 is the harmonic average of precision and recall.

System	Features	Size	WA	UA
Aug	Spectrogram (Baseline)	26 × 129	86.73%	86.40%
Sep	Spectrogram	26 × 129	86.17%	85.46%
Aug	Spectrogram + one-hot gender feature	26 × 131	86.92%	86.24%
Aug	Spectrogram + fixed gender feature	26 × 161	88.22%	87.65%
Aug	**Spectrogram + distributed-gender feature**	26 × 161	88.97%	88.31%
Aug	Spectrogram + LLDs	26 × 161	91.21%	90.76%
Aug	**Spectrogram + gender-driven feature**	26 × 161	**92.71%**	**92.62%**

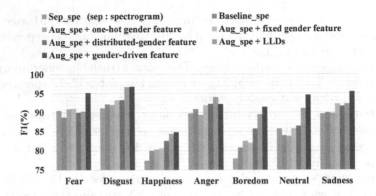

Fig. 4. F1 results of different features on different emotions

more appropriate way. (5) Improvements are shown when LLDs are added into spectrogram. The result reveals that spectrogram and acoustic information are complementary. (6) The gender-driven feature performs better than LLDs. The result shows evidence that the gender-driven feature not only provides gender information but also retains discriminative acoustic information of emotions.

Figure 4 shows the contribution of different features to identify different types of emotions. This figure reveals the following: (1) Although the training data in spectrogram (Sep-System) is less than the baseline, it still performs better on fear and neutral emotions. (2) Use of the distributed-gender feature to represent gender performs better than that of the one-hot gender and fixed gender features on disgust, happiness, anger, boredom and neutral. (3) Adding gender-driven feature to spectrogram contributes to the best results on most emotions, except for anger. Conversely, adding the LLDs to spectrogram achieves the best performance on anger. The reason may be that after the DNN processing, the gender-driven feature is more effective to distinguish gender characteristics. Although the gender-driven feature still keeps acoustic information to classify anger emotion, its contribution is smaller than that of the LLDs. Overall, both the distributed-gender feature and gender-driven feature are effective for SER.

5   Conclusions and Future Work

In this paper, the gender-aware CNN-BLSTM was proposed for speech emotion recognition. We first proposed the distributed-gender feature and gender-driven feature. Then, the two novel features with gender information were individually augmented into spectrogram as additional variables. Finally, the CNN-BLSTM was used to conduct the final classification. The results of evaluations indicated that our proposed features can take advantage of gender information adequately and perform better on SER task. For future work, multi-modal features including textural and visual features will be considered for constructing a SER system.

Acknowledgements. The research was supported by the National Natural Science Foundation of China (No. 61771333 and No. U1736219) and JSPS KAKENHI Grant (16K00297).

References

1. Brody, L.R.: Gender differences in emotional development: a review of theories and research. J. Pers. **53**(2), 102–149 (1985)
2. Hall, J.A., Carter, J.D., Horgan, T.: Gender differences in nonverbal communication of emotion. In: Gender and Emotion: Social Psychological Perspectives, pp. 97–117 (2000). https://doi.org/10.1017/CBO9780511628191.006
3. Sidorov, M., Ultes, S., Schmitt, A.: Comparison of Gender and Speaker-adaptive Emotion Recognition. In: Language Resources and Evaluation Conference, pp. 3476–3480 (2014)
4. Sidorov, M., Ultes, S., Schmitt, A.: Emotions are a personal thing: towards speaker-adaptive emotion recognition. In: IEEE International Conference on Acoustics, Speech and Signal Processing, pp. 4803–4807 (2014)
5. Vogt, T., André, E.: Improving automatic emotion recognition from speech via gender differentiation. In: Language Resources and Evaluation Conference, Genoa (2006)
6. Sidorov, M., Schmitt, A., Semenkin, E., et al.: Could speaker, gender or age awareness be beneficial in speech-based emotion recognition? In: Language Resources and Evaluation Conference (2016)
7. Schuller, B., Steidl S., Batliner, A.: The INTERSPEECH 2009 emotion challenge. In: Tenth Annual Conference of the International Speech Communication Association (2009)
8. Hannun, A., Case, C., Casper, J., et al.: Deep speech: scaling up end-to-end speech recognition. arXiv preprint arXiv:1412.5567 (2014)
9. Amodei, D., Ananthanarayanan, S., Anubhai, R., et al.: Deep speech 2: end-to-end speech recognition in English and mandarin. In: International Conference on Machine Learning, pp. 173–182 (2016)
10. Lim, W., Jang, D., Lee, T.: Speech emotion recognition using convolutional and recurrent neural networks. In: Signal and Information Processing Association Annual Summit and Conference, Asia-Pacific, pp. 1–4. IEEE (2016)
11. Satt, A., Rozenberg, S., Hoory, R.: Efficient emotion recognition from speech using deep learning on spectrograms. In: Proceedings of INTERSPEECH 2017, pp. 1089–1093 (2017)
12. Guo, L., Wang, L., Dang, J., Zhang, L., Guan, H.: A feature fusion method based on extreme learning machine for speech emotion recognition. In: IEEE International Conference on Acoustics, Speech and Signal Processing, pp. 2666–2670 (2018)
13. Scherer, K.R.: Emotion. In: Stroebe, W., Jonas, K., Hewstone, M. (eds.) Sozialpsychologie. Springer-Lehrbuch, pp. 165–213. Springer, Heidelberg (2002). https://doi.org/10.1007/978-3-662-08008-5_6
14. Grezl, F., Fousek, P.: Optimizing bottle-neck features for LVCSR. In: IEEE International Conference on Acoustics, Speech and Signal Processing, pp. 4729–4732 (2008)
15. Petrushin, V.A.: Emotion recognition in speech signal: experimental study, development, and application. In: Sixth International Conference on Spoken Language Processing (2000)

16. Burkhardt, F., Paeschke, A., Rolfes, M., Sendlmeier, W.F., Weiss, B.: A database of German emotional speech. In: Ninth European Conference on Speech Communication and Technology (2005)
17. Yu, D., et al.: Deep convolutional neural networks with layer-wise context expansion and attention. In: INTERSPEECH, pp. 17–21 (2016)
18. Lee, J., Tashev, I.: High-level feature representation using recurrent neural network for speech emotion recognition. In: INTERSPEECH (2015)

Semi-supervised Model for Emotion Recognition in Speech

Ingryd Pereira[1]($\boxtimes$), Diego Santos[2]($\boxtimes$), Alexandre Maciel[1]($\boxtimes$),
and Pablo Barros[3]($\boxtimes$)

[1] Polytechnic School of Pernambuco, University of Pernambuco, Recife, Brazil
{ivstp,amam}@ecomp.poli.br
[2] Fedreal University of Pernambuco, Recife, Brazil
dgs2@ecomp.poli.br
[3] Knowledge Technology, Department of Informatics, University of Hamburg,
Hamburg, Germany
barros@informatik.uni-hamburg.de

Abstract. To recognize emotional traits on speech is a challenging task which became very popular in the past years, especially due to the recent advances in deep neural networks. Although very successful, these models inherited a common problem from strongly supervised deep neural networks: a large number of strongly labeled samples demands necessary, so the model learns a general emotion representation. This paper proposes a solution for this problem with the development of a semi-supervised neural network which can learn speech representation from unlabeled samples and used them in different emotion recognition in speech scenarios. We provide experiments with different datasets, representing natural and controlled scenarios. Our results show that our model is competitive with state-of-the-art solutions in all these scenarios while sharing the same learned representations, which were learned without the necessity of strong labeled data.

Keywords: Emotion recognition · Semi-supervised learning · GAN
Speech representation · Deep learning

1 Introduction

Recent advances in deep learning provided an increase in popularity and robustness on emotion recognition in speech tasks [14, 20, 23]. Such models usually make use of a large number of labeled samples to learn general representations for emotion recognition, providing state-of-the-art results in different speech related scenarios [2, 8, 21].

However, supervised deep learning needs a lot of labeled training data. Another problem with the current supervised deep learning models lies in the nature of emotion description itself. Different persons can express and perceive the same emotion in many ways, which causes a lack of agreement about how to

© Springer Nature Switzerland AG 2018
V. Kůrková et al. (Eds.): ICANN 2018, LNCS 11139, pp. 791–800, 2018.
https://doi.org/10.1007/978-3-030-01418-6_77

annotate samples from different scenarios [7]. One solution for this is the use of an even larger number of labeled samples to represent different emotional states into a general emotion categorization.

The use of unsupervised learning becomes useful to solve this problem since it does not require labeled data to learn general speech representation, which can be transferred to emotions. To work around this problem, recent works like [1,15,16,19] apply semi-supervised training on deep neural networks for image classification in domains where the labeled date is scarcity.

If we train a deep neural model with a dataset from a given domain, the model will specialize in that scenario. But a model specialized on to generate a general representation of the data will be capable of representing the audio in every presented scenario. To be able to be general enough, deep learning models for speech emotion recognition usually rely on a large number of labeled samples. This issue happens because (1) deep neural models need a large number of samples to learn descriptors which are robust enough to generalize the domain where they are applied. (2) Strongly supervised training produces a fast and more focused change on the gradient directions, which usually leads to a better fine-tuning of the descriptors and separation boundaries for classification.

We propose a hybrid neural network, composed of an adversarial autoencoder to learn general speech representations and use it as input to a strongly supervised model to classify emotion expressions in the speech in different scenarios. In the first step, the model learns how to represent the audio through an unsupervised training process. This representation will be the input for the second step where the model learns the separation boundaries and distribution between classes through a supervised learning process. In the unsupervised step, a Generative Adversarial Network (GAN) trains an autoencoder that will be responsible for learning how to represent speech present in the audio. As a GAN has unsupervised training, the model can use unbranded and not emotional data what possibilities that the use of the trained model over different scenarios. After training, the encoder filters can extract prosodic characteristics of the input speech without the necessity of supervised labels. The encoder ends up learning representations based on the data distribution. The second module of the proposed model uses these prosodic characteristics learned by the encoder as low-level feature representations, and, now using a strongly supervised solution, is trained to classify emotion recognition in speech. A set of different filters also composes the classifier. These filters are fine-tuned and learn high-level abstractions of the input signal, which are pertinent to that specific domain.

We make used of an unconstrained and unlabeled corpus to learn general speech representations, which is shared among all our emotion recognition scenario. Our specific classifiers are fine-tuned to specific emotion recognition high-level characteristics. This reduces the training effort and applicability of the model to different emotion recognition scenarios.

So, in emotion recognition task, the use of general speech representation, training in an unsupervised manner, improve the application performance and also build an adaptive model for others scenarios, once the speech representation doesn't be stuck in the scenario of the dataset evaluated. The main contribution of this proposition is the general speech recognition model. This model can fit in different emotional recognition scenarios and different datasets without retraining. In other emotional recognition works the audio representation ends up stuck in the scene obtained from the training dataset. In our proposition the audio representation is more robust, being able to represent different domains, situations, and languages.

We evaluate the performance of our model in three different scenarios: indoor, outdoor and cross-language and compare it with state-of-the-art solutions. We prove that our model learned a general speech representation which is shared among all these scenarios, and the different specific filters learn high-level abstractions which are unique for each of these scenarios. For that, we use three different datasets: the Surrey Audio-Visual Expressed Emotion Dataset (SAVEE) [13] which represents a controlled environment, usually found in indoor scenarios or simple interactions, the OMG Emotion Dataset [3], which represents an in-the-wild, outdoor, unrestricted scenario and finally the Berlin Database of Emotional Speech (EmoDB) [6] which evaluates how well the learned representations learned with speech signals in one language can be transferred to other for emotion recognition. This way, we can prove the universal aspect of emotion recognition, and that our fine-tuning step learns to correlate the emotional aspects of the general speech representation, ignoring the information which is not necessary for this task.

2 Proposed Model

In this work, we propose a semi-supervised model for emotion recognition. The model contains two modules: the first one is the general speech representation and the second one is the classifier model. Figure 1 presents the model illustration.

The training of the first module of our network happens in an unsupervised way. The first model is composed of an autoencoder trained by a GAN. We use the encoder present in the autoencoder model for learning the general speech representation. The GAN was chosen because have an autoencoder in its structure and allows an adversary training with a large amount of unlabeled data. The speech representation generated by the model will be the input for the second part of the model.

The second part is responsible for the distribution between the classes in an emotion classification or for prediction from the values in a dimensional model. The training of this module is in a supervised way. We adapt the output of the classifier accordingly to the task: or we use binary classification for categorical emotions (e.g., anger, fear, happiness, etc.) or we use a double-head one unit structure, for arousal/valence regression.

2.1 Adversarial Autoencoder

The Generative Adversarial Network (GAN) [12] has had a significant impact on data generation, mainly of images, but also in audio applications, for example

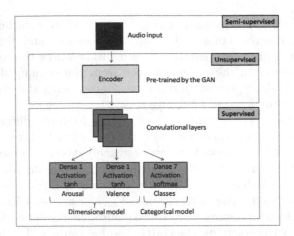

Fig. 1. Abstraction of the classifier and prediction models

for melody generation [22] and noise cleaning [18]. The basic idea of a GAN is to conduct unsupervised adversarial training in two artificial neural networks, a discriminator model (D) and a generator model (G). The training process occurs similarly to a minimax two-player game, in which G captures the data distribution, and D estimates the likelihood of an example coming from G to be real. The G training procedure is to maximize the probability of D making a mistake.

The Boundary Equilibrium Generative Adversarial Networks (BEGAN) [5] is a GAN variation, and have a differential are the use of an autoencoder as a discriminator. Others particularities of BEGAN is the loss derived from Wasserstein's distance; the addition of a γ variable to balance GAN training; and the addition of a new metric called m *global*.

The training of the basic GAN, proposed by Goodfellow [12], G e o D is trained in an The training of the basic GAN, proposed by Goodfellow [12], G and the D are trained in an adversarial way. Figure 2 presents the training representation of a GAN. In this figure, x represents the real samples, $\ddot{x}$ represents the generated samples by the generator and z is the generated noise that is the generator inputs. The training of D has two different moments: first one where the inputs are real samples and the expected output is the real class that example belongs to (i.e., class 1). The second one where the inputs are samples generated by the generator from the noise and the expected output is a fake classification (i.e., class 0). For the generator, the flow is: the generator module receives as input a noisy, and a fake sample generated as an input of the discriminator. The objective is to make this sample be confused with a real sample, so the expected output is a real classification by the discriminator. In this step the discriminator training is frozen, and only training the generator.

A characteristic BEGAN is the application of a balance paired with a loss derived from Wasserstein's distance to the autoencoder training [5]. In the

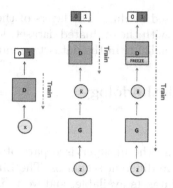

Fig. 2. Training representation of discriminator (D) and generator (G)

training step, the BEGAN has a balancing factor, defined by a variable γ, with a range of 0 to 1. This variable penalizes D training, slowing it down. Since G training is more difficult and slower than D, this penalty balances the algorithms, thus increasing the performance of GAN [5].

GANs were used recently on semi-supervised learning for image classification tasks [1,15,16,19] and was shown to be more effective than strongly supervised classification. That happens because the use of unsupervised training makes possible to the model to learn general representations of the domain, while the supervised fine-tuning specializes in the model to solve the specific tasks. We choose to use a variation of an adversarial autoencoder, the BEGAN [5] because it presented better results than common GANs results on learning general representations.

2.2 Supervised Classifiers

The supervised module of the proposed model varies according to the emotion recognition scenario. But the basic structure is: it receives as input the speech representation obtained by the unsupervised module, then it applies convolutional layers and a softmax classifier which is adapted depending on the scenario.

We optimize the hyper-parameters of the supervised module for each task. For that, we use the Hyperas [4] framework, where is specialized in optimizing search spaces with real, discrete and conditional dimensions.

2.3 Semi-supervised Learning

The adversarial autoencoder will be pre-trained with a database with a larger number of data. Once trained the autoencoder, don't need to retrain this model and this same autoencoder can be reuse in others applications, also without the need of retraining.

The supervised model training happens during the semi-supervised model training process. In this process, we freeze the encoder layers trained previously and train only the supervised module. The layers of the autoencoder are freeze because if it is trained too with the evaluated dataset, lose the nature of general speech representation, specializing in the dataset scenario.

3   Experimental Methodology

3.1   Datasets

We use one dataset to train the unsupervised part of our model, and three to evaluate the whole model in different scenarios. The LibreSpeech [17] dataset is one of the largest audio datasets available, and we use it to train the unsupervised module. We use this dataset because its amount of data and variability of speakers and scenario is interesting to generate a general representation of speech. LibriSpeech is a dataset with approximately 1000 h of English speech.

We use three others datasets, and these datasets are emotional, multimodal and multispeaker. Each one has different characteristics and scenarios, which possibility different analysis. Therefore, we evaluated our model in an indoor, outdoor and cross-language scenarios, witch SAVEE [13], OMG Emotion [3] and EmoDB [6] datasets, respectively.

SAVEE. We used the Surrey Audio-Visual Expressed Emotion Dataset (SAVEE) [13] in our experiments. SAVEE is an emotional audiovisual dataset, with consists of recordings of four male actors speaking phrases in 7 different emotion intonations based on the Universal Emotions [11] with the addition of the neutral emotion, where the speaker not present any of the six universal emotions.

This work uses only the auditive module of the dataset, and has 480 statements in total. The SAVEE database is balanced, recorded in a controlled and noise-free environment and only has male voices. Therefore is considered a simple base and applied as the starting point of the experiments.

OMG Emotion Dataset. The One-Minute Gradual-Emotional Behavior dataset (OMG-Emotion) [3] is the database from the One-Minute Gradual-Emotion Behavior Challenge, which takes place at IJCNN 2018. The dataset contains 567 unique videos totaling 7371 clips each clip consisting of a single utterance. Each video has a different utterance number with an average duration of 8 s by utterance and total average video duration next to 1 min.

The dataset has dimensional and categorical labels, being seven different emotions, based on the Universal Emotions [11] with the addition of the neutral emotion. The dataset also has continuous dimensional label being arousal and valence with values in a range between -1 and 1. OMG emotion dataset is a complex, given its variability of speakers, scenarios, dialogs and videos duration. The dataset labels are either categorical and dimensional, what makes possible to verify the proposed model performance in different emotional recognition tasks.

EmoDB. The Berlin Database of Emotional Speech (EmoDB) [6] is an emotional speech database recorded in German. It contains about 500 utterances spoken by the actors in a happy, angry, anxious, fearful, bored and disgusted manner, as well as in a neutral version. It has statements from 10 different actors and ten different texts. We used the EmoDB dataset to verify it the proposed model can also generalize emotional characteristics from other languages.

3.2 Preprocessing

Our first preprocessing step was to change the audio frequency to 16 kH. Then each audio track was decomposed into 1-s chunks without overlapping. After that, the raw audio was converted to a spectrogram via Short Time Fourier Transform, with an FFT of size 1024 and a length of 512.

3.3 Experiments Setup

To evaluate our model on the SAVEE dataset, we train the BEGAN with part of the LibreSpeech dataset but evaluating the emotion classification model with SAVEE dataset. To be possible to compare with another work, this experiment follows the same protocol of Ashwin work et al. [2], where perform the job of classifying emotions present in audio and video proposing a novel hybrid SVM-RBM classifier. We compare just with the audio module. Ashwin et al. perform the experiment called dependent speaker, which uses each speaker sets for training, and for each evaluated test of each speaker (DC, JE, JK, KL). The division of the base is approximately 60% for training and 40% for testing.

Experiments were also carried out with the OMG Emotion dataset, with categorical and dimensional labels, which allows the evaluation of two emotion recognition tasks: the classification of static emotion and prediction of dimensional values arousal and valence. For all experiments with OMG Emotion dataset, the training process of BEGAN uses part of the LibreSpeech dataset, and the division of the training and testing process follows the same distribution made available in the database itself.

The experiments performed on EmoDB dataset follow the Leave One Speaker Out protocol (LOSO) to be possible perform the comparative with other works that follow the same protocol. In the experiment, we train the BEGAN with part of the LibreSpeech dataset recorded in English and the model evaluated on EmoDB dataset which is one German language recorded database.

We train the algorithms in each experiment with 100 epochs, with a batch size of 16. The discriminator and the generator of the BEGAN used the Adam optimizer with a learning rate of 0.00005. The BEGAN also has a *gamma* value that balances the generator and the discriminator with a value of 0.7.

4   Results and Discussion

Table 1 shows the accuracy averages achieved with ten executions of the model and the best results obtained in Ashwin's work [2]. The results obtained with this proposal are bigger than the related work. The standard deviation is small, so this means that the model proves to be stable.

Table 1. Comparison between the accuracy (%) averages

	DC	JE	JK	KL
Ashwin et al. [2]	79	78	76	80
This work	80.69 (±2.96)	80.96 (±3.41)	80.15 (±1.85)	82.46 (±2.70)

Table 2 presents the summary of the executions of the model when tested with the OMG Emotion Dataset, the baseline results [3], and the best result obtained in the challenge in audio modality[1]. The table has the F-score of the classifier and also has the CCC of the arousal and valence values predicted. The result F-score obtained with the classifier model was higher than the baseline, and has the advantage that a general speech representation was used and that it can be reused without the need of re-training in other datasets. The CCC obtained in our experiments is smaller than the result obtained in the challenge, but is better than baseline work. We obtained this result with the same model of the classification experiments, without specific treatment for this task and still the result is better than the baseline.

Table 2. Results with the OMG emotion dataset

	F-score	Arousal CCC	Valence CCC
Barros et al. [3]	0.39	0.07	0.04
OMG emotion challenge	-	0.29	0.36
This work	0.73	0.17	0.16

Table 3 presents the results from the executions with the EmoDB dataset and the comparison with other works that use the same experimentation protocol. As can be seen, our proposal is above of the related works. But considering that our model learns how to represent the emotional data in another language, the results can still be relevant for being next of the related works.

The BEGAN trained with LibreSpeech database used in our experiments perform the training process only once. After saving the model, it can execute different experiments without the need for retraining. The no reed of retraining is one of the principal advantages of the proposed approach since once trained the model; we can use it for different databases and several tasks without the need for retraining.

---

[1] https://www2.informatik.uni-hamburg.de/wtm/OMG-EmotionChallenge/.

Table 3. Results with EmoDB dataset

	Accuracy
Deb and Dandapat [10]	83.80%
Deb and Dandapat [9]	85.10%
This work	72%

5 Conclusion

The work proposed is the development a new semi-supervised model for emotion recognition tasks. The use of this algorithm can help overcome one of the common challenges of emotion recognition field, which is the speech representation.

We propose a general speech representation model, which is constructed with a GAN and trained in an unsupervised way and then incorporated into the models, thus building the semi-supervised model. From a set of experiments, with different datasets in the same algorithm, it was possible to verify that the use of GAN can help in the training of an emotion recognizer, that besides needing a smaller amount of training data in the supervised part, also achieves superior performance and provides a more stable algorithm.

In this work, experiments were performed with the SAVEE dataset, which is a simple dataset, and also with the OMG Emotion Dataset, which is a complex database, given its speakers and scenarios variability, and has categorical and dimensional labels. In the experiments, it was possible to verify that the proposed model is superior to the baseline, and also the benefit of using a speech representation model that can be reused in other models and other databases.

Experiment with a dataset of other language was performed. The speech representation module was trained with one dataset of the English language and was performed the emotion classification in a Germany dataset. The results were similar to related works used how baseline. This experiment proves that unsupervised model represents the speech emotional characteristics independent of the language.

As a continuation of this work will be carried out sets of experiments where BEGAN will be trained with different datasets, and the semi-supervised learning model will be evaluated with other datasets with different domains (e.g., a dataset with only children's voices, a dataset in other languages, etc.).

References

1. Adiwardana, D.D.F., Matsukawa, A., Whang, J.: Using generative models for semi-supervised learning
2. Ashwin, T., Saran, S., Reddy, G.R.M.: Video affective content analysis based on multimodal features using a novel hybrid SVM-RBM classifier. In: 2016 IEEE Uttar Pradesh Section International Conference on Electrical, Computer and Electronics Engineering (UPCON), pp. 416–421. IEEE (2016)

3. Barros, P., Churamani, N., Lakomkin, E., Siqueira, H., Sutherland, A., Wermter, S.: The OMG-emotion behavior dataset. arXiv preprint arXiv:1803.05434 (2018)
4. Bergstra, J., Yamins, D., Cox, D.D.: Hyperopt: a python library for optimizing the hyperparameters of machine learning algorithms. In: Proceedings of the 12th Python in Science Conference, pp. 13–20. Citeseer (2013)
5. Berthelot, D., Schumm, T., Metz, L.: Began: boundary equilibrium generative adversarial networks. arXiv preprint arXiv:1703.10717 (2017)
6. Burkhardt, F., Paeschke, A., Rolfes, M., Sendlmeier, W.F., Weiss, B.: A database of German emotional speech. In: Ninth European Conference on Speech Communication and Technology (2005)
7. Cabanac, M.: What is emotion? Behav. Process. **60**(2), 69–83 (2002)
8. Chang, J., Scherer, S.: Learning representations of emotional speech with deep convolutional generative adversarial networks. arXiv preprint arXiv:1705.02394 (2017)
9. Deb, S., Dandapat, S.: Emotion classification using segmentation of vowel-like and non-vowel-like regions. IEEE Trans. Affect. Comput. (2017)
10. Deb, S., Dandapat, S.: Multiscale amplitude feature and significance of enhanced vocal tract information for emotion classification. IEEE Trans. Cybern. (2018)
11. Ekman, P.: An argument for basic emotions. Cogn. Emot. **6**(3–4), 169–200 (1992)
12. Goodfellow, I., et al.: Generative adversarial nets. In: Advances in Neural Information Processing Systems, pp. 2672–2680 (2014)
13. Haq, S., Jackson, P.J.: Multimodal emotion recognition. In: Machine Audition: Principles, Algorithms and Systems, pp. 398–423 (2010)
14. Huang, Z., Dong, M., Mao, Q., Zhan, Y.: Speech emotion recognition using CNN. In: Proceedings of the 22nd ACM International Conference on Multimedia, pp. 801–804. ACM (2014)
15. Kingma, D.P., Mohamed, S., Rezende, D.J., Welling, M.: Semi-supervised learning with deep generative models. In: Advances in Neural Information Processing Systems, pp. 3581–3589 (2014)
16. Odena, A.: Semi-supervised learning with generative adversarial networks. arXiv preprint arXiv:1606.01583 (2016)
17. Panayotov, V., Chen, G., Povey, D., Khudanpur, S.: LibriSpeech: an ASR corpus based on public domain audio books. In: 2015 IEEE International Conference on Acoustics, Speech and Signal Processing (ICASSP), pp. 5206–5210. IEEE (2015)
18. Pascual, S., Bonafonte, A., Serrà, J.: SEGAN: speech enhancement generative adversarial network. arXiv preprint arXiv:1703.09452 (2017)
19. Springenberg, J.T.: Unsupervised and semi-supervised learning with categorical generative adversarial networks. arXiv preprint arXiv:1511.06390 (2015)
20. Trigeorgis, G., et al.: Adieu features? End-to-end speech emotion recognition using a deep convolutional recurrent network. In: 2016 IEEE International Conference on Acoustics, Speech and Signal Processing (ICASSP), pp. 5200–5204. IEEE (2016)
21. Weißkirchen, N., Bock, R., Wendemuth, A.: Recognition of emotional speech with convolutional neural networks by means of spectral estimates. In: 2017 Seventh International Conference on Affective Computing and Intelligent Interaction Workshops and Demos (ACIIW), pp. 50–55. IEEE (2017)
22. Yang, L.C., Chou, S.Y., Yang, Y.H.: MidiNet: a convolutional generative adversarial network for symbolic-domain music generation. In: Proceedings of the 18th International Society for Music Information Retrieval Conference (ISMIR 2017), Suzhou, China (2017)
23. Zheng, W., Yu, J., Zou, Y.: An experimental study of speech emotion recognition based on deep convolutional neural networks. In: 2015 International Conference on Affective Computing and Intelligent Interaction (ACII), pp. 827–831. IEEE (2015)

Real-Time Embedded Intelligence System: Emotion Recognition on Raspberry Pi with Intel NCS

Y. Xing[1(✉)], P. Kirkland[1], G. Di Caterina[1], J. Soraghan[1],
and G. Matich[2]

[1] University of Strathclyde, Glasgow, UK
{yannan.xing, paul.kirkland, gaetano.di-caterina,
j.soraghan}@strath.ac.uk
[2] Leonardo MW Ltd, Sigma House, Christopher Martin Road,
Basildon, Essex SS143EL, UK

Abstract. Convolutional Neural Networks (CNNs) have exhibited certain human-like performance on computer vision related tasks. Over the past few years since they have outperformed conventional algorithms in a range of image processing problems. However, to utilise a CNN model with millions of free parameters on a source limited embedded system is a challenging problem. The Intel Neural Compute Stick (NCS) provides a possible route for running large-scale neural networks on a low cost, low power, portable unit. In this paper, we propose a CNN based Raspberry Pi system that can run a pre-trained inference model in real time with an average power consumption of 6.2 W. The Intel Movidius NCS, which avoids requirements of expensive processing units e.g. GPU, FPGA. The system is demonstrated using a facial image-based emotion recogniser. A fine-tuned CNN model is designed and trained to perform inference on each captured frame within the processing modules of NCS.

Keywords: CNN · Embedded system · Low power system · SWaP profile

1 Introduction

Size, Weight and Power (SWaP) profile are important factors in many applications of real-time embedded systems. However, it is difficult to incorporate the benefits of deep learning (DL) in real-time embedded systems due to the limited computation capability and power. One solution is to use cloud computing [1]. This paper shows the first comparison between typical DL hardware and an edge device, which is applicable to any DL model that does not require any online learning. Hoping to show how the NCS can help bridge the gap between the two. The next phase of the Internet of Things (IoT) development will be adding intelligence to the devices. This will not only allow each device to share more in-depth information, but it will also require less information to be sent off the device which provides a greater level of security. These devices are

---

Y. Xing and P. Kirkland—contributed equally to first author.

V. Kůrková et al. (Eds.): ICANN 2018, LNCS 11139, pp. 801–808, 2018.
https://doi.org/10.1007/978-3-030-01418-6_78

typically unable to run DL models due to the amount of processing required, which we show is no longer the case.

The remainder of the paper is organised as follows. Section 2 introduces the background of DL on embedded systems. Section 3 describes the proposed Ras-Pi NCS system with details on system configuration working with a very simple self-designed CNN based on public emotion recognition dataset. The runtime speed and power consumption of system are presented in Sect. 4 and compared to several DL evaluation platforms. Section 5 concludes the paper.

2 Background

Advances in Smart devices and Internet of Things have led to a plethora of devices with the potential to have real-time embedded intelligence. As traditional DL research concentrated on GPUs, the focus was on computational runtime, accuracy and not power use [2]. However, low powered edge devices are an important area of research.

Nvidia to date has arguably the most popular embedded DL devices with the Jetson range. With the NVidia Jetson range TK1, TX1 and TX2 have featured in up to 1,000 research publications (Google Scholar Search) in a broad range of applications [3–5]. Benchmarks compared to PCs have shown there are good use cases for these devices, with power savings of 15–30 times, with a reduction in throughput by one-tenth, a net increase of 5–15 times [6].

Other chip manufacturers have introduced their own version of low powered embedded DL accelerators, such as Qualcomm with their Snapdragon Neural Processing Engine and Intel with both their Nervana Neural Network Processor and the device featured in this paper, the Movidius Myriad Visual Processing Unit (in the form of the Neural Compute Stick). Pena et al. [7] presented the first benchmarking results of the NCS, Raspberry Pi 3, and the Intel Jolue 750x development board. All tests are measuring the amount of time taking and power used to complete one pass of the network, with the NCSs results being averaged over both boards. It also showed how the different systems handled a variety of differing complexity networks. Figure 1 gives an illustration of the design system. The NCS, Webcam and Power Bank are connected via USB, while the touchscreen is connected via the GPIO pins to the Raspberry Pi. The actual system showing how all the components are connected and how the UI appears on the screen are shown on the right of Fig. 1.

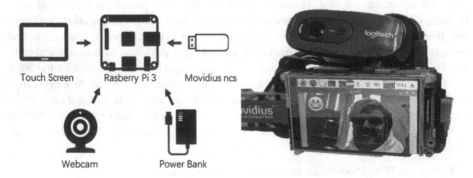

Fig. 1. The Raspberry Pi – NCS system.

3 The System

As is shown in Fig. 1 a Raspberry Pi 3 model B development board with 40 GPIO pins and four USB2.0 ports is used as the main processing unit in the proposed system. The power of board is supplied by a 5 V/2 A mobile DC power bank to make the whole system fully portable. The Raspberry Pi contains a 1.2 GHz 64-bit quad-core ARM Cortex-A53 CPU with 1 GB of RAM, running standard RASPBIAN Jessie desktop OS that supports required Python programming environment for the Intel NCS SDK to run in API mode. A Logitech C270 HD (720p) webcam is used via one USB2.0 port to provide desired video input. A 3.5" TFT touchscreen is set to satisfy general user interaction and visualising the online-processing results. The Intel NCS is used exclusively for the neural network model, with the information being transferred over the USB interface.

3.1 The CNN for Emotes

The architecture of the network had to be a reduced and cut down version of the state of the art architectures, as the inference models that are runnable on the NCS cannot resolve the unknown placeholders/variables. Very often these placeholders are employed for training specific parameters but are not necessary for NCS inferencing. Before trying to compile the NCS model, the Tensorflow model can be trained to generate three saved model files: index file as model indexing, data file as the network parameters and meta file which contains the network structure. These files will be further used in the shrunken version of the network to generate another set of inference-only network models. The original network is reduced with dropout layers and training specific code removed which usually contains: reading/importing data, loss function and accuracy computation definition, placeholders except for the input tensor of the network etc. The name for the input and output layer always requires to be set to make sure the compiler is easier to determine and recognise from the structure of the network.

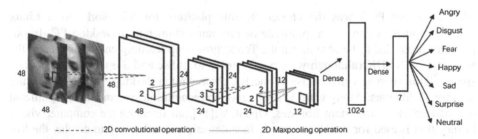

Fig. 2. The designed CNN architecture for facial expression recognition, the stride of convolution kernel is set to be 1 and the stride of polling kernel is set to be 2.

The facial based emotional recogniser network illustrated in Fig. 2 contains a total of 6 layers: 2 convolutional, 2 pooling, and 2 fully-connected. The Rectified linear unit (ReLU) activation function [8] is employed for each layer. The CNN inputs are grayscale 48×48 images and followed by 2 convolutional layers with 32 and 64 filters with the size of both being 3×3. The convolution operation in each layer is set to be 1-pixel strides with the same padding. The max-pooling layers with 2×2 kernel size is placed behind each convolutional layer to perform a subsampling for feature maps from the previous layer. The final stage is a fully connected dense layer with 1024 neurons, the network output layer is comprised of 7 neurons performing the softmax [9] calculation which indicates the number of facial emotions.

Training Phase. The training data utilises the FER2013 database [10]. According to the results from previous work, we consider that the order of the original dataset represents an unbalanced training set., which can lead to obvious overfitting and underfitting issues. We randomly initialised the order of the originally given dataset as well as correspond labels and split it into required data batches. The learning of the CNN employed the backpropagation incorporating cross-entropy as target loss function and the Adam stochastic optimiser [11]. In order to prevent the network suffering from overfitting, the Ridge Penalisation (L2 regularisation) is implemented among the cross-entropy function. The dropout technique [12] also well known as an effective regularisation to prevent network overfitting. In the training phase, the fully connected layer is set to randomly dropout with rate 0.5.

Result. The designed convolutional network was validated on the self-defined (shuffled) testing set and validation set. The Extended Cohn-Kanade(CK+) [13] dataset was also used to evaluate the actual performance of the network with the same model which trained by the FER2013 dataset. After 100 epochs the model converged at 90.99% testing accuracy and 87.73% validation accuracy based on the shuffled FER2013 dataset. The model showing a 70.51% test accuracy on the CK+ dataset with a very good performance in recognising happy with 100%, supervised with 92% and neutral with 84%. The confusion matrix on the FER2013 test set shows nearly perfect accuracy on each emotion.

3.2   Embedded Device

The Raspberry Pi 3 was the chosen flexible platform for this work. As a Linux microcomputer, it can run a multitude of programs similar to a Desktop PC. In our problem, it needed to be able to run the Tensorflow deep learning environment and the full Intel NCS SDK (although we are only going to utilise and use the API to save on space). This approach makes use of the Raspbian stretch desktop OS while utilising another 18 libraries. Along with API, the emotion recognition system makes significant use of two other important libraries, OpenCV [14], an open source computer vision library that is used for the Haar cascade face detection function and to display the live emotion recognition feed to the display. The decision to use the inbuilt Haar cascade was due to the speed at runtime compared to similar models, once optimised, for example, the dlib [15] libraries Histogram of Gradients (HoG) face detector. The Haar classifier was able to produce a robust detection of a face at 3–4x the speed of the HoG classifier. The Haar classifier is known to be the faster and less accurate classifier but proves to be robust enough as the face cropper within this system. The well-established Multi-Task Cascaded Convolutional Network (MTCNN) [16] deep learning approach to face detection and alignment was also tested, as a recent implementation had appeared on the NCS GitHub page called the NCS App Zoo. This network requires the use of a further 2 Intel NCS units to run but would allow an end-to-end deep learning approach to the emotion recognition. However, due to the bounding box regression stages of the network, it proved to be slower with an average runtime similar to that of the dlib HoG classifier.

The other important library to ensure real-time operation is imutils [17]. This convenience library helps with a significant speed up with one of the bottleneck areas of image acquisition. Compared to the OpenCV function, the imutils function utilises the multi-threading of the Raspberry Pi's quad-core processor having a function able to collect the image from the webcam as soon as it is available and then store it to a queue of images. The result is the time taken to acquire the next image reduces from 10 s of milliseconds to 10 s of nanoseconds.

3.3   Intel NCS

DL is appearing in an increasing number of mobile devices without the necessity for cloud computing. The NCS used in this paper is from chipmaker Intel's Movidius department, which incorporates one Myriad 2 machine vision processing unit into a small USB stick, Movidius announced that it delivers more than 100 gigaflops of performance. It can locally run neural networks inference model using Caffe and Tensorflow framework. A general development process of NCS based embedded system is illustrated in Fig. 3. The training process does not need to utilise the NCS stick or SDK but only standard DNN development on a desktop PC. Using the software SDK of the NCS, the user should subsequently perform training, profiling, tuning and compiling a DNN model on the NCS and a PC that runs x86 64bit ubuntu 16.04 OS. The provided SDK can check the validity of designed DNN and API for python and C languages. After that, any developer system (e.g. a raspberry pi) that runs a compatible OS with neural compute API can accelerate neural network inferences.

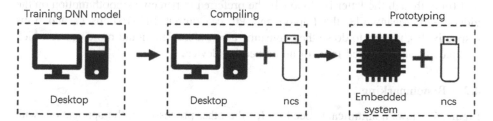

Fig. 3. Illustration of using the Intel NCS to develop for a DNN based embedded system

4   Evaluation

This section looks at the running of the emotion recognition program and delivers the results in terms of processing time. The Raspberry Pi 3 is compared against two other devices running the same application both running Ubuntu 16.04. An Alienware 15

Laptop with an Intel i7 6820HK Quad-core CPU @ 2.7 GHz with 16 GB of RAM and a GTX 980m GPU. The other machine was a Desktop PC with an AMD Ryzen 1700X Octa-core CPU @ 3.4GHZ with 32 GB of RAM and a GTX 1080Ti., with the added measure of how much power is being used to deliver the results.

4.1   Real Time Running on Pi

The actual system with all devices is illustrated in Fig. 1. Figure 4 shows runtimes, for 10 runs of the code averaged, each running for 300 frames. The times for the non-deep learning parts are combined and averaged so as not to influence the overall results as only minor fluctuations appear between runs. Figure 4, breaks down the timing into sections:

- *Camera Read* – the time taken for reading an image from the camera
- *Image Show* – the time taken to display the image onto the touchscreen with emotion emoji,
- *Haar Face Detection* – the time taken for the detector to crop the image around a found face
- *Inference Runtime* – the time taken for the CNN model to run and
- *Loop Runtime* – the total time taken to process one image of the video capture.

The graph highlights which parts of the process are slow, especially on an embedded device, with the time axis given in a log format to allow for the differing magnitudes of time taken for different tasks to be represented equally. Only one section differs from the previously mentioned arrangement which is the R-Pi (opt) which is the optimised version to allow the system to run in true real-time (sub 33 ms), while still displaying the camera feed to the user. Modifications included running the Haar face detector only every 3rd frame. Also removing the emoji image to the image displayed on the device and instead, printing the emotion to the terminal. This resulted in a saving of 20 and 12 ms respectively. Therefore, while the Pi with NCS can run at 14 fps (66 ms) the optimised code can run at 30 fps (33 ms), both of which can be classed as real-time, though the latter is obviously the preferred to perceive smooth motion on the video feed. Meanwhile, the Laptop and PC can output 142–167 fps (7 and 6 ms respectively), though to do so they consume a considerable amount more power which is typically an undesired trait for an embedded device.

4.2   Benchmarking

Figure 4, shows a significant speed up for the other processes in the application, with the GPUs managing to run the TensorFlow models with the fastest time as expected. A better comparison though is to see how the systems perform in terms of Inference per Second per Watt, which would be an important factor to consider with a minimal SWaP profile. Table 1 shows how the results for the 6 system types, with the new value given the term RP (Run-Power is the coefficient - inference/second/Watt).

The results of the final experiment show that the Intel NCS given its low power usage of 1.2 W, rates highly when given these SWaP constraints. Which vary per

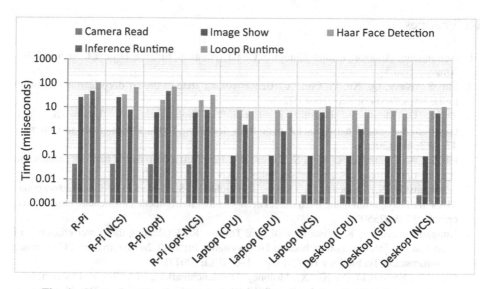

Fig. 4. Chart of results showing each device's running time for the given section

Table 1. Results of power related inferences.

System	Time (ms)	Power (watt)	RP (inf/s/W)
R-Pi (+NCS)	45.26 (7.57)	5 (6.2)	4.42 (21.31)
Intel CPU (+GPU)	1.92 (1.04)	45 (167)	11.57 (5.76)
AMD CPU (+GPU)	1.30 (0.73)	95 (345)	8.10 (3.97)

application in many of the DL use cases of Robotics, Human-Computer Interaction, Healthcare Application and several other Autonomous Systems. Given size and weight or even cost as extra parameters, the NCS would perform even higher than shown.

5 Conclusion

This paper presented a novel design concept, that shows how the Intel NCS device can help to bring state of the art DL to low powered edge devices. The combination of Raspberry Pi and NCS demonstrated the potential of these devices to help carry out complex image processing in real time similar to the Nvidia Jetson, the Intel NCS can be applied to almost any DL research area. This shows the ability of this low-cost inference model runner, to bridge the gap between current edge devices and desktop PCs for DL applications. With growing research into low powered embedded intelligence devices, this paper highlights the usefulness of this type of device.

References

1. Announcing Amazon Elastic Compute Cloud (Amazon EC2) – Beta, 24 August 2006. Amazon.com
2. Shi, S., Wang, Q., Xu, P., Chu, X.: Benchmarking state-of-the-art deep learning software tools. https://arxiv.org/abs/1608.07249
3. Tomè, D., Monti, F., Baroffio, L., Bondi, L., Tagliasacchi, M., Tubaro, S.: Deep convolutional neural networks for pedestrian detection. Signal Process.: Image Commun. **47**, 482–489 (2016)
4. Paszke, A., Chaurasia, A., Kim, S., Culurciello, E.: ENet: a deep neural network architecture for real-time semantic segmentation. https://arxiv.org/abs/1606.02147
5. Smolyanskiy, N., Kamenev, A., Smith, J., Birchfield, S.: Toward low-flying autonomous MAV trail navigation using deep neural networks for environmental awareness. https://arxiv.org/abs/1705.02550
6. Rungsuptaweekoon, K., Visoottiviseth, V., Takano, R.: Evaluating the power efficiency of deep learning inference on embedded GPU systems. In: 2017 2nd International Conference on Information Technology (INCIT), pp. 1–5. IEEE (2017)
7. Pena, D., Forembski, A., Xu, X., Moloney, D.: Benchmarking of CNNs for low-cost, low-power robotics applications. In: RSS 2017 Workshop: New Frontier for Deep Learning in Robotics (2017)
8. Nair, V., Hinton, G.E.: Rectified linear units improve restricted boltzmann machines. In: Proceedings of the 27th International Conference on Machine Learning (ICML-10), pp. 807–814 (2010)
9. Nasrabadi, N.M.: Pattern recognition and machine learning. J. Electron. Imaging **16**(4), 049901 (2007)
10. Goodfellow, I.J., et al.: Challenges in representation learning: a report on three machine learning contests. In: Lee, M., Hirose, A., Hou, Z.G., Kil, R. (eds.) ICONIP 2013. LNCS, vol. 8228, pp. 117–124. Springer, Heidelberg (2013). https://doi.org/10.1007/978-3-642-42051-1_16
11. Kingma, D., Ba, J.: Adam: a method for stochastic optimization. https://arxiv.org/abs/1412.6980
12. Srivastava, N., Hinton, G., Krizhevsky, A., Sutskever, I., Salakhutdinov, R.: Dropout: a simple way to prevent neural networks from overfitting. J. Mach. Learn. Res. **15**(1), 1929–1958 (2014)
13. Lucey, P., Cohn, J., Kanade, T., Saragih, J., Ambadar, Z., Matthews, I.: The extended Cohn-Kanade dataset (CK+): a complete dataset for action unit and emotion-specified expression. In: 2010 IEEE Computer Society Conference on Computer Vision and Pattern Recognition - Workshops (2010)
14. Bradski, G., Kaehler, A.: OpenCV. Dr. Dobb's Journal of Software Tools, 3 (2000)
15. King, D.E.: Dlib-ml: A machine learning toolkit. J. Mach. Learn. Res. **10**(Jul), 1755–1758 (2009)
16. Zhang, K., Zhang, Z., Li, Z., Qiao, Y.: Joint face detection and alignment using multitask cascaded convolutional networks. IEEE Signal Process. Lett. **23**(10), 1499–1503 (2016)
17. Imutils Library. https://github.com/jrosebr1/imutils, 27 May 2018

Short Papers

Improving Neural Network Interpretability via Rule Extraction

Stéphane Gomez Schnyder[1,2]([✉]), Jérémie Despraz[1,2],
and Carlos Andrés Peña-Reyes[1,2]

[1] School of Business and Engineering Vaud (HEIG-VD),
University of Applied Sciences of Western Switzerland (HES-SO),
Yverdon-les-Bains, Switzerland
[2] Computational Intelligence for Computational Biology (CI4CB),
SIB Swiss Institute of Bioinformatics, Lausanne, Switzerland
{stephane.schnyder,jeremie.despraz,carlos.pena}@heig-vd.ch

Abstract. We present a method to replace the fully-connected layers of
a Convolutional Neural Network (CNN) with a small set of rules, allowing
for better interpretation of its decisions while preserving accuracy.

Keywords: Convolutional neural network · Deep-learning
Rule extraction · Random forests · Interpretability

1 Introduction

Convolutional neural networks (CNNs) perform extremely well in many visual
classification and object detection tasks. However, interpreting neural networks
is still a challenging task and many studies propose to visualize, analyze, or
label the feature representations hidden in the internal layers. Such studies seek
to obtain insights about the process that happens inside the neural networks
when it classifies an image. Extracting simple IF-ELSE rules has been tackled
in previous works, for instance by plugging deep Neural Decision Forests on a
CNN [3] and more recently by interpreting CNNs with decision trees [7]. Herein
we present a method to replace part of a neural network with an interpretable
algorithm while preserving a similar level of accuracy.

2 Methodology

In our methodology, see Fig. 1, we: (1) use a trained CNN to extract features
from a set of images, (2) train a Random Forest (RF) [1] to create a set of rules
based on these features, and (3) rank the rules according to their utility, i.e., how
much they contribute to the prediction, by applying a form of preference learning
[5]. An analyst can then select the top-N rules allowing for an interpretation.

First, we present a dataset of 30.000 imageNet [4] images covering 26 different
classes to a pretrained VGG-16 CNN [6] and discard all the images classified

© Springer Nature Switzerland AG 2018
V. Kůrková et al. (Eds.): ICANN 2018, LNCS 11139, pp. 811–813, 2018.
https://doi.org/10.1007/978-3-030-01418-6

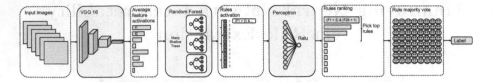

Fig. 1. Schematic summary of the proposed methodology

wrongly. We then consider the average activations of the 512 features for all the images of a target class, and complete it with the same number of images from the other classes. This is the training set for a RF classifier that reproduces the behavior of the fully-connected layers of the CNN. Each root-to-leaf path in the trees of the forest corresponds to a rule. These rules are ranked, according to their predictive accuracy, by a simple perceptron. The perceptron is trained to classify the images by weighting the rule outputs, and minimize a small ℓ_1 penalty to mitigate rule correlations. The rules with the largest weights are kept as the top rules for the target class and may then be used as an approximation of the CNN for the class of interest, classifying any input image by majority vote.

3   Results and Discussion

Figure 2a shows that the accuracy of the selected rules quickly reaches an acceptable threshold and that only 3 rules are often enough for 85–95% accuracy.

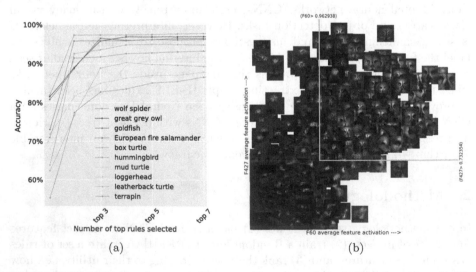

(a)   (b)

Fig. 2. (a) Classification accuracy (on test set) per number of top rules selected. (b) Top rule for the 'Great Grey Owl' class with example images. Images are embedded according to their average filter activation.

The rule shown in Fig. 2b discriminates a class based on two relevant features. The most characteristic images of the class are grouped together as they have similar filter activations. We can also get the intuition for visual patterns that are present in one class but absent in all other classes.

These results show that it is possible to reduce the complexity of the CNN (fully-connected layers) to a small set of relevant rules, without a great loss in accuracy. Furthermore, these rules can be interpreted by looking at how they split the input data. Such a combined analysis helps us to better understand the global behavior of the network.

Further results can be found under our Github repository [2].

References

1. Breiman, L.: Random forests. Mach. Learn. **45**(1), 5–32 (2001)
2. Gomez, S., Despraz, J., Peña-Reyes, C.A.: Improving neural network interpretability via rule extraction (2018). https://github.com/stephster/perceptron-rule-ranking
3. Kontschieder, P., Fiterau, M., Criminisi, A., Bulo, S.R.: Deep neural decision forests. In: 2015 IEEE International Conference on Computer Vision (ICCV), pp. 1467–1475. IEEE, December 2015. http://icccxplore.ieee.org/document/7410529/
4. Krizhevsky, A., Sutskever, I., Hinton, G.: Imagenet classification with deep convolutional neural networks. In: Advances in Neural (2012). http://papers.nips.cc/paper/4824-imagenet-classification-with-deep-convolutional-neural-networks
5. Ribeiro, G., Duivesteijn, W., Soares, C., Knobbe, A.: Multilayer perceptron for label ranking. In: Villa, A.E.P., Duch, W., Érdi, P., Masulli, F., Palm, G. (eds.) ICANN 2012. LNCS, vol. 7553, pp. 25–32. Springer, Heidelberg (2012). https://doi.org/10.1007/978-3-642-33266-1_4
6. Simonyan, K., Zisserman, A.: Very deep convolutional networks for large-scale image recognition. arXiv preprint arXiv:1409.1556 (2014)
7. Zhang, Q., Yang, Y., Wu, Y.N., Zhu, S.C.: Interpreting cnns via decision trees. arXiv preprint arXiv:1802.00121 (2018)

Online Multi-object Tracking Exploiting Pose Estimation and Global-Local Appearance Features

Na Jiang[✉], Sichen Bai, Yue Xu, Zhong Zhou, and Wei Wu[✉]

State Key Laboratory of Virtual Reality Technology and Systems,
Beihang University, Beijing, China
{Jiangna, wuwei}@buaa.edu.cn

Abstract. Multi-object tracking is a challenge in intelligent video analytics (IVA) due to possible crowd occlusions and truncations. Learning discriminant appearance features can alleviate these problems. An online multi-object tracking method with global-local appearance features is thus proposed in this paper. It consists of a pedestrian detection with pose estimation, a global-local convolutional neural network (GLCNN), and a spatio-temporal association model. The pedestrian detection with pose estimation explicitly leverages pose cues to reduce incorrect detections. GLCNN extracts discriminative appearance representations to identify the tracking objects, which implicitly alleviates the occlusions and truncations by integrating local appearance features. The spatio-temporal association model incorporates orientation, position, area, and appearance features of the detections to generate complete trajectories. Extensive experimental results demonstrate that our proposed method significantly outperforms many state-of-the-art online tacking approaches on popular MOT challenge benchmark.

Keywords: Multi-object tracking · Pose estimation · Global-local features
Spatial-temporal association

1 Our Method

Online multi-object tracking is a popular topic in computer vision [1–3], which concentrates on identifying object identities at each incoming frame and achieving multiple complete trajectories in single camera. It recently attracts increasing attentions since the advance of detection based on deep learning [4, 5]. Many traditional methods [6, 7] have been revisited and achieved promising performance. Meanwhile, several methods [8–10] based on deep learning network have been proposed to improve multi-object tracking. However, the occlusions or truncations often result in incorrect detection and inconsistent appearance, which significantly decrease the performance of multi-object tracking algorithm. Targeting to solve these problems, an online multi-object tracking exploiting pose estimation and global-local appearance features thus is proposed in this paper, which consists of pedestrian detection with pose estimation, global-local appearance feature extraction, and spatio-temporal association model.

© Springer Nature Switzerland AG 2018
V. Kůrková et al. (Eds.): ICANN 2018, LNCS 11139, pp. 814–816, 2018.
https://doi.org/10.1007/978-3-030-01418-6

Pedestrian detection with pose estimation. The two-stage detection chooses improved Faster RCNN [11] is selected as basic framework, and incorporates pose estimation to reduce the lost objects and incorrect detections. In the first phase, we replace the VGG-16 with ResNet50 as the convolutional module and adopt five-scale anchors instead of feature pyramids. In the second phase, we change four fixed scales to adaptive size for pose estimation inputs. **Global-local appearance feature extraction.** A global-local convolutional neural network (GLCNN) is designed to extract discriminative appearance representations. It integrates two kinds of global features from unshared branches and three local features of different body parts. The first main branch only extracts global features, while the second one is responsible for extracting head, torso, legs, and another global features. The achieved global feature vectors will be merged as appearance representations by concatenation. **Spatio-temporal association model.** Common spatio-temporal features include the IOU between two bounding boxes, the position of person feet and so on. When facing with dense crowds or occlusions, such spatio-temporal features often increases the number of identity switches and fragmented trajectories. To avoid the problems, this paper chooses orientation, central position, and area of bounding boxes as the spatio-temporal features. After achieving the appearance features and spatio-temporal features, the multi-object trajectories are generated by measuring appearance feature similarity and spatio-temporal correlativity of pairwise detections.

We show some qualitative results from static and dynamic cameras in Fig. 1, in which the different color bounding boxes with solid line indicate the tracking objects. Beside, we demonstrate the effectiveness of the proposed online multi-object tracking, referred as FMOT, on MOT benchmark [12]. The evaluation results illustrate that our approach is superior to many state-of-the-art methods.

Fig. 1. Visual Results on the MOT benchmark. (Best viewed in color)

Acknowledgement. This work is supported by the Natural Science Foundation of China under Grant No. 61472020.

References

1. Iqbal, U., Milan, A., Gall, J.: Posetrack: Joint multi-person pose estimation and tracking. In: 35th Proceedings of the IEEE Conference on Computer Vision and Pattern Recognition. IEEE, Honolulu (2017)
2. Insafutdinov, E., Andriluka, M., Pishchulin, L., et al.: Arttrack: Articulated multi-person tracking in the wild. In: 35th Proceedings of the IEEE Conference on Computer Vision and Pattern Recogni-tion, p. 4327. IEEE, Honolulu (2017)
3. Ma, C., Yang, C., Yang, F., et al.: Trajectory factory: tracklet cleaving and re-connection by deep siamese Bi-GRU for multiple object tracking. In: Proceedings of the IEEE International Conference on Multimedia and Expo. IEEE, San Diego (2018)
4. Kim, H.U., Kim, C.S.: CDT: Cooperative detection and tracking for tracing multiple objects in video sequences. In: Proceedings on European Conference on Computer Vision, pp. 851–867. Springer, Cham (2016)
5. Bae, S.H., Yoon, K.J.: Confidence-based data association and discriminative deep appearance learning for robust online multi-object tracking. IEEE Trans. Pattern Anal. Mach. Intell. **40**(3), 595–610 (2018)
6. Reid, D.: An algorithm for tracking multiple targets. IEEE Trans. Autom. Control **24**(6), 843–854 (1979)
7. Fortmann, T., Bar-Shalom, Y., Scheffe, M.: Sonar tracking of multiple targets using joint probabilistic data association. IEEE J. Oceanic Eng. **8**(3), 173–184 (1983)
8. Leal-Taixé, L., Canton-Ferrer, C., Schindler, K.: Learning by tracking: Siamese cnn for robust target association. In: 34th Proceedings of the IEEE Conference on Computer Vision and Pattern Recognition Workshops, pp. 33–40. IEEE, Las Vegas (2016)
9. Schulter, S., Vernaza, P., Choi, W., et al.: Deep network flow for multi-object tracking. In: 35th Proceedings of the IEEE Conference on Computer Vision and Pattern Recognition, pp. 2730–2739. IEEE, Honolulu (2017)
10. Son, J., Baek, M., Cho, M., et al.: Multi-object tracking with quadruplet convolutional neural networks. In: 35th Proceedings of the IEEE Conference on Computer Vision and Pattern Recognition, pp. 5620–5629. IEEE, Honolulu (2017)
11. Ren, S., He, K., Girshick, R., et al.: Faster r-cnn: Towards real-time object detection with region proposal networks. In: 28th International Proceedings on Advances in Neural Information Processing Systems, pp. 91–99. MIT, Montreal (2015)
12. MOT Challenge Benchmark, https://motchallenge.net/results/DukeMTMCT/, last accessed 2018/05/27

Author Index

Printed in the United States
By Bookmasters

Printed in the United States
By Bookmasters